# Gale Encyclopedia of
# Everyday Law

# Gale Encyclopedia of
# Everyday Law

JEFFREY WILSON, EDITOR

VOLUME TWO, second edition

First Amendment Law

to

Travel

THOMSON

GALE

Detroit • New York • San Francisco • New Haven, Conn. • Waterville, Maine • London • Munich

## Gale Encyclopedia of Everyday Law

**Project Editor**
Jeffrey Wilson

**Editorial**
Jeffrey Lehman

**Editorial Standards**
Laurie Andriot

**Product Design**
Jennifer Wahi

**Manufacturing**
Rhonda Williams

**LIBRARY OF CONGRESS CATALOGING-IN-PUBLICATION DATA**

Gale encyclopedia of everyday law / Jeffrey Wilson, editor.—2nd ed.
    p. cm.
    Includes bibliographical references and index.
    ISBN 1-4144-0353-4 (set : hardcover : alk.paper)—ISBN 1-4144-0401-8 (vol 1 : alk. paper)—ISBN 1-4144-0402-6 (vol 2 : alk. paper)
    1. Law—United States—Popular works.　I. Wilson, Jeffrey, 1971-　II. Title: Encyclopedia of everyday law.
    KF387.G27 2006
    349.73—dc22

                                                2006010071

Printed in the United States of America
10 9 8 7 6 5 4 3 2 1

# TABLE OF CONTENTS

# INTRODUCTION

The *Gale Encyclopedia of Everyday Law* is a two-volume encyclopedia of practical information on laws and issues affecting people's everyday lives. Readers will turn to this work for help in answering questions such as, "What is involved in estate planning?" "Do I have any recourse to noisy neighbors?" and "What are the consequences of an expired visa?" This Encyclopedia aims to educate people about their rights under the law, although it is not intended as a self-help or 'do-it-yourself' legal resource. It seeks to fill the niche between legal texts focusing on the theory and history behind the law and shallower, more practical guides to dealing with the law.

This encyclopedia, written for the layperson, is arranged alphabetically by broad subject categories and presents in-depth treatments of topics such as consumer issues, education, family, immigration, real estate, and retirement. Individual entries are organized in alphabetical order within these broad subject categories, and include information on state and local laws, as well as federal laws. In entries where it is not possible to include state and local information, references direct the reader to resources for further research.

The work contains approximately 240 articles of 2,000-5,000 words each, organized within 26 broad subject categories, which are arranged alphabetically. Each article begins with a brief description of the issue's historical background, covering important statutes and cases. The body of the article is divided into subsections profiling the various U.S.

federal laws and regulations concerning the topic. A third section details variations of the laws and regulations from state to state. Each article closes with a comprehensive bibliography, covering print resources and web sites, and a list of relevant national and state organizations and agencies.

## How to Use This Book

This second edition of the *Gale Encyclopedia of Everyday Law* has been designed with ready reference in mind.

- **ENTRIES ARE ARRANGED ALPHABETICALLY WITHIN 24 BROAD CATEGORIES.** All entries are spelled-out in the Table of Contents.

- **BOLDFACED TERMS** direct readers to glossary terms, which can be found at the back of the book.

- A comprehensible **OVERVIEW OF THE AMERICAN LEGAL SYSTEM** details civil and criminal procedure; appeals; small claims court; in pro per representation; differences between local codes and state codes; and the difference between statutes and regulations.

- A list of **STATE AND FEDERAL AGENCY CONTACTS** gives web sites that lead the user to various state and federal agencies and organizations.

- A **GENERAL INDEX** at the back of the second volume, covers subject terms from throughout the encyclopedia, case and statute titles, personal names, and geographic locations.

# ACKNOWLEDGMENTS

## Advisory Board

In compiling this edition, we have been fortunate in being able to call upon the following people, our panel of advisors who contributed to the accuracy of the information in this second edition of the *Gale Encyclopedia of Everyday Law*. To them we would like to express sincere appreciation:

**Matthew C. Cordon**
Assistant Professor of Law & Reference Librarian
Baylor University Law School
Waco, TX

**Jim Heller**
Director of the Law Library and Professor of Law
College of William & Mary
Williamsburg, VA

**Matt Morrison**
Research Attorney and Lecturer in Law
Cornell University
Cornell Law School Library
Ithaca, NY

**Anna Teller**
Associate Director, Law Library
Texas Wesleyan University Law Library
Fort Worth, TX

## Contributors

Lauren Barrow, James Cahoy, Matthew C. Cordon, Richard Cretan, J. Alicia Elster, Mark D. Engsberg, Lauri Harding, Kristy Holtfreter, Sunwoo Kahng, Anne Kevlin, Frances Lynch, George A. Milite, Melodie Monahan, Joe Pascarella, Monica L. P. Robbers, Mary Hertz Scarbrough, Thomas W. Scholl, III, Scott Slick, Sherrie Voss Matthews, Eric L. Welsh

# OVERVIEW OF THE AMERICAN LEGAL SYSTEM

## FRAMEWORK OF GOVERNMENT IN THE UNITED STATES

### Basis of the American Legal System

The legal system of the United States is administered and carried on by the official branches of government and many other authorities acting within their official lawmaking capacity. The original basis of the law in this country is the United States Constitution, which lays the framework under which each of the different branches of government operates. The Constitution also guarantees the basic civil rights of the citizens of the United States. All authority of the federal government originates from the Constitution, and the Constitution serves as the supreme law of the land. The Constitution grants to the federal government certain enumerated powers, and grants to the states any power not specifically delegated to a branch of the federal government. Under this system, states retain significant authority and autonomy. The Constitutions in each of the fifty states contain many similar provisions to those in the U.S. Constitution in terms of the basic structure of government. Under the federal and state constitutions, the United States legal system consists of a system of powers separated among branches of government, with a system of checks and balances among these branches.

### Legislative Branches

The legislative branch is the primary law-making body among the three branches, although authority emanating from the other branches also constitutes law. The legislative branch consists of Congress, and is subdivided into two lower houses, the House of Representatives and the Senate. In addition to the powers granted to Congress, the Constitution sets forth specific duties of both the House and the Senate. Each Congress meets for two sessions, with each session lasting two years. For example, the 107th Congress met in its first session in 2001, and meets in its second session in 2002. State legislatures are structured similarly, with the vast majority of these legislatures consisting of two lower houses.

### Judicial Branches

The judicial branch in the federal system consists of three levels of courts, with the Supreme Court serving as the highest court in the land. The intermediate courts in the federal system are the thirteen Courts of Appeals. The United States is divided by circuits, with each circuit consisting of a number of states. The Fifth Circuit, for example, consists of Texas, Mississippi, and Louisiana. Each Court of Appeals has jurisdiction to decide federal cases in its respective circuit. The trial level in the federal judicial system consists of the District Courts. Each state contains at least one district, with larger states containing as many as four districts. Congress has also established a number of lower federal courts with specialized jurisdiction, such as the bankruptcy courts and the United States Tax Court.

Most state court systems are similar to that of the federal system, with a three-tiered system consisting of trial courts, appellate courts, and a highest court, which is also referred to as a "court of last resort." The names of the courts are similar from state to state, such as superior court, court of appeals, and supreme court. However, some states do not follow this structure. For example, in New York, the trial level court is the Supreme Court, while the court of last resort is the Court of Appeals. Texas, as another example, has two highest courts— the Supreme

Court and the Court of Criminal Appeals. In addition to the trial level courts, small claims courts or other county courts typically hear small claims, such as those seeking recovery of less than $1000.

### Executive Branches

The federal Constitution vests executive power in the President of the United States. The President also serves as the Commander in Chief of the Armed Forces and has the power to make treaties with other nations, with the advice and consent of the Senate. Besides those powers enumerated in Article II of the Constitution, much of the power of the executive branch stems from the executive departments, such as the Department of the Treasury and the Department of Justice. Congress has the constitutional authority to delegate power to administrative agencies, and many of these agencies fall under the executive branch and are known as executive agencies. Congress also has the authority to create agencies independent of the other branches of government, called independent agencies. Authority emanating from executive and independent agencies is law, and it is similar in many ways to legislation created by legislatures or opinions issued by courts. State executive branches and administrative agencies are similar to those of their federal counterparts.

## Constitutional Authority

### Interpretation of the Constitution

The federal Constitution is not a particularly lengthy document, and does not provide many answers to specific questions of law. It has, instead, been the subject of extensive interpretation since its original ratification. In the famous 1803 case of *Marbury v. Madison*, Chief Justice John Marshall wrote an opinion of the Supreme Court, which stated that the judicial branch was the appropriate body for interpreting the Constitution and determining the constitutionality of federal or state legislation. Accordingly, determining the extent of power among the three branches of government, or determining the rights of the citizens of the United States, almost always requires an evaluation of federal cases, in addition to a reading of the actual text of the Constitution.

### Powers of Congress

Most of the enumerated congressional powers are contained in section 8 of Article I of the Constitution. Many courts have been asked to review congressional statutes to determine whether Congress had the constitutional authority to enact such statutes. Among these powers, the power of Congress "to regulate [c]ommerce among the several [s]tates" has been the subject of the most litigation and outside debate. A number of cases during the New Deal era under President Franklin D. Roosevelt considered the breadth of this provision, which is referred to as the Commerce Clause. After the Supreme Court determined that many of these statutes were unconstitutional, Roosevelt, after a landslide election in 1936, threatened to add additional justices to the court, in order to provide more support for his position with respect to the pieces of legislation passed during the New Deal era (the reason he gave to Congress at the time was that many of the justices were over the age of seventy, and could no longer perform their job function, but the general understanding was that he wanted justices that would approve the New Deal legislation as constitutional). The threat of this so-called "Court-packing" plan succeeded, and the Commerce Clause has been construed very broadly since then. Other powers enumerated in Article I are generally construed broadly as well.

### Civil Rights Provisions in the Constitutions

The main text of the Constitution does not provide rights to the citizens of the United States. These rights are generally provided in the many amendments to the Constitution. The first ten amendments, all ratified in 1791, are called the "Bill of Rights," and confer many of the cherished and fundamental rights to the citizens of the United States. Among the rights included in the Bill of Rights are the freedoms of speech and religion (First Amendment); right to keep and bear arms (Second Amendment); right to be free from unreasonable searches and seizures (Fourth Amendment); right to be free from being compelled to testify against one's self in a criminal trial (Fifth Amendment); right to due process of law (Fifth Amendment); right to a jury trial (Sixth Amendment); and right to be free from cruel and unusual punishment (Eighth Amendment).

Between 1791 and 1865, no constitutional amendments were ratified that provided civil rights to citizens. However, at the conclusion of the Civil War and during the reconstruction period following the war, three major amendments were added to the Constitution. The first was the Thirteenth Amendment, ratified in 1865, which finally abolished slavery and involuntary servitude in the United States. The Fourteenth Amendment, ratified in 1868, provided some of the most significant rights to citizens, including the guarantee of equal protection of the laws and prohibited denial of life, liberty, or property without due process of law. The Fifteenth Amendment, ratified in 1870, provided that the right to vote could not be abridged on account of race, color, or previous condition of servitude. Fifty years later, women were guaranteed the right to vote with the ratification of the Nineteenth Amendment in 1920.

### Application of Constitutional Amendments

Like other constitutional provisions, the judicial branch is the appropriate body to interpret the Bill of Rights and other amendments to the Constitution. The plain language of the amendments can cause some confusion, since some, by their own terms, they apply specifically to Congress, while other apply specifically to states. For example, the First Amendment begins, "Congress shall make no law respecting an establishment of religion . . ." Similarly, the Fourteenth Amendment contains a provision that states, "No State shall make or enforce any law which shall abridge the privileges and immunities of the citizens of the United States . . ." Modern courts have resolved some of these questions by ruling that the Due Process Clauses of the Fifth and Fourteenth Amendments incorporate these provisions, so many provisions apply to both the federal and state governments, despite the language in the Constitution.

### State Constitutions

Many state constitutions are structured similarly to the federal Constitution, except that most are more detailed than the federal Constitution. Most citizens are guaranteed basic civil rights by both the federal Constitution and their relevant state constitutions. For example, it is common for state constitutions to include provisions guaranteeing freedom of speech or equal protection, and most are phrased similarly to the provisions in the First and Fourteenth Amendments. Since the federal Constitution is the supreme law of the land, any rights provided in it are guaranteed to all citizens and cannot be lost because a state constitution's provisions conflict with the corresponding provision in the federal Constitution. A state may provide greater rights to citizens than those provided in a federal counterpart, but may not remove rights guaranteed under the federal doctrine. Section 10 of Article I of the Constitution also prohibits states from making certain laws or conducting certain acts, such as passing an ex post facto law or coining money.

## International Treaties

### Authority of Treaties

Article VI of the Constitution provides, "This Constitution, and the Laws of the United States which shall be made in Pursuance thereof; and all Treaties made, or which shall be made, under the Authority of the Untied States, shall be the supreme Law of the Land." An international treaty is generally considered to be on the same footing as a piece of legislation. If a treaty and a federal statute conflict, the one enacted at a later date, or the one that more specifically governs a particular circumstance, will typically govern. State legislation may not contradict provisions contained in a treaty. Similarly, states are forbidden from entering into treaties under the provisions in Article I, Section 10.

### Creation of Treaties and Other International Agreements

The power to enter into treaties is vested in the President, though the executive must act with the advice and consent of the Senate, and receive the concurrence of two-thirds of the Senate before a treaty is ratified. The various Presidents have also entered into executive agreements with foreign nations when the President has not been able to receive approval from two-thirds of the Senate, or has not sought approval from the Senate. While nothing in the Constitution permits or forbids this practice, executives have entered into thousands of such agreements.

## Federal and State Legislation

### Federal Legislative Process

Members of Congress have the exclusive authority to introduce legislation to the floor of either the House of Representatives or Senate. Legislation is introduced to Congress in the form of bills. Most bills can originate either in the Senate or in the House, with the exception of bills to raise revenue, which must originate in the House under Article I of the Constitution. When a bill is introduced, it is designated with a bill number, and these bill numbers run sequentially through two sessions of Congress. For example, the fifty-sixth bill introduced in the House during the 108th Congress will be designated as "H.R. 56" ("H.R." is an abbreviation for House of Representatives). Likewise, the twelfth bill introduced in the Senate during the same Congress will be designated "S. 12." It is not uncommon that bills are introduced in both the House and the Senate simultaneously that address the same subject matter.

These bills are referred to as "companion bills," and the actual law that is passed often contains components from both the enacted bill and its companion bill. Thousands of bills are introduced in the House and Senate each session, and a relatively small proportion is actually passed into law.

After a bill has been introduced, it is sent to one or more appropriate committees in the House or Senate. The committee or committees analyze the provisions of the bill, including the reasoning for such legislation and the expected effect of the bill if it were enacted into law. A committee conducts hearings, where it hears testimony from experts and other parties that can provide information relevant to the subject matter covered by a bill. A committee may also order the preparation of an in-depth study (called a "committee print") that provides additional background information, often in the form of statistics and statistical analysis. A number of additional documents may also be produced during the committee stage, and practically every action is documented, including the production of written transcripts of committee hearings. A committee may amend or rewrite a bill before it approves it, which generally extends the length of time that a bill remains at the committee stage. The vast majority of bills, in fact, never leave the committee stage, and these bills are commonly said to have "died in committee."

When a committee completes its consideration of a bill, it reports the bill back to the floor of the House or Senate. A committee ordinarily accompanies the bill with a report that summarizes and analyzes each bill's provisions, and provides recommendations regarding the passage of the bill. Reports, as well as other documents, are designated with unique numbers and are made available to the public. An example of a report number is "H.R. Rep. No. 108-15," which indicates that it is the fifteenth report submitted to the House of Representatives in the 108th Congress.

Members of the houses of Congress debate the bills on the floor of the relevant house. These debates are transcribed, and the text of the transcription is routinely available to the public. During this period, the relevant chamber may amend the bill. Once the debates and other activities are completed, the chamber votes to pass the bill. If the chamber approves the bill, it is sent to the other chamber, and the entire process is repeated. The version of the bill sent to the other chamber of Congress is called the

"engrossed" version of the bill. The other chamber must pass this version exactly as it appears in the engrossed version, or else the bill, assuming the second chamber passes it, is sent back to the original chamber for future consideration. If the House and Senate cannot agree to a single version of a bill, a conference, or joint, committee may be convened, where members of both chambers may compromise to complete a version of a bill acceptable to both chambers. If this conference committee is successful in doing so, the bill is returned to the House and Senate for another vote.

Once a bill passes both the House and the Senate, it is sent to the President as an "enrolled" bill. The President may sign the bill and make it law. If the President does not sign the bill, and Congress is still in session, the bill becomes law automatically after ten days. If the President does not sign the bill, and Congress adjourns within ten days, the bill does not become law. The President may also reject the bill by vetoing it. Congress may override this veto with a two-thirds majority vote in both chambers.

### Types of Laws Passed by Congress

Laws that apply to and are binding on the general citizenry are called public laws. Each public law is designated with a public law number, and the numbering system is similar to that of reports and other documents described above. For example, Public Law Number 108-1 represents that this is the first public law passed in the 108th Congress. Congress may also pass laws that apply only to individual citizens or small classes of individuals. These laws are called private laws, and are usually passed in the context of immigration and naturalization. Private laws are numbered identically to public laws, such as, for example, Private Law Number 108-2, which is the second private law passed in the 108th Congress.

Congress also passes various types of resolutions, some of which do not constitute law and do not contain binding provisions equivalent to public laws. A single chamber of Congress may pass simple resolutions, which relate to the operations of that chamber or express the opinion of that chamber on policy issues. Both chambers may pass a concurrent resolution, which relate to the entire operation of Congress, or the express opinion of the entire Congress. Neither simple nor concurrent resolutions constitute law, and are not submitted to the President for approval. Joint resolutions, on the other hand, have the same binding effect as bills, and must be submitted to the President for final approval. Appropriations and similar measures often enter Congress as joint resolutions. Some actions, particularly the introduction of a constitutional amendment, require the use of a joint resolution, and many of these actions do not require presidential approval.

### Publication of Federal Legislation

Practically all documents produced by Congress during the legislative process are published by the United States Government Printing Office and made available to the public. Most of items produced since 1995 are now also available on the Internet in electronic formats. Legislation first appears in the form of a slip law, named as such because the Government Printing Office prints these on unbound slips of paper. At the conclusion of a session of Congress, the laws passed during that session are compiled and appear in the form of session laws, organized in chronological order. The official source for federal session laws is the United States Statutes at Large.

Most legislation in force in the United States is organized into a subject matter arrangement and published in the United States Code. A statute contained in the United States Code is called a codified statute. The U.S. Code consists of fifty titles, with each title representing a certain area of law. For example, Title 17 contains the copyright laws of the United States; Title 26 contains the Internal Revenue Code; and Title 29 contains most of the labor laws of the United States.

### Relationship Between Federal and State Legislation

Federal legislation is superior to state legislation under the provisions of Article VI of the U.S. Constitution. Thus, the courts will resolve any potential conflicts between a state statute and a federal statute by enforcing the federal statute. Federal superiority, however, does not mean that states are forbidden from enacting legislation covering the same subject matter as a federal statute; it is common for both federal and state legislation to govern similar areas of law. This is true in such areas as securities regulation, consumer protection, and labor law. Federal labor relations laws, for example, apply specifically to private employers, but do not apply to public employers. Labor relations between public employers and their employees are governed generally by state labor relations laws.

If Congress wants an area of law to be governed solely by federal legislation, Congress may include a provision that such legislation preempts any state law related to the subject matter covered by the federal statute. Congress may preempt state regulation expressly through specific statutory language, or by implication based on the structure and purpose behind a federal statute. Examples of legislation that contain preemption provisions are the Employment Retirement Income Security Act of 1974, the Comprehensive Environmental Response, Compensation and Liability Act, and the Toxic Substance Control Act.

The Tenth Amendment to the federal Constitution reserves any power not delegated to the federal government to the states, or to the people. However, there have been questions among the courts and scholars regarding the extent of this amendment, and it has not generally been construed to grant any special powers to the states through its enactment. Rather, it is a clause that reserves power to the states where Congress has not acted, subject to some limitations.

### Legislative Process in State Legislatures

Most state legislatures follow similar processes as Congress. Each state legislature, with the exception of Nebraska, consists of two chambers. Most legislatures meet in regular session annually, though some meet biannually with special called sessions held periodically. In many states, the process of introducing a bill is streamlined, where only one chamber may introduce certain types of bills. Several states also permit citizens to initiate legislation, which is not possible in Congress. Some states allow citizens to vote directly on a proposed piece of legislation. Other states contain provisions that all citizens, once they have received a requisite number of signatures, may force the legislature to consider and vote on a particular issue.

### Publication of State Legislation

Most states publish enacted legislation in a similar manner as the publication of federal legislation. Laws passed during each session of a respective legislature are compiled as session laws, and laws currently in force are compiled in a subject matter arrangement. In most states, laws in force are compiled according to a numbering system similar to the United States Code, with title or chapter numbers representing the subject matter of the statute. Other states, most notably California and Texas, have created codes that are named to represent the subject matter of the statues contained in them. For example, the California Family Code contains the family law statutes of that state; similarly, the Texas Finance Code contains the statutes governing many of the financial operations in that state.

Bills introduced in every legislature during a current session are now available on the various legislatures' Internet sites, as are the current statutes. However, very little documentation from the legislative process is published in a fashion to make it readily available to interested members of the public. Legal researchers interested in such information must often travel to their respective state capitol to obtain this information.

### Interpretation of Legislation

The language of a statute may be somewhat ambiguous regarding their application, and the courts have the responsibility to interpret or construe the language to determine the proper application of the statute. Courts have developed "canons of construction" to aid in this interpretation. The most basic form of statutory construction is consideration of the text and plain meaning of a statute. This consideration includes the process of defining the terms and phrases used in statute, including the use of a dictionary to derive the common meaning of a term. Courts will also consider the application of the statute in the context of the broader statutory scheme, which can often indicate what the purpose of the statute was when the statute was enacted.

If the plain meaning of a statute cannot be derived from the statute or statutory scheme, courts may look to the history of the legislation to determine the intent of the legislature when it enacted the statute. It is possible that Congress or a state legislature specifically addressed a concern during the legislative process, and members of the legislature may have made statements indicating how the legislature intended for the statute to apply in a particular circumstance. Locating this information requires a legal researcher to locate documentation prepared during the legislative process, in a process called "compiling" a legislative history.

### Substantive vs. Procedural Laws

Many of the laws passed by legislatures are considered "substantive" laws, because they create, define, and regulate legal rights and obligations. If an individual has been harmed and wants to bring litigation against the person or group that harmed him or her, substantive statutes often provide the law that governs that situation, and also include provisions regarding the appropriate damages that can be awarded to the plaintiff should the plaintiff successfully prove his or her case.

By comparison, procedural laws are those that set forth the rules used to enforce substantive laws.

These laws may dictate the steps that a litigant must take to bring a suit to court, or may dictate the appropriate courts where a case may be brought. Some statutes, called statutes of limitations, also limit the amount of time in which a particular case may be brought. Procedural laws are as important as substantive laws in many respects, because a party with a valid claim may nevertheless lose a case if the proper procedures are not followed, or if the claim is not filed in the time required under a statute of limitations.

### Criminal Law vs. Civil Law

Criminal laws are those designed to punish private parties for violating the provisions contained in these laws. Violations of these laws are crimes against society, and are brought as criminal actions against the alleged offenders by state or federal attorneys acting on behalf of the people. All citizens of the United States are guaranteed rights in criminal investigations and criminal trials, and law enforcement officers and prosecutors must follow certain procedures in order to protect these rights. For this reason, criminal procedure differs significantly from the procedures for bringing a civil case to court. Among the most fundamental rights is that all accused individuals are presumed innocent until the state proves them guilty beyond a reasonable doubt. This places the burden of proof in a criminal action on the state, rather than on the defendant. Title 18 of the U.S. Code contains most of the federal criminal laws, while state penal codes generally contain the state criminal laws.

The term "civil law" has different meanings in two distinct contexts. First, it refers to a system of law that differs from the common law system employed by the United States. This is discussed below. Second, it refers to a type of law that defines rights between private parties, and, as such, differs from criminal law. Civil laws are applicable in such situations as when two parties enter into a contract with one another, or when one party causes physical injury to another party. The procedures that must be followed in a civil court case are generally less stringent than those in a criminal case. Some civil laws include provisions designed to punish wrongdoers, usually in the form of punitive, or exemplary, damages that are paid to the other party.

### Municipal Ordinances and Other Local Laws

Local government entities are generally created by the various states, and are typically referred to as municipalities. The powers of a municipality are limited to those granted to it by the state, usually defined in the municipal charter that created the municipality. Charters are somewhat analogous to state constitutions, and usually were created by vote of the voters in the municipality. Local governing bodies may include a city council, county commission, board of supervisors, etc., and these bodies enact ordinances that apply specifically to the locality governed by these bodies. Ordinances are similar to state legislative acts in their function. In many municipalities, ordinances are organized into a subject matter arrangement and produced as municipal codes.

Local laws often govern everyday situations more so than many state or federal laws. These laws include many provisions for public safety, raise revenue through the creation and implementation of sales and other local taxes, and govern the zoning of the municipality. Decisions regarding education are also generally made through local boards of education, though these boards are entities distinct from the municipal government. Local laws cannot contradict federal or state law, including statutory or constitutional provisions.

## Cases and Case Law in the Judicial Systems of the United States

### Adversarial System

The judicial system in the United States is premised largely on the resolution of disputes between adversaries after evidence is presented on both sides to a judge or jury during a trial. Civil cases usually involve the resolution of disputes between private parties in such areas as personal injury, breach of contract, property disputes, or resolution of domestic relations disputes. Criminal cases involve the prosecution by the state or federal government of an individual accused of violating a criminal statute. The rules and procedures that parties must follow differ between criminal and civil trials, although similarities exist between the two types of rules. Some courts, such as probate courts and juvenile courts, have been developed to hear specific types of suits in a particular jurisdiction. Other tribunals, such as small claims courts and justice of the peace courts, have also been established to resolve minor disputes or try cases involving alleged infractions of minor crimes. The systems by which parties appeal decisions are also premised on an adversarial process.

### Civil Trials

A party commences a civil trial by filing a petition or complaint with an appropriate court. The party bringing the suit is usually referred to as the plaintiff, though in some cases the party is referred to as the petitioner. A petition or complaint must generally name the parties involved, the cause of action, the legal theories under which recovery may be appropriate, and the relief sought from the court. Once the petition or complaint is filed with the court, the plaintiff must serve the party or parties against whom the action was brought. The party against whom the case is brought is referred to as the defendant, though in some cases this party is referred to as the respondent. A defendant generally responds to a petition or complaint by filing an answer admitting or denying liability, though the filing of a pre-answer motion or motions may precede this.

A number of events occur between the time a petition or complaint is filed with a court and the time of trial. During the pretrial stage, the parties will usually file a series of motions with the court, requesting the addition or removal of a party, limits on evidence that may be presented at trial, or the complete dismissal of the case in its entirety. Parties also collect information in a process called discovery. During discovery, parties file interrogatories, which are written questions submitted to the other party or parties; seek admissions to certain facts from the other party or parties; and take depositions, which are oral questions asked of witnesses who are under oath. The pretrial stage is very important to the eventual resolution of a dispute, and many cases are settled by the parties outside of court or dismissed before the case actually goes to trial.

When a civil case goes to trial, a judge or a jury may try it. If a judge tries a case, he or she makes findings of facts and rulings of law, and the trial is usually referred to as a bench trial. If a jury tries a case, the jury makes findings of facts, such as whether a contract existed or whether one party assaulted another party. However, the judge makes rulings of law in a jury trial. A plaintiff who wants a jury to try his or her case must usually request it as a jury demand, or else the case will proceed as a bench trial. Some types of cases, such as family law cases, are never tried with juries. If a jury is requested, the case proceeds with the selection of jurors. During this time, a specified number of jurors are selected randomly from a pool of potential jurors. Both parties are permitted to question the jurors in a process called voir dire, and may ask that a certain number of jurors be removed from the final jury.

At the beginning of a trial, both sides give opening statements, providing an overview of the evidence that will be presented during the trial. After opening statements, both sides present evidence by questioning its own witnesses (called direct examination) and introducing physical items into evidence. Each party has the right to cross-examine witnesses produced by the opposing party. All jurisdictions have developed detailed rules of evidence that must be followed by both parties. Many of these rules govern the questions that may be asked on direct or cross-examination of witnesses. If one party enters something into evidence that violates the rules of evidence, the other party must raise an objection to the entry of this evidence, and the judge may sustain or overrule this objection. Some violations of the rules of evidence may result in a mistrial, in which the entire trial process must be repeated because it would be unfair to continue with the case. Even if the rule violation is not enough to cause a mistrial, a party who may wish to appeal an adverse ruling must raise objections during trial to "preserve error" for future consideration by appellate courts. Appellate courts will generally only consider points of possible error when the party seeking the appeal raised an objection and preserved error at the trial level.

A plaintiff generally has the burden to prove a case, and always introduces evidence before the defendant. Because a plaintiff has the burden of proof, a defendant is not required to introduce evidence, though the defendant will almost always do so. After the defendant concludes his or her presentation of evidence, the plaintiff may present evidence that rebuts evidence offered by the defense. Once all evidence has been introduced, both parties make closing arguments. Closing arguments are followed by jury deliberation, in which the jury determines whether the plaintiff or plaintiffs deserve to recover, and what amount of damages is appropriate. A jury relies on jury instructions (or court charges) given to them by the court, which describe the law and procedure that the jury must use to make its decision. The percentage of jurors that must be in agreement to render a decision ranges among different jurisdictions.

Once a jury renders a verdict, the parties may file post-trial motions that may still affect the outcome of the trial. These motions may include motion for new trial, which is usually awarded if something occurred during the trial that rendered the process unfair to one of the parties; or a motion for judgment notwithstanding the verdict (commonly referred to as "JNOV"), where the court renders judgment for one party, though the jury decided in favor of the other party, because the evidence presented at trial did not support the jury's decision. A party who wishes to appeal an adverse decision may also file a notice of appeal with the trial court, indicating that it wishes to appeal the ruling to an appellate court. Filing a notice of appeal within a certain time frame (30 days is common) is required in most jurisdictions in order to appeal a case to a higher court.

### Criminal Trials

State and federal prosecutors initiate criminal cases, which involve charges that an individual has violated a criminal law. In all criminal cases, the state or federal government serves as the plaintiff, while the person charged is the defendant. Criminal laws, which are promulgated by the various legislatures, consist of two major types of laws: felonies and misdemeanors. Felonies consist of the more serious crimes, and carry with them the most serious punishment. Both felonies and misdemeanors can result in jail or prison time, and both will usually result in a significant fine.

Citizens are guaranteed a number of rights in the context of criminal prosecution, and exercise of these rights is often the focus of criminal trials. The Fourth Amendment of the U.S. Constitution requires that law enforcement officials obtain a search warrant, upon showing of probable cause, before conducting searches or seizures of individuals or the property of individuals. The Fifth and Sixth Amendments contain a number of guarantees to all citizens that must be provided in a criminal trial. If a citizen's constitutional rights have been violated, the state may be required to proceed without the introduction of relevant evidence obtained illegally, or may be required to terminate the criminal action altogether.

When a person is arrested for violation of a criminal law, he or she must generally be brought before a judge within twenty-four hours of the arrest. The judge must inform the individual of the charges brought against him or her, and set bail or other condition of release. After other preliminary matters, the defendant is formally charged in one of two ways. First, the prosecutors may file a "trial information," which formally states the charges against the defendant. In more serious cases, such as murder trials, a panel of citizens will be convened as a grand jury to consider the evidence against the defendant. A grand jury, unlike a trial jury, only determines whether sufficient evidence to support the criminal charge exists, and will issue an indictment if evidence is sufficient. Either the filing of a trial information, or the return of an indictment, formally begins the trial process by charging the defendant. Once the defendant has been formally charged, he or she must appear for an arraignment, where the court reads the charge and permits the defendant to enter a plea. The defendant may enter a plea of guilty or not guilty at this time. Where it is permitted or required as a prerequisite to an insanity defense, the defendant may enter a plea of not guilty by reason of insanity. In some jurisdictions, including federal courts, the defendant may plead nolo contendere, or "no contest," which means that the defendant does not contest the charges. Its primary effect is the same as a plea of guilty, and its primary significance is that a plea of nolo contendere cannot be introduced into evidence in a subsequent civil action as proof of the defendant's guilt in the criminal action. Nolo contendere pleadings may usually only be entered with the permission of the court.

The Sixth Amendment guarantees the accused in a criminal prosecution a speedy and public trial. When a defendant enters a plea of not guilty, the trial is usually scheduled within ninety days of the filing of the trial information or indictment. The Sixth Amendment also guarantees citizens accused of crimes the right to a jury trial, though a defendant may waive this right and request a bench trial. During the pre-trial stage, the defendant may file motions with the court, such as those requesting exclusion of evidence from a trial because the evidence may have been obtained illegally. A defendant may also engage in pretrial discovery, including requests to view evidence in the possession of the prosecution. The prosecution and the defendant may engage in plea bargaining, whereby the prosecution may agree to reduce charges against the defendant in exchange for a plea of guilty or nolo contendere.

When a case proceeds to a jury trial, the parties have an opportunity to question prospective jurors, similar to the selection of jurors in a civil case, except that the final number of jurors in a criminal trial is usually larger than the number used in a civil case. Both the state and the defendant have the opportunity to strike jurors from the final jury. Once the final jury is selected and the trial begins, the prosecution reads the indictment or trial information, reads the defendant's plea, and makes an opening statement. The defendant may make an opening statement immediately after the prosecution, or may wait to do so until the time the defense introduces its evidence. Introduction of evidence in a criminal case is similar to that of a civil case, and the prosecution bears the burden of proving that the defendant is guilty beyond a reasonable doubt. Until the state proves otherwise, the defendant is presumed innocent. The defendant is not required to introduce evidence since the prosecution bears the burden of proof, but if the defendant does produce evidence, the prosecution may present rebuttal evidence and cross-examine any witnesses. Once both sides have presented the evidence, each party may give a closing argument.

A jury in a criminal trial must return a unanimous verdict of "guilty" or "not guilty." If a jury fails to reach a unanimous verdict, it is referred to as a "hung" jury, and a mistrial is declared. In such a situation, a new jury must retry the entire case. If the jury returns a unanimous verdict of guilty, then the jury's duty is usually complete, since a jury in most jurisdictions is not involved in the sentencing of the defendant. A judge, when determining an appropriate sentence for a convicted defendant, considers testimony and reports from a number of different sources, such as probation officers and victims. The federal government and many state governments have established detailed sentencing guidelines that must be followed by judges in criminal cases. In addition to a sentence of imprisonment or of a fine, a court may place a convicted defendant on probation, meaning that the defendant is placed under the supervision of a local correctional program. A defendant must comply with specific terms and conditions of the probation in order to avoid time in prison or jail. Similar to probation, a judge may also give the defendant a deferred judgment, or may suspend the defendant's sentence. In either case, the defendant is given the opportunity to remove the crime from his or her criminal record by successfully completing a period of probation.

### Appeals

If a party in a case is not satisfied with the outcome of a trial decision, he or she may appeal the case to a higher court for review. Not all parties have the right to appeal, however, and parties must follow proper procedures for the higher court to agree to hear the appeal. During trial, parties must "preserve error" by making timely objections to violations of the rules of evidence and other procedural rules. After trial, the party seeking an appeal must file a notice of appeal with the trial court. The opposing party may file a notice of cross-appeal if that party is not satisfied with the final judgment from the lower court. The party bringing the appeal is usually referred to as the appellant (though in some cases this party is the petitioner), and the opposing party is referred to as the appellee (or respondent in some cases).

Once a party has filed a notice of appeal, both parties must comply with a series of rules of appellate procedure to continue with the appeal. The appellant usually requests that the transcript of the trial court proceeding from the trial court reporter be sent to the court of appeals. The appellant must also pay a docketing or similar fee with the court of appeals. Both parties then file briefs with the appellate court stating the facts from the case, stating the legal arguments and reasons for appeal, and requesting relief from the appellate court. Both parties have access to the other party's briefs submitted to the court. Parties also request an oral argument, where both sides are given the opportunity to make their legal arguments before the court, and answer questions from the appellate court justices. Appellate courts do not hear testimony from witnesses or consider evidence that was not introduced in the trial. Rather, a court of appeals reviews the trial court proceeding to determine whether the trial court applied substantive or procedural law to the facts of the case correctly. At the end of the appeal, the court will issue an opinion that states the conclusion of the court of appeals.

Almost all judicial systems in the United States consist of three tiers, and an intermediate appellate court hears the first level of appeals. If a party is dissatisfied with an intermediate court's opinion, the party may seek an appeal by its jurisdiction's court of last resort. In many cases, the decision of a court of last resort to hear an appeal is discretionary, and a party must petition the court to hear the appeal (intermediate appellate courts, by comparison, typically do not have this discretion). The United States Supreme Court is the court of last resort for all cases in the United States, including the intermediate federal courts of appeals and the highest state courts. The U.S. Supreme Court only hears cases involving the application of federal law, and in most cases, the decision to grant an appeal is completely discretionary on the part of the Supreme Court. A party seeking review from the Supreme Court must file a petition for writ of certiorari requesting that the Court review the lower court's decision, and if the Court grants the writ, the Court orders the submission of the lower court's case. The Supreme Court grants a writ of certiorari in a very small percentage of cases, usually when there is a controversial issue of federal law in question in the case.

Civil appeals and criminal appeals are similar, with two main exceptions. First, with very few exceptions, the state may not appeal an acquittal of a criminal in a trial court case. Second, in some criminal cases, especially murder cases where the defendant has received the death penalty, the right to appeal is guaranteed and automatic.

### Jurisdiction and Venue

When a party bring a lawsuit in a court in the United States, the party must determine which court has appropriate jurisdiction to hear the case, and which court is the proper venue for such a suit. Jurisdiction refers to the power of a court to hear a particular case, and may be subdivided into two components: subject matter jurisdiction and personal jurisdiction. Venue refers to the appropriateness of a court to hear a case, and applies differently than jurisdiction.

A court has proper subject matter jurisdiction if it has been given the power to hear a particular type of case or controversy under constitutional or statutory provisions. For example, a county court of law may have jurisdiction to hear cases and controversies where the amount in controversy of the claim is less than $5,000. If a claimant brings a case before the county court with an amount in controversy of $7,500, the court lacks jurisdiction to hear the case and will dismiss it. Subject matter jurisdiction is often a difficult issue with respect to the jurisdiction of federal courts, discussed below. Personal jurisdiction is based on the parties or property involved in the lawsuit. In personam jurisdiction refers to the power of a court over a particular person or persons, and usually applies when a party is a resident of a state or has established some minimum contact with that state. In rem jurisdiction, by comparison, refers to the power of a court over property located in a particular state.

Venue is often confused with jurisdiction because it applies when determining whether a particular court may hear a case. A court may have jurisdiction to hear a case, but may not be the proper venue for such a case. Statutes often provide that proper venue in a particular case is the county or location where the defendant or defendants reside. Even if a court in the county where the plaintiff resides has proper jurisdiction to hear the case, it may not be the proper venue because of a provision in a statute regarding venue.

### Jurisdiction of Federal Courts

Federal courts in the United States have limited jurisdiction to hear certain claims, based primarily on provisions in Article III of the U.S. Constitution. Federal courts can hear cases involving the application of the Constitution, federal statutes, or treaties. Federal courts may also hear cases where the amount in controversy is more than $75,000, and all of the parties are citizens of different states. State courts may also hear cases with federal questions or where parties reside in different states. If a party brings a case in state court and a federal court has jurisdiction to hear the case, the opposing party may remove the case to federal court. The federal court generally reviews each case to determine whether jurisdiction is appropriate. If federal jurisdiction is not appropriate, the court remands the case to state court.

Some suits may only be brought in federal court, such as those brought by or against the government of the United States. Other examples are those involving bankruptcy, patents, and admiralty.

### Legal vs. Equitable Remedies

Some remedies available from courts are considered "legal" remedies, while others are considered "equitable" remedies. Legal remedies are usually those involving an award of monetary damages. By comparison, a court through use of an equitable remedy may require or prohibit certain conduct from a party. The distinction between legal and equitable remedies relates to the historic distinction between "law" and "equity" courts that existed in England as far back as the fourteenth century. Law courts traditionally adhered to very rigid procedures and formalities in resolving the outcome of a legal conflict, while equity courts developed a more flexible system where judges could exercise more discretion. This system transferred to the United States, but today, most courts in the United States may hear cases in both law and equity, although the procedure and proof required to request an equitable remedy may differ from the requirements to request a legal remedy. Examples of equitable remedies are specific performance of a contract, reformation of a contract, injunctions, and restitution.

### Procedural Rules of the Courts

In addition to procedural laws promulgated by legislatures, judicial systems also adopt various rules of procedure that must be followed by the courts and parties to a case. Two main types of court rules exist. First, some rules have general applicability over all courts in a particular jurisdiction. Examples of such rules are rules of civil procedure, rules of appellate procedure, rules of criminal procedure, and rules of evidence. Second, some rules apply only to a particu-

lar court, and are referred to as local court rules. Many counties draft local court rules that apply to all courts in those particular counties. Local court rules are generally more specific than rules of general applicability, and both must be consulted in a given case.

### Pro Se Litigants and the Right to Representation

A litigant representing himself or herself, without the assistance of counsel, is called a pro se litigant. It is almost always advisable to seek counsel with respect to a legal claim, if possible. Defendants in criminal cases are entitled to legal representation, and a lawyer will be provided to a criminal if the criminal shows indigence. Such assistance in criminal cases is usually provided by a public defender's office. Claimants in civil cases, on the other hand, are not entitled to attorneys, though any of a number of legal aid societies may be willing to provide legal services free of charge. Many of these legal aid societies are subsidized by public agencies, and will accept a case only if a person meets certain criteria, usually focusing on the income of the party.

In a civil case, a court may appoint counsel after considering a number of factors, including the validity of the party's position, and the ability of the party to try the case. A party who is indigent must usually file a written motion with the court, explaining the party's indigence and need for counsel. An attorney who provides free legal assistance is said to provide a pro bono service. Attorneys are generally free to determine when they will provide pro bono services, and it is common in every jurisdiction for the number of litigants seeking the appointment of counsel to outweigh the number of attorneys willing to provide pro bono services.

If a party must continue pro se, the rules regarding sanctions of attorneys apply equally to this party. A party must verify the accuracy and reasonableness of any document submitted to the court. If any submission contains false, improper, or frivolous information, the party may be liable for monetary or other sanctions. Likewise, a pro se litigant may be held in contempt of court for failure to follow the directions of a court. Many courts provide handbooks that assist pro se litigants in following proper trial procedures.

### Small Claims Courts and Other Local Tribunals

Cases involving a relatively small amount in controversy may be brought before small claims court.

These courts exist only at the state court level. The maximum amount in controversy for a small claims court is usually $1,000 for a money judgment sought, or $5,000 for the recovery of personal property, though these amounts vary among jurisdictions. Witnesses are sworn, as they are in any trial, but the judge in a small claims court typically conducts the trial in a more informal fashion than in a trial at the district court level. Judges may permit the admission of evidence in a small claims action that may not be admissible under relevant rules of evidence or rules of procedure. One major exception is that privileged communication is usually not admissible in a small claims action. A small claims court usually only has the power to award monetary damages. If a party is unsatisfied with the judgment of the small claims court, the party may ordinarily appeal the case to a district court or other trial court.

### Alternative Dispute Resolution

A variety of procedures may be available to parties, which can serve as alternatives to litigation in the court system. Alternative dispute resolution, or ADR, has become rather common, because it is typically less costly and does not involve the formal proceedings associated with a trial. Parties usually enter into one of two types of ADR: arbitration or mediation. If a case is submitted to arbitration, a neutral arbitrator renders a decision that may be binding or non-binding, depending on the agreement of the parties. An arbitrator serves a function analogous to a judge, though the presentation of each party's evidence does not need to follow the formal rules that must be followed in a judicial decision. Though parties are generally not able to appeal an arbitrator's award, parties may seek judicial relief if the arbitrator acts in an arbitrary or capricious manner, shows bias towards one of the parties, or makes an obvious mistake. Arbitration may be ordered by a court, may be required under certain laws, or may be voluntary.

Mediation is similar to arbitration because it involves the use of a neutral third party to resolve a dispute. A mediator assists the parties to identify issues in a dispute, and makes proposals for the resolution of the dispute or disputes. However, unlike arbitrators, a mediator does not have the power to make a binding decision in a case. Also unlike arbitrators, a mediator typically meets with each of the interested parties in private to hold confidential discussions. Mediation may be court-ordered, may be required under certain laws, or may be voluntary. A number of organizations, including state bar associations, offer mediation services.

A number of other forms of ADR exist. For example, parties may employ the use of a fact finder, who resolves factual disputes between two parties. In some jurisdictions, parties may be required to submit a dispute to early neutral evaluation, where a neutral evaluator provides an assessment of the strengths and weaknesses of each party's position.

### Case Law in the Common Law System

Cases play a very important part in the legal system of the United States, not only because courts adjudicate the claims of parties before them, but also because courts establish precedent that must be followed in future cases. The United States adopted the common law tradition of England as the basis for its legal system. Under the common law system, legal principles were handed down from previous generations, first on an unwritten basis, then through the decisions of the courts. Though legislatures possess constitutional power to make law, in a common law system there is no presumption that legislation applies to every legal problem in the area addressed by the legislation. This differs from the legal systems based on the civil law tradition derived from Roman law (the use of the term civil law also refers to non-criminal laws, as discussed below, and the two uses of the term are distinct). In a civil law system, legislatures develop codes that are presumed to apply to all situations relevant to the code, and courts are employed only to adjudicate claims. The only state in the United States that does not consider itself a "common law state" is Louisiana, which adopted the civil law tradition based on its roots in French law. Accordingly, the codes (legislation) in that state are somewhat different than those in other states.

Courts in the United States follow the doctrine of precedent, which was also adopted from the English common law system. Under this doctrine, courts not only adjudicate the claims of the parties before them, but also establish a precedent that must be followed in future cases. The ruling of a court binds not only itself for future cases, but also any courts under which the court has appellate jurisdiction. Though trial level courts make rulings of law that are binding on future cases, the doctrine of precedent is most important in the legal system at the appellate levels.

### Publication of Case Law

Unlike statutes, cases are usually not available in a subject matter arrangement. When a case is first published, it is issued as a "slip opinion," named as such because these are printed on unbound sheets of paper. These opinions are compiled, and eventually published in bound case reporters. Cases from the U.S. Supreme Court and from courts in many jurisdictions are contained in reporters published by government bodies, and are called official reporters. These cases and other cases are also published in the National Reporter System, originally created by West Publishing Company (now West Group) in 1879. Case reporters in this system include state cases, federal cases, and cases from specialized tribunals, such as the bankruptcy courts. Cases may be readily located by finding their citation in the National Reporter System, or in another case reporter. An example of such a citation is "Roe v. Wade, 93 S. Ct. 705 (1973)." "Roe v. Wade" refers to the names of the parties of the case; "93" refers to the volume of the reporter; "S. Ct." is an abbreviation for Supreme Court Reporter; "705" refers to the page in the reporter where the case begins; and "(1973)" refers to year the case was decided.

Cases from all three levels of the federal judicial system are published. With few exceptions, only appellate court opinions from state courts are published. Unlike appellate courts, state trial judges seldom issue formal legal opinions about their cases, although rulings of law may be available in the record of the trial court. Most legal research in case law focuses on location of appellate court decisions.

### Reading a Judicial Opinion

Like other types of law, reading and understanding the meaning of a judicial opinion is more of an art than a science. The opinion of the case includes the court's reasoning in deciding a case, and is binding on future courts only if a majority of the court deciding the case joins the opinion (in which case the opinion is called the majority opinion). If an opinion is written in support of the court's judgment, but is not joined by a majority of justices, then the opinion is termed a plurality. Plurality opinions are not binding on future courts, but may be highly persuasive since they support the judgment of the court. Some justices may agree with the judgment, but may not agree with the majority opinion. These justices may write concurring opinions that state their reasons in support of the judgment. These opinions have no precedential value, but may be persuasive in future cases. Similarly, justices who disagree with the judgment, the opinion, or both, write dissenting opinions that argue against the judgment or majority opinion.

Some components of a majority opinion are binding on future courts, while others are not. The actual holding or reason for deciding (traditionally referred to as the ratio decidendi) provides the rule of law that is binding precedent in future cases. By comparison, dictum is the portion of an opinion that is not essential to a court's holding, and is not binding on future courts. Dicta may include background information about the holding, or may include the judge's personal comments about the reasoning for the holding. Dicta may be highly persuasive and may alter the holdings of future cases.

## Administrative Law and Procedure

### Creation and Empowerment of Government Agencies

Although the branches of government are primarily responsible for the development of law and resolution of disputes, much of the responsibility of the administration of government has been delegated to government agencies. While branches of government may not delegate essential government functions to agencies, agencies may administer government programs, and promulgate and enforce regulations. When a legislature creates a government agency, it does so through the passage of an enabling statute, which also describes the specific powers delegated to the agency. The Administrative Procedure Act (APA) governs agency action at the federal level, and state counterparts to the APA govern state agencies.

### Types of Government Agencies

Some government agencies are formed to carry out government programs, but do not promulgate regulations that carry the force of law. A number of these agencies have been established to administer such programs as highway construction, education, public housing, and similar functions. Other government agencies promulgate rules and regulations that govern a particular area of law. Examples of regulatory agencies include the Environmental Protection Agency and Nuclear Regulatory Commission, both of which promulgate regulations that are similar in function to legislation. Legislatures also create agencies that resolve dispute among parties, similar to the function of a judicial body. Agency decisions are usually referred to as agency adjudications. Examples of agencies that adjudicate claims are the National Labor Relations Board and Securities and Exchange Commission.

### Agency Rulemaking

Most agencies that have regulatory power promulgate regulations through a process called notice and comment rulemaking. Before a regulatory agency can promulgate a rule, it must provide notice to the public. Federal agencies provide notice in the Federal Register, a daily government publication that provides the text of proposed and final agency rules. After considering comments from the public and making additional considerations, the agency may issue a final, binding rule. The promulgation of a final rule can take months, or may take years, to complete. State agencies must follow similar procedures, including publication of proposed rules in a publication analogous to the Federal Register. Agency rules are functionally equivalent to statutes. Federal agency rules currently in force are published in a subject matter arrangement in the Code of Federal Regulations. Each state publishes its rules in force in a state administrative code.

Some agencies at the state and federal levels are required to follow more formal procedures. Agencies may not exceed the power delegated by a respective legislature, and may adopt rules without following the proper procedures provided in the enabling legislation or legislation governing administrative procedures.

### Agency Adjudications

Agencies with power to adjudicate claims operate similarly to a court. Such an agency considers evidence presented in a hearing, and makes a final, binding decision based on an application of the law to the facts in a case. An agency that adjudicates a claim must maintain a record of the hearing, and parties are generally able to seek judicial review of a decision, much like judicial review of a lower court decision. A court may overrule an agency decision if the agency acted in an arbitrary or capricious manner, made a decision unsupported by substantial evidence, or made a decision unsupported by the facts presented to the agency.

## Relationship Among Various Laws and Other Authority

Laws in the United States do not exist in a vacuum, and determining the appropriate outcome of a case may require consultation with several different types of laws. A single case may be governed by application of a statute, an administrative regulation, and cases interpreting the statute and regulation. Understanding the application of laws usually requires an understanding of the nature of legal authority.

Any authority emanating from an official government entity acting in its lawmaking capacity is referred to as primary authority, and this authority is what is binding on a particular case. Primary authority can be subdivided into two types: primary mandatory authority and primary persuasive authority. Primary mandatory authority is law that is binding in a particular jurisdiction. For example, a Fifth Circuit Court of Appeals decision is primary mandatory authority in Texas, Mississippi, and Louisiana, since the Fifth Circuit governs these states. By comparison, primary authority that is not binding in a particular jurisdiction is referred to as primary persuasive authority. It is considered persuasive because though such authority does not bind a decision-maker in a jurisdiction, the decision-maker may nevertheless be persuaded to act in a familiar fashion as the authority from outside the jurisdiction. In the example above, a Fifth Circuit decision in a court in California would be considered primary persuasive authority, and could influence the California tribunal in its decision-making.

A second type of authority—secondary authority—may also be helpful in determining the appropriate application of the law. Secondary authority includes a broad array of sources, including treatises (a term used for law book); law review articles, which are usually written by law professors, judges, or expert practitioners; legal encyclopedias, which provide an overview of the law; and several other items that provide commentary about the law. An individual who is not trained in the law (and in many cases those who are trained in the law) should ordinarily begin his or her legal research by consulting such authority to gain a basic understanding of the law that applies in a particular situation.

A final consideration that cannot be overlooked is that the law constantly changes. If a legal researcher comes across literature describing the law in a given area, he or she must always verify that the discussion in the literature reflects the current state of the law. Legislatures and agencies constantly add new laws, and revise and amend existing laws. Similarly, courts routinely overrule previous decisions and may rule that a statute or regulation is not valid under a relevant constitutional provision. Updating legal authority involves a process of consulting supplements and other resources, and is necessary to ensure that an individual knows the current state of the law.

# FIRST AMENDMENT LAW

## CENSORSHIP

*Sections within this essay:*

## Background

"Congress shall make no law respecting an establishment of religion, or prohibiting the free exercise thereof; or abridging the freedom of speech, or of the press; or the right of the people peaceably to assemble, and to petition the Government for a redress of grievances." Despite the guarantee implicit in the words of the First Amendment to the U.S. Constitution, there have been many attempts in the ensuing two centuries to censor or ban speech, both in print and in other media.

Censorship is at best problematic and at worst dangerous when it tries to silence the voice of the powerless at the behest of the powerful. History has shown that power and influence are not reliable guides for judgment when it comes to information. The Nazi government in Germany in the 1930s and 1940s, and the governments of the Soviet Union and the People's Republic of China, have shown the world what happens when large, powerful nations choose to deprive their own citizens of knowledge and a voice. In the United States, Americans pride themselves on freedom of speech and freedom of the press—but many of them have experienced censorship. Boards of education frequently try to ban certain books from their school districts; television and radio stations ban certain programming; and newspapers may alter certain stories. The reasons for censorship are numerous, but they all share a common goal: protection. Perhaps children are the most frequently protected group. Books are banned when they depict violence or sexually suggestive material. Motion pictures are rated to protect young people from sex and violence on the screen. Internet resources are filtered to ensure that students will be unable to log into pornographic web sites.

Society, and often the courts, have determined that some information does need to be censored, and that not all media deserve First Amendment protection. Deciding which materials fall into which categories is a subject of ongoing debate.

## Early History

Censorship laws existed in ancient Rome and Greece more than 2,500 years ago; ancient societies in the Middle East and China also had censorship regulations. The role of censorship was to establish moral standards for the general population; civilizations that exercised it saw censorship as a means of helping the people by providing them with guidance.

The invention of movable type in the middle of the fifteenth century revolutionized the printing industry; it made more books available and helped literacy spread beyond just the most educated in society. A more literate public meant more need for censorship. The Roman Catholic Church released a list of Prohibited Books, or *Index Librorum Prohibitorum*, in 1559, the first of 20 such lists (the last was issued in 1948). This list included books deemed by the Church to be heretical. Authors such as Galileo were denounced, and some authors (such as Sir Thomas More) were put to death. Prohibitions were not only religious; in 1563, Charles IX of France issued a decree that all printed material required his special permission.

Nonetheless, it became harder to suppress information, and by the end of the seventeenth century there was a movement toward freedom of speech and the press. Sweden established a law guaranteeing freedom of the press in 1766, followed by Denmark in 1770. The newly formed United States put the First Amendment into its Constitution in 1787, and the French government moved in the same direction in 1789 at the dawn of its revolution.

## Censorship in the United States

The First Amendment has long been the standard by which the U.S. government has measured the freedom of individuals to speak or write their opinions without fear of reprisals. That freedom is not absolute; one of the most commonly cited examples warns that people do not have the right to walk into a crowded theater and shout, "Fire!" thus causing people to panic and trample over each other. Through the decaded the government has attempted to determine legitimate curbs to this freedom as opposed to arbitrary or discriminatory prohibitions.

### Book Censorship

Censorship existed in the United States from its beginnings, the existence of the First Amendment notwithstanding. But although there were federal anti-obscenity laws, censorship itself was not mandated by federal or state governments. What codified censorship was the 1873 Comstock Act, which called for the banning of literature deemed sexually arousing, even indirectly. The man for whom the act is named, Anthony Comstock, was the leader of the New York Society for the Suppression of Vice and a special agent for both the U.S. Post Office and the New York state prosecutor's office. The Comstock Act banned the mailing, importation, and transportation of any printed material (even private letters) that contained lewd or lascivious material. It also banned the transport of any sort of contraceptive drug or device, as well as literature describing contraceptive de-

vices. What this meant was that a book that in any way made mention of any sort of birth control could be considered lewd and subject to confiscation. Violators of the Comstock Act (Comstock himself was deputized and arrested many violators himself) faced steep fines and even time in prison.

Other books that were affected by the Comstock Act included *The Decameron* (written by Giovanni Boccaccio in the fourteenth century), Tolstoy's *Kreutzer Sonata,* Hemingway's *For Whom the Bell Tolls,* and D.H. Lawrence's *Lady Chatterley's Lover.*

In Boston, the Watch and Ward Society, which had long championed against what it deemed indecent, organized book bans in the 1920s, which gave the language the phrase "Banned in Boston." Groups such as the American Civil Liberties Union (ACLU) fought to challenge the censorship laws. These groups were successful on several occasions, winning the right in 1933 for James Joyce's *Ulysses* to be imported into the United States and in 1960 when federal courts allowed the full version of *Lady Chatterley's Lover* to be published here.

Beginning in the 1950s, a series of U.S. Supreme Court cases helped change the scope of censorship laws in the United States.

*Butler v. State of Michigan.* The Butler case determined in 1957 that adult reading material did not need to be restricted to protect minors. It struck down a Michigan law that outlawed any printed material with obscene language (which could corrupt children), noting that the material's existence by itself was not a danger to young readers and the law was too sweeping. Justice Felix Frankfurter wrote that the Michigan law limited the entire adult population to "reading only what is fit for children."

*Roth v. United States.* Also decided in 1957, this case upheld a conviction for mailing materials that were deemed to be "in the prurient interest." Although *Roth* made clear that obscene material was not subject to First Amendment protection, the court did note that material that has *some* redeeming social value or importance. (Obscenity, wrote Justice William Brennan, was "utterly" without such value.)

*Jacobellis v. Ohio.* This case was decided in 1964. It held that "national" standards for obscenity determined "community" standards. A Cleveland Heights, Ohio theater had shown a foreign film with an explicit sex scene. The theater owner was arrested for violating the state obscenity statute, but the Supreme

Court held that since the film in question had been screened across the country without incident, it was not obscene. "The Court has explicitly refused to tolerate a result whereby 'the constitutional limits of free expression in the Nation would vay within state lines,'" wrote Justice William Brennan. "We see even less justification for allowing such limits with town or county lines." *Jacobellis* was the case in which Justice Potter Stewart made his famous observation about obscenity: "I know it when I see it."

*Memoirs v. Attorney General of Massachusetts.* This case, decided in 1966, reversed a state court's ruling that the 1749 book *Memoirs of a Woman of Pleasure,* commonly known as *Fanny Hill,* was obscene. The reason, explained the court, was that the book, despite its content (much of which could be construed as offensive) geared toward prurient interest, the book was not "utterly" without redeeming social value. To be obscene, the book would have to have prurient appeal, offensiveness, *and* utter lack of redeeming social value.

*Ginzburg v. United States.* This case was decided in 1966, and the court upheld the conviction of a publisher who had marketed and mailed three sexually explicit publications. The reason the court reached this decision was that the material, though potentially not patently obscene, had been marketed solely as erotic material and thus could be reasonably construed on that basis to be obscene.

*Ginsberg v. State of New York.* In this 1968 case, the Supreme Court upheld a statute that a state can create more stringent obscenity standards for minors than for adults. The defendant had sold two adult magazines to a 16-year-old boy, and argued that the anti-obscenity statute violated that minor boy's right to read under the First Amendment. The court found that there was no violation of the child's rights because the material in question was obscene for children.

*Miller v. California.* This landmark 1973 case established a new definition for obscenity, replacing the standard set by *Roth.* The defendant had been convicted under California's obscenity law for mailing sexually explicit advertisements to sell adult books and films. An appellate court uphend the conviction, but the Supreme Court vacated the appellate court's decision and sent it back for reconsideration using the new definition. Chief Justice Warren Burger, writing for the majority, outlined the definition: "The basic guidelines . . . must be: (a) whether the average person applying contemporary community standards would find that the work, taken as a whole, appeals to a prurient interest; (b) whether the work depicts or describes, in a patently offensive way, sexual conduct specifically defined by the applicable state law; and (c) whether the work, taken as a whole, lacks serious literary, artistic, political, or scientific value."

*Board of Education v. Pico.* Decided in 1982 by a 5-4 majority, this case ruled that school boards do not have the absolute right to remove books from school libraries. A school board in Island Trees, New York removed several books from the school library shelves, including *The Fixer* by Bernard Malamud, *Slaughterhouse Five* by Kurt Vonnegut, *Best Short Stories of Negro Writers* (edited by Langston Hughes), *A Hero Ain't Nothin' But A Sandwich* by Alice Childress, and *A Reader for Writers* (edited by Jerome Archer). The school board, when challenged about its decision, called the books "anti-American, anti-Christian, anti-Semitic, and just plain filthy." Although it was determined by a separate committee that several of the books should be replaced, but the board refused. A group of students sued the district.

Justice William Brennan wrote that "the special characteristics of the school library make that environment especially appropriate for the recognition of First Amendment rights of students." While the court noted that school boards do have discretion in what books to acquire for the school, and it could reject any works deemed to be "pervasively vulgar."

School boards continue to attempt to ban books, with classics such as *The Adventures of Huckleberry Finn* and *Of Mice and Men* among the most frequently challenged, according to the American Library Association. In the early years of the twenty-first century, the Harry Potter series of books, which tell the story of a young aspiring wizard and his adventures in wizard school, have become a focal point for many who oppose the focus on wizardry and magic.

### Music Censorship

Musical lyrics have been the subject of censorship through the years, particularly those that were deemed sexually suggestive or violent. Censorship has affected the works and performances of such disparate artists as Cole Porter, Frank Zappa, Bruce Springsteen, Rosemary Clooney, the Carpenters, Sheena Easton, Perry Como, and Bob Dylan.

In 1954, for example, Cole Porter's "I Get A Kick Out of You" was edited for radio broadcast to remove the line "I get no kick from cocaine" (it was replaced with "I get perfume from Spain"); the American Broadcasting Company bans Rosemary Clooney's performance of "Mambo Italiano," citing inadequate standards for "good taste"; and police in Long Beach, California and Memphis, Tennessee confiscated jukeboxes thought to contain songs with suggestive lyrics (the owners were fined as well).

Sometimes, the censors' rationale had nothing to do with the lyrics. In 1968, a radio station in El Paso, Texas banned the playing of songs performed by Bob Dylan because his lyrics were hard to understand. (The did not ban performances of his lyrics when sung by other artists.) And in 1990, a radio station in Nebraska led a boycott against the music of k.d. lang—not because of what she sang, but because she was a vegetarian.

Although the music industry has frequently come under attack by opponents they deemed too reactionary or literal-minded, mainstream concerns about lyrics were being expressed more openly. In 1985, twenty wives of politicians and business leaders in Washington, D.C. (including Tipper Gore, wife of then-senator Al Gore) formed the Parents Music Resource Center (PMRC). The group's goal was to lobby the music industry for a ratings system for music similar to that used in the film industry, the printing of lyrics on album covers, and an overall reassessment of musicians and lyricists whose work could be deemed violent or explicitly sexual. In 1990, a parental warning sticker system was adopted by the recording industry that would place warning stickers on records deemed explicit. A year later, Wal-Mart, the nation's largest retailer, announced that it would refuse to stock any stickered albums in its stores. In 1995, former U.S. education secretary William Bennett and national Political Congress of Black Women chair C. Delores Tucker addressed a shareholders' meeting of Time-Warner, Inc., deploring rap music lyrics that promoted violence or that degraded women.

After the attacks in New York and Washington, D.C., on September 11, 2001, Clear Channel Communications (the largest broadcast station owner in the United States) released a list of 150 suggested songs it deemed "lyrically questionable" because they had metaphoric references to planes, crashing, and death. The list included Steve Miller, s"Jet Airliner," the Dave Matthews Band's "Crash Into Me," Pat Benatar's "Hit Me with Your Best Shot," and the Jerry Lee Lewis song "Great Balls of Fire."

### Press Censorship

The concept of "freedom of the press" was established in New York when it was still a British colony. In 1734, John Peter Zenger, publisher of the *New York Weekly Journal,* was charged with libel against colonial governor William Cosby when he printed articles critical of Cosby's decision to remove the chief justice of New York from office. He was imprisoned for nine months before his case went to trial. Philadelphia attorney Andrew Hamilton argued that statements could not be libelous if they were true. Although English law did not accept truth as a defense to libel, Hamilton pressed the issue with the jury, which found Zenger not guilty on August 4, 1735. This case set a precedent that truth is an absolute defense to libel.

Over the years, freedom of the press has been an important element of American society. Newspapers have traditionally been given considerable leeway in what they publish, and there has never been a shortage of opinions expressed in print in the United States. Nonetheless, censorship is hardly unknown in the press, or in broadcast news programs.

Often, the press censorship is voluntary. In times of war, for example, the press is careful about publishing material that could provide enemy forces with sensitive information about U.S. troops. On a more personal level, public figures were long afforded the courtesy of not having their private lives printed in newspapers or broadcast through other media. President Franklin D. Roosevelt could not stand unassisted after his 1921 bout with polio, but during his presidency the press voluntarily refrained from publishing photographs or releasing film footage of Roosevelt being assisted or using a wheelchair. (As the twentieth century progressed, this sort of courtesy eroded steadily, which sometimes may have given the public more information than it wanted about the private lives of public figures.)

Also, the press and broadcast media have often felt compelled to be sensitive to advertisers and sponsors. There are countless examples of brave publications running unsympathetic stories about advertisers, who would promptly cancel all future advertising with the offending publication. And there are examples of publications refusing to run stories that could offend a potential advertiser. But these are not examples of government-sanctioned censorship.

That said, there have been charges of government censorship over the years from the press, particularly during war time. One of the most noteworthy examples comes from the Iraq War, which began in March 2003. Not long after the war began, the Pentagon issued an order banning the release of photographs of flag-draped military coffins returning from the battle zone. (The ban had actually been in effect for several years before the war but not enforced.) Proponents of the ban argued that publishing the photos did a disservice to the privacy of the fallen soldiers and their families. Opponents of the ban countered that it was nothing more than a public relations ploy to minimize the true scope of American war casualties.

The Freedom of Information Act (FOIA), enacted in 1966, establishes the public's right to obtain information from any agency of the federal government. Any group or individual (foreign nationals as well as American citizens) can file a request. Each government agency is required by law to provide the public with information on how to file FOIA requests. There are exemptions to FOIA, including national security information, internal personnel information, confidential business information, inter- and intra-agency confidential communications, law enforcement records, financial institutions, and geological information. FOIA was amended in 1996 to allow increased access to electronic information.

## Electronic Censorship

As a resource for information, the Internet has been both exciting and exasperating for precisely the same reason: the volume of unrestricted material that can be accessed instantly from virtually anywhere in the world. This means that inaccurate information can be distributed as quickly and easily as carefully researched material. It also means that offensive material, including pornography, can be posted and accessed. Balancing the First Amendment right to free speech with the need to protect against unprotected material has been a key focus of the U.S. government since the 1990s.

In 1996, Congress passed the Communications Decency Act (CDA), which prohibited the posting of materials deemed "indecent" or "patently offensive." There were already laws prohibiting child pornography and obscenity; CDA went further and ultimately prohibited what opponents claimed was protected speech under the First Amendment. The U.S. Supreme Court unanimously struck down CDA in 1997, claiming that its reach was too broad.

Congress passed the Child Online Protection Act (COPA) in 1998 and the Children's Internet Protec-

tion Act (CIPA) in 2000. COPA established criminal penalties for any one who distributed indecent online material to minors, and CIPA required libraries and schools to place filters on their computers or face the loss of federal funding. COPA was challenged in the courts and in 2003 the Third Circuit Court of Appeals found that is was unconstitutional. The U.S. Supreme court upheld that decision in 2004 by a 5-4 margin. As for CIPA, it withstood a challenge when the Supreme Court found it constitutional by a 6-3 margin, but a plurality of the justices noted that the filtering systems needed to be easy to disable for adults who wish to use public library computers.

First Amendment arguments have also allowed unsolicited e-mail (better known as spam) to clog the e-mail boxes of millions of individuals, not to mention commercial, corporate, and even government e-mail accounts. Proponents of spam claim that it is the electronic equivalent of bulk mail and is protected speech. Opponents claim that spam is far more insidious because many spammers use phony e-mail addresses and subject lines, making it impossible to contact the source to ask to be removed from the mailing list. (Experts on spam advise against sending a reply to "opt-out" links because this merely assures the spammer that the sender's address is active.) In December 2003 President George W. Bush signed the CAN-SPAM Act, which requires all commercial e-mailers to provide an opportunity to opt out, prohibits false headers and subject lines, and imposes civil penalties on offenders. Though well-intentioned, CAN-SPAM did little to make a real impact, in part because it is easy for spammers to find electronic loopholes that allow them to remain uncaught. The Coalition Against Unsolicited Commercial E-mail (CAUCE) is a volunteer nonprofit organization that works to find ways to help reduce spam. Information on consumer guidelines, and on the group's progress, can be found at www.cauce.org.

## Additional Resources

*Banned in the USA: A Reference Guide to Book Censorship in Schools and Public Libraries,* Herbert N. Foerstel, Greenwood Press, 2002.

*Censorship in America: A Reference Handbook,* Mary Hull, ABC-CLIO, 1999.

*The Language Police: How Pressure Groups Restrict What Students Learn,* Diane ravitch, Knopf, 2003.

*Parental Advisory: Music Censorship in America,* Eric Nuzum, Perennial, 2001.

## Organizations

### American Civil Liberties Union (ACLU)

125 Broad Street, 18th Floor
New York, NY 10004 USA
Phone: (212) 344-3005
URL: http://www.aclu.org/
Primary Contact: Anthony D. Romero, Executive
Director

### American Library Association

50 East Huron Street
Chicago, IL 60611 USA
Phone: (800) 545-2433
URL: http://www.ala.org
Primary Contact: Keith Michael Fiels, Executive
Director

### Fairness and Accuracy in Reporting (FAIR)

112 West 27th Street
New York, NY 10001 USA
Phone: (212) 633-6700
Fax: (212) 727-7668
URL: http://www.fair.org

### Federal Communications Commission (FCC)

445 12th Street, SW
Washington, DC 20554 USA
Phone: (866) 225-5322
Fax: (866) 418-0232
E-Mail: fccinfo@fcc.gov
URL: http://www.fcc.gov
Primary Contact: Kevin J. Martin, Chair

# HEALTHCARE

## DOCTOR-PATIENT CONFIDENTIALITY

*Sections within this essay:*

- Background
- Key Points
- The Doctor-Patient Relationship
- Doctor-Patient Privilege
- Constitutional Right to Privacy
- Waiver of Confidentiality or Privilege
- Select Applications
    - Medical Records
    - Death Certificates
    - Duty to Warn Others of Medical Conditions
- Select State Disclosure Laws
- Additional Resources

## Background

The concept of "doctor-patient confidentiality" derives from English **common law** and is codified in many states' statutes. It is based on ethics, not law, and goes at least as far back as the Roman Hippocratic Oath taken by physicians. It is different from "doctor-patient privilege," which is a legal concept. Both, however, are called upon in legal matters to establish the extent by which ethical duties of confidentiality apply to legal privilege. Legal privilege involves the right to withhold **evidence** from **discovery** and/or the right to refrain from disclosing or divulging information gained within the context of a "special relationship." Special relationships include those be-

tween doctors and patients, attorneys and clients, priests and confessors or confiders, guardians and their wards, etc.

The Oath of Hippocrates, traditionally sworn to by newly licensed physicians, includes the promise that "Whatever, in connection with my professional service, or not in connection with it, I see or hear, in the life of men, which ought not to be spoken of abroad, I will not divulge, as reckoning that all such should be kept secret." The laws of Hippocrates further provide, "Those things which are sacred, are to be imparted only to sacred persons; and it is not lawful to impart them to the profane until they have been initiated into the mysteries of the science."

Doctor-patient confidentiality stems from the special relationship created when a prospective patient seeks the advice, care, and/or treatment of a physician. It is based upon the general principle that individuals seeking medical help or advice should not be hindered or inhibited by fear that their medical concerns or conditions will be disclosed to others. Patients entrust personal knowledge of themselves to their physicians, which creates an uneven relationship in that the vulnerability is one-sided. There is generally an expectation that physicians will hold that special knowledge in confidence and use it exclusively for the benefit of the patient.

The professional duty of confidentiality covers not only what patients may reveal to doctors, but also what doctors may independently conclude or form an opinion about, based on their **examination** or **assessment** of patients. Confidentiality covers all medical records (including x-rays, lab-reports, etc.) as well as communications between patient and doctor, and it generally includes communications between the patient and other professional staff working with the doctor.

The duty of confidentiality continues even after patients stop seeing or being treated by their doctors. Once doctors are under a duty of confidentiality, they cannot divulge any medical information about their patients to third persons without patient consent. There are, however, exceptions to this rule.

## Key Points

- There is no duty of confidentiality owed unless a bona-fide doctor-patient relationship exists or existed

- The scope of the duty of doctor-patient confidentiality, as well as the existence of a doctor-patient legal privilege, varies from state to state. No federal law governs doctor-patient confidentiality or privilege

- Generally, what is confidential is information that is learned or gained by a doctor, during or as a result of the doctor's communications with examination of you, or medical assessment of the patient

- The duty of confidentiality continues even after the patient stops seeing or being treated by the doctor

- The duty of confidentiality is not absolute. Doctors may divulge or disclose personal information, against the patient's will, under very limited circumstances

## The Doctor-Patient Relationship

There must be a bona fide "doctor-patient relationship" between individuals and a physician before any duty of confidentiality is created. Generally speaking, individuals must voluntarily seek advice or treatment from the doctor, and have an expectation that the communication will be held in confidence. This expectation of confidentiality does not need to be expressed. It is implied from the circumstances.

If individuals meet a doctor at a party, and in the course of "small-talk" conversation, they ask the doctor for an opinion regarding a medical question that relates to them, the doctor's advice would most likely not be considered confidential, nor would the doctor be considered "the individuals doctor." Likewise, if individuals send an e-mail to an "Ask the Doctor"

website on the Internet, the communication would not be considered confidential, nor would the person who responded to the e-mail be considered he sender's doctor. No doctor-patient relationship was established, and no duty is owed.

If individuals are examined by a physician at the request of a third party (such as an insurance company or their employer), no matter how thorough or extensive the examination, or how friendly the doctor, there is generally no physician-patient relationship and no duty of confidentiality is owed to the patients. This is because they did not seek the physician's advice or treatment, and the relationship is at "arm's-length."

In many states, the privilege is limited to professional relationships between licensed doctors of medicine and their patients. Other states extend the privilege to chiropractors, psychologists, therapists, etc.

## Doctor-Patient Privilege

Once a bona-fide doctor-patient relationship is established, the duty of confidentiality "attaches," and in many states, the doctor can invoke a legal privilege, on the patient's behalf, when asked to disclose or divulge information the doctor may have or know about the patient.

Federal Rule of Evidence (FRE) 501 provides that any permissible privilege "shall be governed by the principles of common law" as interpreted by federal courts. However, in civil actions governed by state law, the privilege of a witness is also determined by the laws of that state. Most states recognize some form of doctor-patient privilege by express law (**statute**), but over time, there have been many exceptions that have chipped away the use or scope of the privilege.

In recent years, many courts have held that doctors also owe duties to protect non-patients who may be harmed by patients. For example, without a patient's permission or knowledge, doctors may warn others or the police if the patient is mentally unstable, potentially violent, or has threatened a specific person. In some states, the duty to report or warn others "trumps" the right to confidentiality or privileged communication with a doctor. Courts will decide these matters by balancing the sanctity of the confidentiality against the foreseeability of harm to a third party.

## Constitutional Right to Privacy

The fundamental right to privacy, guaranteed by the Fifth and Fourteenth Amendments to the U. S. Constitution, protects against unwarranted invasions of privacy by federal or state entities, or arms thereof. As early as in *Roe v. Wade,* 410 U. S. 113 (1973), the U. S. Supreme Court acknowledged that the doctor-patient relationship is one which evokes constitutional rights of privacy. But even that right is not absolute and must be weighed against the state or federal interest at stake.

For example, in *Whalen v. Roe,* 429 U.S. 589 (1977), a group of physicians joined patients in a lawsuit challenging the constitutionality of a New York statute that required physicians to report to state authorities the identities of patients receiving Schedule II drugs (controlled substances). The physicians alleged that such information was protected by the doctor-patient confidentiality, while the patients alleged that such disclosure was an invasion of their constitutional right to privacy. The Supreme Court did not disagree with the lower court's finding that "the intimate nature of a patient's concern about his bodily ills and the medication he takes . . . are protected by the constitutional right to privacy." However, the high court concluded (after balancing the state's interests) that "Requiring such disclosures to representatives of the State having responsibility for the health of the community, does not automatically amount to an impermissible invasion of privacy."

In the *Whalen* case (decided in 1977), the U. S. Supreme Court had (prophetically) added a note about massive computerized databanks of personal information. Said the Court:

"A final word about issues we have not decided. We are not unaware of the threat to privacy implicit in the accumulation of vast amounts of personal information in computerized data banks or other massive government files . . . The right to collect and use such data for public purposes is typically accompanied by a concomitant **statutory** or regulatory duty to avoid unwarranted disclosures . . . We . . . need not, and do not, decide any question which might be presented by the unwarranted disclosure of accumulated private data—whether intentional or unintentional—or by a system that did not contain comparable security provisions. We simply hold that this record [*Whalen*] does not establish an invasion of any right or liberty protected by the Fourteenth Amendment."

## Waiver of Confidentiality or Privilege

A privilege belongs to the patient, not the doctor. Generally, only a patient may waive the privilege. A patient's written consent is needed before a doctor can release any information about the patient. But there are other ways in which a patient may "waive" the privilege of confidentiality. For example, if a patient brings a friend into the examination or consultation with the doctor, the friend may be forced to **testify** as to what transpired and what was said. (On the other hand, nurses or medical assistants in the room are "extensions" of the doctor for purposes of confidentiality and are covered by the privilege.) The patient may also waive the privilege by testifying about his or her communications with the doctor or about his or her physical condition at the time.

Another common way in which a patient waives the confidentiality of the privilege is by filing a lawsuit or claim for **personal injury**. By doing so, the patient has put his or her physical condition "at issue" in the lawsuit. Therefore, the law presumes that the patient has waived all confidentiality regarding his or her medical condition, and there is an implied authorization to the patient's doctor for disclosure of all relevant information. If a patient fails to object to a doctor's **testimony**, the patient has waived the privilege as well.

## Select Applications

### Medical Records

In the past, physicians could physically secure and shield personal medical records from disclosure, absent consent from their patients. Electronic databanks changed all that (as foretold by the Supreme Court in *Whalen,* above). Patchy and varied state laws involving doctor-patient confidentiality left much to be desired. With the passage of the Health Insurance Portability and Accountability Act of 1996 (HIPAA) (which encouraged electronic transmission of patient data), Congress passed concurrent legislation for uniform protection of medical records and personal information. In December 2000, the Department of Health and Human Services (HHS) published its Privacy Rule (65 Fed. Reg. 82462), which became effective on April 14, 2001. The regulation covers health plans, health-care clearinghouses, and health-care providers that bill and transfer funds electronically. The regulation mandates a final compliance date of April 14, 2003 (small health plans have until April 14, 2004 to comply.) The Privacy Rule includes provisions for the following:

- Ensuring patient access to medical records, ability to get copies and/or request amendments

- Obtaining patient consent before releasing information. Health care providers are required to obtain consent before sharing information regarding treatment, payment, and health care operations Separate patient authorizations must be obtained for all non-routine disclosures and non-health related purposes. A history of all non-routine disclosures must be accessible to patients

- Providing recourse for violations through an administrative complaint procedure

### Death Certificates

Under most state laws, birth and death certificates are a matter of public record. The advent of physician-assisted suicides in less than a handful of states (e.g., Oregon) created new concerns for the scope of doctor-patient confidentiality. Some states have addressed this issue by express legislation, e.g., permitting the registration of physician-assisted deaths directly to state offices rather than to local county offices of vital statistics. Others have permitted dual-systems that incorporate specific codes for "cause of death" on public records but more thorough explanations on private state records. Many doctors simply list innocuous language, such as "cardiac-respiratory failure," on public records, and leave blank the secondary or underlying cause. Similar issues of limited disclosure often arise on birth records. In some circumstances, personal details such as **paternity**, marital status, or information regarding a newborn's HIV status may **warrant** the filing of dual records (one requiring more disclosure than the other) for separate purposes and separate viewers, based on a "need to know" criterion.

### Duty to Warn Others of Medical Conditions

Under most state statutes, doctors and health–care providers generally have duties to report incidence of certain sexually transmitted diseases, **child abuse**, communicable diseases, HIV/AIDS, or other conditions deemed to be risks to the health and safety of the public at large. Some states have developed registries to track the incidence of certain conditions, (e.g., certain forms of cancer) that may later help researchers discover causes. In registry cases, personal data about the patients are released only to the necessary local, state, or federal personnel, and the data usually do not contain "patient identifiers."

## Select State Disclosure Laws

ALABAMA: Medical records disclosing "notifiable diseases" (those diseases or illnesses that doctors are required to report to state officials) are strictly confidential. Written consent of patient is required for release of information regarding sexually transmitted disease. (Ch. 22-11A-2, 22).

ALASKA: Mental health records may be disclosed only with patient consent/court order/law enforcement reasons (Ch. 47.30.845). In cases of emergency medical services, records of those treated may be disclosed to specified persons.(Ch. 18.08.086). Express language permits disclosure of financial records of medical assistance beneficiaries to the Dept. of Social Services. (Ch. 47.07.074).

ARIZONA: Statutory privilege for physicians and surgeons (Ch. 12-2235). There are mandatory reporting requirements for malnourishment, physical neglect, **sexual abuse**, non-accidental injury, or other deprivation with intent to cause or allow death of minor children, but the records remain confidential outside judicial matters (Ch. 13-3620). Access to other medical records is by consent or pursuant to exceptions outlined in Ch. 36-664.

ARKANSAS: Arkansas has a special privilege permitting doctors to deny giving patients or their attorneys or guardians certain medical records upon a showing of "detrimentality" (Ch.16-46-106). Otherwise, access by patients and their attorneys are covered under Ch. 23-76-129 and 16-46-106.

CALIFORNIA: California's legal privilege expressly includes psychotherapists and psychiatrists (Section 1010 of Evidence Rules). Patients must expressly waive doctor-patient confidentiality when they become plaintiffs in civil lawsuits (Section 1016 of Evidence Rules). Doctors may withhold certain mental health records from patients if disclosure would have an adverse effect on patient. (H&S Section 1795.12 and.14).

COLORADO: Doctors are permitted to withhold from patients' psychiatric records that would have a significant negative psychological impact; in those cases, doctors may prepare a summary statement of what the records contain (Ch.25-1-801). There are mandatory disclosure requirements for certain diseases (Ch 25-1-122).

CONNECTICUT: There is limited disclosure of mental health records (Ch. 4-105) and limited disclosure to state officials (Ch.53-146h; 17b-225).

DELAWARE: Strict disclosure prohibitions exist about sexually transmitted diseases, HIV infections (Tit. 16-711). No physician-patient privilege exists in child abuse cases (Tit. 16-908).

DISTRICT OF COLUMBIA: D.C. Code 14-307 and 6-2511 address legal privilege of physicians and surgeons and mental health professionals except where they are outweighed by "interests of public justice." Public mental health facilities must release records to patient's attorney or personal physician (21-562).

FLORIDA: Florida Statutes Annotated 455-241 recognizes a psychotherapist-patient privilege. Mental health records may be provided in the form of a report instead of actual annotations (455-241). Patient consent is required for general medical records releases except by **subpoena** or consent to compulsory physical exam pursuant to Civil Rule of Procedure 1.360 (455-241).

GEORGIA: Legal privilege is extended to pharmacists and psychiatrists (Ch. 24-9-21, 9-40). Mandatory disclosure to state officials is required for child abuse and venereal disease. (Ch. 19-7-5; 31-17-2).

HAWAII: Hawaii Revised Statute 325-2 provides for mandatory disclosure to state officials for communicable disease or danger to public health. Names appearing in public studies such as the Hawaii Tumor Registry are confidential and no person who provides information is liable for it (324-11, et seq.).

IDAHO: Physician-patient privilege is found in the Idaho Code 9-203(4). There is mandatory disclosure for child abuse cases within 24 hours (16-1619) and sexually transmitted diseases (39-601). Both doctors and nurses may request protective orders to deny or limit disclosure (9-420).

ILLINOIS: Mandatory disclosure to state officials exists for child abuse and sexually transmitted diseases (325 Illinois Compiled Statutes Annotated 5/4).

INDIANA: Doctor-patient information is protected by Ch.34-1-14-5. Insurance companies may obtain information with written consent (Ch 16-39-5-2). Mandatory disclosure to state officials exists for child abuse and sexually transmitted diseases (31-6-11-3 and 4) (16-41-2-3).

IOWA: Mandatory disclosure to state officials exists of sexually transmitted diseases (Ch. 140.3 and 4).

KANSAS: State law recognizes doctor-patient privilege (Ch. 60-427) and psychologist-patient privilege

(74-5323). Mandatory disclosure of AIDS (65-6002(c) to state health officials is required of AIDS (65-6002(c)).

KENTUCKY: Psychiatrists are included in privilege statute (Ch. 422-330). Either patient or physician may ask for **protective order** (422-315).

LOUISIANA: Louisiana Code of Evidence, Article 510 waives health-care provider-patient privilege in cases or child abuse or molestation. Mandatory disclosure of HIV information is required (Ch.1300-14 and 1300-15).

MAINE: Privilege covers both physicians and psychologists, except in child abuse cases (Ch. 22-4015). Doctors may withhold mental health records if detrimental to patient's health (22-1711). 20-A Maine Revised Statutes Annotated, Section 254, Subsection 5, requires schools to adopt local written policies and procedures.

MARYLAND: Both psychiatrists and psychologists are included in state's privilege statute (Cts. & Jud. Proc. 9-109). Physicians may inform local health officers of needle-sharing partners or sexual partners in cases of transmittable diseases (18-337).

MASSACHUSETTS: Any injury from the discharge of a gun or a burn affecting more than five percent of the body, rape, or sexual **assault** triggers mandatory disclosure law (Ch. 112-12A). No statutory privilege.

MICHIGAN: MCL 600.2157 recognizes a physician-patient privilege. Mandatory disclosure to state officials exists for communicable diseases (MCL.333.5117).

MINNESOTA: Minnesota Statutes Annotated 144.335 authorizes withholding of mental health records if information is detrimental to well-being of patient. Legal privilege expressly includes nurses and psychologists (595-02).

MISSISSIPPI: Mississippi is one of the few states that includes dentists, as well as pharmacists and nurses, in its statutory provisions for privilege (Ch. 13-1-21). Patient **waiver** is implied for mandatory disclosures to state health officials. Peer review boards assessing the quality of care for medical or dental care providers may have access to patient records without the disclosure of patient's identity (41-63-1, 63-3).

MISSOURI: Physicians, surgeons, psychologists, and dentists are included in Missouri's privilege statute (Ch. 491.060).

MONTANA: Doctor-patient privilege is found at Ch.26-1-805, and a psychologist-client privilege is recognized at Ch. 26-1-807. Mandatory Disclosure to state officials is required for sexually transmitted disease. (Ch. 50-18-106).

NEBRASKA: Nebraska Revised Statutes 81-642 requires reporting of patients with cancer for the Dept. of Health's Cancer Registry. The Dept. also maintains a Brain Injury Registry (81-651). Mandatory Disclosure to state officials is required for sexually transmitted disease. (71-503.01).

NEVADA: An express doctor/therapist-patient privilege is recognized under Nevada Statutes (Ch. 49-235 and 248). Mandatory Disclosure to state officials is required for communicable disease. (441A.150).

NEW HAMPSHIRE: The state has a statutorily-recognized doctor-patient privilege (Ch. 329:26) and psychologist-patient privilege (330-A:19). Mandatory Disclosure to state officials is required for communicable disease (141-C:7).

NEW JERSEY: Doctor-patient privilege is found at Ch. 2A:84A-22.1, and a psychologist-client privilege is recognized at Ch. 45:14B-28. Mandatory Disclosure to state officials is required for child abuse (9:6-8.30), pertussis vaccine (26:2N-5), sexually transmitted disease.(26:4-41), or AIDS (26:5C-6).

NEW MEXICO: Doctor-patient privilege (including psychologists) is found in Rules 11-509Ch. 26-1-805 New Mexico, through its 6 N.M. Administrative Code 4.2.3.1.11.3.2(d) requires the supervisory school nurse to develop and implement written policies and procedures for clinical services, including the administration of medication.

NEW YORK: The state includes dentists, as well as doctors and nurses, in its statutory provisions for privilege (Civ. Prac. 4504). Records concerning sexually transmitted disease or **abortion** for minors may not be released, not even to parents (NY Pub. Health 17).

NORTH CAROLINA: North Carolina General Statute 130A-133, et seq. provides for mandatory disclosure to state officials for communicable disease.

NORTH DAKOTA: Statute 31-01-06 and Rule of Evidence No. 503 provides for a physician/psychotherapist-patient privilege. Mandatory Disclosure to state officials is required for child abuse, communicable diseases, or chronic diseases that impact the public (23-07-01, 50-25.1-01).

OHIO: Doctor-patient privilege is found at Ch. 2317-02(B). Mandatory Disclosure to state officials is required for child abuse (2151-421), occupational diseases (3701.25), contagious disease including AIDS (3701.24), or cases to be included on the Cancer Registry (3701.262).

OKLAHOMA: Title 12, Section 2503 and Title 43A, Section 1-109 cover physician and psychotherapist-patient privileges. Mandatory Disclosure to state officials is required for child abuse, and for communicable or venereal diseases (23-07-01, 50-25.1-01).

OREGON: Oregon Revised Statute 146-750 provides for mandatory disclosure of medical records involving suspected violence, and for physical injury with a knife, gun, or other deadly weapon.

PENNSYLVANIA: Pennsylvania has an express physician-patient privilege limited to civil matter only (Title 42-5929).

RHODE ISLAND: Mandatory Disclosure to state officials is required for occupational disease (Ch. 23-5-5), and for communicable or venereal diseases (23-8-1, 23-11-5).

SOUTH CAROLINA: Mandatory Disclosure to state officials is required for sexually transmitted disease (z016744-29-70). There is also express privilege for mental health provider-patient relationships under Ch. 19-11-95.

SOUTH DAKOTA: Physician-patient privilege is expressly recognized in Ch. 19-2-3, but is waived for criminal proceedings or if physical or mental health of person is at issue. Mandatory Disclosure to state officials is required for venereal disease (34-23-2) and for child abuse or neglect (26-8A-3).

TENNESSEE: Tennessee Code Annotated 24-1-207 and 63-11-213 provide express psychiatrist-patient and psychologist-patient privileges, respectively. There are also requirements for mandatory disclosure to state officials for communicable disease (68-5-101) or sexually transmitted diseases (68-10-101).

TEXAS: There are mandatory disclosure requirements for bullet or gunshot wounds (Health & Safety 161.041), certain occupational diseases (Health & Safety 84.003), and certain communicable diseases (Health & Safety 81.041).

UTAH: Utah Code Annotated 78-24-8(4) provides for doctor-patient privilege. There are mandatory disclosure requirements for suspected child abuse (62A-4A-403), and for communicable and infectious diseases (including HIV and AIDS) (26-6-3).

VERMONT: The state includes dentists, doctors, nurses, and mental health professionals in its statutory provisions for privilege (Title 12-1612). Records concerning sexually transmitted disease require reporting (Title 18-1093). Any HIV-related record of testing or counseling may be disclosed only with a court order evidencing "compelling need" (Title 12-1705).

VIRGINIA: Virginia extends legal privilege to any duly licensed practitioner of any branch of the healing arts dealing with the patient in a professional capacity (Ch. 8.01-399). Mental health professionals may withhold records from patient if release would be injurious to patient's health. (8.01-413).

WASHINGTON: Physician-patient privilege is expressly recognized in Ch. 5.60.060 and psychologist-patient privilege is at 18.83.110. Mandatory Disclosure to state officials is required for sexually transmitted disease (70.24.105), child abuse (26.44.030), and tuberculosis (70.28.010).

WEST VIRGINIA: Mandatory Disclosure to state officials is required for venereal, communicable disease (Ch. 16-4-6; 16-2A-5; 26-5A-4), suspected child abuse (49-6A-2), and gunshot and other wounds or burns (61-2-27).

WISCONSIN: Wisconsin Statute 905.04 recognizes privilege for physicians, nurses, and psychologists.

There are mandatory reporting requirements for sexually transmitted diseases (252.11), tuberculosis (252.07), child abuse (48.981) and communicable diseases (252.05).

WYOMING: Rather than expressly create a statutory privilege, Wyoming addresses the matter by limiting doctors' testimony to instances where patients have expressly consented or where patients voluntarily testify themselves on their medical conditions (putting their medical conditions "at issue") (Ch. 1-12-101). There are mandatory reporting requirements for sexually transmitted diseases, child abuse, and communicable diseases (14-3-205, 35-4-130, 35-4-103).

## Additional Resources

"Confidentiality of Death Certificates." *Issues in Law & Medicine,* Winter 1998.

*"Malpractice Consult."* Johnson, Lee J.,. *Medical Economics,* 21 June 1999.

*"Medical Records."* *National Survey of State Law*, 2nd ed., Richard A. Leiter, Ed. Gale:, 1997.

*The Oath of Hippocrates.* Available at http:/www.ftp/ std.com/obi/Hippocrates/Hippocratic.Oath.

*Privacy Rule.* 65 Fed. Reg/ 82462, 2001. Available at http:// gov.news/press/2001pres/01fsprivacy.html.

*"'Shrinking' the Right to Everyman's Evidence: Jaffe in the Military (A)."* Brenner-Beck, Dru, *Air Force Law Review,*, 1998.

*Whalen v. Roe.* 429 U.S. 589 (1977). Available at http:// caselaw.lp.findlaw.com/scripts/getcase.

# HEALTHCARE

## INFORMED CONSENT

*Sections within this essay:*

## Background

The doctrine of "informed consent" within the context of physician-patient relationships goes far back into English **common law**. As early as 1767, doctors were charged with the tort of "battery" (i.e., an unauthorized physical contact with a patient) if they had not gained the consent of their patients prior to performing a surgery or procedure (e.g., *Slater v. Baker and Stapleton*).

Within the United States, the seminal case is generally accepted to be that of *Schloendorff v. Society of New York Hospital,* 211 NY 125 (1914). In that case, involving allegations of unauthorized surgery during an exploratory **examination**, Justice Cardozo's oft-quoted opinion was that "Every human being of adult years and sound mind has a right to determine what shall be done with his own body;

and a surgeon who performs an operation without his patient's consent commits an **assault**, for which he is liable in damages." The court further described the offense as a "trespass" (upon the patient's body and self).

However, requiring that the patient first consented was only half the task. The other half involved the patient's receipt of sufficient information upon which to make a sound decision. Thus, the concept of "informed consent" was developed on the premise of two distinct components: a person's inherent right to determine what happens to his or her body and a doctor's inherent duty to provide a person with enough information so as to ensure that the patient's ultimate decision is based on an appreciable knowledge of his/her condition, the available options for treatment, known risks, prognoses, etc. Importantly, this means that the patient does not have a duty to inquire about risks or options; the duty rests with the treating doctor.

## From Common Law to Statute

Virtually all states recognize, either by express **statute** or common law, the right to receive information about one's medical condition, the treatment choices, risks associated with the treatments, possible outcomes, and prognoses. Generally, the law requires that medical information be in plain language terms that can readily be understood and in sufficient amounts such that a patient is able to make an "informed" decision about his or her health care. If the patient has received this information (and is otherwise competent to receive the information), any consent to treatment that is given will be presumed to be an "informed consent." A doctor who fails to obtain **informed consent** for non-emergency treatment may be charged with a civil and/or criminal offense. In 1972, the American Medical Association (AMA) incorporated the concept of informed consent in its Patient's **Bill of Rights** movement, and almost all state versions of patient rights include provisions related to informed consent.

## Application of the Doctrine

Typically, an "informed consent" issue arises when a patient suffers an injurious or harmful outcome from a treatment, surgery, or procedure. The harmful or injurious outcome does not appear to be the result of any **negligence**. The patient alleges that he or she was never informed of the possibility of occurrence of the resulting injury or harm.

From that point, the causative factor of the harm or injury must be analyzed. If the negative result (injury or harm) was a foreseeable complication or foreseeable risk, but the possibility of its occurrence had not been communicated to the patient in advance, there may be an actionable case of "lack of informed consent."

In order to prevail on a charge that a doctor performed a treatment or procedure without "informed consent," the patient must usually show that, had the patient known of the particular risk, outcome, or alternative treatment allegedly not disclosed, the patient would not have opted for the chosen treatment or procedure and thus, would have avoided the risk. In other words, the patient must show a harmful consequence to the alleged failure to disclose.

There are unique applications of the doctrine of informed consent, such as in cases involving medical subjects for research, patients of minority age, mentally incompetent patients, etc. The basic premises still apply, however, either directly or indirectly through a surrogate decision maker.

### Defenses
Certain injuries or harms may occur inevitably, and even be foreseeable, despite the best of care and the presentation of comprehensive information to the patient regarding options, risks, foreseeable outcomes, and prognoses. In fact, one of the most viable defense to a charge of "lack of informed consent" is that the resulting harm or injury was a "known risk" and that the patient assumed the risk of its occurrence when the patient consented to the surgery, treatment, or procedure. (This would be true if the

patient had been warned of the potential occurrence of the specific harm or injury and chose the surgery, treatment, or procedure anyway.)

Other viable defenses include the unforeseeability of the harm or injury or that its occurrence was so remote that the doctor had no duty to otherwise advise the patient of the possibility of that particular harm or injury. There is no duty to obtain consent in an emergency where attempts to obtain consent would delay vital emergency treatment. Additionally, doctors may withhold information from a patient if, in the doctor's professional judgment, disclosure would be upsetting to the patient or would substantially interfere with effective treatment. This is referred to as "therapeutic privilege."

Finally, a physician may defend that the patient chose not to hear all the information. Some patients do not wish to participate in medical decision-making and simply defer to the physician's best judgment. Under such circumstances, doctors generally have patients sign waivers giving up their rights to full disclosures. If the patient had prior knowledge of the risks (having undergone the surgery or procedure previously), or if the risks are common knowledge (such as pain following suturing a wound), there is generally no duty to repeat or expressly inform of these risks.

## Measuring the Duty to Inform

States are divided in their approach as to how much information a doctor must disclose to a patient in order to facilitate an "informed consent" to the proposed surgery, treatment, or procedure.

### Professional Standard
The professional standard (for judging the scope of a doctor's duty to disclose) is alternately referred to as the "community standard," the "professional community standard," or the "reasonable physician standard." It generally asks: what would a reasonably prudent physician with the same background, training, experience, and practicing in the same community, have disclosed to a patient in the same or similar situation? This standard is the same as that applied to other forms of alleged **medical malpractice**.

### Materiality and Subjective Patient Standards
A significant number of states have employed the use of a standard commonly referred to as the materiality standard. It is alternately referred to as the

"reasonable patient standard," or the "prudent patient standard." It purports to ask: what would a reasonable patient in the same or similar situation need to know in order to make an appropriate decision regarding a proposed surgery, treatment, or procedure? In other words, what information would be "material" to the patient's decision?

Still other jurisdictions have developed a "subjective patient" standard which asks what that particular patient, in his or her own unique set of circumstances and conditions, would need to know, but this has proven to be a hard standard to establish.

## Select State Law Provisions Regarding Disclosure Requirements

ALASKA: Alaska has adopted a reasonable patient (materiality) standard (Alaska Stat. Ann. 09.55.556(a) but articulates four specific defenses that may be raised on the part of the physician.

ARKANSAS: Arkansas Stat. Ann. 16-114-206(b) provides that "the plaintiff shall have the burden of proving... that the medical care provider did not supply that type of information regarding the treatment, procedure, or surgery as would customarily have been given to a patient... by other medical care providers with similar training and experience."

CALIFORNIA: California generally applies the professional community standard, as developed by **case law**. *Cobbs v. Grant,* 8 Cal 3d 229 (1972).

DELAWARE: Delaware applies the professional community standard. Del. Code Ann. Title 18-6852.

FLORIDA: Florida Statute Section 766.103 expressly adopts the professional community standard, providing that actions are barred if "the action of the [physician] in obtaining the consent of the patient... was in accordance with an accepted standard of medical practice among members of the medical profession with similar training and experience in the same or similar medical community."

GEORGIA: Georgia Code Ann. 31-9-6.1 follows a professional community standard but requires that the harm caused from the alleged failures to disclose be associated with "the material risks generally recognized and accepted by the reasonably prudent physician."

HAWAII: Hawaii Rev. Stat. 671-3(a) establishes a board of medical examiners to develop standards en-

suring that a "patient's consent to treatment is an informed consent." It further provides that the standards may be **admissible** in court as **evidence** of the standard of care required of health care providers.

IDAHO: Idaho Code Section 39-4301 et seq., specifically 39-4304, expressly adopts the objective professional community standard.

ILLINOIS: The state of Illinois has adopted the objective professional community standard (Ill. Ann. Stat. Ch. 110, 2-622) and requires that the alleged breach of duty be reviewed and substantiated by a physician reviewing the case (medical expert) prior to filing a complaint.

INDIANA: Indiana Code Ann. 16-9.5.1 adopts a reasonably prudent patient or "materiality" standard, requiring a disclosure of "material risks."

IOWA: Iowa Code Ann. 147.137 follows an objective professional community standard and further requires that the information disclosed include a detailed list of potential outcomes.

KENTUCKY: Kentucky Revised Statutes (KRS) 304.40-320 adopts the objective professional community standard.

LOUISIANA: Louisiana Rev. Stat. Title 40, Section 1299.40, and 1299.50 (Louisiana Medical Consent Law) raise a presumption of informed consent if information is provided in writing and sets forth certain factors (consistent with general requirements of informed consent).

MAINE: Maine Rev. Stats. Ann., Title 24-2905 adopts the professional community standard.

MASSACHUSETTS: Massachusetts recognizes **implied consent** as developed by case law. It generally follows the "materiality" standard, i.e., a doctor must disclose that information which the doctor should reasonably recognize as material to the patient's decision. *Halley v. Birbiglia,* 458 N.E.2d 710 (1983).

MICHIGAN: Michigan recognizes implied consent as developed by case law. It generally applies the professional standard. Michigan also treats, as an **assault and battery**, any physical contact with a patient that exceeds the scope of the granted consent. Patient consent may be expressed or implied. *Werth v. Taylor,* 190 Mich App 141 (1991).

MISSOURI: Missouri recognizes implied consent as developed by case law. It generally follows the professional standard, i.e., that of a reasonably prudent provider (of medical care or treatment) in the medical community.*Baltzell v. VanBuskirk,* 752 S.W.2d 902 (Mo. App. 1988).

NEBRASKA: Nebraska Revised Statutes, Section 44-2816 adopts the objective professional community standard.

NEW HAMPSHIRE: N.H. Rev. Stat. Ann. 507-C:2 adopts the objective professional community standard.

NEW YORK: NY Public Health Laws, Section 2805-d, applies the professional community standard and specifically provides that "[l]ack of informed consent means the failure... to disclose to the patient such alternatives... and the reasonably foreseeable risks and benefits involved as a reasonable medical... practitioner under similar circumstances."

NORTH CAROLINA: North Carolina General Statute 90-21.13(a)(3) applies an objective professional community standard to a physician's duty to inform.

OHIO: The Ohio Revised Code, Section 2317.54 adopts a reasonably prudent patient or materiality standard, expressly requiring the disclosure of "reasonably known risks."

OREGON: Oregon Rev. Stat. 677.097 adopts the reasonably prudent patient or materiality standard and requires a disclosure "in substantial detail."

PENNSYLVANIA: Pa. Stat. Ann. Title 40-1301.103 adopts the "materiality" standard.

TENNESSEE: Tennessee has adopted an objective professional community standard. Tenn. Code. Ann. 29-26-118.

TEXAS: Texas Code Ann. Article 4590i-6.02 adopts the "materiality" standard. Texas law has created the Texas Medical Disclosure Panel, comprised of three attorneys and six physicians, to establish "the degree of disclosure required and the form in which the disclosure will be made."

UTAH: Utah Code Ann. 78-14-5(f) follows an objective reasonably prudent patient standard, i.e., "reasonably prudent person in the patient's position."

VERMONT: Vermont Stat. Ann. Title 12-1909 adopts the objective professional community standard, requiring that the information disclosed be provided in a manner that allows a reasonably prudent patient to "make a knowledgeable evaluation."

WASHINGTON: Washington has adopted the reasonably prudent patient or "materiality" standard under Wash Rev. Code Ann. 7.70.050.

WEST VIRGINIA: West Virginia has abrogated the professional community standard and adopted a materiality standard. W. Va. Stat 55-7B-3

## Additional Resources

*"Exploring the Gray Areas of Informed Consent"* Dunn, Debra, 1999. Available at http://www.findarticles.com.

*"Informed Consent"* Cutter, Mary Ann G. University of Colorado Dept. of Philosophy. Available at http://www.du.edu/-craschke/consent.html.

*"Informed Consent."* Ethics in Medicine. University of Washington School of Medicine. Available at http://eduserv.hscer.washington.edu/bioethics/topics/consent.html.

*"Informed Consent."* Available at http://www.channel1.com/users/medlaw/prm/informed.html.

*"Informed Consent Does Not Mean Rational Consent."* Journal of Legal Medicine. Jon F. Merz and Baruch Fischoff. Hemisphere Publishing Corporation: 1990.

# HEALTHCARE

## INSURANCE

*Sections within this essay:*

## Background

Perhaps there is no area of the law more complex for the average American than insurance law. Health care and **disability** insurance coverage is no longer a luxury; it is a necessity for most individuals. By far, the majority of private health care insurance policies that are underwritten in the United States are those covered by employer group plans. As such, the sheer number of insureds in each group plan helps to reduce the cost of premiums and helps to standardize many provisions of plan coverage. By contrast, personal insurance purchased by individuals tends to be more costly, less comprehensive, but ostensibly more "portable," (remaining in effect despite job changes, periods of unemployment).

## Health Insurance Basics

Health insurance policies are contracts that require the insurer to pay benefits according to the terms of the policy, in return for the payment of premiums and the meeting of other conditions or criteria spelled out in the plan. Payment of benefits (upon the occurrence of a qualifying event such as illness, injury, office visit, etc.) may be reduced by a "deductible" paid by the insured, by a "co-insurance" payment shared with the insured, or by the reaching of a "maximum benefit amount," which caps the amount the insurer will pay for a covered charge. In such circumstances, the provider of the service may agree to accept the insurance payment and drop the remaining balance or may charge the remaining amount to the patient/insured.

Health insurance policy protection comes in many forms, some of the major ones are:

- *Base Plans:* These policy plans cover hospitalization and related charges

- *Medical and Surgical Benefit Plans:* These policy plans cover physician and service charges (radiology, laboratory, etc.) whether received as an "inpatient" or "outpatient"

- *Major Medical or Catastrophic Plans:* These policy plans only cover illnesses or injuries meeting the categorical criteria

- *Comprehensive Major Medical Plans:* Such plans cover all or most of the above under one policy plan

Two other forms of health insurance should be specifically noted and described:

- *Hospital Indemnity and/or Specified Disease Plans:* Instead of paying or reimbursing for a specific hospital charge, indemnity plans reimburse the insured a specified, fixed amount per day of hospitalization, irrespective of the actual hospital charges, and irrespective of any other insurance coverage. Likewise, specified disease plans pay the insured a fixed, flat amount for each day hospitalized as a result of the specified condition(s) or disease(s). It is important to note that these "insurance" plans are not intended to provide insurance coverage, but rather to supplement the needs of insureds who are hospitalized.

- *Blue Cross and Blue Shield Plans:* "Blues" Plans represent a national federation of local, independent community health service **corporations** operating as not-for-profit service organizations under state laws. They contract with individual hospitals (Blue Cross) and physicians (Blue Shield) to provide prepaid health care to insured "subscribers." The "Blues" plans differ from conventional insurance plans in that they have already negotiated contractual charges with health care providers, so they will usually pay for a semi-private hospital room, or for nursing services, etc., in full rather than paying a fixed sum or "indemnity benefit" toward the total charge.

## Employer Provided Health Insurance

At one time, most employers contracted with external insurance companies to provide benefits for their employees under a "group plan." The cost to the employer depended upon the number of employees, among other factors. Increasingly, employers have bought into "self-insured" or "self-funded" plans, wherein they establish trust funds or set aside other revenues to pay insureds' expenses. There are variations of these plans; for example, some provide for companies to pay benefits up to a certain amount, after which an insurer will take over and continue benefits. In some states, "multiple employ-

er trusts" are established to pool funds and reduce costs for employer-paid benefits. Many states also have insurance "guarantee associations" to which employers may or may not contribute (depending on state law) and which ensure benefits for employees/insureds in the event of **insolvency** or failure to pay on the part of the employer plan.

### *Comprehensive Omnibus Budget Reconciliation Act of 1989 (COBRA)*

Seldom do persons remember what the acronym "COBRA" stands for because its provisions relating to health care constitute such a minor part of the entire congressional act. However, there are two main ways that COBRA affects health care coverage. The first relates to conversion and continuation of health care insurance coverage for individuals who leave an employer group plan. The second (and less known) provision guarantees minimum, life-sustaining treatment and stabilization of the physical condition of anyone presenting for emergency care, irrespective of the absence or presence of health care insurance coverage:

- COBRA Continuation or Conversion: Federal law (PL 99-272 as amended) generally requires that employers/plan administrators provide notice to plan beneficiaries (the insured employees) within a specified number of days of the event (termination of employment, reduction of work hours, etc.) that triggers COBRA rights. These rights allow the insured employee and/or covered family members to retain/continue the insurance coverage and health insurance benefits they had when they were covered under the employer's plan. The continuation of coverage is for a specified period beyond employment (e.g., eighteen, twenty-nine, or thirty-six months). Importantly, the share of the premium or cost of the coverage remains the same during the COBRA period as it was during employment. However, there is no extension of coverage beyond the specified period, and insureds must then convert to a private policy or transfer to a new employer's plan (which can be done at any time during COBRA continuation of benefits). Not all employers are subject to COBRA mandates, but many offer their own parallel conversion plans for continuation of benefits. Parallel conversion provisions were also created under changes to ERISA (the Employer Retirement Income Security Act) for self-insured plans.

## Medicare Coverage

Virtually all persons who have been employed and who are 65 years of age or older are eligible for health care benefits under "Medicare." The program is administered by the Health Care Financing Administration, a branch of the U.S. Department of Health and Human Services.

### Eligibility

Although primarily associated with persons 65 years or older (who are otherwise eligible for Social Security benefits), **Medicare** also covers those under 65 who are "disabled" under Social Security Disability Insurance criteria or suffer from permanent kidney failure. There are other ways to qualify (e.g., over 65 and a Railroad Retirement **beneficiary**; under 65 and previously eligible but returned to work in the interim, etc.). It is recommended that one consult a Social Security office for current eligibility criteria.

### Coverage

Medicare "Part A" coverage helps cover hospital costs for medically necessary inpatient services customarily supplied in a hospital or skilled nursing facility, and/or for hospice care for the terminally ill. Also covered is 100 percent of home health care and 80 percent of approved costs for durable medical equipment supplied under the home health care benefit.

Medicare "Part B" helps cover the services of physicians and surgeons and certain other medical services and supplies, irrespective of the setting in which the services are provided (hospital, office, home, etc.) Certain other costs and expenses are Medicare-reimbursable, such as limited prescription drugs, x-rays and laboratory tests, ambulance services, etc.

### Costs

Medicare "Part A" benefits are financed through the Social Security (FICA) tax paid by employees/workers and employers. "Part B" coverage is optional to all beneficiaries who enroll for "Part A" coverage, and a monthly premium is charged to the enrollee. Additionally, persons (over 65 or disabled) may purchase both Parts A and B if not automatically eligible for Part A by way of some other disqualifying factor.

## Medigap Coverage

Private insurance companies often offer supplemental insurance coverage for those medical costs and expenses not covered by Medicare Parts A and B. They are not government sponsored, and consumers should thoroughly review their proposed coverage (for duplicate or overlapping coverage) in conjunction with covered charges, costs, waiting periods, premium increases related to age, etc.

## Medicaid

**Medicaid** coverage is not to be confused with Medicare coverage (although some persons may qualify for both). Both federal and state governments finance Medicaid programs, which are expressly created to serve the needs of low income or "medically-needy" individuals. Eligibility requirements differ among states. However, in addition to financial need, recipients must generally be under the age of 21 or over the age of 65 or blind or disabled. Some states expand criteria to include certain needy children with other profiles or other "categorically needy" persons. Eligibility criteria consider both income and assets (all states exempt a person's house from consideration). Medicaid benefits are paid directly to participating service providers.

## Disability and Long-Term Care

Virtually all health insurance policies have a "maximum liability" clause that caps the amount of money that will be paid under the policy. For those who have been permanently disabled or diagnosed with permanent or terminal illness, benefits may run out, leaving persons with little or no financial resources to cover medical needs.

Separate and distinct from health care insurance policies, "disability insurance" and "long-term care insurance" policies are available for purchase from private companies. Generally, benefits may be in the form of "income" (providing for periodic payments of a fixed amount to cover lost income during extended illness or injury) or in the form of continued payment of medical costs and expenses once conventional health policy coverage has been exhausted.

Long-term disability income insurance must be distinguished from long-term care coverage. In the former, benefits are payable to replace lost income during the expected or normal work career. According to the terms of the policy, benefits will cease once the insured reaches a certain age or after a certain number of years that equal those that would have been worked by the insured had he or she not been disabled by illness or injury. In the latter, benefits are payable, irrespective of age. These policies are generally expensive but provide extended benefits to cover nursing home care, rehabilitation, etc.

It is imperative that persons interested in purchasing private policies of supplemental, disability, or long-term care insurance thoroughly investigate their options and carefully articulate their needs to the agent or provider. Otherwise, duplicate coverage, redundancy, or worse, absence of necessary or intended coverage may result.

## Denial of Claims or Reduced Payment of Benefits

It is important to note that many states permit insurance providers to disclaim paying benefits already payable through other sources or to reduce the amount paid. These state provisions may be referred to as "priority rules" or "collateral source rules." Priority rules stack the order of insurance liability in the event of a claim (common in complex automobile accident cases). **Collateral** source rules also affect whether persons who recover medical costs and expenses from other sources, e.g., a lawsuit, must reimburse the insurance company for benefits paid. In most states this is permitted, but many states require the insurer to play an active role in the **settlement** negotiations and/or contribute toward the legal fees.

Beneficiaries/insureds do have recourse against insurance companies that delay or deny payment of benefits for covered charges. Although the term is often misused or abused, "bad faith" denials of claims by insurers are actionable in most states. However, the patient/insured generally has the burden of proving that the charge was for "medically necessary" care or treatment, and the charge was reasonable. Many states award **punitive damages** to punish insurance companies for **bad faith** denials. Other states have express laws requiring response to a claim (either payment or formal denial) within a specified number of days of receipt.

## Selected State Laws

ARKANSAS: Contracts for health and accident insurance must include those dental services that would have been covered if performed by a physician (23-79-114). Health care plans or disability insurance policies that cover families must include cover-

age for newborn children (23-79-129). Disability insurance may not discriminate between inpatient or outpatient coverage for the same procedure (23-85-133). Exclusions for preexisting conditions are strictly regulated (23-86-304).

CONNECTICUT: The state has extensive provisions governing health and accident insurance. Some key provisions include mandated coverage for some preexisting conditions (38a-476), limitations on offset provisions as defined under 38a-519, and a provision that married couples working for the same employer under the same group policy do not have to pay double premiums unless it results in greater coverage (38a-540, 541).

INDIANA: No policy for accident or health insurance may be issued until a copy of the form, the classification of risk, and the premium rate have been filed with the state commissioner (IC27-8-5-1). The state maintains a Life and Health Insurance Guarantee Association that protects insureds, beneficiaries, annuitants, etc. from insolvency or failure in performance of contractual obligations owed by the insurer that issued the policy (IC27-8-8-1 to 18).

MAINE: The state has a special provision prohibiting **discrimination** in maternity benefits coverage for unmarried women (T. 24-A-2741).

MARYLAND: Specific provisions are for AIDS/HIV positive individuals (15-201 to 205), breast implants (15-105), preexisting conditions (16-214, 15-208) and mental illness (19-703). Self-employed individuals must have annual open enrollment periods (15-411, 15-210).

MASSACHUSETTS: Policies providing supplemental coverage to Medicare must meet certain standards, with exceptions for employers and trade unions (175, Section 205).

MISSOURI: Insurers may not deny or cancel coverage because of **incarceration** of insured (595.047(1)). Health care service claims must be paid within 30 days of receipt by insurer of all necessary documents (376.427).

NEW JERSEY: New Jersey has a **statutory** Life and Health Insurance **Guaranty** Association to protect insureds and beneficiaries against insolvent or defaulting insurers. (T.17B, c. 32A.1) It also has a Health Care Quality Act providing consumer protections through "plain language" disclosure requirements, etc. (T.26. c.25.1).

NEW MEXICO: Health insurance policies must provide coverage for handicapped children, newborns, adopted children, childhood immunizations, home health care options, mammograms, cytologic screening, diabetes, and minimum hospital stays for certain conditions (59A-22-1).

OKLAHOMA: State Health Care Freedom of Choice Act provides certain rights to select the practitioner of choice for providing certain services (36-6053 to 6057). Genetic Nondiscrimination in Insurance Act restricts disclosure and/or use of genetic tests or information by employers or insurers (36-3614.1).

PENNSYLVANIA: Multiple statutory provisions cover various issues. Specific provision mandates coverage for serious mental illnesses (40-764g). False statements in applications are not automatic bars to coverage (40-757).

TENNESSEE: Health benefits coverage cannot be denied to victims of abuse (56-8-301). Policies may not exclude coverage for drugs not yet approved by FDA if the drug is used to treat life-threatening illness (56-7-2352).

WASHINGTON: Group policies must offer optional coverage for temporomandibular joint disorders (TMJ) (48.21-320) and mammograms (48.21.225). Employer-sponsored group contracts must provide coverage for neuro-developmental therapies (48.21-310).

## Additional Resources

*Family Legal Guide* American Bar Association, Times Books, Random House, 1996.

*Health Insurance* 2nd ed. Enteen, Robert, Demos Vermande, 1996.

*Martindale-Hubbell Law Digest* Martindale-Hubbell, 2001.

# HEALTHCARE

## LIMITATIONS OF LIABILITY

*Sections within this essay:*

## Background

Liability refers to the responsibility, under law or equity, for which a party is bound or obliged to make restitution, compensation, or satisfaction to another for loss or harm. A limitation in liability is a limit placed on the terms or nature of responsibility for loss or harm. It may be expressed in terms of maximum percentage of fault, dollar amount, type of harm or loss, or causative factor, beyond which a party openly denies any responsibility.

Limitations in liability may take several forms, the most common of which are written clauses contained in warranties, disclaimers, waivers, insurance policies, and contract terms. They also may take the form of "exculpatory clauses" which clear or tend to clear parties from any fault or liability for loss or harm to others whatsoever. Governmental entities may limit their exposure to liability for claims by citizens and members of the public (See, **sovereign immunity**).

Limitations in liability also differ in what they limit. There may be a cap or ceiling on monetary damages; an exclusion of certain forms of damages (e.g., punitive, incidental); or an exclusion for certain kinds of harm (e.g. those caused by acts of God or forces of nature). In product purchases, liability may be limited to the purchaser only, and not to third persons or subsequent owners/users.

In a way, limitations of liability are, for the most part, actual (or tantamount to) terms of **contract,** and generally enforced under principles of contract law. They generally require actual or implied notice and the consent of all parties to the transaction, —proof of which is generally deemed to be conclusive as to acceptance of the limitations.

States have different laws regarding the extent to which persons or business entities may limit their liability to others. Since each state may have several laws dealing with limitations of liability (according to the application), contacting the subject state's department of insurance is advised for guidance and clarification. (See *Organizations* listed below.)

### Warranties and Disclaimers

Warranties guarantee minimum standards or performance in products or services. They may be express (as in a manufacturer's certificate of warranty that is attached to a consumer product), or implied (as in the common law **implied warranty** of merchantability). Manufacturers' warranties are controlled by federal and state laws, including the **Uniform Commercial Code (UCC)** Warranties are essentially statements of declared limits to liability, e.g., "Five years or 50,000 miles" for some new vehicles.

A disclaimer is a limitation of liability otherwise attaching to an actual or implied warranty. It works as a substitute for what is otherwise warranted, *other than that which is expressly warranted by the drafter of the disclaimer.* Disclaimers of all warranties is common in items or goods sold on an "as is" basis.

### Monetary Ceilings and Caps

One of the most common forms of limiting liability is through the application of monetary caps or ceilings to the amount recoverable in any claim for loss or harm. So widespread and successful is this practice that it is often incorporated into statutory provisions to ensure uniformity and requisite notice to third persons.

Many states have passed legislation capping the available remedies in **tort** cases (tort reform). Such legislation is particularly intended to address those cases in which emotion may cause "runaway juries" to award millions or billions of dollars in cases that play on their sympathy or anger.

Two broad areas of tort litigation undergoing constant reform are **products liability** and **medical malpractice.** In the area of medical malpractice, a majority of states have enacted tort reform legislation, many of which limit non-economic damages (e.g., to $250,000) as a result of lobbying from insurance companies.

Congress and state legislators have enacted many provisions over the years that serve to limit the available remedies in certain cases or controversies (e.g., the Limitation of Liability Act, 46 USC 181 *et seq.,* regarding cargo shipments)or the Federal Tort Claims Act. Other examples in which Congress has eliminated liability for ordinary negligence, but not for intentional or willful misconduct, include the Bill Emerson Good Samaritan Food Donation Act, the Volunteer Protection Act, the Aviation Medical Assistance Act of 1998, and the Paul D. Coverdell Teacher Protection Act of 2001. These statutes grant private parties immunity from suit in many cases, or otherwise limit their exposure to liability, by declaring them federal employees for purposes of the benefit or good they are providing to the public at large. Likewise, in 2005, during a global threat of a particularly virulent form of the flu virus, the 109th Congress worked on legislation to limit the liability of pharmaceutical manufacturers of flu vaccines. This was intended to accelerate the production of new strains of flu vaccines needed to address a potential pandemic, without developers being unduly delayed by fear of liability for untoward complications or negligence in the testing, manufacturing, labeling, distribution, dispensing, prescribing, or administering of the vaccine.

### Insurance "Policy Limits"

By far, the lion's share of monetary damages awarded in jury trials or voluntary settlements comes from insurance money. At one time, insurance companies merely increased their premiums across the board to recoup their losses. However, insurance premiums have reached all-time highs, and consumers are no longer willing to accept this solution. An alternative has been to sharply raise the limitations of coverage offered by insurers. In health insurance, for example, this may take the form of more stringent limitations on pre-existing conditions, or a lower maximum dollar amount payable per injury/illness or per incident. Although insureds may file suit for reimbursement or payment of larger amounts, the stated policy limit will generally be held valid.

For business entities carrying liability insurance, their contracts or business transactions may often expressly state that liability is limited to "policy limits." This means that, should a damages award against the company result in a liability greater than the amount of coverage provided by any insurance against such loss or liability, persons dealing with the business cannot compel the business to liquidate assets or offer other resources to cover the difference.

In lawsuits, the policy limit is often used as a negotiating tool for early settlement of a case. Even though plaintiffs may believe they could be awarded a greater dollar amount by a jury, they may settle the case for the policy limits of any insurance carried by defendants. This removes the uncertainty and protracted litigation often involved in trying to collect money or liquidating assets from the defendant's personal estate after all available insurance has been paid out.

### Contractual Terms

Standard limitation-of-liability clauses are commonplace in all types of contracts. Because courts of law rarely consider the fairness of contract terms, parties to a contract must carefully review its terms and negotiate any limitation of liability.

An example of a limiting clause in a contract might be language similar to "The liability of contractor to customer, whether in tort or in contract and for any reason and upon any cause of action or claim relating to the performance of work under this agreement, shall be limited to the amount paid by customer to contractor pursuant to this agreement."

Limitations-of-liability clauses are one-sided terms (favorable to the drafter of the contract), and should always be reviewed with scrutiny. Unless they are clearly unconscionable or against **public policy,** courts will seldom set them aside, despite their obvious unfairness to an unwary party to the contract.

## Public Policy Exceptions

Whereas the general rule is that the government (legislative or judicial) cannot interfere with a party's right to engage in contracts, such non-interference does not contemplate an unlimited right to exculpate oneself from liability. Courts will seldom uphold a clause in a contract, disclaimer, or waiver that tends to exculpate a party from liability as a result of intentional, wanton, or reckless conduct. Most states limit exculpatory clauses to acts of ordinary negligence. Moreover, most states do not permit parties to limit liability for loss or harm under circumstances normally requiring strict liability (e.g., the handling of dangerous materials like explosives, radioactive materials, etc.)

When courts interfere with the private contractual rights of parties by not enforcing a limitation of liability clause, it is often under the auspices of protecting persons from violations of public policy which effectively void such clauses. Courts will generally strike unconscionable terms that are oppressive because of grossly unequal bargaining power between the parties; are improper because of the imposition of strict liability; or are unenforceable because they are contrary to state-imposed standards of care (as for certain professional licenses or permits). The justification most often cited for the court's interference in private contractual relations is that such a limitation-of-liability clause is "void as against public policy." Public policy is that which tends to safeguard and support the good or betterment of all, as opposed to the individual rights of contracting parties.

## Limited Liability Companies (LLCs)

Most states require that business entities which limit their liability must declare so openly, which is intended to provide notice to those doing business with them. Certain business entities limit their liability right up front, before they even engage in any contracts or business transactions. Limited Liability Com-

panies, or LLCs, combine many facets of corporate structure with the smaller and simpler partnership structure. Third persons are immediately placed on notice of a LLC's liability limitations by the very name of the company, which, in most states, must included the "LLC" designation as part of its company name.

In a LLC, individual owners are not personally liable for company debts and obligations, including monetary damages awarded against the company in a law suit. This means that if company assets are sold off to meet liabilities, the owners do not need to use their personal assets to make good on business losses.

## Limitations on Governmental Liability

The concept of **sovereign immunity** prevents citizens from suing their governments. (As a government by and for "the people," conducted and administered by democratic representation, citizens would theoretically be suing themselves.) Notwithstanding, branches of both federal and state governments permit the imposition of liability for certain losses and damages. By statutory consent, governments will generally compensate for losses caused by non-discretionary acts of their employees or agencies (so as not to inhibit the exercise of discretionary decision-making in perilous or exigent circumstances, for fear of liability exposure). Often, claimants are prohibited from filing suit in a court of law, but must file in a special Court of Claims, the jurisdiction of which is exclusive to suits involving the government as defendant. Other restrictions and limitations may apply, including limitations on fault, form of remedy, amount of damages, or standing to sue.

## Additional Resources

Cohen, Henry. "CRS Report: Pandemic Flu Liability Limitation Legislation." Washington, DC: Library of Congress, Congressional Research Service, 2005.

Grossman, Mark. "Emerging Issues: Limitations of Liability." 15 July 2003. Published by The Institute of Internal Auditors (The IIA).

Kurer, Martin; Stefano Codini; Klaus Gunther; Jorge Santiago Neves; and Lawrence Teh. *Warranties and Disclaimers: Limitations of Liability in Consumer-Related Transactions.* Aspen Publishers, 2005.

## Organizations

### Alabama Department of Insurance
201 Monroe Street, Suite 1700, PO Box 303351
Montgomery, AL 36104
Phone: (334) 269-3550
Fax: (334) 241-4192
URL: www.aldoi.org

### Alaska Department of Community and Economic Development
3601 C Street, Suite 1324
Anchorage, AK 99503
Phone: (907) 269-7900
Fax: (907) 269-7910
URL: www.dced.sta te.ak.us/insurance

### Alaska Department of Community and Economic Development
P.O. Box 110805
Juneau99811
Phone: (907) 465-2515
Fax: (907) 465-3422
URL: www.commer ce.state.ak.us

### Arizona Department of Insurance
2910 North 44th Street, Suite 210
Phoenix, AZ 85018
Phone: (602) 912-8444
Fax: (602) 954-7008
URL: www.state.az. us/id

### Arkansas Department of Insurance
1200 West 3rd Street
Little Rock, AR 72201
Phone: (501) 371-2640
Fax: (501) 371-2749
URL: www.state.ar. us/insurance

### California Department of Insurance
300 Capitol Mall, Suite 1500
Sacramento, CA 95814
Phone: (916) 492-3500
Fax: (415) 538-4010
URL: www.insuranc e.ca.gov

### Colorado Division of Insurance
1560 Broadway, Suite 850
Denver, CO 80202
Phone: (303) 894-7499, ext. 4311
Fax: (303) 894-7455
URL: www.dora.state.co.us/Insurance

### Connecticut Department of Insurance
P.O. Box 816
Hartford, CT 06142
Phone: (860) 297-3984

URL: www.state.ct.us/cid

### Delaware Department of Insurance
841 Silver Lake Blvd., Rodney Building
Dover, DE 19904
Phone: (302) 739-4251
Fax: (302) 739-5280
URL: www.state.de. us/inscom

### District of Columbia Department of Insurance and Securities Regulation
810 First Street, NW, Suite 701
Washington, DC 20002
Phone: (202) 727-8000
Fax: (202) 535-1196

### Florida Department of Insurance
Plaza Level Eleven
Tallahassee, FL 32399
Phone: (850) 922-3130
URL: www.doi.state.fl.us

### Georgia Insurance and Fire Safety
Two Martin Luther King, Jr. Drive
Atlanta, GA 30334
Phone: (404) 656-2070
Fax: (404) 651-8719
URL: www.inscomm.state.ga.us

### State of Hawaii, Department of Commerce and Consumer Affairs
250 South King Street, 5th Floor
Honolulu, HI 96813
Phone: (808) 586-2790
Fax: (808) 586-2806
URL: www.hawaii.g ov/insurance

### State of Idaho Department of Insurance
700 West State Street, P.O. Box 83720
Boise, ID 83720
Phone: (208) 334-4250
Fax: (208) 334-4398
URL: www.doi.state.id.us

### Illinois Department of Insurance
100 West Randolph Street, Suite 15-100
Chicago, IL 60601
Phone: (312) 814-2420
Fax: (312) 814-5435
URL: www.state.il.u s/ins

### Illinois Department of Insurance
320 West Washington Street
Springfield, IL 62767
Phone: (217) 782-4515
Fax: (217) 782-5020
URL: www.state.il.u s/ins/

**Indiana Department of Insurance**
311 W. Washington St., Ste 300
Indianapolis, IN 46204
Phone: (317) 232-2385
Fax: (317) 232-5251
URL: www.state.in.u s/idoi/

**State of Iowa Division of Insurance**
330 Maple Street
Des Moines, IA 50319
Phone: (515) 281-5705
Fax: (515) 281-3059
URL: www.state.ia.u s/government/com/ins/ins.htm

**Kansas Insurance Division**
420 SW 9th Street
Topeka, KS 66612
Phone: (785) 296-7801
Fax: (785) 296-2283
URL: www.ink.org/ public/kid

**Kentucky Department of Insurance**
215 West Main Street
Frankfort, KY 40601
Phone: (502) 564-3630
Fax: (502) 564-1650
URL: htt p://www.doi.state.ky.us/

**Louisiana Department of Insurance**
950 North Fifth Street
Baton Rouge, LA 70804
Phone: (225) 343-4834
Fax: (254) 342-5900
URL: www.ldi.state.l a.us

**Maine Bureau of Insurance**
34 State House Station
Augusta, ME 04333
Phone: (207) 624-8475
Fax: (207) 624-8599
URL: www.maineins urancereg.org

**Maryland Insurance Administration**
525 St. Paul Place
Baltimore, MD 21202
Phone: (410) 468-2000
Fax: (410) 468-2020
URL: www.mia.state.md.us

**Massachusetts Division of Insurance**
South Station, 5th Floor
Boston, MA 02110
Phone: (617) 521-7794
Fax: (617) 521-7772
URL: www.state.ma.us/doi

**Michigan Office of Financial and Insurance Services**
611 West Ottawa Street, 2nd Floor North, P.O. Box 30220
Lansing, MI 48933
Phone: (517) 373-0220
Fax: (517) 335-4978
URL: www.cis.state. mi.us/ofis

**Minnesota Department of Commerce**
133 East 7th Street
St. Paul, MN 55101
Phone: (651) 296-2488
Fax: (651) 296-4328
URL: www.commer ce.state.mn.us

**Mississippi Department of Insurance**
P.O. Box 79
Jackson, MS 39205
Phone: (601) 359-3569
Fax: (601) 359-2474
URL: www.doi.state.ms.us

**Missouri Department of Insurance**
301 West High Street, Room 630
Jefferson City, MO 65102
Phone: (573) 751-4126
Fax: (573) 751-1165
URL: www.insuranc e.state.mo.us

**Montana Department of Insurance**
840 Helena Avenue, P.O. Box 4009
Helena, MT 59601
Phone: (406) 444-2040
Fax: (406) 444-3497
URL: www.state.mt. us/sao

**Nebraska Department of Insurance**
941 O Street, Suite 400
Lincoln, NE 68508
Phone: (402) 471-2201
Fax: (402) 471-4610
URL: www.nol.org/h ome/NDOI

**Nevada Division of Insurance**
1665 Hot Springs Road, #152
Carson City, NV 89706
Phone: (775) 687-7690
Fax: (775) 687-3937
URL: www.doi.state.nv.us

**New Hampshire Department of Insurance**
56 Old Suncook Road
Concord, NH 03301
Phone: (603) 271-2261
Fax: (603) 271-1406
URL: www.state.nh. us/insurance

**New Jersey Department of Banking and Insurance**
20 West State Street
Trenton, NJ 08625
Phone: (609) 633-7667
Fax: (609) 984-5273
URL: htt p://states.nai c.org/nj/NJHOMEPG.HTML

**New Mexico Department of Insurance**
P.O. Box 1269
Santa Fe, NM 87504
Phone: (505) 827-4601
Fax: (505) 827-4734
URL: www.nmprc.st ate.nm.us

**New York State Insurance Department**
Agency Bldg. 1-ESP, Empire State Plaza
, NY 12257
Phone: (518) 474-6600
Fax: (518) 474-6630
URL: www.ins.state. ny.us

**Consumer Services Bureau NYS Insurance Department**
65 Court Street #7
Buffalo, NY 14202
Phone: (716) 847-7618
Fax: (716) 847-7925
URL: www.ins.state. ny.us

**North Carolina Department of Insurance**
430 North Salisbury Street
Raleigh, NC 27611
Phone: (919) 733-7349
Fax: (919) 733-6495
URL: www.ncdoi.ne t

**North Dakota Insurance Department**
600 East Blvd. Avenue, 5th Floor
Bismarck, ND 58505
Phone: (701) 328-2440
Fax: (701) 328-4880
URL: www.state.nd. us/ndins

**Ohio Department of Insurance**
2100 Stella Court
Columbus, OH 43215
Phone: (614) 644-3378
Fax: (614) 752-0740
URL: www.state.oh. us/

**Oklahoma Insurance Department**
3814 North Santa Fe
Oklahoma City, OK 73118
Phone: (405) 521-2828
Fax: (405) 521-6652

URL: www.oid.state.ok.us

**Oregon Insurance Division**
350 Winter Street, NE, Room 440-2
Salem, OR 97310
Phone: (503) 947-7984
Fax: (503) 378-4351
URL: www.cbs.state.or.us/ins

**Pennsylvania Insurance Department**
1321 Strawberry Square, 13th Floor
Harrisburg, PA 17120
Phone: (717) 787-2317
URL: www.insurance.state.pa.us

**Rhode Island Insurance Division**
233 Richmond Street, Suite 233
Providence, RI 02903
Phone: (401) 222-2223
Fax: (401) 222-5475

**South Carolina Department of Insurance**
1612 Marion Street
Columbia, SC 29201
Phone: (803) 737-6180
Fax: (803) 737-6231
URL: www.state.sc. us/doi/

**South Dakota Division of Insurance**
118 West Capitol
Pierre, SD 57501
Phone: (605) 773-3563
Fax: (605) 773-5369
URL: www.state.sd. us/insurance

**Tennessee Department of Commerce and Insurance**
500 James Robertson Parkway, 5th Floor
Nashville, TN 37243
Phone: (615) 741-2241
Fax: (615) 532-6934
URL: www.state.tn. us/commerce

**Texas Department of Insurance**
333 Guadalupe Street
Austin, TX 78701
Phone: (512) 463-6169
Fax: (512) 475-2005
URL: www.tdi.state. tx.us

**Utah Department of Insurance**
State Office Building Rm 3110
Salt Lake City, UT 84114
Phone: (801) 538-3805
Fax: (801) 538-3829
URL: www.insurance.state.ut.us

# HEALTHCARE

## MANAGED CARE/HMOS

*Sections within this essay:*

## Background

"Managed care" refers to that type of health care system under which medical care and treatment is managed by the entity paying the bills, and not the medical care or treatment provider (physician, hospital, etc.). It is a system dominated by acronyms that identify different services or components (e.g., HMOs, PPOs, EPOs). It is also a system that has become so complex that many believe it has lost sight of its original objectives.

Prior to the proliferation of **managed care** plans, medical services and treatments were traditionally provided under what is now referred to as "fee-for-

service" plans. Under fee-for-service medicine, the health care provider (physician, hospital, etc.) decided what treatment or procedure was necessary for the patient. However, insurance companies often engaged in semantic battles with health care providers over what treatments were considered "necessary" and how much they would cost. Often stuck in the middle were the patients, who had to choose between waiting for a decision or paying for the treatment themselves.

Managed care organizations (MCOs) began to proliferate during the 1980s, when the industry began to court employers (who pay the bulk of the nation's health insurance premiums). There had been reports of hospitals and doctors under traditional medical insurance plans performing unnecessary diagnostic tests or prolonging treatments (especially rehabilitative therapies) to maximize their incomes/profits. Employers saw the MCO industry as a way to cut costs for employee health insurance.

The MCO purports to control the cost, quality, and availability of medical care by limiting access to care providers and shifting focus to wellness rather than illness. MCO plans typically employ doctors and statisticians to assess computer-generated data, such as how long a heart attack patient should be hospitalized or what treatments are most effective for a particular illness or injury. These data are then developed into industry standards that are referred to as "best practice" guidelines or benchmarks. The MCO, and not the treating doctor, then decides what treatments will be authorized and how much will be paid for the treatments/hospital stays, etc. In return, the MCO purports to offer lower insurance premiums for subscribing members.

## Types of Managed Care Organizations (MCOs)

There are four basic types of managed care plans that fall under the umbrella of "MCOs."

### Health Maintenance Organizations (HMOs)

By far the most common type, HMOs ostensibly focus on wellness (e.g., by providing for annual physical examinations). Members (who are insured) pay a fixed annual premium in return for health care access that is limited to the HMO's network of physicians and hospitals. Medical care is also limited to a prearranged, comprehensive list of medical services that will be provided to the enrolled group as a whole. Most HMOs require patients to choose (from the HMO network) a physician as a primary care provider (PCP) who must first be consulted for any medical concern. The PCP, and not the patient, then decides if the patient should consult a specialist or get a second opinion. This practice (common to most forms of MCOs in general) is known as "gatekeeping."

### Preferred Provider Organizations (PPOs)

In a PPO, the managing entity is not always the insurer; it also may be an employer or a plan administrator. Discounted rates are negotiated with specific health care providers in return for increased patient volume. However, members may choose providers outside of the PPO network, but they will have to pay more to do so.

### Exclusive Provider Organizations (EPOs)

Under an EPO, the managing entity contracts with a group of health care providers who agree to internally follow utilization procedures, to refer patients only to other specialists within the EPO, and to use only those hospitals contracted with the EPO. Members must use EPO providers.

### Point-of-Service Plans (POS)

The designation of POS refers to the fact that the amount of co-payment an insured pays is dependent upon the "point of service." If an insured member goes outside of the plan network to receive care, the co-payment is higher, as network providers have agreed to accept a discounted rate for services in return for patient volume and patient referral.

## Medicare Managed Care

Less than 15 percent of Medicare beneficiaries are enrolled in Medicare managed care programs, previously known as the Medicare+Choice plan, but now referred to as Medicare Advantage. As part of the Medicare Reform Package [that resulted in the enactment of the Medicare Prescription Drug Improvement and Modernization Act of 2003 (P.L. 108-173)], Congress increased payments to Medicare HMOs for 2004. In 2006, seniors became eligible for a new Medicare option: PPOs. This was expected to meet the demand of "baby-boomers," the first of whom were entering their 60s at that time. Because approximately 80 percent of individuals with private insurance had PPO plans, the transition to Medicare PPO would be a smoother transition.

Traditional Medicare enrollees often need to understand and deal with three different plans: basic Medicare, "medigap" supplemental insurance, and the new Part D prescription drug plan. However, Medicare Advantage enrollees may reduce this burden by combining regular health care and prescription drugs, as well as limiting ou-of-pocket expenses for copays and deductibles.

## The HMO Act of 1973

The early HMOs were idealistic non-profit organizations endeavoring to enhance the delivery of health care to patients while controlling costs. The HMO Act of 1973 changed that premise. It authorized for-profit IPA-HMOs in which HMOs may contract with independent practice associations (IPAs) that, in turn, contract with individual physicians for services and compensation. By the late 1990s, 80 percent of MCOs were for-profit organizations, and only 68 percent or less of insurance premiums went toward medical care. The remainder was paid for MCO executives' and salespersons' salaries.

As a counterbalance against growing concerns that MCOs had transformed from patient-friendly plans to profit-making machines, state legislators around the country began to enact laws limiting certain restrictions imposed by MCOs on their members. Most of these laws are referred to as "HMO laws" but generally govern all MCOs within the state (HMOs being the most common).

State laws vary on such issues as whether HMOs may deny patient access to medical specialists without first going through the designated primary care provider (PCP); "best practice" minimum hospital stays; and whether HMOs may provide financial incentives to health care providers who curb medical costs by limiting medical care. Almost all states now prohibit "gag rules," which are contractual agreements with physicians not to inform their patients of treatment options not covered by the HMO/MCO plan (a common practice in earlier days).

## State Laws

Nineteen states have POS laws. Point-of-service (POS) plans permit enrollees to choose a non-participating provider instead of a participating provider at the time services are needed. A higher copayment or a deductible may apply if a non-participating provider renders services. A POS law mandates that managed care plans provide a point-of-service choice to enrollees. This is often accomplished by providing a HMO plan alongside an indemnity plan. If the enrollee uses a provider who participates in the HMO network, then HMO benefits apply, but the indemnify benefits apply if a non-participating provider is used. State laws vary. Some require a POS offering only for employers with more than 25 or 50 employees or health plans with more than 5,000 or 10,000 enrollees Others might have special provisions that apply to dental plans.

Seventeen states have network adequacy requirements. Such laws mandate that plans establish standards for the creation and maintenance of provider networks that are sufficient to assure that managed care plan enrollees can access necessary services without unreasonable delay. Sufficiency may be determined in terms of provider-to-enrollee ratios, geographic accessibility, waiting time for appointments, and office hours.

Twenty-three states have a freedom of choice laws that preserve a managed care enrollee's right to select any available provider in the network. Many states limit these laws to providers of pharmaceutical services.

Twenty-two states have AWP (any willing provider) laws that require managed care plans to grant network participation to any provider willing to join and meet network requirements. Most states with this requirement limit the application to pharmacies or pharmacists.

Thirty-seven states prohibit discrimination between various classes of providers based on their academic degrees. To do this, the laws typically broaden the definition of physician to include such practitioners as dentists, dental hygienists, optometrists, podiatrists, chiropractors, mental health practitioners, and nurse practitioners.

Thirty-six states have a continuity of care requirement. These address providers that cease participation in a managed care plan's network. For enrollees who are undergoing treatment by a provider at the time of the provider's network termination, continuity of care requires continued coverage for treatment rendered by that provider for (1) pregnancy, (2) acute illness, or (3) chronic illness (e. g., those that are life-threatening, degenerative, or disabling).

Twenty-nine states have a standing referral requirement. These require managed care plans to establish procedures by which an enrollee with a life-threatening, chronic, degenerative, or disabling disease who requires specialized care over a prolonged period of time is given an ongoing authorization (a standing referral) to receive appropriate treatment from a specialist.

Thirty-eight states provide women with direct access to ob/gyn services.

Twenty-two states provide direct access to specialists.

Seventeen states have an ombudsman program.

### Common State Provisions

ALABAMA: See Alabama Code, sections 27-21A-1 et seq. and others. State law does not permit direct access to medical specialists except for ob-gyn. A specialist cannot be designated as (PCP). There are no prohibitions on use of financial incentives by HMOs to induce providers to limit their care. There is no independent review of HMO and managed care denials, and no law to protect consumers from managed care abuses and wrongful denials.

ALASKA: Most of the HMO laws can be found at Alaska **Statute** Annotated, sections 21.86.010 et seq. State law does not permit direct access to medical specialists, including ob-gyn. A specialist cannot be designated as a PCP. Inpatient childbirth care requires a minimum 48 hours after vaginal birth; 96 hours after caesarian. The law does prohibit the use of financial incentives by HMOs to induce providers to limit their care. Independent review of benefit determinations is available. There is no state law to protect consumers from managed care abuses and wrongful denials.

ARIZONA: Arizona Revised Statutes Annotated, Sections 20-1051 et seq. do not provide for direct access to specialists, nor do they permit the designation of a specialist as a PCP. There is no direct access to ob-gyn, nor can a patient designate ob-gyn as PCP.

Inpatient childbirth care requires a minimum 48 hours after vaginal birth; 96 hours after caesarian. Financial incentives by HMOs to providers are prohibited. The law provides for a binding (on plan) independent review of HMO and managed care denials. Moreover, consumers have the right to sue their HMO for acting unreasonably in denying or delaying approval for care.

ARKANSAS: State law (Arkansas Code Annotated, sections 23-76-101 et seq. and others) does not permit direct access to medical specialists except for primary eye care or ob-gyn. A specialist cannot be designated as a PCP. Inpatient childbirth care requires a minimum 48 hours after vaginal birth; 96 hours after caesarian. The law also provides for inpatient care following breast surgery and requires in-patient care of at least 48 hours following a mastectomy. There are no prohibitions on use of financial incentives by HMOs to induce providers to limit their care. There is no independent review of HMO and managed care denials and no law to protect consumers from managed care abuses and wrongful denials.

CALIFORNIA: California Health and Safety Code, sections 1340 et seq and other state laws, do not permit direct access to medical specialists except for ob-gyn. Except for ob-gyn, a specialist may not be designated as a PCP. Inpatient childbirth care requires a minimum 48 hours after vaginal birth; 96 hours after caesarian. There are no prohibitions on use of financial incentives by HMOs to induce providers to limit their care. The law provides for binding independent review of HMO and managed care denials but only for experimental or investigational treatment. Consumers may sue HMOs for managed care abuses and wrongful denials.

COLORADO: State laws (Colorado Revised Statutes Annotated, sections 10-16-401 et seq. and others) do not provide for direct access to specialists nor do they permit the designation of a specialist as a PCP. There is direct access to ob-gyn. Inpatient childbirth care requires a minimum 48 hours after vaginal birth; 96 hours after caesarian. Financial incentives by HMOs to providers are permitted. The law provides for a non-binding independent review of HMO and managed care denials. No laws exist for consumers to sue their HMO for acting unreasonably in denying or delaying approval for care.

CONNECTICUT: Connecticut General Statutes Annotated (38-175 and others) regulate HMOs and managed care. There is no direct access to medical specialists (excepting ob-gyn) and specialists cannot

be designated as PCPs (except ob-gyn). Inpatient childbirth care provides for a minimum 48 hours for vaginal birth and 96 hours for caesarian. There is also minimum inpatient care following breast surgery, requiring at least 48 hours of inpatient care following mastectomy or lumpectomy. Use of financial incentives between providers and HMOs is not prohibited. There is binding independent review of benefit determinations. No law exists to protect consumers from managed care abuses and wrongful denials.

DELAWARE: Delaware Code Annotated (title 16, sections 9101 et seq. and others) does not permit direct access to medical specialists except for ob-gyn. A specialist cannot be designated as a PCP (except for ob-gyn). Inpatient childbirth care requires a minimum 48 hours after vaginal birth; 96 hours after caesarian. There are no prohibitions on use of financial incentives by HMOs to induce providers to limit their care. There is binding independent review of HMO and managed care denials but no law to protect consumers from managed care abuses and wrongful denials.

FLORIDA: Florida Statutes Annotated section 641.17 et seq. does not permit direct access to medical specialists except for ob-gyn and dermatology. A specialist cannot be designated as a PCP (except ob-gyn). If the treating physician recommends inpatient care following childbirth or mastectomy, it cannot be limited. There are no prohibitions on use of financial incentives by HMOs to induce providers to limit their care. There is nonbinding independent review of HMO and managed care denials but no law to protect consumers from managed care abuses and wrongful denials.

GEORGIA: HMO laws can be found at Official Code of Georgia Annotated, sections 33.31-1 et seq. plus insurance laws, etc. State law does not permit direct access to medical specialists except for ob-gyn. A specialist cannot be designated as a PCP. Inpatient childbirth care requires a minimum 48 hours after vaginal birth; 96 hours after caesarian. The law also provides for inpatient care following breast surgery and requires in-patient care of at least 48 hours following a mastectomy. Use of financial incentives by HMOs to induce providers to limit their care is prohibited. There is independent review of HMO and managed care denials, and consumers may sue HMOs for managed care abuses and wrongful denials.

HAWAII: State law (Hawaii Revised Statutes 432-D and others) does not permit direct access to medical specialists, nor can specialists be designated as PCPs. No direct access is allowed to ob-gyn. No prohibitions on use of financial incentives by HMOs exist to induce providers to limit their care. There is possibly binding independent review of HMO and managed care denials but no law for consumers to sue HMOs for managed care abuses and wrongful denials.

IDAHO: HMO laws can be found at Idaho Code 41-3901 et seq. plus insurance laws, etc. State law does not permit direct access to medical specialists except for ob-gyn. A specialist cannot be designated as a PCP (excepting ob-gyn). Inpatient childbirth care requires a minimum 48 hours after vaginal birth; 96 hours after caesarian. Use of financial incentives by HMOs to induce providers to limit their care is prohibited. There is no provision for independent review of HMO and managed care denials and no consumer law for HMO liability for managed care abuses and wrongful denials.

ILLINOIS: Illinois does not permit direct access to medical specialists except for chiropractors and ob-gyn. A specialist cannot be designated as a PCP (excepting ob-gyn). Inpatient childbirth care requires a minimum 48 hours after vaginal birth; 96 hours after caesarian. Use of financial incentives by HMOs to induce providers to limit their care is prohibited. There is independent review of HMO and managed care denials but no provisions for consumers to sue HMOs for managed care abuses and wrongful denials.

INDIANA: Indiana Code Annotated, sections 27-13-1-1 et seq. does not permit direct access to medical specialists except for ob-gyn. However, Indiana is one of the few states that permit specialists to be designated as PCPs. No prohibitions exist on the use of financial incentives by HMOs to induce providers to limit their care. There is independent review of HMO and managed care denials but no law for consumers to sue HMOs for managed care abuses and wrongful denials.

IOWA: State law does not permit direct access to medical specialists, including ob-gyn. A specialist cannot be designated as a PCP. Inpatient childbirth care requires a minimum 48 hours after vaginal birth; 96 hours after caesarian. The law also provides for inpatient care following breast surgery and requires inpatient care of at least 48 hours following a mastectomy. No prohibition exists on the use of financial incentives by HMOs to induce providers to limit their care. There is independent review of HMO and managed care denials but no provision for consumers to

sue HMOs for managed care abuses and wrongful denials.

KANSAS: Kansas Statutes Annotated, sections 40-3201, do not permit direct access to medical specialists, including ob-gyn. A specialist cannot be designated as a PCP. Inpatient childbirth care requires a minimum 48 hours after vaginal birth; 96 hours after caesarian. Laws prohibits use of financial incentives by HMOs to induce providers to limit their care. There is independent review of HMO and managed care denials but no provision for consumers to sue HMOs for managed care abuses and wrongful denials.

KENTUCKY: State law (Kentucky Revised Statutes Annotated, sections 304-38-010 and other provisions) does not permit direct access to medical specialists, excepting chiropractors and ob-gyn. A specialist cannot be designated as a PCP. Inpatient childbirth care requires a minimum 48 hours after vaginal birth; 96 hours after caesarian. The law also prohibits insurers from mandating that mastectomy be done on an out-patient basis. No prohibition exists on the use of financial incentives by HMOs to induce providers to limit their care. There is independent review of HMO and managed care denials (binding on insurers) but no provision for consumers to sue HMOs for managed care abuses and wrongful denials.

LOUISIANA: Louisiana Revised Statutes Annotated 22:2001 et seq. do not permit direct access to medical specialists, except for ob-gyn. A specialist cannot be designated as a PCP, except for ob-gyn. Inpatient childbirth care requires a minimum 48 hours after vaginal birth; 96 hours after caesarian. The use of financial incentives by HMOs to induce providers to limit care is prohibited. There is binding independent review of HMO and managed care denials but no provision for consumers to sue HMOs for managed care abuses and wrongful denials.

MAINE: Maine Revised Statutes Annotated, Title 24-A- 4201 et seq., do not permit direct access to medical specialists, excepting ob-gyn. A specialist (except ob-gyn) cannot be designated as a PCP. No prohibition exists on the use of financial incentives by HMOs to induce providers to limit their care. There is binding independent review of HMO and managed care denials, and consumers may sue HMOs for managed care abuses and wrongful denials.

MARYLAND: State law (Maryland Health-General Code Annotated 19-701 et seq.) does not permit direct access to medical specialists, except for ob-gyn. A specialist cannot be designated as a PCP, except for ob-gyn. Inpatient childbirth care requires a minimum 48 hours after vaginal birth; 96 hours after caesarian. There is a prohibition on the use of financial incentives by HMOs to induce providers to limit their care. There is binding independent review of HMO and managed care denials but no provision for consumers to sue HMOs for managed care abuses and wrongful denials.

MASSACHUSETTS: Massachusetts General Laws Annotated, Ch. 176G-1 et seq. do not permit direct access to medical specialists, excepting ob-gyn. A specialist cannot be designated as a PCP. Inpatient childbirth care requires a minimum 48 hours after vaginal birth; 96 hours after caesarian. Use of financial incentives by HMOs to induce providers to limit their care is prohibited. There is independent review of HMO and managed care denials (binding on the plans) but no provision for consumers to sue HMOs for managed care abuses and wrongful denials.

MICHIGAN: MCL 333.21001 and other provisions do not permit direct access to medical specialists, except ob-gyn. A specialist cannot be designated as a PCP. The state prohibits the use of financial incentives by HMOs to induce providers to limit their care. There is nonbinding independent review of HMO and managed care denials but no provision for consumers to sue HMOs for managed care abuses and wrongful denials.

MINNESOTA: State law (Minnesota Statutes Annotated, sections 62D.01 and other provisions) does not permit direct access to medical specialists, excepting ob-gyn. A specialist cannot be designated as a PCP. Inpatient childbirth care requires a minimum 48 hours after vaginal birth; 96 hours after caesarian. The use of financial incentives by HMOs to induce providers to limit their care is prohibited. There is nonbinding independent review of HMO and managed care denials but no provision for consumers to sue HMOs for managed care abuses and wrongful denials.

MISSISSIPPI: Mississippi Code Annotated, sections 41.7.401 and other provisions do not permit direct access to medical specialists, except ob-gyn. A specialist cannot be designated as a PCP, except ob-gyn. No prohibition exists on the use of financial incentives by HMOs to induce providers to limit their care. There are no provisions for review of HMO and managed care denials and no provisions for consum-

ers to sue HMOs for managed care abuses and wrongful denials.

MISSOURI: State law (Missouri Revised Statutes 354.400 et seq.) does not permit direct access to medical specialists, except for ob-gyn. A specialist cannot be designated as a PCP. Inpatient childbirth care requires a minimum 48 hours after vaginal birth; 96 hours after caesarian. Prohibitions exist the use of financial incentives by HMOs to induce providers to limit their care. There is binding independent review of HMO and managed care denials, and consumers may sue HMOs for managed care abuses and wrongful denials.

MONTANA: Under state law (Montana Code Annotated 33-31-101 et seq.), there is no direct access to specialists except for ob-gyns, chiropractors, osteopaths, physician assistants, practitioner nurses, and dentists. Specialists (excepting ob-gyn) cannot be designated as PCPs. Inpatient childbirth care requires a minimum 48 hours after vaginal birth; 96 hours after caesarian. Prohibition exists on the use of financial incentives by HMOs to induce providers to limit their care. There is independent review of HMO and managed care denials but no provision for consumers to sue HMOs for managed care abuses and wrongful denials.

NEBRASKA: Nebraska Revised Statutes 44-3292 and other state laws do not permit direct access to medical specialists, including ob-gyn. However, an ob-gyn specialist may be designated as a PCP. The use of financial incentives by HMOs to induce providers to limit their care is prohibited. There are no provisions for independent review of HMO and managed care denials and no provision for consumers to sue HMOs for managed care abuses and wrongful denials.

NEVADA: State law (Nevada Revised Statutes 695C.010 et seq.) does not permit direct access to medical specialists, except ob-gyn. A specialist cannot be designated as a PCP. Inpatient childbirth care requires a minimum 48 hours after vaginal birth; 96 hours after caesarian. There is a prohibition on the use of financial incentives by HMOs to induce providers to limit their care. No provisions exist for independent review of HMO and managed care denials and no provision for consumers to sue HMOs for managed care abuses and wrongful denials.

NEW HAMPSHIRE: New Hampshire Revised Statutes Annotated 420-B:1 et seq. do not permit direct access to medical specialists, including ob-gyn. A specialist cannot be designated as a PCP. Prohibition exists on the use of financial incentives by HMOs to induce providers to limit their care. There is independent review of HMO and managed care denials but no provision for consumers to sue HMOs for managed care abuses and wrongful denials.

NEW JERSEY: State law (New Jersey Statutes Annotated, sections 26:2j et seq. and other provisions) does not permit direct access to medical specialists, including ob-gyn. However, a specialist, including ob-gyn, may be designated as a PCP. Inpatient childbirth care requires a minimum 48 hours after vaginal birth; 96 hours after caesarian. Also required is 48 hours of in-patient care after a simple mastectomy; 72 hours after a radical mastectomy. There is a prohibition on the use of financial incentives by HMOs to induce providers to limit their care. There is also nonbinding independent review of HMO and managed care denials but no provision for consumers to sue HMOs for managed care abuses and wrongful denials. Nonetheless, consumer suits have been adjudicated by the courts.

NEW MEXICO: New Mexico Statutes Annotated 59A-46-1 and other state law do not permit direct access to medical specialists, except ob-gyn. A specialist cannot be designated as a PCP, except ob-gyn. Inpatient childbirth care requires a minimum 48 hours after vaginal birth; 96 hours after caesarian. The law also provides for inpatient care following breast surgery and requires in-patient care of at least 48 hours following a mastectomy and 24 hours following a lumpectomy. There is a prohibition on the use of financial incentives by HMOs to induce providers to limit their care. There is also nonbinding independent review of HMO and managed care denials but no provision for consumers to sue HMOs for managed care abuses and wrongful denials.

NEW YORK: New York Article 44: Health Maintenance Organizations and Article 49: Utilization Review law does not permit direct access to medical specialists, excepting ob-gyn. A specialist cannot be designated as a PCP. Inpatient childbirth care requires a minimum 48 hours after vaginal birth; 96 hours after caesarian. No prohibition exists on the use of financial incentives by HMOs to induce providers to limit their care. There is independent review of HMO and managed care denials but no provision for consumers to sue HMOs for managed care abuses and wrongful denials.

NORTH CAROLINA: State law (North Carolina General Statutes 58-67-1 et seq.) does not permit di-

rect access to medical specialists, excepting for ob-gyn. A specialist cannot be designated as a PCP. Inpatient childbirth care requires a minimum 48 hours after vaginal birth; 96 hours after caesarian. No prohibition exists on the use of financial incentives by HMOs to induce providers to limit their care. There is nonbinding independent review of HMO and managed care denials but no provision for consumers to sue HMOs for managed care abuses and wrongful denials.

NORTH DAKOTA: North Dakota Code, sections 26.1-18.1-1-01 et seq. does not permit direct access to medical specialists, including ob-gyn. A specialist cannot be designated as a PCP. Inpatient childbirth care requires a minimum 48 hours after vaginal birth; 96 hours after caesarian. State law prohibits the use of financial incentives by HMOs to induce providers to limit their care. There are no provisions for independent review of HMO and managed care denials and no provision for consumers to sue HMOs for managed care abuses and wrongful denials.

OHIO: Ohio Revised Code Chapter 1756 et seq., as well as other state provisions, does not permit direct access to medical specialists, except for ob-gyn. A specialist cannot be designated as a PCP. Inpatient childbirth care requires a minimum 48 hours after vaginal birth; 96 hours after caesarian. There is a prohibition on the use of financial incentives by HMOs to induce providers to limit their care. There is binding (on the plan) independent review of HMO and managed care denials but no provision for consumers to sue HMOs for managed care abuses and wrongful denials.

OKLAHOMA: Title 63 of the Oklahoma Statutes Annotated, in addition to other separate provisions, does not permit direct access to medical specialists, including ob-gyn. A specialist cannot be designated as a PCP. Inpatient childbirth care requires a minimum 48 hours after vaginal birth. The law also provides for inpatient care following breast surgery and requires in-patient care of at least 48 hours following a mastectomy. No prohibition exists on the use of financial incentives by HMOs to induce providers to limit their care. There is independent review of HMO and managed care denials, but consumers may sue HMOs for managed care abuses, e.g., delays in treatment, and wrongful denials.

OREGON: Oregon Statutes Annotated 750.005 et seq. State law does not permit direct access to medical specialists, excepting ob-gyn. A specialist cannot be designated as a PCP. Inpatient childbirth care requires a minimum 48 hours after vaginal birth; 96 hours after caesarian. No prohibition exists on the use of financial incentives by HMOs to induce providers to limit their care. There are no provisions for independent review of HMO and managed care denials and no provision for consumers to sue HMOs for managed care abuses and wrongful denials.

PENNSYLVANIA: State law (Pennsylvania Statutes Annotated, Title 40, sections 1551 to 1567) does not permit direct access to medical specialists, excepting for ob-gyn. A specialist can be designated as primary care provider if the enrollee has a life-threatening, degenerative, or disabling disease or condition. Inpatient childbirth care requires a minimum 48 hours after vaginal birth; 96 hours after caesarian. State law prohibits the use of financial incentives by HMOs to induce providers to limit their care. There is non-binding independent review of HMO and managed care denials but no provision for consumers to sue HMOs for managed care abuses and wrongful denials.

RHODE ISLAND: State law (Rhode Island General Laws, sections 27-41-1) does not permit direct access to medical specialists, except ob-gyn. A specialist cannot be designated as a PCP. Inpatient childbirth care requires a minimum 48 hours after vaginal birth; 96 hours after caesarian. The law also provides for inpatient care following breast surgery and requires inpatient care of at least 48 hours following a mastectomy. There are provisions prohibiting the use of financial incentives by HMOs to induce providers to limit their care. There is binding independent review of HMO and managed care denials but no provision for consumers to sue HMOs for managed care abuses and wrongful denials.

SOUTH CAROLINA: South Carolina Code Annotated, Sections 38-33-10, does not permit direct access to medical specialists, except for ob-gyn. A specialist cannot be designated as a PCP. Inpatient childbirth care requires a minimum 48 hours after vaginal birth; 96 hours after caesarian. There are prohibitions on the use of financial incentives by HMOs to induce providers to limit their care. There is binding independent review of HMO and managed care denials but no provision for consumers to sue HMOs for managed care abuses and wrongful denials.

SOUTH DAKOTA: South Dakota Codified Laws, Sections 58-41-1, do not permit direct access to medical specialists, including ob-gyn. A specialist cannot be designated as a PCP. Inpatient childbirth care requires a minimum 48 hours after vaginal birth; 96

hours after caesarian. The law also provides for inpatient care following breast surgery and requires inpatient care of at least 48 hours following a mastectomy. No prohibition exists on the use of financial incentives by HMOs to induce providers to limit their care. There is no provision for review of HMO and managed care denials and no provision for consumers to sue HMOs for managed care abuses and wrongful denials.

TENNESSEE: Tennessee Code Annotated 56-32-201 et seq. does not permit direct access to medical specialists, except for ob-gyn. A specialist can be designated as primary care provider but only when the enrollee has a life-threatening, degenerative, or chronic disease or condition. No prohibition exists on the use of financial incentives by HMOs to induce providers to limit their care. There is binding independent review of HMO and managed care denials but no provision for consumers to sue HMOs for managed care abuses and wrongful denials.

TEXAS: State law (Texas Insurance Code Annotated 20A.01 et seq.) does not permit direct access to medical specialists, except for ob-gyn. A specialist can be designated as primary care provider but only when the enrollee has a life-threatening, disabling, or chronic disease or condition. Inpatient childbirth care requires a minimum 48 hours after vaginal birth; 96 hours after caesarian. The law also provides for inpatient care following breast surgery and requires inpatient care of at least 48 hours following a mastectomy and 24 hours following lymph node dissection. There are provisions prohibiting the use of financial incentives by HMOs to induce providers to limit their care. There is binding independent review of HMO and managed care denials. The statute specifically allows suit against HMOs and managed care companies for abuses and wrongful denials.

UTAH: Utah Code Annotated 31A-8-101 does not permit direct access to medical specialists, excepting ob-gyn. A specialist cannot be designated as a PCP. Inpatient childbirth care requires a minimum 48 hours after vaginal birth; 96 hours after caesarian. No prohibition exists on the use of financial incentives by HMOs to induce providers to limit their care. There is independent review of HMO and managed care denials but no provision for consumers to sue HMOs for managed care abuses and wrongful denials.

VERMONT: State law (Vermont Statutes Annotated, Title 8, sections 5101-5115) does not permit direct access to medical specialists, excepting ob-gyn.

A specialist cannot be designated as a PCP. There is a prohibition on the use of financial incentives by HMOs to induce providers to limit their care. There is binding independent review of HMO and managed care denials but no provision for consumers to sue HMOs for managed care abuses and wrongful denials.

VIRGINIA: Virginia Code Annotated 38.2-4300 et seq. does not permit direct access to medical specialists, excepting ob-gyn. A specialist cannot be designated as a PCP. Inpatient childbirth care requires a minimum 48 hours after vaginal birth; 96 hours after caesarian. The law also provides for inpatient care following breast surgery and requires in-patient care of at least 48 hours following a mastectomy. There is independent review of HMO and managed care denials but no provision for consumers to sue HMOs for managed care abuses and wrongful denials.

WASHINGTON: Washington Revised Code 48.46.010 et seq. does not permit direct access to medical specialists, except for ob-gyn. A specialist cannot be designated as a PCP. No prohibition on exists the use of financial incentives by HMOs to induce providers to limit their care. There is no provision for review of HMO and managed care denials. As of June 2001, consumers may sue their HMOs for managed care abuses and wrongful denials.

WEST VIRGINIA: State law (West Virginia Code 33-25A-1) does not permit direct access to medical specialists, except ob-gyn. A specialist cannot be designated as a PCP, excepting ob-gyn. Inpatient childbirth care requires a minimum 48 hours after vaginal birth; 96 hours after caesarian. There is a prohibition on the use of financial incentives by HMOs to induce providers to limit their care. There is no provision for review of HMO and managed care denials, and no provision for consumers to sue HMOs for managed care abuses and wrongful denials.

WISCONSIN: Wisconsin Statutes Annotated, sections 609.001 does not permit direct access to medical specialists, excepting ob-gyn. A specialist cannot be designated as a PCP. No prohibition on the use of financial incentives by HMOs to induce providers to limit their care. There is a provision for binding review of HMO and managed care denials but no provision for consumers to sue HMOs for managed care abuses and wrongful denials.

WYOMING: Wyoming Statutes Annotated 26-34-101 et seq. do not permit direct access to medical specialists, including ob-gyn. A specialist cannot be designated as a PCP. No prohibition exists on the use of financial incentives by HMOs to induce providers to limit their care. There is no provision for review of HMO and managed care denials and no provision for consumers to sue HMOs for managed care abuses and wrongful denials.

## Additional Resources

"*Fighting HMO and Managed Care Abuses and Malpractice: Laws and Cases*" Trueman, David L. Available at http://www.turemanlaw.com/lawsand.htm.

*Health Against Wealth* Anders, George. Houghton Mifflin: 1996.

*Pro-Patient Managed Care Laws.* Kaminski, Janet L. 2004. Available at http://www.cga.ct.gov/2004/rpt/2004-R—0808.htm

"Managed Care Practice and Litigation"*Representing the Elderly Client Law and Practice.* Beglely, Thomas D., Jr., and J-Anne Herina Jeffreys. Aspen Publishers Inc: 1999 (2001 Suppl.).

"What the New Medicare Law Means to Doctors."*Medical News Today,* 4 April 2004. Available at http://www.medicalnewstoday.com/medicalnews.php?newid=7003.

"*Will State Legislators Keep Playing Doctor?*" Wehrwein, Peter. Available at http://www.managedcaremag.com/archives/9710/9710.legislator.shtml.

## Organizations

### *The HMO Page*
URL: http://www.hmopage.org

# HEALTHCARE

## MEDICAID

*Sections within this essay:*

- Background
- History
- Eligibility
- How Medicaid Funds Are Administered
    - Fee-For-Service Medicaid
    - Medicaid Managed Care
- Benefits
- State-By-State Guide To Medicaid
- Additional Resources

## Background

Of the federal governments two major health programs, **Medicare** and **Medicaid**, Medicaid has had by far the rockier history. Medicare has enjoyed fairly broad based support in its goal of covering the elderly and disabled. While there has been controversy over the extent of benefits, the basic coverage of the Medicare program has remained the same since it was it was first enacted, and the federal government has always had primary responsibility for the program.

In contrast, Medicaid has always inspired battles, between the federal government and the states over funding of the program, between conservatives and liberals over what the purpose of the program should be, and between different interest groups whose members argue over how the Medicaid pie should be divided. There have been suggestions

from several quarters that Medicaid be ended entirely, either eliminated or turned into something completely different, and these suggestions have increased since welfare reform was passed in 1996.

In part, these controversies stem from the reason Medicaid was originally set up—to enable each state, as far as practicable, to furnish medical assistance to individuals whose income and resources are insufficient to meet the costs of medically necessary services. The goal is simple, but the arguments on how to best accomplish that goal are complex. Although many commentators argue Medicaid has been one of the most successful government programs, in terms of the number of people it has helped, the eventual fate of the program remains to be seen.

## History

Medicaid was created in 1965 under Title XIX of the Social Security Act, as part of Lyndon Johnson's War on Poverty. It was enacted at the same time the Medicare program was passed.

Unlike Medicare, Medicaid—the brainchild of Congressman Wilbur Mills, the chairman of the House Ways and Means Committee—involved federal funds given to the states to administer their own programs. The federal government set the basic standards for who was covered by the program, and the states could decide if they wanted to broaden the program beyond those standards

Originally, Medicaid categories were defined by welfare recipient status, but this began to change in the mid-1980's and ceased completely with the passage of welfare reform in the mid-1990's. Over its history, the Medicaid program has changed from a program to provide health insurance to the welfare population to a catch-all program that provides health and long term care services to around 40 million people at a cost of $170 billion dollars to federal and state governments. As of 2000, Medicaid was the source of health care insurance for one in four American children and covered 40 percent of all births.

## Eligibility

Medicaid eligibility has evolved over the years. Originally, it was supposed to assist the so-called "deserving poor," those medically needy people who were aged, blind, disabled, or families with dependant children, or falling into some other status of poverty where assistance was favored. Not every person whose income falls below the poverty line qualifies for Medicaid, and this has always been true of the program.

Medicaid recipients have historically been divided into the "categorically needy," persons who were eligible for Supplemental Security Income (SSI) benefits for **disability**, for Aid to Families with Dependant Children (AFDC) benefits, or had been eligible for other government benefit programs; and the "medically needy," persons whose income exceeds financial standards for the above programs but who incur regular medical expenses that, when deducted from their income, bring their income down to the eligibility level for financial assistance. Technically, these categories no longer exist under the current Medicaid system, but state programs that expand Medicaid coverage beyond the traditional categorically needy are still known as "medically needy" programs. Typically these "medically needy" programs cover nursing home and other long-term care.

Currently the program covers the following groups as "categorically needy." For definitional purposes, the poverty level was $8,350 for an individual, and $17,050 for a family of four as of the year 2000:

- Medicaid must cover all pregnant women with incomes of up to 133 percent of the poverty level.

- Medicaid must cover all children under the age of six with family incomes below 133 percent of the poverty level and children under age 19 born after 1983 in families with incomes up to 100 percent of the poverty level.

- Medicaid must cover the Medicare premiums and cost-sharing obligations for "Qualified Medicare Beneficiaries" whose income does not exceed 100 percent of the poverty level. It must also cover Medicare Part B premiums for "Specified Low-Income Medical Beneficiaries", persons whose income is between 100 percent and 120 percent of the poverty level. Medicaid also covers nursing home costs for persons below a certain income level or asset level set by the state, and provides outpatient drug coverage for some qualified Medicare recipients.

- Medicaid covers **disabled persons** whose income falls below a certain level, including children eligible for SSI disability benefits. Coverage of other adult disabled recipients is generally mandatory if they receive SSI and are at 74 percent of the poverty level, although some states have been waived in at lower levels than this, and one state, Mississippi, does not cover SSI benefit recipients at all. Many states provide home and community-based care for disabled utilizing Medicaid funds as well.

Medicaid funds also help finance health coverage in several states for persons below a certain income who otherwise would not qualify for Medicaid. In general, states have much leeway in terms of coverage with Medicaid funds. Nearly two-thirds of all Medicaid spending is attributable to optional benefits and services.

## How Medicaid Funds Are Administered

The Medicaid program has changed over the years in terms of the way medical and other services are paid for. The original Medicaid law guaranteed recipients their choice of providers. However, beginning in the 1980's, states began making consistent requests for waivers to allow them to enter Medicaid recipients in **managed care** programs, and in 1997, the law was finally amended to allow states to do this explicitly. As of 2002, there are two types of ways Medicaid funds are administered, the traditional fee-for-service way and through Medicaid Managed Care (MMC).

### Fee-For-Service Medicaid

This is the traditional way Medicaid made payments for services and was the only way technically allowed until 1997 by federal Medicaid law, which mandated freedom of choice for all Medicaid recipients. However, there was a catch to this freedom of choice—doctors have the option of opting out of the Medicaid system and refusing to accept Medicaid patients.

Medicaid fees for physicians are set by the state and so vary from region to region. However, they are usually low—paying well below private rates for physician services and usually below what Medicare pays. As a result, the argument has been made that Medicaid recipients often do not get the quality care received by other medical insurance recipients. In many areas, it is difficult to find doctors who will treat Medicare patients because of the low payments, and in other cases doctors have sued to force higher payments from Medicaid programs. Hospitals are more limited in their abilities to turn down Medicaid patients, since they are often tax exempt or have obligations under other federal statutes.

Because states are allowed to set payment rates, such rates can be changes at anytime. Thus, when a state undergoes a budget shortfall or other problem, rates can be and often are lowered.

### Medicaid Managed Care

Because of the problems inherent in fee-for-service Medicaid, many states over the years requested waivers from the freedom of choice requirement to allow them to enter Medicaid recipients in managed care programs. Finally, the federal government amended the Medicaid **statute** with the 1997 Balanced Budget Act to permit states to require Medicaid recipients to enroll in a Medicaid Managed Care (MMC) program. A **waiver** is still needed to require Medicare recipients also receiving Medicaid, Native Americans, and special needs children to enroll in an MMC program.

Currently over half of Medicaid recipients receive care through these programs. MMC programs are similar to managed care programs used by the privately insured. The two most common are:

- The Risk-Based Model: Under this model, the MMC program is paid a fixed monthly fee per enrollee and assumes some or all the financial risk for a broad range of services. About four-fifths of Medicaid MMC enrollees receive services under this model.

- Fee-For-Service Primary Care Case Management (PCCM): Under this model, a health care provider acts as "gatekeeper" to approve and monitor the services given to MMC enrollees. These providers do not assume any financial risk and are paid a per-patient monthly case management fee.

## Benefits

Benefits provided under the Medicaid program vary widely from state to state. Twenty-six categories of services are listed under the Medicaid states as services states may cover, in addition to a provision allowing coverage of "any other medical care, and any other type of remedial care, specified by the Secretary."

As of 2002, states must provide Medicaid recipients who are required by federal law to be covered with inpatient hospital services; outpatient hospital services and rural health clinic services; early and periodic screening; other laboratory and X-ray services; nursing facility services; early and periodic screening, diagnostic and treatment services for children; family planning services and supplies, physician services; and nurse-midwife and other certified nurse practitioners services.

Medicaid also covers long-term care. States have considerable flexibility in their long-term care programs. Although states must cover home health services under Medicaid, they have the option of providing personal care services and also may design home and community-based care programs. Medicaid funds half of all nursing home care in this country. Medicaid also pays for much of the care provided by intermediate care facilities for the mentally disabled.

Nursing homes present a special problem for Medicaid, in that many elderly are too well-off to qualify for Medicaid when they go into the nursing home but become impoverished paying for nursing home expenses and other medical expenses. Thirty-six states allow such people to "spend down" their assets until they reach Medicaid asset eligibility levels. At that point, Medicaid assumes the cost of nursing home and medical care. Not all states allow this, only those that cover the medically needy.

Some states cover optional services, such as podiatry, dental care, eyeglasses, or dentures, under Medicaid. These optional services are usually the first to go if there are cutbacks in the program.

## State-By-State Guide To Medicaid

States have different Medicaid eligibility requirements, with some states being more generous than others. Here is a state-by-state guide to what the eligibility requirements are. All eligibility levels are expressed as a percent of the federal poverty level for a specific group. For example, a child 1-5 in Alabama must be part of a family that makes 133 percent of the federal poverty level ($17,050 for a family of four) or less in order to qualify for Medicaid.

- ALABAMA: Infants, Children 1-5, 133%; Children 6-19, 100%; Pregnant Women, 133%; Supplemental Security Income Recipients 74%; No Medically Needy Program.

- ALASKA: Infants, Children 1-5, 200%; Children 6-19, 200%; Pregnant Women, 200%; Supplemental Security Income Recipients, 74%; No Medically Needy Program.

- ARIZONA: Infants, 140%; Children 1-5, 133%; Children 6-16, 100%; Children 17-19, 50%; Pregnant Women, 140%; Supplemental Security Income Recipients, 74%; No Medically Needy Program.

- ARKANSAS: Infants, Children 1-5, 200%; Children 6-19, 200%; Pregnant Women, 133%; Supplemental Security Income Recipients, 74%; Medically Needy, Individual, 16%; Medically Needy, Couple, 24%.

- CALIFORNIA: Infants, 200%; Children 1-5, 133%; Children 6-19, 100%; Pregnant Women, 300%; Supplemental Security Income Recipients, 74%; Medically Needy, Individual, 89%; Medically Needy, Couple, 104%.

- COLORADO: Infants, Children 1-5, 133%; Children 6-16, 100%; Children 17-19, 43%; Pregnant Women, 133%; Supplemental Security Income Recipients 74%; No Medically Needy Program.

- CONNECTICUT: Infants, Children 1-5, 185%; Children 6-19, 185%; Pregnant Women, 185%; Supplemental Security Income Recipients, 69%; Medically Needy, Individual, 71%; Medically Needy, Couple, 70%.

- DELAWARE: Infants, Children 1-5, 133%; Children 6-19, 100%; Pregnant Women, 200%; Supplemental Security Income Recipients 74%; No Medically Needy Program.

- DISTRICT OF COLUMBIA: Infants, Children 1-5, 200%; Children 6-19, 200%; Pregnant Women, 200%; Supplemental Security Income Recipients, 74%; Medically Needy, Individual, 56%; Medically Needy, Couple, 44%.

- FLORIDA: Infants, 200%; Children 1-5, 133%; Children 6-19, 100%; Pregnant Women, 185%; Supplemental Security Income Recipients, 74%; Medically Needy, Individual, 27%; Medically Needy, Couple, 27%.

- GEORGIA: Infants, 185%; Children 1-5, 133%; Children 6-19, 100%; Pregnant Women, 235%; Supplemental Security Income Recipients, 74%; Medically Needy, Individual, 31%; Medically Needy, Couple, 35%.

- HAWAII: Infants, Children 1-5, 200%; Children 6-19, 200%; Pregnant Women, 185%; Supplemental Security Income Recipients, 69%; Medically Needy, Individual, 54%; Medically Needy, Couple, 54%.

- IDAHO: Infants, Children 1-5, 150%; Children 6-19, 150%; Pregnant Women, 133%; Supplemental Security Income Recipients 74%; No Medically Needy Program.

- ILLINOIS: Infants, 200%; Children 1-5, 133%; Children 6-19, 133%; Pregnant Women, 200%; Supplemental Security Income Recipients, 41%; Medically Needy, Individual, 42%; Medically Needy, Couple, 41%.

- INDIANA: Infants, Children 1-5, 150%; Children 6-19, 150%; Pregnant Women, 150%; Supplemental Security Income Recipients 76%; No Medically Needy Program.

- IOWA: Infants, 200%; Children 1-5, 133%; Children 6-19, 133%; Pregnant Women, 200%; Supplemental Security Income Recipients, 41%; Medically Needy, Individual, 72%; Medically Needy, Couple, 53%.

- KANSAS: Infants, 150%; Children 1-5, 133%; Children 6-19, 100%; Pregnant Women, 150%; Supplemental Security Income Recipients, 74%; Medically Needy, Individual, 71%; Medically Needy, Couple, 53%.

- KENTUCKY: Infants, 185%; Children 1-5, 150%; Children 6-19, 150%; Pregnant Women, 185%; Supplemental Security Income Recipients, 74%; Medically Needy, Individual, 32%; Medically Needy, Couple, 30%.

- LOUISIANA: Infants, Children 1-5, 200%; Children 6-19, 200%; Pregnant Women, 133%; Supplemental Security Income Recipients, 74%; Medically Needy, Individual, 15%; Medically Needy, Couple, 21%.

- MAINE: Infants, 200%; Children 1-5, 150%; Children 6-19, 150%; Pregnant Women, 200%; Supplemental Security Income Recipients, 74%; Medically Needy, Individual, 47%; Medically Needy, Couple, 38%.

- MARYLAND: Infants, Children 1-5, 200%; Children 6-19, 200%; Pregnant Women, 200%; Supplemental Security Income Recipients, 74%; Medically Needy, Individual, 52%; Medically Needy, Couple, 43%.

- MASSACHUSETTS: Infants, 200%; Children 1-5, 150%; Children 6-19, 150%; Pregnant Women, 200%; Supplemental Security Income Recipients, 74%; Medically Needy, Individual, 78%; Medically Needy, Couple, 72%.

- MICHIGAN: Infants, 185%; Children 1-5, 150%; Children 6-19, 150%; Pregnant Women, 185%; Supplemental Security Income Recipients, 74%; Medically Needy, Individual, 61%; Medically Needy, Couple, 60%.

- MINNESOTA: Infants, 280%; Children 1-5, 275%; Children 6-19, 275%; Pregnant Women, 275%; Supplemental Security Income Recipients, 70%; Medically Needy, Individual, 70%; Medically Needy, Couple, 64%.

- MISSISSIPPI: Infants, 185%; Children 1-5, 133%; Children 6-19, 100%; Pregnant Women, 133%; No Supplemental Security Income Recipients Program; No Medically Needy Program.

- MISSOURI: Infants, Children 1-5, 300%; Children 6-19, 300%; Pregnant Women, 185%; Supplemental Security Income Recipients 74%; No Medically Needy Program.

- MONTANA: Infants, Children 1-5, 133%; Children 6-16 100%; Children 17-19, 71%; Pregnant Women, 133%; Supplemental Security Income Recipients, 74%; Medically Needy, Individual, 73%; Medically Needy, Couple, 54%.

- NEBRASKA: Infants, Children 1-5, 185%; Children 6-19, 185%; Pregnant Women, 185%; Supplemental Security Income Recipients, 74%; Medically Needy, Individual, 58%; Medically Needy, Couple, 43%.

- NEVADA: Infants, Children 1-5, 133%; Children 6-16, 100%; Children 17-19, 89%; Pregnant Women, 133%; Supplemental Security Income Recipients 74%; No Medically Needy Program.

- NEW HAMPSHIRE: Infants, 300%; Children 1-5, 185%; Children 6-19, 185%; Pregnant Women, 185%; Supplemental Security Income Recipients, 76%; Medically Needy, Individual, 76%; Medically Needy, Couple, 71%.

- NEW JERSEY: Infants, 185%; Children 1-5, 133%; Children 6-19, 133%; Pregnant Women, 185%; Supplemental Security Income Recipients, 74%; Medically Needy, Individual, 55%; Medically Needy, Couple, 48%.

- NEW MEXICO: Infants, Children 1-5, 235%; Children 6-19, 235%; Pregnant Women, 185%; Supplemental Security Income Recipients 74%; No Medically Needy Program.

- NEW YORK: Infants, 185%; Children 1-5, 133%; Children 6-19, 100%; Pregnant Women, 200%; Supplemental Security Income Recipients, 74%; Medically Needy, Individual, 87%; Medically Needy, Couple, 94%.

- NORTH CAROLINA: Infants, 185%; Children 1-5, 133%; Children 6-19, 100%; Pregnant Women, 185%; Supplemental Security Income Recipients, 74%; Medically Needy, Individual, 60%; Medically Needy, Couple, 50%.

- NORTH DAKOTA: Infants, Children 1-5, 133%; Children 6-19 100%; Pregnant Women, 133%; Supplemental Security Income Recipients, 65%; Medically Needy, Individual, 60%; Medically Needy, Couple, 50%.

- OHIO: Infants, Children 1-5, 200%; Children 6-19, 200%; Pregnant Women, 133%; Supplemental Security Income Recipients 64%; No Medically Needy Program.

- OKLAHOMA: Infants, Children 1-5, 185%; Children 6-19, 185%; Pregnant Women,

185%; Supplemental Security Income Recipients, 74%; Medically Needy, Individual, 39%; Medically Needy, Couple, 36%.

- OREGON: Infants, Children 1-5, 133%; Children 6-19, 100%; Pregnant Women, 170%; Supplemental Security Income Recipients, 74%; Medically Needy, Individual, 100%; Medically Needy, Couple, 100%.

- PENNSYLVANIA: Infants, 185%; Children 1-5, 133%; Children 6-16, 100%; Children 17-19, 71%; Pregnant Women, 185%; Supplemental Security Income Recipients, 74%; Medically Needy, Individual, 63%; Medically Needy, Couple, 49%.

- RHODE ISLAND: Infants, Children 1-5, 250%; Children 6-19, 250%; Pregnant Women, 250%; Supplemental Security Income Recipients, 74%; Medically Needy, Individual, 83%; Medically Needy, Couple, 66%.

- SOUTH CAROLINA: Infants, 185%; Children 1-5, 150%; Children 6-19, 150%; Pregnant Women, 185%; Supplemental Security Income Recipients 74%; No Medically Needy Program.

- SOUTH DAKOTA: Infants, Children 1-5, 200%; Children 6-19, 200%; Pregnant Women, 133%; Supplemental Security Income Recipients 74%; No Medically Needy Program.

- TENNESSEE: Infants, Children 1-18 -, eligibility IS based on child's lack of insurance with no upper income limit; Pregnant Women, 185%; Supplemental Security Income Recipients, 74%; Medically Needy, Individual, 26%; Medically Needy, Couple, 21%.

- TEXAS: Infants, 185%; Children 1-5, 133%; Children 6-19, 100%; Pregnant Women, 185%; Supplemental Security Income Recipients 74%; No Medically Needy Program.

- UTAH: Infants, Children 1-5, 133%; Children 6-19, 100%; Pregnant Women, 133%; Supplemental Security Income Recipients, 74%; Medically Needy, Individual, 55%; Medically Needy, Couple, 50%.

- VERMONT: Infants, Children 1-5, 300%; Children 6-19, 300%; Pregnant Women, 200%; Supplemental Security Income Recipients, 74%; Medically Needy, Individual, 110%; Medically Needy, Couple, 82%.

- VIRGINIA: Infants, Children 1-5, 133%; Children 6-19, 100%; Pregnant Women, 250%; Supplemental Security Income Recipients, 74%; Medically Needy, Individual, 37%; Medically Needy, Couple, 34%.

- WASHINGTON: Infants, Children 1-5, 200%; Children 6-19, 200%; Pregnant Women, 185%; Supplemental Security Income Recipients, 74%; Medically Needy, Individual, 78%; Medically Needy, Couple, 65%.

- WEST VIRGINIA: Infants, Children 1-5, 150%; Children 6-19, 100%; Pregnant Women, 150%; Supplemental Security Income Recipients, 74%; Medically Needy, Individual, 30%; Medically Needy, Couple, 30%.

- WISCONSIN: Infants, Children 1-5, 185%; Children 6-19, 185%; Pregnant Women, 185%; Supplemental Security Income Recipients, 74%; Medically Needy, Individual, 86%; Medically Needy, Couple, 65%.

- WYOMING: Infants, Children 1-5, 133%; Children 6-16, 100%; Children 17-19, 67%; Pregnant Women, 133%; Supplemental Security Income Recipients 74%; No Medically Needy Program.

## Additional Resources

"Celebrating 35 Years of Medicare and Medicaid" DeParle, Nancy-Ann Min, *Health Care Financing Review*, Oct. 1, 2000.

*Health Care Law and Ethics, 2nd Edition.* 2nd. ed., Hall, Mark A., Ellman, Ira Mark, Strouse, Daniel S.; West Group, St. Paul, 1999.

*The Law of Health Care Organization and Finance, Fourth Edition.* Furrow, Barry R., Greaney, Thomas L., et. al., West Group, St. Paul, 2001.

"*Medicaid*", Kaiser Family Foundation, 2002. Available at http://www.kff.org/,. Kaiser Family Foundation, 2002.

## Organizations

### *Centers for Medicare and Medicaid Services*
7500 Security Blvd.oulevard
Baltimore, MD 21244-1850 USA
Phone: (410) 786-3000
URL: http://cms.hhs.gov
Primary Contact: Thomas A Scully, Administrator

### *Henry J. Kaiser Family Foundation*
2400 Sand Hill Road

Menlo Park, CA 94025 USA
Phone: (650) 854-9400
Fax: (650) 854-4800
URL: http://www.kff.org
Primary Contact: Drew Altman, President

**U. S. Department of Health and Human Services**
200 Independence Avenue S.W.

Washington, DC 20201 USA
Phone: (877) 696-6775
E-Mail: HHS.Mail@hhs.gov
URL: http://www.hhs.gov/
Primary Contact: Janet Hale, Chief Information Officer

# HEALTHCARE

## MEDICAL MALPRACTICE

*Sections within this essay:*

## Background

**Medical malpractice** is **negligence** committed by medical professionals. For negligence to be "actionable" (having all the components necessary to constitute a viable cause of action), there must be a duty owed to someone, a breach of that duty, and resulting harm or damage that is proximately caused

by that breach. The simplest way to apply the concept of proximate cause to medical malpractice is to ask whether, "but for" the alleged negligence, the harm or injury would have occurred.

When determining whether the conduct of a member of the general public is negligent, the conduct is judged against a standard of how a "reasonably prudent person" might act in the same or similar circumstance. Conversely, when determining whether a medical professional has been negligent, his or her practice or conduct is judged at a level of competency and professionalism consistent with the specialized training, experience, and care of a "reasonably prudent" physician in the same or similar circumstances. This constitutes the "standard of care" or professional "duty" that a physician owes to his or her patient. If the physician breaches the standard of care and his patient suffers accordingly, there is actionable medical **malpractice**.

The term "patient" generally refers to a person who is receiving medical treatment and/or who is under medical care. In many states, other licensed medical professionals such as chiropractors, nurses, therapists, and psychologists, may also be sued for malpractice, i.e., negligently breaching their respective professional duties owed to the patient. The following sections refer generally to medical malpractice as it relates to medical doctors/physicians.

## Actionable Malpractice

State laws govern the viability of causes of action for medical malpractice. The laws vary in terms of time limits to bring suit, qualifications of "expert" witnesses, cognizable theories of liability, and proper party defendants/proper party plaintiffs. Notwithstanding these differences, there are common requisites for all cases.

First and foremost, a physician must owe a duty to patients before his or her competency in performing that duty can be judged. In U. S. **jurisprudence**, a person has no affirmative duty to assist injured individuals, -in the absence of a special relationship with them (such as doctor-patient, attorney-client, guardian-ward, etc.) A doctor dining in a restaurant has no duty to come forward and assist injured others if they suffer a heart attacks while dining in the same restaurant. If the doctor merely continues with his meal and does nothing to help, the ailing others would not have an action for malpractice against him, notwithstanding their harm. However, once a doctor voluntarily decides to assist others or come to their aid, he or she becomes liable for any injury that results from any negligence during that assistance.

Once the requisite doctor-patient relationship is established, the doctor owes to the patient the duty to render care and treatment with that degree of skill, care, and diligence as possessed by or expected of a reasonably competent physician under the same or similar circumstances. The "circumstances" include the area of medicine in which the physician practices, the customary or accepted practices of other physicians in the area (the "locality rule"), the level of equipment and facilities available at the time and in that locality, and the exigent circumstances, if any, surrounding the treatment or medical service rendered. The requisite degree of skill and expertise under the circumstances is established by "expert testimony" from other practicing physicians who share the same or similar skill, training, certification, and experience as the allegedly negligent physician.

### Failure to Diagnose or Erroneous Diagnosis

Generally, a delay or failure to diagnose a disease is actionable, if it has resulted in injury or disease progression above and beyond that which would have resulted from a timely diagnosis. This situation may be difficult to prove. For example, a patient may **allege** that a doctor failed to timely diagnose a certain cancer, resulting in "metastasis" (spread of the cancer to other organs or tissues). But experts may **testify** that "micrometastasis" (spreading of the disease at the cellular level) may occur as much as ten years before a first tumor has been diagnosed, and cancerous cells may have already traveled in the bloodstream and lodged elsewhere, eventually to grow into new tumors. Therefore, it may be difficult

in some cases to establish that a patient has suffered a worse prognosis because of the failure or delay in diagnosis.

If a patient is treated for a disease or condition that he or she does not have, the treatment or medication itself may cause harm to the patient. This is in addition to the harm caused by the true condition continuing untreated.

Most doctors are trained to think and act by establishing a "differential diagnosis." Doing so calls for a doctor to list, in descending order of probability, his or her impressions or "differing" diagnoses of possible causes for a patient's presenting symptoms. The key question in assessing a misdiagnosis for malpractice is to ask what diagnoses a reasonably prudent doctor, under similar circumstances, would have considered as potential causes for the patient's symptoms. If a doctor failed to consider the patient's true diagnosis on his/her differential diagnosis list or listed it but failed to rule it out with additional tests or criteria, then the doctor is most likely negligent.

### Failure to Treat or Erroneous Treatment

The most common way in which doctors are negligent by failing to treat a medical condition is when they "dismiss" the presenting symptoms as temporary, minor, or otherwise not worthy of treatment. This situation may result in an exacerbation of the underlying condition or injury, causing further harm or injury. For example only, an undiagnosed splinter or chip in a broken bone may result in the lodging of a piece of bone in soft tissue or internal bleeding caused by the sharp edge of the splintered bone.

Erroneous treatment is most likely to occur as a result of a misdiagnosis. However, a doctor who has correctly diagnosed a disease or condition may nonetheless fail to properly treat it. Other times, negligence is the result of a doctor attempting a "novel" treatment that fails, when in fact a more conventional treatment would have been successful.

### Substandard Care, Treatment, or Surgery

The standard of care which is owed to people as a patients is that which represents that level of skill, expertise, and care possessed and practiced by physicians found in the same or similar community as the relevant one, and under similar circumstances. However, the advent of "national board" exams for new doctors and "board certifications" for doctor-specialists has resulted in a more uniform and standard practice of medicine not dependent upon geographic locality.

All licensed physicians should possess a basic level of skill and expertise in diagnosing and treating general or recurring types of illnesses and injuries. Thus, a general practitioner who has administered substandard cardio-pulmonary resuscitation (CPR) to a heart attack victim (who subsequently dies as a result of the substandard care) cannot defend that he or she was not a "cardio-pulmonary specialist." A general practitioner from virtually any other area in the United States could most likely testify as to the level of care and expertise that is to be expected under the circumstances. Conversely, a board-certified cardiopulmonary specialist could not testify that the general practitioner should have done everything that the specialist might have done with his advanced skill and training. Nor, under the locality rule, could an oncology specialist in private practice in Smalltown, U. S. A., be held to the same standard of care as an oncology specialist in a large urban university teaching hospital that has state-of-the-art equipment and facilities.

Because doctors are often reluctant to testify against their colleagues (referred to by lawyers as the "conspiracy of silence"), it may be difficult to find an unbiased expert willing to testify against a negligent doctor or label the care as substandard. This is resistance applies even when they practice on opposite sides of the country: they may know one another from the national board certifications or fellowship programs established for specialists. Moreover, truly competent doctors usually communicate with one another for professional "brainstorming" on diagnosing or treating some conditions or may collaborate in research or academic publications.

### Gross Negligence

Within the context of medical malpractice, the term "gross negligence" refers to conduct so reckless or mistaken as to render itself virtually obvious to a layman without medical training. Examples include a surgeon amputating the wrong limb or leaving a surgical instrument inside a body cavity of the patient. Some states will permit a person to establish a cause of action for medical malpractice grounded in **gross negligence** without the need for expert **testimony**. A minority of states still permit an action for "res ipsa loquitur" ("the thing speaks for itself"), meaning that such an accident or injury to the patient could not have occurred unless there was negligence by the doctor's having control over the patient.

### Unauthorized Treatment or Lack of Informed Consent

Virtually all states have recognized, either by express **statute** or **common law**, the right to receive information about one's medical condition, the treatment choices, risks associated with the treatments, and prognosis. The information must be in plain language terms that can readily be understood and in sufficient amounts such that a patient is able to make an "informed" decision about his or her health care. If the patient has received this information, any consent to treatment that is given will be presumed to be an "informed consent." A doctor who fails to obtain **informed consent** for non-emergency treatment may be charged with a civil and/or criminal offense such as a "battery" or an unauthorized touching of the plaintiff's person.

In order to prevail on a charge that a doctor performed a treatment or procedure without "informed consent," the patient must usually show that, had the patient known of the risk or outcome allegedly not disclosed, the patient would not have opted for the treatment or procedure and thus avoided the risk. In other words, the patient must show a harmful consequence to the unauthorized treatment.

### Guaranteed Results or Guaranteed Prognosis

Virtually all states prohibit or disallow claims that a doctor promised a certain prognosis of success or guaranteed a certain result if a patient agreed to undergo the suggested treatment, procedure, or therapy. Some states permit such claims for cosmetic surgery only if the guaranteed result is in writing and contained in the form of an enforceable contract.

### Breaches of Doctor-Patient Confidentiality

Doctor-patient confidentiality is based upon the general principle that a person seeking medical help or advice should not be hindered or inhibited by fear that his or her medical concerns or conditions will be disclosed to others. There is generally an expectation that the physician will hold that special knowledge in confidence and use it exclusively for the benefit of the patient.

The professional duty of confidentiality covers not only what a patient may reveal to the doctor, but also what a doctor may independently conclude or form an opinion about, based on his or her examination or **assessment** of the patient. Confidentiality covers all medical records (including x-rays, lab-reports, etc.) as well as communications between patient and doctor and generally includes communications between the patient and other professional staff working with the doctor.

The duty of confidentiality continues even after a patient has stopped seeing or being treated by the doctor. Once a doctor is under a duty of confidentiality, he or she cannot divulge any medical information about patients to third persons without patients' consent. There are limited exceptions to this, including disclosures to state health officials. However, unauthorized disclosure to unauthorized parties may create a cause of action against the doctor.

### Vicarious Liability

Finally, a doctor who has been negligent may not be the only **defendant** in a subsequent lawsuit. A hospital that has retained the doctor on its staff may be vicariously liable for the doctor's negligence under a theory of "respondeat superior" ("let the master answer") that often holds an employer liable for the negligence of its employees. More often, the doctor has "staff privileges" at the hospital, and the hospital will attempt to prove the limited role it plays in directing or supervising the doctor's work. Importantly, many doctors belong to private medical practices, such as limited partnerships or limited liability companies, that also may be vicariously liable for the negligence of their member doctors.

However, a doctor is generally liable for any negligence on the part of his assistants and staff in carrying out his orders or caring for his patients. Likewise, an attending physician is generally liable for any negligence on the part of interns and medical students under the physician's guidance.

## Patient's Contributory or Comparative Negligence

As malpractice is a form of negligence, defenses that are generally allowed against general claims of negligence are also viable against claims of malpractice. These might include the following defenses:

- The patient was also negligent and caused much of his or her own harm

- The patient failed to mitigate his or her own harm or damage or made them worse

- The patient gave an informed consent and therefore assumed the risk of any [complication or untoward effect]

- The alleged harm or damage was an unavoidable "known risk" that occurs without negligence

- The patient failed to disclose important information to the doctor

- The patient's prognosis or condition was not worsened by the alleged negligence

- The patient engaged in some intervening or superceding conduct following the alleged malpractice that broke the chain of events linking the malpractice to the patient's damages or harm

## Medical Malpractice Tort Reform

Since 2000, increased tension and conflict between patients, their insurers, the medical community and its insurers, trial lawyers, and victims' rights groups have helped spawn a new movement in addressing medical malpractice: tort reform. In 2005 alone, more than 48 states introduced over 400 bills and modified or amended their laws to reflect the need to effect real change. More than half the states now limit damage awards and many have established limits on attorney fees. Moreover, almost all states now have two year statutes of limitation for standard claims, and have eliminated joint and several liability in malpractice law suits. At the federal level, Congress still struggled with the notion of federal legislation that would preempt all existing state laws governing medical malpractice lawsuits.

## State Tort Reform Statutes for Malpractice Actions

State law governs the applicable **statute of limitations** (time within which individuals must file a lawsuit) for medical malpractice suits, as well as the minimum qualifications of expert witnesses (e.g., whether a non-board-certified general practitioner may testify against a specialist, or vice-versa, etc.). Many states have passed legislation imposing limitations or "caps" on monetary damages recoverable in malpractice suits, but the courts in some of these states have declared the laws unconstitutional.

Each state also has its own laws regarding "wrongful death" claims alleging malpractice as the cause of death. Virtually all states allow longer limitations periods for **disability**, **incompetency**, minority, foreign objects left in the body, or **fraudulent** concealment preventing earlier discovery. One of the most recurring provision coming out of the tort reform movement was the inadmissibility of statements made by medical professionals in sympathy or concern, or apologies made by them for treatment rendered, as evidence of fault or malpractice.

ALASKA:SB 67, signed by Governor in 2005, limits noneconomic damages to $250,000. Noneconomic damages for wrongful death or injury over 70% disabling in severe permanent impairment are limited to $400,000. Damages limits are not applicable to intentional misconduct or reckless acts or omissions.

ARIZONA: SB 1036, signed by Governor in 2005, made some changes to expert witness qualifications specific to malpractice actions. Also, apologies and similar gestures by health care providers are not admissible in court as admissions of liability.

ARKANSAS: SB 233, signed by Governor in 2005, creates an insurance policy holder's bill of rights, and amends standards and criteria for medical liability insurance rates, rate administration, rate criteria. Medical liability insurers are to file specific information with Insurance Commissioner, available to public.

CALIFORNIA: SB 231, signed by Governor in 2005, provides that malpractice judgments or settlements over $30,000 must be reported to appropriate licensing board if medical professional does not have liability insurance. Also, must report to Medical Board of indictment, felony conviction, or plea of guilty or no contest of felony or misdemeanor related to medical profession. There will now be an independent commission to study physicians' peer review process. Patients may now access Internet information about physicians relating to status of medical license, current accusations, judgments or arbitration awards, disciplinary action resulting in revocation of privileges, subject to discipline in different state, some specified information may be removed from internet after 10 years. Finally, each complaint filed with Medical Board will be jointly referred to Attorney General and Health Quality Enforcement Section.

CONNECTICUT: SB 1052, signed by Governor in 2005 now requires a "certificate of good faith" to be filed with medical malpractice lawsuits. It also creastes "offer of compromise" guidelines, associated interest rates reduced. Medical liability insurers are to file specified reports to Insurance Commissioner, which are available to public. Medical liability insurers are required to file rate increase request with Insurance Commissioner if over 5%, and insureds may request public hearing. Patients/ public now have access to physician profiles, including adverse licensure actions in other states. Medical liability insurers are to report any claims paid to Insurance

Commissioner, available to public through malpractice database. Expressions of sympathy by health care providers are not admissible in court as admission of liability.

DELAWARE: HB 75, signed by Governor in 2005, creates Board of Medical Practice guidelines, including disciplinary regulation and proceedings. The Board is to receive required reports from both physicians and liability insurance providers of any malpractice judgments, settlements or awards. Medical personnel are not liable for civil damages for emergency medical aid rendered without compensation at scene of emergency. Also, HB 133, signed by Governor in 2005, states that all medical negligence claims settled or awarded against health care providers are to be reported to Commissioner by defendant and associated insurance provider within 60 days of final disposition of claim.

FLORIDA: S 938, signed by Governor in 2005, implements "Patients' Right to Know" constitutional amendment (from the 2004 General Election) Creates a right of access to records relating to adverse medical incidents. Disclosure of identity of patients is prohibited, other privacy restrictions. S 940, also signed into law in 2005, implements constitutional amendment requiring that doctors lose medical license in Florida if found guilty of medical malpractice 3 or more times in 5 years (also adopted from the 2004 General Election). Finally, the Department of Health is to carry out disciplinary action against physicians found guilty of medical malpractice.

GEORGIA: SB 3, signed by Governor in 2005, requires affidavits in medical malpractice complaints, but it also ensures better defendant access to applicable patient health information. Physicians' apologies are not admitted in court as admission of liability. There are changes to expert witness qualifications. Malpractice insurers are to report to state any judgment or settlement over $10,000. If there are two guilty verdicts, report any further judgments to Medical Board; three guilty verdicts in 10 years can have license revoked or required additional education. There is limited liability in emergency room situations unless proven gross negligence. There is a revision of joint/several liability. Now a $350,000 noneconomic damage limit; aggregate limit of $1.05 million.

ILLINOIS: SB 475, signed by Governor in 2005, limits noneconomic damages to $500,000 against an individual; $1 million against hospital. New expert witness standards, and there must be certificates of merit to meet same standards. Apologies by doctors and hospitals not permissible in court as admission of liability. There are public hearings for insurance rate change of more than 6% or at request of insureds. Medical liability insurance data disclosure to public will also be made via internet. There are changes to the Medical Disciplinary Board, including an increase of disciplinary fines and extension of statute of limitations for complaints. The law also creates a Patients' Right to Know. Another bill, SJR 3, also adopted, petitions the state Supreme Court to provide for specific medical malpractice recordkeeping, case designation, and reporting.

INDIANA: SB 54, signed by Governor in 2005, provides that licensed medical practitioners are immune from civil liability when voluntarily providing health care services without compensation at free medical clinics or health care facilities.

IOWA: HR 50, adopted in 2005, provides that the legislative Council will establish an interim committee to provide regulatory agencies and legislature with alternatives for alleviating problems with availability and affordability of medical liability insurance.

KANSAS: SB 100, signed by Governor in 2005, provides that risk management programs may be established in nursing and assisted living facilities. Specified requirements include the reporting of incidents, which are then referred for investigation but are not admissible in civil lawsuit action without court determination that reports are relevant to allegations.

LOUISIANA: SB 184, signed by Governor in 2005, provides that medical information gathered by medical or insurance facility to identify cause of adverse outcome are not admissible as court evidence. Also, expressions of sympathy by medical personnel are not admissible in court. HB 425, also signed in 2005, specifies that statutory civil liability immunity in commitment in mental health or substance abuse cases is expanded to include hospitals and hospital personnel. A general civil immunity is granted for good faith services, but there is no immunity for willful negligence or misconduct. HB 485, also signed, provides that specified information gathered by medical liability insurers or state risk management program for the purpose of reducing medical liability claims is to remain confidential.

MAINE: LD 385, limits liability for ambulance services. LD 1378 provides that expression of apology or sympathy by a medical practitioner is not admissible as admission of liability. LD 1472, clarifies that any physician or hospital without liability insurance is considered self-insured for purposes of the Rural Medical Access Program.

MARYLAND: SB 836, signed by Governor in 2005, made technical changes to the Rate Stabilization Account and Medical Assistance Program Account. It also specified requirements for insurers reporting medical liability claims, and the penalties for failing to report. Made other technical changes to streamline the cancellation process for liability insurers (which is subject to review by Insurance Commissioner), and regarding the reporting and regulatory requirements for Medical Mutual Liability Insurance Society of Maryland.

MICHIGAN: HB 4821, signed by Governor in 2005, provides that medical review entities are to receive information relating to appropriateness or quality of health care rendered or qualifications, competence, or performance of health care provider. Any reports of disciplinary action are to go to the Department of Community Health.

MISSISSIPPI: HB 369, signed by Governor in 2005, creates a Medical Malpractice Insurance Availability Plan to provide a market of last resort. It also creates an advisory committee for the Tort Claims Board on medical liability issues.

MISSOURI: HB 393, signed by Governor in 2005, creates new venue rules for medical malpractice actions, including ones for wrongful death. Discovery of defendant's assets is only after court finds in favor of awarding punitive damages. Punitive damages are limited to the greater of $500,000 or 5 times net amount of total judgment. The liability of defendants is several unless there is more than 51% at fault. Non-economic damages are limited to $350,000. (There was also a repeal of the current annual inflation adjustment.) Courts are required to dismiss any case filed without an affidavit of written opinion of negligence. Physicians providing free health care service in clinics are not civilly liable unless there has been a willful act or omission; and physicians' expressions of sympathy are not admitted in court as admissions of liability. There is now a peer review committee, with spefied procedures for review. The statute of limitations for minors is 2 years from 18th birthday. A related bill, SCR 19, created a Joint Interim Committee on Missouri Health Care Stabilization Fund created to investigate establishment and implementation of fund, feasibility of paying damages to claimants (the primary objective being to assure reasonable medical liability coverage).

MONTANA: SB 21, signed by Governor in 2005, relates to damages awarded based on "reduced chance of recovery." SB 316, specifies that reports from medical liability insurers are to be sent annually to Insurance Commissioner. HB 24 provides that a medical personnel's statement expressing apology or sympathy is not admissible in court as admission of liability. HB 25, states that a health care provider is not liable for employee's act or omission that occurred when employee was not under the jurisdiction of health care provider. A related bill, HB 26, states that a health care provider is not liable for any act or omission committed by someone who purports to be a member of that organization. HB 64 establishes new qualifications for expert witnesses in medical malpractice cases.HB 138 clarifies that a Board of Medical Examiners is to establish disciplinary screening panels to oversee rehabilitation programs for medical personnel. HB 254 makes medical practitioners guilty of a civil offense and fined up to $500 per offense for writing illegible prescriptions. Complaints are to be filed with licensure board. HB 331 provides that the Insurance Commissioner is to conduct market review of malpractice insurers in Montana; based on findings, is to create market assistance plan or joint underwriting association. Bill also contained specifications for potential market assistance plan and joint underwriting association, and specified limits for claimants under policies, underwriting, and reinsurance.

NEVADA: AB 208, signed by Governor in 2005, provides that applicants for medical licenses are required to submit to criminal background check, as well as physicians against whom any disciplinary action is initiated. There are now expanded grounds for initiating disciplinary proceedings against medical personnel. Criminal justice agencies are= to provide criminal histories to Board of Medical Examiners.

NEW HAMPSHIRE: SB 57, signed by Governor in 2005, establishes a cmmission to study ways to alleviate medical malpractice premiums for high risk specialties, but purview does not include examination of civil justice system specific to malpractice claims. SB 214, creates panels for medical injury claims, including conditions for confidentiality and release of information to public, also, the dreation of a panel and insurance oversight committee to study medical liability insurance rates and effectiveness of manda-

tory panel process. Annual reports to Insurance Commissioner are now required from courts. The current hearing panels for medical malpractice complaints are repealed. HB 514 creates a 5-year health care quality assurance commission to provide information sharing among health care providers about adverse outcomes and prevention strategies. The information submitted, proceedings and deliberation results are to be held confidential. HB 584 declares that statements or actions from medical personnel expressing sympathy relating to personal injury are not admissible as admission of liability, and dos not apply to statements of fault.

NEW JERSEY: S 1804, signed by Governor in 2005, now requires medical facilities to report disciplinary action taken by any facility against any health care professional relating to incompetence or professional misconduct. All health care professionals are to undergo criminal history background check when renewing medical license. There will be reporting of health care professionals to state and employers when specified as necessary. Employers of health care professionals are to disclose job performance upon inquiry of another employer.

NEW MEXICO: SM 7, adopted in 2005, creates New Mexico Health Policy Commission and Insurance Division of Public Regulation Commission to convene task force on medical liability insurance; review relevant state statutes, make recommendations to legislature and governor.

NORTH DAKOTA: SB 2199, signed by Governor in 2005, provides that a plaintiff must submit an expert opinion affidavit to individual medical personnel or facility named as defendant within 3 months of commencement of malpractice action.

OREGON: SB 443, signed by Governor in 2005, allows Board of Medical Examiners to require health care providers to take national licensing exam under circumstances of volunteering in charitable health clinics.

SOUTH CAROLINA: S 83, signed by Governor in 2005, limits Noneconomic damages to $350,000, with exceptions specified. Also, new standards for expert witnesses and mandatory mediation for malpractice actions (binding arbitration are permitted). Provisions relating to Joint Underwriting Association and Patients Compensation Fund. Malpractice insurance providers are required to maintain coverage for licensed health care providers. The bill also requires a notice to all locations where health care provider has a medical license to practice, when the South Carolina medical license is suspended or revoked. If there is any percentage of plaintiff fault in a malpractice action, it will not cause reduction of recoverable damages. A related bill, H 3108, covered provisions relating to investigations of complaints against physicians by Medical Disciplinary Commission.

SOUTH DAKOTA: HB 1104, signed by Governor in 2005, provides that damages are limited that may be awarded in malpractice action against a podiatrist. HB 1148 makes statements and actions expressing apology or sympathy made by health care providers admissible as admission of liability.

TENNESSEE: SB 212, signed by Governor in 2005, declares that medical practitioners voluntarily and without compensation providing health care services within scope of state license at health clinics receive civil immunity for rendered services, unless act or omission was gross negligence or willful misconduct.

UTAH: SB 83, signed by Governor in 2005, declares that medical malpractice actions may not be brought against health care providers due to consequences resulting from refusal of child's parent or guardian to consent to recommended treatment.

VIRGINIA: SB 1173, HB 2659 (identical bills) were both signed by Governor in 2005. They require that an expert witness certification of deviation from care standard to be filed before malpractice lawsuit can be filed. Moreover, physician's expression of sympathy is not admissible in court as admission of liability. Admissible evidence is now expanded, to include observations, evaluations and histories in treatment applicable to lawsuit, which now may be disclosed; the definition of "malpractice" is limited to tort or breach of contract; and malpractice liability insurers are required to submit annual reports to State Corporation Commission regarding claims made against medical personnel. Finally, the Board of Medicine is to assess competency of medical personnel with three malpractice claim payments within ten years. SB 1323 and HB 1505, also identical bills, provides a Birth-Related Neurological Injury Compensation Fund definition such that when infant weighs less than 1800 grams at birth or is at less than 32 weeks of gestation, there will be a rebuttable presumption that the alleged injury is a result of premature birth. HB 1556 states that the Board of Medicine is required

to inform licensees about immunity for services to patients of free clinics. HB 2410 provide that Liability insurers are required to provide 90-day notice of policy cancellation or non-renewal, or premium increase of more than 25% for malpractice insurance.

WEST VIRGINIA: HB 2011, signed by Governor in 2005, states that Health care providers are not liable for personal injury caused by prescription drug or medical device used in accordance with FDA regulations. HB 3174, also signed by Governor, makes any expression made by a health care provider of apology or sympathy is not admissible as an admission of liability.

WYOMING: SF 0078, signed by Governor in 2005, requires additional advance notice of medical liability insurance policy cancellation or premium increase. A public hearing is required if insurer requests to raise premium rate by 30% or more. SF 0088 requires additional specified information on medical malpractice claims to be reported. HB 0083 repeals the current Medical Review Panel and recreates a panel according to constitutional amendment adopted in the 2004 general election.

Additionally, a few state court rulings addressed some of the new statutes: In *DeWeese v. Weaver,* a Pennsylvania Commonwealth Court declared that separation of joint and several liability was unconstitutional based on the germane standard of legislation enacted in 2002. In *Ferndon v. Wisconsin,* the Wisconsin Supreme Court held that noneconomic damages in medical injury cases were unconstitutional.

## Additional Resources

*Law for Dummies* Ventura, John, IDG Books Worldwide, Inc., 1996.

*Medical Malpractice* Harney, David M., The Michie Company:, 1993. Excerpt available at http://www.lectlaw.com/files/med33.htm.

"Medical Malpractice" Plymale & Associates. Available at http://www.plymalelaw.com/medmal.htm.

*Law for Dummies.* John Ventura. IDG Books Worldwide, Inc. 1996.

"Summary of Medical Malpractice Law: Index of States." McCullough, Campbell & Lane, 2001. Available at http://www.mcandl.com/states.html.

# HEALTHCARE

## MEDICAL RECORDS

## Background

Medical records are the property of those who prepare them (medical professionals) and not the property of those about whom they are concerned (patients). However, patients have a privacy right in the information contained in the records. These two interests may or may not conflict when it comes to releasing medical records to outside or third parties, who may also have another interest at stake. Once these basic and often competing interests are separated and assessed, it becomes easier to understand the issues that may surround the right to request, view, copy, or protect medical records and medical information.

Although medical records belong to the medical professionals/entities who create or prepare them, patients generally have a right to review them, demand copies of them, and to demand their confidentiality, i.e., prohibit release of information contained in them (with limited and specific exceptions). Where does a patient get the authority to control the release of documents that belong to others? The patient's rights are dependent upon who created the documents, who wants to view them, and why their release is warranted.

## Sources of Protection of Medical Information

### Common Law Duty of Confidentiality

First and foremost, there is the **common law** concept of "doctor-patient confidentiality" that binds a medical professional from revealing or disclosing what he or she may know about a person's medical condition. The professional duty of confidentiality covers not only what a patient may reveal to the doctor, but also what a doctor may independently conclude or form an opinion about, based on his or her **examination** or **assessment** of the patient. Confidentiality covers all medical records (including x-rays, lab-reports, etc.), as well as communications between patient and doctor, and generally includes communications between the patient and other professional staff working with the doctor.

Once a doctor is under a duty of confidentiality, he or she cannot divulge any medical information to third persons without the patient's consent. There are noteworthy exceptions to this, discussed below.

At one time (fairly common through the 1970s), a doctor was considered a mere "custodian" of medical records, which were considered the property of the patient (because the personal information contained in them related only to the patient). It was common practice to release to a patient, upon demand, all original records concerning the patient. However, that practice led to some patients destroying their medical records, denying that they had received certain treatments, misrepresenting their conditions for the purpose of obtaining life or health insurance policies, and (in the case of psychiatric patients) sometimes becoming a threat to the community at large after learning what was contained in their records. **Medical malpractice** suits and liability for harm caused to third persons became a paramount issue that drove the impetus for establishing a refinement of the law (mostly through **case law**).

This change has resulted in a clarification that the actual original medical records belong to those who create or originate them. However, the release to a patient or to third parties of information contained in the medical records (about a particular patient) is generally controlled by the patient (with specific exceptions).

Medical professionals may be required by the request of a patient (or court order, **subpoena**, etc.), to produce original documents and records for inspection, copying, or review. Usually, this is done in a supervised fashion within the offices or facilities of the creator/originator of the records (the doctor or medical facility). For all intents and purposes, it is more common for the original documents to be simply photocopied and forwarded to the patient or to the party whom the patient designates. It is general practice to not charge for copying or reproducing if the records are not extensive and are being requested by the patient, for the patient's own use.

### Constitutional Right to Privacy

The fundamental right to privacy, guaranteed by the Fifth and Fourteenth Amendments to the U.S. Constitution, protects against unwarranted invasions of privacy by federal or state entities, or arms thereof. As early as *Roe v. Wade*, 410 U.S. 113 (1973), the U.S. Supreme Court acknowledged that the doctor-patient relationship is one which evokes constitutional rights of privacy. Because the Supreme Court

has found that a fundamental right of privacy exists as to medical information about a person, private causes of action (against defendants other than federal or state entities) also exist for alleged violations of privacy rights (e.g., "invasion of privacy"). This right would extend to the privacy of any medical information contained in medical records.

But even that right is not absolute, and must be weighed against the state or federal, or outside interest at stake. For example, in *Whalen v. Roe*, 429 U.S. 589 (1977), a group of physicians joined patients in a lawsuit challenging the constitutionality of a New York **statute** that required physicians to report to state authorities the identities of patients receiving Schedule II drugs (controlled substances). The physicians alleged that such information was protected by doctor-patient confidentiality, and their patients alleged that such disclosure was an invasion of their constitutional right to privacy. The Supreme Court did not disagree with the lower court's finding that "the intimate nature of a patient's concern about his bodily ills and the medication he takes... are protected by the constitutional right to privacy." However, the high court concluded (after balancing the state's interests) that "Requiring such disclosures to representatives of the State having responsibility for the health of the community does not automatically amount to an impermissible invasion of privacy."

### Statutory Privacy Laws

Despite the above two recognized areas of law that purported to shield medical information about a person from unauthorized release or disclosure, there continued to be substantial "gray areas" susceptible to varying interpretations and applications. For example, do "medical records" include dental records, pre-employment physical examination records, self-generated records (documents created or completed by the patients themselves, such as healthcare questionnaires), birth and death certificates? And what about records generated by quasi-medical personnel, e.g., physical therapists or mental health counselors? Further, there appeared to be a developing area of case law that permitted, in fact demanded, the unauthorized release of medical information (i.e., against the patient's wishes and/or without the patient's knowledge) if, without the release, there was a substantial risk of harm to a third person (e.g. by violence of the patient or by communicable or sexually transmitted disease).

To address these concerns, all fifty states have enacted laws that govern the release of medical records. They encompass the recognition of any legal privilege (privileged communications between the health care provider and the patient), any prerequisites to the release of records (almost all require patient consent), and the circumstances under which records or information may be released in the absence of consent.

### The Federal Privacy Rule

In the past, physicians could physically secure and shield personal medical records from disclosure, absent consent from their patients. Electronic databanks have changed all that (as foretold by the Supreme Court in *Whalen*, above).With the passage of the Health Insurance Portability and Accountability Act of 1996 (HIPAA) (which encouraged electronic transmission of patient data), Congress passed concurrent legislation for uniform protection of medical records and personal information. In December 2000, the Department of Health and Human Services (HHS) published its Privacy Rule ("Standards for Privacy of Individually Identifiable Health Information", 65 Fed. Reg. 82462), which became effective on April 14, 2001. The regulation covers health plans, health care clearinghouses, and health care providers that bill and transfer funds electronically. The regulation mandates a final compliance date of April 14, 2003 (small health plans have until April 14, 2004 to comply.) The Privacy Rule includes provisions for the following:

- Ensuring patient access to medical records, ability to get copies and/or request amendments

- Obtaining patient consent before releasing information. Health care providers are required to obtain consent before sharing information regarding treatment, payment, and health care operations. Separate patient authorizations must be obtained for all non-routine disclosures and non-health related purposes. A history of all non-routine disclosures must be accessible to patients.

- Providing recourse for violations through an administrative complaint procedure.

In March 2002, the Bush Administration proposed amendments to the Privacy Rule that would address several complaints registered by patients and medical facilities alike. Specifically, the impact of the proposed amendments would remove the requirement for express consent in such communications as pharmacists filling prescriptions, patient referrals to specialists, treatments provided or authorized from telephone communications, and emergency medical care. The relaxed consent requirement would only apply to uses and disclosures for treatment, payment, and health care operations (TPOs) purposes. All other uses and disclosures would continue to require express patient consent.

## Voluntary Consent for Release of Medical Information

Almost all requests for release of medical records contain a requirement that patient consent be obtained in writing. Medical providers or custodians of medical records may or may not accept facsimile (FAX) transmission of authorizations/signed consent forms. In legal matters, the process may be simplified by a patient authorizing his or her attorney to obtain copies of records (or review originals).

## Waiver of Consent for Release of Medical Information

There are ways in which a patient may "waive" the confidentiality of medical records. A common way by filing a lawsuit or claim for **personal injury**. By doing so, the patient has put his or her physical condition "at issue" in the lawsuit. Therefore, the law presumes that the patient has waived all confidentiality regarding his or her medical condition, and there is an implied authorization to the patient's doctor for disclosure of all relevant information and medical records.

## Involuntary Release of Medical Information

In recent years, many courts have held that doctors are supposed to protect third persons who may be harmed by patients. This often results in a duty to release medical records or medical information without either knowledge or consent on the part of the patient. For example, without a patient's permission or knowledge, doctors may warn others or the police if the patient is mentally unstable, potentially violent, or has threatened a specific person. In some states, the duty to report or warn others "trumps" the right to confidentiality or privileged communication with a doctor. Courts will decide these matters by balancing the sanctity of the confidentiality against the foreseeability of harm to a third party.

## Selected Applications

### Death Certificates

Under most state laws, birth and death certificates are a matter of public record. The advent of physician-assisted suicides in less than a handful of states (e.g., Oregon) created new concerns for the scope of privacy and confidentiality. Some states have addressed such matters by express legislation, e.g., permitting the registration of physician-assisted deaths directly to state offices rather than to local county offices of vital statistics. Others have permitted dual-systems that incorporate specific codes for "cause of death" on public records, but more thorough explanations on private state records. Many doctors simply list innocuous language, such as "cardiac-respiratory failure," on public records, and leave blank the secondary or underlying cause. Similar issues of limited disclosure often arise on birth records. In some circumstances, personal details such as **paternity**, marital status, or information regarding a newborn's HIV status may **warrant** the filing of dual records (one requiring more disclosure than the other) for separate purposes and separate viewers, based on a "need to know" criterion.

### Disclosures to State or Federal Authorities

Under most state statutes, doctors and health care providers generally have duties to report incidence of certain sexually transmitted diseases, **child abuse**, communicable diseases, HIV/AIDS, or other conditions deemed to be risks to the health and safety of the public at large. Some states have developed registries to track the incidence of certain conditions, (e.g., certain forms of cancer) that may later help researchers discover causes. In registry cases, personal data about the patients is released only to the necessary local, state, or federal personnel, and the data usually does not contain "patient identifiers."

## Selected State Disclosure Laws

ALABAMA: Medical records of "notifiable diseases" (those diseases or illnesses that doctors are required to report to state officials) are strictly confidential. Written consent of patient is required for release of information regarding sexually transmitted disease. (Ch. 22-11A-2, 22)

ALASKA: Mental health records may be disclosed only with patient consent/court order/law enforcement reasons (Ch. 47.30.845). In cases of emergency medical services, records of those treated may be disclosed to specified persons.(Ch. 18.08.086). Express language permits disclosure of financial records of medical assistance beneficiaries to the Dept. of Social Services. (Ch. 47.07.074)

ARIZONA: There are mandatory reporting requirements for malnourishment, physical neglect, **sexual abuse**, non-accidental injury, or other deprivation with intent to cause or allow death of minor children, but the records remain confidential outside judicial matters (Ch. 13-3620). Access to other medical records is by consent or pursuant to exceptions outlined in Ch. 36-664.

ARKANSAS: Arkansas has a special privilege permitting doctors to deny giving patients or their attorneys or guardians certain medical records upon a showing of "detrimentality" (Ch.16-46-106). Otherwise, access by patients and their attorneys are covered under Ch. 23-76-129 and 16-46-106.

CALIFORNIA: Doctors may withhold certain mental health records from patients if disclosure would have an adverse effect on patient. (H&S Section 1795.12 and.14).

COLORADO: Doctors are permitted to withhold from patients psychiatric records that would have a significant negative psychological impact; in those cases, doctors may prepare a summary statement of what the records contain (Ch.25-1-801). There are mandatory disclosure requirements for certain diseases (Ch 25-1-122).

CONNECTICUT: Limited disclosure of mental health records (Ch. 4-105) and limited disclosure to state officials (Ch.53-146h; 17b-225).

DELAWARE: Strict disclosure prohibitions about sexually transmitted diseases, HIV infections (Tit. 16-711). However, such diseases must be reported to division of Public Health, by number and manner only (Title 16-702).

DISTRICT OF COLUMBIA: Public mental health facilities must release records to the patient's attorney or personal physician (21-562).

FLORIDA: Mental health records may be provided in the form of a report instead of actual annotations (455-241). Patient consent is required for general medical records releases except by subpoena or consent to compulsory physical exam pursuant to Civil Rule of Procedure 1.360 (455-241).

GEORGIA: Mandatory disclosure to state officials for child abuse and venereal disease. (Ch. 19-7-5; 31-17-2)

HAWAII: Hawaii Revised Statute 325-2 provides for mandatory disclosure to state officials for communicable disease or danger to public health. Names appearing in public studies such as the Hawaii Tumor Registry are confidential and no person who provides information is liable for it (324-11, et seq.).

IDAHO: There is mandatory disclosure for child abuse cases within 24 hours (16-1619) and sexually transmitted diseases (39-601). Both doctors and nurses may request protective orders to deny or limit disclosure (9-420).

ILLINOIS: Mandatory disclosure to state officials for child abuse and sexually transmitted diseases (325 Illinois Compiled Statutes Annotated 5/4).

INDIANA: Insurance companies may obtain information with written consent (Ch 16-39-5-2). Mandatory disclosure to state officials for child abuse and sexually transmitted diseases (31-6-11-3 and 4) (16-41-2-3).

IOWA: Mandatory disclosure to state officials of sexually transmitted diseases (Ch. 140.3 and 4).

KANSAS: Mandatory disclosure to state health officials of AIDS (65-6002(c)). Mental health records only released by patient consent, court order, or consent of the head of mental health treating facility (59-2931).

KENTUCKY: Either patient or physician may ask for **protective order** (422-315). Patients must make written requests for records (422.317).

LOUISIANA: Louisiana Code of **Evidence**, Article 510 waives health care provider-patient privilege in cases or child abuse or molestation. Mandatory disclosure of HIV information (Ch.1300-14 and 1300-15).

MAINE: Doctors may withhold mental health records if detrimental to patient's health (22-1711.20-A Maine Revised Statutes Annotated, Section 254, Subsection 5, requires schools to adopt local written policies and procedures).

MARYLAND: Physicians may inform local health officers of needle-sharing partners or sexual partners in cases of transmittable diseases (18-337).

MASSACHUSETTS: Any injury from the discharge of a gun or a burn affecting more than five percent of the body, rape or sexual **assault** triggers mandatory disclosure law (Ch. 112-12A). No **statutory** privilege.

MICHIGAN: Mandatory disclosure to state officials for communicable diseases (MCL.333.5117).

MINNESOTA: Minnesota Statutes Annotated 144.335 authorizes withholding mental health records if information is detrimental to well-being of patient. Sex crime victims can require HIV testing of sex offender and have access to results (611A.07).

MISSISSIPPI: Patient **waiver** is implied for mandatory disclosures to state health officials. Peer review boards assessing the quality of care for medical or dental care providers may have access to patient records without the disclosure of patient's identity (41-63-1, 63-3).

MISSOURI: Information concerning a person's HIV status is confidential and may be disclosed only according to Section 191.656.

MONTANA: Mandatory disclosure to state officials for sexually transmitted disease. (Ch. 50-18-106). Recognized exceptions for release of records without patient consent (e.g. mental **incompetency**) are covered under 50-16-530.

NEBRASKA: Nebraska Revised Statutes 81-642 requires reporting of patients with cancer for the Dept. of Health's Cancer Registry. The Dept. also maintains a Brain Injury Registry (81-651). Mandatory disclosure to state officials for sexually transmitted disease. (71-503.01).

NEVADA: Mandatory disclosure to state officials for communicable disease. (441A.150) There is a state requirement to forward medical records (with or without consent) upon transfer to a new medical facility (433.332; 449,705).

NEW HAMPSHIRE: New Hampshire maintains that medical records are the property of the patient (332:I-1) Mandatory disclosure to state officials for communicable disease (141-C:7).

NEW JERSEY: Limited right of access to mental health records for attorneys and **next of kin**. Mandatory disclosure to state officials for child abuse (9:6-8.30), pertussis vaccine (26:2N-5), sexually transmitted disease.(26:4-41), or AIDS (26:5C-6).

NEW MEXICO: Mandatory disclosure of sexually transmitted diseases (24-1-7).

NEW YORK: Records concerning sexually transmitted disease or **abortion** for minors may not be released, not even to parents (NY Pub. Health 17).

NORTH CAROLINA: North Carolina General Statute 130A-133, et seq. provides for mandatory disclosure to state officials for communicable disease.

NORTH DAKOTA: Mandatory disclosure to state officials for child abuse, communicable diseases, or chronic diseases that impact the public (23-07-01, 50-25.1-01).

OHIO: Mandatory disclosure to state officials for child abuse (2151-421), occupational diseases (3701.25), contagious disease including AIDS (3701.24), or cases to be included on the Cancer Registry (3701.262).

OKLAHOMA: Mandatory disclosure to state officials for child abuse, communicable or venereal diseases (23-07-01, 50-25.1-01).

OREGON: Oregon Revised Statute 146-750 provides for mandatory disclosure of medical records involving suspected violence, physical injury with a knife, gun, or other deadly weapon.

PENNSYLVANIA: Mental health records in state agencies must remain confidential (Title 50-7111).

RHODE ISLAND: Mandatory disclosure to state officials for occupational disease (Ch. 23-5-5), communicable or venereal diseases (23-8-1, 23-11-5).

SOUTH CAROLINA: Mandatory disclosure to state officials for sexually transmitted disease (z016744-29-70). There is also express privilege for mental health provider-patient relationships under Ch. 19-11-95.

SOUTH DAKOTA: Mandatory disclosure to state officials for venereal disease (34-23-2) or child abuse or neglect (26-8A-3).

TENNESSEE: There are also requirements for mandatory disclosure to state officials for communicable disease (68-5-101) or sexually transmitted diseases (68-10-101).

TEXAS: There are mandatory disclosure requirements for bullet or gunshot wounds (Health & Safety 161.041), certain occupational diseases (Health & Safety 84.003) and certain communicable diseases (Health & Safety 81.041).

UTAH: There are mandatory disclosure requirements for suspected child abuse (62A-4A-403), communicable and infectious diseases (including HIV and AIDS) (26-6-3).

VERMONT: Records concerning sexually transmitted disease require mandatory reporting (Title 18-1093). Any HIV-related record of testing or counseling may be disclosed only with a court order evidencing "compelling need." (Title 12-1705).

VIRGINIA: Mental health professionals may withhold records from patient if release would be injurious to patient's health. (8.01-413).

WASHINGTON: Mandatory disclosure to state officials for sexually transmitted disease (70.24.105) child abuse (26.44.030) or tuberculosis (70.28.010).

WEST VIRGINIA: Mandatory disclosure to state officials for venereal, communicable disease (Ch. 16-4-6; 16-2A-5; 26-5A-4), suspected child abuse (49-6A-2), gunshot and other wounds or burns (61-2-27).

WISCONSIN: There are mandatory reporting requirements for sexually transmitted diseases (252.11), tuberculosis (252.07), child abuse (48.981) and communicable diseases (252.05).

WYOMING: Rather than expressly creating a statutory privilege, Wyoming addresses the matter by limiting doctors' **testimony** to instances where patients have expressly consented or where patients voluntarily **testify** themselves on their medical conditions (putting their medical conditions "at issue") (Ch. 1-12-101). There are mandatory reporting requirements for sexually transmitted diseases, child abuse, and communicable diseases (14-3-205, 35-4-130, 35-4-103).

## Additional Resources

*"Confidentiality of Death Certificates"* Issues in Law & Medicine, Winter 1998.

*"Medical Records."* National Survey of State Law, 2nd ed. Richard A. Leiter, Ed. Gale: 1997.

*Standards for Privacy Rule of Individually Identifiable Health Information,* 65 Fed. Reg 82462, 2001. Available at http://gov.news/press/2001pres/01fsprivacy.html.

*"Standards for Privacy Rule of Individually Identifiable Health Information-Proposed Rule Modification."* FDCH Regulatory Intelligence Database, 21 March 2002.

# HEALTHCARE

## ORGAN DONATION

## Background

There is a great need for human organs for transplantation. In fact, the need far exceeds the supply of transplantable organs. This disparity has promulgated legislation and important **case law**. These laws attempt to regulate the scare resource (transplantable human organs) and to help establish an equitable national system to allocate the organs where they can do the most good.

There are Extensive federal and state laws regulating organ and tissue donation and transplantation. These many laws and regulations were promulgated to address a variety of issues, including the complicated medical, legal, and moral issues involved in organ donation and transplantation. One of the main issues deals with the enormous demand for human organs in a context where there is an inadequate supply of usable organs. These laws are generally viewed by lawmakers, members of the medical professions, and by the populace as a way to ensure the most equitable distribution of organs. However, the many laws and regulations in this area can complicate the process of obtaining organs. Consequently, people who have questions about organ donation or transplantation, should seek advice of an attorney knowledgeable about this area of law.

There are several reasons for the shortage of organs. Perhaps the most common reason is that people are hesitant to donate organs. There are other reasons as well: for example, physicians may neglect to inquire of family members whether they would consent to donating organs when their loved one dies. In other cases, the deceased's wishes to donate his or her organs may not be known by those in the position to act on those wishes. Finally, family members may object to the harvesting of organs from their deceased loved one, regardless of the deceased's intent or wishes to the contrary.

## Legislation

Many federal and state statutes closely regulate organ donation. To understand the laws governing organ donation, one needs to understand the trajectory of some of the most important legislation. While there are many laws pertaining to organ donations, perhaps the most important legislation consists of the following:

- Various early federal legislation

- The Uniform Anatomical Gift Act of 1987

- The National Organ Transplant Act

- The Patient Self Determination Act of 1991

• State Anatomical Gift Acts

### Earlier Federal Legislation

Prior to 1968 there were no federal laws dealing with organ and tissue donation. Before the Uniform Anatomical Gift Act of 1968 (AGA), organ and tissue donations were handled at the state level only. Unfortunately, the state laws then on the books differed considerably from state to state. The AGA was intended to address these problems by providing a framework of uniform laws in the United States relating to organ and tissue transplantation. It also attempted to increase the number of available organs by making it easier for individuals to make anatomical gifts.

In 1972, The Uniform Anatomical Gift Act mandated that the Uniform Organ **Donor** Card be recognized as a legal document in all 50 states. This empowered anyone eighteen years or older to legally donate his or her organs upon death.

In 1984, the National Organ Transplant Act (NOTA) created a national computer registry of donated organs. It was to be operated by the United Network for Organ Sharing (UNOS). NOTA also authorized financial support for organ procurement organizations and outlawed the purchase or sale of human organs.

### Uniform Anatomical Gift Act of 1987

This Act overhauled the 1968 Uniform Anatomical Gift Act (UAGA). Even though the 1968 UAGA successfully constructed a consistent pattern for states to follow in revising their own anatomical gift legislation, it failed to increase the number of donated transplantable organs. The 1968 UAGA did not address the issue of commercial sale of organs. Between 1968 and 1987, there were significant advances in transplant science and the practice of organ transplantation. The 1968 UAGA could not have provided for some of these advances. Consequently, the 1968 UAGA did not address many important issues that developed over time.

In an attempt to respond, a new version of the Uniform Anatomical Gift Act was drafted in 1987. The 1987 UAGA attempted to address many of the holes in the 1968 Act. It covered the following:

1. Explicitly prohibited the sale of human organs. Federal law expressly prohibits the sale of human tissue with the exception of blood, sperm, or human eggs.

2. Guaranteed the priority of a decedent's wishes over the decedent's family members with respect to their objections to organ donation.

3. Streamlined the process of completing the necessary documents to effect organ donation.

4. Mandated that hospitals and emergency personnel develop procedures of "routine inquiry/required request." This provision requires hospitals to ask patients, upon admittance to the hospital, or their families, at patient's death, about organ donation. If the patient expresses the intent to donate his or her organs, that information is added to the patient's record.

5. Permitted medical examiners and coroners to provide transplantable organs from subjects of autopsies and investigations within certain conditions.

The 1968 UAGA enjoyed unanimous approval from every state; however, the 1987 UAGA was opposed in many states. The key issues revolved around three of the five new provisions in the 1987 Act. First, the debate focused on the priority of the donor's intent over his or her family's objections. Second, states were concerned about the "routine inquiry/required request" language. Third, there was debate over the new authority that allowed medical examiners to donate a deceased's organs or other body parts. Although it was intended to create uniformity among the disparate state statutes that had been passed to fill gaps left by the 1968 Act, several states enacted transplant legislation on their own, rather than ratify the 1987 UAGA legislation.

Under the 1987 UAGA, medical examiners or coroners may release organs for transplantation only when they have **custody** of a body and the deceased has no next-of-kin. There must be a reasonable search for **next of kin** by competent authorities. Officials may not remove organs or tissue for transplanting unless a specific state law grants this authority.

### The National Organ Transplant Act

In 1984, the National Organ Transplant Act (NOTA) began to provide a comprehensive structure and articulated policy regarding organ transplantation. This legislation reflected Congress's acknowledgement of the advances being made in transplantation technology and procedures. For example, there was now an 80 percent survival rate for those undergoing kidney transplants. And the drug cyclosporin had increased the survival rate of liver transplant patients from 35 to 70 percent for the first year after undergoing a liver transplant. Of course, there was still great concern about the shortage of available organs.

NOTA also provided funds for grants for qualified organ procurement organizations (OPOs) and an Organ Procurement and Transplantation Network (OPTN). The OPTN was intended to assist OPOs in distributing organs that could not be used in the OPO's geographical area. The Act provided grant money for planning, establishing, and operating or expanding organ procurement organizations. To qualify for the grant money, the OPO had to show that it was a nonprofit organization qualified to receive **Medicare** reimbursement for kidney procurement. It also had to describe established procedures to obtain payment for organs (other than kidneys) that were provided to transplant centers. The Act expressly forbade selling human organs across state lines. Apparently, the committee responsible for this provision felt strongly that human body parts should not be viewed as commodities.

One of the most important achievements of the Act was the establishment of a 25-member Task Force on Organ Transplantation. This task force studies human transplant policy issues, including organ procurement and distribution. The Task Force published its first report covering medical, legal, social, ethical, and economic issues related to organ procurement and transplantation in 1986. In this report, the Task Force commented on the relatively small percentage of transplantable organs that were actually harvested for transplantation and the need to increase this supply. It urged the continued development of organ transplant policies that encourage individuals to donate organs.

### *The Patient Self-Determination Act of 1991*

The Federal Patient Self-Determination Act (PSDA) was meant to encourage the use of advance directives such as living wills and durable powers of attorney for health care. The PSDA changes key provisions in federal Medicare and **Medicaid** laws. It mandates that hospitals and other health care providers maintain explicit policies and procedures regarding five issues. The hospital or health care provider must:

1. provide written information regarding the individual's rights under state law to make decisions concerning medical care, includ-

ing the right to formulate advance directives.

2. note in the patient's medical record whether the individual has executed an advance directive

3. not discriminate against a patient in response to the patient's decision on an advance directive

4. comply with state laws concerning advance directives

5. create a policy to provide for education of its staff and community on issues concerning advance directives

## State Anatomical Gift Acts

State law governs postmortem organ donations under the original (1968) or revised (1987) Uniform Anatomical Gift Act. These acts have been adopted in every state, although there are some minor variations among the states' laws. Basically, the laws state that competent adults may make gifts of an organ or organs in the event of their deaths. The organs may be used for transplantation, research, or education. If there is no explicit anatomical gift made by a decedent, the decedent's family may consent to harvesting of the decedent's organs.

The Uniform Anatomical Gift Act (AGA) has been adopted in various forms by all 50 states. These laws state that a wallet-sized donor card, signed by a person over 18 and witnessed by two other adults, is a legal instrument permitting physicians to remove organs after death. These cards are often part of state driver's licenses. When the AGAs were passed, there was great hope that they would help to dramatically increase the supply of organs. Unfortunately, donor cards have not produced a significant increase in the supply of organs. There are at least two reasons for their failure to bring about the hoped-for increase in the supply of transplantable organs:

• Many people do not sign the donor cards or do so incorrectly

• Despite being recognized as a legal document, many medical professionals have been reluctant to rely upon the donor card for permission to remove organs from decedents for transplantation purposes

## Advance Care Directives

There are three kinds of documents that may provide **evidence** of a person's wish to donate his or her organs in the event of that person's death. These are:

- Living wills: Living wills provide instructions for someone's medical care if that person becomes incapacitated or otherwise unable to make decisions himself or herself. State statutes regulate living wills. In most cases, a **living will** can direct that one's organs or tissues be taken and donated if medically appropriate. If individuals execute a living will, it is advisable for them to inform their physicians and their families of its existence.

- Durable powers of attorney for health care. A durable **power of attorney** for health care names someone, the individual's "agent," to make important decisions regarding that person's health care should the person become incapacitated. These documents can instruct the person's agent to donate the person's organs or tissues upon the person's death. As with living wills, the durable power of attorney for medical care is only effective if, in addition to the agent, the family and the person's physician know of its existence.

- Advanced care medical directive: An advance care medical directive (ACMD) combines some features of the living will and the durable power of attorney for health care. An ACMD allows individuals to provide instructions for the type of care they do or do not want in a number of medical scenarios. These documents need to be created in consultation with their physician(s).

Several states have passed laws that presume consent of a decedent (to donate organs or tissues) in certain limited circumstances. These laws are very limited in scope. Despite these **statutory** provisions, the best way to insure that a person's organs or tissues will be made available for transplantation after his or her death is for the person to let relatives know of his or her desire to donate. This is especially true when one considers that medical personnel rely so heavily on the wishes of the next of kin when deciding whether to harvest useful organs.

Competent living persons may donate renewable tissues (e.g. blood, platelets, plasma, and sperm), and those not essential to the donor's health (e.g. eggs). However, a person may not donate organs or tissues necessary for sustaining the donor's life (e.g. heart, lungs, liver). There are two more ways to let others know of about one's decision to donate. First, the person can complete an organ donor card, or sign the back of the person's driver's license. Second, the person can execute a living will, durable power of attorney for medical care, or create an advance care medical directive informing the prospective medical care provider of the extent of care the person wishes to receive prior to the death. This document will also provide specific instructions for the **disposition** of the person's body after death, including donating your organs. By taking these steps, individuals are best assures that their decision to become an organ and/or tissue donor will be fulfilled.

## Additional Resources

*Dying & death in law & medicine: a forensic primer for health and legal professionals* Berger, Arthur S., Praeger, Arthur S., 1993.

*The Ethics of Organ Transplants: The Current Debate* Caplan, Arthur L., and Daniel H. Coelho, eds., Prometheus Books, 1999.

*http://www.organdonor.gov/.* "Organ Donation." FirstGov.com, 2002. Available at http://www.organdonor.gov/.

*Organ and Tissue Donation for Transplantation.* Edited by Chapman, Jeremy R., Wight, Celia, and Deierhoi, Mark, eds., Edward Arnold Publishers, 1997.

*Organ Transplantation: Meanings and Realities.* Edited by Youngner, Stuart J., Stuart J., Fox, Renee C., and O'Connell, Laurence J., eds., University of Wisconsin Press, 1996.

## Organizations

### *The Living Bank*

P.O. Box 6725
Houston, TX 77265 USA
Phone: (800) 528-2971
E-Mail: info@livingbank.org

### *National Transplant Assistance Fund (NTAF)*

3475 West Chester Pike, Suite 230
Newtown Square, PA 19073 USA
Phone: (800) 642-8399
Fax: (610) 353-1616
URL: http://www.transplantfund.org/homepage2.html

### *The Transplant Network*
1130 Ryland
Reno, NV 89502 USA
Phone: (775) 324-4501
Fax: (775) 323-1596
E-Mail: thetransplantnetwork@gbis.com

### *United Network for Organ Sharing (UNOS)*
1100 Boulders Parkway, Suite 500
Richmond, VA 23225-8770 USA
Phone: (804) 330-8576
Fax: (804) 323-3794
URL: http://www.unos.org/frame_Default.asp

### *National Transplant Assistance Fund (NTAF)*
3475 West Chester Pike, Suite 230
Newtown Square, PA 19073 USA
Phone: (800) 642-8399
Fax: (610) 353-1616
URL: http://www.transplantfund.org/
homepage2.html

### *The Transplant Network*
1130 Ryland
Reno, NV 89502 USA
Phone: (775) 324-4501
Fax: (775) 323-1596
E-Mail: thetransplantnetwork@gbis.com

# HEALTHCARE

## PATIENT RIGHTS

*Sections within this essay:*

- Background

- Right to Autonomy and Self-Determination

-

  - History
  - Living Wills
  - Durable Powers of Attorney
  - The Patient Self-Determination Act of 1990
  - Euthanasia and the "Right to Die"
  - Informed Consent

- Right to Privacy

- Right to Receive Treatment

- State Provisions

- Additional Resources

## Background

The advent of the "patient rights" movement and associated legislation is a relatively recent phenomenon, having first taken root in the early 1990s. However, as of January 2006, a divided and partisan U.S. Congress was still grappling with various provisions for a federal **Patients' Rights** Law, and none appeared likely in the foreseeable future. Part of the delay was due to the 2004 U.S. Supreme Court decision in *Aetna v. Davila,* which severely limited patients' rights to sue their HMOs in state courts. (The Court held that the federal Employee Retirement Income Security Act [ERISA] **preempted** state laws in this area.) The decision impacted and invalidated provisions in at least ten state patients' rights laws.

Notwithstanding, all states have enacted some form of health care law addressing "patient rights." The problem remains that there is no uniformity of laws, and the scope of rights afforded patients varies greatly from state to state.

The term "patient" generally refers to a person who is receiving medical treatment and/or who is under medical care. Certain vulnerabilities attach to the status of patient. For this reason, certain laws have been passed at both the national and state levels to protect people's interests which otherwise might be compromised by medical, social, governmental, and/or financial entities. These protective provisions may be in the form of passive guarantees, or they may spring into effect as a result of some affirmative act on an individual's part, such as the **execution** of a legal document, like a Patient Directive or Durable Power of Attorney (see below).

Generally speaking, the rights of a patient fall into a few main categories: the right to autonomy and self-determination (which includes the related right to withhold or grant **informed consent**), the right to privacy concerning medical information, and the right to receive treatment (not be refused treatment). Some hospitals refer to these collectively as a "Patient Bill of Rights," but there is no such "bill of rights" document **per se**, excepting a generally accepted (but not mandated) model version prepared by the American Medical Association and frequently used by hospitals.

## Right to Autonomy and Self Determination

In early 2005, a shocked and empathetic nation watched the private and personal drama of a family in conflict play out on national television, as the parents of quasi-comatose Terri Schiavo fought with her husband over whether to remove her from life support. Ultimately, the husband prevailed, on the notion that his wishes to remove life support were consistent with what she had told him she would want. His sworn testimony was contrary to that of her parents, and the entire controversy served to remind persons of the need to communicate their wishes *prior* to an emergency which may prevent them from communicating.

Considered one of the most important and fundamental of all is patients' right to direct the medical treatment they choose to receive or reject. Patient "autonomy" or self-determination is at the core of all medical decision-making in the United States. It means that patients have the right and ability to make their own choices and decisions about medical care and treatment they receive, as long as those decisions are within the **boundaries** of law. There is a legal presumption that they are fit and competent to make those decisions until a court determines otherwise.

But what happens when they are suddenly incapacitated and unable to express their wishes regarding their medical care? Thanks to a few historical developments, they can now pre-determine the medical care they wish to receive in the event that they become incapacitated by mental or physical injury or condition. By making their wishes and directives known to their doctors and others before they might suffer the loss of fitness or competency, they are able to avoid the circumstance of a court being forced to second-guess what is best for them or what their wishes would be. Additionally or in the alternative, patients may delegate to another person the power to make these medical decisions for them, should they lose consciousness or competency in the future.

These two concepts sound redundant but are actually quite different. In the first instance, patients have declared in advance the medical treatment they wish to receive in the event that they can no longer express those wishes (commonly referred to as a "living will"). In the second instance, patients have authorized another person to make those medical decisions for them in the event that they can no longer make themselves (commonly referred to as a "health care proxy," or "durable **power of attorney** for health care.") Additionally, most "living will" documents address medical care and efforts in the event

of life-threatening or terminal conditions. Durable powers of attorney generally address medical decision-making in any circumstance where patients are unable or not competent to speak for themselves, whether the condition is temporary or permanent.

The modern trend has been to create a "hybrid" of the above, which combines a declaration of the patients' own wishes with an appointment of a durable power of attorney to make decisions for them (which must be consistent with their declared wishes). Any or all of these legal devices are generally referred to as "advance directives for health care."

The Uniform Health-Care Decisions Act (UHCDA), approved in 1993 by the National Conference of Commissioners on Uniform State Laws, constitutes such a "hybrid" law intended to replace the fragmented and often conflicting laws of each state. Because existing laws (often several within each state) must be separately reviewed and compared to those provisions comprehensively collected under the umbrella Act, **adoption** has been slow. As of 2001, only six states had adopted the Act to replace their existing **statutory** provisions (Alabama, Delaware, Hawaii, Maine, Mississippi, and New Mexico) but dozens more have modeled their own comprehensive health care acts after the UHCDA.

Of course, advance directives are useless unless individuals provide copies of them to their doctors and their families or attorneys-in-fact, while they are still competent and before any incapacitation arises. Otherwise, medical personnel cannot effect their wishes if they are not made aware of them. Importantly, individuals should also keep a copy at their residence, in the event an ambulance is called on their behalf if a medical emergency arises. Without direction, ambulance personnel may initiate life-sustaining procedures that are contrary to their wishes. This is often the case for terminally ill patients who choose home hospice care and have not made other persons aware of their advance directives (even though their treating physicians may be aware of them).

One more note: if individuals do not execute an advance directive in any form, many states have passed "surrogate consent acts" which mandate the priority of surrogates permitted to make decisions about their care, should they be incapacitated.

### History

In 1990, the U. S. Supreme Court decided one of the most important cases of the century, with far-reaching consequences for all citizens, when it ruled that every person had a fundamental right of self determination with regard to refusing life-sustaining medical treatment. In the case of *Cruzan v. Commissioner, Missouri Department of Health,* 497 U.S. 261 (1990), the issue centered around who had the right to decide to remove a permanently brain-damaged and comatose patient from life-support systems, in the absence of the patient's own ability to express that determination. (The case included family **testimony** expressing what they felt the patient's wishes would have been.)

In *Cruzan,* the family of comatose Nancy Cruzan, an automobile accident victim, requested that she be removed from life support systems and be allowed to die naturally. The hospital refused to withdraw the life support equipment. Cruzan remained on life support in an irreversible coma for the next nine years, while the case went through several appeals. Following the Supreme Court's decision, Cruzan's life support equipment was discontinued and she died naturally thirteen days later.

The horror of that scenario, combined with the high court's recognition of a constitutional right of self determination, led to a flurry of state enactments of various laws permitting living wills or advance directives for health care. However, state laws vary considerably, and it is imperative that individuals first research the laws of their state or consult an attorney before attempting to create any of these legal documents. That said, many state offices or private organizations provide pre-printed forms that comply with state laws, so it is not always necessary to consult legal **counsel**.

### Living Wills

A **living will** is a form of advance directive that provides specific instructions to health care providers about patient wishes to receive or refrain from receiving life-sustaining medical care in the event of a life-threatening illness, injury, or incapacitation. The document only has effect in the event that individuals are physically and/or mentally incapable of expressing their wishes at the time. Doctors and medical personnel are generally bound to adhere to the wishes patients have articulated in their living will, even if those wishes are contrary to those of the family or loved ones, and even if those wishes are inconsistent with those of the doctors or medical personnel.

Although a majority of states have living will statutes, they vary greatly in how far the law will permit

individuals to dictate the extent of life-sustaining treatment they may refuse to receive. On one end of the spectrum are those states which only permit people to refuse "artificial means" of sustaining life (such as heart-lung machines, respirators, etc.) all the way to the other end of the spectrum, where less than a handful of states permit individuals to request artificial means to accelerate the timing of their death (such as Oregon's Death With Dignity Act, or other "right to die" initiatives).

### Durable Powers or Attorney

Sometimes referred to as a "health care proxy," the more common term for the appointment of a surrogate decision-maker is the creation of a "durable power of attorney." By placing the word "durable" in front of a regular power of attorney, individuals create an "enduring" power for their appointed "attorney-in-fact" that survives and continues in effect, even if they become incapacitated or lose competency. A durable power of attorney for health care decisions can be worded so that it takes effect only under conditions in which where individuals are unable to competently express their own wishes, or it may be worded to have immediate and continuous effect, whether or not they are incapacitated.

### The Patient Self-Determination Act (PSDA) of 1990

In 1990, Congress passed The Patient Self-Determination Act (PSDA) 42 U.S.C. §§ 1395 et seq., a federal law which requires health care providers (that are recipients of federal Medicaid/Medicare funds) to inform all adult patients of their right to accept or refuse medical treatment, and their right to execute an advance directive. This law had particular impact upon nursing homes and assisted living facilities, because it required them to ask each /patient/ resident whether an advance directive was in effect, and if not, if he or she desired one.

### Euthanasia and the "Right to Die" Movement

There are medical, legal, and ethical distinctions between directing the cessation of life-sustaining medical care or treatment, and directing the initiation of medical technique or treatment that accelerates the onset of death. In all but less than a handful of states, "patient rights" do not include the right to choose euthanasia and/or physician-assisted suicide, and these remain patently illegal. In those few states that permit such initiatives, it is imperative that individuals seek legal counsel prior to committing to such a directive, so that they can fully appreciate the ramifications of their decision upon such factors as life insurance benefits exclusions, health care insurance coverage, the right to change their minds, the possibility of failed initiatives, religious considerations, etc.

In the 1997 U. S. Supreme Court case of *Washington v. Glucksberg,* 117 S. Ct. 2258, the nation's highest court concluded that the "right to die" is not a constitutional right, and that a person's right to assistance in committing suicide is not a fundamental liberty interest protected by the Due Process Clause of the Fourteenth Amendment to the U. S. Constitution. The Court cited a state's legitimate government interest in prohibiting intentional killing and preserving human life, among other stated interests. States are, therefore, free to enact laws that treat such assisted suicides as crimes.

### Informed Consent

Directly related to people's right to make decisions about their medical care is the fact that their ability to make such decisions may be limited by the amount of information they have received regarding their choices or alternatives. Therefore, virtually all states have recognized, either by express **statute** or **common law**, their right to receive information about their medical condition and treatment choices, in plain language terms that they can understand, and in sufficient amounts such that they are able to make an "informed" decision about their health care.

People have a right to know what their diagnosis is, and the doctor generally cannot refrain from advising them of the true nature of their condition. A doctor may temporarily withhold some information if the doctor believes in **good faith** that their condition will be substantially worsened by the knowledge of their diagnosis (referred to as "therapeutic privilege"). Also, doctors may have privilege to withhold certain diagnoses or records of mental conditions, if the disclosure of such information would create a risk of harm to patients or others. Although patients generally have a right to review their medical records, doctors may substitute "summary reports" or summary statements under circumstances of limited disclosure.

Before individuals consent to any treatment for a condition, they should receive, at a minimum, an explanation of their health problem, the treatment options available to them (including any standard treatments not available through their particular health care provider), the pros and cons of the various treatment choices, and the expected prognosis or consequence associated with each. If they have received this information, any consent to treatment that they subsequently give will be presumed to be an "informed consent."

During medical emergencies, doctors are not required to obtain permission to save individuals' lives or end the emergency, in the absence of any advance directive from patients notified them of. Also, patient consent for routine treatments or procedures such as having blood drawn or providing a urine sample, is presumed by the fact that the patients have solicited a medical **assessment** and diagnosis from their doctors. On the other hand, their consent cannot be "informed" if they are intoxicated, under chemical influence of drugs or medicine, or (sometimes) in extreme pain or quasi-conscious; the law will presume that their judgment or consent was impaired under those circumstances. A doctor who fails to obtain an informed consent for non-emergency treatment or care may be charged with a criminal offense.

If individuals are incapacitated and have executed an advance directive, their attorneys in fact must consent to their treatment (durable power of attorney) and/or the health care provider must treat them in a manner consistent with their declared wishes (living will).

## Right to Privacy

The fundamental right to privacy, guaranteed by the Fifth and Fourteenth Amendments to the U. S. Constitution, protects against unwarranted invasions of privacy by federal or state entities, or arms thereof. As early as in *Roe v. Wade,* 410 U.S. 113 (1973), the U. S. Supreme Court acknowledged that the doctor-patient relationship is one which evokes constitutional rights of privacy and confidentiality. But even that right is not absolute and must be weighed against the state or federal interest at stake.

For example, in *Whalen v. Roe,* 429 U.S. 589 (1977), a group of physicians joined patients in a lawsuit challenging the constitutionality of a New York statute that required physicians to report to state authorities the identities of patients receiving Schedule II drugs (controlled substances). The physicians alleged that such information was protected by the doctor-patient confidentiality, while the patients alleged that such disclosure was an invasion of their constitutional right to privacy. The Supreme Court did not disagree with the lower court's finding that "the intimate nature of a patient's concern about his bodily ills and the medication he takes—are protected by the constitutional right to privacy." However, the high court concluded (after balancing the state's interests) that "Requiring such disclosures to representatives of the State having responsibility for the health of the community, does not automatically amount to an impermissible invasion of privacy."

There are a few key points to remember about the privacy or confidentiality of medical information:

- Generally, what is considered private is information that is learned or gained by a doctor, during or as a result of a doctor's communications with patients, or **examination** of them, or medical assessment of them. The privacy extends to documents and forms, whether completed by them or their health care providers, that are contained in their personal medical records.

- The scope of the duty of doctor-patient confidentiality, as well as the existence of a doctor-patient legal privilege, varies from state to state. No federal law governs doctor-patient confidentiality or privilege.

- The duty to maintain the privacy of one's own medical information continues even after individuals stop seeing or treating with the health care provider.

- The right to privacy of medical information is not absolute. Doctors may divulge or disclose personal information, against patients' will, under very limited circumstances. Some exceptions include the duty to warn police or third persons of a patient's threats of harm, or the duty to report to health authorities the fact of sexually transmitted or communicable diseases, including HIV or AIDS status. In many states, health care providers are required to report treatments of gunshot or stab wounds and suspected incidence of child abuse.

## The Right to Treatment

If individuals do not carry health insurance, they are still entitled to hospital emergency care, including labor and delivery care, regardless of their ability to pay. The federal Emergency Medical Treatment and Active Labor Act (EMTALA), 42 U.S.C. § 1395, which is a separate section of the more comprehensive 1985 Consolidated Omnibus Reconciliation Act

(COBRA), mandates minimum standards for emergency care by hospital emergency rooms. The law requires that all patients who present with an emergency medical condition must receive treatment to the extent that their emergency condition is medically "stabilized," irrespective of their ability to pay for such treatment.

An emergency medical condition is defined under federal law as one that manifests itself by acute symptoms of sufficient severity (including severe pain, psychiatric disturbance, and/or symptoms of substance abuse) such that the absence of immediate medical attention could reasonably be expected to result in the following:

- placing the health of the individual (or unborn child) in serious jeopardy

- the serious impairment of a bodily function

- the serious dysfunction of any bodily function or part

- the inadequate time to effect a safe transfer of a pregnant woman to another hospital before delivery, or, that the transfer may pose a threat to the health or safety of the woman or unborn child

The law goes on to define "stabilization" as meaning "that no material deterioration of the condition is likely within reasonable medical probability to result from or occur during the transfer of the patient from a facility" (or discharge).

However, once the emergency is over and a patient's condition is stabilized, the patient can be discharged and refused further treatment by private hospitals and most public hospitals. If the individual seeks routine medical care or schedule a doctor's appointment for non-emergency medical problems, doctors have a general right to refuse treatment if they have no insurance or any other means of paying for the provided care.

There are numerous protections for HIV-positive and AIDS patients that prohibit hospitals and facilities from refusing treatment if the facility's staff has the appropriate training and resources. However, most private physicians and dentists are under ethical but not legal obligations to provide treatment.

Individuals also have a **legal right** to not be released prematurely from a hospital. If they are advised to vacate their hospital room because of a standardized "appropriate length of stay" generally approved for their specific condition, they have the right to appeal that discharge if they believe that they are not well enough to leave. They should consult both their doctors and a hospital patient representative for procedural information regarding an appeal. However, the policy generally works in a way that makes them liable for payment of excess hospital stays if they should lose the appeal.

Individuals have the right to refuse treatment and leave a hospital at any time, assuming that they are mentally competent. The hospital may ask them to sign a document releasing it from liability if their medical condition worsens as a result of their refusal to accept the recommended treatment.

If individuals lose mental competency and appear to be a danger to themselves or others, they may be taken to a hospital against their will and held for involuntary "commitment." Most states require an immediate written statement or **affidavit** affirming the reasons for their involuntary commitment. However, within a short period of time (e.g., 72 hours), most states require a full examination by a medical and psychiatric doctor, a diagnosis, and (within a certain number of days) a **hearing** at which they will have the right to be represented by counsel. The purpose of the hearing is to establish whether there is sufficient information to justify their continued commitment or whether they should be released. Also, their attorneys will advise them as to whether there had been sufficient cause to justify holding them against their will in the first place.

## State Provisions

In the following summaries, "DPA" is substituted for "Durable Power of Attorney." The acronym "UHCDA" is substituted for the Uniform Health Care Decisions Act, discussed previously. The reference to "combined advance directives" means that both living wills and proxy or power of attorney directives are authorized.

ALABAMA: Alabama has adopted an Act modeled after the UHCDA at Alabama Code of 1975, Sections 22-8A-2 to 11, enacted in 1997 (amended in 2001). Patients must be in a terminal condition or permanently unconscious. The state also has a DPA Act, Section 26-1-2, revised in 1997.

ALASKA: Alaska Statute Section 13.26.332 to.356 (specifically, 13-22.344(l) generally authorizes DPA for health care.

ARIZONA: Arizona has enacted a Comprehensive Health Care Decisions Act under Arizona Revised Statutes Annotated, Section 36-3231, dated 1992 and amended in 1994. All forms of advance directives permitted in the state are covered under Sections 3201 to 3262. State law was impacted by the Supreme Court's 2004 decision in *Aetna*.

ARKANSAS: Arkansas has a Living Will Declaration Statute, Section 20-17- 202 to 214. The 1999 Arkansas Laws Act 1448 (House Bill 1331) created a special DPA for health care.

CALIFORNIA: California **Probate** Code, Sections 4600 to 4948 (enacted in 1999) and Sections 4711 to 4727 authorize combined advance directives and a Comprehensive Health Care Decisions Act. There is a limitation on DPA power for civil commitments, electro-convulsive therapy, psycho-surgery, sterilization, and **abortion**. State law was impacted by the Supreme Court's 2004 decision in *Aetna*.

COLORADO: Colorado law authorizes health care DPA under Revised Statutes, Section 15-14-501 to 509, enacted in 1992. A separate Surrogate Consent Act is at Section 15-18.5-103.

CONNECTICUT: Connecticut authorizes DPA and combined advance directives under General Statutes, Section 1-43 (1993) and Sections 19a-570 to 575 (1993). Reviewed but not amended in 1998.

DELAWARE: Delaware Code Title 16, Sections 2501 to 2517, revised in 1996 and 1998, authorize combined advance directives modeled after the UHCDA.

DISTRICT OF COLUMBIA: D.C. Code Section 21-2210 (1998) covers the DPA for Health Care Act.

FLORIDA: Florida Statutes Annotated, Sections 765-101 to 404 cover the state's Comprehensive Health Care Decisions Act, last amended in 2000.

GEORGIA: Appointment of a Special DPA is authorized under Georgia Code Annotated, Section 31-36-1 to 13 (1990, amended in 1999). It also has a separate Informed Consent statute under Section 31-9-2 (1998). In 1999, the state enacted the "Temporary Health Care Placement Decision Maker for an Adult Act" which basically expands the Informed Consent Statute. State law was impacted by the Supreme Court's 2004 decision in *Aetna*.

HAWAII: Hawaii Revised Statute Section 327E-1 to 16 covers the state's Comprehensive Health Care Decisions Act, modeled on the UHCDA. (1999, amended in 2000).

IDAHO: Idaho Code 39-4501 to 4509, last amended in 2001, authorizes the appointment of a Special DPA. Section 39-4303 contains the state's Informed Consent statute.

ILLINOIS: (755 Illinois Compiled Statutes 45/1-1 to 4-12, amended in 1999, creates a Special DPA for health care. 755 ILCS 40/25 (1998) addresses the state's Surrogate Consent Act, in the absence of an advance directive.

INDIANA: Indiana Code Section 30-5-1 to 5-10 authorizes a general DPA. Section 16-36-1-1 to 1-14 contains provisions for the Health Care Agency and Surrogate Consent Act.

IOWA: A Special DPA is authorized under Iowa Code Section 144B.1 to B12, enacted in 1991. A separate Living Will Statute is found at Section 144A.7 (1998).

KANSAS: Kansas Statutes Annotated, Sections 58-625 to 632, amended in 1994, create a special DPA for health care.

KENTUCKY: Kentucky Revised Statutes, Sections 311.621 to 643, amended in 1998, provide for a combined advance directive. A separate Living Will Statute is found at Section 311.631 (1999).

LOUISIANA: Louisiana Revised Statutes, 40:1299.58.1 to.10 (1999) provide for a Living Will (with proxy powers addressed in that statute).

MAINE: Maine Revised Statutes, Title 18A, Sections 5-801 to 817 (1995) create a combined advance directive authorization, modeled after the UHCDA. State law was impacted by the Supreme Court's 2004 decision in *Aetna*.

MARYLAND: Maryland Code Annotated, Chapter: Health-General, Sections 5-601 to 608, (amended in 2000) permit combined advance directives.

MASSACHUSETTS: Mass. Gen. Laws Ann., Ch. 201D (1990) provides for the appointment of a special DPA.

MICHIGAN: MCL 333.3651 to 5661 provides for special DPA, with limitations on powers involving pregnancy.

MINNESOTA: Minnesota Statutes Annotated 145C.01 to.16 (1993) (substantially revised in 1998) provides for a combined advance directive. Section 253B.03(Subd 6b) provides for advance directives involving mental health patients.

MISSISSIPPI: Miss. Code Section 41-41-201 to 229 (1998 replacing 1990 law) provides for an combined advance directive modeled after the UHCDA.

MISSOURI: Mo. Ann. Statutes, Sections 404.700 to 735 and Section 800-870 (1991) create a special DPA and DPA for health care.

MONTANA: Montana Code Annotated, Sections 50-9.101 to 111, and 201 to 206 (1991) combine a Living Will statute with a health care proxy authorization.

NEBRASKA: Nebraska Revised Statutes, Sections 30-3401 to 3434 (amended in 1993) permit the appointment of special DPA for health care. Special limitations on the DPA power for pregnancy, life sustaining procedures, and hydration/nutrition.

NEVADA: Nevada Revised Statutes, Sections 449.800 to 860 provide for special DPA for health care. Section 449.626 (1997) contains the state's Living Will Statute.

NEW HAMPSHIRE: The state provides for a Special DPA under Statute Section 137-J:1 to J:16 (1991, revised in 1993).

NEW JERSEY: New Jersey provides for combined advance directives under Statute Section 26:2H-53 to 78 (1991). State law was impacted by the Supreme Court's 2004 decision in *Aetna*.

NEW MEXICO: Statute Sections 24-7A-1 to 16 (1995, amended in 1997) provide for combined advanced directives modeled after the UHCDA.

NEW YORK: N.Y. Public Health Law, Sections 2980 to 2994 (1990) provide for the appointment of a special DPA. Additionally, Section 2695 (1999) adds a specialized Surrogate Consent Statute, for use in "do not resuscitate" (DNR) directives.

NORTH CAROLINA: North Carolina General Statute 32A-15 to 26 (1993, amended in 1998) creates a special authority for DPA. Section 122C-71 to 77 (1997) addresses advance directives for mental health patients. Section 90-322 contains the Living Will Statute. State law was impacted by the Supreme Court's 2004 decision in *Aetna*.

NORTH DAKOTA: Code Section 23-06.5-01 to 18 (amended in 2001) authorizes a special DPA for health care. There is a separate Informed Consent statute under Section 23-12-13.

OHIO: Ohio Revised Code Sections 1337-11 to 17, (1989, 1991) create authority for a special DPA for health care. A separate Living Will Statute is found at Section 2133.08 (1999).

OKLAHOMA: Title 63, Sections 3101.1 to.16 (last amended in 1998) provide for combined advance directives. There is a separate statute provision that addresses experimental treatments at Title 63, Section 3102A. State law was impacted by the Supreme Court's 2004 decision in *Aetna*.

OREGON: Oregon Revised Statute 127-505 to 640 (enacted in 1989, amended in 1993) provides for combined advance directives. Sections 127.700 to 735 address mental health advance directives. Section 127.635 specifically addresses living wills.

PENNSYLVANIA: Pennsylvania has a Living Will statute found at Statute Title 20, Sections 5401 to 5416 (1993). A general DPA (not specific to health care) is permitted under Sections 5601 to 5607.

RHODE ISLAND: Rhode Island General Laws, Sections 23-4:10-1 to 12 (amended in 1998) permit a special DPA for health care decisions.

SOUTH CAROLINA: South Carolina Code Section 62-5-501 to 504 creates a special DPA for health care. Section 44-66-30 (1998) provides separately for the Surrogate Consent Act in the absence of an advance directive.

SOUTH DAKOTA: The state's Codified Laws, Section 34-12C 1 to 8 and Section 59-7-2.1 to 8 (1990) provide for the appointment of a special DPA. There is a separate Surrogate Consent Act under Section 44-66-30 (1998).

TENNESSEE: Tennessee Code Annotated, Sections 34-6-201 to 214 (1990, amended 1991) create the authority for special DPAs.

TEXAS: Texas Health and Safety Code, Sections 166.001 to 166.166 (amended in 1999) authorize a special DPA. In 1997, the state enacted its Advance Directive Act under Section 166.039. State law was impacted by the Supreme Court's 2004 decision in *Aetna*.

UTAH: Utah Code Annotated, Sections 75-2-11-1 to 1118 (amended in 1993) authorizes a special DPA for health care. Since then, it has added its Comprehensive Health Care Decisions Act under Sections 75-2-1105 to 1107 (1998).

VERMONT: Statute Title 14, Sections 3451 to 3467 (1989) authorize the appointment of a special DPA for health care.

VIRGINIA: Virginia Code Sections 54.1-2981 to 2993 (1992, amended in 2000) provides for combined advance directives, including a version of a comprehensive health care decisions act at Section 54.1-2986.

WASHINGTON: Revised Code Sections 11.94.010 to 900 (1990) provide for general DPA, with limitations on power for electro-convulsive therapy, amputation, and psychiatric surgery. A separate Informed Consent statute is contained under Section 7.70.065 (1998). State law was impacted by the Supreme Court's 2004 decision in *Aetna*.

WEST VIRGINIA: W. Va. Code Section 16-30-1 to 21 (2000) provide for combined advance directives, but mandate separate documents for living wills and medical powers of attorney. State law was impacted by the Supreme Court's 2004 decision in *Aetna*.

WISCONSIN: Wisconsin Statutes Annotated, Sections 155.01 to 80 and Section 11.243.07 (6m) (amended 1998) authorize a special DPA.

WYOMING: Wyoming Statutes Annotated, Section 3-5-201 to 214 (specifically Section 3-209) (1991, 1992) authorize appointment of a special DPA. The identical statute is also contained at Section 35-22-105(b) (1998) but is referred to as the Living Will statute.

## Additional Resources

"A Few Facts About the Uniform Health-Care Decisions Act." Available at http://www.alzheimers . . .

"Alzheimer's Disease and Related Dementias: Legal Issues in Care and Treatment, 1994." A Report to Congress of the Advisory Panel on Alzheimer's Disease. Available at http://www.alzheimers

"Federal Laws in Emergency Medicine." Derlet, Robert, M.D. *eMedicine Journal*, 22 January 2002. Available at http://www.emedicine.com/emerg/topic860.htm.

"Health Care Power of Attorney and Combined Advance Directive Legislation." American Bar Association, Commission on Legal Problems of the Elderly. July 2000.

*Law for Dummies*. Ventura, John. IDG Books Worldwide, Inc. 1996.

"Surrogate Consent in the Absence of an Advance Directive." American Bar Association, Commission on Legal Problems of the Elderly. July 2001.

*The Court TV Cradle-to-grave Legal Survival Guide*. Little, Brown and Company: 1995.

## Organizations

### *The American Bar Association (Commission on Legal Problems of the Elderly*

740 15th Street NW
Washington, DC 20005 USA
Phone: (202) 992-1000

### *Choice in Dying*

200 Varick Street
New York, NY 10014 USA
Phone: (800) 989-WILL
URL:

### *The National Association for Home Health Care*

228 Seventh Street SE
Washington, DC 20003 USA
Phone: (202) 547-7424
URL: webmaster@nahc.org

### *The National Association of People with AIDS*

1413 K Street NW
Washington, DC 20005 USA
Phone: (202) 898-0414

### *The Patient Advocacy List*

URL: http://infonet.welch.jhu.edu/advocacy.html

# HEALTHCARE

## TREATMENT OF MINORS

*Sections within this essay:*

- Background

- Informed Consent
  - Generally
  - Family Planning
  - Emergency
  - Sexual Abuse
  - Mental Health and Substance Abuse
  - Sexually Transmitted Diseases
  - Status

- The Mature Minor Doctrine

- Confidentiality of Medical Records

- Additional Resources

## Background

Fifty years ago, the issue of medical treatment of minors—children under the age of 18—would never have been considered controversial. At that time, parental consent was required for almost any type of medical treatment, as it was required for any other situation involving children. Minors were simply not considered competent to make medical decisions.

However, the past 50 years have witnessed a gradual expansion of the rights of minors, and health care has been no exception. Minors who previously had no medical rights now found themselves in the position of making decisions about the most intimate medical procedures.

But the area of medical treatment of minors is still controversial, especially as it relates to certain proce-

dures and conditions such as **abortion** and sexually transmitted diseases. Many states grant minors broad leeway to determine the course of their medical treatment, and others grant them very few rights. There is little agreement by either medical professionals or state lawmakers as to how far minor rights should go regarding medical treatment.

What is at issue in the debate over minor rights to medical treatment is a tension between the parental responsibilities toward the child, the immaturity and vulnerability of children, and the child's right to be emancipated from the decision of the parent. This tension has produced a patchwork of laws and makes it difficult to make any overriding statements about minor and parental rights in regard to medical treatment.

## Informed Consent

The crux of the debate over the treatment of minors is the doctrine of **informed consent**. A person must offer informed consent to any medical treatment given to them, or the physicians involved can risk legal liability. Informed consent has always been a crucial part of the doctor-patient relationship, and has been viewed by courts as a fundamental right.

But in the case of children, the question is, can they offer informed consent, or does that informed consent have to be provided by their parents, who may be seen as more capable of making a knowledgeable decision on a subject as important as medical care. Beyond this simple question are an important set of underlying questions, pertaining for example to the age at which a child may become capable of informed consent, and whether there are certain procedures in which informed consent is more important than others.

### Generally

In general, for most medical procedures, the parent or legal **guardian** of the minor still has to grant consent in order for the procedure to be performed. While the state can challenge a parent's decision to refuse medically necessary treatment and can in some cases win the authority to make medical decisions on behalf of the child, the minor can not make his or her own medical decisions.

This general rule is virtually always the case regarding any sort of medical treatment before the minor enters their teenage years—no state or court has ever authorized minors younger than 12 to make any sort of medical decision for themselves. But after the minor becomes a teenager, states begin to digress in terms of the responsibility the minor can take for medical decisions. Exceptions have been carved out for various medical procedures that allow teenage minors to have final say in their medical care.

### Family Planning

Twenty-five states and the District of Columbia have laws that explicitly give minors the authority to consent to contraceptive services, and twenty-seven states and the District of Columbia specifically allow pregnant minors to the obtain prenatal care and delivery services without parental consent or notification.

The Title X federal family planning program, which supports clinics that provide contraceptive service and other reproductive health care to minors on a confidential basis and without the need for parental consent or notification, has seen efforts made by Congress to require consent or notification before a minor receives these services. All of these efforts, the most recent in 1998, have failed.

Probably the most controversial area of family planning and minors is abortion. Two states—Connecticut and Maine—as well as the District of Columbia have laws that give minors the right to obtain abortions on their own. In contrast, 31 states currently have laws restricting minors' rights to obtain abortions by either requiring them to obtain the permission of one or both parents, or to notify one or both of them of the procedure. The rest of the states either have no laws regarding parental consent and notification and abortion or laws that are currently blocked from going into effect by the courts of the state.

The family planning area and its relation to minors has been a difficult one for the states to tackle because of several Supreme Court rulings that have ruled that minors do have a limited right of privacy in respect to family planning issues. The Court has ruled that if states are going to restrict the right of minors to have an abortion, they have to provide an alternative to the requirement of parental consent, to allow the minor to show she is mature enough to make the decision of having an abortion herself. This alternative is generally in the form of a judicial bypass—permitting a court to make the decision regarding whether the minor can get an abortion. Maryland allows a "physician bypass" that permits a doctor to waive parental notice if the minor is capable of giving informed consent or if notice would lead to abuse of the minor.

States that require consent before a minor may have an abortion include Alabama, Indiana, Kentucky, Louisiana, Massachusetts, Michigan, Mississippi, Missouri, North Carolina, North Dakota, Pennsylvania, Rhode Island, South Carolina, Tennessee, Wisconsin and Wyoming. States requiring notification before a minor's abortion include Arkansas, Delaware, Georgia, Idaho, Iowa, Kansas, Maryland, Minnesota, Nebraska, Ohio, South Dakota, Texas, Utah, Virginia and West Virginia.

Also, because the Supreme Court rulings, states that do not explicitly allow minors to obtain contraceptive and prenatal care services without parental consent still must permit this to happen in practice, as the court has ruled that these are services that are covered by the minors' right to privacy. However, states can still impose limitations on minors' ability to obtain these services, based on factors such as age, marriage status, medical condition or who referred the minors for treatment. In addition, two states—Utah and Texas—prohibit the use of state funds to provide contraceptive services to minors without parental consent.

### Emergency

All states allow parental consent for treatment of a minor to be waived in the event of a medical emergency. The circumstances that should be present in order for such an emergency include the patient being incapacitated to the point of being unable to give an informed choice, the circumstances are life-threatening or serious enough that immediate treatment is required, and it would be impossible or imprudent to try to get consent from someone regarding the patient. In these cases, consent of the parent is presumed, since otherwise the minor would suffer avoidable injury.

### Sexual Abuse

Most states allow minors to seek treatment for **sexual abuse** or **assault** without parental consent; however, many states require the minor's parents or guardian to be notified of the sexual abuse unless the physician has reason to believe the parent or guardian was responsible for the sexual abuse.

### Mental Health and Substance Abuse

Twenty states and the District of Columbia give minors the explicit authority to consent to outpatient mental health services. No state specifically requires parental consent to obtain these services, but many states do impose age requirements or other restrictions in regards to minors who obtain these services.

Forty-four states and the District of Columbia have laws or policies authorizing a minor who abuses drug or alcohol to consent to outpatient counseling without a parent's consent. Again, no states require parental consent for these services, but some restrictions may be imposed on which minors can obtain this counseling.

### Sexually Transmitted Diseases

Every state currently allows minors over the age of 12 to receive testing for sexually transmitted diseases, including HIV, without parental consent. Most of these states allow minors to receive treatment for all sexually transmitted diseases without parental consent; however, three states—California, New Mexico, and Ohio—as of 2002 do not allow minors to receive treatment for HIV without parental consent. One state, Iowa, requires that parents be notified in the event of a positive HIV test. Many states allow doctors to notify the parents of the results of tests and treatment for sexually transmitted diseases, though they do not require the doctor to get a consent.

### Status

In addition to making exceptions to the general rule requiring informed consent for specific medical treatments, states will often allow minors to consent to medical treatment on the basis of their status—whether they are considered emancipated from their parents. Most states determine a child has reached the **age of majority** and is emancipated from his or her parents upon reaching the age of 18, although in Alabama and Nebraska, 19 is considered the age of majority, and in Pennsylvania it is 21. Mississippi

has the age of majority at 21, but 18 as the **age of consent** for health care decisions.

Beyond age, courts can declare a minor emancipated from their parents and thus able to issue consent, if they meet certain conditions, including self-sufficiency, living separate and apart from the parents, receiving money from a business activity not related to the parents, and proven capability of managing their own affairs. Married and divorced minors are often considered automatically emancipated, as are minors on active duty with the armed forces. In addition, minor parents are allowed to make medical decisions for their children. In 29 states and the District of Columbia, this consent is explicitly authorized.

## The Mature Minor Doctrine

The "mature minor" doctrine provides for minors to give consent to medical procedures if they can show that they are mature enough to make a decision on their own. It is a relatively new legal concept, and as of 2002 only a few states such as Arkansas and Nevada have enacted the doctrine into **statute**. In several other states, including Pennsylvania, Tennessee, Illinois, Maine and Massachusetts, state high courts have adopted the doctrine as law.

In the states where it exists, the mature minor doctrine takes into account the age and situation of the minor to determine maturity, in addition to factors and conduct that can prove maturity. The Arkansas statute states, "any unemancipated minor of sufficient intelligence to understand and appreciate the consequences of the proposed surgical or medical treatment or procedures, for himself [may offer consent]." The standard is typical of the requirements of the mature minor doctrine.

The mature minor doctrine has been consistently applied in cases where the minor is sixteen years or older, understands the medical procedure in question, and the procedure is not serious. Application of the doctrine in other circumstances is more questionable. Outside reproductive rights, the U.S. Supreme Court has never ruled on its applicability to medical procedures.

## Confidentiality of Medical Records

States that allow minors to consent to certain medical procedures often provide for confidentiality from parents in regard to those medical procedures. However, this is not always the case. Many states allow the doctor to inform parents of medical procedures, and some states require parental notifications about specific medical procedures done on minors even when the minor has given consent.

When confidentiality is provided for, California's statute is typical of the requirements. It states that except as provided by law or if the minor authorizes it in writing, physicians are prohibited from telling the minor's parents or legal guardian about medical care the minor was legally able to authorize. The physician is required to discuss with the minor the advantages of disclosing the proposed treatment to the minor's parents or legal guardian before services are rendered.

## Additional Resources

"Acknowledging The Hypocrisy: Granting Minors The Right To Choose Their Medical Treatment" *New York Law School Journal of Human Rights*, Summer 2000.

"Informed Consent to the Medical Treatment of Minors: Law and Practice" Schlam, Lawrence, Joseph P. Wood, *Health Matrix: Journal of Law-Medicine*, Summer 2000.

"Medical Care For Minors: How To Consent To Medical Care for Minors" Available at http://www.cmanet.org/, Aug. 7, 2001.

"Minors and The Right to Consent To Health Care"Boonstra, Heather, Elizabeth Nash. Available at http://www.agi-usa.org/, 2000.

## Organizations

### Alan Guttmacher Institute

120 Wall Street, 21st Floor
New York, NY 10005 USA
Phone: (212) 248-1111
Fax: (212) 248-1951
URL: http://www.agi-usa.org
Primary Contact: Sara A. Seims, President

### American Academy of Pediatrics

141 Northwest Point Boulevard
Elk Grove Village, IL 60007-1098 USA
Phone: (847) 434-4000
Fax: (847) 434-8000
URL: http://www.aap.org/
Primary Contact: Louis Z. Cooper, President

### Planned Parenthood Federation of America

810 Seventh Ave.
New York, NY 10019 USA
Phone: (212) 541-7800
Fax: (212) 245-1845
URL: http://www.plannedparenthood.org/
Primary Contact: Gloria Feldt, President

# HEALTHCARE

## TREATMENT WITHOUT INSURANCE

*Sections within this essay:*

- Background
- The Dangers of Being Uninsured
    - Quality of Care
    - Failure to Get Treatment
- How are the Uninsured Protected?
    - EMTALA
    - Other Options
- Government Assistance
- Seeking Quicker Solutions
- Additional Resources

## Background

Nearly 40 million Americans between the ages of 18 and 64 carry no health insurance coverage. In the past, only the poor or the unemployed faced this problem. Today, with health care costs rising dramatically each year, the threat of being uninsured now extends to low- and moderate-income people as well. Between 1980 and 1998, according to the Health Care Financing Administration, the amount of money Americans spent on health care quadrupled. In 1998 Americans spent $1.1 trillion on health care, roughly $4,000 for every person in the United States.

Health insurance costs have continued to rise, a problem that has been particularly difficult for small companies and the self-employed. Small companies often have less clout with insurers because they have a smaller premium base and thus cannot negotiate large-scale deals. For the self-employed it is worse.

Insurance companies that in the past have offered health insurance policies to individuals have gradually been eliminating this coverage. Even if a person is willing to pay high premiums, there is simply less to choose from in the insurance market. Some people get around this dilemma by getting their insurance through professional associations; others get insurance through a spouse. Some take insurance policies with high deductibles of perhaps $5,000 or even $10,000. These are known as "catastrophic coverage" and are meant to protect individuals from unforeseen major medical events (such as cancer). An alarmingly large number of people, however, seem to be saying that it may be easier and more cost-effective to take their chances and go completely without coverage.

The number of uninsured people had actually been falling since the late 1990s, in response to the strong economy. But with the economic downturn beginning in 2000, the belief was that numbers would begin to rise again. Even if those numbers were to remain steady, the grim fact remains that the most recent figures translate into one in four working-age people.

## The Dangers of Being Uninsured

Clearly the greatest danger in having no health insurance is that a serious illness could destroy one's finances. But there are other less obvious dangers whose combined effects can be quite dramatic.

### Quality of Care

Many who are uninsured may receive poorer quality health care simply because they do not carry insurance. According to the Employee Benefit Research Institute (EBRI) in its 2001 *Health Confidence Survey,* more than two–thirds of uninsured Americans are concerned that they will not get top quality care should they need medical treatment. Moreover, they worry about how they would pay for prescription medication (which can be an enormous expense, especially for a chronic condition) if they needed it.

### Failure to Get Treatment

Moreover, perhaps, about 44 percent of the uninsured have consciously delayed getting needed medical treatment or simply foregone care altogether. Not surprisingly, they may also fail to seek preventive care, such as check-ups or follow-up doctor's visits. The failure to seek needed care may cause the person to become sicker, until there is no choice but to seek care. By then, what might have been a minor or easily treatable problem may have turned into something more serious.

The fear of getting lesser care may not be without merit. A number of studies have shown that the uninsured are given less attention than those who have insurance. The Center for Studying Health System Change released a report in 1998 that showed the level of treatment for the uninsured varied depending in part on where they live. Those in large urban areas fare slightly better, even if they are poor, because there are usually more physicians and hospitals, as well as more social programs that might help them take care of their needs. A report released in 2000 by the Consumers Union (the publisher of *Consumer Reports*) revealed that the uninsured in general do receive lesser care than the insured.

This is not necessarily the fault of the health care profession. Part of the difficulty is that, as more people become uninsured, more seek help through the programs that are set up to help them. Eventually such programs get overwhelmed.

## How Are the Uninsured Protected?

### EMTALA

In 1986 Congress passed the Emergency Medical Treatment and Labor Act (EMTALA), part of the 1985 Consolidated Omnibus Reconciliation Act (COBRA). Most people know COBRA as the law that mandates that a company has to let an employee who leaves pay into the health insurance plan and remain covered temporarily. This mandate protects employees from suddenly losing their health insurance after, for example, being laid off. EMTALA focuses on another

issue: the practice of patient "dumping." Dumping occurs when a hospital fails to treat, screen, or transfer patients. Not surprisingly, a patient's ability to pay plays heavily into this treatment. Before EMTALA was passed, hospitals could transfer indigent patients instead of treating them.

Under EMTALA, no patient who arrives in a hospital with an emergency condition will be turned away or transferred unnecessarily. Anyone who shows up in a hospital emergency room will be screened to determine the severity of his or her condition. If the condition is deemed an emergency, the hospital is obligated to stabilize the patient. The hospital can transfer patients only when it lacks the ability to stabilize the patient beyond a certain limit; a transfer to a charity hospital merely to avoid treating the patient is a violation.

A woman who is in labor is deemed to be in an emergency medical situation and cannot be denied care or unnecessarily transferred.

The hospital does have the right to inquire whether the patient can pay. It is a violation, however, if **examination** or treatment is delayed while the hospital asks the question. The hospital is not permitted to base its decision to treat a patient on whether there is an expectation of payment.

The hospital has no obligation to the patient if an emergency condition does not exist. Nor does the hospital have an obligation to a patient who refuses examination, treatment, or transfer. The hospital is required to keep a record of this and also must try to get the patient's refusal in writing. The patient should also be told about the risks incurred in leaving the hospital.

EMTALA imposes harsh penalties for hospitals that violate the law. The hospital may face fines of up to $50,000 per incident; attending physicians can also be fined if they are found to have hidden the true nature of a patient's condition.

While laws like EMTALA are helpful, they ignore the issue of how uninsured people can pay for non-emergency care. Uninsured people have to pay full price for their prescription medication, for any routine doctor's visit, and for elective procedures. Some uninsured individuals try to get around the law by showing up at a hospital's emergency room for non-emergency care, in the hope that the emergency staff will provide some degree of assistance. Trying to use the emergency room for more routine health problems still provides inadequate care to these people, and it also ties up staff and resources needed for true emergencies

### Other Options

What options are there for those who are uninsured, short of paying out-of-pocket or trying to use the emergency room for routine care? Part of the difficulty in sorting out the health care dilemma is that there are so many groups with agendas that may not necessarily converge. On the surface, everyone wants the same thing: top-quality health care at the most reasonable cost possible. How to get to that point is what keeps the different sides so far apart. The attempts by the Clinton Administration to create a more comprehensive health care system in the early 1990s showed just how firmly entrenched different groups are in their own beliefs and opinions on the subject.

Physicians want to have more freedom to make choices without being beholden to insurance companies that are forever trying to place cost containment over patient well-being. Insurance companies want to find ways to cut the cost of medical care instead of letting physicians take control of the industry and price the insurers out of business.

Health advocacy groups have suggested a number of options:

- Tax credits for the poor to help them pay for their health insurance

- Greater access to "medical savings accounts" (MSAs). These accounts allow people to set aside money for medical costs. Typically, a person with a high **deductible** insurance policy will use an MSA to cover the cost of that deductible

- Overhauling the entire health care system to eliminate waste and inefficiency

- Encouraging all Americans to adopt healthier lifestyles, thus making the public healthier in general and reducing the overall need for complicated medical care

To be sure, each of these ideas may have some merit. From the standpoint of the would-be patient who has no insurance and who cannot afford a trip to the doctor, however, the issue is more immediate: how to get decent medical care *now*.

### Government Assistance

Examining the dozens of resources that are available through the U. S. Government alone is enough to leave one's head spinning. The U.S. Department of Health and Human Services has tried to streamline the information overload through the Center for **Medicare** and **Medicaid** Services (formerly the Health Care Financing Administration). This group oversees not only Medicare and Medicaid, but also children's insurance through the State Children's Health Insurance Program (SCHIP).

Medicaid, which is designed to cover the health costs of those whose income falls beneath a certain minimum number, can be helpful for some people. But each state determines how Medicaid is distributed and individual levels of eligibility. For someone who is struggling but not quite poor enough to receive Medicaid, the program offers little consolation.

The SCHIP offers more leeway, trying to **redress** the problem of what to do when a family makes too much money for Medicaid but not enough to pay for private coverage. In **fiscal** year 2000, some 3.3 million children were covered by SCHIP. Again, each state administers its own program, with oversight by the U. S. Department of Health and Human Services. Some states will do a better job than others, and no system is foolproof, but at least SCHIP begins to address what for many families is the most unnerving drawback to lack of coverage: how to pay for their children's needs.

One of the problems that Medicaid, SCHIP, and other programs to help the uninsured pay for medical expenses is that there is a surprising lack of knowledge of these programs among the very people they are designed to serve. In 1999, according to EBRI, only 22 percent of uninsured Americans were aware of low-cost or free insurance or medical programs for uninsured adults and children in their state. That number rose to 37 percent in 2000 and dropped to 31 percent in 2001. Part of the reason for the rise and then drop is that the economy began a downward shift in 2000; more people lost their jobs and more companies cut back on health care offerings, which left more people uninsured.

### Seeking Quicker Solutions

For the person who is suddenly uninsured and who may not have time to wait for the health care system to be reformed, what are the options?

The first step is to gather information from the U. S. Department of Health and Human Services as well as state and local agencies, to find out precisely what options might be available to individuals and their families. Whether out of embarrassment or fear of inadequate care, many people will fail to explore these options. In fact, depending on the state or local initiatives, there may be ways to get low-cost or no-cost services without fear of substandard care. The resources exist, but it will take research on the individual's part to find out what the options are.

Another option may be to seek out a professional organization that offers its members health insurance at group rates. These programs can offer relatively reasonable coverage. More important, since the coverage is group rather than individual, there is less danger that the insurance company will discontinue the program (many companies that used to make individual private insurance available have stopped, citing rising costs). Local business associations, community organizations, Chambers of Commerce, and similar groups may have something to offer. It is hardly a perfect solution, but it is better than carrying no insurance.

Unfortunately, this is a problem that has no easy answers and many, many different approaches to "fixing" the problem. The most important step that anyone, insured or uninsured, can take is to try to keep informed about the options. There is no shortage of information, and identifying the best sources will at least provide some of the tools necessary to better understand an increasingly complex issue.

## Additional Resources

*Covering America: Real Remedies for the Uninsured.* Meyer, Jack A., project director; Elliot K. Wicks, editor.; Economic and Social Research Institute, 2001.

*The Future U. S. Healthcare System: Who Will Care for the Poor and Uninsured?*Altman, Stuart H., et al, editors., Health Administration Press, 1998.

*System in Crisis: The Case for Health Care Reform.*Blendon, Robert J., and Jennifer N. Edwards, editors., Faulkner & Gray, 1991.

## Organizations

### American Medical Association
515 N. State Street
Chicago, IL 60610 USA
Phone: (312) 464-5000
URL: http://www.ama-assn.org
Primary Contact: Michael D. Maves, M.D., CEO

### Consumers Union
101 Truman Road
Yonkers, NY 10703 USA
Phone: (914) 378-2455
Fax: (914) 378-2928
URL: http://www.consumersunion.org
Primary Contact: Jim Guest, President

### Employee Benefit Research Institute (EBRI)
2212 K Street NW, Suite 600
Washington, DC 20037 USA
Phone: (202) 659-0670
Fax: (202) 775-6312
URL: http://www.ebri.org
Primary Contact: Dallas L. Salisbury, President and CEO

### U. S. Department of Health and Human Services

### Center for Medicare and Medicaid Services
7500 Security Boulevard
Baltimore, MD 21244 USA
Phone: (410) 786-3000
URL: http://cms.hhs.gov
Primary Contact: Tom Scully, Administrator

# HOMELAND SECURITY

## DEPARTMENT OF HOMELAND SECURITY

*Sections within this essay:*

## Background

As a response to terrorist attacks that took place on U.S. soil on September 11, 2001, Congress in November 2002 approved the creation of the Department of Homeland Security. This executive branch department aims to detect and prevent terrorist attacks in the United States by performing functions that were previously preformed by more than twenty federal agencies. The department has developed a series of broad strategic goals related to the fulfillment of its mission. These goals are as follows:

- Raise awareness of threats of and vulnerabilities to terrorist attacks

- Detect, deter and mitigate terrorist threats to the United States

- Safeguard the United States, including its people, critical infrastructure, property, and economy, from acts of terrorism, as well as natural disasters and other emergencies

- Lead, manage, and coordinate a national response to acts of terrorism, as well as natural disasters and emergencies

- Lead efforts among national, state, local, and private entities to recover from acts of terrorism, natural disasters, and emergencies

- Serve the public by facilitating lawful trade, immigration, and travel

- Achieve organizational excellence

The Department of Homeland Security facilitates communication between federal agencies as well as state and local government entities. Moreover, each state has developed its own office or commission to address security and terrorism within its own border.

## September 11th Terrorist Attacks

On the morning of September 11, 2001, 19 terrorists, working in teams of four or five, hijacked four commercial airliners. The terrorists crashed two of the planes into the World Trade Center in New York City, which eventually destroyed the structure. A third plane crashed into and seriously damaged the Pentagon in Washington, D.C., while a fourth crashed in a field in Pennsylvania. The hijackings killed nearly 3000 people.

The investigation into the attacks focused almost immediately on the activities of Osama Bin Laden, leader of the al-Qaeda terrorist organization. Investigators determined that the terrorists who staged the hijackings had lived in the United States for several months prior to the attacks. Several U.S. agencies, such as the Central Intelligence Agency (CIA), Federal Bureau of Investigation (FBI), and the Department of Defense, later fell under harsh criticism for failing to communicate effectively with one another in a manner that could have prevented the terrorism from taking place.

## Creation of the Office of Homeland Security

Nine days after the September 11th attacks, President George W. Bush in an address to Congress announced that he would create the Office of Homeland Security. The goal of this agency was to coordinate the efforts of more than 40 federal agencies in order to prevent further terrorist attacks. Bush created this office nearly a month after the attacks. Tom Ridge, the former governor of Pennsylvania, became the first director of the office, which fell within the Executive Office of the President.

The Office of Homeland Security served primarily as a coordinating body. In other words, the president charged the office with coordinating efforts of other agencies, in addition to the development of a national strategy to prevent terrorism. Because of its limited mandate, several government officials and commentators called for the creation of a stronger department that could be responsible for combating terrorism.

## Passage of the Homeland Security Act

Within months of the creation of the Office of Homeland Security, Republicans in Congress in January 2002 introduced the Homeland Security Act. The House and Senate approved the statute in November 2002, and Bush signed the bill into law that month. The statute called for the largest restructuring of federal administrative agencies since the creation of the

Department of Defense in 1947. The act created the Department of Homeland Security as a cabinet-level department, under which more than 20 existing agencies would merge.

The president nominates a secretary to lead the department. The Senate must approve the nominee. Bush appointed Ridge to be the secretary of this new department, and Ridge served in this capacity until 2005. On February 15, 2005, Michael Chertoff, a former federal judge in the Third Circuit Court of Appeals, was sworn in as secretary, replacing Ridge.

## Restructuring of Federal Agencies into Directorates

The Homeland Security Act brought together 22 federal agencies to serve a myriad of functions. The department took control of such entities as the Immigration and Naturalization Service, the U.S. Coast Guard, the U.S. Customs Service, and the Federal Emergency Management Agency (FEMA). In order to fulfill the department's mission, the department was divided into five teams, referred to as directorates. These directorates include the following: Border and Transportation Security, Emergency Preparedness and Response, Information Analysis and Infrastructure Protection, Science and Technology, and Management.

## Components of the Department of Homeland Security

Several components make up the Department of Homeland Security. Most of the activities focus on fulfilling the responsibilities of the five directorates, along with the Office of the Secretary and other offices.

### Office of the Secretary

Staff members within the Office of the Secretary perform a variety of tasks that contribute to the overall mission of the department. The components of the Office of the Secretary include the following: Office of the Chief Privacy Officer, Office of Civil Rights and Civil Liberties, Office of Counter Narcotics, Office of General Counsel, Office of the Inspector General, Office of Legislative Affairs, Office of National Capital Region Coordination, Office of the Private Sector, Office of Public Affairs, Office of Security, and Office of State and Local Government Coordination and Preparedness.

### Border and Transportation Security

The Border and Transportation Security directorate, the largest of the directorates in the department, brought together several agencies from such departments as the Treasury Department, the Department of Justice, the Department of Transportation, and the Department of Agriculture. The mission of this directorate is to secure the borders and transportation systems of the United States and to enforce immigration laws. This directorate consists of four main agencies: the Transportation Security Administration, Customs and Border Protection, Immigration and Customs Enforcement, and the Federal Law Enforcement Training Center.

### Emergency Preparedness and Response

The Emergency Preparedness and Response directorate oversees the federal government's national response and recovery strategy. This directorate works closely with FEMA in coordinating the first response to a catastrophe. This directorate is also responsible for the development of vaccines, antidotes and treatments in the event of a biological attack on the United States.

### Information Analysis and Infrastructure Protection

The Information Analysis and Infrastructure Protection directorate assesses vulnerabilities to terrorist attacks in the United States. This directorate is also responsible for disseminating accurate information about terrorist threats to federal, state, local, private, and international entities. The three bodies that carry out these missions are the Homeland Security Operations Center, Information Analysis, and Infrastructure Protection.

Information disseminated by the Information Analysis and Infrastructure Protection directorate is probably the most widely identified by the general public due to the public's familiarity with the color-coded terrorist warnings. This warning system, which consists of five levels representing the severity of the threat of terrorism, are frequently displayed on news broadcasts, in the print media, and on the Internet.

### Science and Technology

The Science and Technology directorate studies the use of scientific and technological resources to combat terrorism and protect the United States. The three entities that comprise this director include the Office of National Laboratories, Homeland Security Laboratories, and the Homeland Security Advanced Research Projects Agency.

### Office of Management

The Office of Management oversees the budget and allocation of funds within the Department of Homeland Security.

### U.S. Citizenship and Immigration Services

U.S. Citizenship and Immigration Services (USCIS) assumed many responsibilities previously carried out by the Immigration and Naturalization Service (INS). The USCIS manages U.S. policy towards visitors, refugees, immigrants, asylum seekers, and new citizens, while also protecting against acts of terrorism, unlawful entrants, and illegal residents.

### U.S. Coast Guard

The U.S. Coast Guard protects U.S. ports and waterways.

### U.S. Secret Service

The U.S. Secret Service protects the President, the leaders of the United States, and the country's financial and critical infrastructures.

## State Offices of Homeland Security

In addition to the federal Department of Homeland Security, each state had developed its own department, office, commission, or task force responsible for overseeing homeland security within that state. The following is a listing of these state offices:

ALABAMA: Department of Homeland Security.

ALASKA: Division of Homeland Security and Emergency Management.

ARIZONA: Homeland Security Planning Office.

CALIFORNIA: Office of Homeland Security.

COLORADO: Office for Preparedness, Security, and Fire Safety.

CONNECTICUT: Division of Homeland Security, Department of Public Safety.

DELAWARE: Department of Safety and Homeland Security.

FLORIDA: Florida Department of Law Enforcement.

GEORGIA: Office of Homeland Security.

HAWAII: Hawaii State Civil Defense.

IDAHO: Bureau of Homeland Security.

ILLINOIS: Illinois Homeland Security.

INDIANA: Indiana Counter-Terrorism and Security Council.

IOWA: Iowa Homeland Security and Emergency Management.

KANSAS: Division of Emergency Management.

KENTUCKY: Office of Homeland Security.

LOUISIANA: Office of Homeland Security and Emergency Preparedness.

MAINE: Emergency Management Agency.

MARYLAND: Governor's Office of Homeland Security.

MASSACHUSETTS: Executive Office of Public Safety.

MICHIGAN: Michigan Homeland Security.

MINNESOTA: Office of Homeland Security.

MISSISSIPPI: Office of Homeland Security.

MISSOURI: Missouri Homeland Security.

MONTANA: Disaster and Emergency Services Division.

NEBRASKA: Emergency Management Agency.

NEVADA: Homeland Security Commission.

NEW HAMPSHIRE: Department of Safety.

NEW JERSEY: Office of Emergency Management.

NEW MEXICO: Office of Homeland Security.

NEW YORK: State Emergency Management Office.

NORTH CAROLINA: Department of Crime Control and Public Safety.

NORTH DAKOTA: Department of Emergency Services.

OHIO: State of Ohio Security Task Force.

OKLAHOMA: Office of Homeland Security.

OREGON: Office of Homeland Security.

PENNSYLVANIA: Office of Homeland Security.

RHODE ISLAND: Emergency Management Agency.

SOUTH CAROLINA: Law Enforcement Division.

SOUTH DAKOTA: Office of Homeland Security.

TENNESSEE: Office of Homeland Security.

TEXAS: Office of Homeland Security.

UTAH: Department of Public Safety's Division of Emergency Services and Homeland Security.

VERMONT: Department of Public Safety Homeland Security Unit.

VIRGINIA: Office of Commonwealth Preparedness.

WASHINGTON: Emergency Management Division.

WEST VIRGINIA: Division of Homeland Security and Emergency Management.

WISCONSIN: Homeland Security Council.

WYOMING: Office of Homeland Security.

## Additional Resources

*Homeland Security Law and Policy.* William C. Nicholson, Charles C. Thomas, Publisher, Ltd., 2005.

*Homeland Security Law Handbook..* ABS Consulting, Government Institutes, 2003.

National Conference of State Legislatures: State Offices of Homeland Security, 2005. http://www.ncsl.org/programs/legman/nlssa/sthomelandoffcs.htm.

*West's Encyclopedia of American Law.* 2d ed., Thomson/Gale, 2004.

## Organizations

### *Department of Homeland Security*
Washington, DC 20528 USA
Phone: (202) 282-8000
URL: http://www.dhs.gov

### *Homeland Security Institute*
2900 South Quincy Street, Suite 800
Arlington, VA 22206 USA
Phone: (703) 416-3550
URL: http://www.homelandsecurity.org

# HOMELAND SECURITY

## EMERGENCY MANAGEMENT

*Sections within this essay:*

- Background
- Early Efforts with Emergency Management
- First Responders
- Government Agencies
    - Department of Homeland Security
- Civilian Agencies
    - Private Sector
- Additional Resources

## Background

The attacks on September 11, 2001 that destroyed the World Trade Center in New York and the Pentagon in Washington were disasters of an almost unimaginable scale. Still, even in the panic and devastation that ensued, orderly emergency procedures needed to be maintained to prevent further damage and to spare as many additional lives as possible. Emergencies on a smaller scale may not require as much sustained effort as the September 11 attacks did, but they, too, require effective emergency management procedures.

Emergencies that can warrant either a local, state, or federal effort can include a variety of situations:

- *Natural disasters* include earthquakes, floods, tornados, hurricanes, blizzards, mudslides, and volcanoes.

- *Fires* can be set accidentally (by lightning storms or by careless campers) or they can be set deliberately by arsonists.

- *Transportation* disasters include airline crashes, train crashes and derailments, boat accidents, highway pileups and accidents, and anything that disrupts the ability of people to move from one place to another.

- *Hazardous materials* emergencies include oil spills, hazardous waste spills, and nuclear accidents.

- *Invasions and attacks* could come from military or terrorist sources.

Depending on the size and location of the emergency, local municipalities may take the primary charge, with state and federal agencies providing backup. Emergency management can also come from the private or corporate sector; mining accidents, for example, are usually handled primarily by the mining company (whose on-site miners are most familiar with the safest and most efficient rescue procedures).

## Early Efforts with Emergency Management

Until the twentieth century, there was no formal government response system for emergency situations. The fear of an attack on U.S. soil, for example was almost nonexistent; the last foreign troops in the United States had been the British during the War of 1812. By the twentieth century, attitudes had changed, but it was not until the 1940s that the federal government felt compelled to take action. President Franklin D. Roosevelt created the first Office of Civilian Defense in 1941, in anticipation of possible attacks on U.S. soil by the Axis forces in Germany and Japan. By 1950,when President Harry S. Truman created the Federal Civil Defense Administration, the main focus of emergency management was guarding against a possible invasion from Communist forces.

During the Cold War years following World War II, civil defense administrators worked with citizens to help them prepare against possible enemy attacks. A major fear was nuclear attack. The devastation of the bombings at Hiroshima and Nagasaki in Japan were still fresh in people's minds. During the 1950s, many families installed bomb shelters underground or in their basements to guard not only against bombs but also against nuclear fallout. Municipal buildings, schools, and large private office buildings and apartment houses often displayed placards with the Civil Defense logo and the words "Fallout Shelter" (many older buildings still sport these placards). Up until the 1960s, students were led through air-raid drills in which they were instructed to "duck and cover" by ducking under their desks and covering their heads with their arms.

By the 1970s there were more than 100 federal agencies handling various aspects of disaster relief and emergency management. These included the National Fire Prevention and Control Administration, the Federal Insurance Administration, the Federal Preparedness Agency of the General Services Administration, and the U.S. Defense Department's Civil Preparedness Agency. In addition, each state and many municipalities had individual disaster relief and emergency management programs. There was concern that in the event of an emergency situation, there would be so many organizations scrambling to take charge that no one would be able to get anything done in the ensuing disorder. In 1979, President Jimmy Carter signed an executive order that merged the numerous disaster relief agencies into one central agency, the Federal Emergency Management Agency (FEMA). FEMA's role is "responding to, planning for, recovering from, and mitigating against disasters." One of FEMA's first innovations was the creation of an Integrated Emergency Management System to provide warning systems in the event of disasters. FEMA can provide information and guidance for messages broadcast through the Emergency Alert System (which is actually maintained by the Federal Communications Commission).

## First Responders

When an emergency situation develops, the first people on the scene are usually police officers, firefighters, and paramedics, or emergency medical technicians (EMT). These are the *first responders,* and they are trained to react quickly in emergencies. The first responders' primary task is to make sure people are safe. This includes evacuation, rescue, crowd control, and medical attention. They also make sure that the area where the emergency is occurring has been secured. They redirect traffic and they keep onlookers away. In addition, they try to serve as a calming force, keeping panic and disorder to a minimum.

First responders have a unique perspective because they know their localities well. They know street plans and landmarks firsthand, and they also understand the local residents and the municipal structure. Despite this, and despite their training, first responders are not equipped to handle large emergencies alone.

## Government Agencies

Military agencies play a role in emergency management, most often through the Army National Guard, the Air National Guard, and the U.S. Coast Guard. The Army National Guard was formed in 1636 by the Massachusetts Bay Colony. Currently it has 340,000 members. They receive military training with the understanding that during wartime they can be mobilized. The Air National Guard, formed in 1947, serves essentially the same function and can also be called into active duty in time of war. The Coast Guard is made up of active duty, reserve, and civilian personnel and protects the coastal boundaries of the United States.

During wartime, the National Guard is under the jurisdiction of the federal government, but in peacetime the troops are under the jurisdiction of state governments. Each state maintains its own National Guard bureau that works with local authorities during emergency situations. In its role as a state-run agency, the National Guard' role is to mobilize where a crisis has occurred and use its training to help local authorities deal with the crisis situation. National Guard troops help reinforce dams and dikes threatened by floods, help contain forest fires, and offer emergency aid after hurricanes and tornadoes. The Coast Guard assists with ocean disasters (such as oil spills).

There are more than 1,800 National Guard units located in 2,700 communities across the United States. Guard members can fly helicopters and drive trucks that transport supplies, injured and sick people, and emergency materials (such as sandbags to help combat rising waters in flood situations).

## Department of Homeland Security

After the September 11 attacks, the Bush Administration decided that, as with the dozens of pre-FEMA organizations in the 1970s, there were too many government entities that were inefficient. In part this was because there was no formal structure that allowed these various agencies to communicate with each other on a regular basis. The result was a system that was inefficient. The various agencies might be in touch during times of national crisis, but their unfamiliarity with one another might only serve to hinder their efforts. President George W. Bush was convinced that one way to make the nation safer from future attacks was to streamline the government structure and combine several departments that should have a logical connection under one umbrella cabinet-level organization, the Department of Homeland Security (DHS). Bush proposed the new agency in June 2002, and it was created in March 2003. The first Secretary of Homeland Security was former Pennsylvania governor Tom Ridge.

Among the government agencies that were gathered under the Homeland Security umbrella were the U.S. Customs Service, the Immigration and Naturalization Service, the Federal Emergency Management Agency, the Transportation Security Administration, the Office for Domestic Preparedness, the Environmental Measurements Laboratory, and the Nuclear Incident Research Team. The Secret Service and the U.S. Coast Guard were also located in the Department of Homeland Security, although remaining intact as independent agencies.

The Department of Homeland Security offers a wide array of information about emergencies and how the public and local officials can deal with them on its web site (www.dhs.gov). It has a special site, www.ready.gov, that offers information on a variety of emergencies such as explosions, attacks, and natural disasters. Through FEMA, DHS also sponsors the Emergency Management Institute. This training program for interested and qualified civilians provides a series of courses on how to deal with emergencies, including preparedness, response, and recovery. It operates two campuses, one in Emmitsburg, Marlyand and one in Anniston, Alabama. Each year more than 5,000 people take courses at the two campuses, while an additional 100,000 take local courses through Emergency Management Institute-sponsored programs.

## Civilian Agencies

Civilian agencies can offer a great deal of aid during emergencies, in part because they are able to mobilize supplies and volunteers quickly thanks to large networks. Two of the oldest and best known are the American Red Cross and the Salvation Army.

The American Red Cross, founded in 1881 by Clara Barton, has been providing emergency assistance for more than a century. With nearly 1,300 chapters across the United States, the Red Cross is able to get volunteers to disaster sites within two hours of being notified of the crisis, The Red Cross provides needed essentials such as food, clothing, and shelter to victims of crises, and it also provides health care services as an adjunct to whatever local doctors or hospitals can provide. The Red Cross also maintains a national blood bank and can provide blood for much-needed transfusions. One of the important supports the Red Cross provides is mental health service. Understanding that the trauma of disasters can produce devastating emotional reactions, even if those suffering are unaware, and trained licensed mental health professionals are provided to offer assistance. They work with local mental health providers and professionals to coordinate both short- and long-term care.

The Salvation Army, founded in 1878, offers services similar to those of the Red Cross. It provides food, clothing, and shelter, and it also assists with cleanup and restoration. It distributes brooms, mops, shovels, buckets, and detergent, and it also sets up warehouses to house and distribute reconstruction supplies such as lumber. Because the Salvation Army is a religious organization, it can also offer spiritual comfort by providing chaplain services to disaster workers, emergency personnel, and disaster victims. Salvation Army counselors who are ordained as clergy can conduct funeral and memorial services.

## Private Sector

The private sector can play a vital role in emergency management, both during and after the emergency event. Businesses that have specialized training (transportation, for example) can provide trained volunteers to assist in emergency management efforts, as well as equipment. A food services business could provide meals for emergency personnel. Companies with excess space could house equipment or people.

The DHS has a special service for businesses that want to donate goods or services toward emergency relief, the National Emergency Resource Registry. Interested business can register at the web site www.nerr.gov. The registry is a feature of DHS's Homeland Security Information Network, which is designed to provide the DHS Operations Center with round-the-clock access to "a broad spectrum of industries, agencies and critical infrastructure across both the public and private sectors."

## Additional Resources

*Homeland Security Law and Policy,* William C. Nicholson, Charles C. Thomas, 2005.

*Introduction to Emergency Management,* George D. Haddow and Jane A. Bullock, Elsevier/Butterworth/Heinemann, 2006.

*Living with Hazards, Dealing with Disasters: An Introduction to Emergency Management,* William L. Waugh, Jr., M. E. Sharpe, 2000.

### *American Red Cross*
2025 E Street, NW
Washington, DC 20006 USA
Phone: (202) 303-4498
URL: http://www.redcross.org

Primary Contact: Jack McGuire, Interim Director and CEO

### *Federal Emergency Management Agencu (FEMA)*
500 C Street, SW
Washington, DC 20472 USA
Phone: (800) 621-3362
Fax: ()
URL: http://www.redcross.org
Primary Contact: R. David Paulison, Acting Director

### *Salvation Army*
615 Slaters Lane
Alexandria, VA 22313 USA
Phone: (703) 684-5500
Fax: (703) 684-5538
URL: http://www.salvationarmyusa.org
Primary Contact: W. Todd Bassett, National Commander

### *U.S. Department of Homeland Security*
Washington, DC 20528 USA
Phone: (202) 282-8000
URL: http://www.dhs.gov
Primary Contact: Michael Chertoff, Secretary of Homeland Security

# HOMELAND SECURITY

## NATURAL DISASTERS

*Sections within this essay:*

- Background
- Charting Disasters
    - Early Agencies
    - FEMA
    - NOAA
    - U.S. Geological Survey
- First Responders
- National Guard and Coast Guard
- Department of Homeland Security
- Additional Resources

## Background

Any disaster that arises from the physical phenomena—hurricanes, floods, earthquakes, tornadoes, tsunamis—can be deemed a natural disaster. So-called "man-made" disasters are often the direct result of natural conditions. The floods that devastated New Orleans during Hurricane Katrina in August 2005 were caused by levees that burst, but it was the hurricane's wind and rain that caused the excess of water. Likewise, fires destroyed large sections of San Francisco in April 1906, but they were caused by broken gas lines resulting from a major earthquake.

Natural disasters can strike anywhere, and they can destroy wealthy communities as easily as they destroy poorer ones. The poor usually suffer more than the rich, however, because they lack the resources to rebuild or to relocate. Government agencies can assist those who have lost their homes and

possessions, but often that assistance covers only part of what is needed. Moreover, it is difficult for people to get protection such as homeowner's **insurance** in areas prone to damage from floods or hurricanes.

Nonetheless, there are numerous agencies (federal and state government as well as non-governmental) that provide help to those in need when disaster strikes. Anyone who is a victim of natural disaster needs to know which agencies can help and how to contact them.

## Charting Disasters

The disaster considered the most deadly in American history is the hurricane that devastated Galveston, Texas, on September 8, 1900. Galveston, an affluent and rapidly growing island city on the Gulf of Mexico, was also a popular tourist community, and many residents and tourists ignored warnings by the U.S. Weather Bureau to seek higher ground. Instead, they chose to stay put and watch the huge waves. What they failed to realize was that Galveston was no match for those waves (up to fifteen feet high), accompanies by winds reaching 130 miles per hour. The hurricane slammed directly into Galveston and swept away more than half the structures. The storm claimed more than 8,000 lives.

The first federal legislation directed toward disaster relief was passed by Congress in 1803 during the presidency of Thomas Jefferson. That legislation provided assistance for a New Hampshire community that had been ravaged by fire. Although the federal government continued to provide disaster relief, (more than 100 times through the nineteenth century), that relief was primarily given on a case-by-case basis. There was no formal procedure for obtaining aid.

It was during the nineteenth century that the American Red Cross was established by Clara Barton, who served as a battlefield nurse during the American Civil War. Modeled after the International Red Cross, which provided battlefield aid during wartime, the American Red Cross visualized by Barton was created to provide disaster relief during peacetime. The American Red Cross was formally established in 1881. The Salvation Army, which had been established three years earlier, offers disaster relief assistance as well, both material and spiritual. Many Salvation Army members are ordaind clergy and can serve in chaplain roles at disaster sites.

### Early Agencies

The nineteenth century also saw the advent of "physical science" agencies, which focused on studying the atmosphere and better understanding and using natural resources. The U.S. Coast Survey was established in 1807, the U.S. Weather Bureau in 1870, and the U.S. Commission of Fish and Fisheries in 1871. It was the U.S. Weather Bureau that developed the measurement and observation tools used to track changes in the weather, including severe events such as hurricanes and blizzards.

In the 1930s, the federal government began to take a more formal role in disaster relief. The Reconstruction Finance Corporation was the first step; it made disaster loans for the reconstruction of public facilities damaged by earthquakes. The Bureau of Public Roads received the authority to provide money to repair highways and bridges damaged by natural disasters. Other laws such as the Flood Control Act authorized the U.S. Army Corps of Engineers to create flood control projects.

Despite these advances, disaster relief was still a fairly disjointed activity, with some federal help, some help from state governments, and some help from organizations such as the American Red Cross. During the 1960s the United States was hit with several severe hurricanes including Carla in 1962, Betsy in 1965, and Camille in 1969. More legislation was passed, such as the National Flood Insurance Act in 1968 (which provided additional protection to homeowners hit by floods) and the Disaster Relief Act of 1974 (which formalized the President's power to declare national emergencies. Even with these efforts to streamline procedures, however, there were still major obstacles. During the 1970s the govern-

ment began implementing programs to deal with possible disasters involving hazardous waste and nuclear plants. By the end of the 1970s there were more than 100 federal agencies handling various aspects of disaster relief. These included the National Fire Prevention and Control Administration, the Federal Insurance Administration, the Federal Preparedness Agency of the General Services Administration, and the U.S. Defense department's Civil Preparedness Agency. In addition, each state and many municipalities had individual disaster relief programs.

### FEMA

In 1979, President Jimmy Carter signed an executive order that merged the numerous disaster relief agencies into one central agency, the Federal Emergency Management Agency (FEMA). Its stated purpose is "responding to, planning for, recovering from, and mitigating against disasters." One of FEMA's first innovations was the creation of an Integrated Emergency Management System to provide not only direction and control of disasters but also warning systems.

FEMA provides relief to disaster victims in the form of financial assistance, temporary shelter, and loans to business owners (provided through the Small Business Administration). It does not duplicate payments received from insurance companies that cover such things as damage to one's home. Grants from FEMA's Individual and Households Program do not have to be repaid.

### NOAA

Improved technology in measuring atmospheric changes also became a part of the disaster management equation. In 1970, the Bureau of Commercial Fisheries, Weather Bureau, Coast and Geodetic Survey, Environmental Data Service, and several related agencies were combined to form the National Oceanic and Atmospheric Administration (NOAA). A division of the U.S. Department of Commerce, NOAA's role is to provide research and information about the atmosphere, as well as to educate the public about the conditions that could prompt natural disasters to take place.

One way NOAA measured atmospheric conditions was through satellites. The first NOAA satellite was launched in 1975; a polar-orbiting satellite was launched four years later. At present, NOAA operates 16 meteorological satellites. These satellites measure cloud cover, storm activity, and heat indices as aids in predicting the weather across the United States.

Predicting storms is one of NOAA's most important jobs. Often, when storms hit, the deaths and injuries that result are caused by inadequate warning. A quick-moving hurricane or thunderstorm can wreak severe damage with little time for people to escape its path. In 1999 NOAA launched its StormReady program for cities across the United States. StormReady is a hazard preparedness program in which NOAA works with local governments to establish emergency operations centers that include local warning systems and a means of receiving up-to-date weather reports. In 2002 NOAA added TsunamiReady to the StormReady program. TsunamiReady measures ocean activity and helps increase preparedness of coastal cities that are in potential danger in case of tsunami activity. As of January 2006 nearly 1,000 communities had StormReady programs and 26 communities on both the East and West Coast were deemed TsunamiReady cities.

### U.S. Geological Survey

Although earthquakes cannot be predicted, seismic activity can be monitored and particularly active regions can be measured. People think of major earthquakes such as those in California when they think of earthquakes, but in fact there is seismic activity across the nation. In fact, 500,000 earthquakes occur each year, with 100,000 strong enough to be felt.

The United States Geological Survey (USGS), an arm of the the Department of the Interior, measures earthquakes and activity and provides information on earthquake-prone regions, as well as potential tsunami activity. USGS also provides the public with information about safety during and after an earthquake.

## First Responders

When an emergency situation such as a natural disaster develops, the first people on the scene are usually police officers, firefighters, and paramedics, or emergency medical technicians (EMT). These are the *first responders,* and they are trained to react quickly in emergencies. The first responders' primary task is to make sure people are safe. This includes evacuation, rescue, crowd control, and medical attention. They also make sure that the area where the emergency is occurring has been secured. They redirect traffic and they keep onlookers away. In addition, they try to serve as a calming force, keeping panic and disorder to a minimum.

First responders have a unique perspective because they know their localities well; they are familiar with street plans and landmarks, and they also understand the local municipal structure. This can give them an advantage if the disaster that strikes does not devastate the community's infrastructure. An earthquake or hurricane that levels an entire community leaves little for first responders to work with. Yet they still form an integral component of the disaster relief framework.

## National Guard and Coast Guard

The Army National Guard, the Air National Guard, and the U.S. Coast Guard can provide vital support during natural disasters. The Army National Guard was formed in 1636 by the Massachusetts Bay Colony. Currently it has 340,000 members. There are more than 1,800 National Guard units located in 2,700 communities across the United States. Members of the National Guard receive military training with the understanding that during wartime they can be mobilized. The Air National Guard was formed in 1947. The Coast Guard is made up of active duty, reserve, and civilian personnel and protects the coastal boundaries of the United States.

The National Guard is under the jurisdiction of the federal government during war time, but in peacetime the troops are under the jurisdiction of state governments. Each state maintains its own National Guard bureau that works with local authorities during emergency situations such as natural disasters. In its role as a state-run agency, the National Guard' role is to mobilize where a crisis has occurred and use its training to help local authorities deal with the crisis situation. National Guard troops help reinforce dams and dikes threatened by floods, help contain forest fires, and offer emergency aid after hurricanes and tornadoes. The Coast Guard assists with ocean disasters. Guard members can fly helicopters and drive trucks that transport supplies, injured and sick people, and emergency materials.

## Department of Homeland Security

After the September 11 attacks, the Bush Administration decided to streamline the disaster relief organizational structure within the federal government and give the many agencies that handle emergencies an opportunity to work together more effectively. In June 2002 President George W. Bush proposed a new agency, the Department of Homeland Security

(DHS), and with widespread support the agency was launched in March 2003. The first Secretary of Homeland Security was former Pennsylvania governor Tom Ridge.

FEMA was one of the agencies that were placed under the umbrella of Homeland Security. The others were the U.S. Customs Service, the Immigration and Naturalization Service, the Transportation Security Administration, the Office for Domestic Preparedness, the Environmental Measurements Laboratory, and the Nuclear Incident Research Team. The Secret Service and the U.S. Coast Guard were also located in the Department of Homeland Security, although remaining intact as independent agencies.

The DHS provides an opportunity for businesses that want to donate goods or services toward emergency relief during and after disasters, the National Emergency Resource Registry. The private sector can play a vital role in emergency management, both during and after the emergency event. Businesses that specialize in transportation, ground transportation, for example, could provide trained volunteer drivers to assist in emergency management efforts. Interested business can register at the web site www.nerr.gov.

The events surrounding Hurricane Katrina, which struck the southern United States in August 2005, led many people to wonder whether putting FEMA under the stewardship of DHS was a wise decision. Residents of New Orleans, which was devastated by floods after several levees broke, complained that the emergency response system that should have provided basic items such as food and water for stranded citizens, had failed. Although FEMA was blamed in part for the bottleneck, local, state, and federal governments were also held responsible. The scope of the New Orleans devastation took everyone by surprise, but FEMA pledged to improve its response time and streamline any bureaucratic problems in the future.

## Additional Resources

*Confronting Catastrophe: New Perspectives on Natural Disasters,* David E. Alexander, Oxford University Press, 2000.

*Natural Hazards,* Edward Bryant, Cambridge University Press, 2005.

### American Red Cross
2025 E Street, NW
Washington, DC 20006 USA
Phone: (202) 303-4498
URL: http://www.redcross.org
Primary Contact: Jack McGuire, Interim Director and CEO

### Federal Emergency Management Agencu (FEMA)
500 C Street, SW
Washington, DC 20472 USA
Phone: (800) 621-3362
URL: http://www.redcross.org
Primary Contact: R. David Paulison, Acting Director

### National Oceanic and Atmospheric Administration (NOAA)
Fourteenth Street and Constitution Avenue, NW
Washington, DC 20230 USA
Phone: (202) 482-6090
Fax: (202) 482-3154
URL: http://www.noaa.gov
Primary Contact: Conrad C. Lauterbach, Director

### Salvation Army
615 Slaters Lane
Alexandria, VA 22313 USA
Phone: (703) 684-5500
Fax: (703) 684-5538
URL: http://www.salvationarmyusa.org
Primary Contact: W. Todd Bassett, National Commander

### U.S. Department of Homeland Security
Washington, DC 20528 USA
Phone: (202) 282-8000
URL: http://www.dhs.gov
Primary Contact: Michael Chertoff, Secretary of Homeland Security

### U.S. Geological Survey
12201 Sunrise Valley Drive, MS 905
Reston, VA 20192 USA
Phone: (888) 275-8747
URL: http://usgs.gov
Primary Contact: Pat Leahy, Acting Director

# HOMELAND SECURITY

## TERRORISM

*Sections within this essay:*

- Overview
- Methods of Attack
- Terrorism in the United States
    - Anti-government
    - Race-based
    - Anti-war and Nationalist
    - Eco-terrorism
- The USA PATRIOT Act
- Department of Homeland Security
- FBI and NCTC
- Additional Resources

## Overview

No event in American history touched the nation or the world more than the attacks on New York and Washington on September 11, 2001. The destruction caused by 19 hijackers who flew three of four planes into buildings (the fourth never reached its target thanks to passengers who overwhelmed the hijackers), and the loss of more than 3,000 lives, drove home to the United States the true horrors of terrorism.

Yet, terrorism on American soil is not unknown. In fact, the same World Trade Center that was destroyed in 2001 had been the victim of a terrorist attack in 1993. Miraculously, only six people died in that attack, but the damage to the Twin Towers was significant. Moreover, not all terrorism is caused by

foreign operatives. The destruction of a government office building in Oklahoma City in 1995 was the work of a former U.S. soldier. And so-called "eco-terrorists" have destroyed buildings and businesses in the name of saving the environment.

*The American Heritage College Dictionary* defines terrorism as "the unlawful use or threatened use of force or violence to intimidate or coerce societies or governments, often for ideological or political reasons." Most terrorists are determined to use force and violence almost always without warning and often indiscriminately. Most governments and societies neither condone terrorism nor capitulate to it; yet, attacks still occur. For that reason, society must find ways to protect itself. The question of how to do this is not easy to answer, but failing to address it will not make terrorism go away.

## Methods of Attack

Terrorism can reach the public in a number of ways:

- *Bombings.* Terrorists use bombs to inflict damage on buildings or vehicles as well as to kill or injure. Some bombs are hidden by terrorists and set off with timers, while others are detonated by "suicide bombers" who have chosen to sacrifice their lives along with those of their victims.

- *Bioterrorism.* Chemical or biological agents are released into the atmosphere with the intent of contaminating or killing people. Examples are the attack using poisonous gas on the Tokyo subway system in 1995 and the series of anthrax-laced letters mailed in the United States in 2001.

- *Kidnapping.* Individuals or groups can be kidnapped and held hostage in return for some demand. Often terrorists demand the release of other terrorists from prison as a requirement for releasing their hostages. Government officials, members of the press, and foreign nationals are the most frequent victims of kidnapping.

- *Assassination.* Terrorists often carry out assassinations of government leaders or diplomats, with the intention of causing a government or a powerful political movement to collapse.

The element of fear is what makes terrorism so difficult to tackle. Once a community has been victimized by a terrorist attack, people become fearful that more attacks will occur. Societies that fall prey to numerous terrorist attacks often develop a sense of resignation, going about their daily business despite any potential danger. For a community that experiences terrorism for the first time, or isolated incidents of terrorism, fear comes from another key element: surprise.

## Terrorism in the United States

### Anti-government

Political and anti-government activism is nothing new in the United States. In 1886, eight labor radicals bombed Haymarket Square in Chicago, killing seven and injuring 70. Labor radicals in 1910 were also responsible for the bombing of the Los Angeles Times building in California, which killed 20. Anarchists were suspected when a bomb went off on Wall Street in New York City in 1920. The blast killed 34 people and injured more than 200.

### Race-based

Groups such as the Ku Klux Klan were infamous for terrorizing individuals during the twentieth century. In 1963, four Klan members exploded a bomb in a Baptist church in Birmingham, Alabama, killing four young black girls.

### Anti-war and Nationalist

In 1970, anti-war protesters attacked the University of Wisconsin's campus in Madison, killing one person and damaging more than 50 buildings. During the 1970s and 1980s, Puerto Rican nationalist groups claimed responsibility for several bombings, includ-

ing one at New York's Fraunces Tavern in 1975 that killed four people.

Many consider assassinations as terrorism, depending on the assassin's reason for committing the crime. Two Presidential assassinations could be considered acts of terrorism: Abraham Lincoln's assassination in April 1865 at the hands of Confederate sympathizer John Wilkes Booth, and William McKinley in September 1901 at the hands of anarchist Leon Czolgosz.

Until the September 11 bombings, the April 1993 bombing of the Murrah Federal Building in Oklahoma City was the most deadly terrorist attack on American soil. The bombing killed 168 people; several victims were children because there was a day care center in the building. The bomber, Timothy McVeigh, was a Gulf War veteran who claimed his act was one of revenge on the U.S. government for killing members of a fringe militia group in Waco, Texas.

### Eco-terrorism

There are numerous environmental groups and animal rights groups whose work and commitment to fostering better understanding about their issues is above reproach. Unfortunately, there are also extremist groups whose goal, far from fostering understanding, is to coerce the public into accepting their beliefs. Two such groups, the Earth Liberation Front (ELF) and the Animal Liberation Front (ALF) have engaged for several years in "eco-terrorism"—acts of arson for the purpose of destroying targets including meat-packing companies, timber companies, ski resorts, and private residences. Federal investigators estimate that groups like ELF and ALF may be responsible for as many as 1,200 such crimes for the period 1990–2004.

Typically, these groups fashion incendiary devices using flammable liquids and other fuels, which they set on timers and use to destroy buildings. Their targets are chosen on the basis of the damage they believe those targets are doing to the environment. For example, destroying the offices of a timber company could save trees, and destroying a meat-packing plant could save cattle. Destroying large private homes, they reason further, keep people from moving into pristine areas and harming the environment.

In January 2006, eleven suspected arsonists were indicted on charges of arson, sabotage, and **conspiracy**. They were allegedly responsible for seventeen incidents over a five-year period from 1996 to 2001. What makes suspects like these difficult to find and arrest is that they are extremely secretive. Members of groups such as ELF and ALF pledge secrecy and also pledge never to reveal the names of any of their co-conspirators.

## The USA PATRIOT Act

On October 26, 2001, just weeks after the September 11 attacks, Congress passed the USA PATRIOT Act (Uniting and Strengthening America by Providing Appropriate Tools Required to Intercept and Obstruct Terrorism). which gave the government greater ability to seek out for and combat terrorist activity in the United States.

The PATRIOT Act grants the Secretary of the Treasury with new regulatory powers to fight money laundering from foreign countries in U.S. banks; secures national borders against foreign nationals who are terrorists or who support terrorism; eases restrictions on interception and surveillance of correspondence and communication that may link to terrorist activity; stiffens penalties against money laundering, counterfeiting, charity **fraud**, and similar crimes; and creates new crimes and penalties for such acts as harboring terrorists and giving terrorists material support.

Civil liberties groups complained that the PATRIOT Act granted the federal government too much power to investigate innocent people or to track private records. Section 215 of the Act, which gives the FBI permission to examine business records for foreign intelligence and international terrorism investigations, has been called the "library provision" because some have read it to mean that libraries will be required to turn over lists of who has checked out which books.

As of the end of 2005 certain provisions of the PATRIOT Act were slated to sunset by February 2006, although members of Congress were planning to seek renewal or compromise on certain sections that were controversial, such as Section 215.

Efforts such as the PATRIOT Act illustrate part of the difficulty of confronting terrorism. On the one hand, people want to feel safe in their own communities, not fearful that their lives are in constant danger. Many people believe that safety is so important that putting some minor constraints on personal freedom is worth the price. On the other hand, many people feel that the short-term gains of giving up some freedom could have a long-term impact be-

cause there is no guarantee that other freedoms could not be compromised. In the end, it is a matter of striking a balance that provides safety without taking away the rights of the innocent.

## Department of Homeland Security

After the September 11 attacks, the Bush Administration decided to take definitive domestic action by revamping its security apparatus. President George W. Bush believed that one way to make the nation safer from future attacks was to streamline the government structure by combining several departments under one umbrella cabinet-level organization, the Department of Homeland Security (DHS). Bush proposed the new agency in June 2002, and it was created in March 2003. The first Secretary of Homeland Security was former Pennsylvania governor Tom Ridge.

Among the government agencies that were gathered under the Homeland Security umbrella were the U.S. Customs Service, the Immigration and Naturalization Service, the Federal Emergency Management Agency, the Transportation Security Administration, the Office for Domestic Preparedness, the Environmental Measurements Laboratory, and the Nuclear Incident Research Team. The Secret Service and the U.S. Coast Guard were also located in the Department of Homeland Security, although remaining intact as agencies.

DHS developed a six-point agenda to ensure that its "policies, operations, and structures are aligned in the best way to address the potential threats—both present and future—that face our nation." The department's's agenda includes:

- Increasing overall preparedness, especially for catastrophic events.

- Creating and implementing better transportation security to move people and goods more securely.

- Strengthening border security and reforming the immigration process.

- Improve the sharing of information with other agencies.

- Making sound financial management, human resource development, and information technology top priorities.

- Making sure that the organization's structure makes the best and most efficient use of its resources.

An example of DHS's proactive agenda is its work with other cabinet agencies to make the nation's borders more secure. DHS worked with the State Department and the Department of Justice to create the Terrorist Screening Center, which coordinates terrorist watchlist information across all government agencies, thus making it harder for potential terrorists to sneak into the U.S. as ordinary tourists. Tied to this is the Human Smuggling and Trafficking Center, which aims to thwart human smugglers, traffickers, and those who facilitate terrorist travel. DHS and the State Department have reached out to foreign governments to assist in creating an exchange of watchlists and other information that could curb terrorist travel. While screening terrorists out is important, so is tourism and business and educational travel. DHS has recommended extending the length of student visas from 90 days to 120 days and to allow students to enter the country 45 days before their studies begin instead of 30 days. Also DHS worked with the State department to streamline the application process for business and temporary worker visas. A new Business Visa Center helps U.S. businesses that have upcoming travel or events that require people to travel to the United States. At American embassies and consulates in more than 100 countries, DHS has worked to expedite business visas, in part wit the help of local Chambers of Commerce.

As with the PATRIOT Act, there have been critics of DHS's procedures and progress. Systems that were meant to streamline travel have sometimes made travel, even domestic travel, more problematic. The five-color Alert System, meant to let citizens know the current terror threat level based on possible terrorist activity, did not move the public to feel more secure; a disaster readiness program that advocated the use of duct tape to seal windows against poisons likewise did not encourage the public. Yet DHS also introduced US-VISIT, which screens foreign passengers through an integrated database system that spits individuals with criminal histories or possible terrorist connections. From the beginning of 2004 to the end of 2005, more than 45 million people were processed through US-VISIT, more than 970 were intercepted based on their data, and no terrorist attacks took place on U.S. soil.

## FBI and NCTC

The Federal Bureau of Investigation enforces anti-terrorist action through its Joint Terrorism Task Force (JTTF). As of the end of 2005 there were 100 JTTFs throughout the United States; sixty-five of them were created after the September 11 attacks. The JTTF includes more that 3,700 law enforcement and investigative specialists including FBI agents, state and local law enforcement officers, and professionals (including analysts, diplomats, and linguists) from other agencies including DHS and the Central Intelligence Agency (CIA). Begun in New York in 1980, the JTTF program helps find and break up terrorist cells, trace sources of terrorist funding, and investigate potential terrorist threats.

The National Counterterrorism Center (NCTC) is in charge of integrating and analyzing counterterrorism intelligence. It works much line the FBI's Joint Terrorism Task Force in that it comprises employees of several cabinet departments plus the FBI, the CIA, the Nuclear Regulatory Commission, and the Capitol Police.

Individuals who want information about terrorism and the government's efforts at battling terrorist activities can find additional information at the DHS web site (www.dhs.gov) the FBI web site (www.fbi.gov) and the NCTC web site (www.nctc.gov)

*At War with Civil Rights and Liberties,* Thomas E. Baker and John F. Stack, Jr., eds. Rowman and Littlefield Publishers, 2006.

*In the Name of Terrorism: Presidents on Political Violence in the Post-World War II Era,* Carol K. Winkler, State University of New York Press, 2006.

*The 9/11 Commission Report: Authorized Version,* W.W. Norton, 2004.

### Federal Bureau of Investigation

J. Edgar Hoover Building, 935 Pennsylvania Avenue NW
Washington, DC 20535 USA
Phone: (202) 324-3000
URL: http://www.fbi.gov
Primary Contact: Robert Mueller, Director

### U.S. Department of Homeland Security

Washington, DC 20528 USA
Phone: (202) 282-8000
URL: http://www.dhs.gov
Primary Contact: Michael Chertoff, Secretary of Homeland Security

### U.S. Department of Justice

950 Pennsylvania Avenue, NW
Washington, DC 20530 USA
Phone: (202) 514-2000
URL: http://www.usdoj.gov
Primary Contact: Alberto R. Gonzales, Attorney
General

# IMMIGRATION

## ASYLUM

*Sections within this essay:*

- Background

- Qualifying for Asylum
    - Who Can Stay
    - Who Cannot Stay

- The Asylum Process
    - Derivative Asylum
    - Torture

- Appealing a Rejected Application

- Additional Resources

## Background

The concept of asylum is not new; the Old **Testament** mentions "cities of refuge" and in all likelihood the idea goes back farther than that. Asylum, as we understand it today, differs somewhat from refuge; the asylum-seeker (or asylee) seeks his or her status after arriving in what is hoped will be the welcoming country. The refugee is given that status before traveling to the final destination. The basic premise, however, is the same: People who face persecution, torture, or even death in their home country are sometimes compelled to seek shelter and protection in another land.

Asylum is a complex issue because people have many different reasons for leaving their homeland and not all asylum seekers **warrant** protection from another government. A person who leaves a country in which people are routinely tortured or killed for their political or religious beliefs may seem at first

blush a prime candidate for asylum. If, however, that person was one of the torturers and merely wishes to avoid **imprisonment** when a new government takes over, asylum may not be justified. For this and other reasons, the process of obtaining asylum is a complicated one involving a series of interviews and paperwork that to many can seem daunting.

The history of asylum in the United States goes back to the days when America was still a group of British colonies. Roman Catholics, Jews, and certain Protestant sects (such as the Quakers from England and the Huguenots from France) sailed to America to seek the freedom to practice their religion without fear of recrimination. Historically, the United States has stood stands as a symbol of freedom and has attracted persecuted men and women from other shores. At times, the influx has been so great that legal restrictions have had to be imposed. Historical events, such as World Wars I and II, revolutions in other countries, and the attacks in New York and Washington D. C. on September 11, 2001, also play a role in how, when, and to whom asylum is granted.

## Qualifying for Asylum

A person who has been granted asylum by the U. S. **Immigration** and Naturalization Service (INS) is free to remain in the United States. and will not be returned to his or her home country. That same person entering the United States. as an illegal alien, with no fear of persecution from another country, can be removed from the United States. This explains why some people attempt to seek asylum when in fact they have no need for this protection.

The U.S. Government is quick to point out that admission to the United States is a privilege, not a right, and INS has developed a series of regulations and guidelines for handling asylum or potential asylum cases.

### Who Can Stay

Anyone who seeks asylum in the United States must be able to prove that he or she will be subject to persecution if returned home. That persecution may be based on race, religion, or political beliefs. In countries where local tribes or clans vie for power, a member of one such group may fear persecution if another group gains political control. Women are persecuted in a number of countries, particularly if they oppose their country's position on such issues as **abortion** and **birth control**. Homosexuals are a frequent target of persecution, especially in strongly religious countries. Students are another common target of persecution, especially if they engage in political or social activism (either at home or abroad).

Those who wish to emigrate to the United States solely for economic purposes (in other words, better job opportunities) must go through normal immigration procedures, not the asylum process. Trying to find a better job, while perhaps laudable, is not a reason to fear one's government.

### Who Cannot Stay

A number of people are considered "inadmissible" by the United States. These individuals cannot enter the country as immigrants, refugees, or asylum seekers because they failed to meet the requirements for admissibility. Among the primary reasons for inadmissibility are the following:

- *Communicable diseases:* These include tuberculosis, AIDS, and other serious diseases that can easily be transmitted. The reason is obvious; someone carrying a serious or deadly disease can infect others and potentially endanger the health of large numbers of people. It is possible for someone with a serious communicable disease to have a finding of inadmissibility overturned, if he or she can prove that the disease in question has been cured. For some incurable diseases, such as AIDS, it is possible to get a **waiver**.

- *Criminal record:* Those found to have committed "aggravated felonies" are generally denied admission to the United States. Aggravated felonies include serious crimes such as murder, rape, and drug trafficking; they also include **treason**, **espionage**, and terrorist activities. Clearly the U.S. Government does not want to admit people who may commit violent crimes or engage in subversive activities. In some cases an asylum seeker can get a waiver, also known as a "Withholding of Removal." Someone **accused** of an aggravated **felony** but whose sentence ran less than five years and whose crime has been deemed "not serious" by a judge may be eligible for this protection.

- *Physical and mental disorders:* As with communicable diseases, decisions based on physical or mental disorders can be overturned if the asylum seeker can prove that the condition has been cured or is under control. In some cases, as well, waivers may be granted.

- *People likely to become dependent on welfare:* The United States does not wish to encourage people to seek asylum if they are unwilling to become productive citizens. While it is not obligatory for the asylum seeker to have a job waiting, it is important that those seeking asylum are doing so for legitimate reasons, not merely to gain entry into a country with more benefits for the jobless.

- *Terrorists and spies:* Anyone who is likely to engage in subversive activity against the United States will be denied asylum. There are no waivers available under these circumstances.

Individuals who wish to obtain a waiver of inadmissibility do not need to disprove the grounds of inadmissibility; in other words, the premise is that the asylum seeker will be granted asylum despite a situation that would normally result in inadmissibility. Asylum seekers who do wish to disprove their inadmissibility may do so. For example, those undergoing an INS medical exam may challenge the findings if INS says there are certain medical conditions that would prohibit asylum. The key to making a successful appeal is having strong documentation.

## The Asylum Process

Individuals who seek asylum in the United States must meet the definition of "refugee" as provided by the Immigration and Nationality Act: essentially, a refugee is anyone who is either unwilling or unable to return to his or her home country because persecution (or well-founded fear of persecution) on the basis of race, religion, or social or political beliefs awaits the individual.

A person can apply for asylum at a port of entry into the United States (ports of entry include airports, seaports, and border crossings) or any time up to one year from the date of entry. The standard application, known as INS Form I-589, is the first step. There is no fee for filing this form. After the form is filled out, it must be sent to a processing center (which center depends on the place from which it is mailed.) All questions on the form must be answered, even if the answer is "none" or "unknown." If even one question is left blank, the entire form will be deemed incomplete and mailed back to the applicant. Applicants who do not speak English must find a competent translator to complete the form; INS does not supply translation services.

Applicants who wish to go to work while waiting for their application to be approved must wait 150 days from the date the application was *accepted* by INS. Accepting work also requires filling out a separate Employment Authorization Form.

Once the application has been received and processed, the applicant will be called in for an interview with an asylum officer. Applicants are allowed to bring legal **counsel** and witnesses to the interview. (As with the application, the asylum seeker is responsible for providing a translator if he or she does not speak English.) Usually the asylum officer will issue a decision that will be reported to the applicant at a later date, although officers sometimes announce their decision at the end of the interview.

### Derivative Asylum

Frequently an asylum seeker will have a spouse and children who are also seeking asylum Anyone seeking asylum may include a spouse and children on his or her Form I-589. Individuals who have already been granted asylum may apply for *derivative asylum* for a spouse and all children under the age of 21. Stepchildren are also eligible if the applicant and spouse married before the child's 18th birthday. Adopted children must have been adopted before their 16th birthday and the applicant must have been the legal parent for at least two years. If an applicant has a child by a woman to whom he is not married, he can apply for derivative asylum for the child, but not for the mother unless he was married to her by the date he was granted asylum. Derivative asylum must be requested within two years of the applicant's own grant of asylum.

### Torture

One type of "withholding of removal" is offered in response to the United Nations Convention Against Torture and Other Cruel, Inhuman, or Degrading Treatment or Punishment. Under the terms of this 1999 Convention, a person who can show that he or she is more likely than not to be tortured if returned home can be granted asylum unless deemed to be a serious criminal or a potential subversive. Applicants who wish to be considered for this status are advised to check the box on the first page of Form I-589; an INS Immigration Judge will make the decision based on the **evidence** submitted.

Although Article 3 of the Convention Against Torture prohibits the United States from returning an asylum seeker to a country in which torture is likely, it does *not* prevent the United States from sending the applicant to a third country where there is no danger of torture.

## Appealing a Rejected Application

The asylum officer may decide to refer an application to an Immigration Judge for a final decision. If the judge denies the application, the asylum seeker will get a letter explaining how to appeal. The appeal is sent to the Board of Immigration Appeals (it must be received within 33 days of receiving the denial notice), where a final decision will be made.

A derivative asylum application that is denied cannot be appealed, but the person who made the application may submit a motion to reopen or reconsider the case. A motion to reopen must be accompanied by new documentation that could change the decision. A motion to reconsider, however, needs to show that the denial was based on incorrect application of the law or of INS policy.

Asylum law and the procedures are complex, involved in seeking and getting protection are complex and the process of seeking asylum can leave people confused at a particularly vulnerable time. INS provides comprehensive information on its web site, http://www.ins.usdoj.gov. There are INS district offices throughout the country, and they are usually able to offer information about not–for–profit groups that help immigrants and asylum seekers through the process. The United Nations High Commissioner for Refugees, whose Washington D. C. phone number is (202) 296-5191, can also provide advice. Those who can afford legal counsel would do well to seek the advice and assistance of an experienced immigration lawyer.

## Additional Resources

*Emigrating to the USA: A Complete Guide to Immigration, Temporary Visas, and Employment.* Beshara, Edward C., and Richard & Karla Paroutard, Hippocrene Books, 1994.

*The Immigration and Naturalization Service* Dixon, Edward H., and Mark A. Galan, Chelsea House, 1990.

*Immigration Made Simple: An Easy-to-Read Guide to the U. S. Immigration Process.* Brooks Kimmel, Barbara, and Alan M. Lubiner, Next Decade, 2000.

*Meeting the Challenge through Innovation.* U. S. Department of Justice, Immigration and Naturalization Service, 1996.

*Refugee Law and Policy: International and U. S. Responses.* Nanda, Ved P., editor, Greenwood Press, 1989.

*Refugee Rights and Realities: Evolving International Concepts and Regimes* Nicholson, Frances, and Patrick Twomey, editors, Cambridge University Press, 1999.

## Organizations

### United States Association for the United Nations High Commissioner for Refugees (UNHCR)

1775 K Street, NW, Suite 290
Washington, DC 20006 USA
Phone: (202) 296-1115
Fax: (202) 296-1081
URL: http://www.usaforunhcr.org
Primary Contact: Jeffrey Meer, Executive Director

### United States Department of Justice

### Immigration and Naturalization Service (INS)

425 I Street, NW
Washington, DC 20536 USA
Phone: (202) 514-2648
Phone: (800) 375-5283
Fax: (202) 514-1776
URL: http://www.ins.usdoj.gov
Primary Contact: James W. Ziglar, Commissioner

# IMMIGRATION

## DEPORTATION

*Sections within this essay:*

- Background

- History of Deportation in the United States

- The Deportation Process
    - Voluntary Departure
    - Inadmissible Aliens

- Ways to Avoid Deportation
    - Waivers, Cancellation, and Suspension
    - Asylum Seekers

- The Changing Role of INS

- Additional Resources

## Background

**Deportation**, according to the U.S. **Immigration** and Naturalization Service, is "the formal removal of an alien from the United States when the alien has been found removable for violating immigration laws." Throughout the history of the United States individuals have been deported for such reasons as committing subversive acts against the government, fraudulently obtaining legal residency, and having a criminal record. In the last two decades of the twentieth century, for example, a number of immigrants to the United States were deported when it was determined that they had been prison guards in Nazi concentration camps during the 1930s and 1940s. Sometimes these individuals had been living quietly in the United States for nearly half a century.

Until nearly the end of the twentieth century, deportation was considered separate from *exclusion,*

the act of denying an alien entry into the United States With the passage of the Illegal Immigration Reform and Immigrant Responsibility Act in 1996, deportation and exclusion procedures were consolidated, effective April 1, 1997.

## History of Deportation in the United States

The first deportation law in the United States was the Alien Act of 1798. Under this law, the president could deport any alien who was deemed dangerous. (A Naturalization Act was also passed that raised from five to 14 years the length of time an immigrant had to reside in the United States before being eligible for naturalization.) These measures were the result of growing hostility between the United States and France; with the accession to power of Napoleon Bonaparte, tensions eased dramatically, and no one was ever deported under the Alien Act.

Toward the end of the nineteenth century the Chinese Exclusion Act was passed to limit the number of Chinese immigrants into the United States, but it was not a deportation law. During the first decades of the twentieth century, however, a number of potentially subversive **aliens** were deported, particularly in light of the proliferation of anarchists and the spread of socialism. Events such as World War I and the 1918 Bolshevik revolution in Russia helped shape opinions in the United States, and immigration was viewed less and less favorably.

In the 1920s the issue was not so much deporting aliens as keeping them out; quota systems limited the number of immigrants to the United States. After World War II, the Cold War and a growing fear of

Communist infiltration into the U.S. government resulted in more deportations for several years.

In the 1980s and 1990s an increasing number of illegal immigrants from South and Central America, Haiti, and Cuba tried to enter the United States. Most deportation cases today, in fact, are illegal immigration cases.

## The Deportation Process

In general, a person who is a *lawful permanent resident* (LPR) need not fear deportation, unless it can be proven that he or she entered the United States fraudulently or committed a serious crime (ex-Nazi prison guards, for example). One of the more familiar ways for ordinary people to remain in the United States by **fraud** is to marry a U.S. citizen. When someone who is about to be sent back to his or her country (because a **visa** has expired, for example) suddenly gets married, INS requires that both spouses be questioned. The typical movie depiction of this is of a desperate alien who loves the U.S. and is able to stay after finding a kindhearted and selfless person who agrees to a fake marriage. In real life these marriages are not always based on such altruistic motives.

The first step in deporting an alien is to issue an "Order to Show Cause." This document establishes the government's reasons for deporting the person in question. The alien is usually detained, although he or she can be released by posting bond. The alien is then scheduled to attend a **hearing** before an immigration judge. The government is represented at these hearings by an attorney; the alien can also have legal representation, but it must be "at no expense to the government." In many jurisdictions, there are lawyers and legal agencies who will work for the alien for reduced fees or **pro bono**.

The judge hears the **evidence** on both sides and makes a ruling, which can be appealed by both sides to the Board of Immigration Appeals (BIA). Once BIA makes this ruling, the losing side can appeal through federal courts, although the likelihood of an alien appealing would depend on his or her financial resources.

### Voluntary Departure

Some aliens fear that deportation will forever ruin their chances of returning to the United States. A less punitive measure that serves the same effect (getting the alien out of the country) is "voluntary departure." This is usually the final step before deportation hearings, and it allows the alien to leave with somewhat less of a stigma. Voluntary departure candidates must possess good moral character and must be capable of paying their own transportation costs (including air and ship travel).

### Inadmissible Aliens

Some potential immigrants are barred from entering the United States. **Inadmissible** aliens cannot enter the country as immigrants, refugees, or asylum seekers because they fail to meet the necessary requirements. Reasons for inadmissibility include:

- *Communicable diseases.* Carriers of diseases such as tuberculosis, AIDS, typhoid fever, and other serious ailments that can easily be transmitted are not allowed to emigrate. The reason is obvious: Someone carrying a serious or deadly disease can infect others and create a severe health crisis. (It is possible for someone with a serious communicable disease to have a finding of inadmissibility overturned, but only if he or she can prove that the disease in question has been cured. For some incurable diseases, such as AIDS, a **waiver** may be granted.)

- *Criminal record.* Anyone who has committed crimes classified as "aggravated felonies" are generally denied admission to the United States. Aggravated felonies include serious crimes such as murder, rape, and drug trafficking. Other aggravated felonies are **treason**, **espionage**, and terrorist activities. (In certain cases, some ex-convicts who seek asylum can get a waiver, but they have to be able to prove to a judge that their crime was not serious or that the charges had been trumped up by their government.).

- *Physical and mental disorders.* Certain conditions bar aliens from immigrating to the United States, although aliens can try to prove that the condition in question has been cured or is under control.

- *Terrorist and or espionage threat.* In addition to those who have been convicted of aggravated felonies, anyone deemed likely to engage in subversive activity against the United States will be denied entry.

As covered under the Illegal Immigration Reform and Immigrant Responsibility Act, inadmissible aliens can be deported through the procedure known as *expedited removal.* Aliens who possess no entry documents or whose documents are either fraudulently obtained or **counterfeit** are subject to expedited removal. So are aliens who have entered (or attempted to enter) the United States without having first been admitted by an immigration officer at a standard port of entry. Aliens have the right to make claim to legal status in the United States, or they can ask for asylum. While the INS can allow an alien to appear before an immigration judge, there is no obligation to do so, and the alien may simply be ordered removed.

## Ways to Avoid Deportation

Deportation is a complex issue that many immigrants cannot understand, especially if they are expected to gain all the necessary knowledge through a relatively small window of opportunity. Finding an immigration lawyer or service is probably the best step anyone facing deportation can take. In larger cities with significant immigration populations, there may be organizations in place to help immigrants. Contacting local bar associations may be a useful first step in finding lawyers who specialize in immigration law, including those who charge reduced fees or no fees at all.

### Waivers, Cancellation, and Suspension

Among the ways to avoid deportation are the following:

- *Waivers.* In certain cases, immigrants can apply for waivers from deportation if they can prove that deporting them would pose an undue hardship (the government uses the phrase "extreme hardship") to his or her spouse, children, or parents. (This assumes that these relatives are either U.S. citizens or LPRs). The granting of a waiver depends on the reason for deportation, and immigration officials have considerable leeway in making a decision.

- *Cancellation of Removal.* If someone who is already an LPR is targeted for deportation, he or she can apply for a cancellation of removal from the United States. The individual must have been a resident of the United States for at least seven years and an LPR for at least five and cannot have committed any serious crimes (called "aggravated felonies" by the government). It is helpful if the per-

son has family ties to the United States, has a good employment history or owns a business, has engaged in community service, has served in the U.S. Armed Forces, and has no criminal record (or has been rehabilitated if a criminal record exists). In short, if the person displays "good moral character," it weighs in his or her favor. Non-permanent residents can also apply for cancellation of removal, but they must have been in the United States for a minimum of 10 years. (This is done in part to prevent illegal aliens from marrying American citizens simply to stay in the United States.)

- *Suspension of Deportation.* This is another means by which an illegal alien can apply not only to remain in the United States but also obtain LPR status. Again, family ties, good moral character, and the threat of hardship are key factors. (The United States only issues 4,000 cancellation of removal and suspension of deportation grants per year.).

If an alien is allowed to stay in the United States on any of these grounds, the deportation order will be canceled and the case will be closed.

### Asylum Seekers

Asylum seekers often have a bit more leeway, depending on where they are coming from and whether a significant danger of **imprisonment**, torture, or **execution** awaits them if they are returned to their home country. Asylum seekers who wish to obtain a waiver of inadmissibility do not need to disprove the grounds of inadmissibility, but they do have to prove that their particular situation warrants a waiver.

Anyone who seeks asylum in the United States must be able to prove that he or she will be subject to persecution if returned home. That persecution may be based on race, religion, gender, sexual orientation, or political beliefs. Sometimes, an alien in danger of being deported will make a claim of "credible fear of persecution" in his or her native country. INS is required to make information about this option available to those who may be able to avail themselves of it. An INS asylum officer determines whether each such case warrants further action.

If it does, the claimant will appear before an immigration judge to make a case during a full hearing. It should be understood that a credible fear of persecution ruling is not the same as being granted asylum. The credible fear ruling is merely the first step in the process; it may or may not result in a granting of asylum.

In addition, an alien seeking asylum may be granted a "withholding of deportation" instead. This is similar to asylum, except that it does not allow the alien to apply for permanent resident in the United States, and it only prohibits deportation to the country in question.

## The Changing Role of INS

Particularly since the 1990s, INS has come under increasing attacks from a number of fronts. Civil liberties and **human rights** organizations have charged that such measures as the Illegal Immigration Reform and Immigrant Responsibility Act have been used not to streamline the organization, as INS claims. Rather, they say, such laws have allowed INS to exercise its authority to deny due process to innocent aliens. A number of articles have appeared that explore the plight of an immigrant who had led a productive life while in the United States, only to be detained and threatened with deportation on account of a minor **infraction** committed many years earlier. While it would be unfair to characterize the entire INS by cases such as these, it is fair to say that efforts to streamline the agency fell short of expectations.

Charges of INS inefficiency have been exacerbated by the growing sense of unrest and anti-American sentiment throughout the world. The destruction of the World Trade Center and the attack on the Pentagon in September 2001 drove home the point to Americans of all political persuasions that immigration issues demand better scrutiny. Among other concerns, many Americans worried that INS had been unable to keep the hijackers out of the country; the primary fear was that more such criminals could be living in the United States without the knowledge of INS.

A push to reorganize the functions of INS to make the agency run better resulted in Congressional action in the spring of 2002, when the House of Representatives voted to authorize significant changes to the agency. (Those seeking updated information on current progress at INS can obtain comprehensive information from the agency's website,http://www.ins.usdoj.gov.) A streamlined organization will be better equipped to handle the huge number of illegal immigration, exclusion, and deportation hearings that will continue as long as the United States is seen as a country in which opportunities are so much more abundant than in other parts of the world.

## Additional Resources

*Deportation Officer's Handbook* U.S. Department of Justice, Immigration and Naturalization Service, 1986.

*Historical Guide to the U.S. Governments* GeorgeT. Kurian, ed., Oxford University Press, 1998.

*The Immigration and Naturalization Service* Dixon, Edward H., and Mark A. Galan, Chelsea House, 1990.

*Immigration Made Simple: An Easy-to-Read Guide to the U.S. Immigration Process* Kimmel, Barbara Brooks, and Alan M. Lubiner, Next Decade, 2000.

*Meeting the Challenge through Innovation* U.S. Department of Justice, Immigration and Naturalization Service, 1996.

*Refugee Rights and Realities: Evolving International Concepts and Regimes* Nicholson, Frances, and Patrick Twomey, editors, Cambridge University Press, 1999.

## Organizations

***United States Association for the United Nations High Commissioner for Refugees (UNHCR)***
1775 K Street, NW, Suite 290
Washington, DC 20006 USA
Phone: (202) 296-1115
Fax: (202) 296-1081
URL: http://www.usaforunhcr.org
Primary Contact: Jeffrey Meer, Executive Director

***United States Department of Justice, Immigration and Naturalization Service (INS)***
425 I Street, NW
Washington, DC 20536 USA
Phone: (800) 375-5283
Fax: (202) 514-1776
URL: http://www.ins.usdoj.gov
Primary Contact: James W. Ziglar, Commissioner

# IMMIGRATION

## DUAL CITIZENSHIP

*Sections within this essay:*

- Background

- What Is A Dual National?
    - Pros and Cons

- Significant Court Cases
    - *Perkins v. Elg*
    - *Kawakita v. U.S.*
    - *Afroyim v. Rusk*

- Renouncing Citizenship
    - United States
    - Other Countries
    - Staying Informed

- Additional Resources

## Background

One of the more intriguing concepts in **immigration** law is dual citizenship or **dual nationality**. In its simplest form, dual nationality means allegiance to more than one country. Although some countries place strict controls on who is and who is not considered a citizen, a surprising number (including the United States) have no actual restrictions on dual nationality. It is not unheard of for individuals to claim citizenship in as many as five countries, although this is hardly common.

Why would a person need or want to be a citizen of more than one country? In some cases it may be simply a matter of cultural attachment. Some individuals who live in one country but were raised in another may see dual citizenship as a way of connecting with their heritage. For others, dual citizenship may be a matter of convenience: holding more than one **passport** can make travel easier when a country places restrictions on visitors from certain countries. Still others, having more unsavory motives, see dual citizenship as a way to evade the law; fugitives from one country with passports from another could theoretically travel on their "safe" passports.

The truth is that most people do not even know that dual nationality exists, and of those who do, their knowledge is limited. A visit to the Internet can yield all manner of incorrect information about dual nationality and why it is either a dream come true or a terrible nightmare. What people need to know about dual nationality, first and foremost, is that only information that comes directly from government sources can be considered accurate. That said, it is important to remember that regulations and restrictions can change and that each nation's government has the right to set its own requirements for citizenship.

## What Is A Dual National?

Many people are under the impression that most governments do not allow their citizens to be nationals of more than one country. Some countries, such as Germany and Japan, have strict requirements, especially regarding naturalization. But for the most part, while no country actually encourages dual citizenship, many tolerate it. Israel provides Jews around the world with the "right of return," which means that they can come to Israel and assume Israeli citizenship without going through a naturalization process. In Australia, naturalized citizens may maintain the nationality of their native country, which gives them dual citizenship. Native-born Australians, however, cannot become dual citizens of another country without giving up their Australian citizenship. (There is a strong **lobbying** effort going on in Australia to **rescind** this law.)

The United States does not prohibit dual nationality. The State Department recognizes that U. S. citizens can acquire the citizenship of another country through marriage, for instance, or that naturalized U. S. citizens may not automatically lose their native country's citizenship. In fact, a U. S. citizen does not automatically relinquish his or her citizenship by acquiring another. Losing one's U. S. citizenship requires a formal renunciation and proof that the individual is making that decision freely and voluntarily.

### Pros and Cons

Along with the legal aspects of dual citizenship are the practical ones; there are also ethical considerations. Should people be allowed to claim more than one nationality? If not, why not? There are legitimate arguments on both sides.

People who favor the existence of dual citizenship explain that it can be useful to people traveling through countries in which one nationality is more welcome than another. The rise around the world in anti-American sentiment has a number of people genuinely concerned that an American passport could actually endanger the life of its holder. On a less ominous note, having a second nationality may make it easier for people to work abroad. Someone with dual citizenship in the United States and any European Union country, for example, could work in any European Union nation without having to secure permits.

For some, the issue is as simple as money. Belize, a small Caribbean nation known mostly for its beaches, initiated an Economic Citizenship Program that grants Belizean citizenship to anyone willing to pay the equivalent of $50,000. This "purchase" of nationality (which does not require renunciation of a former nationality) allows the new Belizean to reap the benefits of a lenient tax law structure that does not collect taxes on capital gains, estates, or money earned overseas.

Those who oppose the concept of dual citizenship say that it is antithetical to the ideal of loyalty to one's homeland. Citizenship is a privilege, they argue. In many countries, it is a privilege for which people fought and gave their lives. If citizenship requirements are eased too much, opponents of dual

nationality say, eventually the concept of citizenship will have little or no meaning. Citizenship connotes a powerful emotional bond for many that should not be taken lightly. Those who may not feel this way may instead recognize the more pressing concern that becoming a dual national could mean having to serve in a foreign country's armed services or pay taxes to its government.

Dual nationals need to remember that they are subject to the laws of both countries. That may include some benefits, but it also may include tax and military responsibilities. This does not mean that a dual national living in the United States will be required to travel to the other country in which he holds citizenship to serve in the army there. If, however, he visits that country, the government may have the **legal right** to compel him to serve out his military obligation if there is one.

## Significant Court Cases

A number of cases, some of which reached the Supreme Court of the United States, have helped frame immigration law regarding dual nationals. Here are some of the most noteworthy.

### Perkins v. Elg (1939)

This case involved Marie Elizabeth Elg, who was born in the United States in 1907 to Swedish parents and raised in Sweden. When she turned 21 she acquired a U.S. passport and returned to live in the United States. Later, the U. S. government tried to deport her, claiming that under Swedish law she had become a Swedish citizen when she and her parents returned to Sweden. The U. S. Supreme Court ruled unanimously that Elg was in fact a U. S. citizen because her parents' action did not take away her right to reclaim U. S. citizenship when she reached her majority. While this is not technically a dual citizenship case (since Elg did not try to maintain her Swedish citizenship), it nonetheless was important for those who did not wish to lose their right to U. S. citizenship through no fault of their own.

### Kawakita v. United States (1952)

Tomoya Kawakita, born in the United States to Japanese parents, was in Japan when World War II broke out. During the war he supported the Japanese cause. He went to work in a factory where he supervised and also abused American prisoners of war who were forced to work there. After the war he returned to the United States on a U. S. passport, whereupon he was arrested for **treason**, convicted, and sentenced to death. Kawakita appealed the sentence, arguing that he had registered as a Japanese national during the war and therefore was not a traitor. The Supreme Court ruled that Kawakita had neither acquired Japanese citizenship nor renounced U. S. citizenship, since he was already a dual national. Kawakita lost the appeal but instead of **execution** he was stripped of his U. S. citizenship and deported to Japan.

### Afroyim v. Rusk (1967)

Beys Afroyim immigrated from Poland to the United States in 1912 and became a naturalized citizen some years later. He became fairly well known in art circles as a modernist painter in the 1930s and 1940s. In 1950 he emigrated to Israel, and ten years later he tried to renew his U. S. passport. The State Department refused, explaining that Afroyim had voted in an Israeli election in 1951 and had thus given up his citizenship in the United States.

Afroyim sued the State Department, and the case reached the U.S. Supreme Court, which ruled in his favor in a 5-to-4 vote. Interestingly, the Court invoked the Fourteenth Amendment to the U.S. Constitution. Although intended to guarantee citizenship rights to freed slaves, the Court held that in effect it protected *all* American citizens from losing their citizenship without proof of intent to do so. True, Afroyim had voted in an Israeli election. But this was not a formal renunciation of his U. S. citizenship.

## Renouncing Citizenship

### United States

The U. S. Immigration and Nationality Act (INA) stipulates that anyone wishing to renounce U. S. citizenship must do more than merely claim allegiance to another government. Americans who face prosecution in the United States or who owe back taxes, for example, cannot merely become naturalized citizens of a country that does not have an **extradition** agreement with the United States. Under the terms of INA, anyone who wishes to renounce U. S. citizenship must appear in person before a U. S. consular or diplomatic official and sign an oath of renunciation. This must be done in a foreign country (usually it can be done at a local U. S. Embassy or consulate); the renunciation cannot be executed in the United States proper. Failure to follow these conditions will render the renunciation useless for all practical purposes. Moreover, those who renounce their U. S. citizenship are still liable for any tax obligations they

have incurred and may still be liable for military service. If they have committed a crime in the United States, they can still be prosecuted.

### Other Countries

Each country has its own policies regarding dual citizenship and renunciation of nationality. Although the oath of allegiance that new U. S. citizens take states that they are renouncing all other governments, often that has as much weight in their home country as a similar oath taken by an American would have in the eyes of the U. S. government. Just as those wishing to renounce U. S. citizenship must follow specific steps, so must those who are giving up another nationality.

In the case of those who have citizenship ties to another country through means other than birth or naturalization, it is a good idea to check with that country. If a country recognizes as a citizen anyone who had one parent who was a citizen, it is possible that a lifelong American could inadvertently possess dual citizenship. This fact does not suggest that countries are lying in wait for innocent tourists who, on a visit to their ancestral home, find out that they must serve three years in the military before they can leave. But depending on the stability of the government in question, it may be a good idea to speak to someone in the consular offices in the United States to make sure there will be no unforeseen problems. If, for example, a particular country recognizes a dual national solely as one of its citizens and that person is charged with a crime while in that country, U.S. citizenship will be of little if any value.

### Staying Informed

Problems can be avoided by taking commonsense precautions before traveling. If people who believe they may be dual nationals and do not wish to be, they will need to find out from the government whose citizenship they do not desire exactly what they need to do to renounce that citizenship. If they have questions about whether a particular country is safe for travel, the State Department posts travel warnings and consular information sheets at http://www.travel.state.gov/travel_warnings.html. Clearly issues like this are unlikely to come up between countries that have good relations. But if there is any question, it is best to be armed with more information rather than not enough.

## Additional Resources

*"As Rules Ease, More Citizens Choose to Fly Two Flags."* Cortese, Amy, *The New York Times,*, July 15, 2001.

*The Congressional Politics of Immigration Reform.* Gimpel, James G., and James R. Edwards, Jr. Allyn and Bacon, 1999.

## Organizations

### U. S. Department of State, Bureau of Consular Affairs

2201 C Street NW

Washington, DC 20520 USA

Phone: (202) 647-4000

Fax: (202) 647-5225 (Overseas Citizens Services)

URL: http://travel.state.gov

Primary Contact: Mary A. Ryan, Assistant Secretary for Consular Affairs

# IMMIGRATION

## ELIGIBILITY FOR GOVERNMENT SERVICES

*Sections within this essay:*

- Background

- Pre-1996

- Welfare Reform and Its Impact

- Benefits for Legal Immigrants
    - Temporary Assistance for Needy Families
    - SSI
    - Food Stamps
    - Medicaid
    - Exceptions

- Sponsor Deeming

- Public Charge Finding

- State-by-State Guide to Government Benefits for Immigrants

## Background

For many immigrants, the United States has seemed like a land of bountiful wealth. Traditionally, it has been generous with that wealth, at least in respect to legal immigrants. The Supreme Court has ruled repeatedly that resident **aliens** are entitled to the same constitutional protections as normal citizens. Resident aliens have been entitled in the past to participate in federal welfare programs on an equal basis with U.S. citizens.

But in 1996, with the passage of the Personal Responsibility and Work Opportunity Reconciliation

Act (PRWORA), also known as the welfare reform bill, conditions changed dramatically for legal immigrants. As of 2002, legal immigrants face a patchwork of laws in the various states that may or may not give them the right to benefit from various public assistance programs.

By contrast, illegal immigrants are banned from any sort of public assistance under PRWORA, including the very limited services that some states may have chosen to provide them before the act was passed. States giving out public benefits must now verify that immigrants are legal before they receive such benefits. In addition, state and local governments may not restrict their employees from reporting any immigrants to the **Immigration** and Naturalization Service, providing a further disincentive to illegal immigrants in trying to receive benefits. But for legal immigrants, trying to sort out the maze of public benefit regulations has become much more difficult since welfare reform.

## Pre-1996

The first social welfare programs, such as Social Security, made no distinctions at all between citizens and resident aliens. Legal aliens were allowed to participate in that program, and other programs such as **Medicare**, **Medicaid** and Aid to Dependant Children on an equal basis with U.S. citizens.

As immigrants began to arrive in this country during the 1980s and 1990s at levels unseen since the turn of the century, however, concern began to focus on how the new arrivals were straining the net of social welfare programs. In 1994, California passed Proposition 187, which eliminated all public assistance for illegal immigrants and banned the children of illegal immigrants from public schools in the state, requiring that such children be reported. It also required state facilities to refuse health care treatment for illegal immigrants. Passage of this law was considered a sign of the public's increasing intolerance of the effects of immigration.

## Welfare Reform and Its Impact

In 1996, after much debate, Congress passed the PRWORA. An important result of this law was that states were no longer required to provide most forms of public benefits to legal immigrants. Subsequent legislation softened some of the laws concerning treatment of legal immigrants in areas such as Supplemental Security Income (SSI) benefits and food stamps. But the ability of legal immigrants to receive public assistance has clearly changed after passage of the PRWORA

Previous to the PRWORA, the federal government set most of the eligibility requirements for federal welfare programs. The PRWORA allowed states to set the requirements for many of these programs. This was particularly true for immigrants. States were allowed to decide whether immigrants could participate in programs such as Medicaid and the newly formed Temporary Assistance For Needy Families, which replaced the Aid to Families with Dependant Children.

As a result of the PRWORA, different states treat immigrants in different ways. Some states are generous with the benefits they provide to immigrants; others are not. What legal immigrants can receive depends on where they reside.

## Benefits For Legal Immigrants

Under the PRWORA, legal immigrants are treated differently than illegal immigrants and also differently than citizens. The restrictions on the benefit rights for legal immigrants have proven to be the most controversial aspects of the PRWORA, and several provisions have been reworked since it was passed in 1996. But the PRWORA still places restrictions on legal immigrants' access to the same benefits as normal citizens.

Although the PRWORA cuts off legal immigrants from access to means tested programs involving federal funds, states are still allowed to set up their own programs using their own funds to cover immigrants who were cut off by the PRWORA. Many states have decided to do just that, so what kind of benefits immigrants are actually eligible for is determined by what state they reside in.

### Temporary Assistance for Needy Families

Among the changes wrought by the PRWORA was the replacement of the Aid to Families with Dependant Children (AFDC) program with Temporary Assistance for Needy Families (TANF). One of the chief effects of this change for immigrants was to put the states in charge of administering the program. Regarding immigrants who arrived before the PRWORA became law—August 22, 1996—states have the options of allowing them to continue to collect benefits.

Immigrants who arrived after August 22, 1996 are banned from receiving any sort of TANF benefits for five years after arrival. After five years, states have the option to bar immigrants from receiving benefits until citizenship. The bar not only applies to grants under TANF but also to any means-tested benefit or service provided with TANF funds, including job training and work support.

### SSI

For SSI, immigrants who resided in the United States as of August 22, 1996 are still eligible for benefits, either if they are already receiving them or if they become disabled. Immigrants residing in the United States as of August 22, 1996 who turn 65 but are not disabled are not eligible for benefits. Originally, the PRWORA cut off SSI benefits for all legal immigrants, but they were restored for the above categories by the 1998 budget reconciliation law.

As with TANF, immigrants who arrive in the United States after August 22, 1996 are barred from all SSI benefits for a term of five years. After the five-year bar, immigrants may qualify for SSI.

### Food Stamps

Legal immigrants lost their eligibility for food stamps under the PRWORA. Unlike with SSI, eligibility for food stamps has not been restored across the board. In 1998, eligibility for food stamps was restored for children of immigrants, for disabled immigrants, and for immigrants over 65 years of age. All other immigrants, including those who entered before August 22, 1996, must be credited with 40 quarters (10 years) worth of work or become U.S. citizens before they can qualify again for food stamps.

## Medicaid

Access to Medicaid is controlled by the same rules that govern the TANF program. For immigrants in the United States before August 22, 1996, states may determine if they are eligible for the program. Immigrants who arrived after that date are barred for a term of five years, after which states may again decide on including immigrants in the Medicaid program. Immigrants are automatically eligible for Medicaid again once they become citizens or have worked for 40 quarters.

## Exceptions

There are exceptions for these restrictions on immigrant's qualifications for means-tested benefits. Perhaps the most important is for refugees and asylum seekers, who remain eligible during their first five years in the United States for TANF benefits, after which states may continue benefits or limit their eligibility and for their first seven years for food stamps and SSI benefits.

Other exceptions to the bar on means-tested benefits for immigrants include immigrants who have worked in the United States for 40 quarters or more, veterans and those on active duty, persons with deportation/removal withheld, Cuban-Haitian entrants, Amerasians, Hmong and highland Lao tribe members and certain Native Americans born in Canada or Mexico who are entitled by treaty to live in the United States.

In addition, many programs are exempt from the general five-year bar for means tested government assistance. This includes emergency medical assistance; emergency disaster relief; national school lunch benefits; child nutrition act benefits; public health assistance for immunizations, testing and treatment of symptoms of communicable diseases; foster care and **adoption** assistance; programs specified by the attorney general; higher education; means-tested programs under the Elementary and Secondary Education Act; Head Start, and the Job Training Partnership Act.

## Sponsor Deeming

Immigrants who come to the United States under the auspices of sponsors—whether a family member or any other person who signs a legally enforceable **affidavit** of support—are subject to "sponsor deeming." Sponsor deeming refers to taking into account the income and resources of the sponsor in determining the immigrant's eligibility for government benefit programs.

The 1996 immigration law requires new family-related immigrants to produce affidavits of support from their sponsors, and these affidavits are legally enforceable. Sponsors are required to have an income of 125 percent of the federal poverty level, unless they are active duty personnel, in which case they must have an income of 100 percent of the federal poverty level. If an immigrant receives government benefits without meeting sponsor deeming requirements, the agency that provided the benefits may sue the sponsor for reimbursement.

Sponsor deeming now applies to immigrant eligibility for TANF, SSI, Food Stamps and Medicaid. It remains in effect until the immigrant receives citizenship or has been employed for 40 quarters in the United States.

## Public Charge Finding

A public charge is an immigrant who is considered likely to become primarily dependant on the government for subsistence. The Immigration and Naturalization Service (INS) designates who is a public charge. Immigrants who are hoping to become legal permanent residents are subject to public charge scrutiny. Immigrants who are already legal permanent residents of the United States may also be subject to public charge scrutiny but rarely ever are unless they leave the country for more than 180 consecutive days.

In general, merely receiving a government benefit, with the sole exception of institutionalization for long-term care at government expense, is not a factor in determining whether an immigrant will become a public charge. Refugees and asylum seekers are not subject to public charge determination.

A finding by the INS of being a public charge can result in the denial of permission to enter the United States or the denial of an attempt to change status to become a legal permanent resident of the country. In certain extreme cases, it can result in **deportation**, although this is very rare and subject to numerous regulations.

## State-by-State Guide to Government Benefits for Immigrants

The following state-by-state guide for immigrants lists whether the states provide TANF to immigrants who arrived before the enactment of PRWORA;

whether the state funds TANF for immigrants during five-year bar of PRWORA; whether the state provides TANF following the five-year bar; whether the state has an SSI substitute program for immigrants; whether there is a state funded food program for immigrants cut off from food stamps; whether the state provides Medicaid to immigrants who arrived before the enactment of PRWORA; and whether the state provides Medicaid during five-year bar under PRWORA.

ALABAMA: No TANF to pre-enactment immigrants, no state funded TANF during five-year bar; no TANF following five-year bar; no SSI substitute program for immigrants; no state funded food program for immigrants; Medicaid to pre-enactment immigrants; no state funded Medicaid during five-year bar.

ALASKA: TANF to pre-enactment immigrants, no state funded TANF during five-year bar; TANF following five-year bar; no SSI substitute program for immigrants; no state funded food program for immigrants; Medicaid to pre-enactment immigrants; no state funded Medicaid during five-year bar.

ARIZONA: TANF to pre-enactment immigrants, no state funded TANF during five-year bar; TANF following five-year bar; no SSI substitute program for immigrants; no state funded food program for immigrants; Medicaid to pre-enactment immigrants; no state funded Medicaid during five-year bar.

ARKANSAS: TANF to pre-enactment immigrants, no state funded TANF during five-year bar; no TANF following five-year bar; no SSI substitute program for immigrants; no state funded food program for immigrants; Medicaid to pre-enactment immigrants; no state funded Medicaid during five-year bar.

CALIFORNIA: TANF to pre-enactment immigrants, state funded TANF during five-year bar; TANF following five-year bar; SSI substitute program for immigrants; state funded food program for immigrants; Medicaid to pre-enactment immigrants; state funded Medicaid during five-year bar.

COLORADO: TANF to pre-enactment immigrants, no state funded TANF during five-year bar; TANF following five-year bar; no SSI substitute program for immigrants; no state funded food program for immigrants; Medicaid to pre-enactment immigrants; no state funded Medicaid during five-year bar.

CONNECTICUT: TANF to pre-enactment immigrants, state funded TANF during five-year bar; TANF following five-year bar; no SSI substitute program for immigrants; state funded food program for immigrants; Medicaid to pre-enactment immigrants; state funded Medicaid during five-year bar.

DELAWARE: TANF to pre-enactment immigrants, no state funded TANF during five-year bar; TANF following five-year bar; no SSI substitute program for immigrants; no state funded food program for immigrants; Medicaid to pre-enactment immigrants; state funded Medicaid during five-year bar.

DISTRICT of COLUMBIA: TANF to pre-enactment immigrants, no state funded TANF during five-year bar; TANF following five-year bar; no SSI substitute program for immigrants; no state funded food program for immigrants; Medicaid to pre-enactment immigrants; no state funded Medicaid during five-year bar.

FLORIDA: TANF to pre-enactment immigrants, no state funded TANF during five-year bar; TANF following five-year bar; no SSI substitute program for immigrants; state funded food program for immigrants; Medicaid to pre-enactment immigrants; no state funded Medicaid during five-year bar.

GEORGIA: TANF to pre-enactment immigrants, state funded TANF during five-year bar; no TANF following five-year bar; no SSI substitute program for immigrants; no state funded food program for immigrants; Medicaid to pre-enactment immigrants; no state funded Medicaid during five-year bar.

HAWAII: TANF to pre-enactment immigrants, state funded TANF during five-year bar; TANF following five-year bar; no SSI substitute program for immigrants; no state funded food program for immigrants; Medicaid to pre-enactment immigrants; state funded Medicaid during five-year bar.

IDAHO: TANF to pre-enactment immigrants, no state funded TANF during five-year bar; TANF following five-year bar; no SSI substitute program for immigrants; no state funded food program for immigrants; Medicaid to pre-enactment immigrants; no state funded Medicaid during five-year bar.

ILLINOIS: TANF to pre-enactment immigrants, no state funded TANF during five-year bar; no TANF following five-year bar; SSI substitute program for immigrants; state funded food program for immigrants; Medicaid to pre-enactment immigrants; state funded Medicaid during five-year bar.

INDIANA: TANF to pre-enactment immigrants, no state funded TANF during five-year bar; Undecided on TANF following five-year bar; no SSI substitute program for immigrants; no state funded food program for immigrants; Medicaid to pre-enactment immigrants; no state funded Medicaid during five-year bar.

IOWA: TANF to pre-enactment immigrants, no state funded TANF during five-year bar; TANF following five-year bar; no SSI substitute program for immigrants; no state funded food program for immigrants; Medicaid to pre-enactment immigrants; no state funded Medicaid during five-year bar.

KANSAS: TANF to pre-enactment immigrants, no state funded TANF during five-year bar; TANF following five-year bar; no SSI substitute program for immigrants; no state funded food program for immigrants; Medicaid to pre-enactment immigrants; no state funded Medicaid during five-year bar.

KENTUCKY: TANF to pre-enactment immigrants, no state funded TANF during five-year bar; TANF following five-year bar; no SSI substitute program for immigrants; no state funded food program for immigrants; Medicaid to pre-enactment immigrants; no state funded Medicaid during five-year bar.

LOUISIANA: TANF to pre-enactment immigrants, no state funded TANF during five-year bar; no TANF following five-year bar; no SSI substitute program for immigrants; no state funded food program for immigrants; Medicaid to pre-enactment immigrants; no state funded Medicaid during five-year bar.

MAINE: TANF to pre-enactment immigrants, state funded TANF during five-year bar; TANF following five-year bar; SSI substitute program for immigrants; state funded food program for immigrants; Medicaid to pre-enactment immigrants; state funded Medicaid during five-year bar.

MARYLAND: TANF to pre-enactment immigrants, state funded TANF during five-year bar; TANF following five-year bar; no SSI substitute program for immigrants; state funded food program for immigrants; Medicaid to pre-enactment immigrants; state funded Medicaid during five-year bar.

MASSACHUSETTS: TANF to pre-enactment immigrants, state funded TANF during five-year bar; Undecided on TANF following five-year bar; no SSI substitute program for immigrants; state funded food program for immigrants; Medicaid to pre-enactment immigrants; state funded Medicaid during five-year bar.

MICHIGAN: TANF to pre-enactment immigrants, no state funded TANF during five-year bar; TANF following five-year bar; no SSI substitute program for immigrants; no state funded food program for immigrants; Medicaid to pre-enactment immigrants; no state funded Medicaid during five-year bar.

MINNESOTA: TANF to pre-enactment immigrants, state funded TANF during five-year bar; TANF following five-year bar; no SSI substitute program for immigrants; state funded food program for immigrants; Medicaid to pre-enactment immigrants; state funded Medicaid during five-year bar.

MISSISSIPPI: TANF to pre-enactment immigrants, no state funded TANF during five-year bar; no TANF following five-year bar; no SSI substitute program for immigrants; no state funded food program for immigrants; Medicaid to pre-enactment immigrants; no state funded Medicaid during five-year bar.

MISSOURI: TANF to pre-enactment immigrants, state funded TANF during five-year bar; TANF following five-year bar; no SSI substitute program for immigrants; state funded food program for immigrants; Medicaid to pre-enactment immigrants; no state funded Medicaid during five-year bar.

MONTANA: TANF to pre-enactment immigrants, no state funded TANF during five-year bar; TANF following five-year bar; no SSI substitute program for immigrants; no state funded food program for immigrants; Medicaid to pre-enactment immigrants; no state funded Medicaid during five-year bar.

NEBRASKA: TANF to pre-enactment immigrants, state funded TANF during five-year bar; TANF following five-year bar; no SSI substitute program for immigrants; state funded food program for immigrants; Medicaid to pre-enactment immigrants; state funded Medicaid during five-year bar.

NEVADA: TANF to pre-enactment immigrants, no state funded TANF during five-year bar; TANF following five-year bar; no SSI substitute program for immigrants; no state funded food program for immigrants; Medicaid to pre-enactment immigrants; no state funded Medicaid during five-year bar.

NEW HAMPSHIRE: TANF to pre-enactment immigrants, no state funded TANF during five-year bar; TANF following five-year bar; SSI substitute program for immigrants; no state funded food program for immigrants; Medicaid to pre-enactment immigrants; no state funded Medicaid during five-year bar.

NEW JERSEY: TANF to pre-enactment immigrants, no state funded TANF during five-year bar; TANF following five-year bar; no SSI substitute program for immigrants; state funded food program for immigrants; Medicaid to pre-enactment immigrants; no state funded Medicaid during five-year bar.

NEW MEXICO TANF to pre-enactment immigrants, no state funded TANF during five-year bar; TANF following five-year bar; no SSI substitute program for immigrants; no state funded food program for immigrants; Medicaid to pre-enactment immigrants; no state funded Medicaid during five-year bar.

NEW YORK: TANF to pre-enactment immigrants, no state funded TANF during five-year bar; TANF following five-year bar; no SSI substitute program for immigrants; state funded food program for immigrants; Medicaid to pre-enactment immigrants; no state funded Medicaid during five-year bar.

NORTH CAROLINA: TANF to pre-enactment immigrants, no state funded TANF during five-year bar; TANF following five-year bar; no SSI substitute program for immigrants; no state funded food program for immigrants; Medicaid to pre-enactment immigrants; no state funded Medicaid during five-year bar.

NORTHA DAKOTA: TANF to pre-enactment immigrants, no state funded TANF during five-year bar; TANF following five-year bar; no SSI substitute program for immigrants; no state funded food program for immigrants; Medicaid to pre-enactment immigrants; no state funded Medicaid during five-year bar.

OHIO: TANF to pre-enactment immigrants, no state funded TANF during five-year bar; no TANF following five-year bar; no SSI substitute program for immigrants; state funded food program for immigrants; Medicaid to pre-enactment immigrants; no state funded Medicaid during five-year bar.

OKLAHOMA: TANF to pre-enactment immigrants, no state funded TANF during five-year bar; no TANF following five-year bar; no SSI substitute program for immigrants; no state funded food program for immigrants; Medicaid to pre-enactment immigrants; no state funded Medicaid during five-year bar.

OREGON: TANF to pre-enactment immigrants, state funded TANF during five-year bar; TANF following five-year bar; SSI substitute program for immigrants; no state funded food program for immi-

grants; Medicaid to pre-enactment immigrants; no state funded Medicaid during five-year bar.

PENNSYLVANIA: TANF to pre-enactment immigrants, state funded TANF during five-year bar; TANF following five-year bar; no SSI substitute program for immigrants; no state funded food program for immigrants; Medicaid to pre-enactment immigrants; state funded Medicaid during five-year bar.

RHODE ISLAND: TANF to pre-enactment immigrants, state funded TANF during five-year bar; TANF following five-year bar; no SSI substitute program for immigrants; state funded food program for immigrants; Medicaid to pre-enactment immigrants; state funded Medicaid during five-year bar.

SOUTH CAROLINA: TANF to pre-enactment immigrants, no state funded TANF during five-year bar; Undecided on TANF following five-year bar; no SSI substitute program for immigrants; no state funded food program for immigrants; Medicaid to pre-enactment immigrants; no state funded Medicaid during five-year bar.

SOUTH DAKOTA: no TANF to pre-enactment immigrants, no state funded TANF during five-year bar; no TANF following five-year bar; no SSI substitute program for immigrants; no state funded food program for immigrants; no Medicaid to pre-enactment immigrants; no state funded Medicaid during five-year bar.

TENNESSEE: TANF to pre-enactment immigrants, state funded TANF during five-year bar; TANF following five-year bar; no SSI substitute program for immigrants; no state funded food program for immigrants; Medicaid to pre-enactment immigrants; no state funded Medicaid during five-year bar.

TEXAS: TANF to pre-enactment immigrants, no state funded TANF during five-year bar; no TANF following five-year bar; no SSI substitute program for immigrants; state funded food program for immigrants; Medicaid to pre-enactment immigrants; no state funded Medicaid during five-year bar.

UTAH: TANF to pre-enactment immigrants, state funded TANF during five-year bar; no TANF following five-year bar; no SSI substitute program for immigrants; no state funded food program for immigrants; Medicaid to pre-enactment immigrants; no state funded Medicaid during five-year bar.

VERMONT: TANF to pre-enactment immigrants, state funded TANF during five-year bar; TANF following five-year bar; no SSI substitute program for immigrants; no state funded food program for immigrants; Medicaid to pre-enactment immigrants; no state funded Medicaid during five-year bar.

VIRGINIA; TANF to pre-enactment immigrants, no state funded TANF during five-year bar; Undecided on TANF following five-year bar; no SSI substitute program for immigrants; no state funded food program for immigrants; Medicaid to pre-enactment immigrants; state funded Medicaid during five-year bar.

WASHINGTON: TANF to pre-enactment immigrants, state funded TANF during five-year bar; TANF following five-year bar; no SSI substitute program for immigrants; state funded food program for immigrants; Medicaid to pre-enactment immigrants; state funded Medicaid during five-year bar.

WEST VIRGINIA: TANF to pre-enactment immigrants, no state funded TANF during five-year bar; TANF following five-year bar; no SSI substitute program for immigrants; no state funded food program for immigrants; Medicaid to pre-enactment immigrants; no state funded Medicaid during five-year bar.

WISCONSIN: TANF to pre-enactment immigrants, state funded TANF during five-year bar; TANF following five-year bar; no SSI substitute program for immigrants; state funded food program for immigrants; Medicaid to pre-enactment immigrants; no state funded Medicaid during five-year bar.

WYOMING: TANF to pre-enactment immigrants, state funded TANF during five-year bar; TANF following five-year bar; no SSI substitute program for immigrants; no state funded food program for immigrants; no Medicaid to pre-enactment immigrants; no state funded Medicaid during five-year bar.

## Additional Resources

"Bridging the Gap Between Rights and Responsibilities: Policy Changes Affecting Refugees and Immigrants in the United States Since 1996" Fredriksson, John, *Georgetown Immigration Law Journal*, Spring, 2000.

"Immigration and Welfare Reauthorization" Fremstad, Shawn, Center on Budget and Policy Priorities, 2002. Available at http://www.cbpp.org/

"The INS Public Charge Guidance: What Does It Mean For Immigrants Who Need Public Assistance" Fremstad, Shawn, Center on Budget and Policy Priorities, 2000. Available at http://www.cbpp.org/, Shawn Fremstad,

"Q&A on Immigrant Benefits" Morse, Ann D., Health Policy Tracking Service, 1999. Available at http://www.stateserv.hpts.org/

"State Snapshots of Public Benefits for Immigrants" Urban Institute, 1999. Available at http://newfederalism.urban.org/html/occa24_sup.html

## Organizations

### Immigration and Naturalization Service

425 I Street, NW
Washington, DC 20536 USA
Phone: (800) 375-5283
URL: http://www.ins.gov
Primary Contact: James W. Ziglar, Commissioner

### National Immigration Law Center

3435 Wilshire Blvd., Suite 2850
Los Angeles, CA 90010 USA
Phone: (213) 639-3900
Fax: (213) 639-3911
E-Mail: info@nilc.org
URL: http://www.nilc.org/
Primary Contact: Susan Drake, Executive Director

### U.S. Department of Health and Human Services

200 Independence Avenue S.W.
Washington, DC 20201 USA
Phone: (877) 696-6775
E-Mail: HHS.Mail@hhs.gov.
URL: http://www.hhs.gov/
Primary Contact: Janet Hale, Chief Information Officer

# IMMIGRATION

## RESIDENCY/GREEN CARDS/ NATURALIZATION

*Sections within this essay:*

- Background

- Becoming a Lawful Permanent Resident
    - Immigration Petition
    - Immigrant Visa Number
    - Special Situations
    - Working in the United States

- Naturalized Citizens
    - Requirements for Naturalization
    - The Application Process

- Appealing INS Decisions

- Immigration Reform
    - Passport Technology

- Additional Resources

## Background

The United States is a nation of immigrants; anthropologists believe that even Native Americans (American Indians) crossed an early land bridge from Asia into North America. Many people who come to the United States choose to keep their citizenship, sometimes as a source of connection to their native country; sometimes because they see no need to become naturalized citizens. Those who choose this option can become *legal permanent residents* (LPRs), identified by the wallet-sized identification popularly known as the "green card."

Many people, especially those who have made their homes in the United States, want to be able to

enjoy the same benefits as native-born Americans. To do this, they can become *naturalized citizens.* A naturalized citizen holds all the rights and privileges afforded to any U.S. citizen, including the right to vote, the right to hold a U.S. **passport**, and the right to the protection of the U.S. government while abroad. The only right a naturalized citizen does not have, to all intents and purposes, is to become president or vice president of the United States. Naturalized citizens can hold Cabinet posts, however; two of the best known are former Secretaries of State Henry Kissinger and Madeleine Albright. There are a number of steps involved in applying for temporary residence, permanent residence, and naturalization.

## Becoming a Lawful Permanent Resident

There is much more to obtaining permanent residency than leaving one's home country and finding housing and employment in the United States. Each year thousands of people apply for LPR status, but the United States limits the number of immigrants that it admits. It is not unheard of for an immigrant to wait several years to receive an immigrant **visa** number, which identifies the immigrant as an LPR.

Some people do not need to get LPR status. Students or people working on temporary projects can get temporary visas that allow them to live and work freely in the United States. Many people who enter the country on temporary visas choose not to leave after the visa runs out; people who do this are in violation of the law and subject to **deportation**. People who come from another country and wish to make the United States their permanent home need to go through the residency process.

---

### Immigration Petition

The first step in obtaining permanent residency is to have an immigrant petition approved by the U.S. **Immigration** and Naturalization Service (INS). This step is usually taken by a family member or an employer. In certain cases, such as workers with special skills who have come from overseas for specific projects, the immigrant can petition INS directly. Once the application is approved, INS will contact the person who filed the petition

### Immigrant Visa Number

After the immigration petition has been approved and accepted by INS, the next step is to obtain an immigration visa number. The petitions are processed in chronological order; the date on which the original petition was filed is known as the priority date. Because so many people apply for permanent residence, the process can take a long time. People can check with the U.S. State Department to get a general idea of how long the process will take. The department publishes a bulletin that notes the current month and year of petitions currently being processed.

Once individuals are assigned an immigrant visa number, they must apply to have their status adjusted to permanent resident. If they are outside the United States when they receive an immigrant visa number, they can complete the process at the nearest U.S. Consulate office.

### Special Situations

Immigrant visa numbers are actually awarded on the basis of a preference system. First of all, anyone who is an immediate relative of a U.S. citizen (parent, spouse, unmarried child under the age of 21) does not have to wait for a number; it is granted as soon as INS approves the petition. All other family members are ranked in the following order of highest preference:

- Unmarried adult children (INS classifies adults as those 21 and above).

- Spouses of LPRs and their unmarried children of any age.

- Married children of U.S. citizens, their spouses, and their minor children.

- Brothers and sisters of adult U.S. citizens, their spouses, and their minor children.

For those seeking LPR status based on employment there is a separate preference system; in order of highest preference it is as follows:

- Priority workers (people with special skills and abilities, noted professors and researchers, selected multinational executives)

- Professionals who hold advanced degrees or otherwise have demonstrated exceptional ability in their career.

- Highly skilled workers and professionals

- Certain special immigrants, including those in various religious vocations

- Employment Creation Immigrants, or Immigrant Investors (people with a specific plan to come to the United States and establish a business that will employ at least 10 people)

Another special situation applies to those who qualify for the *Diversity Visa* program. Every year the United States sets aside 55,000 visas for immigrants from countries that are considered under-represented in terms of immigration volume (typically a country from which fewer that 50,000 people emigrate each year). Anyone who is from one of these under-represented countries can enter the "Diversity Lottery." The application submission instructions and dates are usually posted by INS in August and the lottery is usually held in October.

Those who receive LPR status based on their marriage to a U.S. citizen are considered *conditional* permanent residents if the marriage is less than two years old on the day LPR status was granted. This is to cut down on the number of people who enter into marriages of convenience simply to remain in the United States.

### Working in the United States

Unless an immigrant has won a very different kind of lottery, chances are that he or she will need to work while waiting for an immigration visa number. These people are able to work in the United States if they apply for an *employment authorization document* (EAD). The EAD proves that the holder is allowed to work in the United States. EADs can be renewed; a person who is waiting for an EAD but has not received it yet may ask for an interim EAD after 90 days. Generally, INS makes its decision sooner than that.

In some cases, a person who is not an LPR may not need an EAD, for example, someone who is authorized to work for a specific employer such as a foreign government.

The EAD is a protection for both the employer and the employee. It is illegal for employers to hire non-citizens who do not have either LPR status or an EAD. As for employees, having an EAD prevents them from being forced to take a job with someone who knows they are not authorized to work and exploits them by paying them below **minimum wage**, for example.

Once Lawful Permanent Resident status has been granted and a **green card** issued, individuals may live and work in the United States and travel freely into and out of the country. If they wish to become naturalized U.S. citizens, however, they must prove that they were in the United States consecutively for a specific period of time. A person who travels to an overseas family home every three months and spends three months at a time there cannot apply for naturalization, even if he or she considers the U.S. home.

Individuals who are employed outside of the United States as executives, managers, or specialized consultants may qualify for a L-1 intracompany transfer work visa. If the individual is already in the United States at the time of application, a change of status may be possible. There are no quota restrictions for L-1 work visas.

## Naturalized Citizens

### Requirements for Naturalization

Only those age 18 or older can apply for naturalization. After that, the first requirement for anyone who wishes to become a naturalized U.S. citizen is residency. An applicant for naturalization must have been an LPR for at least five years. At least half of that time must have been spent *continuously* in the United States. The applicant cannot have spent more than one continuous year outside the United States during his or her permanent residency and must have lived in the current state or district of residence for at least three months.

The applicant must be able to read and write basic English, and, not surprisingly, must be favorably disposed toward the United States. Moreover, he or she must be deemed to possess "good moral character." People who fail to meet this requirement include the following:

- Those who have committed a crime, whether against an individual, property, or the government

- Those who have a record of substance abuse (alcohol and other drugs)

- Anyone involved in illegal gambling or prostitution

- Anyone who practices polygamy

- Anyone who has violated a court order to pay **alimony** or child support

- Anyone who has lied to gain immigrant benefits

- Anyone who has persecuted others (based on race, religion, national origin, or political opinion) while a resident of the United States

- Anyone who has been deported

- Anyone who has spent more that 180 days in jail

### The Application Process

Anyone who meets the above criteria can make application for citizenship. The first step is filling out the proper forms and submitting the correct accompanying documentation. INS Form N-400 is the standard naturalization form. Applicants must complete the form and send it, along with a fingerprint card, a Biographic Information form (not always required), and two unsigned photographs to the nearest INS office. The fee as of 2001 was $260 (not including any possible charges for the **fingerprints**).

Once the form has been examined and accepted by INS, the applicant will be contacted for an appointment with a naturalization **examiner**. Upon arriving at the application **examination**, the applicant must fill out another form, the Petition for Naturalization (for which a processing fee is paid). It is during the examination that applicants are asked about the United States, about why they wish to become naturalized citizens, and what they feel their responsibilities will be as U.S. citizens. Some of the questions are quite basic, while others are more involved. Among the possible questions are the following:

- How many branches are there in the U.S. government?

- Who was the first president of the United States?

- How many judges serve on the U.S. Supreme Court?

- Into which branches is Congress divided?

- Who is the Congressional representative from the applicant's district?

- How many amendments are there to the U.S. Constitution?

- Can the applicant summarize one amendment from the **Bill of Rights**, other than the First Amendment?

- Can the applicant recite the Pledge of Allegiance?

If the application examiner determines that the applicant is eligible for citizenship, the applicant must appear before a judge for a final **hearing**. Applicants who are denied citizenship may appear at the hearing and petition the judge, who will then make a final decision.

If all the conditions for naturalization are met, the judge will ask the applicant to take the oath of allegiance to the United States. Often, a number of people take the oath together in the courtroom. Each new U.S. citizen is given a naturalization certificate; once naturalization takes place the applicant no longer needs to carry or renew a green card.

New U.S. citizens need to understand that many countries do not recognize naturalization as entailing the loss of citizenship in another country. Some people may actually be "dual nationals" whose governments do not recognize them as Americans. In some cases, the individual must actually appear at his or her embassy and renounce citizenship in the native country.

One little-known type of naturalization is *posthumous citizenship*. This is an honorary citizenship given to non-U.S. citizens who died in the service of the United States (in the armed forces, for example). This is strictly honorary and does not confer any citizenship rights upon the person so honored.

### Appealing INS Decisions

In the wake of the attacks on the World Trade Center in New York and the Pentagon in Washington, D.C., on September 11, 2001, immigration officials have become even more vigilant. A push to reorganize the functions of INS to make the agency run better resulted in Congressional action in the spring of 2002, when the House of Representatives voted to authorize significant changes to the agency. Those seeking updated information on current progress at INS can obtain comprehensive information from the agency's web site, http://www.ins.usdoj.gov.

INS Executive Office for Immigration Review (EOIR) includes the Office of the Chief Administrative Judge (whose office oversees some 220 Immigration Judges across the country), the office of the Chief Administrative Hearing Officer (responsible for hearing cases mostly about illegal employment practices), and the Board of Immigration Appeals (the highest administrative body dealing with immigration law). Many appeals of rejected applications can be handled at one of the 512 regional INS offices across the country, where an immigration judge can issue a ruling.

Because immigration issues are so specialized and complicated, it is a good idea to find either an immigration lawyer (some of whom may offer **pro bono** services) or an organization that deals with immigration issues. The INS website, in addition to providing updated news, offers a wide variety of explanatory documents on all aspects and phases of the immigration process.

### Immigration Reform

As of 2005, there was an estimated backlog of 5.5 million persons who had applied for legal immigration benefits. The 2000 census had previously indicated some 500,000 to 700,000 illegal aliens were settling in the United States each year. Alarmingly, more immigrants came to the United States illegally from 2000 to 2004 than the number admitted with legal status, undermining the efficacy of the entire INS. The cumulative number of illegal immigrants in the United States is estimated at 11 million.

In a post-9/11 world, the Bush Administration made immigration reform a priority. One contentious issue has been the 2,000-mile southwest border of the United States. President Bush proposed a "guest worker" effort for legalizing the status of illegal Mexican immigrants, comprising half of all U.S. illegal aliens. The proposal would grant permanent residency to persons living in the United States for five years, who worked 24 months, passed a background check and medical examination, and demonstrated proficiency in the English language. The Bush proposal also required background checks, but workers would have to apply separately for "green cards" (residency) with no special consideration.

In 2004, Democratic lawmakers unveiled their own similar plan. Both plans required employers to certify that U.S. workers were not available, but one proposal added a requirement that the U.S. Department of Labor first find that employment of foreign workers would not adversely affect the wages and working conditions of U.S. workers. The key difference between the two plans was that the Democratic proposal aimed for permanent residency status of illegal aliens and encouragement of legal immigration for their family members; whereas the Bush proposal for temporary status offered a tax-sheltered account for workers to set aside monies to return home (although they would get credit for Social Security contributions. In return for such a program, Mexico would assist in tightening security along the border.

Meanwhile, the House Judiciary Committee toughened its stance on illegal immigration and was considering legislation to criminalize illegal status (currently treated as a violation of civil immigration law). Increased security measures, including the use of unmanned aerial vehicles (UAVs) (the drone Predator B), electronic sensors, night-vision goggles, and increased manpower. By 2006, Congress had approved the construction of a high fence along the entire border, intended to control drug cartels, with additional benefits in controlling illegal immigration.

### Passport Technology

In 2005, the United States began testing biometric electronic passports (e-passports). The new passports contain embedded computer chips that hold the same information that is written in regular passports, in addition to a unique digital signature designed to protect the data from tampering or unauthorized access. Two more features were added to later issues, including a digital antenna embedded in the passport cover that will allow remote reading devices to capture the stored chip data. The State Department received several thousand comments that were overwhelmingly opposed to the new passport, primarily based on fears that terrorists with remote readers could identify and target them as U.S. citizens. Additionally, 27 countries resisted the technology, citing privacy concerns.

## Additional Resources

*DAR Manual for Citizenship* National Society, Daughters of the American Revolution, 1998.

*Emigrating to the USA: A Complete Guide to Immigration, Temporary Visas, and Employment* Beshara, Edward C., and Richard & Karla Paroutard, Hippocrene Books, 1994.

*The Immigration and Naturalization Service* Dixon, Edward H., and Mark A. Galan, Chelsea House, 1990.

*Immigration Made Simple: An Easy-to-Read Guide to the U.S. Immigration Process* Kimmel, Barbara Brooks, and Alan M. Lubiner, Next Decade, 2000.

*Meeting the Challenge through Innovation* U.S. Department of Justice, Immigration and Naturalization Service, 1996.

*U.S. Immigration Newsletter.* Various 2004-2006 issues. U.S. Department of Justice, Immigration and Naturalization Service. Available online at http://www.usimmigrationsupport.org/newsletter/

*Refugee Law and Policy: International and U.S. Responses* Ved P. Nanda, editor, Greenwood Press, 1989.

## Organizations

### United States Association for the United Nations High Commissioner for Refugees (UNHCR)

1775 K Street, NW, Suite 290
Washington, DC 20006 USA
Phone: (202) 296-1115
Fax: (202) 296-1081
URL: http://www.usaforunhcr.org
Primary Contact: Jeffrey Meer, Executive Director

### United States Department of Justice, Immigration, and Naturalization Service (INS)

425 I Street, NW
Washington, DC 20536 USA
Phone: (800) 375-5283
Fax: (202) 514-1776
URL: http://www.ins.usdoj.gov
Primary Contact: James W. Ziglar, Commissioner

# IMMIGRATION

## U.S. IMMIGRATION AND NATURALIZATION

*Sections within this essay:*

## Background

As a result of the terrorist attacks on the U.S. on September 11, 2001, the Immigration and Naturalization Service (INS) ceased to be an agency of the Department of Justice, as it had been for more than six decades. Along with 21 other federal agencies, INS was reorganized and brought under the aegis of the newly-created Department of Homeland Security (DHS) in 2003.

Immigration laws, both pre- and post-September 11, fall into two distinct categories. One category is enforcement. Enforcement includes border control and security, removal of illegal **aliens**, and investigation and enforcement of other immigration laws, such as document fraud, alien smuggling, and work authorization. The other category of immigration laws has to do with benefits, such as **asylum**, **naturalization**, and admission to the U.S.

When Ellis Island opened as an immigration processing center in New York Harbor in 1892, INS (then known as the Immigration Service) employed fewer than 200; by the beginning of the twenty-first century INS employed some 29,000. In fiscal year 2004, statistics showed:

- Legal immigration of 705,827 (down from 1,063,732 in 2002)
- 537,151 people were sworn in as U.S. citizens
- More than 1.2 million aliens were apprehended
- Nearly 203,000 aliens were formally removed from the U.S.; more than 1 million others agreed to voluntarily depart the country
- 88,897 criminal aliens were removed
- Nonimmigrant admissions amounted to nearly 31 million
- 32,682 applications for asylum were received; about one-third were granted
- Refugee arrivals totaled 52,835 (up from 28,306 in 2003)

## Brief History

### Pre-1900

There was no perceived need for an immigration service in the United States in its early days. Immigration was welcome. In fact, the first immigration law in the United States, passed in 1864, was actually intended to encourage immigration by making the process easier by assisting in transportation and **settlement**. Most immigration matters were handled by individual states until nearly three decades later, when the number of immigrants was growing rapidly and the state laws were competing with federal statutes.

The Immigration Act of 1891 gave control of the immigration process to the federal government. Under the law, the new Office of Immigration (then a branch of the U. S. Treasury Department) was able to consolidate the process and thus streamline it as well. Soon after the office was established, 24 inspection stations were opened at various ports of entry (both on the borders and at seaports). The most famous of these inspection stations was Ellis Island, in New York Harbor. Opened in 1892, it processed hundreds of thousands of immigrants for more than 60 years. (Today, the site is a museum dedicated to the immigrants who came to New York.) In fact, in 1893, of the 180 employees at Immigration, 119 (nearly two-thirds) worked at Ellis Island. While Ellis Island remained the best known immigrant station, others were built or expanded, and former state customs officials were hired to serve as immigration inspectors.

During these early years the basic structure of the U. S. immigration service was formulated and formalized. It was at Ellis Island that the process of choosing who would and who would not gain admission was refined. Boards of Special Inquiry were developed to hear individual exclusion cases and determine whether a decision to deport could be reversed.

### 1900 to 2002

In 1895 the office was restructured to reflect its growing importance and was renamed the Bureau of Immigration. Over the next several years the Bureau's duties expanded as the U. S. government worked to further consolidate national immigration policy. In 1903 the Bureau of Immigration was transferred from the Treasury Department to the newly formed Department of Commerce and Labor. The federal government also sought to consolidate the process of naturalization. Naturalization had been handled by individual state and local courts; in 1905 more than 5,000 courts across the United States conducted naturalization proceedings. In 1906 Congress passed the Basic Naturalization Act and gave responsibility for naturalization to the Bureau of Immigra-

tion, which was renamed the Bureau of Immigration and Naturalization.

Immigration and naturalization were separated in 1913 after the Bureau was transferred to the Department of Labor (which had separated from Commerce). The two bureaus were reunited in 1933 and called the Immigration and Naturalization Service. By 1940, with World War II engulfing the globe, immigration and naturalization were deemed to be issues of national security instead of economics. As a result, INS was transferred once more, this time to the **Department of Justice**.

After World War II, Congress consolidated all existing immigration and naturalization laws under the Immigration and Nationality Act of 1952. During the 1950s INS began to focus on the growing problem of illegal aliens. Admission of refugees from post-war Europe was another major issue. The Immigration and Nationality Act was amended and revised in 1965, and additional laws were passed in the ensuing decades. The Refugee Act of 1980 consolidated several refugee laws into one standardized process. Additional laws passed in the 1980s and 1990s further consolidated immigration procedures and also addressed problems such as companies that knowingly hired illegal aliens. A 1986 law gave legal status to nearly three million aliens who were in the country illegally.

## Immigration Challenges

Immigration issues often meant that INS was precariously balanced between competing concerns. On the one hand, the United States has built itself on its reputation of welcoming newcomers. On the other hand, that openness has sometimes made it difficult to protect the nation's interests. Throughout its history INS has reflected the national mood, even when the national mood was overly suspicious. The September 11 terrorist attacks underscore the crucial, yet often controversial role immigration laws have played throughout U.S. history, but it is by no means the only example.

In 1882, Congress passed the Chinese Exclusion Act. The law arose out of anti-Chinese sentiment which resulted after a heavy influx of immigrants from China. Originally intended as a temporary measure to limit the number of Chinese immigrants, the act was kept in force until 1943. After World War I, the U.S. government passed laws assigning quota numbers to each nationality based on immigration and **census** figures from past years. This action was in response to a post-war increase in immigration. (The increase in illegal entries by aliens in the 1920s led to the establishment of the Border patrol in 1924.)

In another example, after the United States entered World War II in 1941, INS initiated a program to document and fingerprint every alien residing in the United States. It was one of several organizations that operated internment camps that housed Japanese-Americans and Japanese who were long-time U.S. residents. INS-run camps were supposed to house "enemy aliens," but many internees were imprisoned only because of their Japanese heritage.

In light of unrest around the world in the 1990s and early in the twenty-first century, civil liberties and **human rights** organizations kept a close watch on INS activity. Laws For instance, the Illegal Immigration Reform and Immigrant Responsibility Act of 1996 stirred criticism when groups claimed it gave INS the power to deny due process to innocent aliens.

## Reorganization after September 11, 2001

Over the years, INS was repeatedly criticized for its seemingly unmanageable bureaucracy. Border Patrol agents and INS investigators developed reputations of being undertrained and overworked. People applying for immigration benefits often encountered backlogs that stretched for years. Many suggestions were made for reorganization, but the terrorist attacks of 2001 finally precipitated major change. In the wake of September 11, INS was criticized for its failure to prevent the terrorists from entering the country. Calls for change became more strident after the revelation that several of the hijackers had received visas to come to the U.S. to attend flight-training schools.

On November 19, 2002, President George W. Bush signed legislation that established the Department of Homeland Security, a cabinet-level department. DHS encompassed 22 agencies and 190,000 employees. Along with INS, the Coast Guard and the Customs Service came under DHS jurisdiction on March 1, 2003.

Under the auspices of DHS, the U.S. Citizenship and Immigration Services (USCIS) has assumed the responsibility for administering benefits, including oversight over:

- Immigrant and nonimmigrant admission to the country
- Work authorization and other permits
- Naturalization of qualified applicants for U.S. citizenship
- Asylum and refugee processing

Immigration enforcement now comes within the purview of the Directorate of Border and Transportation Security. Duties are further divided between the Bureau of Immigration and Customs Enforcement (ICE), and the Bureau of Customs and Border Protection (CBP). ICE is responsible for the enforcement of immigration laws within the U.S. CBP is responsible for inspections of people coming to the country, and for patrolling the border. Enforcement responsibilities for ICE and CBP include:

- Preventing aliens from entering the country unlawfully
- Detection and removal of aliens who are living in the U.S. unlawfully
- Preventing terrorists and other criminal aliens from entering or residing in the U.S.

## Immigration Law Highlights

### Temporary Visitors

The "US-Visit" program was created to address the challenges of inspecting and admitting millions of people who wish to visit the U.S. every year. US-Visit applies to most people who wish to come to the U.S. as nonimmigrants (i.e., they seek temporary admission for a specific purpose). Nonimmigrant classes include tourists, visitors coming for business purposes, and students. The US-Visit program typically begins overseas, at the U.S. consular office that issues a person's visa. There, biometric information is collected in the form of digital fingerscans and photographs. The information is checked against a database of known criminals and suspected terrorists.

When the visitor arrives at a port of entry in the U.S., the biometric information is checked to make sure that the person entering the country is the same person who received the visa. Officials still review a traveler's passport and visa, and ask questions about the intended stay. Eventually, all visitors leaving the country will also be asked to check out using US-Visit. In late 2005, the US-Visit exit procedures had been implemented on a limited basis.

There is no limit to the number of nonimmigrant admissions each year, although some limits are placed on the number of temporary workers who may enter. Nearly 34 million nonimmigrant visitors were admitted in 2000, the highest recorded number ever. The number fell after the September 11 terrorist attacks.

### Illegal Immigration Activities

The U.S. shares nearly 8,000 miles of border with Canada and Mexico. There are approximately 300 official ports of entry. The daunting goal is to ensure the efficient flow of people and commerce, while preventing terrorists and other criminals from entering the country.

Millions of visitors enter the U.S. legally every year, but many others try to enter illegally. They may either attempt to cross the border without detection, or they may try to enter the country with fraudulent documents or by misrepresenting their intentions. Because the United States is seen by many as a "land of opportunity," many people wish to live here, but are unable to legally emigrate. This results in a steady stream of undocumented or "illegal" aliens who take low-paying jobs offered by unscrupulous employers. The working conditions for these aliens are often just as oppressive as what they left behind. However, employers hold all the power and often threaten to report any illegal aliens who complain.

To address these challenges, CBP Border Patrol agents employ a "prevention through deterrence" strategy. This means that the Border Patrol's major objective is to deter illegal entry into the U.S., rather than apprehending aliens who are already illegally in the country. Border enforcement takes place by air, sea, and land. Some patrolling is done on horseback or on foot.

CBP operations are divided into 21 sectors. Nine sectors cover much of the four southern border states (California, Arizona, New Mexico, and Texas). Border apprehensions in the southwest accounted for 98 percent of all Border Patrol apprehensions in 2004 (Border Patrol apprehensions totaled 1,160,395). The remaining sectors are in:

- Livermore, California
- New Orleans, Louisiana
- Miami, Florida
- Havre, Montana
- Blaine and Spokane, Washington
- Grand Forks, North Dakota
- Buffalo, New York

- Swanton, Vermont
- Detroit, Michigan
- Ramey, Puerto Rico
- Houlton, Maine

While much immigration activity centers on deterring aliens from entering the country illegally, every year thousands of other immigration investigations take place. ICE Special agents plan and conduct investigations into possible civil and criminal violations involving immigration issues. The investigators often work in multi-agency task forces on issues such as document fraud, narcotic trafficking, terrorism, and various forms of organized crime. Investigators also inspect work sites to make sure employers are not employing undocumented workers; criminal and civil sanctions may be imposed for employers who violate these laws. In 2004, immigration investigators initiated nearly 59,000 investigations into activities such as identity and benefit fraud, alien smuggling, counter terrorism, and other crimes.

An alien who has been identified by the Border Patrol or by ICE investigators as being in the U.S. illegally is typically placed in **removal** proceedings. Removal means the expulsion of an alien from the U.S. Most removal proceedings are conducted before an immigration judge. However, noncriminal illegal aliens may be given the option of **voluntary departure**. Voluntary departure means that an alien agrees that the entry was illegal. The alien waives the right to a hearing, and pays the expenses of departing the country. The advantage of voluntary departure is that an alien may be able to obtain lawful admission at a later date. An alien who has been ordered removed, on the other hand, will be barred from legally reentering the country for a period of years, or even for life, depending on the circumstances. An alien who agrees to voluntary departure must verify that the departure actually occurred, in order to be eligible for lawful admission at a later time. Aliens who are apprehended at the border and are offered voluntary departure are typically escorted by authorities back across the border.

Some inadmissibile aliens may be subject to **expedited removal**. Expedited removal allows authorities to quickly remove certain inadmissible aliens from the country. Expedited removal includes aliens who arrive with no entry documents, or those that have used counterfeit, altered, or otherwise fraudulent or improper documents. Under expedited removal procedures, an alien typically is not allowed to a hearing before an immigration judge.

### Asylum and Refugee Status

A person who is unable or unwilling to return to his or her country of nationality because of persecution, or a well-founded fear of persecution, is called an **asylee**. The persecution or fear of persecution must be based upon the alien's race, religion, nationality, membership in a particular social group, or political opinion.

An asylee may already be in the U.S., or may be seeking entry at a port of entry. According to statute, it is irrelevant for purposes of asylum whether an alien is in the country legally or illegally. Aliens who have been apprehended apply with an immigration judge; others apply to a USCIS asylum officer. Aliens must establish past persecution or a well-founded fear of persecution if they return to their country. If the USCIS denies an alien's claim for asylum, the claim may be renewed before an immigration judge.

A **refugee** meets the same criteria as an asylee but is located outside the United States, and outside his or her country of nationality. DHS officers in overseas offices make refugee approvals. Only a certain number of refugees may be admitted in any given year; the number is set by the President after consultations with Congress. Both asylees and refugees may later adjust their status to **lawful permanent resident** status.

### Lawful Permanent Residents

Aliens who wish to live lawfully and permanently in the U.S. seek *lawful permanent resident* status. A lawful permanent resident either obtains an immigrant visa overseas from the State Department, or adjusts from a nonimmigrant status (or, in certain cases, they may be undocumented immigrants) to an immigrant status, through application to the USCIS. Once granted lawful permanent resident status, the immigrant is issued an Alien Registration Receipt Card, more popularly known as a "green card" (even though they have not been green for many years). The **green card** allows aliens with permanent resident status to travel outside the U. S. and return freely, as long as they maintain their permanent home in the U. S. It also confers employment authorization.

Not everyone who wishes to emigrate to the U.S. can do so. U.S. immigration law gives preferential status to people with a close family relationship with a U.S. citizen or lawful permanent resident. Close family relationships are defined as: :

- unmarried sons or daughters of U.S. citizens and their children

- unmarried sons and daughters of lawful permanent residents

- married sons and daughters of U.S. citizens and their spouses and children

- brothers and sisters, including spouses and children, of U.S> citizens ages 21 and over

Other aliens may be eligible for permanent residency because of certain employment characteristics. Persons with needed job skills, certain ministers and religious workers, and aliens with "exceptional ability" are included in employment based preferences. Those who qualify as refugees also receive preferential status.

Furthermore, the number of persons who may be admitted as lawful permanent residents in any year ranges by law from 421,000 to 675,000. This number depends upon the number of admissions the previous year. However, *immediate relatives* of U.S. citizens are not subject to a numerical limitation. Immediate relatives are defined as spouses of U.S. citizens, children (under 21 years of age and unmarried) of citizens, and parents of citizens 21 years of age or older.

Lawful permanent residency is the first step toward U.S. citizenship, for those who wish to become citizens. Lawful permanent residents who have been in the U.S. for five years (four in certain cases) are allowed to apply for U.S. citizenship; upon acceptance of their application they are sworn in and become naturalized citizens.

## Additional Resources

*Historical Guide to the U. S. Governments.* Kurian, George T., ed., Oxford University Press, 1998.

*2004 Yearbook of Immigration Statistics.* The Department of Homeland Security, 2005. Available at http://uscis.gov/graphics/shared/statistics/yearbook/index.htm., The Department of Homeland Security, 2005.

*Immigration and Borders..* The Department of Homeland Security, 2005. Available at http://www.dhs.gov/dhspublic/theme_home4.jsp., The Department of Homeland Security, 2005.

## Organizations

### U.S. Department of Homeland Security

Washington, DC 20528 USA

Phone: (202) 282-800
URL: http://www.dhs.gov/dhspublic/
Primary Contact: Michael Chertoff, Secretary

# INTELLECTUAL PROPERTY

## COPYRIGHT

*Sections within this essay:*

## Background

### Definition of Copyright

A **copyright** is an intangible right granted by **statute** to the originator of certain literary or artistic productions, including authors, artists, musicians, composers, and publishers, among others. For a limited period of time, copyright owners are given the exclusive privilege to produce, copy, and distribute their creative works for publication or sale.

Copyright is distinct from other forms of legal protection granted to originators of creative works such as **patents**, which give inventors exclusive rights over use of their inventions, and **trademarks**, which give businesses exclusive rights over words, symbols, and other devices affixed to goods for the purpose of signifying their authenticity to the public. All three types of legal protection comprise an area of law known as intellectual property.

### History of Copyright

U. S. copyright law is an outgrowth of English **common law**. When the printing press was created in the fifteenth century, rights were at first granted to printers rather than to authors. The English common law protected printers' intellectual property rights until 1710, when Parliament passed the Statute of Anne, which conferred upon authors the right to control reproduction of their works after they were published. The right lasted for 28 years, after which an author's work was said to enter the **public domain**, meaning that anyone could print or distribute the work without obtaining the author's permission or paying the author a royalty for the right to distribute it.

By the late eighteenth century, protecting intellectual property interests was considered an important means of advancing the **public interest** in both Great Britain and the United States. Granting a **monopoly** to the originator of a creative work provided incentive for authors and inventors to make things the public found valuable enough to buy for personal, commercial, and governmental uses. The **Patent** and Copyright Clause, contained in Article I, Section 8, Clause 8 of the U. S. Constitution, recognized the growing importance of protecting intellectual property interests. It empowers Congress to "promote the Progress of Science and useful Arts, by securing for limited Times to Authors and Inventors exclusive Right to their respective Writings and Discoveries."

Congress passed the first copyright statute in 1790 and has substantially revised it several times, most notably in 1831, 1870, 1909, 1976, 1998, and 2005. In 1831, musical compositions were granted copyright protection over objections made by opponents who claimed that such works did not fall within the Constitution's definition of a "writing." In 1870 Congress granted copyright protection to paintings, statues, and other works of fine art. In 1909 copyright owners were given the right to renew a copyright for 28 years beyond the initial 28-year term established by the first statute.

In 1976 Congress brought unpublished works within the ambit of federal copyright law. Prior to 1976, unpublished works were only afforded protection by state common law. The protection was perpetual in nature, meaning that authors could prevent others from copying their works during their lifetimes, and then pass this right on to their heirs. However, once an authorized person published a work, the common law copyright was extinguished, and the only protection afforded was by federal statute. The 1976 act abolished nearly every significant aspect of common law copyright, creating a unified system for both published and unpublished works (see 17 U.S.C. § 102[a]). The 1976 act also made U. S. copyright law conform more to international standards, particularly with regard to the duration of copyright protection and the formalities of copyright registration.

In 1998 Congress passed the Digital Millennium Copyright Act (DMCA) to address a number of concerns relating to copyright **infringement** in the computer age. The DMCA limited the liability of Internet service providers (ISPs) for copyright infringement by Internet content providers, enabled Internet content providers to require immediate removal of infringing material, and made it illegal to circumvent encryption technologies designed to protect copyrighted works from unauthorized **appropriation**. Legal observers expect more intellectual property legislation to follow in the new millennium.

Congress enacted the Family Entertainment and Copyright Act in 2005 to address several concerns. This act incorporated several other acts that had been introduced in previous congressional sessions. One component, dubbed the Artists' Rights and Theft Prevention Act of 2005, renders the unauthorized use of a video camera at a movie theater an offense punishable by a term of imprisonment. A second component, called the Family Movie Act of 2005,

clarifies that those who alter movies to remove objectionable content are not liable to copyright owners. This statute protects companies that edit movies to remove or alter scenes on DVD movies such that families can watch the films without having to watch or listen to objectionable scenes.

## Copyrightable Works

### *What is Copyrightable*

Applicants seeking copyright protection for their works must establish that the works are original and have been reduced to "tangible medium of expression." (see 17 U.S.C. § 102[a]). The phrase, "tangible medium of expression," means that the work must be reduced to some concrete form, as when something is written on a piece of paper, recorded on an audiotape, captured on a videotape, or stored on a computer disk or hard drive.

"Originality" does not mean "novelty" for the purposes of copyright law. It simply means that the work in question is the work of the person seeking copyright protection and not the creation of a third-party from whom the work was copied. The law allows for old works to be recreated with new themes or characters, adapted to new settings, or updated with fresh data so long as the new variation is something more than trivial and reflects the creator's contribution. However, courts will not sit in judgment of a work's artistic merits or aesthetic qualities.

### *What is Not Copyrightable*

Copyright protects the expression of an idea but not the idea itself. Concepts, plots, procedures, processes, systems, methods of operation, principles, and discoveries are thus not copyrightable until they have been reduced to some **tangible** form, no matter how original they might be. Nor is everything that has been reduced to a tangible form eligible for copyright protection. Words, phrases, slogans, blank forms, phone listings, and standard calendars will not receive copyright protection without proof that the originator contributed something new to the work. However, a reproduction of an original copyrighted work constitutes a violation of copyright law. Thus, one commercial entity may not simply reproduce another entity's phone directory without running afoul of copyright law. But each entity is free to gather the same facts and arrange them in nearly the same manner, so long as both entities invest some original labor.

# Copyright Ownership

## *Registration, Deposit, and Notice*

Registration of copyright requires applicants to record the existence of authored works and the identity of their authors with the Copyright Office in the Library of Congress. Copyright deposit involves placing the work in its written, recorded, or other physical form with the same office. Notice of copyright means marking the authored work with the word "Copyright," the abbreviation "Copr.," or the letter "C" in a circle, along with the year of first publication and the name of the copyright owner.

For nearly two centuries after the U. S. Constitution was ratified by the states, several major copyright acts required that applicants register and deposit their works with a federal district court or the Library of Congress before a copyright could be enforceable. The Copyright Act of 1976 eliminated these requirements, giving authors exclusive federal copyright protection from the moment they reduce their work to a tangible medium of expression.

Nonetheless, registration, deposit, and notice still have significant legal and practical consequences. Copyright owners may not sue for infringement unless they have first registered the copyright (see 17 U.S.C. §§ 411, 412). Although deposit is not a precondition to bringing a suit for infringement, federal law requires that two copies of a published work be deposited within three months of publication, and failure to deposit a copy after it has been demanded by the Copyright Office is a criminal offense punishable by a fine. Notice provides immediate warning that a work is protected by copyright and may help stave off legal disputes with potential infringers.

## *Identifying Ownership*

The author of an original work is the copyright owner, except in the case of a "work for hire." A work for hire can arise in two situations: (1) when an employee creates a work within the scope of his or her employment; (2) when two parties enter a written agreement designating the work as a work for hire and the work falls within certain categories designated by copyright law. If a work qualifies as a work for hire, the employer owns the copyright and enjoys the same rights of copyright ownership as if the employer had created the work itself. If a work does not qualify as a work for hire, then the employee who authored the work retains copyright ownership and transfer of the copyright can only be accomplished through a written assignment of copyright.

## *Attributes of Ownership*

Copyright affords an author of an original work five exclusive rights: (1) to reproduce or copy the work; (2) to prepare new works that derive from the copyrighted work; (3) to distribute the work to the public by sale or other arrangement; (4) to perform the work publicly; and (5) to display the work publicly. The last three rights are infringed only when violated publicly, that is, before a "substantial number of persons" outside family and friends (see 17 U.S.C. § 101). The first two rights are infringed whether violated in public or in private. In general, copyright of popular works can be extremely lucrative for the owner, since it includes the right to any profits from dramatizations, abridgements, and translations. It also includes the right to sell, license, or transfer one or more of the exclusive rights afforded by copyright law.

## *Duration of Ownership*

Protection from copyright infringement for works created after 1977 extends throughout the life of the author who created the original work, plus 50 years after the author's death (see 17 U.S.C. § 302[a]). When an original work is joint-authored, the copyright expires 50 years after the death of the last surviving author. Copyright is considered **personal property** that may be transferred to the author's heirs upon his or her death. For works created prior to 1977, the duration of ownership depends upon the law that was in effect at the time a work was created. In many cases, original works were protected for only 28 years and have long since passed into the public domain, unprotected by U. S. copyright law.

# Copyright Infringement

## *Definition of Infringement*

Copyright infringement is the violation of any exclusive right held by the copyright owner. Infringement may be intentional or unintentional. Often called "innocent infringement," unintentional infringement occurs when an author creates an ostensibly new work that later proves to be a mere reproduction of an existing work, though the author was unaware of the identity between the two at the time the copy was made. For example, former Beatle musician George Harrison was guilty of innocent infringement when he released the song "My Sweet Lord," which a court found was the same song as the Chiffons' "He's So Fine," only with different words. The court said that Harrison had "subconsciously" borrowed the Chiffons' unique motif (see *Bright*

*Tunes Music Corp. v. Harrisongs Music, Ltd.,* [S.D.N.Y. 1976]).

### Defense to Infringement: Fair Use

Fair use is a judicial doctrine that refers to a use of a copyrighted work that does not violate the exclusive rights of the copyright owner. Examples of fair use include the reproduction of original works for the purpose of criticism, comment, news reporting, teaching, scholarship, or research (see 17 U.S.C. § 107). Whether a particular use is "fair" depends on a court's application of the following factors: (1) the purpose and character of the use, including whether the use is of a commercial nature or is for nonprofit educational purposes; (2) the nature of the copyrighted work; (3) the amount and substantiality of the portion used in relation to the copyrighted work as a whole; and (4) the effect of the use upon the potential market for the copyrighted work, including the extent to which the use diminishes the economic value of the work. Courts have ruled that the fair use doctrine allows individuals to use video cassette recorders (VCRs) to tape television shows and movies for home use without fear of being sued for copyright infringement.

However, in a case closely watched by the public, the U. S. Court of Appeals for the Ninth Circuit ruled that the fair use doctrine does not allow an Internet service to store digital audio files of copyrighted sound recordings for downloading by service subscribers who pay no fee to the copyright owners (see *A&M Records, Inc. v. Napster, Inc.,* [9th Cir. 2001]). Recognizing that the individual subscribers were mostly high school and college students downloading the music for personal consumption, the court still found that the purpose and character of their use was commercial in nature. "Napster users get for free something they would ordinarily have to buy," the court observed. The court said that Napster's service reduced audio CD sales among those students, thereby diminishing both the size of the copyright owners market and the value of the copyrighted work.

The recording and movie industries won another victory in 2005 when the U.S. Supreme Court ruled that an Internet file-sharing service named Grokster committed copyright infringement by providing a service that allowed users to share files directly with one another. Grokster argued that it was not liable because, unlike Napster, it did not store files on its own servers but rather only served as a medium to allow users to share directly with one another. The Court, in a unanimous decision in *Metro-Goldwyn-Mayer Studios, Inc. v. Grokster* (2005), disagreed, ruling that this type of file sharing violated copyright laws. In November 2005, Grokster agreed to shut down its services until it could provide a legal service.

### Remedies for Infringement

Copyright is valuable to the extent it protects an author's investment in an original work. Infringement directly injures the copyright owner by depriving the owner of the revenue that is generated by the infringer's work and indirectly injures the owner by softening demand for his work. A copyright owner who has been injured by an infringing work may file a law suit requesting one of two types of remedies. First, the owner may ask the court to grant an injunction ordering the offending party from continuing to infringe on the copyright. Or the owner may instead choose to receive **statutory** damages for the infringement, which range from as little as $100 for innocent infringement to as much as $50,000 for willful infringement.

Willful infringement is also a federal criminal offense, a **misdemeanor** punishable by a fine of up to $10,000 and up to a year in prison (see 17 U.S.C.A. § 506[a]). However, the law requires that the prosecution demonstrate that the infringement was willful and that it was for the purpose of "commercial advantage or private financial gain." Mass **piracy** of sound or motion picture recordings without permission of the copyright owner is a separate criminal offense, punishable by a fine of up to $250,000 and five years in prison under the Piracy and **Counterfeiting** Amendments Act of 1982 (see 18 U.S.C. § 2318).

## State Laws Related to Copyright

Although copyright law is an area of law mostly governed by federal statute, certain state laws also related to copyright law. Most states have anti-bootlegging and anti-piracy statutes, many of which mirror corresponding federal statutes. The following is a description of state laws that relate to copyright:

ALABAMA: The state's anti-bootlegging statute and anti-piracy statute are both located in title 13A of the Alabama Code.

ALASKA: The state's anti-piracy statute is located in title 45 of the Alaska Statutes.

ARIZONA: The state's anti-bootlegging statute and anti-piracy statute are both located in title 13 of the Arizona Revised Statutes.

ARKANSAS: The state's anti-piracy statute is located in title 5 of the Arkansas Code.

CALIFORNIA: The state's anti-bootlegging statute and anti-piracy statute are both located in the California Penal Code.

COLORADO: The state's anti-piracy statute is located in title 18 of the Colorado Revised Statutes.

CONNECTICUT: The state's anti-piracy statute is located in title 53 of the Connecticut General Statutes.

DELAWARE: The state's anti-piracy statute is located in title 11 of the Delaware Code.

DISTRICT OF COLUMBIA: The anti-bootlegging statute and anti-piracy statute are both located in title 22 of the D.C. Code.

FLORIDA: The state's anti-bootlegging statute and anti-piracy statute are both located in chapter 540 of the Florida Statutes.

GEORGIA: The state's anti-piracy statute is located in title 16 of the Georgia Code.

HAWAII: The state's anti-piracy statute is located in chapter 482C-1 of the Hawaii Revised Statutes.

IDAHO: The state's anti-piracy statute is located in title 18 of the Idaho Code.

ILLINOIS: The state's anti-bootlegging statute and anti-piracy statute are both located in chapter 720 of the Illinois Compiled Statutes.

INDIANA: The state's anti-bootlegging statute is located in title 35 of the Indiana Code.

IOWA: The state's anti-piracy statute is located in chapter 714 of the Iowa Code.

KANSAS: The state's anti-bootlegging statute and anti-piracy statute are both located in title 21 of the Kansas Statutes.

KENTUCKY: The state's anti-bootlegging statute and anti-piracy statute are both located in title 434 of the Kentucky Revised Statutes.

LOUISIANA: The state's anti-bootlegging statute and anti-piracy statute are both located in title 14 of the Louisiana Revised Statutes.

MAINE: The state's anti-piracy statute is located in title 10 of the Maine Revised Statutes.

MARYLAND: The state's anti-bootlegging statute and anti-piracy statute are both located in article 27 of the Maryland Code.

MASSACHUSETTS: The state's anti-bootlegging statute and anti-piracy statute are both located in chapter 266 of the Massachusetts Laws.

MICHIGAN: The state's anti-bootlegging statute and anti-piracy statute are both located in chapter 752 of the Michigan Compiled Laws.

MINNESOTA: The state's anti-piracy statute is located in chapter 325E of the Minnesota Statutes.

MISSISSIPPI: The state's anti-bootlegging statute and anti-piracy statute are both located in title 97 of the Mississippi Code.

MISSOURI: The state's anti-bootlegging statute and anti-piracy statute are both located in chapter 570 of the Missouri Revised Statutes.

MONTANA: The state's anti-bootlegging statute and anti-piracy statute are both located in title 30 of the Montana Code.

NEBRASKA: The state's anti-piracy statute is located in chapter 28 of the Nebraska Revised Statutes.

NEVADA: The state's anti-piracy statute is located in chapter 205 of the Nevada Revised Statutes.

NEW HAMPSHIRE: The state's anti-bootlegging statute and anti-piracy statute are both located in chapter 352-A of the New Hampshire Revised Statutes.

NEW JERSEY: The state's anti-bootlegging statute and anti-piracy statute are both located in title 2C of the New Jersey Statutes.

NEW MEXICO: The state's anti-bootlegging statute and anti-piracy statute are both located in chapter 30 of the New Mexico Statutes.

NEW YORK: The state's anti-bootlegging statute and anti-piracy statute are both located in the New York Penal Law.

NORTH CAROLINA: The state's anti-bootlegging statute and anti-piracy statute are both located in chapter 14 of the North Carolina General Statutes.

NORTH DAKOTA: The state's anti-bootlegging statute and anti-piracy statute are both located in title 47 of the North Dakota Century Code.

OHIO: The state's anti-piracy statutes are located in chapters 1333 and 2913 of the Ohio Revised Code.

OKLAHOMA: The state's anti-bootlegging statute and anti-piracy statute are both located in title 21 of the Oklahoma Statutes.

OREGON: The state's anti-bootlegging statute and anti-piracy statute are both located in chapter 164 of the Oregon Revised Statutes.

PENNSYLVANIA: The state's anti-bootlegging statute and anti-piracy statute are both located in title 18 of the Pennsylvania Statutes.

RHODE ISLAND: The state's anti-bootlegging statute and anti-piracy statute are both located in title 6 of the Rhode Island General Laws.

SOUTH CAROLINA: The state's anti-bootlegging statute and anti-piracy statute are both located in title 16 of the South Carolina Code.

SOUTH DAKOTA: The state's anti-piracy statute is located in title 43 of the South Dakota Codified Laws.

TENNESSEE: The state's anti-bootlegging statute and anti-piracy statute are both located in title 39 of the Tennessee Code.

TEXAS: The state's anti-bootlegging statute and anti-piracy statute are both located in the Texas Business and Commerce Code.

UTAH: The state's anti-piracy statute is located in title 13 of the Utah Code.

VIRGINIA: The state's anti-bootlegging statute and anti-piracy statute are both located in title 59.1 of the Virginia Code.

WASHINGTON: The state's anti-bootlegging statute and anti-piracy statute are both located in title 19 of the Washington Revised Code.

WEST VIRGINIA: The state's anti-bootlegging statute and anti-piracy statute are both located in title 61 of the West Virginia Code.

WISCONSIN: The state's anti-bootlegging statute and anti-piracy statute are both located in chapter 943 of the Wisconsin Statutes.

WYOMING: The state's anti-bootlegging statute and anti-piracy statute are both located in title 40 of the Wyoming Statutes.

## Additional Resources

*American Jurisprudence.* West Group, 1998

*Copyright Law in Business and Practice.* Hazard, John W., Jr., West Group, 1998.

*Intellectual Property and Unfair Competition in a Nutshell, 5th Edition.* McManis, Charles R., Thomson/West, 2004.

*West's Encyclopedia of American Law, 2nd Edition.* Thomson/Gale, 2004.

## Organizations

### United States Copyright Office, The Library of Congress
101 Independence Avenue, SE
Washington, DC 20559-6000 USA
Phone: (202) 707-3000
Fax: (202) 707-2600
URL: http://lcweb.loc.gov/copyright

### Intellectual Property Owners Association
1255 23rd St., NW, # 200
Washington, DC 20037 USA
Phone: (202) 466-2396
Fax: (202) 466-2366
URL: www.ipo.org.

### Recording Industry Association of America
1330 Connecticut Ave., NW, Suite 300
Washington, DC 20036 USA
Phone: (202) 775-0101
Fax: (202) 775-7253
URL: http://www.riaa.com

# INTELLECTUAL PROPERTY

## PATENTS

*Sections within this essay:*

## Background

Article I of the United States Constitution provides Congress with the power to "promote the progress of science and useful arts, by securing for limited times to—inventors the exclusive right to their—discoveries." Pursuant to this provision, Congress established rules and regulations governing the granting of **patents**. Congress delegated the administration of these duties to the **Patent** and Trademark Office. The **statutory** provisions are contained in Title 35 of the United States Code. The federal statutory scheme was modified considerably in 1995 with the **adoption** of the General Agreement on Tariffs and Trade (GATT), which aligned U. S. patent law with patent laws in other countries.

Issuance of patents is exclusively a federal concern, so state governments cannot issue patents to protect inventions. However, some state laws may provide protection to inventors if the inventor does not attain a patent.

Only certain types of inventions may be patented. The three major types of patents are utility, design, and plant patents, definitions of which appear in the federal **statute**. If an invention falls within one of the appropriate types of patents, the invention must still be patentable. First, the invention must be novel, meaning no other prior invention description anticipates or discloses the elements of the new invention. Second, the invention must have utility, that is, usefulness. Third, the new invention must not be obvious to those skilled in an art relevant to the invention. The latter requirement is referred to as "nonobviousness."

Congress and the Patent and Trademark Office require that applicants follow specific steps in order for a patent to be issued. Once a patent has been issued, the right is considered the **personal property** of the inventor, so it can be sold, assigned, etc. The length of the patent depends on the type of patent issued. Generally, the length is either 20 years (utility and plant patents) or 14 years (design patents). Damages for patent **infringement** are rather severe, thus providing greater incentive for inventors to follow proper procedures to apply for a patent.

## Types of Patents

Not all inventions may be patented, even those that are novel and unique. The most basic restriction is that while the application of a certain idea may be appropriate for a patent, the mere idea cannot be patented. Thus, **discovery** of a scientific formula may not be patented, but development of a method using this formula may be patented. The restriction against patenting ideas is often referred to as the "law of nature" doctrine.

### Utility Patents

Perhaps the most familiar of the types of patents, utility patents may be issued for "any new and useful process, machine, manufacture, or composition of matter, or any new and useful improvement thereof." In the patent application, an inventor must include a detailed description of how to make and use an invention, "claims" that define the invention, and drawings of the invention, in addition to other procedures required by the Patent and Trademark Office and the federal patent statute.

### Design Patents

Design patents may be issued for a new, original, or ornamental design for an article of manufacture. This type of patent is limited to the unique shape or design of an object and only applies to the ornamental or aesthetic value of the object. If the shape serves some function, then the inventor should apply for a utility patent. The design cannot be an adaptation of a known form or ornament to a different article. The patent application for a design patent is similar to a utility patent, though the description and "claim" that defines the design are usually very short.

### Plant Patents

A plant patent may be issued to someone who invents or discovers a unique variety of plant and asexually reproduces such a plant. This category includes cultivated spores, mutants, hybrids, and newly found seedlings, subject to some restrictions. Plant patents do not apply to sexually reproducible plants, but the Plant Variety Protection Act may provide protection for these types of plants.

## Patentability

An applicant for a utility patent must satisfy three basic requirements for a patent to be patentable: novelty, nonobviousness, and utility. Requirements for a design patent or a plant patent are similar, except that ornamentality (design patent) or distinctiveness (plant patent) is required instead of utility.

### Novelty

The patent statute requires that each invention is novel as a condition for the issuance of a patent. For an invention to be considered "novel," no other reference in "prior art" may anticipate or disclose each of the elements of the invention in the patent application. The term "prior art" is somewhat confusing, as it refers to the state of knowledge existing or publicly available at some time before the application for the patent is filed. Prior art may include prior printed publications from anywhere in the world, patents filed prior to the current patent application, publicly available knowledge or use of an invention in the United States, a foreign patent filed by the applicant, a prior invention in the United States, or the previous sale of an item. The time frame in which prior art refers to an invention is set forth in the statutory section defining prior art. The question in most common cases is whether the publication, patent, etc., existed prior to the earliest provable date of invention or more than one year before the patent application was filed.

Even if prior art exists that relates to an invention, a variation in prior art will likely satisfy the novelty requirement. The most common method to prove the difference between prior art and an invention is to demonstrate physical differences between the two. Other methods for proving novelty may include a showing that a new combination of components of an existing item was used or that the invention is a new use for an existing item.

### Nonobviousness

Even if a patent satisfies the novelty requirement, it must still satisfy the requirement of nonobviousness. Under this requirement, if the differences between the subject matter of a new invention and the subject matter of prior art would have been obvious to a person of ordinary skill in the art relevant to the subject matter of the invention, then the nonobvious requirement has not been met. In other words, a new invention must be more than different from prior art; the difference (or different use) must not be obvious to someone who has ordinary skill in using such an invention.

### Utility, Distinctiveness, or Ornamentality

A final requirement for a utility patent is that the invention has utility, which refers generally to the usefulness of the invention. Practically any level of utility is sufficient; the invention must provide some identifiable benefit. However, if an invention can be used only for a scientific curiosity or could only be used for illegal purposes, the patent application is more likely to be denied.

An applicant for a plant patent needs to demonstrate that the plant is clearly distinguishable from existing plants but does not need to prove usefulness or utility of the new plant. An applicant must similarly prove ornamentality rather than utility. Thus, the inventor must show that the invention serves some ornamental or aesthetic purpose.

## Obtaining a Patent

### Inventors Entitled to Patents

Under the Patent Act, only the original and authentic inventors may claim patent rights. Even if an invention may be patentable, the patents will not be granted if the wrong individual applies for the patent. The idea for an invention cannot generally be assigned to another person; only the original inventor may apply for the patent. Thus, if an employee invents an item, he or she cannot assign the right to patent the item to an employer in the name of the employer, even if the original inventor used the employer's resources and created the invention during the inventor's employment. The only permitted assignment is one that permits the assignee to obtain a patent in the name of the original inventor. Note that it is common for employees to agree to assign patents to employers.

### Provisional Patent Application

The Patent statute permits an inventor to file an abbreviated version of a patent application, called a **Provisional** Patent Application (PPA). The PPA allows an inventor to establish a filing date earlier than the filing date of a Regular Patent Application (RPA). The PPA must be filed within one year of the filing of the RPA. The PPA is beneficial to an inventor if he or she is concerned that someone else may develop the invention, or the inventor does not want to build and test an invention immediately.

The PPA must describe the invention, including a description of how to make and use it; drawings of the invention, if these are necessary to describe how to make and use the invention; a cover sheet; pay-

ment of a fee; and a filing of a small entity declaration, if applicable. If a PPA is filed, and the RPA is filed at a later date, the length of the patent is measured by date of the filing of the RPA.

### Joint Inventions

Two or more inventors can be granted a patent for a joint invention; in fact, if a joint invention is appropriate, none of the joint inventors can claim to be the original inventor individually. Should an application omit parties erroneously or the application otherwise names a wrong party, the application could fail. The Patent Act does allow parties to correct mistakes in some circumstances, such as exclusion of an original inventor from the application.

The determination of the appropriate inventor or inventors in a particular case may not be clear. For example, two individuals may have collaborated throughout a project in which something is invented, while a third individual may have assisted from time to time but added nothing by way of original thought or contribution. The appropriate test for determining whether an individual should be included as an inventor is whether the individual worked on the subject matter and made some original contribution to the thought and final result of at least one claim in the application. In the example above, the first two inventors would most likely be considered joint inventors, while the third most likely would not.

### Specifications and Claims

The Patent Act includes two main requirements in a patent application: a specification and a claim. The specification generally requires the applicants to describe why the invention differs from prior art, show that the invention is, in fact, useful, and show that the invention would not be obvious to someone skilled in the art relevant to the invention. The patent statute requires that the application describe the invention in its "best mode" to enable an individual skilled in the art relevant to the invention to be able to repeat the invention. The specification cannot be indefinite and must be "clear, concise, and exact." Moreover, the specification must disclose specifically how to use the invention, including specific times, dosages, etc., that are necessary to use the invention.

A claim defines the inventor's right and illustrates how the invention meets the three requirements for patentability: novelty, nonobviousness, and utility (note that these are described in the specification). The claim should describe the invention and should not merely include functional language. Functional language would include, for example, how a new chip performs in a computer system without describing the chip itself or indicating specifically why it is patentable. Functional language cannot establish patentability, and the application will be rejected because the claim is barred.

### Patent Oath and Fees

An inventor must include with a patent application a signed statement indicating that the applicant is the original and first inventor of the subject matter claimed in the application. The application must also identify each inventor by full name, the country in which each applicant is a citizen, plus several requirements related to foreign applications. Moreover, an applicant must acknowledge that he or she is aware of the necessity to disclose information that is material to the review of the application and must state that he or she understand and has reviewed the specifications and claims.

The applicant must sign the application and be sworn to under oath or include a declaration. The inventor or inventors must make the oath or declaration personally. A **legal representative** may satisfy these requirements only in certain circumstances described by the Patent Act and the regulations of the Patent and Trademark Office. Fees must accompany the application, as set forth in the statute and the regulations.

### Review by the Patent and Trademark Office

When the Patent and Trademark Office receives an application, it can make an initial allowance, a partial rejection, or a complete rejection. If an application is rejected, the inventor may contest the rejection by introducing **evidence** in reply to the rejection, amend or modify the specification and/or claim, or both. If the application is rejected twice, the applicant must appeal the decision.

The first appeal of a rejected application is to the Patent and Trademark Office's Board of Appeals. The Patent Office will engage in informal communications and interviews with both the **examiner** and the applicant. The Board will generally raise all issues that give rise to the rejection, including discovery of prior art or problems with patentability. The applicant must refute these problems with particularity. This means the applicant must state precisely why the application is satisfactory, why the invention is indeed patentable, etc. The process may continue through several cycles of rejection, amendments, and refiling of an application (though the amendments are limited after a second rejection). The Pa-

tent Office may declare a final rejection any time after a second **examination** on the merits.

If the Board rejects the application then the applicant may appeal to the United States District Court for the District of Columbia or the United States Court of Appeals for the Federal Circuit. However, courts typically give a considerable amount of deference to the decision of the Patent Office, so prevailing in an appeal is unusual.

## Inventors' Rights to Patented Items

### Duration of Patents

The duration of a patent depends on the type of patent that has been granted. One of the more significant effects of the General Agreement on Tariffs and Trade was the duration of a patent in the United States. Prior to 1995 (and dating back to 1861), the length of a typical patent was 17 years. After GATT came into effect in 1995, the length increased to 20 years.

Utility patents filed after June 8, 1995 extend 20 years from the date the application was filed. Plant patents also extend 20 years from the date of filing. Design patents extend 14 years from the date the patent was granted. Once the term of the patent has expired, the invention becomes public property and may be used, sold, and reproduced. In some limited cases, such as proceedings to determine the priority of an invention, the length of a patent may be extended up to five years.

### Assignment and Licensing

The original and authentic inventor or inventors are preserved to be the owner of any patent application, unless this right has been assigned. An application may be assigned before or after the application is filed, and the assignment must be recorded with the Patent and Trademark Office. The right to sue for present or past infringement cannot be assigned, except as it relates to the assignment itself. An assignment transfers all rights of the inventor, and the assignee takes the application subject to licenses granted by the assignor.

An inventor may also issue a license, which gives the license holder permission to make, use, or sell the invention. The rights transferred in a license depend on the actual transfer. For example, a license may be for exclusive or non-exclusive use of the license. A joint owner of a patent may generally give a valid license without the permission of the other joint owners, unless the joint owners agree otherwise. As noted above, even if the rights to a patent are assigned, the license nevertheless survives according to the terms of the license agreement.

### Abandonment

The applicant through an express writing that is signed by the applicant and filed with the Patent and Trademark Office may abandon a patent application. The Patent Office will also consider an application abandoned if the inventor fails to **prosecute** the application within six months of the filing. A patent may also be abandoned if the applicant fails to pay required fees within three months of a notice of allowance sent to the applicant.

**Abandonment** of an application differs from an abandonment of an invention. An abandonment of an application does not transfer right to the public, while an abandonment of an invention surrenders or dedicates the invention to the public. Abandonment of an invention may be express or implied.

### Infringement

A patent owner may protest his or her invention by suing for patent infringement, which is a tort for the unauthorized making, using, selling, offering to sell, or importing the subject matter of the patent. To determine whether an infringement has occurred, a court will compare the infringing subject matter with the subject matter covered by the patent. Infringement cannot occur before the issuance of a patent, but an individual may infringe a patent right even if he or she does not know the existence of a patent. Infringement may be direct; indirect, where the infringer encourages someone else to infringe the patent; or contributory, where an individual knowingly sells or supplies a component of a patented machine or other invention to another.

### Damages

A patent owner may recover significant damages in a successful action for patent infringement. The Patent Act permits a court to award treble damages, which means the court can increase damages by up to three times the amount of the actual damages. Courts may also award attorneys fees in exceptional cases.

The minimum award a patent owner may receive for patent infringement is a reasonable royalty, plus costs and interest fixed by the court. A patent owner may also recover the profit the patent holder would have made on sales of the subject matter relevant to the patent. Profits earned by the patent infringer constitute a factor for determining the appropriate royalty or other damages.

## Applicability of State Law to Patents

An inventor may have rights based on state law in addition to patent rights to protect the intellectual property related to an invention. However, the Patent Act preempts many state causes of action, especially because Congress is granted the right to issue patents in the United States Constitution. The Supreme Court has held that state **unfair competition** laws are generally preempted by the Patent Act insofar as the state law provides a cause of action that is functionally similar to recognition of a patent right and a cause of action for patent infringement.

State law governing trade secrets are generally not preempted, so an inventor may be able to protect his or her rights through this cause of action. On the other hand, the protection offered through this cause of action is considerably weaker than the rights protected when a patent is granted. More specifically, a patent right is a **monopoly** to make, use, and sell an invention, while trade secrets law focuses on the conduct of a party that violates the trade secrets of a party. Stated simply, obtaining a patent right is virtually always preferable.

## Additional Resources

*Code of Federal Regulations, Title 37: United States Patent and Trademark Office, Department of Commerce.* U. S. Government Printing Office, 2001. Available at http://www.access.gpo.gov/nara/cfr/waisidx_01/37cfrv1_01.html#101.

*Intellectual Property: Patents, Trademarks, and Copyright in a Nutshell.* Miller, Arthur R., and Michael H. Davis, West Group, 2000.

*McCarthy's Desk Encyclopedia of Intellectual Property, Second Edition.* McCarthy, J. Thomas, Bureau of National Affairs, 1995.

*Patent It Yourself, 4th Edition.* Pressman, David, Nolo Press, 1995.

*Patent Law Precedent: Key Terms and Concepts.* Aisenberg, Irwin M., Little, Brown, and Company, 1991.

*U.S. Code, Title 35: Patents.* U.S. House of Representatives, 1999. Available at http://uscode.house.gov/title_35.htm.

## Organizations

### American Intellectual Property Law Association (AIPLA)

2001 Jefferson Davis Highway, Suite 203
Arlington, VA 22202 USA
Phone: (703) 415-0780
Fax: (703) 415-0786
URL: http://www.aipla.org/
Primary Contact: Mike Kirk, Exec. Dir.

### National Association of Patent Practitioners (NAPP)

4680-18i Monticello Ave., PMB 101
Williamsburg, VA 23188 USA
Phone: (800) 216-9588
Fax: (757) 220-3928
E-Mail: napp@napp.org

URL: http://www.napp.org

### National Congress of Inventor Organizations (NCIO)

P.O. Box 93669
Los Angeles, CA 90093-6690 USA
Phone: (888) 695-4455
Fax: (213) 947-1079
URL: http://www.inventionconvention.com/ncio
Primary Contact: Stephen Paul Gnass, Exec. Dir.

### U.S. Patent & Trademark Office (USPTO), General Information Services Division

Crystal Plaza 3, room 2C02
Washington, DC 20231 USA
Phone: (800) 786-9199
E-Mail: usptoinfo@uspto.gov
URL: http://www.uspto.gov

# INTELLECTUAL PROPERTY

## TRADEMARKS

*Sections within this essay:*

- Background
- Trademark Law
    - The Lanham Act
    - Trademark Registration
    - Trademark Infringement
- State Court Decisions Interpreting State Trademark Statutes
- Additional Resources

## Background

A trademark is a device used by businesses to distinguish their goods and services from competitors' goods and services. It may consist of a word, a symbol, a logo, or any combination thereof, so long as it clearly signifies the source of ownership for a product or service. Adidas is an example of a trademarked name, McDonald's golden arches is an example of a trademarked symbol, and the NIKE name written above the "swoosh" symbol is an example that combines two types of trademark devices. When a trademark is used to distinguish a service, it is usually called a service mark. "American Express" is the service mark for a well known provider of credit card services.

Consumers rely on **trademarks** when making their purchases. Trademarks can reflect a product's authenticity, quality, and accumulated customer good will. When a product or service is defective, of poor workmanship, or otherwise unpopular with consumers, its trademark can reflect those undesir-

able qualities as well. Even when two products are of seemingly equal quality, like two cola soft drinks, their trademarks simply communicate to customers which is which.

Moreover, trademarks serve to protect a business owner's investment in a particular product by preventing competitors from capitalizing on the reputation affiliated with a particular name in the marketplace. They also save new companies from wasting their time trying to market a product under an existing trademark. Before individuals or entities start selling products or services that bear a certain name or logo, they often hire an attorney to investigate prior or existing marks that are in any way the same or similar to the mark they intend to use. Companies that fail to conduct this kind of search or blatantly ignore the existing use of a trademark risk being sued for **infringement** and ordered by a court to cease promoting their products with a particular mark.

The presence of trademark protection for a good or service is often indicated by a small "R" inside a circle placed near the trademark. The "R" means that the mark has been registered with the U. S. **Patent** and Trademark Office and serves as a warning against unauthorized use of the mark. Individuals may also claim rights to a particular trademark by displaying the letters "TM" near the mark. Trademarks bearing the "TM" symbol are not registered, but the symbol indicates the owner's intent to register it.

Trademarks are distinct from trade names or **trade dress**. A **trade name** is the name or designation used by a business to identify itself and distinguish it from other businesses. By contrast, a trademark distinguishes the line of products from all other product lines, particularly those offered by competing businesses. For example, Ford Motor Company is the trade name for a particular maker of automobiles, trucks, and vans that bear the trademark "Ford." Trade dress is the manner in which a business distinguishes a product's appearance from the appearance of a rival's product. Something as simple as a grille on the front end of an automobile may constitute trade dress if it is sufficiently distinctive and the manufacturer takes deliberate and **tangible** steps to market the grille over a long period of time.

## Trademark Law

### The Lanham Act

Trademark law in the United States is governed by the Trademark Act of 1946, also known as the **Lanham Act** (15 U.S.C.A. section 1051 et seq). The Lanham Act codified much of the then existing **common law** of trademarks, and it also clarified some areas where jurisdictions differed in their approach to particular issues. Congress has since amended the Lanham Act several times, addressing new concerns as they are presented by both trademark owners and consumers. Many states have enacted trademark statutes of their own, which may be applied to legal issues that are not pre-empted by Lanham.

Lanham defines trademarks to include words, names, symbols, and logos that businesses use or intend to use in commerce for the purpose of distinguishing their goods from those made or sold by competitors. The key to any claim for trademark rights is the distinctiveness of the proposed mark. Roughly analogous to the originality requirement for **copyright**, the distinctiveness requirement for trademarks may be satisfied by proof that the mark is descriptive, suggestive, arbitrary, or fanciful. Proof that a mark is generic will defeat a claim for trademark protection.

A generic name is the common name for a product and thus does nothing to distinguish itself from other products of the same genre. Shoe, ball, hat, and lightbulb are all generic product names that will never receive trademark protection. Conversely, trademarks that are distinctive and have qualified for trademark protection may lose that protection by becoming generic in the mind of the public. This transition happens when a substantial segment of consumers in the relevant market adopt a trademark as the general name for an entire line of products. Examples of once distinctive trademarks that have since become generic include aspirin, cellophane, escalator, and thermos. The trademark owners of Kleenex, Xerox, Sanka, and Teflon have successfully prevented their marks from becoming generic, despite many consumers' strong identification of their individual products with the product lines as a whole.

For a trademark to receive and retain its distinctiveness, the mark must fall into one of four categories: descriptive, suggestive, arbitrary, or fanciful. One level more distinctive than a generic mark, descriptive marks will not receive trademark protection unless they have acquired a secondary meaning, which happens when a significant portion of consumers identify the mark as signifying a particular manufacturer's good. Suppose the Jones Sport and Recreation Company sought trademark protection for their line of bicycles known as the "blue bike." The word blue does almost nothing to distinguish Jones' product from other bikes with the same color being sold by competitors. But now suppose that Jones has spent millions of dollars over the last several years marketing its product, and sales of the "blue bike" have grown to such a degree that bicycle-buying Americans now identify blue bikes as originating from the Jones' company. Then Jones' mark may have acquired secondary meaning, and thus its "blue bike" is much more likely to receive federal trademark protection.

Suggestive marks imply a quality or characteristic of a product that goes beyond merely describing it. These kinds of marks require consumers to use their imaginations to make the connection between the mark itself and the product it represents. As a result, suggestive marks can receive federal trademark protection immediately upon their first use. Examples of suggestive marks include Orange Crush (orange-flavored soft drink), Playboy (sexually oriented magazine for men), Ivory (white soap), and Sprint (long-distance telephone company).

The strongest marks are arbitrary and fanciful marks. Their strength lies in the fact that they bear little or no obvious relationship to the products with which they are affiliated, and yet they serve as a source of immediate authenticity in the minds of consumers. As a result, arbitrary and fanciful marks most effectively serve the dual role of trademarks, promoting fair competition between rivals in the marketplace and communicating the source and ownership of products to potential buyers. Arbitrary marks can be actual words that have their own meaning, but when associated with a particular product they do not describe the product or suggest anything about it. Examples of arbitrary marks include Pledge for furniture polish, Camels for cigarettes, and Dial for soap. Fanciful marks are not words at all and have no meaning apart from their affiliation with a good or service. They are inherently distinctive. Examples of fanciful marks include Kodak, Exxon, and Rolex.

### Trademark Registration

Trademark registration begins with an application to the commissioner of **patents** and trademarks at the U. S. Patent and Trademark Office (USPTO). One may apply with either the principal register or the supplemental register of the USPTO. The principal register records descriptive, suggestive, arbitrary, and fanciful marks that have acquired secondary meaning. The supplemental register records descriptive marks that are capable of acquiring secondary meaning but have not yet acquired that meaning in the minds of many consumers. Once a mark acquires secondary meaning, however, it can be transferred from the supplemental register to the principal register.

Registration with the principal register is proof that the mark is valid, registered, and the intellectual property of the registrant, who has exclusive rights to use the mark in commerce. Registration with the principal register is deemed to put potential infringers on constructive notice of the registrant's ownership interests in the trademark and entitles the owner to bring an infringement suit against the bearers of any offending marks. Individuals or entities who **counterfeit** registered trademarks also face criminal and civil penalties.

Applications for offensive, immoral, deceptive, or scandalous marks will be denied (see 15 U.S.C.A. 1052[a]). Marks such as "bubby trap" for a brassiere is an example of an offensive mark, *In re Riverbank Canning Co.*, 95 F.2d 327 (Cust. & Pat.App. 1938), **as is** the mark "a breast in the mouth is better than a leg in the hand" for a chicken restaurant, *Bromberg, Et Al. v. Carmel Self Service, Inc.*, 198 U.S.P.Q. 176 (Trademark Tr. & App. Bd. 1978). Offensive marks cannot be cured by acquiring a secondary meaning that is inoffensive, unless the secondary meaning entirely replaces the primary, literal, or obvious meaning.

Despite the advantages of registration, it is actually the use or intended use of a mark that confers upon the mark federal trademark protection. As a general rule, conflicting claims to a trademark are resolved according to priority of **appropriation**. The first to use a mark will normally be given **proprietary** rights over the mark. Although this rule seems clear cut, demonstrating first use or first intended use can often prove difficult in court. Consequently, the law gives businesses incentive to register their marks concomitantly with the date of first use by presuming that registered marks have been in continuous use from the date the trademark application was filed and by prohibiting court challenges to trademarks that have been in continuous use for five years from the date of registration. Registration also demonstrates to a court that the user has done everything to protect its mark.

A rule favoring the first user of a trademark protects what is assumed to be an established identification between consumers and a trademarked product. Nonetheless, it is possible that a second user may establish stronger consumer identification with its product in a geographical market different from the market where the first user is doing business. When this happens, courts will often recognize the trademark rights of both the first and second users, so long as the second user established its mark in **good faith** and confines its use to a market distant from the first user.

Trademark registrants can **forfeit** their rights to a mark by using them in a **fraudulent** or deceptive manner. They can also lose their rights by abandoning the mark. However, nonuse by itself does not constitute **abandonment**. Acts of abandonment must also be accompanied by an intent not to use the mark again. Finally, registrants can lose their rights to a trademark if the public adopts a trademark as the general name for a type of goods, as happened with the aspirin and cellophane examples mentioned above. Trademark owners typically take great efforts to prevent their marks from becoming generically used by the public. Rollerblade, for example, spent millions of dollars in advertising and law suits to prevent its new brand of roller skate from becoming the generic name used to describe in-line skates, after both consumers and rivals began referring to all such skates as rollerblades regardless of who made them.

### Trademark Infringement

Trademark infringement suits generally involve claims that the bearer of an allegedly offending similar mark is creating the likelihood of customer confusion over competing products, diluting the distinctiveness and value of an existing mark or **counterfeiting** an existing mark with an identical "knock-off" mark.

Likelihood of confusion is shown by proof that the allegedly offending mark is causing "probable" confusion among consumers, such that buyers in the relevant market are mistaking the defendant's name or logo for the plaintiff's trademark. Proof that confusion among consumers is only possible will not suffice to establish an infringement claim. On the other hand, the **evidence** need not rise to the level of actual confusion. Instead, courts will evaluate claims of customer confusion on a case-by-case basis in light of the following factors: (1) the similarity of the marks; (2) the similarity of the products; (3) the degree in which the markets for the competing products overlap; (4) the degree of care likely to be exercised by consumers; (5) the strength of the marks; (6) the amount of actual confusion; and (7) wrongful intent.

Trademark dilution is shown by proof that the defendant's use of an allegedly offending mark is likely to tarnish, degrade, or lessen the individuality, distinctiveness, or consumer impact of the plaintiff's mark. Trademark dilution suits seek to protect the advertising value of particularly strong and well-recognized trade symbols by stopping other businesses from using similar symbols to promote their products, even though no consumer confusion affects actual results and even though the rivals' products are not in direct competition with each other. Thus, Polaroid could successfully prevent an Illinois company from using the word "polaroid" in marketing its refrigerator and heating installation business (see *Polaroid Corp. v. Polaroid, Inc.,* 319 F.2d 830 [7th Cir. 1963]).

The Lanham Act defines a counterfeit mark as a "spurious mark that is identical with, or substantially indistinguishable from, a registered mark" (see 15 U.S.C.A. § 1127). All counterfeit marks are infringements, unless the offending mark is associated with a type of product or service that is wholly different from the plaintiff's mark. Individuals who intentionally traffic in counterfeit trademarks or attempt to traffic in them also face criminal punishment, including fines up to $2 million, **imprisonment** up to ten years, or both (see 18 USCA § 2320).

Defendants can raise several defenses against infringement suits, many of which are addressed briefly above. First, a **defendant** can claim that the plaintiff's mark is generic and thus not of sufficiently distinctive quality to qualify for federal trademark protection. Second, a defendant can offer proof that the plaintiff abandoned its trademark and thus is no

longer the owner of the mark. Third, a defendant can charge that it had first use of a mark and thus that the plaintiff is actually engaging in infringement of the defendant's mark. Fourth, a defendant can claim that it is making "fair use" of the defendant's mark, meaning essentially that the defendant is using the plaintiff's mark for non-commercial purposes, as when a teacher uses a mark for the educational benefit of students. Finally, the defendant may plead that the plaintiff has unclean hands, meaning the plaintiff has acted in an illegal, unfair, or deceptive manner that should prevent the court from enforcing the plaintiff's trademark.

## State Court Decisions Interpreting State Trademark Statutes

In addition to relying on federal law when enforcing a claim against an alleged trademark infringer, trademark owners may turn to state trademark law as well, unless the state law governs an area that is pre-empted by federal law. Below are a sampling of cases decided at least in part based on the court's interpretation of a state's trademark law.

ARKANSAS: The state's Trademark Act does not empower the Secretary of State to register trademarks or service marks for a limited geographical area within the state so as to accommodate similar marks used by businesses that are not directly competing with each other over the same consumers (see A.C.A. §§ 4-71-101 to 4-71-114; *Worthen Nat. Bank of Batesville v. McCuen,* 317 Ark. 195, 876 S.W.2d 567 [Ark. 1994]).

ILLINOIS: A maid service that was named "Maid To Order" was not entitled to injunction prohibiting the showing of a film by the same name, even if its name was deemed to be "distinctive" under state antidilution law, absent proof that the maid service would be irreparably harmed by consumers seeing the film (see Ill.Rev.Stat.1987, ch. 140, par. 22; *Kern v. WKQX Radio,* 175 Ill.App.3d 624, 529 N.E.2d 1149, 125 Ill.Dec. 73, [Ill.App. 1 Dist. 1988]).

NEW MEXICO: The state's trademark **statute** specifically preserves the common-law rights of trademark owners, such that the rights of a trademark owner registered with the state trademark office could be qualified by the bona fide rights of common-law users (see NMSA 1978, § 57-3-12; *S & S Investments, Inc. v. Hooper Enterprises, Ltd.,* 116 N.M. 393, 862 P.2d 1252 [N.M.App. 1993].

UTAH: The Lanham Act does not pre-empt the state's criminal simulation statute which prohibits anyone from selling or possessing with intent to sell a counterfeited object or from authenticating or certifying such an object as genuine (see U.S.C.A. Const. Art. 1, § 8, cl. 8; Art. 6, cl. 2; U.C.A.1953, 76-6-518; Lanham Trade-Mark Act, §§ 1-45, 15 U.S.C.A. §§ 1051-1127).

WASHINGTON: Under the state's trademark laws, the remote possibility of future competition between a national bank and a federal **savings and loan association** in a county where the national bank was located and where the savings and loan conduct incidental business did not justify enjoining the national bank's use of the same name as the savings and loan association (see *Pioneer First Federal Sav. and Loan Ass'n v. Pioneer Nat. Bank,* 98 Wash.2d 853, 659 P.2d 481 [Wash. 1983])

## Additional Resources

*West's Encyclopedia of American Law.* St. Paul: West Group, 1998.

*American Jurisprudence.* St. Paul: West Group, 1998.

*Intellectual Property in a Nutshell: Patents, Trademarks, and Copyright.* St. Paul, West Group. [no year given]

*http://www.findlaw.com/01topics/23intellectprop/ 03trademark.*FindLaw for Legal Professionals: Trademark Law.

*McCarthy on Trademarks and Unfair Competition.* St. Paul: West Group, 2001.

## Organizations

### U. S. Patent and Trademark Office
Crystal Plaza 3, Room 2C02
Washington, DC 20231 USA
Phone: (800) 786-9199
Fax: (703) 305-7786
URL: http://www.uspto.gov
Primary Contact: Nicholas Godici, Director

### Intellectual Property Owners Association
1255 23rd St., NW, # 200
Washington, DC 20037 USA
Phone: (202) 466-2396
Fax: (202) 466-2366
URL: www.ipo.org
Primary Contact: Ronald E. Myrick, President

### International Trademark Association
1133 Avenue of the Americas
New York, NY 10036 USA
Phone: (212) 768-9887
Fax: (212) 768-7796
URL: http://www.inta.org
Primary Contact: Nils Victor Montan, President

# INTELLECTUAL PROPERTY

## UNFAIR COMPETITION

*Sections within this essay:*

- Background

- The Law of Unfair Competition
    - Free Market Theory Underlying the Law
    - Interference with Business Relations
    - Infringement upon Trademarks, Trade Names, and Service Marks
    - Infringement upon Copyrights and Patents and Theft of Trade Secrets
    - False Advertising, Trade Defamation, and Misappropriation of a Name or Likeness

- State Law of Unfair Competition

## Background

**Unfair competition** means any **fraudulent**, deceptive, or dishonest trade practice that is prohibited by **statute**, regulation, or the **common law**. It consists of a body of related doctrines that gives rise to several different causes of actions, including (1) actions for **infringement** of **patents**, **trademarks**, or copyrights; (2) actions for wrongful **appropriation** of trade names, **trade dress**, and trade secrets; and (3) actions for publication of defamatory, false, or misleading representations.

The law of unfair competition serves five purposes. First, it seeks to protect the economic, intellectual, and creative investments made by businesses in distinguishing themselves and their products. Second, the law seeks to preserve the good will that businesses have established with customers over time. Third, the law seeks to deter businesses from appropriating the good will of their competitors. Fourth, the law seeks to promote clarity and stability by encouraging customers to rely on a merchant's **trade name** and reputation when evaluating the quality and prices of rival products. Fifth, the law of unfair competition seeks to increase competition by providing businesses with incentives to offer better goods and services than others in the same field.

Although the law of unfair competition helps protect consumers from injuries caused by deceptive trade practices, the remedies provided to **redress** such injuries are generally only available to business entities and proprietors. Consumers who are injured by deceptive trade practices normally must avail themselves of the remedies provided by **consumer protection** laws. Businesses and proprietors, however, may typically avail themselves of two remedies offered by the law of unfair competition, injunctive relief (a court order restraining a competitor from engaging in a particular unlawful action) and money damages (compensation for any losses caused by the unlawful practice). These remedies may be available in both state and federal court, depending on the circumstances surrounding the unlawful act.

## The Law of Unfair Competition

### *Free Market Theory Underlying the Law*

The freedom to pursue a livelihood, operate a business, and otherwise compete in the marketplace is essential to any free enterprise system. Competition creates incentives for businesses to earn customer loyalty by offering quality goods at reasonable prices. At the same time, competition can also inflict harm. The freedom to compete gives businesses the right to lure customers away from their competitors. When one business entices enough customers away from a competitor, the competitor may be forced to shut down its business or move to a different location.

The law of unfair competition will not penalize a business merely for being successful in the marketplace and will not subsidize a business for failing in the marketplace. Liability will not be imposed for aggressive, shrewd, or otherwise successful marketing tactics that are not deceptive, fraudulent, or dishonest. The law will assume, however, that for every dollar earned by one business, a dollar will be lost by a competitor. Accordingly, the law prohibits businesses from unfairly profiting at a rival's expense. What constitutes an "unfair" trade practice varies according to the cause of action asserted in each case.

### Interference with Business Relations

No business can effectively compete without establishing good relationships with its employees and customers. In some instances the parties execute a formal contract to memorialize the terms of their relationship. In other instances business relations are based on a less formal oral agreement. Most often, however, business relations are conducted informally with no contract or agreement at all. Grocery shoppers, for example, typically have no contractual relationship with the supermarkets that they patronize. The law of unfair competition regulates all three types of relationships, formal, informal, and those falling somewhere in between.

Many businesses depend on formal written contracts to conduct business. Employer and employee, wholesaler and retailer, and manufacturer and distributor all frequently reduce their relationships to writing. These contractual relations create an expectation of mutual performance, meaning that each party will perform its obligations according to the terms of the agreement. Protecting these relationships from outside interference facilitates performance and stabilizes commercial undertakings. Interference with contractual relations upsets commercial expectations and drives up the cost of doing business by involving competitors in squabbles that can find their way into court.

Virtually every contract, whether written or oral, qualifies for protection from unreasonable interference under the law of unfair competition. Noncompetition agreements are a recurrent source of **litiga-**

**tion** in this area of the law. These types of agreements are generally struck up in professional employment settings where an employer requires a skilled employee to sign an agreement promising not to go to work for a competitor in the same geographic market. Such agreements may also expressly prohibit the employee from taking client files, customer lists, and other **tangible** and intangible assets from the employer.

Noncompetition agreements are generally enforceable, unless they operate to deprive the employee of the right to meaningfully pursue a livelihood. Employees who choose to violate the terms of a noncompetition agreement may be sued for breach of contract, but the business that enticed the employee away from the employer may be held liable for tortious interference with an existing business relationship. The elements of this tort are: (1) the existence of a business relationship or contract; (2) the wrongdoer's knowledge of the relationship or contract; (3) the wrongdoer's intentional action taken to prevent contract formation, procure contractual breach, or terminate the business relationship; (4) lack of justification; and (5) resulting damages.

Informal trade relations that have not been reduced to contractual terms are also protected from outside interference by the law of unfair competition. Businesses are forbidden from intentionally inflicting injury upon a competitor's informal business relations through improper means or for an improper purpose. Improper means include the use of violence, undue influence, or **coercion** to threaten competitors or intimidate customers. For example, it is unlawful for a business to blockade an entryway to a competitor's shop or impede the delivery of supplies with a show of force. The mere refusal to deal with a competitor, however, is not considered an improper means of competition, even if the refusal is motivated by spite.

Malicious or monopolistic practices aimed at injuring a rival may constitute an improper purpose of competition. Monopolistic behavior includes any agreement between two or more people that has as its purpose the exclusion or reduction of competition in a given market. The Sherman Anti-Trust Act of 1890 makes such behavior illegal by proscribing the formation of contracts, combinations, and conspiracies in restraint of trade. 15 U.S.C.A sections 1 et seq. **Corporate** mergers and acquisitions that suppress competition are prohibited by the **Clayton Act** of 1914, as amended by the Robinson-Patman

Act of 1936. 15 U.S.C.A. sections 12 et seq. The Clayton Act also regulates the use of predatory pricing and unlawful tying agreements. Predatory pricing is the use of below-market prices to inflict pecuniary injury on competitors. A tying agreement is an agreement in which a vendor conditions the sale of one product upon the buyers promise to purchase an additional or "tied" product. For example, the U. S. Department of Justice sued Microsoft Corporation for allegedly tying its Internet Explorer web-browsing product to the sale of its Windows operating system. U. S. v. Microsoft Corp., 253 F.3d 34 (D.C.Cir. 2001). The case was settled before the issue was finally resolved by a court.

### Infringement upon Trademarks, Trade Names, and Service Marks

Before a business can establish commercial relations with customers and other businesses, it must create an identity for itself, as well as for its goods and services. Economic competition is based on the premise that consumers can intelligently distinguish between products offered in the marketplace. Competition is made difficult when rival products become easily mistaken for each other, since one business may profit from the sale of a product to consumers who believe they are buying a rival's product. Part of a business's identity is the good will it has established with customers, while part of a product's identity is the reputation it has earned for quality and value. As a result, businesses spend tremendous amounts of resources identifying their goods, distinguishing their products, and cultivating good will.

The four principal devices businesses use to distinguish themselves are trademarks, service marks, trade names, and trade dress. Trademarks consist of words, logos, symbols, slogans, and other devices that are affixed to goods for the purpose of signifying their origin and authenticity to the public. The circular black, blue, and white emblem attached to the rear end of motor vehicles manufactured by Bavarian Motor Works (BMW) is a familiar trademark that has come to signify meticulous craftsmanship to many consumers. Whereas trademarks are physically attached to the goods they represent, service marks are generally displayed through advertising. "Orkin" is the service mark for a well-known pest-control company.

Trade names are used to identify **corporations**, partnerships, sole proprietorships, and other business entities. A trade name may be the actual name of a business that is registered with the government,

or it may be an assumed name under which a business operates and holds itself out to the public. For example, a husband and wife might register their business as "Sam and Betty's Bar and Grill," while doing business as "The Corner Tavern." Both names are considered trade names under the law of unfair competition.

Trade dress refers to a product's physical appearance, including its size, shape, texture, and design. Trade dress can also include the manner in which a product is packaged, wrapped, presented, or promoted. In certain circumstances particular color combinations may serve as trade dress. For example, the trade dress of Chevron Chemical Company includes the red and yellow color scheme found on many of its agricultural products. Chevron Chemical Co., v. Voluntary Purchasing Groups, Inc., 659 F.2d 695 (5th Cir. 1981).

When a business uses a trademark, service mark, trade name, or trade dress that is deceptively similar to competitor's, a cause of action for infringement of those intellectual property interests may exist. The law of unfair competition forbids companies from confusing customers by using identifying trade devices that make their businesses, products, or services difficult to distinguish from others in the market. Actual confusion need not be demonstrated to establish a claim for infringement, so long as there is a likelihood that consumers will be confused by similar identifying trade devices. Greater latitude is given to companies that share similar identifying trade devices in unrelated fields of business or in different geographic markets. A court would be more likely to allow two businesses to use the identifying trade device "Hot Handguns," when one business sells firearms downtown and the other business runs a country western dance hall in the suburbs.

Claims for infringement of an identifying trade device are cognizable under both state and federal law. At the federal level, infringement claims may be brought under the Lanham Trademark Act. 15 U.S.C.A. sections 1051 et seq. At the state level, claims for infringement may be brought under analogous intellectual property statutes and miscellaneous common-law doctrines. Claims for infringement can be strengthened through registration of the identifying trade device. For example, most states require that businesses register their trade names with the government and provide protection against infringement to the business that registers its trade name first.

### Infringement upon Copyrights and Patents and Theft of Trade Secrets

The intangible assets of a business include not only its trade name and other identifying trade devices but also its inventions, creative works, and artistic efforts. Broadly defined as trade secrets, this body of commercial information may consist of any formula, pattern, process, program, tool, technique, mechanism, or compound that provides a business with the opportunity to gain an advantage over a competitor. Although a trade secret is not patented or copyrighted, the law of unfair competition awards individuals a property right in any valuable trade information they discover and attempt to keep secret through reasonable steps

The owner of a trade secret is entitled to its exclusive use and enjoyment. A trade secret is valuable not only because it enables a company to gain advantage over a competitor, but also because it may be sold or licensed like any other property right. On the other hand, commercial information that is revealed to the public, or at least to a competitor, retains limited commercial value. Consequently, courts vigilantly protect trade secrets from disclosure, appropriation, and theft. Businesses may be held liable for any economic injuries that result from their theft of a competitor's trade secret, as may other opportunistic members of the general public. Employees may be held liable for disclosing their employer's trade secrets, even if the disclosure occurs after the employment relationship has ended.

Valuable business information that is disclosed to the public may still be protected from infringement by **copyright** and **patent** law. Copyright law gives individuals and businesses the exclusive rights to any original works they author, including movies, books, musical scores, sound recordings, dramatic creations, and pantomimes. Patents give individuals and businesses the exclusive rights to make, use, and sell specific types of inventions, such as mechanical devices, manufacturing processes, chemical formulas, and electrical equipment. Federal law grants these exclusive rights in exchange for full public disclosure of an original work or invention. The inventor or author receives complete legal protection for his or her intellectual efforts, while the public obtains valuable information that can be used to make life easier, healthier, or more pleasant.

Like the law of trade secrets, patent and copyright law offers protection to individuals and businesses who have invested considerable resources in creating something useful or valuable and who wish to exploit that investment commercially. Unlike trade secrets, which may be protected indefinitely, patents and copyrights are granted protection only for a finite period of time. Applications for copyrights are governed by the Copyright Act, 17 U.S.C.A. section 409, while patent applications are governed by the Patent Act, 35 U.S.C.A. section 111.

### False Advertising, Trade Defamation, and Misappropriation of a Name or Likeness

A business that successfully protects its creative works from theft or infringement may still be harmed by **false advertising**. Advertising need not be entirely false in order to be actionable under the law of unfair competition, so long as it is sufficiently inaccurate to mislead or deceive consumers in a manner that it inflicts injury on a competitor. In general businesses are prohibited from placing ads that either unfairly disparage the goods or services of a competitor or unfairly inflate the value of its own goods and services. False advertising deprives consumers of the opportunity to make intelligent comparisons between rival products. False advertising also drives up costs for consumers who spend additional resources in examining and sampling products.

Both state and federal laws regulate deceptive advertising. The Lanham Trademark Act, 15 U.S.C.A. section 1051, regulates false advertising at the federal level, while many states have adopted the Uniform Deceptive Trade Practices Act (UDTPA), which prohibits three specific types of representations: (1) false representations that goods or services have certain characteristics, ingredients, uses, benefits, or quantities; (2) false representations that goods or services are new or original; and (3) false representations that goods or services are of a particular grade, standard, or quality. Advertisements that are only partially accurate may give rise to liability if they are likely to confuse prospective consumers. Ambiguous representations may require clarification to prevent the imposition of liability. For example, a business which accuses a competitor of being "untrustworthy" may be required to clarify that description with additional information if consumer confusion is likely to result.

Trade **defamation** is a close relative of false advertising. The law of false advertising regulates inaccurate representations that tend to mislead or deceive the public. The law of trade defamation regulates communications that tend to lower the reputation of a business in the eyes of the community. A species of **tort law**, trade defamation is divided into two categories, **libel and slander**.

Trade libel generally refers to written communications that tend to bring a business into disrepute, while trade slander refers to defamatory oral communications. Before a business may be held liable under either category of trade defamation, the First Amendment requires proof that a defamatory statement was published with "actual malice," which the Supreme Court defines as any representation that is made with knowledge of its falsity or in reckless disregard of its truth. New York Times v. Sullivan, 376 U.S. 254, 84 S. Ct. 710, 11 L. Ed. 2d 686 (1964). The actual **malice** standard places some burden on businesses to verify, prior to publication, the veracity of any attacks they level against competitors.

It is also considered tortious for a business to appropriate the name or likeness of a famous individual for commercial advantage. All individuals are vested with an exclusive property right in their identity. No person, business, or other entity may appropriate an individual's name or likeness without permission. Despite the existence of this common law tort, businesses occasionally affiliate their products with popular celebrities without first obtaining consent. Although movie stars and televisions actors can lend prestige to the goods and services they promote, a business which falsely suggests that a celebrity has sponsored or endorsed one of its products will be held liable for money damages in amount equal to the economic gain derived from the wrongful appropriation.

## State Law of Unfair Competition

The body of law governing unfair competition is comprised of a combination of federal and state legislation and state common law. Below is a sampling of state court decisions decided at least in part based on their own state's **statutory** law, common law, or both.

CALIFORNIA: A manufacturer's price policy, which set minimum resale prices for its products and informed retailers that the manufacturer would refuse to sell products to any retailer who did not comply, was permissible under the state's unfair competition law. West's Ann.Cal.Bus. & Prof.Code §§ 16720 et seq. *Chavez v. Whirlpool Corp.,*—- Cal.Rptr.2d ——, 2001 WL 1324737 (Cal.App. 2 2001).

HAWAII: Where the seller of a solar water heating unit incorrectly represented to a purchaser that it had been in business for 16 years and that it had licensed engineers on its staff, and then failed to scien-

tifically tailor an efficient water heating system for the purchasers' home, installed the system knowing it was defective in design, and failed to provide a reasonable and effective service and repair program to correct the faulty system after its installation, the seller's conduct and representations constituted acts or practices violating the state's statute governing unfair competition and deceptive trade practices. HRS § 480-2. *Rosa v. Johnston,* 3 Haw.App. 420, 651 P.2d 1228 (Hawaii' App. 1982).

ILLINOIS: A competitor of a flashlight bulb distributor was free to copy the bulb's information chart and reorder card that was used by the distributor in connection with the sale to retail merchants of bulbs that were not copyrighted, and the only restriction imposed by the state law of unfair competition was that the competitor sufficiently identify the source of the chart and card to customers by providing proper labeling. S.H.A. ch. 121 =, § 312. 15. *Duo-Tint Bulb & Battery Co., Inc. v. Moline Supply Co.,* 46 Ill.App.3d 145, 360 N.E.2d 798, 4 Ill.Dec. 685, (Ill.App. 3 Dist. 1977)

INDIANA: The appropriate remedy for the misappropriation of a university's name or likeness by a professor for his website and e-mail addresses was under the state's unfair competition law, trademark statutes, and the common law of tortious interference with business relations. West's A.I.C. 24-2-1-1 et seq. *Felsher v. University of Evansville,* 755 N.E.2d 589, (Ind. 2001).

NEW JERSEY: The "rule of reason" analysis, rather than a "per se" approach, is required for restraint of trade claims alleging **conspiracy** to damage or eliminate a competitor by unfair means, and thus a distributor's failure to establish probable or actual injury to competition caused by a processor's conduct precluded the imposition of liability upon the processor. *Ideal Dairy Farms, Inc. v. Farmland Dairy Farms, Inc.,* 282 N.J.Super. 140, 659 A.2d 904, (N.J.Super.A.D. 1995).

NEW YORK: The plaintiff's allegations failed to state a claim for unfair competition arising out of miscellaneous business relations, where the complaint did not state the requisite elements of a confidential business relationship between the parties or indicate that the parties had entered a valid agreement to refrain from the alleged acts of unfair competition. *Ponte and Sons, Inc. v. American Fibers Intern.,* 222 A.D.2d 271, 635 N.Y.S.2d 193 (N.Y.A.D. 1 Dept. 1995).

OHIO: Actions under the state's deceptive trade practice and unfair competition law have been restricted by court interpretation of federal copyright law to lawsuits seeking to redress violations of a company's trade dress and labeling so as to prevent purchasers from being misled as to the source of goods. 17 U.S.C.A. § 301. *George P. Ballas Buick-GMC, Inc. v. Taylor Buick, Inc.,* 5 Ohio Misc.2d 16, 449 N.E.2d 805, 1983 Copr.L.Dec. P 25,550, 5 O.B.R. 236 (Ohio Com.Pl., 1981).

WASHINGTON: A state court's issuance of an injunction against a national bank's use of a name was inconsistent with the authority of the **Comptroller** of Currency to approve names for national banks, and thus the court's reliance on the state's law of unfair competition was preempted by the Comptroller's congressionally-approved discretion to approve bank names. National Bank Act, 12 U.S.C.A. § 30. *Pioneer First Federal Sav. and Loan Ass'n v. Pioneer Nat. Bank,* 98 Wash.2d 853, 659 P.2d 481 (Wash. 1983).

## Additional Resources

*American Jurisprudence* West Group, 1998.

*http://profs.lp.findlaw.com/copyright/index.html* FindLaw for Legal Professionals: Copyright Law.

*http://www4.law.cornell.edu/uscode/17/index.text.html* Title 17 United States Code: Copyrights.

*http://www.findlaw.com/01topics/23intellectprop/03trademark* FindLaw for Legal Professionals: Trademark Law.

*Intellectual Property in a Nutshell: Patents, Trademarks, and Copyright* West Group.

*McCarthy on Trademarks and Unfair Competition* West Group, 2001.

*West's Encyclopedia of American Law* West Group, 1998

## Organizations

### *Intellectual Property Owners Association*
1255 23rd St NW # 200
Washington, DC 20037 USA
Phone: (202) 466-2396
Fax: (202) 466-2366
URL: www.ipo.org.
Primary Contact: Ronald E. Myrick, President

### *Recording Industry Association of America*
1330 Connecticut Avenue NW, Suite 300
Washington, DC 20036 USA
Phone: (202) 775-0101
Fax: (202) 638-0862
URL: http://www.riaa.com
Primary Contact: Hilary B. Rosen,CEO

### *U. S. Patent and Trademark Office*
Crystal Plaza 3, Room 2C02
Washington, DC 20231 USA
Phone: (800) 786-9199
Fax: (703) 305-7786
URL: http://www.uspto.gov
Primary Contact: Nicholas Godici, Director

# INTERNET

## ADVERTISING

*Sections within this essay:*

## Background

The number of people who see an advertisement on the Internet and click on it to get more information is growing. For these people, the Internet is a means of streamlining commerce. Depending on the sophistication of the ad, the viewer may be able to get product information, comparison information on other products, a listing of current vendors who sell the product (along with the price each charges), and an electronic order form. The Internet allows people to purchase anything from travel tickets to groceries online, and people are drawn to online products via ads.

It is also true that people who have clicked on an online ad have in all likelihood provided the advertis-er with a way to collect information about them. Some of this information may seem innocuous—a favorite hobby, product preferences. In some cases, however, the site may gather more information about viewers than they realize, and it may do so more actively than they wish.

Because the Internet is a relatively new phenomenon (having become popular as a communications tool in the 1990s), there are still a number of questions about how to use it effectively. Moreover, because the Internet exchanges information between computers, it allows users to be "tracked" to varying degrees. Not surprisingly, this ability has made the Internet a particularly attractive tool for advertisers and marketers. An advertisement placed on the Internet has the potential to reach literally millions of people anywhere in the world, at a fraction of the cost of traditional print or broadcast advertising. As with traditional advertising, some people welcome the information, while others simply wish to be left alone. In most cases this is not a problem; an Internet user who sees an ad has the option of clicking it and being put on an electronic mailing list if he or she chooses, while someone who is not interested can ignore the ad. In fact, many people do wish to be placed on such lists. Being on these lists might allow a consumer to receive information about new products and special offers via email. To some, this is seen as a convenience.

Some Internet sites, however, are set up to collect information about visitor usage patterns. They use this information to target potential customers via mail, telephone, and email. For every person who sees this as a convenience, there is someone else who views it as a threat to security and privacy. Although the issue will likely be a work in progress for some time, various groups in the government and the private sector are working to ensure that Internet advertising is safe and secure and that it respects the privacy of viewers and customers.

## Before the Internet

Using advertising as a means of tracking customers and their preferences is hardly new. The twentieth century witnessed the growth of targeted marketing based on information supplied, willingly, by consumers. This could be accomplished by many means, with the dual goal of finding out which advertising is most effective and which customers are most receptive.

### Print, Radio, and TV Advertising

A simple example is a print advertisement in a newspaper or magazine that includes the line, "Mention this ad and receive an additional discount on our services." The advertiser had an accurate and cost-effective way of determining how successful the ad was; if hundreds of people mentioned it, the ad was working, but if no one mentioned it, the ad needed to be changed or dropped. Ads of this type also appear on radio and television.

An ad that asks people to list their name and address and asks them to send that information to the advertiser is designed to perform two functions. First, it allows the advertiser to track individuals and reach them directly with product and service offers. Second, it allows the consumer to receive targeted information about products that he or she may be interested in purchasing. For a consumer who sees this as a service, this works well for everyone concerned. A consumer who has no interest in getting mail or telephone calls from advertisers can simply ignore requests for additional information.

### Advertising Becomes More Intrusive

As technology made it easier for records to be kept, it became increasingly difficult for people to remain anonymous. As marketing became a more definitive science in the latter half of the twentieth century, more people found themselves subjected to ads in the mail and on the telephone. Anyone with a telephone number and a mailing address could expect to be contacted by advertisers. People who did business with a company and paid by credit card or people who submitted their names to local businesses offering free prizes, might find themselves being targeted with specific offers. Junk mail, junk phone calls, and even junk faxes have become a fact of life for virtually everyone. People who switch to unlisted telephone numbers often find that they get calls for the last person before them to hold that number. Organizations such as the Direct Marketing Association (DMA) can help consumers get off mail and telephone lists, but other lists do continue to crop up.

## Benefits of Internet Advertising

Despite the negative aspects of Internet ads, they do actually serve a useful function for both consumers and those who have websites. For consumers, Internet advertising provides them with one enormous advantage: free access to websites. Many websites use the revenue generated by ads to pay for the web hosting service that allows them to appear in the Internet in the first place.

From the website's perspective, accepting ads allows people to have free access. Without the ads, the sites would likely need to charge a fee to remain viable and pay for web hosting services (which include the space on the Internet to run the site).

Advertising can be done via email as well. This is a highly cost-effective way for companies to reach customers or potential customers. Typically, a company will collect the email addresses of customers and ask them whether they wish to be sent special offers or company news via email. Those who say yes will get periodic product updates and special purchase officers delivered electronically. Customers can opt into or out of the system. Email has the advantage of quick delivery and minimal cost; even a company that has no website can send e mail.

## Advertising Caveats

### Website Advertising

Anyone who has visited a website on the Internet is familiar with the ad that flashes across the screen, known as the *banner ad*. Banner ads often have some sort of graphic element that catch the viewer's attention, along with an invitation to learn more about the product being advertised.

Banner ads are often considered intrusive and many people simply ignore them. Other ads that are less easy to ignore actually pop up on the screen while the viewer is looking at a website. Some of these ads open up in a new window, and the viewer must physically close these windows to get rid of the ad.

What many people fail to realize is that by clicking on to an Internet ad, they are authorizing a tracking device to be placed on their computer. This device will allow the advertiser to monitor the potential customer's computer use, including other sites visited and purchases made. Many people who believe they are safe from Internet advertisers are surprised to find themselves getting offers online or in the mail because they are unaware that clicking onto a banner ad launches this tracking device, known as a *cookie.*

### Cookies

Despite the whimsical name, cookies are a powerful tracking tool for advertisers. They are designed to store small pieces of information on a computer to make it easier for websites to remember the computer user. In its most innocuous form the cookie is a useful item. Cookies are used to save passwords and user ID information, which is useful for people who visit websites of organizations they belong to. Thanks to cookies, the computer can "remember" this information instead of forcing the user to type it in each time he or she visits a site.

Cookies can also be used, however, to gather more personal information about users, including what they purchase, how much time they spend at different sites, what they click on, and what they purchase. Often, banner ads include cookies, so anyone who clicks on a banner ad gets a cookie placed on his or her computer. That may be fine if the cookie only tracks the user's visits to that particular ad. Unfortunately, many banner ad companies actually collect data from cookies for all their member companies. This is how clicking on one particular ad can generate junk email, phone calls, or print mail.

### Spam

Unsolicited electronic advertising, or spam, has become an increasingly common nuisance to anyone with an email account. Spam is essentially electronic junk mail. Those who send spam may purchase email lists, or they may use technology that sends to random email names in a particular domain name (in much the same way computerized telemarketing will dial different telephone numbers at random). Spam may advertise anything at all from magazines to electronic equipment to travel packages. One of the most pervasive, and offensive, uses of spam is advertising of pornographic websites and literature.

Spam is popular with advertisers because it is convenient and because it costs a fraction of what mass mailings cost. With an actual mailing, the advertiser has to pay for paper, printing, and postage. With email advertisements, none of those costs exists. As with telemarketing, the danger of offending potential customers is offset many times over by the number of new customers who see email marketing as a convenient way to receive information.

A number of companies offer spam-filtering services that are designed to identify mail that looks like spam and prohibit its delivery. Usually the spam is stored where the would-be recipient can view it at his or her leisure and delete as necessary. Some Internet service providers (ISPs) also offer anti-spam functions. Electronic communication experts recommend that those who wish to minimize the amount of spam they get can send complaints to the ISP's postmaster (for example, if the domain name is sample.com, the complaint would be sent to postmaster@sample.com.) Often the ISP has no idea that a customer is using spam and will be only too happy to remove that client from its roster. Replying to a spam message, even when there are instructions for getting off of a list, is not recommended because even an angry note tells the sender that they have reached a live person, and they may continue to send spam anyway.

## Internet Advertising and Children

Children are particularly vulnerable when it comes to advertising. Marketers have long known that television advertising can be highly effective in reaching children, who are not savvy enough to understand that ads can be misleading.

Congress enacted legislation in 2000 to protect children, as well as their parents, from unscrupulous or unwitting advertisers who try to solicit information. Known as the Children's Online Privacy Protection Act (COPPA), it requires websites to obtain verifiable parental consent before collecting data from children. This data could include names, mailing addresses, email addresses, birth dates, and other private or personal information that children may not realize should not be shared online.

There have been cases, for example, in which children have been asked to provide this sort of information to websites as part of the entry rules for an online contest. COPPA mandates that in the case of such contests, children cannot be asked for information that is not deemed reasonably necessary. Companies that violate COPPA can face large fines. COPPA covers all websites for children ages 13 and under, as well as any website that collects data from children.

In fairness to these websites, many of them were ignorant about the problem and its potential fallout. Through increased education and compliance efforts, COPPA has helped children's websites to be more careful. For example, a 1998 survey of 144 children's websites revealed that only 24 percent had some sort of privacy policy to ensure that children's information would not be given to other sources. A second survey, released in 2001, revealed that the number of sites with a privacy policy had risen to nearly 90 percent.

## Making Internet Advertising Work for Users

Used properly, Internet advertising can be appealing to consumers and cost-effective to advertisers. Consumers who wish to get the most out of Internet advertising can follow some simple guidelines to ensure that they are not being placed unwittingly on mailing lists.

- *Learn how to reject and remove cookies.* Internet browsers (such as Netscape, Internet Explorer, and Opera) allow users to set their preferences to accept only certain cookies, or no cookies at all. This can be helpful, but it sometimes makes it cumbersome to access websites that use cookies to store member ID and password names. Each browser does provide instructions on how to do this, and also on how to selectively delete cookies currently residing on a computer.

- *Provide only the necessary information to conduct online transactions.* Some websites ask for name, mailing address, home and work phone numbers, email address, date of birth, etc. Users probably do not need to divulge all this information. In most online forms, "required fields" (those that must be filled out for the form to be accepted) are marked with an asterisk; everything else is optional.

- *If users belong to any online lists or frequent any sites where they make purchases, they can check their preferences to see what information is available.* About 2001 Yahoo, which offers services such as listserve hosting, upgraded its technology. In so doing, it set all Yahoo customers to a **default** setting in which they all consented to receiving solicitations by mail, phone, and

email. Yahoo did notify its customers and provided instructions on how to change those preferences, but if they belong to other list groups or if they make purchases from a particular site they should periodically check their settings.

- *Do not respond to spam.* Sending a reply to spam asking to be removed from a list almost never works. Users can contact their Internet service provider to find out if it can help them track down spam; there is also software on the market that can screen some spam.

Some organizations on the Internet provide information about online privacy issues, advertising, legal action, and spam. The Electronic Frontier Foundation (http://www.eff.org) offers a variety of information and also has links to other information.

Ultimately, dealing with Internet advertising is like dealing with any other type of advertising. Understanding how it works may not eliminate ads, but it will help users know how to minimize their impact.

## Additional Resources

*Advertising and Marketing on the Internet: Rules of the Road* Federal Trade Commission, Bureau of Consumer Protection, 1998.

*Advertising on the Internet* Zeff, Robbin Lee, and Brad Aronson, Wiley, 1999.

*Advertising on the Web* Sterne, Jim, Que, 1997.

*Cybermarketing* Keeler, Len, AMACOM, 1995.

*E-Advertising and E-Marketing: Online Opportunities* Haegele, Katie, Rosen Publishing Group, 2001.

## Organizations

### Electronic Frontier Foundation (EFF)
454 Shotwell Street
San Francisco, CA 94110 USA
Phone: (415) 436-9333
Fax: (415) 436-9993
URL: http://www.eff.org
Primary Contact: Shari Steele, Executive Director and President

### Federal Communications Commission (FCC)
445 12th Street SW
Washington, DC 20554 USA
Phone: (888) 225-5322

Fax: (202) 418-0232
URL: http://www.fcc.gov
Primary Contact: Michael K. Powell, Chairman

**_Federal Trade Commission (FTC)_**
600 Pennsylvania Avenue NW

Washington, DC 20580 USA
Phone: (202) 382-2537
URL: http://www.ftc.gov
Primary Contact: Frederick J. Zirkel, Inspector
General

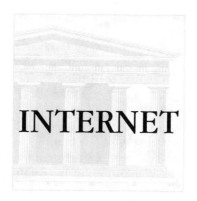

# INTERNET

## CONSUMER RIGHTS AND PROTECTION

*Sections within this essay:*

- Background
- Development of the Internet
- Consumers and Privacy
    - Computer Fraud and Abuse Act
    - Electronic Communications Privacy Act
    - Children's Online Privacy Protection Act
    - FTC Actions
- Cybersquatting
- Electronic Signatures and E-Sign
- Additional Resources

## Background

The Internet has raised a variety of legal issues since it first became widely used in the mid-1990s, most in the area of consumer rights and protections. But because the Internet is relatively new, regulations affecting consumer rights have often lagged behind the development of e-commerce as important new revenue source for businesses in the United States.

At the end of the 1990s and beginning of the twenty-first century, legislation affecting consumer and business rights in areas such as privacy, cybersquatting, and electronic signatures was passed. This legislation marked some of the first attempts to regulate the Internet marketplace. Because the Internet is still changing and developing, these new laws will almost certainly not be the last in terms of Internet regulation. It remains to be seen what will develop for this extraordinarily powerful marketing and selling tool.

## Development of the Internet

The Department of Defense first created the Internet in the late 1960s as a way of making sure communications between different facilities could withstand a war. It was originally called APRAnet, and in time this network came to link **corporations** and educational institutions as well. As this system developed, its aptitude for commercial applications became more and more apparent. The introduction of the first Internet browsers, along with the development of domain names—the names used by their owners to identify specific Internet addresses (e.g. www.gale.com)—and hypertext transfer protocols (HTTP), hastened this changeover. By 1995, when the National Science Foundation finally stopped supervising the Internet and Netscape introduced the first commercial Internet browser, it was clear that the Internet was going to become something big.

Since that time, companies offering various commercial services have popped up all over the Internet. Amazon, E-Bay, and Yahoo are the most widely known of the thousands of retail companies that have taken advantage of the Internet's lack of overhead and its ease of use. Internet commerce exploded from less than $100 million in 1995 to $33 billion in 2001.

But with this tremendous increase in trade has come concern for the rights of consumers who use the Internet to buy everything from soap to cars. Because the Internet has grown so fast in a relatively short while, many unusual consumer issues have arisen that have required both regulatory agencies such as the FTC and the legislative branches to pass new rules and laws specifically adapted to the situation.

## Consumers and Privacy

One of the most controversial issues facing consumers using the Internet has been privacy. Consumers have been concerned not just about having important information such as credit card numbers given out to the wrong people but also other information such as addresses and phone numbers.

One of the biggest controversies over privacy and the Internet has concerned so-called informational databases that companies accumulate when individuals buy something or registers on their sites. These databases contain personal information that can be sold to other corporations wishing to target those consumers. Corporations have traditionally treated these databases as a normal business asset. Recently Congress has stepped in to enact legislation making it more difficult to sell or purchase these databases without the consent of the consumer providing the information. There are questions about the reach of some of this legislation, however.

### Computer Fraud and Abuse Act

The Computer **Fraud** and Abuse Act (CFAA), first passed in 1984, was amended in 1996 to punish anyone who "intentionally accesses a computer without authorization or exceeds authorized access and thereby obtains information from any protected computer." Computers used for e-mail communication between states or used for online purchases from online vendors from other states are presumably included under the definition of protected computer that states that it includes any computer "which is used in interstate or foreign commerce or communication."

Thus, any user who covertly collects personal information of web-users engaged in transactions is in violation of this act. However, the CFAA has been used sparingly in prosecutions so far, and there are questions about its reach in regard to Internet privacy issues.

### Electronic Communications Privacy Act

Like the CFAA, the Electronic Communications Privacy Act (ECPA) was originally passed in the 1980s. The ECPA prohibits the intentional interception of electronic communications, the intentional disclosure of electronic communications wrongfully obtained, and the intentional use of electronic communications wrongfully obtained.

Observers have suggested that the EPCA could limit the use of "online profiling." Profiles are compiled by tracking users' movements online, usually by the use of cookies (pieces of code that are placed on users' computers when they visit a website that compiles information about users the websites use when the users make return visits). These cookies are often traded between sites so that online profiles of Internet users can be built, and marketing information can be targeted as specific users.

The ECPA contains an exception to its general rules about electronic communications that allows the interception and dissemination of electronic communications when one party to the communication has given consent. This would limit the use of EPCA in terms of online profiling since the site the user is in direct contact with would be allowed to use the consumer's information under this exception.

### Children's Online Privacy Protection Act

The Children's Online Privacy Protection Act (COPPA), passed in 1998, marks the first action by the government specifically limiting companies' dissemination of private information over the Internet. COPPA prohibits an operator of a website or online service directed at children or any operator that has actual knowledge that children are using its website, from collecting personal information from a child, unless the operator meets certain regulatory requirements.

These regulatory requirements include providing notice on the website as to what information is collected from the children and how the operator plans to use the information. In addition, the operator must obtain verifiable parental consent for the collection, use, or disclosure of personal information from children. Finally, operators are required, upon the request of a parent, to provide a description of the specific types of personal information collected from the child by that operator and an opportunity to prevent further collection or use of such information.

COPPA applies to websites and online services that are specifically directed at children under the age of thirteen and to operators of websites where the operators have actual knowledge they are collecting information from children under the age of thirteen. In 2000, the Federal Trade Commission filed its first action under COPPA, against a website called Toysmart. After it declared **bankruptcy**, Toysmart had attempted to sell the data it had collected selling toys. The FTC and Toysmart eventually agreed to a consent degree which allowed Toysmart to sell its database but only to a qualified buyer who focused its business in the same area that Toysmart did and agreed to the same limitations on that information that Toysmart had to follow under COPPA.

### FTC Actions

Beyond the above-mentioned acts, the FTC has made clear to Internet service providers they are expected to abide by the privacy policies posted on their websites. Recently, the FTC took action against at least one "virtual community website"—consisting of the home pages of millions of members—which was providing information to third parties compiled from members in violation of its own privacy policies. The FTC suggested in a release after the case was settled that "statements about information practices must be accurate and complete." If a retailer or other service provider states in a privacy policy it will not disseminate information, the FTC will step in if that policy is violated.

## Cybersquatting

Cybersquatting refers to the registration of a domain name in which the person has no legitimate interest. Cybersquatting is the attempt to profit by reserving and later reselling the domain name to the companies or individuals that have the trademarked right to the domain name. This can happen because domain names are registered on a first come, first serve basis. As an example, a cybersquatter may register the name "Exxon.com" and attempt to sell this name back to the Exxon corporation, or alternatively, may attempt to block Exxon from using Exxon.com as an address to conduct business on the Internet. The cybersquatter may use the Exxon.com address to post disparaging information about Exxon or to try to **defraud** consumers wishing to do business with Exxon into thinking they have accessed the official Exxon site.

In response to the tremendous amount of **litigation** that occurred as a result of cybersquatting, the Anticybersquatting **Consumer Protection** Act (ACPA) was passed in 1999. This law provides that persons are liable for civil damages if they register, use, or traffic in domain names that are identical or confusingly similar to a distinctive or famous mark

owned by the plaintiff and the person has a **bad faith** intent to profit from such activity.

The ACPA is a fairly broad act that prevents many of the actions of cybersquatters discussed above. To assist in the bad faith determination, the court provides a non-exhaustive list of factors the court may examine in looking at a person's registration of a domain name. These include:

- The trademark or other intellectual property rights of the person in the domain name

- The extent to which the domain name consists of the legal name of the person or a name that is commonly used to identify that person

- The person's prior use of the domain name for a commercial purpose

- The person's prior use of the domain name for noncommercial purposes

- The person's intent to divert consumers from the mark owner's online location to a site that could harm the good will represented by the mark, either for commercial gain or with the intent to tarnish or disparage the mark

- The person's offer to transfer, sell, or otherwise assign the domain name to the mark owner or any third party for financial gain without having used the domain name in the bona fide offering of any goods or services

- The person's provision of material and misleading false contact information when applying for the registration of the domain name

- The person's registration or acquisitions of multiple domain names that the person knows are identical or confusingly similar to the marks of others

- The extent to which the mark incorporated in the person's domain name registration is or is not distinctive and famous.

## Electronic Signatures and E-Sign

One of the most difficult issues to resolve in the area of consumer rights and the Internet is the role of "electronic signatures." Traditionally, signatures have had a hallowed place in the arena of contract law, where they have been seen as crucial to making a valid contract between parties. But on a computer, it is impossible to sign a name; at least in the traditional way it has been done. Yet consumer transactions between parties require some sort of indication of agreement even over the Internet, some sort of indication there has been a "meeting of the minds."

On Oct. 1, 2000, in answer to these concerns, the E-Sign Act took effect. E-Sign established a uniform federal framework for validating electronic commerce transactions. E-Sign allows electronic signatures for two scenarios: a transaction that occurs in "electronic form," and a transaction that utilizes an electronic signature or electronic record. In both of these scenarios, E-sign upholds the effects of electronic transactions regardless of the type of method of electronic record or signature employed by the transacting parties.

E-Sign applies only to transactions where parties have agreed to do business electronically—through the Internet or other electronic methods. In addition, where an existing law requires that information relating to a transaction be made available to a consumer in writing, a consumer must affirmatively consent to an electronic record in place of the written record, and must be provided with an easy to understand way to withdraw such consent.

E-Sign does not change existing state law regarding the necessity or effect of signatures. It merely provides one more way for such signatures to be recorded.

## Additional Resources

*"Consumer Protection and Antitrust Enforcement at the Speed of Light: The FTC Meets the Internet"* Graubert, John, Jill Coleman, Canada-United States Law Journal, 1999.

*"Fighting Back on the Internet: A Primer on the Anticybersquatting Consumer Protection Act"* Toth, Justin T., Utah Bar Journal, November, 2001.

*"From Wax Seals to Hypertext: Electronic Signatures, Contract Formation and a New Model for Consumer Protection in Internet Transactions"* Balloon, Anthony M., Emory Law Journal, Summer 2001.

*"The New Economania: Consumer Privacy, Bankruptcy, and Venture Capital at Odds in the Internet Marketplace"* Wingate, John M., George Mason Law Review, Spring 2001.

*"The Rise and Fall of Internet Fences: The Overbroad Protection of the Anticybersquatting Consumer Protection Act"* Ward, Jonathon M., Marquette Intellectual Property Law Review, 2001.

## Organizations

### Electronic Frontier Foundation (EFF)
454 Shotwell Street
San Francisco, CA 94110-1914 USA
Phone: (415) 436-9333
Fax: (415) 436-9993
URL: http://www.eff.org/
Primary Contact: Brad Templeton, Chairman of the Board

### Federal Trade Commission (FTC)
600 Pennsylvania Avenue, N.W.
Washington, DC 20580 USA
Phone: (202) 326-2222
URL: http://www.ftc.gov
Primary Contact: Timothy J. Muris, Chairman

### National Consumer Law Center
77 Summer Street, 10th Floor
Boston, MA 02110-1006 USA
Phone: (617) 542-8010
Fax: (617) 542-8028
URL: http://www.consumerlaw.org/
Primary Contact: Willard P. Ogburn, Executive Director

# INTERNET

## FREE SPEECH

*Sections within this essay:*

- Background

- Radio, Television, and the Internet

- The Communications Decency Act of 1996
  - *Reno v. ACLU*
  - The Child Online Protection Act

- Filters
  - The Children's Internet Protection Act
  - The Yahoo! Case

- Anonymity

- Additional Resources

## Background

In the United States, **freedom of speech** is guaranteed by the First Amendment of the U.S. Constitution, the highest law in the land. This law protects what individuals say, what they write, and their right to meet freely with other people in just about any forum: clubs, demonstrations, organizations, and rallies. This cherished protection applies to everyone in the United States.

The advent of the Internet and the huge variety of data it makes accessible has been hailed by free speech advocates as an incredible boon to the United States and the world. On the other hand, the notion that such a vast array of speech can be disseminated so easily and broadly, all without any restrictions or review, concerns and offends many individuals and groups. Some groups have called for an

array of content regulations and restrictions, for example, legislative initiatives that would force electronic communications providers to censor the material they distribute or to deny access to various potential users. On the other side of the debate, there are concerns that such regulation contravenes the protections of the First Amendment, ultimately providing control at the cost of free speech.

The Internet poses certain challenges to traditional First Amendment law. Some groups assert that the Internet should be allowed to regulate itself. These groups assert that government regulations would lag behind the rapidly developing technology. Even so, there have been many attempts to regulate the Internet, and these have frequently raised legal questions and challenges.

## Radio, Television, and the Internet

To use television or radio airtime, get ideas published in a newspaper or magazine, or use traditional types of communications media to share thoughts with thousands or millions of listeners, people must first obtain the approval and assistance of publishers and broadcasters. But, such concerns are not as relevant in cyberspace. On the Internet, people can publish themselves, and their messages are instantly distributed around the globe. Through the Internet and the World Wide Web, individuals now possess an unprecedented degree of freedom regarding the words and images shared with others.

The urge to regulate new communication technologies is certainly nothing new. Practically every new technological communications development has been subjected to the same legislative fervor for review in its earliest days. Even though the U.S. Supreme Court has traditionally vigorously supported First Amendment rights, the Court has been somewhat inconsistent when it applies the First Amendment to providers of mass communications. A typical maneuver is for the Court to find differences in the characteristics of the new medium that it uses to justify different treatment in the First Amendment standards that apply to it.

Previously, radio and television broadcasters encountered similar problems. In the early days of radio, there were calls for restricting broadcasting only to persons licensed by the federal government, and only on the frequencies and at the times assigned to them. Laws such as the Radio Act of 1927 required broadcasters to censor obscene and profane language from their programs. At the same time, the Radio Act purported to prohibit the government's control over the content of broadcasts. In the 1940s, radio broadcasters asserted that such regulations violated their First Amendment rights. But the Supreme Court cited the difference between radio and other forms of communication because it is not available universally. This difference, the Court found, made radio subject to government regulation. One of the consequences of such regulation has been less stringent First Amendment protection for providers of mass communications media. This restricted view dominated legal discourse on the subject for the second half of the twentieth century.

Similar to the legislative and regulatory challenges prior communications media providers endured, there are as of 2002 numerous appeals for legislation and regulation of electronic media. Current events outside the communication industries have also driven the impetus to regulate. For example, after the Oklahoma City bombing, some groups demanded that government control Internet sites on which individuals can learn about making bombs. Following a Carnegie Mellon study on Internet **pornography** and a subsequent Time Magazine article that brought the study's findings to mainstream America, there were fresh calls for immediate legislative and regulatory crackdowns on the content available on electronic networks. These regulations were intended to protect children from seeing materials that would harm them. This Carnegie Mellon study quickly attracted intense criticism for flawed research and distorted statistics of the quantity of porn to be found on the Internet. But public concern pushed attempts by Congress to do something to address these con-

cerns. What resulted was the Communications Decency Act of 1995 (CDA).

The federal courts have helped to provide guidelines for First Amendment rights of online services. The courts have ruled on various challenges to Internet providers and groups who provide content for Web sites. Of course, judicial protection can never be guaranteed. But generally, it is safe to say that the First Amendment allows restriction of speech that is obscene or defamatory in certain situations and the First Amendment does not protect speech that is an imminent threat of action.

The Courts are nevertheless striking out into new territory. For example, in 1991, the Supreme Court case of *Cubby v. CompuServe* helped clarify the parameters of First Amendment protections extended to businesses that provide digitized information. The court held that an online service provider is acting as a kind of digital, profit-based library when it makes publications available online as long as the service provider has no editorial control over the content. This extends First Amendment protections given to news distributors and conventional libraries. In arguing its case, CompuServe asserted that in this age of cyber-publication, there is no way that an online service provider can have knowledge of the content of each message or communication transacted over its service. CompuServe also argued that to do so would be to inappropriately assume editorial control of the speech of its users, and doing so would make the service more like a publisher than a distributor.

## The Communications Decency Act of 1996

The Communications Decency Act of 1996 (CDA) was enacted as a means to prevent the transmission of indecent and patently offensive materials to minors over the Internet. There were two key provisions to the CDA:

1. The first prohibited companies or individuals from knowingly transmitting obscene or indecent messages to anyone under 18.

2. The second prohibited companies or individuals from knowingly sending or displaying patently offensive communications.

The CDA imposed broadcast-style content regulations on the Internet; many felt that this severely restricted the First Amendment rights of U.S. Internet users. Some claimed that the Act threatened the very existence of the Internet itself. A major problem for the CDA, despite its good intentions, was its impracticability. How can such a law be effective at controlling content on a global communications medium when a website in the Netherlands is as accessible as a site in Tulsa?

Soon after the CDA was enacted, the activist group, Citizens Internet Empowerment Coalition (CIEC), was assembled to challenge the CDA. CIEC is a broad coalition of the following groups: book associations, libraries, civil liberties groups, magazines newspapers, online service providers, over 56,000 individual Internet users, and recording industry associations. In terms of composition, CIEC is a fairly good representation of the breadth of the Internet community. CIEC asserted that the Internet is a unique communications medium deserving broad First Amendment protections. Basically, CIEC argued that the inability of Internet users and providers to reliably verify the age of information recipients prevented them from engaging in indecent speech, which traditionally has received strong protection under the First Amendment.

It is important to keep in mind that the CDA was not intended to outlaw child pornography, **obscenity**, or **stalking** children. These acts were made crimes many years earlier under other laws. Rather, the CDA prohibited users from posting indecent or obviously offensive materials in public forums on the Internet. These included chat rooms, newsgroups, online discussion lists, or web pages. Under the CDA, books such as the *Catcher in the Rye, Ulysses, Fanny Hill,* and many other texts, although offensive to some people, have the full protection of the First Amendment if they are published in a newspaper, magazine, or a book, or posted in the public square.

After a lengthy **hearing** that included many examples and on-line demonstrations, a special three-judge district court (which was created by the CDA in anticipation of constitutional challenges) agreed with the groups and ruled that the provisions violated the First Amendment. This decision went to the Supreme Court on appeal.

### Reno v. ACLU

A major U.S. Supreme Court case on Internet free speech is *Reno v. ACLU*. In that case, the Supreme Court struck down the CDA. As part of its ruling, the Court granted the highest level of First Amendment protection to speech conducted over the Internet. In *Reno*, the Court distinguished the Internet which has much weaker First Amendment protections from

broadcast media and placed the Internet squarely among traditional media such as books and newspapers. By doing so, the Court helped establish unequivocally that the Internet is entitled to the broadest First Amendment protections.

In 1997, the Supreme Court held unanimously in *Reno v. American Civil Liberties Union* that the CDA constituted an unconstitutional restriction on speech on the Internet. The court found the Internet to be a "unique and wholly new medium of worldwide human communication" deserving of full First Amendment protection. Lawmakers may only regulate obscenity; consequently, the regulations contained in the CDA would reduce the constitutionally protected material available to adults "to only what is fit for children." According to the Supreme Court, the unique features of Internet communications such as its availability and ease of use were critical to its decision.

### The Child Online Protection Act

In October of 1998, the federal government enacted the Child Online Protection Act (COPA). In some ways, COPA can be described as the "sequel" to CDA. COPA provides criminal penalties for any commercial distribution of information harmful to minors. The law was challenged almost immediately, and in February 1999, the plaintiffs obtained an injunction that prevented the government from enforcing COPA. Eventually, COPA was declared unconstitutional by the Supreme Court on the grounds that each individual who tries to disseminate speech over the Internet would have to conform that speech to the most restrictive and conservative state's standard of what constitutes material harmful to minors.

## Filters

Internet users can publish material that can reach millions of people at very low cost. This differs greatly from television and radio, which have a limited channel capacity and cede little control to viewers or listeners. Additionally, Internet users can control a great deal of the content they receive online. For example, Internet users can prevent their children from viewing certain material by employing inexpensive and easy-to-use technologies that can block or filter content based on the individual tastes and values of parents.

### The Children's Internet Protection Act

In December 1999 Congress passed the Children's Internet Protection Act (CIPA). This legislation requires schools and libraries receiving federal funds for Internet access to install filtering software on their computers in order to block access to materials that are obscene or otherwise harmful to minors. **Civil Rights** and Free Speech advocates filed suit to block implementation of the law citing the potential that filtering software would block protected, harmless, or innocent speech. As of 2002, the case had been argued and the court's opinion was pending.

The plaintiffs in the CIPA case caution that software limiting the availability of electronic material may jeopardize free expression and facilitate government **censorship**. Proponents of filters and rating systems frequently characterize these systems as features or tools. On the other hand, filters and rating systems also are seen as fundamental architectural changes that may actually suppress speech far more than laws ever could. For example, several popular Internet filters block the Web sites of benign **human rights** organizations. Basically, the problem with filters appears to be their inability to consider context. What troubles free speech advocates far more than inadvertent context-based blocking is blocking legitimate sites based on a set of morals or political points of view. In a similar fashion, blocking software at libraries can prevent adults as well as children from getting access to valuable speech in the areas of sex education, abuse recovery discussions, and protected speech concerning lesbian and gay issues.

### The Yahoo! Case

In 2000, a French court ruled that the Internet company, Yahoo!, must ban its French users from English-language sites that auctioned Nazi books and other paraphernalia. Basically, the court was asking Yahoo! to filter out French users to certain parts of its many sites. Yahoo! claimed that because Yahoo.com services are governed by U.S. law, auctions of such materials cannot be barred because of the U.S. constitutional right to freedom of speech. In November 2001, a U.S. District Court ruled that this French decision could not be enforced in U.S. courts. The court held that the First Amendment protects content created in the United States by American companies from regulation by countries that have more restrictive free speech laws. Subsequently, the League Against Racism and Anti-Semitism and the French Union of Jewish Students have sought an appeal claiming that French law should not be overruled by U.S. law.

## Anonymity

Anonymity in the context of communications is the ability to hide one's identity while communicating. Doing so helps individuals to express their political ideas without fear of government intimidation or public retaliation in three important areas:

1. participate in governmental processes

2. membership in political associations

3. the practice of religious belief

In three cases between 1960 to 1999, the Supreme Court reaffirmed the notion that sacrificing anonymity "might deter perfectly peaceful discussions of public matters of importance." Additionally, the Supreme Court has upheld disclosure laws (laws that reduce anonymity in political contexts) only in cases in which the government can demonstrate the existence of a compelling government interest. For example, a compelling governmental interest exists in assuring the integrity of the election process by requiring campaign contribution disclosures.

The feature of anonymity has been embraced by a huge number of Internet users. Some of the venues especially suitable for anonymity are message boards, chatrooms, and various informational sites. Anonymity allows individuals to consume and/or provide unpopular, controversial, or embarrassing information without sacrificing privacy or reputations. But such anonymity is increasingly being assailed as civil litigants have begun using the adversarial **discovery** process to get around online anonymity measures. Since 1998, there have been many **defamation** lawsuits filed against "John Doe" defendants by plaintiffs who **allege** they have been harmed by anonymous Internet postings.

As of 2002, any civil litigant may allege defamation against an Internet poster and bring a civil suit. If, during discovery, the court approves a **subpoena** calling for the identity of a poster, the Internet service provider must disclose the individual's name, even before the poster's statement is proven defamatory. This enables companies or other powerful groups to use the legal discovery process to intimidate anonymous users. This issue has been litigated in New Jersey; that court imposed strict rules to protect the identities of anonymous Internet posters in the discovery process. Nationally, the law is far from settled:

## Additional Resources

*Code and Other Laws of Cyberspace* Lessig, Lawrence, Basic Books, 1999.

*Governance in 'Cyberspace': Access and Public Interest in Global Communications* Grewlich, Klaus W., Kluwer Law International, 1999.

*Issues in Cyberspace: Communication, Technology, Law, and Society on the Internet Frontier* Samoriski, Jan, Allyn and Bacon, 2002.

*The Law of the Internet* 2nd ed. Delta, George B., and Jeffrey H. Matsuura, Aspen Publishers, Inc., 2002.

*Liberating Cyberspace: Civil Liberties, Human Rights, and the Internet* Edited by Liberty (National Council for Civil Liberties), Pluto Press, 1999.

## Organizations

### Computer Professionals for Social Responsibility (CPSR)
PO Box 717
Palo Alto, CA 94302 USA
Phone: (650) 322-3778
Fax: (650) 322-4748
URL: http://www.cpsr.org/

### The Center for Democracy & Technology (CDT)
1634 Eye Street NW, Suite 1100
Washington, DC 20006 USA
Phone: (202) 637-9800
Fax: (202) 637-0968
E-Mail: feedback@cdt.org
URL: http://www.cdt.org/speech/

### Electronic Frontier Foundation (EFF)
454 Shotwell Street
San Francisco, CA 94110-1914 USA
Phone: (415) 436-9333
Fax: (415) 436-9993
URL: http://www.eff.org/

### Freedom Forum
1101 Wilson Blvd.
Arlington, VA 22209 USA
Phone: (703) 528-0800
Fax: (703) 284-3770
E-Mail: news@freedomforum.org
URL: http://www.freedomforum.org/

### People for the American Way (PFAW)
2000 M Street NW, Suite 400
Washington, DC 20036 USA
Phone: (202) 467-4999
Fax: (202) 293-2672
E-Mail: pfaw@pfaw.org
URL: http://www.pfaw.org/

# INTERNET

## INTERNET CRIME

*Sections within this essay:*

## Background

Internet crime is among the newest and most constantly evolving areas of American law. Although the Internet itself is more than three decades old, greater public usage began in the late 1980s with widespread **adoption** only following in the 1990s. During that decade the Net was transformed from its modest military and academic roots into a global economic tool, used daily by over 100 million Americans and generating upwards of $100 billion in domestic revenue annually. But as many aspects of business, social, political, and cultural life moved online, so did crime, creating new challenges for lawmakers and law enforcement.

Crime on the Net takes both old and new forms. The medium has facilitated such traditional offenses as **fraud** and child **pornography**. But it has also given rise to unique technological crimes, such as electronic intrusion in the form of hacking and computer viruses. High-speed Internet accounts helped fuel a proliferation of **copyright infringement** in software, music, and movie **piracy**. National security is also threatened by the Internet's potential usefulness for **terrorism**. Taken together, these crimes have earned a new name: when FBI Director Louis J. Freeh addressed the U. S. Senate in 2000, he used the widely-accepted term "cybercrime."

Lawmakers have scrambled to keep up with cybercrime. The skyrocketing growth of Internet usage and the rapid advance of technology quickly revealed the inadequacy of existing laws, particularly those drafted to fight **computer crime** in the mid-1980s. In the 1990s, headlines frequently announced high-profile cyber crimes such as the estimated $80 million in damages caused by the nationwide outbreak of the computer virus Melissa in 1999, unauthorized intrusion into military computer systems, and brazen hacker attacks that ranged from denying service to major **corporate** websites to defacing U. S. government websites of the CIA, FBI, and others. Simultaneously, the computer software industry announced massive losses due to piracy, $12 billion in 1999 alone, according to the Washington-based Business Software Association (BSA), the leading U.S. software industry watchdog. Regarding these concerns, Congress acted repeatedly. Its legislative response ranges from provisions governing hacking, viruses, and denial of service attacks to fraud, **obscenity**, copyright infringement, and terrorism.

- The **Counterfeit** Access Device and Computer Fraud and Abuse Act of 1984 launched federal cybercrime law. The law safeguarded classified government information as well as certain financial information stored digitally, while also creating offenses for malicious damage of computer systems and trafficking in stolen computer passwords. It was superseded by the Computer Fraud and Abuse Act of 1986, which was amended significantly in 1994, 1996, and 2001, and remains the backbone of federal Internet law.

- The Electronic Communications Privacy Act of 1986 was passed to prevent the unauthorized interception of digital communications and later amended to specifically bar unauthorized reading of e-mail by third parties, network operators, and Internet access providers.

- The National Information Infrastructure Protection Act of 1996 expanded the Computer Fraud and Abuse Act. Amendments covered the confidentiality, integrity, and availability of computer networks, essentially broadening the definition of computer hacking punishable under federal law.

- The No-Electronic Theft Act (NET Act) of 1997 tightened restrictions on the reproduction and dissemination of copyrighted intellectual property like software, music, and movies, while the Digital Millennium Copyright Act (DMCA) of 1998 prohibited the circumvention of copyright protection systems.

- The Communications Decency Act (CDA) of 1996 criminalized the dissemination of obscene or indecent material to children over computer networks. It was ruled unconstitutional under the First Amendment in 1997.

- The Child Online Protection Act (COPA) of 1998 modified the scope of the CDA by criminalizing the use of the World Wide Web to sell material harmful to minors. It, too, was ruled unconstitutional in a case that has since been granted review by the Supreme Court.

- The Protection of Children from Sexual Predators Act of 1998 included Internet-specific provisions for reporting child pornography to authorities and prohibiting federal prisoners from unsupervised Internet usage.

- The Patriot Act of 2001 was passed in response to terrorist attacks upon the United States. Modifying the Computer Fraud and Abuse Act, it provides new investigative powers to the U. S. attorney general to order monitoring of Internet communication and usage for the purpose of protecting national security.

## Fraud

Fraud is the broadest category of cybercrime. Fraud includes many types of criminal activity, ranging from credit card abuse, wire fraud, and business fraud to misrepresentation and the failure to deliver purchases. The Federal Trade Commission monitors and regulates Internet commerce, and it maintains advice for avoiding fraud at its website:http://www.ftc.gov/bcp/menu-internet.htm. The Federal Bureau of Investigation investigates and prosecutes cybercrimes. In partnership with several federal agencies, the FBI maintains the Internet Fraud Complaint Center online for accepting complaints at http://www1.ifccfbi.gov/index.asp.

Traditional **consumer protection** laws apply to fraud on the Internet, but federal law also contains specific Internet-related laws as well. First among these is fraud involving access devices. Federal law defines access devices as cards, codes, account numbers, serial numbers, and so forth that are used to obtain money, goods, and services or to initiate a transfer of funds. A typical example is the **fraudulent** use of another person's credit card over the Internet.

The law targets several forms of fraud regarding the use of access devices:

- Producing, using, or trafficking in access devices

- Obtaining anything of value aggregating $1,000 or more during a one-year period

- Possessing fifteen or more counterfeit or unauthorized access devices

- Possessing or controlling **counterfeiting** access device equipment

- Effecting transactions with access devices issued to another person

- Offering to sell access devices or information on how to obtain them

- Possessing equipment modified to obtain unauthorized use of telecommunications services

- Possessing "scanning receivers" capable of intercepting wire or electronic communication

- Possessing hardware or software that modifies telecommunications identifying information in order to obtain unauthorized telecommunications service

- Unauthorized charges to credit cards

Penalties for violations range from fines to **imprisonment** from between five to 10 years per offense.

## Unauthorized Computer Access

### Types of Unauthorized Access

Popularly known as hacking, unauthorized computer access is a crime punishable under the Computer Fraud and Abuse Act (as codified in 28 U.S.C. ¤ 1029). The law begins by defining hacking in two ways:

- Unauthorized access to computer systems

- Access that exceeds a person's authorized limits

The prohibition thus covers trespassers who have no right at all to use a given computer, as well as those who are allowed to use a given computer but manage to access parts of the system that are off limits.

### National Security

The Computer Fraud and Abuse Act creates a separate offense of unauthorized or exceeded authorization in access for purposes that are damaging to national security. These crimes include obtaining state secrets protected by **statute** or Executive order, along with military data or any information governed by the Atomic Energy Act of 1954, when such information could be used to injure the nation or to provide an advantage to a foreign nation. Minimum penalties may include fines, imprisonment for up to ten years, or both.

### Illegally Obtaining Information

Federal law broadly prohibits hacking in order to gain information. It criminalizes obtaining three categories of information from different types of computer systems:

- Financial data, including records of financial institutions, credit card companies, and credit bureaus

- Information from any department or agency of the United States

- Information from any computer used in interstate or foreign communication

These are known in the Computer Fraud and Abuse Act as "protected" computer systems. The last category—computers used in interstate or foreign communication - essentially covers most computers connected to the Internet. The law does not go into detail on the types of information it intends to protect; instead, the intent is to prohibit unauthorized access to any information on protected systems. Minimum penalties may include fines, imprisonment for up to one year, or both.

### Affecting U.S. Government Computers

The law forbids any unauthorized access of computers belonging to, or used by, a department or agency of the U. S. Government if the access merely "affects" their usage. As with the prohibition on gaining unauthorized information, the law is generally written in broad language to encompass the widest range of possible offenses. Minimum penalties may include fines, imprisonment for up to one year, or both.

### Intent to Defraud

A separate offense occurs when a person gains unauthorized access with the intent to **defraud**. The law is violated if anything of value is obtained. Minimum penalties may include fines, imprisonment for up to five years, or both.

### Damaging Computers

Damage is defined as any impairment to the integrity or availability of data in any of four ways:

- The damage causes loss aggregating at least $5,000 in value during any 1-year period to one or more individuals

- The damage modifies or impairs, or potentially modifies or impairs, medical diagnosis, treatment, or care of one or more individuals

- The damage causes physical injury to a person

- The damage threatens public health or safety

Three grades of damage to computer systems are defined. In increasing degree of severity, these are:

- Damage

- Reckless damage

- Intentional damage

Damage is distinguished by criminal intent. Mere damage involves all forms of injury to data or equipment that were not intended yet still occurred. Reckless damage involves **negligence**, the result of the criminal's carelessness. The third category, intentional damage, involves knowingly transmitting "a program, information, code, or command" that leads to damage. Examples of intentional damage include maliciously deleting files on a computer or releasing a computer virus or worm.

Convictions on any of the offenses can lead to fines, imprisonment, or both, with the prison sentences scaling upwards depending upon intent. Damage carries a **penalty** of one year of imprisonment. Reckless damage carries a penalty of up to five years imprisonment. Intentional damage is a **felony** and carries a penalty of up to five years.

### Password Trafficking

Typically, passwords for computer access or online accounts are restricted to individuals. Since computer hackers often need to obtain them in order to enter systems without being detected, the law targets the illegal acquisition, sharing, or dealing in passwords. Two conditions trigger an offense:

- The trafficking must affect interstate or foreign commerce

- The computer is used by or for the U. S. Government

Minimum penalties may include fines, imprisonment for up to one year, or both.

### Extortion

**Extortion** occurs when a person communicates a threat to damage a protected computer system with the goal of obtaining some reward, such as money. This element of the law addresses a widely publicized trend in the 1990s involving hackers who sought to profit from their ability to infiltrate the security of computer systems.

Unauthorized access with intentional extortion is an offense when committed upon any of the following:

- Person

- Firm

- Association

- Educational Institution

- Financial Institution

- Government entity

- Other legal entity

Minimum penalties may include fines, imprisonment for up to five years, or both.

### Additional Penalties and Legal Recourse

The Computer Fraud and Abuse Act prescribes penalties for either attempting or actually committing its offenses. The minimum penalties for each offense are only available to first-time offenders who are not convicted in conjunction with other offenses under the law. For multiple and repeat offenses, the law doubles the prescribed imprisonment time.

Besides these criminal penalties, the law specifically provides for civil lawsuits. Thus anyone who suffers damage or loss through a violation of the Computer Fraud and Abuse Act can bring suit against the violator and seek **compensatory damages**, court orders to end specific behavior, or other forms of relief. Such lawsuits must be brought within two years of the date of the complaint or the date of the **discovery** of the damage.

## Damaging Communications Lines, Stations, or Systems

In addition to the damage provisions under the Computer Fraud and Abuse Act, broad protections to the nation's communication infrastructure are found in Federal law at 18 U.S.C. ¤ 1362. The law criminalizes damaging any of the communications systems operated or controlled by the United States. These crimes include maliciously obstructing, hindering, or delaying the transmission of any communication. Penalties may include fines, imprisonment for up to ten years, or both.

## Interception and Disclosure of wire, Oral, or Electronic Communications

Federal law protects communication over the Internet in much the same way it protects communication by the more traditional means of telephone and mail. Just as it has long been a federal offense to intercept another person's telephone calls or mail, it is illegal to intercept or disclose communications that occur over the Internet as e-mail, voice mail, Internet-based telephone calls, or any other private Internet-based communication.

Under 18 U.S.C. ¤ 2511, federal law specifically protects individuals from eavesdropping and companies from industrial **espionage**. All third parties are prohibited from unauthorized interception or disclosure of private communications, except under certain exceptions. Exceptions to the prohibition cover employees of the Federal Communications Commission (FCC), law enforcement personnel, and the employees of Internet service providers. FCC employees may intercept communications in the course of monitoring responsibilities for enforcement of federal communications law. Generally, law enforcement personnel require court approval in order to intercept private communications; however, in certain cases involving national security, this is not required. Employees of Internet service providers are banned from intercepting private communications except in the normal course of their employment under certain exceptions:

- The interception is necessary incident to the rendition of his or her service or to the protection of the rights or property of the Internet provider

- Observing or random monitoring is only permissible for mechanical or service quality control checks

- The service has been ordered by law enforcement officials to intercept communications in the course of a criminal investigation

Penalties may include fines, imprisonment from one to five years, or both.

## Terrorism

In response to terrorist attacks upon the United States on September 11, 2001, Congress passed the Patriot Act of 2001. This law provides several new powers to the U.S. attorney general to combat terrorism. Several provisions relate to cybercrime and electronic **evidence**:

- Expanded authority for ordering wiretapping in a wider range of criminal investigations

- Relaxed restrictions for obtaining access to voice-mail and stored voice communications

- Expanded scope of data that can be subpoenaed, such as Internet access logs and other digital records of Internet usage

- Expanded authority for obtaining access to cable Internet records previously kept private by cable TV laws

- Provided grounds for Internet service providers to make voluntary emergency disclosures to law enforcement about customer records in emergencies involving immediate risk of death or serious physical injury to any person

- Removes geographical restrictions on tracing Internet and other electronic communication

- Expands authority to monitor actions of computer trespassers

- Permits federal courts to issue nationwide search warrants for e-mail

- Raises certain penalties for computer hackers to prevent and deter "cyberterrorism"

- Creates a new offense for damaging computers used for national security and criminal justice

Because of concerns about civil liberties, several of the new powers are temporary. Subject to so-called sunset provisions, they expire on December 31, 2005 unless renewed by Congress. Lawmakers built in these limitations in recognition of the potential for abuse of such powers, which they wished to limit to usage in combating the extraordinary dangers presented by the war on terrorism.

## Unlawful Access to Stored Communications

Besides criminalized illegal interception of communication as it occurs, federal law prohibits unauthorized access to stored communications. Under 18 U.S.C. ¤ 2701, it is illegal to intentionally gain access or exceed authorized access to a facility that provides an electronic communication service, such as an Internet provider that handles e-mail. The law spells out two main offenses:

- Accessing the service without authorization or exceeding authorization

- Obtaining, altering, or preventing proper access to the service's stored communications

Minimum penalties include fines and prison sentences of six months. However, if the offense is committed for purposes of commercial advantage, malicious destruction or damage, or private commercial gain, prison sentences may range from one to two years.

## Pornography and Sexual Predators

Federal law regarding pornography on the Internet remained tied up in the courts in 2001. During the previous decade, Congress twice enacted laws aimed at protecting children from exposure to pornography. The Communications Decency Act of 1996 broadly criminalized the dissemination of obscene or indecent material to minors over computer networks but was ruled unconstitutional the following year in Reno v. ACLU. In response, Congress modified the law, enacting the Child Online Protection Act (COPA) of 1998. COPA narrowed the scope of the previous law by criminalizing the act of selling material harmful to minors over the World Wide Web. Following a ruling that it was also unconstitutional, the case was on appeal to the Supreme Court with a decision expected in 2002.

However, while pornography remains widely available on the Internet, child pornography is treated severely under the law. Both federal and state law enforcement agencies routinely target child pornography online, and both U. S. Customs and the FBI maintain programs that encourage citizen reporting of criminal images of minors found on websites.

Specific Internet offenses are targeted in portions of the Protection of Children From Sexual Predators Act of 1998:

- Provides for the prosecution of individuals for the production of child pornography if the materials have been mailed, shipped, or transported in interstate or foreign commerce, including by computer

- Requires Internet service providers to report evidence of child pornography offenses to law enforcement agencies

- Prohibits Federal prisoners from being allowed Internet access without supervision

by a government official, and urges that state prisons adopt the same policy

- Directs the attorney general to request that the National Academy of Science study technological approaches to the problem of the availability of pornographic material to children on the Internet

## Copyright Violations

The problem of piracy — unauthorized storage, copying, or dissemination of copyrighted material such as computer software, music, movies and books — burgeoned along with the growth of the Internet. Existing federal copyright law makes it a crime to duplicate, store, or disseminate copyrighted materials for profit. But under the No Electronic Theft Act of 1997, it is also illegal merely to reproduce or distribute copyrighted works even without the defendant's having a commercial purpose or private financial gain. This aspect of the law targets the popular free trade of copyrighted material on the Internet.

Federal copyright law provides for both criminal and **civil action** against offenders. Criminal penalties may include fines, jail sentences up to three years, or both. Civil penalties can reach as high as $150,000 per violation.

The Digital Millennium Copyright Act (DMCA) of 1998 marked the first significant revision of federal copyright law in a generation. Among its chief reforms, the law made it a criminal offense to bypass or defeat security provisions built into products by manufacturers to prevent copying. The applicability of that aspect of the law to the Internet was shown in Universal City v. Reimerdes (2001). In that high-profile case, a federal appeals court upheld a lower court verdict that a hacker website violated the DMCA by publishing information about defeating the anti-copying protection software built into movie DVDs.

## State Laws and Policing

Most states have enacted Internet laws. Generally, these laws have evolved alongside and therefore mirror federal law. Most state Internet laws criminalize fraudulent use of computer systems for hacking, damage to computer systems, and unauthorized interception of communication. Several laws have enacted statutes that extend their existing laws on traditional crimes to the Internet, such as a 1995

Connecticut state law that targets online **stalking**: the law creates criminal liability for sending messages with intent to harass, annoy, or alarm another person. And while Congress in 2000 and 2001 often debated the issue, most states have enacted their own laws to ban online gambling.

More than a dozen states have passed laws targeting online pornography and sexual predators. Generally, these laws have sought to protect minors from access to porn or other material deemed harmful, such as California's 1997 law, or they have extended state child pornography laws to cover Internet images, as Kansas and Georgia both did as early as 1995. But as with federal legislation in this area, not all state laws have survived legal challenges. In 1997, a federal court overturned New York State's anti-pornography law in ALA v. Pataki, ruling that its ban on sending "indecent" materials to minors over the Internet was an unconstitutional regulation of commerce. Georgia was also prohibited in 1997 from enforcing a statute that made it a criminal offense to communicate anonymously over the Internet in an attempt to protect children from sexual predators; the law was held unconstitutionally vague and overbroad in ACLU v. Miller.

In the twenty-first century, states are also adopting proactive law enforcement policies. Examples include Washington State, which in 2000 launched a combined federal-state program called the Computer Law Enforcement of Washington (CLEW) initiative. Under CLEW, local, state and federal law enforcement agencies share information, maintain a high-tech crime strike force, and publish tips online to help fight fraud and other crime. Several states, such as New Jersey, established special cybercrime units in order to investigate crimes from industrial espionage to drug trafficking. Because of the cross-jurisdictional nature of much Internet crime, state attorneys general have also pursued innovative information-sharing programs. Legal observers expect to see further law enforcement cooperation among states.

## Additional Resources

*A Parent's Guide to Internet Safety* FBI, 2001. Available at: http://www.fbi.gov/publications/pguide/pguide.htm.

*Computer Crime and Intellectual Property Section (CCIPS)* Criminal Division of the U. S. Department of Justice, 2001. Available at: http://www.cybercrime.gov.

*Consumer Protection: E-Commerce and the Internet.* Federal Trade Commission, 2001. Available at: http://www.ftc.gov/bcp/menu-internet.htm.

*Cybercrime.* Statement by Louis J. Freeh, Director of Federal Bureau of Investigation, in Senate testimony, February 16, 2000. Available at: http://www.fbi.gov/congress/congress00/cyber021600.htm.

*Internet Fraud Preventive Measures* FBI Internet Fraud Complaint Center, 2001. Available at: http://www1.ifccfbi.gov/strategy/fraudtips.asp.

*Software Piracy and the Law* Business Software Alliance, 2001. Available at: http://www.bsa.org/usa/freetools/consumers/swandlaw_c.phtml.

*U. S. Code, Title 18, Section 1029: Fraud and Related Activity in Connection with Access Devices.* U.S. Congress. Available at: http://www.usdoj.gov/criminal/cybercrime/usc1029.htm.

*U. S. Code, Title 18, Section 1030: Fraud and Related Activity in Connection with Computers* Available at: http://www.usdoj.gov/criminal/cybercrime/1030_new.html.

*U. S. Code, Title 18, Section 1362: Communication Lines, Stations, or Systems* Available at: http://www.usdoj.gov/criminal/cybercrime/usc1362.htm.

*U. S. Code, Title 18, Section 2511: Interception and Disclosure of Wire, Oral, or Electronic Communications Prohibited.* Available at: http://www.usdoj.gov/criminal/cybercrime/usc2511.htm.

*U. S. Code, Title 18, Section 2701: Unlawful Access to Stored Communications* Available at: http://www.usdoj.gov/criminal/cybercrime/usc2701.htm.

*U. S. Code, Title 18, Section 2702: Disclosure of Contents* Available at: http://www.usdoj.gov/criminal/cybercrime/usc2702.htm.

*West Encyclopedia of American Law* West Group, 1998.

## Organizations

### Business Software Alliance (BSA)
1150 18th St. NW, Suite 700
Washington, DC 20036 USA
Phone: (888) 667-4722
URL: http://www.bsa.org
Primary Contact: Robert Holleyman, President

### Federal Bureau of Investigation
J. Edgar Hoover Building, 935 Pennsylvania Avenue, NW
Washington, DC 20535-0001 USA
Phone: (202) 324-3000
Fax: ()
URL: http://www.fbi.gov
Primary Contact: Robert S. Mueller III, Director

## Federal Trade Commission

CRC-240
Washington, DC 20580 USA
Phone: (877) 382-4357
Fax: ()
URL: http://www.fbi.gov
Primary Contact: Timothy J. Muris, Chairman

## National Infrastructure Protection Center

J. Edgar Hoover Building, 935 Pennsylvania
Avenue, NW
Washington, DC 20535-0001 USA
Phone: (888) 585-9078
Fax: (202) 323-2079
URL: http://www.nipc.gov
Primary Contact: Ron Dick, Director

# INTERNET

## INTERNET FILTERS IN SCHOOLS AND LIBRARIES

*Sections within this essay:*

- Background

- Filtering Restrictions
    - Institutions Affected
    - Compliance
    - Internet Safety Policy
    - Filtering
    - Disabling Filters
    - Timetable
    - Enforcement
    - Expedited Legal Review

- State and Local Restrictions on School and Library Internet Usage

- Additional Resources

## Background

Internet filters are software programs that control what is shown while a computer user is viewing pages on the World Wide Web. Emerging on the commercial market for home use in the mid-to-late 1990s, the filters are designed to protect minors from viewing **pornography**, hate speech, and other controversial online content. They work by intercepting and blocking attempts to view particular web pages and their controls cannot be disabled except by an administrator. Marketed primarily toward parents who wish to allow their children to surf the Internet without constant adult supervision, filters currently available include Cyber Patrol, Net Nanny, and Cyber Snoop.

Government interest in filters emerged after early, unsuccessful attempts to directly regulate Internet content. Prompted by the explosion of popularity in Internet usage in the early 1990s, lawmakers responded to public complaints about the accessibility of pornography. While such imagery represented only a small percentage of web sites, studies have shown it amounts to as little as 2%, Internet search engines made locating the material easy even for young people. Thus, unlike with printed material controlled at the point of sale in newsstands and bookstores, minors using the Internet could obtain or accidentally suffer exposure to hard core pornography. In an effort to combat this problem, Congress first sought to control what could be shown on web pages.

- The Communications Decency Act of 1996 (CDA) was passed to prohibit Internet users from communicating material that would be deemed offensive to minors under contemporary community standards. The controversial law carried fines and **imprisonment** for offenders, but enforcement was immediately blocked by a federal court. Attacked by critics as **censorship**, the law was later overturned unanimously by the Supreme Court as an unconstitutional violation of the First Amendment in Reno v. ACLU in 1997.

- The Child Online Protection Act of 1998 (COPA) was passed to meet the objections of the Supreme Court to the CDA. The new law attempted to be more specific in order to overcome constitutional problems, this time targeting commercial purveyors of material deemed harmful to minors. However, in 1999, it, too, was immediately blocked by a court injunction, and subsequently a district court and federal appeals court both found the law unconstitutional because it would require every Web page to abide by the most restrictive community standards. The Supreme Court agreed to hear an appeal, ACLU v. Ashcroft, scheduled for 2002.

- When the courts proved unwilling to allow federal control of what was communicated, lawmakers pursued a new avenue. Internet filtering offered a mechanism by which the law could control what was received on publicly–funded computers connected to the Internet. In December 2000, Congress passed both the Children's Internet Protection Act (CIPA) and the Neighborhood Internet Protection Act (Neighborhood Act), highly similar bills that were added to an appropriations measure, signed by President William J. Clinton and enacted as **Public Law** 106-554. Together, the two acts place restrictions on Internet usage in public libraries and public schools that receive federal funding. For enforcement, the law employs a carrot and stick approach: continued computer and Internet funding depends upon libraries and schools using filtering software and, in some cases, establishing broader controls as part of a new, comprehensive Internet safety policy.

Federally-required Internet filtering in schools and libraries immediately proved as controversial as earlier congressional measures. In particular, critics argued that Internet filtering software is highly imprecise; it has the tendency to erroneously block harmless, non-pornographic material as well because it cannot determine the context in which the material it filters appears. As the law went into effect in Spring 2001, **litigation** promptly followed. Separate lawsuits brought by the American Library Association (ALA) and another by a coalition including publishers and civil liberties groups challenged the law on First Amendment grounds similar to those brought successfully against the CDA and COPA. After a court found that both challenges have valid legal grounds to continue, trial was scheduled to begin in February 2002.

## Filtering Restrictions

### Institutions Affected

Public elementary and secondary schools and public libraries are required to certify annual compliance with the law if they wish to maintain eligibility for federal funding for computers and/or Internet access. The extent to which they are regulated depends upon what types of federal funding they already receive. There are three distinct federal programs that provide subsidies to institutions for Internet access, service, internal connections, and personal computers:

- Universal Service (E-rate) discounts for Internet access, Internet service, or internal connections.

- Library Services and Technology Act (LSTA) state grant funding to buy computers used to access the Internet or to pay direct Internet access costs.

- Title III funding under the Elementary and Secondary Education Act (ESEA) to buy computers used to access the Internet or to pay direct Internet access costs.

The libraries and schools that receive E-rate funding face the broadest range of new requirements, including installation of filters, public notification and participation, and other measures. The law governs all such federal funding, whether it is disbursed directly or through a state intermediary agency. However, it does not apply to academic or college libraries, which do not qualify for the types of federal funding in question.

### Compliance

Lawmakers gave the Federal Communications Commission (FCC) regulatory authority over the law. In the broadest possible application of the rules for eligibility, institutions must meet three requirements:

- Adopt an Internet safety policy.

- Provide notice and hold at least one public meeting on the proposed Internet safety policy.

- Certify that they have adopted and implemented the policy, which must include Internet filters.

For eligibility for E-rate funding, institutions must meet all three requirements. However, those institutions receiving only LSTA or ESEA funding must only meet the filter requirement.

## Internet Safety Policy

The Internet safety policy requirement covers five areas. It is designed to be a comprehensive policy governing Internet usage by minors in public schools and libraries and, as such, goes beyond the issue of filtering web pages. More broadly, libraries and schools must monitor several types of Internet usage. Under FCC rules, the policy must address five key areas.

- Access by minors to "inappropriate matter" on the Internet and the World Wide Web.

- The safety and security of minors when using electronic mail, chat rooms, and other forms of direct electronic communications.

- Unauthorized access, including so-called "hacking," and other unlawful online activities by minors.

- Unauthorized disclosure, use, and dissemination of personal information regarding minors.

- Measures designed to restrict minors' access to materials harmful to minors.

Prior to adopting an Internet safety policy, schools and libraries must provide public notice of the process and hold at least one public **hearing** or meeting on the proposed policy. The actual adopted policy must be available for review by the FCC.

## Filtering

The Internet safety policy must include what the law defines as a "technology protection measure," i.e., a software filter or blocker that prevents the display of certain visual depictions, photographs, and illustrations. No particular brand of filter is required, however, but the filter must perform specific duties. It must govern Internet access by both adults and minors and block three types of visual depictions.

- **Obscenity**.

- Child pornography.

- Material that is "harmful to minors."

The law does not provide an express definition of obscenity. Under Miller v. California in 1973, the Supreme Court laid out its famous three-part "community standards" test now typically used to determine what is obscene. The test requires a court determination of three parts:

- Whether "the average person, applying contemporary community standards," would find that the material, taken as a whole, appeals to the prurient interest.

- Whether the work depicts or describes, in a patently offensive way, sexual conduct specifically defined by the applicable state or federal law to be obscene.

- Whether the work, taken as a whole, lacks serious literary, artistic, political, or scientific value.

The Internet law goes into some specific detail as to what constitutes material "harmful to minors," who are defined as anyone under the age of 17. It states that the term "means any picture, image, graphic image file, or other visual depiction" that has the following characteristics:

- Taken as a whole and with respect to minors, appeals to a prurient interest in nudity, sex, or excretion.

- Depicts, describes, or represents in a patently offensive way with respect to what is suitable for minors, an actual or simulated sexual act or sexual contact, actual or simulated normal or perverted sexual acts, or a lewd exhibition of the genitals.

- Taken as a whole, lacks serious literary, artistic, political, or scientific value as to minors.

Adults are not subject to the restrictions on material harmful to minors. Text on web pages is not regulated under the law like visual depictions are.

The law makes a further distinction between what is "harmful" to minors and what is merely "inappropriate" for minors. While it carefully defines harmful material, it leaves the definition of inappropriate material up to local community control. The FCC declined to be more specific in this area in its rule-making capacity, instead leaving such definitions up to school boards, library boards, and other local authorities.

## Disabling Filters

Under some circumstances, Internet filters may be legally disabled. While forbidding Internet users to disable the filters themselves, the law permits a school or library administrator to disable filtering software in order to allow bona fide research or other lawful use by an adult. However, the law does not specify what constitutes such usage. In its April 2001 rules, the FCC acknowledged criticism of this measure: libraries complained that the law's vagueness meant they would be required to spend considerable time determining the validity of each adult request for filter disabling. Nevertheless, the FCC here, too, declined to be more specific. The commission noted that prescribing rules would "have a chilling effect" on adults' Internet usage and "significantly impinge" on library staff time and resources. As such all libraries must develop their own policies.

### Timetable

Congress and the FCC do not expect these changes to occur overnight. In each affected federal program, the law phases in its requirements over two years. For the first year, the deadline of October 28, 2001, was established for schools and libraries to certify that they are taking steps to put in place their Internet safety policy. In the second year, these institutions must demonstrate that their policies and the required filtering technology is in place. As such, some library patrons may not encounter filtering software until 2002 or later.

### Enforcement

The law prescribes different types of enforcement. In each case, the responsible funding agencies must make determinations about compliance. For institutions receiving E-rate funding, failure to submit certification annually will result in ineligibility, and failure to comply with the law can result in institutions being suspended or required to reimburse funding. For those receiving funds under ESEA or LSTA programs, the responsible funding agency may withhold further payments, suspend the funding, or issue a complaint to compel compliance; recovery of funding is, however, specifically prohibited.

Complaints about an institution could lead to an agency finding that it is out of compliance. However, legal analysts are in doubt as to whether the law creates a cause of action —legal grounds that may serve as the basis for litigation—for citizens to sue institutions over failure to comply.

### Expedited Legal Review

Foreseeing likely legal challenges to the law, Congress provided for any litigation contesting its constitutionality to receive expedited **judicial review** first by a three-judge federal appeals panel and, if necessary, by the Supreme Court.

## State and Local Restrictions

Even before enactment of the 2000 federal law, five states had passed their own statutes. Nearly 20 states had some form of legislation under consideration in 2001. Most of these laws are directed at libraries, some at schools, and at least one mandates that no filters be used at all in public libraries.

During the late 1990s, cities, counties, and library boards began enacting Internet usage policies that varied widely and often differed from community to community in the same state. Michigan demonstrates this variety. In Holland, Michigan, where the nation's first ballot measure on library Internet filters was held in February 2000, residents of the 32,000-strong city voted 55 percent to 45 percent against the proposal, despite heavy spending by proponents such as the American Family Association in a controversial political battle that attracted national attention. Nearby Georgetown Township, which is slightly larger, installed filters. And then later in the year, the state enacted a law requiring filters, rendering local differences moot.

For the nation's nearly 9,000 public libraries, the issue is still clearly unsettled. Some had already begun installing filters independently in the late 1990s, and the American Library Association estimated that as many as 25 percent had done so by 2001. However, most had resisted filtering. The ALA reported that many had adopted resolutions similar to its 1997 anti-filtering declaration, which holds that federally-mandated filtering is unconstitutional and violates the organization's Library **Bill of Rights**. For thousands of libraries, the ALA's pending litigation against the federal filtering law is closely watched and will ultimately shape future policies.

In two cases, filtering advocates have lost legal challenges. In 1998, in Mainstream Loudoun V. Board of Trustees of Loudoun County, a federal district court in Virginia ruled that a library violated the First Amendment by using filtering software. In 2001, a California federal appeals court upheld a ruling that rejected a parent's lawsuit against a library where her 12-year-old son downloaded sexually-explicit photos on the library's Internet connection. The court in Kathleen R. v. City of Livermore held that the city is not subject to suit for damages, nor could it be forced to censor the Internet usage of its library patrons.

Not all legal action on library filtering has focused upon the needs of library patrons. In a Minneapolis, Minnesota dispute that attracted national attention, twelve librarians filed **sexual harassment** claims based on unwanted exposure to patrons viewing pornography on the library's Internet computers.

They argued that such exposure subjected them to a so-called "hostile work environment," one of the legal standards commonly pursued under sexual harassment law. In June 2001, the U. S. Equal Employment Opportunity Commission agreed with their complaint.

More broadly than public libraries, a majority of schools have adopted restrictive Internet policies. In 2000, a national survey by Quality Education Data Inc. found that more than 90 percent of teachers reported that schools had established acceptable use policies for Internet usage. Often these policies have involved installing software solutions, whether fitting each computer with off-the-shelf filters, blocking data at the school server level, or monitoring student Internet activity with so-called "sniffing" software that inspects their communication for behavior such as illegally downloading copyrighted music or seeking weapons information.

The following states and cities have enacted specific filtering legislation. However, other state and local laws may also apply to Internet usage on public computers. Concerned individuals can check with their school or library for a copy of its Internet usage policy.

ARIZONA: Public schools are required to filter Internet services to prevent minors from accessing harmful material, with each school district prescribing its own standards and rules. Public libraries must equip computers with Internet filters, implement policies, and follow statewide library rules. Schools and libraries in compliance with the law are protected from criminal liability and liability for damages.

KENTUCKY: Public schools are required to be filtered via so-called proxy software installed on Internet servers. However, schools and districts are free to exercise control over what they consider inappropriate.

MICHIGAN: Public libraries are required to choose from three options for preventing children from accessing inappropriate Internet sites. They may install filters, monitor children's behavior, or require adult supervision.

MINNESOTA: Public and school libraries are required to block Internet access for obscenity and child pornography for both adults and children. They may choose between using either filtering software or "other effective methods."

SAN FRANCISCO: The city banned the use of Internet filters on most public-access library computers, thus codifying a 1999 San Francisco Public Library policy in opposition to filters.

SOUTH CAROLINA: Public and school libraries must filter computers for pornographic pictures or text; those not in compliance face losing half their state funding.

TENNESSEE: All public school computers have Internet web pages filtered system wide, making the state the first in the nation to employ this approach.

## Additional Resources

*Children's Internet Protection Act and the Neighborhood Internet Protection Act, as contained in Public Law 106-554* Available at: http://www.ala.org/cipa/Law.PDF

*"CIPA's Internet Filter Software Mandate Takes Effect."* Brian Matross. InternetLawJournal.com. June 3, 2001. Available at: http://www.tilj.com/content/ecomheadline06030101.htm

*"Digital Chaperones for Kids: Which Internet Filters Protect the Best? Which Get in the Way?"* Consumer Reports Online. March 2001. Available at: http://www.consumerreports.org

*"Filth, Filtering, and the First Amendment: Ruminations on Public Libraries' Use of Internet Filtering Software"* Bernard Bell. Federal Communications Law Journal. March, 2001.

*"Fahrenheit 451.2: Is Cyberspace Burning? How Rating and Blocking Proposals May Torch Free Speech on the Internet."* Ann Beeson, et al. American Civil Liberties Union. 1997 Available at: http://www.aclu.org/issues/cyber/burning.html

*"The Internet Filter Farce."* Geoffrey Nunberg. The American Prospect. Volume 12, Issue 1. January 1-15, 2001.

## Organizations

### American Library Association (ALA)
1301 Pennsylvania Avenue NW, Ste. 403
Washington, DC 20004 USA
Phone: (202) 628-8410
Fax: (202) 628-8419
URL: http://www.ala.org/cipa/
Primary Contact: Emily Sheketoff, Exec. Dir. Washington Office

### American Civil Liberties Union (ACLU)
125 Broad Street, 18th Floor
New York, New York 10004 USA
Phone: (212) 549-2500
URL: http://www.aclu.org
Primary Contact: Nadine Strossen, Pres.

### American Family Association

P.O. Box 2440
Tupelo, MS 38803 USA
Phone: (662) 844-5036
Fax: (662) 842-7798
URL: http://www.afa.net
Primary Contact: Donald E. Wildmon, Pres.

### Electronic Frontier Foundation

454 Shotwell Street
San Francisco, CA 94110 USA
Phone: (415) 436-9333
Fax: (415) 436-9993
URL: http://www.eff.org
Primary Contact: Brad Templeton, Chm.

# INTERNET

## INTERNET PRIVACY

*Sections within this essay:*

## Background

Among the many legal issues presented by the Internet, privacy is a leading problem. In fact, Internet privacy covers a broad range of concerns: fears about the safety of children in chat rooms and on the World Wide Web, the privacy of e-mail, the vulnerability of web users to having their Internet use habits tracked, the collection and use of personal information, the freedom of people to chat and post messages anonymously. Moreover, the rapid evolution of the Internet has frequently brought such privacy concerns before lawmakers and the courts.

Privacy concerns are frequently newsworthy. During the 1990s, child safety advocates highlighted special online dangers for children following high-profile abuse cases. Internet commerce has also been affected, too. The Federal Trade Commission (FTC) report noted in 2000 in its annual report to Congress that survey data demonstrated 92% of consumers are concerned about the misuse of personal information online. Privacy concerns over unsolicited commercial messages arose as Internet users battled to keep this so-called "spam" out of their e-mail inboxes, while in 2001, civil liberties advocates opposed potential abuse by the Federal Bureau of Investigation of its Carnivore hardware, a data-collecting technology attached to Internet services for criminal investigation.

Congress has been reluctant to enact legislation, relying upon a privacy law last revised in 1986 and passing only one new Internet privacy law in the 1990s. This was not for want of ideas. Numerous bills proposing Internet privacy protections were submitted in Congress during the late 1990s and early 2000s, and the Federal Trade Commission (FTC) also proposed legal reform. But lawmakers showed deep reservations about trifling with Internet regulation of privacy, expressing fears about hurting online commerce and creating an unenforceable regulatory scheme. Internet crime laws passed, but these criminalized intrusive and destructive behaviors without directly creating privacy rights.

The legal framework for online privacy thus rests largely on two federal laws, a subdued federal regulatory approach, a mixture of state laws, and contradictory **case law** from the courts:

- In 1986, Congress significantly updated the Electronic Communications Privacy Act (ECPA), originally enacted two decades earlier in 1968 to prevent telephone **wiretapping**. The law protects the privacy of much online communication, such as e-mail and other digital messaging, but far from all of it. The law offers little privacy protection to electronic communication in the workplace, which courts have further restricted.

- The Children's Online Privacy Protection Act of 1998 was passed amid complaints that websites frequently sought too much personal information from children. The law requires website operators to maintain privacy policies, grants parents powers to control information gleaned from their children by websites, and grants regulatory power to the FTC.

- Throughout the 1990s, the FTC studied and recommended proposals for new Internet privacy laws. The commission made such recommendations again in its annual 2000 report on the issue, but in 2001 new FTC leadership called for more study of the issue and a continued emphasis on self-regulation by business.

- Passed in response to the September 11, 2001 terrorist attacks upon the United States, the Patriot Act of 2001 appeared likely to significantly impact online privacy. The law dramatically increases federal police investigatory powers, including the right to intercept e-mail and track Internet usage.

- Courts have offered mixed verdicts on anonymity on the Internet. In 1997, Georgia was prohibited from enforcing a **statute** that barred anonymous communication in ACLU v. Miller. In subsequent cases, courts have allowed plaintiffs to force disclosure of the identities of anonymous users of Internet message boards, but some have required that strict evidentiary standards are met by plaintiffs first.

## Electronic Communication Privacy Act

### Purpose of the law

The Electronic Communication Privacy (ECPA) of 1986 creates limited **statutory** privacy rights for Internet users. First enacted in 1968, the law originally sought to prevent wiretapping by determining limits on electronic surveillance. By 1986, growing federal concern about privacy in an age of new communication technology led to a major overhaul. Lawmakers amended the ECPA to extend its privacy protection to several forms of contemporary electronic communication, from cell phones and pagers to computer transmissions and e-mail.

On the Internet the ECPA protects both digital transmissions and stored messages. In general, the law prohibits their interception or disclosure by third parties. It spells out several separate offenses:

- Intercepting or endeavoring to intercept communication

- Disclosing communication without consent

- Using electronic, mechanical, or other devices to intercept communication

- Intercepting communication for commercial purposes

- Intercepting communication for the purpose of impeding criminal investigations

Besides criminal penalties, the statute authorizes that injured parties may bring civil suits for any damages suffered, **punitive damages**, and other relief.

### Protected Internet Communication

Electronic communication is defined in broad terms as "any transfer of signs, signals, writing, images, sounds, data, or intelligence of any nature transmitted in whole or in part by a wire, radio, electromagnetic, photo electronic or photo optical system." Thus the ECPA extends privacy protection to everything from e-mail to drawings, pictures, and sounds as well. For communication to receive the law's protection, it cannot be simply sent between two computers: the communication must take place in the course of interstate or foreign commerce.

However, numerous exceptions are spelled out in the law. These fall into three categories:

- Limited exceptions allowing employees of network services access to communication under specific circumstances

- Broad workplace exceptions allowing employers access to employee e-mail

- Conditional government authority to carry out criminal investigations

### Exceptions for Employees of Network Services

The ECPA prohibits employees of Internet providers from eavesdropping on subscribers' e-mail or other communication. However, it is not unlawful for these employees to intercept or disclose communication in the normal course of employment under two conditions:

- While engaged in the normal required performance of their jobs

- For the protection of the rights or property of the provider of the service

The statute further restricts how such exceptions may occur, specifying that "service observing" and "random monitoring" may only be carried out for mechanical or quality control checks.

### Exceptions for Employers

In contrast to private home usage of the Internet, Internet communication in the workplace is given far less privacy protection under the ECPA. Underpinning this difference are philosophical assumptions about how much privacy individuals may expect at home as opposed to what they may normally expect at work. As courts have long recognized, several factors influence this question: the nature of the workplace, the relationship between employees and employers, and the legal concerns of employers are all issues that shape why the employee has a lesser expectation of privacy at work than at home.

The law permits private employers to monitor worker e-mail usage in two main ways:

- In the ordinary course of business

- When employees have given consent

Because employer monitoring of employees has been at the heart of much **litigation**, the courts have helped to define what these conditions mean. In determining whether monitoring is legal in the ordinary course of business, courts generally examine the reasons that businesses conduct the monitoring. Generally, workplace monitoring has been held to be legal under the ECPA where employers have provided notice of the policy to conduct monitoring and limited it to monitoring communication that is business-related rather than personal.

Private business and public sector employees come under different laws. While employees may give consent to monitoring, the courts have also found that "implied consent" may exist. This consent occurs when employees know or should have known that their employers intercept their electronic communications. Public sector employers are subject to a different legal standard. Monitoring in a government workplace may trigger constitutional issues such as the First Amendment right to free speech or the Fourth Amendment right to be free from an unreasonable search or seizure.

### Exceptions for Government Authorities

The ECPA governs law enforcement access to private electronic communication. This statutory privacy is not absolute; however, the law recognizes that law enforcement must be able to conduct its work. But the government's power to have access to electronic communication unlimited. Like protections afforded by the Fourth Amendment to the U.S. Constitution, the law spells out limits upon government intrusion in this area of private life.

Government agents must take specific steps before intercepting communication over the Internet, gaining access to stored communication, or obtaining subscriber information such as account records and network logs from Internet service providers. Generally, they must issue subpoenas or seek and execute court orders such as search warrants. Greater degrees of invasiveness require court authority. Thus investigators can **subpoena** basic subscriber information, but they must obtain a **search warrant** for **examination** of the full content of an account.

An additional exception is created for employees or agents of the Federal Communications Commission (FCC). They may intercept or disclose communications in the normal course of employment duties or in discharging the FCC's federal monitoring responsibilities spelled out in Chapter 5 of Title 47 of the United States Code.

### Additional Exceptions Under the Patriot Act of 2001

Signed into law by President George Bush on October 26, 2001, the Patriot Act of 2001 authorizes new investigatory powers for law enforcement in response to terrorist attacks upon the nation. Not all of its powers are limited to use in fighting **terrorism**, however. The 350-page law amends over one dozen existing statutes, including the ECPA, for use in investigations of **computer crime** and other offenses. Some of the ECPA changes relate to the law's protections for technologies other than the Internet, but a few circumscribe the existing privacy protections for

Internet communications and usage. Not all are permanent. Many are subject to sunset provisions provided by lawmakers out of concern over potential long-term harm to civil liberties.

Under the changes, law enforcement agents are able to conduct investigations with fewer legal hindrances:

- Agents may use the ECPA to compel cable Internet service providers to disclose customer Internet records without obtaining court orders.

- Agents have broader authority to obtain stored voice communications. This change to the ECPA allows agents to use a search **warrant** for examining all e-mail as well as any attachments to e-mail that might contain communication without having to seek further court authority. This change will sunset on December 31, 2005.

- Internet service providers may voluntarily make so-called "emergency disclosures"of information involving information previously prohibited from disclosure under the ECPA. This information includes all customer records and customer communications. The disclosures are permitted in situations involving immediate risk of death or serious physical injury to any person. However, the law merely permits such disclosure but does not create an obligation to make them. This change will sunset on December 31, 2005.

Without altering the ECPA, other provisions of the Patriot Act also increase police powers that potentially impact Internet privacy. These include:

- Extending the authority to trace communications on computer networks in a manner similar to tracing telephone calls, along with giving federal courts the power to compel assistance from any communication provider

- Allowing agents to obtain nationwide search warrants for e-mail without the traditional requirement that the issuing court be within the relevant **jurisdiction**. This change will sunset on December 31, 2005

## The Children's Online Privacy Protection Act

### *Purpose of the law*

Designed to protect minors who use the Internet, the Children's Online Privacy Protection Act (COPPA) governs how websites and online services may interact with children under 13 years of age. COPPA restricts the online collection of personal information from these young Internet users and creates certain statutory rights for their parents. Effective April 21, 2000, the law grants regulatory and enforcement authority to the Federal Trade Commission (FTC).

### *Who Must Comply*

Businesses, groups, and individuals that collect information from children must comply with COPPA. Two broad categories exist:

- Operators of commercial websites and online services "directed to children" that collect personal information from children

- Operators of general audience websites that have actual knowledge that the site collects personal information from children

The FTC weighs several factors in determining whether a site is directed to children:

- Subject matter

- Visual or audio content

- The age of models on the site

- Language

- Whether advertising on the site is directed to children

- Information regarding the age of the actual or intended audience

- Whether a site uses animated characters or other child-oriented features

The FTC determines whether someone is a website operator by considering the following:

- Ownership and control of the information.

- Payment for the collection and maintenance of information

- Pre-existing contractual relationships

- What role the website plays in collecting or maintaining information

### Basic Compliance Provisions

Under COPPA, website and online service operators must meet three main forms of compliance:

- Post their privacy policy

- Send a direct notice to parents and obtain parental consent before collecting information from children

- Obtain new consent when the site's information practices change in a material way

### Privacy Policy

Operators must post a link to their privacy policy on the home page of the website or online service, as well as at each point where the site collects personal information from children. The policy must be clear and prominent and must specify the following:

- Types of personal information collected, such as name, home address, email address, or hobbies

- How the site will use the information

- Whether the information is given to advertisers or third parties

- A person who may be contacted at the site

### Obtaining Parental Consent

In many cases, a special notice seeking parental consent must be sent to the child's parents. The operator must notify a parent:

- That it wishes to collect personal information from the child

- That the parent's consent is required for the collection, use, and disclosure of the personal information

- How the parent can provide consent

The notice may be sent by e-mail or regular postal mail. Replies via e-mail are acceptable when the operator merely wishes to collect personal information from the child. When answers are delayed, operators may seek confirmation of consent by letter or telephone call.

Consent requirements are more strict when the operator wants to disclose a child's personal information to a third party or make the information publicly available. In such cases, the FTC requires a more reliable form of consent. Forms of consent include:

- A signed form from the parent via postal mail or fax

- Acceptance and verification of a credit card number

- Acceptance of calls from parents through a toll-free number

- E-mail accompanied by a so-called digital signature

Whenever operators make material changes to their information policies, they must send a new notice and request for consent to parents.

### Exceptions Not Requiring Consent

Consent is not required when obtaining a child's e-mail address for several limited purposes:

- Responding to a one-time request from the child

- Providing notice to the parent

- Ensuring the safety of the child or the site

- Sending a newsletter of other information regularly provided parents are notified and allowed to refuse the arrangement

### Parental Rights

COPPA creates two kinds of statutory rights for parents:

- Parents may compel a site to disclose both general and specific kinds of personal information they collect online from children

- Parents may revoke their consent at any time, refuse to allow further use of the child's information, and direct the operator to delete the information

### Verifying Parental Identity

In order to protect children, operators must take reasonable steps to verify the parent's identity before divulging personal information:

- A signed form from the parent via postal mail or fax

- Acceptance and verification of a credit card number

- Acceptance of calls from parents through a toll-free number

- E-mail accompanied by a so-called digital signature or a PIN number or password

The law provides protection from liability under federal and state law for inadvertent disclosures of a child's information to someone who purports to be a parent.

### Safe Harbors

Under COPPA, industry groups and others can create self-regulatory programs to meet compliance with the law. These so-called safe harbors require approval from the FTC.

### Violations

Violations FTC rules for COPPA are treated as unfair or deceptive trade practices, punishable under the Federal Trade Commission Act.

## Anonymity

The Internet has popularized the use of anonymous online identities. For privacy purposes when communicating with strangers, using public message boards, or in Internet gaming, many people avoid using their legal name and instead choose aliases. Advocates of online privacy such as the American Civil Liberties Union strongly back protections for this anonymity. Publishing anonymously has a long tradition at **common law**, but anonymity is not guaranteed by statute.

Legal battles over anonymity have become increasingly common since the late-1990s. In particular, companies have sought to discover the identities of their online critics by issuing subpoenas to force their disclosure. Civil liberties advocates have argued that the threat of legal action by powerful plaintiffs can stifle online speech, which, they say, depends upon anonymity. Opponents have regarded anonymity as merely cover for **defamation** and libel.

Courts have provided different results, and no consistent body of law exists. In an October 2000 ruling in Hvide v. John Does, a Florida appeals refused to overturn a lower court order that Yahoo and America Online must divulge the identities of eight anonymous message posters sought by a subpoena in a defamation lawsuit. Courts in other jurisdictions have responded differently, articulating tough evidentiary standards for obtaining subpoenas. In November 2000, a Pittsburgh state court ruled in Melvin v. Doe against a public official seeking to discover the identity of anonymous critic. And in Dendrite International v. John Does, the Superior Court of New Jersey ruled in November 2000 against a company seeking to compel disclosure of anonymous critics **accused** of making false statements, holding that the right of companies to sue "must be balanced against the legitimate and valuable right to participate in online forums anonymously or pseudonymously." Case law on anonymity thus remains in flux

in the early 2000s, and it is hard to predict how this area of online privacy law will develop in future years.

## State Laws

Several states have enacted Internet privacy laws. Since most crime is prosecuted in state courts rather than at the federal level, states have commonly tried to keep pace with the federal government's protections. As a result, many have modeled e-mail privacy laws upon the federal Electronic Communications Privacy Act, such as New Jersey's and Pennsylvania's respective Wiretapping and Electronic Surveillance Control Acts. A number of other states protect children's privacy online, much in the way that the federal Children's Online Privacy Protection Act does. In another respect, state courts recognize common law claims involving the tort of invasion of privacy, so not all privacy rights depend upon statutory protections.

Demonstrating a strong approach to new technology issues, state legislatures have gone further than Congress in protecting e-mail privacy. Several states, such as Arkansas and Maryland, prohibit harassment through e-mail. A few address workplace concerns, with recent legislation emerging that protects employee rights. Under a Delaware law that took effect in August 2001, employers who monitor employee e-mail or Internet transmissions must inform workers about the monitoring before it begins.

Following the lead of pioneering legislation like Washington State's 1998 law, at least eighteen states have passed laws restricting how e-mail may be used by companies that send unsolicited commercial messages to consumers. Popularly known as "spam," this digital equivalent of junk mail has raised widespread concerns among private individuals who prefer not to receive it and companies that prefer not to pay the costs associated with processing it.

Anti-spam laws protect Internet service providers as well as consumers. Two of the toughest laws were passed in the late 1990s in Washington State and California. Washington State's law forbids sending commercial e-mail messages using a third party's domain name without permission, containing false or missing routing information, or with a false or misleading subject line. California's law allows Internet Service Providers to sue companies that mail spam in violation of the service's anti-spam policy, while also requiring spam to contain so-called opt-out instructions and clear labeling in the subject line describing the spam as an advertisement.

But state anti-spam laws have faced difficulties with enforcement as well as challenges to their constitutionality. Courts have reached different verdicts. In Ferguson v. Friendfinder, a San Francisco Superior Court judge ruled in June 2000 that key portions of California's anti-spam law were violations of the federal constitution's Commerce Clause. But in June 2001, the Washington Supreme Court upheld the constitutionality of its state anti-spam law: State of Washington v. Jason Heckel marked the first appeals court ruling on such cases. In October 2001, the U.S. Supreme Court declined to hear an appeal to the case, allowing the verdict to stand.

## Additional Resources

*"Cyber Liberties"* American Civil Liberties Union, 2001. Available at: http://www.aclu.org/issues/cyber/hmcl.html

*FBI Develops Eavesdropping Tools* Bridis, Ted, Associated Press, November 22, 2001.

*"Kidz Privacy"* Federal Trade Commission, 2001. Available at: http://www.ftc.gov/bcp/conline/edcams/kidzprivacy/inde x.html.

*Privacy Rights in a High-Tech World: Monitoring Employee E-Mail, Voicemail, and Internet Use.* Morgan Lewis Counselors at Law, June 2001. Available at http://www.morganlewis.com/wpprivacyrights.htm.

*U.S. Code, Title 13, Section 1301: Children's Online Privacy Protection Act of 1998.* Available at http://www.ftc.gov/ogc/coppa1.htm.

*U.S. Code, Title 18, Section 2510 et seq.: Electronic Communications Privacy Act of 1986.* Available at http://www.usdoj.gov/criminal/cybercrime/cclaws.html.

*You've Got Spam.* Stim, Rich, Nolo.com, 2001. Available at http://www.nolo.com/encyclopedia/articles/ilaw/gotspam.html.

*West Encyclopedia of American Law.* West Group, 1998.

## Organizations

### American Civil Liberties Union (ACLU)
125 Broad Street, 18th Floor
New York, NY 10004 USA
Phone: (212) 549-2500
URL: http://www.aclu.org
Primary Contact: Nadine Strossen, President

### Electronic Frontier Foundation
454 Shotwell Street
San Francisco, CA 94110 USA
Phone: (415) 436-9333
Fax: (415) 436-9993
URL: http://www.eff.org
Primary Contact: Brad Templeton, Chairman

### Federal Bureau of Investigation
J. Edgar Hoover Building, 935 Pennsylvania Avenue, NW
Washington, DC 20535-0001 USA
Phone: (202) 324-3000
Fax: ()
URL: http://www.fbi.gov
Primary Contact: Robert S. Mueller III, Director

### Federal Trade Commission
CRC-240
Washington, DC 20580 USA
Phone: (877) 382-4357
Fax: ()
URL: http://www.fbi.gov
Primary Contact: Timothy J. Muris, Chairman

# INTERNET

## INTERNET REGULATION

*Sections within this essay:*

## Background

The Internet is an immense labyrinth of more than 200 million computers, computer networks, and databases interconnected across the world. Through its user interface, known as the World Wide Web, the Internet gives users access to a vast amount of information, including typewritten text, tabular and graphic material, sound recordings, video images, pictures, and computer programs, which are stored at locations called "Web sites." Each Web site has a unique address, identified by its alphabetic Universal Resource Locator (URL) and its numeric Internet Protocol (IP). For example, http://www.montana.edu is the URL for Montana State University's Web server, while 153.90.2.1 is the IP for the school's Web site. The Internet also enables users to communicate to each other through e-mail, instant messaging, chat rooms, and message boards.

Most users do not access the Internet directly but instead go through an Internet Service Provider (ISP). ISPs typically charge subscribers an hourly or monthly fee for the service they provide. In addition to providing users with a connection to the Internet, many ISPs offer content of their own, ranging from e-mail and video games to personal banking, home shopping, tax, and research services. Subscribers connect to ISPs in a variety of ways, including cable modems and satellite uplinks. However, the most common means of accessing an ISP is over a telephone line. ISPs provide subscribers with telephone numbers that dial into servers that are connected to the Web.

Once connected, users literally have the world at their fingertips. Web sites today are as diverse as they are countless. Governments, governmental watchdogs, non-profit organizations, commercial entities, **consumer protection** groups, educational institutions, religious institutions, news media, and members of the sports and entertainment industries are just a few of the entities hosting Web sites on the Internet. The group of users visiting these Web sites is similarly large and diverse. In September 2001 researchers estimated that approximately 420 million people were accessing the Internet each day in at least 27 countries. Despite the enormous amount of daily global Internet traffic, no single authority exists to regulate it.

In fact, the Web was designed in part to thwart outside control and withstand foreign attack. The Internet evolved from the Advanced Research Project Agency Network (ARPANET), which was created by the U. S. Department of Defense in 1969 to function as a decentralized, self-maintaining national communications network that permitted computer-to-computer transmissions across vast distances in case the United States came under nuclear attack. ARPANET was programmed to work without human intervention, and sometimes in spite of it. For example, if a communications processing hub became disabled, ARPANET would re-route all transmissions through a different hub.

In the early 1980s the National Science Foundation relied on Internet technology to create the NSF Network (NFSNET), a high-speed communication network that facilitates research at remote academic and governmental institutions. NFSNET now serves as the technological backbone for all Internet communications in the United States. In 1989 English computer scientist Tim Berners-Lee developed the first prototype of the World Wide Web as means for the general populace to access the Internet. A year later he invented the concept of hypertext browsing, a method for imbedding shortcuts into on-screen text, a look that still defines the Internet today. In 1991 the World Wide Web debuted on the Internet, and by 1995 16 million people were reported "surfing" it each day.

As more people posted content on the Web and more people used the Web for personal, governmental, and business purposes, the Internet soon opened the door to an array of lawsuits and legal disputes. In one sense, the legal disputes were as novel as the Internet itself. But in another sense, the disputes merely presented new variations on long-standing legal controversies. As the millennium approached, law schools, lawyers, and judges were recognizing a distinct area of **jurisprudence** known as Internet law.

Internet law consists of state and federal statutes, **case law**, and other legal norms that regulate activity on the World Wide Web. Although the law governing the Internet is in many ways no different than the law governing other areas of life in the United States, legal disputes involving the Internet have generally centered on four bodies of law: (1) intellectual property; (2) free speech; (3) privacy; and (4) contracts.

## Intellectual Property

### Trademark Law

**Trademarks** consist of words, logos, symbols, slogans, and other devices that are used to signify the origin and authenticity of a good or service to the public. Established trademarks symbolize the quality of the goods or services they are associated with, and enable consumers to make effective and reliable buying decisions. For example, the circular black, blue, and white emblems attached to both ends of motor vehicles manufactured by Bavarian Motor Works (BMW) represent a familiar trademark that has come to signify meticulous craftsmanship to many consumers. However, the federal Trademark Act only protects marks that are distinctive and not merely generic. 15 U.S.C.A. sections 1051 et seq. Once a mark is sufficiently distinctive, competitors are prohibited from luring customers away from each other by using confusingly similar marks in commerce. Competitors are also prohibited from using marks that dilute or tarnish the value of another's mark in commerce.

Most Internet trademark **litigation** has revolved around domain name disputes. A domain name is the portion of a URL that follows the "http://www" prefix. A domain name can be reserved for use on the Internet by registering it with any one of several registrars that are accredited by the Internet Corporation for Assigned Names and Numbers (ICANN). Domain-name litigation typically arises when a business that has invested heavily in developing good will for a famous trademark is thwarted from using that mark for its Web site by a so-called "cybersquatter." Cybersquatters are individuals who intentionally reserve a third-party's trademark as a domain name for the purpose of selling it back to the owner for a profit.

A leading case on this issue is *Panavision Intern., L.P. v. Toeppen*, 141 F.3d 1316 (9th Cir. 1998), in which the **defendant** was sued after reserving approximately 240 domain names that were extremely similar to the trademarks of famous commercial entities, including "deltaairlines.com," "britishairways.com," "crateandbarrel.com," and "ussteel.com." One of the commercial entities sued the defendant. The defendant admitted he had no intention of ever using the marks to sell goods or services, and thus the plaintiff could not claim that consumers were likely to be confused by the similar names. Instead, the court found that the defendant diluted the plaintiff's trademark by curtailing the exploitation of its value on the Internet.

A year later Congress codified the rights of Trademark owners against cybersquatters, passing the Anti-Cybersquatting Act of 1999 (ACPA). The Intellectual Property and Communications Omnibus Reform Act of 1999, PL 106-113, 113 Stat 1501 (November 29, 1999). ACPA imposes civil liability upon defendants who have registered, trafficked in, or used a domain name that is identical to or confusingly similar to a trademark owned by the plaintiff, so long as the mark is distinctive and the defendant acted with a **bad faith** intent to profit from the plaintiff's mark. Bad faith can be shown in a number of ways, including a pattern of registering widely known trademarks as domain names to divert Internet users from the trademark owner's Web site. 15 U.S.C.A. section 1125(d). The law empowers courts to dispose of a domain name when the owner cannot be found or served with a **summons** and complaint in the United States.

### Copyright Law

A **copyright** is an intangible right granted by **statute** to the originator of certain literary or artistic productions, including authors, artists, musicians, composers, and publishers, among others. For a limited period, copyright owners are given the exclusive privilege to produce, copy, and distribute their creative works for publication or sale. Applicants seeking copyright protection for their work must establish that the work is original and has been reduced to a "tangible medium of expression." 17 U.S.C.A section 102(a). "Originality" does not mean "novelty" for the purposes of copyright law. It simply means that the work in question is the work of the person seeking copyright protection and not the creation of a third party from whom the work was copied. The phrase "tangible medium of expression" means that the work manifests itself in a concrete form, as when something is written on a piece of paper, recorded on an audiotape, captured on a videotape, or stored on a computer disk, hard drive, database, or server.

There are a number of defenses to copyright **infringement** suits, but "fair use" is the most frequently asserted. Fair use refers to the use of a copyrighted work that does not violate the exclusive rights of the copyright owner. The defense allows original works to be reproduced for the purpose of criticism, comment, news reporting, teaching, scholarship, research, and personal consumption. 17 U.S.C.A. section 107. Whether a particular use is "fair" depends on a court's application of the following factors: (1) the purpose and character of the use,

including whether the use is of a commercial nature or is for nonprofit educational purposes; (2) the nature of the copyrighted work; (3) the amount and substantiality of the portion used in relation to the copyrighted work as a whole; and (4) the effect of the use upon the potential market for the copyrighted work, including the extent to which the use diminishes the economic value of the work.

Copyright thus has important implications for the Internet. It is not uncommon for Web sites to make copyrighted works available to Internet users or for users to alter copyrighted works downloaded from the Internet. Nor is it uncommon for either Web site owners or Internet users to distribute original or altered copyrighted works across the Internet. But unless they are doing so with the permission of the copyright owner, both Web site owners and Internet users face possible claims for infringement, even if the distribution does not directly profit the distributor and even if the recipients are using copyrighted works for personal pleasure.

For example, in the case of *A&M Records, Inc. v. Napster, Inc.*, 239 F.3d 1004 (9th Cir. 2001), where the U.S. Court of Appeals for the Ninth Circuit ruled that the fair use doctrine does not allow an Internet service to facilitate the transfer of copyrighted MP3 digital audio files between service users who pay no fee to the copyright owners. Napster, the defendant Web service, created a system whereby service users interested in obtaining MP3 files, which reproduce high-quality music in a compressed and easily transferable format, could connect to Napster and contact others interested in exchanging digital recordings. The users would then send MP3 files to each other through the Internet, but the files would never pass through Napster's servers. Recognizing that the individual users were mostly high school and college students exchanging the music for personal consumption, the court still found that the purpose and character of their use was commercial in nature. "Napster users get for free something they would ordinarily have to buy," the court observed. The court said that Napster reduced audio CD sales among those students who used its service, thereby diminishing both the size of the copyright owners' market and the value of the copyrighted work.

### Patent Law

**Patents** give individuals and businesses the exclusive rights to make, use, and sell specific types of inventions, such as software programs, mechanical devices, manufacturing processes, chemical formulas, and electrical equipment. Federal law grants these exclusive rights in exchange for full public disclosure of an original work or invention. The inventor or author receives complete legal protection for his or her intellectual efforts, while the public obtains valuable information that can be used to make life easier, healthier, or more pleasant. For example, U.S. **Patent** No. 5,625,781 gives International Business Machines Corporation (IBM) the exclusive rights over a Web browsing tool that allows users to navigate through a list of hypertext links that are displayed on a Web site and then return to the list without having to backtrack through the intermediate links. Were another company to make the same technology available for its own Web-browsing product, IBM would have a viable claim for patent infringement.

## Free Speech

### Obscenity and Pornography

The Supreme Court has always had difficulty distinguishing obscene material, which is not protected by the First Amendment, from material that is merely salacious or titillating, which is protected. Justice Potter Stewart once admitted that he could not define **obscenity**, but quipped, "I know it when I see it." *Jacobellis v. Ohio*, 378 U.S. 184, 197, 84 S.Ct. 1676, 1683, 12 L.Ed.2d 793 (1964). Nonetheless, the Supreme Court has articulated a three-part test to determine when sexually oriented material is obscene. Material will not be declared obscene unless (1) the average person, applying contemporary community standards, would find that the material's predominant theme appeals to a "prurient" interest; (2) the material depicts or describes sexual activity in a "patently offensive" manner; and (3) the material lacks, when taken as a whole, serious literary, artistic, political or scientific value. *Miller v. California*, 413 U.S. 15, 93 S.Ct. 2607, 37 L.Ed.2d 419 (1973).

The Internet added new challenges to free speech regulation by making hardcore **pornography** readily available to Web users young and old. Congress tried to curb children's access to indecent and offensive material by passing the Communications Decency Act of 1996 (CDA). Pub.L. 104-104, 110 Stat. 56 (1996). The CDA made it unlawful to knowingly transmit indecent messages or "patently offensive" displays or images to all persons under 18 years of age. But the CDA failed to withstand scrutiny in *Reno v. American Civil Liberties Union*, 521 U.S. 844, 117 S.Ct. 2329, 138 L.Ed.2d 874 (1997), where the U. S. Supreme Court declared the law violative of the First Amendment. The Court reasoned that the law imposed a blanket restriction on the targeted speech, and thus was not narrowly tailored to accomplish the government's objective of curtailing minors' access to obscene material.

Congress attempted to refine its approach by passing the Child Online Protection Act (COPA). Pub. L. No. 105-277, § 231, 112 Stat. 2681-2736 (1999). COPA called for the implementation of an age-verification system that would shield minors from accessing hard core pornography on the Internet. This law was also successfully challenged in court. The U. S. District Court for Eastern District of Pennsylvania issued an injunction barring enforcement of COPA. In affirming the district court's decision, the U. S. Court of Appeals for the Third Circuit said that the law would allow the most conservative communities in the country to dictate the level of **censorship** for the rest of the country, a result directly contrary to the Miller test that required a community-by-community approach to obscenity. *American Civil Liberties Union v. Reno*, 217 F.3d 162 (3rd Cir. 2000). However, the case was appealed to the Supreme Court, which is expected to rule on it in 2002.

Meanwhile, Congress passed Children's Internet Protection Act (CIPA)in 2000. Pub. L. No. 106-554, 114 Stat. 2763 (2000). The law requires public schools and libraries that receive federal technology funding to block objectionable material on the Internet by installing filtering software. CIPA was challenged in March of 2001 when the American Civil Liberties Unions (ACLU) filed a lawsuit in federal court. However, the trial is not slated to begin until sometime in 2002.

### Commercial Speech

The First Amendment permits governmental regulation of commercial speech so long as the government's interest in doing so is substantial, the regulations directly advance the government's asserted interest, and the regulations are no more extensive than necessary to serve that interest. The Supreme Court has ruled that the government has a "substantial interest" in regulating false, deceptive, and misleading advertisements. However, the Supreme Court had not been asked to consider whether the First Amendment allows the government to regulate the distribution of unwanted advertisements. It may be asked shortly to do so with the prevalent use of "spamming" on the Internet.

Spamming is a term that describes the mass distribution of unwanted and unsolicited e-mail that advertises the sale of goods and services. Large-scale delivery of electronic advertisements on the Internet is not only annoying to users but also to ISPs and Web site owners whose mail servers can be overburdened by bulk e-mail. Sixteen states have banned spamming to some extent, and Congress has several bills before it aimed at achieving the same purpose. However, legal challenges are slowly creeping into courts across the country.

The Washington State Supreme Court, for example, upheld the state's anti-spamming law. *State v. Heckel*, 143 Wash.2d 824, 24 P.3d 404 (Wash. 2001). The court concluded that the law served the legitimate purpose of banning cost-shifting inherent in the sending of deceptive unsolicited bulk e-mail, and the only burden it placed on spammers was in prohibiting the distribution of e-mail with misleading subject lines. RCWA 19.190.010 et seq. The court found that this prohibition was consistent with other state statutes outlawing false and deceptive advertising. However, not all courts agree on this issue. The U. S. District Court for the Southern District of Ohio found that spamming constitutes an illegal form of **trespass**. *CompuServe, Inc. v. Cyber Promotions, Inc.*, 962 F.Supp. 1015 (S.D.Ohio 1997).

### Defamation

The law of **defamation** addresses harm to a party's reputation or good name through the torts of **libel and slander**. The **common law** rules underlying the doctrines of libel and slander have developed over time and typically vary from state to state. At common law libel law governed injurious written communications, while slander law governed injurious oral communications. In general the elements for libel and slander are a false and defamatory statement concerning another, made in a negligent, reckless, or malicious manner, and which is communicated to at least one other person in such a fashion as to cause sufficient harm to **warrant** an award of **compensatory damages**. As long as these elements are satisfied, a suit for defamation will not offend the First Amendment to the U. S. Constitution. A stricter set of elements must be satisfied when the allegedly injured party is a public official or a **public figure**. *New York Times v. Sullivan*, 376 U.S. 254, 84 S.Ct. 710, 11 L.Ed.2d 686 (1964).

The Internet makes it easier than ever before to disseminate defamatory statements to a worldwide audience. The risk of liability associated with defamatory statements is an important consideration for parties seeking to communicate with others on the Internet, as well as for parties that provide the technological means for such communications. Even satirical or humorous communication can give rise to a cause of action for libel or slander if the communication reasonably asserts a factual charge that is defamatory. However, the U. S. Court of Appeals for the Fourth Circuit limited the liability of ISPs, when it ruled that 47 U.S.C.A. § 230(c)(1) insulates them from libel or slander claims stemming from defamatory statements that are made by persons using the Internet through their service. *Zeran v. America Online, Inc.*, 129 F.3d 327 (4th Cir. 1997).

## Privacy

### Privacy Concerns on the Internet

Advances in technology now allow Web site operators, advertisers, and others to intercept, collect, compile, and distribute personal information about users browsing the Internet. Every time individuals browse the Internet they leave a trail of electronic information along the way, and most Web sites employ a variety of devices to automatically gather this trail and analyze it, sometimes offering it for sale to third parties who may use the information for targeted marketing. Known as "clickstream data," this information may include the user's e-mail address, the type of computer, and the browsing software.

Information about a user's activities may also be obtained through the use of Persistent Client-Side Hypertext Transfer Protocol files, commonly referred to as Internet "cookies." A cookie is a small file generated by a Web server and stored on a user's hard drive. Internet sites use cookies to count the users visiting their Web pages, and collect information about a user's personal preferences based on the other sites they visit. Most Web browsers allow users to prevent cookies from being stored on their hard drives, though Internet sites can in turn deny access to users who block cookies from being deposited on their hard drives.

Privacy may also be compromised on the Internet by "hackers" who unlawfully intercept Web transmissions without authorization or consent. In the early days of the Internet it was far more common to hear reports of individuals breaking into commercial, governmental, academic, or private sites or transmissions for the purpose of stealing credit card numbers, social security numbers, phone numbers, passwords, and other information that could facilitate a **fraudulent** scheme to make money. While such incidents still occur, encryption software is now widely deployed to keep hackers out. By and large, encryption software is effective. However, some experts predict that the next generation of computer viruses will allow hackers to take over control of infected operating systems from remote locations.

### Laws Regulating Privacy on the Internet

There is no comprehensive legislation in the United States that regulates the collection, storage, transmission, or use of personal information on the Internet. As new technologies have developed, the response has been to enact laws designed to target specific privacy-related issues on an **ad hoc** basis. As a result, the law governing privacy issues on the Internet consists of an assortment of state and federal legislation, regulations, and court decisions interpreting them.

In 1999 Congress enacted the Financial Modernization Act (FMA), which requires federal agencies to issue regulations implementing restrictions on a financial institution's ability to disclose nonpublic personal information about consumers to nonaffiliated third parties. Pub. L. No. 106-102, 113 Stat. 1338 (1999). Affected agencies include the Federal Trade Commission (FTC), **Securities** and Exchange Commission(SEC), and the Federal Reserve. Pursuant to the act, the FTC issued a final rule requiring financial institutions to provide notice to consumers about its privacy policies and practices and set forth the conditions under which a financial institution may disclose nonpublic personal information about consumers to nonaffiliated individuals and entities.

The Electronic Communications Privacy Act (ECPA) regulates intrusions into electronic communications and computer networks. 18 U.S.C.A sections 2510 et seq. Subject to various exceptions, ECPA makes it illegal to intercept e-mail at the point of transmission, while in transit, when stored by an e-mail router or server, or after receipt by the intended recipient. ECPA specifically prohibits the intentional interception, disclosure, or use of any wire, oral, or electronic communication. The act provides both criminal and civil penalties for its violation. However, one federal court ruled that ECPA could not be interpreted to support a **class action** alleging that an advertising corporation had unlawfully stored cookies on the hard drives of Web users who had visited particular Internet sites. **In re** DoubleClick Inc. Privacy Litigation, 154 F.Supp.2d 497 (S.D.N.Y. 2001)

The **Fair Credit Reporting Act** (FCRA), as amended by the Consumer Reporting Reform Act of 1996, regulates the collection and use of personal information by consumer reporting agencies. Fair Credit Reporting Act of 1970, 15 U.S.C.A sections 1681-1681u (1997); Consumer Credit Reporting Reform Act of 1996, Pub. L. No. 104-208, 110 Stat. 3009-426 (1996). The law requires that consumer reporting agencies establish "reasonable measures" addressing the commercial need for consumer credit information in a manner that ensures "confidentiality, accuracy, **relevancy**, and proper utilization" of the information. Among other things, the law prohibits the disclosure of a consumer report in the absence of written consent from the consumer, unless the disclosure is made pursuant to a court order or for legitimate business purposes.

Many states have enacted laws that mirror or expand upon the above federal acts. For example, Article 250 of New York's Penal Law prohibits intercepting or accessing electronic communications without the consent of at least one party to the communication. N.Y. Penal L. sections 250 et seq. States have also enacted privacy legislation relating to medical records and employment records. Conn. Gen. Stat. Ann sections 13-128a et seq. One state has modified its existing privacy laws so they apply to information collected over the Internet. Va. Code Ann. § 2.1-379. Another state passed a law prohibiting gambling on the Internet to quell concerns over the kinds of information that might be exchanged to partake in such activity. 720 ILCS 5/28-1.

## Contracts

At the heart of electronic commerce is the need for parties to form valid and legally binding contracts online. Basic questions relate to how contracts can be formed, performed, and enforced as parties seek to replace paper documents with electronic equivalents. It is often difficult, if not impossible, to be certain about the identity of the party with whom one is dealing on the Internet. Web transactions, particularly consumer-oriented transactions, often occur between parties having no preexisting relationship. Not knowing the identity of a party to an online transaction can raise concerns about whether a seemingly valid contract is actually enforceable. Appropriate use of digital signatures has been one solution to this problem.

The term "digital signature" describes a technology that is not based upon hand-signed instruments but rather on complex mathematical algorithms that facilitate the verification, integrity, and authenticity of electronic communications to make them non-reputable. "Non- reputable" means that **evidence** exists to link the identity of a party to the substance of an electronic message or data and that the evidence is sufficient to prevent a party from falsely denying having sent the message or data. The evidence usually comes in the form an electronic "seal" on a digital work, which typically requires that the parties signing a contract have access to cryptographic software.

The Uniform Electronic Transactions Act (UETA) endorses the use of digital or electronic signatures. UETA provides that "a record or signature may not be denied legal effect or enforceability solely because it is in electronic form." It also provides that electronic records may substitute for typewritten or handwritten records when the law requires that a document be in writing. Finally, for contracts and agreements that require a signature to be enforceable UETA provides that an electronic or digital signature will suffice. UETA has been adopted in 22 states.

## Other Legal Considerations

The four areas of law discussed above are amongst the most heavily litigated for cases involving Internet-related issues. But by no means are they the exclusive and definitive source for Web jurisprudence. Depending on the circumstances of a particular case, Internet law and regulation can be nearly as inclusive and encompassing as the entire corpus of all U. S. law. If a Web site fails to accommodate a blind person with voice-recognition software, handicapped users might have a claim for **disability discrimination**. If another Web site entices users to visit it and then preaches anti-race and anti-gender sentiments, visitors may have a claim under relevant harassment or hate speech laws. Stockowners desiring to trade shares over the Internet will need to determine what disclosure rules they must comply with before consummating a deal. Consumers living in one state and buying goods over the Internet in another state should be aware of applicable sales taxes in both jurisdictions. Protestors condemning a foreign government's behavior on an Internet message board might want to consider if they are in violation of foreign or international laws by doing so.

But the biggest challenge facing the future of Internet regulation may come from random attacks by computer viruses and worms unleashed by Web terrorists. The increase of virus outbreaks over the past two years has been highlighted by the widespread recognition they have received. "SirCam," "Melissa," and "Love Bug" are just three widely known viruses that experts estimate to have caused more than a billion dollars in damage worldwide. Security breaches by hackers cost U. S. companies another $10 billion every year. Private companies, government agencies, and academic institutions invest millions more in developing technology and educating their employees to protect their computer systems from these dangers. Nonetheless, the dangers persist. As a result, many federal lawmakers have urged changing the focus from preventing the spread of worms and viruses to developing effective means of identifying the individuals who have released them and then punishing those individuals severely enough to deter others from engaging in similar behavior.

## Additional Resources

*American Jurisprudence* West Group, 1998.

*Doing Business on the Internet: Forms and Analysis* Millstein, Jullian S., Jeffrey D. Neuburger, and Jeffrey P. Weingart, American Lawyer Media, 2000.

*Intellectual Property in a Nutshell: Patents, Trademarks, and Copyright* West Group.

*McCarthy on Trademarks and Unfair Competition* West Group, 2001.

*West's Encyclopedia of American Law* West Group, 1998.

*U. S. Constitution: First Amendment* Available at: http://caselaw.lp.findlaw.com/data/constitution/amendment01.

## Organizations

### *The American Bar Association*
740 15th Street, NW
Washington, DC 20002 USA
Phone: (202) 544-1114
Fax: (202) 544-2114
URL: http://w ww.abanet.org
Primary Contact: Robert J. Saltzman, President

### *Free Speech Coalition*
904 Massachusetts Ave NE
Washington, DC 64196 USA
Phone: (202) 638-1501
Fax: (202) 662-1777
URL: http://w ww.freespeechcoalition.com/home.htm

Primary Contact: Jeffrey Douglas, Director

### United States Copyright Office, The Library of Congress

101 Independence Avenue, SE
Washington, DC 20559-6000 USA
Phone: (202) 707-3000
Fax: (202) 707-2600
URL: http://lcweb.loc.gov/copyright

Primary Contact: Marybeth Peters, Register of Copyright

### U. S. Patent and Trademark Office

Crystal Plaza 3, Room 2C02
Washington, DC 20231 USA
Phone: (800) 786-9199
Fax: (703) 305-7786
URL: http://www.uspto.gov
Primary Contact: Nicholas Godici, Director

# INTERNET

## ONLINE BUSINESS

*Sections within this essay:*

## Background

At the beginning of the Internet revolution, many proclaimed the World Wide Web would "change everything." Although it was impossible for the Internet to live up to the dizzying expectations and frenzied hype it garnered at its inception, its contribution to the business world cannot be understated. The exponential explosion of the Internet in the mid-1990s spawned an entirely new creature: the online business. Whether one calls the wired business world the dot–coms, the new economy, or e–biz, the Internet has definitely made it easier and relatively inexpensive for these businesses—big or small, new or old, local or international—to reach out to a larger population and customer base.

Because of the ease and economics of the Internet, thousands of brand-new ventures have been created exclusively online and "old economy" businesses have branched out to form online extensions of their "brick–and–mortar" bases. The following projections and facts illustrate this trend.

- Forrester Research projects that by 2003, business-to-consumer e-commerce revenues will total $108 billion in the United States while business-to-business revenues will total $1.3 trillion in the United States

- International Data Corp. (IDC) projects that business-to-business purchases through e-commerce will total $4.3 trillion by 2005

- Jupiter Media projects that there will be 120 million online buyers in the United States by 2005, an increase from 65 million buyers in 2001

- Donaldson, Lufkin & Jenrette projects that by 2003, there will be 183 million worldwide online purchasers

- Keenan Vision projects that total online purchase revenues will equal $1.4 trillion by 2004

- According to IDC, nearly 75% (5 million) of small businesses with PCs are on the Internet; while 2 million small firms maintain their own homepage and Website

- IDC found that 725,000 small companies were actively selling online by 2001

With the influx of thousands of online businesses, legal issues that entrepreneurs and seasoned business executives never had to consider, or could have even imagined, just a few years ago are now crucial to starting and maintaining an online business. Obscure or even nonexistent to the traditional business, issues such as domain names, customer privacy, links, metatags, and digital signatures have become an everyday concern. Further, entirely new rules, statutes, laws, and the fresh application of old laws have been created or modified to fit the landscape of the emerging online business world. At the local, state, federal, and international levels, laws are being debated and passed every day, and these new enactments are being tested regularly in courts of law. The online business must know these latest legal rules and the ramifications of starting and doing business on the Net in order to survive and thrive.

## General Legal Issues Confronting Those Starting and Maintaining an Online Business

### Domain Names and Trademarks

One of the first tasks in starting an online business is to purchase a domain name, such as aol.com, amazon.com, and ebay.com. The top-level domain is the.com,.gov,.cc.,.net, etc., of a web address. The second-level domain can be a company name, trademark, or industry buzzword. Obviously, no two domain names are the same. Over 33,000,000 domain names have already been registered, so finding a unique and unused name may be more difficult than appears at first glance.

The legal problems surrounding the registration of domain names most often involve trademark and service mark violations. **Trademarks** and service marks are words, names, symbols, or devices used by businesses to identify their products and services. Even if one finds a domain name that has not yet been registered, that does not mean that it will not run afoul of trademark law. Typically, the first to register a domain name is entitled to keep it. However, if one registers a domain name that has been previously registered as a trademark, he or she may be in violation of the Anticybersquatting **Consumer Protection** Act (ACPA), which created a new cause of action under Section 43(d) of the **Lanham Act**, 15 U.S.C. ¤ 1125(d). The ACPA contains penalties for bad-faith use of another's trademark of up to $100,000 per domain-name violation. This law applies even if the trademark owner has not registered it as a domain name.

Similarly, if someone has used another person's trademark for a domain name, legal action may be necessary. All domain names registered after January 1, 2000 contain ICANN's (International Corporation for Assigned Names and Numbers) Uniform Domain Name Dispute Resolution Policy (UDNDRP), which requires all such disputes to be determined by an administrative panel. The only remedy under the UDNDRP for the **bad faith** use of another's trademark is transfer of the domain name to the trademark owner. Even after such a determination, though, one may still seek **redress** in a court of law.

Sound legal advice is for a new online business to protect its domain name by registering it as a trademark first. A trademark may be obtained electronically at the **Patent** and Trademark Office web site using the Trademark Electronic Application System. Once individuals obtain trademarks, they may also then want to monitor the Internet for cybersquatters improperly using their trademarks. There are fee-based firms that will monitor usage of your trademark in the United States. Trademark owners may also avoid costs associated with hiring such a firm by doing manual searches for trademarks using search engines. Whois.net will find all domain names that contain the string of words a person's wishes to check and may also provide the registrar's name, address, email address, and other useful information that can be used to begin an investigation as to whether such entity is cybersquatting.

However, the holder of a trademark right is not automatically entitled to the same domain name that uses the trademark. In Strick Corp. v. Strickland (E.D.Pa. Aug. 27, 2001), 162 F.Supp.2d 372, Strick Corp., a provider of transportation equipment and trademark holder of the name, sued a provider of computer consulting services that had registered the domain name Strick.com. Strick Corp. claimed there was blurring and dilution of trademark occurring when Internet searches using "Strick" as a search term encountered the alleged diluter's web page and concluded that the trademark holder had no Internet presence. The federal court found that the use of Strick.com by the computer consulting company did not dilute the trademark and did not violate the Lanham Act or state law. The court determined that any initial confusion that arose from the defendant's use of the domain name was not substantial enough to be legally sufficient. The judge also found that there was not "dilution by blurring" because a reasonable consumer would not associate the two uses of the trademark in his or her own mind. The sensible practice to avoid an inevitable lawsuit for using another's trademark in a domain name is first either to hire an attorney to run a trademark search or check with the U. S. Patent and Trademark Office database at www.uspto.gov before registering the domain name.

### Privacy Issues

Through their own analyses or the help of online advertising agencies, online businesses can track users' buying, what they look at, how long they look at it, what the referring site was, what other sites were visited, the time of day they browse, and where they live, not to mention the detailed information the browser supplies voluntarily through registration and purchases. Indeed, the browsing public knows the threat of websites gathering their personal information. PriceWaterhouseCoopers found that nearly 77% of those surveyed said that the disclosure of personal details was a barrier to purchasing online. Another 48% stated they do not shop online because they do not trust web retailers. Twenty-seven percent of Internet users surveyed by CyberDialogue said they had abandoned an online purchase because of privacy concerns regarding the abuse of personal data. This apprehension and mistrust have not gone unnoticed by lawmakers. As a result, online businesses must now pay careful attention to an array of privacy laws.

Several federal laws affect privacy issues for online businesses. The Federal Trade Commission (FTC) Act, 15 U.S.C. 41 et seq., has only limited effect on online businesses. The FTC's power under the FTC Act is generally to ensure that a website follows its own stated privacy policy. The FTC Act gives no power to the FTC to demand any specific privacy policy be followed or that any policy even be posted. The FTC does, however, use its wide-ranging power under Section 5 of the FTC Act to take action against "deceptive acts or practices." It should be noted, though, that the FTC Act provides no right of legal action for individual consumers wishing to obtain damages for privacy policy violations by a website.

The Children's Online Privacy Protection Act (COPPA), 15 U.S.C. 6501 et seq., enacted in 1998, applies only to web sites that target children under 12 years old as users or have actual knowledge that information is being collected from a child. COPPA requires that such a web site post privacy policies describing what personal information it collects and what it may do with such information. The law further requires that the online operator get prior "verifiable parental consent" before collecting, maintaining, or disclosing information about the child. The law also provides a "safe harbor" for those web sites that act in compliance with a self-regulatory program approved by the FTC. Any online business that may be marketing toward children must be aware of COPPA and its requirements.

The Electronic Communications Privacy Act of 1986 (ECPA), 18 **USC** 2510 et seq. and 2701 et seq., also has application to certain web site practices. The ECPA prohibits the interception or disclosure of electronic communications. Although the ECPA provides an exemption for those who are parties to a communication, a web site that considers collecting or distributing information obtained via emails to its site or through monitoring forum or chat-room services it provides should be wary of the prohibitions of the ECPA. Merely posting a privacy policy that explains that users of the service implicitly consent to collection and disclosure of their communications may not be enough. To be certain, web sites should obtain specific consent from those parties involved directly with the communications.

### The Uniform Commercial Code and Online Business

Article Two of the **Uniform Commercial Code** (UCC) applies to all contracts, both business-to-business and business-to-consumer, for the sale of goods, unless the parties agree to vary the terms of their agreement. Louisiana is the only state that has not adopted Article Two, and versions of Article Two vary from state to state. Further, unless otherwise agreed upon, if two parties are from countries that have joined the United Nations Convention on the International Sale of Goods (UNCISG), the UNCISG may have control over the UCC with regard to their transaction. Four general provisions are particularly important to online businesses: the writing requirement, contract formation, warranties, and remedies.

The writing requirement of Article Two requires that for the sale of goods over $500, there must be some writing sufficient to indicate a contract. For online businesses, it is likely sufficient for there to be an electronic record of the acceptance of the terms by the buyer or an indication of acceptance via email. A typed name on the email or the filling-in of the name on the online order is also likely to constitute sufficient signatures. (See UCC Section 1-201(39): "signed" includes any symbol that demonstrates the intention of a party. See also "Electronic and Digital Signatures" below.)

The requirement of contract formation requires that an offer can be accepted in any reasonable manner. An acceptance by e-mail is acceptable if the offer was by e-mail. If the offer was made by another medium, it is suggested that one first inquire if acceptance by e-mail is acceptable.

The **warranty** requirements of Article Two provide that there is an express warranty, **implied warranty** of merchantability, implied warranty of fitness for particular purpose, and implied warranty of title and noninfringement. Many online businesses limit these warranties through "clickwraps," which are a set of contract terms that an online customer accepts by clicking on an "accept" or similar button, usually on a separate screen. Online businesses should allow the consumer to agree to the limitations before completing the transaction. Under the remedies requirement of Article Two, buyers may obtain from sellers after a breach of contract certain remedies, including actual damages, incidental damages, and consequential damages. Many online sellers limit the buyer's remedy in the clickwraps to the damages of repair, refund, or replacement of the purchased goods. Consequential damages, however, may not be limited or excluded if "unconscionable."

### Electronic and Digital Signatures

An electronic signature is generally any electronic data used to validate and authenticate the parties to a transaction. A digital signature, which is a form of an electronic signature, is a unique, encrypted code affixed to an electronic document or contract that authenticates the signor. The use of such electronic signatures allows parties to use the Internet to conduct transactions quickly and securely while reducing paperwork.

The most important federal legislation on electronic signatures is the Electronic Signatures in Global and National Commerce Act (E-SIGN), 15 U.S.C. sec. 7001 et seq., which became effective on October 1, 2000. E-SIGN provides that a signature or contract may not be denied legal effect "solely because it is in electronic form," except as provided in the Act itself. See section 101(a)(1) and (2). An electronic signature is defined as any "electronic sound, symbol, or process, attached to or logically associated with a contract or other record and executed or accepted by a person with the intent to sign the record." Al-

though E-SIGN does not apply to all transactions and writings, it applies to "any transaction in or affecting interstate or foreign commerce." Because a "transaction" is defined as "an action or set of actions relating to the conduct of business, consumer, or commercial affairs site, and place it on the page." For example, an online businesses may use an HREF link to link to a manufacturer's web site or use an IMG link to insert images of a product from the manufacturer's web site onto its own web site. Generally, there are no laws against HREF linking to another web page because the HREF link merely contains the coded information of the target's address. Because the code is pure information, no **copyright** or any other intellectual property laws provide protection. However, online businesses should keep in mind several issues related to the practice of HREF and IMG linking.

When one incorporates content from another's page via an unauthorized IMG link, there is no direct copyright **infringement** by the creator of the link because the image is not copied. As explained above, the visiting browser has provided the user's browser with instructions to retrieve the image. It is actually only the web viewer who has copied the image. However, the creator of the link may still be liable under copyright law for contributory infringement, which occurs when one knowingly makes an infringement possible. Further, it is possible that a web site could be liable for copyright infringement if IMG links use several copyrighted images to form an entirely new "derivative work" on its web site. Generally, it is considered proper protocol for a web site to get permission from a copyright owner before placing an IMG link on its own web site. Web site operators should also be certain to properly attribute works or images that may be reached or created with links and not misrepresent the ownership of the work. Online businesses must also be careful not to infringe on the trademarks of others. If a web site falsely leads the user to believe that the web site is affiliated, approved, or sponsored by the trademark owner, it could be liable for trademark infringement.

A link to another's page or image may also be potentially defamatory if it communicates a false and damaging statement about a person or entity. Further, even if a statement alone is not defamatory, it could become defamatory by providing a link within, before, or after the statement that directs the viewer to further information or identification.

Framing is a technique that puts a frame, or several frames, on a webpage that stays in place even when the viewer links to another site. The practical purpose of a frame is to be able to see information from several different sources on one display. However, because the original web site's logo, color scheme, design, or other characteristics may still be on the frame(s), viewers may be led to believe that they are still on the original web site and seeing content created by the original web site. This situation creates a problem for some situations, such as when a web site that is being framed by another web site does not want to be associated with the framing web site but appears to be so because of the frame. Thus, framing can raise the same issues as HREF and IMG linking. Although the legality of framing is not certain, web site operators should appreciate the potential legal liability of linking other's pages into frames without permission.

It should also be noted that some consider "deep-linking" to be web **piracy** if it is done on a large scale. Deep-linking is when a link is provided to a specific web page within another's web site and not merely to the homepage. Some web operators are angered by this practice because the link takes the viewer directly to the page and bypasses its homepage, eliminating the ability of the homepage to build brand recognition, to supply important information, and to serve advertising functions. However, there is no law against deep-linking, and it is an extremely common practice that most see as not problematic, as long as it is not deceptive. Deep-linking has also been found legal by at least one federal court. See Ticketmaster Corp. V. Tickets.Com, Inc. (C.D.Cal. Mar. 27, 2000), No. CV-99-7654 (use of deep links to Ticketmaster.com did not violate copyright law because there is no copying involved, and the online ticket consumer is openly and obviously transferred to Ticketmaster's website; deep-linking also did not constitute **unfair competition** because a disclaimer negated any confusion as to the true source of the ticket purchase).

### E-mailing and "Spamming"

Many online businesses use e-mail as an advertising and marketing tool because of the potentially vast reach it has and the very inexpensive cost of sending e-mail. Some e-mail used for these purposes is targeted to a specific group of consumers who have requested such useful information. However, an ever-growing amount of commercial e-mail is unsolicited, bulk e-mail sent en masse. This latter type is often referred to as "spam." One commentator from Spam.abuse.net cites several reasons for the maligning of spam: the receiver pays more in aggra-

vation than the sender does in time and money; as spam grows, it will crowd out mailboxes and render them unusable; many spammers send their junk e-mail via innocent intermediate systems to avoid filters; spam clogs providers' systems; spam messages are nearly exclusively worthless, deceptive, and partially or totally **fraudulent**; and some spam may be illegal.

While the annoyance of having an e-mail inbox filled to the virtual brim with these clogging and often useless solicitations has raised the ire of millions of e-mail users, it apparently has not touched the federal legislators enough for them to enact federal laws directly pertaining to it. Several Federal laws were pending at the time of this writing in the 107th Congress, including the Anti-Spamming Act of 2001 (H.R. 718), Anti-Spamming Act of 2001 (H.R. 1017), Controlling the **Assault** of Non-Solicited **Pornography** and Marketing (CAN SPAM) Act of 2001 (S. 630), Netizens Protection Act of 2001 (H.R. 3146), Unsolicited Commercial Electronic Mail Act of 2001 (H.R. 95), and Wireless Telephone Spam Protection Act (H.R. 113). However, as discussed below, many states have enacted legislation regulating unsolicited e-mails.

Therefore, although spamming is generally not in violation of any federal laws at this time, it may soon be and is considered an extremely poor, if not unethical and despicable, business practice. Any business that wishes to use targeted, solicited e-mail as an advertising tool should be careful to steer clear of sending bulk, unsolicited advertising to unwitting recipients because doing so may tarnish its reputation and run afoul of the many state laws on the subject, as discussed below.

### Metatags

Metatags are invisible HTML programming codes that contain commands to search engine programs that index web pages. In normal practice they provide keywords relating to the content of the page so a search engine will display the page in its results when a user inserts them as search terms. Thus, by successfully using metatags, a web operator can increase the frequency a search engine will index a site.

However, website operators quickly figured out that by using metatags unrelated to their own content or metatags that contained a competitor's company or product name, they could increase their own traffic. Even though metatags are not visible on the page (they may be viewed by clicking "View" and then "Source"), this deceptive practice has been the basis for numerous lawsuits brought by individuals, companies, and web sites asserting that unrelated websites are illegally using metatags.

In general, courts have enjoined the use of trademarks in a non-owner's metatag when the parties were competitors or when the use of the trademark in a metatag was used to divert business to the site for profit. The key factor courts consider in determining whether a website has infringed on another's trademark through its use in a metatag seems to be whether there could be consumer confusion. See, e.g., Playboy Enterprises, Inc. v. Calvin Designer Label (N.D. Cal. 1997), 985 F.Supp. 1220 (web site may not use "Playboy" and "Playmate" in metatags on web site because web site was attempting to profit by confusing consumers and diverting business to the site).

The improper use of metatags by online businesses can also raise issues of unfair competition or trademark dilution. Unfair competition prohibits a company from deceptively claiming a connection with or endorsement from another. Trademark dilution occurs when one uses the trademark of another in such a manner that it blurs the significance of the mark or when using a similar mark in an objectionable manner tarnishes the meaning of the mark. For an example, see Ken Roberts Co. v. Go-To.com (N.D. Cal. May 10, 2000), No. C99-4775-THE (competitor's use of plaintiff's name in metatags interfered with plaintiff's prospective economic advantage by knowingly diverting plaintiff's current or potential customers from plaintiff's website to competitor's, constituting unfair competition and trademark dilution).

However, businesses may use another company's trademark under certain circumstances. An online business may generally use another company's trademark as a metatag on a webpage with a comparison advertisement. Of course, an online business would also be permitted to use another's trademark as a metatag if it was a distributor of the trademark owner's product and had a license from the manufacturer to use the trademark. Courts have also refused to find trademark infringement when the metatag is used to indicate content that provides a description of goods or services of the mark owner or their geographic origin. Such are permitted as a "fair use" of a trademark. See, e.g., Playboy Enterprises v. Welles (S.D. Cal. 1998), 7 F.Supp.2d 1098, aff'd without opinion, (9th Cir. 1998), 162 F.3d 1169 (it was "fair use" for former Playboy Playmate of the Year to use "playboy" and "playmate" in metatags of her web-

site because they were key words that identified her source of recognition to the public). However, outside these limited circumstances, online businesses should not use a trademark as a metatag without permission, particularly if the trademark belongs to a competitor. Many companies and trademark owners regularly search the Internet for metatag trademark violations, and such searches are simple to conduct.

### Internet Sales Tax

On November 28, 2001, President George W. Bush signed H.R. 1552, the Internet Tax Non-Discrimination Act. The Act extends the moratorium on new, special, and discriminatory Internet taxes and Internet access taxes originally enacted in October 1998 as part of the Internet Tax Freedom Act (47 U.S.C. 151). The new legislation extends through November 1, 2003.

## Special State Law Considerations

### Electronic and Digital Signatures and E-SIGN

As the Internet grew in popularity, many states quickly moved to enact legislation pertaining to electronic and digital signatures. When E-SIGN took effect in October 2000, the question that then arose was whether E-SIGN preempted such state laws on the subject. Preliminarily, it is clear that E-SIGN preempts state laws that conflict with or frustrate E-SIGN's basic policy, as spelled out in Section 101(a)(1) and (2), that electronic signatures and records cannot be denied legal effect solely because they are in electronic form. However, E-SIGN clearly does not preclude other laws that do not conflict with the validation principles contained in Section 101 of E-SIGN.

In 1999, to combat problems that could arise when parties from two jurisdictions entered into an electronic transaction, the National Conference of Commissioners on Uniform State Laws recommended the Uniform Electronic Transactions Act (UETA) for enactment in all states. UETA recognized electronically-based transactions and records as the "functional equivalent" of paper transactions where the parties agreed to use electronics. In formulating E-SIGN, the drafters clearly took UETA into account. Indeed, Section 102 of E-SIGN specifically recognizes UETA and acknowledges that individual states, through the enactment of UETA, can modify, limit, or supersede the effect of the validation provisions in Section 101 of E-SIGN without federal preemption. However, the state must enact UETA in its "pure" form (without modification) and express its intention to supersede E-SIGN. Still, because UETA only applies when the parties agree to use electronics, E-SIGN would apply in cases where there was no mutual agreement. Thus, these "opt-out" provisions provide for uniformity of state law, even though the provisions in UETA may differ from E-SIGN. E-SIGN also provides that a state may modify, limit, or supercede the validation terms of Section 101 if the state law specifies the alternative procedures for use of electronic signatures or records and those procedures are consistent with E-SIGN and do not validate only a particular type of technology. Therefore, online businesses should note that, although E-SIGN must be followed, individual states could enact additional laws affecting electronic signatures.

### E-mailing and "Spamming"

Although Congress has failed to enact any legislation specifically regulating unsolicited, bulk, commercial e-mailing, many laws have been passed at the state level. In July 1997, Nevada became the first state to enact an anti-spam law. The following states have also passed spam laws: California, Colorado, Connecticut, Delaware, Idaho, Illinois, Iowa, Louisiana, Missouri, North Carolina, Oklahoma, Pennsylvania, Rhode Island, Tennessee, Virginia, Washington, and West Virginia. The statutes in these states are variously worded and provide a wide range of protection against unsolicited, commercial e-mail. The anti-spam laws in the following states require "opt-out" instructions, and most also require that the opt-out requests be honored: California, Colorado, Idaho, Iowa, Missouri, Nevada, Rhode Island, and Tennessee. The anti-spam legislation in the following states applies to e-mails that are delivered to a resident of that state via a provider's facilities or equipment located in that state: California, Colorado, Connecticut, Illinois, Iowa, Oklahoma, Tennessee, and Virginia. The anti-spam legislation in Delaware and Rhode Island applies to e-mails originating outside the state if the recipient is located in that state and the sender is or should have been reasonably aware that the recipient is a resident of that state. North Carolina's law applies to e-mails sent into or within the state. In Washington and West Virginia, the anti-spam laws apply if a message is sent from within the state or if the sender knows that the recipient is a resident of that state. The following states require unsolicited, bulk, commercial e-mail to have certain labels in the subject line, such as "ADV" (advertisement) or "ADLT" (adult): California, Colorado, Nevada, Pennsylvania, and Tennessee.

### Internet Sales Tax

In Quill Corp. v. Heitkamp (1992), 504 U.S. 298, the United States Supreme Court found that states cannot require out-of-state retailers to collect sales taxes unless they have a physical presence, or nexus, within the state. Thus, online sellers do not have the power to collect tax on Internet sales to customers in other states, as such taxes are considered an interference with interstate commerce. However, if an online business is selling **tangible personal property**, it is likely required to collect **sales tax** in the state where its inventory is located or where it has a "bricks–and–mortar" store. Also, although no state may require out-of-state e-businesses to collect and remit taxes on sales to its residents, states may still require residents to remit such taxes themselves. Such a tax is referred to as a "use" tax. The difficulty is that it is nearly impossible for states to enforce such laws, so states have no choice but to rely on the honor system in collecting use taxes.

States have complained about their lack of ability to collect sales tax for Internet purchases, citing lost taxes as high as $13 billion for 2001. However, exclusively online e-tailers argue that if they are required to collect sales taxes and pay them to the proper taxing authorities, it will be extremely difficult to comply with nearly 8,000 state and local taxing jurisdictions, each with different rates and rules. One proposal that the National Governors' Association (NGA) has countered with is for the establishment of a "trusted third party," which would calculate and collect for the online businesses the appropriate local and state sales taxes. However, the NGA's **lobbying** efforts to allow states to tax such online purchases from remote sellers has yet been to no avail, as indicated by the passage of the Internet Tax Non-Discrimination Act.

## Additional Resources

*101 Things You Need to Know About Internet Law.* Bick, Jonathan, Three Rivers Press, 2000.

*The E-Business (R)Evolution: Living and Working in an Interconnected World.* Amor, Daniel, Prentice Hall, 2000.

*Internet Law and Business Handbook: A Practical Guide.* Brinson, J. Dianne, and Mark F. Radcliffe, Ladera Press, 2000.

## Websites

***About.com***
URL: http://law.about.com/cs/cyberspacelaw/

***Alan Gahtan's Cyberlaw Encyclopedia***
URL: http://www.gahtan.com/cyberlaw/

***Bitlaw***
URL: http://www.bitlaw.com/

***Findlaw for Legal Professionals***
URL: www.findlaw.com/01topics/10cyberspace/
index.html

***Gigalaw***
URL: www.gigalaw.com

***The Internet Law Journal***
URL: http://www.tilj.com

***The John Marshall Law School***
URL: http://www.jmls.edu/cyber/index/index.html

***Megalaw***
URL: http://www.megalaw.com/top/internet.php3

***Nolo Law for All***
URL: www.nolo.com

***Spam Laws***
URL: http://www.spamlaws.com/

# INTERNET

## PIRACY AND FILE-SHARING

*Sections within this essay:*

- Background
- Federal Laws
    - Digital Millennium Copyright Act
    - No Electronic Theft Act
- Napster
- After Napster
    - Grokster
    - Campus Crackdowns

## Background

Movies, computer software, and music are all forms of **intellectual property**—products of human intelligence. As technology has evolved from analog technology to digital technology, it has become easier to store and transmit types of intellectual property over the Internet from one computer user to another. This new technology sometimes results in a collision between quickly evolving technology and decades-old copyright law.

Computer technology makes it easy to share digital files between users. A file is a block of information stored on a magnetic media, such as on a hard disk, a tape, or a flash drive; examples of files are computer programs, documents, music, and movies. The practice of sharing files illegally exploded when a format for audio compression produced a type of file known as an MP3 file. This audio compression was important because it significantly reduced the amount of data that needed to be sent over computer networks, but did not affect the perceived quality of the sound or image being transmitted. For example, the MP3 format can reduce the digital recording of a song by a ratio of up to 12 to 1.

File-sharing services allow web users to find and download files from hard drives of other computers. File-sharing is often accomplished through peer-to-peer networks. Pure peer-to-peer computer networks use the computing power of its participants, rather than relying on servers. However, other peer-to-peer networks use a server to communicate the host user's Internet address to a requesting user. The requesting user utilizes this information to connect to the host user's computer. Once the connection is made, a copy of an MP3 file may be downloaded to the requesting user's computer. In a peer-to-peer network, anyone on the network may access files stored on other network computers. Legal issues arise when peer-to-peer networks and other methods are used for the unauthorized transfer and copying of **copyrighted** materials, such as music, books, and movie files. The illegal duplication and distribution of copyrighted files is known as **piracy**.

Copyright **infringement** issues also arise with regard to streaming media. Streaming media is the transmission or transfer of data that is delivered to an online viewer in a steady stream in near real time. Copyrighted content may not be streamed without the express authorization of the copyright holder.

Copyright infringement and piracy issues implicate both criminal and civil law. Most issues are handled under federal law, although state laws sometimes play a part. On the civil side, copyright holders may sue for monetary or statutory damages. In addition, the government may file criminal charges.

The scope of piracy and illegal file-sharing is vast. According to the Motion Picture Association of America (MPAA), more than 1.8 million illegal movies and 3,059 duplicating machines were seized in North America in 2004.

On October 12, 2005, the United States Attorney's Office of the Northern District of California handed down indictments charging several individuals with a scheme to pirate more than 325,000 illegal copies of copyrighted CDs and software. Reportedly the largest CD manufacturing seizure in the country to date, authorities allege that counterfeit copies were made with sophisticated replicating equipment that made the copies look legitimate in every way, even down to affixing the FBI Anti-Piracy warning label that states, "Unauthorized copying is punishable under federal law. "

Piracy issues are by no means confined to the United States. For example, in December 2005, officials in Jakarta, Indonesia, announced that they had seized 2.35 million pirated optical discs in three raids over a ten-day period. In the Asia-Pacific region alone, the MPA (the international counterpart of the MPAA) estimated annual losses of approximately $900 million. In 2004, approximately 49,000,000 illegal optical discs were seized in the area..

## Federal Laws

### Digital Millennium Copyright Act

President Bill Clinton signed the Digital Millennium Copyright Act (DMCA) on October 28, 1998. The law was designed to address problems in copyright laws created by evolving technology. The law was also passed to address international concerns regarding copyright. In 1996, the World Intellectual Property Organization (an agency of the United Nations) passed the Copyright Treaty and the Performances and Phonograms Treaty. This treaty provided for increased protection for copyrighted materials that are in digital form. Signers of the treaty agreed to implement laws to enforce the treaties. The United States is a signatory to the treaty, and the DMCA implemented the treaty on behalf of the U.S.

DMCA goes beyond prior copyright infringement laws. It provided for enhanced penalties for copyright infringement on the Internet. DMCA also criminalizes production and dissemination of technology that is used to circumvent measures taken to protect copyright.

Title I contains provisions that focus on conduct that is intended to circumvent technological measures protecting copyrighted works. It is illegal to "manufacture, import, offer to the public, provide, or otherwise traffic any technology, product, service, device, component, or part thereof," when its primary purpose is to circumvent "a technological measure that effectively controls access to" a copyrighted work. DMCA imposes criminal penalties for such circumvention.

Circumvention devices may be either actual physical medium or digital files that allow for content protection devices put on films, videos, music CDs and the like. An example of unauthorized circumvention devices is the software utility DeCSS, which can break copy protection on DVDs. Using DeCSS, a movie can be decrypted and illegally copied on a computer's hard drive. Two other circumvention devices are the so-called "black boxes" and macrovision defeaters.

Two cases demonstrate DMCA's dual role with civil and criminal provisions. In a ruling in a civil case in early 2004, a federal judge from the Northern District of California halted a company from selling DVD copying software, in the case of *321 Studios v. Metro Goldwyn Mayer Studios*. Judge Susan Ilston enjoined 321 from manufacturing, distributing or otherwise trafficking in DVD circumvention software. Another case, also from the Northern District of California, involved a criminal prosecution under DMCA. In *U.S. v. Elcom Ltd.*, the government obtained a conviction against a company that marketed a product for the unauthorized reproduction and distribution of electronic books.

### No Electronic Theft Act

President Clinton signed the No Electronic Theft Act (NET) in 1997. The law provides for enhanced criminal remedies for copyright infringement. NET was intended to stem the widespread theft of computer software.

The NET Act amended provisions in titles 17 and 18 of the U.S. Code. It permits federal prosecution in cases of large scale, willful copyright infringement even where the purpose is not for a commercial purpose or private financial gain. The law allows for the prosecution of anyone who copies, distributes, or receives software worth more than $1,000, in violation of copyright. Violation is a **misdemeanor** for the $1,000/six months, but becomes a **felony** where the value exceeds $2,500.

The law closed a loophole in prior law, which permitted criminal prosecution only for violations that result in financial gain. In 1994 a college student and computer hacker named David LaMacchia used an electronic bulletin board to distribute many commercial software programs. His actions allegedly cost software companies more than $1 million, but LaMacchia himself did not profit. Using pre-NET Act law, a federal judge dismissed the charges against LaMacchia.

## Napster

Originally, file-sharing was an unorganized activity. The launch of Napster in 1999 changed everything. That year, college student Shawn Fanning developed a system that made peer-to-peer sharing of MP3 music files easy to do. Named after Fanning's nickname, the development caused an explosion in the popularity of peer-to-peer sharing. College students loved it, but they were by no means the only ones using Napster. Practically overnight, millions were using Napster.

Napster's system allowed music on one computer hard drive to be copied by other Napster users. Digital MP3 files are created from an audio compact disk CD by a process called "ripping." Ripping software allows a CD user to compress the audio information on the CD into the MP3 format, and copy it directly onto a computer's hard drive. Napster users used Napster's centralized servers to search for MP3 files stored on other computers. Then, exact copies of the MP3 file could be transferred from one computer to another via the Internet. The compressed format of the MP3 file is what makes the rapid transmission from one computer to another feasible. Napster's MusicShare software made this all possible. The software was available for free download at the Napster web site. Napster also provided technical support for users. Some estimates estimate up to sixty million people used Napster at the height of its popularity.

Major record companies quickly realized Napster's threat to their profits. They brought suit, charging Napster with contributory and vicarious copyright infringement. A federal district judge in California entered a preliminary injunction against Napster. The judge ordered the company to block users from exchanging copyrighted material.

Napster appealed to the Ninth Circuit Court of Appeals. In 2001, the appellate court upheld most of the lower court's ruling. The Ninth Circuit found that

**plaintiffs** had established a prima facie case of direct copyright infringement. To establish their case, the record labels needed to show ownership of the allegedly infringed material. They also needed to demonstrate that the alleged infringers violated at least one exclusive right granted to copyright holders. The record companies' evidence showed that they owned approximately 70 percent of the files available through Napster. They also established that a majority of Napster users used the Napster system to download and upload copyrighted material.

Napster argued that it had engaged in **fair use** of the copyrighted material. If so, Napster did not violate copyright laws. The doctrine of fair use first developed in court decisions, but it was later made a part of copyright law, in section 107 of U.S. copyright law. According to the law, a reproduction of a particular work may be considered "fair" if used for purposes such as criticism, comment, news reporting, teaching, scholarship, or research. The law also provides four factors to be used in determining whether or not a particular use is fair:

- The purpose and character of the use, including whether such use is of commercial nature or is for nonprofit educational purposes;

- The nature of the copyrighted work;

- The amount and substantiality of the portion used in relation to the copyrighted work as a whole; and

- The effect of the use upon the potential market for or value of the copyrighted work.

Determining whether a use is fair use or an infringement of copyright is often difficult. For example, when examining the amount of a work that has been used, there is no specific number of words, lines, or notes that may safely be taken without permission. Moreover, merely acknowledging the source of copyrighted material is not a substitute for obtaining permission from the copyright holder.

Napster contended that its system was fair use, rather than infringement. It supported this argument with claims that Napster users used the service to make temporary copies before purchasing music ("sampling"), and to access music its users already owned in CD format ("space shifting"). The district and appellate court rejected both these claims. Sampling was a commercial use, the court ruled, even if some of the users eventually purchased the music.

Moreover, although wholesale copying does not preclude a claim of fair use, it militates against such a finding. In addition, the recording industry established that its marketability had been affected by Napster.

The appellate court found that Napster could be liable for contributory copyright infringement. Contributory copyright infringement is defined as "one who, with knowledge of the infringing activity, induces, causes or materially contributes to the infringing conduct of another." The Ninth Circuit determined that the district court did not err when it concluded that plaintiffs would likely prevail on this point: "Napster, by its conduct, knowingly encourages and assists the infringement of plaintiffs' copyrights."

The recording companies were ordered to provide Napster with lists of recordings. Once that had been done, Napster had the burden to promptly remove those recordings from its system. In 2001 Napster agreed to use screening technology to block distribution of files identified by the recording companies.

## After Napster

### Grokster

The legal rulings against Napster signaled its virtual demise, but the sharing of copyrighted material over the Internet adapted and continued. Other companies developed services that did not rely on centralized servers to facilitate the file-sharing. Grokster, StreamCast, and other companies distributed free software that allowed users to connect directly with one another. Since the software was free, the companies made money through sales of advertisements included with the software.

Companies in the music industry and the motion picture industry sued to stop these new file-sharing services. The plaintiffs alleged that copyright infringement accounted for 90 percent of the activity on these peer-to-peer networks. Evidence in Grokster showed that the companies marketed themselves to former Napster users and that they did not offer any way to filter copyrighted material that passed through their software.

When the Grokster case was filed in the latter part of 2001, the controlling law was found in the 1984 ruling in *Sony Corp. of America v. Universal City Studios, Inc.,* more commonly called the Betamax case.

In Betamax, the entertainment industry sued Sony for selling videocassette recorders (VCRs), because they could be used to record copyrighted movies. The Supreme Court held that Sony was not liable for damages of contributory copyright infringement. It ruled that where a product may be used for "substantial" or "commercially significant noninfringinguses" it was not liable for infringement. This was true even where VCR owners used the product in a manner that constituted copyright infringement, because the VCRs could be used for other noninfringing purposes.

The Grokster litigation reflected the everchanging face of technology, and the laws' attempts to keep up with those changes. Initially, a federal district court judge in California ruled against the music and movie industries, and declined to distinguish between Betamax and Grokster. Moreover, Judge Stephen Wilson distinguished the Ninth Circuit decision in the Napster case. Wilson found that Napster was different because it actually provided a network for the infringement to take place; these defendants did not. On appeal, the Ninth Circuit agreed, ruling that Grokster and the other defendants did not have actual knowledge of copyright infringement, nor the right or ability to supervise its users.

The Ninth Circuit opinion in Grokster conflicted with a ruling from the Seventh Circuit Court of Appeals. In the case of In re Aimster Copyright Litigation, the Seventh Circuit held that Aimster, which provided services similar to Grokster and StreamCast, was liable for violation of copyright laws.

The plaintiffs in Grokster filed a **writ** of certiorari to the Supreme Court, and the case was accepted for review. The court's unanimous decision settled the conflict between the Seventh and Ninth Circuit rulings. On June 27, 2005, in *Metro-Goldwyn-Mayer Studios Inc. v. Grokster Ltd.,* the U.S. Supreme Court ruled that companies providing peer-to-peer Internet file-sharing programs could be held liable for the copyright infringement by the users of their service. The opinion, written by Justice David Souter held that the Ninth Circuit had misread the Betamax decision. The high court determined that most of the evidence in the case indicated the defendants' purpose was to facilitate a way for users to share files illegally.

The Supreme Court returned the case to the federal district court for final resolution. Rather than continue with the litigation, the parties came to an agreement, which was announced on November 7, 2005. Grokster agreed to immediately discontinue its former business operations, and agreed to have a judgment and a permanent injunction entered against it in favor of the plaintiffs. The Grokster website in December 2005 included the following announcement: "There are legal services for downloading music and movies. This service is not one of them. Grokster hopes to have a safe and legal service available soon." The nearly-bare website also included some information and links about copyright laws.

### Campus Crackdowns

Shutting down Napster, Grokster, and other file-sharing systems has not made the problem of illegal file-sharing disappear. Moreover, illegal file-sharing has always enjoyed immense popularity among college students, so music industry officials began to concentrate anti-piracy efforts against these individuals. In December 2002, the Recording Industry Association of America (RIAA) sent letters and other warning messages to colleges and universities. College administrators pledged to work with the recording industry to prevent illegal file sharing. RIAA also announced an amnesty plan, available to persons who admitted to illegal sharing of files. Dubbed "Clean Slate ", the system required those seeking amnesty to destroy or delete all illegally downloaded copyrighted sound recordings, to refrain from downloading illegal recordings in the future, and to certify that they have not been sued for copyright infringement nor performed any downloading for a commercial purpose.

RIAA has also filed civil lawsuits against students who build their own Napster-like systems on campus. In April 2003, the RIAA filed civil lawsuits against four individual students at Princeton University, Michigan Technological University, and Rensselaer Polytechnic Institute. According to allegations in these complaints, copyright infringement at universities is a serious problem. RIAA alleged that students made between 27,000 and a million songs available through their universities' networks. The music industry also contended that statistics indicated that nearly 50 percent of the available computer resources at some universities were being used for unauthorized copying and distribution of copyrighted material. These cases were settled; defendants paid damages reported to range from $12,500 to $17,000.

The music industry continues to fight against unauthorized file-sharing. On December 15, 2005, RIAA announced copyright infringement lawsuits against 751 individuals, including students at Drexel University, Harvard University, and the University of Southern California. This announcement followed filings of more than 800 such suits in November 2005. Some of the RIAA lawsuits have been filed against unknown persons, so-called "John Doe" lawsuits. This initial approach is necessary because in 2003, the U.S. Court of Appeals for the District of Columbia ruled that RIAA could not require Internet service providers (ISPs) to provide the identities of users who had allegedly engaged in illegal file-sharing. Thus, RIAA initially files against the John Does where an individual cannot be identified. RIAA then requests a court order to force the ISPs to release the names.

## Additional Resources

*Media, Technology, and Copyright,* Michael A. Einhorn, Edward Elgar Publishing, Inc., 2004.

*Prosecuting Intellectual Property Crimes Manual,* Computer Crime and Intellectual Property Section, Criminal Division, U.S. Department of Justice, 2001, available at http://www.cybercrime.gov/ipmanual.htm

*NET Act, Summary of Changes to the Criminal Copyright and Trademark Laws, Department of Justice,* Feb. 18, 1988, available at http://www.usdoj.gov/criminal/cybercrime/netsum.htm.

## Organizations

### Motion Picture Association of America (MPAA)
15503 Ventura Blvd.
Encino, CA 91436 USA
Phone: (818) 995-6600
URL: http://www.mpaa.org
Primary Contact: Dan Glickman, Chair and CEO

### Recording Industry Association of America(RIAA)
URL: http://www.riaa.com
Primary Contact: Mitch Bainwol, Chair and CEO

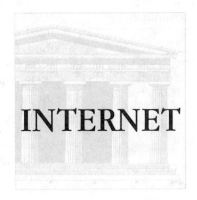

# INTERNET

## PORNOGRAPHY

*Sections within this essay:*

- Background
- Federal Restrictions on Cyber Porn
    - Child Pornography
    - Disseminating Cyber Porn to Minors
    - Filtering in Federally-funded Public Schools and Libraries
- State Laws
- Additional Resources

## Background

Internet **pornography** is a battlefield in U.S. law. Since the explosion of **public interest** in the Net in the 1990s, the public, lawmakers, and the courts have argued over how to control online porn. Congress and state legislatures have passed several laws aimed at protecting children from exposure to so-called cyber porn, but the most sweeping of these have often failed to pass constitutional tests. The failure of these laws in court means this popular yet controversial medium faces few regulations.

According to the Internet Filter Review (an industry group advocating pornography filtering), Internet pornography accounts for $2.5 billion of the $57 billion worldwide pornography market. The Review found that in 2003 there were 4.2 million pornography Web sites allowing access to 72 million worldwide visitors, of which 40 million of them were Americans. One fourth of the search engine requests every day (68 million) are for pornographic material.

In some respects, the issue continues a legal struggle many decades old. Opponents of pornography have long tried to control it on moral grounds, even as proponents sought to protect it as a valid expression of free speech. Traditionally, opponents won these battles. The Supreme Court established that **obscenity** is not protected by the First Amendment, but the difficult question in each case has been defining what is and what is not obscene. Court rulings gradually shifted from a broad, forbidding position of the late 1950s to holding, in the 1970s, that communities could set their own standards for obscenity. Replayed in countless courtrooms, the tug-of-war between these camps has continued ever since.

But the fight over cyber porn carries traditional arguments into new areas shaped by technology. A chief concern is that the Internet allows minors easy access to it through search engines—sometimes even accidentally. U.S. **Solicitor General** Ted Olson contended that minors could stumble upon or intentionally enter 28,000 commercial porn websites. Also of worry is the Internet's ability to facilitate the illegal dissemination of child pornography. And the ubiquity of Internet access has raised new social problems by introducing pornography into new settings, such as public libraries and the workplace.

Milestones in the development of Internet pornography law include the following.

- The Supreme Court established that obscenity is not protected by the First Amendment in *Roth v. United States* (1957), declaring obscenity to be "utterly without redeeming social importance."

- After subsequent cases showed the difficulty of finding a conclusive definition of obscenity, the Court restated its definition in *Miller v. California* (1973). It substituted a detailed three-part test ultimately to be used by each locality—the so-called "community standards" test.

- The Court ruled that child pornography is not a form of expression protected under the constitution in *New York v. Ferber* (1982). It has also upheld a state law prohibiting the possession and viewing of child porn in *Osborne v. Ohio* (1990).

- Seeking to control Internet porn, Congress first passed legislation in 1996. The Communications Decency Act (CDA) criminalized the dissemination over computer networks of obscene or indecent material to children.. Immediately blocked from enforcement by the courts, it was ruled unconstitutional under the First Amendment in 1997.

- Seeking to update federal child pornography law for the Internet, Congress passed the Child Pornography Prevention Act (CPPA) of 1996. Among other features, the law criminalized any visual depiction that "appears to be" child pornography, including so-called virtual porn created by computer. After lower courts struck down provisions of the **statute**, the U.S. Supreme Court agreed to hear an appeal. In *Ashcroft v. Free Speech Coalition*, (2002), the high court agreed with the Ninth Circuit that two key provisions of the CPPA were unconstitutionally overbroad (affecting both legal and illegal speech) under the First Amendment. The law was struck down.

- Congress responded by passing the Child Online Protection Act (COPA) of 1998. More narrowly written, COPA took aim at commercial online porn sites that disseminate material to minors. And, anticipating constitutional objections, it mandated that criminal cases brought under it would be tried according to contemporary community standards. The law set stiff penalties of $150,000 for each day of violation and up to six months in prison. However, COPA suffered similar setbacks in court after the ACLU and several non-pornographic online websites successfully contested it, first in federal district court in Philadelphia and then before the U.S. Court of Appeals for the

3rd Circuit. As before with the CDA, the **Justice Department** continued to appeal; this time, it argued that online porn is even more readily accessible to children and thus in need of urgent control. However, in 2004, the U.S. Supreme Court rejected Congress' version of the Child Online Protection Act (COPA), in that it did not sufficiently protect the rights of adults to consensually view sexually explicit material on the Internet. *Ashcroft v. ACLU,* No. 03-0218 (2004). The Court, by a close 5-4 vote, concluded that the government had not shown why less-restrictive alternatives (such as software filters) could not be equally or more effective. The high court noted that filtering software had come a long way in just five years, and that two less restrictive laws had passed muster, one prohibiting misleading domain names, and another creating a child-safe kids.domain, and that these and similar actions may be sufficient to protect children. The case was remanded to a lower court for further investigation and action.

- In response to this, the Department of Justice began issuing subpoenas to Google, Yahoo, and MSN, to obtain one million random Web addresses and records of all searches for a one-week period in order to prove the superiority and necessity of COPA, and the ineffectiveness of filtering technology.

As these federal cases suggest, recent outcomes have favored those who regard federal control of Internet pornography as **censorship**. That does not mean the issues are settled, as indeed partisans on both sides of the issue eagerly anticipate forthcoming proposed legislation and judicial review thereof..

## Federal Restrictions on Cyber Porn

### Child Pornography

Child pornography has long been treated severely under both federal and state law. Congress first addressed the issue with the Protection of Children Against Sexual Exploitation Act of 1977. Lawmakers later toughened restrictions in the Child Protection Act of 1984, the Child Protection and Obscenity Enforcement Act of 1988, and the Child Protection Restoration and Penalties Enhancement Act of 1990.

In the 1990s, lawmakers twice passed legislation targeting child porn online. The first was the Child

Pornography Prevention Act (CPPA) of 1996, designed both to close loopholes in existing federal child pornography law and address new technological issues by the following:

- Criminalizing the act of knowingly possessing, selling, receiving, sending, or transmitting child pornography via the internet or e-mail.

- Criminalizing so-called "virtual, or morphed" depictions of child pornography, those that appear to involve minors and those created by computer graphics software.

The law was struck down by the U.S. Supreme Court, which held that it was overbroad and would also have hurt artistic expression. *Ashcroft v. Free Speech Coalition,* (2002).

The Protection of Children from Sexual Predators Act of 1998 contains further anti-child porn provisions. Title II of the law contains the following provisions:

- Provides for the prosecution of individuals for the production of child pornography if the visual depiction was produced with materials that have been mailed, shipped, or transported in interstate or foreign commerce, including by computer.

- Tightens previous federal law by making it a criminal offense to possess for even one depiction of child pornography

- Outlines responsibilities for Internet Service Providers in reporting child pornography to authorities

- Increases federal criminal penalties for child pornography, which include fines and prison sentences ranging from 15 to 30 years

### Disseminating Cyber Porn to Minors

Although several federal laws have sought to control Internet porn, none has specifically tried to forbid it. In large part this is a recognition of the legal protections pornography enjoyed toward the end of the twentieth century. **Case law** has established that much pornography is protected speech under the First Amendment. Obscenity is not protected. However, as the Supreme Court's "community standards" doctrine acknowledges, communities measure obscenity differently: what is likely to be considered obscene by a jury in Utah is not guaran-

teed to similarly move a jury in New York. The difficulty of formulating one broad standard of obscenity for all communities is made even greater by the Internet's being a global network, available everywhere at once.

Thus rather than trying to eliminate cyber porn, Congress has twice sought to protect children from exposure to it. These laws have yet to be enforced. Both wound up in court, where sections of each were ruled unconstitutional. Crucially, the fate of one law still remains as of 2002 on appeal.

The Communications Decency Act (CDA) of 1996 was lawmakers' first attempt to regulate the availability of indecent and obscene material online to minors. The CDA prohibited the "knowing" dissemination of such material to minors over computer networks or telephone lines, establishing penalties for violations of up to five years **imprisonment** and fines of up to $250,000. But it quickly fell to a legal challenge brought by the American Civil Liberties Union (ACLU) and a coalition of major publishers. Bringing a traditional First Amendment case against censorship, they argued successfully that the law was too broad: in trying to protect kids, its prohibitions would have limited the speech of adults to a level suitable for children. After a special three-judge panel ruled against the law in Philadelphia in 1996, the Supreme Court by 7-2 vote in *American Civil Liberties Union v. Reno* (1997) held that the law unconstitutionally abridged **freedom of speech**, and thus struck down key provisions.

### Filtering in Federally-funded Public Schools and Libraries

In another attempt to protect children from exposure to cyber porn, Congress passed two laws in 2000 aimed at public schools and public libraries. Federally-funded institutions of this kind are required to put in effect Internet safety policies in order to continue qualifying for federal support. They must install so-called Internet filters on their public computers: these are commercially-available software programs, with names like Cyber Patrol and Net Nanny, that intercept and block pornographic materials. Under the terms of the Children's Internet Protection Act (CIPA) and the Neighborhood Internet Protection Act (NCIPA), filters had to be in place by 2001, although libraries were ultimately given extra time to comply.

Proving as controversial as the CDA and COPA, the laws were challenged by the American Library Association and civil liberties groups. They argued that the law will result in censorship because it relies upon inaccurate technology, citing **evidence** that some software filters erroneously block non-pornographic material, too. In *U.S. v. American Library Association,* No. 02-361 (2003), the U.S. Supreme Court upheld CIPA s constitutional.

## State Laws

State laws on Internet pornography have evolved rapidly. Prior to the rise in popularity of the Internet, most states already had laws on the books regulating age limits for purchasing pornography as well as statutes criminalizing child pornography. Many legislatures saw a need for legislation to respond to the vicissitudes of new technology. Between 1995 and 2002, nearly two dozen states considered bills that would control in some fashion access to Internet pornography. More than a dozen states enacted them.

Closely resembling federal law, state laws break down into two broad categories. In the first and broadest, the laws forbid the access by minors to what the laws usually call "harmful materials"—verbal and visual information that includes, but is not necessarily limited to, pornography. Sometimes these laws target "indecent" material; for example, Oklahoma and New York law each criminalize the transmission of indecent materials to minors.

Most state laws on transmission of indecent materials target exposure in public schools and libraries. Their remedy is to require, and in at least one case merely recommend, that these facilities install so-called Internet filtering software on their computers. At least six states have passed such laws: Arizona, Kentucky, Michigan, Minnesota, South Carolina, and Tennessee. Twenty more states were considering such legislation in 2001-2002.

Like federal law, a second category of state law targets virtual child pornography. Aggressively defining this new category of criminal offense, these laws treat so-called virtual porn as severely as actual photography of minors. In the mid-1990s, for instance, both Kansas and Montana expanded their existing statutes to prohibit transmission and possession of such images, while other states such as Missouri and Minnesota enacted new laws.

In early court challenges, much more sweeping state cyber porn laws failed to pass constitutional tests in three states. In *American Library Associa-*

*tion v. Pataki* (1997), a federal judge blocked enforcement of a New York statue prohibiting online indecency that had been modeled on the federal Communications Decency Act, ruling that it violated the Constitution's Commerce Clause. In *ACLU v. Johnson* (1998), a federal district judge ruled on First Amendment grounds that New Mexico could not enforce a law criminalizing the online dissemination of any expression that involves nudity or sexual content. And in another victory for First Amendment advocates, a federal judge blocked Michigan's 1999 law criminalizing online communications deemed harmful to minors in *Cyberspace v. Engler* (1999).

In September 2004, a federal district judge struck down Pennsylvania's 2002 law requiring Internet service providers (ISPs) to disable or block access to child pornography Websites. The law also imposed criminal sanctions on ISPs who failed to comply. In *CDT v, Pappert,* No. 03-5051 (U.S.D.C. Eastern District PA, 2004), the district court ruled that the Internet Child Pornography Act, 18 Pa. Cons. Stat., Sections 7621-7630, failed to pass muster under both First Amendment and Commerce Clause challenges under the U.S. Constitution. In summary, because the Act blocked access to legitimate Internet content far outside of the state, it could not be viewed as the least restrictive means for furthering a legitimate governmental interest under the First Amendment. Moreover, because the Act involved Internet communications, it necessarily and substantially affected interstate commerce, prohibited under the Dormant Commerce Clause of the Constitution as well.

## Additional Resources

*Constitutional Amendments: 1789 to the Present* Kris E. Palmer, ed., Gale Group, 2000.

*Cyber Liberties* American Civil Liberties Union Website. Available at http://www.aclu.org/issues/cyber/hmcl.html.

*Petitioner's Brief, Ashcroft v. Free Speech Coalition* U.S. Department of Justice, 2000. Available at http://www.usdoj.gov/osg/briefs/2000/3mer/2mer/2000-0795.mer.aa.html.

*State Internet Laws Face a Different Constitutional Challenge* Kaplan, Carl S., The New York Times, July 2, 1999.

*U.S. Supreme Court Considering Law on 'Virtual Child Porn.'* Kleder, Martha, Culture and Family Institute. Available at http://cultureandfamily.org/report/2001-11-08/n_childporn.shtml

*West Encyclopedia of American Law.* Theresa J. Lippert, ed., West Group, 1998.

## Organizations

### American Civil Liberties Union (ACLU)

125 Broad Street, 18th Floor
New York, NY 10004 USA
Phone: (212) 549-2500
URL: http://www.aclu.org
Primary Contact: Nadine Strossen, Pres.

### American Family Association

P.O. Box 2440
Tupelo, MS 38803 USA
Phone: (662) 844-5036
Fax: (662) 842-7798
URL: http://www.afa.net
Primary Contact: Donald E. Wildmon, Pres.

### Federal Bureau of Investigation

J. Edgar Hoover Building, 935 Pennsylvania
Avenue, N.W.
Washington, DC 20535-0001 USA
Phone: (202) 324-3000
Fax: ()
URL: http://www.fbi.gov
Primary Contact: Robert S. Mueller III, Dir.

# LABOR LAW

## AT-WILL EMPLOYMENT

*Sections within this essay:*

- Background
- History
- Application of the Doctrine
- Exceptions
    - Public Policy
    - Written Employment Contracts
    - Oral Contracts
    - Employee Handbooks and Manuals
    - Good Faith and Fair Dealing
    - Statutes
- Selected State Laws Concerning At-Will Employment
- Additional Resources

## Background

In many employment situations, the law generally considers the employment relationship to be terminable at the will of either party. That is, an employer may terminate an employee at the will of an employer, while an employee may quit at any time. When either of these events occur, the party that ends the relationship is not liable to the other, even if this termination causes damage to the other party. This type of relationship is termed employment at-will.

Although rules governing at-will employment remain largely intact today, courts and legislatures have crafted some exceptions to these rules. Some of these exceptions apply when the employer and the employee have entered into a contract. Other excep-

tions apply when the discharge violates a mandate of public policy or when an employer violates a duty to exercise good faith and fair dealing with the employee. Though these exceptions do not prohibit an employer from terminating an employee, they will allow the employee to recover damages. Individual states vary regarding protections offered to employees in an at-will employment relationship.

The United States remains the only major industrial power that adheres to the at-will employment doctrine. Other nations, including Great Britain, France, Italy, Germany, and Japan, each have statutes that require employers to show good cause before the employers can terminate employees.

## History

Historically, courts in England did not adhere to rules that recognized an employment relationship as one that could be terminated by either party at any time. In fact, ancient statutes and early decisions sought to protect employees by presuming that the employment relationship would last for a certain period of time, such as one year. This type of rule prevented employers from hiring employees for a short period of time, such as for the duration of a harvest season, and then firing the employee during the winter season, when the employee would not have food or shelter.

Courts in the United States during the 19th century began to follow the rule that where an employee did not have a contract for a fixed length of time, the employer could terminate the employment relationship at any time. H.G. Wood, an author of a leading treatise on the relationship between master and servant, formulated a rule in 1886 that set forth the employment at will doctrine. Nearly every state eventually adopted the at-will doctrine as the law governing employment relationships.

## Application of the Doctrine

The employment at will doctrine contains three major rules. The first general rule is that an employer is not liable for any alleged damages suffered by an employee who is fired arbitrarily. Until courts in the 1980s began to recognize exceptions to the at-will doctrine (see below), the courts generally refused to award damages to discharged employees, even in situations where the employer did not follow its own procedures or where the employer acted with malice. The second general rule is that an employee who alleges that his or her employment contract was for a specified term has the burden of proving that the contract was for a defined term. The third general rule is that a court will construe an employment contract for an indefinite period of time, including a contract for "permanent" employment, to mean that the employment relationship is at will.

## Exceptions

The employment at will doctrine often leads to harsh results. Employees often feel a strong need for security in their jobs, but the doctrine provides no such security since an employer can terminate an employee without any recourse in the law. Civil rights legislation enacted in the 1960s provided support for the idea that employers should not have unfettered rights to hiring and firing of employees. Discharged employees challenged the at-will doctrine in courts during the 1970s and 1980s and eventually experienced some success. Courts began to allow employees to recover damages in suits for wrongful discharge.

The major exceptions to the employment at will doctrine are as follows:

## Public Policy

The first recognized exception to the employment at will doctrine applies when an employer terminates an employee in a manner that violates public policy. This exception generally applies in four circumstances: (1) an employee refuses to perform an illegal act at the request of an employer; (2) an employee attempts to exercise a legal right provided by statute, such as filing a workers' compensation claim; (3) the employee reports on an employer's illegal acts, also known as "whistleblowing;" and (4) an employee attempts to perform a public duty, such as serving on a jury.

The majority of states recognize at least some form of a public policy exception. Courts are generally more likely to recognize a public policy exception that is based on a statute than one based on some other authority, such as a constitutional right. Thus, for instance, employees who have attempted to argue that they were wrongfully discharged for engaging in actions allegedly protected by the First Amendment to the U.S. Constitution have not had significant success in the courts.

This exception does not eliminate the employment at will doctrine, but rather allows employees to recover for wrongful discharge.

## Written Employment Contracts

Some employees enter into employment relationships by signing employment contracts, although the number of employees in general who have such contracts is relatively small. Company executives, highly paid employees, and highly skilled employees are examples of those who may receive written employment agreements. These contracts contain the terms of employment, including salaries, the length of the employment contract, provisions regarding early termination, and so forth.

An employee who has a written contract with his or her employer must first prove the existence of the contract. Once the employee has proven this, then the employee must prove that the employer has breached the agreement. Whether an employer has breached a contract depends on the terms of the agreement itself. In some instances, a contract may restrict an employer from terminating an employee except for certain reasons or by following certain procedures. The employee must prove that the employer breached the agreement in order to recover.

## Oral Contracts

In some instances, an employer may make oral promises to an employee regarding job security. These promises often take place before the employee is hired and are often intended to entice the employee to work for the employer. Although employees may have difficulty proving that an employer has made an oral promise, courts frequently enforce such promises of job security.

As is the case with a written contract, the specific language than an employer uses when making an oral promise will determine whether a court will enforce the contract or treat the relationship as one that is at will. Courts are more likely to enforce a contract that states a more definite period of time. Such a period of time may be very specific, such as a promise for employment for one year, or it may be determined in some objective manner, such as a promise that an employee will remain employed until the completion of a particular project. Courts have struggled with other types of promises, such as a promise of "permanent" or "lifetime" employment. Some courts treat an employment relationship under such a promise merely as an employment at will relationship, while other courts view such a promise as a commitment to continued employment so long as the employee remains alive.

## Employee Handbooks and Manuals

Employees often provide standardized instructions to employees through the use of employee handbooks or manuals. These handbooks allow the employers to train a large number of employees without the use of individual training. These handbooks can set forth the employer's standard employment practices and establish the expectations of employees. Provisions in a handbook or manual may include descriptions of the following examples:

- Compensation of employees
- Health and other benefits offered to employees
- Work hours
- Overtime
- Leaves of absence
- Holidays
- Vacation time
- Rules of expected behavior
- Discharge
- Discipline and disciplinary procedures
- Grievance
- Promotion

Until the 1980s, courts seldom enforced the terms of an employee handbook as a contract. In many instances, handbooks do not contain language that a court would construe as promissory in nature. However, courts in the 1980s began to recognize that language in these handbooks may bind the employer contractually. The majority of jurisdictions now recognize an employee handbook as an exception to at-will employment.

A number of issues may arise in the context of employee handbooks. Many cases involve a question of whether an employer may fire an employee and, if so, whether the employer followed the proper procedures in firing the employee. Cases involving employee handbooks often turn on whether the language in a handbook is sufficiently specific. For instance, if a handbook sets forth a list of reasons why an employer may fire an employee, courts will likely find that this language binds the employer. On the other hand, if a handbook is vague about reasons for a discharge, courts are more likely to determine that the relationship is at will.

Where an employer includes language indicating that an employee handbook does not constitute a promise or a contract, courts usually rule in favor of the employer. In such an instance, the courts require that the disclaimer is clear and unequivocal, that it is placed conspicuously, and that the disclaimer is communicated to the employee.

## Good Faith and Fair Dealing

A minority of states recognize that an employment contract may give rise to an implied covenant of good faith and fair dealing. Although this concept applies generally to all contracts, courts traditionally did not apply this covenant in cases involving employment contracts. This situation often arises where an employee has accrued benefits and the employer takes an action that effectively deprives the employee of these benefits. For instance, assume that an employee of a company has just completed a large sale, and the company will owe a large commission to the employee. On the following day, the company fires the employee, thus avoiding the requirement of paying the commission. In states that recognize an implied covenant of good faith and fair dealing, a court may apply the covenant to require payment of the commission.

## Federal Statutes

A number of federal statutes restrict employers from discharging employees on certain grounds. A listing of these statutes is as follows:

- Age Discrimination in Employment Act
- Americans with Disabilities Act
- Civil Rights Act of 1964
- Clean Air Act
- Consumer Credit Protection Act
- Employee Retirement Income Security Act
- Energy Reorganization Act of 1974
- Fair Labor Standards Act
- Family and Medical Leave Act
- Federal Water Pollution Control Act
- Judiciary and Judicial Procedure Act
- National Labor Relations Act
- Occupational Safety and Health Act of 1970
- Railroad Safety Act
- Vietnam Era Veterans Readjustment Assistance Act
- Vocational Rehabilitation Act of 1973

### Selected State Laws Concerning At-Will Employment

The vast majority of states recognize at least one exception to the employment at will doctrine. The most commonly accepted exception is the public policy exception; the only states that do not recognize this exception include Alabama, Florida, Georgia, Louisiana, Maine, New York, and Rhode Island. A few states have enacted piecemeal legislation related to at-will employment, though only Montana has enacted a comprehensive statute on the subject.

The following provides summaries of some selected state laws regarding application of the doctrine of at will employment and its exceptions:

ALABAMA: The Alabama Supreme Court has held that even where an employment contract has been made with reference to and subject to workers' compensation laws, this did not restrict an employer's right to terminate the contract at will. Several cases have reaffirmed the employment at will doctrine.

CALIFORNIA: The California Supreme Court has recognized that an employer who has violated a mandate of public policy may be liable under a contract in tort.

CONNECTICUT: The Connecticut Supreme Court in a 1980 case held that an at-will employee could recover for wrongful discharge after the employer fired the employee for insisting that the employer comply with the Food, Drug, and Cosmetics Act.

IDAHO: In 1996, the Idaho Supreme Court ruled that a teacher could recover for wrongful discharge after the state department of education fired her for missing work when she responded to a subpoena. According to the court, the firing violated public policy because failure to comply with a subpoena could be punished by contempt under a state statute.

INDIANA: Indiana courts have recognized that an employee may have a cause of action when an employer retaliates after an employee has exercised a statutorily-conferred right, an employee has refused to perform an unlawful act, or the employee has breached a statutorily-imposed duty.

IOWA: The Iowa Supreme Court recognizes two exceptions to the general rule of at-will employment. First, an employee may recover when a discharge violates a well-established and well-defined public policy. Second, an employee may recover when an employee handbook creates an implied contract.

KANSAS: The Kansas Supreme Court has recognized that an employee may recover for wrongful discharge where the employee is terminated for filing a workers' compensation claim.

MASSACHUSETTS: The Supreme Judicial Court of Massachusetts has stated that an employee may be terminated at any time, for any reason, or for no reason at all.

MONTANA: Montana has enacted the Wrongful Discharge from Employment Act. In most instances, an employee may only be discharged for "good cause." The statute defines good cause as reasonable job-related grounds for dismissal based on failure to satisfactorily perform job duties, disruption of employer's operation, or other legitimate business reasons.

NEW HAMPSHIRE: The New Hampshire Supreme Court has held that termination of an at-will employment relationship that is motivated by bad faith or malice on the part of the employer is not in the best interest of the legal system and constitutes a breach of contract.

NEW JERSEY: The New Jersey Supreme Court has held that an employee may have a cause of action for wrongful discharge when the discharge is contrary to a clear mandate of public policy. Such a mandate may appear in the form of legislation; administrative rules, regulations, or decisions; or judicial decisions.

OHIO: Ohio courts recognize the tort of wrongful discharge in derogation of public policy. This tort has four elements, including the following: (1) the clarity element, which requires that a clear public policy existed and was manifest under state or federal law; (2) the jeopardy element, which requires that the dismissal of employees like those involved in the plaintiff's dismissal would jeopardize public policy; (3) the causation element, under which a plaintiff must prove that the dismissal was motivated by conduct related to the public policy; and (4) the overriding justification element, where a plaintiff must prove that the employer lacked a legitimate business justification for the dismissal.

SOUTH DAKOTA: A South Dakota statute defines termination of employment at will as follows: "An employment having no specified term may be terminated at the will of either party on notice to the other, unless otherwise provided by statute."

VERMONT: The Vermont Supreme Court has held that the dismissal of an at-will employee on the basis of age contravened public policy and established a cause of action under the public policy exception to at-will employment.

WISCONSIN: The Wisconsin Supreme Court held that an employee could recover under the public policy exception to at-will employment when the employer was terminated for refusing to drive a company truck after telling the company that he did not have a required license to operate the truck.

## Additional Resources

*Employment Law in a Nutshell.* Covington, Robert N. and Kurt H. Decker, St. Paul: West Group, 2002

*Employment Law.* 3rd Edition, Rothstein, Mark A., Charles B. Craver, Elinor P. Schroeder, and Elaine W. Shoben, St. Paul: Thomson/West, 2005.

*West's Encyclopedia of American Law* 2nd Edition, Thomson/Gale, 2004.

## Organizations

### American Bar Association Section of Labor and Employment Law
321 N. Clark Street
Chicago, IL 60610 USA
Phone: (312) 988-5813
Fax: (312) 988-5814
URL: http://www.abanet.org/labor/home.html

### National Employment Law Project
55 John Street, 7th Floor
New York, NY 10038 USA
Phone: (212) 285-3025
Fax: (212) 285-3044
URL: http://www.nelp.org

### National Employment Lawyers Association
44 Montgomery Street, Suite 2080
San Francisco, CA 94104
Phone: (415) 296-7629
Fax: (415) 677-9445
URL: http://www.nela.org/home.cfm

### U.S. Department of Labor
200 Constitution Avenue, NW
Washington, DC 20210 USA
Phone: (866) 4-USA-DOL
URL: http://www.dol.gov

# LABOR LAW

## BENEFITS

*Sections within this essay:*

- Background
- Federal Laws that Impact Employee Benefits
    - Laws that Mandate Certain Benefits
    - Laws that Impact Employee Benefits
- Optional Employee Benefits
    - Nontraditional and Emerging Employee Benefits
    - Employee "Cafeteria Plan" Benefits
- Benefit Incidence Among Medium to Large Employers
- Additional Resources

## Background

Employee benefits are those incentives, amenities, or perquisites ("perqs") that employees receive above and beyond their basic salaries or wages. Certain benefits are required by law (such as overtime pay or excused absences under the Family and Medical Leave Act). Additional benefits or "benefit packages" are generally negotiated as employment terms and conditions between employer and employee. They may be negotiated individually between the parties or through labor-management contract negotiations affecting classes of employees as a whole. Importantly, if employees are represented by bargaining units within a union, they cannot negotiate directly with employer representatives for any change, addition, or deletion of a benefit (this statement does not relate to employee "choice" benefits packages, popularly referred to as "cafeteria plans," discussed below).

An employee benefit may be something as simple as free soft drinks during working hours or as complex as stock options or profit sharing plans. Typically, benefits include such advantages as health and life insurance, paid vacation or time off, flexible work hours, holiday pay, and retirement or **pension** pay.

## Federal Laws that Impact Employee Benefits

### Laws that Mandate Certain Benefits

There are certain employee benefits, above and beyond wages, that are legally required of all employers. These include social security contributions, federal and state unemployment insurance, and worker's compensation. The unemployment insurance program was established under Title IX of the federal **Social Security Act of 1935** (42 **USC** 1101), which also governs social security contributions. Minimum working conditions and working environments are mandated by the federal Occupational Safety and Health Act (OSHA).

### Laws that Impact Employee Benefits

- The **Employee Retirement Income Security Act** (ERISA) regulates employers who offer pension or retirement benefit plans to their employees. One of the most important components of ERISA as it relates to employee benefits is that certain employers and plan administrators must pay premiums to the federal government for insurance to protect employee retirement benefits.

- The Comprehensive Omnibus Budget Reconciliation Act (COBRA) has an important provision requiring the continuation of health-care benefits for employees whose employment is terminated (voluntarily or involuntarily) for a certain number of months, which may be further extended if employees pay the associated costs.

- The National Labor Relations Act (NLRA) guarantees freedom of choice and majority rule for employees in choosing exclusive bargaining representatives to negotiate benefits for covered bargaining unit employees.

- The Labor-Management Reporting and Disclosure Act of 1959 (also known as the Landrum-Griffin Act) protects employee contributions to union funds by requiring labor organizations to file annual financial reports.

- The Family and Medical Leave Act (FMLA) requires employers with 50 or more employees to allow up to 12 weeks of unpaid, job-protected leave for the birth or **adoption** of a child or the serious illness of an employee or a spouse, child, or parent.

- Veterans' Preference laws permit special employment preference rights for eligible veterans applying for governmental jobs. The preferential factors apply only at the time of initial hiring and/or in the event of a reduction in force.

## Optional Employee Benefits

Following is a list of some of the more common employee benefits, sometimes referred to as fringe benefits, negotiated between employers and employees as conditions of employment. No law or constitution requires the offering of any of these benefits. However, once they have been contractually negotiated as part of the terms and conditions of employment, the failure to provide such benefits may expose employers to liability for breach of contract claims.

- Health and Life Insurance: Contrary to popular belief, no federal law requires employers to grant health and life insurance coverage to their employees. Health insurance coverage may be totally provided by the employer but is more often based on co-payment of insurance premiums with the employee. Spousal and/or dependent coverage is also an option. Long-term **disability** insurance is a premium benefit that most employers do not offer without substantial contributions from the employee toward the cost of the premiums.

- Paid Holidays: Contrary to popular belief, no federal law requires employers to grant paid holiday benefits to their employees. Paid holiday benefits are generally in the form of receiving full pay for a non-worked holiday or receiving premium pay for having worked on the holiday. The number of days designated as holidays varies from employer to employer, although certain ones are considered "standard," irrespective of an employee's personal beliefs or customs. They include: New Year's Day, Memorial Day, the Fourth of July, Labor Day, Thanksgiving, and Christmas Day. There are a handful of other days that employers may consider holidays, including Presidents' Day, Veterans' Day, Martin Luther King Day, etc.

- Pension and Retirement Benefits: This area of benefits, although optional on the part of the employer, invokes the greatest federal and state governance. Pension programs are covered in a separate entry. However, if a private employer does not provide a pension plan, the federal Internal Revenue Code permits individual workers to establish their own individual retirement accounts (IRAs) with registered financial institutions and to set aside a certain percentage of **earned income** each year as tax-deferred contributions to the accounts. Self-employed persons may establish Keogh retirement accounts, which accomplish the same purpose.

- Paid Leave: This benefit may be in the form of vacation pay, paid sick leave, "personal days," funeral leave, military leave, or jury duty.

- Supplemental Pay: This benefit is used as an incentive for working less than desirable days or shifts. It includes overtime, weekend, or holiday pay, shift differentials, and nonproduction bonuses.

### Nontraditional and Emerging Employee Benefits

In a way to induce employee hiring and retention, a number of employers have resorted to fewer common benefits packaging or offerings. These may include such desirable amenities as employee stock ownership plans (ESOPs), tuition reimbursement or paid higher education, dental or optical insurance coverage, child daycare services, paid parking or other commuting subsidies, fitness center or private club memberships, legal aid plans, company cars, flextime hours, casual work attire, home office assignments, and "domestic partner" benefits. A common benefit in the retail industry is a percentage discount on employee purchases of company products.

### Employee "Cafeteria Plan" Benefits

Cafeteria plans, created by the Revenue Act of 1978 and governed by Section 125 of the Internal Revenue Code, are tax-qualified flexible benefit plans that offer employees choices in putting together their own benefits package by choosing from a list of options (thus, the term "cafeteria," indicating a pick-and-choose approach to individualized benefits). The popular plan program allows employees to choose between taxable benefits (such as cash or vacation pay) and at least two nontaxable benefits (such as term-life, dental, or health insurance).

Cafeteria plans are characterized by "open enrollment" periods during which plan participants must choose and enroll for selected benefits. The plans are renewed on a yearly basis, and mid-year alterations or amendments are only permitted when there is a "change in status" of an employee (e.g., change in marital status, number of dependents, a change in residence, a change in employment status, or a return from unpaid leave).

Section 125 benefits plans, including cafeteria plans, allow pre-tax allocation of employee wages toward benefit contributions, thus reducing the employee's **taxable income**. Another benefit plan qualified for Section 125 tax treatment is the Flexible Spending Account (FSA) which allows employees to set aside pretax monies to help pay for unreimbursed medical expenses and/or dependent care. However, in both forms of plans, unused benefits and unspent funds are forfeited.

## Benefit Incidence Among Medium to Large Employers

The National Compensation Survey (NCS) of the U.S. Bureau of Labor Statistics tracks and publishes data on benefit incidence (expressed in terms of percentages of workers with access to or participation in employer-provided benefit plans). According to the last published NCS Survey (2001, based on 1999

data), the most prevalent employee benefit available to workers in the private sector was paid time off (with paid vacation and paid holidays being the most recurrent benefits).

Paid sick leave and term life insurance was an employee benefit enjoyed by more than half of all private-sector workers (in the 70s percentile for both). Fifty-three percent of employees participated in health care plan benefit programs, and 48 percent were covered by retirement or pension plans (most of which were contribution plans). Short- and long-term disability benefits were available to 36 and 25 percent of employees, respectively. The other frequently offered benefits were non-production bonuses (available to 42 percent of employees) and job-related education assistance (available to 41 percent of employees).

Benefit coverage in general was much more prevalent (predictably) among full-time employees: 64 percent of full-time, versus 14 percent of part-time employees, were covered by health care plans (overall, 53 percent of all employees were covered). Likewise 56 percent of full-time (versus 21 percent of part-time) employees were covered by retirement benefits plans (with 48 percent of all employees enrolled).

The greatest disparity in benefit incidence was in relation to the size of the company or establishment. For example, 81 percent of workers in companies with more than 2,500 employees had a retirement plan, compared with just 30 percent of workers with small establishments of 50 employees or less. Paid holidays were offered to 82 percent of employees in large establishments, compared to 66 percent in the smallest establishments.

Blue-collar and service workers were more likely to have their health care benefits fully paid for by their employers than their counterparts in professional or technical jobs. Goods-producing industries had a higher incidence of benefits coverage than did service-producing industries. Finally, geographic location affected benefits coverage, although less dramatically: 53 percent of workers in the Northeast and Midwest—compared with 47 percent in the West, and 43 percent in the South—were covered by retirement benefits. Overall incidence of benefits, expressed by specific benefit, was as follows. (All fifty states were included in the NCS survey.)

- Retirement benefits: Forty-eight percent of all workers were participating in retirement plans. This number included 79 percent of union employees and 44 percent of non-union employees. Employee contribution plans outweighed defined benefits by approximately 15 percent.

- Health care benefits: Fifty-three percent of all workers were covered by health insurance plans. This number included 73 percent of all union members and 51 percent of non-union members.

- Dental care benefits: Fifty-two percent of all workers enjoyed dental care insurance benefits, and 52 percent of union workers had dental coverage.

- Life insurance: Fifty-six percent of all workers had term life insurance as an employee benefit. This number included 78 percent of union members and 76 percent of those in professional or technical fields. The retail trade had the lowest incidence of life insurance benefits.

- Paid sick leave: Only 53 percent of all workers had paid sick leave, parallel with a 54 percent union member benefit incidence. Incidence (occurrence of available benefits, not occurrence of use of the paid sick leave) was highest among professional and technical employees (81 percent).

- Short-term disability insurance: Thirty-six percent of all workers were covered under short-term disability plans, with highest incidence among union employees (66 percent).

- Paid vacation: Just under 80 percent of all employees enjoyed paid vacations, higher among union members (86 percent) and professional/technical employees (88 percent) (75 percent for blue-collar or service employees). Forty-three percent of part-time employees were eligible for vacation benefits.

- Paid holidays: Seventy-five percent of all employees were paid for holidays. This number included 82 percent of union employees and 75 percent of non-union employees, but 36 percent of part-time employees. The retail industry faired poorly, with only 50 percent of employees being paid for holidays; manu-

facturing and utilities companies offered paid holidays to approximately 92 percent of their workers.

- On-site **child care**: Only three percent of all workers participated in this benefit, with highest incidence (ten percent) in companies employing 2,500 or more. Prevalence of this benefit was slightly higher in the Northeast and lowest in the West.

- Severance pay: Twenty-two percent of all workers were protected with severance pay benefits, slightly higher (28 percent) among union members. The benefit most often occurred in companies employing 2,500 or more (53 percent), and the benefit appeared most frequently in the finance, insurance, and real estate industries (44 percent).

- Educational assistance: Work-related education assistance appeared as an available benefit most often in companies employing 2,500 or more (70 percent) and in the finance, insurance, and real estate industries (69 percent). Overall benefit incidence was 41 percent. Ten percent of employees received an education benefit that was not work-related.

- Savings and thrift plans: Of those establishments with 100 or more workers, 87 percent of participating employees may choose how their funds are invested and 65 percent may choose how the employer's matching funds are invested. The most recurring investment choices were company stock funds, **common stock** funds, bond funds, government **securities**, and guaranteed investment contracts.

## Additional Resources

*"Employee Benefits in Private Industry."* United States Department of Labor, Bureau of Labor Statistics, National Compensation Survey. 1999. Available at http://www.bls.gov/news/release/ebs2.t01.htm.

"Kinder, Simpler Cafeteria Rules" Hirschman. Carolyn. *HR Magazine*, January 2001.

*Summary of American Law* Weinstein, Martin. The Lawyers Cooperative Publishing Company: 1988.

"Summary of DOL Laws and Programs." U.S. Dept. of Labor. Available at http://www.dol.gov/opa/aboutdol/lawsprog.htm.

# LABOR LAW

## DISCRIMINATION

*Sections within this essay:*

- Background

- Federal Laws Prohibiting Employment Discrimination
    - National Labor Relations Act of 1935
    - Fair Labor Standards Act of 1938
    - Equal Pay Act of 1963
    - Title VII of the Civil Rights Act of 1964
    - Age Discrimination in Employment Act of 1967
    - Rehabilitation Act of 1973
    - Civil Service Reform Act of 1978
    - Pregnancy Discrimination Act of 1978
    - Immigration Reform and Control Act of 1986
    - Americans With Disabilities Act of 1990
    - Family Medical Leave Act of 1993

- State Laws and Statutes Prohibiting Employment Discrimination

## Background

Over the course of the last 150 years, the majority of laws in the United States to protect employees from unfair labor practices perpetrated by employers were enacted as a result of the labor movement and realization of workers' rights. As the workers' role in mass production became vital to the capitalist market economy during the Industrial Revolution that commenced in Europe and spread to the United States in the 1820s, protection of workers' rights and government intervention (particularly the Federal government) to regulate employers to protect workers became a necessity to prevent exploitation of workers (including child laborers) in often dangerous working conditions. An outgrowth of this movement to protect employees and employees' rights from dangerous conditions and unfair wages and hours was the protection of employees from **discrimination** by employers. More specifically, laws were enacted and enforced to prevent discrimination of targeted groups such as women and racial minorities and ensuring all employees are granted equal rights with respect to hiring, promotion, and termination decisions.

Laws specifically designed to protect workers commenced in earnest during the New Deal policies of Franklin Delano Roosevelt's presidential administration. New Deal policies, intended to ease the hardships caused by the depression, included laws to assist workers. The most prominent laws enacted by the Federal Government to protect workers during this period were the National Labor Relations Act of 1935 and the **Fair Labor Standards Act** of 1938. Provisions of the National Labor Relations Act of 1935 were initially part of the National Industry Recovery Act of 1933. However, employers and leaders in the business community did not embrace the provisions of the act. Employers and business leaders felt that the National Recovery Act of 1933 gave the Federal government too much power to regulate the operations and administration of businesses and would ultimately stifle competition. A contentious court battle ensued after passage of the act and the United States Supreme Court declared the National Industry Recovery Act of 1933 invalid in the case of *A.L.A.*

*Schechter Poultry Corporation v. United States* (1935). Provisions of the National Recovery Act of 1933 that mandated that workers receive a **minimum wage** salary and rights to join unions were then incorporated into the National Labor Relations Act of 1935. The validity of the National Labor Relations Act of 1935 was challenged before the Supreme Court in 1937 in *National Labor Relations Board v. Jones & Loughlin Steel Corporation* (1937). The Supreme Court, however, upheld the National Labor Relations Act of 1935 (also referred to as the Wagner Act) in a landmark decision that began an era of intervention by the Federal government to address unfair labor practices.

Labor laws pertaining specifically to discrimination have endeavored to protect workers from discrimination by their employer(s) based upon the employees race, gender, religion, national origin, age, marital status or physical **disability**. These laws were enacted as a derivative of both the greater labor movement and the "civil rights revolution" of the 1960s that sought to end discrimination in all social institutions, including the workplace. Labor discrimination may take several forms, but laws specifically prohibiting employment practices, such as discriminatory hiring, promotion, job assignment, termination, compensation and various types of harassment, were enacted by Federal law beginning in the early 1960s. There are also laws prohibiting retaliation against employees who initially lodge complaints. These laws are designed to protect employees. Some federal laws, however, do not always apply to state and local governments. In some late 1990s cases, the Supreme Court ruled that the federal laws place undue regulatory powers on state and local governments. In those instances, employees are protected by state and local laws but not federal laws.

## Federal Laws Prohibiting Employment Discrimination

### National Labor Relations Act of 1935

The National Labor Relations Board (NLRB) was created by passage of the National Labor Relations Act of 1935. The NLRB allows workers to anonymously vote to unionize their workplace. The provisions of the NLRB apply to all employers engaged in interstate commerce although airlines, railroads, agriculture, and government employers are exempt. The five board members are appointed by the president of the United States. There are two principle aims of the NLRB: to determine the free-will choice of employees to be represented by unions by means of secret-balloting and to deter and remedy unfair labor practices by employers and unions. The NLRB investigates complaints of unfair labor practices. If the NLRB determines there is reasonable cause to suspect a violation, an attempt is made by the NLRB to settle the complaint between the disputing parties. If there is no agreeable **settlement**, a formal complaint is issued and the complaint is heard before a NLRB administrative law judge. The judge issues an opinion that may be appealed to the board of the NLRB. The board's decision is subject to review by the United States **court of appeal**. About 35,000 charges are filed annually with the NLRB.

### Fair Labor Standards Act of 1938

The principle aim of the Fair Labor Standards Act (FLSA) was to ensure minimum wage and maximum hour requirements for all nonunion workers. The initial intent was to protect children, particularly those exploited and working in bad factory conditions. The FLSA helps entry level workers in low wage jobs, such as manufacturing and agriculture, by establishing minimum wage and maximum hour provisions. As of 2002, the minimum wage is $5.15 per hour worked and workers who work more than 40 hours in a 168-hour seven day workweek cycle must be compensated at one and one-half times their regular hourly wage.

The FLSA was amended in 1974 to extend to all employees of States and local governments. However, an organization of municipalities and state governments sued, proclaiming that the new amendments exceeded congressional authority to extend the minimum wage and maximum hours provisions of the FSLA. In a landmark decision, the United States Supreme Court held in the 1976 decision of *National League of Cities et al. v. Usery, Secretary of Labor* (1976) that the 1974 amendments of the FLSA did exceed congressional power and were therefore unconstitutional. The case limited Federal power to regulate state and local employers concerning minimum wage and maximum hours provisions.

### Equal Pay Act of 1963

The Equal Pay Act of 1963 amended the FLSA by prohibiting wages based upon gender. According to the act, "equal work in jobs requiring equal skill, effort and responsibility and performed under similar working conditions" should be compensated equally, regardless of gender. Provisions of the Equal Pay Act of 1963 are enforced by Equal Employment Opportunity Commission (**EEOC**).

### Title VII of the Civil Rights Act of 1964

Title VII of the **Civil Rights** Act of 1964 (CRA) prohibits employment discrimination based on race, color, religion, sex, and national origin. There have been several notable amendments to the original CRA enactment in 1964. The act protects prospective and incumbent employees against those prohibited acts of failing or refusing to hire or discharging or discriminating with respect to promotion decisions.

The most practical legislation to ensure compliance regarding these matters was the creation of the Equal Employment Opportunity Commission. The Equal Employment Opportunity Commission (EEOC) seeks to prevent unlawful discriminatory employment practices by investigating complaints and advocating on behalf of complainants. If the respondent is a public organization such as a public agency or government agency, and the EEOC finds an unlawful employment practice, the EEOC requests the organization to refrain. If the responding organization does not agree with the findings of the EEOC, the EEOC may commence a **civil action**. The court adjudicating the case then makes a determination. The court may reinstate or hire employees with or without back pay or any other relief. Discrimination may also be remedied by altering policies. Respondents may also appeal adverse rulings.

According to the CRA, employers may not engage in practices that may have a "disparate impact" on employees of a particular race, gender, religion, or national origin. Disparate impact occurs when a particular group is not hired or promoted at the same rate as another group. Proving a disparate impact practice may be difficult. The employee (the "plaintiff") must prove prima facie **evidence** of disparate impact. If the plaintiff is successful, the burden of proof then shifts to the employer, the "respondent," who must then claim that the selection methods and decisions are job related. Bonifide occupational qualifications (BFOQs) are requirements necessary for specific employment. For example, people who want to be public safety workers such as police officers and firefighters must be physically fit.

Unlawful employment practices may consist of discriminating against a particular race by not hiring or promoting because of race or not hiring or promoting members of that race at the same rate of other races hired or promoted. Violations involving national origin may consist of "English-speaking only" work rules. Employers may not discriminate because of accent or manner of speaking. Employers

may not schedule examinations or other selection or promotional exams in conflict with employees' days of worship. The employer may not also maintain a restrictive dress code in conflict with specific religious attire. Also, mandatory "new age" training programs such as yoga or meditation may conflict with the non-discriminatory provisions of the religious. As of 2002, the EEOC handled between 75,000 and 80,000 complaints each year.

The Civil Rights Act (and subsequent amendments) grants power to recover **compensatory damages** and **punitive damages** for violations of other laws, such as the Americans with Disabilities Act of 1990 and the Rehabilitation Act of 1973. The Civil Rights Act of 1991 amended several provisions of Title VII including extending the category aggrieved parties to include United State citizens working in foreign countries and clarifying what is necessary for the plaintiff to prove.

### Age Discrimination in Employment Act of 1967

Discrimination based upon age has been the subject of numerous debates. The debate involves classification of age discrimination within discrimination based upon race, color, sex, national origin, or religion. The idea that older persons are not targeted because everyone ultimately ages is central to the debate. That is to say, since everyone ages, there is no separate class for aging individuals. Older persons do not form a unique and distinct class. The resistance to classifying age with race, gender, and religion caused it to be omitted from the original Civil Rights Act of 1964. Subsequently there were numerous challenges of the ADEA. The ADEA was originally intended for private employers; however, in 1974, amendments extended it to local and state governments. There have been two landmark Supreme Court cases regarding the application of the ADEA to state employers. In 1983, the Supreme Court held in the case of *EECO v. Wyoming* (1983) that the ADEA was a valid exercise of congressional authority. However, the Supreme Court later ruled in *Kimel et al. v. Florida Board of Regents* (2000) that persons could not sue state and local employers for violations.

### Rehabilitation Act of 1973

The Rehabilitation Act of 1973 protects employees with "handicaps" from discriminatory practices by their employers. Persons are defined as handicapped by the Rehabilitation Act of 1973 if they have a physical or mental impairment that substantially limits one major activity or has a record of such impairment or is regarded as having such an impairment. The Rehabilitation Act of 1973 also provides money to states for employment training and counseling for persons with handicaps. Several provisions of the Rehabilitation Act of 1973 specify groups protected and rights granted. Section 504 prohibits organizations that receive federal assistance from discriminating against qualified persons with handicaps. The 1992 amendments brought the Rehabilitation Act of 1973 into compliance with the Americans with Disabilities Act (ADA). The act required states to provide access devices for persons with handicaps. The amendments in 1998 require access to electronic and information technology provided by the Federal government unless doing so causes an "undue burden." Provisions of the Rehabilitation Act of 1973 are enforced by the Office of Civil Rights (OCR).

### Civil Service Reform Act of 1978

The Civil Service Reform Act of 1978 (CSRA) prohibits any employee with the authority to make personnel decisions from discriminating against applicants or incumbent employees based on the person's race, color, national origin, religion, sex, age, or disability. The CSRA also grants certain protections against personnel actions based upon a person's marital status or political affiliation. Provisions of the CSRA are enforced by the Federal Office of Special **Counsel** (OSC) and the Merit Systems Protection Board (MSPB).

### Pregnancy Discrimination Act of 1978

The Pregnancy Discrimination Act (PDA) is an amendment to Title VII of the Civil Rights Act of 1964 enacted in 1978, requires employers not to discriminate because of pregnancy, childbirth, or medical conditions related to pregnancy and childbirth. The PDA also applies to all females regardless of marital status. Provisions of the PDA are enforced by the EEOC.

### Immigration Reform and Control Act of 1986

The **Immigration** Reform and Control Act of 1986 (IRCA) is not primarily focused on prohibitions against unlawful employment practices; however, one provision requires employers who require employee verification prior to hiring not to discriminate against national origin. Provisions of the IRCA are enforced by the Office of Special Counsel for Immigration-Related Unfair Employment Practices.

### Americans With Disabilities Act of 1990

ADA prohibits private employers, state and local governments, employment agencies and labor unions with 15 or more employees from discriminating against qualified employees with disabilities. An employer is prohibited from discriminating against persons with disabilities in hiring, firing, advancement, compensation, training and other benefits related to employment. According to the ADA, a person with a disability has a physical or mental impairment that substantially limits one or more major life activities, has a record of such impairment, or is regarded as having such impairment. The ADA protects employees with disabilities prior to initial employment and employees that develop disabilities while employed by the employer.

In addition to prohibition against unlawful employment practices, the employer must also make "reasonable accommodations" for qualified employees who can perform "essential functions" of the job. A reasonable accommodation may consist of making existing facilities readily accessible to persons with disabilities or modifying equipment, training examinations, and policies, or requiring readers or interpreters. However, an employer is not required to lower quality or production standards to make accommodations.

The Supreme Court held in *Board of Trustees of the University of Alabama et al. v. Garrett et al.* (2000) that suits in federal court by state employees to recover money damages by reason of the State's failure to comply with Title I of the ADA are barred by the Eleventh Amendment. Essentially, the court ruling held that state employers are not bound by the ADA. Another recent Supreme Court ruling, *Ella Williams v. Toyota* (2001) also restricted the definitions of a person with a disability by adding that the disability must be in one or more major life activity which prevents the person "from performing tasks that are of central importance to most people's daily lives." The United States Supreme Court, with this ruling, attempted to clarify the broad language of the ADA to more precisely define when a person is to be considered disabled as opposed to impaired.

### Family Medical Leave Act of 1993

The Family Medical Leave Act of 1993 (FMLA) protects employees against possible disruption in their employment caused by leave from work needed to care for a newborn or a sick family member. The FMLA applies to all public federal, state, and local municipal employers. The FMLA also applies to private employers who employ 50 or more employees in 20 or more workweeks in the current or proceeding year. Private employers must also be engaged in commerce or any industry affecting commerce.

The employee is entitled to specific benefits if employed by a public or private employer covered by the FMLA. The employee is entitled to 12 workweeks of unpaid leave during a 12-month period for: the birth and care of a newborn child of the employee, for placement with the employee of a son or daughter for **adoption** or foster care, for care of an immediate family member (defined by the FMLA as a spouse, child, or parent) with a serious health condition (defined by the FMLA as "any period of incapacity or treatment connected with inpatient care in a hospital or hospice or residential medical-care facility or continuing treatment by a health care provider which includes any period in which the employee is unable to work, attend school, or perform regular activities due to a health condition, a pregnancy-related absence, a chronic serious health condition or a permanent long-term condition.") The employee may take leave intermittently, meaning that the 12 week block does not have to be taken consecutively. However, intermittent leave, when used for birth and care for adoption or foster care must be approved by the employer. When the leave is used to care for a seriously ill family member, the intermittent leave may be taken only when medically necessary.

When the employee returns from FMLA leave, the employer must restore the employee to the original job or equivalent job with equivalent pay. The employer must also maintain health benefits while the employee is on FMLA leave.

Employees must meet certain requirements before they are eligible for benefits afforded by the FMLA. Employees must work for a covered employer for a total of 12 months and have worked for at least 1,250 hours in the 12-month period. The employee must provide 30-days advanced notice for the need to take FMLA leave. Employers may also require employees to provide medical documentation to validate the medical condition claimed. Employers (at their expense) may require employees to seek a second or third opinion. Employees also must furnish their employers with status reports and intent to return to work.

The provisions of the FMLA are enforced by the United States Secretary of Labor's Wage and Hour Division. Thus far, there have not been any challenges to the provisions of the FMLA heard before the United States Supreme Court.

Although employees of state and local employers cannot sue their employers for discriminatory practices involving provisions of some Federal laws (most notably the ADEA and ADA), below is a list of the applicable state laws prohibiting employment discrimination.

## State Laws and Statutes Prohibiting Employment Discrimination

ALABAMA: Title 25 of the Code of Alabama 1975

ALASKA: Title 23 of Alaska Statutes

ARIZONA: Title 23 of Arizona Revised Statutes

ARKANSAS: Title 11 of Arkansas Department of Labor Laws and Regulations

CALIFORNIA: Chapter 98.75 of the California Labor Code

COLORADO: Title 8 of Colorado Department of Labor and Employment

CONNECTICUT: Title 31 of the Connecticut Department of Labor

DELAWARE: Title 19 of the Delaware Code

DISTRICT of COLUMBIA: Title 36 of the District of Columbia Code

FLORIDA: Title 31 of the Florida Statutes

GEORGIA: Title 34 the Georgia Code

HAWAII: Title 21 of the Hawaii Revised Statutes

IDAHO: Title 44 of the Idaho Statutes

ILLINOIS: Chapter 820 of the Illinois State Employment Law

INDIANA: Title 22 of the Indiana Code

IOWA: Title 3 of the Code of Iowa

KANSAS: Chapter 44 of the Kansas Statutes

KENTUCKY: Title XXVII of the Kentucky Revised Statutes

LOUISIANA: Title 23 of the Louisiana Revised Statutes

MAINE: Title 26 of the Maine Revised Statutes

MARYLAND: Labor and Employment Article of the Maryland State Statutes

MASSACHUSETTS: Part I, Title XXI of the General Laws of Massachusetts

MICHIGAN: Chapter 408 of the Michigan Compiled Laws

MINNESOTA: Chapter 175 through 186 of the Minnesota Statutes

MISSISSIPPI: Title 71 of the Mississippi Code

MISSOURI: Title XVIII of the Missouri Revised Statutes

MONTANA: Title 39 of the Montana Code

NEBRASKA: Chapter 48 of the Nebraska Statutes

NEVADA: Title 53 of the Nevada Revised Statutes

NEW HAMPSHIRE: Section 275 of New Hampshire Revised Statutes

NEW JERSEY: Title 34 of New Jersey Statutes Annotated

NEW MEXICO: Chapter 50 of New Mexico Statutes Annotated

NEW YORK: Executive Law Article 15, New York State **Human Rights** Law

NORTH CAROLINA: Chapter 95-240 through Chapter 95-245 of the North Carolina General Statutes

NORTH DAKOTA: Chapter 14 of the North Dakota Century Code

OHIO: Section 4112.02 of the Ohio Revised Code

OKLAHOMA: Title 40 of the Oklahoma Statutes

OREGON: Title 51, Chapters 651-663 of the Oregon Revised Statutes

PENNSYLVANIA: Title 43 of the Pennsylvania Consolidated Statutes

RHODE ISLAND: Title 28 of the Rhode Island General Laws

SOUTH CAROLINA: Title 41 of the South Carolina Code of Laws

SOUTH DAKOTA: Title 60 of the South Dakota Codified Laws

TENNESSEE: Title 50 of the Tennessee Code

TEXAS: Texas Labor Code

UTAH: Title 34 of the Utah Code

VERMONT: Title 21 of the Vermont Statutes

VIRGINIA: Title 40.1 of the Code of Virginia

WASHINGTON: Title 49 of the Revised Code of Washington

WEST VIRGINIA: Chapter 21 of the West Virginia Code

WISCONSIN: Chapter 111 of the Wisconsin Statutes

WYOMING: Title 27 of the Wyoming Statutes

## Additional Resources

"*An Overview of the Fair Labor Standards Act*" United States Office of Personnel Management. Available at www.opm.gov/flsa.htm.

"*Employment Discrimination: An Overview*" Legal Information Institute, Cornell Law School. Available at http:// www.law.cornell.edu/topics/employment_ discrimination.htm.

"*Federal Laws Prohibiting Job Discrimination Questions and Answers*" United States Equal Employment Opportunity Commission. Available at www.eeoc.gov/facts/ qanda.html.

*A Guide To Disability Rights Laws* United States Department of Justice, Civil Rights Division, Disability Rights Section. Washington, DC: Government Printing Office, 2001.

Jacob, M. C. "*Industrial Revolution*" World Book Online Americas Edition, 2002. Available at http:// www.aolsvc.worldbook.aol.com/wbol/wbPage/na/ar/co/ 275880.

"*Labor and Employment Laws of the Fifty States, District of Columbia and Puerto Rico*" Legal Information Institute, Cornell Law School. Available at http:// www.law.cornell.edu/topics/Table_Labor.htm.

"*Labor Movement,*" Mills, D. Q., World Book Online Americas Edition, 2002. Available at http:// www.aolsvc.worldbook.aol.com/wbol/wbPage/na/ar/co/ 306670.

"*Title VII of the Civil Rights Act of 1964*" United States Equal Employment Opportunity Commission. Available at www.eeoc.gov/laws/vii.html

*Troubled passage: The Labor Movement and the Fair Labor Standards Act* Samuel, H. D., Monthly Labor Review, 123 (12) 32-37, 2000.

"*United States Equal Employment Opportunity Commission: An Overview*" United States Equal Employment Opportunity Commission. Available at www.eeoc.gov/ overview.html.

# LABOR LAW

## DRUG TESTING

*Sections within this essay:*

- Background
- Federal Law
- Constitutional Protections
- Key Provisions
- Special Considerations
    - Mandatory vs. Optional Testing
    - "For Cause" vs. "Random" Testing
    - Testing Union vs. Non-union Employees
    - Testing Employees vs. Applicants
- Select State Laws
- Additional Resources

## Background

Testing employees or job applicants for drug or alcohol use invokes a controversial area of policy and law that is still establishing its parameters. No one denies that employee drug and alcohol abuse costs employers billions of dollars each year in decreased productivity, increased liability exposure, and higher **workers' compensation** insurance premiums. Employers clearly have a substantial and vested interest in not only providing, but also ensuring, a drug-free workplace, for the safety and welfare of both employees and employers.

Controversy enters the picture when employers either ineptly or aggressively impose drug testing in a manner that may violate personal or constitutional rights, such as privacy rights or protections against unlawful searches and seizures. While drug testing is permitted in most states, it is not always mandated. For those employers who implement drug testing programs, it is imperative that the programs follow state and federal guidelines in order to ensure protection of employee rights.

## Federal Law

The drug-testing movement began in 1986, when former President Ronald Reagan signed Executive Order 12564, requiring all federal employees to refrain from using illegal drugs, on or off-duty, as a condition of federal employment. Two years later, Congress passed the Drug-Free Workplace Act of 1988. That, in turn, spawned the creation of federal Mandatory Guidelines for Federal Workplace Drug Testing Programs (Section 503 of **Public Law** 100-71). The mandatory guidelines apply to executive agencies of the federal government, the uniformed services (excepting certain members of the armed forces), and contractors or service providers under contract with the federal government (excepting the postal service and employing units in the judicial and legislative branches).

Although the Act only applies to federal employees, many state and local governments followed suit and adopted similar programs under state laws and drug-free workplace programs.

## Constitutional Protections

The U.S. Constitution does not prohibit drug testing of employees. However, in the U.S. Supreme

Court case of *Treasury Employees v. Von Raab*, 489 U.S. 656 (1989), the high court ruled that requiring employees to produce urine samples constituted a "search" within the meaning of the Fourth Amendment to the U.S. Constitution. Therefore, all such testing must meet the "reasonableness" requirement of the Fourth Amendment (which protects citizens against "unreasonable" searches and seizures). The Court also ruled that positive test results could not be used in subsequent criminal prosecutions without the employee's consent.

The other major constitutional issue in employee drug testing involves the Fifth Amendment (made applicable to the states by the Fourteenth Amendment), which prohibits denial of life, liberty, or property without "due process of law." Since the majority of private-sector employees in the United States (excepting mostly union employees) are considered "at-will employees," an employer need not articulate a reason for termination of employment. However, under certain circumstances, the denial of employment or the denial of continued employment based on drug test results may invoke "due process" considerations, such as the validity of the test results, the employee's right to respond, or any required notice to an employee.

Finally, under the same constitutional provisions, persons have a fundamental right to privacy of their person and property. Drug testing, although in itself deemed legal, may be subject to constitutional challenge if testing results are indiscriminately divulged, if procedures for obtaining personal specimens do not respect the privacy rights of the person, or if testing is unnecessarily or excessively imposed.

## Key Provisions

Under state and federal drug-free work place programs include the following:

- Both employees and applicants may be tested.

- Tests may be conducted pre-employment, "upon reasonable suspicion" or "for cause," at random, routinely, and/or post treatment or rehabilitation. Random testing involves unannounced, "suspicionless," and/or non-routine testing that may be indiscriminately applied to some, but not all, employees.

- Basic tests screen for amphetamines (speed, meth, ecstasy, crank, etc.), cannabinoids (marijuana, hashish), cocaine (coke or crack), opiates (heroin, morphine, opium, codeine), or phencyclidine (PCP).

- Extended tests might screen for barbiturates, benzodiazepines, ethanol, hallucinogens, inhalants, or anabolic steroids.

- Tests may involve urine samples, saliva tests, hair samples, sweat patches, breathalyzers, or blood tests.

## Special Considerations

### Mandatory vs. Optional Testing

Under federal law, jobs that involve safety or security functions generally require mandatory drug testing of applicants or employees. The U.S. Department of Transportation adopted revised regulations in August 2001, and other agencies are free to adopt their own internal regulations. Likewise, many states expressly mandate drug testing for similar jobs, for example, jobs in the medical and health related fields, jobs requiring the use of machinery or vehicles, security positions, food handling jobs, or physically demanding jobs such as utilities cable line installation or climbing.

### "For Cause" vs. "Random" Testing

Generally, employers are permitted to engage in "for cause" or reasonable-suspicion testing under drug-free workplace programs. State law may limit or prohibit random ("suspicionless") testing of employees unless the job position warrants such an intrusion, such as in "safety sensitive" positions. It is important to remember that private-sector employees do not always enjoy Fourth Amendment rights protecting them against unwarranted or unreasonable searches and seizures (only Fifth amendment rights are extended to the states by the Fourteenth Amendment). Nevertheless, many state constitutions incorporate such rights into their own constitutions, so private sector employees may have the same protections.

### Testing Union vs. Non-union Employees

Union employees are protected by the National Labor Relations Act (NLRA), which mandates that private sector employers must bargain collectively over terms and conditions of employment. The NLRA has ruled that drug testing of current employees (but not applicants) is a term or condition of employment. Unionized public sector employers may unilaterally decide to impose drug testing, but must negotiate the procedures (e.g., chain of **custody** of samples, notice to employees, confidentiality, consequence of positive results, etc.).

### Testing Employees vs. Applicants

Since applicants are generally deemed to have a lesser expectation of privacy than current employees, employers enjoy greater freedom to test applicants, without the same concerns being invoked. However, to contain costs, many employers limit drug testing to those applicant whom they expect to offer a position to, as a condition of hire. While there is no requirement to notify an applicant in advance of a drug test, he or she is free to refuse to submit to it. Refusal to submit, of course, may be grounds to terminate the application process.

## Select State Laws

ALABAMA: Alabama's Drug-Free Workplace Program is codified under Ala. Code 25-5-330 et seq. Employers who implement a Drug-Free Workplace Program qualify for a 5 percent discount under the employer's workers' compensation policy.

ALASKA: Alaska's law for drug and alcohol testing of employees is codified at Alaska Stat. 23.10.600 et seq. Employers who comply with the **statute** are protected from civil liability if they take disciplinary action in **good faith** based on the results of positive tests. However, persons who are injured by a drug or alcohol-impaired employee may not sue the employer for failing to test for drugs or alcohol.

ARIZONA: Ariz. Rev. Stat. Ann. 23-493 et seq. requires employers to adopt a written policy distributed to every employee who is subject to testing or printed as part of a personnel handbook or manual.

ARKANSAS: Arkansas has not enacted any laws regarding the testing of employees for drugs or alcohol. The Arkansas Supreme Court has upheld dismissals of employees who violate an employer's substance abuse policy.

CALIFORNIA: Under California Drug-Free Workplace Act of 1990, Cal. Gov. Code 8350 et seq. (modeled after the federal act), only employers who are awarded contracts or grants from any state agency must certify to the contracting or granting agency that they will provide a drug-free workplace. The contractors must also have a written policy for their employees.

COLORADO: Colorado has not enacted any employment drug or alcohol testing laws. However, the Colorado Supreme Court has upheld testing if the employee's supervisor had a reasonable suspicion that the employee was either using or was under the influence of illegal drugs or alcohol.

CONNECTICUT; Connecticut's law, codified at Conn. Gen. Stat. 31-51 et seq., provides express language protecting the privacy of employee testing. Reasonable suspicion is required before an employer may compel testing, and the employer must show that the use was adversely affecting the employee's job performance.

DELAWARE: No specific laws have been enacted.

FLORIDA: Employee drug testing is voluntary in Florida. However, Fla. Stat. 440.101 et seq. gives incentives to employers that implement drug-free workplace policies. Florida law parallels federal law on the subject. If a governmental unit receives two or more equal bids for services or goods, preference is given to the business that has implemented a drug-free workplace program. The state also gives a worker's compensation premium discount to employers who have implemented a drug-free workplace.

GEORGIA: Georgia has a Drug-free Workplace Act, Ga. Code 50-24-1. All state contractors holding contracts of at least $25,000 must certify that they will provide a drug-free workplace. If a contractor fails to comply with the Act, the state may suspend payments or terminate the contract, so the contractor has an incentive to comply.

IDAHO: The Idaho Private Employer Alcohol and Drug-Free Workplace Act, Idaho Code 72-1701 et seq. provides voluntary drug and alcohol testing guidelines for private employers. If an employer follows the guidelines, employees testing positive for drugs or alcohol will be guilty of misconduct and will be denied unemployment benefits.

ILLINOIS: Illinois has not enacted its own legislation, but it allows private employers to require all employees to conform to the requirements of the federal Drug-free Workplace Act of 1988.

INDIANA: Indiana has not enacted its own legislation, but it allows private employers to require all employees to conform to the requirements of the federal Drug-free Workplace Act of 1988.

IOWA: Under Iowa Code 730.5 et seq., random testing is prohibited. An employer may require preemployment drug tests for peace officers or state correctional officers. An employer may require a specific employee to submit to a drug test only if certain conditions are met, as outlined in the statute.

KANSAS: Kansas has not enacted any workplace drug and alcohol testing laws.

KENTUCKY: Kentucky has no legislation governing employment drug or alcohol testing. However, 702 Ky. Admin. Regs. 5:080 requires all school bus drivers working for any county school district in Kentucky to be drug-tested after an accident resulting in bodily injury or $1,000 worth of property damage.

LOUSIANA: Under Louisiana Rev. Stat. 49:1001 et seq., private employers do not need a written policy to implement a drug testing policy, there need not be reasonable cause to test an employee, and employers need not offer rehabilitation to offenders prior to termination from employment. Same-gender direct observation is permitted in certain circumstances, as where there is reason to believe an employee may alter or substitute urine specimens, etc.

MAINE: Rev. Stat. 26 -681 et seq., protects the privacy rights of individual employees from undue invasion by employers but permits the use of tests when the employer has a compelling reason to administer them.

MARYLAND: Under Md. Code Ann., Health-Gen. 17-214, employers may test their employees for drugs and alcohol for any "legitimate business purpose." However, the statute outlines specific procedural requirements and employee rights in cases where positive results may be used for discipline.

MASSACHUSETTS: Massachusetts has no specific employment drug and alcohol testing laws.

MICHIGAN: No specific law, except that under Mich. Comp. Laws 37.1211(a **civil rights** law) established employment policies, programs, procedures or work rules regarding the use of alcoholic liquor or the illegal use of drugs will not be considered to violate an individual's civil rights.

MINNESOTA: Minnesota was one of the first states to enact employment drug and alcohol testing laws in the country, entitled "Authorized Drug and Alcohol Testing" and codified at Minn. Stat. 181.951 et seq. Employers may not conduct drug and alcohol tests without a written drug and alcohol testing policy. Employers may not require employees or job applicants to undergo drug and alcohol testing on an "arbitrary and capricious basis."

MISSISSIPPI: Under Miss. Code Ann. 71-7-1 et seq, all employers who participate in Mississippi's workers' compensation program are required to establish and implement a written drug and alcohol-testing program. That virtually covers all employers.

MISSOURI: Missouri's Drug-Free Public Work Force Act is codified at Mo. Rev. Stat.105.1100 et seq. Only state employees under the **executive branch** of the Missouri state government are subject to the Act. No provisions mandate compliance from private employers.

MONTANA: Mont. Code Ann. 39-2-205 et seq. ("Montana Workforce Drug and Alcohol Testing Act") requires that any testing of employees by private employers be done in accordance with written policies and procedures established by the employer.

NEBRASKA: Neb. Rev. Stat. 48-1901 et seq. states that no disciplinary or administrative action is allowed unless an initial positive test has been confirmed by gas chromatography/mass spectrometry technique. Attempts to alter the results of a drug or alcohol test are punishable as Class I criminal misdemeanors.

NEVADA: No state law regulates private employer drug or alcohol testing. State employees do not include members of the Nevada National Guard or employees of state penal, mental, and correctional institutions.

NEW HAMPSHIRE: New Hampshire has not enacted any employment drug or alcohol testing laws.

NEW JERSEY: New Jersey has no express law relating to employment drug or alcohol testing.

NEW MEXICO: New Mexico has no statutes regulating the testing of employees for drugs or alcohol.

NEW YORK: New York has no express employment drug or alcohol testing laws. Random drug and alcohol testing of city transit authority bus drivers, police officers and corrections officers has been upheld by courts.

NORTH CAROLINA: North Carolina has a "Controlled Substance **Examination** Regulation" codified at Gen. Stat. 95-230 et seq. The law purports to protect individuals from "unreliable and inadequate examinations and screening for controlled substances" and to preserve an individual's dignity to the extent practical, and focuses on chain-of-custody and laboratory testing procedures more than policy guidelines.

NORTH DAKOTA: No statute expressly addresses employment drug and alcohol testing in North Dakota, and there is little, if any, **case law** in the area.

OHIO: Ohio does not have any employment drug and alcohol testing laws.

OKLAHOMA: Oklahoma's "Standards for Workplace Drug and Alcohol Testing Act", Okla. Stat. 40-551, applies to both public and private employers. No unusual provisions.

OREGON: No specific employment drug or alcohol testing laws.

PENNSYLVANIA: Pennsylvania has not enacted any employment drug and alcohol testing laws.

RHODE ISLAND: Rhode Island's "Urine and Blood Tests as a Condition of Employment" provision under R.I. Gen. Laws 28-6.5-1 and 28-6.5-2. prohibits the termination from employment of any person who tests positive for drugs or alcohol. Instead, the employee must be referred to a substance abuse professional for treatment or evaluation.

SOUTH CAROLINA: South Carolina's law, modeled after the federal law, affects those doing business with the State. Codified at S.C. Code Ann. 44107-10 et seq. offers a 5 percent reduction in worker's compensation premiums to participating employers (private employers are not required to implement such programs).

SOUTH DAKOTA: No employment drug and alcohol testing laws.

TENNESSEE: Tenn. Code Ann. 50-9-103 et. seq., gives a discount on workers' compensation premiums and shifts the burden of proof to employees in case of an accident.

TEXAS: Under Tex. Code Ann. 411.091, the "Policy for Elimination of Drugs in the Workplace," employers with fifteen or more employees with workers' compensation insurance coverage are required to adopt a policy of their own choosing but directed at the elimination of drug abuse and its effects in the workplace.

UTAH: Utah Code Ann. 34-38-1 et seq. employers may test employees or prospective employees as a condition of hire or continued employment. In a twist of the law, employers and management must submit to the testing themselves.

VERMONT: Vt. Stat. Ann. 21 § 511 et seq. prohibits random testing for drugs or the drug testing of employees as a condition of continued employment, promotion, or change in employee status.

VIRGINIA: No express law governs employment drug testing.

WASHINGTON: Washington Rev. Code 49.82.010 et seq. models the federal law. Private employers who adopt a drug-free workplace program will receive a 5 percent discount on their workers' compensation premiums.

WEST VIRGINIA: West Virginia has not enacted any employment drug or alcohol testing law, and in a 1990 case, the Supreme Court of West Virginia prohibited random testing by a private employer.

WISCONSIN: No express statute governs employment drug and alcohol testing.

WYOMING: Wyoming has no express statute governs employment drug and alcohol testing.

## Additional Resources

"*Drug Testing in the Workplace.*" Available at http://jobsearchtech.about.com/library/weekly/aa090301-2.htm

"*Drug Testing State Laws.*" March 2002. Available at http://www.urineluck.com.

"*Mandatory Guidelines for Federal Workplace Drug Testing Programs.*" Available at http://workplace.samhsa.gov/Resource/Center/r362.htm.

"*Small Business Workplace Kit: Alcohol and Drug Testing.*" U.S. Dept. of Labor. Available at http://www.dol.gov/asp/programs/drugs/workingpartners/Screen5.htm.

*Treasury Employees v. Von Raab,* 489 U.S. 656 (1989) Available at http://caselaw.lp.findlaw.com.

"*Your Questions Answered - Drug Testing.*" Stanton, Hughes. March 2002. Available at http://www.stantonhughes.com/qa0203.html.

# LABOR LAW

## EMPLOYEE'S RIGHTS/EEOC

*Sections within this essay:*

- Background

- Employee-Employer Relationships

- Types of Employment Discrimination

- The EEOC
    - Make-Up Of The EEOC
    - Filing a Charge
    - Procedures
    - Enforcement and Relief

- Additional Resources

## Background

Claims of employee rights and **discrimination** have become almost commonplace over the course of the last 30 years. Since the passage of the main civil right legislation in the 1960s—the Equal Pay Act, the **Civil Rights** Act of 1964, and the Age Discrimination Employment Act (ADEA)—federal law has explicitly protected the rights of employees. The 1973 Rehabilitation Act and the 1990 Americans with Disabilities Act (ADA) added the disabled to the list of protected employees, and the 1991 Civil Rights Act expanded relief possibilities for all groups.

During the course of the last 40 years of employee rights law, the federal Equal Employment Opportunity Commission has come to play a primary role in the enforcement of federal civil rights statutes. The **EEOC** was created in 1964, as part of Title VII of the Civil Rights Act. Virtually all discrimination complaints against employers at the federal level must go through the EEOC first before a lawsuit may be filed. Thus the agency is of paramount importance to both employers and employees.

Considering this, it is important for both employees and employers to know how the EEOC works, what kind of complaints the commission handles, and what is needed to bring a complaint before the EEOC.

## Employee-Employer Relationships

At **common law**, employee-employer relationships that were not controlled by a formal contract were considered at-will relationships. Employees could be dismissed for any reason at all, whether the reason was discriminatory or not.

Today, the at-will relationship between employee and employer is still a common one with employees not working under a union contract or some other form of agreement. However, the at-will term has become somewhat misleading, since a host of federal laws and rules now govern the employee-employer relationship. Perhaps the most important in terms of protecting employees against arbitrary **dismissal** by employers are the civil rights laws.

When arguably the most important of these laws—the Civil Rights Act of 1964— was drawn up, many advocates of the law felt a gatekeeper was needed to prevent the courts from being clogged with employee lawsuits under the new law. This led to the creation of the EEOC, which was given primary responsibility for the enforcement of these laws. Subsequently, the EEOC was entrusted with the enforcement of practically all civil rights laws, with the exception of federal employees, who are protected under the 1978 Civil Service Reform Act. Enforcement of that act is entrusted with the Office of Special **Counsel** and the Merit Systems Protection Board.

The size of the employer determines if it falls under EEOC authority. Employers of 15 or more employees are covered under both Title VII of the Civil Rights Act and the Americans With Disabilities Act (ADA). Employers of 20 or more are covered under the Age Discrimination Employment Act (ADEA), and the Equal Pay Act has no limit in terms of the size of employers it covers.

## Types of Employment Discrimination

There are many types of discrimination covered by the civil rights laws the EEOC is charged to enforce. Some of them include:

- Discrimination on the basis of race or color: Title VII of the Civil Rights Act prohibits race discrimination.

- Discrimination on the basis of sex: Title VII of the Civil Rights Act prohibits discrimination on the basis of sex. Title VII prohibitions against **sex discrimination** also prohibit **sexual harassment** (practices ranging from direct requests for sexual favors to workplace conditions that create a hostile environment for persons of either gender, including same sex harassment). In addition, the federal Equal Pay Act, which the EEOC also enforces, prohibits discrimination on the basis of sex in the payment of wages or benefits, where men and women perform work of similar skill, effort, and responsibility for the same employer under similar working conditions.

- Discrimination on the basis of pregnancy: Pregnancy, childbirth, and related medical conditions must be treated in the same way as other temporary illnesses or conditions.

- Discrimination on the basis of national origin: Title VII of the Civil Right Act makes it illegal to discriminate against an individual because of birthplace, ancestry, culture, or linguistic characteristics common to a specific ethnic group. For example, a rule requiring that employees speak only English on the job may violate Title VII unless an employer shows that the requirement is necessary for conducting business.

- Discrimination on the basis of religion: Title VII prohibits religious discrimination. An employer is required to reasonably accommodate the religious belief of an employee or prospective employee, unless doing so would impose an undue hardship.

- Discrimination on the basis of age: The ADEA prohibits any discrimination in regards to age. Among the acts covered by the ADEA are: statements or specifications in job notices or advertisements of age preference and limitations; discrimination on the basis of age by apprenticeship programs, including joint labor-management apprenticeship programs; and denial of benefits to older employees.

- Discrimination on the basis of **disability**: The ADA prohibits discrimination on the basis of disability in all employment practices. An individual with a disability under the ADA is a person who has a physical or mental impairment that substantially limits one or more major life activities, has a record of such an impairment, or is regarded as having such an impairment. The employer is required to make reasonable accommodations for such an employee, unless the employer can prove such accommodation would impose undue hardship on the operation of the employers business. Reasonable accommodation may include, but is not limited to, making existing facilities used by employees readily accessible to and usable by persons with disabilities; job restructuring; modifying of work schedules; providing additional unpaid leave; reassigning to a vacant position; acquiring or modifying equipment or devices; adjusting or modifying examinations, training materials, or policies; and providing qualified readers or interpreters. An employer may not ask job applicants about the existence, nature, or severity of a disability, though applicants may be asked about their ability to perform job functions.

Under all the major civil rights laws, it is illegal to discriminate in any aspects of employment. The EEOC lists the following as examples of functions in which it is illegal to discriminate:

- Hiring and firing

- Compensation, assignment, or classification of employees

- Transfer, promotion, layoff, or recall

- Job advertisements

- Recruitment

- Testing

- Use of company facilities

- Training and apprenticeship programs

- Fringe benefits

- Pay, retirement plans, and disability leave

- Other terms and conditions of employment

- Harassment on the basis of race, color, religion, sex, national origin, disability, or age

- Retaliation against an individual for filing a charge of discrimination, participating in an investigation, or opposing discriminatory practices

- Employment decisions based on stereotypes or assumptions about the abilities, traits, or performance of individuals of a certain sex, race, age, religion, or ethnic group, or individuals with disabilities

- Denying employment opportunities to a person because of marriage to, or association with, an individual of a particular race, religion, national origin, or an individual with a disability. Title VII also prohibits discrimination because of participation in schools or places of worship associated with a particular racial, ethnic, or religious group

All employers within the United States are required to post notices advising workers of their rights under the EEOC, and the notices are required to be accessible and posted so all workers can see them.

## The EEOC

Once employees determine they have been the victim of illegal discrimination by the employer, they must go about filing a complaint with the EEOC in order to state a federal civil rights claim. The EEOC then follows procedures to make a determination about the validity of the claim and what actions it should take to resolve the claim.

### Make-Up of the EEOC

The EEOC is composed of five commissioners and a general counsel appointed by the president and confirmed by the Senate. Commissioners are appointed for five-year staggered terms; the general counsel's term is four years. The president designates a chair and a vice-chair. The chair is the chief executive officer of the commission. The commission has authority to establish equal employment policy and to approve **litigation**. The general counsel is responsible for conducting litigation. The EEOC also has 50 field offices located across the nation.

### Filing a Charge

A discrimination complaint with the EEOC should be filed with the nearest EEOC office to the complainant. The EEOC lists its offices on its website at http://www.eeoc.gov/teledir.html. Complaints may be filed by mail, telephone, or in person. A toll free number, 800-699-4000, may be used to find this information.

Federal civil rights laws contain time frames when discrimination complaints must be filed. To preserve the ability of the EEOC to act, these time frames must be met. If they are not met, the complainant will lose any right to a federal civil rights claim. Under Title VII, the ADA, or ADEA, a complaint must be filed with the EEOC within 180 days of the alleged discriminatory act.

In states or localities where there is an antidiscrimination law and an agency authorized to grant or seek relief, a complaint must be presented to that state or local agency. In such jurisdictions, the complainants may file charges with EEOC within 300 days of the discriminatory act, or 30 days after receiving notice that the state or local agency has terminated its processing of the charge, whichever is earlier.

For a complaint under the Equal Pay Act, individuals are not required to file a complaint with the EEOC before filing a private lawsuit, so the time limits do not apply. Individuals with an Equal Pay Act claim must decide whether they would be better off filing a complaint with the EEOC or going directly to court.

### Procedures

After the complaint is filed with the EEOC, the employer is notified of the complaint. At that point, the EEOC can handle the complaint in a number of ways. According to the EEOC, the following are ways the complaint can be disposed of:

- A complaint may be assigned for priority investigation if the initial facts appear to support a violation of law. When the **evidence** is less strong, the complaint may be assigned for follow up investigation to determine whether it is likely that a violation has occurred.

- The EEOC can seek to settle a complaint at any stage of the investigation if the charging party and the employer express an interest in doing so. If **settlement** efforts are not successful, the investigation continues.

- In investigating a complaint, the EEOC may make written requests for information, interview people, review documents, and, as needed, visit the facility where the alleged discrimination occurred. When the investigation is complete, the EEOC will discuss the evidence with the charging party or employer, as appropriate.

- The complaint may be selected for the EEOC's **mediation** program if both the charging party and the employer express an interest in this option. Mediation is offered as an alternative to a lengthy investigation. Participation in the mediation program is confidential, voluntary, and requires consent from both charging party and employer. If mediation is unsuccessful, the complaint is returned for investigation.

- A complaint may be dismissed at any point if, in the agency's best judgment, further investigation will not establish a violation of the law. A complaint may be dismissed at the time it is filed, if an initial in-depth interview does not produce evidence to support the claim. When a complaint is dismissed, a notice is issued in accordance with the law which gives the charging party 90 days in which to file a lawsuit on his or her own behalf. This notice is known as a "right to sue." Under Title VII and the ADA, a charging party also can request a notice of right to sue from the EEOC 180 days after the charge was first filed with the Commission, and may then bring suit within 90 days after receiving this notice. Under the ADEA, a suit may be filed at any time 60 days after filing a charge with the EEOC and no right to sue notice is required.

Once the EEOC investigation is finished, the commission makes a determination over how to proceed. The EEOC lists the following as actions it can take to resolve a discrimination complaint:

- If the evidence obtained in an investigation does not establish that discrimination occurred, this will be explained to the charging party. A required notice is then issued, closing the case and giving the charging party 90 days in which to file a lawsuit on his or her own behalf.

- If the evidence establishes that discrimination has occurred, the employer and the charging party will be informed of this in a letter of determination that explains the finding. The EEOC will then attempt **conciliation** with the employer to develop a remedy for the discrimination.

- If the case is successfully conciliated, or if a case has earlier been successfully mediated or settled, neither EEOC nor the charging party may go to court unless the conciliation, mediation, or settlement agreement is not honored

If the EEOC is unable to successfully conciliate the case, the agency will decide whether to bring suit in federal court. If the EEOC decides not to sue, it will issue a notice closing the case and issue a right to sue notice giving the charging party 90 days in which to file a lawsuit on his or her own behalf.

The EEOC is empowered to file a judicial action against non-governmental employers. The U. S. attorney general is authorized to sue state and local governments. The federal government cannot be sued. The EEOC actually files suit on only a small number of cases.

### Enforcement and Relief

Relief the EEOC may seek against discrimination include: back pay, hiring, promotion, reinstatement, front pay, reasonable accommodation, or other actions that will make an individual "whole" (in the condition he or she would have been but for the discrimination). Relief also may include payment of attorneys' fees, expert witness fees, and court costs. In addition, and employer may be required to post notices to all employees addressing the violations of a specific charge and advising them of their rights under the laws the EEOC enforces and their right to be free from retaliation.

Under most EEOC-enforced laws, compensatory and **punitive damages** also may be available where intentional discrimination is found. Damages may be available to compensate for actual monetary losses, for future monetary losses, and for **mental anguish** and inconvenience. Punitive damages also may be available if an employer acted with **malice** or reckless indifference. Punitive damages are not available against state or local governments.

The employer also may be required to take corrective or preventive actions to cure the source of the identified discrimination and minimize the chance of its recurrence, as well as discontinue the specific discriminatory practices involved in the case.

## Additional Resources

"Facts About Mediation" The Equal Employment Opportunity Commission, 2001. Available at http://www.eeoc.gov.

*Federal Law of Employment Discrimination.* Mack Player, Mack, St. Paul, West Group, 1989.

*"Federal Laws Prohibiting Job Discrimination Question and Answers,"* The Equal Employment Opportunity Commission, 2001. Available at http://www.eeoc.gov., The Equal Employment Opportunity Commission, 2001.

*"Filing A Charge,"* The Equal Employment Opportunity Commission, 2001. Available at http://www.eeoc.gov., The Equal Employment Opportunity Commission, 2001.

## Organizations

### Department of Justice, Civil Rights Division
950 Pennsylvania Avenue, N.W.
Washington, DC 20530 USA
Phone: (202) 514-4609
Fax: (202) 514-0293
URL: http://www.usdoj.gov/crt/crt-home.html
Primary Contact: Ralph Boyd, Assistant Attorney General

### U. S. Department of Labor
200 Constitution Avenue, NW
Washington, DC 20210 USA
Phone: (866) 4-USA-DOL
URL: http://www.dol.gov/
Primary Contact: Elaine Chao, Secretary of Labor

### U. S. Equal Employment Opportunity Commission (EEOC)
1801 L Street, NW
Washington, DC 20507 USA
Phone: (202) 663-4900
URL: http://www.eeoc.gov/
Primary Contact: Cari M. Dominguez, Chair

# LABOR LAW

## FAMILY AND MEDICAL LEAVE ACT (FMLA)

### Background

The Family and Medical Leave Act (FMLA) was signed into law in 1993 as a means of addressing the changing needs of workers' family responsibilities. Under the law, anyone who works in a company that employs 50 or more people can take up to 12 weeks of medical leave per year without threat of losing his or her job. FMLA covers both pregnancy and **adoption**, as well as caring for a seriously ill relative. It also covers the individual employee's own serious illnesses.

Many companies already had leave policies in place before the enactment of FMLA. Some companies, not surprisingly, are more generous than others. The need for federally mandated protection stems from several issues. First is the fact that families are changing. The two–parent one–income family, once the norm in American society, is less and less common. Two–income families and single–parent families have to deal with pregnancy, childhood illness, and a host of other situations that may require time away from work. In addition, a growing number of people are serving as caregivers for elderly parents. Whether in their home or the parent's home, this service can turn into a significant expenditure of time.

Second is the changing structure of the workplace. With medical costs skyrocketing and wide economic shifts, some companies may be inclined to cut back on the amount of leave they want their employees to take. Or they may wish to withhold payment of medical benefits while an employee is on leave, even if that leave is related to a medical condition. Some companies may allow employees to take several weeks of medical leave and then not reinstate them. FMLA offers protection to employees so that they can take the time off they need without fear of recriminations.

### The Basics of FMLA

Simply stated, FMLA guarantees employees that they can take up to 12 weeks of either family leave (to handle adoption proceedings, for example) or medical leave (to take care of a recuperating parent) per year. Anyone who has worked for an employer for at least 1,250 hours and 12 months is entitled to leave under FMLA. Employees can take both family and medical leave during the year, but the total amount of time cannot exceed 12 weeks. If an employee requesting leave under FMLA has accrued sick time and vacation time, the employer can require that this time be included in the 12–week leave. In other words, if an employee has two weeks of paid vacation time accrued, he or she cannot automatically take those two weeks *and* an additional 12 weeks; the employer can be generous and allow that but is not obligated to do so.

Under FMLA, the employee taking leave is entitled to reinstatement upon returning to work. If the employee's old job is not available, he or she is entitled to another job at a similar level of responsibility. A company cannot punish an employee who takes FMLA leave by firing or demoting that person simply for taking the time off.

It is important to understand that FMLA is not an extended personal leave program Employers have a right to know the specific reasons the employee is applying for leave under FMLA. If an employee requests leave because of illness, the employer has a right to ask for proof from a physician. Moreover, the employer also has a right to ask for proof from a physician that an employee is able to return to work.

### Having or Adopting a Baby

Anyone who is pregnant or who is adopting a baby (or taking in a foster child) can take FMLA leave. A woman who takes her leave for pregnancy can use her accrued sick time as part of her leave; those who are adopting cannot. FMLA leave for the arrival of a baby is not limited to women. Men who want to take time off after a child is born and single men who decide to adopt a child are entitled to the same 12 weeks of FMLA leave that women can get. Moreover, a married couple can take 12 weeks *apiece*, so that, for example, a new baby could have at least one parent home for 24 weeks. If the couple works for the same company, however, they are only entitled to a total of 12 weeks between them.

### Family Members and Serious Illness

FMLA allows employees to take up to 12 weeks off to take care of an immediate family member who is seriously ill. A child who is recuperating from major surgery, a parent suffering from Alzheimer's disease, or a spouse recovering from an auto accident are examples. The stipulation is that the person being cared for must be immediate family; an in-law or a favorite second cousin would not count. Serious illness can include stroke and heart attack, complications from pregnancy, pneumonia, sever arthritis, and epilepsy. Clearly not every condition will require the full 12–week leave to be used up at one time. But

FMLA allows employees to break up their leave time, so long as it does not exceed 12 weeks per year.

### Employee's Illness

Employees who suffer serious illness are also covered under FMLA. If, for example, a worker needs to stay home for six weeks to recuperate from back surgery but the worker only has two weeks sick leave, that worker is entitled to FMLA leave. The employer has the right to require the employee to take accrued paid time as part of the 12–week leave.

## FMLA, ADA, and Title VII

With the existence of the Americans with Disabilities Act (ADA) and Title VII of the **Civil Rights** Act (both of which predate FMLA), why bother with a family medical leave act at all? While there is some overlap between the three, each plays a different role.

ADA focuses on people who have disabilities that affect their ability to perform activities that are regarded as part of normal everyday life. A person who cannot walk or see is covered under ADA. Title VII prohibits **discrimination** on the basis or race, color, sex, religion, or national origin. A company cannot provide leave to one group and not another.

Why FMLA? The most important difference between it and ADA and Title VII is probably that it has a more direct effect on an employee's family. Neither ADA nor Title VII provide guarantees to individuals who wish to take leave to look after a sick child or spouse. Nor do they provide for full medical insurance coverage the way FMLA does. Under ADA, an employee who chooses to work part-time because of a **disability** is only entitled to whatever insurance is provided to other part-timers. Under Title VII, an employer cannot provide one employee with insurance and another with none solely on the basis of race, color, religion, sex, or nationality. But there is no provision guaranteeing insurance.

Under FMLA, employers must maintain the employee's insurance at its current level (that includes covering a spouse and children who are on the plan), so long as the employee keeps making his or her regular contribution (if any) into the policy.

## The Employer's Perspective

It may seem as though FMLA and similar laws are all designed to protect employees and not those who hire them. While protection of workers' rights is clearly important, no law is designed with the intention of crushing businesses under a mountain of untenable regulations.

It is important to understand that laws such as FMLA serve as a framework for minimum acceptable standards. Many companies offer more than 12 weeks leave to employees, and a number also offer at least partial paid leave. Interestingly, a survey of 1,000 employers conducted by the research firm Hewitt Associates just at the time FMLA was becoming law in 1993 indicated that some 63 percent already had some sort of family leave program in place, and 56 percent had medical leave programs. To be sure, many of these companies were not offering benefits at the same level guaranteed under FMLA. But they were not ignoring employee needs, either.

During the economic boom of the 1990s, many companies found that they had to offer more and better benefits to attract employees from a shrinking applicant pool. In leaner economic times that line of reasoning does shift, but top companies have long known that one of the best ways to attract the best employees is to give them good benefits.

Sometimes it is difficult to get employees to take their full benefits. For example, even though FMLA allows men to take time off during and after the arrival of a baby, far fewer men take time off than women. Part of the reason is that in many companies there is still a perception that someone who takes time off to raise a child is not committed to his or her career. For men this is still a more difficult hurdle, since even in the most enlightened companies there is still the perception that men should exhibit an almost overriding commitment to their job. One thing that laws such as FMLA may ultimately do is help break down stereotypes like these, so that more people can benefit.

Laws such as FMLA, ADA, and Title VII are geared toward protecting employees, but that does not mean employers must bankrupt themselves to accommodate only a few employees who choose to take advantage of such protections. For example, under FMLA an employer has the right to know precisely what the leave is intended for. Lack of protection would give companies the right to terminate employees rather than give them even unpaid leave. But protection without requirements and guidelines could be misused by unscrupulous employees.

In the years since FMLA was enacted, a number of business groups have asked for adjustments and clarifications. Although there is much support for the spirit of FMLA, many say that as a practical matter there is too much room for abuse. Reports of people taking FMLA time off for the flu or a simple cold, or taking their FMLA leave time in small increments (so-called "intermittent leave" that allows people to take an hour at a time off, or even less, under the current regulations) only fuel the complaints of skeptics.

Ideally, the company and the employee should work together to find arrangements that are suitable to both. FMLA allows such flexibility. For example, an employee may choose to take FMLA-approved leave intermittently (perhaps a few days or a week at a time) during the year instead of in one 12-week chunk. Or the employee may be able to work on a part-time schedule.

## Other Elements of FMLA

### Federal vs. State Regulations

Under the terms of FMLA, state regulations that are more generous than FMLA accommodations will take precedence over FMLA regulations. Where this is not the case, FMLA regulations will supersede the state rules. Each state has its own department of labor and its own set of guidelines for employee rights. Those who wish to know about the rules in a specific state should contact that state's labor department to find out precisely how its regulations work and how they mesh with FMLA and other federal laws.

Currently, 18 states, as well as the District of Columbia and Puerto Rico, have laws that are more comprehensive than FMLA. For example, in Vermont, Oregon, and the District of Columbia, the 50-employee minimum is significantly lower. In Hawaii and Montana, companies with one or more employees must offer leave for maternity disability. An employee can take leave to care for an in-law in the District of Columbia, Hawaii, Oregon, and Vermont. In Massachusetts, employees receive 24 hours leave per year to accompany a child or relative to routine medical or dental appointments. Louisiana and Tennessee provide four months leave for maternity disability.

### Proposed Changes to FMLA

In 2001, two amendments to FMLA with very different outcomes were introduced in Congress. The Right Start Act is designed to expand FMLA by including employers with 25 or more employees instead of the current 50. It would also offer employees 24 extra hours of leave per year to visit their children's school (for parent-teacher conferences or literacy programs, for example). A quite different measure, the Family Leave Clarification Act, would toughen the rules on what constitutes a "serious illness" and set the minimum increment of leave time to one half-day. Both of these bills were pending action in early 2002, and each has strong supporters and opponents.

Employers and employees should work together as much as possible, but they also need to know enough of the regulations to avoid making an inadvertent mistake. Organizations such as the U. S. Department of Labor, the Equal Employment Opportunity Commission, and the Society for Human Resource management can provide useful information. Employers that seek legal **counsel** would do well to remember that for a subject this complex it makes sense to look for attorneys or firms who specialize in employment law.

## Additional Resources

*Family and Medical Leave in a Nutshell.* Decker, Kurt H., West Group, 2000.

*Paid Family Leave: At What Cost?* Hattiangadi, Anita U., Employment Policy Foundation, 2000.

*Taking Time: Parental Leave Policy and Corporate Culture.* Fried, Mindy, Temple University Press, 1998.

## Organizations

### Society for Human Resource Management (SHRM)
1800 Duke Street
Alexandria, VA 22314 USA
Phone: (703) 548-3440
Fax: (703) 535-6490
URL: http://w ww.shrm.org
Primary Contact: Helen G. Drinan, President and CEO

### U. S. Department of Labor, Employment Standards Administration, Wage and Hour Division
200 Constitution Avenue NW
Washington, DC 20210 USA
Phone: (866) 487-9243
URL: http://www.dol.gov/dol/esa
Primary Contact: Tammy D. McCutchen, Administrator

### Work in America Institute
700 White Plains Road
Scarsdale, NY 10583 USA
Phone: (914) 472-9600
Fax: (914) 472-9606
URL: http://www.workinamerica.org
Primary Contact: Jerome M. Rosow, Chairman and CEO

# LABOR LAW

## LABOR UNIONS/STRIKES

*Sections within this essay:*

- Background

- Parties Involved in Labor Relations
    - Employees
    - Employers
    - Unions

- Forming and Joining a Union to Bargain Collectively
    - Bargaining Units
    - Representation Procedures
    - The Duty to Bargain
    - Good Faith in Bargaining

- Subjects for Collective Bargaining

- Conflict Resolution
    - Impasse
    - Picketing
    - Boycotts
    - Strikes and Lockouts

- State Provisions Regarding Labor Unions and Strikes

- Additional Resources

## Background

Congress in 1935 passed the National Labor Relations Act (Wagner Act), which was the first of the three federal laws that govern labor relations in the United States. The other two laws, passed in 1947 and 1959, respectively, were the **Taft-Hartley Act** and the Landrum-Griffin Act. These statutes guarantee the right of private employees to form and join unions in order to bargain collectively. The vast majority of states have extended union rights to public employees.

Additional federal statutes affect the labor rights of employees. A summary of the major federal labor statutes is as follows:

- The Norris-LaGuardia Anti-Injunction Act, passed in 1932, restricted federal courts from issuing injunctions in labor disputes except in some very limited conditions.

- The Wagner Act in 1935 set forth many of the basic protections offered under the labor statutes, including the restriction against employers interfering with or otherwise restraining the ability of employees to organize to bargain collectively.

- The Brynes Anti-Strikebreaking Act of 1938 restricted the interstate transportation of anyone being used to interfere with peaceful picketing in the process of **collective bargaining** or labor dispute.

- The Hobbs Anti-Racketeering Act of 1946 prevented unions from extorting money from nonunion employees.

- The Taft-Hartley Act in 1947 brought a balance between the rights of employees and employers, which was believed to favor employees and unions over employers. Among the provisions included restrictions on unfair labor practices by unions.

- The Labor-Management Reporting and Disclosure of 1959, or Landrum-Griffin Act, established a code of conduct for unions and contained significant amendments to the Taft-Hartley Act. The code of conduct guaranteed certain rights to union members, which was necessary after findings of wrongdoing by unions and their officers. The amendments to the Taft-Hartley Act added some rights to unions and union members but also placed restrictions on union strikes, picketing, and boycotts.

## Parties Involved in Labor Relations

### Employees

The National Labor Relations Act employs a broad definition of "employee." The term includes anyone currently on a company's payroll and anyone whose employment has ceased due to a current strike or **unfair labor practice** and who has not obtained regular employment elsewhere. Several classes of workers are specifically exempted from this definition, including the following:

- Agricultural laborers

- Persons employed in a family's or persons' domestic service in the home

- Persons employed by a spouse or parent

- Independent contractors

- Persons employed by businesses subject to the Railway Labor Act

- Supervisors

The inclusion of supervisory employees on this list is most significant, because supervisors are not protected if they choose to participate in union activity. In some very limited circumstances, however, a supervisor may be protected from termination, if an employer terminates a supervisor to intimidate other employees from exercising their rights.

### Employers

The NLRA's definition of "employer" includes any employer that affects interstate commerce. "Affecting interstate commerce" is traditionally a very broad term, and the vast majority of employers fall within this definition. The NLRA excludes several groups of employers from its scope, including the following:

- The Federal Government

- Any wholly owned government corporation or federal reserve bank

- Any state government or political division of a state

- Employers subject to the Railway Labor Act

- Labor organizations, with some exceptions

### Unions

Much of the NLRA focuses on the relationship between the employees joining together to bargain collectively and the election of the union that acquires the right to represent these employees through a vote of the employees.

## Forming and Joining a Union to Bargain Collectively

A series of complex laws governs the labor representation process. Forming and joining a union to bargain collectively must be completed before the collective bargaining process. The process of forming a union involves numerous considerations, such as the types of employees who would constitute an appropriate bargaining unit, and the selection of the appropriate union to represent the employees.

### Bargaining Units

Employees must define an appropriate collective bargaining unit or units to determine how the employees should be represented in collective bargaining. Under the NLRA and other labor statutes, only those individuals who share a sufficient "community of interest" may comprise an appropriate bargaining unit. Community of interests generally means that teachers have substantial mutual interests, including the following:

- Wages or compensation

- Hours of work

- Employment benefits

- Supervision

- Qualifications

- Training and skills

- Job functions

- Contact with other employees

- Integration of work functions with other employees

- History of collective bargaining

Many state statutes set forth requirements or considerations with respect to determinations of bargaining units in the public sector. Moreover, some statutes set forth specific bargaining units.

### Representation Procedures

The NLRA provides formal processes for designation and recognition of bargaining units. State statutes include similar provisions. When disputes arise with respect to union representation, many states direct parties to resolve these disputes with the public employment relations board in that state. Once employees organize bargaining units, members may file a petition with the appropriate labor board. The labor board will generally determine that **jurisdiction** over the bargaining unit is appropriate, that the proposed bargaining unit it appropriate, and that a majority of employees approve the bargaining unit through an election. **Statutory** provisions and other rules generally ensure that the votes are uncoerced and otherwise fair. After this election, the labor board will certify the union as the exclusive representative of the bargaining unit. Once a union is certified, usually for a one-year period, neither employees nor another union may petition for a new election.

### The Duty to Bargain

Once a union has been elected, both public and private employers are bound to deal exclusively with that union. The elected union must conversely bargain for the collective interests of the members of the bargaining unit. However, neither the union nor the employer is required to agree to any proposal or to make any concessions in the bargaining process.

### Good Faith in Bargaining

Both employers and unions must bargain with one another in **good faith**. The duty of parties to bargain in good faith is very important to the collective bargaining process, since negotiations between employers and unions can become very intense and heated. Interpretations of the term "good faith" under the NLRA typically focus an openness, fairness, mutuality of conduct, and cooperation between parties. Many state statutes define "good faith" similarly, though some states provide more specific guidance regarding what constitutes good faith bargaining. Some statutes also provide a list of examples of instances that are considered bargaining in **bad faith**. Failure or refusal to negotiate in good faith constitutes an unfair labor practice under the NLRA and many other statutes.

## Subjects for Collective Bargaining

The NLRA provides that an employer and union must bargain on issues concerning wages, hours, and other terms and conditions of employment. The National Labor Relations Board has established three sets of rules for the following three categories of bargaining issues: (1) illegal subjects, which would be forbidden by the NLRA; (2) voluntary subjects, which fall outside the mandatory subjects; and (3) mandatory subjects that in the category of wages, hours, and other terms and conditions of employment.

The National Labor Relations Board has determined that a number of topics fall within the category of mandatory subjects. Examples of these subjects are as follows:

- Employee discharge
- Working schedules
- Seniority
- Grievances
- Vacations and individual merit raises
- Christmas bonuses and profit-sharing retirement plans
- Plant rules on breaks and lunch periods
- Safety rules
- Physical examinations of employees

In the absence of statutory language specifying the scope of collective bargaining, unions and employers must consult relevant **case law** and labor board decisions to determine whether a subject is mandatory or voluntary. Other limitations to collective bargaining may also be present. A **collective bargaining agreement**, for example, cannot violate or contradict statutory law or constitutional provisions. Similarly, the collective bargaining agreement should recognize contractual rights that may already exist.

## Conflict Resolution

### Impasse

When good faith efforts between unions and employers fail to resolve the dispute or disputes between the parties, a legal impasse has occurred. Once this occurs, active bargaining between the union and the parties will typically be suspended, and parties go through a series of options to resolve the impasse.

The first option after an impasse is declared is **mediation**. A mediator is employed to act as a neutral third party to assist the two sides in reaching a compromise. Mediators cannot make binding decisions and are employed only to act as advisors. Many state statutes require use of mediators in the public sector upon declaration of an impasse. Private sector unions and schools may employ a federal mediator, though federal labor laws do not prescribe further options regarding dispute resolution.

Should mediation fail, many states require the employment of a fact-finder, who analyzes the facts of the bargaining process and seeks to recognize a potential compromise. Parties are not bound by recommendations of the fact-finder, though a fact-finder may influence public opinion regarding an appropriate resolution of a dispute. In some states, fact-finding is the final stage of impasse resolution, leaving the parties to bargain among themselves.

### Picketing

Union employees often resort to picketing when there is a conflict between the union and the employer. Picketing in its simplest form is used to provide information to employees and the public that there is a dispute between the union and the employer. However, picketing is also used to coerce action on the part of the employer or to dissuade customers from patronizing the employer.

The National Labor Relations Board permits picketing for purely informational purposes. However, it is unlawful for a union to picket where it seeks recognition for a union or seeks for employees to accept the union when another union has been recognized, and the NLRB would not conduct a new election; a valid election has been conducted within the past 12 months; or no election petition has been filed, and picketing has been conducted for a period of time not to exceed 30 days.

Questions are sometimes raised when the picketing seeks to provide information and seeks recognition of the union. The NLRB has set forth a number of rules, some of which hinge on whether the picketing disrupts pickup from or delivery to the employer.

### Boycotts

Unions also employ boycotts when conflicts occur. A primary or simple **boycott** occurs when a union refuses to deal with, patronize, or permit union members to work for the employer with whom the union has a conflict. A secondary boycott occurs when a union refuses to deal with, or pickets, customers or suppliers of the employer. Many secondary boycotts are banned, and others are lawful only when limited conditions are met.

### Strikes and Lockouts

Employees may resort to strike in the event of a conflict where other measures have failed. A lockout by an employer is the counterpart to the strike. The right to strike in the private sector is guaranteed under the NLRA. However, only about half of the states extend this right to employees in the public sector. Where public employees are not permitted to strike, state statutes often impose monetary or similar penalties on those who strike illegally. In states where strikes by public employees are permitted, employees must often meet several conditions prior to the strike. For example, a state may require that a bargaining unit has been properly certified, that methods for impasse resolution have been exhausted, that any existing collective bargaining agreement has expired, and that the union has provided sufficient notice to the school board. The purpose of such conditions is to give the parties an opportunity to avoid a strike, which is usually unpopular with both employers and employees.

## State Provisions Regarding Labor Unions and Strikes

The NLRA governs labor relations of private employers, subject to some limitations. A union of a private employer should determine whether the NLRA applies to its business. State labor statutes generally govern labor relations between public employers and unions. These provisions are summarized below.

ALABAMA: All employees have the general right to join or not to join a labor organization.

ALASKA: Public employees are permitted to join to bargain collectively, and, subject to restrictions, public employees may strike.

ARKANSAS: It is **public policy** in Arkansas that employees should be free to organize to bargain collectively. However, the **statute** has been held not to apply to public employees, and public employees are prohibited from striking.

CALIFORNIA: California provides an extensive statutory scheme governing collective bargaining in that state. Collective bargaining by employees of public employers is generally permitted.

COLORADO: Collective bargaining is permitted by statute, which also provides a limited right to strike.

CONNECTICUT: Connecticut permits bargaining by state and municipal employees, with some exceptions.

DELAWARE: Most public employees are permitted to bargain collectively, but strikes by public employees are generally prohibited.

FLORIDA: Right for public employees to bargain collectively is guaranteed by statute, but public employees are forbidden to strike. Public employers are required to recognize employee organizations with majority status.

HAWAII: Statute permits collective bargaining by all public employees. During impasse, mediation, fact-finding, and binding **arbitration** are provided by statute. Strikes are permitted only after other conflict resolution provisions have been completed without success.

ILLINOIS: Public employees are generally permitted to bargain collectively. Strikes are permitted only after certain conditions are met.

INDIANA: Most public employees permitted to bargain collectively, but strikes are generally prohibited.

IOWA: Statute allows bargaining by all public employees. The statute provides a number of procedures for conflict resolution, including mediation, fact-finding, and binding arbitration. Strikes by public employees are prohibited.

KANSAS: Collective bargaining is permitted by all public employees, but subject to some limitations in the process. Strikes by public employees are prohibited.

LOUISIANA: Collective bargaining is neither prohibited nor required in Louisiana.

MAINE: Statue permits collective bargaining by all public employees. Strikes by all state employees are prohibited.

MASSACHUSETTS: Statute allows collective bargaining by all public employees. Strikes or other strike-related activity are prohibited by public employees.

MICHIGAN: Statute permits bargaining by public employees. Strikes by public employees are prohibited.

MINNESOTA: Statute allows collective bargaining by all public employees. Strikes are permitted only after certain conditions have been met.

MISSOURI: Some public employees are granted a right to bargain collectively. Statute does not grant a right to strike.

MONTANA: Statute permits all public employees to bargain collectively. Courts have construed this statute to permit strikes.

NEBRASKA: Statute permits bargaining by all public employees. Nebraska restricts supervisors from joining a bargaining unit, with some exceptions. Strikes by teachers are prohibited.

NEVADA: Statute permits bargaining by all public employees. Strikes by public employees are illegal by statute.

NEW HAMPSHIRE: Statue permits collective bargaining by all public employees. Impasse resolution procedures must be implemented within the same time period specified by the statue. Strikes by public employees are illegal by statute.

NEW JERSEY: Statute permits bargaining by all public employees but excludes standards of criteria for employee performance from the scope of negotiation.

NEW YORK: Statute permits bargaining by all public employees. The statute limits the scope of negotiations to matters related to wages, employment hours, and other terms and conditions of employment. Arbitration is required by statute when an impasse is declared. Strikes by public employees are prohibited.

NORTH CAROLINA: Statute prohibits collective bargaining by all public employees. Statute also prohibits strikes by public employees.

NORTH DAKOTA: Statute permits mediation of disputes between public employees and employees. The statute also specifies the rights of public employees, including membership in a union.

OHIO: Statute permits collective bargaining by public employees. Strikes by public employees are prohibited.

OKLAHOMA: Statutes generally permit collective bargaining by public employees.

OREGON: Statue permits collective bargaining by all public employees. Impasse resolution procedures include mediation and fact-finding. Strikes are permitted after conflict resolution procedures have been implemented.

PENNSYLVANIA: Statute permits bargaining by all public employees under the Public Employee Relations Act. Statute limits which employees may be included in a single bargaining unit. Strikes by public employees are permitted only after conditions set forth in the statute are met.

RHODE ISLAND: Statute generally permits collective bargaining by state and municipal employees. Strikes by some public employees are prohibited.

SOUTH DAKOTA: Statute permits bargaining by all public employees. Strikes by public employees are prohibited.

TEXAS: Statute prohibits public employees from entering into collective bargaining agreements. Strikes by public employees are generally prohibited.

UTAH: Statute permits union membership by public employees.

VERMONT: Statute permits bargaining by all state and municipal employees. Strikes by state employees are generally prohibited.

VIRGINIA: Strikes by public employees are prohibited by statute.

WASHINGTON: State permits collective bargaining by public employees. Strikes by public employees are prohibited by statute.

WISCONSIN: Statute permits collective bargaining by municipal employees. Impasse resolution procedures include mediation and arbitration. Strikes are permitted after impasse resolution procedures have been exhausted.

WYOMING: Statute permits right to bargain collectively as a matter of public policy.

## Additional Resources

*Foundations of Labor and Employment Law.* Estreicher, Samuel, and Stewart J. Schwab, Foundation Press, 2000.

*Labor Law in a Nutshell, Fourth Edition.* 4th ed., Leslie, Douglas L., West Group, 2000.

*Outline of Law and Procedure in Representation Cases.* National Labor Relations Board, 2000. Available at http://www.nlrb.gov/outline.html.

*Primer of Labor Relations, Twenty-Fourth Edition.* 23rd ed., Kenny, John J., and Linda G. Kahn, Bureau of National Affairs, 1989.

*U. S. Code, Title 29: Labor, Chapter 7, Labor-Management Relations,* U. S. House of Representatives, 1999. Available at http://uscode.house.gov/title_29.htm.

## Organizations

### AFL-CIO
815 16th Street, N. W.
Washington, DC 20006 USA
Phone: (202) 637-5000
Fax: (202) 637-5058
URL: http://www.aflcio.org/home.htm

### Industrial Relations Research Association (IRRA)
University of Illinois, 121 Labor and Industrial Relations, 504 E. Armory, MC-504
Champaign, IL 61820 USA
Phone: (217) 333-0072
Fax: (217) 265-5130
E-Mail: irra@uiuc.edu
URL: http://www.irra.uiuc.edu/

### National Labor Committee
275 Seventh Avenue, 15th Floor
New York, NY 10001 USA
Phone: (212) 242-3002
Fax: (212) 242-3821
E-Mail: nlc@nlcnet.org
URL: http://www.nlcnet.org/

### National Labor Relations Board (NLRB)
1099 14th Street
Washington, DC 20570-0001
Phone: (202) 273-1770
Fax: (202) 273-4270
URL: http://www.nlrb.gov

# LABOR LAW

## OCCUPATIONAL HEALTH AND SAFETY

*Sections within this essay:*

## Background

The Occupational Safety and Health Act, 29 U.S.C. 651 et seq. (1970) is the federal law that "assure[s] so far as possible every working man and woman... safe and healthful working conditions." The Act is administered by the correlative federal agency, the Occupational Health and Safety Administration (OSHA).

OSHA applies to all private sector employers engaged in any business affecting commerce (which, by way of the Commerce Clause of the U.S. Constitution [Art. I, Sec. 8], Congress derived its authority to exercise OSHA control over states). OSHA does not apply to public sector employees.

Employers with fewer than ten employees are exempt from some of OSHA's record-keeping requirements, as well as some of OSHA's penalties and enforcement measures. However, small employers must still comply with OSHA standards and provide a safe workplace for their employees.

The following are not covered by the OSH Act:

- Self-employed persons

- Farms at which only family members work

- Public sector employees (unless they are included in a State OSHA-approved plan)

- Those working conditions regulated by other federal agencies under other statutes. Examples include workplaces in the mining industry, nuclear energy and nuclear weapons industry, and much of the transportation industry.

## Providing a Safe Workplace

OSHA mandates impose three obligations on employers. First, they are required to furnish a workplace "free from recognized hazards that are causing or are likely to cause death or serious physical harm" to employees. Second, they are required to comply with OSHA standards for workplace safety and health. Third, they are required to maintain records of employee injuries, deaths, illnesses, and exposures to toxic substances. They must also preserve all employee medical records.

### Accident Prevention Programs

OSHA requires that every employer establish and maintain an Accident Prevention Program. The program must include training that will inform workers of hazards and teach them about safe work practices, including special instructions peculiar to their industry or peculiar to any special hazards.

An approved accident prevention program includes general training applicable to all workers, such as providing examples of the best ways to lift objects or the fastest way to exit a building. Instructions on the use of personal protective equipment, especially respirators, is a common subject for training.

A second part of an employer's accident prevention program involves the establishment of procedure to conduct internal inspections or reviews to help detect unsafe conditions and correct them before accidents happen. Many larger companies maintain a "Risk Assessment" office or have an employee whose entire job may be to detect and correct potential safety risks and hazards.

### Workers' Right to Know

OSHA's Federal Hazard Communication Standard (29 CFR 1910.1200) requires employers to set up "hazard communication programs." Such programs are designed to inform employees about the health effects of toxic or chemical exposure and ways to prevent such exposures.

### Hazardous Materials

The Hazard Communication Standard requires that Material Safety Data Sheets (MSDS) be made available at the workplace for each and every chemical or hazardous product that an employee may come in contact with, and the ingredients of which may cause physical or health hazards. MSDS are prepared and supplied by the product's manufacturer and generally summarize the ingredients, the hazards to humans, and safe handling techniques when using the product. At the worksite, containers holding the product must have warning labels and/or other written signs describing the product's hazards.

Employers are also required to instruct employees on how to read the MSDS and make proper use of the information they contain. Employees must be trained on proper use of the hazardous product, safe handling methods, containment of the product (against leaks, spills, fumes, or spreads), personal protective gear, and emergency procedures.

Most employers must submit written information regarding their hazard communication programs, how they intend to disseminate information and conduct training, and what particular products or hazardous materials are at their workplace. MSDS must always be given to union officials or employees' physicians when requested.

### Personal Protective Equipment

The OSHA standard covering personal protective equipment (which may vary for each industrial category) requires that employers provide, at no cost to employees, personal protective equipment as needed to protect them against certain hazards found at the workplace. Such equipment may include protective helmets, eye goggles, hearing mufflers or other hearing protection, hard-toed shoes, respiratory masks or shields, respirators, or gauntlets for iron workers.

### Recordkeeping and Reporting

Two main records are required by OSHA to be kept by covered employers: OSHA Form 200 and OSHA Form 101. OSHA Form 200 is an injury/illness log. There are separate line entries for each recordable incident of illness or injury. The ongoing log also captures (by line entry) such information as whether the illness/injury required offsite or onsite medical treatment, whether there was a loss of consciousness, whether there were any restrictions of work or motion, and whether the employee was transferred to another job. At year's end, a summary Form 200, capturing the totals of illness and injury incidents, must be posted for the entire month of February in the following year.

OSHA Form 101 is the form used to record data involving each accident, injury, or illness. The form provides room for added detail about the facts surrounding the event. **Workers' compensation** claims forms or insurance claims forms may be substituted for the OSHA 101.

Employers are also required to report to the nearest OSHA office within eight hours of any accident that results in death or hospitalization of three or more employees. Periodically, employers may be contacted and notified that they have been selected to participate in the Department of Labor's Bureau of Labor Statistics (BLS) survey. Special recording and reporting forms may be required as part of the survey.

### Training and Education

OSHA maintains more than 70 field offices that function as full-service centers offering a variety of safety-related information and assistance. This may include the dissemination of printed material, audio-visual aids on workplace hazards, lecturers available to speak to employees, and technical assistance.

OSHA also maintains and operates its Training Institute in Des Plaines, Illinois, where basic and advanced training in federal and state OSHA compliance is offered, and compliance officers, state consultants, and other agency personnel are certified. OSHA also provides funds and grants to organizations for conducting workplace training and education. It submits an annual report identifying areas of unmet needs and solicits grant proposals to address those needs.

### Access to Records

OSHA Standard 3110 provides workers with the right to see, review, and copy their own medical records and records of exposure to toxic substances. Additionally, employees have a right to see and copy records of other employees' exposure to toxic substances if they have had similar past or present jobs or working conditions. Employees also may review employer information from the National Institute for Occupational Safety and Health (NIOSH) Registry of Toxic Effects of Chemical Substances (although this information is usually incorporated in the MSDS). "Exposure records" include:

- workplace monitoring or measurement records

- MSDS or other information which identifies substances or physical agents and their characteristics

- biological monitoring results (e.g., blood tests which monitor levels of absorbed substances in the body, etc.)

"Medical records" include:

- results of medical exams, laboratory tests and other diagnostic tests

- medical and employment questionnaires or histories

- medical opinions, recommendations, diagnoses, and progress notes

Generally, a free copy is provided at the request of employees or access to a place where copies may be made is provided. Employees are permitted to establish a designated representative to review records on their behalf, such as a union representative. Written authorization for release of personal information is routinely required. Employers must preserve and maintain both exposure records and medical records for at least 30 years.

### Protection From Retaliation for Reporting Violations

The Act expressly protects employees from adverse employment action (discharge or discipline) for exercising rights under the OSH Act. Employers are prohibited from discriminating against an employee as a result of that employee's having filed a complaint with OSHA, requested an OSHA inspection, talked with OSHA officials, or otherwise assisted OSHA with an investigation. Similar provisions are also incorporated in many states' "Whistleblowers" laws.

The Act also protects employees who refuse to perform a job task that is likely to cause death or serious injury. Such protection requires that the employee's refusal be based on a **good faith** belief of real danger of death or serious injury, that a reasonable person in the employee's position would conclude the same, that there was/is insufficient time to eliminate the danger through OSHA channels, and the employee had unsuccessfully requested that the employer correct the hazard or risk.

## Complying with OSHA Standards

OSHA standards are categorized by industry sectors. Those applicable to general industry are contained in 29 CFR 1910. Those applicable to the construction industry are contained in 29 CFR 1926. Maritime, marine terminals, longshoring standards are found at 29 CFR 1915 to 1919. Agricultural industry standards are found at 29 CFR 1928. As of 2002, OSHA regulations filled five volumes of the CFR (**Code of Federal Regulations**).

### OSHA Inspections

Workplace inspections are authorized under the Act and are generally conducted by OSHA compliance safety and health officers (CSHOs), who are trained by OSHA. Programmed inspections are of a periodic or routine nature, while unprogrammed inspections are in direct response to a specific complaint or catastrophes.

### Penalties and Consequences of OSHA Violations

- Serious Violations: Any violation which creates a substantial probability that death or serious physical harm could result and the employer knew or should have known of the hazard. For such violations, a mandatory **penalty** of up to $7,000 for each occurrence may be imposed. Serious violations may be downgraded by OSHA personnel, based upon employer good faith, lack of previous violations, the size of the business, etc.

- Other than Serious Violations: Any violation directly related to workplace safety or health, but would unlikely cause serious physical harm or death. OSHA may propose a discretionary penalty of up to $7,000. These violations also may be downgraded by OSHA personnel, based upon employer good faith, lack of previous violations, the size of the business, etc.

- Willful Violations: Any violation that an employer intentionally and knowingly commits. The employer must either know that he or she is committing a violation, or be aware that a serious hazardous condition exists and makes no reasonable effort to eliminate it. The Act assesses a civil penalty of not less than $5,000 for such violations. Moreover, if the violation results in the death of an employee, a court-imposed criminal fine of up to $250,000 for individuals and/or **imprisonment** for up to six months; or $500,000 for **corporations** as a criminal fine may be imposed.

- Repeated Violations: Repeat violations may result in fines up to $70,000 each. To be considered a "repeat" offense or violation, the **citation** for the original violation must have been issued in final form.

- Failure to Correct a Prior Violation: Such failures may bring civil penalties of up to $7,000 if the violation extends beyond the prescribed **abatement** date.

### Appeals

Appeals may be initiated by employers or employees. Employees may not contest citations, amendments to citations, penalties, or the lack thereof. If the inspection was the result of an employee complaint, that employee may informally appeal any decision to not issue a citation. Employees may also appeal their employers' petitions for modifications of abatement (PMAs).

Employers may appeal both citations and penalties. At the first level, employers may request meet-ings with area directors and may send representatives authorized to enter into **settlement** agreements. However, a formal notice of contest must be in writing and be delivered within 15 days of receipt of the citation or proposed penalty. A copy of the employer's Notice of Contest must be given to the employees' authorized representative.

## State OSH Laws and Programs

States must obtain express permission from the Secretary of Labor to promulgate their own laws regulating any area directly covered by OSHA regulation. States are free to regulate any area not covered by federal OSHA regulations. Federal approval of a state OSHA plan has been effected in two-thirds of states as of 2002. The following states have substituted approved state OSH plans for the federal OSHA plan:

- ALASKA
- ARIZONA
- CALIFORNIA
- CONNECTICUT
- HAWAII
- INDIANA
- IOWA
- KENTUCKY
- MARYLAND
- MICHIGAN
- MINNESOTA
- NEVADA
- NEW JERSEY
- NEW MEXICO
- NEW YORK
- NORTH CAROLINA
- OREGON
- SOUTH CAROLINA
- TENNESSEE
- UTAH
- VERMONT
- VIRGINIA
- WASHINGTON

- WYOMING

## Additional Resources

*Family Legal Guide* American Bar Association. Times Books, Random House: 1996.

*"The Occupational Safety and Health Act"* Small Business Handbook. Available at http://www.dol.gov/asp/programs/handbook/osha.htm.

*"State Plans"* Published by OSHA, U.S. Department of Labor. 16 January 2002. Available at http://www.osha.gov.

*"Workers Have a Right to Know."* Undated. Available (May 2002) at http://www.lungsusa.org/occupational/workers.html.

# LABOR LAW

## PRIVACY

*Sections within this essay:*

- Background

- Federal Law Governing Workplace Privacy
    - Federal Constitutional Law
    - Federal Legislation

- State Law Governing Workplace Privacy
    - State Constitutional Law
    - State Legislation
    - State Common Law

- Conclusion

- Additional Resources

## Background

Employers have a legitimate and important interest in maintaining an efficient and productive workforce and a safe workplace. Most employers establish rules governing workplace conduct to ensure that employees stay on task and earn their wages. Yet, these rules are often broken, and that in turn increases the need for employers to monitor their employees. Prior to the present era of technology and computers, employer supervision typically took the form of hands-on monitoring, a supervisor patrolling the workplace to make sure that employees were doing their jobs. In some employment settings hands-on supervision remains common place. For example, many manufacturers still employ supervisors to monitor assembly-line workers as they toil each day. In a host of other employment settings, human supervision has been replaced at least in part by technological supervision.

Technological innovations, particularly computers, have drastically altered the nature of the employer-employee relationship. Where once a human supervisor could only monitor employee activity in one place at one time, networked computers now allow employers to monitor nearly everything, nearly all the time, and without employees knowing whether they are being watched. Internet usage can be monitored by employers seeking to compile data about the websites being visited by their employees. Files stored on employees' hard drives can be scanned for format and content. Surveillance cameras can monitor workers' activity throughout the workplace. Telephone lines can be monitored and telephone conversations recorded.

There are two kinds of workplace electronic surveillance, quantitative and qualitative. One type involves monitoring records and analyzes quantitative information, such as the number of keystrokes per hour and the number of minutes spent on the telephone each day. The other type of monitoring analyzes the quality of performance in whatever qualitative terms an employer defines. For example, many employers monitor the content of incoming and outgoing email to make sure the messages exchanged are work-related.

Balanced against employers' interests in maintaining an efficient, productive, and safe workplace are employees' interest in privacy. Workers have a legitimate and important interest in being able to perform their jobs without fear of embarrassment or stigma that might result from an employer's unreasonable intrusion into their workspace. It is also reasonable for employees to expect that their employers will not disclose personal information they obtain via pre-employment applications, honesty tests, **polygraph** examinations, criminal background checks, urine or blood analyses, and the like.

The interests of employers and employees are not always at odds. The quality of the work environment is a concern to both groups. Employees do not generally appreciate having to worry about constant electronic surveillance. Respect for employee privacy is one factor people consider when deciding whether to apply for a job, take a job, or keep a job, and employers generally take heed of this reality. Consistent with employers' goal of maintaining a productive workforce is their goal of attracting good employees and keeping them happy. Accordingly, most employers understand that they must offer a professional work environment in which employees can exercise a certain amount of liberty free from the watchful eye of a supervisor. However, the line separating a reasonable intrusion on employee privacy from one that is unreasonable is often neither clear nor bright, and courts are routinely asked to draw the line for labor and management as a whole.

In the United States the right to privacy traces it origins to the nineteenth century. In 1890 Samuel D. Warren and Louis D. Brandeis published "The Right to Privacy" (4 Harv. L. Rev. 193), an influential article that postulated a general **common law** right of privacy. Before publication of this article, no U. S. court had ever expressly recognized a right to privacy. Since the publication of the article, courts have recognized a general right to privacy that Americans enjoy to varying degrees in different contexts.

Today privacy in the labor context is regulated at both the state and federal levels by a combination of constitutional provisions, federal statutes, and common law. Depending on the **jurisdiction**, the laws can regulate both private employees and public employees (i.e., employees working for a governmental entity). Companies doing business in multiple states must stay familiar with the privacy laws in each state.

## Federal Law Governing Workplace Privacy

Federal law governing workplace privacy generally falls into two categories, constitutional law or **statutory** law. There is no federal common law governing workplace privacy, other than the **case law** interpreting the U. S. Constitution and federal statutes.

### Federal Constitutional Law

The Fourth Amendment to the U. S. Constitution prohibits the federal government from conducting unreasonable searches and seizures, and searches or seizures conducted without a **warrant** are presumptively invalid. The U. S. Supreme has repeatedly held that public employees are protected by the strictures of the Fourth Amendment precisely because they are employed by the government. O'Connor v. Ortega, 480 U.S. 709, 107 S.Ct. 1492, 94 L.Ed.2d 714 (1987). Workers employed by private companies enjoy no such constitutional protection.

The Supreme Court and lower courts have also consistently ruled that the Fourth Amendment right protecting public employees from unreasonable searches and seizures conducted by their employers is more limited than the right protecting the rest of society from searches and seizures conducted by law enforcement officials investigating criminal activity. The Fourth Amendment only protects individuals who have a "reasonable expectation of privacy" in the place to be searched or the thing to be seized. However, in the public employment context courts have recognized that they must balance the alleged invasion of an employee's privacy against the employer's need for control of a smoothly running workplace.

One consequence of this balancing is that employers typically do not need a **search warrant** or **probable cause** to search an employee's work space, so long as the search is for work-related reasons. Even when the search is for **evidence** relating to employee misconduct, the employer's intrusion need not be made pursuant to a search warrant or probable cause unless the alleged misconduct rises to the level of criminal activity, at which point the employee is entitled to full protection of the Fourth Amendment.

Thus, it is generally recognized that most work-related intrusions by an employer comply with the Fourth Amendment's reasonableness requirement. Courts have said that requiring a warrant for work-related searches would be disruptive and unduly burdensome. To ensure the proper, ongoing operation of governmental agencies, entities, and units, courts interpret the Fourth Amendment as giving public employers wide latitude to enter employee offices, search their desks, and open their drawers and file cabinets for work-related reasons.

Drug testing of government employees (or of private employees pursuant to government regulation) has been addressed by several courts. Upon weighing the competing public and private interests, most lower courts have concluded that such testing is constitutional at least in those instances where the employer possessed a reasonable suspicion that a particular employee was using drugs and that the drugs affected the employee's job performance. For example, employers can compel workers to undergo blood, breath, or urine tests to check for drug use following a serious workplace accident that injured or imperiled others, so long as the employer has reason to believe that the accident was caused in part by an employee's drug use. Courts allowing drug testing in these situations have emphasized that the reasonable suspicion test fairly accommodates employees' privacy interests without unduly compromising workplace safety or the safety of the public.

### Federal Legislation

For certain employees, drug testing is not only constitutionally permissible, but statutorily mandated. Under the Federal Drug-Free Workplace Act of 1988, drug testing is required of both public and private employees who are engaged in work that creates high risks of danger to the health and safety of other workers or the health and safety of the public. 41 U.S.C.A. sections 701 et seq. Employees targeted for mandatory drug testing include those employed in the following industries: mass transit, motor carriers (taxi cabs and buses), aviation, railroads, maritime transportation, and natural gas and pipeline operations. In addition, the Americans with Disabilities Act (42 U.S.C.A. section 12210) and the Rehabilitation Act of 1973 (29 U.S.C.A. sections 701 et seq) allow employers to establish drug testing programs for former drug users who are currently enrolled in a drug rehabilitation program or have completed one in the past. Because courts have interpreted these laws as effectively placing former and present substance abusers on notice, employees subject to their provisions typically understand the very limited privacy rights they enjoy when it comes to employer-mandated drug tests.

Less clear cut is the application of the National Labor Relations Act (NLRA) to privacy issues in the employment setting. The NLRA guarantees employees the right to "self-organize, to form, join, or assist labor organizations, to bargain collectively . . . and to engage in other concerted activities for . . . mutual aid or protection." 29 U.S.C.A. sections 101 et seq. The act also prohibits employers from committing "unfair labor practices" that would violate these rights. An **unfair labor practice** is any action or statement by an employer that interferes with, restrains, or coerces employees in the exercise of their rights to self-organize.

Employer surveillance of employee activities may constitute an unfair labor practice if the surveillance interferes with, restrains, coerces, or intimidates employees who are exercising one of their rights protected by the NLRA. At the same time, the NLRA permits employers to enforce company rules aimed at guaranteeing employee productivity and safety, and federal courts have acknowledged that workplace surveillance is sometimes necessary to achieve these objectives. However, employee surveillance will not normally withstand scrutiny under the NLRA unless a rule is actually in place before the surveillance begins.

Once a rule is in place, the lawfulness of a particular surveillance method will be evaluated on a case-by-case basis. Where union or non-union employees conduct their activities openly on or near company property, employers may lawfully observe their activities without running afoul of the NLRA, even if there is no pre-existing rule in place authorizing such observation. N.L.R.B. v. C. Mahon Co., 269 F.2d 44 (6th Cir. 1959). However, an illegal intent may be inferred from an employer's surveillance of open activities if the surveillance is combined with other forms of employer harassment, interference, or intimidation, and the employee under surveillance is subsequently discharged. A history of anti-union animus will also weigh against an employer who is engaged in what would otherwise be deemed lawful surveillance. Conversely, what otherwise might be deemed an unfair labor practice can be made lawful if the surveillance is isolated, not accompanied by a threat, and the employer gives assurances that the employee's job is safe.

Before conducting surveillance of its employees, employers also need to familiarize themselves with the Omnibus Crime Control and Safe Streets Act of 1968. Pub.L. No. 90-351, 82 Stat. 197, June 19, 1968; 18 U.S.C.A. sections 2510-2520. Title III of the act prohibits any person from intentionally using or disclosing information that has been knowingly intercepted by electronic surveillance without consent of the persons under surveillance. As originally conceived, the act applied only to the "aural" acquisition of information by recording, bugging, **wiretapping**, or other devices designed to intercept and transmit sound.

Congress updated the act by passing the Electronic Communications Privacy Act of 1986 (ECPA).

Pub.L. 99-508, Title I, Oct. 21, 1986, 100 Stat. 1848. ECPA governs the interception of data transmissions, which comprise the bulk of modern electronic communications. ECPA prohibits anyone from intercepting, accessing, or disclosing electronic communications without first getting authorization from the parties to the communication. However, ECPA does permit employers to monitor employees' electronic communications if the monitoring is done in the regular course of business, regardless of whether the communication involves a data or sound transmission, so long as the employer is the provider of the communication system being monitored. Thus, an employee's use of intra-company email is generally fair game for employers' to monitor. However, employees who transmit messages from work via a third-party email provider, such as Yahoo!, may create a reasonable expectation of privacy that insulates their communications from employer monitoring.

## State Law Governing Workplace Privacy

State law governing workplace privacy generally falls into one of three categories, constitutional law, statutory law, or common law. Like their federal counterparts, state courts are cognizant of every employer's need to maintain an efficient, productive, and safe workplace. Nonetheless, state law often affords more protection for the privacy interests of both public and private employees,

### State Constitutional Law

Many state constitutions guarantee a right to privacy independent of the right to privacy found in the federal constitution. Those states include Alaska, California, Florida, Hawaii, Illinois, Louisiana, Montana, South Carolina, Texas, and Washington. Some of these state constitutional provisions apply only to public sector employees, while others have been interpreted to apply generally to all state residents. Although it is difficult to make meaningful generalizations about each of these state constitutional provisions, employees' privacy interests are frequently afforded greater protection under state constitutional law than they are under the federal constitution.

For example, the Texas Supreme Court invalidated a state agency's mandatory polygraph testing policy on the grounds that it violated the employee's privacy rights protected by the Texas constitution. Texas State Employees Union v. Texas Department of Mental Health & Mental Retardation, 746 S.W.2d

203 (1987). The court found that the test was "highly offensive" to the average employee because of the extremely personal nature of the questions asked. The court also concluded that the test was not accurate enough to provide a reliable way of identifying misbehaving, inefficient, or unproductive employees.

A California court reinstated a railroad employee who was fired for refusing to take a random drug test. The court noted that an employee's right to privacy in refusing a drug test is not absolute under the state constitution but must be weighed against the employer's competing interests. Luck v. Southern Pac. Transp. Co., 218 Cal. App. 3d 1, 267 Cal. Rptr. 618 (1990), rehearing denied 489 U.S. 939, 112 L. Ed. 2d 309, 111 S. Ct. 344 (1990). Conceding that the employer had a compelling interest in maintaining a safe workplace, the court noted that the discharged employee was simply a clerk who had no direct involvement with the railway operations. As a result, the court determined that the employee's privacy interests were more substantial than the employer's countervailing interests.

At the same time, state courts are pragmatic. They are normally disinclined to interpret a general right to privacy as a guarantee of specific individual freedoms that might be exercised to disrupt the workplace or interfere with an employer's legitimate interest in gathering relevant information about employees and job applicants. Thus, the Florida Supreme Court rejected a prospective employee's claim that she was not required to disclose whether she was a smoker on a pre-employment application. City of North Miami v. Kurtz, 653 So.2d 1025 (1995). The court found that the applicant did not enjoy a reasonable expectation of privacy regarding her use of tobacco.

### State Legislation

Several states and U. S. territories have enacted statutory provisions that prohibit employers from spying on employees who are exercising certain protected rights. They include Connecticut, Hawaii, Kansas, Minnesota, New York, Rhode Island, the Virgin Islands, and Wisconsin. Most of the prohibitions contained in these statutes closely mirror or expand upon the prohibitions contained in the NLRA. Specifically, the statutes regulate employer surveillance of workers who are engaging in union-related activities, and each **statute** permits employer surveillance that is done pursuant to clearly defined rules and in furtherance of legitimate business objectives.

A number of states have also enacted statutes that prohibit employers from disclosing certain personal information about employees gathered during the employment relationship. Minnesota, for example, forbids public employers from disclosing information contained in an employee's personnel file. M.S.A. sections 13.01-13.99. Georgia makes it unlawful for employers to obtain certain criminal history information about an employee or prospective employee without that person's consent. OCGA section 35-3-34(A). Alaska makes it unlawful for employers to require employees or job applicants take a polygraph **examination**. Alaska Stat. Section 23.10.037. However, no state prohibits an employer from requiring an employee or job applicant to undergo a psychological evaluation for the purpose of assessing the test-taker's propensity for truthfulness or deceit.

Several states limit the right of healthcare providers to release medical information to a patient's employer. For example, a Maryland statute generally requires the patient's consent before healthcare providers can disclose medical information to employers. Md Health General Code Ann., section 4-305. Similar statutory restrictions in Maryland prohibit insurance carriers from disclosing medical information to an insured's employer without the insured's consent. Md. Ins. Code Ann., section 4-403.

### State Common Law

The state common law of torts generally recognizes three discrete rights of privacy that are regularly asserted during employment **litigation**. First, the common law affords individuals the right to sue when their seclusion or solitude has been intruded upon in an unreasonable and highly offensive manner. Second, individuals have a common law right to sue when information concerning their private life is disclosed to the public in an extremely objectionable fashion. Third, tort liability may be imposed on individuals or entities who publicize information that places someone in a false light.

A valid cause of action for invasion of privacy will not arise for any of these common law torts unless the employer's intrusion is so outrageous or pervasive as to offend the sensibilities of the average, reasonable person. Merely calling an employee at home, for example, will not give rise to a claim for invasion of privacy, unless the employer making the calls is doing so in a persistent and extremely offensive manner. Johns v. Ridley, 245 Ga.App. 710, 537 S.E.2d 746 (Ga.App. 2000). However, a claim for invasion of privacy may be supported by the allegations of female employees who claim that their supervisor has poked holes in the ceiling to watch them disrobe in the women's restroom. Benitez v. KFC Nat. Management Co., 305 Ill.App.3d 1027, 714 N.E.2d 1002, 239 Ill.Dec. 705 (Ill.App. 2 Dist. 1999).

At the same time, an employer who merely reveals an employee's credit problems to co-workers may not be held liable for invasion of privacy. Dietz v. Finlay Fine Jewelry Corp., 754 N.E.2d 958 (Ind.App. 2001). Nor may an employer be held liable for common law invasion of privacy by circulating a sexually suggestive photograph of a male employee, if the photograph accurately depicts the employee in a place open to the public. Branham v. Celadon Trucking Services, Inc., 744 N.E.2d 514 (Ind.App. 2001). Similarly, an employer does not invade an employee's privacy during an office meeting by suggesting that the employee stole from the employer, if the employer's suggestion is made during an investigation of office thefts and the employee's possible role in them. Zielinski v. Clorox Co., 215 Ga.App. 97, 450 S.E.2d 222. (Ga.App. 1994)

### Conclusion

It is telling that much of the law governing privacy in the workplace actually protects employers from liability for invasion of privacy claims brought by employees. In this way the law reflects a general understanding among the American public that the workplace is essentially a place for commerce, productivity, and human interaction, but normally not a place for privacy or seclusion.

For the most part, employees themselves realize that the employer owns the company and expends the resources to make it profitable. Employees generally want to be efficient and productive so they can receive better reviews and better raises. Consequently, the law gives employers wide latitude and ample discretion in dictating how their businesses will be run. On the other hand, an individual does not abandon his or her privacy rights at the employer's front door. Instead, the law puts in place certain checks to prevent employers from overstepping **boundaries**, abusing their positions of power and authority, and running their businesses in a manner deemed highly offensive or objectionable to the average person.

### Additional Resources

*American Jurisprudence* West Group, 1998.

*West's Encyclopedia of American Law* St. Paul: West Group, 1998.

## Organizations

### The American Bar Association
740 15th Street, NW, Floor 8
Washington, DC 20005-1019 USA
Phone: (202) 662-1000
Fax: (816) 471-2995
URL: http://www.abanet.org
Primary Contact: Robert J. Saltzman, President

### Electronic Privacy Information Center
1718 Connecticut Avenue, NW, Suite 200
Washington, DC 20009 USA
Phone: (202) 483-1140
Fax: (202) 483-1248
URL: http://www.epic.org

Primary Contact: Marc Rotenberg, Executive Director

### National Lawyers Association
P.O. Box 26005 City Center Square
Kansas City, MO 64196 USA
Phone: (800) 471-2994
Fax: (202) 662-1777
URL: http://www.nla.org
Primary Contact: Mario Mandina, CEO

### National Organization of Bar Counsel
515 Fifth Street, N.W.
Washington, DC 2001-2797 USA
Phone: (202) 638-1501
Fax: (202) 638-0862
URL: http://www.nobc.org
Primary Contact: Barbara L. Margolis, President-Elect

# LABOR LAW

## SEXUAL HARASSMENT

*Sections within this essay:*

## Background

Unheard of until the 1970s, **sexual harassment** has become a dominant concern of employers, schools, and other organizations throughout the country. It is one of the most litigated areas of sexual **discrimination** law, and virtually all major companies, government organizations, colleges and universities and even the military now have sexual harass-ment policies in place. Even the president of the United States has been subject to a sexual harass-ment lawsuit.

The definition of sexual harassment has always been controversial. Black's Law Dictionary defines it as ""A type of employment discrimination consisting in verbal or physical abuse of a sexual nature," and it has also been held to exist in educational situa-tions. But beyond this, there is the question of what kind of behavior translates into sexual harassment and what the relationship of the parties must be for sexual harassment to occur.

These issues have been fought over at the federal level for many years. Although sexual harassment law is still not clearly defined, there has emerged over the years a consensus of the basic outlines of what sexual harassment is and what needs to be done by companies and other groups to prevent it.

## Types of Sexual Harassment

The Equal Employment Opportunity Commission (**EEOC**) defines sexual harassment this way: "Unwel-come sexual advances, requests for sexual favors, and other verbal or physical conduct of a sexual na-ture constitute sexual harassment when (1) submis-sion to such conduct is made either explicitly or im-plicitly a term or condition of an individuals employment; (2) submission to or rejection of such conduct by an individual is used as the basis for em-ployment decisions affecting such individual or (3) such conduct has the purpose or effect of unreason-ably interfering with an individual's work perfor-mance or creating an intimidating, hostile or offen-sive work environment."

Generally speaking, the EEOC guidelines divide sexual harassment into two different types:

- **Quid Pro Quo** sexual harassment is the easiest kind of sexual harassment to understand. Quid pro quo is a Latin term that translates as "something for something," and quid pro quo sexual harassment is simply an employer or other person in a position of power demanding sexual favors in return for advancement or as the basis for some other employer decision. To establish a case of quid pro quo sexual harassment, individual employees must show that they were subjected to conduct of a sexual nature that was unwelcome, unsolicited, and not incited or instigated by the employee; that the conduct was based on their sex; and that the employees' reaction to the conduct was used as the basis for an employment decision involving compensation, privileges, or conditions of employment. An example of quid pro quo sexual harassment would be a boss demanding his employee to have sex with him in return for a promotion. Quid pro quo sexual harassment is the easiest kind of sexual harassment to prove, but it is also uncommon compared to the other type of sexual harassment.

- Hostile-environment sexual harassment is created in situations in which an employee is subject to unwelcome verbal or physical sexual behavior that is either extreme or widespread. There is no threat to employment in this kind of harassment, but the harassment causes the employee subject to it enough psychological strain as to alter the terms, conditions and privileges of employment. Hostile environment harassment includes such circumstances as hearing sexual jokes, seeing pornographic pictures, and receiving repeated invitations to go on dates. This type of sexual harassment **litigation** currently is most seen by courts and is the kind most difficult to prove. Most recent Supreme Court and appeals court cases regarding sexual harassment have been hostile-environment cases.

## History

Sexual harassment law has had a history in the United States only since the 1964 **Civil Rights** Act,

and even then, the first sexual harassment cases were not brought under the Act until the 1970s. Since then, the trend has been for courts to broaden their interpretation of what constitutes sexual harassment under the law, with some exceptions.

### Title VII and EEOC Guidelines

Title VII of the Civil Rights Act of 1964 marked the first time sexual discrimination was banned in employment. Title VII prohibits discrimination by employers, employment agencies, and labor organizations with 15 or more full-time employees on the basis of race, color, religion, sex, or national origin. It applies to pre-interview advertising, interviewing, hiring, discharge, compensation, promotion, classification, training, apprenticeships, referrals for employment, union membership, terms, working conditions, working atmosphere, seniority, reassignment, and all other "privileges of employment."

In the years immediately following the passage of Title VII, sexual harassment claims were rarely brought under the **statute**, and when they were, courts dismissed their claims as not applying to the statute. Finally in the mid-1970s, courts began to accept sexual harassment as a form of gender discrimination under Title VII.

This trend received an enormous boost with the EEOC's passage of the first guidelines against sexual harassment in 1980. The guidelines - which courts are not required to follow, specifically stated for the first time that "harassment on the basis of sex is a violation of Title VII," and then the guidelines go on to define sexual harassment. However, these standards remained ambiguous enough as to create some disagreement among appeals courts as to what actually constitutes sexual harassment and defines hostile environment sexual harassment.

### Meritor Savings Bank v. Vinson

*Meritor Savings Bank v. Vinson,* decided in 1986, marked the first time the Supreme Court considered a sexual harassment case under Title VII. The case involved a female employee at a bank who alleged she was forced to have sex by her supervisor, fearing the loss of her job if she refused. The **evidence** showed the employee had repeatedly advanced through the bank by merit, that she had never filed a complaint about the supervisor's behavior, and that she was terminated only because of lengthy sick leave absence. Yet the Supreme Court ruled that she had a case against her former employer on the basis of hostile environment sexual harassment.

For sexual harassment to be actionable, the court declared, it must be "sufficiently severe or pervasive to alter the conditions of [the victim's] employment and create an abusive working environment." In this case, the Court held, the facts were "plainly sufficient to state a claim for 'hostile environment' sexual harassment." The Court also added that on the facts of the case, the plaintiff had a claim for quid pro quo sexual harassment as well.

The *Meritor* case was a landmark for sexual harassment rights in that it established the legal legitimacy of both quid pro quo and hostile environment sexual harassment claims before the Supreme Court. It also rejected the idea that there could be no sexual harassment just because the sexual relations between the plaintiff and the **defendant** were voluntary. The results opened a floodgate of sexual harassment litigation.

### Harris v. Forklift Systems, Inc.

The 1993 case of Theresa Harris marked the Supreme Court's next foray into sexual harassment law. Harris was a manager who claimed to have been subjected to repeated sexual comments by the company's president, to the point where she was finally forced to quit her job. The question before the Court was whether Harris had to prove she had suffered **tangible** psychological injury or whether her simply finding the conduct abusive was enough to prove hostile environment sexual harassment.

In allowing Harris to proceed with her case, the Court took a "middle path" between allowing conduct that was merely offensive and requiring the conduct to cause a tangible psychological injury. According to the Court, the harassment must be severe or pervasive enough to create an environment that a reasonable person would find hostile or abusive and also is subjectively perceived by the alleged victim to be abusive. Proof of psychological harm may be relevant to a determination of whether the conduct meets this standard, but it is not necessarily required. Rather, all of the circumstances must be reviewed, including the "frequency of the discriminatory conduct; its severity; whether it is physically threatening or humiliating, or a mere offensive utterance; and whether it unreasonably interferes with an employee/s work performance." The Harris case further broadened sexual harassment law, making it much easier for plaintiffs to prove harm from sexual harassment.

### Oncale v. Sundowner Offshore Services, Inc.

*Oncale,* a 1998 case, marked the Supreme Court's **ratification** of the same-sex sexual harassment case. The Court held that male-on-male and female-on-female sexual harassment violated Title VII in the same way a male-female sexual harassment situation would violate it. The Court said harassing conduct did not have to be motivated by sexual desire to support an inference of discrimination on the basis of sex.

### Faragher v. Boca Raton and Burlington Industries, Inc. v. Ellerth

Faragher and Burlington Industries both stood for the same proposition: employers are vicariously liable for the actions of their supervisors in sexual harassing employees even if they did not ratify or approve of their actions, or even if they had policies prohibiting sexual harassment in place. However, the Supreme Court, decided in these two 1998 cases that employers could defend themselves against supervisor sexual harassment cases by proving (a) that the employer exercised reasonable care to prevent and correct promptly any sexually harassing behavior; and (b) that the plaintiff employee unreasonably failed to take advantage of any preventive or corrective opportunities provided by the employer or to avoid harm. Even with these two caveats, however, the Supreme Court expressly held that these defenses were not available "when the supervisor's harassment culminates in a tangible employment action, such as discharge, demotion, or undesirable reassignment."

### Clark County School District v. Breeden

The 2000 case of *Clark County School District v. Breeden* was the first time the Supreme Court narrowed the scope of Title VII sexual harassment claims. Ruling in the case of an employee who said she had been retaliated against for reporting a sexually offensive mark made by a supervisor, the Court ruled that for sexual harassment conduct to be severe and offensive enough to be actionable, it had to be more than teasing, offhand comments, or an isolated incident, unless that incident was extremely serious. The case served notice that courts had to be careful to find a balance in sexual harassment cases in the process of determining what constitutes creating a hostile environment.

### Other Legal Issues

Although the Supreme Court has the final word on sexual harassment cases, litigation has proved broad enough that there are many unsettled questions that still remain in regards to sexual harassment. These questions include the proper standard to be imposed in sexual harassment cases, whether a "reasonable person" should be more like a reasonable man or a reasonable woman. Also, whether employers can be held liable for "second-hand sexual harassment," sexual harassment not directed at the plaintiff. Another issue is whether is constitutes sexual harassment when a supervisor creates an equally hostile environment for both men and women. These are just some of the issues currently unresolved in the area of sexual harassment law.

## Education and Sexual Harassment

Employers are not the only ones who have to deal with sexual harassment issues. Educators also deal with sexual harassment cases, in both the areas of teacher-student sexual harassment and student-on-student sexual harassment. Until very recently, it was unclear whether such cases were legitimate, but two important Supreme Court cases dealing with education and sexual harassment decided in the 1990s seem to have settled the matter.

### Title IX

Unlike employment sexual harassment cases brought under Title VII, cases involving sexual harassment of students are brought under Title IX of the Educational Amendments of 1972. Title IX states that "no person in the United States shall, on the basis of sex, be excluded from participation in, be denied the benefits of, or be subjected to discrimination under any education program or activity receiving Federal financial assistance."

For many years, there was confusion as to whether a sexual harassment case could be brought under Title IX. Some courts allowed them, and others did not. Then in 1992, the Supreme Court decided the case of *Franklin v. Gwinnett County Schools,* the first time the court had given an opinion in on the matter.

### Franklin v. Gwinnett County Public Schools

In this case, the Supreme Court determined for the first time that a high school student who was allegedly subjected to sexual harassment and abuse could seek monetary damages under Title IX for alleged intentional gender-based discrimination. The case involved a high school girl who claimed a coach at her school was persistently harassing her, including at one point forcing her to have intercourse with him. The girl claimed that school officials knew about the harassment but made no efforts to stop it. Eventually, the girl switched to another school.

The Court said that damages were available for an action brought to enforce Title IX prohibiting exclusion from participation in, denial of benefits of, or discrimination under any education program or activity receiving Federal financial assistance, since there was no indication in text or history of statute that Congress intended to limit available remedies. In this case, the coach's action in harassing the girl prevented her from fully participating in educational opportunities at her school, thus violating Title IX.

### Davis v. Monroe County Board of Education

In this 1999 case, the Supreme Court expanded the reach of Gwinnett to cover student-on-student sexual harassment. A narrow majority of the court ruled that a school district could be held liable for damages if the school district acts with deliberate indifference to known student-on-student sexual harassment that is so severe as to effectively deny the victim access to an educational program or benefit.

The Court did rule that school districts retain flexibility when it comes to sexual harassment and that damages were not available for acts of teasing and name-calling, even where these comments target differences in gender. But in this case, involving physical contact and sexual slurs allegedly so harsh and pervasive it caused the victim to consider suicide, a claim under Title IX could be established.

### State Laws and Sexual Harassment

Although most sexual harassment claims are brought under federal law, many states have civil rights laws that cover much of the same ground as Title VII and provide an additional state cause of action for sexual harassment. These states often require such complaints to be adjudicated before a specific board or court. States that have civil rights laws prohibiting discrimination on the basis of gender and, therefore, providing a possible cause of action for sexual harassment, include in the following:

- ALASKA: Complaint to be filed before Alaska Commission for **Human Rights**, also provides for private state action

- ARIZONA: Complaints filed with Civil Rights Division

- ARKANSAS

- CALIFORNIA

- COLORADO:Complaints filed with Colorado Civil Rights Commission

- CONNECTICUT: Complaints filed with Commission on Human Rights and Opportunities

- DELAWARE: Complaints filed with state's labor department
- DISTRICT OF COLUMBIA
- FLORIDA: Complaints filed with Florida Human Relations Commission
- GEORGIA
- HAWAII: Complaints filed with State Civil Rights Commission
- IDAHO: Complaints filed with Idaho Commission on Human Rights
- ILLINOIS: Complaints filed with the Department of Human Rights
- INDIANA: Complaints filed with Indiana Civil Rights Commission
- IOWA: Complaints filed with Civil Rights Commission
- KANSAS: Complaints filed with Kansas Commission on Civil Rights
- KENTUCKY: Complaints filed with Commission on Human Rights
- LOUISIANA
- MAINE: Complaints filed with Human Rights Commission
- MARYLAND
- MASSACHUSETTS: Complaints filed with Commission Against Discrimination
- MICHIGAN: Complaints filed with Civil Rights Commission
- MINNESOTA: Complaints filed with Commission of the Department of Human Rights
- MISSOURI: Complaints filed with Commission on Human Rights
- MONTANA: Complaints filed with Commission on Human Rights
- NEBRASKA: Complaints filed with Equal Opportunity Commission
- NEVADA: Complaints filed with Nevada Equal Rights Commission
- NEW HAMPSHIRE: Complaints filed with Commission on Human Rights
- NEW JERSEY: Complaints filed with Division of Civil Rights
- NEW MEXICO: Complaints filed with Commission on Human Rights

- NEW YORK: Complaints filed with Commission on Human Rights
- North Dakota
- OHIO: Complaints filed with Commission on Civil Rights
- OKLAHOMA: Complaints filed with Commission on Human Rights
- OREGON: Complaints filed with Bureau of Labor and Industries
- PENNSYLVANIA: Complaints filed with Human Relations Commission
- RHODE ISLAND: Complaints filed with Commission on Human Rights
- SOUTH CAROLINA: Complaints filed with Commission on Human Affairs
- SOUTH DAKOTA: Complaints filed with Division of Human Rights
- TENNESSEE
- TEXAS: Complaints filed with Commission on Human Rights
- UTAH: Complaints filed with State Industrial Commission
- VERMONT
- WASHINGTON: Complaints filed with Commission on Human Rights
- WEST VIRGINIA: Complaints filed with Commission on Human Rights
- WISCONSIN: Complaints filed with Department of Industry, Labor, and Human Relations
- WYOMING: Complaints filed with Fair Employment Commission

## Additional Resources

"Davis v. Monroe County Board of Education: Title IX Recipients' 'Head In The Sand' Approach to Peer Sexual Harassment May Incur Liability," Romano, Patricia, Journal of Law and Education, January, 2001.

Draw the Line: A Sexual Harassment Free Workplace Lynch, Frances, Oasis Press, 1995.

Sex, Power and Boundaries: Understanding and Preventing Sexual Harassment Rutter, Peter, Bantam Books, 1996.

"So Much for Equality in the Workplace: The Ever-Changing Standards for Sexual Harassment Claims Under Title VII," Rushing, Emily E., St. Louis University Law Journal, Fall 2001.

*U. S. Code, Title 20: Education, Chapter 38: Discrimination Based on Sex or Blindness* U. S. House of Representatives, 1999. Available at: http://uscode.house.gov/title_20.htm

*U. S. Code, Title 42: The Public Health and Welfare, Chapter 21: Civil Rights, Subchapter VI: Equal Employment Opportunities* U. S. House of Representatives, 1999. Available at: http://uscode.house.gov/title_42.htm

*"What the General Practitioner Needs to Know to Recognize Sexual Harassment Claims,"* Miller, Gerald L., Alabama Lawyer, July, 2001.

## Organizations

### Feminist Majority Foundation
1600 Wilson Blvd., Suite 801
Arlington, VA 22209 USA
Phone: (703) 522-2214
Fax: (703) 522-2219
E-Mail: femmaj@feminist.org
URL: URL: http://www.feminist.org/911/1_supprt.html
Primary Contact: Eleanor Smeal, President

### National Organization For Women (NOW)
733 15th St. NW, 2nd Floor
Washington, DC 20005 USA
Phone: (202) 628-8NOW (8669)
Fax: (202) 785-8576
URL: http://www.now.org/
Primary Contact: Kim Gandy, President

### U. S. Equal Employment Opportunity Commission
1801 L Street, NW
Washington, DC 20507 USA
Phone: (202) 663-4900
URL: URL: http://www.eeoc.gov/
Primary Contact: Cari M. Dominguez, Chairperson

# LABOR LAW

## UNEMPLOYMENT INSURANCE/ COMPENSATION

*Sections within this essay:*

- Background

- Program Overview

- Federal Preemptive Laws

- Federal Unemployment Tax Act (FUTA)

- State Unemployment Provisions

- Additional Resources

## Background

The U.S. Constitution does not recognize any right to work for pay. However, by virtue of a myriad of federal and state laws, persons who work for pay but lose their employment through no fault of their own and are unable to immediately secure other employment are generally eligible for temporary monetary assistance.

"Unemployment compensation" is generally paid to eligible persons through mandatory state programs designed to protect workers from interruption of wages or income due to loss of work. Compulsory, state-imposed unemployment insurance is generally carried at the expense of employers. Unemployment insurance shifts the burden of unemployment from the taxpayer at large to industry and business. It also alleviates the burden of financing public assistance for unemployed persons.

## Program Overview

The unemployment insurance program was established under Title IX of the federal **Social Security Act of 1935** (42 **USC** 1101). Correlative with that act is the Federal Unemployment Tax Act (FUTA) (26 USC 3301 et seq.) Under this law, each state administers a separate unemployment insurance program that must be approved by the Secretary of Labor based on federal standards (42 USC 503; 20 CFR 640.1 et seq.). Federal standards apply because the state programs are made applicable to areas normally regulated by federal law (under labor, **commerce**, and general welfare clauses). Special federal rules apply for nonprofit organizations and governmental entities.

Under FUTA, a combination of federal and state taxes is levied upon employers. Although they are imposed as "taxes," the amounts paid are, in reality, akin to "premiums" that are paid for unemployment insurance coverage.

Proceeds from the taxes are deposited in the U.S. Treasury's Federal Unemployment Trust Fund (the Fund) and each state has a separate account in the Fund. The funds are generally invested by the Secretary of the Treasury in government **securities** similar to those for social security trust funds. The use of these funds for any purpose other than payment of unemployment benefits is strictly prohibited. (42 USC 1104).

The Fund itself holds revenues in three separate federal accounts:

- The Employment Security Administration Account covers federal and state administrative costs for unemployment insurance and other employment services, such as for veterans. This account also contains federal grants to states under 42 USC 1101 et seq. for **unemployment compensation** administration.

- The Extended Unemployment Compensation Account contains the federal share of revenues which are drawn upon for extended unemployment benefits during periods of high unemployment.

- The Federal Unemployment Account advances moneys to depleted state trust funds to ensure that benefit obligations are met. These funds are repayable by the states to this account.

As long as a state maintains minimum standards required under the federal Act, it remains eligible to participate in the federal-state collaboration that provides it with access to the above funds and grants (in the form of replenishment of exhausted funds, advances, special assistance when economic crises exist, etc.). While states are not required to conform to every federal **statutory** provision, they may not preempt federal law with respect to those areas where federal law is express. Thus, while state law generally governs eligibility requirements, amounts received, and maximum eligibility periods for benefits, these provisions must not conflict with any expressed federal provisions.

## Federal Preemptive Laws

- The Railroad Unemployment Insurance Act (45 USCS 351) expressly governs unemployment compensation for workers in the railroad industry.

- The Trade Act (19 USCS 2271) provides special payments to workers unemployed or facing unemployment as a result of imported goods and products that compete in the domestic market with goods or products produced by the workers' employers. Special federal rules also apply for nonprofit organizations and governmental entities.

## Federal Unemployment Tax Act (FUTA)

The FUTA tax is in the form of a payroll tax imposed upon (and paid by) employers. It is not withheld from employee wages. The amount that employers must pay is based on the amount of wages they pay to employees (excluding agricultural and domestic workers). Generally, employers are liable for FUTA taxes if one of the following applies:

- they have paid wages totaling at least $1,500 in any calendar quarter

- they have at least one employee on any given day in each of 20 calendar weeks (the 20 weeks need not be consecutive, and the "one employee" need not be the same person).

Once an employer is liable for FUTA under the above criteria, the employer must pay FUTA tax for the current calendar year as well as the next calendar year. The FUTA tax is currently at 6.2 percent, scheduled to decrease to 6.0 percent in 2008. The FUTA tax is imposed as a single flat rate on the first $7,000 of wages for each employee; no tax liability is incurred beyond the $7,000.

FUTA taxes are reported annually on Form 940, "Employer's Annual Federal Unemployment Tax Return," due every January 31 for the preceding year. On an annual basis, the Secretary of Labor reviews and certifies each state unemployment insurance program to the Secretary of the Treasury. The certification is necessary in order for employers who contribute to state unemployment funds to obtain FUTA tax credits. Employers who pay their state unemployment taxes on time are permitted to claim a credit equal to 5.4 percent of federally taxable wages, which effectively reduces the FUTA tax rate to 0.8 percent (6.2 minus 5.4).

## State Unemployment Provisions

State tax rates (for the next calendar year) are proportional to the amount of benefits received in past years by employees drawing from the funds. The taxes, in the form of payroll taxes against the employer, are not deducted from employee wages. States may provide additional unemployment benefits above minimum requirements, e.g. for disabled workers or those with dependents, for which additional taxes may apply.

In order for claimants to receive unemployment insurance benefits (paid weekly), all states generally require that they not have left employment voluntarily without good cause and/or that they were not discharged from employment for "fault" (misconduct). Additionally, states generally require that claimants have met the following qualifying factors in order to receive benefits:

1. They have made a claim;

2. They have registered for work and reported to an employment office;

3. They are capable of doing work and is available to do it;

4. They have been totally or partially unemployed for the benefit week;

5. They have made reasonable and active effort to secure work for which they are qualified.

The formula used to calculate benefits varies from state to state, but some general principles and terms apply. A "base period" usually refers to the work period (consisting of four to five quarters of annual employment, i.e., there are four calendar quarters in a year) last worked by claimants. The claimants' prior work must have been "insured work," that is, work performed for an employer who paid into the unemployment insurance fund.

ALABAMA: In addition to the above qualifying criteria, Alabama requires that claimants, during the base period, have been paid wages for work equal to or exceeding one and a half times the total of wages for work paid to them in the quarter of the base period in which the total wages were the highest. Persons who have received benefits in a preceding benefit year shall not be eligible to receive benefits in a succeeding benefit year unless, after the beginning of the preceding benefit year, they have earned wages equal to at least 8 times the weekly benefit amount established for them in the preceding benefit year. See Alabama Code 25-4-77.

ALASKA: In addition to the above criteria, Alaska statutes provide that benefits are payable to individuals who have earned at least $1000 during the base period and which amount was paid over at least two of the calendar quarters of the base period. Claimants are disqualified for the first six weeks of unemployment if termination of employment was for misconduct. See Alaska Stat. 23.20.350-406).

ARIZONA: In addition to the above criteria, Ariz. Rev. Stat. Ann. 23-601 et seq. provides that benefits are payable for a maximum of 26 weeks and may not exceed one-third of the yearly base pay. **Child support** payments are automatically deducted from benefits.

ARKANSAS: In addition to the above criteria, Arkansas statutes provide that claimants must have earned wages of at least 27 times their weekly benefit during at least two quarters of the base period. The unemployment must not be the result of a labor dispute. Claimants are eligible for benefits in the amount of 1/26th of total wages paid during one quarter of the base period in which highest wages were paid. Code Ann. 11-10-100 et seq.

CALIFORNIA: In addition to the above qualifying criteria, California's Unemployment Insurance Code also provides for benefits to persons unable to work because of nonindustrial **disability** resulting from illness or injury ("Unemployment Compensation Disability" or UCD).

COLORADO: In addition to the above criteria, Colorado's Employment Security Act (8-70-101) limits the maximum benefit period to 26 weeks. Claimant are ineligible if unemployment was due to a strike in which the claimants had direct interest. Illegal **aliens** are not eligible for benefits. Severance pay may reduce or postpone benefits. Full benefits are available where an employer disregards its own discharge policy (677 P.2d 447).

CONNECTICUT: In addition to the above criteria, Connecticut has a one week "waiting" period. Claimants are disqualified for benefits if they were discharged for committing **larceny**. All employees may be eligible for benefits if they voluntarily quits due to **domestic violence**, but employers' accounts are not charged for the claim See Section 31-222. et seq.

DELAWARE: In addition to the above criteria, Del. Code Ann, Title 19.3300 et seq. provides that claimants must have earned wages equal to at least 36 times their weekly benefit amount during the base period. Claimants are disqualified for voluntary termination, discharge for good cause, refusal to accept work for which they are reasonably qualified, for strikes, for illegal alien status, for temporary breaks in athletic employment, and **incarceration**.

DISTRICT OF COLUMBIA: In addition to the above criteria, District of Columbia requires minimum earnings during base period of at least $1,300 in one quarter or $1,950 in two quarters and total wages during base period equal to one and a half times the highest wages in any quarter. See Code Section 46-108. Pregnancy creates no presumption of inability to work. Benefits are denied to illegal aliens and those who fail to attend training or retraining programs.

FLORIDA: In addition to the above criteria, Florida provides for benefits equal to 1/26th of total wages paid during quarter in which highest wages were paid during base period. See Fla. Stat. Ann, Section 443.001 et seq. Since 2000, Florida has been paying an extra five percent of weekly benefit for the first eight weeks. Automatic child support payments are deducted. Employers who must lay off workers may qualify for a state program which permits them to shorten work weeks for employees, who will then qualify for benefits for the time they are not working (443.111(6)).

GEORGIA: No information available. See generally, Georgia Statutes 34-8 et seq.

HAWAII: In addition to the above criteria, Hawaii requires claimants to have earned wages at least five times their weekly benefit amount. Maximum benefit is 2/3 of statewide average weekly wage. Benefits are limited to 26 weeks but may be extended 13 weeks by the state governor. Hawaii has some unusual exemptions; for example, companies that only employ family members who own at least 50 percent of the company are exempt from the statutes. One week waiting period occurs before claimants receive benefits. See Hawaii Rev. Stat. 383-7 et seq.

IDAHO: Follows general requirements; no unusual provisions. See Idaho Code 72-1316 et seq.

ILLINOIS: In addition to the above criteria, Illinois requires that claimants have earned at least $1,600 in wages, of which at least $440 of wages paid during base period must have been paid outside of the calendar quarter in which wages were the highest. Illinois adjusts the amount of benefits according to the number of dependents wage-earners have. (820-405/401 to 405/403). 805 and 820 Ill. Comp. Stat. Ann.

INDIANA: In addition to the above criteria, Indiana law provides that persons retired under compulsory provisions of a **collective bargaining** unit are nonetheless eligible for benefits if otherwise qualified (IC22-2-14-1) See Ind. Code Ann. 22-4-12-2 for benefit rates.

IOWA: No unusual requirements are in effect in addition to the above criteria.

KANSAS: No unusual requirements are in effect in addition to the above criteria. See Kansas Stat. Ann.44-706 for benefits rates.

KENTUCKY: In addition to the above criteria, there is a one week waiting period under Kentucky law. Benefits may not exceed the lesser of 26 times the weekly benefit or one-third of base period wages. See KRS 341.350 et seq.

LOUISIANA: In addition to the above criteria, Louisiana requires a one-week waiting period and earned wages equaling at least one and a half times the wages paid in the calendar quarter in which wages were the highest. Disqualifications include receiving payments under a private **pension** or retirement plan. (Title 23, Section 1600 et seq.)

MAINE: In addition to the above criteria, Maine has a one week waiting period and disqualifies claimants who are receiving pensions, terminal pay, vacation pay, or holiday pay. Claimants are not disqualified if they voluntarily leave work because of illness, spousal transfer, acceptance of another job that failed to materialize, or domestic abuse, if claimants have reasonably attempted to preserve employment. (Title 26, Sections 1191-1193.)

MARYLAND: In addition to the above criteria, Maryland requires that claimants have been paid wages for two calendar quarters that total one and a half times the upper limit of division of highest quarter wages. Additional benefits for up to five dependent children under 16 years of age. Benefits may be extended during periods of high state or national unemployment. See Md. Code Ann., 8-800 to 8-1110.

MASSACHUSETTS: In addition to the above criteria, Massachusetts requires that claimants have earned a minimum of $2000 during base period. The maximum benefits are for 30 weeks or 36 percent of total wages for preceding year, whichever is less. See Mass. Gen. Laws, Ch. 151A.

MICHIGAN: In addition to the above criteria, Michigan law provides that weekly benefits shall be 4.1 percent of claimants' wages paid in calendar quarter in which claimants earned their highest wages, plus $6 per dependent, up to five. Maximum benefit is $300 weekly. See MCL 421.20 et seq. Child support is withheld.

MINNESOTA: In addition to the above criteria, Minn. Stat. Ann. 268.01 et seq. provides that weekly benefit amount is the higher of (1) 50 percent of average weekly wage during the base period up to a maximum of 66 2/3 percent of state's average weekly wage; or (2) 50 percent of average wage during the higher quarter up to a maximum of 50 percent of the state's average weekly wage, whichever is higher. Generally, 26 weeks is the benefit maximum.

MISSISSIPPI: In addition to the above criteria, Mississippi requires that a claimant have earned wages equal to 40 times his/her weekly benefit during two quarters of the base period. Weekly benefit amounts are 1/26th of the total wages for highest quarter of base period, but not more than $165 per week. If weekly benefit computes to less than minimum, individual is not entitled to benefits. See Miss. Code Ann. 71-5-501 et seq.

MISSOURI: In addition to the above criteria, Missouri requires earned wages of at least $1000 in at least one quarter of base period and a one week waiting period. Since 2001, maximum weekly benefit is $250. See Vernon's Ann. Mo. Stat. 288.030 et seq.

MONTANA: In addition to the above criteria, Montana Code Ann. 39-51-2101 et seq. provides that claimants may be required to participate in reemployment service. Maximum benefit is 60 percent of average weekly wage. Maximum benefit weeks depends upon amount of earnings during base period.

NEBRASKA: In addition to the above criteria, Nebraska law establishes an "unemployment benefit" table. Since 1999, individuals must have earned wages of not less than $1600 during two quarters of base period ($800 each quarter) and must have worked. Child is support automatically withheld. See Neb. Rev. Stat. 48.601 et seq.

NEVADA: In addition to the above criteria, Nevada law provides that weekly benefits are equal to 1/25th of total wages during highest wage quarter, with a maximum of 50 percent of state's average weekly wage. See Nev. Rev. Stat. Ann. 612.340 et seq.

NEW HAMPSHIRE: No unusual requirements are in effect in addition to the above criteria. See N.H Stat. Ann. 282-A, Section 31.

NEW JERSEY: In addition to the above criteria, New Jersey statutes permit benefits if claimants have worked at least 20 weeks or earned at least 12 times the state average weekly wage or 1,000 times the **minimum wage** of the year prior to benefits. (These rules are different for agricultural workers.) Maximum benefits of 26 weeks. See N.J. Stat. Ann. Title 43, Ch. 21.

NEW MEXICO: In addition to the above criteria, weekly benefit is 1/26th of wages in highest quarter. Maximum benefit is for the lesser of 26 times weekly benefit or 60 percent of base period wages. See N.M. Stat. Ann. 51-1-1.

NEW YORK: In addition to the above criteria, New York permits the accumulation of days for the purpose of benefits, with benefit rate based upon claimants' average weekly wages. The maximum weekly benefit is $365. Benefits are available for victims of domestic violence who have left employment for good cause. See N.Y. Labor Laws Section 590 et seq.

NORTH CAROLINA: In addition to the above criteria, North Carolina has substantial **penalty** waiting periods for leaving employment voluntarily or being fired for substantial fault. See N.C. Gen. Stat. 96-01 et seq.

NORTH DAKOTA: In addition to the above criteria, North Dakota has no exceptional or unusual requirements. See, generally, N.D. Cent. Code 52-01-01 et seq.

OHIO: In addition to the above criteria, Ohio has no exceptional or unusual requirements. See, generally, Ohio Revised Code (ORC) 4141.01 et seq.

OKLAHOMA: In addition to the above criteria, Oklahoma requires that claimants have earned at least minimum wage during base period. See Okla. Stat. Ann. Title 40-2-201 et seq.

OREGON: In addition to the above criteria, Oregon requires claimants to have worked for subject employers at least 18 weeks with wages of $1,000. Claimants must have earned six times the weekly benefit amount in base period. Benefit amounts are based on state average weekly covered wages. See Or. Rev. Stat. 657.101 et seq.

PENNSYLVANIA: In addition to the above criteria, Pennsylvania law requires that claimants have earned not less than 20 percent of total base year wages in one or more quarters of the base period. Benefits are based on the greater of either an amount based on highest quarterly wage or 50 percent of full time weekly wage. Benefits are reduced for retirement pensions, severance pay, etc. See Pa. Cons. Stat. Ann. 43.751 et seq.

RHODE ISLAND: In addition to the above criteria, no unusual requirements are in effect. Benefits are available in addition to tuition benefits. See R.I. Gen. Laws 28-42 to 28-48.

SOUTH CAROLINA: In addition to the above criteria, South Carolina requires earned wages in the first four of previous five calendar quarters exceeding 1 1/2 times total of wages paid in highest earnings quarter. See S.C. Code Ann. 41-27-10 to 41- 41-50.

SOUTH DAKOTA: In addition to the above criteria, South Dakota requires base period wages (in other than highest quarter) equal to or exceeding 20 times the weekly benefit amount. Weekly benefits are equal to 1/26th of wages paid in quarter of highest earnings. Special formula and waiting period exist for persons leaving employment voluntarily. See S.D. Codified Laws Ann. 61-6-1 et seq.

TENNESSEE: In addition to the above criteria, Tennessee has no unusual requirements. Maximum benefit as of 1999 was $255 weekly. See Tenn. Code Ann. 50-7-101 et seq.

TEXAS: In addition to the above criteria, Texas has a lengthy list of exclusions based on the nature of employment (e.g., insurance agents or solicitors if earnings are solely by commission, newscarriers under age 18, etc.) See Tex. Labor Code, 207.001 et seq.

UTAH: In addition to the above criteria, Utah requires that claimants have earned wages in preceding benefit year equal to at least six times the weekly benefit amount. Weekly benefits are reduced by 100 percent of retirement income attributable to that week. See Utah Code Ann. 35A-4-401 et seq.

VERMONT: In addition to the above criteria, Vermont law provides that claimants be paid one half of average weekly wages, based on 20 weeks of highest earnings during base period. See Vt. Stat. Ann., 21-1330 et seq.

VIRGINIA: In addition to the above criteria, Virginia law requires that claimants have earned wages during the highest two quarters of the base period an amount exceeding that specified in a table contained in Va. Code Ann. 60.2-602.

WASHINGTON: In addition to the above criteria, Washington law provides that weekly benefits are payable in an amount equal to 1/25th of the wages of the two highest average quarters. Maximum benefit is 55 percent of state average weekly wage for prior calendar year preceding June 30. Maximum benefits are lesser of 1/3 of base year earnings or 30 times weekly benefit. See Wash. Rev. Code Ann. 50.01 et seq.

WEST VIRGINIA: In addition to the above criteria, West Virginia requires that claimants have earned at least $2,200 during more than one quarter of base period. Maximum benefit is 66 2/3 percent of state average weekly wage. Alabama requires See W. Va. Code art. 6 et seq.

WISCONSIN: In addition to the above criteria, Wisconsin requires that claimants have earned at least 30 times the weekly benefit during the base period and four times weekly benefit outside of the quarter with the highest wages in the base period. See Wis. Stat. Ann. 108.01 et seq.

WYOMING: In addition to the above criteria, Wyoming has no unique requirements. See Wyo. Stat. Ann. 27-3-101 et seq.

## Additional Resources

*Martindale-Hubbell Law Digest* Martindale-Hubbell: 2000.

*Summary of American Law* Weinstein, Martin, The Lawyers Cooperative Publishing Company: 1988.

"Unemployment Compensation" *American Jurisprudence,* 2nd ed.Lawyers Cooperative Publishing: 1992.

# LABOR LAW

## WAGE AND HOUR LAWS

*Sections within this essay:*

- Background
- History
- Fair Labor Standards Act
- Exempt Employees
- Child Labor
- Overtime
- State Wage and Hour Laws
- Additional Resources

## Background

The **Fair Labor Standards Act**, enacted by Congress in 1938 and amended numerous times since then, requires most employers in the United States to comply with **minimum wage** and hour standards. The law's basic requirements govern the payment of a minimum wage, payment of overtime pay for employees working more than 40 hours per work week, employment limitations for children, and mandated record keeping by employers.

## History

At the end of the nineteenth century, the industrial age was spurring the growth of factories known as sweatshops. Sweatshops routinely employed women, children, and recent immigrants who had no choice but to accept inferior wages and harsh working conditions. Social activists pushed for laws at the state level to pay all workers, regardless of social status or gender, wages that would allow them to maintain an adequate standard of living.

Massachusetts, in 1912, became the first state to enact a law mandating a minimum wage. Other states soon followed suit. Widespread poverty during the Great Depression increased public awareness of the need for wage standards, and by 1938, twenty-five states had enacted minimum wage laws. Some states established commissions to determine the minimum wage based on what the commission perceived to be a "living" wage for employees. Some of these commissions also took into account the employer's financial conditions in determining appropriate wages. Other states simply established flat minimum wage rates for all employees in those states.

Eventually, however, the success of state wage statutes was tempered by court decisions, including a U. S. Supreme Court decision that held state minimum wage laws to be unconstitutional. According to the courts, these laws violated the rights of employers and employees to freely negotiate and form contracts over appropriate wages. President Franklin D. Roosevelt responded by attempting to enact federal legislation granting the president the authority to regulate a minimum wage as part of the federal government's right to regulate interstate commerce. The Supreme Court found President Roosevelt's first attempt at such legislation to be unconstitutional, but the Court upheld his second attempt, the 1938 Fair Labor Standards Act (FLSA), as constitutional.

## Fair Labor Standards Act

The FSLA requires that most U. S. workers are entitled to receive a minimum hourly wage. This federally enacted minimum wage changes only when Congress passes a bill and the president signs it into law, which happens periodically in keeping with U. S. economic conditions. When the FSLA was enacted, the minimum wage was 25 cents an hour. In 2002, the minimum wage was $5.15 an hour.

The FSLA also requires that most U. S. workers are entitled to receive one and one half times their hourly rate of pay, even if that rate is above the minimum wage, for hours worked in excess of 40 hours per work week. This is known as overtime. The FSLA also contains child labor restrictions and mandates certain working conditions for children under the age of 18. Finally, to ensure that employers comply with the federal law, the FSLA requires them to keep detailed employment records. The FSLA does not require employers to provide sick or severance pay to employees. It does not require employers to provide employees with vacation time or holidays, fringe benefits, or increases in pay beyond the minimum wage. Employers, however, do have to comply with state employment laws that deal with issues not covered by the FSLA.

## Exempt Employees

Not all employees are protected by the FSLA. Some employees are exempt from minimum wage protections, and some employees are exempt from overtime pay requirements. Employers may try to avoid the FSLA requirements by categorizing their employees as exempt, but courts narrowly construe whether an employee is exempt and place the burden of proof on the employer.

There are numerous examples of employees who are exempt from the protections of the FSLA. Employees who earn more than half of their total earnings from sales commissions are usually exempt from FSLA overtime requirements. Computer professionals who earn at least $27.63 per hour are not entitled to overtime pay, either. Drivers and mechanics whose jobs affect the safety of vehicles that transport people or property are exempt from the overtime pay requirement. Farm workers on small farms are exempt from both minimum wage and overtime pay requirements. Most employees of car dealerships are exempt from overtime pay requirements. Seasonal and recreational employers do not have to comply with minimum wage or overtime requirements of the FSLA. Finally, white collar workers—employees whose job duties are executive, administrative, professional, or involve outside sales—are exempt from

minimum wage and overtime pay requirements. The FSLA lists numerous other exemptions, as well.

## Child Labor

The FSLA protects workers under the age of 18 to ensure that they are safe at work and that work does not jeopardize their health or their ability to receive an education. States also have **child labor laws**, some of which are more restrictive than the FSLA. Child workers generally receive the same protections and usually greater protections, than adult workers under the FSLA. The FSLA's child labor provisions do not apply to children under the age of 16 who work for their parents, children who work as actors, children who deliver newspapers, or children who work at home making evergreen wreaths.

Workers under the age of 20 are entitled to receive minimum wage under the FSLA, but during the first 90 days of employment, an employer is allowed to pay these workers a lesser wage of $4.25 per hour. Certain students, apprentices, and disabled workers also may receive less than minimum wage under special allowances by the Department of Labor. Restaurant servers and other workers who receive tips may be paid $2.13 per hour so long as the additional money made in tips adds up to at least minimum wage.

Under the FSLA, workers at least 16 years old may work unlimited hours unless the job is deemed hazardous by the Secretary of Labor. Workers who are 14 or 15 years old may not work during school hours except in career exploration programs through the school. They may not work before 7 a.m. or after 7 p.m. during school months; they may not work after 9 p.m. from June 1 through Labor Day. Workers who are 14 or 15 years old may not work more than three hours per school day, more than eight hours per non-school day, more than eighteen hours per school week, or more than forty hours per non-school week. Children who work as professional sports attendants are exempted from the maximum hours requirements but still may not work during school hours.

Workers who are 14 or 15 years old may not work in certain occupational areas, such as manufacturing, mining, food processing, transportation, warehousing, construction, or any occupation deemed hazardous by the Secretary of Labor. These workers may work in most retail, food service, and gasoline service occupations but may not perform work in an engine or boiler room, maintain or repair machines or equipment, work on ladders or scaffolds or perform outside window washing, cook or bake, operate food slicers or grinders, work in freezers or meat coolers, load or unload goods from trucks or conveyors or railroad cars, or work in warehouses.

Children under the age of 18 are prohibited from driving occupations, but workers who are 17 may drive cars and trucks as part of their work on an occasional and incidental basis. Driving must take place during daylight hours, and the worker must hold a valid state license to drive and have no record of moving violations. The car or truck must have a seat belt, and the worker must use the seat belt when driving. The driving may not include towing cars or other vehicles, route deliveries or sales, transporting more than three people, urgent deliveries, or more than two trips away from the employer per day.

Employers who violate the FSLA's child labor protections are subject to civil penalties of up to $10,000 per child laborer. The Wage and Hour Division of the Department of Labor's Employment Standards Administration enforces the FSLA and has investigators stationed throughout the country to ensure that employers comply with the law.

## Overtime

Some employers attempt to avoid the requirement to pay one and a half of an employee's hourly rate for overtime hours. The FSLA is very strict in defining what constitutes overtime and requires that anytime an employer requires or allows the employee to work, that work counts toward the employee's weekly hours. This means that even if an employer does not require an employee to work, but the employee works anyway, those hours count toward the overtime determination. For example, assume that the manager of a copy center asks her employee to work on a copying project. The employee's shift ends at 7 p.m., so the manager tells him that he can leave work when his shift ends and can then complete the project the following day if necessary. Nevertheless, the employee continues to work on the project after his shift ends and manages to complete it that evening. His efforts, however, take an additional three hours beyond the forty hours he has already worked that week. The employee is entitled to receive three hours of overtime pay, at one and a half times his usual hourly wage, for the additional work he did. If the employer knows or has reason to believe that an employee is continuing to work and if

the employer benefits from the work being done, that time counts toward the overtime calculation.

Also included in the overtime calculation is time spent by an employee correcting mistakes, even when the employee does so voluntarily. Time spent by an employee merely waiting for something to do or doing nothing counts toward hours worked, assuming the employer requires the employee to be present. Work performed by the employee at home or at another location other than the employer's premises also counts toward hours worked.

## State Wage and Hour Laws

ALASKA: State minimum wage is $5.65. Workers employed as school bus drivers receive at least two times the Alaska minimum wage.

ARKANSAS: Employers of workers who receive board, lodging, apparel, or other items as part of the worker's employment may be entitled to an allowance for such board, lodging, apparel or other items, not to exceed 30 cents per hour, credited against the minimum wage.

INDIANA: An employer must pay a base wage of $2.13 per hour for tipped employees (any employee who receives more than $30 a month in tips) and the employer must pay the difference between the base wage and federal minimum wage if applicable.

MICHIGAN: Workers under the age of 18 are entitled to a 30 minute meal break after five hours of work. Michigan law does not require a meal break for workers over the age of 18.

NEW HAMPSHIRE: An employer cannot require a worker to work more than five hours without a thirty minute meal break. An employee who reports to work at the employer's request is entitled to be paid a minimum of two hours wages.

NEW JERSEY: Workers under the age of 18 are entitled to a 30 minute meal break after five hours of work. New Jersey law does not require a meal break for workers over the age of 18.

OREGON: State minimum wage is $6.50 per hour. State law prohibits employers from taking a credit against minimum wage for tips. Employees are entitled to thirty minute meal periods for work shifts six hours or longer, and ten minute work breaks during each four hour work shift.

VERMONT: State minimum wage is $6.25 per hour. State minimum wage for restaurant servers is

$3.44 per hour with a maximum tip credit allowance of $2.81 per hour.

WEST VIRGINIA: Minors 14 or 15 years of age must receive work permits before working. The permit is forwarded to the Division of Labor, which has the responsibility of ensuring that minors are not working in hazardous or unsuitable conditions.

WASHINGTON: State minimum wage is $6.90 per hour. No employer may employ a minor without a work permit from the state along with permission from the minor's parent or **guardian** and school.

## Additional Resources

*Child Labor Bulletin 101.* U. S. Department of Labor, Employment Standards Administration, Wage and Hour Division WH-1330. Revised March 2001.

*West's Encyclopedia of American Law.* West Group, 1998.

## Organizations

### U. S. Department of Labor
200 Constitution Avenue NW
Washington, DC 20210 USA
Phone: (866) 487-2365
URL: www.dol.gov

### GotTrouble.com
12439 Magnolia Blvd. Suite 204
Studio City, CA 91607 USA
URL: www.gottrouble.com

### U. S. Bureau of Labor Statistics, Office of Compensation and Working Conditions
2 Massachusetts Avenue NE
Washington, DC 20212-0001 USA
Phone: (202) 691-6199
URL: www.bls.gov/ncs/

# LABOR LAW

## WHISTLEBLOWERS

*Sections within this essay:*

- Background
- Federal Whistleblower Statutes
    - False Claims Act
    - Other Federal Laws
- State Whistleblower Statutes
    - General State Whistleblower Statutes
    - Public Policy Exception
    - Federal Preemption
    - State-by-State Guide to Whistleblower Coverage
- Additional Resources

## Background

The protection of whistleblowers exposing **fraud** or wrongdoing perpetrated by individuals or **corporations** has been an issue for centuries. Under English **common law**, suits brought on behalf of the government by individuals alleging fraud were known by the Latin phrase describing them, "qui tam pro domino rege quam pro si ipso in hac parte sequitur," meaning "who sues on behalf of the King as well as for himself."

The first **statute** to protect whistleblowers in the United States was the federal False Claims Act, inspired by the corruption and fraud that resulted from the Civil War. Passed in 1863, the act allowed private parties to bring suits against those corporations or individuals trying to **defraud** the government, with the bringer of the lawsuit entitled to half the recovery from the fraud, which included a $2,000 fine for each

violation and damages amounting to double the loss from the fraud.

States also began to pass their own versions of whistleblower laws. By the 1980s, such legislation had become common at the state and federal level, and in 1986 the federal False Claims Act was strengthened to give whistleblowers more rights. Despite being unpopular with businesses, the federal False Claims Act has withstood Supreme Court scrutiny and today serves as the most important of the many federal and state laws protecting whistleblowers.

State and federal whistleblower statutes generally fall into two categories: those that encourage whistleblowers by giving them some form of compensation for their action, such as the False Claims Act, and those that protect the whistleblower from retaliation, which constitute the majority of state and federal statutes. As of 2002, all 50 states provide some sort of whistleblower protection.

## Federal Whistleblower Statutes

Federal whistleblower statutes are included in a wide range of laws, governing activities ranging from employee safety to environmental protection. The first of all federal whistleblower statutes, and still considered the most important, is the federal False Claims Act.

### False Claims Act

The 1863 federal False Claims Act (FCA) has gone through many changes. The act was revised in 1986, which strengthened it and made it the prime federal whistleblower statute. FCA reports of fraud have increased from an average of six per year pre-revision to 450 per year in 1998.

Lawsuits brought under the FCA are known as "qui tam" actions. Under the 2002 FCA, a successful lawsuit brought by a whistleblower will net the whistleblower between 25 and 30 percent of all money recovered by the action if the government decides not to join in the lawsuit. If the government does join the lawsuit, the whistleblower can net between 15 and 25 percent of the total proceeds of the suit. This is in addition to reasonable expenses and attorneys fees.

Under the False Claims Act, a business found guilty of defrauding the federal government can be fined from a minimum of $5,000 to a maximum of $10,000 for each violation. In addition, a business found liable under the act must pay three times the amount of damages that the government sustains as a result of the violation. There is a **statute of limitations** under the act of 10 years. An employee can also file a separate lawsuit if the person is fired, demoted, or harassed at work as a result of bringing an FCA action against the employer.

FCA lawsuits can be very lucrative. Since 1986, over 3,000 FCA cases have been filed and about $3 billion has been recovered. The average recovery in an FCA case is $5.8 million, and the average whistleblower's reward has been about $1 million. The government intervenes in only 21 percent of the FCA cases. The only limitations the FCA puts on these types of suits is that a member of the armed forces is precluded from asserting a claim against another member of the armed forces.

FCA cases generally include three common elements in order to prove fraud under the act. The **defendant** must present a claim for payment to the federal government, or the defendant must cause a third party to submit a claim; that claim must be made knowingly; and the claim must be false or **fraudulent**.

Claim is defined under the FCA as any request or demand, whether under a contract or otherwise, for money or property which is made to a contractor, grantee, or other recipient if the United States Government provides any portion of the money or property which is requested or demanded, or if the government will reimburse such contractor, grantee, or other recipient for any portion of the money or property which is requested or demanded.

"Knowingly" is defined as actual knowledge of the false information; acts in deliberate ignorance of the truth or falsity of the information; or acts in reckless disregard of the truth or falsity of the information.

The Supreme Court recently upheld the FCA. In the 2000 case of Vermont Agency of Natural Resources v. United States, the high court determined that citizens have standing to file whistleblower suits under the act, though the court also ruled that states and their agencies are not liable under the provisions of the act.

### Other Federal Laws

Other federal laws with whistleblower provisions generally take a different approach to whistleblowers than the FCA, providing protections to those who act as whistleblowers rather than incentives. These statutes prohibit any retaliatory discharge of or **discrimination** against the whistleblower and punish violators of the statute.

Within this context, the statutes can take different approaches to protecting the worker. Some provide the whistleblower with a private cause of action against the employer and allow the person to bring suit himself. These statutes include: the Clean Air Act, the Energy Reorganization Act, the Federal Deposit Corporation Improvement Act, and the Vessels and Seamen Act.

Other federal laws require the Secretary of Labor or other government official to bring action in a case of retaliatory discharge or discrimination against a whistleblower. Those statutes include: the Age Discrimination in Employment Act, the Civil Service Reform Act, the Comprehensive Environmental Response, Compensation and Liability Act, the Employee Retirement Investment **Securities** Act, the Federal Surface Mining Act, the Family and Medical Leave Act, the Job Training and Partnership Act, the Migrant and Seasonal Agricultural Worker Protection Act, the Mining Safety and Health Act, the Occupational Safety and Health Act, the Safe Drinking Water Act, the Solid Waste Disposal Act, the Surface Transportation Assistance Act, the Toxic Substance Control Act and the Water Pollution Control Act. These acts do not allow the whistleblower to bring his or her own private cause of action.

Generally speaking, these acts cover whistleblowers when they file a complaint or institute or cause to be instituted any proceeding under or related to the law the provision exists under, or when the whistleblower has testified or is about to **testify** in any proceeding related to the law. If an employer is determined to be liable for discharging or discriminating against an whistleblower employee under one of these laws, the employer can often be fined and required to reinstate the employee to his or her former position; to pay **compensatory damages**; or take other appropriate actions to remedy any past discrimination.

## State Whistleblower Statutes

While some states had whistleblower statutes during the early part of the twentieth century, most of the action in regards to state legislation to protect whistleblowers occurred in the latter half of the century. In the 1980s, for example, 15 states passed general whistleblower statutes, and many state courts further developed a **public policy** exception to the at-will employment doctrine for whistleblowers. The result is that state courts have become a major arena for whistleblower cases.

### General State Whistleblower Statutes

As a rule, state whistleblower statutes differ from federal whistleblower statutes in several significant ways. The first is that with only a couple exceptions, state whistleblower statutes do not follow the compensation model of the federal False Claims Act. Those exceptions are Illinois, Florida, Oregon, South Carolina, and Wisconsin. Only Illinois and Florida provide compensation for whistleblowers anywhere near what the federal law provides, with the other three states providing less satisfactory compensation.

State whistleblower statutes instead provide protection from retaliation for **whistleblowing**. Unlike the federal governments, the majority of state governments have whistleblower statutes that generally protect all employees who report violations of the law by their employers, in addition to having whistleblower statutes covering the violations of specific laws. In many states, these general whistleblower protections are limited to public employees, although other states have protections for both private and public employees.

States with general whistleblower statues that protect both private and public employees include: Arizona, California, Connecticut, Florida, Hawaii, Illinois, Louisiana, Maine, Michigan, Minnesota, Montana, New Hampshire, New Jersey, New York, Ohio, Oregon, Rhode Island, and Tennessee.

States with general whistleblower statutes that protect only public employees include Alaska, Colorado, Delaware, District of Columbia, Georgia, Idaho, Indiana, Iowa, Kentucky, Maryland, Massachusetts, Mississippi, Missouri, Nebraska, Nevada, North Caro-

lina, North Dakota, Oklahoma, Pennsylvania, South Carolina, South Dakota, Texas, Utah, Washington, West Virginia, Wisconsin, and Wyoming.

Many of the state laws provide employees with a private cause of action, providing another contrast with federal whistleblower statutes. This allows the employee to sue directly in the courts, rather than having to go through an agency of the state.

### Public Policy Exception

In addition to specific statutes protecting whistleblowers, many state courts have enunciated a public policy exception for whistleblowers to the at-will employment doctrine which allows employees who are not under contract to be dismissed by their employers at any time.

The public policy exception for whistleblowers usually holds that employers should not be able to use their power as employers to subvert public policy as established by the legislatures or the courts. Employees who are fired, demoted, or harassed for refusing to violate a law, rule or regulation, or who report a violation of such, can sue their employer under this theory.

State courts can read this public policy exception either narrowly or broadly, depending on the particular court. More conservative courts may insist on showing the act of the employer caused actual harm to the **public interest** before allowing a public policy exception. But some state courts will award **punitive damages** if they find a strong public policy violation.

### Federal Preemption

When federal and state whistleblower laws conflict, the federal laws preempt the state laws. Because states tend to have traditionally been responsible for employment issues, courts have been leery of finding preemption when it comes to whistleblower statutes. However, in some instances they have found such preemption exists. The test seems to be whether the federal law concerns an area of strong enough federal concern that it did not leave room for state regulation. Preemption cases involving whistleblower statutes have yielded mixed results over the past two decades.

### State-by-State Guide to Whistleblower Coverage

Besides statutes protecting whistleblowers in general, most states protect whistleblowers in specific areas, such as employment of minors, abuse of children, nursing home violations, or wage and hour violations. Whether the whistleblower is protected in a specific area depends on the state.

The following is a state-by-state guide to some of the different areas where whistleblowers are protected if they report violations in those areas:

- ALABAMA: Child labor violations.

- ALASKA: Occupational safety and health violations, the Alaskan Railroad Company violations, **child care** facilities violations, assisted living homes violations, legislative employees violations.

- ARIZONA: Water quality control violations, occupational safety and health violations.

- ARKANSAS: **Civil rights** violations, fair housing violations, long term care violations.

- CALIFORNIA: State universities violations, savings associations violations, health care facilities violations, elderly care facilities violations, occupational safety and health violations, toxic substances violations, fraudulent unemployment actions violations, mental health facilities violations.

- COLORADO: **Minimum wage** law violations, false disclosures to the state violations.

- CONNECTICUT: Environmental violations, information to auditors or public accountants violations, child care violations, violations committed by leaders or employees of a foundation violations, civil rights violations, **collective bargaining** for state employees violations, public schools violations, nursing homes violations, minimum wage violations, Labor Relations Act violations, **child abuse** violations.

- DELAWARE: Public and private schools violations, nursing homes violations, civil rights violations, workers compensation fraud violations, long term care facilities violations, child labor violations, minimum wage violations, firefighters violations, public works contractors violations, hazardous chemical control.

- DISTRICT of COLUMBIA: Procurement issues violations, discrimination and civil rights violations, unfair labor practices violations, workers compensation fraud violations, minimum wage violations, occupational safety and health violations, long term care facilities violations.

- FLORIDA: Child abuse violations, long term care facilities violations, continuing care facilities violations.

- GEORGIA: Fraud in state programs violations, unfair labor practices violations, gender discrimination in minimum wage laws violations.

- HAWAII: Unfair labor practices violations, elder care violations, minimum wage laws violations, civil rights violations, occupational safety and health violations.

- IDAHO: Sanitation violations on farms violations, fair wage law violations, environmental protection violations, PCB waste disposal violations, minimum wage laws violations, state **human rights** law violations, long term care facilities violations.

- ILLINOIS: Field sanitation for agricultural workers violations, prevailing wage law violations, disclosures by transportation authority workers violations, civil rights laws violations, migrant worker conditions violations, unfair labor practices violations, public and private schools violations, elder care violations, nursing home facilities violations, minimum wage laws violations, equal pay laws violations, occupational safety and health violations, toxic substances violations.

- INDIANA: Elder care violations, health care facilities violations, long term care facilities violations, education violations, political subdivisions violations.

- IOWA: Collective bargaining violations, public health facility personnel violations, civil rights violations.

- KANSAS: Reporting disease violations, child abuse violations, elder care violations, working conditions violations.

- KENTUCKY: Occupational safety and health violations, long term facilities violations, firefighters violations.

- LOUISIANA: Health care providers violations, lead hazard reduction licensing of certification violation violations, insurance code violations, hospitals violations, long-term care facilities violations, environmental laws violations.

- MAINE: Human rights law violations, occupational safety and health violations, employment practices violations, state universities violations, judicial branch violations, agricultural violations, public utility violations.

- MARYLAND: Occupational safety and health violations, civil rights violations.

- MASSACHUSETTS: Domestic service violations, health care violations, asbestos **abatement** violations, hazardous substances violations, child care violations, minimum wage violations, civil rights violations.

- MICHIGAN: Adult care provider violations, civil rights violations, long-term care facility violations, occupational safety and health violations.

- MINNESOTA: Child care facility violations, **unfair labor practice** violations, civil rights violations, occupational safety and health violations, health services violations, asbestos abatement violations.

- MISSISSIPPI: Workers compensation violations, vulnerable adult violations.

- MISSOURI: Nursing home violations, public health violations, Department of Correction violations, mental health facility violations, in home care provider violations, long term care facility violations.

- MONTANA: Unlawful discrimination violations.

- NEBRASKA: Occupational safety and health violations, unlawful discrimination violations, Industrial Relations Act violations, nursing home violations.

- NEVADA: Long term care facility violations, occupational safety and health violations, mental health care facility violations.

- NEW HAMPSHIRE: Hazardous waste law violations, human rights law violations, asbestos management and control violations, elder care violations, dog and horse racing facility violations, toxic substance control violations, child care facility violations.

- NEW JERSEY: Ski tow lift and tramway violations, hazardous substance violations, civil rights violations, child abuse violations, occupational safety and health violations, minimum wage violations, elder care violations.

- NEW MEXICO: Long term care facility violations, residential care facility violations, oc-

cupational safety and health violations, radiation control violations.

- NEW YORK: Civil rights violations, elder care facility violations, occupational safety and health violations, minimum wage violations, Labor Relations Act violations, toxic substances control violations, health care facility violations.

- NORTH CAROLINA: Long term care facility violations, violations of state law by department, agency or local political subdivision.

- NORTH DAKOTA: Child abuse and welfare violations, adult care facility violations, mentally and physically handicapped violations, minimum wage law violations, long-term facility care violations, agency misuse of funds violations.

- OHIO: Long term care facility violations, child care facility violations, minimum wage law violations, nursing home violations, health care facility violations, abuse of mentally handicapped adult violations.

- OKLAHOMA: Children's group home violations, civil rights violations, violations occurring in group homes for person with developmental or physical disabilities, child abuse violations, foster care violations, occupational safety and health violations, nursing home violations.

- OREGON: Adult care facilities violations, long term care facilities violations, collective bargaining violations, occupational safety and health violations, civil rights violations.

- PENNSYLVANIA: Occupational safety and health violations, radioactive waste violations, Community Right to Know Act violations, toxic substances violations, civil rights violations, seasonal farm workers rights violations, public utility company violations.

- RHODE ISLAND: State hospital violations, long-term care facility violations, asbestos abatement violations, insurance company violations, HMO violations, non-profit hospital violations.

- SOUTH CAROLINA: Occupational safety and health violations, long-term care facility violations.

- SOUTH DAKOTA: Civil rights violations, collective bargaining violations.

- TENNESSEE: State educational system violations, nursing home facility violations, child care facility violations, mental health and **disability** facilities violations, adult care facilities violations, minimum wage violations, occupational health and safety violations.

- TEXAS: Agricultural laborer violations, worker health and safety violations, immediate-term care facility violations, treatment facility violations, hospital and health care facility violations.

- UTAH: Minimum wage law violations, occupational safety and health violations, long term care facility violations.

- VERMONT: Occupational safety and health violations, **Polygraph** Protection Act violations, fair employment practices violations, state labor practices violations, long term care facilities violations.

- VIRGINIA: Occupational safety and health violations, adult care facilities violations, child welfare protection violations, nursing home facilities violations.

- WASHINGTON: Agricultural laborer violations, long-term care facility violations, minimum wage law violations, nursing home violations, state hospital violations.

- WEST VIRGINIA: Miners health, safety and welfare protection violations, nursing home violations, personal care home violations, residential care violations, asbestos abatement violations, occupational safety and health violations, equal pay law violations, minimum wage law violations.

- WISCONSIN: Residential care facility violations, long-term care facility violations, rural medical center violations, collective bargaining violations, solid waste facility violations.

- WYOMING: Long-term care violations, equal pay act violations, occupational safety and health violations.

## Additional Resources

*"Bringing Rogues to Justice: The Qui Tam Provisions of the False Claims Act,"* Androphy, Joel, Adam Peavy, Texas Bar Journal, February 2002.

*"The State of State Whistleblower Protection"* Callahan, Elletta Sangrey, Terry Morehead Dworkin, American Business Law Journal, Fall 2000.

*"State Whistleblower Statutes and The Future of Whistleblower Protection"* Vaughn, Robert G., Administrative Law Review, Spring 1999.

*"Silencing the Whistleblower: The Gap Between Federal and State Retaliatory Discharge Laws"* O'Leary, Trystan Phifer, Iowa Law Review, January 2000.

## Organizations

### *National Whistleblower Center*
P.O. Box 3768
Washington, DC 20007 USA
Phone: (202) 342-1902
Fax: (202) 342-1904
URL: http://www.whistleblowers.org
Primary Contact: Kris Kolesnik, Executive Director

### *Office of Administrative Law Judges: United States Department of Labor*
Suite 400 North, 800 K Street, NW
Washington, DC 20001-8002 USA
Phone: (202) 693-7300
Fax: (202) 693-7365
URL: http://www.oalj.dol.gov
Primary Contact: P.J. Soto, Director, Office of Program Operations

### *U.S. Department of Labor*
200 Constitution Avenue, NW
Washington, DC 20210 USA
Phone: (866) 487-2365
URL: http://www.dol.gov/
Primary Contact: Elaine Chao, Secretary of Labor

# LABOR LAW

## WORKERS' COMPENSATION

*Sections within this essay:*

- Background
- History
- Rationale
- Third Party Negligence
- Procedure
- Compensable Injuries
- Types of Benefits
- State Workers' Compensation Laws
- Additional Resources

## Background

**Workers' compensation** is a system that requires employers, typically through their insurance companies, to pay lost wages, medical expenses, and certain other benefits to employees who are injured on the job. Because employers pass on the costs of workers' compensation benefits or insurance premiums in the pricing of their products, consumers ultimately fund the workers' compensation system.

Workers' compensation is different from other types of torts in that it is not based on fault or **negligence**. A worker who is injured due to her own negligence or that of her employer typically is entitled to the same workers' compensation benefits as a worker whose injury did not result from negligence at all. The idea behind workers' compensation is not to right a wrong or punish negligence; rather, it is a

way to protect employers from negligence lawsuits and injured workers from destitution. The goal is to return injured employees to work efficiently and economically without damaging the employer's business.

Workers' compensation is legislated by every state, and the laws vary among jurisdictions but carry many of the same features. An employee who sustains an occupational disease or **personal injury** arising out of and in the course of employment is entitled automatically to certain benefits. These benefits may include lost wages, payment of medical treatment, provision of vocational rehabilitation or job placement assistance, and in the case of an employee's work-related death, benefits to the employee's dependents. Some workers, such as independent contractors, are excluded from workers' compensation protection.

## History

Workers' compensation came about in the United States in the early 1900s, a product of the industrial age and a result of increasing numbers of job-related injuries and deaths. Until the development of workers' compensation laws, workers had little or no recourse against their employers for injuries sustained on the job. When job injuries led to the inability to work and the inability to pay for medical care, these workers frequently were left destitute.

The system of workers' compensation grew from the law of vicarious liability, an English law developed in approximately 1700. The law of vicarious liability made a master or employer liable for the negligent acts of a servant or employee. An 1837 English case, Priestly v. Fowler, modified the law of vicarious liability with the fellow servant exception, which relieved a master or employer of liability for a negligent employee who caused injury to a co-employee. Following the example set in Priestly, U. S. courts continued to modify the law of vicarious liability and provide the employer with greater protections against liability resulting from negligence. The doctrine of assumption of the risk presumed, often incorrectly, that employees could refuse dangerous job assignments, thereby relieving the employer of liability when those job assignments caused injury or death. Employers could also rely on the defense of contributory negligence, which completely absolved them of liability when the employer's negligence along with the employee's negligence caused his injury.

Workers were left with inadequate remedies against their employers for injuries resulting from work. At the same time, the industrial age was spawning an increase in work injuries. States began to recognize a problem by the end of the nineteenth century and looked to the compensation systems of other countries for guidance. In 1884, Germany, with its socialist traditions, had developed a compensation system whereby employers and employees shared the cost of subsidizing workers disabled by injury, illness, or old age. Next was England, which in 1897 developed a similar system called the British Compensation Act. Finally, in 1910, representatives from various states met in Chicago and drafted the Uniform Workmen's Compensation Law. This uniform law was not widely adopted, but states used it as a model to draft their own workers' compensation statutes. Most states had such laws in place by 1920, and when Hawaii passed its **statute** in 1963, all fifty states had workers' compensation laws.

## Rationale

Workers' compensation is a no-fault law, meaning that it is irrelevant whether the employer was not negligent or whether the employee was negligent. No-fault law differs from most types of personal injury lawsuits, which require the injured party to prove the negligence of another party before recovering money and which allow a **defendant** who was not negligent to escape liability.

The rationale behind a no-fault workers' compensation system can be illustrated by imagining what would happen without it. Assume, for example, that an employer owned a loading dock and instructed its employees how to safely lift heavy merchandise on the dock, requiring them to use a forklift to lift any carton weighing more than 100 pounds. A worker, hurrying to complete his shift, negligently ignored the forklift requirement and attempted to lift a carton weighing 110 pounds and badly injured his back as a result. He had to undergo surgery and became disabled from working at all for six months.

Without workers' compensation, society would have essentially two different options in dealing with this injured worker. It could decline any assistance and force the worker to fund his own medical care and unemployment, which could be impossible and could leave him destitute. Or, it could provide government assistance such as **Medicaid**, welfare, or food stamps. This option would guarantee the injured worker's survival, but at the expense of local taxpayers regardless of any ties to the employer or injury.

With workers' compensation, the injured worker receives an income and payment for medical care from a private source rather than at government, or taxpayer, expense. It is not the goal of workers' compensation to punish or hurt the employer, and that is why state laws require employers either to establish a self-insured fund or to buy workers' compensation insurance. Employers fund the costs of the system but pass those costs along to the consumers of the products or services that cause or contribute to the worker's injury. The goals of the workers' compensation system are therefore accomplished: the worker retains his dignity, receives appropriate financial and medical benefits, and the consumer becomes the ultimate source of payment.

## Third Party Negligence

In exchange for workers' compensation protection, an injured worker loses the right to sue the employer under the **common law** for negligence. An injured worker retains the right, however, to sue a third party whose negligence caused or contributed to the worker's injury, even if the worker receives workers' compensation. A common example of this involves a sales employee whose job duties include driving to customers throughout a certain territory. If that employee, while making a sales call, is injured by a negligent motorist who runs a red light, the employee is covered by workers' compensation but can additionally sue the motorist under a common law tort theory. If the worker recovers money from the negligent third party motorist, the worker must repay the employer or insurer who paid workers' compensation benefits and keep only what is left. In some jurisdictions, the employer or insurer paying workers' compensation benefits may sue a negligent third party on behalf of an injured worker with the hopes of recovering part or all of those benefits from the third party. This is known as subrogation.

## Procedure

Workers' compensation disputes in most states are resolved in an administrative court rather than a judicial court. This is in keeping with the goal of returning the injured worker to productive employment quickly and efficiently. Workers' compensation courts often follow their own rules of procedure and **evidence**, and the administrative system typically is more relaxed and speedy than the judicial system. As with judicial courts, parties can represent themselves but frequently hire attorneys for representation.

Workers' compensation laws require employers to either be self-insured, meaning they must have enough verifiable financial resources to be able to pay workers' compensation benefits directly to their injured employees, or to purchase private workers' compensation insurance. Many major insurance companies in the United States offer workers' compensation policies in various states. Other insurance companies are smaller and may provide coverage in only one or a few states. Some states choose to fund their own insurance companies, either as the state's exclusive provider or in competition with other private insurers.

## Compensable Injuries

Various types of injuries are covered by workers' compensation. Perhaps the most typical type of injury involves a specific trauma or event; for example, a painter who falls off a scaffold or a car mechanic who injures his back after lifting an engine. Another type of injury is a cumulative trauma injury, an injury caused by repetitive work over time. An example of cumulative trauma injury is carpal tunnel syndrome caused by using a computer keyboard. A third type of compensable injury is occupational disease, and an example of that would be lung disease caused by exposure to asbestos at work.

Mental illness caused by work is compensable in some, but not all, jurisdictions. Mental illness such as stress, anxiety, or depression, even when caused by work, is not compensable in most states. However, mental illness that accompanies a work-related physical injury is compensable in most states. For instance, a nurse who develops depression related to his work in an emergency room typically would not be entitled to workers' compensation, but a nurse who is attacked and physically injured by a patient and as a result develops anxiety could receive workers' compensation benefits for the physical as well as the mental injury in most states.

Injuries are deemed to be work-related and compensable under workers' compensation if they arise out of and in the course of employment. The requirement that the injury arises out of employment ensures a causal relationship between the injury and the job, and it is usually the employee's burden to prove that an increased risk of the job caused a compensable injury.

There are three general categories of risks that determine whether an injury is compensable. The first type of risk is one that is associated directly with the employment, such as a when a roofer falls off a roof. An injury like this clearly arises out of employment and is always compensable.

The second category of risk involves personal risk. An example of personal risk is an employee with high blood pressure who suffers a stroke while on the job. Assuming nothing on the job caused the stroke, or assuming the stroke would have occurred notwithstanding the employment, the stroke would be considered personal rather than arising out of employment. Purely personal risks are not compensable.

It is more difficult to determine compensability with the third category of risk called neutral risk. Neutral risks are those that are neither distinctly personal nor distinct to the employment. Examples of neutral risks include a worker who has an allergic reaction to a bee sting sustained while on the job, or an employee who is struck by lightening while on the job. Whether neutral risks are compensable depends on the **jurisdiction** and the fact surrounding the injury and the job duties. In general, an employee trying to collect workers' compensation must demonstrate that the job increased the risk of the injury and that the risk was greater than that to which the general public was exposed. The risk of being injured by lightning, for example, is greater for an employee working on the top of a metal communication tower than it is for the general public. Therefore, a lightning strike would be a compensable injury for that employee. **Assault** is another neutral risk injury. If a worker is assaulted on the job and injured, courts generally look at whether the nature of the job increased the risk of assault, such as the case of a prison guard. If an argument led to a workplace assault, the court would determine whether the argument was work-related or personal. Other common forms of neutral risk injuries include sunstroke, frostbite, heart attacks, and contagious diseases.

To be compensable, the injury must not only arise out of, but also in the course of, employment. This means that the injury must occur at the place of employment, while the employee is performing the job and within the period of employment. Employees who are injured while traveling to or from their jobs typically are not covered by workers' compensation, although there are exceptions to that rule.

## Types of Benefits

There are two general categories of workers' compensation benefits, medical and indemnity. Medical treatment that is medically reasonable and necessary and serves to cure or relieve the effects of the injury is compensable. Disputes may arise over the kind of treatment the injured worker receives, and courts and legislators try to strike a balance between the patient's right to select medical care and the employer's right to curb excessive or unnecessary treatment.

Indemnity benefits are those that attempt to compensate the injured employee for lost earnings or earning capacity caused by the work injury. Some injured workers never lose time from work and may be entitled only to medical benefits. Other injured workers are out of work temporarily and receive temporary total **disability** payments, usually two-thirds of the worker's average wage. Injured workers who are able to return to a job only part time or at a reduced wage receive temporary partial disability payments, which supplement the worker's reduced paychecks. Workers who sustain injuries that cause permanent disability are entitled to permanent partial disability payments if they are able to return to work. The calculation of permanent partial disability payment varies among states but usually depends on a disability rating given by a doctor. If a worker is permanently precluded by a work injury from ever working again, that worker is deemed permanently and totally disabled and may receive workers' compensation benefits until retirement or death. When a work injury causes death, most states require the payment of dependency benefits to the employee's spouse, children, or both.

The workers' compensation system is criticized at times for being outdated in a post-industrial age world. Workers' compensation premiums and expenses drive up the cost of products, and the system is made more expensive by **fraud** and **litigation**. Disputes often arise between employers and employees regarding the legitimacy of workers' compensation claims. Yet proponents of the system say it is effective in returning injured workers to work and that it promotes safe workplaces.

## State Workers' Compensation Laws

ALABAMA: For temporary or permanent total disability, an injured worker receives 66 2/3 percent of the wage with a minimum and maximum wages established by law. The employer selects the employee's physician.

ARIZONA: Disability rate is 66 2/3 percent of the wage with no minimum weekly payments but maximum payments established by law. The employee selects the physician.

CALIFORNIA: A state agency oversees the selection of the physician.

DISTRICT OF COLUMBIA: The employee selects the physician from a list created by the District of Columbia.

FLORIDA: After employee reaches maximum medical improvement, a $10 co-payment is required to be paid by the employee for all medical services.

GEORGIA: Maximum period of temporary total disability payments is 400 weeks.

ILLINOIS: No limit on duration of temporary total disability payments.

IOWA: Disability rate for temporary or permanent total disability is 80 percent of "spendable earnings."

KANSAS: Temporary total disability capped at $100,000. Permanent total disability capped at $125,000. Workers' compensation benefits subject to offset for unemployment and social security benefits.

MASSACHUSETTS: Disability rate is 60 percent of wage.

MISSISSIPPI: Maximum period of temporary disability is 450 weeks. Cap on temporary total disability is $131,787. Cap on permanent total disability is $136,507.

NEVADA: Injured worker can waive the right to workers' compensation.

NEW YORK: Disability rate is 66 2/3 percent of wage. Employee selects physician from state's list of workers' compensation physicians.

OREGON: Duration of temporary disability payments is duration of disability.

TEXAS: Employers are not required to purchase workers' compensation insurance.

WEST VIRGINIA: State funded insurer is the exclusive workers' compensation insurer in West Virginia.

## Additional Resources

*West's Encyclopedia of American Law. West Group, 1998.*

## Organizations

### U. S. Department of Labor

200 Constitution Avenue NW
Washington, DC 20210 USA
Phone: (866) 487-2365
URL: www.dol.gov

# REAL ESTATE

## BOUNDARY/PROPERTY/TITLE DISPUTES

## Background

The concept of land estates in American law arose out of the feudal system in England which consisted of present interests and future interests in estates which were parcels of land. These concepts developed into the modern law of possessory rights.

## Forms of Title

### Fee Simple

The most common form of ownership, when a homeowner purchases a home, is the fee simple absolute. The holder of a title in fee simple has full possessory rights now and in the future for an infinite duration. There are no limitations on its inheritability. The holder of the estate can sell the entire estate or any part of it and dispose of it by will at time of death. When a condominium or townhouse is purchased, the owner typically purchases the residential unit in fee simple and obtains the right to use the common areas. Each unit has its own tax bill, **deed**, **mortgage** and ownership rights but shares in the maintenance of the common areas.

### Joint Tenancy with Right of Survivorship

In this type of title each owner holds an undivided share of the estate. There is a right of survivorship which means on the death of one joint owner, the surviving owner or owners retain an undivided right to the entire estate, which is not subject to the rights of the heirs of the deceased co-owner.

### Tenancy in Common

In a title held as a **tenancy** in common, each owner has an undivided interest in the entire property. Each tenant has the right to possession of the whole property. There is no right of survivorship. Each tenant has a distinct proportionate interest in the property, which passes by **succession**. There is a presumption that a conveyance to two or more persons is a tenancy in common.

### Tenancy in the Entirety

This is a marital estate, which can only be created between a husband and wife. It is similar to a joint tenancy except that the right of survivorship cannot be destroyed, since severance by one tenant is not possible. An existing marriage is requisite for a tenancy by the entirety. In many states there is a presumption that a tenancy by the entirety is created in any conveyance to a husband and wife. This type of title is considered somewhat archaic and the majority of states have abolished this type of tenancy, favoring instead that the couple take title to the property as joint tenants with right of survivorship.

## Obtaining Title to Property

A purchaser of real estate has the right to receive a clear, marketable title to the property being purchased absent an agreement to the contrary. In most jurisdictions, a buyer obtains a title **examination** and **title insurance** through a title company. If the purchase is financed through a bank, the bank will require title insurance to protect the bank against loss resulting from claims by third parties against the real estate. In some states, attorneys offer title insurance as part of their services in examining title and providing a title opinion. The attorney's fee may include the title insurance premium. In other states, a title insurance company or title agent directly provides the title insurance. A lender's title insurance policy will not protect a purchaser. The purchaser must buy an owner's policy in order to obtain protection, and doing so is generally less expensive if acquired at the same time and with the same insurer as the bank's policy.

Banks and title insurance companies often require a survey to mark the **boundaries** of the property. A survey is a drawing of the property showing the perimeter boundaries and the location of any buildings or structures on the property. The total cost of a title insurance policy varies depending on several factors including, the amount insured and the searches requested.

The actual transfer of title to real property typically occurs via a deed at the closing of the transaction. There are various types of deeds:

- *Quitclaim Deeds:* These deeds contain no covenants by the grantor. These are typically used when two owners hold title to a property and one owner releases the other, perhaps due to sale of the property or a **divorce** of the parties.
- *Warranty Deeds:* These deeds contain covenant or warranties from the grantor, includ-

ing that the grantor has the right to convey the property and that there are no encumbrances on the property. A general **warranty deed** warrants title against defects arising before as well as during the time the grantor has title. A special **warranty** deed contains the same covenants, but only warrants against defects arising during the time the grantor has title.

A deed must be in writing and should clearly identify the parties and the land involved. In order to protect a purchaser or lender from the subsequent rights of third parties over the real estate, it is essential to record the relevant documents by filing in a county recording office. Significant differences with regard to recording procedures and requirements exist from county to county. Most recording statutes provide that the deed must be acknowledged before a **notary public** to be recorded.

In addition to putting others on notice regarding ownership of the property, recording also tracks chain of title. When title insurance is purchased, the title insurer checks the chain of title to determine whether any defects occurred in prior conveyances and transfers. Such defects can then be put right or excluded from coverage.

## Ownership of Land by Aliens

The regulation of the rights to hold real property of individuals who are not citizens of the United States is left to the states. Generally, any alien or non-national may take, hold, convey and devise real property. There are not many federal restrictions on non-nationals owning or investing in real property in the United States.

## Forms of Leaseholds

A leasehold is an estate in land with an ascertainable period of possession. The tenant has a present possessory interest in the premises, and the landlord/owner has a future interest. When a tenant signs a **lease**, the type of right that tenant has in the property is known as a leasehold.

### Periodic Tenancy

This is a tenancy for a term of successive periods such as year-to-year or month-to-month. There is no definite termination date, and it continues until terminated by either the **landlord** or tenant. It is terminated by proper notice, which is usually statutorily prescribed. This tenancy may be created by express written agreement, by oral agreement, or by operation of law.

### Tenancy at Will

The **landlord and tenant** both have the right to terminate the tenancy at will. The parties must have an agreement or understanding that either party can terminate at any time. The tenancy has no stated duration and lasts as long as the landlord and tenant desire. In most states, the acceptance by the landlord of regular rent will cause the courts to consider the tenancy to be a periodic tenancy. No notice is required to terminate a tenancy at will at **common law**. However, in most states, statutes require notice of termination to be given at least one month in advance.

### Tenancy for Years

This tenancy continues for a fixed period of time and has certain beginning and termination dates. Since the parties know when the tenancy will end, the term expires at the end of the period without notice required by either party.

### Holdover Tenant

A tenant who was lawfully in possession of a leasehold and stays too long at the end of the tenancy is called a tenant at sufferance, commonly known as a holdover tenant. This tenancy lasts until the tenant is evicted or until the landlord elects to hold the tenant to an additional term.

## Partition Actions

If two or more people who own a property as tenants in common or if people who are not married to each other own a property as joint tenants with right of survivorship develop a dispute concerning the property, any owner may bring a partition action with the court to get the property divided between owners. While the lawsuit is pending, all owners will have equal access to and interest in the property. This arrangement applies regardless of whether the mortgage is in one owner's name or the name of all owners.

## Boundary Disputes

### Identifying Property Boundaries

If a survey was done when at the time of the purchase of the property, the survey should reflect the boundary lines. Prior to erecting a fence on a boundary line, an updated survey could be ordered which reflects the accurate boundary lines. This may be impossible, due to perhaps the age of the property or the wording of the deed. (Some older deeds can contain legal descriptions such as "52 feet from the bend in the stream" on a piece of land, which has only a dry riverbed where a stream once existed.) In such a situation, the owner may file a quiet title lawsuit and request the judge determine the boundary lines of the property. This procedure is generally more expensive than a survey due to the legal filing fees. Another perfectly acceptable alternative is for adjacent property owners to agree on a physical object, such as a fence, which could serve as the boundary line between the properties. Each owner would then sign a quitclaim deed to the other, granting the neighbor ownership to any land on the other side of the line both owners had agreed upon.

### Adverse Possession Issues

If the piece of property in dispute has been used by someone other than the owner for a number of years, the doctrine of adverse possession may apply. State laws vary with respect to time requirements; however, typically, the possession by the non-owner needs to be open, notorious, and under a claim of right. In some states, the non-owner must also pay the property taxes on the occupied land. A permissive use of property eliminates the ability to claim adverse possession.

### Fences

Local fence ordinances usually regulate height and location, and sometimes the material used and appearance. Residents of subdivisions are often subject to even stricter Homeowners' Association restrictions. In residential areas, local rules typically restrict backyard fences to a height of six feet and front yards to a height of four feet. Exceptions exist and a landowner can seek a variance if there is a need for a higher fence. While some jurisdictions have specific aesthetic **zoning** rules with respect to fences, as long as a fence complies with local laws it cannot be taken down simply because it is ugly. In fact, unless the property owners agree otherwise, fences on a boundary line belong to both owners when both are using the fence. Both owners are responsible for keeping the fence in good repair, and neither may remove it without the other's permission. In the event that trees or other vegetation hangs over the fence, most states agree that the property owner may cut tree limbs and remove roots where they cross over the property line, provided that such pruning will not damage the basic health and welfare of the tree.

### Trees

Sometimes disputes arise between neighbors when trees belonging to one property owner fall on and damage or destroy adjacent property. In such cases, the tree owner is only responsible for damage if some failure to maintain the tree contributed to the damage. If the damage was solely the result of a thunderstorm or act of God, the tree owner will not be responsible as the damage could not have been foreseen. If, however, the tree owner allows the tree to grow so that it uproots the fence, it would be considered an **encroachment** onto the adjacent property. In that instance, the tree owner would be required to remove the offending tree. Leaves, bean pods, or acorns which fall off and end up on adjacent property are considered a natural occurrence and are the responsibility of the landowner on whose property they ultimately come to rest.

### Animals

In the old courts of England, the owner of livestock was held strictly liable for any damages to person or property done by the livestock straying onto the property of another. The mere fact that they strayed and damaged crops, other livestock or **personal property** was sufficient to hold the owner liable for the injuries inflicted by cattle, sheep, goats, and horses. This strict liability position made sense in the confines of a small island such as England, but in the United States with herds of livestock wandering over vast expanses of land, a different process developed. The legislatures enacted statutes which provided that livestock were free to wander and that the owner was not responsible for damage inflicted by those livestock unless they entered land enclosed by a legal fence. These became known as open range laws. Subsequently, certain states reversed the open range laws and required the owners of livestock to fence in their livestock. This position was similar to the common law position, only instead of strict liability, the livestock owner could be held liable only upon a showing that the livestock escaped due to the owner's **negligence**.

## Additional Resources

*Modern Law of Deeds to Real Property.* Natelson, Robert, Aspen Law, 1992.

*Neighbor Law: Fences, Trees, Boundaries and Noise.* Jordan, Cora, Nolo Law, 2001.

## Organizations

### American Land Title Association

1828 L Street, NW
Washington, DC 20036-5104 USA
Phone: (800) 787-ALTA
Fax: (888) FAX-ALTA
URL: http://www.alta.org/

### American Society for Photogrammetry & Remote Sensing

5410 Grosvenor Lane, Suite 210
Bethesda, MD 20814-2160 USA
URL: http://www.asprs.org/

### National Society of Professional Surveyors (NSPS)

6 Montgomery Village Avenue, Suite #403
Gaithersburg, MD 20879 USA
Phone: (240) 632-9716
E-Mail: info@acsm.net
URL: http://www.acsm.net

# REAL ESTATE

## BUYING AND SELLING/MORTGAGES

*Sections within this essay:*

- Background
- Types of Mortgages
    - Fixed Rate Mortgage
    - Adjustable Rate Mortgage
    - Owner Carryback and Financing
    - Home Equity Loan
    - Second Mortgage
    - Reverse Mortgage
- Deed of Trust
- Escrow
    - Abstract of Title
    - Prepayment Penalty Clause
    - Mortgage Contingency Clause
- Types of Lenders
    - Mortgage Brokers and Bankers
    - Direct Lenders
    - Secondary Lenders
- Defaults and Foreclosures
    - Anti-Deficiency laws
    - Mortgage Insurance
- Tax Credit
- State Laws
- Additional Resources

## Background

Most people borrow money in order to purchase their home. A loan for this purpose is commonly called a home loan or **mortgage**. The term mort-

gage originates from two Latin words. The first, "mort" is from the Latin word for death. The second, "gage" means pledge or promise. The word "mortgage" literally means "dead promise." While this may seem nonsensical at first, it actually makes sense: the property was considered forfeited or "dead" to the borrower if the loan were not repaid. Similarly, once the loan was satisfied, the promise itself was dead or unenforceable.

Typically, a mortgage is secured by a **lien** on the property. The mortgagor is the party transferring the interest in land. The mortgagee is the provider of the loan. A mortgage is paid in installments that include both interest and a payment on the principle amount borrowed. With respect to which entity has title to the property, a number of possibilities exist. Under the title theory, title to the security interest rests with the mortgagee. Most states follow the lien theory under which the legal title remains with the mortgagor unless there is **foreclosure**. The intermediate theory applies the lien theory until there is a **default** on the mortgage whereupon the title theory applies.

## Types of Mortgages

A mortgage involves the transfer of an interest in land as security for a loan. The mortgagor and the mortgagee generally have the right to transfer or assign their respective interest in the mortgage. Standard contract and property law provisions govern the transfer or assignment of any interest. There are several different types of mortgages available.

### Fixed Rate Mortgage

A fixed rate mortgage carries an interest rate that will be set at the inception of the loan and remain constant for the length of the mortgage. A 30-year mortgage will have a rate that is fixed for all 30 years. At the end of the 30th year, if payments have been made on time, the loan is fully paid off. To a borrower the advantage is that the rate will remain constant and the monthly payment will remain the same throughout the life of the loan. The lender is taking the risk that interest rates will rise and it will carry a loan at below market interest rates for some or part of the 30 years. Because of this there is usually a higher interest rate on a fixed rate loan than the initial rate and payments on adjustable rate or balloon mortgages. If the rates fall, homeowners can pay off the loan by refinancing the house at the then lower interest rate.

### Adjustable Rate Mortgage

An adjustable rate mortgage (ARM) provides a fixed initial interest rate and a fixed initial monthly payment for a short period of time. With an ARM, after the initial fixed period, which can be anywhere from six months to six years, both the interest rate and the monthly payments adjust on a regular basis to reflect the then current market interest. Some ARMs may be subject to adjustment every three months while others may be adjusted once a year. Also, some ARMs limit the amount that the rates can change. While an ARM usually carries a lower initial interest rate and lower initial monthly payment, the purchaser is taking the risk that rates may rise in the future.

### Owner Carryback and Financing

An alternative form of financing, usually a last resort for those who cannot qualify for other mortgages, is owner financing or owner carryback. The owner finances or "carries" all or part of the mortgage. Owner financing often involves balloon mortgage payments, since the monthly payments are frequently interest only. A balloon mortgage has a fixed interest rate and fixed monthly payment, but after a fixed period of time, such as five or ten years, the whole balance of the loan becomes due at once. This means that the buyer must either pay the balloon loan off in cash or refinance the loan at current market rates.

### Home Equity Loan

A home equity loan is usually used by homeowners to borrow some of the equity in the home. Doing so may raise the monthly housing payment considerably. More and more lenders are offering home equity lines of credit. The interest may be tax **deductible** because the debt is secured by a home. A home equity **line of credit** is a form of revolving credit secured by a home. Many lenders set the credit limit on a home equity line by taking a percentage of the home's appraised value and subtracting from that the balance owed on the existing mortgage. In determining the credit limit, the lender will also consider other factors to determine the homeowner's ability to repay the loan. Many home equity plans set a fixed period during which money can be borrowed. Some lenders require payment in full of any outstanding balance at the end of the period.

Home equity lines of credit usually have variable rather than fixed interest rates. The variable rate must be based on a publicly available index such as the prime rate published in major daily newspapers or a U. S. Treasury bill rate. The interest rate for borrowing under the home equity line will change in accordance with the index. Most lenders set the interest rate at the value of the index at a particular time plus a margin, such as 3 percentage points. The cost of borrowing is tied directly to the value of the index. Lenders sometimes offer a temporarily discounted interest rate for home equity lines. This is a rate that is unusually low and may last for a short introductory period of merely a few months.

The cost of setting up a home equity line of credit typically includes a fee for a property **appraisal**, an application fee, fees for attorneys, **title search**, mortgage preparation and filing fees, property and **title insurance** fees, and taxes. There may also be recurring maintenance fees for the account or a transaction fee every time there is a draw on the credit line. It might cost a significant amount of money to establish the home equity line of credit, although interest savings can justify the cost of establishing and maintaining the line.

The federal Truth in Lending Act requires lenders to disclose the important terms and costs of their home equity plans, including the APR, miscellaneous charges, the payment terms, and information about any variable-rate feature. If the home involved is a principal dwelling, the Truth in Lending Act allows 3 days from the day the account was opened to cancel the credit line. This right allows the borrower to cancel for any reason by informing the lender in writing within the 3-day period. The lender must then cancel its security interest in the property and return all fees.

### Second Mortgage

A second mortgage provides a fixed amount of money repayable over a fixed period. In most cases the payment schedule calls for equal payments that will pay off the entire loan within the loan period. A second mortgage differs from a home equity loan in that it is not a line of credit, but rather a more traditional type of loan. The traditional second mortgage loan takes into account the interest rate charged plus points and other finance charges. The **annual percentage rate** for a home equity line of credit is based on the periodic interest rate alone. It does not include points or other charges.

### Reverse Mortgage

A reverse mortgage works much like traditional mortgages, only in reverse. It allows homeowners to convert the equity in a home into cash. A reverse mortgage permits retired homeowners who own their home and have paid all of their mortgage to borrow against the value of their home. The lender pays the equity to the homeowner in either payments or a lump sum. Unlike a standard home equity loan, no repayment is due until the home is no longer used as a principal residence, a sale of the home, or death of the homeowner.

## Deed of Trust

A **Deed of Trust** is similar to a mortgage, with one important exception. If the borrower breaches the agreement to pay off the loan, the foreclosure process is typically much quicker and less complicated than the formal mortgage foreclosure process. While a mortgage involves a relationship between the borrower/homeowner and the bank/lender, a **Deed** of Trust involves the homeowner, the lender, and a title insurance company. The title insurance company holds legal title to the real estate until the loan is paid in full, at which time the title company transfers the property title to the homeowner.

## Escrow

An **escrow** company or agent is an independent third party who handles aspects of the purchase and related loan transaction. The escrow company will often hold the **down payment** until the closing, receive the amount of the loan from the lender, transfer the down payment and mortgage money to the seller, transfer and record the deed of title to the buyer or title company, and make sure the lender is protected by filing and recording the mortgage with the local county recorder of deeds. In some states the escrow functions are handled by a licensed title insurance company or an escrow company, while in other states an attorney handles the transaction. The purchase is said to be held in escrow pending certain investigations, inspections, and contingencies.

### Abstract of Title

An abstract is a document that a title insurance company or, in some states, an attorney, will prepare giving the history of the home. The document usually lists who owned the property all the way back to its first original owner. The document will also disclose any liens or encumbrances on the title which may affect whether lenders will provide a loan or whether the new homeowner will want to take title to the property.

### Prepayment Penalty Clause

A prepayment **penalty** is a charge the borrower pays when a mortgage is repaid before a certain period of time elapses. Not all lenders impose a prepayment penalty. From a mortgage lender's perspective a prepayment penalty helps the lender at least recoup some or all of the significant expense it incurs in putting a new loan on the books. If the loan is to be repaid quickly due to a refinance, the lender may have a significant loss. A prepayment penalty provision must be set out in the mortgage contract in order for the lender to collect one.

### Mortgage Contingency Clause

A mortgage contingency clause is a provision in the home purchase contract that says that if the prospective buyer cannot get a mortgage within a fixed period of time, the buyer may cancel the entire transaction.

## Types of Lenders

### Mortgage Bankers and Brokers

A mortgage broker can submit a loan to many different lenders and typically has access to several types of loan programs. A mortgage broker can shop for the best and most competitive mortgage rates and terms available tailored to meet a borrower's needs. Some charge processing or origination fees. Mortgage bankers are lenders that are large enough to originate loans and create pools of loans. Some companies do not sell directly to those major investors but sell their loans to the mortgage bankers. They often refer to themselves as mortgage bankers as well.

### Direct Lenders

A direct lender loans the money directly to the borrower. Banks and credit unions are often direct lenders.

### Secondary Market Lenders

Federal National Mortgage Association (FNMA or Fannie Mae), Government National Mortgage Association (GNMA or Ginnie Mae) and Federal Home Loan Mortgage Corporation (FHLMC or Freddie Mac) are all secondary market lenders. Many retail lenders actually receive their funds from a secondary market lender. These secondary lenders have assisted the national mortgage market by allowing money to move easily from state-to-state. The movement of loan funds helps to avoid a situation where mortgages are only available in certain areas or states. Also, the secondary lenders have established regulations and guidelines that help the general public.

## Defaults and Foreclosures

If a homeowner fails to make payments upon the mortgage, the lender may foreclose on the property. Foreclosure allows the mortgagee to declare that the entire mortgage debt is due and must be paid immediately. This action is accomplished through an acceleration clause in the mortgage. Many states regulate acceleration clauses and allow late payments to avoid foreclosure. Depending upon the terms and agreements made in the mortgage contract, the lender may do a **statutory** foreclosure or a judicial foreclosure. A statutory foreclosure can be performed without bringing a court action. The lender does have to follow strict state regulations as to the proper notices and opportunities to provide payment by the homeowner before a sale of the property occurs. This procedure is relatively quick. If a judicial foreclosure action is required, the lender must file a complaint with the court system and go through the **litigation** process to obtain the right to foreclose on the property. In several state jurisdictions, the homeowner is allowed the right to stay in possession of the home until the foreclosure process is finalized or a sale of the home occurs.

Since lenders want to avoid the cost of foreclosure, the lender will sometimes work out an agreement with the homeowner whose payments have fallen behind. The lender may accept interest only payments or partial payments for a while in order to assist the homeowner. There are detailed regulations regarding foreclosure procedures. Filing a Chapter 7 **bankruptcy** temporarily stalls a lender's right to foreclosure, until it gets court permission to go forward with the foreclosure proceedings. Under a Chapter 13 plan, it is possible for a homeowner to make up the missed payments. Liens do not automatically go away in any bankruptcy. A bankruptcy discharge does not extinguish a lien on property.

### Anti-Deficiency Laws

Some states have anti-deficiency laws which protect purchasers of residential real property used as primary residence. If the purchaser fails to make the mortgage payment the property is foreclosed and title is obtained by the lender through a legal procedure. The property is then typically sold to pay the mortgage and a deficiency between the sale price and the outstanding balance of the mortgage usually exists. Under anti-deficiency laws, if the mortgage is a purchase money mortgage for the purchase of a dwelling occupied by the purchaser, the purchaser will not be held responsible for any deficiency. The lender can only recover the property and the proceeds of a subsequent sale. The purchaser does not pay any deficit between the sale proceeds and the outstanding loan balance. This allows the purchaser to walk away from a property without owing a deficiency judgment amount. Anti-deficiency laws typically provide no protection for second mortgages or home equity lines. Also, there is no protection when the property is not used as the primary residence of the purchaser.

### Mortgage Insurance

Private mortgage insurance and government mortgage insurance protect the lender against default and enable the lender to make a loan which the lender considers a higher risk. Lenders often require mortgage insurance for loans where the down payment is less than 20% of the sales price. Mortgage insurance should not be confused with mortgage life, credit life, or **disability** insurance, which are designed to pay off a mortgage in the event of the borrower's death or disability.

With lender paid mortgage insurance (LPMI), the lender purchases the mortgage insurance and pays the premiums to the insurer. The borrower cannot cancel LPMI or government mortgage insurance during the life of the loan. However, it may be possible to cancel private mortgage insurance at some point, such as when the loan balance is reduced to a certain amount.

## Tax Credit

A mortgage interest credit is available for first-time home buyers whose income is generally below the median income for the area in which they live. The credit is intended to help lower-income individuals afford home ownership. A tax credit is allowed each year for part of the home mortgage interest paid. Any mortgage interest **deduction** is reduced by the amount of the credit taken. The interest on home mortgages is typically tax deductible.

## State Laws

ALASKA: Alaska has a broad form of anti-deficiency **statute** that precludes a deficiency judgment following the completion of a nonjudicial foreclosure.

ARIZONA: Arizona's anti-deficiency statutes prevent a lender from suing a person for any losses on a home after foreclosure. A person may not be sued by the lender for property located on 2.5 acres or less that is a single family residence or duplex. This provision is only applicable if the decrease in value is not due to the home owner's neglect. If a lender seeks a deficiency judgment, it has 90 days after the sale of the property to begin judicial proceedings to recover any losses. Failure to do so may result in the lender's loss of its right to recover the deficiency. In the event the property is something other than the foregoing, a deficiency judgment may still be avoided by deeding the property back to the lender prior to foreclosure. This is known as a deed-in-lieu of foreclosure. By accepting the deed, the lender is agreeing to accept the property for the amount that the borrower owes, thus eliminating any potential deficiency. However, when a person deeds the property back to the lender, he or she may be taxed on the amount of the deficiency that was forgiven by the lender. The only exception to Arizona's anti-deficiency statutes are VA loans. VA is allowed to obtain a deficiency judgment despite current state laws that prohibit such actions.

CALIFORNIA: California's anti-deficiency law applies only to funds used to purchase a residence. The anti-deficiency law does not apply to additional financing such as second mortgages or home-equity loans. California requires foreclosure on real property trust deeds and mortgages instead of a suit on the note. No deficiency judgment is possible where the seller takes back a purchase money note and deed of trust as part of the sale financing. If a third-party lender finances the purchase, the third party cannot recover a deficiency judgment if that loan is given and used for paying all or part of the purchase price, is secured by the property purchased, is a property for use by no more than four people, and is owner occupied. A deficiency judgment is not available if

the lender forecloses by private sale by **trustee** instead of a judicial foreclosure law suit. Federally made or guaranteed loans are generally not subject to the anti-deficiency laws of the state. V. A., FHA and Small Business Administration loans may subject the borrower to a deficiency judgment. A third-party refinance of a purchase money loan is not a purchase money loan and the buyer could be personally liable for payment of the seller's note after a judicial foreclosure.

FLORIDA: In Florida, mortgages must be foreclosed by filing a lawsuit in court. Florida is unusual in that the state has passed few statues regulating foreclosures. A sale can be set aside if there is an error in the procedure to foreclose; however, it cannot be set aside because of a too low sale price. After the sale takes place, the sale terms must be confirmed by the court. If the terms of the sale order are met, title in the buyer's name can become complete by filing a certificate of title. At the discretion of the court, junior lien holders can redeem the property, up to the time of the confirmation of the sale. The **equity of redemption** is cut off when the sale is confirmed, but it exists prior to that time. The borrower can redeem the property from foreclosure by curing the default prior to confirmation. Any action for a deficiency must be filed within four years from the foreclosure.

MASSACHUSETTES: Under the Massachusetts Uniform **Fraudulent** Conveyance Act if the foreclosure sale took place for less than **market value**, it may be ruled to be a fraudulent conveyance. Therefore the lender should have the property appraised at the time of foreclosure. In Massachusetts, there are two methods by which a mortgage may be foreclosed. The lender may enter and take possession of the premises and then wait three years for title to become final in the name of the lender. The other method is that the lender may complete a nonjudicial sale under a power of sale clause. Unless the borrower can come up with enough money to pay off the mortgage within three years, however, the lender's ownership becomes final and the borrower's right to redeem the property is cut off. Despite this provision, the usual method of foreclosure is through sale under a power of sale clause in the mortgage. The sale must be conducted in accordance with the requirements specified in the power of sale clause. Notice of the foreclosure must be given. There is no requirement for the borrower to actually receive the notice, merely for the lender to make a diligent effort to locate the borrower. If there is any money left from the foreclosure sale after paying off the lender, the surplus goes to the borrower. A proper sale prevents the borrower from exercising any right to reclaim the property through redemption. If the foreclosure sale proceeds are not enough to pay off the lender, then the borrower is liable for the deficiency.

NORTH DAKOTA: In North Dakota, a lawsuit may be brought in district court for foreclosure or for satisfaction of a mortgage on real estate. Prior to bringing any lawsuit, the lender must give the borrower advance notice. This notice must be sent no later than 90 days before the suit is filed. The notice must state a description of the real estate, the date and amount of the mortgage, the amount due for principal, interest, and taxes. The notice must also state the time period for redemption, which is either one year, or, for small tracts with substantial balances and the properly worded mortgages, six months. The notice must be served by registered or certified mail addressed to the owner of record. If the borrower brings in the missing payments any time within 30 days after receipt of the notice, the loan must be reinstated. North Dakota law requires the lawsuit paperwork to include several allegations that are unusual. First, North Dakota law requires the attorney bringing the suit to hold a **power of attorney** to act on behalf of the lender. Second, the lender must also declare in the original lawsuit whether the lender will pursue a deficiency judgment against the borrower if the foreclosure sale does not bring in enough money to pay off the outstanding loan balance. The lender may not ask for a deficiency in the foreclosure suit if it has already brought another suit just to collect on the loan. If the borrower can bring in the missed payments plus foreclosure costs before the **decree** of sale is issued by the court, then the lender's lawsuit to foreclose must be dismissed. Whenever the real estate is sold at foreclosure, the sheriff or deputy must give the buyer a certificate of sale, and at the expiration of the redemption time period, a deed must be given to the buyer. Any cash surplus from the sale, beyond that needed to pay off the mortgage and the foreclosure costs, must be paid to the borrower.

OREGON: Foreclosure in Oregon may be either by court action or by advertisement and sale. The borrower, or any junior lien holder, can cure the default prior to foreclosure. A deficiency judgment cannot be obtained through a non-judicial deed of trust foreclosure by advertisement. A person who was entitled to receive notice of the foreclosure but did not receive it may sue to invalidate the foreclosure at any time within five years of the sale. On a judicial foreclosure, the borrower or a successor in interest may redeem property within 180 days after sale.

SOUTH CAROLINA: South Carolina uses judicial foreclosure. The lender must file a lawsuit and seek either an order of sale or a judgment for the loan balance against the borrower or both. Deficiency judgements are permitted. Within 30 days after the sale, a borrower who was sued for a deficiency can apply to the court for an order of appraisal. The **defendant** appoints one **appraiser**, the judgment **creditor** appoints another, and the judge appoints another. If the appraised value is greater than what remains owed on the loan, after subtracting the foreclosure sale proceeds, then there is no deficiency. However if it is less, then the borrower still gets credit against the judgment for the higher appraised value of the property.

TEXAS: Texas has laws which make foreclosure easy. Deficiency judgments can only be for the difference between **fair market value** and the balance owed on the loan. There is no right of redemption.

## Additional Resources

*All about Escrow and Real Estate Closings* Gadow, Sandy, Escrow Publishing Company, 1999.

*How to Find a Home and Get a Mortgage on the Internet* Johnson, Randy, Wiley, John & Sons, Incorporated, 2000.

*Owner Will Carry: How to Take Back a Note or Mortgage without Being Taken*Broadbent, Bill, Dry Bones Press, 2000.

## Organizations

### National Association of Mortgage Brokers
8201 Greensboro Drive, Suite 300
McLean, VA 22101 USA
Phone: (703) 610-9009
Fax: (703) 610-9005
Primary Contact: President, Joseph L. Falk
URL: http://www.namb.com

### National Association of Mortgage Planners
3001 LBJ Freeway, Suite 110
Dallas, TX 75234 USA
Phone: (972) 241-0927
Fax: (972) 241-7046
URL: http://www.namp.org

# REAL ESTATE

## CONDOMINIUMS/CO-OPS

## Background

While home ownership is a dream most people aspire to, for some it is a difficult one to reach. As housing costs continue to rise, the hope of affording even what was once called a "starter home" seems out of reach for many people. Many people see renting as a better alternative to buying, but renting provides no equity. The answer for people who want to own their own home or who want equity but like the convenience of apartment-type living is to purchase a condominium or a cooperative apartment.

**Condominiums and cooperatives** are known as *common interest communities*. All the common space, including hallways and corridors, lobbies and common rooms, and exterior grounds, are commonly owned or maintained by all the tenants in the development. Although condominium ownership differs in significant ways for cooperative ownership, both afford the buyer with the opportunity to achieve equity at a relatively reasonable price without giving up some of the amenities of apartment living, such as on-site repair people.

## Condominiums

Condominiums, also known as "condos," offer many of the same amenities as home ownership, except that the development is managed by an "association" that acts much like a cooperative's board of directors (see below). Individual owners of condominium units share in ownership of common areas, such as corridors and recreation rooms indoors and courtyards outdoors. The association makes sure that the common areas are kept in good repair. There may be an on-site superintendent, or there may be a maintenance crew on call.

Condominium sales are treated just like house sales; the buyer secures a **mortgage** and on the day of purchase signs an actual **deed** for the dwelling. That deed does not grant the same level of ownership that a deed to a house would provide. All the buyer really owns is the air space within the unit. Because the common space is jointly held by all the residents, they are restricted and often prohibited from making any changes, even beneficial ones. Thus, a condominium owner who wants to renovate indoors can install new fixtures, tear out non-supporting walls, even install a new kitchen or bathroom. That same owner is probably not allowed to do any exterior painting or do any gardening outdoors, not even moving a bush or planting a tree. (In some complexes, property is set aside for this purpose, but even then any plantings must conform with the overall character of the development.)

Condominiums can take many forms structurally. They may be like regular apartments, or they may be townhouses. In fact, many are converted apartment houses or townhouse complexes. Some condominium communities actually offer individual standalone houses; these communities look like typical housing tracts, but again the residents own only the air space inside their homes. Even though each may have a fair amount of property, that property is managed by the association and not the individual owners.

## Cooperatives (Co-ops)

A cooperative, more commonly known as a co-op, is generally much more like apartment living that a condo. A large number of co-op buildings actually started out as rental buildings but were later converted. Co-ops are more restrictive than condominiums, but they also offer residents greater say in several aspects of how the property is managed.

The owner of a co-op does not own his or her unit. The co-op is a corporation, complete with a **corporate** board of directors, and each resident is a "shareholder." Co-op buyers do not sign a deed. Instead, they purchases shares of the corporation, shares that include a **lease** granting use of a specific unit. The number of shares owned is based on the size of the unit.

The "mortgage" that one receives when making a co-op purchase is not really a mortgage but rather a loan to purchase shares. To all intents and purposes, however, it functions as a mortgage.

In addition to the selling price for a co-op, there is also a monthly maintenance fee for upkeep of the property. It can include utilities, maintenance and repairs, and property taxes. This fee can range from a small amount to levels higher than mortgage payments. Parts of the maintenance fee may be tax **deductible**.

Because they do not own their individual units, co-op owners are generally not allowed to do anything inside their apartments beyond simple maintenance. A co-op owner cannot put in a new kitchen or bathroom or tear down any walls. In this regard, co-op living is very much like apartment living. The positive side of this is that residents are not responsible for making their own repairs; the on-site maintenance crew or superintendent handle those.

## Advantages of Condominiums and Co-ops

Why choose to live in a condominium or a co-op over renting or private home ownership? There are a number of reasons, and ultimately the answer depends on a person's circumstances and goals.

### Affordability

A renter who wishes to build equity in his or her home but who has no desire to incur the responsibilities of maintaining a home may choose condominium or co-op ownership because it provides many of the same maintenance services as a rental unit would. A single person who wishes to own property but who cannot afford a house may turn to the generally more reasonable condominium or co-op market. Older homeowners who wish to give up what has become a large and unwieldy house but who have no desire to spend their equity on a rental unit often see condominiums or co-ops as an attractive alternative.

Although condominium and co-op owners are responsible for the maintenance in their own units (more so for co-op owners), the comfort of knowing that someone else will do the landscaping, the exterior painting, and the snow removal is often more than enough to make this option more attractive than home ownership.

### Stability

Condominiums and co-ops also offer more stability than apartment houses. In years past, people moved into apartment houses and stayed for many years; they would start with a small apartment, move to a larger one in the same building as their family grew, and move back into a smaller one when their children had moved out. Today, most people who live in apartments do not stay long. This may be the result of higher rents, or it may be because apartment houses are often maintained with less than stellar reliability. A condominium or co-op offers a stronger sense of community to residents because they are owners; they are less likely to move after only a few years. Also, because they are owners, they will probably assume more responsibility in making sure the common areas are well-maintained.

## Disadvantages of Condominium and Co-op Living

For all their advantages, condominiums also have a number of disadvantages that should make potential buyers weigh their decision carefully.

### Ongoing Costs

A condominium or co-op owner has to pay not only a monthly mortgage but also the maintenance fee. In an expensive unit, this can run into thousands of dollars over the course of a year. Granted, some of that is probably tax deductible, and the money goes for maintenance and other common costs. Nevertheless, some people see the combination mortgage/maintenance fee as similar to paying double rent. Thus, the older couple who wants to trade their large house for a small co-op might find the various costs prohibitively expensive when they are all added up.

Because many condominium and co-op buildings are older, converted apartment houses, chances are that maintenance and repair costs will be quite high. For the condominium owner, this means higher repair costs within his or her own unit. For the co-op owner, this means higher monthly fees to pay for repairs throughout the building.

### Restrictions

The extent of restrictions in condominiums depends on the layout of the development. If the development consists of free-standing homes or townhouses, residents may have a fair amount of leeway as far as landscaping, for example. For buildings, the restrictions will probably be more comprehensive and more carefully enforced.

Restrictions in co-ops are far more all-encompassing. Co-op residents who wish to sell their unit, or rather, their shares, often find that the co-op **bylaws** are extremely strict about whom they can sell to. People who fail to meet a minimum income may be ineligible to live in a particular co-op, even if they have enough money to make the purchase. For that matter, co-op apartments in wealthy neighborhoods will sometimes refuse to sell to celebrities, citing their fear that the presence of a celebrity will draw too many fans and other celebrities to the building.

Co-op **subletting** is also subject to significant restrictions. Some co-ops only allow a set number of subleases per year. Thus, a person who has been transferred to another state will need to seek approval to sell the co-op or to sublet it, and that approval may not be forthcoming.

Particularly in co-ops, the board of directors wields considerable power; often the only way to gain some influence within the development is to join the board. The politics involved in decision-making is literally brought home to co-op residents, and many do not enjoy the experience.

Because many people are unwilling to put up with the restrictions found in condominium and co-op communities, it can be much harder to find a buyer to begin with. Condominiums and co-ops do not rise in value the same way houses do, so while they preserve equity they do not build as much as a private home would.

## Conversions to Condominiums or Co-ops

It is not uncommon for rental buildings to be converted to condominiums or co-ops; in fact, most of the older buildings that are condominium or co-op developments started out as rentals.

Frequently the first sign that a building's owner is considering a conversion is a series of improvements to the building—new windows, new kitchens and bathrooms, redecorated common space (corridors, lobby). The sponsor of the conversion (usually but not necessarily the owner) will contact all the tenants and give them the opportunity to purchase their own units, usually for a good price. If enough tenants decide to take the sponsor up on the offer, the conversion can go through. Although there is a fairly low minimum number, sponsors like to get as high a percentage of tenants to buy in as possible, because it means more money to pay for upkeep and keep maintenance fees down.

### Example: Conversions in New York

In New York City and some of its outlying suburbs, many rental apartment buildings are subject to rent regulation laws that prohibit landlords from raising rents beyond a certain percentage. Buildings constructed before 1974 are subject to rent stabilization, which allows only small increases each time the lease is renewed (every year or every two years). Buildings constructed before 1974 may be protected under rent control laws that further restrict the amount of rental increases. Rent-controlled and rent-stabilized tenants have a **legal right** to have their leases renewed as long as they are paying their rent on time and as long as the apartment is their primary residence. If a rental building is converted to a condominium or co-op, these tenants are still allowed to stay in their apartments.

Clearly for a building seeking a conversion from rental to co-op, it would be important to convince a reasonably high percentage of tenants to buy in. Otherwise, the renters would continue to pay their artificially low rents (they do not have to pay monthly maintenance fees) while shareholders would have to pick up more of the common costs. Since it only requires 15 percent of the current tenants to approve a co-op conversion, this could leave the sponsor of the conversion (often the **landlord**) with carrying 85 percent of its units as rentals. (In most cases, apartment house owners will wait until they have a much higher percentage before they proceed with a co-op conversion.)

Not surprisingly, many tenants choose to remain renters because it costs less than buying. For elderly tenants in particular, who have no need for the equity of an owned residence, continuing to rent may make sense.

Rent-controlled apartments are deregulated as soon as the tenant moves out, but rent- stabilized apartments remain stabilized no matter how often they change hands. Some apartment owners have tried to "warehouse" apartments by not renting stabilized apartments as they become available. The fewer apartments rented when the co-op conversion takes place, the fewer renters the building will have to carry. The practice of warehousing apartments is illegal.

Also illegal is trying to force renters to leave by curtailing services to them or by harassing them. Many co-op boards enact strict regulations in the hope of driving away renters. Some of these restrictions, such as no-pets clauses, may be imposed with the idea that renters with pets would rather leave than give up their companions. While co-op boards have a great deal of latitude when enacting rules or guidelines, those guidelines cannot be unduly unfair or onerous to the renters.

## Buying a Condominium or Co-op

People interested in condominium or co-op ownership should pay close attention to a number of factors at each development they visit:

- They should ask about the financial condition of the association or corporation that

manages the property. They may request a copy of the latest financial statements and budgets. They can find out about the ratio of owners to renters, the stability of the maintenance fees, and recent unit sales.

- They should find out whether there are any pending lawsuits against the development. Builders, neighbors, and even former owners might have filed suit. If anyone did, they can find out why and find out the outcome.

- They should ask about the bylaws and the restrictions. If they are particularly strict, prospective buyers may not wish to purchase a home there. Even if they have no trouble with the restrictions, potential subsequent buyers might when it comes time to sell later on.

- Prospective buyers should hire an inspector to check the structural condition of the building (including electrical, heat, and plumbing). They should find out the condition of the roof and the common areas. Also, they need to find out about how soundproof the building is.

- Prospective buyers should talk to current or former owners if possible. They may be able to find out from the owners what are the pros and cons of the development in question—what they like and what they wish they could change.

Condominium and co-op ownership is not for everyone. If people think it will meet their needs, however, they will do themselves an enormous favor simply by making a checklist of the items above and being prepared when it comes time to discuss an actual deal.

## Additional Resources

*The Co-op Bible: Everything You Need to Know About Co-ops and Condos* Shapiro, Sylvia, St. Martin's Griffin, 1998.

*How to Buy a House, Condo, or Co-op* Thomsett, Michael C., and the Editors of Consumer Reports. Consumer Reports Books, 1996.

*Keys to Purchasing a Condo or Co-op* Friedman, Jack P., and Jack C. Harris. Barron's Education Series, 2000.

## Organizations

### National Association of Realtors
P. O. Box 10598
Chicago, IL 60610 USA
Phone: (800) 874-6500
Fax: (312) 329-5960
URL: http://www.realtor.org
Primary Contact: Terrence M. McDermott, CEO

### Urban Homesteading Assistance Board
120 Wall Street, 20th Floor
New York, NY 10005 USA

Phone: (212) 479-3300
URL: http://www.uhab.org
Primary Contact: Andrew Reicher, Executive Director

### U.S. Department of Housing and Urban Development (HUD)
451 Seventh Street, SW
Washington, DC 20410 USA
Phone: (202) 708-1112
Fax: (202) 708-1455 (TTY)
URL: http://www.hud.gov
Primary Contact: Mel Martinez, HUD Secretary

# REAL ESTATE

## CONTRACTORS/LIENS

*Sections within this essay:*

## Background

A **lien** is a claim to property for the payment of a debt, typically one connected to the property. Because a lien is something that is filed with the local recorder's office, it can be a powerful legal tool. It is a public record, available to anyone, that alleges a valid, unpaid debt against the specific real estate named in the lien.

There are several types of liens, all of which could cloud the title and prevent the seller from conveying marketable title to the buyer. In some states, a **mortgage** is regarded as a lien, not a complete transfer of title, and if not repaid the debt is recovered by **foreclosure** and sale of the real estate. Real estate can also be affected by liens for federal income taxes. Additionally, liens can be placed on property for the non-payment of real estate taxes and special assessments, including homeowners' association dues. Contractors, subcontractors, material suppliers, and laborers can place liens against property for the value of work or materials installed on that property. The filing requirements and statutes of limitation for these liens vary according to the law of each state.

The word lien, derived from the French, means "knot or binding." The person to whom the debt is owed, the one who binds the property, is known as the lien holder. In certain circumstances, the lien holder may foreclose on the property if the debt is not paid in full. Liens can generally be removed by the payment of the amount owed. This payment can occur at any time up to and including the stage at which the closing documents for the sale of the property are signed.

## Types of Liens

### Contractor's Lien

A contractor's lien, often known as a mechanic's lien, or a construction lien, is a claim made by contractors or subcontractors who have performed work on a property who have not yet been paid. A supplier of materials delivered to the job may also file a mechanic's lien. In some states, professionals such as architects, engineers, and surveyors may also be entitled to file a lien for services rendered.

The priority of liens on a construction project does not depend upon the time of completion of the particular job, but rather everything relates back to the first visible commencement of the work. This stipulation means the final work, such as painting, is equal in priority to the initial work of laying a cement foundation. Therefore, during the entire work of construction, the owner must obtain lien releases or waivers of lien from each **subcontractor** and material supplier. Without these waivers or releases the real estate is subject to liens of all the subcontractors, even if the general contractor, though paid in full, fails to pay the subcontractors.

In some states, contractors and subcontractors must notify the property owner prior to filing a lien, but in other states such liens can be filed without any notification to the owner. Lien claimants who are contractors or subcontractors are protected under this legal doctrine because all their materials and labor are "buried" in the real estate, having become part of it. Unlike mortgage liens, however, the liens of these claimants cannot force a foreclosure.

### Divorce Liens

In a **divorce**, one party may be awarded the right to live in the marital house. When that spouse sells the property, the ex-spouse may be entitled to half of the equity. That ex-spouse could file a lien to ensure receipt of his or her share of the sales proceeds. In some states, although a lien is not part of a divorce proceeding, it can be placed on property of parents for unpaid **child support** payments.

### Judgment Liens

A judgment lien can be filed if an actual judgment in a lawsuit is obtained from a court. Such cases include failure to pay a debt, including credit cards, bank loans, or deficiency judgements on repossessed vehicles. In some circumstances, judgments can be enforced by sale of property until the amount due is satisfied.

### Homeowners' Association Liens

Homeowners' Association Liens are commonly filed against property when Homeowner Association Dues assessed against that property are not paid on time. When a house or condominium belonging to a homeowners' association sells, the title or **escrow** company will request a certificate of payment from the homeowners' association to be sure that all due and assessments have been paid and are current. If these payments have not been made, the dues will need to be brought current at the time the closing transaction papers are signed.

### Federal Tax Liens

A tax lien can sometimes be placed on a property for past taxes due to the government by the taxpayer/owner. In order for a Federal Tax Lien to be filed by the Internal Revenue Service (**IRS**), the IRS must file a Notice of Federal Tax Lien. Prior to even filing a notice, however, the IRS must do all of the following:

- The IRS must determine and assess the exact amount of tax liability

- The IRS must send the taxpayer a notice and demand for payment

- The taxpayer must neglect or refuse to fully pay the liability within 10 days of the notice and demand

If the taxpayer pays the lien or posts a bond guaranteeing payment, the IRS must issue a Release of the Notice of Federal Tax Lien within 30 days. A lien will release automatically if the IRS does not refile the lien before the time expires to legally collect the tax. A taxpayer may sue the federal government for damages if the IRS knowingly or negligently fails to release a Notice of Federal Tax Lien provided the taxpayer first exhausts all administrative appeals within the IRS and the suit is filed within two years from the date the IRS should have released the lien.

A taxpayer can also get a Lien Release by entering into an **installment** agreement with the IRS to satisfy the liability. Finally, the IRS can withdraw a filed Notice of Tax Lien if the withdrawal will facilitate collection of the tax or if it is determined by the IRS that the withdrawal would be in the best interest of both the taxpayer and the government.

A Federal Tax Lien is incorrect and may be appealed if any of the following occurs:

- The taxpayer paid the entire amount owed before the lien was filed

- The IRS assessed the tax and filed the lien when the taxpayer was in **bankruptcy** and subject to the automatic stay during bankruptcy (although the bankruptcy filing may not absolve the taxpayer of the tax liability, the filing of the lien during that time would not be permissible)

- The IRS made a procedural, administrative, or mathematical error in making an assessment

- The **statute of limitations** had expired prior to the time the IRS filed the lien

### Equitable Liens

An equitable lien is a legal fiction created by courts in certain circumstances in which justice may require the creation of a lien. Courts of equity have the power to create so-called equitable liens on property to correct some injustice. For example, a person who lived on the property and contributed a substantial amount to the improvement of the property may be able to, with the assistance of the court, obtain a lien on the property by suing for a constructive trust.

## Lien Releases

People having a home built can require contractors and subcontractors to provide lien releases or waivers as part of a written project contract. The contract can mandate a lien release be issued before the contractor receives payment for services, in which case it is called a lien **waiver**. If payments are made to a general contractor in stages for work performed by subcontractors, the homeowner can obtain lien releases from the various subcontractors as their part of the project is completed.

Sometimes, construction loan documents drafted by a bank may indicate that the bank will obtain lien releases, but the bank may do this solely for its own benefit. Therefore, the property owner's requiring lien releases should be clearly stated and independent of any agreement made by or with the bank.

Often contractors will have waiver and release forms available. If not, sample waivers and releases can usually be obtained from local or state **consumer protection** organizations. In addition to signed lien releases, those building homes should keep records of what has been paid to contractors, which contractors worked on the job site and when. Unfortunately, unethical contractors can easily file **fraudulent** liens for incorrect amounts. Accurate record keeping can help the homeowner ensure lien releases from all necessary parties.

## Lien Waivers

Although the terms lien waiver and lien release seem to be interchangeable, a release demonstrates completion and payment, so as to prove any claim has been satisfied, while a waiver demonstrates a relinquishment of a known right. Waivers are typically obtained prior to commencement of any work, whereas releases are subsequently obtained. Waivers of lien must be in writing, give a sufficient description of the real estate, and be signed by the one with authority to file or claim a lien. No payment needs to be made in advance if the subcontractor agrees to release the land from the lien and rely only on the credit of the owner or general contractor for payment of the debt.

## Discharging Liens

Liens can be discharged after a certain length of time. Therefore, if a property owner is in no hurry to sell the property, and the lien holder is not seeking to foreclose, it may make sense to do nothing and wait until the lien expires. If the lien is not renewed, the cloud on the title will no longer exist. If a person pays and satisfies a lien in order to have it discharged, it is imperative that a written, legally sufficient release or satisfaction be obtained and recorded in the appropriate government office. Doing so ensures clear title to the property.

## State Rules Regarding Contractor's Liens

ALABAMA: All potential lienors, with the exception of an original contractor (a contractor with a direct contract with the owner who is exempted from the notice requirement), must fulfill three basic steps prior to perfecting a lien: provide **statutory** notice to the owner, file a verified statement of lien in the **probate** office of the county where the improvement is located, and file suit to enforce the lien. The verified statement of lien must be filed in the office of the judge of probate of the county where the subject property is located. When the property is located in more than one county, the statement must be filed in each county.

ARKANSAS: Unlicensed contractors cannot take legal action to enforce their contracts.

ARIZONA: Unlicensed contractors cannot take legal action to enforce their contracts.

CALIFORNIA: A subcontractor or supplier must give notice to the owner. Unlicensed contractors cannot take legal action to enforce their contracts. Design professionals may file liens, and lien rights may exist even when the design was not used.

DISTRICT OF COLUMBIA: Although the mechanic's lien has no priority over a prior recorded construction loan, it does have priority over any security interest filed after the mechanic's lien even though it is not necessary to file suit to enforce the mechanic's lien until one year after it is filed.

FLORIDA: In cases where the contractor does work and is not paid by the owner for the full amount that is due, the contractor can file a lien against the owner's property. The Claim of Lien must be filed with the Clerk of the Circuit Court in the county where the property is located within 90 days of the date the contractor last performed any labor or services or furnished materials. The contractor is not required to give a Notice To Owner as a condition for obtaining a lien against the owner's property. However, if the contractor is entitled to receive his final payment, the contractor must give the owner a Contractor's **Affidavit** before any lien can be effective. A Contractor's Affidavit must state that all subcontractors, sub-subcontractors, and material suppliers have been paid. If all subcontractors have not been paid, the Contractor's Affidavit must list those who remain unpaid and the amounts due. If the final payment is due, the contractor has no lien rights until the Contractor's Affidavit is given to the owner.

If the direct contract for the entire job between the owner and the contractor is less than $2,500, subcontractors and suppliers who do not have a direct contract with the owner have no lien rights on the job. Only the contractor (the person with a direct contract with the owner) can file a lien on jobs of less than $2,500. Design professionals may file liens, and lien rights may exist even when the design was not used.

GEORGIA: A lien can only be filed if the contractor filing the lien is in substantial compliance in the underlying contract with the owner. All liens must be filed with the clerk of the superior court of the county where the property is located within three months after completion of the work. When filing a lien, the contractor must send a copy of the lien by registered or certified mail to the owner of the property or the contractor as the agent of the owner. The party filing the lien has 14 days to file the lien with the clerk of the superior court in the county where the property is located. This notice must refer to the then-owner of the property against which the lien was filed and refer to a **deed** or other recorded instrument with the chain of title of the affected property.

HAWAII: A lien may be filed for design work and supervision, but only if the design is used to improve the property.

IOWA: A lien may be filed for design work and supervision, but only if the design is used to improve the property.

KANSAS: Posting a bond is permitted; however, the court determines the amount of the bond. No advance notice requirements prior to filing a lien.

LOUISIANA: Subcontractors, laborers, employees, suppliers, and lessors may file claims against both the owner and the general contractor. All claims of suppliers and subcontractors rank equally and ahead of the privilege of contractor and surveyors, architects and engineers, which also rank equally. If no claimant conclusively establishes prior claim superior to others, a pro rata distribution is assumed.

MARYLAND: A lien cannot be filed unless the value of the improvements equals at least 15 percent of the property value. A contractor cannot obtain a lien until suit is filed and a court orders the lien. Once obtained, however, the lien has priority over other liens filed after this court determination.

MASSACHUSETTS: A design professional may lien only for work done supervising construction, but not for design.

MINNESOTA: Liens are filed with the recorder of deeds.

MISSISSIPPI: All parties claiming liens on the same property shall be made parties to the suit. Any sale of property made shall be by a special **writ** of **execution** and all liens paid pro rata. Subcontractors and laborers may bond amount due by general by written notice to owner. Owner may pay amount due into court for final distribution according to rights of parties.

MISSOURI: The owner cannot put up a bond to fight the lien. The lien is filed with the clerk of the court rather than in the recorder's office. A lien may be filed for design work and supervision, but only if the design is used to improve the property.

NEBRASKA: Lien waivers are invalid. Design professionals may file liens, and lien rights may exist even when the design was not used.

NEW YORK: Unlicensed contractors cannot take legal action to enforce their contracts.

NORTH CAROLINA: All claims of lien must be filed in the office of the clerk of superior court in each county wherein the real property subject to the claim of lien is located. Claims of lien may be filed at any time after the obligation becomes due, but not later than 120 days after the last furnishing of labor or materials.

OHIO: A design professional may lien only for work done supervising construction, but not for design.

PENNSYLVANIA: Advance Lien Waivers are permitted. Subcontractors must serve a Formal Notice on owner at least 30 days before filing a lien claim. Subcontractors performing alterations or repairs must serve an additional notice on the owner before work completed. All contractors must file liens in the court clerk's office within four months of the last work and serve notice of the lien claim on the owner within one month after that. Lawsuits to enforce liens must be filed within two years of lien filing. A General Contractor can file stipulation against liens with court before the project begins waiving all subcontractor mechanic's lien rights. Third tier or sub-subcontractors have no lien rights. A design professional may lien only for work done supervising construction, but not for design.

SOUTH CAROLINA: A person furnishing labor or material actually used in improving real property by agreement with or consent of the owner shall have a lien on such property and on the interest of the owner up to the amount due in contract. South Carolina defines consent to require a contract between the mechanic and owner before labor and material is furnished. Notice is required.

The Notice of Intent to Lien must include:

- The name of the claimant

- The name of the person with whom the claimant contracted or was employed

- A general description of the labor, services, or materials furnished and their contract price or value

- A description of the project sufficient for identification

- The first and last dates on which materials, labor, or services were provided or scheduled to be provided

- The amount due

TENNESSEE: Advance Lien Waivers are permitted. A lien claimant has no lien if the claimant makes even a minor mistake in filing this notice of lien. A single mistake can be **fatal** to the mechanics' lien. The lien attaches only to whatever interest the owner has in the land. Thus, if an owner is leasing property, the lien can only be asserted against the leasehold interest, not the ownership interest of the **lessor**.

A contractor who contracts directly with the owner need not give any formal notice to the owner in order to preserve lien rights against the owner.

However, if the contractor desires to perfect the lien against someone who purchases the owner's land without notice of the lien, then the contractor must file a sworn statement. Submitted within 90 days after the project is completed or within 90 days from the contractor's last work on the project, this statement must include the amount due and a complete legal description of the land.

The contractor without a direct contract with the owner must give two separate and distinct notices (although there is no reason why they cannot be done in the same document, if within the proper time period) to the owner and the contractor. Within 60 days of the last day of the month in which work was performed or materials were furnished, the contractor must send a notice of nonpayment to the owner and the contractor who has a contract with the owner. The notice of nonpayment must contain all of the following information: the name and address of the contractor sending the notice of nonpayment; a general description of the work, services or materials provided; a statement of the last date the contractor performed work or furnished materials; and a legal description of the real property. In addition to the notice of nonpayment, the contractor must also send to the owner a notice that the lien is claimed. This notice to the owner must be sent within 90 days from either the time the work is complete or within 90 days from the completion of the improvements. The lien of a contractor who did not contract directly with the owner is valid for 90 days from the date of the notice claiming the lien. The lien continues to be valid until the final termination of any suit for enforcement brought within the 90-day period. A contractor without a direct contract with the owner must also file a sworn statement and notice of the lien in order to be protected from purchasers without notice.

TEXAS: The contractor must file an affidavit claiming a lien no later than the fifteenth day of the fourth month following the month in which the original contract was materially breached or terminated, completed, finally settled, or abandoned. The affidavit must contain the following information: sworn statement of the claim, a legally sufficient description of the real property, a description of the work performed by the claimant, the amount due, the name and address of the reputed owner, and the name and address of the claimant. The affidavit must be filed with the county clerk in the county in which the property is located. The original contractor must send a copy of the lien affidavit to the owner at his last known business or residential address no later than the deadline for filing the affidavit or the tenth day following the filing of the affidavit, whichever is earlier.

There are two types of statutory liens for subcontractors. Fund Trapping occurs when a claimant can obtain a lien on the property and subject the property owner to personal liability to the extent that the owner has received the requisite statutory notice and fails to withhold any further payments from the contractor in an amount sufficient to cover the stated claim. In other words, when an owner receives the required "fund-trapping" notice, any unpaid contract funds (up to the amount of the claim as stated in the notice) are "trapped" in the hands of the owner. The claimant has a lien on the real property and a claim against the owner personally for the funds that were "trapped" by the notice letter. There is a significant problem with this method, however. If the owner has already paid all of the contract funds by the time it receives the "fund-trapping" notice letter, there may be no contract funds trapped. In that case, the claimant does not have a valid lien on the property. Statutory Retainage is handled the following way. To ensure that at least some contract funds will be available to satisfy claims arising toward the completion of construction, the property code requires an owner to retain ten percent of the contract amount (or value of the work then completed) during the course of construction and for 30 days following final completion. The statutory obligation to retain contract funds is commonly known as "statutory retainage." This required retainage creates a fund for the benefit of claimants who have filed lien affidavits within 30 days after the completion of the original contract and who have sent the required notices. If an owner fails to retain sufficient funds as required by the code, the owner will be personally liable and his property subject to a lien to the extent of the funds that should have been retained.

The requirements for a subcontractor's lien where the subcontractor's contract is not directly with the owner are the same but also require notice to the owner. The second-tier contractor is required to furnish the owner with a written notice of its claim. The notice letter must be sent to the owner no later than the fifteenth day of the third month following each month during which the claimant performed work for which payment is sought. For the subcontractor's lien to "trap any contract funds," the letter must contain a specific statutory warning which advises the owner that he will be personally liable and his prop-

erty will be subject to a lien if he fails to withhold sufficient contract funds to pay the claim. The letter must also be sent to the original contractor by actual delivery or certified mail.

Requirements for a third-tier subcontractor are the same as for a second-tier subcontractor, except that the third-tier subcontractor must also send a letter of notice to the original contractor. Design professionals may file liens, and lien rights may exist even when the design was not used.

UTAH: Unlicensed contractors cannot take legal action to enforce their contracts. State law protects homeowners from having a lien maintained on their home and from civil judgment by persons other than the original contractor, provided the following conditions are met:

- The homeowner used the services of a licensed contractor

- The homeowner has a written contract with the original contractor

- The homeowner pays the original contractor(s) in full according to the terms of the written contract and any amendments to that contract

If a lien is incorrectly placed on a property, it is the owner's responsibility to notify the lien claimant in writing that the above listed requirements have been met and to provide all relevant documentation.

VIRGINIA: The contractor's lien holder has partial priority over even the construction lender. Therefore, banks in Virginia are typically concerned about contractor's lien waivers. All persons performing labor or furnishing materials of the value of $50 or more for the construction, removal, repair, or improvement of any structure may file a lien upon the structure. The contractor seeking a lien must file a Memorandum of Mechanic's Lien with the land records of the county where the real property is located. The general contractor may file a lien at any time after the work is commenced or materials furnished but not later than 90 days from the last day of the month in which the contractor last performs labor or furnished materials.

The main elements of a lien memorandum are as follows: name of owner, address of owner, name of claimant, address of claimant, type of materials or services furnished, amount claimed, type of structure on which work done or materials furnished, brief description and location of real property, date from which interest on the above amount is claimed and signature of claimant or its authorized agent. In addition, the memorandum must contain an affidavit by the claimant or its agent that the owner is justly indebted to the claimant in the amount claimed by the lien.

WASHINGTON: Unlicensed contractors cannot take legal action to enforce their contracts.

## Additional Resources

*A Simplified Guide to Construction* Acret, James, Building News, Inc., 1997.

*Construction Nightmares* O'Leary, Arthur, and James Acret, Building News, Inc., 1997.

*Federal Tax Liens* Schmudde, David A., American Bar Association, 2001.

*Fix the Lien Law Hodgepodge* McGreevy, Susan, Engineering News-Record, 2000.

*National Mechanics Liens Handbook: The Mechanics Lien Laws of the 50 States and the District of Columbia* Acret, James, BNI Publications, Incorporated, 2001.

*Selecting and Working with Architects, Engineers and Contractors* Williams, David J., 1st Books Library, 2001.

## Organizations

### *American Society of Home Inspectors, Inc.*
932 Lee Street, Suite 101
Des Plaines, IL 60016 USA
Phone: (847) 759-2820
Fax: (847) 759-1620
URL: http://www.ashi.com/
Primary Contact:

### *California Contractors State License Board*
9821 Business Park Drive
Sacramento, CA 95827 USA
Phone: (800) 321-2752
Fax: (916) 255-4016
URL: http://www.cslb.ca.gov/offices1.html
Primary Contact:

### *National Association of Home Builders*
1201 15th Street, NW
Washington, DC 20005
Phone: (202) 822-
URL: http://www.nahb.com
Primary Contact:

# REAL ESTATE

## EASEMENTS

*Sections within this essay:*

## Background

An **easement** is a property interest, which entitles the owner of the easement to the privilege of a specific and limited use of the land of another. A right of way is a form of an easement granted by the property owner that gives another the right to travel over and use the owner's land as long as it is not inconsistent with the owner's use and enjoyment of the land. These principles had their origins in traditional **common law** which governed matters such

as the free flow of water and which allowed neighboring landowners to traverse, often by horseback or on foot, an informal "road system." Early courts reasoned that while absolute ownership rights of property can be lessened by an easement, society as a whole benefits from the resulting freedom of movement.

## Types of Easements

### *Affirmative Easements*

An affirmative easement is a requirement to do something, such as allowing another access to or across a certain piece of property. Most easements fall into this category.

### *Negative Easements*

A negative easement is a promise not to do something with a certain piece of property, such as not building a structure more than one story high or not blocking a mountain view by constructing a fence. There are not many negative residential easements in existence today as such architectural specifications are typically covered by rules and regulations promulgated by homeowners' associations. These documents are usually entitled *Codes, Covenants, and Restrictions,* often referred to as CC&Rs. A negative easement is sometimes referred to as an easement of light and air and in most states cannot be created by implication.

## Creation of Easements

There are five ways to create an easement: by an express grant, by implication, by strict necessity, by permission, and by prescription.

### Express Easements

An express easement is created by a **deed** or by a will. Thus, it must be in writing. An express easement can also be created when the owner of a certain piece of property conveys the land to another but saves or reserves an easement in it. This arrangement is known as an easement by reservation.

### Implied Easements

To create an easement by implication, three requirements must be met:

- The easement must be at least reasonably necessary to the enjoyment of the original piece of property.

- The land must be divided (or "severed"), so that the owner of a parcel is either selling part and retaining part, or subdividing the property and selling pieces to different new owners.

- The use for which the implied easement is claimed must have existed prior to the severance or sale.

### Necessity Easements

The courts will find an "easement by necessity" if two parcels are so situated that an easement over one is strictly necessary to the enjoyment of the other. The creation of this sort of easement requires that at one time, both parcels of land were either joined as one or were owned by the same owner. Prior use of the easement, however, is not required. The most common example of an easement by necessity is landlocked property, so that access to a public road can only be gained by having a right of way over an adjoining parcel of land. The legal theory is the landlocked parcel was accidentally created, and the owner forgot to include an easement appurtenant to reach the road.

### Permissive Easements

A permissive easement is simply an allowance to use the land of another. It is essentially a license, which is fully revocable at any time by the property owner. In order to be completely certain that a permissive easement will not morph into a prescriptive easement, some landowners erect signs stating the grant of the permissive easement or license. Such signs, often found on private roadways, typically state: "This is a private roadway. Use of this road is permissive and may be revoked at any time by the owner."

### Prescriptive Easements

Most litigated easements are those created without permission. An easement by prescription is one that is gained under principles of adverse possession. Prescriptive easements often arise on rural land when landowners fail to realize part of their land is being used, perhaps by an adjoining neighbor. Fences built in incorrect locations often result in the creation of prescriptive easements. If a person uses another's land for more than the **statute of limitations** period prescribed by state law, that person may be able to derive an easement by prescription. The use of the land must be open, notorious, hostile, and continuous for a specified number of years as required by law in each state.

The time period for obtaining an easement by adverse possession does not begin to run until the one seeking adverse possession actually trespasses on the land. Thus, a negative easement cannot be acquired by prescription because no **trespass** takes place. The use of the easement must truly be adverse to the rights of the landowner of the property through which the easement is sought and must be without the landowner's permission. If the use is with permission, it is not adverse. There must be a demonstration of continuous and uninterrupted use throughout the **statute** of limitations period prescribed by state law. If the use is too infrequent for a reasonable landowner to bother protesting, the continuity requirement will probably not be satisfied.

Subsequent parties in the same position to the land using the right of way adversely can add up the time to meet the required statute of limitations. This situation is known as tacking. Thus, a prescriptive easement need not be exclusive; it can be shared among several users.

### Conservation Easements

A conservation easement, a type of express easement, is created by a voluntary legal agreement between a landowner and another party, usually the government, which restricts the development of a piece of land. Under certain specific conditions, conservation easements are recognized by the U. S. Internal Revenue Service (**IRS**). If IRS requirements are met, the landowner may qualify for certain tax incentives. The requirements for a conservation easement approved by the IRS are as follows:

- The easement must have a valid conservation purpose; that is, the easement holder must be satisfied that protection of the land or resources is justified for conservation reasons. Different land trusts and government entities have different requirements that must be satisfied. Generally, the IRS requires purposes such as the following:

- Outdoor recreation by, or the education of, the general public

- Protection of a relatively natural habitat of fish, wildlife, or plants

- Preservation of open space

- Preservation of historically important land area or buildings

- The agreement must be completely voluntary: no one can force a landowner to enter into a conservation easement agreement. A conservation easement may be either donated or sold by a landowner to an easement holder.

- The agreement must be legally binding. It is recorded as a Deed of Conservation Easement. The agreement is binding on both present and future owners of the property. Both the landowner and the qualified easement holder must be in a position to enforce the terms of the agreement. This requirement recognizes the easement holder's responsibility for periodic inspection of the property with the landowner.

- The agreement must be permanent and irrevocable. A conservation easement must be permanent in order to qualify for the income and estate tax benefits provided by the IRS. If a conservation easement is valid for a set period of time only, for instance, ten years, the landowner may be eligible for certain property tax benefits but is not eligible for federal and state income and estate tax benefits.

- The easement must be held by a qualified easement holder, i.e., a government entity or a land trust. While any government entity can hold an easement, those most likely to hold conservation easements include city and county governments and certain federal agencies, such as the U. S. Forest Service and the U. S. Fish and Wildlife Service. A land trust is a private, nonprofit corporation.

- The easement must restrict development of the land. Ownership of land includes a number of legally recognized rights, including the rights to subdivide, sell, farm, cut timber, and build. The goal of devising a conservation easement is the landowner's voluntary agreement to give up one or more of these rights in order to protect certain natural resources. Prohibitions could include such matters as limitations on roads, structures, drilling, or excavating. The landowner could retain certain rights as long as those rights did not interfere with the conservation goals of the easement. For example, the landowner could retain the right to use the land, to restrict public access, and even to construct additional structures on certain sites.

When a landowner donates a permanent conservation easement to a land trust, the landowner may deduct the value of the easement from federal and state income taxes. The value of an easement is the difference between the **fair market value** of the land without the restriction and the fair **market value** after the restriction. If the value of the parcel exceeds $5000.00, the value of the conservation easement must be computed by a certified **appraiser**. The landowner can deduct up to 30 percent of the **adjusted gross income** over a period of six years until the value of the easement is exhausted, if the property has been held for investment purposes for more than twelve months.

The organization that holds the easement has the right to enter and inspect the property and is legally obligated to assure that the property is in compliance with the terms of the easement.

### Preservation Easements

Similar to conservation easements, preservation easements protect against undesirable development or indirect deterioration. Preservation easements may provide the most effective legal tool for the protection of privately owned historic properties. Such easements are usually expressly created and incorporated into formal preservation easement deeds. Preservation easements can prohibit such actions as alteration of the structure's significant features, changes in the usage of the building and land, or subdivision and topographic changes to the property. The property continues on the tax rolls at its current use designation rather than its value if developed, thereby giving the property owner a certain tax benefits.

The same standards are used as in conservation easements to determine the qualified tax **deduction**. The **donor** is entitled to a charitable contribution deduction in the amount of the fair market value of the donated interest. However, an easement to preserve a historic structure must protect a structure or area listed in the National Register or located in a National Register district and certified by the Secretary of the Interior as being of historic significance to the district. The donation of an easement over an historically important land area includes land that is either independently significant and meets National Register criteria for evaluation or is adjacent to a property listed individually in the National Register of Historic Places in a case where the physical or environmental features of the land area contribute to the historic or cultural integrity of the property.

The definition of a historically important land area includes structures or land area within a registered historic district, except buildings that cannot reasonably be considered as contributing to the significance of the district. To qualify as a preservation easement the donation must be protected in perpetuity. Because of this point, rights of mortgagers must be carefully set out in the easement to avoid loss of the easement in the event of **foreclosure**.

## Uses of Easements

Once an easement is created, the owner of the easement has the right and the duty to maintain the easement for its purpose unless otherwise agreed between the owner of the easement and the owner of the underlying property. The owner of the easement can make repairs and improvements to the easement, provided that those repairs or improvements do not interfere in the use and enjoyment of the easement by the owner of the property through which the easement exists.

## Transfer of Easements

### Easement Appurtenant

When the title is transferred, the easement typically remains with the property. This case is known as an easement appurtenant. This type of easement ldquo;runs with the landrdquo; which means that if the property is bought or sold, it is bought or sold with the easement in place. The easement essentially becomes part of the legal description.

If a parcel of property with an easement across it is sub-divided into smaller lots and sold to different people, and the geography is such that each of the smaller lots can benefit from the easement, then each will usually be permitted to use the easement.

### Easement in Gross

Traditionally, easements in gross were easements that could not be transferred and were not tied to a particular piece of land. A person could grant an easement across a residence to a neighbor, but this type of easement would not continue with the new neighbor if the neighbor holding the easement sold the property. Today, courts typically refer to these types of easements as ldquo;personalrdquo; easements. Nevertheless, an easement that began as personal may be transferable, particularly if it is a commercial easement, such as a utility easement.

## Termination of Easements

Unlike other types of interests in land, easements may be terminated by **abandonment** under certain circumstances. Simply stating a desire to abandon the easement is not be enough. Words alone are legally insufficient to constitute abandonment. However, if the easement holder intends to abandon an easement and also takes actions which manifest that intent, that is sufficient to show abandonment of the easement, and it can be terminated. One action that qualifies as manifesting intent is non-use of the easement for an extended period of time, despite the holder of the easement's having had an extended period of access to the easement.

## Additional Resources

*Holding Our Ground: Protecting America's Farms and Farmland.* T. Daniels and D. Bowers, Island Press, 1997.

*Pennsylvania Land Trust Handbook.* Thomas A. Coughlin, Chesapeake Bay Foundation, 1991.

*Preserving Family Lands: Essential Tax Strategies for the Landowner.* S. J. Small, Landowner Planning Center, 1992.

*Property.* Jesse Dukeminier and James E. Krier, [no publisher given], 1998.

*Saving the Forests for the Trees and Other Values* Laurie A. Wayburn, The Newsletter of Land Conservation Law. Vol. 4, No. 5, 1994.

*.The Conservation Easement Handbook* J. Diehl and T. Barnett, eds., Land Trust Alliance and Trust For Public Land, 1988.

## Organizations

### American Farmland Trust
1920 N Street NW, Suite 400

Washington, DC 20036 USA
Phone: (202) 659-5170

**Land Trust Alliance**
1319 F St. NW, Suite 501
Washington, DC 20004 USA

Phone: (202) 638-4725

**Trust for Public Land**
116 New Montgomery St.,4th Floor
San Francisco, CA 94105 USA
Phone: (415) 495-4014

# REAL ESTATE

## EMINENT DOMAIN

*Sections within this essay:*

## Background

Grounded in the Fifth Amendment to the U.S. Constitution, the concept of eminent domain refers to the government's right to condemn and appropriate private property for public use. Other terms meaning essentially the same thing include "condemnation" (but that has additional implications, see below) and "expropriation." Through application of the Fourteenth Amendment, the power to exercise eminent domain is vested in both federal and state governments and subdivisions thereof (counties, cities, and towns, etc.). Such power also may be delegated to political subdivisions such as governmental agencies and local governments, as well as private persons or corporations that provide services or benefits to the public.

For years, the accepted scope of the term "public use" contemplated property being taken for such purposes as public roadways, bridges, parks, libraries, governmental buildings, utilities, etc. However, in the 2005 landmark case of *Kelo v. City of New Landen*, the U.S. Supreme Court made clear that the government could also appropriate property to private, for-profit real estate developers, if such development would result in economic growth for the betterment of the community.

## Substantive Due Process

The Fifth Amendment (made applicable to the states through the Fourteenth Amendment), which protects individual liberties from unwarranted governmental intrusion, states in relevant part, "...nor shall private property be taken for public use, without just compensation." Importantly, the provision does not preclude such government action, as long as there has been "just compensation."

### Property to be Taken

Although most often applied to real property (real estate, including buildings), in fact, any kind of property may be taken. This includes both tangible and intangible property, such as franchises and contracts.

However, not all property can be appropriated or condemned for any purpose. Many states prohibit the exercise of eminent domain for property currently being used for such purposes as cemeteries, gardens and orchards, or factories. A landowner cannot convert the use of property to one of these uses in order to avoid condemnation, once proceedings have begun (notice of intent).

Often, governmental units, particularly at the local level, begin condemnation proceedings for private property that is not needed for public use, but rather, has been deemed a risk to the public health or safety. This, in fact, is the more appropriate use of the term "condemnation," although the authority or power invoked to condemn the property is that of eminent domain.

A "dedication" of land is a similar form of appropriation of private land (or an **easement** therein) for public use, but is effected voluntarily by the landowner, rather than through an adverse process of condemnation. A dedication may be express or implied through the landowner's conduct and the facts and circumstances related to the property. Notwithstanding, a dedication also may arise following an adverse (to the interests and/or use of the landowner) and exclusive use by members of the public under a claim of right. Such claim, by an adverse public user, is similar to a common law "adverse possession" claim between private parties, and is predicated upon the knowledge, actual or imputed, and acquiescence of the owner. Many states provide for both common-law and statutory dedications.

### What Constitutes a Taking

What is necessary in order for a "taking" to occur is not always a formal transfer of interest in the property. Rather, what is required is a destruction of a personal *interest* in property, or such a drastic interference with the use and enjoyment of that property so as to constitute a taking. In other words, the impairment is so severe that it is tantamount to the assertion of a servitude on the property for the benefit of the government.

It is often the case that a landowner is not completely deprived of his property, but instead suffers a restriction or impairment of his or her right to use it. For example (and as is frequently the case), a government may need to run a utility through private property, or need to alter a shoreline such that the property is no longer on the waterfront. The property may need to be flooded to create a dam, or a building on the property may need to be relocated to make access to another point. In such cases, a partial taking may be effected, and the landowner is entitled to proportional compensation.

Still another form of taking may occur when there is no actual property being taken from a person. Instead, governmental activity on one property may so severely deplete the value of adjacent or neighboring property so as to constitute a "constructive taking,"

often referred to as inverse or reverse condemnation. Fumes, noises, vibrations, changes in flow of ground water, or toxic pollutants are some of the more common interferences that may constitute constructive takings. Examples include properties affected by airport noise and fumes, waterfront properties affected by rerouted water, or livestock farms affected by nearby noise or ground vibration. In each of these circumstances, property owners may be entitled to compensation from the governmental entity.

Finally, a taking need not be permanent; it may be effected and justified only under limiting circumstances. For example, in time of war or insurrection, a government may need to exercise control and dominion over lands otherwise not needed for public welfare or safety. Again, a landowner may be compensated for the temporary impairment or deprivation in his or her use of private property.

### Public Use

A "public use" is generally one which confers some benefit or advantage to the public, and the term does not necessarily imply, and is not confined to, actual "use" by the public. Moreover, the purported benefit to be derived from the taking of property need not be available to the entire public; it may benefit a smaller sector of members of the public in a particular locality, i.e. a subdivision of the general public. In other words, it is not necessary that the intended users be all members of the public; rather, it is the purpose for the taking that must be for the public, and not for the benefit of any particular individuals.

The use (purpose) must be a needed one, which cannot be surrendered without obvious general loss or inconvenience. However, the parameters of such needed public use move along a spectrum, and defy absolute definition or parameter because of changing needs of society, increases in population, and developing modes of transportation and communications.

In *Kelo v. City of New Landen*(2005), the U.S. Supreme Court was called upon to determine whether that changing parameter was broad enough to include for-profit development of real estate which would ostensibly result in needed economic growth for the community. In a decision that surprised many, the Court agreed.

### Justification or Necessity

It is the legislature that has the power to determine the necessity of taking property for public use, as well as the amount of property to be taken. Most takings must comport with legislative language that mandates under what circumstances such an action is justified or necessary. A formal court action objecting on grounds of taking property not strictly needed for public use, or for taking more property than needed for public use is generally referred to as an action for "excess condemnation."

If a local government deems certain property to be a hazard to the public, e.g. a health or safety risk, it may condemn the property as unfit for human occupancy following formal inspection and assessment. Usually this is accomplished by citation of violations involving local ordinances, building codes, or federal public safety regulations. During the time between condemnation and bringing the property back into conformity with relevant laws, a landowner is generally*not* entitled to compensation, even though a deprivation of property rights has occurred.

### What Compensation is Considered Just

Whether a proffered compensation is just or not is a judicial question. Generally, an appropriate measure is the fair market value of the property at the time of the taking, plus any subsequent accrued interest. An objecting claimant will not succeed in arguing speculative value, or the fact that the property could be used for a special purpose which would tend to enhance its value. Instead, an objective assessment of the property in its present state is the correct measure, although consideration may include assessment of market value at its best and most profitable use.

Notwithstanding, the compensation must be fair to both the property owner and the public. This assessment involves consideration of such factors as the cost of reproducing the property, its present market value, and the resulting damage or decrease in value to any remaining/residual property of the owner. It also may include consideration of the price originally paid for the property, and any buildings, crops, timber, or minerals located on the property. Additional compensation may be added for any delay in payment, as interest is recoverable when payment is not made at the time of the taking.

## Procedural Due Process

An aggrieved party who objects to a government taking must have an opportunity to receive fair notice (a reasonable time to obtain legal advice and prepare a formal objection). Additionally, there must be

opportunity for a fair hearing before the award (of compensation) becomes final. The hearing provides a forum to adjudicate whether or not there had been an actual taking (in the question of less than total deprivation of interest); whether the taking was for a public use; and/or whether just compensation had been made.

### Notice

Prior to any governmental action to exercise its right of eminent domain, the government must negotiate in good faith with the land owner for an acceptable price for the land. Initially, most governments notify landowners of prospective action by serving a notice of intent. The contents generally describe the parameters of the property in question, the proposed use, and an offer (in dollars) of purchase. Extensive mediation and offers/counteroffers usually precede court action. A formal condemnation action only follows if an agreement cannot be reached.

### Hearing

Not all condemnation proceedings are the same. State laws differ on the number of hearings and the procedural structure of each, depending on the type of property in question or the intended use. Generally, a landowner may contest both the proposed taking and the amount of compensation offered. Ultimately, if administrative appeals fail, the landowner may petition in court, under the auspices of violation of constitutional rights.

Both sides may offer witness testimony and other evidence in support of their positions. Both sides may call attention to the fair market value (by expert testimony) of similar properties for comparison. Following court decision, appeals may take years, but generally does not stay the taking; if a landowner ultimately prevails on appeal, only money damages are generally available.

### Remedies

Initially, an objecting landowner may request either or both injunctive and monetary relief. However, if the government's action meets the legislative and constitutional criteria, the landowner may be responsible for court costs if the objection was not well-grounded or appears to have been motivated by excessive pecuniary interest.

In cases of partial takings or excessive takings, adjudication includes a determination of the percentage interest in a property which is adversely affected, and monetary award is prorated accordingly. Likewise, if the complaint is for devalued property which is not directly taken, but is adversely affected because of governmental activity or use on nearby property, adjudication includes a determination as to whether other factors have devalued the property and the monetary difference between the devalued property and its fair market value without the alleged adverse effect.

Compensation is required, effective from the date of the alleged taking. Payments not made at that time accrue interest, to which the landowner is entitled. Occasionally, subsequent actions or objections are filed months or years after the initial determination. This is especially true in the case of partial takings, e.g., easements. Over time, a government entity may engage in additional activity that exceeds in scope of the initial taking. If this causes further decrease in residual use or enjoyment still vested in the original property owner, both injunctive and monetary relief may be available.

## Additional Resources

Bhatnagar, Parija. "Eminent Domain: A Big Bonanza?" CNN News, 24 June 2005. Available at http://www.cnn.com

Eminent Domain information available at http://www.eminentdomainonline.com

# REAL ESTATE

## FORECLOSURE

*Sections within this essay:*

## Background

**Foreclosure** is the **legal right** of a **mortgage** holder or other third-party **lien** holder to gain ownership of the property and/or the right to sell the property and use the proceeds to pay off the mortgage if the mortgage or lien is in **default**. It is a concept that has existed for centuries.

Initially, the law had it that a mortgage default resulted in the automatic ownership of the property by the holder of the mortgage (sometimes referred to as the mortgagee). But the law developed over the years so as to allow mortgagors time to pay off mortgages before their property was taken away. This process of taking away the mortgagor's property because of default is what constitutes foreclosure.

Today, numerous state laws and regulations govern foreclosure to protect both the mortgagor and the holder of the mortgage from unfairness and **fraud**. In the United States, although states have their own variations, the basic premises of foreclosure law remain the same.

## Types of Foreclosure

The mortgage holder can usually initiate foreclosure anytime after a default on the mortgage. Within the United States, there exist several types of foreclosure. Two are widely used, with the rest being possibilities only in a few states.

The most important type of foreclosure is foreclosure by judicial sale. This is available in every state and is the required method in many. It involves the sale of the mortgaged property done under the supervision of a court, with the proceeds going first to satisfy the mortgage, and then to satisfy other lien holders, and finally to the mortgagor. Because it is a legal action, all the proper parties must be notified of the foreclosure, and there will be both pleadings and some sort of judicial decision, usually after a short trial.

The second type of foreclosure, foreclosure by power of sale, involves the sale of the property by the mortgage holder not through the supervision of a court. Where it is available, foreclosure by power of sale is generally a more expedient way of foreclosing on a property than foreclosure by judicial sale. The majority of states allow this method of foreclosure. Again, proceeds from the sale go first to the mortgage holder, then to other lien holders, and finally to the mortgagor.

Other types of foreclosure are only available in limited places and are therefore considered minor methods of foreclosure. Strict foreclosure is one example. Under strict foreclosure, when a mortgagor defaults, a court orders the mortgagor to pay the mortgage within a certain period of time. If the mortgagor fails, the mortgage holder automatically gains title, with no obligation to sell the property. Strict foreclosure was the original method of foreclosure, but today it is only available in New Hampshire and Vermont.

## Acceleration

The concept of acceleration is used to determine the amount owed under foreclosure. Acceleration allows the mortgage holder the right when the mortgagor defaults on the mortgage to declare the entire debt due and payable. In other words, if a mortgage is taken out on property for $10,000 with monthly payments required, and the mortgagor fails to make the monthly payments, the mortgage holder can demand the mortgagor make good on the entire $10,000 of the mortgage.

Virtually all mortgages today have acceleration clauses. However, they are not imposed by **statute**, so if a mortgage does not have an acceleration clause, the mortgage holder has no choice but to either wait to foreclose until all of the payments come due or convince a court to divide up parts of the property and sell them in order to pay the **installment** that is due. Alternatively, the court may order the property sold subject to the mortgage, with the proceeds from the sale going to the payments owed the mortgage holder.

## Foreclosure by Judicial Sale

Foreclosure by judicial sale requires the mortgage holder to proceed carefully in order to ensure that all affected parties are included in the court case, so the purchaser of the foreclosed property receives valid title to the property.

### Parties and Omissions

A mortgage holder bringing a suit for foreclosure in court must join any "necessary" parties to the case. To understand what a necessary party is, it must be realized that the purpose of a foreclosure sale is to sell the property as it was when the mortgage was first taken out. Anyone who acquired an interest in the property after the mortgage was taken out must be dealt with in the court case before the property can be sold.

Necessary parties include parties who acquired easements, liens, or leases after the mortgage being foreclosed was executed. They can be added, or "joined" to the case as parties without their consent. The intent is to terminate their interest in the property. If a party is not joined, then their interest in the property is not affected by the foreclosure, and the purchaser does not acquire an interest in the property fee of their rights.

For example, if party A takes out a mortgage from party B and then takes out a second mortgage from party C, and party B decides to foreclose on the property and sell the property to party D at foreclosure, party B must extinguish the interest of party C to sell the property to party D. Otherwise party C can enforce their mortgage on party D.

The other type of party involved in a foreclosure case is called a "proper" party. A proper party is a party that is useful, but not necessary, to a foreclosure case. An example would be a party who had an interest in the property before the mortgage was executed. Since this party would not be affected by the foreclosure, the individual is considered a voluntary party to a case and normally cannot be included in the case without consenting to it. However, often courts will require these parties to be joined anyway to the case to clarify their status with respect to the mortgage being foreclosed upon.

### Procedures

The procedure for a judicial sale varies from state to state, but generally calls for a court appointed official or a public official such as the sheriff to conduct the actual sale of the foreclosed property. The mortgage holder can bid for the mortgaged property.

If a lien holder who acquired the lien after the mortgage was executed (also known as a junior lien holder) is not named as a party in the foreclosure, the individual can either foreclose the lien subject to the mortgage sold at foreclosure or redeem the lien and acquire the property by paying the purchaser the mortgage debt. In the case of a omitted junior lien holder, the purchaser of the property has the option of paying the lien holder outright for their interest in the property, or reforeclosing on the original mortgage to eliminate the junior lien holder, - in which case there would be another foreclosure sale.

### Deficiency Judgments

When the foreclosure sale is not enough to satisfy the amount of the mortgage, the mortgage holder may bring a deficiency judgment against the mortgagor to make up the difference. For example, a mortgage holder of a $10,000 mortgage, who only receives $8,000 in a foreclosure sale, may sue the mortgagor for the remainder of the amount due under the mortgage.

Deficiency judgments are tempered in many jurisdictions by "fair value" legislation. This requires the deficiency to be calculated using the difference between the mortgage debt and the fair value of the real estate. In the above example, a court in a fair value **jurisdiction** might determine that the fair value of the property was $9,000. In that case, the mortgage holder could only obtain a deficiency judgment of $1,000.

## Foreclosure By Power of Sale

Foreclosure by the power of sale, where law allows it, usually saves time and money over foreclosure by judicial sale. It accomplishes the same thing as a judicial sale. However, there are also some difficulties associated with this method of foreclosure.

### Availability and Disadvantages

Today, 29 states (Alabama, Alaska, Arizona, California, Colorado, the District of Columbia, Georgia, Hawaii, Idaho, Maine, Maryland, Massachusetts, Michigan, Minnesota, Mississippi, Missouri, Montana, Nevada, New Hampshire, North Carolina, Oregon, Rhode Island, South Dakota, Tennessee, Texas, Utah, Washington, West Virginia and Wyoming) allow foreclosure by the power of sale.

However, foreclosure by the power of sale is often subject to **judicial review** at a later date because there are issues about title that must be resolved by the court. These would include actual defects in the **deed**, and the priority of various lien holders and lessees on the property. In addition, in many jurisdictions the mortgage holder is prohibited from seeking a deficiency judgment if the holder chooses to sell the property through extra-judicial means. Also, the mortgage form must generally allow for power of sale and cannot be in the form of an absolute deed for a foreclosure by the power of sale to take place.

### Deed of Trust

In many jurisdictions, a **deed of trust** is required in order to conduct a foreclosure by the power of sale. A deed of trust conveys the property from the mortgage holder to the **trustee**, who holds the property in trust for the mortgage holder. In the instance of foreclosure, the trustee, not the mortgage holder, conducts the sale of the mortgaged property. The trustee is generally instructed by the mortgage holder to foreclose on the mortgage and is under no obligation to determine whether this foreclosure is justified.

A deed of trust and trustee supervised foreclosure allows the mortgage holder to bid for the foreclosed property, provided the trustee and the mortgage holder are not closely associated. Otherwise, a mortgage holder cannot bid for the mortgaged property when the foreclosure is by power of sale.

### Constitutional Issues

Foreclosure by power of sale requires notice of the sale to interested parties. Generally speaking, this is done by taking out an advertisement in a local newspaper in the jurisdiction in which the property is located. Many states also require notice be given to the mortgagor.

This procedure has resulted in some constitutional controversy. It has been argued in several cases that foreclosure by power of sale legislation fails to comply with the notice and **hearing** requirements of the Fourteenth Amendment of the U. S. Constitution. Courts have consistently rejected this theory when it comes to private foreclosure actions with no public official conducting the foreclosure sale, ruling that there is no state action necessary to invoke the terms of the Fourteenth Amendment. However, there have been rulings indicating that if the mortgage holder is a government entity or if a public official conducts the foreclosure sale, the Fourteenth Amendment might be invoked and stricter notice requirements might apply. The **case law** on this issue is so far unsettled.

## Federal Laws Affecting Foreclosure

While the Fourteenth Amendment has a debatable nexus to foreclosure actions, at least two federal laws clearly apply to foreclosure actions

### Bankruptcy

The filing of any **bankruptcy** action automatically stays a foreclosure proceeding, regardless of type. At that point, whether the stay will be lifted depends on whether the mortgagor has equity in the mortgaged property. If the bankruptcy has been filed under a Chapter 11 petition, the bankruptcy court may "terminate, annul, modify or condition such stay" for cause, including the lack of adequate protection of an interest in property of the mortgage holder, or if the mortgagor does not have equity in the property and the property is not necessary for an effective reorganization.

If it has been filed as a straight bankruptcy petition, asking for discharge of all debts, the mortgage holder will be allowed to foreclose if the bankrupt **debtor** has no equity in the property. If there is equity in the property, the property can be sold by the bankruptcy court.

### Soldier and Sailors Relief Act

The Soldiers and Sailors Relief Act of 1940 gives special protection to mortgagors on active duty in the armed forces for mortgage loans executed prior to when they went into service. The Act provides that a service person can apply to a court to set aside a **default judgment** leading to a foreclosure action. Because of this provision, a mortgage holder initiating a foreclosure action against a mortgagor who fails to answer the foreclosure complaint must file an **affidavit** with the court stating the mortgagor is not on active duty in the armed services.

If the mortgagor is in the armed services, the individual must be present or represented at the foreclosure hearing, meaning foreclosure by power of sale is not available. If a court finds that the mortgagor's ability to meet the terms of the mortgage has been affected by their service in the armed forces, they can stay the foreclosure action as long as the person is in the service.

## Statutory Redemption

**Statutory** redemption allows the mortgagor to redeem the mortgage even after foreclosure sale. About one-half the states have statutory redemption laws. Generally, these laws give anywhere from six months to a year for the mortgagor to redeem the mortgage by payment of the foreclosure sale price

plus a statutory rate of interest to the sale purchaser. Junior lien holders also have a right to redeem under these statutes, in order of their priority, though not until the period for the mortgagor to redeem runs out. As a rule, the mortgagor can retain possession of their property during this statutory redemption period.

## Additional Resources

*"The Constitutionality of Texas Nonjudicial Foreclosure: Protecting Subordinate Property Interests From Deprivation Without Notice"* Krock, Kenneth M., *Houston Law Review*, Fall 1995.

*How To Save Your Home From Foreclosure* RJM Marketing, 1998.

*Land Transactions and Finance* Nelson, Grant, and Dale Whitman, West Group, 1998.

*Real Estate Finance in a Nutshell.* Bruce, Jon W., West Group, 1997.

### Federal Home Loan Mortgage Corporation (Freddie Mac)

8200 Jones Branch Drive
McLean, VA 22102-3110 USA
Phone: (703) 903-2000
URL: http://www.freddiemac.com
Primary Contact: Leland C. Brendsel, Chairman

## Organizations

### Federal National Mortgage Association (Fannie Mae)

3900 Wisconsin Avenue, NW
Washington, DC 20016-2892 USA
Phone: (202) 752-7000
E-Mail: headquarters@fanniemae.com
URL: http://www.fanniemae.com
Primary Contact: Primary Contact, Franklin Raines, Chairman

### Mortgage Bankers Association of America (MBAA)

1919 Pennsylvania Avenue, NW.
Washington, DC 20006-3438 USA
Phone: (202) 557-2700
URL: http://www.mbaa.org
Primary Contact: John Courson, Chairman

# REAL ESTATE

## HOMEOWNERS ASSOCIATIONS

*Sections within this essay:*

- Background

- History of Homeowners Associations
  - Levittown Breaks New Ground
  - Disputes

- Homeowners Associations and Government

- Getting Involved with Your Homeowners Association

- Additional Resources

## Background

Most cities and towns have **zoning** requirements that prohibit homeowners from making unrestricted changes to their houses. This keeps people from adding third stories to two-story structures, building three-car garages up to the neighbor's property line, or simply tearing down a house to make room for two houses on the same lot. Most communities, however, have no power to require homeowners to choose attractive colors for their exterior walls, keep their lawns well-manicured, or repair broken steps or walkways. For people who prefer a consistently well-kept neighborhood, there are a number of residential options, known as *common interest developments* (CIDs). The CID (sometimes called a *planned unit development*)combines the security of home ownership with the convenience of minimal maintenance. Often they provide residents with self-contained communities with shared amenities such as swimming pools, parks, tennis courts, and buildings for community events. Some CIDs have actual single-unit houses, while others had attached houses or townhomes. Oversight of the common areas is the responsibility of the homeowners association, whose responsibilities include maintaining common areas, managing the CID's budget (residents pay monthly maintenance fees), and ensuring that residents abide by the community's regulations.

The CID differs somewhat from a *condominium* or a *cooperative*. The condominium owner owns only the interior space of the unit; the exterior walls are considered part of the common space (and thus are maintained by a condominium owners' association). In a cooperative, owners hold shares in a corporation that owns the property; each resident actually owns shares that correspond to a specific unit. The cooperative fees pay for building maintenance inside and out. With a CID, the resident owns the entire structure and the land on which it sits. CID residents are thus responsible for the exterior upkeep of their own homes. But the community is responsible for maintaining the common amenities; many also take care of mowing lawns.

The convenience is clearly a big selling point. According to the Community Associations Institute (CAI), a national advocacy and education group, there were 274,000 association-governed communities in the United States in 2005, with 22.1 million housing units and 54.6 million residents. In contrast, in 1970 there were only 10,000 such communities, with 701,000 housing units and 2.1 million residents. A survey conducted for CAI by polling group Zogby International in 2005 showed strong satisfaction among CID owners. Some 71 percent of survey respondents reported CID living as a positive experience, as opposed to only 10 percent who said it was a negative experience. More than half of respondents said they were satisfied with their homeowners association, and 90 percents said they were on friendly terms with association board members. In addition, 78 percent of respondents said that the association rules and regulations enhanced the CID's property values.

It is those rules and regulations, known as *covenants, conditions, and restrictions* (CC&Rs), that make CIDS popular—but CC&Rs are also the basis for many resident complaints. The CC&Rs generally cover the exterior appearance of each residence and their goal is to create a uniform environment. The difficulty arises when the homeowners association and individual residents have a different idea of what "uniform" actually means. Some CIDs have very general guidelines that allow people to express a certain degree of individuality (landscaping, for example, or exterior paint colors) as long as their homes are well-kept. Other CIDs have CC&Rs that prohibit residents from choosing their own paint trim colors, planting their own shrubs in their front lawn, or even hanging an non-approved color of curtains or blinds in their windows. Often, the CC&Rs are included in the property **deeds**, which means removing a particular regulation can be time-consuming and cumbersome.

Among the items a typical homeowners association may regulate:

- pets
- shingles, siding, and exterior paint
- fences, shrubs, and hedges
- landscaping (what flowers can be planted, for instance)
- swing sets, basketball hoops, and other structures for children
- mailboxes
- noise
- tool sheds
- home-based business

Thus, one CID may allow residents to plant their own gardens but not to fence off their gardens. Another CID may allow cats or small dogs but not large dogs. Still another might allow children's swing sets in the back yard but not a basketball hoop in the front.

Along with the CC&Rs, fees are something that can vary considerably. Some CIDs charge a nominal monthly fee to maintain common areas, while others can charge significantly higher fees. In addition, CIDs can levy assessments on residents for major renovations or repairs. These charges can quickly add up, and the fee policy depends on what the CID and the governing association determine it to be. In some cases, residents who either cannot or will not pay required fees can face foreclosure.

Those who want to explore the option of living in a community development should do their homework before they commit to purchasing a home. The need to know what the restrictions are, and they need to know whether they can live with those restrictions.

## History of Homeowners Associations

In the nineteenth century, the United States began to transform itself from a primarily agricultural society to an industrial society. A growing number of people took jobs in cities, but most cities were overcrowded, dusty, and noisy. The advent of commuter rail lines allowed people to work in the city and live outside the city. A series of "railroad communities" grew up along rail stations. Usually these communities were populated by middle-class families.

The twentieth century made people even more mobile, thanks to the automobile. This led to a series of planned communities around the country. In some, the houses would look essentially the same; in others, several designs would be built. These communities attracted more affluent families; there were few restrictions, but people who lived in these communities generally shared common ideas of how streetscapes should look. Homeowners associations as we know them today did not really exist; if similar associations existed in any of these early communities, their purpose was often to restrict residency based on race or religion.

### Levittown Breaks New Ground

The first modern planned development was Levittown, built on the site of a potato field on Long Island, off the coast of New York. Builder William Levitt constructed a series of inexpensive but attractive homes that veterans could purchase with low-interest loans guaranteed by the federal government under the Servicemen's Readjustment Bill of 1944 (better known as the GI Bill). Between 1947 and 1951 more than 17,000 houses were built in and around the original Long Island community. Although Levittown residents were subject to restrictive covenants in their deeds, prohibiting such items as laundry lines in front yards, there was no formal homeowners association.

As suburban living continued to become a more attractive option, other developments were built, albeit on a smaller scale than Levittown. These developments were often more self-contained than the large-scale communities in that they maintained stricter standards regarding the appearance of the homes (both the structures and the landscaping). The general idea was that people who were looking for certain amenities (whether restrictions on pets or rules governing hedge planting) would be drawn to these communities; those who sought other amenities would look at other developments. Despite the logic behind this, it is not uncommon for residents of a CID to find themselves in disputes with other neighbors, or with the homeowners association, over seemingly minor infractions of the rules.

### Disputes

Some of the disputes between homeowners and their associations are clearly misunderstandings, others are amusing, and still others are considerably more serious. Residents have been sued by their homeowners associations for using the wrong shade of paint; in one Atlanta case in 2003, the homeowner took paint chips with her to match the paint, but because the colors chosen were not specifically listed as "approved" colors by the homeowners association, she was ordered to repaint her house. A couple near Coeur d'Alene, Idaho was instructed to remove six pink flamingoes they had placed on they front lawn; they admitted freely that the birds had been placed there in protest of the homeowners association's arbitrary rules regarding lawn ornaments.

After the attacks of September 11, 2001 and the government's decision to invade Iraq in 2003, many people across the country adorned their homes with American flags and signs reading "Support Our Troops." In a number of cases, residents of CIDs found that they were barred from doing so under the rules set forth by their homeowners association.

### Homeowners Association and Government

Can government get involved in resolving homeowners association disputes? The answer depends on the issue at hand. For general resident-association disputes, most government agencies are unlikely to get involved. In an information package distributed to CID residents by the State Attorney General's office in New York, the answer is clear: "In most cases there is no government agency that can help unhappy owners who are having problems with their homeowners association." That does not mean governments are never able to get involved. When homeowners associations clearly overstep their bounds, government does sometimes step in. In June 2005 Colorado passed a measure known as Senate Bill 100, which prohibits homeowners associations from adopting rules that prevent residents from displaying the American flag or political signs. It also limits the availability of **foreclosures** and requires homeowners associations to give potential buyers a copy of the rules that govern the CID.

One reason government is often reluctant to get involved with these disputes is that often for every one resident who has a complaint about a particular rule there are dozens of residents who value that rule. (The CAI survey results cited above illustrate this.) Many people choose to live in a community that guarantees them a sense of structure and uniformity, because along with structure and uniformity also comes security and peace of mind.

Regardless of the legal standing, most people would say that there is a difference between a resident who inadvertently violates a CID rule and one who deliberately does so. Colorado's Senate Bill 100 was actually less stringent when it was signed into law than it had originally been. Governor Bill Owens explained that taking too much authority away from homeowners associations ignored the fact that many CID residents had chosen to live there because they wanted a neighborhood with clear regulations.

### Getting Involved with Your Homeowners Association

One way residents can help ensure that their homeowners associations set reasonable rules is to get involved themselves by joining their association board. Homeowners association boards (likewise condominium and cooperative boards) are made up of residents and the positions are acquired through elections. In fact, more than 1.25 million CID residents nationwide serve on their community association boards, with an additional 300,000 serving on board committees.

Depending on the structure of the organization, the board can have fairly sweeping power, and often that power is exercised arbitrarily. Often, these are the boards that find themselves the subject of legal action. Homeowners association boards can in fact work effectively and harmoniously, but it takes work. Many of the people who serve on these boards, after all, may have no governance experience.

Those who have no interest in joining a board should stay involved nonetheless. The best way to know what is going on within the community is to attend board meetings and to hold members accountable. As with any community, the best way to ensure that one's agenda is put forth is to be active within that community.

Groups such as the Community Associations Institute (CAI) are useful for new or established board members. They provide data about CIDs and homeowners associations, and they also advocate on behalf of homeowners associations. In addition, CAI offers a series of educational programs, both nationally, and locally, for board members, property managers, and CID residents. The goal is to make the governance of the CID a good experience for all involved. This serves a practical goal as well as a humanitarian one. From a practical standpoint, the well-run homeowners association whose regulations are understood and respected within the community is a more attractive place to live, which means that property values remain more stable. From a human standpoint, a harmonious repatinship between the homeowners association and the residents adds to the quality of life—which, after all, is the primary reason people move into community developments in the first place.

## Additional Resources

*Privatopia: Homeowner Associations and the Rise of Residential Private Governments,* Evan McKenzie, Yale University Press, 1994.

*Working with Your Homeowner's Association: A Guide to Effective Community Living,* Marlene Coleman, Sphinx Publishing, 2003.

## Organizations

### Community Associations Institute (CAI)
225 Reinekers Lane, Suite 300
Alexandria, VA 22314
Phone: (703) 548-8600
Fax: (703) 984-1581
URL: www.caionline.org
Primary Contact: Ross W. Feinberg, President

### National Board of REALTORS
430 North Michigan Avenue
Chicago, IL 60611
Phone: (800) 874-6500
URL: www.realtor.org
Primary Contact: Dale Stinton, Executive Vice President and CEO

# REAL ESTATE

## HOMEOWNER'S LIABILITY/SAFETY

## Background

Premises liability involves the responsibility of property owners to maintain safe conditions for people coming on or about the property. Homeowners can be and often are held liable for injuries which occur on their property. If a person slips, trips, or falls as a result of a dangerous or hazardous condition, the property owner may be fully responsible. Property owners are generally held accountable for falls as a result of water, ice, or snow, as well as abrupt changes in flooring, poor lighting, or a hidden hazard, such as a gap or hard to see hole in the ground. Several categories of persons to whom a property owner may be liable exist, and the duties of protection owed to each group are specific.

## Homeowner Liability

### Invitees

Where a homeowner, by express or implied invitation, induces or leads others to come upon the premises for any lawful purpose, a duty to exercise ordinary care arises to keep the premises safe. The invitation may be express, implied from known and customary use of portions of the premises, or inferred from conduct actually known to the homeowner. Workers or contractors are typically considered invitees.

### Licensees

A licensee is a person who has no contractual relation with the owner of the premises but is permitted, expressly or implicitly, to go on the premises. A social guest at a residence is normally considered a licensee. The homeowner is liable to a licensee only for willful or wanton injury. It is usually willful or wanton not to exercise ordinary care to prevent injuring a licensee who is actually known to be, or is reasonably expected to be, within the range of a dangerous act or condition.

### Trespassers

Surprising to many homeowners is the fact that a duty is also owed to those without permission to be on the premises. A trespasser is a person who enters the premises of another without express or implied permission of the owner, for the trespasser's own benefit or amusement. The duty of the owner to a trespasser is not to prepare pitfalls or traps for the trespasser nor to injure the trespasser purposely. Once the owner is aware of the trespasser's presence or can reasonably anticipate such presence from the circumstances, (**evidence** of skateboarders in an unfinished swimming pool would fall into this category) then the owner has a duty to exercise ordinary care to avoid injuring the trespasser.

### Insurance Coverage

Homeowner's Insurance policies cover this form of legal liability in the event that anyone suffers an injury while on the insured property. Certain actions of the policyholder, which occur away from the insured property, may also be covered. Even if a house is under construction and has no contents to be protected, the homeowner should obtain liability insurance to protect against claims of workers and even trespassers.

When a homeowner purchases liability insurance, part of the insurance company's obligation is to provide a defense in the event of a lawsuit. Even though the insurance company selects the lawyer and must approve the payment of all legal fees and other expenses of the lawsuit, the lawyer represents the policyholder. Under most types of liability insurance, the insurance company has the contractual right to settle or defend the case as it sees fit. The homeowner has an opportunity to express opinion, but the company typically has no obligation to obtain the policyholder's consent or approval.

A suit against a homeowner may involve several different claims, some of which may be covered by the liability insurance policy and some of which may not be covered. The insurance company is obligated to provide a defense for any claim, which could be covered, but the company may not be obligated to pay the damages for certain types of claims. Since liability policies typically do not provide coverage for intentional acts, there may be a question as to whether the policyholder acted intentionally. Negligent or accidental acts are generally covered, however, papers filed in court might **allege** both negligent and intentional actions. In such a situation, the insurance company may send the homeowner a Reservation of Rights letter, a notice that the company is paying for the defense for the claim but is not agreeing that it is required to pay for any and all losses under the terms of the policy.

Limitations and exclusions can alter the provisions of coverage in a policy. A limitation is an exception to the general scope of coverage, applicable only under certain circumstances or for a specified period of time. An exclusion is a broader exception which often rules out coverage for such cases as intentional acts, when the policy covers damages due to negligent acts.

Insurance companies and policyholders have contractual obligations which must be satisfied to ensure resolution of claims. Insurance policies list specific things a policyholder must do in order to perfect a claim once a loss has taken place. These duties are known as contract conditions. Policies typically require an insured to give prompt notice of any loss or the time and place of an accident or injury. Liability claims require the policyholder to give the insurance company copies of any notices or legal papers received.

The insurance company may ultimately refuse to pay part or all of a claim. The insurance company may take the position that the loss is not covered by the policy, perhaps because it was the result of some intentional act. Or the insurance company may allege that the policyholder took some type of action that rendered the policy void. Because insurance policies are contracts and open to interpretation by the courts, policyholders may be able to use the legal system to reverse such decisions. If an insured homeowner opts to consult an attorney to pursue such remedies, the chosen attorney ought to be one other than the one hired by the insurance company to represent the homeowner.

## Safety Considerations

In addition to considering the welfare of those in the home and visitors to the home, safety precautions can reduce potential liability for homeowner's and in some cases attention to these issues may even lower the cost of homeowner's insurance.

### Smoke Alarms and Fires

Fire kills more Americans than all natural disasters combined and over 80 percent of all fire deaths occur in residences. Direct property loss due to fires in the United States is estimated at $8.6 billion per year. Cooking and smoking are the leading causes of residential fires, followed by heating fixtures. A smoke alarm is a battery operated or electrically connected device that senses the presence of visible or invisible particles produced by combustion and is designed to sound an alarm within the room or suite within which it is located. There are two types of household smoke alarms in common use: ionization and photoelectric smoke alarms. An ionization alarm uses a small amount of radioactive material to ionize air in the sensing chamber. As a result, the air chamber becomes conductive, permitting current to flow between two charged electrodes. When smoke particles enter the chamber, the conductivity of the chamber air decreases. When this reduction in conductivity is reduced to a predetermined level, the alarm is set off. Most smoke alarms in use are this type. A photoelectric smoke alarm consists of a light emitting diode and a light sensitive sensor in the sensing chamber. The presence of suspended smoke particles in the chamber scatters the light beam. This scattered light is detected and sets off the alarm. Smoke alarms should be maintained in accordance with the manufacturers' instructions. Occasional light vacuuming will keep the air vents clean. Long life smoke alarms have been designed to use lithium batteries where the battery life is predicted to last 10 years with the normal low battery drain of ionization smoke alarms. The smoke alarms are still designed to provide a low battery audible signal as the battery charge is reduced to a level that may make the smoke alarm inoperable. Although these batteries are designed to last 10 years, ongoing testing and maintenance is required as per manufacturers' instructions.

### Furnace, Fireplace, and Chimney Maintenance

Carbon monoxide is an odorless, colorless gas that interferes with the delivery of oxygen in the blood to the rest of the body. This gas can impede coordination, worsen cardiovascular conditions, and produce fatigue, headache, weakness, confusion, disorientation, nausea, and dizziness. High levels result in death. The symptoms are sometimes confused with the flu or food poisoning. Fetuses, infants, elderly, and people with heart and respiratory illnesses are particularly at high risk for the adverse health effects of carbon monoxide. An estimated 1,000 people die each year as a result of carbon monoxide poisoning and thousands of others end up in hospital emergency rooms. Carbon monoxide is produced by the incomplete combustion of carbon-containing fuels including coal, wood, charcoal, natural gas, and fuel oil. It can be emitted by combustion sources such as unvented kerosene and gas space heaters, furnaces, wood stoves, gas stoves, fireplaces and water heaters, automobile exhaust from attached garages, and tobacco smoke. Problems can arise as a result of improper installation, maintenance, or inadequate ventilation.

Chimneys blocked by birds' or squirrels' nests can cause deadly carbon monoxide gas to enter a home. This danger can be lessened by having the chimney professionally cleaned each year. A carbon-monoxide alarm will provide added protection, but such alarms are not a replacement for proper use

and maintenance of fuel-burning appliances. Proper placement of a carbon monoxide detector is important. Because victims of carbon monoxide poisoning will slip deeper into unconsciousness as their condition worsens, a loud alarm is necessary to wake them. Additional detectors on every level and in every bedroom of a home provide extra protection. Homeowners should not install carbon monoxide detectors directly above or beside fuel-burning appliances, as appliances may emit a small amount of carbon monoxide upon start-up. A detector should not be placed within fifteen feet of heating or cooking appliances or in or near very humid areas such as bathrooms. Carbon monoxide rises with warmer air temperatures and so mounting the device on or near the ceiling is often recommended.

### Swimming Pools

Drowning is the second leading cause of unintentional injury-related deaths to children ages 14 and under. A temporary lapse in supervision is a common factor in most drownings and near-drownings. Child drownings can happen in a matter of seconds—in the time it takes to answer the phone. There is often no splashing to warn of trouble. Children can drown in small quantities of water and are at risk in their own homes from wading pools, bathtubs, buckets, diaper pails, and toilets as well as swimming pools, spas, and hot tubs. Pool and spa owners can take practical steps to make their pool and spa less dangerous and reduce their potential liability.

All doors which give access to a swimming pool should be equipped with an audible alarm which sounds when the door and/or screen are opened. The alarm should have an automatic reset feature. The alarm can be equipped with manual means, such as touchpads or switches, to temporarily deactivate the alarm for a single opening of the door from either direction. This arrangement allows adults to pass through without setting off the alarm. Such deactivation should last for no more than 15 seconds. The deactivation touchpads or switches should be located at least 54 inches above the threshold of the door.

A non-climbable, five-foot fence that separates the pool/spa from the residence should be installed. Openings should be no more than four inches wide so children cannot squeeze through the spaces. A fence or barrier completely surrounding the pool can prevent many drowning accidents. The area adjacent to the outside of the fence must be free of objects such as chairs, tables, and playground equipment that children could use to climb over the fence.

Other safety measures can include:

- Self-closing and self-latching gates and doors leading to the pool should have latches above a child's reach. Gates should open outward.

- Pool safety covers can be installed. Power operated covers are the safest and easiest to use.

- A telephone can be installed near the pool. Emergency numbers as well as the address of the property should be posted near the phone so that it is visible to callers.

- Constant supervision of swimmers of all ages is the most effective means of drowning prevention.

### Wiring Systems and General Maintenance

The improper use of extension cords can cause shocks, fires, and other electrical hazards, which is another area of potential danger and liability for homeowners. Electrical cords and wiring systems should be inspected on a periodic basis. General maintenance, not only for electrical devices, but for other items and conditions which may be unsafe or dangerous, is helpful to prevent potential liability.

## Additional Resources

A *Glossary of Insurance, Development and Planning Terms.* Davidson, Michael, American Planning Association, 1997.

*The Legal Edge for Homeowners, Buyers, and Renters.* Bryant, Michel J., Renaissance Books, 1999.

## Organizations

### Environmental Health Center
1025 Conn. Ave., NW, Suite 1200
Washington, DC 20036 USA
Phone: (202) 293-2270
URL: http://www.nsc.org/ehc.htm

### National Swimming Pool Foundation
PO Box 495
Merrick, NY 11566 USA
Phone: (516) 623-3447
Fax: (516) 867-2139
URL: http://www.nspf.com/

### National Safety Council
1121 Spring Lake Drive
Itasca, IL 60143 USA
Phone: (630) 285-1121
Fax: (630) 285-1315
URL: http://www.nsc.org/index.htm

### U.S. Fire Administration
16825 S. Seton Ave
Emmitsburg, MD 21727 USA
Phone: (301) 447-1000
URL: http://www.usfa.fema.gov

# REAL ESTATE

## HOUSING DISCRIMINATION

*Sections within this essay:*

- Background
- The Fair Housing Act
- The Civil Rights Act
- Anti-Discrimination Provisions for Sales and Rentals
- Anti-Discrimination Provisions for Mortgage Lending
- Other Provisions
- Disability Issues
    - Unlawful Questions
    - Accessibility Requirements
- Families
- Discrimination Complaints
- Lawful Discrimination
- State and Local Laws
- Additional Resources
- Organizations

## Background

Title VIII of the **Civil Rights** Act of 1968, as amended in 1988, also known as the Fair Housing Act, and the Civil Rights Act of 1866 prohibit **discrimination** in a wide array of real estate practices, including housing sale and rental, provision of homeowner's insurance, and **mortgage** lending.

## The Fair Housing Act

The Fair Housing Act identifies seven classes protected by the law: race, color, national origin, religion, sex, familial status, and **disability**. State and local laws often extend these protected classes to include such characteristics as sexual preference, age, and even student status. The Fair Housing Act is a federal law, which covers most housing in the United States. In some circumstances, the Act exempts owner-occupied buildings with no more than four units, single-family housing sold or rented without the use of a broker, and housing operated by organizations and private clubs that limit **occupancy** to members. For purposes of the Fair Housing Act, sexual discrimination includes **sexual harassment** which is defined as deliberate or repeated unsolicited verbal comments, gestures, or physical contact that creates an offensive environment and sexual favors sought in return for housing. With regard to familial status, families are defined as at least one child under the age of eighteen living with at least one parent or appointed **guardian**. It also includes pregnant women and those in the **adoption** process.

## The Civil Rights Act

The provisions of the Civil Rights Act of 1866 are extremely broad. Section 1981 protects the right of all persons to make and enforce contracts free from racial discrimination. Section 1982 protects the rights of citizens to **inherit**, purchase, **lease**, sell, hold and convey real and **personal property**. The act only covers racial discrimination, however, and section 1982 only protects United States citizens.

## Anti-Discrimination Provisions for Sales and Rentals

No one may take any of the following actions based on race, color, national origin, religion, sex, familial status or disability:

Refuse to rent or sell housing

Refuse to negotiate for housing

Make housing unavailable

Deny a dwelling

Set different terms, conditions or privileges for sale or rental of a dwelling

Provide different housing services or facilities

Falsely deny that housing is available for inspection, sale, or rental

For profit, persuade owners to sell or rent (blockbusting)

Deny anyone access to or membership in a facility or service (such as a multiple listing service) related to the sale or rental of housing

### Anti-Discrimination Provisions for Mortgage Lending

No one may take any of the following actions based on race, color, national origin, religion, sex, familial status or disability

Refuse to make a mortgage loan

Refuse to provide information regarding loans

Impose different terms or conditions on a loan, such as different interest rates, points, or fees

Discriminate in appraising property

Refuse to purchase a loan

Set different terms or conditions for purchasing a loan

### Other Provisions

Additionally, it is illegal for anyone to threaten, coerce, intimidate, or interfere with anyone exercising a fair housing right or assisting others who exercise that right. It is also unlawful to advertise or make any statement that indicates a limitation or preference based on race, color, national origin, religion, sex, familial status, or disability. This prohibition against discriminatory advertising applies to single-family and owner-occupied housing that is otherwise exempt from the Fair Housing Act.

## Disability Issues

Because persons with disabilities face negative stereotypes and prejudice that limit them from housing options along with physical barriers, federal and local governments have amended fair housing laws to include persons with disabilities as a protected class. The broadest protections originate from the Federal Fair Housing Act Amendments of 1988 and Section 504 of the Rehabilitation Act of 1973.

Disability can encompass either a physical or mental disability. Disability can include hearing, mobility and visual impairments, chronic alcoholism, chronic mental illness, AIDS, AIDS Related Complex, and mental retardation, or it can be any other condition that substantially limits one or more major life activities. However, housing need not be made available to a person who is a direct threat to the health or safety of others or who currently uses illegal drugs. If a person either has a disability or is regarded as having a disability, a **landlord** may not refuse to allow the tenant to make reasonable modifications to the dwelling or common use areas at the tenant's expense. The landlord also must make reasonable accommodations in rules, policies, practices, or services if necessary for the disabled person to use the housing. These actions includes the permitting of assistive animals and the designation of disabled parking spaces.

Newly constructed, multi-family housing of four or more units require at least one building entrance to have an accessible route, public and common areas readily accessible to and usable by people with disabilities, and doors sufficiently wide for use by persons in wheelchairs. Accessibility guidelines are issued by HUD to provide technical assistance in meeting the design requirements.

A reasonable modification is a structural or other physical change to the unit or housing structure to provide a person with a disability physical access. A common example is a ramp to a building's entrance. It is the responsibility of the consumer to make an accommodation or modification request. A landlord should not be expected to predict or anticipate a person's needs. Accommodation or modification letters should be in written form to document the request.

According to Fair Housing laws, "reasonable" means that the action requested by the individual with the disability does not cause an undue financial or administrative burden to the housing provider, does not cause a basic change in the nature of the housing programs available, will not cause harm or damage to others, and is technologically possible. An accommodation or modification request will be denied if it is not reasonable according to the above standards.

Under fair housing and civil rights laws, landlords can request verification from a medical professional or professional service provider (such as a social worker) that indicates a tenant requires a reasonable accommodation or modification. For a modification, a landlord may ask to inspect or review site plans and demand that they are completed in a workmanlike or professional manner. Aesthetics is not a defense in denying a modification request. While a modification or accommodation request only requires a minimal disclosure of disability (to identify oneself as protected under the law), disclosure may hasten the request process. However, it is not required.

### Unlawful Questions

It is an illegal inquiry for a landlord, leasing or sales agent to ask a tenant the following questions:

What is your disability?

What is the nature of your disability?

How severe is your disability?

How was your disability acquired?

What medications do you take?

Can you live independently?

Do you have AIDS?

Why do you need this reasonable accommodation or modification?

Are you a fire hazard?

### Accessibility Requirements

In buildings that have an elevator and four or more units, public and common areas must be accessible to persons with disabilities. This means that doors and hallways must be wide enough for wheelchairs. Additionally, all units must have an accessible route into and through the unit, accessible light switches, electrical outlets, thermostats and other environmental controls, reinforced bathroom walls to allow later installation of grab bars, and kitchens and bathrooms that can be used by people in wheelchairs. These requirements are federal minimum standards only and do not replace any more stringent standards in State or local law.

## Families

Unless a building or community qualifies as housing for older persons, it may not discriminate based on familial status. That is, it may not discriminate against families in which one or more children under 18 live with a parent, a person who has legal **custody** of the child or children, or the designee of the parent or legal custodian, with the parent or custodian's written permission. Familial status protection also applies to pregnant women and anyone securing legal custody of a child under 18.

Housing for older persons is exempt from the prohibition against familial status discrimination if the Housing and Urban Development (HUD) Secretary has determined that it is specifically designed for and occupied by elderly persons under a Federal, State or local government program, or it is occupied solely by persons who are 62 or older, or it houses at least one person who is 55 or older in at least 80 percent of the occupied units, and adheres to a policy that demonstrates an intent to house persons who are 55 or older.

## Discrimination Complaints

Individuals with complaints of discrimination can have HUD investigate to determine whether there is reasonable cause to believe the Fair Housing Act has been violated. A one-year **statute of limitations** exists after an alleged violation for filing a complaint with HUD. HUD will notify the alleged violator of the complaint and permit that person or entity to submit an answer. HUD will try to reach an agreement through **conciliation**, but if HUD has reasonable cause to believe that a conciliation agreement is breached, HUD will recommend that the Attorney General file suit.

State and local agencies also exist to enforce fair housing laws. HUD may refer complaints to those agencies for investigation. HUD may also authorize the attorney general to go to court to seek temporary or preliminary relief, pending the outcome of a complaint, if irreparable harm is likely to occur without HUD's intervention. If HUD finds reasonable cause to believe that discrimination occurred, the matter will go to an administrative hearing at which HUD attorneys litigate the case on behalf of the complainant. Alternately, complainants can hire an attorney. An Administrative Law Judge (ALA) will consider the **evidence** and if ALA decides that discrimination occurred, the respondent can be ordered to pay damages, including actual damages, and damages for humiliation, pain and suffering. The respondent may also be order to make the housing available, pay attorney's fees, and pay fines to the Federal Government.

The matter can also proceed to Federal District Court with private **counsel** where the court may order relief, which could include **punitive damages**. The **statute** of limitations in federal court is two years from the date of an alleged violation. The Attorney General may file a suit in a Federal District Court if there is reasonable cause to believe a pattern or practice of housing discrimination is occurring.

## Lawful Discrimination

Only certain kinds of discrimination are covered by fair housing laws. Landlords are not required by law to rent to any tenant who applies for a property. Landlords can select tenants based on objective business criteria, such as the applicant's ability to pay the rent and take care of the property. Landlords can lawfully discriminate against tenants with bad credit histories or low incomes. Landlords must be consistent in the screening, treat all tenants in the same manner, and should document any legitimate business reason for not renting to a prospective tenant.

## State and Local Laws

Along with the federal laws against housing discrimination, a few states and cities jurisdictions provide additional protection under local laws.

CALIFORNIA: Fair Employment and Housing Act, which includes the California Fair Housing Law often called the Rumford Fair Housing Act, is the primary state law banning discrimination in housing accommodations because of race, color, religion, sex, marital status, national origin, ancestry, disability, and familial status. The Civil Rights Act of 1959 provides for the right to be free from discrimination in public accommodations. This Act has been interpreted by the courts to prohibit arbitrary discrimination by business establishments on any basis other than economic status such as level of income.

BERKELEY: Berkeley Municipal Code prohibits discrimination against families with children, discrimination based on sexual orientation, and discrimination based on the fact potential applicants have of having AIDS or associated conditions.

OAKLAND: Oakland **Ordinance** prohibits discrimination against families with children and against persons who have the medical condition known as AIDS or ARC or AIDS related conditions (ARC).

RICHMOND: Richmond Ordinance prohibits discrimination in housing against people with AIDS and related conditions.

SAN FRANCISCO: San Francisco prohibits discrimination on the basis of race, color, creed, religion, national origin, ancestry, age, sex, sexual orientation, gender identity, domestic partner status, marital status, disability or AIDS/HIV status, familial status, source of income, weight and height.

NEW YORK: New York State law adds marital status and age to the list of protected categories. New York City law adds sexual orientation, lawful occupation, and citizenship status.

## Additional Resources

*Fair Housing Compliance Guide* Daniels, Rhonda, Home Builder Press, 1995.

*Fair Housing Litigation Handbook* Zuckerman, Howard, Wiley, John & Sons, Inc.orporated, April 1993.

## Organizations

### U.S. Department of Housing and Urban Development
451 7th Street S.W.
Washington, DC 20410
Phone: (202) 708-1112
URL: http://www.hud.gov/offices/fheo/index.cfm
Primary Contact: Mykl Asanti

### Arizona Center for Disability Law
3839 N. Third Street, Suite 209
Phoenix, AZ 85012
Phone: (602) 274-6287
Fax: (602) 274-6779
URL: http://www.acdl.com

### Cleveland Tenants Organization
2530 Superior Avenue
Cleveland, OH 44115
Phone: (216) 621-0540
URL: http://little.nhlink.net/nhlink/housing/cto/cto.htm
Primary Contact: Mike Foley

**Metropolitan St. Louis Equal Housing Opportunity Council**
1027 South Vandeventer Ave.nue, Fourth Floor
St. Louis, MO 63110
Phone: (314) 534-5800
Fax: (314) 534-2551

**Cleveland Tenants Organization**
2530 Superior Avenue
Cleveland, OH 44115
Phone: (216) 621-0540
URL: http://little.nhlink.net/nhlink/housing/cto/cto.htm
Primary Contact: Mike Foley

**South Bay Fair Housing Project**
2 W. Santa Clara Street, 8th Floor
San Jose, CA 95109

Phone: (408) 283-3700
URL: www.clscal.org

**Arizona Center for Disability Law**
3839 N. Third Street, Suite 209
Phoenix, AZ 85012
Phone: (602) 274-6287
Fax: (602) 274-6779
URL: http://www.acdl.com

**U. S. Department of Housing and Urban Development**
451 7th Street S.W.
Washington, DC 20410
Phone: (202) 708-1112
URL: http://www.hud.gov/offices/fheo/index.cfm
Primary Contact: Mykl Asanti

# REAL ESTATE

## INSURANCE (HOMEOWNER'S AND RENTER'S)

*Sections within this essay:*

## Background

Insurance is a legally binding contract, typically referred to as an insurance policy. The contractual relationship is between the insurance company and the person or entity buying the policy, the policyholder. The policyholder makes payments to the insurance company, which can be monthly, quarterly or yearly. The insurance company agrees to pay for certain types of losses under certain conditions, which are set forth in the policy.

One requirement for insurance is that the policyholder needs to possess an insurable interest in the subject of the insurance. A policyholder either owning or renting property is said to have such an interest in the property. Insurance policies compensate an insured party for the cost of monetary damages in the event of economic loss or in the event of damages leveled against a policyholder who is liable for damages to another. Liability insurance pays damages up to the dollar amount of liability coverage purchased and protects the personal assets of the policyholder in the event of a judgement against the policyholder for damages.

## Types of Insurance

### Homeowner's Insurance

Homeowner's insurance includes both property and liability coverage, many of which cover activities away from and not in any way connected with a policyholder's residence. Homeowner's insurance covers repair or rebuilding of a house which is damaged by natural causes such as fire, fallen trees, or heavy winds. It also covers acts of theft and **vandalism**. This type of policy also typically pays for replacement of the personal items inside a residence if those items are damaged by the same causes that damage the house or if such items are stolen.

Homeowner's policies also cover legal liability in the event that anyone suffers an injury while on the insured property. Certain actions of the policyholder, which occur away from the insured property may also be covered. Even if a house is under construction and has no contents to be protected, the homeowner can insure the structure against damages for fire and liability.

### Title Insurance

**Title insurance** provides coverage to a homeowner if it is discovered in the future that there was a defect in the title and the homeowner did not get clear title to the property. Coverage is provided if a dispute arises that was not discovered during the **title search**. The title insurance will pay attorney fees, as well as all other costs in defending the title. The lender will usually require title insurance until the loan is paid in full.

### Mortgage Insurance

**Mortgage** insurance is only for the benefit of the lender. It protects the lender against the risk of non-payment by the buyer. It is generally required by a lender to protect it against **default** by a borrower who makes a low **down payment**. If the borrower defaults, the mortgage insurer pays the lender its money and then seeks to recover from the borrower or forecloses on the property.

### Mortgage Life Insurance

Mortgage life insurance is not the same as mortgage insurance. It is simply a life insurance policy that pays off the mortgage balance if the policyholder dies.

### Renter's Insurance

Although renting a property is not subject to the same liability as owning a property, renters can still benefit from property insurance. Renter's insurance typically covers the cost of replacing personal items that are stolen, damaged, or destroyed. Additionally, renters, like owners, have potential liability to anyone injured on the occupied property. Renter's insurance policies are similar to homeowners' insurance policies but have no coverage for buildings or structures. Although renter's insurance is not usually required by the terms of some leases, tenants may be required to have insurance to cover their liability exposure if someone is injured on the premises, or if damages occur from items owned by the renter, such as waterbeds.

## Insurance Coverage

### Exclusions and Limitations

Limitations and exclusions can alter the provisions of coverage in a policy. A limitation is an exception to the general scope of coverage, applicable only under certain circumstances or for a specified period of time. An exclusion is a broader exception which often rules out coverage for such things as intentional acts, when the policy covers damages due to negligent acts.

### Rates and Applications

State insurance laws dictate the manner in which insurance companies may conduct marketing, underwriting (determining which policyholders or risks to accept or reject for coverage), and rate activities. Insurance underwriting decisions must be based on reasons that are related in some way to the risk to be insured. Some states have laws limiting an insurance company's ability to cancel or discontinue coverage once a policy has been issued. In all states, it is illegal to refuse insurance on the basis of race, color, sex, religion, national origin or ancestry. In many states this list is expanded to include marital status, age, occupation, language, sexual orientation, physical or mental impairment, or the geographic area a person resides. An individual has a **legal right** to be promptly informed of the reasons for a refusal to issue an insurance policy.

Insurance companies determine the premium, or payment to charge, based on numerous circumstances known as rating factors. These rating factors must be reasonably related to the risk being insured. The rates and rating factors for insurance must be filed with the state insurance regulatory agency for each state where the insurance is to be sold. In certain states, the rates must get regulatory approval before they can be used.

### Cancellations

Generally, once a policy is issued, it can be cancelled only for failure to make premium payments or for misrepresentation or **fraud** by the policyholder. State laws typically limit items an insurance company can include in the cancellation provisions of its policies. Most property and liability policies are issued for a stated policy term. The limitation on cancellation applies only during the policy term. Insurance companies can decide to discontinue or not renew these policies at the end of the term for any reason except a reason that would be prohibited by law. In most states, an insurance company is required to provide the policyholder with written notice if it intends not to renew a renter's or homeowner's policy.

A policyholder may cancel an insurance policy at any time by giving notice to the insurance company. Some clauses include financial penalties for early cancellation by the policyholder. Most property and liability policies require what is known as a short rate **penalty** when a policyholder requests cancellation, which gives the insurance company the ability to retain a larger, disproportionate amount of the premium.

A cancellation notice usually must be sent to the policyholder several days prior to the effective date of cancellation. State law usually requires at least 10 days advance written notice, with a reinstatement period. Once the time period has expired, reinstatement after termination of coverage is discretionary by the insurance company.

## Payment of Claims

Insurance companies and policyholders have contractual obligations which must be satisfied to ensure resolution of claims. Insurance policies list specific things a policyholder must do in order to perfect a claim once a loss has taken place. These duties are known as contract conditions. Policies typically require an insured to give prompt notice of any loss, information about what property was damaged or the time and place of an accident or injury. In the case of property damage, the policyholder will be required to take steps to protect the property from further destruction. In the event of theft, policies usually require a police report. Liability claims require the policyholder to give the insurance company copies of any notices or legal papers received.

The insurance company may deny or refuse to pay a claim. The insurance company may take the position that the loss is not covered by the policy or that the claimant was not insured under the policy. In some cases, the insurance company may conclude that the policyholder took some type of action that rendered the policy void. Because insurance policies are contracts which are open to interpretation by the courts, policyholders may be able to use the legal system to reverse such decisions.

### Good Faith Payment of Claims

All insurance policies are contracts and all contracts contain an implied obligation of **good faith** and fair dealing. When a claim is presented, this implied obligation means that an insurance company must make a thorough, good faith investigation of the claim. This investigation includes an obligation for the insurance company to review potential reasons and circumstances that could justify the claim.

If an insurance company breaches this implied covenant of good faith and fair dealing and refuses to pay a claim that it legally should be pay or denies a claim without adequate investigation, the policyholder may have a **bad faith** claim against the company. If the company is found to have acted in bad faith in its handling of a claim, the policyholder

would be entitled to damages. If the conduct by the insurance company is outrageous and totally unconscionable, the insured also may be entitled to recover **punitive damages**.

## Insurance Regulation

No federal regulatory agency exists to monitor insurance companies and so companies selling insurance are regulated by individual state agencies. These state regulatory groups are designed to assure that insurance companies operating in the state have the financial ability to pay claims. The state regulatory agency is typically empowered to take various actions against an insurance company that fails to conduct its business in a financially sound manner, including actions to prohibit the company from doing business in the state.

Most states have laws regarding the conduct of insurance business to ensure lawfulness and fairness to applicants for insurance and policyholders. State agencies can investigate complaints by consumers and **sanction** companies with unfair practices. State agencies also review policy forms used by insurance companies and rates charged for various types of insurance for compliance with state law.

Unlike car insurance, there is no law that requires a homeowner to have insurance. However, banks and lending institutions usually require that a borrower carry such insurance to protect the interest of the lender until the loan is repaid. A mortgage or **deed of trust** typically requires enough insurance to cover the repair or rebuilding of the house in the event it is destroyed. Mortgages can be structured so that the lending company pays the insurance directly, and the cost is taken out of the homeowner's monthly mortgage payment.

## Additional Resources

*A Glossary of Insurance, Development and Planning Terms* Davidson, Michael, American Planning Association,1997.

*The Legal Edge for Homeowners, Buyers, and Renters* Bryant, Michel J., Renaissance Books, 1999.

## Organizations

### The American Homeowners Resource Center
P.O. Box 97
San Juan Capistrano, CA 92693

Phone: (949) 366-2125
Fax: ()
URL: www.ahrc.com

**Alabama Department of Insurance**
201 Monroe Street, Suite 1700, PO Box 303351
Montgomery, AL 36104
Phone: (334) 269-3550
Fax: (334) 241-4192
URL: www.aldoi.org

**Alaska Department of Community and Economic Development**
3601 C Street, Suite 1324
Anchorage, AK 99503
Phone: (907) 269-7900
Fax: (907) 269-7910
URL: www.dced.sta te.ak.us/insurance

**Alaska Department of Community and Economic Development**
P.O. Box 110805
Juneau, AK 99811
Phone: (907) 465-2515
Fax: (907) 465-3422
URL: www.commer ce.state.ak.us

**Arizona Department of Insurance**
2910 North 44th Street, Suite 210
Phoenix, AZ 85018
Phone: (602) 912-8444
Fax: (602) 954-7008
URL: www.state.az. us/id

**Arkansas Department of Insurance**
1200 West 3rd Street
Little Rock, AR 72201
Phone: (501) 371-2640
Fax: (501) 371-2749
URL: www.state.ar. us/insurance

**California Department of Insurance**
300 Capitol Mall, Suite 1500
Sacramento, CA 95814
Phone: (916) 492-3500
Fax: (415) 538-4010
URL: www.insuranc e.ca.gov

**Colorado Division of Insurance**
1560 Broadway, Suite 850
Denver, CO 80202
Phone: (303) 894-7499, ext. 4311
Fax: (303) 894-7455
URL: www.dora.state.co.us/Insurance

**Connecticut Department of Insurance**
P.O. Box 816

Hartford, CT 06142
Phone: (860) 297-3984
URL: www.state.ct.us/cid

**Delaware Department of Insurance**
841 Silver Lake Blvd., Rodney Building
Dover, DE 19904
Phone: (302) 739-4251
Fax: (302) 739-5280
URL: www.state.de. us/inscom

**District of Columbia Department of Insurance and Securities Regulation**
810 First Street, NW, Suite 701
Washington, DC 20002
Phone: (202) 727-8000
Fax: (202) 535-1196

**Florida Department of Insurance**
Plaza Level Eleven
Tallahassee, FL 32399
Phone: (850) 922-3130
URL: www.doi.state.fl.us

**Georgia Insurance and Fire Safety**
Two Martin Luther King, Jr. Drive
Atlanta, GA 30334
Phone: (404) 656-2070
Fax: (404) 651-8719
URL: www.inscomm.state.ga.us

**State of Hawaii, Department of Commerce and Consumer Affairs**
250 South King Street, 5th Floor
Honolulu, HI 96813
Phone: (808) 586-2790
Fax: (808) 586-2806
URL: www.hawaii.g ov/insurance

**State of Idaho Department of Insurance**
700 West State Street, P.O. Box 83720
Boise, ID 83720
Phone: (208) 334-4250
Fax: (208) 334-4398
URL: www.doi.state.id.us

**Illinois Department of Insurance**
100 West Randolph Street, Suite 15-100
Chicago, IL 60601
Phone: (312) 814-2420
Fax: (312) 814-5435
URL: www.state.il.u s/ins

**Illinois Department of Insurance**
320 West Washington Street
Springfield, IL 62767
Phone: (217) 782-4515

---

Fax: (217) 782-5020
URL: www.state.il.u s/ins/

**Indiana Department of Insurance**
311 W. Washington St., Ste 300
Indianapolis, IN 46204
Phone: (317) 232-2385
Fax: (317) 232-5251
URL: www.state.in.u s/idoi/

**State of Iowa Division of Insurance**
330 Maple Street
Des Moines, IA 50319
Phone: (515) 281-5705
Fax: (515) 281-3059
URL: www.state.ia.u s/government/com/ins/ins.htm

**Kansas Insurance Division**
420 SW 9th Street
Topeka, KS 66612
Phone: (785) 296-7801
Fax: (785) 296-2283
URL: www.ink.org/ public/kid

**Kentucky Department of Insurance**
215 West Main Street
Frankfort, KY 40601
Phone: (502) 564-3630
Fax: (502) 564-1650
URL: htt p://www.doi.state.ky.us/

**Louisiana Department of Insurance**
950 North Fifth Street
Baton Rouge, LA 70804
Phone: (225) 343-4834
Fax: (254) 342-5900
URL: www.ldi.state.l a.us

**Maine Bureau of Insurance**
34 State House Station
Augusta, ME 04333
Phone: (207) 624-8475
Fax: (207) 624-8599
URL: www.maineins urancereg.org

**Maryland Insurance Administration**
525 St. Paul Place
Baltimore, MD 21202
Phone: (410) 468-2000
Fax: (410) 468-2020
URL: www.mia.state.md.us

**Massachusetts Division of Insurance**
South Station, 5th Floor
Boston, MA 02110
Phone: (617) 521-7794
Fax: (617) 521-7772

URL: www.state.ma.us/doi

**Michigan Office of Financial and Insurance Services**
611 West Ottawa Street, 2nd Floor North, P.O. Box 30220
Lansing, MI 48933
Phone: (517) 373-0220
Fax: (517) 335-4978
URL: www.cis.state. mi.us/ofis

**Minnesota Department of Commerce**
133 East 7th Street
St. Paul, MN 55101
Phone: (651) 296-2488
Fax: (651) 296-4328
URL: www.commer ce.state.mn.us

**Mississippi Department of Insurance**
P.O. Box 79
Jackson, MS 39205
Phone: (601) 359-3569
Fax: (601) 359-2474
URL: www.doi.state.ms.us

**Missouri Department of Insurance**
301 West High Street, Room 630
Jefferson City, MO 65102
Phone: (573) 751-4126
Fax: (573) 751-1165
URL: www.insuranc e.state.mo.us

**Montana Department of Insurance**
840 Helena Avenue, P.O. Box 4009
Helena, MT 59601
Phone: (406) 444-2040
Fax: (406) 444-3497
URL: www.state.mt. us/sao

**Nebraska Department of Insurance**
941 O Street, Suite 400
Lincoln, NE 68508
Phone: (402) 471-2201
Fax: (402) 471-4610
URL: www.nol.org/h ome/NDOI

**Nevada Division of Insurance**
1665 Hot Springs Road, #152
Carson City, NV 89706
Phone: (775) 687-7690
Fax: (775) 687-3937
URL: www.doi.state.nv.us

**New Hampshire Department of Insurance**
56 Old Suncook Road
Concord, NH 03301
Phone: (603) 271-2261

Fax: (603) 271-1406
URL: www.state.nh. us/insurance

**New Jersey Department of Banking and Insurance**
20 West State Street
Trenton, NJ 08625
Phone: (609) 633-7667
Fax: (609) 984-5273
URL: htt p://states.nai c.org/nj/NJHOMEPG.HTML

**New Mexico Department of Insurance**
P.O. Box 1269
Santa Fe, NM 87504
Phone: (505) 827-4601
Fax: (505) 827-4734
URL: www.nmprc.st ate.nm.us

**New York State Insurance Department**
Agency Bldg. 1-ESP, Empire State Plaza
, NY 12257
Phone: (518) 474-6600
Fax: (518) 474-6630
URL: www.ins.state. ny.us

**Consumer Services Bureau NYS Insurance Department**
65 Court Street #7
Buffalo, NY 14202
Phone: (716) 847-7618
Fax: (716) 847-7925
URL: www.ins.state. ny.us

**North Carolina Department of Insurance**
430 North Salisbury Street
Raleigh, NC 27611
Phone: (919) 733-7349
Fax: (919) 733-6495
URL: www.ncdoi.ne t

**North Dakota Insurance Department**
600 East Blvd. Avenue, 5th Floor
Bismarck, ND 58505
Phone: (701) 328-2440
Fax: (701) 328-4880
URL: www.state.nd. us/ndins

**Ohio Department of Insurance**
2100 Stella Court
Columbus, OH 43215
Phone: (614) 644-3378
Fax: (614) 752-0740
URL: www.state.oh. us/

**Oklahoma Insurance Department**
3814 North Santa Fe
Oklahoma City, OK 73118

Phone: (405) 521-2828
Fax: (405) 521-6652
URL: www.oid.state.ok.us

**Oregon Insurance Division**
350 Winter Street, NE, Room 440-2
Salem, OR 97310
Phone: (503) 947-7984
Fax: (503) 378-4351
URL: www.cbs.state.or.us/ins

**Pennsylvania Insurance Department**
1321 Strawberry Square, 13th Floor
Harrisburg, PA 17120
Phone: (717) 787-2317
URL: www.insurance.state.pa.us

**Rhode Island Insurance Division**
233 Richmond Street, Suite 233
Providence, RI 02903
Phone: (401) 222-2223
Fax: (401) 222-5475

**South Carolina Department of Insurance**
1612 Marion Street
Columbia, SC 29201
Phone: (803) 737-6180
Fax: (803) 737-6231
URL: www.state.sc. us/doi/

**South Dakota Division of Insurance**
118 West Capitol
Pierre, SD 57501
Phone: (605) 773-3563
Fax: (605) 773-5369
URL: www.state.sd. us/insurance

**Tennessee Department of Commerce and Insurance**
500 James Robertson Parkway, 5th Floor
Nashville, TN 37243
Phone: (615) 741-2241
Fax: (615) 532-6934
URL: www.state.tn. us/commerce

**Texas Department of Insurance**
333 Guadalupe Street
Austin, TX 78701
Phone: (512) 463-6169
Fax: (512) 475-2005
URL: www.tdi.state. tx.us

**Utah Department of Insurance**
State Office Building Rm 3110
Salt Lake City, UT 84114
Phone: (801) 538-3805
Fax: (801) 538-3829

URL: www.insurance.state.ut.us

**Vermont Department of Banking, Insurance, Securities and Health Care Administration**
89 Main Street, Drawer 20
Montpelier, VT 05620
Phone: (802) 828-3302
Fax: (802) 828-3301
URL: www.state.vt.us/bis

**Virginia Bureau of Insurance**
P.O. Box 1157
Richmond, VT 23218
Phone: (804) 371-9967
URL: www.state.va.us/scc

**Washington Office of the Commissioner of Insurance**
14th Avenue and Water Street
Olympia, WA 98504
Phone: (360) 753-3613
Fax: (360) 586-3535
URL: www.insuranc e.wa.gov

**West Virginia Department of Insurance**
1124 Smith St.
Charleston, WV 25301
Phone: (304) 558-3354
Fax: (304) 558-0412
URL: www.state.wv.us/insurance

**Wisconsin Office of the Commissioner of Insurance**
121 East Wilson Street, P.O. Box 7873
Madison, WI 53707
Phone: (608) 266-0103
Fax: (608) 266-9935
URL: bad ger.state.w i.us/agencies/oci

**Wyoming Department of Insurance**
122 West 25th Street, 3rd Floor East
Cheyenne, WY 82002
Phone: (307) 777-7401
Fax: (307) 777-5895
URL: www.state.wy.us/~insurance/

# REAL ESTATE

## LANDLORD/TENANT RIGHTS

*Sections within this essay:*

- Background

- Leases and Rental Agreements

- Parties to a Lease
  - Landlord
  - Tenant
  - Roommates

- Standard Lease Provisions
  - Unenforcable Clauses

- Landlord Obligations

- Tenant Obligations

- Security Deposits

- Eviction and Unlawful Detainer

- Defenses to Eviction Proceedings
  - Improper Notice
  - Acceptance of Partial Rent
  - Failure of the Landlord to Maintain the Premises
  - Retaliatory Eviction
  - Constructive Eviction
  - Fair Housing

- State and Local Laws

## Background

Landlord–tenant law governs the rental of property. The basis of the legal relationship between a **landlord and tenant** is derived from both contract and property law. The tenant has a temporary possessory interest in the premises. The rental premises may be land, a house, a building, or an apartment. The length of the **tenancy** may be for a specific period of time, for an indefinite but renewable period of time (this would include a month–to–month tenancy). During the term of the tenancy, the tenant has the right to possess the premises, and to restrict the access of others. A landlord–tenant contract may alter and define rights allowed under law. Landlord–tenant contracts are typically known as rental agreements or leases. What provisions may be contained in a **lease** is normally regulated by state law. Standard in all leases is the implied covenant of quiet enjoyment which gives the tenant the right to possess the rental premises without interference from or disturbance by others, including the **landlord**. Another standard lease provision for residential rental units is the **warranty** of **habitability**. If the landlord causes the rental to become uninhabitable or fails to make repairs so that the premises are uninhabitable, a constructive **eviction** may occur. This may allow the tenant to withhold rent, repair the problem and deduct the cost from the rent, or recover damages. Federal law prohibits **discrimination** in housing and the rental market. Landlords are also typically restricted by state laws from evicting tenants in retaliation of action the tenant may have taken to enforce a provision of the lease, a housing code compliance, or other applicable law.

## Leases and Rental Agreements

A lease or rental agreement is a contract between a landlord and a tenant which gives the tenant the right to use and occupy rental property for a certain period of time. When a tenant turns over the right or the partial right to use and occupy rental property to a roommate or subtenant, that agreement is sometimes referred to as a sublease. A lease can be a verbal agreement or a written agreement. At the end of the lease, use and possession of rental property must be returned to the landlord. A lease requires the tenant to pay a specified amount of money each month in return for the use and enjoyment of the premises. This payment is called rent.

## Parties to a Lease

### Landlord

A landlord is the owner the rental property or the agent of the owner of rental property. Often real estate management companies will act as landlords for private or **corporate** entities. The landlord allows a tenant to use and occupy the rental property in exchange for payment of rent.

### Tenant

A tenant is the person or entity that has the right to occupy rental property in accordance with a rental agreement or lease. In addition to provisions set out in the lease, state law typically outlines tenant rights with its own Landlord and Tenant law.

### Roommates

If roommates are listed on the lease, each roommate is considered a tenant and each one will be individually fully responsible for the total amount of the rent due to the landlord, unless the lease specifically states otherwise. If only one roommate is listed on the lease and the others have not signed the lease, only the roommate listed is considered the tenant. The others are considered subtenants. Only roommates who sign the lease are responsible for the full amount of the rent to the landlord. The roommates who signed may have some separate claims against their non-signing, non-paying roommates, but such claims would typically be covered by contract law rather than landlord tenant law.

## Standard Lease Provisions

Most lease have standard provisions which set forth landlord and tenant rights and obligations. Such provisions include:

1. The names of the parties
2. A description of the rental property
3. The term, or length, of the lease
4. The amount of rent
5. The due date of the rent
6. The amount of the security deposit
7. Whether the tenant is subject to late fees
8. Maintenance responsibilities
9. Options to renew
10. Termination notice requirements
11. When the landlord may enter the rental property
12. Rules concerning pets

While leases or rental agreements do not have to be in writing to be valid, the terms of the agreement will be easier to enforce and the responsibilities of the parties will be clearer if the rental agreement is in writing.

### Unenforceable clauses

Some clauses that appear in a written lease or rental agreement are, by the nature of the clause, unenforceable. These include agreements that the landlord can repossess property if the tenant falls behind in the rent, agreements allowing the landlord to enter the rental unit any time, without notice, agreements that tenants will pay for all damages to the rental unit without regard to fault, and agreements that court action entitles the landlord to more money than can be order by the court.

## Landlord Obligations

Landlords have the responsibility to maintain residential rental property and repair any defects. Under most state law, there is an **implied warranty** of habitability, which is defined as the minimum standard for decent, safe, sanitary housing suitable for human habitation. This warranty applies throughout the lease. Most jurisdictions that ordinances or laws that require owners of real property to maintain the property and make any necessary repairs. These codes typically require that any rental property offered by a landlord must meet the minimum standards established in the codes. The landlord's obligation is to deliver the rental property to the tenant in compliance with the housing codes and to maintain compliance with the housing codes throughout the time the tenant has possession of the rental property.

## Tenant Obligations

The responsibilities of tenants are typically spelled out in the lease; however, basic responsibilities include timely payment of rent, reasonable use and care of the premises, and a duty not to disturb or disrupt surrounding neighbors with excessive noise.

## Security Deposits

A security deposit is an amount of money given by the tenant to the landlord to ensure that reimbursement is available for any damage done to the premises by the tenant. Some leases require additional deposits for pets or waterbeds. State laws require the return of the security deposit within a certain period of time. If the entire security deposit is not returned, the landlord should provide the tenant with a written explanation regarding any deductions made from the security deposit. Some states have laws with steep financial penalties for landlords that fail to return the security deposit within the amount of time allowed by law. A security deposit typically cannot be credited toward the payment of the final month's rent. Some state laws require the landlord to keep the security deposit in a separate interest bearing account.

## Eviction and Unlawful Detainer

Eviction is a legal process by which a landlord may terminate a tenant's right to remain on the rental property. Ultimately, the tenant may be forcibly removed from the property by the sheriff or other law enforcement official; however, doing so requires a formal court order. A tenant can be evicted for numerous reasons, but typically evictions take place where the tenant is in violation of one or more provisions of the lease agreement. Valid reasons for eviction may include:

1. Failure to pay rent on time

2. Harboring pets or persons not authorized to reside at the premises under the lease

3. Illegal or criminal activity taking place within the rental premises

A landlord cannot forcibly evict a tenant without proper notice. The landlord must provide written notice to the tenant of the **default**. If the tenant does not fix the default within a reasonable amount of time, the landlord must file for a formal court eviction proceeding. Courts commonly refer to eviction actions as "forcible entry and detainer" or "unlawful detainer" actions. The legal theory is that the landlord alleges the tenant unlawfully continues to detain

or have use and possession of the rental property, and the landlord seeks the assistance of the court to have the tenant removed. The first step is for the landlord to file a complaint or petition with the local court and pay a small filing fee. The tenant must be served with the court documents. An **unlawful detainer** action is typically a proceeding which, unlike many civil trials, can move quickly through a court system; however, in some jurisdictions, tenants are entitled upon request to a jury trial in which the jury determines whether the tenant should be evicted.

In most jurisdictions, once the landlord has filed the required paperwork, a court **hearing** on the unlawful **detainer** will be set. In some jurisdictions, the tenant is required to file a written notice or answer. In those jurisdictions, if the answer is not filed, the landlord will prevail without a hearing ever being set. In jurisdictions that do require a hearing, if the tenant does not attend the scheduled court hearing, the landlord will prevail. If the tenant does attend, the court will determine whether the tenant should be evicted and will take into account any defenses the tenant may have. The landlord may be given a monetary judgment for the amount of money owed for rent, attorney fees and costs, and may be granted a **writ** for possession of the premises. A writ will typically issue a few days after the judgement, allowing the tenant the opportunity to move voluntarily. Once the writ is issued, it may be executed by local law enforcement officials (never the landlord directly) so that the tenant is removed from the rental property and then the landlord is given possession.

## Defenses to Eviction Proceedings

### Improper Notice

Each state has its own requirements for the notice of eviction and the method the tenant receives the notice. If the landlord did not provide sufficient notice prior to filing a court action or did not correctly deliver or serve the notice to the tenant, the tenant may have a defense to the eviction, even if the tenant has not paid the required rent. If this argument is successful, the landlord will usually be forced to redo the procedure from the beginning.

### Acceptance of Partial Rent

If the landlord accepts partial rent from the tenant, knowing that the tenant is in noncompliance with the lease agreement, either because of nonpayment of rent or due to some other reason, the right to evict the tenant during that rent period is usually waived. The landlord could have the tenant sign a paper indicating that partial acceptance on the part of the landlord waives any rights the tenant would otherwise have to claim partial payment. Such waivers are valid in many jurisdictions.

### Failure of the Landlord to Maintain the Premises

A tenant seeking to use this theory as a defense to eviction should provide written notice to the landlord that there is a defect in the property. The notice to the landlord typically must provide the landlord with a reasonable amount of time to accomplish the repairs. If the landlord is nonresponsive, the tenant may then hire and pay for a professional to make the necessary repairs, then deduct the cost of the repairs from the rent paid to the landlord. Some states restrict this repair and deduct tactic and provide that the cost of the repair must not be more than one month's rent.

### Retaliatory Eviction

This type of eviction happens when the landlord takes an action against a tenant for acting as an tenant activist. If the landlord seeks to evict the tenant for informing government agencies of code violations or requesting that the landlord make repairs and maintain the rental property in fit and habitable condition, a retaliatory eviction claim may be a valid defense to an eviction action.

### Constructive Eviction

Constructive eviction occurs when residential rental property is in an uninhabitable condition. When rental property is uninhabitable, it is said to create circumstances under which the tenant has been deprived of the full use and possession of the rental property and has therefore been "evicted." The theory of constructive eviction is that since the tenant did not received what was contracted for, the tenant is not obligated to continue paying rent to the landlord. In order for such a claim to be effective, the tenant should give the landlord written notice of reasons for the constructive eviction and provide the landlord with a reasonable amount of time to correct the problems. If the landlord does not fix the problems within a reasonable amount of time, the tenant may leave the rental property and not be responsible for payment of rent which would have otherwise been due.

### Fair Housing

In 1968 the federal government passed the Fair Housing Act which has since been modified and adopted by states and various localities. The Fair Housing Act as amended prohibits discrimination in housing and related transactions on the basis of race, color, national origin, sex, religion, **disability**, and familial status (the presence or anticipated presence of children under 18 in a home). The Act covers discrimination in all types of housing-related transactions, including rentals and leases.

## State and Local Laws

Most states and some jurisdictions have Landlord Tenant Acts specific to the area. These laws vary significantly and state laws will govern the provisions of any lease.

ALASKA: Except for units renting for more than $2,000 per month, security deposits and prepaid rents may not total more than two months' rent. Security deposits and prepaid rent must be deposited by the landlord or the property manager in a trust account in a bank or **savings and loan association** or with a licensed **escrow** agent. Exceptions can be made in rural Alaska, if there is no bank in town, and it would be impractical to bank the money. A trust account can be any separate savings or checking account labeled "trust account" and used only for deposits and prepaid rents. There is no requirement that the trust account earn interest. However, if the rental property is managed by a property manager, the interest in the trust account belongs to the tenant, under the terms of the real estate license law, unless the tenant agrees in writing that the interest is payable to the property owner. A seven-day written notice is required to terminate a tenancy for nonpayment of rent. The tenant can cure by paying the rent within seven days. The notice must tell tenants that they have the choice of paying or moving.

ARIZONA: Security deposits cannot exceed one and a half times the monthly rent. To bring an eviction action, the landlord must first serve a five-day notice to vacate the premises in person, by certified mail, or at the premises. If notice is sent by certified or registered mail, the tenant is assumed to have received the notice on the date the tenant signs for it or five calendar days after it was mailed, which ever occurs first. State law mandates that the trial be held no sooner than three and no later than six business days after the complaint was filed. If the complaint is for non-payment of rent and the landlord accepts payment of all rent due and reasonable late fees identified in the written agreement, attorney fees and court costs, the rental agreement is reinstated and the case will be automatically be dismissed. An eviction order is issued no earlier than the sixth calendar day after judgment if the tenant has not moved out of the rental unit. The order instructs the sheriff or constable to evict the tenant. Lockouts and utility shutoffs by the landlord prior to 24 hours after the issuance of a writ are unlawful. Unlawful lockouts and utility shutoffs may entitle the tenant two months' free rent. Security deposits must be returned within 14 business days from the time the tenant vacates the premises.

ARKANSAS: Tenants have few rights under Arkansas law. Rental units can lawfully be rented in "as is" condition. The landlord does not have to provide additional maintenance to the dwelling. Security deposits cannot be in excess of two months rent. Security deposits must be returned within 30 days. A landlord may withhold the entire amount of the security deposit for damages or unpaid rent. There are two types of eviction procedures: "unlawful detainer" (a civil eviction) and "failure to vacate" (a criminal eviction). "Unlawful detainer" requires three days written notice to vacate after which the landlord can file a complaint. If the tenant does not object in writing to the eviction within five days, the sheriff can removed the tenant from the rental property. "Failure to vacate" method of eviction, requires ten days written notice. This method of eviction applies only to non-payment of rent. Tenants who do not leave the premises within ten days can be charged with a criminal **misdemeanor** and could be fined $25 a day for each day the tenant remains on the rental property. A landlord is not permitted to change the locks, move furniture out, turn off utilities or use any other "self-help" method of eviction; however, all property left in the dwelling by the tenant will be considered abandoned and may be disposed of by the landlord as the landlord sees fit and without recourse by the tenant. All property left on the premises by the tenant is subjected to a **lien** in favor of the landlord for the payment of all sums agreed to be paid by the tenant.

CALIFORNIA: The landlord must pay five percent interest on all security deposits and deposits must be returned to the tenant within 21 days after the tenant vacates the rental property. State law requires a 60 day notice for any rent increases which, alone or cumulatively, raise a tenant's rent by more than 10 percent within a 12 month period. This law covers both rent controlled and non-rent controlled units. Lockouts are illegal, and the landlord can be liable for $100 a day in penalties on an illegal lockout. There is a three day notice requirement. Tenants must an-

swer a complaint for forcible detainer within five days or lose the right to trial.

SAN FRANCISCO: Under the San Francisco Housing Code, landlords must provide heat capable of maintaining a room temperature of 68 degrees (at a point three feet above the floor). This level of heat must be provided for at least thirteen hours, specifically from 5:00 AM to 11:00 AM and 3:00 PM to 10:00 PM.

COLORADO: There is a three day requirement on non-payment of rent notices. Colorado law provides that in certain situations a landlord may have a lien on a tenant's **personal property** for rent the tenant owes the landlord. In certain circumstances, the landlord may enter the tenant's residence at a reasonable time and in a peaceable manner to take possession of the property covered by the lien. Under this law, a landlord can take only certain property of the tenant to pay back rent. A landlord cannot take personal items, cooking utensils, bedding, beds, or clothes; however, the landlord can take such items as stereos, computers, and televisions. If the landlord takes a tenant's property and the tenant doesn't pay money owed to the landlord within 30 days, then the landlord must file a **foreclosure** action in court. After a complex legal procedure set forth in Colorado law, the landlord may sell the tenant's property to recover the money owed by the tenant. If the landlord sells or otherwise disposes of the tenant's property without properly complying with Colorado law, the tenant is entitled to bring a court action to recover the value of the property or $100 (whichever is greater) and reasonable attorney's fees. The landlord may be liable to the tenant for actual and **punitive damages** if the landlord wrongfully takes the tenant's property. Lockouts by landlords are illegal, but a tenant who is unlawfully locked out could still be arrested for disturbing the peace if an argument with the landlord erupts in the process of re-entry.

CONNECTICUT: By law the temperature of the rental unit must stay above 65 degrees in the winter. The landlord must also keep the rental unit free of rat and roach infestations. No peeling paint or broken windows are allowed. Security deposits must be returned within 30 days from date of move-out. Security deposits must be kept in an escrow account in a Connecticut bank. Security deposit cannot exceed two months rent. This limit is reduced to one month's rent if a tenant is 62 years of age or older.

DELAWARE: Rental agreements for period longer than one year must be in writing. The security deposit may not be more than one month's rent if the rental agreement is for one year or more. A security deposit must be held in a federally insured bank with an office within the State of Delaware. The account must be called a security deposit account and cannot be used in the operation of the business of the landlord. The landlord must disclose to the tenant the location of the security deposit account within 20 days of the receipt of a written request for that information, or the landlord forfeits the security deposit. A landlord may not charge any non-refundable fee as a condition for the tenant living in the rented unit, unless that fee is an optional service fee for actual services rendered to the tenant. Delaware has special provisions whereby a tenant may terminate a rental agreement early by giving the landlord 30 days written notice. These provisions include job transfer in excess of 30 miles, serious illness, admission into a senior citizens facility or retirement home, admission into a subsidized rental unit, military service, and death.

FLORIDA: A landlord may not prohibit waterbeds, unless the local building code bans them. However, renters with waterbeds must carry a "reasonable amount" of liability insurance on the bed payable to the building owner. **Deduction** notices regarding security deposits must be sent to the tenant within 15 days of move-out; otherwise the landlord loses the right to take any deductions at all. If the landlord has the security deposit in an interest-bearing account, the landlord must pay the tenant either 5% interest or 75% of the account's interest rate.

GEORGIA: Georgia law requires that before the tenant pays a security deposit and moves into the rental unit the landlord must give the tenant a complete list of all existing damages. Georgia law does not require the landlord to place the security deposit in an interest bearing account nor does the law require that any interest that is earned be paid to the tenant. The landlord has 30 days to return the security deposit after the tenant terminates the lease.

HAWAII To bring an eviction action, the landlord must first serve a five day notice to vacate the premises. This notice can be posted on the rental premises

IDAHO: Idaho law says nothing as to whether the landlord has the right to enter the premises. If the rental agreement does not address the landlord's right to enter the premises, the landlord should notify the tenant as to the necessity of entry, requesting permission to enter in a reasonable manner. Security

deposits should be returned within 21 days but in no case later than 30 after the tenant vacates. If a tenant fails to pay rent or violates any term of the rental agreement, the landlord must give the tenant written notice of the violation and provide three days in which the tenant can remedy the problem. The notice informing the tenant of the violation must be delivered to the tenant personally, or a copy of the notice may be left with some person of suitable age and discretion at either the tenant's residence or place of business. If this form of communication proves impossible, the landlord may post the notice in a conspicuous place on the property and a copy must be mailed to the tenant at the address where the property is situated. If a landlord pursues formal **legal proceedings** for the purpose of evicting a tenant due to nonpayment of rent, the trial must be held within 12 days from the time the lawsuit is filed in court.

ILLINOIS: The Illinois Retaliatory Eviction Act prohibits landlords from evicting tenants for complaining to any governmental authority. There is no limit on the amount of security deposit a landlord can require; however, the landlord must pay the tenant interest on the security deposit if it is held for at least six months and there are at least 25 rental units in the complex. The landlord must pay the interest to the tenant or apply the interest as a credit to rent every 12 months. Security deposits must be returned within 45 days of tenant move out. Any security deposit wrongfully withheld by the landlord is subject to double damages. Leases running year-to-year require a 60-day written notice. Evictions require a 10 day notice. Lockouts and utility shutoffs are prohibited.

KANSAS: "Party shack" laws prohibit certain activities in rental unit, including gambling, promoting **obscenity**, prostitution, or the use or possession of controlled substances. Under these laws, unlawful activities can subject a tenant to eviction. The three-day notice used for non-payment of rent has been narrowly defined as any 72-hour period with additional time requirements when mailed. Security deposits must be returned with 14 days of tenant move out with wrongfully withheld amounts being subject to damages of one and a half times the amount of the security deposit.

MAINE: Evictions require a seven-day notice, and the tenant can cure within the seven days by paying the rent. The tenant can also cure prior to the court case being held by paying all rent, cots and fees due.

The notice cannot be served until the tenant is seven days or more behind in rent. It can be served personally. If the tenant owes back rent, the landlord can keep any property left on the premises and may ultimately sell it.

MARYLAND: Tenants can cure by paying the rent owed, plus court costs, up until the time the sheriff arrives to evict the tenant. This is known as the tenant's "right to redeem." The tenant can exercise this right three times within a 12 month period, at which point the landlord no longer has to accept the rent. Security deposits must be returned within 45 days of tenant move out.

MASSACHUSETTS: If there is a security deposit, the landlord must give a written statement of the condition of the rental property to the tenant within ten days after the beginning of the tenancy and must deposit the money in a separate interest bearing account. The landlord must also give the tenant a signed receipt listing the name of the bank and account number where the security deposit is held. If the landlord fails to do so within 30 days, the tenant is entitled to get the security deposit immediately returned. Late charges are not permissible unless the rent is more than 30 days late. Massachusetts has designated Housing Courts with judges specializing in this area. Either party can request eviction cases be transferred to the Housing Court; however, doing so may limit the parties' **appellate** rights.

MICHIGAN: The landlord must provide a seven-day notice prior to bringing an eviction action. Lockouts, shutting of utilities, and physically moving out tenant possessions are illegal landlord actions, and the tenant may sue the landlord for such acts. State law prohibits the renting of cellars for living purposes. A cellar is defined as having 50% or more of the outside walls below ground level. A basement where more than 50% of the outside walls are above ground can be lawfully rented, but a cellar must meet specific minimum standards before being rented. The only way a cellar can be legally rented is if it has received a variance from the local housing or health department. Security deposits are regulated by the Michigan Security Deposit Act. This law applies to all tenants in the state and to all subtenants and encompasses both verbal and written leases. The total security deposit charged cannot exceed one and a half times the monthly rental rate. The landlord must deposit the security deposit into a regulated financial institution. The name and address of the institution must be given to the tenant upon rental and the land-

lord may only use the money if a bond is posted with the Secretary of State's Office. Even if a bond is posted, the deposit remains property of the tenant. Landlords must return the security deposit to the tenant within 30 days of the tenant's moving. Landlords may keep the interest earned on security deposits.

ANN ARBOR: It is illegal for the landlord to include a cleaning **waiver** as part of the lease without compensation to the tenant. Ann Arbor City Housing Code prohibits cleaning waivers; however, it does not prohibit agreements between landlord and tenant that provide for the tenant to clean the unit in return for compensation.

NEBRASKA: Evictions require a three-day notice, and tenants must respond to any **summons** and complaint in writing. If the tenant does not respond in writing, the landlord can obtain a **default judgment**. No unit may be rented until it contains safe heating equipment, which heats the entire unit. Security deposits cannot exceed one month's rent unless there is a pet and the landlord requires a pet deposit. The landlord must return security deposits within 14 days after a tenant requests it.

OMAHA: A city code inspector may not come out to a rental unit to inspect unless the tenant has given the landlord a 14 day notice of the problems.

NEW HAMPSHIRE: New Hampshire law requires landlords to provide safe, sanitary housing for tenants. By law, rental properties will not meet this standards if any of the following are present: bugs, mice, or rats, (unless the landlord is conducting a routine inspection and extermination program; internal plumbing that does not work or a back-up of sewage caused by a faulty septic or sewage system; bad wiring, such as exposed wires, the wrong connectors, bad switches or outlets, or other conditions that create a danger of electrical shock or fire; leaking roof or walls; falling plaster from the walls or ceilings; large holes in floors, walls, or ceilings; porches, stairs, or railings are not structurally sound; insufficient water, or broken water heater; leaks in the gas lines; improperly installed heating facilities or heating facilities which cannot safely and adequately heat all livable rooms and bathrooms to an average temperature of at least 65 degrees or if heat is included in the rent, the premises are not actually kept at a minimum average temperature of 65 degrees in all livable rooms.

NEW MEXICO: A landlord cannot charge a tenant more than one month's rent as a deposit on any lease of less than a year. If the lease is for a year or more, the landlord may collect a deposit of more than one month's rent but must pay the tenant current passbook interest on the whole deposit. The landlord has 30 days from the end of the tenancy in which to return the security deposit. Evictions for non-payment require that the landlord give a three-day notice then go to court to file for a "writ of **restitution** of property." The landlord may not lock the tenant out or remove tenant property without a court order. If a tenant does not request any type of service to be performed in the residence, the landlord must provide the tenant with a written 24 hour written notice before entering the premises.

NEW YORK: In New York City, landlord-tenant disputes generally fall into two categories: non-payments, where the tenant has not paid rent, and holdovers, where the landlord alleges the tenant has violated the terms of the lease. These disputes are generally heard in New York City Housing Court which is part of the New York City Civil Court system. If the Housing Court orders an eviction, a 72-hour Notice of Eviction is sent by a city marshal. New York City residents can call the number on the notice to find out what day the marshal has scheduled the eviction. The eviction could take place at any time within the 72 hours.

NORTH CAROLINA: Security deposits cannot be more than two months' rent. Late charges cannot exceed $15 or 5% of the rent payment, whichever is more. Late charges cannot be assessed unless the tenant is at least five days late on the rent. The landlord is required to maintain in good and safe working order and promptly repair all electrical, plumbing, sanitary, heating, ventilating, air conditioning, and other facilities and appliances supplied, but only if the tenant first advises the landlord of needed repairs in writing. If the repairs are emergency ones, the landlord must fix the problem once the landlord becomes aware of the problem, regardless of whether the tenant has given written notification. If the tenant repairs an emergency problem, the landlord must reimburse the tenant, regardless of prior notice. The tenant can agree to perform some or all of the landlord's maintenance duties, but the parties must make an agreement separate from the lease, and the tenant must be compensated.

NORTH DAKOTA: The security deposit cannot exceed the amount of one month's rent or $1,500. This amount includes any extra pet deposits. The landlord must deposit the money in a federally insured interest-bearing savings or passbook account. The landlord may apply the security deposit money and accrued interest upon termination of the lease toward any damages suffered through the **negligence** of the tenant, unpaid rent, or costs of cleaning and repairs which were the tenant's responsibility. Any tenant property with a total estimated value of no more than $1,500, which has been left for at least 30 days in the vacated premises, becomes the property of the landlord to dispose of or sell, without notice to the tenant. Additionally, expenses for storing or moving the property which exceed proceeds from the sale can be deducted from the security deposit. Security deposits must be returned with 30 days of the termination of the lease or the landlord may be subject to treble damages for amounts wrongfully withheld.

OHIO: To bring an eviction action, the landlord must first serve a three-day notice to vacate the premises in person, by mail, or at the premises. A landlord may enter a tenant's unit only after giving a 24-hour notice, except in case of emergency. Landlords may not enter at an unreasonable time or in an unreasonable manner. Tenants may seek injunctive relief from the courts if landlords abuse their right of access. State law requires landlords to evict tenants when the landlord has information from a law enforcement officer, based on a legal search, that the tenant, the tenant's guest, or a member of the tenant's household is involved in drug activity in connection with the premises. In some areas of the state, landlords may be held liable for repeated drug violations in their properties.

OKLAHOMA: All security deposits must be kept in an escrow account by the landlord. When the lease is terminated, any security deposits may be used to pay the balance of rents due or for repairs to the dwelling; however, the landlord must provide an itemized statement of what is kept and for what the amount is kept delivered to the tenant. The balance of the deposit must be returned within 30 days of the termination date of lease or termination of tenancy if the tenant sends a written demand for the return of the deposit. If the tenant fails to demand in writing the return of the deposit within six months, the deposit becomes the landlord's money.

OREGON: A landlord may evict a tenant based on a 72-hour notice for non-payment of rent, if the tenant fails to pay rent within seven days of its due date.

If the tenant fails to pay the rent within the 72 hours, the landlord may immediately file a court eviction proceeding. In calculating the seven-day period, the day the rent is due counts. The landlord may not evict a tenant on 72 hours' notice for non-payment of rent when the only money owed is a late charge. If a written agreement states the landlord can give notice after four days, only four days of default are required. The notice must give the tenant 144 hours to pay the rent in that case. Notices may be served by either personal delivery or by first class mail. Oregon law does require that the landlord return the deposit within 31 days after the tenancy ends.

PENNSYLVANIA: For evictions, notice time should be written in the lease. For verbal leases, the landlord must give 15 days' notice prior to filing for eviction for non-payment of rent. State law allows the tenant to pay the amount of the money judgment up to the time of the scheduled eviction to save the tenancy; however, this money must be paid to the constable not directly to the landlord. Even after a court ordered eviction, tenants have 21 days before the tenant is required to move out. Lockouts and utility shutoffs are not allowed. Security deposits limited to no more than two months' rent as a security deposit in the first year of residence and no more than one month rent thereafter. The landlord has 30 days to return the security deposit and if this is not done, the tenant can collect double the amount that would have been due after any damages are taken into account.

RHODE ISLAND: Evictions require that the landlord send the tenant a five-day notice. An elderly (age 65 or older) tenant may terminate a written lease agreement if entering a residential care/assisted living facility, a nursing facility, or a private or public housing complex designated by the federal government as housing for the elderly. A landlord must give a minimum two-day verbal or written notice when needing to enter a tenant's rental unit. Entry should be during reasonable hours and only for such legitimate business reasons such as inspections, repairs, alterations, supplying necessary services, or showing the unit to potential buyers or renters.

SOUTH CAROLINA: Security deposits must be returned with 30 days of the termination of tenancy. A five-day written notice is required unless the lease provides that no such notice need be given. Lockouts and utility shutoffs are illegal. Once a tenant is served with eviction papers, the tenant has ten days to answer. If the tenant does not answer in court, the landlord can obtain an ejectment order to evict the tenant without further court proceedings.

TENNESSEE: The landlord cannot turn off utilities while a tenant is living in the rental unit, even if the tenant is in default on the lease. Lockouts are not permitted. If the landlord refuses to make repairs within 14 days after a written request from the tenant, the tenant can break the lease and can sue the landlord for damages caused by the landlord's refusal to make repairs. A 30-day notice is required prior to filing for eviction for non-payment of rent unless the lease provides for a waiver of notice.

TEXAS: Texas law requires a three-day notice for eviction for breach of the lease unless the notice provides for a shorter or longer notice period. If utilities are part of the rent payment, the landlord can cut off the utilities but must give a five-day written notice of intent to do so, and the tenant must be at least seven days late in paying the rent. The landlord may legally change the lock on the tenant's door when rent is delinquent but must first give the tenant at least three days advance written notice of intent to change the locks if the rent is not paid. The landlord must also leave a statement attached to the outside of the door explaining where the tenant may acquire a new key. By law, the landlord must give the tenant the key when requested, even if the tenant has not paid rent. The landlord has 30 days to return the security deposit after termination of the lease.

VERMONT: Evictions require a 14-day notice, which may be hand delivered to the tenant. A landlord can enter a rental unit only with 48 hours advanced notice, only 9:00 a.m. and 9:00 p.m., and only to either, inspect the premises, make necessary repairs, or show the unit. Landlords must supply heating facilities capable of safely and adequately heating all habitable rooms. Heating facilities must be able to maintain the heat at the minimum temperature of 65 degrees Fahrenheit when the outside temperature is 15 degrees Fahrenheit. The Code forbids the use of space heaters with a flame that is not properly vented to a chimney or duct leading to the outdoors. If heat is included in the rental charge, it is the landlord's responsibility to provide adequate heat whenever the outside temperature is below 55 degrees Fahrenheit, regardless of the time of year. The Code forbids a landlord to turn off required utilities, "except for such temporary interruption as may be necessary while actual repairs or alterations are in process or during temporary emergencies." Thus, it is illegal for a landlord to shut off a tenant's heat, water, or electricity under most circumstances.

BURLINGTON: People who suffer discrimination in rental units may file a complaint either under the Burlington Housing Discrimination **Ordinance** with the Burlington city attorney's office or under the Vermont Fair Housing Act with the **Human Rights** Commission. If a tenant complains about problems to a housing inspector, and the inspector determines that the problems are code violations, any attempt by the landlord to evict the tenant within 90 days after the landlord has repaired the problems is presumed to be an act of retaliation. Security deposits can be no more than one month's rent and must be placed into an interest-bearing account, with an interest rate at least equivalent to a current Vermont bank passbook savings account. The tenant is entitled to the interest.

BARRE: Security deposits are limited to one month's rent, and tenants are entitled to the interest.

VIRGINIA: Evictions require a five-day notice, which may be sent with a certificate of mailing or posted on the door by the county sheriff's department. The notice should name each person on the lease and specify the sum due. Until the court date a tenant has the **legal right** to avoid eviction by paying the landlord the full amount due (including reasonable attorney's fees and late charges as well as rent). A tenant may exercise this right only once in any 12-month period with the same landlord. The Virginia Residential Landlord and Tenant Act protects tenants from certain types of retaliatory eviction. A tenant otherwise in compliance with the lease cannot be evicted simply for complaining to the landlord about a violation of state law or the county housing code, complaining to County Community Inspections about a serious code violation, organizing or joining a tenants' association, or testifying against the landlord in court.

WASHINGTON: All leases beyond one month must be in writing. Leases of more than one year must also be notarized.

SEATTLE: The Rental Agreement Regulation Ordinance declares that month-to-month rental agreements cannot contain minimum stay requirements, and requires landlords to provide tenants with a summary of landlord-tenant laws. Seattle's Just-Cause Ordinance protects city renters from retaliatory evictions. Additionally, landlords of city tenants are required to give at least 60 days written notice when housing costs are increased by 10% or more in a year.

WISCONSIN: Landlords may not advertise or rent condemned property. Landlords must disclose any uncorrected housing code violations of which they have received notice and must also reveal any other defects which may be a substantial hazard to health or safety, such a structural defects, a lack of hot and cold running water, or serious plumbing or electrical problems. If the heating unit is incapable of maintaining temperature of at least 67 degrees Fahrenheit, this fact must also be disclosed. If the dwelling unit is one of several units, which are not individually metered, the landlord must disclose how utility charges will be allocated among the individual dwelling units. A landlord has the right to inspect, repair, and show the premises at reasonable times. Except for emergency situations, the landlord may only enter after a 12-hour advance. There are no state-wide rent controls in Wisconsin. There is no state law limiting amount of a rent increase. Month-to-month tenancy requires a notice of termination at least 28 days prior to the next rent due date. An initial five days notice is required prior to filing eviction proceedings with the tenant having the option to pay and/or cure the default. But on a second default, the landlord can terminate on 14 days notice without giving the tenant an opportunity to pay or cure the default. Holdover tenants can be obligated to pay twice the amount of the rent, prorated on a daily basis, for each day of unlawful occupation of the premises. The landlord must return security deposits within 21 days and may deduct for unpaid rent or physical damages for which the tenant is responsible. State law does not require payment of interest on security deposits.

## Additional Resources

*Landlording: A Handy Manual for Scrupulous Landlords and Landladies Who Do It Themselves,* Robinson, Leigh, ExPress Publishing, 2001

*Guide to Being a Smart Landlord.* Edwards, Casey F. and Susanna Craig, Macmillan Publishing, 2000

*How to Negotiate Real Estate Leases: For Landlords and Tenants* Warda, Mark, Sourcebooks, 1998

## Organizations

**National Housing Institute**
439 Main Street, Suite 311
Orange, NJ 07050 USA

Phone: (973) 678-9060
Fax: (973) 678-8437
URL: http://www.nhi.org/index.html

**_The Tenants Union_**
3902 S. Ferdinand St.

Seattle, WA 98118 USA
Phone: (206) 723-0500
Fax: (206) 725-3527
URL: http://www.tenantsunion.org

# REAL ESTATE

## NEIGHBOR RELATIONS

*Sections within this essay:*

## Background

Probably as soon as humans shifted from nomadic to agricultural, neighbors have had disputes. Through the centuries, these conflicts have been resolved numerous ways. In early history the resolution was sometimes amicable and other times it was literally a fight to the death. Modern conflict resolution of neighbor disputes is generally not so dangerous as in ancient times. However, the concept that one's home is one's castle is an idea ingrained deeply enough to create strong and sometimes seemingly uncompromising positions when neighbors face off.

Legal disputes in the area of neighbor relations can be unreasonably costly as disputes are typically about rights rather than monetary damages. Attorneys fees can run higher than any potential damage award by a court, and this fact can lead to both parties coming away dissatisfied and financially and emotionally drained. Thus, **mediation** is often recommended as a means to resolve these types of disputes.

## Neighbor Conflicts

Good neighbors communicate, resolving problems to their mutual benefit. However, conflicts can develop over a number of common issues.

### Boundary Disputes

Surveys done at the time of any property purchase, should reflect the boundary lines. Prior to erecting a fence on a boundary line, an updated survey could be ordered which reflects the accurate boundary lines. This may be impossible, due to perhaps the age of the property or the wording of the **deed**. (Some older deeds can contain legal descriptions such as "52 feet from the bend in the stream" on a piece of land, which has only a dry riverbed where a stream once existed.) In such a situation, the owner may file a quiet title lawsuit and request the judge determine the boundary lines of the property. This procedure is generally more expensive than a survey due to the legal filing fees. An acceptable alternative is for adjacent property owners to agree on a physical object, such as a fence, which could serve as the boundary line between the properties. Each owner would then sign a quitclaim deed to the other, granting the neighbor ownership to any land on the other side of the line both owners had agreed upon.

If the piece of property in dispute has been used by someone other than the owner for a number of years, the doctrine of adverse possession may apply. State laws vary with respect to time requirements, however, typically, the possession by the non-owner must be open, notorious, and under a claim of right. In some states, the non-owner must also pay the property taxes on the occupied land. A permissive use of property eliminates the ability to claim adverse possession.

### Fences

Good neighbors should agree to split the cost of the repair of fences or common boundary walls. Local fence ordinances usually regulate height and location and sometimes the material used and appearance. Residents of subdivisions are often subject to even stricter Homeowners' Association restrictions. In residential areas, local rules typically restrict backyard fences to a height of six feet and front yards to a height of four feet. Exceptions exist and a landowner can seek a variance if there is a need for a higher fence. While some jurisdictions have specific aesthetic **zoning** rules with respect to fences, as long as a fence complies with local laws it cannot be taken down simply because it is ugly. In fact, unless the property owners agree otherwise, fences on a boundary line belong to both owners when both are using the fence. Both owners are responsible for keeping the fence in good repair, and neither may remove it without the other's permission. In the event that trees hang over the fence, most states agree that the property owner may cut tree limbs and remove roots where they cross over the property line, provided that such pruning will not damage the basic health and welfare of the tree.

### Trees

Sometimes disputes arise between neighbors when trees belonging to one property owner fall on and damage or destroy adjacent property. In such cases, the tree owner is only responsible for damage if some failure to maintain the tree contributed to the damage. If the damage was solely the result of a thunderstorm or act of God, the tree owner will not be responsible, as the damage could not have been foreseen. If a tree limb appeared precarious and the owner failed to maintain the tree after warnings, the owner may well be responsible for resulting damage when a storm causes the limb to fall. If, however, the tree was well maintained and a storm causes a tree limb to crash into a neighbor's roof, the tree owner is not responsible. If, however, the tree owner allows the tree to grow so that it uproots the fence, it would be considered an **encroachment** onto the adjacent property. In that instance, the tree owner would be

required to remove the offending tree. A boundary tree is one planted on the boundary line itself and should not be removed without mutual agreement. Leaves, bean pods, or acorns which fall off and end up on adjacent property are considered a natural occurrence and are the responsibility of the landowner on whose property they ultimately come to rest.

Property owners in every state have the right to cut off branches and roots that stray into their property, in most cases this is the only help that is provided by the law, even when damage from a tree is substantial. A property owner who finds a neighbor's tree encroaching must first warn or give notice to the tree owner prior to commencing work and give the tree owner the chance to correct the problem. If the tree owner does nothing, the tree can still be trimmed. As a general rule a property owner who trims an encroaching tree belonging to a neighbor can trim only up to the boundary line and must obtain permission to enter the tree owner's property, unless the limbs threaten to cause imminent and grave harm. Additionally, the property owner cannot cut the entire tree down and cannot destroy the structural integrity or the cosmetic symmetry and appeal of a tree by improper trimming.

### Animals

In the old courts of England, the owner of livestock was held strictly liable for any damages to person or property done by the livestock straying onto the property of another. The mere fact that they strayed and damaged crops, other livestock, or **personal property** was sufficient to hold the owner liable for the injuries inflicted by cattle, sheep, goats, and horses. This strict liability position made sense in the confines of a small island such as England, but in the United States with herds of livestock wandering over vast expanses of land, a different process developed. The legislatures enacted statutes which provided that livestock were free to wander and that the owner was not responsible for damage inflicted by those livestock unless they entered land enclosed by a legal fence. These became known as open range laws. Some years later, certain states reversed the open range laws and required the owners of livestock to fence in their livestock. This position was similar to the **common law** position, only instead of strict liability, the livestock owner could be held liable only upon a showing that the livestock escaped due to the owner's **negligence**. Dogs or other animals inflicting bites may make their owners both civilly and criminally liable for such behavior. In some jurisdictions, an animal can be declared dangerous by a court and a judge may order the animal be confined or destroyed. If the issue is that the neighbor has too many pets, the neighbor could be in violation of a zoning, health code, or noise **ordinance**.

### Views

Disputes sometimes arise between neighbors about changing views. If a tree entirely on a neighbor's property grows so large that it blocks a property owner's view or even natural sunshine, the best tactic is to discuss the matter with the neighbor. The homeowner probably has no **legal right** to get the neighbor to alter the tree unless a local ordinance or Homeowners' Association rule exists regarding such an issue.

### Structural Additions/Changes

Sometimes structural additions or changes ruin views and may potentially damage property values. Local zoning and building departments typically require permits and set rules for any building or structural changes. If the neighbor meets the legal requirements, generally nothing can be done. Homeowners' Associations and CC&Rs may be of some assistance, particularly if the change is unusually hideous and more cosmetic than structural.

### Water

Natural water runoff from a neighbor's property due to rain or snow is not actionable. However, natural runoff is uncommon in city areas. Any grading or building which alters the natural runoff and may cause the neighbor to be liable for damages. If a neighbor's home improvement project causes a water line to burst, creating flood or water damage, the neighbor will likely be responsible. Fortunately, most homeowner's insurance policies cover this type of negligence.

### Parking

Parking is governed by local laws and ordinances and typically enforced by the local municipality. If a car is parking in a no-parking zone, fire lane, or parked unlawfully in any manner, a citizen can simply call the local parking enforcement authorities and have the vehicle ticketed and/or towed. A car parking on private property without permission can be considered abandoned and can be towed away by order of the property owner; however, unless the property owner has some arrangement with the towing company, a charge will likely be assessed at the time of the tow. Broken cars or unsightly recreational vehicles parked on any property may violate a provision of the zoning code or perhaps Homeowner's Association rules. If not, and the vehicle is parked either on

a neighbor's property or a public street, not much can be done to remedy the matter other than convincing the neighbor that such items detract from the neighborhood. There must be a written agreement to enforce any agreement for sharing maintenance and/or towing expenses for a shared driveway.

### Noise

Excessive noise is usually a criminal **misdemeanor** violation. Police can be called to quiet a noisy event; however, it is difficult to measure damages for any type of civil suit for continued noise violations. It may be possible to appear at the trial for a noise violation and, once the neighbor is found guilty of the violation, ask the judge to order no excessive noise as a condition of the violator's **probation**.

### Weeds

Homeowner's Associations, health codes, local ordinances, and nuisance laws may prohibit unmaintained yards. Homeowner's Associations sometimes have provisions in which, after adequate notice, the association may hire a landscaper to maintain the property and assess the homeowner.

### Home Business

Although thousands of people work out of their homes, home-based businesses can cause traffic congestion, noise, unwelcome smells, unsightly signage, and general neighborhood upheaval. Local ordinances regulate home businesses and may require specific business licenses. Zoning ordinances may prevent home based businesses in residential areas altogether.

## Alternative Dispute Resolutions

Increasingly widespread in recent years, alternative dispute resolution may be helpful in resolving neighborhood disputes. In lieu of costly **litigation**, parties involved in a dispute may settle their differences through a mediation or **arbitration**. This is known as alternative dispute resolution, the alternative to litigation and court. Essentially, arbitration differs from mediation in that arbitration uses a neutral third person who makes a decision after **hearing** from all sides. A mediator is also a neutral third party, but a mediator assists the parties in reaching an agreement rather than making the decision for the parties involved. Mediation, and arbitration to a degree, give the parties greater control in the outcome of the situation. The parties can also agree upon a framework in which any future disputes may be resolved.

## Mediation

Mediation is an attempt by the parties to resolve a dispute with the aid of a neutral third party known as a mediator. The mediator is often an attorney or retired judge, but the parties may use any mediator. The mediator may offer advice or creative resolutions, but mediation is a non-binding process in which the parties must agree in order to reach some type of resolution. If the mediator is a licensed attorney, mediation proceedings can be fully confidential. In a mediation, the parties are not bound to award only monetary damages as a court might be but instead can fashion a process and a solution especially well suited to the dispute between them.

## Additional Resources

*The Legal Edge for Homeowners, Buyers, and Renters* Bryant, Michel J., Renaissance Books, 1999.

Jordan, Cora. *Neighbor Law: Fences, Trees, Boundaries and Noise* Nolo Law, 2001.

Natelson, Robert. *Modern Law of Deeds to Real Property* Natelson, Robert, Aspen Law, 1992.

## Organizations

### American Arbitration Association
335 Madison Avenue, Floor 10
New York, NY 10017 USA
Phone: (212) 716-5800
Fax: (212) 716-5905
URL: http://www.adr.org

### International Centre for Dispute Resolution
1633 Broadway, Floor 10
New York, NY 10019 USA
Phone: (212) 484-4181
Fax: (212) 246-7274
Primary Contact: Luis Martinez, Vice President

### Neutrals' Services
3200 North Central Avenue, Suite 2100
Phoenix, AZ 85012 USA
Phone: (602) 734-9300
Fax: (602) 279-3077
Primary Contact: Harry Kaminsky, Vice President

### The Tenants Union
3902 S. Ferdinand St.
Seattle, WA 98118 USA
Phone: (206) 723-0500
Fax: (206) 725-3527
URL: http://www.tenantsunion.org

### Environmental Health Center
1025 Conn. Ave., NW, Suite 1200
Washington, DC 20036 USA
Phone: (202) 293-2270
URL: http://www.nsc.org/ehc.htm

# REAL ESTATE

## NEIGHBORHOOD COVENANTS

## Background

Technically (and within the context of residential neighborhoods), a covenant is a rule governing the use of real property. However, in common usage, it may also refer to a promise or agreement (as formalized in a **deed**) concerning the use of the land, as where a purchaser of land "covenants" to abide by certain restrictions associated with the use of the land. Essentially, such covenants are promises made by a prospective purchaser as a condition of purchasing the land in question.

When properly recorded on a deed conveying land, a covenant ("restrictive deed covenant") has the legal effect of a binding **contract** term, and may be so enforced. When covenants are instead signed privately among neighbors, as in a mutual compact or agreement, they are still binding upon the signatories and may be litigated if breached.

Most planned developments (subdivisions of homes built by a particular builder), including closed or gated residential areas, as well as condominium associations and housing cooperatives, make use of covenants for the benefit of all residential owners and their neighbors. Neighborhoods with properly drafted and enforced covenants or architectural standards have been shown to retain property value better than those with poorly enforced covenants or no standards at all. Neighborhoods that follow their covenants and standards tend to be safer, look better, maintain better relationships with local governments, and better retain or increase the investments that homeowners have made in their properties.

Covenants differ from **zoning** ordinances in that they are between private parties rather than between a governmental entity and a private party. Thus, a neighborhood association or single homeowner may enforce a covenant as against another homeowner, rather than a city or county enforcing a zoning ordinance as against a private citizen. Another difference is that zoning ordinances are regulations recorded as local laws "on the books," whereas covenants are recorded in private deeds, either as deed restrictions or as neighborhood compacts between private parties. Because covenants are voluntary, they may be more restrictive that zoning ordinances.

## General Purpose

Property owners agree to stringent covenants and conditions that restrict the use and enjoyment of their own property for two main reasons. First, and most importantly, homeowners want to maintain or enhance the property's value. Second, homeowners want to use and enjoy their property without annoyance, distraction, or offensive use by their neighbors that falls short of being an actual violation of any existing law. Zoning ordinances are limited in what they can control; they cannot control what type of person moves into a neighborhood and/or how he will maintain his property. Although it is true that most counties and local governments do have laws protecting residents from unsafe or unhealthy conditions on neighboring property, there is little they can do to prevent clutter, poor appearance, or just "bad taste." These indiscretions can cost a neighboring property thousands of dollars in appraised value, and can also impair home buyers' interest in it, should the owners attempt to move away from the offending property.

Covenants regulate what property owners in a particular area can or cannot do with their property. When a geographically-restricted group of homeowners are bound by neighborhood covenants, individual homeowners are better insulated from the possibility that one errant homeowner will bring down the value of surrounding properties because of the appearance of his or her house. Covenants ostensibly ensure that a residential area will remain a desirable one to live in; that the properties contained therein will retain their value; and that, in return for some minor sacrifices, homeowners will be able to better enjoy their own properties. Zoning laws can change, leaving residents unprotected from the possibility that a strip club or deer-processing plant might move in.

Covenants can range in subject matter from the prohibition of flagpoles in the front yard to restrictions in outdoor music during certain hours. They may limit the colors a homeowner may paint a house or the type of shrubs and trees used to landscape

around it. They may control pets, vehicle parking, security lights and alarms, mailboxes, or remote-control toys. While many people are accustomed to such restrictions when renting or leasing residential properties, they do not realize that such limitations also can be placed on properties they own. "It's my property and I can do what I want with it" is a common retort that provides little defense for a homeowner who has breached a covenant attaching to his or her property.

In order for covenants to be binding, they must be legal. For example, in the early 1900s, racially restrictive covenants were used to exclude minorities from white neighborhoods. Since civil rights laws (prohibiting discrimination) did not come into being until many years later, state courts reviewed challenges to these covenants under the **Due Process** Clause and the Rule Against Restraints on Alienation. In some courts, neither of these grounds proved sufficient to strike down such racially restrictive covenants, and many continued for years (although restrictions on alienation of property are generally void). The practice was finally outlawed by the U.S. Supreme Court in *Shelley v. Kraemer,* 334 U.S.1 (1948). Other covenants that attempt to restrict otherwise legal rights can always be challenged, but, buyer beware, a homeowners' association is a private one in which buyers voluntarily agree to the covenants.

## Covenants, Conditions, and Restrictions (CC&Rs)

Covenants are often lumped together under the collective term of "covenants, conditions, and restrictions" or CC&Rs, a term commonly found in real estate documents. Since most covenants involve some kind of condition or restriction placed upon the buyer, the collective term "CC&Rs" has been more widely used in recent years to indicate the existence or future existence of limitations associated with the use of the purchased land.

Many home buyers are so charmed by the appearance of a house for sale that they fail to take the time to read the CC&Rs that come with the property. They are so pleased with a nice kitchen or a fenced-in back yard that they sign a purchase agreement without realizing that existing CC&Rs may prevent them from keeping their boat or truck on the property, or erecting a basketball hoop in the driveway. Often, title companies will not have copies of the CC&Rs affecting the property until the day of closing, and they are often overlooked at that point. However, CC&Rs are binding upon the purchaser, and the purchaser will become subject to them, whether or not they have been reviewed, read, or understood. The general rule of "constructive notice" applies in these cases. No real estate contract should be signed until a purchaser has reviewed all the CC&Rs (and zoning laws) affecting the property.

### Builders' Restrictions

Real estate developers generally purchase large parcels of land, which they then subdivide into individual lots for home construction. Most developers will build homes in a subdivision that are fairly similar in appearance, so as to convey an attractive incentive for would-be purchasers that they will be living in a community of fine homes. Developers have a vested interest in ensuring that the character of the neighborhood and the appearance of the subdivision remains attractive, at least until their construction project loans have been repaid and they have turned a profit.

To that end, developers will often file, generally at the same time that the land plat is being approved for subdivision and development, a declaration of covenants that will be applicable to all parcels of land (lots) sold within the development. Once the zoning authority approves of the development as presented, the covenants (conditions and restrictions) will become binding on any purchaser of land in the subdivision. In other words, these covenants generally "run with the land" (see below).

The important thing to remember is that the builder's covenants are binding on all persons purchasing property within the builder's subdivision. Such covenants are made "of record" in the county or city where the land is located, and will be referred to in any deed transferring land to a purchaser. Language in a deed most often refers to the conveyance of land "subject to any existing CC&Rs and **easements** of record" or similar wording.

Specific restrictions and covenants are generally *not* enumerated in the deed itself, but will be contained in a separate document referred to in the deed. It is important that a prospective purchaser inquire about and review any such separate documents containing these covenants prior to purchasing the land in question.

### Homeowners or Condominium Associations

Most homes in a subdivision or development, as well as most condominiums existing today, are sub-

ject to CC&Rs. If the legal description of property contained in a deed refers to a certain "lot," especially if followed by a number, e.g., "Lot No. 24," that lot is most likely part of a subdivided plot that is subject to CC&Rs.

The declaration of covenants filed by a developer for a particular subdivision project will generally contain language that delegates control and enforcement authority to a newly-formed homeowners' association or an architectural control board. Until all the homes in the subdivision are sold, the builder may retain control and enforcement of the CC&Rs, or may delegate it to the association. In any event, once the developer has sold all the homes and no longer has a vested interest in the subdivision or project, overseeing the CC&Rs will transfer directly to the homeowners. The newly authorized association will continue the existing covenants but may eventually create new ones, depending on the specifics contained in its bylaws.

Importantly, purchasing a lot or existing home may require that the purchaser pay dues or fees for membership in a homeowners' or condominium owners' association. Bylaws for these associations generally provide for the election of officers and outline voting rights of the property owners affected by the adopted covenants. Voting rights of homeowners or condominium owners may be delegated to an appointed or elected board or panel of fellow homeowners or condominium owners. As with all delegated authority, their decisions regarding CC&Rs will be binding, whether or not individual property owners agree with them. The only recourse may be to wait until the next general election of officers or panel members.

### Voluntary Neighborhood Covenants

Often, homeowners whose individual homes are not part of any organized association and/or are not subject to any CC&Rs, will voluntarily form an association to promote the maintenance or enhancement of their property values. By forming a group united by concerns that other homeowners may share, the homeowners will draft covenants binding on all homeowners within a geographically defined area. This form of voluntary covenant can be more difficult to create or enforce, for two specific reasons. First, a single homeowner who holds back consent or refuses to join the association can prevent the formation of binding covenants. Secondly, because the covenants were formed after the fact of purchase, they are not "deed restrictions" and will not run with the land. Since they are voluntary commitments among current owners, the sale of a single property to a subsequent purchaser can end the covenants for all properties.

Notwithstanding, a group of residents may voluntarily agree to adopt permanent covenants and choose to have them subsequently added to their property descriptions and deeds. This often occurs when they are concerned that, if one of them sells his or her home, the remaining residents will be adversely affected by what a subsequent purchaser will do with/to the property.

## Creation and Termination of Covenants

Binding neighborhood covenants are created by written documents (e.g., a declaration of covenants). In most cases, they will already be in existence at the time a purchaser takes interest in a parcel of land or house. If they are simple and brief, they may appear in a deed transferring property, but in most cases, a deed will only refer to covenants and incorporate them by reference, e.g., the deed will convey the land from grantor to grantee "subject to all existing CC&Rs or easements of record," (or similar language).

### Covenants Running With the Land

Most neighborhood covenants "run with the land." This means that they subject the property itself, and not its current owners, to the conditions or restrictions contained in them. Thus, the liability to perform a covenant, refrain from doing something, and/or take advantage of a covenant passes with the land itself to any subsequent owners.

In order for covenants to run with the land, they must be included in a deed transferring property, and they become part and parcel of the "chain of titles." The covenants remain binding on each successive owner of the property, whether or not the new owner has been advised of them.

In order for a benefit or burden to run with the land, requirements under the **Statute of Frauds** must be met. However, if any covenants are contained in the deed itself, acceptance of the deed constitutes satisfaction of the Statute of Frauds, as though the purchaser had signed the covenants himself.

### Expiration or Termination

Neighborhood covenants may be permanent, expire naturally, or have a declared term of existence.

For example, a builder will often initiate covenants running with each lot in a subdivision, that address such restrictions as type of dwelling that can be constructed on a lot (e.g. single family structure only) or setback from street (e.g. minimum of 100 feet). Once the houses have been built upon the lots, the covenants regarding setback and type of dwelling naturally expire *as between the builder and the purchasers of the lots.* However, more likely than not, a homeowners' association will adopt the prior covenants to prevent subsequent homeowners from either converting their homes to multiple-family dwellings or building additions to the home that are closer than 100 feet to the street. In such an example, the builder is no longer a party to the covenants, but they nonetheless will be binding among subsequent homeowners represented by the association.

Such a transfer of covenants is most often provided for by the developer in the initial covenants filed with the city or county at the time the subdivision development is approved. An example contained in a declaration of covenants might read something like, "After 50 percent of the total lots in the Subdivision have been sold by the undersigned developer, or after ten (10) years, whichever occurs first, the "Triple Crown Homeowners Association" shall be established as a not-for-profit corporation. The owners of each lot shall collectively own one share in the Homeowners Association. It shall be the duty of The Homeowners Association to enforce these covenants and restrictions, majority rule shall prevail except as otherwise stated herein_"

Commonly, CC&Rs have a declared term of existence, after which they expire naturally. The positive side of having covenants with fixed terms of life is that subsequent property owners are not burdened with restrictions that have become arcane, dated, or no longer desirable. For example, in 1950, a homeowners association wanted to preserve the charm of a residential area and created covenants restricting the sale of any properties for use only as single-family homes. But as the area grew, commercial properties surrounded the residential area, making it unattractive to prospective homebuyers. A well-written covenant with a term life would have contemplated this scenario and limited the restriction to 25 or 30 years, for example. At that time, new owners could voluntarily agree to extend the life of the covenants or adopt new ones. Or, with expired covenants, they could petition local zoning boards to rezone their neighborhood as commercial or multiple-family residential properties, to maximize the return on their investments.

It is also possible that some expired covenants are converted into new zoning laws affecting the residential area, and will therefore be binding on subsequent property owners as well.

## Types of Covenants

### Appearance and Maintenance

Probably the single most controlling covenant found in those adopted by homeowners' associations is that which addresses the appearance and maintenance of private properties.

It is important to note that, even in the absence of CC&Rs, many of these same issues are regulated by local zoning or blight ordinances. However, because covenants are voluntary in nature (a purchaser agrees to abide by the covenants as a condition of purchasing the property), they can impose more strict obligations upon homeowners than those required under zoning ordinances.

### View

Covenants addressing views are often found in both CC&Rs and (less commonly) local zoning laws. Homeowners pay top dollar for property "with a view," and the privilege of gazing at an appealing scene from the comfort and privacy of one's own home is a highly prized commodity. This, in turn, manifests in enhanced dollar value of the real estate.

Importantly, there is no natural or common law right to light, fresh air, or a view. (There are exceptions for the deliberate and malicious blocking of another's view with a structure that has no reasonable use or benefit to the one who constructed it.)

Such a right must therefore be granted in writing by a special law or CC&Rs. Generally speaking, the view that becomes protected by a CC&Rs is the view that existed at the time that the property was purchased (taking into account any pending impairments to view in existence at that time, such as the construction of additional homes in the area).

There are three common view obstructions that become the subject of CC&Rs: fences, trees, and freestanding outbuildings/sheds. Since each of these is normally associated with a homeowner's right to use and enjoy his property, CC&Rs seldom prohibit these improvements, but rather try to restrict them.

### Noise

A common covenant is one controlling noises, particularly during certain hours of the day, e.g., between 10:00 p.m. and 7:00 a.m. Violation of such a covenant often parallels local ordinances, so neighbors may simply contact police to immediately address the problem, then later file a complaint with the association for covenant violation.

### Fences

Fence heights are generally controlled by local ordinance but may also be a subject covered in neighborhood covenants. Commonly, they restrict fence heights to six feet in back yards, and three to four feet in front yards.

Natural fences are more burdensome. Bushes or trees used as natural borders or fences (or deemed to constitute same) become overgrown and tend to encroach on neighbors' properties. In addition to the encroachment (which may constitute a trespass), overgrown natural fences also tend to obstruct views, thereby possibly violating another covenant.

### Pets

Clearly, covenants may address the number and type of pets that residents may keep on their property. It is imperative that prospective residents seek out the nature of any such covenants prior to purchasing the property or bringing animals or pets onto the property. Property associations do have the right to compel removal of pets in violation of covenants. However, this generally can only be done after proper notice and hearing, followed by judgment in a court of law to enforce the covenant. Members of homeowners' associations do not have authority to enter the property of another and remove pets.

### Home Businesses

Neighbors often complain about the noise and traffic of home-based businesses. They may also resent the presence of outsiders constantly coming into the residential area, which may enhance burglaries, robberies, and other crime. They may fear the consequences that home businesses have on property values or zoning regulations.

In truth, most home businesses are discreet and unobtrusive. They may involve computer work, arts and crafts, writers, or consultants, so the negative effect on neighboring properties is minimal or nonexistent. Covenants attempting to restrict them may fail as unjustified restrictions on private rights to be gainfully employed. For this reason, most covenants involving home-based business address corollary issues, such as noise, traffic, pollution, etc.

### Personal Conduct

Covenants may address personal conduct, particularly concerning dress codes when entering common areas, such as swimming pools, tennis courts, etc. Drunk or disorderly conduct, entering another's property unannounced, or disturbing the peace may also be prohibited in particular covenants.

Miscellaneous covenants may address or prohibit other activities or issues that tangentially touch on personal conduct. These topics may also be addressed under appearance and maintenance covenants. Storing or working on disabled or older, broken-down vehicles in one's yard, or keeping a backdoor floodlight (or front door light) may be prohibited, even though they impinge on a resident's right to his own use and enjoyment of his property. The legal concept relied upon to enforce such covenants is the argument that the proscribed activities also impinge upon neighboring properties and the use and enjoyment of them as well. Since residents voluntarily agree to covenants, their conduct can be thus restricted.

### Common Areas

Covenants addressing common areas generally deal with maintenance, repairs, conduct, and use. Restrictions may be placed on the number of visitors or guests a resident may bring into a common area. Parking spaces are frequently addressed in covenants, including restrictions on parking in front of others' property.

## Enforcement and Remedy

All neighborhood covenants include procedures for handling violations of CC&Rs, or requests for relief thereof. Since covenants are created by homeowners' or neighbor associations, internal notice and hearing requirements will be spelled out in the covenants themselves. It is important to remember that homeowners' associations cannot evict residents, remove personal property belonging to residents, or violate residents' personal rights in attempting to enforce covenants or control alleged violations.

### Variances

The most common and easiest form of attempted compliance with a CC&Rs is to request a variance. A request for variance is a request for permission to depart from the literal requirements of a covenant. Variances are usually granted where enforcement would cause undue or unfair hardship on the requesting individual or resident. Examples include outdoor lighting at night for vision-impaired residents, pets that exceed the size, weight, breed, or limit on number as contained in a covenant, or keeping extra vehicles on the property or street.

### Association Hearings

Almost all requests for variances are handled by hearings before the association. Notice generally goes to all other residents, or at a minimum, to residents whose properties may be affected by a committee or board decision.

Alleged violations of existing covenants are generally first handled by progressive action. After verbal and written warnings, as outlined in the covenants, associations will generally hold hearings on the matter. Alleged violators will have this forum to present their defenses or objections to the allegations. Some hearings are more formal in nature, in which residents may present witnesses or "cross-examine" those who allege violations. Decision and resolution is generally controlled by vote.

### Court Action

For alleged violations that are not resolved, associations may decide to bring legal action against a resident for enforcement of a covenant. A court of law which has jurisdiction over the parties and the subject matter may render a formal judgment for or against the resident. Importantly, courts cannot enforce covenants for which they cannot determine a binding contract between the parties. The petitioning party must be able to show that the resident, in agreeing to the covenant(s), received some form of consideration in return for the promise. This may be inferred from circumstances evidencing increased property value, etc., but may also be a stumbling block for the association if its cause of action is not properly articulated. To overcome this possibility, associations tend to back up their lawsuits with citations of common law that parallel the covenants, e.g., public and private nuisance, interference with the use and enjoyment of property, disturbance of the peace, etc.

Courts of law may award monetary damages, impose injunctions, impound vehicles, or compel removal of personal property such as pets, in upholding CC&Rs. They may empower the association itself to take action, or compel relief through other resources, such as local police.

## Additional Resources

Jordan, Cora. *Neighbor Law*. 4th Edition, 2001. Berkeley: Nolo Press

Warda, Mark. *Neighbor v. Neighbor*. 2nd Edition, 1999. Clearwater, FL: Sphinx Publishing.

# REAL ESTATE

## RENTERS' LIABILITY

*Sections within this essay:*

- Background
- Renters' Obligation
    - Invitees
    - Licensees
    - Trespassers
- Insurance
    - Renter's Insurance
    - Moving Insurance
- Additional Resources

## Background

Premises liability involves the responsibility of property owners to maintain safe conditions for people coming on or about the property. Those responsible for the premises can be held liable for injuries, which occur on the property, even if another person or entity is the lawful owner of that property. If a person slips, trips, or falls as a result of a dangerous or hazardous condition, the renter and property owner may both be responsible in some manner. Several categories of persons to whom property owners and those renting the premises may be liable exist, and the duties of protection owed to each group are different.

## Renters' Obligation

### Invitees

Where, by express or implied invitation, a person induces or leads others to come upon a particular premises for any lawful purpose, a duty to exercise ordinary care arises to keep the premises safe. The invitation may be express, implied from known and customary use of portions of the premises, or inferred from conduct actually known. Workers or contractors are typically considered invitees.

### Licensees

A licensee is a person who has no contractual relation with the premises but is permitted, expressly or impliedly, to go on the premises. A social guest at a residence is normally considered a licensee. Liability to a licensee only arises for willful or wanton injury. It is usually willful or wanton not to exercise ordinary care to prevent injuring a licensee who is actually known to be, or is reasonably expected to be, within the range of a dangerous act or condition.

### Trespassers

Surprising to many is that a duty is also owed to those without permission to be on the premises. A trespasser is a person who enters the premises of another without express or implied permission, for the trespasser's own benefit or amusement. The duty to a trespasser is not to prepare pitfalls or traps for the trespasser nor to injure the trespasser purposely.

## Insurance

Insurance is a legally binding contract, typically referred to as an insurance policy. The contractual relationship is between the insurance company and the person or entity buying the policy, the policyholder. The policyholder makes payments to the insurance company, which can be monthly, quarterly, or yearly. The insurance company agrees to pay for certain types of losses under certain conditions, which are set forth in the policy.

One requirement for insurance is that the policyholder needs to possess an insurable interest in the subject of the insurance. A policyholder renting property is said to have such an interest in the property. Insurance policies compensate an insured party for the cost of monetary damages in the event of economic loss or in the event of damages leveled against a policyholder who is liable for damages to another. Liability insurance pays damages up to the dollar amount of liability coverage purchased and protects the personal assets of the policyholder in the event of a judgement against the policyholder for damages. Some renters' policies cover legal liability in the event that anyone suffers an injury while on the insured property. Certain actions of the policyholder, which occur away from the insured property may also be covered.

When a renter purchases liability insurance, part of the insurance company's obligation is to provide a defense in the event of a lawsuit. Even though the insurance company selects the lawyer and must approve the payment of all legal fees and other expenses of the lawsuit, the lawyer represents the policyholder. Under most types of liability insurance, the insurance company has the contractual right to settle or defend the case as it sees fit. The policy owner has an opportunity to provide input, but the company typically has no obligation to obtain the policyholder's consent or approval.

The entity that the renter is leasing from typically has some type of liability insurance also. This may, in some circumstances, cover the renter. Liability suits may involve several different claims, some of which may be covered by the liability insurance policy and some of which may not be covered. The insurance company is obligated to provide a defense for any claim, which could be covered, but the company may not be obligated to pay the damages for certain types of claims. Since liability policies typically do not provide coverage for intentional acts, there may be a factual question as to whether the policyholder acted intentionally. Negligent or accidental acts are generally covered; however, papers filed in court might **allege** both negligent and intentional actions. In such a situation, the insurance company may send a Reservation of Rights letter. This is a notice that the company is paying for the defense for the claim but is not agreeing that it is required to pay for any and all losses under the terms of the policy.

Limitations and exclusions can alter the provisions of coverage in a policy. A limitation is an exception to the general scope of coverage, applicable only under certain circumstances or for a specified period of time. An exclusion is a broader exception which often rules out coverage for such things as intentional acts, when the policy covers damages due to negligent acts.

Insurance companies and policyholders have contractual obligations which must be satisfied to ensure resolution of claims. Insurance policies list specific things a policyholder must do in order to perfect a claim once a loss has taken place. These duties are known as contract conditions. Policies typically require an insured to give prompt notice of any loss or the time and place of an accident or injury. Liability claims require the policyholder to give the insurance company copies of all notices or legal papers received.

The insurance company may ultimately refuse to pay part or all of a claim. The insurance company may take the position that the loss is not covered by the policy, perhaps because it was the result of some intentional act. Or the insurance company may allege that the policyholder took some type of action that rendered the policy void. Because insurance policies are contracts and open to interpretation by the courts, policyholders may be able to use the legal system to reverse such decisions. If an insured opts to consult an attorney to pursue such remedies, it should be an attorney other than the one hired by the insurance company to represent the policyholder.

### Renter's Insurance

Although renting a property is not usually subject to the same liability as owning a property, renters can still benefit from property insurance and renters can purchase separate liability insurance. Renter's insurance typically covers the cost of replacing personal items that are stolen, damaged, or destroyed. Additionally, renters, like owners, have potential liability to anyone injured on the occupied property. Renters' insurance policies are similar to homeowners' insurance policies but have no coverage for buildings or structures. Although renter's insurance is not usually required, by the terms of some leases, tenants may be required to have insurance to cover their liability exposure if someone is injured on the premises, or if damages occur from items owned by the renter, such as waterbeds. And, the **landlord** can, in fact, require the renter to have liability insurance. When signing a new **lease** or after proper legal notice for a month-to-month rental agreement the landlord can even lawfully change the terms of the agreement to require renter's insurance. This may be particularly important if the renter has animals or the property contains a pool. The landlord's insurance will probably not cover tenant property losses unless the tenant can specifically demonstrate that the landlord was negligent in some manner.

### Moving Insurance

There are a variety of costs associated with a move and most moving companies will provide a free written estimate. Estimates are typically based on shipment weight and length of travel. Professional moving companies are required by federal law to provide some level of insurance; however, additional insurance can be purchased. Basic liability insurance results in a standard coverage of about $.60 per pound per item. Thus, a 100 pound item would create a liability for the mover on that item of $60. With declared value protection or **actual cash value** insurance, the value of the goods is pre-determined by the owner of the goods, and the mover is liable for this declared value, or the purchase price less **depreciation**. If all the items are lost or stolen, the mover's liability would be the total pre-determined worth of the goods as stated in the moving agreement. Moving companies can take up to 120 days after receipt of any complaint to make a decision about paying on the claim.

## Additional Resources

A *Glossary of Insurance, Development and Planning Terms.* Davidson, Michael, American Planning Association,1997.

*The Legal Edge for Homeowners, Buyers, and Renters.* Bryant, Michel J., Renaissance Books, 1999

## Organizations

### The Tenants Union
3902 S. Ferdinand St.
Seattle, WA 98118 USA
Phone: (206) 723-0500
Fax: (206) 725-3527
URL: http://www.tenantsunion.org

### U. S. Department of Transportation Office of Motor Carriers
400 7th Street, S.W.
Washington, DC 20590 USA
Phone: (202) 366-4000
URL: http://www.dot.gov/

### The Tenants Union
3902 S. Ferdinand St.
Seattle, WA 98118 USA
Phone: (206) 723-0500
Fax: (206) 725-3527
URL: http://www.tenantsunion.org

# REAL ESTATE

## TIMESHARES

## Background

Timeshares are created when a developer purchases or builds one or more condominium type units and then completes the required legal steps to be allowed to sell week stays in these units. Some states consider some **timeshare** arrangements to be actual pieces of real estate, making other real estate laws applicable to timeshare owners.

## Types of Timeshare Ownerships

### Deeded Timeshares

In this timeshare, the timeshare owner purchases an ownership interest in a particular piece of real es-

tate. Usually, the buyer purchases a particular unit and a particular week in the year. That owner will always stay in that same unit on the same week of every year, unless an exchange is made through an exchange company. This arrangement is usually called Fixed Time or Fixed Unit.

### Non-deeded Timeshare

In a non-deed timeshare, the timeshare owner purchases a **lease**, license, or club membership to use the property for a specific amount of time each year for a stated number of years. This is sometimes called a Floating Time arrangement. The purchaser has to contact the resort to make reservations for the exact week required. Some resorts have limitations on how early units can be reserved. Seasonal Floating is the same as Floating Time except that the owner can only reserve time within a particular season

## Considerations in Purchasing a Timeshare

Numerous factors should be taken into account prior to purchasing a timeshare. A review of the background of the seller, developer, and management company, along with a review of the current maintenance budget, will assist the prospective seller in making an informed decision. Local real estate agents, Better Business Bureaus, and **consumer protection** offices also are good sources of information. While many reputable builders do exist, purchasing an undeveloped property carries additional risks. One means of protection is to hold money in an **escrow** account in case the developer defaults. The commitment from the seller that the facilities will be finished as promised should be written into the purchase contract with a date certain.

### Practical Factors

Timeshares provide the convenience of pre-arranged vacation facilities, however future circumstances may alter future planning ability. Timeshare plans typically do not include recession provisions for poor health or job loss. Vacationing tastes and favored activities may also change over time. These factors should be considered in evaluating a purchase.

### Investment Potential

Timeshare resales usually are difficult and often sold at a loss to the seller. Therefore, timeshares are typically not considered an investment as a second or vacation home might be. There are many investment options in the property area, but investment should not be a major factor when purchasing a timeshare. Renting is also difficult and many timeshare owners pay advance fees to rental agencies which may not be able to find any renters for that time frame.

### Total Costs

Total costs include **mortgage** payments and expenses, as well as travel costs, annual maintenance fees and taxes, closing costs, broker commissions, and finance charges. Annual timeshare maintenance fees can be high depending on the amenities of the resort. The larger and more upscale the resort, the higher the fees. These fees cover all of the costs of operation but are typically several hundred dollars a year. These fees can and do rise over time. All of these expenses should be incorporated when determining the overall cost of purchasing a timeshare.

### Document Review

Purchase documents for any type of real estate transaction are binding legal contracts and should be reviewed by an attorney. The contract may provide for, and some states require, a set "cooling-off" period during which the purchaser may cancel the contract and obtain a refund. The contract may include a non-disturbance clause and/or a non-performance clause. A non-disturbance provision ensures continued use of the unit in the event of **default** and subsequent third party claims against the developer or management firm. A non-performance protection clause allows the purchaser to retain ownership rights, even if a third party is required to buy out the contract. All promises made by the salesperson should be written into the contract. If not, such provisions will almost certainly be unenforceable in a court of law.

### Exchange Programs

These programs allow trades with other resort units in different locations for an additional fee. However, these trades usually cannot be guaranteed. There also may be some limits on exchange opportunities. Most developers are affiliated with large exchange companies. Two major companies are Resort Condominiums International (RCI) and Interval International (II). When a developer affiliates with the exchange company, the exchange company allows all of the buyers who purchase at that development to be able to join the exchange company. The developer pays an initial fee to the exchange company, and thereafter the individual timeshare owners are usually assessed an annual fee. The exchange company provides owners with a directory of hundreds of resorts. The exchange company is a huge computerized reservation system that is also licensed as a travel agency. An individual can deposit the week that they own and trade it for a week at another resort anywhere in the world, provided that one is available. There is usually a fee for the exchange, and there are also size rules, which allow trades equal or down. In most exchanges, a two bedroom can exchange for a two bedroom, but a three bedroom would likely require additional charges. Both of the major exchange companies rate their resorts. Usually, one needs to be giving up a week at a top resort to get a week at another top resort. In RCI the top rated resorts are called Gold Crown. In II top resorts are known as Five Star. There are a number of smaller exchange companies that are available to timeshare owners. These smaller companies are often regionally based.

## Foreign Properties

Timeshares and vacation club memberships in foreign countries are subject to the law of the **jurisdiction** in which the timeshare is located. A contract outside the United States for a timeshare located in another country will not be protected under U. S. federal or state contract property laws.

## Sales Incentives

Timeshare resorts sometimes offer free lodging to potential buyers in exchange for their attendance at a presentation about properties the developer has for sale. A free Vacation Certificate may be offered by telephone, mail, or from the Internet. Offers vary, but they are often for a three day, two night stay at the resort itself or a nearby hotel. Nearly all offers are subject to certain conditions, including age and income requirements. Both spouses must usually attend a sales presentation and upon arrival participants are often asked to provide proof of identity. Advance deposits, which may not be refundable, are often required to guarantee the time. Any charge termed a processing fee is probably nonrefundable. If deposit funds are actually called a deposit, refunds may be given at the location or at the end of the stay.

## State Regulation

Most states now regulate timesharing, either under existing state land sale laws or under laws that were specifically enacted for timesharing. The regulating authority is usually the Real Estate Commission in the state where the timeshare property is located.

FLORIDA: Under the Florida Vacation Plan and Timesharing Act, purchasers may cancel Timeshare contracts within 10 calendar days after the date the contract is signed if the seller is notified of the cancellation in writing. Any attempt by the seller to obtain a **waiver** of the cancellation right is void and of no effect. While closing documents may be executed, the closing cannot actually take place until the 10 day cancellation period has expired.

HAWAII: Hawaii state law requires the purchaser to have a seven-day right of rescission of any timesharing sales contract. Hawaii law also outlines specific guidelines for developers, acquisition agents, and sales agents of timeshare units, providing that failure to fully disclose certain actions as sales solicitations constitutes unfair and deceptive business practices. The law is also quite severe with respect to seller misrepresentations.

MARYLAND: A time-share purchaser shall have the right to cancel the sales contract until midnight of the tenth calendar day following, the contract date, or the day on which the time-share purchaser received the last of all documents required to be provided as part of the public offering statement, which ever is latest. This right of cancellation cannot be waived by the purchaser or by any other person. Although documents may be signed in advance, closing cannot occur until the purchaser's cancellation period has expired. Any false representation made by or on behalf of a developer that a purchaser may not exercise the right of cancellation or any attempt to obtain a waiver of the purchaser's cancellation rights or a closing prior to the expiration of the cancellation

period shall be unlawful, and the transaction is voidable at the option of the purchaser for a period of one year after the expiration of the cancellation period.

MASSACHUSETTS: In Massachusetts, timeshares are considered real estate. Notices of assessments and bills for taxes are required to be furnished to and paid by the managing entity or if there is no managing entity, to each timeshare owner. The managing entity is required by law to give notice of such **assessment** to the timeshare owners.

NEVADA: In Nevada, the purchaser of a timeshare may cancel, by written notice, the contract of sale until midnight of the fifth calendar day following the date of **execution** of the contract. The contract of sale must include a statement of this right. This right of cancellation may not be waived. Any attempt by the developer to obtain a waiver results in a contract that is voidable by the purchaser. The notice of cancellation may be delivered personally to the developer or sent by certified mail or telegraph to the business address of the developer. The developer shall, within 15 days after receipt of the notice of cancellation, return all payments made by the purchaser.

NEW MEXICO: The contract of sale is voidable by the purchaser within seven days after execution of the contract of sale. The contract shall conspicuously disclose the purchaser's right to cancel under this subsection and how that right may be exercised. An instrument transferring a timeshare shall not be recorded until seven days after the execution of the contract of sale. Advertisements which include the offer of a prize or other inducement must fully comply with the provisions of the Unfair Practices Act.

NEW HAMPSHIRE: The law requires that buyers' deposits must be held in escrow until the closing. Some projects must present a public offering statement to each buyer before or at the time of purchase. In addition, under the law buyers usually may cancel their purchase within five days after signing the purchase contract or five days after receiving the public offering statement whichever is later.

OREGON: A seller offering an exchange program to a purchaser in conjunction with a timeshare plan must provide specific written information to the purchaser about the exchange program, including whether participation is voluntary. A purchaser from a developer may cancel, for any reason, any contract, agreement or other **evidence** of indebtedness associated with the sale of the timeshare within five calendar days from the date the purchaser signs the first written offer or contract to purchase. A notice of cancellation given by a purchaser need not take a particular form and is sufficient if it indicates in writing the purchaser's intent not to be bound by the contract or evidence of indebtedness. Notice of cancellation, if given by mail, shall be given by certified mail, return receipt requested, and is effective on the date that the notice is deposited with the United States Postal Service, properly addressed and postage prepaid. Upon receipt of a timely notice of cancellation, the developer shall immediately return any payment received from the purchaser. If the payment was made by check, the developer shall not be required to return the payment to the purchaser until the check is finally paid. Upon return of all payments the purchaser shall immediately transfer any rights the purchaser may have acquired in the timeshare to the developer, not subject to any encumbrance created or suffered by the purchaser. No act of a purchaser shall be effective to waive the right of cancellation.

SOUTH CAROLINA: Contracts must inform the purchaser of the right to cancel the contract within four days, not including Sunday if that is the fourth day, from the date of the contract. Additionally, the purchaser may cancel at any time if the accommodations or facilities are no longer available as provided in the contract. Cancellation notice must be sent to the seller by certified mail, return receipt requested.

TEXAS: Under the Texas Timeshare Act, a purchaser may cancel a contract to purchase a timeshare interest before the sixth day after the date the contract is signed. If a purchaser does not receive a copy of the contract at the time the contract is signed, the purchaser may cancel the contract to purchase the timeshare interest before the sixth day after the date the contract is received by the purchaser. A purchaser may not waive the right of cancellation under this section. A contract containing a waiver is voidable by the purchaser.

## Additional Resources

*Blaggers: Adventures inside the Sun-Kissed but Murky World of Holiday Timeshare* Ley, Barry, Mainstream Publishing, 2001.

*Setting up Home in Florida: How to Buy, Rent or Timeshare Residential Property in the Sunshine State* Ray, Michael, Trans-Atlantic Publications, 1996.

## Organizations

### American Resort Development Association
15th Street NW, Suite 400
Washington, D.C. 20005
Phone: (202) 371-6700
Fax: (202) 289-8544
URL: http://www.arda.org

### State Legislative Affairs Office
201 South Orange Avenue Suite 525
Orlando, FL 32801
Phone: (407) 245-7601
Fax: (407) 872-0771

### Federal Trade Commission
600 Pennsylvania Ave, NW
Washington, DC 20580
URL: http://www.ftc.gov

# REAL ESTATE

## TRESPASSING

## Background

Trespassing is a legal term that can refer to a wide variety of offenses against a person or against property. Trespassing as it relates to real estate law means entering onto land without consent of the landowner. There are both criminal and civil **trespass** laws. Criminal trespass law is enforced by police, sheriffs, or park rangers. Civil trespass requires that the landowner initiate a private enforcement action in court to collect any damages for which the trespasser may be responsible, regardless of whether a crime has been committed. Traditionally, for either type of trespass, some level of intent is required. Thus, the trespasser must not simply unwittingly traverse another's land but must knowingly go onto the property without permission. Knowledge may be inferred when the owner tells the trespasser not to go on the land, when the land is fenced, or when a "no trespassing" sign in posted. A trespasser would probably not be prosecuted if the land was open, the trespasser's conduct did not substantially interfere with the owner's use of the property, and the trespasser left immediately on request.

## Landowner Consent

### Express Consent

The landowner may indicate, verbally or in writing, permission to enter onto the land.

### Implied Consent

The existence of consent may be implied from the landowner's conduct, from custom, or from the circumstances. Consent may be implied if these factors exist: the landowner was unavailable to give consent and immediate action is necessary to save a life or prevent a serious injury. Additionally, some states may extend this protection to animals.

## Hunting

A hunting license is not a license to trespass, but state laws treat hunters differently when it comes to trespassing. Some states have laws that specifically address trespassing while hunting, and others rely simply on the general trespassing statutes of the state. In about half of the states posting is not required to prevent trespassing; that is, it is against the law for hunters to trespass on private property without the landowner's permission even if the land is not posted. Where posting is required, some states have laws specifying how to post land. In some states, trespass while in possession of a firearm is a **felony** punishable by **imprisonment** for up to five years and/or a fine up to $5,000. A few states have laws that address hunters trespassing to retrieve dogs or wounded animals. In most states, however, hunters may not retrieve dogs or wounded animals if they cannot legally hunt on that land.

## Adverse Possession

Sometimes a trespasser continues trespassing for such a long time, the law permits the trespasser to have the right to stay on the land. This right ranges from the right to live on the land to the right to pass across it to get somewhere else. If the piece of property in dispute has been used by someone other than the owner for a number of years, the doctrine of adverse possession may apply. State laws vary with respect to time requirements; however, typically, the possession by the non-owner needs to be open, notorious, and under a claim of right. In some states, the non-owner must also pay the property taxes on the occupied land. A permissive use of property eliminates the ability to claim adverse possession. One common form of trespassing is when a neighbor's driveway or fence encroaches onto someone else's land. Sometimes the owner will not want to make an issue of the encroachment—either because it seems to be a minor problem or because the neighbor is a friend. To avoid problems later, however, the owner should give the "trespasser" written permission to keep the **encroachment** for as long as the owner continues to authorize it. If properly handled, this document will prevent the trespasser from acquiring a right to continue the encroachment and from passing along this right to future owners.

## Trespass By Animals

In the old courts of England, the owner of livestock was held strictly liable for any damages to person or property done by the livestock straying onto the property of another. The mere fact that animals strayed and damaged crops, other livestock, or **personal property** was sufficient to hold the owner liable for the injuries inflicted by cattle, sheep, goats, and horses. This strict liability position made sense in the confines of a small island such as England, but in the United States with herds of livestock wandering over vast expanses of land, a different process developed. The legislatures enacted statutes which provided that livestock were free to wander and that the owner was not responsible for damage inflicted by those livestock unless they entered land enclosed by a legal fence. These became known as open range

laws. Subsequently, certain states reversed the open range laws and required the owners of livestock to fence in their livestock. This position was similar to the **common law** position, only instead of strict liability, the livestock owner could be held liable only upon a showing that the livestock escaped due to the owner's **negligence**.

## State Laws

All city, county, and state law enforcement officers are authorized to enforce the hunter trespass laws. In 40 states, wildlife officers from the state's wildlife management agency are also authorized to enforce the trespassing laws. In 22 states posting is not required which means it is against the law for hunters to trespass on private property without the landowner's permission even if the land is not posted. Where posting is required some states have laws specifying how to post land. Only a few states have statutes that specifically address hunters trespassing to retrieve dogs or wounded animals. In all other states hunters may not retrieve dogs or wounded animals if the hunter cannot legally hunt on that land.

ALABAMA: All hunting requires permission of the landowner. There are no requirements for posting by property owners

ALASKA: Trespassing notices must be printed legibly in English, be at least 144 square inches in size, give the name and address of the person under whose authority the property is posted and the name and address of the person who is authorized to grant permission to enter the property, be placed at each roadway and at each way of access onto the property that is known to the land owner. In the case of an island, signage must be placed along the perimeter at each cardinal point of the island. The sign must explicitly state any specific prohibition that the posting is directed against.

ARIZONA: Hunters are permitted to enter onto land unless lawfully posted. Signs must be at least eight inches by eleven inches with plainly legible wording in capital and bold-faced lettering at least one inch high. The sign must have the words "no hunting", "no trapping" or "no fishing" either as a single phrase or in any combination. The signs must be conspicuously placed on a structure or post at least four feet above ground level at all points of vehicular access, at all property or fence corners and at intervals of not more than one-quarter mile along the property boundary. A sign with one hundred square inches or more of orange paint may serve as the interval notices between property or fence corners and points of vehicular access. The orange paint shall be clearly visible and shall cover the entire above ground surface of the post facing outward and on both lateral sides from the closed area.

FLORIDA: Trespass while in possession of a firearm is a felony punishable by imprisonment for up to five years and/or a fine up to $5,000. A person who knowingly propels or causes to be propelled any potentially lethal projectile over or across private land without authorization also commits felony trespass. A potentially lethal projectile includes any projectile launched from any firearm, bow, crossbow or similar tensile device.

IOWA: The unarmed pursuit of game or fur-bearing animals lawfully injured or killed which come to rest on or escape to the property of another is an exception to the trespass law.

KANSAS: Trespassing is permitted by licensed hunters in order to pursue a wounded game bird or animal, except that if the owner of the land instructs the hunter to leave, the hunter must leave immediately. Any person who fails to leave such land when instructed is subject to the provisions of the criminal trespass law.

LOUISIANA: Trespass is permitted in order to retrieve a dog or livestock, provided the trespasser is unarmed. Posting by landowners is required. Trespass on marshlands to trap or hunt fur bearing animals without permission is strictly prohibited

MARYLAND: It is unlawful to hunt on private lands in all counties without permission of the landowner or the landowner's **lessee**. Written permission is required from the property owner to hunt on private property in Allegany, Anne Arundel, Baltimore, Calvert, Carroll, Cecil, Charles, Frederick, Garrett, Harford, Howard, Montgomery, Prince George's, St. Mary's, and Washington Counties. Written permission is required from the property owner to hunt deer on private property in Somerset, Wicomico, and Worcester Counties. Written permission is required from the property owner to trap on private and **public lands** in all counties. The landowner is not liable for accidental injury or damage to the hunter, whether or not the landowner or the landowner's agent or lessee have given permission to hunt.

MICHIGAN: A person other than a person possessing a firearm may, unless previously prohibited in writing or orally by the property owner, enter on foot upon the property of another person for the sole purpose of retrieving a hunting dog. The person shall not remain on the property beyond the reasonable time necessary to retrieve the dog.

MINNESOTA: Law allows hunters to trespass unless no trespassing signs are posted along the **boundaries** every 1000 feet or less, or in wooded areas where boundaries are less clear, at intervals of 500 feet or less, or at the primary corners of each parcel of land and at access roads or trails at points of entrance. Furthermore, the law mandates that the lettering should be at least two inches high and the name and phone number of the landowner or occupant should be listed. Lands that are cropped or grazed and show signs of tillage, crops, crop residue, or fencing for livestock containment do not require posting of signs. Hunters must ask permission to enter these lands. A person on foot may, without permission of the owner, enter land to retrieve a wounded animal that was lawfully shot. The hunter must leave the land immediately after retrieving the wounded game. A person on foot may, without permission of the owner, enter private land without a firearm to retrieve a hunting dog. After retrieving the dog, the person must immediately leave the premises.

NEW YORK: A person may enter and remain upon unimproved and apparently unused land, which is neither fenced nor otherwise enclosed in a manner designed to exclude intruders, unless notice against trespass is personally communicated to by the owner.

NORTH CAROLINA: In Halifax and Warren counties, no arrests for trespassing can be made without the consent of the owner the land.

NORTH DAKOTA: Any hunter may enter upon legally posted land to recover game shot or killed on land where the hunter had a lawful right to hunt.

OKLAHOMA: Signs are required at all entrances and all corners and at 200 yard intervals along property lines.

OREGON: No person shall hunt upon the cultivated or enclosed land of another without first obtaining permission from the owner or lawful occupant thereof, or the agent of such owner or occupant. The boundaries of enclosed land may be indicated by wire, ditch, hedge, fence, water or by any visible or distinctive lines that indicate a separation from the surrounding or contiguous territory.

SOUTH CAROLINA: Any person entering upon the lands of another for the purpose of hunting, fishing, trapping, netting; for gathering fruit, wild flowers, cultivated flowers, shrubbery, straw, turf, vegetables or herbs; or for cutting timber on such land, without the consent of the owner or manager, is guilty of a **misdemeanor**.

SOUTH DAKOTA: In the part of the Black Hills fire protection district lying south of Interstate Highway 90, no person may enter upon any private land with intent to take or kill any bird or animal, after being notified by the owner or lessee not to do so. Such notice may be given orally or by posting written or printed notices to that effect at the residence or where the buildings are located thereon, and at the gates or entering places therein, and in conspicuous places around the land posted. All such notices shall contain the name and address of the owner or lessee posting the lands.

TEXAS: It is against the law to hunt or fish on privately owned lands or waters without the permission of the owner or owner's agent. No person may pursue a wounded wildlife resource across a property line without the consent of landowner of the property where the wildlife resource has fled. Under the trespass provisions of the Penal Code, a person on a property without the permission of the landowner is subject to arrest.

UTAH: Written permission is required from the owner or person in charge to enter upon private land that is either cultivated or properly posted and must include the signature of the owner or person in charge, the name of the person being given permission, the appropriate dates, and a general description of the property.

VERMONT: Notices prohibiting the taking of wild animals shall be erected upon or near the boundaries of lands to be affected with notices at each corner and not over 400 feet apart along the boundaries thereof. Notices prohibiting the taking of fish shall show the date that the waters were last stocked and shall be maintained upon or near the shores of the waters not over 400 feet apart. Legible signs must be maintained at all times and shall be dated each year.

VIRGINIA: Fox hunters and coon hunters, when the chase begins on other lands, may follow their dogs on prohibited lands, and hunters of all other game, when the chase begins on others lands, may go upon prohibited lands to retrieve their dogs, but may not carry firearms or bows and arrows on their persons or hunt any game while thereon. The use of vehicles to retrieve dogs on prohibited lands shall be allowed only with the permission of the landowner.

WEST VIRGINIA: Written permission must be in the possession of anyone who will shoot, hunt, fish, or trap upon the fenced, enclosed or posted grounds or lands of another person. Written permission is also required to peel trees or timber, build fires or do any other act or thing thereon in connection with or auxiliary to shooting, hunting, fishing or trapping. Hunters who kill or injure any domestic animal or fowl, destroy or damage any bars, gates, or fence, or leave open any bars or gates resulting in damage to the owner, can be held criminally liable as well as liable to the landowner. The landowner may personally arrest any such person found violating this law and take the hunter before a **justice of the peace** for trial. In such instances, the landowner is vested with all the powers and rights of a game warden.

## Additional Resources

*The Legal Edge for Homeowners, Buyers, and Renters.* Bryant, Michel J., Renaissance Books, 1999.

*Modern Law of Deeds to Real Property.* Natelson, Robert, Aspen Law, 1992.

*Neighbor Law: Fences, Trees, Boundaries and Noise.* Jordan, Cora, Nolo Law, 2001.

## Organizations

### Environmental Health Center
1025 Conn. Ave., NW, Suite 1200
Washington, DC 20036 USA
Phone: (202) 293-2270
URL: http://www.nsc.org/ehc.htm

### The Fund for Animals
200 West 57th Street
New York, NY 10019
Phone: (212) 246-2096
Fax: (212) 246-2633
URL: http://www.fund.org
Primary Contact: Marian Probst, President

# REAL ESTATE

## ZONING

*Sections within this essay:*

- Background
- Types of Zoning
    - Residential Zoning
    - Commercial Zoning
    - Industrial Zoning
    - Agricultural Zoning
    - Rural Zoning
    - Combination Zoning
    - Historic Zoning
    - Esthetic Zoning
    - Permitted and Accessory Uses
- Zoning Changes
    - Change of Zoning
    - Variances
    - Non-Conforming Uses
    - Conditional Use Permits
    - Eminent Domain
- Additional Resources

## Background

**Zoning** is the way the local governments control the physical development of land and the kinds of uses for different parcels of property. State and local governments have the power to enact statutes and ordinances, known as zoning regulations, in order to control the use of land for the protection of the public health, safety, and welfare. Zoning laws place significant limitations on the uses of the property within the defined areas or "zones" established in the particular zoning **ordinance**. Zoning laws typically specify the areas in which residential, industrial, rec-

reational or commercial activities may take place. These could be residential, rural, commercial, industrial or a combination. Zoning laws often use numerical or alphabetical designations, such as CR-1; however the designation are not standard and differ from one community to another.

In addition to limiting land uses, zoning laws can also regulate the dimensional requirements for lots and for buildings on property located within the community, the density of development, and what livestock can inhabit the parcel of land. Zoning ordinances may designate certain spaces for hospitals, parks, schools, and buildings with historical significance. Zoning can also provide for restrictions on parts of certain parcels of land, such as those parcels which lie within protected peaks and ridges.

Zoning ordinances and maps are public records. The zoning information is listed on the tax records in most localities. These records can be located at the local tax assessor's office and are often online.

## Types of Zoning

Zoning categories and symbols vary among communities. A C-1 zone in one city is not necessarily the same as a C-1 in another. Typically, jurisdictions use letters of the alphabet as code abbreviations to identify the use allowed in a physical geographic area, such as R for residential, C for commercial, and I for industrial. These symbols are usually paired with some number. The number can specify the level of use, or it may indicate a certain amount of acreage or square footage for that particular property.

### Residential Zoning

Residential zoning can include Single Family Residences (SFR), Suburban **Homestead** (SH), or any number of other designation which cover homes, apartments, duplexes, trailer parks, co-ops, and condominiums. Residential zoning can cover the issues as to whether mobile homes can be placed on the property and the number of such structures.

Zoning laws typically limit the type of animals allowed at a residence. While domestic pets, such as dogs, birds, and cats, are generally not regulated, chickens, sheep, horses, llamas, pigs, and cows are subject to certain requirements. Many ordinances prohibit keeping these farm animals in residential neighborhoods. Others limit the number of animals based on the size of the property.

Zoning laws on home-based businesses can depend on the nature of the business, whether there are employees or business invitees, the hours of operation, signage, parking and delivery concerns, and noise issues. Some zoning ordinances prohibit all in-home businesses in residential areas. Others restrict the type of business, the hours, and may require separate parking and entrance facilities. Rules regarding home-based businesses for condominiums are typically even more restrictive than private residences.

### Commercial Zoning

Commercial zoning usually has several categories and is dependant upon the business use of the property and often the number of patrons. Office buildings, shopping centers, nightclubs, hotels, certain warehouses, some apartment complexes, as well as vacant land that has the potential for development into these types of buildings can all be zoned commercial. Almost any kind of real estate except single-family home and single-family lots can be regarded as commercial real estate.

The availability of parking may affect the type of commercial zoning that is permitted. Additionally, there can be rules regarding the proximity of certain types of businesses to others. Many zoning laws prohibit or restrict adult entertainment establishments to a certain geographical area. Others bar such establishments within a certain distance of existing schools or churches.

### Industrial Zoning

Like commercial zoning, industrial zoning can be specific to the type of business. Environmental factors including noise concerns usually are issues in determining into which industrial level a business falls. Manufacturing plants and many storage facilities have industrial zoning. Certain business, such as airports, may **warrant** their own designation.

Industrial Zoning is often dependent upon the amount of lot coverage, which is the land area covered by all buildings on a lot, and building height. Additionally, set-back requirements are higher for industrial zoned properties.

### Agricultural Zoning

Agricultural zoning is generally used by communities that are concerned about maintaining the economic viability of their agricultural industry. Agricultural zoning typically limits the density of development and restricts non-farm uses of the land. In many agricultural zoning ordinances, the density is controlled by setting a large minimum lot size for a residential structure. Densities may vary depending upon the type of agricultural operation. Agricultural zoning can protect farming communities from becoming fragmented by residential development. In many states, agricultural zoning is necessary for federal voluntary incentive programs, subsidy programs and programs that provide for additional tax abatements.

### Rural Zoning

This designation is often used for farms or ranches. In certain parts of the country, this designation will include residences zoned to allow horses or cattle.

### Combination Zoning

Any of the designations can be combined to form some sort of combination zone, many of which are unique to the community adopting the particular designation.

### Historic Zoning

Homes and buildings over fifty years old are often included in historic zones. These zones have regulations, which prevent the alteration of the structures from the original conditions, although there are allowances for repair and restoration in keeping with the historic plan. Frequently, buildings in these areas can qualify for governmental tax incentives.

The National Register of Historic Places is the U. S. official list of cultural resources worthy of preservation. Authorized under the National Historic Preservation Act of 1966, the National Register is part of a national program to coordinate and support public and private efforts to identify, evaluate, and protect historic and archeological resources. Properties listed in the Register include districts, sites, buildings, structures, and objects that are significant in U. S. history, architecture, archeology, engineering, and culture. The National Register is administered by the National Park Service, which is part of the U. S. Department of the Interior. The National Register accepts applications for buildings, which meet certain specific historic requirements.

Owners of properties listed in the National Register may be eligible for a 20% investment tax credit for the certified rehabilitation of income-producing certified historic structures such as commercial, industrial, or rental residential buildings. This credit can be combined with a straight-line **depreciation** period of 27.5 years for residential property and 31.5 years for nonresidential property for the depreciable basis of the rehabilitated building reduced by the amount of the tax credit claimed. Federal tax deductions are also available for charitable contributions for conservation purposes of partial interests in historically important land areas or structures.

### Esthetic Zoning

Increasingly popular in upscale communities, this sort of zoning covers color schemes, landscaping, mailboxes, fences, solar panels, decks, satellite dishes, and types of materials. Esthetic zoning ordinance may require that building plans be submitted and approved by an architectural review committee. Wireless communication receiving devices can often be impacted by these types of zoning rules.

### Permitted and Accessory Uses

Permitted and **Accessory** uses are built-in exceptions within a certain zoning category. For example, a property which is not zoned for a bar may have a bar which is connected to the hotel as accessory or permitted use.

## Zoning Changes

### Change of Zoning

If the zoning on a parcel of land is inconsistent with the use the land owner desires, the owner may apply to the local **jurisdiction** for a change of zoning. Each jurisdiction has its own rules and regulations. However, there is typically an application and a fee, followed by some type of **hearing** at which the owner presents the request and the reasons for the requested change. Surveys, drawings, photographs, and even models can be used to convey the proposed plan. Many owners hire engineers or lawyers to assist with the rezoning process.

If the owner is unsuccessful in obtaining the change, there may be a possibility to appeal the action either within the administrative structure of the governmental body or in a court of law.

### Variances

A variance is a request to deviate from current zoning requirements. If granted, it permits the owner to use the land in a manner not otherwise permitted by the zoning ordinance. It is not a change in the zoning law. Instead, it is a specific **waiver** of requirements of the zoning ordinance.

Typically, variances are granted when the property owner can demonstrate that existing zoning regulations present a practical difficulty in making use of the property. Each jurisdiction municipality has rules for variance requests. Usually, the land owner seeking the variances files a request or written application for a variance and pays a fee. Normally, the requests go first to a zoning board. The zoning board notifies nearby and adjacent property owners. The zoning **examiner** may then hold a hearing to determine if the variance should be granted. The applicant may then be required to appear before the governing body of the municipality, such as a city council, for the final determination.

### Non-Conforming Uses

A nonconforming use is a permitted use of property which would otherwise be in violation of the current zoning ordinance. The use is permitted because the land owner was using the land or building for that use before the zoning ordinance became effective. Nonconforming uses are often referred to as being "grandfathered in" to a zoning code. In order to qualify for nonconforming use, the property almost always needs to have had the use continuously. Thus, if the businesses closes and the use lapses for any time, the permission for the nonconforming use could vanish.

### Conditional Use Permits

Similar to variances, conditional use permits allow an otherwise non-permitted use of the property that the zoning code does not include. Conditional use permits are usually granted at a public hearing before a political body, usually with the conclusion that the new use of the property will be in the **public interest**.

### Eminent Domain

Eminent domain is the power of government to take private property and use it for public purposes. The power of eminent domain is recognized in the

United States Constitution, which prohibits the taking of private property "without just compensation." The federal constitutional provision recognizing the power of eminent domain implies the requirement that property be taken for a "public use."" Public use includes the traditional government activities of building roads, government and public facilities such as government buildings and parks, as well as more generally beneficial activities assured through protection of scenic areas, wetlands, and historic landmarks.

If the government zones a piece of property such that the property owner can no longer effectively use the parcel of land, this provision may be applicable. The property owner may be able to sue for compensation because the land has been "taken" by the government. This is commonly referred to as "a taking." Just compensation is difficult to determine. By definition, it is the **fair market value** that a property owner would receive if the property were being sold without the zoning restrictions in place. If the government and the property owner are unable to agree on the fair **market value**, the property owner can file suit and hire a certified **appraiser** to give **testimony** concerning the value.

## Additional Resources

Daniels, Thomas L. and Keller, John W., Lapping, Mark B.*The Small Town Planning Handbook.* American Planning Association, 1995.

Davidson, Michael*A Glossary of Zoning, Development and Planning Terms* American Planning Association,1997.

Fischel, William A. *The Economics of Zoning Laws: A Property Rights Approach to American Land Use Controls.* Johns Hopkins University Press, 1987.

Harr, Charles Monroe and Kayden, Jerold S. *Zoning and the American Dream: Promises Still to Keep.* American Planning Association, 1989.

Siegan, Bernard H.*Property and Freedom: The Constitution, the Courts, and Land-Use Regulation.* Bowling Green State University,1997.

## Organizations

### American Association of Home Based Businesses (Residential Zoning)
PO Box 10023
Rockville, MD 20849 USA
Fax: (301) 963-7042
URL: http://www.aahbb.org
Primary Contact: Beverley Williams, President

### National Register of Historic Places
1849 C Street, NW NC400
Washington, DC 20240 USA
Phone: (202) 343-9536
URL: http://www.cr.nps.gov/nr

### National Trust for Historic Preservation.(Historic Zoning)
1785 Massachusetts Ave, NW
Washington, DC 20036 USA
Phone: (202) 588-6000
Fax: (202) 588-6038
URL: http://www.nationaltrust.org

### Urban Planning Institute
2100 M Street, NW
Washington, DC 20037 USA
Phone: (202) 833-7200
URL: http://www.urban.org

# RETIREMENT AND AGING

## ASSISTED LIVING FACILITIES

*Sections within this essay:*

- Background
- Federal Purview
- Resident Rights
- Funding
- State Provisions
- Additional Resources

## Background

The concept of "assisted living" as a unique program of care or service for elderly/minimally impaired persons has been slow, in the eyes of legislators and practitioners, to distinguish itself from other existing forms of services. The distinction becomes important for purposes of funding and financial assistance from state and federal entities. But more importantly, the distinction becomes important in the eyes of the residents and their families.

Assisted living is often described as a statement of philosophy which differentiates itself from other forms of "residential care" by focusing on a model of living that promotes independence, autonomy, privacy, and dignity for residents in a facility. In other words, the concept relates more to an approach toward care rather than to the actual care received. Moreover, families struggling with the less appealing option of placing their loved ones in traditional "nursing homes" are more soothed by the option of knowing that assisted living strives to maintain the current level of independence enjoyed by residents, but with supervision or support when needed.

In general, the term "assisted living" is used transitionally with that of "board and care" services. However, assisted living statutes and regulations usually contain language referring to "independence," "autonomy," "privacy," etc. Assisted living is also different from other residential programs (e.g., homes for the aged, board and care facilities, residential care facilities, etc.) in that it is more likely to involve apartment-like settings and (if living space is to be shared) choice of apartment mates. Finally, assisted living facility staff will often make arrangements for external entities rather than internal staff members to provide nursing care or health related services to residents. This arrangement makes such services more likely to be reimbursable as "home health care services" under **Medicaid** or other funding initiatives.

But when assisted living residents need nursing care, the distinction between "assisted living" and other forms of residential care becomes more nebulous. In many states, assisted living facilities may admit or retain residents who meet "level of care" criteria used for admission to nursing facilities. At the same time, many nursing homes divide their beds into wards or designated areas, so as to accommodate varying levels of resident needs. They may have a skilled care area, an intermediate care area, and an "assisted living" area all within the same facility. Generally, such an arrangement is mutually beneficial to facility and patient. It keeps **occupancy** rates high at the facility and allows residents to move internally from one area of care to another without the need to move to another facility altogether.

Semantics aside, assisted living generally refers to a residential living arrangement in which residential amenities are combined with "as needed" assistance with "activities of daily living" (ADLs) (eating, dressing, bathing, ambulating, toileting, etc.) and personal care. Although only about half of all states actually use the term "assisted living" in their regulations or statutes, a vast majority of states have either reviewed existing legislation or enacted new laws to address the growing demand for assisted living facilities. This action occurred particularly during the years of 1995 through 2000.

## Federal Purview

All assisted living facilities accepting state or federal funds must be licensed. For those accepting federal funds, most of the applicable regulations and rules are incorporated into those applicable to nursing homes in general. They include:

- The Nursing Home Reform Act is absorbed in a massive piece of legislation known as the Omnibus Budget Reconciliation Act of 1987 (OBRA 1987). The Act imposes more than just minimum standards; it requires that a facility provide each patient with a level of care that enables him or her "to attain or maintain the highest practicable physical, mental and psychosocial well-being." Importantly, OBRA 87 makes each state responsible for establishing, monitoring, and enforcing state licensing and federal standards. Under the Act, states must fund, staff, and maintain investigatory and Ombudsman units as well.

- The Patient Self Determination Act of 1990 is absorbed in the Omnibus Budget Reconciliation Act of 1990 (OBRA 1990). Applicable to more than just nursing homes, it essentially mandates that facilities provide written information to patients regarding their rights under state law to participate in decisions concerning their medical care. This includes the right to execute advance directives and the right to accept or reject medical or surgical treatments. The facilities must also provide a written policy statement regarding implementation of these rights, and must document in each patient's record whether or not an advance directive has been executed.

## Resident Rights

States are required to effect bills of rights for nursing home residents. Generally, the same rights attach to residents in assisted living facilities as those in nursing homes. Most state declarations of rights parallel the federal ones, codified at 42 **USC** 1395i-3(a) to (h); and 1396r(a) to (h) (1988 supplement to the U.S.C.). They are enumerated in the section addressing nursing homes.

## Funding

Public subsidies for elders in residential settings take different courses in different states. Older persons qualifying for low-income subsidies may apply their federal SSI benefits, as well as any state supplemental SSI benefits, toward assisted living charges for room and board. Medicaid generally pays for nursing or medical services provided to qualified individuals. In most states, this is done through Home and Community Based Services (HCBS) (Section 1915(c)) waivers. **Waiver** programs acknowledge that many individuals at high risk for being institutionalized can be cared for in their own homes or communities, thus preserving their independence and ties to family and community, at no more cost than that of institutional care. Thus, a person eligible for institutional care may "waive" that right and apply the funds toward home care or assisted living arrangements. Waivers are generally granted for three years and may be renewed for five years.

Finally, many states are developing policies that combine SSI with Medicaid benefits to provide one level of care appropriate for the resident. This encourages "aging in place" rather than the stressful alternative of finding another facility should the resident's health decline and he or she needs more than what assisted living can offer.

## State Provisions

The following information summarizes state approaches to assisted living arrangements. The absence of certain information in the summary for a particular state (e.g. a mention of minimum staffing ratios or room sizes) is not to be construed as meaning that no requirements exist for that state regarding that element or factor. Rather, the information focuses on some of the important or distinguishing points from state to state.

ALABAMA: See Ala. Code Chapter 420-5-4. Revisions to existing regulations were issued in 1999. The state recognizes three categories of assisted living facilities: congregate (17 or more adults), group (4 to 16 adults), and family (2 to 3 adults). The regulations provide that residents must be "ambulatory adults who do not require acute, continuous, or extensive medical or nursing care and are not in the need of hospital or nursing home care." Staffing ratio requirements are one staff member per six residents, 24 hours a day. Minimum room size is 80 square feet for single or 130 square feet for double occupancy. No public financing is available other than SSI.

ALASKA: See Alaska Stat. 47.33.005 et seq; also Reg. 7 AAC 75.010 et seq. In addition to private facilities, the state operates six Pioneer Homes that provide supportive living services. Alaska's "general relief" program does offer limited financial support in combination with a Medicaid HCBS waiver for certain qualified individuals. Alaska has minimal facility and staff requirements, but requires a written contract between home and resident that covers all conditions, charges, policies, duties and rights, etc. The state continually reviews its regulations.

ARIZONA: Ariz. Adm. Rules, R9-10-701 et seq. The Arizona Long Term Care System (ALTCS) has expanded its Supportive Residential Living Center (SRLC) state-run project, which consolidated adult care homes, support residential living, supervisory care homes, and adult family care into a single "assisted living" category. The state now has three licensed classifications (facilities assisting ten or fewer residents, eleven or more residents, and adult foster care homes with one to six residents). Minimum room size, 80 square feet for bedroom units, 220 square feet for residential units. There are no minimum staffing ratio requirements, but facilities must be able to meet the needs and handle crisis intervention on a 24-hour basis. Minimum one toilet/lavatory per eight residents.

ARKANSAS: Ark. Ann. Code 20-76-201 et seq. requires that tenants be 18 years of age or older and be independently mobile (physically and mentally capable of vacating the facility within three minutes). There are numerous other requirements regarding minimum physical and mental conditions. Single units must have at least 100 square feet; double units must be 80 square feet. There must be a minimum of one toilet/lavatory per six residents. Staffing requirements are scaled for daytime, evening, and night shifts.

CALIFORNIA: Cal. Code of Reg, Title 22; Division 6, Chapter 8 governs "residential care facilities for the elderly (RCFE)," of which the state has approximately 6,000 facilities. In 1995, special legislation was passed to permit RCFEs serving persons with Alzheimer's Disease to develop secure perimeters (exterior doors or perimeter fences, delayed egress doors, etc.) One toilet/sink per six residents. Minimum staffing requirements for facilities with fewer than 100 residents is one person. Medicaid coverage is not available.

COLORADO: Colorado regulates "personal care boarding homes" under Chapter VII, Section 1.1 et seq. Minimum requirements include one toilet/lavatory per six residents, no more than two residents to a room, and a 100 square foot single occupancy room size.

CONNECTICUT: Conn. Gen. Stat.192-490 and Agency Regulation 19-13-D105 address the state's unique approach of permitting "managed residential communities" (MRCs) to offer assisted living services through assisted living services agencies (ALSAs). The state has about 25 licensed ALSAs. Minimum requirements include at least one RN on-call 24 hours a day and one toilet/lavatory per six residents. Medicaid reimbursement is available for assisted living services in elderly housing complexes. Residents may receive temporary nursing services through an external agency.

DELAWARE: Under state law, assisted living agencies (Del. Code Ann, Title 16, Part II, Ch. II, 63.0 et seq) are distinguished from "rest residential homes" (Part II, 59.0 et seq.) in that the latter is intended for those who only need shelter, housekeeping, board, personal surveillance or direction in activities of daily living. Persons with income less than 250 percent of the SSI level are eligible for fee waiver service. In residential homes, there must be one toilet and bathtub or shower for every four residents.

DISTRICT OF COLUMBIA: All community residential facilities are governed by D.C. Code Ann. 32-1301 et seq, 34-3400 et seq., and DC Law 5-48. The DC Housing Code (DCMR) establishes minimum square footage and bathing/toilet requirements. However, no more than four persons may share one sleeping room. Short term nursing care is permitted (72 hours or less).

FLORIDA: Florida law maintains three levels of assisted living: standard, limited nursing services, and "extended congregate care (ECC)," (requiring a higher level of assistance/care). See Fla. Stat. Ann., Ch. 400 Part III and Admin. Code Ch. 58-A-5. The general rule is that facilities serving more than 17 residents must have staff on duty 24 hours a day; fewer than 17 residents requires staff on duty or monitoring mechanisms to ensure the safety of residents. There is a minimum requirement of one bathroom per three residents. There is an optional state supplement to federal SSI and SSDI assistance and a Medicaid home and community based services waiver. RNs must visit ECCs twice a year to monitor residents and review state compliance.

GEORGIA: See Ga. Code Ann. 31-2-4, 31-7-2, and Regulation 290-5-35.07 et seq. "Personal Care Homes" serve any adult over 18 years of age who is ambulatory and does not require continuous medical, nursing, or mental health monitoring or care. The maximum facility size is for 24 residents or less. Bedrooms must have at least 80 square feet of usable floor space per resident. A Medicaid waiver is available. Facilities must have at least one staff person to 15 residents during waking hours, and one to 25 during non-waking hours.

HAWAII: See Hawaii Admin. Rules 11-90 to 11-101. The state distinguishes between "assisted living" facilities (for independent living) and "adult residential care" facilities (Types I and II) whose residents require at least minimal assistance in ADLs. Neither can accept persons who need nursing care, although adult residential care facilities may obtain an "extended care license" to serve residents who meet the nursing home level of care. Assisted living facilities must have a minimum of 220 square feet of living space, while residential care homes only require 90 square feet for single rooms or 70 square feet per occupant of a multiple occupancy room.

IDAHO: See Idaho Code 39-3301 et seq. and Admin. Rule Title 4, Ch. 22-70. The state has one designation of "residential care facility" that is broken down into three categories by level of care: minimum, moderate, or maximum. A state fund is maintained to assist in reimbursement costs for eligible persons. Facilities must have at least one staff person available to residents at all times.

ILLINOIS: Under Illinois law (77 IAC 330 and Title 89, Ch. 1, Subchapter d, Part 146) "shelter care facilities" are licensed for maintenance and personal care but not routine nursing care. "Supportive living facilities" (SLFs) offer 24-hour supervision and assistance and is most consistent in definition with the accepted definition of "assisted living." The state has set up a third option, "community based residential facilities" (CBRFs) intended to provide short or long term

needs in order to relieve family caregivers. SLFs require licensed and certified staff.

INDIANA: Indiana law only provides recommendations for assisted living facilities, although it has several laws that impact residential care facilities in general.(See, e.g., 410 IAC 16.2 et seq.). For example, all facilities must have at least one staff member on duty at all times (for facilities with fewer than 100 residents) and an additional staff member for each 50 residents above 100. Medicaid coverage is not available but is being assessed.

IOWA: See Iowa Code Ann 231C and 321 IAC Chapter 27; IAC 661-5.626. Licensed facilities serve at least six residents and may provide health related care in addition to personal care and assistance. Minimum staffing is left up to the facility, but each tenant must sign an occupancy agreement that explains services, charges, etc., and whether or not staff are available 24 hours a day. Each dwelling unit must have 190 square feet of living space. Multiple occupancy quarters must have at least 80 square feet of living space per bed.

KANSAS: Kan. Stat. Ann. 28-39-144 et seq. addresses assisted living facilities (caring for six or more individuals). Health care attendants provide assistance and services up to 12 hours a day. Medicaid waivers are available to elderly persons who meet the nursing home level of care criteria and have income below 300 percent of the federal SSI payment.

KENTUCKY: See 905 KAR 5:080 and 902 KAR 20:036. The state has a voluntary certification program for assisted living facilities. For certification, the maximum number of beds per room is four; there must be one toilet/lavatory for every eight residents, with separate bathrooms for each sex on each floor. No room size requirements. There is no Medicaid funding available.

LOUISIANA: See La. Rev. Stat. Ann 2151 et seq. Assisted living homes refer to facilities that provide room, board, and personal services to two or more residents who reside in individual living units. Personal care homes offer the same but have congregate living settings of two to eight residents. Shelter care homes are larger scale personal care homes with congregate living and dining services. There must be at least one awake staff on duty at night and sufficient staff to cover resident needs during daytime hours. Elderly Medicaid beneficiaries who can no longer live at home may qualify for assistance.

MAINE: See Me. Rev. Stat. Ann. Tit 22. Section 7902. Laws finalized in 1998 provide for Level I residential care facilities (formerly known as adult foster care homes or six bed boarding houses) and Level II residential care facilities for more than six residents. Levels I and II facilities must have 100 square feet for single or 80 square feet for double rooms. Bathrooms must be provided for every six residents, and showers/bathtubs for every 15 residents. Medicaid funds are available for eligible residents. Staffing rules require a ratio of 1:12 residents during day shifts; 1:18 for evening hours, and 1:30 for night shifts.

MARYLAND: Assisted living programs are covered under Md. Code Ann., Title 10.07.14. Facilities may not serve persons who require more than intermittent nursing care. Medicaid does not reimburse for assisted living beyond the existing Senior Assisted Housing Program. Assisted living programs have three levels of care distinctions for purposes of staffing requirements and services provided.

MASSACHUSETTS: See Mass. Code of Regulations, 651 CMR 12.00. Persons needing 24-hour skilled nursing supervision are not eligible for assisted living facilities. Medicaid's Group Adult Foster Care (GAFC) provides some subsidizing of services for low income residents. The state has created a special SSI living arrangement for assisted living.

MICHIGAN: Michigan distinguishes homes for the aged (supervised personal care facilities under MCL 333.20106) from adult foster care homes (large group homes). Neither type of facility may accept residents who require continuous nursing care. There are staffing ratio requirements for adult foster homes. Medicaid waivers are available if services are delivered by community agencies and not the facility's staff. Toilet/lavatory ratios are one to eight residents.

MINNESOTA: See Minn. Stat. Ann. 144 et seq. and 144A and D. Minnesota covers assisted living through its funded Alternative Care (AC) program and Medicaid waiver programs. The AC program serves persons whose income exceeds Medicaid eligibility but who would spend down to Medicaid levels within six months of admission to a nursing home. There are no unit size requirements for facilities, nor are there minimum staffing requirements.

MISSISSIPPI: See Mississippi Regulations 1201.1 et seq. "Personal care homes" are licensed to provide care to ambulatory residents who are not in need of nursing care. Separate toileting facilities are required for each sex on each floor, with a ratio of one to six residents. Residents may not be required to access one bedroom by entering another. There is a maximum of four beds per room and a minimum of 80 square feet per resident. Medicaid funding is not available for assisted living.

MISSOURI: See Vernon's Ann. Mo. Stat. 198.003 to 198.186, and regulations, title 13, Section 15-10.010 et seq. Missouri law recognizes Type I and Type II residential care facilities (RCFs). Type II involves a higher level of care under the direction of a licensed physician. Both types require that residents be of such mental and physical capability as to be able to negotiate a normal path to safety, using assistive devices or aides when necessary. There is Medicaid reimbursement for personal care services. All licensed facilities must have a minimum of 70 square feet per resident, irrespective of whether in single or shared quarters. State requires one toilet/lavatory for every six residents.

MONTANA: Personal care facilities (PCFs) are governed by Subchapter 9, Section 16.32.902. Adult foster care homes are covered under Chapter 16, Subchapter 1, Section 11.16. Both are eligible for Medicaid HCBS waiver reimbursements. Single dwelling bedrooms must be at least 100 square feet, multi-tenant bedrooms must contain at least 80 square feet per resident. One toilet is required for every four residents. In PCFs, residents are classified as either A or B categories (B involves incontinence, under chemical or physical restraint, ventilator dependent, etc.; facilities may have up to five B residents).

NEBRASKA: Assisted living facilities are covered under NAC Title 174, Chapter 4. In 1998, state legislators approved $40 million in grants or loan guarantees to nursing homes to convert wings or entire facilities to assisted living. This action followed a law passed in 1997 that replaced residential care facilities and domiciliary facilities with the new distinction of assisted living. All facilities must be licensed. Minimum room size of 100 square feet is required for single apartments or dormitory-like rooms; 80 square feet per resident for shared room space. A toilet and sink must adjoin each resident's bedroom. Medicaid waivers are available.

NEVADA: See Nev. Rev. Stat. Ann. 449.017 et seq. and administrative code section 449.156. Residential care facilities may be in the form of an adult group home or an Alzheimer's group home. Single occupancy rooms must be at least 80 square feet in size; maximum shared quarters of three residents with at least 60 square feet each. Alzheimer's facilities must have sprinkler systems and 24-hour awake staff, as well as exit doors with alarms or time-delay locks and fenced yards. Residents are assessed as "care category 1" (ambulatory) or "care category 2" (non-ambulatory). Personal care services are Medicaid reimbursable if residents meet SSI eligibility criteria. Facilities with more than 20 residents must have at least one awake staff around the clock, with a second available within ten minutes.

NEW HAMPSHIRE: Supported residential care facilities are covered under Chapter He-P 805; residential care home facilities are covered under Chapter He—804. RCFs are defined as offering services beyond room and board to two or more individuals. No resident may require 24-hour nursing services. A minimum room size of 80 square feet for single residents or 140 square feet for double occupancy is required. Residents must be mobile and able to self-evacuate. Medicaid reimbursement is available.

NEW JERSEY: See N.J. Admin. Code Chapter 8:36. Regulations effective in 1996 created assisted living programs in subsidized housing sites, as well as licensing of "service agencies" to deliver assisted living services to subsidized elderly housing projects. No more than two persons may occupy an assisted living residential unit. There must be at least one awake personal care assistant and one additional staff member available at all times.

NEW MEXICO: Adult residential care is covered under New Mexico's Administrative Code, Title 7, Ch.8, Part 2. The state offers assisted living as a Medicaid waiver service. Private rooms must have at least 100 square feet of useable floor space.

NEW YORK: See NY Social Law 461-1 et seq., as well as NY Comp. Codes R & Regulations, Title 18, Section 485.1 et seq. Assisted living programs are Medicaid-reimbursable and are available in both "adult care homes" and "enriched housing programs" (which offer congregate services but independent housing units). No more than three persons may share independent units.

NORTH CAROLINA: See N.C. Admin Code Title 10, Ch. 42, and N.C. Gen. Stat. 131D-2. In 1995, state law combined former "adult care or domiciliary homes" and multi-unit assisted housing with services, under the new umbrella of "assisted living residences." Adult homes may have up to four residents

share bedroom space, with a minimum 80 square feet per bed. Personal care services are reimbursable as state plan services through Medicaid. Staffing requirements vary with facility size.

NORTH DAKOTA: North Dakota funds assisted living programs that require apartment like settings in basic care facilities. While licensing is not required, the public welfare **statute** contains a clear definition of assisted living that must be met in order to qualify for monetary assistance. Assisted living participants in the state's Service Payments for Elderly and Disabled (SPED) program must have impairments in four ADLs or five IADLs and not be eligible for the Medicaid HCBS waiver. Adult day care and respite care is Medicaid reimbursable. Awake staff must be on duty 24 hours a day in basic care facilities. See Chapter 50-24.5 and Chapter 23-09.3.

OHIO: See ORC. 3721.01 et seq. (residential care facilities) and ORC 3722 et seq (adult care facilities). Most assisted living facilities in Ohio are licensed as residential care facilities. RCF residents may receive up to 120 days of nursing services on a part-time or intermittent basis. Adult care facilities provide fewer services (e.g., no administration of medication or wound care, etc.). RCFs must offer a minimum of 100 square feet for single or 80 square feet per resident in multiple occupancy rooms. Toilets/lavatories are required for every eight residents, including separate toilets for the sexes if there are more than four of a sex on any floor. RCFs require one staff person on site at all times.

OKLAHOMA: Oklahoma has both residential care homes and assisted living centers. See Okla. Stat. Ann. Title 63, 1-819. An assisted living category was legislatively created in 1997, and all such facilities require licensing. No more than two residents may share bedrooms. There is a minimum square footage of 80 for single rooms or 60 square feet per bed in multiple occupancy rooms. Residents cannot have needs greater than intermittent or unscheduled nursing care. Staffing requirements are a minimum of 3/4 hour of personnel per day per resident, based on the average daily **census**. Limited Medicaid reimbursements are available for certain services.

OREGON: See Or. Admin Reg Division 56: 411-056-0000 and 56: 411-55-000. Assisted living is handled as a program within a physical structure, which may be a "residential care facility." RCFs operate with two categories of residents: Class I residents must be ambulatory and only need assistance with ADLs; Class II residents have higher needs. Payments are available for services to Medicaid recipients residing in assisted living settings who meet the nursing home level of care criteria. Staffing ratios are established in the regulations on a sliding scale according to time of day and number of residents.

PENNSYLVANIA: Personal care homes are governed by PC Title 55, Chapter 2620. Single occupancy rooms must have 80 square feet of floor space; multiple occupancy rooms require 60 square feet per person, with a maximum of four. Residents who are not ambulatory may nonetheless be admitted if they do not require nursing care.

RHODE ISLAND: Regulations R23-17.4 SCF. Regulations use the term "residential care and assisted living facilities," and the state does have Medicaid waiver provisions for certain service arrangements. There are general requirements that resident rooms must have no more than two beds with a minimum floor space of 100 square feet per single or 80 per person double occupancy. No more than eight persons may share toilet/lavatory facilities. Residents must not require medical or nursing care but may require medication administration. A responsible staff member must be on the premises at all times.

SOUTH CAROLINA: See S.C. Regulation R61-84, Community Residential Care Facilities. Minimum bedroom size is 80 square feet for single or 60 square feet per bed for double occupancy, with one toilet/lavatory for every eight residents. Minimum staff requirements are one staff member for every ten residents during daytime hours and one per 44 residents at night. Medicaid waiver reimbursement is available.

SOUTH DAKOTA: Article 44:04 et seq. governs assisted living centers. Medicaid waiver reimbursements are available. All must be seen by a physician at least once a year. For facilities with more than ten residents, one staff person who is awake is required during sleeping hours; if fewer than ten residents, staff may sleep if there are adequate fire alarm systems and staff call systems in place. See S.D. Codified Laws Ann. 34-12-1.

TENNESSEE: The Tennessee Rules of the Dept. of Health, Ch. 1200-8-9 et seq. cover assisted living facilities and homes for the aged. Homes for the aged must have contract agreements with a physician who is available to render care and with a nursing home that will accept residents who must be discharged from the home for the aged because of medical or care needs that surpass those provided by the home.

TEXAS: Texas law provides for "personal care homes" under Tex. Rev. Health and Safety Stat. 247.001 et seq. and Administrative Code Title 25-146.321 et seq. Medicaid waiver reimbursement is available for services provided in personal care facilities licensed by the Texas Dept. of Human Services. There are required staffing ratios of 1 to 16 residents for day shifts, 1 to 20 for evening, and 1 to 40 for night shifts. Room sizes must be a minimum of 80 square feet for single bedrooms and 60 square feet per bed for multiple occupancy rooms (maximum of four persons).

UTAH: Assisted living facilities are covered by Regulation 432-270. Residents must be ambulatory to the extent of being able to evacuate a facility without assistance. Pets are permitted according to local ordinances. Direct care staff members are required on site 24 hours a day. Minimum room size for congregate facilities is 100 square feet for single or 160 square feet for double occupancy. Medicaid waiver reimbursement is available.

VERMONT: Residential care homes are licensed under Regulation Section 7102 Medicaid waiver coverage is available. Residential care homes differ from assisted living residences in that they include more extensive personal care services, whereas assisted living generally provides "supportive services." Under certain criteria, residential care homes may retain persons who need nursing services for 60 days or less.

VIRGINIA: 22 Virginia Administrative Code Section 40-71-10 et seq. covers for adult care residences (ACRs). Medicaid HCBS waivers are available. ACRs may offer single rooms (minimum 100 square feet) or multiple occupancy rooms (80 square feet per resident, with a maximum of four). One toilet/lavatory is required for every seven persons. Staffing ratios are based on resident needs.

WASHINGTON: Medicaid assisted living in covered under the Washington Administrative Code Chapter 388-110. Boarding homes in general are covered under Chapter 246-316. Assisted living services are those contracted with a licensed boarding home to be provided to residents, and Medicaid recipients may be required to move when their needs exceed the level of contracted services.

WEST VIRGINIA: Personal care homes are covered under 64 CSR 14, et seq.; residential care homes (for ambulatory residents) are covered under 64 CSR 65; and residential care communities (congregate facilities/apartment units for ambulatory residents) are covered under Section 16-5N-1 et seq. Awake staff are optional in personal care facilities with ten or fewer residents. Larger facilities must have one awake staff per floor in multi-story buildings (with limited exceptions).

WISCONSIN: In Wisconsin, there are two categories of facilities available. First, there are residential care apartment complexes (RCACs) provide for residents "not more than 28 hours per week" services that are supportive, personal, and nursing care related. Conversely, "community based residential facilities" focus more on care and treatment services above the level of room and board and which serve as primary functions of the facility. Both categories require ambulatory residents. State funding is available for Medicaid recipients who meet the nursing home level of care criteria. See Wis. HFS Chapters 83 and 89.

WYOMING: In Wyoming, assisted living facilities are distinguished from boarding homes by the fact that they provide limited nursing care. Neither type provides habilitative care. Rooms must have at least 120 square feet for single or 80 square feet per person for double occupancy. Toilets/lavatories are required for every ten residents. At least one awake staff is required for all facilities with more than ten residents.

## Additional Resources

*Legal Guide for Older Americans* American Bar Association. Random House:1998.

"Nursing Home Law Overview." Available at http://www.elderlibrary.org/nursing%20home%20law%20overview.htm.

"Nursing Home Resident Rights." Edson, Gail, 1996. Available at http://www.keln.org/bibs/edson2.html.

*State Assisted Living Policy: 1998* Mollica, Robert L., National Academy for State Health Policy:1998.

## Organizations

### *American Association of Retired Persons (AARP)*
601 E Street, NW
Washington, DC 20049 USA
Phone: (800) 424-3410
URL: www.aarp.org

### *The American Bar Association (Commission on Legal Problems of the Elderly)*
740 15th Street, NW
Washington, DC 20005 USA
Phone: (202) 992-1000

### *The National Citizens' Coalition for Nursing Home Reform*
1424 16th St., NW, Suite 202
Washington, DC 20036 USA
Phone: (202) 332-2275

# RETIREMENT AND AGING

## ELDER ABUSE

*Sections within this essay:*

## Background

As the population of elderly people in the United States increases, so does the incidence of what is known as elder abuse. Estimates put the number of cases in which elderly victims are abused as high as half a million annually. The number of reported incidents, however, is barely 15 percent of that.

As with all forms of abuse, elder abuse affects people from all socioeconomic backgrounds. The more frail the individual, the more likely he or she will be a victim of abuse. Abuse can be physical or emotional, subtle or blatant. Most frightening is that abuse is most likely to come at the hands of someone the victim trusts: a child, a spouse, a caregiver.

With elder abuse more pervasive, the issue has garnered increased attention, and a number of groups, along with federal, state, and local agencies, are taking steps to reverse the trend. Part of the challenge is to find ways to get people to report abuse when it happens. This means educating people to know and watch for warning signs, and it means encouraging victims to speak out without fear of recrimination.

## Types of Elder Abuse

The word "abuse" carries a number of interpretations; legal definitions may differ from researchers' definitions, and experts frequently disagree among themselves. Abuse can manifest itself in any of several forms; as a practical matter, we can define abuse here as deliberate maltreatment or mistreatment. The most pervasive forms of mistreatment include the following:

### Physical Abuse

Any use of physical force that results in injury, pain, or any sort of impairment constitutes physical abuse. It includes striking, pushing, and shoving, shaking, kicking, punching, and slapping. Some abusers will strike the victim with an object. Others will inflict burns on the victim. Force-feeding or withholding food, administering inappropriate drugs, and applying physical restraints all come under the heading of abuse. There will often be visible signs of physical abuse, such as bruises, swellings, burn marks, scratches, or broken bones. Not infrequently, these injuries will be attributed to carelessness (a fall, standing too close to the stove).

### Emotional Abuse

There are no overtly physical signs of emotional or psychological abuse, but that does not make it any less serious than actual physical abuse. A victim may be subjected to angry verbal tirades, harassment, threats, and humiliation. Affecting an over-protective manner toward the victim, as though to imply that the victim is in capable of caring for him- or herself, can be a more subtle form of emotional abuse. Sometimes the abuser will isolate the victim from family and friends or much-enjoyed activities (even something as simple as a daily outing to the local newspaper stand). A person who is being emotionally abused may become either strangely agitated or overly withdrawn.

### Sexual Abuse

Sexual activity that is non-consensual is abuse, and unfortunately the elderly are not immune to this sort of victimization. It could be anything from unwanted touching and groping to forced posing for explicit photographs to rape and **sodomy**. Unexplained genital bruising, bleeding, or infection can be a sign that **sexual abuse** is taking place.

### Financial Exploitation

In the 1935 play *Kind Lady,* an elderly woman is befriended by a family that subsequently robs her of her money and possessions. Unfortunately, this crime happens in real life all too frequently. This form of abuse includes cashing the victim's **pension** checks and keeping the money, forging the victim's signature, misusing a **power of attorney**, coercing the victim to sign a will or a **deed** to property, and outright stealing. An elderly person who makes any sudden changes in legal documents such as wills or deeds or who transfers large sums of money out of a bank account for no apparent reason, may well be the victim of exploitation.

### Neglect and Abandonment

Neglect of an elderly person's needs, especially by one who has been entrusted to take care of that person, is sadly not as uncommon as it should be. A relative may ignore much-needed repairs at the victim's home, or a caregiver may neglect to feed and bathe a victim properly. An abusive caregiver may not bother to make sure that the victim's home has such necessities as heat and hot water. Some caregivers will simply abandon an elderly person, much the same way one might abandon a newborn. They may leave the victim at a hospital or nursing home, or they may leave the victim at a shopping mall.

If caregivers neglect an elderly person who is frail or confused, that person will become neglectful of his or her own needs. Ill health, coupled with loneliness and depression, may rob the person of any desire to eat, to go outside, to bathe, or to see old friends. This can put the person's life in danger; he or she may become malnourished or ignore serious medical problems, for example.

## Scope of the Problem

In the fall of 1998 a study examining the number of elder abuse incidents in the United States painted an alarming picture of the true scope of abusive behavior. Called the National Elder Abuse Incidence Study, it was funded by two branches of the U. S. Department of Health and Human Services: the Administration on Aging and the Administration for Children and Families. Conducted by the National Center on Elder Abuse and a survey research firm, the study found that for the year 1996 some 450,000 elderly persons in domestic settings were abused or neglected. That figure is frightening enough, but more frightening is the fact that only a fraction of those cases were reported to local Adult Protective Services (APS) agencies. Through several methodologies including local reports from "sentinels" (specially trained people in community agencies who have contact with and access to the elderly), they were able to arrive at the 450,000 number. The actual number of cases reported by APS agencies in 1996 was 70,942. That represents a mere 16 percent of the estimated figure.

### Problems Reporting Abuse

Why would a problem so pervasive, and so potentially deadly, be so easily hidden? Part of the answer lies in the victims themselves.

Many elderly people are both physically and emotionally healthy. They enjoy rewarding lives and remain independent. Others are not so fortunate. They may be mentally alert but physically frail. Or they may be suffering from Alzheimer's disease or the effects of circulatory problems, both of which reduce mental awareness. Some elderly people who might otherwise be mentally alert suffer from depression, which makes them appear listless and apathetic. These individuals may be victims of abuse and neither fully comprehend nor care. Thus, they make no effort to protect themselves.

Other elderly victims of abuse are no doubt quite aware of what is happening to them. There are a number of reasons why these people might fail to speak out. Often they are embarrassed to admit that they are being abused; they feel that it makes them appear helpless. Some may be protective of those who are abusing them. Being abused may be the preferable option when the only other choice is turning one's own child in to the local police. Finally, a number of elderly victims are afraid of their abusers. Fear of bodily harm or of **abandonment** keeps them from taking action.

As with any type of abuse (such as **child abuse** or **domestic violence**), the issue is often more complex than simply identifying behavior and taking action. A family that is locked in a cycle of violent behavior may see elder abuse as acceptable despite the obvious reasons why it is not. Substance abusers create a special problem because they may be violent only when they are under the influence of alcohol or other drugs. The elderly parent, like the spouse or the child, may keep quiet as a means of denying that an addiction exists. Sometimes, family members who are put in the role be serving as caregivers react violently out of total frustration with a situation they are totally unprepared to handle. The elderly victim may feel guilty for putting the caregiver in such a stressful position and consequently say nothing. It is also likely, in some cases, that since abuse can take its toll quickly, an elderly person in otherwise reasonable health may go downhill quickly once abuse starts and thus be unwilling or unable to speak out forcefully.

## Federal, State, and Local Action

Federal legislation protecting elderly people, such as the Older Americans Act of 1975, do not address specific issues related to elder abuse. (The Older Americans Act was amended in 1987 to include definitions of abuse, but those definitions are meant to serve primarily as a guideline.) Elder abuse is handled primarily by state laws, and each state has different regulations. All agree, however, that obvious abuse of an elderly person demands quick action, and all 50 states have some method of reporting abuse.

Usually it is the local or state APS agencies that handle reports of elder abuse. In some communities, the responsibility falls to other government agencies, such as a county social services department. Usually the state's human services agency has responsibility for programs for the aging. Many states have a toll-free 24-hour hotline number for those who wish to report instances of abuse.

The Administration on Aging works closely with state and local agencies to provide support, to help train APS workers to recognize and work with elder

abuse, and to develop informational materials such as posters, videos, and public service announcements. It also helps state agencies coordinate their efforts as a means of streamlining their work. It also funds the National Center on Elder Abuse, which serves as a clearinghouse for public and private agencies, as well as individuals, who are seeking information on elder abuse and its prevention. The Center's web site (http://www.elderabusecenter.org) includes a listing of toll-free telephone numbers for each state, as well as access to a variety of information on abuse.

Typically, a report of elder abuse is followed up by someone from an APS agency, which will investigate the charge. If the report turns out to be accurate, the agency will work with other community groups to ensure the safety of the victim. If a victim is competent and refuses to be helped, the APS can do nothing. But if the victim asks for help, or if the victim has been declared incapacitated by a court and a **guardian** has been appointed, the APS can initiate action. Other advocacy groups such as AARP offer guidelines and advice to elderly people who may fall prey to abuse.

## Striking a Balance

Elderly people who are frightened and confused are often stereotyped and, consequently, not listened to when they complain. While many elderly individuals may indeed be suffering from Alzheimer's disease or other conditions that affect brain functions, (a series of small and apparently insignificant strokes, for example, can affect cognitive skills and memory), others may merely be suffering from the effects of over or under medication. Spouses, children, and caregivers need to understand this and be willing to help determine the cause of confusion, mood swings, or memory loss. Local agencies provide support and counseling for caregivers, especially first-time caregivers who have no understanding of how to take care of a frail elderly person. APS agencies may have information on community programs, so may local hospitals or senior citizen recreation centers. Educating caregivers helps those whose frustration might push them over an unacceptable edge to know how and when to step back and reevaluate their actions before they become abusive.

For those whose abusive tendencies are more deeply rooted, any help that can be given to them is a step in the right direction. That said, people who for whatever reason cannot be trusted to care properly for an elderly person should not be allowed to do so. If they violate the law through their abuse, they must be dealt with. So should those who are motivated not by deep-seated problems but rather such base instincts as greed (those who try to exert control over an elderly person's finances, for example).

When an elderly person complains of abuse, he or she should be listened to. For those who are being abused but cannot or will not admit it, they, too, must be listened to, in the chance that they might say something that backs up suspicions of abuse. Elderly people need to feel that they are taken seriously. Community service providers who can develop a feeling of trust with them will be providing an invaluable service.

As for those elderly who suffer from self-neglect, if it turns out that they are truly unable to care for themselves, their advocates must ensure that anyone who seeks a power of attorney or conservatorship is acting in the individual's best interest.

## Additional Resources

*Abuse and Maltreatment of the Elderly: Causes and Interventions*Kosberg, Jordan I., editor., Wright-PSG, 1983.

*Abuse, Neglect, and Exploitation for Older Persons: Strategies for Assessment and Intervention.* Baumhover, Lorin A., and S. Colleen Beall, editors., Health Professions Press, 1996.

*Family Crimes Against the Elderly: Elder Abuse and the Criminal Justice System.* Brinell, Patricia J., Garland Publishing, 1998.

*Issues in Intimate Violence.*Kennedy Bergen, Raquel, editor, Sage Publications, 1998.

## Organizations

### AARP
601 E Street NW
Washington, DC 20049 USA
Phone: (202) 434-2257
Fax: (202) 434-2588
URL: http://www.aarp.org
Primary Contact: William Novelli, CEO

### National Council on the Aging
409 Third Street, Suite 200
Washington, DC 20024 USA
Phone: (202) 479-1200
Fax: (202) 479-0735
URL: http://www.ncoa.org
Primary Contact: James P. Firman, President and CEO

### National Council on Elder Abuse
1201 15th Street NW, Suite 350
Washington, DC 20005 USA
Phone: (202) 898-2586
Fax: (202) 898-2583
URL: http://www.elderabusecenter.org
Primary Contact: Sara Aravanis, Director

### U. S. Department of Health and Human Services

### Administration on Aging
330 Independence Avenue SW
Washington, DC 20201 USA
Phone: (202) 619-0724
Fax: (202) 260-1012
URL: http://www.aoa.gov
Primary Contact: Josefina G. Carbonell, Assistant Secretary for Aging

# RETIREMENT AND AGING

## HEALTHCARE/MEDICARE

*Sections within this essay:*

- Background
- Medicare: Part A
- Medicare: Part B
- Medicare: Part C
- Medicare: Part D
- Payment, Notice, and Appeals
- The Future of Medicare

## Background

**Medicare** is the federal health insurance program for persons 65 and older and certain disabled persons. Congress established Medicare in 1965 as Title XVIII of the Social Security Act. It is now codified as 42 U.S.C.A sections 1395 et seq. Pub.L. No. 89-97, 79 Stat. 291. Medicare is an entitlement program for qualified beneficiaries and not a need-based program like **Medicaid**, the federal-state health insurance program for low-income persons. Thus, the rich, the poor, and the middle class all may receive Medicare benefits, so long as they satisfy the eligibility criteria.

Medicare is administered by the Centers for Medicare & Medicaid Services (CMMS), formerly known as the Health Care Financing Administration (HCFA). It oversees issues concerning eligibility requirements, extent of coverage, and termination of benefits. CMMS is a division of the U. S. Department of Health and Human Services. Its main office is located in Baltimore, Maryland, and there are nine regional offices throughout the United States.

The Medicare program is divided into four parts: (1) Medicare Part A covers inpatient hospital services, skilled nursing facility services, home health services, and hospice services; (2) Medicare Part B covers other reasonable and necessary medical services, including outpatient hospital care and physician services; (3) Medicare Part C provides an array of private health insurance plans that are mandated to cover the same items and services offered by Medicare Parts A and B. Depending on the plan, Part C may also contain additional costs and offer additional benefits to those in Parts A and B. (4) The Medicare Prescription Drug Improvement and Modernization Act of 2003 (P.L. 108-173) effectively became Medicare Part D, and covers prescription drug benefits. Its first benefit began in 2004 with the introduction of Medicare-Approved Drug Discount Cards, which phased out when permanent prescription drug benefits went into effect in 2006.

Part A Medicare is largely funded by mandatory payroll taxes paid by employers and employees. Part B is an elective program financed in part through premiums paid by Medicare beneficiaries and in part through government contributions. Part C is essentially a medical savings plan that is also funded partly by **beneficiary** premiums and partly by government contributions. Each part has its own trust fund. Part A payroll taxes are maintained in the Federal Hospital Insurance Trust Fund, while Part B premiums and contributions are maintained in the Supplementary Medical Insurance Trust Fund. Part C premiums and contributions are maintained by the Medicare+Choice (now called Medicare Advantage) MSA Trust Fund.

Individuals are generally entitled to coverage under any of the three parts if they are 65 years or older and (1) qualify for Social Security or Railroad Retirement benefits; (2) have received Social Security or Railroad Retirement **disability** benefits for at least 24 months; (3) or suffer from end-stage renal disease. Individuals who elect retirement at age 62 are not eligible for Medicare until they turn 65, even if they qualify for Social Security or Railroad Retirement benefits earlier. Individuals who are eligible for Social Security retirement benefits and postpone retirement to continue working after age 65 can begin receiving Medicare benefits at age 65.

The largest group of Medicare recipients qualify for coverage based on their entitlement to Social Security benefits. Sometimes called Old Age, Survivors, and Disability Insurance (OSADI) benefits, these benefits are paid to workers eligible to retire, survivors of workers eligible to receive these benefits, and disabled workers. Workers are eligible to retire at age 62 (with reduced benefits) if they are "fully insured," which means that they have worked and paid Social Security taxes for the requisite amount of time specified by **statute**. Survivors are entitled to Social Security benefits according to their relationship with the deceased worker (i.e., widow, divorced spouse, child, or parent). Workers are "disabled" and entitled to Social Security benefits if they are unable to engage in any substantial gainful activity by reason of a medically determinable physical or mental impairment that can be expected to result in death or that has lasted or can be expected to last for a continuous period of not less than twelve months. 42 U.S.C.A. section 1382c.

Health care providers may participate in Medicare and receive Medicare payments if they satisfy state and federal licensing requirements and comply with the standards promulgated by CMMS. A health care provider must also enter into an agreement with the Secretary of Health and Human Services. The agreement designates the amounts the provider will charge Medicare patients and the manner in which it will provide medical services. Hospitals, skilled nursing facilities, home health agencies, clinics, rehabilitation agencies, public health agencies, comprehensive outpatient rehabilitation facilities, hospices, critical access hospital, and community mental health centers (CMHCs) may generally seek to participate in Medicare under a provider agreement. However, clinics, rehabilitation agencies, and public health agencies may enter into provider agreements only for services involving outpatient physical therapy and speech pathology. CMHCs may only enter into provider agreements to furnish certain hospitalization services.

## Medicare: Part A

The hospital insurance program established under Part A of Medicare provides qualified individuals with basic protection against the costs of the following services: (1) inpatient hospital care; (2) extended care services furnished to skilled nursing facility inpatients; (3) home health care; and (4) hospice care for terminally ill persons. Inpatient hospital care may generally be provided by urban hospitals, most rural hospitals, certain psychiatric institutions, and Christian Science sanatoriums. 42 U.S.C.A. sections 1395c et seq. Specifically, the costs covered by Medicare include: bed and board at the hospital; most physician, nursing, and related services; most drugs, supplies, appliances, and equipment furnished by the hospital; diagnostic and rehabilitative services; occupational, respiratory, physical, and speech therapy; and social services for personal, emotional, and financial issues related to covered medical care. Anesthesia services provided by a certified registered nurse anesthetist, however, are expressly excluded from coverage.

Individuals who are ineligible for OASDI or railroad retirement benefits may establish entitlement to hospital insurance benefits under Medicare Part A if they have worked in Medicare qualified government employment or meet the requirements for "deemed entitlement" to OASDI benefits. Individuals who lack "fully insured" status are "deemed" entitled to OASDI benefits for the purpose of obtaining Part A coverage if they are 65 years old, are residents of the United States, are U. S. citizens or **aliens** lawfully admitted to the United States for permanent residence, and have filed an application for Medicare hospital insurance benefits. Individuals who cannot otherwise qualify for hospital insurance benefits may obtain Medicare Part A coverage by paying a premium.

Part A coverage is based on "benefit periods." An episode of illness is termed a benefit period and starts when the patient enters the hospital or nursing home facility and ends sixty days after the patient has been discharged. A new benefit period starts with the next hospital stay, and there is no limit to the number of benefit periods a person can have. Medicare will pay the cost of hospitalization for up to 90 days. The patient must pay a one-time **deductible** for the first sixty days of a benefit period and an additional daily fee called a co-payment for hospital care provided during the following thirty days. Apart from these payments, Medicare covers the full cost of hospital care.

So long as the premiums and deductibles are fully paid in a timely manner, beneficiaries remain entitled to Medicare coverage through the later of (1) the month of the individual's death, if the individual would have been entitled to OASDI or Railroad Retirement benefits if he or she had not died, or (2) the month in which the individual no longer meets Part A entitlement requirements. Individuals who die during the month in which they would have turned 65 are entitled to hospital insurance benefits for that month, even if death occurs before the individual's birthday, provided the individual would have met conditions for Medicare Part A entitlement had he or she not died.

## Medicare: Part B

Medicare Part B provides benefits that supplement the coverage provided by Part A. It makes voluntary supplementary medical insurance (SMI) available to most individuals age 65 or over and to disabled individuals under age 65 who are entitled to hospital insurance under Medicare Part A. The SMI program is financed in part by beneficiaries who pay a monthly premium and a yearly deductible. The program also receives federal funding. As of 2005, new enrollees in Medicare Part B are eligible for a one-time initial wellness physical examination within six months of enrollment, as part of enhanced preventive service benefits under Part B.

SMI is administered by insurance companies, referred to as carriers, which have entered into contracts with CMMS to perform designated functions as agents of CMMS. Those functions include receiving, disbursing, and accounting for funds in making payments for covered services; providing an opportunity for a **fair hearing** if CMMS denies an enrollee's request for payment; and assisting enrollees in locating physicians participating in the Medicare Part B program.

Not every physician provides services covered by Medicare. Physicians must agree to participate in the Medicare program, promise to accept the Medicare approved charge as payment in full, and then submit only charges that are reasonable and necessary for treating the patient. 42 U.S.C.A section 1395u. Federal law prohibits physicians from charging more than

115% of Medicare's approved charge. Medicare will reimburse the beneficiary 80% of Medicare's approved charge, and the beneficiary is responsible for the remainder. 42 U.S.C.A. section 1395w-4(g)(2)(C). Fines and penalties apply to physicians who charge above the 115% cap, including exclusion from the Medicare program and monetary penalties of up to $2,000 per violation.

Persons entitled to Part A benefits are enrolled automatically in Part B, unless they indicate that they do not want to participate in Part B. Persons who do not apply for Social Security benefits and are therefore not automatically enrolled in Medicare can apply at the local Social Security Administration office or by mail. Generally, individuals can enroll in Medicare Part B during an initial seven-month enrollment period that begins 3 months before their 65th birthday and ends 3 months after it. Individuals who miss their initial enrollment period may only enroll during a general enrollment period, which lasts from January through March of each year. Coverage then becomes effective on July 1st of that year.

Individuals who enroll during the first three months of the initial enrollment period are eligible for Part B entitlement beginning in the first month of their eligibility to enroll. If an individual enrolls during the fourth month of the initial enrollment period, entitlement begins the following month. Individuals who enroll during the fifth month of the initial enrollment period are eligible for Part B entitlement beginning with the second month after the month of enrollment. For individuals who enroll in either of the last two months of the initial enrollment period, entitlement begins with the third month after the month of enrollment.

Part B beneficiaries may terminate their enrollment at any time by giving CMMS written notice that they no longer wish to participate in the SMI program. Entitlement to benefits under the program terminates at the end of the month after the month in which the individual files the disenrollment request. Entitlement also terminates upon death, termination of entitlement to Medicare Part A benefits, or nonpayment of premiums. Termination upon death ends SMI entitlement on the last day of the month in which the individual dies.

Part B covers the services of physicians and other health practitioners; supplies furnished incidental to physicians' services; outpatient hospital services; rural health clinic services; comprehensive outpatient rehabilitation facility services; physical and occupational therapy services; speech pathology services; prosthetic devices and durable medical equipment; ambulance services; X-ray treatment; and diagnostic and other laboratory tests. 42 U.S.C.A. section 1395k(a); 42 U.S.C.A. sections 1395x et seq.

The Part B program is not comprehensive. Excluded items include dentures and other dental care; most outpatient drugs, except where the drugs are physician-administered during covered treatment; routine physical examinations; hearing aids; orthopedic shoes; and eyeglasses and eye examinations. 42 U.S.C.A. section 1395y(a). Medicare covers limited preventive care services, such as pap smears, pelvic exams, mammograms, colorectal cancer screening, prostate cancer screening, bone mass measurement tests, and flu, pneumococcal, and hepatitis B shots. It also covers diabetes glucose monitoring and diabetes education.

## Medicare: Part C

Congress significantly restructured the Medicare program with the establishment of Medicare Part C, the Medicare+Choice program (now referred to as Medicare Advantage). Medicare offers beneficiaries the following private health care delivery options: Medicare health maintenance organizations (HMOs), medical savings accounts (MSAs), preferred provider organizations (PPOs) (regionally expanded in 2006), private fee-for-services (PFFS), and provider sponsored organizations (PSOs). However, individuals are only eligible to elect a Medicare Advantage plan offered by a Medicare Advantage organization (MCOs, referring to the prior designation of Medicare+Choice) if the plan serves the geographic area in which the individual resides.

Beneficiaries who reside in an area served by a Medicare Part C plan may opt out of either Part A or Part B and elect to enroll in Medicare Part C, except those with end-stage renal disease. Beneficiaries may only enroll during November of each year, and plan elections become effective in January of the following year. Beneficiaries who do not elect any option will automatically be enrolled in traditional fee-for-service Medicare. If a beneficiary does not make an election for a particular year and is already enrolled in Part C from the previous year, he or she will automatically be re-enrolled in that plan. Beneficiaries can also change plans if their plan contract terminates or if they move from their plan's service area. 42 U.S.C.A. section 1395w-21(e)(3).

The Secretary of Health and Human Services has established a process through which elections under Medicare Part C are made and changed. Individuals seeking to elect a an must complete and sign an election form, provide the information required for enrollment, and agree to abide by the rules of the Medicare Advantage program. Within 30 days from receipt of the election form, MCOs transmit the information necessary for CMMS to add the beneficiary to its records as an enrollee of the MCO. A beneficiary's enrollment may not be terminated unless the beneficiary engages in disruptive behavior, provides **fraudulent** information on the election form, permits abuse of the enrollment card, or fails to pay premiums in a timely fashion. Part C monthly premiums are calculated based on the rules set forth in 42 U.S.C.A. section 1395w-24(b)(1)(A).

A plan offered by an MCO satisfies the basic requirements for benefits and services if the plan provides payment in an amount that is equal to at least the total dollar amount of payment for such items and services as would otherwise be authorized under Medicare Parts A and B. The plan must also comply with (1) CMMS's national coverage decisions and (2) written coverage decisions of local carriers and intermediaries for jurisdictions handling claims in the geographic area for which services are covered under the plan.

## Medicare: Part D

Medicare Part D Prescription Drug Benefits were phased in by the enactment of the Medicare Prescription Drug Improvement and Modernization Act of 2003 (MIMA), 42 U.S.C.A. 1395w-101 et seq. Starting in 2004, Medicare-Approved Drug Discount Cards became available to all Medicare enrollees. The card did not pay the cost of prescription drugs, but reduced the amount paid for medications by 10 to 20 percent. Cards expired with the implementation of Medicare's permanent prescription drug program in 2006.

Enrollment in Medicare Part D began in November 2005 and was scheduled to end on May 15, 2006 (although the program was available for use on January 1, 2006). Penalty for late enrollees is one percent per month of the Part D premium charged by the prescription drug plan ultimately chosen. 42 U.S.C.A. section 1395w-101 Section 1860D-13(b).

All those enrolled in Medicare are eligible to enroll for Part D benefits. Enrollees must choose a prescription drug plan offered by a number of Pharmacy Benefit Managers (PBMs) that best fits their health profile and anticipated prescription drug use. Monthly benefit premiums are approximately $35 (as of 2006). Enrollees pay a $250 deductible, after which Part D benefits begin. Part D benefits will pay 75 percent of prescription drug costs between $250 and $2,250. Enrollees then pay 100 percent of costs above $2,250 up to a maximum of $3,600 in out-of-pocket spending. Part D will again pay approximately 95 percent of costs above $3,600. Those drugs for which payment could be made under Medicare Part A are excluded from Part D coverage. 42 U.S.C.A. 1395w-102(e)(1).

## Payment, Notice, and Appeals

Medicare payments can be sent directly to the health care provider or to the patient. Regardless of the method of payment, the patient must receive notice that the provider has filed a medical insurance claim. The notice should detail the medical services provided, identify the expenses that are covered and approved by Medicare, and **itemize** any expenses that have been credited toward the annual deductible and any expenses Medicare has already paid in full. Patients or providers who are dissatisfied with a decision made regarding a Medicare claim may ask CMMS or the insurance carrier to reconsider the decision, depending on the nature of the claim. Following reconsideration, either party may request a formal hearing before an administrative law judge, though no formal hearing will be granted for claims made under Part B unless the claim is for at least $100. Once the administrative law review process has been completed, aggrieved parties may appeal to federal district court. Part B claims must total at least $1,000, however, before a federal district court will hear the appeal.

## The Future of Medicare

Approximately 76 million Americans born between 1946 and 1964 are expected to retire in the next 28 years. In 2001 about 39 million Americans were enrolled in Medicare, and that number is expected to swell to 77 million in 2030. Meanwhile, the ratio of workers to beneficiaries is expected to decline by over 40 percent between 2001 and 2030, and thus the number of persons who help finance Medicare through payroll taxes will decrease as the number of persons receiving Medicare benefits increases.

According to a Bush Administration Fact Sheet, cash flow deficits in the Medicare program may begin as early as 2016.

These figures have alarmed both politicians and voters, who have demanded that something be done to save Medicare from possible future of **bankruptcy** and chaos. Proposals to "fix" the system have varied from conservative efforts aimed at "privatizing" Social Security and Medicare by allowing workers to invest their payroll deductions in the **securities** market to more liberal efforts aimed at placing Social Security and Medicare funds in a "lock box" to keep them safe from tampering and theft.

Following the inauguration of George W. Bush as the 43rd president of the United States, Congress began debating the future of Social Security and Medicare. However, much of the nation's domestic social agenda was temporarily placed on hold after the terrorist attacks in New York City and Washington, D. C., on September 11, 2001. Nonetheless, in December of 2001 the U. S. House of Representatives unanimously passed the Medicare Regulatory and Contracting Reform Act. H.R. 3391. The bipartisan bill was intended to streamline the complex and cumbersome rules governing Medicare so that doctors spend more time with patients and less time on paperwork. However, the bill did not address any issues concerning Medicare's long-term financial **solvency**. With the enactment of the Medicare Prescription Drug Improvement and Modernization Act of 2003, legislators hoped to contain the costs associated with prescriptive drugs by making the system more competitive, ultimately helping to contain overall costs of Medicare.

## Additional Resources

*American Jurisprudence* West Group, 1998

*http://guide.biz.findlaw.com/01topics/17govbenefit/gov_laws.ht ml* FindLaw: Government Benefits Law

*Medicare: Nuts and Bolts* Baker, Joe, 101 PLI/NY 203, Practicing Law Institute, 2001.

"What You Need to Know: The New Medicare Prescription Drug Coverage." American Association of Retired Persons (AARP), 2005. http://www.aarp.org/health/medicare/drug_coverage/medicarepdfl.html

*West's Encyclopedia of American Law* West Group, 1998

## Organizations

### *Social Security Administration*

6401 Security Blvd.
Baltimore, MD 21235-6401 USA
Phone: (800) 772-1213
Fax: (800) 325-0778
URL: http://w ww.ssa.gov
Primary Contact: Jo Anne B. Barnhart,
Commissioner

### *Centers for Medicare & Medicaid Services*

7500 Security Boulevard
Baltimore, MD 21244-1850 USA

Phone: (410) 767-8392
Fax: (410) 333-5185
URL: http://www.hcfa.gov
Primary Contact: Tommy G. Thompson, Secretary
of Health and Human Services

### *American Association of Retired Persons*

601 E St NW
Washington, DC 20049 USA
Phone: (202) 434-2277
Fax: (202) 434-7710
URL: http://www.aarp.org/index.html
Primary Contact: William Novelli, CEO

# RETIREMENT AND AGING

## NURSING HOMES

*Sections within this essay:*

## Background

With more people living longer and with the first of the Baby Boom generation reaching retirement age,, it is hardly surprising that the number of people requiring some sort of long-term nursing care is growing. According to the American Association of Homes and Services for the Aging (AAHSA), people who reach the age of 65 have a 40 percent likelihood of entering a nursing home; by 2020, approximately 12 million older Americans will need long-term care. The type of care available today fills a variety of needs; traditional nursing care for the infirm or incapacitated, assisted living for people who are still somewhat independent, adult day care for those who need supervision when the family is not available, and home health care for those who want or need to remain in their own homes.

Until the twentieth century, elderly people who could no longer take care of themselves were taken in by family members; those without money or family were placed in almshouses. Older Americans today have much better options and can expect a much better quality of life. With so many facilities (17,000 nursing homes alone), choosing the right one can be a challenge. Those who must reside in nursing homes—and their families—need to determine the best option based on quality of care, comfort level, location, and cost. The smart consumer will do enough research to know exactly what to look for in choosing a nursing facility.

## History of Nursing Homes

The concept of a residence set aside solely for the elderly and infirm was unknown until the nineteenth century. Before that, it was understood that elderly people would be taken in by family once they were unable to care for themselves. Those who had no family could rely on servants if they had the financial resources, but for those who were alone and poor the only choice was the local almshouse.

As the Industrial Revolution brought more people to cities, families spread out and often people had no local extended family to fall back upon when they were in need. The result was a growing number of single and widowed people who had no one to take care of them in their old age. The first homes for the elderly were established by churches and women's groups, catering to widows and single women who had limited resources. Homes such as the Indigent Widows' and Single Women's Society in Philadelphia and the Home for Aged Women in Boston were a far better option than an almshouse. These early homes were not open to all. Many of them required entrance fees, and some asked for certificates of good character. Requirements like these shut out the neediest, who were still relegated to the almshouse.

By the beginning of the twentieth century, sensibilities about caring for the poor and incapacitated had begun to change. Specialized facilities were built for children, the mentally ill, and younger infirm individuals. But little was done for the elderly, and they merely became a larger percentage of the almshouse population. In 1880, one third of the residents of almshouses in the United States were elderly; by 1923, two thirds were elderly.

### Social Security

It was not until the 1930s that things began to change for older people in need. The Social Security Act of 1935, part of President Franklin D. Roosevelt's New Deal, provided monthly payments to those over the age of 65. Although the payments were relatively small, they were an important step. Some older people were able to leave the almshouses and live on their own. Others were able to enter private facilities.

There was an unforeseen downside. Private facilities were unregulated, which meant that many were poorly run—dirty, overcrowded, unresponsive to residents' needs. Public facilities were at least regulated, but part of the Social Security legislation mandated that recipients were not eligible to live in them; only the truly indigent could stay in public homes.

By the 1950s, Congress realized that the situation needed to change. The Social Security Act was amended so that recipients could be eligible for public accommodations. The Medical Facilities Survey and Construction Act of 1954 mandated the construction of public facilities for the elderly.

### Medicare and Medicaid

It was the creation of **Medicare** and Medicaid in 1965 that provided regulation for nursing homes. Congress set the first set of standards for nursing homes in 1967 and differentiated between "skilled nursing facilities" and "intermediate care facilities." (Skilled nursing facilities provide nursing and rehabilitation services; intermediate care facilities provide care to people who do not need immediate nursing care.) Congress periodically updated the standards, notably in 1987 as part of the Omnibus Budget Reconciliation Act (OBRA) and again as part of the 1990 OBRA.

The 1987 OBRA standards require that skilled nursing facilities and intermediate care facilities pro-

vide a level of care that will allow patients "to attain or maintain the highest practicable physical, mental, and psychosocial well-being." Among the specifics:

- Facilities must allow patients (or their proxies) to make their own choices in activities, schedules, and health care decisions.

- Facilities must have around-the-clock licensed practical nurse care and at least one registered on duty at least eight hours every day. Nurse's aides are required to receive specialized training.

- State agencies must create, monitor, and enforce both state and federal standards, in part through the establishment of investigatory units and ombudsman units.

The Patient Self Determination Act of 1990, part of OBRA 90, governs long-term facilities that participate in Medicare or Medicaid:

- Facilities must provide patients with information in writing that outlines their rights to participate in medical care decisions (including the right to accept or refuse treatment).

- Facilities must provide written statements outlining their policies.

- Patients have a right to issue advance directives, and facilities must document this in their records.

- Facilities must comply with state laws on advance directives and cannot discriminate against patients who have or have not issued them.

- Facilities must provide education for staff and the general community on advance directive issues.

## Choosing A Nursing Home

Deciding to opt for nursing home care is a difficult experience for the patient and for the family. Ideally, a nursing home should be a place that combines the benefits of modern health care with the amenities of a home-like atmosphere. A nursing home that is sterile and hospital-like may suit some people but probably not most, likewise a nursing home whose staff is pleasant but whose facilities are in poor repair. Most experts in nursing care advise people to explore the options before the need arises, but few people plan ahead to the day when they may need long-term care.

The Medicare web site (www.medicare.gov) includes a useful comparison tool called *Nursing Home Compare*. This tool provides information on Medicare- and Medicaid-certified nursing homes throughout the United States. Visitors can get information on nursing homes by geographic region, community, or ZIP code. They can compare facilities, patient-to-staff ratio, various programs offered within each home, and so forth.

While tools such as Nursing Home Compare can break down general information about nursing homes, they cannot provide information such as whether a particular facility met only the minimum standards or exceeded all standards. Experts recommend that the patient (if possible) and the family members involved in the decision-making process visit several nursing homes before making a choice. This is important because nursing home care is usually long-term, and also because it is particularly traumatic for elderly, infirm people to have to move. Moving from one nursing home to another is physically and emotionally taxing for patients and families.

Often, the decision to move to a nursing home is one that must be made quickly—often, the patient is sent to a nursing home after a hospital stay and must be transferred immediately after being discharged from the hospital. In some cases it may be better to pay for a longer stay in the hospital or arrange for temporary home care instead of taking the first available nursing home even if it seems less than ideal.

### Paying for Nursing Home Care

Few people can pay out-of-pocket for nursing home care; the specialized round-the-clock full-service costs can run up very quickly. People who have financial assets can pay on their own, but those assets get used up rapidly. For those who have limited assets (such as a small pension), there are a number of payment options.

*Medicaid* pays the expenses of nearly two thirds of all nursing home residents. It is distributed jointly by federal and state agencies Each state has a State Health Insurance Assistance Program (SHIP) that determines Medicaid payments. You can reach yor state's SHIP by visiting the Medicare web site (www.medicare.gov). *Medicare* does not usually pay much toward nursing care; it functions as health insurance for those over 65, but not as long-term insurance. Check www.medicare.gov or call 1-800-MEDICARE to get clarification.

Medicaid does not cover assisted living or continuing care retirement communities. However, 22 states do offer assistance for these services under a program called Program of All-Inclusive Care for the Elderly (PACE). An individual must be at least 55 years old and be screened by doctors and other medical professionals to determine whether such care is available. For a list of PACE organizations state-by-state, visit the web site www.cms.hhs.gov/pace/pacesite.asp.

Private health insurance may cover some long-term care, but often it has limits. Managed care plans are useful only if the nursing home in question is covered by the plan. An option worth exploring is long-term care insurance. The costs vary, but the national Association of Insurance Commissioners (www.naic.org) offers information on long-term care including a free Shopper's Guide.

## Nursing Home Abuse

With some 17,000 nursing homes serving 1.6 million individuals, it is expected that standards will vary, even among homes ostensibly adhering to the same standards. Unfortunately, in some nursing homes, abuse exists. Homes that are overcrowded, or homes with staff shortages or minimally trained staff, are susceptible, but it would be wrong to say that any specific condition makes abuse more likely. Under no circumstances is abuse excusable or acceptable in any way.

The greatest danger of nursing home abuse is that its victims are often either too frightened or too disoriented to report it, or even to tell friends or family. Those with family members in a nursing home should be aware of what to look for when trying to determine whether abuse exists:

- The patient appears fearful or agitated, depressed or withdrawn.

- The patient is isolated with no justification.

- The staff is rude or makes humiliating or derogatory comments to patients.

- Patients are making complaints.

- Patients' rooms are not kept clean by staff.

- Common areas are unsanitary.

- Patients appear unkempt or dirty.

- Patients have bed sores or other untreated medical conditions.

- Patients have unexplained wounds, cuts, scrapes, sprains, or broken bones.

- Patients experience sudden unexplained weight loss.

- Patients are restrained without explanation as to why.

- Patient's personal property is missing.

- Money is missing from patient's accounts.

- Staff restricts or refuses visitors.

- Patient makes sudden changes in a will or other financial documents.

If you find abuse in a nursing home, you should report it at once. The U.S. Administration on Aging has a National Center on Elder Abuse web site (www.elderabusecenter.org) that links to individual state agencies. You can also call the Elder Care Locator at 1-800-677-1116. In an extreme emergency (if a patient's life is in danger, for example), dialing 911 may be the best idea.

## Alternatives to Nursing Homes

Although good nursing homes provide comprehensive care in a comfortable setting, a skilled nursing facility may not be the right choice. It is important, both for the patient and the patient's family, to explore other options.

For those with adequate funds, of course, private nurses, cooks, housekeepers, and drivers are not difficult to obtain. Most elderly people, however, live on fixed incomes and have limited resources. For these people, alternatives to nursing home care, if covered by insurance or Medicare, may be less expensive than long-term care in a skilled nursing facility.

Home health care may be a better option, particularly for elderly people who are in reasonable health but who need assistance. A home health care worker can assist the patient with everything from shopping for groceries to physical therapy to bathing. For patients who are in reasonable health but for whom living at home is impractical (even with home health aides), assisted living facilities or continuing care retirement communities (CCRCs) may provide a good alternative. Some of these facilities are run like hotels; residents live in small apartments an are independent, but meals and housekeeping services are provided. While best-suited to people who are still independent, they can also accommodate people suffering from conditions such as Alzheimer's disease.

Adult day care services are often useful for those caring for elderly relatives who cannot be left alone during the day, (for example, Alzheimer's disease patients). The typical adult day care facility works much like a child day care center; the participants are dropped off and kept occupied during the day with a variety of activities. Along with those activities, the participants are fed and also given the opportunity to socialize with others. Adult day care provides caregivers (usually adult children) an opportunity to continue working or taking care of other matters during the day while being able to watch their loved one at home overnight.

Some elderly individuals may benefit simply from a medical transportation program, which provides door-to-door transportation to doctor's appointments and outpatient treatment, for example. This is helpful for people who can take care of their basic needs but who no longer drive.

## Additional Resources

*Guide to Choosing a Nursing Home,* Centers for Medicare and Medicaid Services, 1994.

*Old Age and the Search for Security,* Carole Haber and Brian Gratton, Intiana University Press, 1994.

*Social Froces and Aging,* Robert C. acthley, Wadsworth, 1994.

## Organizations

### Centers for Medicare and Medicaid Services (CMS)
7500 Security Boulevard
Baltimore, MD 21244 USA
Phone: (877) 267-2323
URL: www.cms.hhs.gov
Primary Contact: Mark B. McClellan, Administrator

### National Family Caregivers Association
10400 Connecticut Avenue, Suite 500
Kensington, MD 20895 USA
Phone: (301) 942-6430
Fax: (301) 942-2302
URL: www.nfcacares.org
Primary Contact: Suzanne Mintz, President

### U/S/ Administration on Aging
One Massachusetts Avenue
Washington, DC 20201 USA
Phone: (202) 619-0724
Fax: (202) 357-3555
URL: www.aoa.gov.org
Primary Contact: Josefina G. Carbonell, Assistant Secretary on Aging

# RETIREMENT AND AGING

## RETIREMENT PENSION PLANS

*Sections within this essay:*

## Background

A **pension** plan is an organized investment program designed to provide income during older age or retirement years. Pension plans may be individually arranged or come through an employer. Because most qualified programs and plans offer a form of social insurance, the federal government treats them favorably, with deferred **taxation** and portability benefits.

- Tax Treatment: Pension fund contributions from both individuals and contributing employers are tax **deductible**. Fund earnings on the invested contributions are tax deductible. Benefits are not taxed until they are actually paid out—during retirement years when retirees would presumably be in a lower tax bracket. It is this treatment that provides the incentive for most persons to invest in pension plans rather than savings accounts or other investments, which are taxed when the interest is earned or the investment growth is "realized."

- Portabililty: Formal pension plan administrators may invest pension funds in various portfolio schemes and may move funds around to maximize investment return. Likewise, individuals may "roll-over" funds from one account to another, without invoking a tax penalty (in most cases) and without losing the funds' distinction as constituting part of a "pension plan."

## Employer Provided Pension Plans

A pension plan is a contract between employer and employee. However, an employer can modify or alter the plan unilaterally in most cases. In the United States, most employer-provided pension plans are "defined benefit plans"; the other major type is referred to as a "defined contribution plan."

- DEFINED BENEFIT PLANS: Under such plans, employees receive benefits based on a formula, usually years of service and percent of salary. This arrangement promises the employee a benefit in the form of a specific dollar amount per payment period during retirement. For example, the plan might specify that a worker will receive an annual pension equal to 1.5 percent of his or her average salary over the most recent five years, times the years of service. Upon retirement, the employer or plan administrator pays that specific amount.

- DEFINED CONTRIBUTION PLANS: Under these plans, employers pay a specific amount or percentage into a pension fund annually. The funds are allocated to individual employee accounts. Retiring employees receive benefits according to how much money they have in their fund upon retirement. This may be taken as a lump sum or used to purchase an **annuity** that will pay monthly benefits for a set number of years. The amount of annuity benefit and the years payable depends on how much was in the fund at retirement.

- EMPLOYEE STOCK OPTION PLANS (ESOPs): ESOPs are considered defined contribution plans. In such plans, employees either earn (as an employee benefit) or purchase company stock. At least 51 percent of the assets of an ESOP must be invested in the company. (Conversely, regular defined benefit or defined contribution pension programs may not invest more than ten percent of funds into company stock, excepting some 401(k) plans.) ESOPs enhance employee motivation and productivity but also create risk because a large portion of an employee's retirement wealth is all in one investment.

- SIMPLIFIED EMPLOYEE PENSION PLANS (SEPs): Under these plans, employers merely contribute to employees' private individual retirement accounts (IRAs).

### Plan Termination

Pension plan terminations may be standard, distress, or involuntary in nature. The Single Employer Pension Plan Act of 1986 provides extensive detail regarding the conditions of each, not relevant here. What is relevant is that all terminations must be reviewed by the Pension Benefit Guarantee Corporation (PBGC) (see below).

When plans are terminated by employers, benefit accrual ceases. With defined contribution plans, the employer may cease contributions and pass fund management responsibilities to an insurance company. With defined benefits plans, the options are more complex, as well as controversial if fund assets do not at least equal the present value of promised benefits. However, if fund assets exceed pension liabilities, the excess assets may legally be reverted back to the company, although that practice has been severely hampered by the Pension Protection Act of 1990. (As of 2002, companies must pay a 50 percent **excise** tax on any surplus funds pulled out of pension plans.)

### Employee Rights

Under provisions of the **Employee Retirement Income Security Act** of 1974 (ERISA), employees that are part of a pension program are entitled to certain information and/or access to certain information regarding their individual accounts and the entire fund or plan. Generally, employees are entitled to the following:

- a copy of the plan within 90 days of enrollment

- notice regarding any changes in the plan (an updated version must be furnished every five years

- an accounting of the total benefit to which the employee is entitled at any given point

- notification of the specific vesting schedule being used

- final statement of account upon leaving employment with the company

## Individual Retirement Pension Plans

For those persons who do not have employer-sponsored pension programs, the federal Internal Revenue Code (IRC) offers comparable advantages to private pension fund participants. It is intended to encourage individual workers to set aside a percentage of their earnings, tax-free, until retirement.

### Individual Retirement Accounts (IRAs)

Individual Retirement Accounts (IRAs) are private accounts into which persons may contribute up to $2000 (for individuals) or $2250 (for individuals and a non-working spouse) annually. Starting with the 2002 tax year, the amounts are $3000 for individual accounts, and $3500 for persons over 50 years old. The contributions are tax-deductible. As with other plans, benefits are taxed upon withdrawal at retirement.

### 401(k) Plans

Officially, these are cash or deferred profit sharing plans, more often referred to as "401(k) plans," after the section in the Internal Revenue Code, discovered by a pension consultant in 1978, that provided a tax loophole permitting the creation of these plans. Under 401(k) plans, participants contribute portions of their earnings (which are matched or enhanced by employer contributions) to private pension accounts. Participants elect to receive direct cash or stock payments from the employers or choose to have them contributed to a trust. All taxes on the contributions, as well as any investment earnings, are tax deferred until the funds are withdrawn at retirement. Like ESOP plans, 401(k) plans put "many eggs in one basket." That is risky and yet may prove extremely profitable.

### Keogh Retirement Plans

Keogh Plans, also known as H.R. 10 plans, are intended for self-employed individuals who want to establish private pension plans. A self-employed individual may contribute up to 15 percent of earned annual income into a Keogh account, with yearly caps.

## Pension Fund Protections

### Employee Retirement Income Security Act of 1974 (ERISA)

ERISA is the controlling body of law governing retirement plans, and preempts ("trumps") any state law addressing them. The original goal of ERISA was to reform defined benefit plans by ensuring diversification of invested funds. It prohibited the investment of any more than ten percent of a pension fund's assets in company stock (ESOPs and other profit-sharing plans such as 401(k) plans are exempted.) Some of the many protections that ERISA affords are:

- Employers can no longer decide who is qualified to belong to a pension program. Under ERISA, any worker aged 21 or older who has worked for at least one year qualifies for participation.

- Employers can no longer withhold "vesting" rights (the percentage of benefit an employee is entitled to receive after a specified period of employment) until retirement. ERISA established three vesting schedules that employers must follow.

- Prior to ERISA, there were no rules regarding proper funding for pensions; thus, underfunded programs became every retiree's nightmare. ERISA now formulates funding of

pension programs to ensure that fund assets cover accrued liabilities. Under complex rules, it permits companies to amortize funding deficiencies over several years.

- Under ERISA, widows and widowers are generally protected by survivor's rights to pensions. These protections are afforded through "joint and survivor annuity" provisions, which must be affirmatively elected by the plan participant.

- ERISA creates **fiduciary** duties (duties of trust and confidence, requiring that the person act primarily for the benefit of another and not for himself/herself) on the part of plan administrators, who must act in the interest of plan beneficiaries.

- ERISA requires that investment funds be diversified to minimize risk to plan participants.

- ERISA imposes severe penalties for underfunding of pension plans.

### Pension Benefit Guarantee Corporation (PBGC)

A provision in ERISA created the non-profit Pension Benefit Guarantee Corporation (PBGC) to afford certain protections against insolvent pension plans. Importantly, PBGC remedies and assistance only come into play for defined benefit plans. PBGC insures vested pension benefits up to the legally established amounts and guarantees payment of benefits under certain types of employer insolvencies.

### Other Remedies

The U.S. Supreme Court has ruled that a company's pension plan liability is a debt that cannot be transferred to the PBGC while the corporation continues to operate following Chapter 11 **bankruptcy** proceedings and reorganization. Companies who under-fund their pension programs or companies that are financially troubled may be forced to **liquidate** in Chapter 7 bankruptcies.

## Federal Laws that Impact Pension Plans and Pension Programs

The following federal laws (not a comprehensive list) affect a variety of issues relating to pension benefits and underscore the scope and complexity of pension plan programs. Persons are encouraged to seek legal **counsel** for any issue relating to pension plans or fund participation.

- Employee Retirement Income Security Act of 1974 (ERISA)

- Welfare and Pension Plans Disclosure Act of 1958 (WPPDA)

- Labor-Management Reporting and Disclosure Act of 1959 (LMRDA)

- Tax Reform Act of 1976

- Revenue Act of 1978

- Multi-Employer Pension Plan Amendments Act of 1980 (MPPAA)

- Economic Recovery Act of 1981 (ERTA)

- Tax Equity and **Fiscal** Responsibility Act of 1982 (TEFRA)

- Retirement Equity Act of 1984 (REA)

- Deficit Reduction Act of 1984 (DRA)

- Consolidated Omnibus Budget Reconciliation Act of 1985 (COBRA)

- Single Employer Pension Plan Amendments Act of 1986 (SEPPA)

- Omnibus Budget Reconciliation Act of 1986 (OBRA)

- Tax Reform Act of 1986 (TRA)

- Pension Protection Act of 1987 (PPA)

- Worker Adjustment and Retraining Act of 1989 (WARA)

- Uniformed Services Employment and Re-employment Rights Act

- Pension Protection Act of 1990 (PPA)

- Economic Growth and Tax Relief Reconciliation Act of 2001 (EGTRRA)

- Pension Security Act of 2002 (As of 2002 Pending)

## Additional Resources

*"A Predictable Secure Pension for Life"* Federal Consumer Protection Information Center. Available at http://www.pueblo.gsa.gov/cic_text/money/secure-4life/secure-pension.htm.

*Fundamentals of Employee Benefits Programs* 5th ed., Employee Benefit Research Institute (EBRI), 1997.

*Managing Corporate Pension Plans* Logue, Dennis E., HarperCollins Publishers, 1991.

*"Pensions"* McMillan, Henry. Available at http://www.econlib.org/library/Enc/Pensions.html.

## Organizations

### Employee Retirement Benefit Institute
Suite 600, 2121 K Street NW
Washington, DC 20037-1896 USA
Phone: (202) 659-0670
URL: http://www.ebri.org

# RETIREMENT AND AGING

## SOCIAL SECURITY

*Sections within this essay:*

## Background

Social Security is a program created by the **Social Security Act of 1935** to provide old age, survivors', and **disability** insurance benefits to workers and their families in the United States. 42 U.S.C.A. sections 301 et seq. The program is administered by the Social Security Administration (SSA), an independent federal agency. Unlike welfare, which is financial assistance given to persons who qualify on the basis of need, Social Security benefits are paid to individuals on the basis of their employment record and the amount they contributed to Social Security during their employment careers. In 1965 Social Security was expanded to include health insurance benefits under the **Medicare** program. 42 U.S.C.A. sections 1395 et seq.

As a more general term, "social security" refers to any plan designed to protect society from the instability caused to workers and their families by the unemployment or death of a wage earner. Statistics show that unemployment will affect at least 4 per-

cent of U. S. workers each year. But it is impossible to know in advance which workers will lose their jobs. A government-run plan of social insurance helps spread the risk of unemployment among all members of society so that no single family will be completely ruined by the interruption of incoming wages.

### History

Germany was the first industrial nation in Europe to adopt a general program of social security that extended beyond military veterans. In the 1880s Chancellor Otto von Bismarck instituted a plan of compulsory sickness and old age insurance to protect most wage earners and their dependents. Over the next thirty years, other European and Latin American countries created similar plans with various features to benefit different categories of workers.

In the United States the federal government first provided insurance only to veterans who had been disabled in war. During the late eighteenth and early nineteenth centuries the U. S. federal government provided pensions to veterans disabled in the American Revolution. In 1820 the federal government established a **pension** for needy or disabled veterans of the War of 1812. After the Civil War, the U. S. government broadened the category of veterans eligible for governmental assistance, paying pensions not only to needy and disabled veterans but also to most veterans age 65 or older.

However, Congress did not take any significant legislative action to create an old-age pension for the rest of America's workforce until the early twentieth century. Until that time, retired, unemployed, and chronically ill workers were left to manage by resorting to their personal savings, relying on private charities, or forming beneficial associations that provided a modicum of sickness, old-age, and funeral insurance to workers who joined the association.

Yet membership in these associations was never widespread. Nor were such associations designed to address the catastrophic effects of the Great Depression. Triggered in part by the stock market crash of 1929, the Great Depression was ravaging the U.S. economy by 1932, when businesses reported losses of approximately $6 billion, wages suffered declines of close to 60 percent, and 13 million workers headed for the unemployment lines. A year later another million Americans lost their jobs, and the unemployment rate hit 25 percent for the entire economy and 38 percent outside farm-related industries. By 1934 nearly every state was home to at least a few communities comprised of penniless and hungry families living in squalor, including many families with members who were senior citizens.

Congress tried to ameliorate some of these conditions by enacting the Social Security Act of 1935, which was part of the economic-stimulus and social-reforms package of President Franklin D. Roosevelt's New Deal. The act provided for the payment of monthly benefits to qualified wage earners who were at least 65 years old or the payment of a lump-sum death benefit to the estate of a wage earner who died before reaching age 65. In 1939 Congress added dependent spouses, widows, widowers, and parents of wage earners to the class of beneficiaries entitled to Social Security benefits upon the retirement or death of a working family member.

Social Security originally protected only workers in industry and commerce. Other classes of workers were excluded as beneficiaries after Congress concluded that it would be too expensive and inconvenient to collect their contributions. For example, household workers, farmers, and workers in family businesses were excluded as Social Security beneficiaries because Congress believed that these three classes of workers were unlikely to maintain adequate employment records. By the 1950s Congress had reversed its position, extending Social Security protection to most self-employed individuals, most state and local government workers, members of the armed forces, and members of the clergy. Federal employees, who had their own retirement and benefit system, were given Social Security coverage in 1983.

## Old Age, Survivors', and Disability Insurance

Federal Old Age, Survivors', and Disability Insurance (OSADI) benefits are monthly payments made to retired workers, to families whose wage earner has died, and to workers who are unemployed because of sickness, injury, or disability. Workers qualify for these benefits by having been employed for the mandatory minimum amount of time and by having made contributions to Social Security. There is no financial need requirement that must be satisfied. Once a worker qualifies for OSADI benefits, his family is entitled to those benefits as well. The entire program is geared toward helping families as a matter of social policy.

Two large funds are held in trust to pay benefits under OASDI: the Old Age and Survivors' Trust Fund (OASTF) and the Disability Insurance Trust Fund (DITF). As workers and employers make payroll contributions to these funds, money is paid out in benefits to people currently qualified to receive monthly checks. The OASTF provides benefits to retired workers, their spouses, their children, and other survivors of deceased workers, such as parents and divorced spouses. The DITF provides benefits to disabled workers, their spouses, and their dependent children. DITF also pays for rehabilitation services provided to the disabled.

The OASDI program is funded by payroll taxes levied on employees, employers, and the self-employed. The tax is imposed upon the employee's **taxable income**, up to a maximum amount, with the employer contributing an equal amount. Self-employed workers contribute twice the amount levied on employees. However, to put self-employed individuals in approximately the same position as employees, self-employed individuals can deduct half of these taxes for both Social Security and **income tax** purposes.

### Old Age Benefits

There are three requirements for an individual to be eligible to receive old age Social Security benefits. First, the individual must have attained the age of 62. Second, the individual must file an application for old age benefits. Third, the application must demonstrate that the individual is "fully insured." The extent to which an individual is insured depends on the number of quarters of coverage credited to his or her Social Security earnings record. 20 CFR section 404.101(a). A quarter is a three-month period ending March 31, June 30, September 30, or December 31.

A worker becomes "fully insured" when the individual has been credited with working the requisite number of quarters. 42 U.S.C.A. section 414(a). The Social Security Administration's regulations contain a table specifying by birth date the quarters of coverage required to obtain fully insured status. 20 CFR § 404.115. But irrespective of birth date, any worker who has 40 quarters (i.e., 10 years) of coverage is fully insured.

Workers born before 1950 can retire at age 65 with full benefits based on their average income during their working years. For workers born between 1950 and 1960, the retirement age for full benefits has increased to age 66. Workers born in 1960 or later will not receive full retirement benefits until age 67. However, any worker, regardless of birth date, may retire at age 62 and receive less than full benefits. At age 65, a worker's spouse who has not contributed to Social Security receives 50 percent of the amount paid to the worker.

Workers who continue to work past retirement age may lose some benefits because Social Security is designed to replace lost earnings. If earnings from employment do not exceed the specified amount exempted by law, persons working past the age of retirement will receive full benefits. If earnings are greater than the exempt amount, one dollar of benefit is withheld for every two dollars in wages earned above that amount. Once a worker reaches age 70, however, he or she no longer has to report earnings to SSA, and thus his or her Social Security benefits will cease to be reduced.

Since 1975 Social Security benefits have increased annually to offset inflation. Known as cost of living adjustments (COLAs), these increases are based on the annual increase in consumer prices as reflected by the **consumer price index** (CPI). Allowing benefits to increase automatically eliminated the need for Congress to pass special acts each year to address the issue. However, critics complain that COLAs are responsible for unnecessarily driving up the costs of Social Security. They contend that the CPI overestimates current rates of inflation, and, as a result, Social Security benefits are overadjusted upward.

### Survivors' Benefits

Survivors' benefits are paid to family members when a worker dies. Survivors can receive benefits if the deceased worker was employed and contributed to Social Security long enough for someone his or her age to qualify. Surviving spouses of deceased wage earners are the primary class of beneficiaries

entitled to survivors' benefits under the Social Security Act. Although sometimes referred to asb "widow's" or "widower's" benefits, beneficiaries also include surviving divorced spouses who have minor or disabled children in their care. However, neither a surviving spouse nor a surviving divorced spouse may collect survivors' benefits if they have remarried following the death of the wage earner. Surviving spouses and surviving divorced spouses can begin collecting survivors' benefits at age 60, unless the surviving spouse or surviving divorced spouse is disabled, then he or she can begin collecting survivors' benefits at age 50. In addition to monthly checks, a worker's widow or widower may receive a lump-sum payment of $255 upon the worker's death.

Survivors' benefits are also payable to unmarried, dependent children under age 18 and to unmarried children of any age who are disabled prior to age 22. Thus, if a disabled, unmarried, dependent child of a worker became disabled prior to age 22, he or she will be entitled to receive survivors' benefits for the duration of the disability. However, if the disabled surviving child remarries, his or her survivors' benefits will be terminated, unless the disabled child marries another Social Security recipient.

### Disability Benefits

The original Social Security Act of 1935 included programs for needy elderly persons and blind persons. In 1950 a program for needy **disabled persons** was created under the act. Known as the "adult categories," these three programs were administered by state and local governments with partial federal funding. By the late 1960s, studies showed that the programs were being unevenly administered by more than 1,300 state and local agencies, resulting in a gross disparity of benefit payments to beneficiaries in different jurisdictions. These disparities were eliminated in 1972, when Congress federalized the "adult categories" by creating Supplemental Security Income (SSI). 42 USCA sections 1381 et seq.

SSI is payable to workers who become "disabled," which the law says occurs when a worker is unable to engage in substantial gainful activity by reason of a medically determinable physical or mental impairment that can be expected to result in death or that has lasted or can be expected to last for a continuous period of not less than twelve months. 42 USCA section 1382c. Courts have said that "substantial gainful activity" means more than the ability to find a job and physically perform it. It also requires the ability to hold the job for a significant period of time. *Andler v. Chater*, 100 F.3d 1389 (8th Cir. 1996). Examples of disabilities that meet the criteria set forth in the Social Security law include brain damage, heart disease, kidney failure, severe arthritis, and mental illness.

In cases where the gravity of a disability is less clear, the SSA uses a sequential evaluation process to decide whether a person's disability is serious enough to justify awarding SSI benefits. If the impairment is so severe that it significantly affects a "basic work activity," the worker's medical records are compared with a set of guidelines known as the Listing of Impairments. 42 USCA APP., 20 CFR § 404.1529. A claimant found to suffer from a condition on this listing is entitled to receive SSI benefits. If the condition is less severe, the SSA will make a determination as to whether the impairment prevents the worker from doing his or her former work. If not, the application will be denied. If so, the SSA proceeds to the final step, in which it determines whether the impairment prevents the applicant from doing other work available in the economy.

In making this determination, the SSA relies on a series of medical-vocational guidelines that consider the applicant's residual functional capacity as well as the applicant's age, education, and experience. The guidelines look at three types of work, "sedentary work," "light work," and "medium work." Sedentary work involves lifting no more than 10 pounds at a time and occasionally lifting or carrying articles like **docket** files, ledgers, and small tools. Light work involves lifting no more than 20 pounds at a time with frequent lifting or carrying of objects weighing up to 10 pounds. Medium work involves lifting no more than 50 pounds at a time with frequent lifting or carrying of objects weighing up to 25 pounds. 42 USCA APP., 20 CFR § 404.1567.

If the SSA finds that an applicant can perform work that falls into one of these three categories, benefits will be denied. A claimant may appeal this decision to an administrative law judge (ALJ), who will then hear **evidence** presented by both the claimant and the SSA. If the ALJ denies the claim for benefits, the claimant may appeal to the SSA's Appeals Council. Claimants who lose this appeal may file a **civil action** in federal district court seeking review of the appeal's council decision. 42 U.S.C. section 405(g).

Workers who meet the disability eligibility requirements may receive three types of benefits, monthly cash payments, vocational rehabilitation, and medical insurance. Monthly cash payments begin with the sixth month of disability. The amount of a monthly benefit payment depends upon the amount of earnings on which the worker has paid Social Security taxes and the number of the worker's eligible dependents. The maximum payment for a family is roughly equal to the amount that the disabled worker is entitled to receive as an individual, plus allowances for dependents.

Vocational rehabilitation services are provided through a joint federal-state program. A person receiving cash payments for a disability may continue to receive them for a limited time after beginning to work at or near the end of a vocational rehabilitation program. Called the "trial work period," this period may last for as long as nine months.

Medical insurance is available through the Medicare program (a federally sponsored program that provides hospital and medical insurance). A recipient of disability benefits may begin to participate in Medicare twenty-five months after the onset of a disability. The Medicare program is discussed in more detail in the next section.

Disabled workers are eligible for disability benefits even though they have not reached the age of retirement, so long as they have worked enough years under Social Security prior to the onset of the disability. The number of work years required to qualify for SSI depends on the worker's age at the time of the disability. For workers under 24 years of age, the number of work years can be as few as one and a half years of work in the three years before the onset of the disability. However, the number of work years required for SSI eligibility can never exceed ten for any worker, regardless of his or her age.

A waiting period of five months after the onset of the disability is imposed before SSI payments begin. A disabled worker who fails to apply for benefits when eligible can sometimes collect back payments. But no more than twelve months of back payments may be collected. Even if a worker recovers from a disability that lasted more than twelve months, the worker can apply for back benefits within fourteen months from the date of recovery. If a worker dies after a long period of disability without having applied for SSI, his or her family may apply for disability benefits within three months from the date of the worker's death. Family members are also eligible for survivors' benefits.

The Contract with America Advancement Act of 1996 changed the basic philosophy underlying the disability program. Pub.L. No. 104-121, March 29, 1996, 110 Stat 847. The act provides that new applicants for Social Security or SSI disability benefits will no longer be eligible for SSI benefits if drug addiction or alcoholism is a material factor in their disability. Unless new applicants can qualify on some other medical basis, they will not receive Social Security disability benefits. Individuals who were receiving Social Security disability benefits prior to the act's passage had their benefits terminated as of January 1, 1997.

Congress also narrowed the class of beneficiaries eligible for SSI payments when it passed the Personal Responsibility and Work Opportunity Reconciliation Act of 1996. Pub.L. No., 104-193, August 22, 1996, 110 Stat 2105. The law terminated SSI eligibility for most non-citizens, including most non-citizens who were receiving SSI payments at the time the law was passed. Before its enactment, nearly all **aliens** lawfully admitted to the United States could receive SSI if they met certain other requirements.

## Medicare

Medicare is a federal program that provides health insurance to the elderly and the disabled. 42 U.S.C. sections 1395 et seq. It is funded through the Social Security Trust Fund and is administered by the Centers for Medicare & **Medicaid** Services (CMMS), formerly known as the Health Care Financing Administration (HCFA). However, Medicare is not like other federal programs that have large organizational hierarchies. Instead, the federal government enters into contracts with private insurance companies for the processing of Medicare claims made by qualified patients.

The concept of federal health insurance was first proposed in the United States during the late 1940s by President Harry S. Truman. However, the proposal languished in Congress for parts of the next two decades. President Lyndon B. Johnson revived the proposal during his administration, and it came to fruition in 1965, when Congress passed the Health Insurance for the Aged Act (Medicare Act), Pub. L. No. 89-97, 79 Stat. 343 (1965). As originally enacted, Medicare provided health insurance only to the elderly. In 1972 Congress expanded coverage to include disabled persons.

A patient's eligibility for Medicare does not depend on his or her income. Patients generally qualify for Medicare coverage if they are 65 years or older

and (1) qualify for Social Security or Railroad Retirement benefits; (2) have received Social Security or Railroad Retirement disability benefits for at least 24 months; (3) or suffer from end-stage renal disease. Individuals who have not worked long enough to receive Social Security benefits may still enroll in Medicare by paying a monthly premium. Individuals who are too poor to pay the monthly premium may apply for Medicaid, a state and federal health insurance program for low income persons.

Health care providers may participate in Medicare and receive Medicare payments if they satisfy state and federal licensing requirements and comply with any standards set by CMMS. A health care provider must also enter into an agreement with the Secretary of Health and Human Services. The agreement designates the amounts the provider will charge Medicare patients and the manner in which it will provide medical services. Hospitals, skilled nursing facilities, home health agencies, clinics, rehabilitation agencies, public health agencies, comprehensive outpatient rehabilitation facilities, hospices, critical access hospital, and community mental health centers (CMHCs) may all generally seek to participate in Medicare under a provider agreement. However, clinics, rehabilitation agencies, and public health agencies may enter into provider agreements only for services involving outpatient physical therapy and speech pathology. CMHCs may only enter into provider agreements to furnish certain hospitalization services.

Medicare is divided into three programs, a hospital insurance program, a supplementary insurance program, and a Medicare+Choice program. The hospital insurance plan is funded through a 2.9 percent Social Security payroll tax. The money is placed in a trust fund and invested in U.S. Treasury **securities**. The hospital insurance plan covers reasonable and medically necessary treatment in a hospital or skilled nursing home, meals, regular nursing care services, and the cost of necessary special care.

The hospital insurance plan offers coverage for in-patient hospital services based on "benefit periods." An episode of illness is termed a benefit period and starts when the patient enters the hospital or nursing home facility and ends sixty days after the patient has been discharged. A new benefit period starts with the next hospital stay, and there is no limit to the number of benefit periods a person can have. Medicare will pay the cost of hospitalization for up to 90 days. The patient must pay a one-time **deductible** for the first sixty days of a benefit period and an additional daily fee called a co-payment for hospital care provided during the following thirty days. Apart from these payments, Medicare covers the full cost of inpatient hospital care.

Medicare's supplementary medical insurance program is primarily financed by the federal government out of general tax revenues. The balance of the program is funded by those enrolled in it. Persons enrolled in Medicare pay a regular monthly premium and a small annual deductible for any medical costs incurred above the amount of the deductible during a given year.

Once the deductible and premiums have been paid, the supplementary medical insurance program covers 80 percent of any bills incurred for physician's services, including surgery, laboratory and diagnostic tests, consultations, and home, office, and institutional calls, but excludes services that constitute inpatient hospital care under the hospital insurance plan. Chiropractic services are covered by the program if the chiropractor meets specified regulatory requirements relating to education. 42 C.F.R. section 410.22(a). However, the supplementary medical insurance program does not cover routine physical checkups, eyeglasses, hearing aids, dentures, or orthopedic shoes. Nor does it cover the cost of drugs or medicines that can be self-administered.

Medicare computes its 80 percent responsibility based on the medical expenses and charges it deems reasonable for each kind of service provided to the patient pursuant to the supplementary insurance plan. Under the reasonable charge system, Medicare reimburses the lowest of the actual charge in question, the physician's customary charge for the service, or the applicable prevailing charge for the service. A physician's customary charge is based on the physician's actual charges for the same service during a twelve-month historical data collection period. When the charges vary during the historical period, the charges are then arrayed, weighted by frequency, and a customary charge is established at a level equal to the median of the charges. The prevailing charge is determined by a similar methodology, applied to all charges in the charge location by all physicians, with the prevailing charge fixed at an amount that would cover the full customary charges of the physicians whose billings accounted for at least 75 percent of the charges in the array.

The Medicare+Choice program is essentially a privatized medical savings plan that is funded partly by **beneficiary** premiums and partly by government contributions. The premiums and contributions are maintained by the Medicare+Choice MSA Trust Fund. As of January 1, 1999, beneficiaries are offered the following private health care delivery options under the program: Medicare health maintenance organizations (HMOs), medical savings accounts (MSAs), preferred provider organizations (PPOs), private fee-for-services (PFFS), and provider sponsored organizations (PSOs). However, individuals are only eligible to elect a Medicare+Choice plan offered by a Medicare+Choice organization (MCO) if the plan serves the geographic area in which the individual resides.

Beneficiaries who reside in an area served by a Medicare+Choice plan may opt out of either the health insurance or supplementary insurance plans and elect to enroll in Medicare+Choice, except those with end-stage renal disease. Beneficiaries may only enroll during November of each year, and plan elections become effective in January of the following year. Beneficiaries who do not elect any option will automatically be enrolled in traditional fee-for-service Medicare. If a beneficiary does not make an election for a particular year and is already enrolled in a Medicare+Choice plan from the previous year, he or she will automatically be re-enrolled in that plan. Beneficiaries can also change plans if their plan contract terminates or if they move from their plan's service area. 42 U.S.C.A. section 1395w-21(e)(3).

The Secretary of Health and Human Services has established a process through which elections under the Medicare+Choice program are made and changed. Individuals seeking to elect a Medicare+Choice plan must complete and sign an election form, provide the information required for enrollment, and agree to abide by the rules of the plan. Within 30 days from receipt of the election form, MCOs transmit the information necessary for CMMS to add the beneficiary to its records as an enrollee of the MCO. A beneficiary's enrollment may not be terminated unless the beneficiary engages in disruptive behavior, provides **fraudulent** information on the election form, permits abuse of the enrollment card, or fails to timely pay premiums. Monthly premiums for Medicare+Choice plans are calculated based on the rules set forth in 42 U.S.C.A. section 1395w-24(b)(1)(A).

A Medicare+Choice plan offered by an MCO satisfies the basic requirements for benefits and services if the plan provides payment in an amount that is equal to at least the total dollar amount of payment for such items and services as would otherwise be authorized under the health insurance or supplementary insurance plans. The Medicare+Choice plan must also comply with (1) CMMS's national coverage decisions; and (2) written coverage decisions of local carriers and intermediaries for jurisdictions handling claims in the geographic area for which services are covered under the plan.

Payments provided under the health insurance plan, supplementary insurance plan, or the Medicare+Choice plan can be sent directly to the health care provider or to the patient. Regardless of the method of payment, the patient must receive notice that the provider has filed a medical insurance claim. The notice should detail the medical services provided, identify the expenses that are covered and approved by Medicare, and **itemize** any expenses that have been credited toward the annual deductible and any expenses Medicare has already paid in full. Patients or providers who are dissatisfied with a decision made regarding a Medicare claim may ask CMMS or the insurance carrier to reconsider the decision, depending on the nature of the claim. Following reconsideration, either party may request a formal hearing before an administrative law judge, though no formal hearing will be granted for claims made under supplementary medical insurance plans unless the claim is for at least $100. Once the administrative law review process has been completed, aggrieved parties may appeal to federal district court. Supplementary medical insurance claims must total at least $1,000, however, before a federal district court will hear the appeal.

### The Future of Social Security and Medicare

Approximately 76 million Americans born between 1946 and 1964 are expected to retire in the next 28 years. In 2001 39 million Americans were enrolled in Medicare, and that number is expected to swell to 77 million in 2030. In 2001 35 million Americans were eligible to collect Social Security, while in 2030 more than 70 million will be eligible. The ratio between employed workers and Social Security recipients is expected to drop from 3.4 in 2001 to 2.1 in 2030.

These figures have alarmed both politicians and voters, who have demanded that something be done to save Social Security from a possible future of **bankruptcy** and chaos. Proposals to "fix" the system have varied from conservative efforts aimed at "privatizing" Social Security by allowing workers to invest their payroll deductions in the securities market to more liberal efforts aimed at placing Social Security funds in a "lock box" to keep them safe from tampering and theft.

Following the inauguration of George W. Bush as the 43rd President of the United States, Congress began debating the future of Social Security. In December of 2001 the Presidential Commission on Social Security put forward three proposals that would allow workers to invest varying portions of their payroll taxes in stocks and **bonds**. Comprised of 16 members handpicked by the White House, the commission disclosed that it would probably take $2 trillion to $3 trillion of new revenue to shore up Social Security for 75 years, money that could only come from increased borrowing, higher taxes, or spending cuts in other programs. It is now up to Congress and the president, members of the commission said, to make tough decisions about choosing among the approaches, apportioning the associated benefit cuts, and coming up with the trillions of dollars necessary to improve Social Security's long term financial condition.

### Additional Resources

*American Jurisprudence* West Group,1998.

*http://guide.biz.findlaw.com/01topics/17govbenefit/gov_laws.html* FindLaw: Government Benefits Law.

*West's Encyclopedia of American Law* West Group, 1998.

### Organizations

#### American Association of Retired Persons (AARP)
601 E St., NW
Washington, DC 20049 USA
Phone: (202) 434-2277
Fax: (202) 434-7710
URL: http://www.aarp.org/index.html
Primary Contact: William Novelli, CEO

#### Centers for Medicare & Medicaid Services
7500 Security Blvd.
Baltimore, MD 21244-1850 USA
Phone: (410) 767-8392
Fax: (410) 333-5185
URL: http://www.hcfa.gov
Primary Contact: Tommy G. Thompson, Secretary of Health and Human Services

***Social Security Administration***
6401 Security Blvd.
Baltimore, MD 21235-6401 USA
Phone: (800) 772-1213

Fax: (800) 325-0778
URL: http://www.ssa.gov
Primary Contact: Jo Anne B. Barnhart,
Commissioner

# TAXES

## CAPITAL GAINS

### Background

The United States Tax Code is a complicated document. The power to levy taxes on the U. S. population belongs to Congress, and the authority to collect those taxes rests with the **Executive branch**. The Internal Revenue Service is the agency within the executive branch of the federal government that collects the taxes. But states also have the power to levy taxes on their own populations in addition to whatever the federal government does. One part of an individual's or **corporate** entity's financial profile which is subject to **taxation** is capital gains. To determine taxation of capital gains, one must also consider capital losses. Gains are taxable, and losses may help offset tax liability.

When individuals sell or dispose of property and realize an amount over the adjusted basis of that property they have gain. When they sell or dispose of property and realize an amount below the adjusted basis of the property they have loss.

Capital gains are gains from the sale or exchange of capital assets. Capital losses are losses or reductions in value resulting from the sale or exchange of capital assets. To more fully understand the concepts of capital gains or losses, individuals need to understand the concepts of capital assets and basis. Once they understand these two concepts, then they can begin to see how they function within the broader context of the tax rules for capital gains and losses.

### Capital Assets

Almost everything individuals own and use for personal purposes or investment qualifies as capital assets. Homes, household furnishings, store equipment, computers, stocks and **bonds** are all capital assets. When a person sells a **capital asset**, the difference between the sale price and the basis in the property, which is usually its previous cost, is either a capital gain or a capital loss. A capital gain occurs when property sells for more than the basis. A capital loss occurs if the asset sells for less than the basis. Losses from the sale of property that was acquired for personal use such as a home or a vehicle are not **deductible** as capital losses.

Capital assets are any property held by a taxpayer except property that falls in one of the following categories:

- used in business and is depreciable
- stock in trade or inventory

- held primarily for sale to customers in the ordinary course of taxpayer's trade or business

- certain copyrights, compositions, letters, and memorabilia

Basically, most assets not used in business are capital assets. Assets used in a business are capital assets unless they may be depreciated or are inventory items.

Whether an asset is held primarily for sale is a question subject of much **litigation**. If an owner is unsure of the status of an asset, he should consult his attorney or tax advisor. People need to remember that transactions involving stocks and bonds by someone who is not a dealer or an underwriter will always result in capital gain or loss, regardless of the frequency of sales. This rule affects so-called "day traders," many of whom may not be aware of the tax laws as applied to their small-scale trading.

## Basis

The basis of a capital asset is usually equal to the cost of the asset. Two exceptions to this general rule have to do with how the asset was acquired:

- Inheritance:—the basis will be equal to the estate tax value in the decedent's estate. This amount is usually calculated on the value of the property on the date of death.

- Gift: —the basis is the same as it would have been for the person who gave you the gift (the **donor**) or its **fair market value**, whichever is lower. If the recipient had to pay a gift tax on the gift, the amount of that tax gets added to the basis of the gift. This is true even though the tax is imposed on, and usually paid by, the donor.

In the end, gain or loss is measured against adjusted basis, and many things may adjust the basis of a capital asset. **Depreciation** and rules relating to capitalizing property are some of the more common factors that adjust the basis of property.

## Capital Gains and the Sales of Homes

Changes to the tax laws in 1997 provided a new exclusion for gain from the sale of a principal residence. The law applies only to homes that qualify as a principal residence. This specification eliminates

vacation homes, timeshares, or other types of real estate. The home must have actually been lived in as a principal residence for two of the five years immediately preceding its sale. For taxpayers in the categories of single **head of household**, or married filing separately, the exclusion is $250,000. For married taxpayers filing a joint return, the exclusion is $500,000. The exclusion can be used only once every two years. Gain in excess of the exclusion is taxable, usually as long-term capital gain.

## Mortgaged Property

There is a long-standing general principle in tax law: borrowing money is not taxable. Thus, if individuals sell a parcel of mortgaged property, the amount they realize is the **net** purchase price. This is true regardless of whether they actually get to pocket any equity or profit in the sale of the property. For example, assume a person buys a house for $100,000 and uses $50,000 of his own money and borrows the remaining $50,000 from a bank., The bank's $50,000 is secured by a **mortgage**. Later, he sells it for $200,000, and assuming that his basis is then $80,000 after depreciation, his gain is $120,000, being the amount realized ($200,000) minus the basis. The amount of cash he receives will be $200,000 minus the amount of the mortgage, but that amount will have no particular bearing on the amount of gain.

## Long-Term and Short-Term Capital Gains

To determine the tax consequences that result from transferring capital assets one must first determine the rate his capital gains will be taxed. The tax rate that applies to capital gains depends on how long he holds a given capital asset. To calculate these rates, first separate the short-term capital gains and losses from the long-term gains and losses. While short-term gains are taxed as ordinary income, the taxes on long-term gains (assets held for more than one year) can range from 8 percent to 28 percent. Short-term assets are those investments held for one year or less. The government taxes short-term capital gains like any other income. These rates can be as high as 38.6 percent. On the other hand, short-term gains are taxed at the regular rate. The regular rate falls within a range of 10 percent to 39.1 percent for 2001. The rate is between 10 and 38.6 percent for 2002.

Long-term investments are those held for more than one year. Long-term gains are taxed at special rates. In 1998, the tax law was amended to reduce the holding period for the 20 percent rate to just 12 months. The holding period begins to run on the day after one acquires the investment asset. It ends on the day the asset is sold. Basically, the day an asset is bought does not count, although the day the asset is sold does. Long-term gains are taxed at lower capital gains rates. But there are exceptions to these rate rules. For example, a taxpayer in a low **income tax** brackets will have lower maximum tax rates. Also, if he had other regular losses, he may end up having to pay no tax at all.

In fact, there are six additional long-term capital-gains rates; the rates go from 8 percent to 28 percent. Which category applies in any case depends on the seller's income-tax bracket, the type of asset you sold, and how long the seller held it. There are many rules concerning capital gains and losses and with the holding period for assets. People should check with their attorney or tax or financial advisor to see if any of these apply in their case.

## Netting

The capital gains tax rules apply to net capital gains or losses. Capital gains and losses for any taxable year must first be netted, or calculated, so that the losses are subtracted from the gains. First the net of short-term gains and losses are calculated; next the net of long-term gains and losses are calculated against each other. The net short-term gain or loss and the net long-term gain or loss are calculated against each other for the net. This number is relevant to the tax year.

Taxpayers report capital gains and losses on Schedule D of Form 1040. If a taxpayer has a "net capital gain," that gain may be taxed at a lower tax rate. Net capital gain is the amount that results when net long-term capital gain for the year is more than net short-term capital loss. If capital losses exceed capital gains from the sale of capital assets, the amount of the losses that exceed the gains that may be claimed is limited to $3,000, or $1,500 if the taxpayer is married filing separately. If net capital loss is greater than this limit, the taxpayer can carry the loss forward to subsequent tax years.

Each gain or loss is calculated first by subtracting the purchase price of the asset from the sales proceeds. Then these figures are combined to come up with a net short-term gain or loss figure. Next, the same procedure is done with long-term assets. The result is either a net long-term loss or a net long-term gain. Next, the short- and long-term figures are netted to come up with a final tally.

## Lower Capital Gains Tax Rates and Low-Income Tax Bracket Taxpayers

There is a new, lower, capital-gains rate on investments held for more than five years. These rates are 8 percent or 18 percent, depending on the taxpayer's income. This can save you a lot of tax money if you plan to hold your investment long-term.

Taxpayers in the 15 percent federal tax bracket are eligible for a capital gains tax rate of only 8 percent on sales of stock and other investment **securities** held more than five years. This is a reduction from the standard 10 percent rate taxpayers in the lower tax bracket paid on long-term gains from investments held more than one year but not more than five years.

For gifts of stock or other investment securities, calculating the length of time the asset is held depends on the donor's ownership period added to the recipient's period of ownership. In these cases, it can be much easier to meet the more-than-five-year rule and thereby qualify for the 8 percent rate. This rate applies only to five-year gains triggered by sales of assets on or after Jan. 1, 2001.

### Eligibility for the 8 Percent Rate

To take advantage of the 8 percent rate on a 2001 return, the **taxable income** had to be less than the following amounts:

- $27,050 if single
- $45,200 if filing jointly
- $36,250 if head of household
- $22,600 if married but filing separately

To take advantage of the 8 percent rate on a 2002 return, the taxable income had to be less than the following amounts:

- $27,950 if single
- $46,700 if filing jointly
- $37,450 if head of household
- $23,350 if married but filing separately

It is important to remember that taxable income is the figure which results from subtracting personal exemptions and the standard **deduction** or itemized deductions. In this way, a taxpayer can be in the 15 percent bracket even if the person has a substantial salary.

### The 18 Percent Rate

There is a capital gains rate of 18 percent taxpayers in the 28 percent bracket and above. This is a reduction in the tax rate, although there is a substantial delay before a taxpayer may reap any tax savings. Gains from investments acquired on or after Jan. 1, 2001, and that were held for more than five years will be taxed at a maximum rate of only 18 percent. For investments acquired before 2001, a taxpayer may make a special one-time election with the 2001 return and thereby become eligible for the 18 percent rate. By doing so, taxpayers proceed as though they sold the investment for its Jan. 2, 2001 **market value**. The taxpayers also act as though they repurchased the investment for the same price on that same day. Resulting capital gains tax from the imaginary profit on the imaginary sale are reported on the 2001 **tax return**. The benefit of this complicated scheme is that any future **appreciation** of the value of the asset will be subject to an 18 percent tax rate (instead of 20 percent). To reap this benefit, taxpayers must hold on for at least another five years before selling the asset. This is where the delay comes in. They must wait until at least 2006 to actually realize any tax savings.

## Additional Resources

*Basic federal income taxation, 5thEdition.* 5th ed., Andrews, William D., Aspen Law & Business Publishers, 1999.

*Capital Gains, Minimal Taxes: The Essential Guide for Investors and Traders.* Thomas, Kaye A., Fairmark Press Inc., 2000.

*http://www.irs.gov/* "The IRS" Department of the Treasury, 2002.

*http://www.taxadmin.org/fta/link/link.html* "2001 State Tax Forms" Federation of Tax Administrators, 2002.

*The Labyrinth of Capital Gains Tax Policy: A Guide for the Perplexed* Burman, Leonard E., Brookings Institute, 1999.

*Taxes for Dummies 2002.* Tyson, Eric, David J. Silverman. Hungry Minds, Inc., 2001.

*The Labyrinth of Capital Gains Tax Policy: A Guide for the Perplexed.*Leonard E. Burman. Brookings Institute, 1999.

*http://www.taxadmin.org/fta/link/link.html* "2001 State Tax Forms" Federation of Tax Administrators, 2002.

*http://www.irs.gov/*"The IRS" Department of the Treasury, 2002.

## Organizations

### Council On State Taxation
122 C Street, NW, Suite 330
Washington, DC 20001-2109 USA
Phone: (202) 484-5222
Fax: (202) 484-5229
URL: http://www.statetax.org/index.html

### Federation of Tax Administrators (FTA)
444 N. Capital St., NW, Suite 348
Washington, DC 20001 USA
Phone: (202) 624-5890
URL: http://www.taxadmin.org/

### National Tax Association (NTA)
725 15th St., NW #600
Washington, DC 20005-2109 USA
Phone: (202) 737-3325
Fax: (202) 737-7308
E-Mail: natltax@aol.com
URL: http://ntanet.org/

# TAXES

## CORPORATE TAX

### Background

There are four basic types of business entity:

1. **corporations** (C and S)
2. limited liability companies
3. partnerships (general and limited)
4. sole proprietorships

Basically, if someone is the only owner of a business, that person will be able to form any of the types except a partnership. If there are two or more owners, they will be able to form any business type except a **sole proprietorship**. Tax law is a large and complicated subject.

### How Corporations Are Taxed

Corporations are taxed in a different manner than other business entities. In fact, corporations are the only types of business that pay income taxes on their profits. Conversely, partnerships, sole proprietorships, and limited liability companies (LLCs) are not taxed on business profits. Rather, the business profits "pass through" to the business' owners, who in turn report the business income (or losses) on their personal **income tax** returns.

Corporations are taxed separately from their individual owners. If a taxpayer's business is not incorporated, all the profits from the business will be taxed on the taxpayer's personal income **tax return** in the year that the profits were earned. Incorporating such a business may prove to be a good way to save on taxes, especially if the taxpayer intends to reinvest the profits in the business. For example, if a taxpayer's business is incorporated, the first $75,000 of the business's profits will be taxed at a lower rate than if the taxpayer claimed them on his or her personal income tax return. However, there are exceptions: personal service corporations like legal, accounting, consulting, and medical groups must pay a flat tax rate of 35 percent on their **taxable income**.

Corporations can deduct employee benefits, such as health insurance, **disability**, and up to $50,000 in life insurance. This **deduction** applies to owners who are also employees of the company. The **IRS** permits incorporated businesses to treat their owners as employees for benefits purposes, allowing these owners to take the tax deduction on their own as well as their employees' benefits. Conversely, owners of unincorporated businesses and sole-proprietorships cannot deduct their own benefits.

Taxpayers cannot immediately claim on their personal income tax **corporate** losses on their incorporated businesses. Rather, they must wait until they can offset their losses by profits. This is particularly problematic for newer businesses because most new businesses produce very little revenue in their first few years and losses are common.

### Corporate Tax Payments

Corporations must file corporate tax returns every year. They are taxed on their profits at a corporate income tax rate. If a corporation expects to owe taxes, the IRS requires it to estimate the amount of tax due for the year and make payments to the IRS on a quarterly basis—in the months of April, June, September, and January.

### Shareholder Tax Payments

If the corporation's owners work for the corporation, they will pay individual income taxes on their salaries and bonuses, just like regular employees of any business. Salaries and bonuses are **deductible** business expenses to the corporation, so the corporation can deduct those costs and does not pay taxes on them.

### Dividends

For corporations that distribute dividends to its owners, the owners must report and pay personal income tax on these amounts. Dividends are not tax-deductible, unlike salaries or bonuses. Moreover, the corporation must also pay taxes on dividends. Thus, dividends are taxed twice—once to the corporation and again to the shareholders.

### Retained Earnings

Corporations frequently want or need to retain some of their profits at the end of the year. These funds can be used for a wide range of business activities such as expansion, development, or other purposes related to growth in the business. If the corporation does retain some of its profits, the corporation will be liable for taxes on that money at the appropriate corporate income tax rate. A corporation's owners can save money by retaining a portion of corporate profits in the company because the initial corporate income tax rates are lower than most owners' marginal income tax rates for the same amount of income. In contrast, owners of sole proprietorships, as well as partnerships and LLCs, are taxed on all business profits at their individual income tax rates, whether they take the profits out of the business or not.

The IRS permits corporations to retain a limited amount of profits within the corporation. Most corporations can legally retain up to $250,000 at any one time in the corporation without facing negative tax consequences. There is an exception for some professional corporations that may not retain more than $150,000.

### Fringe Benefits

C corporations can deduct the full cost of the fringe benefits it provides to its employees—including the business's owners in most instances. This factor provides shareholders of C corporations with a slight advantage over other types of business owners because owners of limited liability companies, partnerships, and sole proprietorships may not take as many fringe benefit deductions. For example, sole proprietors, owners of partnerships, and LLCs cannot currently deduct 100 percent of their health insurance premiums (although the limit increases by increments through 2003 until these other businesses will be able to deduct the full cost of their health insurance premiums).

As we have seen, corporations are separate entities from their owner-shareholders. They are established as either C corporations or as S corporations (sometimes known as subchapter S corporations), and the tax laws apply to each of these differently.

### Tax-Deductible Expenses

To help offset taxable profits, a corporation can deduct its business expenses. These include basically any money the corporation spends in the ordinary and legitimate pursuit of profit. Some of the principal business deductions include:

- Costs associated with medical plans
- Ordinary operating expenses
- Product and advertising outlays
- Retirement plans for employees
- Salaries and bonuses
- Start-up costs

## C Corporations

C corporations are formed when corporations are created. If those forming the corporation do not elect to be treated as an **S corporation**, their corporation will continue to be a C corporation. Like other business entities, C corporations are taxable entities and file tax returns (Form 1120). They pay tax on **net** profits each year. Any profits remaining after taxes can be distributed to the shareholders as dividends.

## Tax Advantages of C Corporations

In many instances, C corporations can be more flexible than S corporations. For example,

- owners of C corporations can choose a **fiscal** tax year

- C corporations are not limited to the numbers or types of shareholders

- C corporations can deduct contributions to charities. Other types of business entities must pass charitable expenses through to the owners, who then might be able to deduct them on individual tax returns

- Until recently, C corporations enjoyed the most options in choosing retirement plans

Because of this flexibility, C corporations are the entity of choice for most tax-free mergers and acquisitions

## Tax Disadvantages of C Corporations

Perhaps the most significant tax disadvantage for owners of C corporations is that these entities have a form of double **taxation**. The corporation itself is taxed, as are the dividends it earns. These taxes are collected before the shareholders receive their after-tax shares of the profits. This is the main reason that many people choose to create a different kind of business entity such as an S corporation or a partnership.

There are three other significant tax disadvantages to C corporations:

1. If there is any taxable gain from the **liquidation** or sale of corporate assets, there will also be double taxation to the shareholders

2. In terms of special allocations of profits or expense items, C Corporations are less flexible than partnerships

3. Losses to the corporation cannot be passed through to the shareholders

## S Corporations

At its foundation, an S corporation is a C corporation that has elected to be taxed as a "pass through" entity. The election is made on Form 2553 and must be filed with the IRS no later than 60 days after the beginning of the year in which the election is to be effective. The election is revocable. Once the business owners have made the election, it remains in effect until the business's owners revoke it. Instead of being taxed on its income, the S corporation passes the income through to the shareholders, where it is taxed as part of their personal income. S corporations file Form 1120S, a different return from that used by C corporations.

## Tax Advantages of S Corporations

In the most basic sense, S corporations do not pay taxes on income. Rather, income, losses, deductions, and credits pass through the corporations to shareholders. S corporations provide shareholders with liability protection that comes with being incorporated, yet business profits and losses pass through to the owner's personal income tax returns.

S corporations can be an especially good idea for start-up companies. For example, if new businesses sustain losses in some years, their owners can claim those losses in the current year of the loss on their personal tax returns.

There are other benefits to electing to be taxed as an S corporation. For example, if a taxpayer incurs interest in order to purchase S corporation stock, the taxpayer may deduct that interest as an investment interest expense. And when selling an S corporation business, the owners' taxable gain on the sale may be less than it would be if the business had been a C corporation.

The IRS permits most but not all small businesses to incorporate as S corporations. In order for a small business to qualify for S corporation status, the business must meet these three requirements:

- It must be a U. S. company

- It must have only one class of stock

- It must have no more than 75 shareholders, all of whom must be legal residents or U. S. citizens and not also part of partnerships or other corporations

The tax reporting rules for S corporations are similar to those of partnerships. However, the IRS treats shareholders of S corporations as employees for payroll tax purposes. An S corporation must provide its employees a Schedule K-1, which lists the relative share of income or loss, deductions, and credits that must be reported on the employees' income tax returns. And the IRS treats health insurance premiums paid by an S corporation for more than 2 percent stockholders as wages; these are deductible on Form 1120S by the corporation and reported to the stockholder on Form W-2.

However, there are limitations on deductions. For example, taxpayers may only deduct losses in the same amount that they put into their companies on their personal tax returns. Additionally, there is potential for problems when it comes to claiming losses from passive activities if taxpayers do not actively work in the taxpayers' S corporation. These can only be used to offset passive income.

### Tax Disadvantages of S Corporations

S corporations are less flexible than partnerships in terms of allocating profits and expenses for tax advantages. Also, if an S corporation liquidates an asset, it can result in taxable gain for its shareholders.

Other issues associated with S corporations that give rise to tax disadvantages include the following:

- Accounting: Accounting rules that apply to S corporations can be extremely complex which can result in higher accounting and tax preparation fees for S corporations

- Complex tax preparation: Tax preparations and filing become complicated when an S corporation has out-of-state shareholders or conducts business in multiple states. Shareholders who live in states other than the one in which the corporation is located must file tax returns in their home states, as well as filing in the state or states in which the business is located. If an S corporation conducts business in multiple states, each shareholder may have to file tax returns to each of the states in which the corporation does business

- Minimum tax: Tax preference items reported on shareholders' personal income tax returns can trigger an unexpected minimum tax problem for some.

- Recognition: Not all states recognize the S corporation as a legitimate business entity

- Salaries for shareholders: The IRS watches closely the salaries of shareholder-employees. If warranted, it may claim that the corporation is underpaying its shareholders to save in paying FICA taxes

## Corporate Tax Credits

In most cases, tax credits for corporations are more beneficial than deductions. The amount of tax credits remains constant regardless of the income level and tax bracket of a corporation. By contrast, the amount of money a taxpayer actually saves through deductions depends to a great extent on the taxpayer's income level and tax bracket. For example, one company with the same amount or type of deduction as another corporation may end up with a larger or smaller deduction than the first corporation because of the relative tax brackets of the individual businesses. Additionally, tax credits reduce a taxpayer's taxes more than a tax deduction of the same amount. Thus, tax credits are almost always more beneficial to taxpayers.

Some of the credits that may be available to corporations are as follows:

- Credit for federal tax on fuels used for certain purposes: Taxpayers may claim this credit when they have paid tax on nontaxable forms of aviation fuel or gasoline, diesel fuel, gasohol, gasoline, kerosene, and liquefied petroleum gas

- Credit for prior year minimum tax: Corporations can claim this credit to figure the minimum tax credit if any for the alternative minimum tax they incurred in previous tax years and to figure any minimum tax credit to carry forward

- Foreign tax credit: When a foreign country or a U. S. possession imposes a tax upon the income or profits of a U. S. domestic corporation, the corporation can claim a credit for those foreign taxes it paid

- Possessions tax credit: Corporations may take this credit when the corporation uses the profit split method or the cost sharing method of computing taxable income for a particular product

- Qualified electric vehicle credit: Corporations may claim a tax credit for a qualified electric vehicle it places in service during the tax year. The corporation can make this choice regardless of whether the vehicle is used in a trade or a business

In conclusion, reporting and paying taxes on a separate corporate tax return can be time consuming. However, it is clear that there are some real benefits to having a separate level of taxation. Taxpayers should consult a tax expert for a complete explanation of corporate taxation as it applies to their situations.

## Additional Resources

*Abrams and Doernberg's Federal Corporate Taxation* 4th ed., Abrams, Howard E., and Richard L Doernberg, Foundation Press, 1998.

*"E-Commerce Tax News."* Hardesty, David E., 2001. Available at http://www.ecommercetax.com/.

*Federal Corporate Taxation* 4th ed., Doernberg, Richard L., and Howard E. Abrams, Foundation Press, Inc., 1999.

*Federal Income Taxation of Corporations and Stockholders in a Nutshell* 4th ed., Burke, Karen C., and Peter P. Weidenbruch, West, 1996.

*How to Form Your Own S Corporation and Avoid Double Taxation* Friedman, Robert, Dearborn Financial Publishing, Inc., 1999.

"TaxGaga Consumer's Site" TaxGaga, Inc. 2002. Available at http://www.taxgaga.com/.

"Tax Information for Corporations" Internal Revenue Service, 2002. Available at http://www.irs.gov/businesses/corporations/display/0,,i1=2&i2=14&genericId=15020,00.ht ml.

*"Tax Statistics: Corporations."* Internal Revenue Service, 2002. Available at http://www.irs.gov/taxstats/display/0,,i1%3D40%26genericId%3D16805,00.html. Internal Revenue Service, 2002.

"United States Tax Court" United States Tax Court, 2002. Available at http://www.ustaxcourt.gov/.

## Organizations

### Council on State Taxation
122 C Street, NW, Suite 330 NW
Washington, DC 20001-2109 USA
Phone: (202) 484-5222
Fax: (202) 484-5229
URL: http://www.statetax.org/index.html

### Federation of Tax Administrators (FTA)
444 N. Capital St., NW, Suite 348 NW
Washington, DC 20001 USA
Phone: (202) 624-5890
URL: http://www.taxadmin.org/

### National Tax Association (NTA)
725 15th St. NW #600 NW
Washington, DC 20005-2109 USA
Phone: (202) 737-3325
Fax: (202) 737-7308
E-Mail: natltax@ aol.com
URL: http://ntanet.org/

### U. S. Chamber of Commerce
1615 H Street, NW
Washington, DC 20062-2000 USA
Phone: (202) 659-6000
E-Mail: custsvc@uschamber.com
URL: http://www.uschamber.com/default.htm

# TAXES

## INCOME TAXES

## Background

Income **taxation** has a long history in the United States. During the Civil War, President Lincoln and Congress created the commissioner of Internal Revenue and enacted an **income tax** to pay war expenses in 1862. This first income tax was repealed a decade later. In 1894, Congress attempted to revive the income tax, but the next year the Supreme Court ruled it unconstitutional.

The Sixteenth Amendment to the U.S. Constitution, ratified in 1916, authorized Congress to tax "in-comes, from whatever source derived, without **apportionment** among the several States, and without regard to any **census** or enumeration." That same year, Congress introduced the first form 1040. It levied a 1 percent tax on **net** personal income above $3,000, and it placed a 6 percent **surtax** on incomes of more than $500,000. This top rate of income tax later rose as high as 77 percent as the United States looked for revenues to help finance the World War I effort. World War II ushered in legislation to mandate payroll withholding and quarterly tax payments.

After World War II, the **IRS** was reorganized to replace the patronage system with career, professional employees. As of 2002, only the top IRS official, the IRS commissioner, and the IRS's chief **counsel** are selected by the president and confirmed by the Senate.

The Internal Revenue Code (IRC) is contained in Title 26 of the United States Code (26 U.S.C.). This is the body of **statutory** law that governs federal income taxation. Congress created the Internal Revenue Service (IRS) to function as the nation's tax collection agency. It administers the IRC. The IRS is a branch of the Department of Treasury, an executive agency. It deals directly with more U.S. citizens than any other public or private institution.

All residents and all citizens of the United States are subject to the federal income tax. Most states also tax the income of their residents, although there are a few states that do not have an income tax. However, not everyone is required to file a return. The general purpose of income tax is to generate revenue for the federal, state, and local budgets. These funds are necessary to shape and preserve the free market economy. Along with individuals, **corporations** file income tax returns. While they are subject to many of the same rules as are individual taxpayers, they are also covered by an intricate body of rules addressed to the peculiar nature of corporations.

## Personal Income Taxes

While most people automatically think of federal income tax when the subject of personal income tax is raised, not many people know that personal income tax was first introduced by the states. The state of Wisconsin has the dubious distinction of being the first to introduce a form of the personal income tax system in 1911. As of 2002, most states have some form of personal income tax. There are two basic methods to determine income tax, the graduated income tax and the flat rate income tax. Both methods require taxpayers to figure their **taxable income**.

## Federal Income Taxes

The federal income tax is levied on taxable income of U.S. citizens and residents for the taxable year. It also applies to estates, trusts, partnerships, corporation, and other entities. The federal income tax and all other income tax laws, provide for annual returns of income. These are usually remitted to the appropriate department of revenue and cover the preceding **fiscal** or calendar year by the taxpayer or his representative.

There are four main steps to calculating federal income tax. These are:

1. Calculating total income

2. Subtracting deductions

3. Applying the right tax rate to taxable income

4. Subtracting withholding and other payments and credits

### Calculating Total Income

A taxpayer's total income can include many kinds of income:

- **alimony**

- amounts received from IRAs and **pension** plans

- business and partnership income

- dividends

- interest

- lottery winnings

- wages

- all other sources of income

The list also includes profit from the sale of stock or real property, otherwise known as capital gain. There are a few sources that are not included, such as gifts and life insurance proceeds.

### Subtracting Deductions

After they calculate their deductions and exemptions, taxpayers subtract that amount from their **gross income**. The sum is their taxable income. Deductions reduce taxable income; credits reduce tax. There are four principal types of deductions:

- Business deductions: These are claimed as part of a business's income tax.

- Adjustments: These are deductions a taxpayer may claim even if the taxpayer does not claim itemized deductions. Adjustments include alimony and contributions to IRAs or Keogh plans. After subtracting these adjustments from total income, taxpayers arrive at their **adjusted gross income**.

- Itemized or standard **deduction**: Taxpayers may claim a list of specifically itemized deductions, or taxpayers may take the standard deduction, whichever is larger. There are quite a few things one can add to the list of itemized deductions, including medical expenses, state and local taxes, **mortgage** interest, and investment expenses. If taxpayers' itemized deductions do not have a large enough total, the taxpayers may claim the standard deduction instead. The standard deduction depends on filing status; it is adjusted each year for inflation.

- Exemptions: Taxpayers get a personal exemption in addition to an exemption for each person who qualifies as the taxpayer's dependent. Like the standard deduction, the exemption deduction is adjusted each year for inflation.

Individuals arrive at taxable income after they subtract these four categories of deductions from their total income.

### Applying the Right Tax Rate to Taxable Income

People need to find the tax rate appropriate for them and apply it to their taxable income, the result is their tax. Perhaps the simplest way to do this is to use the tax table supplied with their tax form.

### Subtracting Withholding and Other Payments and Credits

The result of this step is the tax owed. This is the place where people learn the amount they owe to the government in additional tax. When individuals overpay their taxes they are entitled to a refund. This is the basic system used by the federal government; it is also the process used in the vast majority of states. In fact, many states require a copy of taxpayers' federal income **tax return** when they file state income tax returns.

## Filing Status

Federal income tax is a **progressive tax**. This means that the more money earned by taxpayers, the more income taxes taxpayers pay. Taxpayers' filing status is crucial to figuring out their ultimate tax liability.

Filing status is tied to taxpayers' marital status. However, filing status can depend upon when the taxpayer married, when the taxpayer's spouse died, or who else lives in the taxpayer's home. A mistake in determining filing status can be expensive. There are five filing statuses:

1. Single: A taxpayer's marital status at the end of the year applies for the entire tax year. If a taxpayer is unmarried on Dec. 31, that taxpayer generally must file as a single person for that year.

2. Married filing jointly: If a taxpayer is married at end of the year, the taxpayer can file a joint return with his or her spouse. The taxpayer may also file under the status of married filing separately. The latter status requires preparing two 1040s (one for each spouse). Note: the 2004 tax act extended relief for many married taxpayers. Through 2010, the basic standard deduction for joint returns is twice the standard deduction. In addition, the married filing jointly 10 to15 percent rate brackets will be twice those of single filers in respective brackets. This partially alleviates the marriage penalty but does not eliminate it.

3. Married filing separately: Married people are not absolutely required to file a joint return with their spouses. Instead, they have the option to file separate income tax returns, with each return listing that spouse's share of the couple's income and deductions. This can be advantageous for some couples, though most find it the least advantageous way to file. And state laws also affect the bottom line. For example, in some states, a married couple's income is deemed by law to be split 50/50; this is true regardless of who actually earns the income. In other words, the laws of a state may make it unattractive to file separate federal returns.

4. Qualifying widow/widower: If taxpayers' spouses die, they may be able to continue to file under the status of married filing jointly for up to two years after the spouse's death. The taxpayer must remain single during those two years. Additionally, the taxpayer must pay over half the cost of maintaining a home for a dependent child. After the initial two years, such taxpayers may qualify to file as **head of household**.

5. Head of household: Generally a taxpayer must be single to file as a head of household (HOH). A taxpayer who qualifies for this status is entitled to more favorable tax brackets and a more generous standard deduction. The Working Families Tax Relief Act of 2004 modified the definition of this status. The definition is detailed, but in general, a taxpayer may qualify for this filing status if the individual was unmarried on the last day of the year; file a separate return; furnished more than one-half the cost of maintaining the household during the tax year; and during the last six months of the tax year, did not have a spouse who was a member of the household. The only exception to the general rule that a taxpayer must be single to be a HOH is the "abandoned spouse rule." A taxpayer may qualify for HOH if the individual was married at the end of the year and lived with the taxpayer's child but apart from the person's spouse for at least the last half of the year

In addition to federal income tax, most individuals must pay state income tax, and in some cases local income tax, depending on their place of residence. Besides the various income taxes, employers are required to withhold 6.2 percent of their employees' income for Social Security and another 1.45 percent for **Medicare**. Individuals with J, F, M and Q visas are exempt from Social Security and Medicare withholdings.

## State and Local Taxes

In the United States, individual states have maintained their right to levy taxes, and the federal government has always recognized this right. When the U.S. Constitution was ratified, the federal government was also granted the power to levy taxes. The right to impose taxes—except those taxes that are expressly forbidden by the Constitution and their own state constitutions—was retained by the states. In addition to money from the federal government, the fifty states get the money they need to provide essential services through taxes, fees, and licenses.

Some of the most common types of taxes imposed by states include:

- **corporate** income tax
- personal income tax
- real and **personal property** tax
- **sales tax**

In the 1930s and 1940s, personal income tax and sales tax were introduced in many states. The depression prompted the need for new ways for states to bring in additional revenue to finance public services.

Unlike personal income taxes, the tax on real property has a very long history in the United States. As early as 1646, the Massachusetts Bay Colony taxed settlers who owned land. After independence, many states introduced new systems of property taxes. Eventually, local governing bodies assumed the power to tax property. Property tax is generally paid to a local government, a school district, a county government, or a water district, but not to a state or the federal government.

State individual income taxes generally apply to all natural persons as individuals, partners, fiduciaries and beneficiaries. Most states use a system of graduated tax rates, but six states have a flat rate tax. They are:

1. Colorado
2. Illinois
3. Indiana
4. Massachusetts
5. Michigan
6. Pennsylvania

Taxpayers conducting business as partnerships are liable for income tax only in that taxpayers' individual capacity, but the taxpayers must report partnership income they received. Estates and trusts are taxed in much the same way as individuals. Basically, the entire income of an estate or trust must be reported on a return filed for it by the **fiduciary** (the personal representative of the estate or the trustee(s) of a trust).

There are few constitutional limits to a state's power to tax net income of its residents. In fact, most states impose a variety of taxes upon their residents, as well as those conducting business within their borders. In most states, individual residents are taxed on their entire net incomes. There are seven states that do not collect individual income taxes. They are:

1. Alaska
2. Florida
3. Nevada
4. South Dakota
5. Tennessee (only taxes interest and dividend income)
6. Texas
7. Washington
8. Wyoming

Nonresidents are taxed on their net income earned from property located or business carried on in the state.

## State Corporate Income Taxes

Most states impose a corporate income tax in addition to personal income tax. This makes corporations subject to income tax in the same way as individuals although rates, deductions, and other important rules differ between individuals and corporations. Some state corporate income tax systems use a graduated method, and some states use a flat rate method. To help attract businesses to their states, some states purposely keep their corporate income tax rates lower than other states. Other incentives can include certain tax exemptions, also designed to attract new businesses to these states.

## Deductions

Individual taxpayers may claim deductions for alimony, medical expenses, dividends from income otherwise taxed, and charitable contributions or gifts. Many states allow an optional standard deduction in lieu of other deductions, much like the federal option for standard or itemized deductions. But states seldom offer this option in lieu of business expenses; this deduction is a percentage of gross or adjusted gross income. There is no state deduction for personal, living, or family expenses.

## Credits and Exemptions

Several state personal income tax laws allow taxpayers to deduct certain amounts of money from their net income according to filing status: single, heads of families, and individuals with dependents. And a few states permit the taxpayer to take the personal exemption in the form of a credit against the tax.

While there are some limitations, residents of states with income taxes are usually permitted to take a credit for taxes paid on income paid to another state. The tax must arise from personal services or business carried on in the other state. In terms of income earned in the state, nonresidents are often given a credit for taxes paid to their state of residence.

## Reciprocal Personal Income Tax Agreements

Several states have adopted income tax reciprocity agreements with one or more sister states—including the District of Columbia. These agreements allow income to be taxed in the state of residence even though it is earned in another state, as long as the state where the income was earned is a party to the reciprocity agreement. Such reciprocity agreements are an exception to the rule stating that the state in which income is earned has the primary right to tax that income.

In addition to reducing administrative reporting burdens, states with these agreements do not anticipate significant revenue loss because of them. Even considering the number of nonresidents working in a given state, its tax rate, and taxpayer income levels, the taxable revenue shared between the states may be about the same in both states.

Generally, reciprocal agreements only cover compensation, such as wages, salaries, tips, commissions, and bonuses a taxpayer receives for personal and professional services. But states may specify that certain income, such as lottery winnings, is not covered under reciprocity agreements.

Reciprocity agreements can simplify tax filing for some taxpayers. But in general, U.S. tax laws are very complicated. Fortunately, there are inexpensive tax preparation programs that people can use to make the annual tax filing chore easier. Taxpayers may also consult experienced tax professionals or attorneys for in-depth answers to more complex issues or for other specific tax advice.

## Additional Resources

*All States Tax Guide* Research Institute of America, Inc., 1960.

*"IRS.com"* http://www.irs.com/index.htm?DAID=10001. DotCom Corporation, 2002.

*Local Government Tax and Land Use Policies in the United States: Understanding the Links (Studies in Fiscal Federalism and State-Local Finance)* Edited by Helen F. Ladd and Wallace E. Oates, 1998.

*"National Conference of State Legislatures"* National Conference of State Legislatures, 2002. Available at http://www.ncsl.org/.

*State Taxation* 3rd ed., Hellerstein, Jerome R., and Walter Hellerstein, The RIA Group, 1998.

*State & Local Taxation: What Every Tax Lawyer Needs To Know* Hyans, Hollis L. and Diann L. Smith, Practicing Law Institute, 2001.

*State and Local Tax Policies* Hy, Ronald John, and William L., Jr. Waugh, 1995.

"Tax Filing Status."*Forbes.* January 2006. Available at http:/www.forbes.com/2006/01/13/taxes-ernstandyoung-ircs_sr_0117taxes2.html

*Taxing Powers of State and Local Government* Organization for Economic Co-Operation and Development, 1999.

## Organizations

### *ABA Section of Taxation*
740 15th Street NW, 10th Floor
Washington, DC 20005-1009 USA
Phone: (202) 662-8670
Fax: (202) 662-8682
URL: http://www.abanet.org/tax/home.html

### Council on State Taxation (COST)
122 C Street, NW, Suite 330280
Washington, DC 20001-2109 USA
Phone: (202) 484-5222
Fax: (202) 484-5229
URL: http://www.statetax.org/index.html

### Federation of Tax Administrators (FTA)
444 N. Capital St., NW, Suite 348280
Washington, DC 20001 USA
Phone: (202) 624-5890

E-Mail: webmaster@taxadmin.org
URL: http://www.taxadmin.org/

### Institute for Professionals in Taxation (IPT)
One Capital City Plaza, 3350 Peachtree Road, NE,
Suite 280
Atlanta, GA 30326 USA
Phone: (404) 240-2300
Fax: (404) 240-2315
E-Mail: ipt@ipt.org
URL: http://www.ipt.org/

# TAXES

## IRS AUDITS

*Sections Within This Essay*

- Background

- Types of Audits

- How the IRS Selects Taxpayers to Audit

- Time Limits for the IRS

- What Happens at an Audit

- Contesting the Audit

- The Small Case Division of the Federal Tax Court

- Audit Findings

- Additional Resources

## Background

The Internal Revenue Service (**IRS**) **audit** is an expansive subject. One needs to know a few of the basics of the U. S. history of the **income tax** to gain perspective on IRS audits. The history of income **taxation** in the United States is nearly as old as the United States itself. George Washington's administration levied the first taxes based on income. But there were three later major developments in the income tax law in the United States that made it a permanent fixture in U. S. political, economic, and legal culture.

The first major development occurred when Congress created the Office of the Commissioner of Revenue in 1862. The second major development came after the Civil War and various financial and economic crises of the late nineteenth century with the Six-

teenth Amendment of the U. S. Constitution, ratified in 1913. This amendment states that "The Congress shall have the power to lay and collect taxes on incomes, from whatever source derived, without **apportionment** among the several states, and without regard to any **census** or enumeration." The income tax was permanently established shortly thereafter. The third major development came in the middle of World War II. In 1942, Congress enacted a law that required employees to withhold taxes owed by their employees from the employees' wages and salaries.

Besides mandated withholding, Congress provided the IRS with an extensive array of powers to persuade the American people to meet their tax obligations. Tax returns must be:

- Accurate

- Filed

- Paid on time

The IRS has a variety of ways to choose which returns to audit, but only a relatively small number of individual taxpayers are actually selected for audits.

The prospect of an Internal Revenue Service (IRS) audit can create a good deal of anxiety in any taxpayer. An audit is a type of investigation used to determine whether the information provided to the government on the information/tax return is accurate. The audit is used in turn to determine whether the taxpayer paid the proper amount of tax. Audits are also used to uncover **fraud**. The taxpayer bears the burden of proof during an audit. That is, the taxpayer must prove to the IRS that the information the taxpayer reported on the income **tax return** is true and correct.

Whether taxpayers need outside assistance such as an accountants or an attorneys when they are faced with an audit depends on their particular circumstances. If their tax matters are fairly simple, they may be able to handle the audit entirely on their own. But if the tax issues are complex or if they do not fully understand taxes, it is a good idea for them to hire a professional to assist them.

## Types of Audits

Some audits are fairly routine, and some result in only minor changes for the taxpayer. Some audits do result in additional taxes, penalties, or interest that the taxpayers must pay, but some audits do result in refunds. These results come from any of three basic types of audits:.

- The mail audit: In these cases, the IRS will send a letter requesting an explanation or additional information. Note that an "Automatic Adjustment Notice," simply states that a taxpayer owes a certain amount of additional tax. These are usually the result of a calculating error.

- The interview audit: Here, a taxpayer appears at an IRS office with all receipts and crucial documents ready for the audit.

- The field audit: The IRS schedules field audits at the taxpayer's home or business. This is the usual form of audit for small businesses and for businesses operated from the home.

In some audit situations, a taxpayer may not need to actually meet in person with an IRS agent. These kinds of audits are conducted entirely by mail (sometimes known as "correspondence audits"). In an audit by mail, a taxpayer is commonly requested to justify or explain some part of a tax return by providing additional information through the mail.

If taxpayers are asked to provide documents to the IRS through the mail, they must send copies, as the IRS may misplace the originals. It is also a good idea to use certified mail, return receipt requested, to mail documents to the IRS. This method will provide proof that the response was mailed by the deadline the IRS gave the taxpayer. While phone calls can be more expeditious in some cases, that is not usually the case with the IRS. However, if taxpayers find it necessary to call the IRS about their audit, they should be sure to keep a detailed log of the call. They should record the date and time of the call, the name and title of any IRS employee with whom they speak, the general content of their discussion, and any advice or directions that they receive.

When taxpayers first hear from the IRS about an audit, they will receive a copy of the IRS publication, "Your Rights as a Taxpayer." This pamphlet contains an explanation of the Taxpayers' **Bill of Rights**, which has been enacted by Congress. It will also describes how the IRS conducts audits and collects unpaid taxes.

It is a very bad idea to ignore correspondence from the IRS about taxes. Doing so may expose taxpayers to **negligence** penalties; it may also lead to a full-blown audit that might otherwise have been unnecessary.

If the IRS determines that an audit should be conducted in person, it will either take place in an IRS office or in the taxpayer's home or business. The IRS conducts most field audits in offices, which are preferable often preferable to taxpayers. Even if the IRS asks to conduct the audit in the taxpayer's home or business, the taxpayer can keep the auditor away by providing all of the financial records to the tax adviser and asking that the audit be conducted at the tax advisor's place of business. If the IRS seems insistent that the audit takes place at the taxpayer's home or office, individuals need to keep in mind that they cannot be compelled to admit them to their home or place of business. In cases where this is an issue, taxpayers may need to show that an audit would be disruptive to their home or business to keep the auditor away from these places.

The IRS will allow taxpayers several weeks to prepare for an audit. Individuals need to use this time to gather the documents they will need to support the entries on their return. If taxpayers need extra time to prepare or to retrieve documents, they may request a change from the original appointment time set by the IRS. If their request is reasonable, the IRS is likely to grant it.

## How the IRS Selects Taxpayers to Audit

The IRS conducts audits on approximately 2% to 3% of individual tax returns submitted every year. Because there are about 130 million tax returns individual tax returns filed annually, about 4 million of them will be audited.

There are several methods the IRS uses to determine if which tax returns to audit. Three of the most common are:

1. The Differential Income Factor (DIF) Method. Each tax return filed with the IRS is assigned a score based on the amount of income reported and the kind and amount of deductions claimed. The IRS will include tax returns in the pool of returns for auditing if the DIF score a tax return receives exceeds a particular threshold for income reported on the return. The higher the expenses relative to the income, the higher the DIF score.

2. The Information Returns Factor Method. The IRS receives copies of all W-2s and 1099s every year. The IRS also records the social security numbers from these documents and matches them to the social security numbers on the tax returns that are filed. If a taxpayer fails to report all of the income from their forms W-2 or 1099 on their tax return, the IRS will catch this discrepancy. This discrepancy will help to select that taxpayer's tax return for audit.

3. The Random Selection Method. All tax returns receive a random, computer-generated number. Tax returns with high DIF scores and non-matched information are taken out. A certain number of these tax returns are picked at random to audit.

Once the IRS has selected a pool of tax returns for auditing, they are assigned to Internal Revenue agents and revenue officers. When a tax return is chosen for audit, it is assigned a certain transaction code (TC). The TC identifies it as being selected for audit.

Every taxpayer who submits tax returns to the IRS has a record that is maintained by the IRS. These records are known as Individual Master Files (IMF). Since 1974 the **Freedom of Information Act** has allowed taxpayers to access their IMFs. The IMF provides data on a computer-generated report concerning each taxpayer the IRS has on record. The IMF can reveal whether a taxpayer's return

- has been received by the IRS
- has been selected for audit
- has been assessed additional taxes
- what the final collection date is for the tax return

Agents are assigned individual audits up to six months before the taxpayer is even notified of an audit. Therefore, a copy of the taxpayer's IMF can tell him or her whether the taxpayer's tax return has been selected for audit.

The most likely groups to be audited are taxpayers who own sole proprietorships. These taxpayers file a Schedule C that is attached to their Form 1040. Taxpayers with high incomes are also frequently targeted for audits. Others likely to be targets of auditors are taxpayers who work in businesses that conduct a lot of businesses in cash, for example, owners of bars, restaurants, vending machine services, or laundromats. This is true whether or not the taxpayer files Form 8300 (Report of Cash Payments Over $10,000 Received in a Trade or Business). On the average, cash businesses are subject to auditing much more than other types.

## Time Limits for the IRS

IRS auditors must complete audits within 28 months of the date the audited taxpayer filed the tax return, or by the date it was due, April 15, whichever is later. Actually, the law gives the IRS eight additional months after that (for a total of 36 months, or three years), but auditors need to leave at least eight months in which the IRS can process appeals. This means that taxpayers need to keep their tax records and supporting documents for at least that long. This three-year limit does not apply, however, if they underreported their income by more than 25 percent. In those cases, the IRS has six years in which to conduct an audit and assess additional taxes if they are warranted. There is no time limit at all for audits in cases where taxpayers file **fraudulent** returns. Given these factors, the common wisdom says that taxpayers should retain tax records for at least six years.

Sometimes the IRS is not able to complete an audit within its three-year time limit. In such cases, the IRS may extend this time limit. Taxpayers do not have to agree to an extension, but the IRS can make the audit very unpleasant if they do not get an extension. The IRS will typically respond to a refusal by disallowing every questionable item on the return being audited. It may be a better strategy to negotiate an extension with a definite expiration date and to restrict the extension to only those items in question when the extension is granted. This keeps the IRS from expanding its audit to other areas of the return during the extension period.

Occasionally a taxpayer will be notified by the IRS about an impending audit, but then the taxpayer will not hear from the auditor for a long time. This can mean several things. For example, the auditor may no longer work for the IRS or may have changed jobs within the IRS. It is possible that the taxpayer's file is being processed somewhere else within the IRS. If and when the file again comes to the IRS's attention, it may be assigned to a new auditor who is working under a shortened deadline to close the audit. This can work in the taxpayer's favor. So, although the taxpayer may be tempted to inquire about the status of the audit, it may be best to remain silent.

It may be a good idea for the taxpayer to have the person who prepared the taxes (if the taxpayer had a paid tax preparer) appear at the audit with him to explain how the taxes were figured. If an attorney, **CPA**, or an "enrolled agent" prepared the tax return, that person can even appear in the taxpayer's place. Other kinds of tax preparers may accompany their clients to an audit, but they cannot represent clients at the audit. In some cases where permissible, it may be better for the taxpayer not to attend the audit, since the professional representing the taxpayer has no emotional involvement in the outcome of the audit. These people may be less likely to irritate or raise the suspicions of the auditor.

Perhaps the best advice about audits is never to provide more information than the IRS requests. Most audits are limited to specific areas of a return, which the taxpayer knows in advance. At the audit, the taxpayer should limit his response only to inquiries the auditor makes about these specified areas. If the auditor attempts to examine other areas of the return, the taxpayer should refuse to discuss them until he has received a formal request to audit that portion of the return. Although most audits are limited in scope, there are a small number of taxpayers (about 50,000) that are subjected to a Tax Compliance Measurement Audit. This kind of audit examines every item on the tax return. Naturally, these taxpayers must respond to all of the auditor's inquiries.

## What Happens at an Audit

For any audit, IRS agents must review the following four issues:

- Income: The IRS will want to see bank statements, records from the sale of assets, documents relating to prizes, **alimony**, pensions, and state and federal tax refunds.

- Previous audits: If the taxpayer previously had an audit, the agents will review information about when the previous audit took place, the results, and any recent correspondence the taxpayer has had with the IRS.

- Other returns: Agents will examine whether the taxpayer filed subsequent and prior years' returns on time and whether adjustments were necessary.

- Penalties: IRS agents must inquire whether the taxpayer has previously been assessed tax penalties. Of course, they will determine whether penalties should be assessed as a result of the current audit.

All audits begin with the taxpayer receiving a notice in the mail from the IRS. People should not panic if they do receive correspondence from the IRS in the mail. In fact, what they receive may not even be an audit notice at all, but an "automated adjustment notice," (also called a CP2000) informing them about additional taxes they owe. Automated adjustment notices reveal errors taxpayers made in computing income or taxes. The IRS sends automated adjustment notices to certain taxpayers because they failed to report some income to the IRS which was reported to it on a 1099 form, such as dividends or interest.

Even though a taxpayer receives an automated adjustment notice does not mean that the taxpayer must pay the amount assessed without question. In fact, the IRS itself makes miscalculations of taxes or enters income data about incorrectly. Federal law gives taxpayers the right to appeal an automated adjustment notice in writing within 60 days of receipt of the notice.

If people receive a notice from the IRS that they will be audited, they should first contact the revenue agent assigned to their case to schedule a mutually convenient time to meet. The taxpayer bears the burden of proof, which means the taxpayer must prove that the tax return in question, as well as the taxpayer's records are accurate and complete. The taxpayer will be assessed additional taxes if the taxpayer cannot prove the questionable aspects of the reported income and/or deductions. This possibility makes it important to maintain organized and accessible financial records.

Audited taxpayers should expect the IRS to ask some or all of the following questions or look into the following issues:

- Did the taxpayer report all of his or her business sales and receipts?

- Did the taxpayer write off any personal living expenses as business expenses?

- Does the taxpayer's lifestyle seem to exceed the amount of reported self-employment income?

- Did the taxpayer write off automobile expenses for travel that was not business-related?

- Did the taxpayer claim large business entertainment expenses?

- Are the taxpayer's workers classified as independent contractors when they are really employees?

- Does the taxpayer make payroll tax deposits in a timely manner?

- Did the taxpayer report all cash transactions — especially large cash transactions?

When the IRS revenue agent completes the audit, the taxpayer will get a report describing the agent's recommendation and a statement of the amount of money the taxpayer owes. The agent will probably ask the taxpayer to sign a **waiver** of the appeal rights at that time. When the agent asks the taxpayer to sign the waiver the taxpayer has three options:

1. Go ahead and pay the additional tax; if the taxpayer disputes the additional amount, the taxpayer can file for a refund.

2. The taxpayer requests an appeal with the IRS **appellate** division. The taxpayer does not pay the tax bill and interest on the tax bill continues to accumulate during the appeal process. Even so, this is a small item compared to the tax savings that result from most appeals.

3. The taxpayer signs the waiver and pays the tax.

Occasionally the IRS will conclude that a taxpayer knowingly violated the tax laws. In these cases the IRS can recommend to the U. S. Department of Justice that the taxpayer be charged with a crime. Some of these taxpayers are prosecuted for specific tax violations, including knowingly failing to file a return or knowingly filing a fraudulent return. Recently, the IRS criminal referrals have been increasingly based on statutes relating to **money laundering**, drugs, and other currency violations.

It is important to remain as objective as possible during an audit. The audit is, after all, strictly about numbers. However, taxpayers need not be subject to an auditor who is rude or unpleasant. In such cases, taxpayers are legally entitled to request the assignment of a different auditor.

## Contesting the Audit

At the audit, the taxpayer will need to **substantiate** the information on the return. This means that the taxpayer will need plenty of **documentary evidence**. The taxpayer will need cancelled checks, receipts, bank statements, and all other documented financial records related to the tax return. Of course, the taxpayer can also **testify** in person about information on the return. While some of the proof may not be sufficient for the actual audit, it may be accepted on appeal or even before the tax court, though the audit appeal may be the easiest, quickest, and least expensive route to at least partial success.

There are three principal reasons for appealing an audit:

1. The appeals process is relatively simple and costs the taxpayer nothing (unless the individual hires a tax attorney or accountant, which are not required).

2. In most cases, appeals result in some tax, **penalty**, or interest savings, although appeals rarely result in a total victory for the taxpayer.

3. An appeal can delay for months a tax bill based on the audit; this can buy individuals time to raise the money they may owe under the audit.

The IRS agent's financial conclusions are not absolutely binding. Taxpayers can appeal by sending a protest letter to the IRS within 30 days of receiving the audit report. In fact, taxpayers may question the auditor's report at a number of levels:

- before an appeals' officer

- before the agent's manager

- before the U. S. Tax Court

If a taxpayer requests an appeal, the taxpayer will be granted a meeting with an Appeals Officer. This person will not be part of the IRS division that performed the taxpayer's audit. There are important time limitations related to each of these levels of appeal. Taxpayers need to make sure they know what they are and that they stay within them so that their rights to appeal an audit are not lost through such a technicality.

Although it is very unusual, the appeals officer may raise issues the auditor may have missed. So, if a taxpayer is concerned that a particular item will be discovered and the taxpayer will owe even more in taxes, it may be advisable for the taxpayer to go directly to Tax Court where new issues cannot be raised. Before the taxpayer bypasses an appeal, however, it is wise for the taxpayer to consult a tax or legal professional.

If the appeal does not result in a change in the audit report, an aggrieved taxpayer can file a petition in tax court. For audit bills less than $50,000, this is a fairly inexpensive and simple process. If the audit bill is more than $50,000, taxpayers are well advised to seek the services of a tax attorney. It is generally a good idea to contest an audit report. Appeals and **litigation** in tax court result in a lower tax bill for about half the people who challenge their audit report.

In some cases, a particularly aggrieved taxpayer may consider taking his appeal to the U. S. Supreme Court. However, it is unlikely that the Supreme Court will hear the case unless the tax issue is one that will have a far-reaching effect.

## The Small Case Division of the Federal Tax Court

The federal Tax Court has a special ''small case'' division. This division has **jurisdiction** over cases in which the IRS claims that amount of taxes and penalties for a taxpayer in any one tax year is $50,000 or less. Cases that qualify for **adjudication** in the small case division are known as ''small cases'' and receive an ''S'' designation.

Most people who file a small case in Tax Court end up getting their taxes reduced by some amount. And some taxpayers never even make it to court. In almost every case, before the trial date, the IRS will ask the taxpayer to meet with its lawyer to try to reach a **settlement**. It is quite possible that the taxpayer may be able to settle for an amount that is less than the additional tax originally imposed by the auditor. This is because Appeals Division officers weigh the cost of litigation and the risk that the IRS might lose a court appeal against the chances of success. Statis-

tics have shown that most cases (9 out of 10, in fact) heard by the Appeals Division are settled.

If a taxpayer does not settle with the IRS or otherwise proceeds to court, that taxpayer will discover that the small case division of the tax court operates much like a small claims court. One simply tells the judge his or her story and shows whatever **evidence** he or she may have. Laypersons need not know legal procedures or technical legal jargon. Conversely, the IRS will send a lawyer to advocate for its side. A typical case lasts just an hour or two. Of course, the taxpayer can always hire someone to represent him. A lawyer, especially one with training and experience in tax law, can represent the taxpayer; so can an enrolled agent or CPA who has been admitted to practice before the Tax Court.

The odds are that about half of all taxpayers will be audited at least once, and the odds increase with the amount of income the taxpayer reports. In the end, the best way to avoid an IRS audit is to minimize the possibility that the income tax return raises questions when the taxpayer files it with the IRS. To do this, the taxpayer should be sure to file all the required forms and answer all the questions asked on the return, even if they seem unrelated to the taxpayer's situation. Finally, the taxpayer should check the accuracy of W-2 and 1099 forms and report all the income on these forms to the IRS.

## Audit Findings

In 2005, the IRS released preliminary results from a major research project that assessed U.S. citizens' (including business entities) compliance with tax laws. The findings revealed that the vast majority of Americans paid taxes in a timely and accurate manner. However, there still remained a substantial tax gap, which is the difference between what taxpayers should pay and what was actually paid on a timely basis. According to the report, this gap exceeds $300 billion per year. IRS enforcement activities, along with late payments, recoup approximately $55 billion per year.

Other significant findings:

- Underreporting of income constituted the largest component of the tax gap, and accounted for approximately 80 percent of total noncompliance. Non-filing and underpayment of taxes each contributed about ten percent to the total tax gap.

- Individual income tax is the single largest source of the annual tax gap. More than 80 percent of underreporting of income comes from understated income, not overstated deductions. Most understated income comes from business activities and not wages or investment income.

- Compliance rates are highes where there is third-party reporting or withholding. Preliminary findings estimate less than 1.5 percent of wages and salaries are misreported.

## Additional Resources

*Disagreeing with the IRS.* Edited by Crouch, Holmes F. and Irma J. Crouch, eds. Allyear Tax Guides, 1998.

*http://www.irs.gov/* "The IRS" Department of the Treasury, 2002.

*http://www.taxfables.com/Columns/List_Audits.html* "A. J.'s Tax Fables: A Syndicated Newspaper Column," A. J. Cook, 2002.

*"New IRS Study Provides Preliminary Tax Gap Estimate."* IR-2005-38, issued 29 March 2005. Available at http://www.irs.gov/newsroom.

*http://www.irs.ustreas.gov/pub/irs-utl/tbor2.pdf* "Taxpayer's Bill of Rights." Internal Revenue Service, 2002.

*Stand Up to the IRS, 6th Edition.* 6th ed., Frederick W. Daily, Frederick W., and Robin Leonard, Nolo Press, 2001.

*Surviving an IRS Tax Audit.* Frederick W. Daily, Frederick W., Nolo Press, 1999.

*What the IRS Doesn't Want You to Know: A CPA Reveals the Tricks of the Trade.* Martin A. Kaplan, Marin A., Marty Kaplan, and Naomi Weiss, Random House, 2001.

## Organizations

### Council On State Taxation
122 C Street, NW, Suite 330
Washington, DC 20001-2109 USA
Phone: (202) 484-5222
Fax: (202) 484-5229
URL: http://www.statetax.org/index.html

### Federation of Tax Administrators (FTA)
444 N. Capital St., NW, Suite 348
Washington, DC 20001 USA
Phone: (202) 624-5890
URL: http://www.taxadmin.org/

### National Tax Association (NTA)
725 15th St., NW #600
Washington, D.C., DC 20005-2109 USA
Phone: (202) 737-3325
Fax: (202) 737-7308
E-Mail: natltax@aol.com
URL: http://ntanet.org/

# TAXES

## PROPERTY TAXES

## Background

Some taxes are based on a proportion of the value of the property being taxes. These are known as "ad valorem" taxes. To arrive at an accurate amount of tax, an **appraisal** of the taxable subject matter's value needs to be done periodically. When the property owner's property value changes, so does their assessed or appraised value. Most property taxes are this **ad valorem** variety. Ad valorem property taxes are based on ownership of the property. Property owners must pay these taxes whether they actually use the property or not or whether it generates income for them or not.

There are many types of property subject to property tax although the tax is most commonly based on the value of real property (land). Municipal governments use property taxes to collect revenue probably more than any other taxing authority. Municipalities gain their authority to levy property taxes from state law. Property taxes are used to help finance local government services. These include public schools, fire and police protection, roads, parks, streets, sewer and/or water treatment systems, garbage removal, public libraries, and many other local services.

Taxing land and buildings is one of the oldest forms of **taxation** in the United States. Before income and sales taxes, local governments used property-based taxes to finance most of their activities. Property taxes remain a major source of revenue for local governments. Most local governments collect taxes on both real and **personal property**, but they have been moving away from taxing intangible property such as bank accounts and **corporate** stocks and **bonds**.

Both state and local government agencies are authorized to levy taxes, but the way they conduct assessments, collection, and compliance can differ widely. In some states, a single state agency has primary responsibility for obtaining all appraisals, making assessments, and collecting taxes. In most states, certain agencies assess some or all railroads and utilities properties.

Generally, responsibility for the three phases of property tax—levy, appraisal, and collection—rests almost exclusively on the taxing authorities within local governments. A taxing authority like a county, city, town, hospital, refuse collection, school, or other special district, is a legal entity of the government with elected or appointed officers who serve a distinct geographic area.

## Types of Property

There are two basic categories of property: real and personal. The **assessment** procedures and the tax rate will vary between these two categories. Real property, in general, is land and anything permanently affixed to land (e.g. wells or buildings). Structures such as homes, apartments, offices, and commercial buildings (and the land to which they are attached) are typical examples of real property.

Basically, personal property is any property that is not real property. Personal property is not permanently attached to land. In most cases, it is moveable and does not last as long as real property. It comprises nearly everything that is perceptible to the senses. Personal property includes vehicles, farm equipment, jewelry, household goods, stocks, and bonds.

Personal property is divided into "tangible" and "intangible" forms. **Tangible** personal property is just that: it has a physical form. It can be seen, touched, and moved. Examples of tangible personal property include clothing, books, and computers. On the other hand, the notion of intangible personal property is an abstraction. They do not have physical forms. These include assets such as **patents**, **trademarks**, stocks, and bonds.

In addition to the basic types of property, property is grouped into various classes and subclasses for purposes of tax assessment. These classes are based on the use of the property. These schedules of classes vary considerably from state to state. For example, a state may have the following classes of property:

- Class 1. Agriculture, grazing, livestock, notes, bonds, stocks, accounts receivable
- Class 2: Commercial properties
- Class 3: Motor vehicles
- Class 4: Personal property, except motor vehicles
- Class 5: Residential, farm homes
- Class 6: Swamp and waste

Property classification according to various uses or types serves as a basis for adjusting the rate of tax.

## Determining Tax Rates

Tax dollars help support the functions and services of specific local organizations. The local taxing authority (e.g. the county or municipal government) uses one of two methods to calculate the tax rate:

1. In the first method, the taxing authority estimates its total expenditures over a given time period. Then, it divides that figure by the taxable or assessed value of all property within its **jurisdiction**. The result is the tax rate. This rate is sometimes expressed using mills or percentages; sometimes it is expressed as a dollar amount ($1 per $100).

2. In the second method, the taxing authority estimates the amount of taxes available from property tax levied at a specific rate. The taxing authority will either increase or decrease its budget based on increases or decreases in the total value of the property's taxable or assessed value.

State constitutions or statutes commonly impose rate limitations. Many states set a maximum rate for each class of government (e.g., school, city, or county). Because real property can be located in overlapping tax districts (e.g. schools and towns), the total tax rates will vary from one neighborhood to another. This results in more than one local taxing authority calculating tax rates for the property. Many jurisdictions aggregate these rates, resulting in a single tax levy called a consolidated, overall, or composite levy.

## Exemptions

Basically, all real and personal property is subject to tax unless specifically exempted. Exemptions come in many forms. These exemptions include its use, such as for religious or charitable purposes, and the form of its ownership, such as household goods. Exemptions are used by state and local governments to help attract new businesses or to encourage certain types of development, such as low-income housing or reclamation of historic sites.

Exemptions range from full to partial tax relief. One town may provide a full exemption for personal or business property, whereas another town may provide only a partial exemption for these types of property. The limitations can be expressed in terms of dollar amounts or by a percentage of value. Homeowners' exemptions are an example of this kind of partial exemption. Other forms of exemptions exist for the following:

- Certain municipal levies
- County city, town and school purposes

- Government property (these are required by state law)
- Persons over age 65
- Veterans.

An important issue in property tax law deals with the location of property or its "situs" for tax purposes. If a taxpayer owns property in more than one area, or if the taxpayer owns property that is moveable, like a car or a trailer, it can be difficult to determine the most appropriate location from which to determine the property tax on those items. Because the law can be so variable from one place to the next, this issue is often in dispute.

The general rule states that land will be taxed according to the laws of the county where the land is located, regardless of where the owner resides. On the other hand, moveable property is generally taxable according to the laws of the county where the taxpayer resides. These are general rules. For information specific to a person's own situation, the person should check with an accountant, tax advisor, or lawyer.

## Tax Assessments

An assessment is basically an estimate of what a piece of property is worth. This valuation of the property helps decide what part of the local property tax levy will be billed to the property. Once this has been determined, the value is multiplied by the tax rates, sometimes known as the "mill rate," to determine how much tax the owner must pay on that piece of property. Many states use full **market value** (or a fraction of it) as a basis for their assessments.

Assessors "value" property for tax appraisal purposes. "Value" is also known as the following:

- Actual value
- Appraisal value
- Fair and reasonable market value
- Fair cash value
- Full and fair value
- Full value
- Just value
- Market value
- True value

Despite these similar terms, most states focus on "market value." Market value is the amount of money a typical, knowledgeable, buyer (unrelated to the seller) would pay for a given parcel of property. To calculate the market value of a piece of property, an assessor will determine if there have been changes in the real estate market where the property is situated. The assessor will examine what different types of property are selling for, local construction costs, normal operating expenses like utilities, nearby rental rates, and inflation. Changes in these factors may change the assessed value of the property.

## Assessing Personal Property

To make assessments of most personal property, appraisers use information contained on personal property statements filed by the property owner. If the property owner does not provide information about the value of his or her personal property, the assessor estimates the property's value using acceptable appraisal data and techniques, taking into consideration factors such as the age, cost, and type of property. Depending on the state or locality, tax rates for personal property may be the same as that for real property or may differ.

## Assessing Real Property

There are three principal methods for assessing the value of real property. These differ based on the kind of property being assessed.

1. The cost (or replacement) method. This method is used for assessing buildings or other structures. Assessors estimate how much it would cost, using current rates for material and labor, to replace a given structure. An assessor will deduct the reasonable **depreciation** of the property but add the value of the land. This approach is most appropriate when the assessment is of a new and unique or specialized property. It is also useful when there are no meaningful sales of comparable properties.

2. The income method. Under this method, assessors estimate the amount of income from a piece of property if the property is used to produce an income. This method is used for apartments, stores, warehouses, shopping centers, and office buildings. To arrive at an assessment, the assessor considers the business taxes, the

amount of income the property may generate, insurance costs, rates of vacancy, operating expenses, maintenance costs, and the current interest rate charged for borrowing money for making improvements or repairs on such a property.

3. The market or sales comparison method. Here, sales of similar properties are compared to each other and adjusted for differences. Most residential real estate is appraised by using the market or sales comparison method. This approach is similar to the method banks employ to value property when they consider issuing a **mortgage**.

Most states appraise various classes or types of real estate using other approaches to value. For example, farmland or timberland may be appraised on its use or level of productivity. Business inventories may be assessed on the basis of the business's records, as well as the state of its machinery and equipment. And assessors may even combine approaches to arrive at a fair appraisal of a piece of property.

Taxpayers have a right to fair appraisals. Furthermore, no class of property should be over–or under–valued in relation to similar properties within a given area. Even so, it is up to individual property owners to monitor their assessments. To find out which appraisal method was used in a situation owners should contact their local assessor's office.

## Changing Property Values

Individuals may pay more in property tax if the tax rate increases, or if the value of their property increases. Their property tax rate can increase because their taxing district needs to raise revenue in order to provide services. The tax rate may also rise as a result of voter-approved bonds and override levies. If their district's budget increases while the assessed value of all property remains the same, in most cases the tax rate will rise and they will pay higher taxes.

Even if the tax rate remains the same, individuals' taxes may rise if their property value increases. Some other factors that will adjust the value upward include the following:

- Adding a new bathroom
- Adding a fireplace
- Adding a terrace
- Adding an extra room

- Expanding or adding a garage
- Finishing the basement

Besides reflecting added features to the home, the property's value is a part of the economy of the area. Thus, a development of upscale homes nearby can make their property more valuable. If individuals live in a community with rapid growth, and the demand for housing increases, their property's value will most likely go up.

The opposite is true as well. If the owner's property is in poor repair or becomes damaged by a fire, earthquake, or flood, or if a major structural problem develops or their neighborhood deteriorates, the assessed value of their home would probably decrease as well. A poor local economy, slow growth, and low demand for homes in their area will probably depress their property's value.

## Payment

The due date for property tax is due depends on location. The deadlines vary considerably. Some property taxes are paid annually, and some are paid in two, three, or four installments. Some jurisdictions allow for monthly tax payments. The collection office nearest the property owner will have more information on payment options. A few of these are:

- Credit card payments
- Discounts for early payment
- **Escrow** agreements
- Extensions
- Partial payments
- Split payments

In some areas, homeowners pay their property tax through escrow accounts. The tax bill is incorporated with the mortgage payment. Thus, the mortgage-holder pays the tax bill out of these combined funds.

## Challenging the Valuation of One's Property

Because the effects of an assessment can be quite expensive to property owners, challenges to the valuations of properties are quite common. In most cases, owners are free to meet with the assessor to present their cases. Owners need to keep in mind that any changes must be based on **evidence**. Mere complaints that the owners think their taxes are too high will not lead to a reduction.

Property owners will need all the records pertinent to the valuation of their property in order to make a successful argument for changing the valuation. Make sure they scrutinize the accuracy of the assessor's information for obvious errors. If the assessor accidentally added an extra bedroom or bath in his assessment of the property, or figured the tax using the wrong taxing authority are mistakes that can make an enormous difference in the owner's property tax. Owners should also request copies of the comparable sales information the assessor used to value their property. Examine these documents and closely compare their property's assessed value and those of nearby properties.

An appeal may be successful if the appraisal overlooked hidden conditions such as a pest infestation, a cracked foundation, or other undesirable environmental conditions. These factorss could adversely lower the property's value, and hence adjust the owner's appraisal downward. Additionally, certain exemptions in the property may negatively impact its value. These include veterans', POW, and homeowner exemptions.

In most cases, the best evidence of property value are comparisons of recent property sales within the same neighborhood. Because this is public information, it is not difficult to obtain; however, analyzing it and applying it to the owner's particular situation can be difficult. For example, the motivations of buyers and sellers can influence sales prices, but this information is very difficult to obtain. If there are no recent property sales within the property owner's neighborhood from which the owner can make comparisons, the next best alternative is to check for areas of comparison between the owner's property and property that is reasonably similar to sit. Consider factors like location, style, age, and physical factors like square footage, lot size, number of rooms, and so forth.

Every state provides formal and informal methods to challenge tax bills. In both, adherence to procedure and time limitations are critical. Note that in most jurisdictions, they must pay the assessed taxes even while their appeal is pending. If they do not, the taxing authority (municipal or county government, in most cases) may charge the owner interest and penalties on the unpaid balance.

The laws and procedures for disputing a tax bill vary considerably from state to state, although there are some common mechanisms for appeals. For example, most states have between two and four steps for appeals. The level of appeal after a complaint to the local assessor usually occurs at an administrative agency (e.g., county review board, county commissioner). Here, property owners may present evidence that supports their contrary opinion of an assessment or of a tax bill. Should they not convince the authorities at that level, there are usually additional procedures at a higher state level, or even recourse to courts. If **litigation** is the owner's next step, it is wise to hire an attorney whose specialty is representing property owners in these types of disputes.

If property owners feel that they cannot afford the taxes assessed on their property, they have little recourse. Personal hardships, such as living on a fixed income or inability to pay are not considered in the assessment of taxes. The property's worth is the only criterion for assessing taxes on that property. Property taxes are not based on earnings, the original price of a piece of property (except in California), disposable income, or one's ability to pay. If property owners receive a large tax bill that strains their ability to pay the tax, about the only recourse they have is to apply for a hardship exemption or a tax deferral. Not all states have these procedures. If they cannot pay their taxes, they may check with their local collection office for the options that are available to them.

## Additional Resources

"2001 State Tax Forms" Federation of Tax Administrators, 2002. Available at ttp://www.taxadmin.org/fta/link/link.html.

"The IRS" Department of the Treasury, 2002. Available at http://www.irs.gov/.

*State and Local Taxation and Finance in a Nutshell, 2nd Edition.* 2nd, M. David Gelfand, M. David, and Peter W Salsich, Jr., West Publishing, 2000.

*http://www.taxsites.com/state.html* "Tax and Accounting Sites Directory: State and Local Tax" Schmidt Enterprises, LLC, 2002. Available at http://www.taxsites.com/state.html.

*Taxes for Dummies 2002.* Eric Tyson, Eric, and David J. Silverman., Hungry Minds, Inc., 2001.

*http://www.taxadmin.org/fta/link/link.html* "2001 State Tax Forms" Federation of Tax Administrators, 2002.

*http://www.irs.gov/* "The IRS" Department of the Treasury, 2002.

## Organizations

### American Society of Appraisers (ASA)
555 Herndon Parkway, Suite 125
Herndon, VA 20170 USA
Phone: (703) 478-2228
Fax: (703) 742-8471
E-Mail: asainfo@appraisers.org
URL: http://www.appraisers.org/

### The Appraisal Foundation
1029 Vermont Avenue, NW, Suite 900
Washington, DC 20005-3517 USA
Phone: (202) 347-7722
Fax: (202) 347-7727
E-Mail: info@appraisalfoundation.org
URL: https://www.appraisalfoundation.org/
default.asp

### Council On State Taxation
122 C Street, NW, Suite 330
Washington, DC 20001-2109 USA
Phone: (202) 484-5222
Fax: (202) 484-5229
URL: http://www.statetax.org/index.html

### Federation of Tax Administrators (FTA)
444 N. Capital St., NW, Suite 348
Washington, DC 20001 USA
Phone: (202) 624-5890
URL: http://www.taxadmin.org/

### National Tax Association (NTA)
725 15th St. NW #600
Washington, DC 20005-2109 USA
Phone: (202) 737-3325
Fax: (202) 737-7308
E-Mail: natltax@aol.com
URL: http://ntanet.org/

# TAXES

## SALES TAXES

*Sections within this essay:*

- Background

- General Sales Tax

- Use Tax

- Excise and Other Special Sales Taxes

- Gross Receipt Taxes

- Sales Tax Issues
    - National Sales Tax
    - Internet Taxes

- Listing of State Sales Tax Rates

- Additional Resources

### Background

Of all the taxes Americans are subjected to, **sales tax** is the more often than not considered the least controversial. Rarely does it inspire the debate of the **income tax** or property tax. Thus, a useful tax for funding everything from schools to ballparks.

The general sales tax has only been in effect since 1932, when it was imposed on the state of Mississippi and the municipalities of New York City and New Orleans. Special sales taxes, or **excise** taxes, have been used for much longer: the famous Boston Tea Party of 1773 was held as a protest over such a tax on tea, and the United States first imposed an excise tax on whiskey in 1790.

Within the context of tax revenues, the state sales tax is an important tax. In fact, it is currently the larg-est source of total state revenues in the country—45 states and the District of Columbia now impose a sales tax, and hundreds of municipalities and local government entities across the United States impose their own sales taxes. Cuts in income taxes and property taxes over the past 10 years have made states and local governments even more dependent on the sales tax.

### General Sales Tax

Although most people assume sales taxes are paid by the purchaser, the general sales tax is considered to be imposed on the seller, and is considered a tax on the privilege of doing business in the state or municipality. It is imposed when the seller completes a sale of **tangible personal property** or services.

The goods and services covered by a sales tax are generally extensive—virtually any transaction within the state or municipality where money changes hands is covered by the general sales tax, including all consumer goods, entertainment such as movies or sports events, hotels, restaurants, and even items such as phone charges or electrical bills.

Although the seller is required to collect the sales tax, the tax is imposed upon the purchaser as part of the final purchase price. The seller is usually considered ultimately responsible for the collection of the tax as the primary tax collector.

The sales tax is identified in percentage terms within the measure of a dollar—a 4 percent sales tax means for every dollar spent, there will be a four-cent tax. Most government entities utilize a bracket system to identify how much tax is to be paid on specific goods. The bracket system allocates how much sale tax is to be paid to a specific dollar amount. For example, the six percent sales tax in Michigan results in the following brackets: no tax due on amounts from $0.00 to $0.10, one cent due from $0.11 to $0.24, two cents due from $0.25 to $0.41, three cents due from $0.42 to $0.58, four cents due from $0.59 to $0.74, five cents due from $0.75 to $0.91, six cents due from $0.92 to $0.99, and for $1.00 and each multiple of $1.00, 6 percent of the sale price. Like Michigan, many states have these specific bracket calculations set out in their **statute**, although some states delegate this power to an administrative agency.

Sellers are generally required to remit the sales tax on a periodic basis, usually quarterly, sometimes more frequently if the amount of the tax reaches a certain point. Most states allow sellers to keep a small portion of the tax as a payment for the work they do in collecting the tax.

General sales taxes usually contain exclusions and exemptions. These exclusions and exemptions can be quite broad, often including sales of intangible personal property and goods meant for resale. Goods used in production are also often exempted from sales tax to prevent multiple taxations. Most states exempt professional and personal services such as those provided by doctors and lawyers from sales taxes.

The sales tax is a regressive tax—that is, its burdens fall more heavily on poorer people. Because of this fact, basic goods such as food, clothing, and medicine are many times exempted from sales tax. Some states also declare "tax holidays" exempting persons shopping within a specific time frame from having to pay sales tax.

Most states allow local government entities within the state to impose their own general sales taxes. Usually, doing so requires the approval of both the state and municipal government, although in some states with strong home rule provisions, these taxes can be passed without state approval. The same exclusions and exemptions of the state sales tax are usually present for these local sales taxes, though state law sometimes allows local governments to override these exclusions with their own taxes. Local governments are also commonly restricted in the rates they can impose.

A problem that often arises when local government entities impose their own sales taxes in multiple sales taxes for businesses located in several differ-

ent places. States solve this problem by declaring the sales tax is to be imposed at the place of business of the seller. If there is more than one place of business, then the place where the initial transaction occurs determines the imposition of the tax.

## Use Tax

A **use tax** differs from a sales tax in that a sales tax is assessed on the purchase price of property and is imposed at the time of sale; a use tax is assessed on the storage, use, or consumption of property and takes effect only after such use begins.

Another way of looking at this point is to observe that the taxable event for **assessment** of the sales tax occurs at the time of sale. The taxable event for assessment of the use tax occurs when possession of the property is transferred to the purchaser within the taxing state for storage, use, or consumption.

The use tax is considered supplementary to the sales tax. It ensures that purchasers who attempt to avoid the sales tax by buying outside of the area of the sales tax will still have to pay the use tax when they use the product or service they have purchased within the taxing area.

Use taxes are almost always imposed at the same rate as the sales tax. If a sales tax has already been paid on the good or service in question in the place where it was purchased, the use tax will generally not be imposed. The person using the good or service is liable for the tax, although responsibility for collecting the tax is often imposed on the seller.

Use taxes have been fought in court, particularly by mail order companies required to collect the tax. The Supreme Court has ruled that in order to collect a use tax from a business, a company's activity must have a "substantial nexus" with the taxing state. Thus, the court ruled that a mail order company with no office in the taxing state does not have a substantial nexus with the state, and therefore, the state cannot impose its use tax.

Use taxes, by their nature, can be hard to collect, because many times purchasers of goods or services has no idea that they owe a use tax. If the state or local government entity cannot impose the tax directly, they often have no recourse in collecting the tax unless there is a separate registration requirement (as with a car).

## Excise and Other Special Sales Taxes

Excise taxes are sales taxes targeted at a specific item, such as cigarettes or alcohol. They are imposed in a different way than sales tax, although responsibility for collecting them is still with the seller.

For example, the cigarette tax is usually imposed as an amount per cigarette or per specific number of cigarettes. Payment of the tax by the seller is designated by the use of stamps, which are attached to the cigarette carton. In the same way, motor vehicle taxes are usually by the gallon, and alcohol taxes are also assessed on a per gallon basis, generally varying by alcohol content.

Excise taxes are among the oldest taxes and are generally imposed only by the state, although some municipalities, such as New York City, are allowed to impose these special taxes. These taxes have to treat all products they tax equally—they cannot favor products made locally. For example, it would be unconstitutional for North Carolina to tax differently cigarettes made from tobacco grown locally different from cigarettes from tobacco grown out of state.

There are other examples of special sales taxes that are not considered excise taxes, since they do not target products but rather services. One example is the hotel/motel tax, which is a tax on the rental of hotel and motel rooms. Also, many states impose various entertainment taxes on restaurants, theaters and other tourist attractions. These taxes are often passed by local government entities and many times do not need the approval of the state in order be imposed.

## Gross Receipt Taxes

Gross receipt taxes are charged to businesses and are based on the total revenues of a business. The tax is imposed on an annual or other periodic basis and is required on top of the sales tax. A gross receipt tax differs from a general sales tax in that it is a tax on the business activity itself and is assessed as a percentage of revenues received, regardless of the source of the revenue. The occupational license tax is a good example of such a tax: states require businesses to pay this tax in order to do business in the state.

## Sales Tax Issues

The sales tax has been the focus of several important debates over the past 10 years. Two of the most important are over imposing a national sales tax and over taxing goods sold over the Internet.

### National Sales Tax

Proponents of a national sales tax have suggested that substituting a national sales tax for the income tax would result in many positive benefits. Such a tax would result in doing away with complicated tax forms, and (some proponents suggest) with the Internal Revenue Service. It would be easier to collect, and, therefore, would result in less cheating. It would also give taxpayers a greater sense of control over the tax, since by their purchases they would determine when the tax would be imposed.

Despite these arrangements, and the endorsement of local and national political candidates of the idea, the national sales tax has never caught on. Opponents of the idea suggest it has **fatal** flaws. For example, the tax would have to be too high to make up for the loss of income tax; it would be regressive unlike the income tax, which is currently administered in a progressive way; and the exemptions and exceptions that would be granted would make it just as difficult and complicated to administer as the income tax.

### Internet Taxes

One current area of controversy is the issue of sales taxes for goods sold over the Internet. When the Internet first began to be widely used, there was a debate over whether goods sold over cyberspace should be subjected to a use or tax alternatively, a sales tax if the company selling the goods did business within the state.

In 1998, President Bill Clinton signed the Internet Tax Freedom Act (ITFA). The ITFA imposed a moratorium on all taxes of goods and services sold over the Internet for three years, until a decision was made on what kind of tax system to impose on Internet shopping and use. States could not collect sales or use taxes from Internet sellers unless the seller had a sufficient nexus with the state. The ITFA has now been extended until November, 2003. As of 2002, however, no decision has been made on what kind of sales or use tax system to allow states to impose on Internet goods.

With electronic commerce growing quickly many states believe it would be difficult to continue to lose revenue from Internet commerce not subject to **taxation**. On the other hand, Internet vendors worry that they may face the nightmarish prospect of having to deal with multiple taxes required by a host of states. It remains to be seen whether the federal government will do anything about this situation or will simply let the ITFA expire and let the states go their separate ways.

## Listing of State Sales Tax Rates

The following is a listing of state sales tax rates, as of 2001:

- ALABAMA: 4.00 %
- ALASKA: no sales tax
- ARIZONA: 5.60 %
- ARKANSAS: 5.125 %
- CALIFORNIA: 6.00 %
- COLORADO: 2.90 %
- CONNECTICUT: 6.00 %
- DELAWARE: no sales tax
- DISTRICT of COLUMBIA: 5.75 %
- FLORIDA: 6.00 %
- GEORGIA: 4.00 %
- HAWAII: 4.00 %
- IDAHO: 5.00 %
- ILLINOIS: 6.25 %
- INDIANA: 5.00 %
- IOWA: 5.00 %
- KANSAS: 4.90 %
- KENTUCKY: 6.00 %
- LOUISIANA: 4.00 %
- MAINE: 5.00 %
- MARYLAND: 5.00 %
- MASSACHUSETTS: 5.00 %
- MICHIGAN: 6.00 %
- MINNESOTA: 6.50 %
- MISSISSIPPI: 7.00 %
- MISSOURI: 4.225 %
- MONTANA: no sales tax
- NEBRASKA: 5.00 %
- NEVADA: 4.25 %
- NEW HAMPSHIRE: no sales tax
- NEW JERSEY: 6.00 %
- NEW MEXICO: 5.00 %
- NEW YORK: 4.00 %
- NORTH CAROLINA: 4.50 %
- NORTH DAKOTA: 4.50 %
- OHIO: 5.00 %
- OKLAHOMA: 4.50 %
- OREGON: no sales tax
- PENNSYLVANIA: 6.00 %
- RHODE ISLAND: 7.00 %
- SOUTH CAROLINA: 5.00 %
- SOUTH DAKOTA: 4.00 %
- TENNESSEE: 6.00 %
- TEXAS: 6.25 %
- UTAH: 4.75 %
- VERMONT: 5.00 %
- VIRGINIA: 3.50 %
- WASHINGTON: 6.50 %
- WEST VIRGINIA: 6.00 %
- WISCONSIN: 5.00 %
- WYOMING: 4.00 %

## Additional Resources

*State and Local Taxation and Finance In A Nutshell.* Gelfand, M. David, Joel Mintz, Peter W. Salsich, West Group, 2000.

*"State And Local Sales Tax On Internet Commerce: Developing A Neutral And Efficient Framework"*Way, Kashi M., *Virginia Tax Review,*Summer, 1999.

"State Tax Rates" Sales Tax Institute, Available at http:/// www.salestaxinstitute.com, 2001.

*"Questioning The Viability Of The Sales Tax: Can It Be Simplified To Create A Level Playing Field?"* McKeown, Rich, *Brigham Young University Law Review,* 2000.

*"State Tax Rates,"* Sales Tax Institute, http:/// www.salestaxinstitute.com, 2001.

## Organizations

### *The National Retail Sales Tax Alliance*

8094 Rolling Road, PMB 905

Springfield, VA 22153 USA
Phone: (703) 644-9859
Fax: (703) 644-4687
URL: http://www.salestax.org/
Primary Contact: Neal White, President

**Sales Tax Institute**
220 S. State Street
Chicago, IL 60605 USA
Phone: (312) 986-1086
Fax: (312) 986-1087

E-Mail: info@salestaxinstitute.com
URL: http://www.salestaxinsitute.com

**Sales Tax Resource Group**
16882 Bolsa Chica, Suite 206
Huntington Beach, CA 92649 USA
Phone: (714) 377-2600
Fax: (714) 377-2605
E-Mail: info@salestaxresource.com
URL: http://www.salestaxresource.com
Primary Contact: Graham Hoad, President

# TAXES

## SELF EMPLOYMENT TAXES

*Sections within this essay:*

- Background
- Social Security
- Self Employment
    - Trade or Business
    - Independent Contractors
    - Religious Workers
- Income For Self-Employment Tax
- Deductions
- Social Security Credits
- Correcting Social Security Earnings
- Family Business Arrangements
- Estimated Tax
- Additional Resources

## Background

Self-employment tax is a Social Security and **Medicare** tax primarily for individuals who work for themselves. It is similar to the Social Security and Medicare taxes withheld from the pay of most wage earners. Social Security benefits are available to self-employed persons just as they are to wage earners. Most people who pay into Social Security work for someone else. Their employer deducts Social Security taxes from their paycheck, matches that contribution, and sends wage reports and taxes to the Internal Revenue Service (**IRS**) and Social Security. But self-employed people must report their earnings and pay the taxes directly to the IRS.

The main source of Social Security income is the taxes that employees, employers, and the self-employed pay. This is the primary method of financing Social Security. Both benefit amounts and Social Security taxes are based on the worker's earnings under the program.

## Social Security

The Social Security program is a system of social insurance under which workers (and their employers) contribute a part of their earnings in order to provide protection for themselves and their families if certain events occur. Since each worker pays Social Security taxes, each worker earns the right to receive Social Security benefits without regard to need. The fact that Social Security benefits go to some people who have high incomes has been a source of criticism. However, these persons pay into the program and play an important role in its financial base. Moreover, benefits of higher earners are subject to the **income tax** as a result of the 1983 Social Security amendments. Social Security taxes and benefit amounts are related to a person's level of earnings during working years. As people earn more money and pay more in Social Security taxes, they are earning a right to higher benefits. There is, however, a limit on the amount of yearly earnings on which Social Security taxes must be paid and on which program benefit payments are figured.

## Self-Employment

According to the IRS, an individual is self-employed if that person operates a trade, business, or profession, either alone or with partners. Yearly earnings in excess of $400 must be reported on Schedule SE for Social Security purposes.

### Trade or Business

A trade or business is generally an activity carried on for a livelihood or in **good faith** to make a profit. The facts and circumstances of each case determine whether an activity is a trade or business. The regularity of activities and transactions and the production of income are important elements; however, making a profit is not essential to being in a trade or business as long as the business has a profit motive. The business does not have to be full-time in order for an individual to be self-employed. Having a part-time business in addition to a regular job may be sufficient for self-employment for IRS purposes.

### Independent Contractors

Independent contractors often include doctors, dentists, veterinarians, lawyers, accountants, contractors, subcontractors, public stenographers, or auctioneers who are in an independent trade, business, or profession offering specific services. Generally, an individual is an **independent contractor** if the payer has the right to control or direct only the result of the work and not what will be done and how it will be done. The earnings of a person who is working as an independent contractor are subject to SE tax.

### Religious Workers

For income tax purposes, a licensed, commissioned, or ordained minister is generally treated as a **common law** employee of his or her church, denomination, or sect. There are, however, some exceptions such as traveling evangelists who may be treated as independent contractors. The **gross income** of a licensed, commissioned or ordained minister does not include the fair rental value of a home (a parsonage provided), or a housing allowance paid, as part of the minister's compensation for services performed that are ordinarily the duties of the minister. The fair rental value of a parsonage or the housing allowance can be excluded from income only for income tax purposes. No exclusion applies for self-employment tax purposes. For Social Security purposes, a duly ordained, licensed, or commissioned minister is self-employed. Religious workers can request an exemption from self-employment tax, if they can prove they are conscientiously opposed to public insurance for religious reasons. The exemption is not permitted solely for economic reasons. A previously elected exemption from Social Security coverage and self-employment tax can be revoked; however, once it is revoked, it cannot be elected again.

## Income for Self-Employment Tax

Self-employment tax is based solely on the business income reported on Schedule C of an individual's **tax return**. It is 15.3 percent of the individual's **net** earnings from self-employment as reported on Schedule SE and consists of two portions: 12.4 percent is for Social Security, and 2.9 percent is for Medicare. The Social Security portion of the self-employment tax is satisfied once the self-employed earner has at least $80,400 of income; however, the Medicare portion of the self-employment tax is unlimited. For an individual who has wages and is also self-employed, the tax on the wages is paid first. This rule is only relevant when the individual has total earnings over $84,900.

## Deductions

Income tax deductions can reduce the self-employment tax liability. These deductions are intended to make sure self-employed people are treated in much the same way as employers and employees for Social Security and income tax purposes. Net earnings from self-employment are reduced by an amount equal to half of the individual's total Social Security tax. This is similar to the way employees are treated under the tax laws because the employer's share of the Social Security tax is not considered income to the employee. Also, half of a self-employed individual's Social Security tax can be deducted on the face of the IRS Form 1040. This means the **deduction** is taken from gross income in determining **adjusted gross income**. It cannot, however, also be an itemized deduction and must not be listed on Schedule C.

Along with these deductions self-employed persons may deduct numerous business expenses including the cost of computers and computer-related equipment, furniture, office supplies, postage costs, and telephone bills. If the individual works from home, a home-office deduction may be advantageous. Additional potential deductions include business use of a car, health insurance, certain travel and entertainment expenses, 50 percent of meals and entertainment, and attorney and accounting fees that are directly related to the business.

## Social Security Credits

Social Security in the United States is designed to act as a safety net for all citizens of the United States. In addition to retirement benefits, those that are disabled, dependent for support upon someone who receives Social Security income, and those who are a widow, widower, or child of someone who has died may be eligible for benefits. When an individual works and pays Social Security taxes, called FICA (Federal Insurance Contributions Act) on some pay stubs, that worker earns Social Security credits. Most people earn the maximum of four credits per year. The number of credits required to earn retirement benefits depends on the date of birth. Those born after 1929 need 40 credits. Social Security taxes pay for Retirement Benefits, **Disability** Insurance, Family Insurance, Survivors Benefits, and Medicare Insurance. Net earnings of $3,480 or more earns an individual four credits—one for each $870 of earnings. Net earnings for Social Security are gross earnings from a trade or business, minus the allowable business deductions and **depreciation**.

## Correcting Social Security Earnings

Workers 25 and older are mailed Social Security Statements each year. The Statement shows the earnings that appear for each year of work on the individual worker's Social Security record. It is important Social Security earnings records be correct so that workers can get all of the credits earned. Every year, Social Security receives reports of earnings that cannot be credited to anyone because the name and number on the reports do not match the name and number on its records. These records can, however, be claimed by the worker contacting Social Security.

## Family Business Arrangements

Family members may operate a business together. A husband and a wife may be partners or be running a **joint venture**. Each member of a couple who has such a business should report a share of the business profits as net earnings on separate self-employment returns (Schedule SE), even if they file a joint income tax return. The partners must decide the amount of net earnings each should report (for example 50 percent and 50 percent). Each spouse should include his or her respective share of self-employment income on a separate Form 1040 Schedule SE. Self-employment income belongs to the person who is the member of the partnership and cannot be treated as self-employment income by the nonmember spouse, even in **community property** states. This generally does not increase the total tax on the return, but it does give each spouse credit for Social Security earnings on which retirement benefits are based. However, this may not be true if either spouse exceeds the Social Security tax limitation.

## Estimated Tax

**Estimated tax** is the method used to pay tax (including SE tax) on income not subject to withholding. An individual must make estimated tax payments if the individual expects to owe tax, including self-employment tax, of $1,000 or more for the year. A person who is both self-employed and an employee, can avoid paying estimated tax by having the employer increase the income tax taken out of wages using Form W-4, Employee's Withholding Allowance Certificate. There are penalties for underpayment of estimated taxes.

## Additional Resources

*Mercer Guide to Social Security and Medicare* Treanor, Robert J. and Dale Mercer Myers, Mercer, 2002.

*Smart Tax Write-Offs: Hundreds of Tax Deduction Ideas for Home-Based Businesses, Independent Contractors, All Entrepreneurs* Ray, Norm, Rayve Productions, Incorporated, 2000

*Taxes Made Easy for Your Home-Based Business* Carter, Gary, Wiley, John & Sons, 2000.

## Organizations

*National Association for the Self-Employed*
P.O. Box 612067
Dallas, TX 75261-2067 USA
Phone: (800) 232-NASE
URL: http://www.nase.org

*The Social Security Administration*
6401 Security Blvd.
Baltimore, MD 21235-0001 USA
Phone: (800) 772-1213
URL: http://www.ssa.gov

# TAXES

## SMALL BUSINESS TAX

*Sections within this essay:*

- Background
- Business Income
- Small Business Tax Deductions
- Other Deductions
- Types of Expenses
    - Current Expenses
    - Capitalized Expenses
- Depreciation or Amortization of Expenses
- Independent Contractors and Employees
- Employee Taxes
- Partnerships
- Getting Help
- Additional Resources

## Background

There are several important tax issues that arise for owners and managers of small businesses. These issues occur at the federal, state, and local levels. Because the state and local issues vary so widely, this entry focuses primarily on federal tax issues.

To understand the many tax issues that arise for small businesses, one must first know the different types of business entities one may create. The Internal Revenue Service (**IRS**) and the U. S. tax laws—codified in the Internal Revenue Code (IRC)—treats each of these entities in significantly different ways. The four basic forms of businesses are:

1. Sole proprietorships
2. Partnerships (general and limited)
3. **Corporations** and S)
4. Limited liability companies

Generally, taxpayers who own their businesses alone can form any one of these types of businesses except partnerships. Multiple owners of a business may form any type of business except a **sole proprietorship**.

Most of the many kinds of business income are taxable. The Internal Revenue Service (IRS) taxes the income generated by a business the same as it does an individual's income. Similarly, businesses can minimize their tax liabilities through deductions and credits the same way individuals can.

## Business Income

Regarding the topic of small business taxes, it is necessary to understand the IRS definition of "income" before turning to a discussion of deductions, credits, or other aspects of small business taxes. It may actually be better to understand the concept of "gross income." In section 61 of the Internal Revenue Code (IRC), the phrase is defined thus: "Except as otherwise provided . . . gross income means all income from whatever source derived." Obviously, this is a very broad definition.

Section 162 of the IRC is the section of the Tax Code used to determine the deductibility of business expenditures. This is a lengthy section, but the first sections contain the most important language. Here are the principal provisions:

(a) In general, there shall be allowed as a **deduction** all the ordinary and necessary expenses paid or incurred during the taxable year in carrying on any trade or business, including:

(1) a reasonable allowance for salaries or other compensation for personal services actually rendered;

(2) traveling expenses (including amounts expended for meals and lodging other than amounts which are lavish or extravagant under the circumstances) while away from home in the pursuit of a trade or business;

(3) rentals or other payments required to be made as a condition to the continued use or possession, for purposes of the trade or business, of property to which the taxpayer has not taken or is not taking title or in which he has no equity.

Apparently, the IRC can be quite vague at times. For example, the IRC does not go on to define "ordinary" or "necessary," even though these terms are very important concepts in small business **taxation**. In the most general sense, a business's **net** income is the product of "ordinary and necessary expenses" subtracted from "gross receipts." In an effort to define these important concepts, the federal courts have held "ordinary" to mean "normal, common and accepted under the circumstances by the business community." And according to the courts, "necessary" means "appropriate and helpful." Thus, the two terms generally mean the purpose for which an expense is made.

Basically, gross receipts are all the money earned by the small business entity. And although "ordinary and necessary" expenses are left up to the courts to define, they are not particularly abstract or unusual concepts. Practically every expense that a small business owner reasonably needs to run a business qualifies as "ordinary and necessary." Rent, wages, marketing, and office supplies are some typical examples. But other expenses such as interest on business-related loans and insurance premiums can also qualify.

For tax purposes, income can take many forms. It need not be just cash. Services, good, and other types of property received in exchange for goods or services may qualify as income. If the business owner exchanges goods or services for someone else's goods or services (a process also known as bartering) the owner needs to report the **fair market value** of the goods or services received. Basically, anything of value the owner or the business receives is income, unless it specifically falls within one of the following IRS exclusions such as gifts and inheritances and some "fringe benefits" provided by businesses to owners and employees.

It is particularly important to owners and investors of businesses that the return of a capital investment is not taxed as income. If a business owner sells a business or an asset and receives money for the asset, the business has not earned any **taxable income**. Only the profit, if there is any, will be taxed.

When the IRS audits business deductions, one of its primary concerns is that personal expenses are claimed as business expenses. Because these tactics are so common among taxpayers, the IRS auditors are especially vigilant when it comes to business expense deductions.

## Small Business Tax Deductions

Business owner/taxpayers can deduct most of what they spend in the course of conducting their businesses which makes an enormous difference in their final tax bills. The IRC allows business owners and investors to deduct the costs of conducting the business from their **gross income**. What remains is the net business profit, the amount subject to taxation. The taxpayer/business owner who can legitimately claim the most **deductible** business expenses will lower his taxable profits. Generally, if something is necessary for the business, it can be deductible. There are, of course, limitations. Home telephone expenses, traffic tickets, and clothing (except required uniforms) that are worn on the job are not deductible expenses.

The type of business entity can make a big difference when a taxpayer sits down to calculate and file a small business **tax return**. Some expenses may or may not be deductible, depending on the type of business entity. A common example is that of charitable contributions, which can be deducted by a C corporation, but not by other types of business entities.

Home businesses offer other potential for deductions. A taxpayer can deduct the portion of the taxpayer's home used for a business as long as the taxpayer conducts administrative or management activities of the business there. And whether the home is owned or rented, the taxpayer can also deduct certain related costs such as utilities, insurance, and remodeling expenses.

## Other Deductions

Business taxes will be lower depending on the number of tax deductions the business can legitimately take. How successful the business owner is at reducing business's tax liability depends largely on paying strict attention to IRS rules on just what is and what is not deductible.

When business owners calculating their business's expenses, they need to keep these 13 business deductions in mind:

1. Advertising and Promotion: The costs associated with advertising the business are deductible as a current expense.

2. Auto Expenses: If a vehicle is used for the business, the business owner can deduct the cost of owning, maintaining, and operating it.

3. Bad Debts: The rules differ depending on whether the business sells goods or services. If the business sells products, the owner can deduct the cost of goods that sell but for which the owner has not been paid. If, however, the business sells services, the owner may not deduct the loss associated with a transaction for which a client or customer has not paid.

4. Business Entertaining: Owners may deduct 50 percent of the cost of entertaining either present or prospective clients or customers.

5. Business Start-up Expenses: The costs of starting a business are capital expenses for tax purposes. These expenses must be deducted over the first five years of the business's operation.

6. Charitable Contributions: Limited liability businesses and S corporations (corporation that have elected to be taxed like a partnership) can make charitable contributions and pass the deductions through to the business owner(s). These can be claimed on the owner(s) individual tax returns. If the business is a standard (C) corporation, the deduction does not pass through and the corporation itself deducts the charitable contributions.

7. Computer Software: The general rule states that the business owner must depreciate software over a 36-month period for use in that is bought for the business. There are some important exceptions to this rule, however. Owners may want to check with their tax advisor or IRS publications for more complete information.

8. Education Costs: Owners may deduct the expense to maintain and enhance their qualifications for their present job, or training required by their employers. Owners may NOT deduct the expenses of a degree or other education program that qualifies them for a new job.

9. Interest: Owners can deduct the interest charges incurred to finance business purchases.

10. Legal and Other Professional Fees: Generally, owners can deduct in the year they incur them, attorney fees and fees they pay to tax professionals or consultants.

11. Moving Expenses: To claim this deduction, the move must have been made in connection with work, the new workplace is at least 50 miles farther from the old home than the old home was.

12. Taxes: Generally, owners may deduct the taxes they incur from running their business. There are many exceptions to this generality though. Taxpayers should check with their tax advisor or IRS publications for more detailed information.

13. Travel: Many expenses from business travel are deductible, including airfare, ground transportation, meals and lodging, mailing or shipping business materials, clothes cleaning, telephone calls, faxes, and gratuities. If others accompany the owner on a business trip, the owner may only deduct the owner's own travel.

## Types of Expenses

Knowing whether a business expense is current or capitalized will help to determine when owners may deduct the expense from their business's taxes. The IRC dictates what expenses can be deducted and even in what year they can be deducted. Owners can deduct some business expenses the year they incur them; these are called "current" expenses. They can deduct other business expenses in increments over a certain number of years in the future; these are known as "capitalized" expenditures. It is important to understand the differences between the two types of expenses and the tax rules that apply to each.

### Current Expenses

Basically, current expenses include the common expenses of running a taxpayer's business. These include costs such as utility bills, **mortgage** or rent expenses, copy paper supplies, and so on. The IRC rules for deducting current expenses are fairly clear. In most cases, a taxpayer merely subtracts the amount spent on current expenses from the business's gross income in the year the expenses were incurred.

### Capitalized Expenses

Some business owner purchases are meant to help the business create revenue in future years. These are known as "capitalized" expenses because they actually become assets of the business over time. As a business uses capitalized assets, the assets' cost is "matched" to the revenue they help the business to earn. In theory, this helps the business to more accurately account for its real profitability from one year to the next.

Sometimes it is unclear which kind of expense rules to apply to a particular expense. For example, routine costs for equipment repairs seem to be obvious current expenses. But, the IRC states that the cost of making improvements to a business asset must be capitalized if the improvement

- adapts it to a different use

- increases its value

- significantly extends the time a business can use it

If the routine repair to, say, a computer or phone line does any of the above three things, then the expense should be capitalized

The costs associated with acquiring business equipment are usually considered capital expenses if the equipment will have a useful life of more than one year. However, Section 179 of the IRC permits taxpayers to deduct a certain amount (up to $24,000 in 2001) of its capital assets per year against the business's income. Taxpayers should check with their tax advisor about the rules, advantages, and disadvantages for making this sort of deduction.

## Depreciation or Amortization of Expenses

Generally, taxpayers cannot deduct the cost of items with a ldquo;useful life"—at least not in the

same way as they can deduct current expenses. Instead, when they buy an asset for their business, the IRS treats the purchase as an investment in their business. Taxpayers must deduct the cost over a number of years, specified in the tax code (with one important exception, discussed below). This deduction is usually known as "depreciation." It is occasionally known as a "depreciation expense" or an "amortization expense." Despite the terminology, these terms describe the same thing: spreading out the deduction of these types of asset purchases over the course of several annual tax cycles.

The rules for depreciating or amortizing expenses can be confusing, and taxpayers need to know the rules that apply to each different type of property. The IRC sets absolute limits for some **depreciation** deductions, and it sets the number of years that businesses can depreciate assets. IRC § 179 contains an important exception to the long-term write-off rules: small businesses can deduct most of their capital expenditures in one year.

## Independent Contractors and Employees

There are certain financial and tax advantages that arise from having workers classified as independent contractors instead of employees. For example, a business with employees must pay payroll taxes, keep employee records, and file payroll tax forms for its employees. A business need not perform these tasks for its workers who are independent contractors.

The IRS pays careful attention to the classification of workers in a business. Generally, if the business owner or manager instructs its workers when, where, and how to do their jobs, the business owner is treating these workers as employees. Business owners or managers may treat workers as independent contractors only if the workers have their own businesses and offer their services to several contractors. If a business owner or manager is unsure of the status of its workers, it is best to treat them as employees.

It may be tempting to classify workers as independent contractors. Owners might even save money in the short run. However, doing so may get them into big trouble in an IRS **audit**. The IRS may decide that their "independent contractors" really are employees. This could result in their having to pay an **assessment** of back taxes, penalties, and interest.

## Employee Taxes

There are two types of employee-related taxes:

1. Taxes paid by the employer (employer taxes)
2. Employee taxes withheld by the employer (withheld taxes)

While the employer pays these taxes to the IRS, note that employee taxes actually come out of the employees salary or wages. Most employers deposit these amounts with a bank every month. Once every three months, the employer reports on IRS Form 941 the amounts paid and withheld to the IRS.

The employer taxes come from the business income. Employer taxes include the employer's share of Social Security and **Medicare**, as well as an amount for federal unemployment taxes.

Self-employed business owners do not have the same tax liabilities—such as Medicare and Social Security—as a business's employee. Instead, self-employed persons must pay the self-employment tax, which amounts to the combined portion of taxes for employees. Self-employed individuals report their taxes on Form 1040 under the "Other Taxes" category. In addition, self-employed people must also file quarterly **estimated tax** payments for both their individual income and self-employment taxes. When they file their annual **income tax** returns, if they have not paid enough estimated tax, they may have to pay a **penalty** to the IRS.

## Partnerships

If a taxpayer is in business with other people and all of them share the expenses and profits (even unequally), the IRS deems these people to be in a partnership. This is true whether the parties have entered a formal agreement or not. Consequently, the business must file a yearly partnership tax return (Form 1065). In addition to individual tax returns, the taxpayer and the other people involved in the business must file Form 1065, the annual partnership tax return. A formalized partnership agreement will not affect a taxpayer's tax status, but it is a good idea to consult an attorney and to prepare a partnership agreement in order to clarify the various partners' rights and responsibilities in the business.

## Getting Help

The federal tax laws that apply to most small businesses are fairly straight-forward, although they can be confusing in some cases. Keeping good financial records, following directions carefully, and preparing complete and honest tax returns is the best way to avoid trouble with the IRS. For many businesses this can be done without the advice of legal or tax professionals.

In most cases, it is not necessary for taxpayers to hire a legal or tax professional to help them establish a sole proprietorship or to start operating their business. If they plan to establish a general partnership or a C corporation, they may need to seek professional tax advice, especially concerning the many state and local laws with which their business may need to comply. However, it may be a good idea to hire a tax expert if they expect to need complex tax advice. This is a good general guideline, but it is especially true if they plan to do minute comparisons between the various types of business entities.

## Additional Resources

*Don't Let the IRS Destroy Your Small Business: Seventy-Six Mistakes to Avoid* Savage, Michael, Perseus Publishing, 1998.

*J. K. Lasser's New Rules for Small Business Taxes.* Barbara Weltman, Barbara, John Wiley & Sons, 2001.

"Small Business/Self-Employed" Internal Revenue Service, 2002. Available at http://www.irs.gov/businesses/small/display/0,,i1=2&i2=23&genericId=20005,00.html.

*Small Time Operator: How to Start Your Own Business, Keep Your Books, Pay Your Taxes, and Stay Out of Trouble* 25th ed., Kamoroff, Barnard B., Bell Springs Publishing, 2000.

*422 Tax Deductions for Businesses & Self-Employed Individuals, 3rd Edition.* 3rd ed., Bernard B. Kamoroff, Barnard B., Bell Springs Publishing, 2001.

"Tax Information for Businesses" Internal Revenue Service, 2002. Available at http://www.irs.ustreas.gov/businesses/display/0,,i1%3D2%26genericId%3D15019,00.html.

*Tax Savvy for Small Business: Year-Round Tax Strategies to Save You Money, 5th Edition.* 5th ed., Nolo Press, 2001.

## Organizations

### *American Small Businesses Association (ASBA)*

8773 IL Rte. 75E. NW
Rock City, IL 61070 USA
Phone: (800) 942-2722
URL: http://www.asbaonline.org/index.html

### Council On State Taxation

122 C Street, NW, Suite 330 NW
Washington, DC 20001-2109 USA
Phone: (202) 484-5222
Fax: (202) 484-5229
URL: http://www.statetax.org/index.html

### Federation of Tax Administrators (FTA)

444 N. Capital St., NW, Suite 348 NW
Washington, DC 20001 USA
Phone: (202) 624-5890
URL: http://www.taxadmin.org/

### National Tax Association (NTA)

725 15th St. NW #600 NW
Washington, DC 20005-2109 USA
Phone: (202) 737-3325
Fax: (202) 737-7308
E-Mail: natltax@aol.com
URL: http://ntanet.org/

### U. S. Chamber of Commerce

1615 H Street, NW
Washington, DC 20062-2000 USA
Phone: (202) 659-6000
E-Mail: custsvc@uschamber.com
URL: http://www.uschamber.com/default.htm

# TAXES

## TAX EVASION

*Sections within this essay:*

- Background
- The Criminal Investigation Division
- Tax Evasion, Tax Fraud, and Other Tax Crimes
- Tax Fraud Prosecution
- Failing to File Returns
- Additional Resources

## Background

The law does not require taxpayers to arrange their finances in order to maximize their taxes. All taxpayers are entitled to take all lawful steps that apply to their individual situations in order to minimize their tax liabilities. For example, it is lawful to take tax deductions that are available, and a taxpayer may avoid taxes on a certain amount of income by making charitable contributions.

Contrasted with legal efforts to minimize tax liabilities, **tax evasion** is a crime. Tax evasion typically involves failing to report income, or improperly claiming deductions that are not authorized. Some of the most common forms of tax evasion include the following:

- Failing to report the cash income
- Taking unauthorized deductions for personal expenses on a business's **tax return**
- Falsely claiming charitable deductions—or inflating the amount of charitable deduc-

tions—when there have in fact been none or there have been significantly less than claimed

- Overestimating the value of property donated to charity
- Filing a false tax return, improperly omitting property and knowingly and significantly underreporting the value of an estate

According to section 7201 of the Internal Revenue Code (IRC), it is a federal crime for anyone to willfully attempt to evade or defeat the payment of federal income taxes. A taxpayer can be found guilty of that offense when all of the following facts are proved beyond a reasonable doubt:

1. The **defendant** owed substantial **income tax** in addition to that declared in the defendant's tax return

2. The defendant knowingly and willfully attempted to evade or defeat the tax

The prosecution need not show the exact amount of the taxes due, but it must prove that the defendant knowingly and willfully attempted to evade or defeat a substantial portion of the additional tax charged in the **indictment**.

In this context, the word "attempt" means that the defendant knew or understood that he had **taxable income** which he was required by law to report to the Internal Revenue Service (**IRS**) during the particular tax year or years involved. Nevertheless, the defendant attempted to evade or defeat the tax, or a significant part of the tax on that income, by willfully failing to report all of the income the defendant earned during that year.

## The Criminal Investigation Division

During an **audit**, if an IRS revenue agent suspects **fraud**, he can impose penalties himself, or he can refer the case to the Criminal Investigation Division (CID). The CID is part of the enforcement mechanism for the IRS. It is divided into two parts—General Enforcement (for ordinary taxpayers) and Special Enforcement (for unions, organized crime, and cases involving drugs).

The CID has broad powers. In fact, a taxpayer may not even know the CID is investigating him until the taxpayer is formally charged. The CID takes its job very seriously and conducts extremely thorough investigations. In pursuit of **evidence**, CID agents may contact a taxpayer's friends, employer, co-workers, neighbors, and bankers, and spouse. There are CID offices throughout the United States. CID agents are federal investigators who have been trained in law enforcement techniques. Most CID agents are also accountants, and many have earned their **CPA**.

The CID may monitor mail and may apply for a court order for a phone tap. For example, In October, 2000, prompted by the IRS, the U. S. District Court ordered American Express and MasterCard to provide credit and **debit** card information pertaining to U. S. taxpayers involving banks in Antigua, the Bahamas, and the Cayman Islands for the 1998 and 1999 tax years. The IRS has estimated that some $70 million in annual taxes is lost through offshore tax evasion activities. The banks of Antigua, the Bahamas, and the Cayman Islands are favorite locations in which to conceal revenue from the IRS.

If taxpayers fail to report transactions and pay taxes on those transactions, they could be guilty of tax fraud, tax evasion, and **money laundering** under U. S. law. U. S. citizens must inform the IRS whether they have earned interest on an account deposited in a foreign bank on Form 1040, Schedule B. If they do, then they must complete TD F90-221 if the aggregate amount held in all foreign accounts exceeds $10,000 at any time during the tax year. Additionally, currency transactions involving more than $10,000 must be reported on Form 4789, and international transportation of currency or monetary instruments (such as bearer **bonds**) must be reported on Form 4790. By focusing on the records of U. S. credit card companies, the IRS has found an effective means to investigate offshore tax havens. Thus, many U. S. tax evaders have cause to be uneasy about their offshore activities.

Because of the many resources it takes to conduct a CID investigation, only a very small percentage of taxpayers or tax evaders are investigated by the CID. The IRS will use the CID only when it has strong implications of serious wrongdoing. Even in these cases, the CID will recommend prosecution only if it has built an airtight case against the suspect.

The CID will usually **prosecute** cases it determines are very strong. On the other hand, if the case may generate a lot of publicity, the CID may decide to prosecute anyway. The CID and IRS view high publicity prosecutions against high profile people as being a major deterrent for others contemplating committing a tax crime. The CID also considers the amount of money involved in a tax crime when deciding whether to prosecute a case. The average amount of money owed in most criminal tax cases exceeds $70,000. Once the decision to prosecute has been made by officials in the CID, and the **Justice Department** accepts the case, the chances of obtaining a **conviction** are about 80 percent. About half of those convicted will be incarcerated, irrespective of any prior criminal record in their past.

## Tax Evasion, Tax Fraud, And Other Tax Crimes

When the CID completes an investigation and recommends that a taxpayer be prosecuted for a tax crime, IRS lawyers will conduct at least two stages of before there is final approval to proceed with a prosecution:

1. After the IRS decides to prosecute, it forwards the case to the United States Department of Justice Tax Division in Washington, D. C. Federal prosecutors with special training in prosecuting criminal tax violations review the case and determine whether or not to authorize prosecution.

2. If the Department of Justice Tax Division in Washington approves prosecution, the case is sent to U. S. attorney's office located near the suspect. It is instructed to prepare indictments and to prosecute the individual or individuals for the alleged offenses.

The Tax Division's principal function is to provide legal advice for its main client, the IRS. The Division handles almost all civil **litigation** arising under the internal revenue laws except for those cases that are docketed in the U. S. Tax Court. The Division also enforces the criminal tax laws by supervising or directly handling all criminal tax cases.

In tax crime cases, the prosecution approval process can work to a suspected taxpayer's advantage. The process allows several opportunities to derail a federal criminal case before it ever gets presented to a **grand jury**. Assuming a taxpayer is aware that a case is being prepared against him, his lawyer will have the opportunity to confer with the government's lawyers and try to convince them not to prosecute his client. If the government has a strong case against the suspected taxpayer, it is unlikely that the IRS can be dissuaded from pursuing the case. However, if the case involves mere misunderstandings that can be explained and the IRS can be convinced that there really was no criminal conduct, the taxpayer may be able to convince the government to decline prosecution prior to grand jury.

In a tax crime case, a defendant is well advised to hire a lawyer who is experienced in federal criminal matters and who also has significant experience in federal criminal tax cases. If a defendant in a tax crime case cannot find a lawyer with this combination of training and experience, the defendant may want to consider hiring a former CID agent to help with the defense. In short, it is sound policy to have both federal criminal defense and tax crime experience on the defense team.

## Tax Fraud Prosecution

After the (CID) has conducted an investigation and has recommended prosecution to the Justice Department, there are three crimes with which an individual may be charged:

- Tax evasion: This is an intentional violation of tax laws. It is a broad category, encompassing any cheating of the government in taxes. Tax evasion is a **felony** and a very serious crime. A conviction for tax evasion can carry with it up to a five-year prison sentence and/or fines up to $100,000.

- Filing a false return: Prosecution for this crime is appropriate when a taxpayer has provided the government with false or misleading information on the taxpayer's tax return. In such cases, the government does not have to prove the taxpayer intended to evade tax laws. Rather, it merely must prove

that the taxpayer filed a false return. Filing a false return is a felony. Punishment for this crime can consist of up to three years in prison and/or up to $100,000 in fines.

- Not filing a tax return at all: Failing to file a tax return is the least serious of the three tax crimes. It is a **misdemeanor**. The consequences for being found guilty is a maximum of 1 year in prison and/or fines totaling up to $25,000 for each year a taxpayer failed to file.

A taxpayer may be arrested once the taxpayer has been charged with one of these three crimes. If so, the taxpayer may be required to post **bail** or may be released on his or her own recognizance. Once charged, it is imperative that the **accused** taxpayer retain a tax attorney as soon as possible. The lawyer will need time to study the client's case and formulate a defense. Taxpayers need to keep in mind that the IRS has already completed their investigation and has most likely built a strong case against the accused taxpayer.

## Failing to File Returns

The vast majority of taxpayers do file their tax returns with the IRS every year. However, according to some estimates, about three percent of taxpayers do not file tax returns at all. If a taxpayer does not owe any taxes, the penalties are not severe. But failing to file a tax return in years where one does owe taxes is a crime. The penalties can be quite severe. For example, for each year a taxpayer fails to file a return, the IRS can fine that taxpayer up to $25,000, or the taxpayer can be sentenced to one year in prison. And this is just for being negligent. If a taxpayer does not file a return in an effort to evade taxes, the IRS can pursue felony charges, including a fine up to $100,000 or a maximum of 5 years in jail. While **incarceration** is rare, the threat is real and should deter those considering evading taxes.

It is wise to file a return even in cases where a taxpayer may not have enough resources to pay the entire tax bill. The IRS will work out a payment plan with taxpayers in these cases. There is a six-year **statute of limitations** for filing criminal charges based on failing to file a tax return, but there is no **statute** of limitations on how long the IRS can seek taxpayers and demand payment or taxes owed on non-filed returns.

The IRS may penalize taxpayers for filing tax returns late. Depending on the circumstances, there can be criminal or civil trials. At the very least, the IRS may withhold refunds to the taxpayer. If the taxpayer actually owes taxes from a late return, the IRS can levy a late filing **penalty** of 5 percent per late month to a maximum of 25 percent. Additionally, the IRS may impose a = percent to 1 percent late payment penalty to the late filing penalty. In the meantime, interest is accumulating on the debt to the IRS. Thus, it is in taxpayers' best interests to file late returns before they are contacted by the IRS.

The IRS usually does not pursue criminal charges against taxpayers who file of their own volition before the IRS has contacted them. The IRS also tends to be more sympathetic in collecting taxes from taxpayers who volunteer their late returns than taxpayers the IRS had to investigate and "catch." If the IRS identifies an errant taxpayer before the taxpayer has a chance to file a late return, the manner in which they contact the taxpayer is an indication of how seriously they may treat the particular case. The IRS uses four ways to notify taxpayers of fraud or other criminal tax behavior:

1. Most non-filers receive a non-threatening written request from the IRS Service Center.

2. A letter or personal call from a Taxpayer Service Representative gives taxpayer a deadline for filing (usually 30 days).

3. A call or personal visit from a Revenue Agent or Officer gives the taxpayer a deadline by which to file returns directly to the agent. The agent may even offer to assist in preparing the missing returns. Note that if a taxpayer refuses to file, the IRS can legally prepare a return, which is never in a taxpayer's best interest.

4. The worst way to be notified is by a visit by a Special Agent in which the taxpayer is informed that he or she has become the subject of a criminal investigation.

Considering all the above, it appears crucial to file one's tax returns within the deadlines. If a taxpayer needs more time to file, the IRS has a fairly simple method to request an extension for time to file. But do not fail to file at all. If one has failed to file returns in the past, it is best to go ahead and file late returns before coming to the attention of the IRS. If one owes taxes from late returns, it is advisable to go ahead and pay the debt as soon as possible, even if one must borrow the amount. It costs more to owe the IRS than it does almost anybody else. If a taxpayer has not filed returns in many years, the taxpayer should not worry about being caught if the taxpayer resumes filing. The IRS computers do not search for such taxpayer information. Besides, the IRS wants to encourage non-filers to start filing again.

## Additional Resources

*The Cheating of America: How Tax Avoidance and Evasion by the Super Rich Are Costing the Country Billions, and What You Can Do About It* Lewis, Charles, and Bill Allison, William Morrow & Company, 2001.

*The Ethics of Tax Evasion* McGee, Robert W., ed. Dumont Institute for Public Policy, 1998.

*Great American Tax Dodge: How Spiraling Fraud and Avoidance Are Killing Fairness, Destroying the Income Tax, and Costing You* Steele, James B., and Donald L. Barlett, Little Brown & Company, 2000.

*Ill-Gotten Gains: Evasion, Blackmail, Fraud, and Kindred Puzzles of the Law* Katz, Leo, University of Chicago Press, 1996.

"Internal Revenue Service Criminal Investigation." Internal Revenue Service, 2002. Available at http://www.ustreas.gov/irs/ci/index.htm.

*The Layman's Guide to Tax Evasion* Holzer, Henry Mark, iUniverse.com, 2000.

*Tax Evasion and Firm Survival in Competitive Markets* Palda, K. Filip, Edward Elgar Publishing, 2001.

*Tax Procedure and Tax Fraud in a Nutshell* Morgan, Patricia T., West, 1998.

"United States Department of Justice Tax Division Criminal Tax Manual — 1994 Edition." Department of Justice, 1998. Available at http://www.usdoj.gov/tax/readingroom/criminal/toc.Htm.

## Organizations

### ABA Section of Taxation
740 15th Street NW, 10th Floor
Washington, DC 20005-1009 USA
Phone: (202) 662-8670
Fax: (202) 662-8682
URL: http://www.abanet.org/tax/home.html

### Institute for Professionals in Taxation (IPT)
One Capital City Plaza, 3350 Peachtree Road, NE, Suite 280
Atlanta, GA 30326 USA
Phone: (404) 240-2300
Fax: (404) 240-2315
E-Mail: ipt@ipt.org

URL: http://www.ipt.org/

## Council on State Taxation (COST)
122 C Street, NW, Suite 330
Washington, DC 20001-2109 USA
Phone: (202) 484-5222
Fax: (202) 484-5229
URL: http://www.statetax.org/index.html

## Tax Division, U. S. Department of Justice (DOJ)
950 Pennsylvania Avenue, NW
Washington, DC 20530-0001 USA
Phone: (203) 514-2901
E-Mail: AskDOJ@usdoj.gov
URL: http://www.usdoj.gov/tax/

# TELECOMMUNICATIONS

## FCC REGULATIONS

*Sections within this essay:*

## Background

The Federal Communications Commission (FCC) is a large, independent United States government agency. On June 19, 1934, Congress enacted legislation establishing the Federal Communications Commission (FCC). This important legislation made the administrative duties of regulating broadcasting and wired communications into a single agency. The FCC had three divisions: broadcast, telegraph, and telephone. Its prime directive was to create "a rapid, efficient, nationwide, and worldwide wire and radio communication service." The FCC's first seven commissioners and 233 employees soon began to consolidate the rules and procedures from three other agencies:

- Federal Radio Commission

- Interstate Commerce Commission

- Postmaster General into one agency

FCC has **jurisdiction** in all 50 states, the District of Columbia, and U.S. possessions such as Puerto Rico, Guam, American Samoa, and the American Virgin Islands.

The FCC has grown a great deal over the years. With more than nearly 2,000 employees, it had added to its original mandate, with oversight responsibilities in new communications technologies such as satellite, microwave, and private radio communications. There are six major sections of the 1934 Act, called "titles." They are:

- Title I: This section describes the administration, formation, and powers of the FCC.

- Title II: This section is about common carrier regulation.

- Title III: This section concerns broadcast station requirements.

- Titles IV and V: These two sections deal with **judicial review** and enforcement of the Act.

- Title VI: This section describes various provisions of the Act including amendments to the Act and the emergency war powers of the president. It also extends FCC power to regulate cable television.

The 1934 Act restricts FCC regulatory authority to interstate and international common carriers. For purposes of the Act, telephone and microwave communications are deemed common carriers.

Many of the prototypes for broadcasting regulations were created before the 1934 Act by the Federal Radio Commission. Sections 303-307 defines many of the FCC's powers related to broadcasting. Other sections either put limits on FCC's authority or some of the activities of broadcasters:

- The FCC may not censor broadcast stations.

- Individuals may not uttering obscene or indecent language over a broadcast station.

- The "Equal Time Rule" requires broadcasters to provide an equal opportunity to candidates seeking political office.

- Under the "Fairness Doctrine," broadcasters must allow for rebuttal of controversial viewpoints.

The 1934 Act has been amended many times. Communication technology has changed dramatically during the FCC's history. These changes include the introduction of the following:

- television

- satellite and microwave communications

- cable television

- cellular telephone

- PCS (personal communications) services

FCC responsibilities have increased to accommodate the regulatory issues presented by these new technologies. Consequently, it now shares regulatory power with other federal, executive, and judicial agencies.

The FCC oversees all broadcasting regulation. The FCC can license operators of telecommunication services and has recently used auctions as a means of determining who would be awarded licenses for personal communications services. The FCC enforces the requirements for wire and wireless communications through its rules and regulations. The FCC handles major issues at its monthly meetings; it deals with less important issues by circulating them among the commissioners for action. The language of the Act is flexible, sufficient to work as a framework for the FCC to promulgate new rules and regulations related to a huge variety of technologies and services.

## Organization

The president appoints and the Senate confirms the FCC's five commissioners. They serve 5-year terms, unless appointed to fill an unexpired term. One of the five commissioners is designated by the president to serve as chairperson. The chairperson delegates management and administrative responsibility to the managing director of the FCC. To preserve a certain degree of political equilibrium, one political party may only have three commissioners at any one time. No commissioner may have a financial interest in any business related to the work of the commission. The five FCC commissioners supervise all of their organization's official activities and delegate agency responsibilities to staff units and bureaus.

## Bureaus and Offices

The FCC contains four key branches and divisions:

1. Mass Media Bureau, which oversees licensing and regulation of broadcasting services

2. Common Carrier Bureau, which handles interstate communications service providers

3. Cable Bureau, which oversees rates and competition provisions of the cable act of 1992

4. Private Radio Bureau, which regulates microwave and land mobile services

And there are special offices within the FCC that help support the four bureaus:

- The Field Operations Bureau, which provides enforcement, engineering and public outreach programs.

- The Office of Engineering and Technology, which provides engineering expertise and knowledge to the FCC and tests equipment for compliance with FCC standards.

- The Office of Plans and Policy, which functions as a sort of think tank for the FCC.

The FCC contains six Bureaus and ten Staff Offices, arranged by function. The sixteen bureaus and offices are:

1. Consumer & Governmental Affairs Bureau

2. Enforcement Bureau

3. International Bureau

4. Media Bureau

5. Office of Administrative Law Judges

6. Office of Communications Business Opportunities

7. Office of Engineering And Technology

8. Office of Inspector General

9. Office of Legislative Affairs

10. Office of Media Relations

11. Office of Plans And Policy

12. Office of The General Counsel

13. Office of The Managing Director

14. Office of Work Place Diversity

15. Wireless Telecommunications

16. Wireline Competition Bureau.

These bureaus' responsibilities include:

- analyzing complaints and conducting investigations

- developing and implementing regulatory programs

- participating in hearings

- processing applications for licenses and other filings

Although these various divisions within the FCC have individual functions, they frequently join to address issues that affect the entire FCC.

## The Fairness Doctrine

First Amendment issues have been the most active areas of public controversy among broadcasters since the Communications Act of 1934. The FRC and then the FCC have maintained that "scarcity" requires a licensee to operate a broadcast station in the public trust; a station is not meant to be an exclusive means to promote its owners' views. This controversial doctrine formed the basis of many FCC rules up through the mid-1980s.

The **Fairness Doctrine** withstood constitutional challenges. For example, in 1969 the Doctrine was held to be constitutional by the Supreme Court in *Red Lion Broadcasting v. FCC* (395 U.S. 367). Broadcasters had complained vociferously about the doctrine, complaining that it produces a chilling effect on free speech. Despite the potential for conflict,

though, the FCC determined a station's fairness record on the overall programming record of the licensee. The U.S. Supreme Court also reaffirmed that as long as a licensee met its public **trustee** obligations, the licensee was not obligated to sell or give time to specific opposing groups to meet Fairness Doctrine requirements. Eventually, the FCC commissioners pursued policies of deregulation and began looking for ways to eliminate the Fairness Doctrine.

In 1985, an FCC report concluded that scarcity was no longer a valid argument and the Fairness Doctrine unduly prevented broadcasters from airing more controversial material. Two subsequent federal court cases finally allowed the FCC to eliminate the Fairness Doctrine in 1987. The FCC revoked the Fairness Doctrine, with the exception of the personal attack and political editorializing rules that remain in effect.

## The FCC and Broadcasting

Since the FCC's founding, the act of determining whether a licensee has fulfilled its responsibilities under the "public interest, convenience and necessity" standard of the Act has varied a great deal depending upon the composition of Commission and the various orders or requests from Congress. The FCC enjoys broad authority under section 303 to do the following:

- approve equipment and set standards for levels of interference

- assign frequencies and power

- classify stations and prescribe services

- issue cease and desist orders

- levy fines and forfeitures

- make regulations for stations with network affiliations

- prescribe qualifications for station owners and operators

Perhaps the FCC's most important powers are those associated with licensing. These powers allow the FCC to license or short-license broadcast licenses. It can also withhold, fine, revoke or renew broadcast licenses and construction permits based on its own evaluation of whether the station has served in the **public interest**. Even though the FCC can revoke a license, it has not used this authority much over its 60-year history.

Before the era of deregulation, the FCC had a set of complicated rules and regulations for broadcasters. At the same time, it also gave licensees a lot of scope to determine what constituted service in the public interest based on local needs; this was known as the "Ascertainment Policy." Once the FCC licensed a station, the station's operator had to monitor the technical, operational, and programming functions of the station. It also had to maintain files on all aspects of station operations for several years.

The requirements for filing for and renewing licenses for broadcasters are greatly reduced today. But when two or more applicants compete for the same license or when someone challenges a Petition to Deny, the FCC determines which of the rival applicants is the most qualified to own and operate the broadcasting facility. There are strict procedures for hearings that ensure that the applicants' rights are protected. Consequently, the FCC's adjudicative process can be expensive and time-consuming.

## Broadcast Regulation and FCC Policy Decisions

Because the 1934 Act does not enumerate specific powers to regulate networks, the FCC has sought to regulate the relationship between affiliated stations and broadcast networks. Following the promulgation of the FCC's Chain Broadcasting Regulations, major radio and television networks challenged the Commission's authority to promulgate such rules. Their 1943 suit, *National Broadcasting Co., Inc. et al. v. United States* (319 U.S. 190) resulted in the Supreme Court upholding the constitutionality of the 1934 Act as well as the FCC's rules related to business alliances. In its opinion, the Court pointed out the broad and flexible powers granted to the FCC by Congress. The FCC has used the network case as a precedent to justify its broad discretionary powers in numerous subsequent rulings.

The FCC promulgated the seven-station rule, multiple-ownership and cross-ownership restrictions, and cable television-broadcast television cross-ownership rules to promote a diverse group of owners and opinions in various markets and geographical areas. But as the FCC licensed more radio and television stations, restrictions that limited ownership to a few stations made less sense to the FCC. Thus, recognizing greater market competition, the Commission relaxed ownership rules in 1985. Subsequently, the FCC eased restrictions on the following areas:

- Anti-Trafficking
- Ascertainment
- Duopoly and Syndication
- Financial Interest Rules
- Limits on Commercials
- Ownership

In the U.S. Supreme Court case of *National Cable & Telecommunications Assn v. Brand X Internet Services*, the high court ruled that the FCC acted within its discretion in deciding to classify "high speed Internet connections" as non-telephonic. In so finding, the Court ruled that cable providers do not have to allow ISPs to use their services.

## Regulating Broadcast Television and Radio

To broadcast radio or TV signals in the United States, an owner or operator must obtain a license from the FCC. The FCC licenses all transmitters whose signal can travel distances, although there are a few exceptions for very low power radio transmitters, such as those in CB radios and walkie-talkies.

The FCC licenses radio transmitters according to geography and certain other common ownership rules that are intended to help prevent radio stations from interfering with the signals of other stations. The spectrum of available radio and television frequencies is limited, so the FCC can issue only a limited number of licenses. Therefore, broadcast licenses are extremely valuable, particularly in large cities.

The FCC limits individuals or **corporate** entities from acquiring more than a certain number of stations in order to promote diverse viewpoints over the airwaves. The Telecommunications Act of 1996 relaxed these limits, sparking a wave of recent broadcast mergers and acquisitions.

## Wireless "Cellular" And "PCS" Communications

The FCC administers licensing for wireless communications. This industry is growing rapidly, evidenced by the many new products and services using wireless frequencies that are announced every week. Cellular creates a system of mobile communications through "cells," which are small, linked service areas that operate using analog technologies.

Personal communications services (PCS) are essentially mobile phones that operate with digital technologies. PCS units can provide a range of services and features such as paging, answering services, and text messaging. The newest PCS versions even permit users to send and receive text e-mail.

Communications law is a broad field covering many issues that arise from the transmission of information. But every communications law issue involves problems with either "content" or "distribution."Some of the most common problems associated with content include:

- copyright
- libel/slander
- patents
- trademark

## Getting Involved in FCC Rulemaking

When the FCC considers changes to its rules, it seeks comments from interested parties. These filings are known as "comments." The FCC then allows for a period—usually around 30 days- for interested individuals or groups to respond to the comments of others; these responses are known as "reply comments."

The FCC encourages comments from members of the public on its proceedings and proposed rulemakings. Comments are either formal or informal. Formal comments are those that have a specific deadline and require a certain number of copies—usually four. Additionally, the FCC places formal comments in the **docket**. Docket numbers are crucial to make sure that an individual's comments are considered, no matter how they are submitted. To locate a docket number, people can contact the Office of Public Affairs, Public Service Division, or the bureau or office responsible for the item.

All of the FCC's decision-makers read and consider formal comments. But informal comments are those that do not meet deadline or copy requirements. While they are placed in the docket, they will not be as widely distributed within the FCC for review. There is no guarantee that informal comments will be read. If individuals file formal comments, they must deliver an original plus four copies of their comments to the FCC's Office of the Secretary. If they want their formal comments to be sent to the commissioners themselves, they need to submit an original and nine copies.

Unfortunately, many people do not comment on issues of interest to them because they think that comments must be prepared and filed by an attorney. This is not true; individuals need not hire an attorney to prepare comments. There is no set format for comments, and anyone may prepare and file comments. People can prepare comments as they would a short statement or a brief letter. Of course, comments may also be detailed documents prepared by an outside law firm or other professional.

When preparing comments for the FCC, people should try to prepare sound arguments. Well-argued comments are the most helpful to the Commission when it is formulating new rules. In the end, new rules must stand the test of petitions of reconsideration by the parties involved, and sometimes they also face court challenges.

### Making a Personal Presentation

Any communication directed to the merits or outcome of an FCC proceeding is considered an "ex parte" presentation. Citizens may appear in person before FCC officials to make an ex parte presentation. Ex parte presentations may also be made in writing. The FCC has specific disclosure requirements associated with different forms of ex parte presentations:

1. Oral ex parte presentations: If individuals want to make oral ex parte presentations and present data or arguments in that proceeding that are not already reflected in their written comments, they must provide an original and one copy of a written memorandum to the Secretary (with a copy to the Commissioner or staff member involved) that summarizes the data and arguments they intend to present. Their memoranda must clearly indicate on its face the docket number of the particular proceeding(s) to which it relates, the fact that an original and one copy have been submitted to the Secretary, and it must be labeled or captioned as an ex parte presentation. Individuals can file their memoranda on the date of their oral presentations.

2. Written ex parte presentations: Individuals must provide two copies of the written presentation to the Commission's Secretary to be included in the public record. This must occur on the same day the presentation is submitted. They need to be sure to include the docket number on the face of the presentation to which it relates,

and that two copies of it have been submitted to the Secretary, and label it as an ex parte presentation.

It is a good idea to contact the FCC staff member associated with the proceeding before planning an ex parte presentation. Because some proceedings are restricted, staff can let people know if they can make a presentation and can explain the rules for doing so.

### Electronic Filing

The FCC actively encourages participation in its rulemaking process. One way it does so is by urging the public to submit comments on proposed rules through electronic mail and fax. If individuals file comments via email and want it to be treated as "formal," they should also print out their comments and send the original plus four copies to the Secretary's office by the stated deadline. If they cannot make the deadline this way, or if they are faced with the prospect of commenting informally or not commenting at all, they should go ahead and submit their comments any way they can, then follow up with a phone call to ensure the FCC received them. If they merely file their comments via email or fax or in the form of a letter without the extra four copies, the FCC will consider them to be "informal" comments.

## Other First Amendment Issues

The FCC has recently been confronted with several controversial issues concerning indecent or obscene broadcasts. And increasingly suggestive music lyrics prompted the FCC to take action against several licensees in 1987. In a formal Public Notice, the FCC restated a generic definition of indecency, which was subsequently upheld by the U.S. Court of Appeals. With encouragement by Congress, the FCC increased its efforts to limit the broadcast of indecent programming material. This action includes such instances as the graphic depiction of aborted fetuses in political advertising. Various FCC enforcement rules, including a 24-hour ban and a "safe harbor period" from midnight to 6 a.m., have been challenged in court.

Currently the FCC has come under criticism on several fronts. Its critics claim that the agency is unnecessary and the Communications Act of 1934 is outdated. Sweeping changes in communications technology are placing new burdens on the commission's resources. But it remains to be seen whether the FCC will be substantially changed in the future.

## Additional Resources

*The ARRL's FCC Rule Book: Complete Guide to the FCC Regulations* Hogerty, Tom, ed. American Radio Relay League, Incorporated, 1998.

*The Broadcaster's Survival Guide: A Handbook of FCC Rules and Regulations for Radio and TV Stations* Whitley, Jack W. and Gregg P. Skall, St. Martin's Press, Inc., 1990.

*Communications Deregulation and FCC Reform: Finishing the Job* Eisenach, Jeffrey, and Randolph J. May, eds. Kluwer Academic Publishers, 2001.

*Electronic Media and Government* Smith, F. Leslie, Milan Meeske, and John W. Wright II, Longman, 1995.

*Electronic Media Law and Regulation* Creech, Kenneth, Focal Press/Butterworth Legal Publishers, 1993.

*FCC: The Ups And Downs of Radio-TV Regulation* Ray, William B., Iowa State University Press, 1990.

"Hypertext FCC Rules Project" Available at http://www.hallikainen.com/FccRules/, hallikainen.com, 2002.

*Mass Communications Law in a Nutshell* Carter, T. Barton, Harvey L. Zuckman, and Juliet Lushbough, West Publishing, 1994.

## Organizations

### Federal Communications Commission (FCC)
445 12th St., S.W.
Washington, DC 20554 USA
Phone: (888) 225-5322
Fax: (202) 418-0232
E-Mail: fccinfo@fcc.gov
URL: http://www.fcc.gov/

### National Association of Broadcasters (NAB)
1771 N Street, NW
Washington, DC 20036 USA
Phone: (202) 429-5300
Fax: (202) 429-4199
E-Mail: nab@nab.org
URL: http://www.nab.org/

### National Exchange Carrier Association (NECA)
80 South Jefferson Road
Whippany, NJ 07981-1009 USA
Phone: (800) 228-8597
Fax: (973) 884-8469
E-Mail: webmastr@neca.org
URL: http://www.neca.org/

**Telecommunications Industry Association (TIA)**
2500 Wilson Blvd., Suite 300
Arlington, VA 22201 USA

Phone: (703) 907-7700
Fax: (703) 907-7727
E-Mail: tia@tia.eia.org
URL: http://www.tiaonline.org/

# TELECOMMUNICATIONS

## SATELLITE AND CABLE

*Sections within this essay:*

## Background

To begin to comprehend the issues and the many laws and regulations related to satellite and cable industries in the United States, one must first understand a bit about the Federal Communications Commission (FCC). Congress created the FCC when it enacted the Communications Act of 1934. The Act was intended in part to help regulate interstate and foreign commerce in communications via wire and radio to help make available a rapid, efficient, nationwide, and worldwide wire and radio communications service. Note that the term "radio" has been interpreted in its most inclusive sense to also apply to television. The FCC has grown into a very large gov-

ernmental agency, and its functions have expanded to include oversight of the satellite and cable telecommunications media. Questions about satellite or cable laws or regulations are most likely addressed by the FCC.

## The FCC

The FCC has five commissioners, appointed by the president and confirmed by the Senate, who oversee the operations of the agency. There are various operating bureaus under the commissioners, one of which is the Mass Media Bureau. Different bureaus within the FCC regulate different aspects of telecommunications media. For example, the Mass Media Bureau regulates amplitude and frequency modulation, low-power television, and direct broadcast satellite. The Common Carrier Bureau regulates telephone and cable operations.

The FCC licenses new broadcast stations based on the needs of communities in a given region and on technical engineering considerations that prevent interference between stations. The FCC must approve a host of activities by broadcasters, including allocations of new stations and applications to build, modify, renew, or sell a station. When the FCC considers an application for any of these activities, it tries to determine if granting the request serves the **public interest**. This kind of review is required by the Communications Act.

### *The FCC and Censorship*

The FCC expects stations to manifest an awareness of the important problems or issues in the communities they serve by presenting programming and/or announcements about local issues. In the end, though, it is broadcasters and not the FCC (or any other government agency) who are responsible for selecting all the content of their programs. The Communications Act and parts of the U.S. Constitution prohibit the FCC from censoring broadcast content. These considerations limit the FCC's role in overseeing the content of programming. But the FCC is permitted to levy fines on a station or revoke its license if the station has violated any of the following three considerations:

1. restrictions on indecent programming

2. limits on the number of commercials aired during children's programming

3. rules involving candidates for public office

### Other FCC Enforcement Functions

The FCC's authority differs greatly regarding standard broadcast television stations and other types of television channels such as cable television. Cable television channels are available by subscription only; they cannot be received over the air. Consequently, cable operators are subject to a different set of FCC rules than broadcast television stations. A broadcast television station on a cable system is regulated as a broadcast station.

The FCC enforces regulations designed to promote competition among cable companies, satellite companies, and other firms offering video programming services to the general public. This competition-promotion function includes a variety of issues such as the following:

- commercial availability of set-top boxes

- commercial leased access

- mandatory carriage of television broadcast signals

- open video systems

- over-the-air reception devices

- program access

- the accessibility of closed captioning and video description on television programming

More specific information about these functions can be found on the FCC's website, http://www.fcc.gov.

## Problems with Cable Operators

Basically, decisions concerning what services to offer and most other programming decisions are within the discretion of the cable operator. The FCC is powerless to address most complaints against cable companies other than specific violations concerning indecent programming, the limit on the number of commercials aired during children's programming, and the rules involving candidates for public office.

To meet the requests for "family-friendly" programming, cable and satellite companies have begun voluntarily to make changes in their offerings. In December 2005, FCC chair Kevin J. Martin announced that some cable companies may "respond to consumer demand and begin to voluntarily offer family tiers." Early in 2006, satellite provider DirecTV announced that it would offer a family package that included 40 channels providing children's programming, educational programming, and public interest channels.

Interference is occasionally a problem for cable subscribers. One common source of interference is home electronics equipment. To receive the clearest signals, the equipment must be adequately designed with circuitry or filtering technologies that reject unwanted signals emitted from nearby transmitters. The FCC recommends that users contact the manufacturer and/or the store where the equipment was purchased to resolve the interference problem.

If users have a complaint about cable rates or poor service, they should direct their communication to their local franchise authority. A franchising authority is the municipal, county, or other government organization that regulates certain aspects of the cable television industry at the local or state level. There are approximately 30,000 franchising authorities in the United States. The name of the franchising authority is often found on the front or back of a cable bill. If the name of the franchising authority is not on the bill, users can contact their cable company or their local town or city hall.

## Signal Bleed

The cable television industry goes to great lengths to protect its programs from theft. Theft most often occurs when consumers are able to receive content over cable channels for which they have not paid in their subscription account. To block these signals, cable television firms encrypt or scramble their signals so that the subscriber receives only the services for which they have paid. Occasionally, some scrambling techniques employed by cable companies do not block the entire audio and video signals. "Signal bleed" occurs when consumers are able to view such inadequately blocked broadcast material. Signal bleed may cause concern for parents because it may permit children in homes with a cable subscription to view programming that contains objectionable material.

## Blocking Programs or Channels

Cable television operators determine the channels that are available on their cable systems. To help increase the number of subscribers, a cable operator will select channels that appear likely to attract a broad spectrum of viewers. Because of this, a cable subscriber may receive programs as part of a programming package that he or she does not wish to view.

Federal law now requires broadcasters of most programming available on television to alert viewers if a program contains violence, inappropriate language, or other material that a viewer may find offensive. Generally, the broadcaster and not the cable operator is responsible for the programming that is shown on a particular channel. The cable operator usually does not have the right to prevent the transmission of a program containing objectionable material. Individual subscribers, however, have two important tools that they may use to prevent programs or channels from being viewed on their television sets.

1. Lockboxes. These are devices a subscriber may buy or **lease** from the subscriber's cable company. They are also available from some retail electronic stores. A lockbox can literally lock particular channels so that the programming cannot be viewed.

2. V-chip. A V-chip is circuitry in a television capable of identifying governmental ratings and blocking the programming that an individual finds inappropriate. Depending on its technical specifications, the V-chip may block individual programs, or it may be used to block one or more channels entirely. All television screens that are 13-inches or larger and that are manufactured or imported for use in the United States are required by law to be equipped with the V-chip. The law required manufacturers to produce 50% of their televisions with the V-chip by 1999, and the remaining 50% were to contain the v-chip by 2000. Televisions not equipped with a V-chip may be fitted with one.

## The Satellite Home Viewer Improvement Act of 1999

The Satellite Home Viewer Improvement Act of 1999 (SHVIA) provides significant modifications to the Satellite Home Viewer Act of 1988, the Communications Act, and the U.S. **Copyright** Act. SHVIA was enacted to promote competition among multi-channel video programming distributors. These include satellite companies and cable television operators. It was also intended to encourage an increase in programming choices.

SHVIA allows satellite companies to broadcast local TV signals to their subscribers who live in the local TV station's market. SHVIA also allows satellite companies to provide "distant" network broadcast stations to certain eligible satellite subscribers. The satellite company has the option of providing local TV signals into a local TV station's market, but it does not have to do so. Some satellite companies have opted to provide this service in some viewing markets. Users can contact their satellite company to determine whether and when the service is available in their market.

### Satellite Radio

Radio listeners now have the option of bypassing traditional broadcasts and getting programs via satellite radio. The twenty-first century saw the advent of two companies in the United States, XM Satellite Radio and Sirius Satellite radio. As of 2005, XM had more than 5 million subscribers and Sirius had more than three million. The programming offered on each satellite radio station includes more than 120 stations covering everything from news to talk shows to sports to all varieties of music. The programming is commercial-free, but listeners must have special antennas—and they must pay a monthly subscription fee. The satellite radio stations believe that enough people will appreciate the variety and convenience of satellite radio that the monthly subscription price (less than $15 as of 2006) will be money well spent.

## Satellite Antennas

Generally, users may install a satellite dish that is 1 meter (39.37 inches) or less on their own property or property on which they have the exclusive use, such as leased or rented property. In Section 207 of the Telecommunications Act of 1996, Congress adopted the Over-the-Air Reception Devices Rule. This rule applies to governmental and non-governmental restrictions imposed on a consumer's ability to receive video programming signals from direct broadcast satellites, wireless cable providers, and television broadcast stations. The rule outlaws restrictions intended to prevent a consumer from installing, maintaining, or using an antenna. The rule applies to a broad range of potential regulatory bodies, laws, or regulations:

- building regulations
- condominium or cooperative association restrictions
- homeowner association rules
- land-use regulations
- lease restrictions
- other restrictions on property within the exclusive use or control of the antenna user where the user has an ownership or leasehold interest in the property
- private covenants
- Zoning regulations

There is a three-part test to determine whether a particular restriction is illegal under the rule. It must:

1. unreasonably delay or prevent the use of the antenna
2. unreasonably increases the cost of the antenna or service
3. prevent a person from receiving or transmitting an acceptable quality signal

The rule does not prohibit restrictions based on legitimate safety concerns, nor does it prohibit restrictions intended to preserve designated or eligible historic or prehistoric properties. In such cases, the restriction must be no more burdensome than necessary to accomplish its safety or preservation purposes.

## Some Activities Not Regulated by the FCC

The FCC licenses individual stations only; it does not license radio or television networks, which are organizations composed of multiple stations. Exam-ples of networks include ABC, NBC, CBS, and Fox. The FCC does license the owners of particular stations within those networks. The FCC does not regulate information provided over the Internet.

The FCC cannot regulate closed-circuit radio or television, which means that it cannot control what is carried over closed-circuit systems in, for example, department stores, airports, or casinos. In addition, the FCC has no authority over the following:

- bullfights
- exhibitions
- promoters of prizefights
- rodeos
- sports teams or leagues

Arrangements for broadcasting these events and other exhibitions are made privately between owners of the rights (such as sports teams or leagues) and the stations and/or network involved.

Finally, the FCC cannot regulate:

- companies that measure the size and other characteristics of radio and TV audiences
- music-licensing organizations
- news-gathering organizations (such as AP or UPI) that provide stations with news and comment
- record companies
- the manufacture and distribution of audio and video recordings
- the production, distribution and rating of motion pictures
- the publishing of newspapers, books, or other printed material

## Additional Resources

*American Broadcast Regulation and the First Amendment: Another Look* Tillinghast, Charles H., Iowa State University Press, 2000.

*The Cable and Satellite Television Industries* Parsons, Patrick R., Robert M. Frieden, and Rob Frieden, Allyn & Bacon, 1997.

*"Consumer & Governmental Affairs Bureau."* Available at http://www.fcc.gov/cgb/consumers.html. Federal Communications Commission, 2002.

*The First Amendment and the Fifth Estate: Regulation of Electronic Mass Media* 5th ed., Carter, T. Barton, Marc A. Franklin, and Jay B. Wright. Foundation Press, 1999.

*Satellite Communications Regulations in the Early 21st Century: Changes for a New Era* Salin, Patrick-André, M. Nijhoff, 2000.

*Selling the Air: A Critique of the Policy of Commercial Broadcasting in the United States* Streeter, Thomas, University of Chicago Press, 1996.

*Telecommunications Law and Policy* Benjamin, Stuart Minor, Douglas Gary Lichtman, and Howard A. Shelanski, Carolina Academic Press, 2001.

*Video Scrambling & Descrambling for Satellite & Cable TV* Graf, Rudolf F., and William Sheets, Newnes, 1998.

## Organizations

### Advanced Television Systems Committee (ATSC)
1750 K Street NW, Suite 1200
Washington, DC 20006 USA
Phone: (202) 872-9160
Fax: (202) 872-9161
E-Mail: atsc@atsc.org
URL: http://www.atsc.org
Primary Contact: Mark Richer, President

### Federal Communications Commission (FCC)
445 12th Street, SW
Washington, DC 20554 USA
Phone: (866) 225-5322
Fax: (866) 418-0232
E-Mail: fccinfo@fcc.gov
URL: http://www.fcc.gov

Primary Contact: Kevin J. Martin, Chair

### National Telecommunications and Information Administration (NTIA)
1401 Constitution Ave., NW
Washington, DC 20230 USA
Phone: (202) 482-7002
URL: http://www.ntia.doc.gov/
Primary Contact: Michael D. Gallagher, Assistant Secretary for Commerce for Communications and Information

### North American Association of Telecommunications Dealers (NATD)
131 NW First Avenue
DelRay Beach, FL 33444 USA
Phone: (561) 266-9440
Fax: (561) 266-9017
E-Mail: jmarion@NATD.com
URL: http://www.natd.com/
Primary Contact: Joseph Marion, Executive Director

### Satellite Industry Association (SIA)
1730 M Street NW, Suite 600
Washington, DC 20036 USA
Phone: (202) 349-3650
Fax: (202) 349-3622
E-Mail: info@sia.org
URL: http://www.sia.org/
Primary Contact: David Cavossa, Executive Director

# TELECOMMUNICATIONS

## TELEPHONE

*Sections within this essay:*

- Background
- Federal Regulation of Telephone Companies and Telephone Services
    - The Communications Act of 1934
    - Recent Amendments to the Communications Act of 1934
- State Regulation of Telephone Companies and Telephone Services

A "telephone" is an apparatus for the transmission of human speech or other sounds over distances greater than the limits of ordinary human audibility. The business of transmitting information by telephone is quasi-public in character. The law treats telephone companies both as common carriers of information and as **public utilities**. As such, telephone companies are regulated by the Federal Communications Commission (FCC) at the federal level and by public utility commissions at the state level. Telephone systems may generally be owned and operated by a partnership, an individual, or a corporation.

## Background

Invented by Alexander Graham Bell in 1876, the original telephone was described as a mere improvement upon the magnetic telegraph, which sent data as fast as electrons could move along wires. Unlike telegraph companies, however, telephone companies do not receive, transmit, or deliver messages in the ordinary sense of these terms. Instead, tele-phone companies furnish customers with networks, facilities, and devices through which conversations can take place over long distances.

The telephone-services sector began to develop in the late nineteenth century when several **patents** registered by Bell began to expire, while independent local telephone companies began to proliferate in major cities. At first, telephone service in the United States was predominantly local because satisfactory technology for transmitting long-distance calls did not exist. However, American telephony witnessed an explosion in technological innovations during the early twentieth century, including the invention of a "vacuum tube," which allowed phone conversations to be transmitted over distances of several miles.

The Bell telephone companies—under the parentage of the American Telephone and Telegraph Company (AT&T)—patented and deployed this technology across state lines. But they typically refused to allow independent telephone companies to interconnect with their long-distance service. As a result of this handicap and the intense price competition with the Bell companies, many independent telephone service providers chose to sell their companies to AT&T. By the advent of the 1930s, AT&T controlled approximately 80% of local exchange lines in the United States. These practices placed AT&T in the cross hairs of antitrust authorities, who convinced Congress of the need for regulation in this area.

## Federal Regulation of Telephone Companies and Telephone Services

### The Communications Act of 1934

After conducting a series of hearings on AT&T's growing dominance over American telephoning, Congress determined that AT&T and its competitors were public service **corporations** whose facilities and instruments were devoted to public use, which made them subject to two kinds of legislative control, state and federal. States may regulate the transmission of telephone communications wholly within state **boundaries**, Congress said, so long as such intrastate communications do not substantially affect interstate commerce. Once a telephone communication crosses state boundaries or substantially affects commerce in more than one state, Congress observed, the Commerce Clause of the U.S. Constitution gives only federal authorities the power to regulate such interstate communications. U.S.C.A.Const.Art. I, section 8, clause 3. Congress formalized these findings in the Communications Act of 1934.

The Communications Act of 1934 establishes a dual system of state and federal regulation for telecommunications services. 47 USCA sections 151 et seq. The act grants the FCC broad authority, but also clearly delineates a strict separation between interstate and intrastate **jurisdiction**, and denies the FCC authority over most intrastate communications. The act also establishes the Federal-State Communications Joint Board to hear disputes that involve questions concerning both interstate and intrastate telephone transmissions, and any other telecommunications dispute deemed to involve a mixture of state and federal concerns.

In determining whether the FCC has jurisdiction to regulate a particular telephone service provider, the focus is on the nature of the service at issue, since the FCC may regulate telephone services only to the extent of their interstate use. However, purely intrastate telephone facilities and services that are used to complete even a single interstate call can fall under FCC jurisdiction depending on the nature of that phone call. Thus, the FCC has authority to regulate use of an intrastate call made on a Wide Area Telecommunications Service (WATS) when that service is used as part of an interstate communications network. National Association of Regulatory Utility Commissioners v. F.C.C., 746 F.2d 1492 (D.C. Cir. 1984). Similarly, where a telephone company has all of its facilities within one state and solely engages in

intrastate telephone communication except for its physical connection with carriers doing business in other states, it is still subject to federal regulation under the Communications Act as a connecting carrier. At the same time, the FCC does not have authority to order connecting carriers to continue interconnection agreements with interstate telecommunication service providers. Accordingly, connecting carriers are free to remove their interconnection with any interstate carrier, and thereby remove themselves completely from jurisdiction of the FCC.

### Recent Amendments to the Communications Act of 1934

Telephone companies that are subject to federal jurisdiction under the Communications Act are also subject to any other applicable laws, regulations, or rules enacted by Congress or promulgated by a federal agency. On three occasions during the 1990s Congress amended the Communications Act of 1934, updating its provisions in light of technological developments and market conditions. In 1991 Congress passed the Telephone **Consumer Protection** Act (TCPA) to give Americans greater freedom at home from unsolicited commercial advertisements. 47 U.S.C.A. section 227. The TCPA generally imposes restrictions on unsolicited advertisements made through automatic telephone dialing systems, artificial or prerecorded voice messages, and telephone facsimile machines.

The FCC began fleshing out these restrictions when it promulgated a regulation requiring telemarketers to create do-not-call lists for consumers who ask not to receive further **solicitation**. The FCC also limited the hours during which telemarketers may call a consumer's residence (not prior to 8 a.m. or after 9 p.m.). Additionally, the FCC issued a rule flatly prohibiting the transmission of unsolicited advertisements via telephone facsimile machines. Finally, the FCC published a regulation requiring all artificial or prerecorded messages delivered by an auto-dialer to clearly identify the caller at the beginning of the message.

In 1992 Congress again amended the Communications Act of 1934, when it passed the Telephone Disclosure and Dispute Resolution Act (TDDRA). 15 U.S.C.A. section 5701. The TDDRA regulates how telephone carriers may offer pay-per-call services (e.g., 900 numbers), and prohibits unfair and deceptive practices undertaken by telephone carriers in connection with pay-per-call services, including misleading and **fraudulent** billing and collection practices.

Specifically, the TDDRA provides that any interstate telephone service, other than a telephone company directory assistance service, that charges consumers for information or entertainment must be provided through a 900 number unless it is offered under what is termed a "pre-subscription or comparable arrangement." That pre-subscription or comparable arrangement may be a preexisting contract by which the caller has "subscribed" to the information or entertainment service. The arrangement may also be made through the caller's authorization to bill an information or entertainment service call to a prepaid account or to a credit, **debit**, charge, or calling card. Telephone companies may not disconnect local or long-distance telephone service for failure to pay 900 number charges, and must offer consumers the option of blocking access to 900 number services if technically feasible. Telephone companies that bill consumers for pay-per-call and pre-subscribed information or entertainment services must show those charges in a portion of the bill that is separate from local and long-distance charges.

Despite increased regulation at the federal level, the telephone service market in the United States remained largely monopolistic for most of the twentieth century, continuing to be dominated by a few small companies in each region of the country. Congress attempted to increase competition by passing the Telecommunications Act 1996 (the "1996 Act"), which allows multiple "local exchange carriers" (LECs) to compete for customers. 1996 Pub.L. No. 104-104. The 1996 Act amends the 1934 Act by distinguishing between incumbent LECs (ILECs) and competing LECs (CLECs). ILECs are existing telephone service providers that have established a telecommunications network in a given market. CLECs are telephone service providers that seek access to an ILEC's market.

One way in which the 1996 Act attempts to improve competition is through "interconnection agreements" and "reciprocal compensation agreements." 47 U.S.C.A. section 251. "Interconnection agreements" require ILECs to make their telecommunications networks available (via purchase or **lease**) to CLECs so that a phone call initiated by the customer of an ILEC may be connected to the customer of a CLEC, and vice versa. "Reciprocal compensation agreements" require the carrier for the customer who initiates a phone call to share some

of its revenues from that call with the carrier of the customer who receives the call (the telecommunications industry describes the LEC of the customer who receives the call as the one that "terminates" the call and not the one that "receives" it). These requirements were challenged and upheld in federal court on two separate appeals, and are now under consideration by the U.S. Supreme Court. Illinois Bell Telephone Co. v. Worldcom Technologies, Inc., 179 F.3d 566 (7th Cir. 1999); Bell Atlantic Maryland, Inc. v. MCI WorldCom, Inc., 240 F.3d 279 (4th Cir. 2001). In a related case, the U.S. Supreme Court upheld FCC rules that require ILECs to lease their networks to competitors at heavily discounted rates. Verizon Communications, Inc. v. F.C.C., —U.S.—, — S.Ct. —, — L.Ed.2d —, 2002 WL 970643 (U.S., May 13, 2002).

## State Regulation of Telephone Companies and Services

State law regulates intrastate telephone services that do not substantially affect interstate commerce. It is the policy of each state to protect the **public interest** in having adequate and efficient telecommunications services available to every state resident at a just, fair, and reasonable rate. To carry out this policy and to regulate rates, operations, and services, state public utility commissions (PUCs) have the general power to regulate and supervise the business of each public utility within its jurisdiction and to do anything that is necessary and convenient in the exercise of its power. For example, state PUCs are typically given exclusive jurisdiction to determine whether a telephone utility should be permitted to close a business office in a given community.

PUCs are also commonly charged with the exclusive responsibility to enhance competition by adjusting regulation to match the degree of competition in the marketplace so that costs associated with running a utility do not deter new telephone service providers from entering the market. State PUCs must ensure that telephone rates are not unreasonably preferential, prejudicial, predatory, or discriminatory and are applied equitably and consistently throughout its jurisdiction. Additionally, PUCs may supplement federal law by enacting their own rules and regulations governing pay-per-call services, unsolicited advertisements, automatic dial announcing devices, or any other feature of local telephone service that might adversely affect consumers.

An individual, partnership, or corporation may not normally offer local telephone service without complying with PUC rules and regulations. In most states, the PUC requires that before a telephone company may provide local service each company must obtain (1) a certificate of convenience and necessity; (2) a certificate of operating authority; or (3) a service provider certificate of operating authority. PUCs may revoke or amend a certificate of convenience and necessity, a certificate of operating authority, or a service provider certificate of operating authority after notice and **hearing** if it finds that the certificate holder has never provided or is no longer providing service in all or any part of the certificated area. PUCs may also require one or more public utilities to provide service in an area affected by the revocation or amendment of a certificate held by a public utility.

Organized for public purposes to more efficiently serve its customers, telephone companies are usually granted special privileges and powers in addition to those that they possess as private corporations. For example, telephone corporations, telephone cooperatives, and foreign telephone companies are often given the power of eminent domain, which gives these entities a right-of-way to erect, construct, and maintain necessary stations, plants, equipment, or lines upon, through, or over private land. The delegation of the state's power of eminent domain has been held valid because of the public good derived from installing telecommunications systems on private property.

On the other hand, local telephone companies have no absolute right to use city streets to erect telephone poles or configure their facilities and networks. Instead, telephone companies must first obtain consent from the municipal authorities of the city in which they are seeking to provide telephone service. This consent is commonly manifested by the grant of a franchise from the governing municipal authority, and PUCs should not unreasonably restrict the rights and powers of municipalities in granting or refusing a telephone company the right to use city streets. However, cities, towns, and villages have no right to deny telephone companies all use of their streets, and when a municipal corporation unlawfully rejects a telephone company's application to erect poles and string wires along certain public streets, it abandons the right to prescribe the streets on which the line will be constructed.

## Additional Resources

*West's Encyclopedia of American Law* St. Paul: West Group, 1998

*American Jurisprudence* St. Paul: West Group, 1998

## Organizations

### Federal Communications Commission

445 12th Street S.W.
Washington, DC 20554 USA
Phone: (888) 225-5322
Fax: (202) 835-5322
E-Mail: fccinfo@fcc.gov
URL: http://www.fcc.gov
Primary Contact: Michael K. Powell, Chairman

### Public Utility Commission of Texas

1701 N. Congress Avenue
Austin, TX 78711-3326 USA
Phone: (512) 936-7000
E-Mail: customer@puc.state.tx.us
URL: http://www.puc.state.tx.us/about/index.cfm
Primary Contact: Lane Lanford, Executive Director

# TELECOMMUNICATIONS

## TELEVISION

*Sections within this essay:*

## Background

American businesses pour billions of dollars each year into marketing their services and products on television. Transmitted to viewers through electromagnetic airwaves, satellite feeds, optical fibers, and cable lines, television programming often transcends state lines. The interstate character of this commercial activity brings regulation of television within the purview of the Commerce Clause of the U. S. Constitution. U.S.C.A. Const. Art. I, section 8, cl. 3. Under the Commerce Clause, federal courts have ruled that Congress has the power to regulate "radio communications," including the power to control the number, location, and activities of broadcasting stations around the country.

Pursuant to this power Congress passed the Communications Act of 1934, which expanded the definition of "radio communication" to include "signs, signals, pictures, and sounds of all kinds, including all instrumentalities, facilities, apparatus, and services . . . incidental to such transmission.". With the advent of television in the late 1930s and its growth in popularity during the 1940s and 1950s, "radio communication" was eventually interpreted to encompass television broadcasts as well.

The rapid growth of telecommunications also prompted Congress to create the Federal Communications Commission (FCC), an **executive branch** agency charged with overseeing the telecommunications industry in the United States. The FCC has exclusive **jurisdiction** to grant, deny, review, and terminate television broadcast licenses. The FCC is also responsible for establishing guidelines, promulgating regulations, and resolving disputes involving various broadcast media. The FCC does not, however, typically oversee the selection of programming that is broadcast. There are exceptions for this general rule, including limits on indecent programming, the number of commercials aired during children's programming, and rules involving candidates for public office. Five commissioners, appointed by the president and confirmed by the Senate, direct the FCC. Commissioners are appointed for five-year terms; no more than three may be from one political party. Within the FCC, the Media Bureau develops, recommends and administers the policy and licensing programs relating to electronic media, including cable and broadcast television in the United States and its territories.

The FCC enacts and enforces regulations addressing competition among cable and satellite companies and other entities that offer video programming services to the general public. This jurisdiction includes issues such as:

- Mandatory carriage of television broadcast signals

- Commercial leased access

- Program access

- Over-the-air reception devices

- Commercial availability of set-top boxes

- Accessibility of closed captioning and video description on television programming

In 1978 Congress established the National Telecommunications and Information Administration (NTIA) to serve as the policy arm for federal regulation of telecommunications. Together with the FCC, the NTIA formulates and presents official White House positions on a variety of domestic and international telecommunication-related issues.

Federal regulation of television broadcasting preempts any conflicting state or local regulation. However, the federal government's power to regulate television is not absolute. In regulating television, both Congress and the FCC must do so to advance the public interest. Congress and the FCC also must be sensitive to First Amendment concerns. Television broadcast companies are entitled to exercise robust journalistic freedom that is consistent with the right of the public to participate in a diverse marketplace of ideas, a marketplace that itself is tempered by appropriate social, political, esthetic, moral, and cultural values.

## Federal Regulation of Licenses, Content, and Advertising

### Regulation of Television Broadcast Licenses

The Communications Act of 1934 confers upon the FCC the sole authority to examine applications for television broadcast licenses and to grant, refuse, or revoke them as the public interest, convenience, or necessity requires. Each license granted for the operation of a television station lasts for a term of not to exceed eight years and may be renewed for a term of not to exceed eight years, measured from the expiration date of the preceding license.

Pursuant to provisions in the Telecommunications Act of 1996, television in the United States must convert from analog signal broadcast to digital signal. During the transition period, the FCC has temporari-

ly assigned each television station a second station to broadcast the digital signal, while continuing to broadcast the analog on the original channel. Total conversion is expected to be completed in 2006, unless the FCC approves an extension. The FCC is not accepting any applications for new stations until television broadcasting has completed the conversion to digital.

The FCC has broad discretion to establish the qualifications for applicants seeking a television broadcast license and for licensees seeking renewal. The FCC has exercised this discretion to prescribe an assortment of qualifications relating to citizenship, financial **solvency**, technical prowess, and moral character, and other criteria the commission has deemed relevant to determine the fitness of particular applicants to run a television station. The FCC will also compare the programming content proposed by an applicant to the content of existing programming. The FCC favors applicants who will make television entertainment more diverse and competitive.

To limit the concentration of power in television broadcast rights, the FCC has promulgated rules restricting the number of television stations that a licensee may operate. An applicant who has reached the limit may seek an amendment, **waiver**, or exception to the rule, and no licensee may be denied an additional license until he or she has been afforded a full **hearing** on the competing public interests at stake. Applicants or licensees who are dissatisfied with a decision issued by the FCC may seek review from the U. S. Court of Appeals for the District of Columbia Circuit, which has exclusive jurisdiction over appeals concerning FCC decisions granting, denying, modifying, or revoking television broadcast licenses. Decisions rendered by the appellate court may be appealed to the U. S. Supreme Court.

The FCC is authorized to assess and collect a schedule of license fees, application fees, equipment approval fees, and miscellaneous regulatory assessments and penalties to cover the costs of its enforcement proceedings, policy and rulemaking activities, and user information services. The commission may establish these charges and review and adjust them every two years to reflect changes in the **Consumer Price Index**. Failure to timely pay a fee, **assessment**, or **penalty** is grounds for dismissing an application or revoking an existing license.

### Content Regulation: The Fairness Doctrine

The original rationale for federal regulation of telecommunications was grounded in the finite number of frequencies on which to broadcast. Many Americans worried that if Congress did not exercise its power over interstate commerce to fairly allocate the available frequencies to licensees who would serve the public interest, then only the richest members of society would own television broadcast rights and television programming would become one-dimensional, biased, or slanted. Only by guaranteeing a place on television for differing opinions, some Americans contended, would the truth emerge in the marketplace of ideas. These concerns manifested themselves in the **fairness doctrine**.

First fully articulated in 1949, the fairness doctrine had two parts: it required broadcasters to (1) cover vital controversial issues in the community; and (2) provide a reasonable opportunity for the presentation of contrasting points of view. Violation of the doctrine could result in a broadcaster losing its license. Not surprisingly, licensees grew reluctant to cover controversial stories out of fear of being punished for not adequately presenting opposing views. First Amendment advocates decried the fairness doctrine as chilling legitimate speech. The doctrine came under further scrutiny in the 1980s when the explosion of cable television stations dramatically expanded the number of media outlets available.

In 1987 the FCC abolished the fairness doctrine by a 4-0 vote, concluding that the free market and not the federal government is the best regulator of news content on television. Individual media outlets compete with each other for viewers, the FCC said, and this competition necessarily involves establishing the accuracy, **credibility**, reliability, and thoroughness of each story that is broadcast. Over time the public weeds out news providers that prove to be inaccurate, unreliable, one-sided, or incredible.

### Content Regulation: Rules Underlying the Fairness Doctrine

Despite the death of the fairness doctrine in 1987, two underlying rules that were developed during its existence remained in effect for another 13 years: the personal attack rule and the political editorial rule. The personal attack rule required broadcast licensees to notify persons who were maligned or criticized during their station's coverage of a controversial public issue and allow the attacked persons to respond over the licensees' air waves. If the attack was made upon the honesty, character, or integrity of another person, the licensee was required to provide a script or tape of the attack to the person identified before giving that person a reasonable opportunity to respond. The political editorial rule afforded political candidates notice of and opportunity to respond to editorials opposing them or endorsing another candidate.

The personal attack and political editorial rules fell by the wayside in 2000, when the Court of Appeals for the District of Columbia ordered the FCC to either provide a detailed justification for their continued application or abandon them. Initially, the FCC suspended the rules on a temporary basis, but later formally repealed both rules.

Proponents of both the personal attack and political editorial rules, as well as the fairness doctrine, have sometimes called for reinstatement. For example, during the 2004 presidential campaign, a furor erupted when some stations decided to broadcast "Stolen Honor", a documentary critical of presidential candidate John Kerry. However, none of the rules have been reinstated.

Although the demise of the Fairness Doctrine and its underlying rules have given broadcasters greater control over the content of their programming, broadcasters still may not discriminate among candidates for public office. Once a broadcaster permits one candidate for public office to use its facilities, it must afford equal opportunities to all other candidates for the same office. Broadcast stations that willfully or repeatedly fail to provide a legally qualified candidate for elective office reasonable access to their airwaves may subject themselves to sanctions, including revocation of their licenses. The FCC "equal time" provisions apply only to the candidates themselves and not to appearances made by campaign managers or other supporters. The determination of what constitutes a legally qualified candidacy is made by reference to state law.

### Content Regulation: Obscene, Profane, and Indecent Broadcasts

Within the universe of First Amendment protection, broadcast radio and television stations have been subjected to greater regulation than any other verbal, visual, or printed medium of expression. The licensing process by itself gives the federal government more power over the content of television and radio broadcasts than it has over any print medium. Radio and television stations have been required to carry public service messages that they might not otherwise have chosen to carry, and they have been subjected to censure for broadcasting materials that would not have been punishable if they had been published in another medium.

The United States Code prohibits the broadcast of any material that is "obscene, indecent, or profane," but offers no definition for those terms. Instead, that task is left to the FCC through its rulemaking and adjudicatory functions. Essentially, it is illegal to air obscene programming at any time. To determine what is obscene, the U.S. Supreme Court crafted a three-prong test:

- An average person, applying contemporary community standards, would find that the material, as a whole, appeals to the prurient interest

- The material depicts or describes, in a patently offensive way, sexual conduct specifically defined by applicable law

- The material, taken as a whole, lacks serious literary, artistic, political, or scientific value

Federal law also prohibits the broadcast of indecent programming or profane language during certain hours. According to the FCC, indecent programming involves patently offensive sexual or excretory material that does not rise to the level of obscenity. Indecent material cannot be barred entirely, because it is protected by the First Amendment. The FCC has promulgated a rule that bans indecent broadcasts between the hours of 6:00 a.m. and 10:00 p.m. The FCC defines profanity as "including language so grossly offensive to members of the public who actually hear it as to amount to a nuisance". Profanity is also barred from broadcast between 6:00 a.m. and 10:00 p.m.

In 1978 in *FCC v. Pacifica Foundation,* the U. S. Supreme Court upheld an FCC order finding that a pre-recorded satirical monologue constituted indecent speech with the repeated use of seven "dirty words" during an afternoon broadcast.. The Supreme Court acknowledged that the monologue was not obscene and thus could not have been regulated had it been published in print. But the Court distinguished broadcast media from print media, pointing out that radio and television stations are uniquely pervasive in Americans' lives, and are easily accessible by impressionable children who can be inadvertently exposed to offensive materials without adult supervision. Print media, the Court said, do not intrude upon Americans' privacy to the same extent or in the same manner. Thus, the Court concluded that the FCC could regulate indecent speech on radio and television but cautioned that the commission must do so in a manner that does not completely extinguish such speech.

When a station airs obscene, indecent, or profane material, the FCC may revoke the station's license, impose a monetary forfeiture, or issue a warning. One of the highest profile cases in the last few years came after a half-time performance with Janet Jackson and Justin Timberlake at the 2004 Super Bowl. In August 2004, the FCC ordered CBS Broadcasting to pay $550,000 for its broadcast of indecent material. The FCC issued $7.9 million in indecency fines in 2004.

The FCC undertakes investigations into alleged obscene, profane, and indecent material after receiving public complaint. The FCC reviews each complaint to determine whether it appears that a violation may have occurred. If so, the FCC will begin an investigation. The context of the broadcast is the key to determine whether a broadcast was indecent or profane. The FCC analyzes what was aired, the meaning of it, and the context in which it aired. Complaints can be made online, via e-mail or regular mail, or by calling 1-888-CALL-FCC (voice) or 1-888-TELL-FCC (TTY).

As cable television gained prominence during the 1980s, it became unclear whether the FCC's rules on indecency and profanity applied to this burgeoning medium. Cable operators do not use broadcast spectrum frequencies, but they are licensed by local communities in the same way broadcast television station operators are licensed by the FCC. Moreover, cable operators partake in the same kind of First Amendment activities as do their broadcast television counterparts.

Congress tried to clarify the responsibilities of cable operators when it passed the Cable Television **Consumer Protection** and Competition Act of 1992 (CTCPCA). CTCPCA authorized cable channel operators to restrict or block indecent programming. The authorization applied to leased access channels, which federal law requires cable systems to reserve for **lease** by unaffiliated parties, and public access channels, which include educational, governmental, or local channels that federal law requires cable operators to carry. Cable operators claimed that the **statute** was fully consistent with the First Amendment because it left judgments about the suitability of programming to the editorial discretion of the operators themselves. But cable television viewers filed a lawsuit arguing that the statute violated the First Amendment by giving cable operators absolute power to determine programming content.

In 1996 the case was appealed to the U. S. Supreme Court, which issued an opinion that was as badly divided as the litigants. In handing down its 5-4 decision in *Denver Area Educational Telecommunications Consortium, Inc. v. F.C.C,* the Court first noted that cable television shares the same characteristics of broadcast television that were discussed in the Pacifica case, namely that it is uniquely pervasive, is capable of invading the privacy of viewers' homes, and is easily accessible by children. Despite the similarities, the Court held that CTCPCA had violated the First Amendment by giving cable operators the power to prohibit patently offensive or indecent programming transmitted over public access channels. The court reasoned that locally accountable bodies comprised of community members are better capable of addressing programming concerns, and thus creating a "cable operator's veto" was not the least restrictive means of addressing the appropriateness and suitability of cable television programming.

With respect to leased access channels, the Court ruled that CTCPCA also violated the First Amendment by requiring cable system operators to segregate patently offensive programming on separate channels and then requiring the operators to block those channels from viewer access until individual cable subscribers requested access in writing. The Court said that these requirements had an obvious speech-restrictive effect on viewers and were not narrowly or reasonably tailored to protect children from exposure to indecent materials. The Court cited the V-chip, as one less restrictive means of accomplishing the same objective.

## Regulation of Advertising

The law governing television advertising is more settled than that of obscene, indecent, or profane materials. The First Amendment permits governmental regulation of television advertising and other forms of commercial speech so long as the government's interest in doing so is substantial, the regulations directly advance the government's asserted interest, and the regulations are no more extensive than necessary to serve that interest. This test affords advertisers more First Amendment protection than does the public-interest test under which federal courts review most FCC content-related regulations. In a free enterprise system the law recognizes that consumers depend on unfettered access to accurate and timely information regarding the quality, quantity, and price of various goods and services.

Conversely, society is not served by false, deceptive, or harmful advertisements, and thus regulations aimed at curbing such advertising are typically found to serve a substantial governmental interest. The best example involves the federal ban on cigarette advertising. In 1967 the FCC acted upon citizen complaints against the misleading nature of tobacco advertisements by implementing a rule that required any television station carrying cigarette advertisements to also air public service announcements addressing the health risks posed by tobacco. The rule withstood a court challenge. In addition, two years later Congress passed the Public Health and Cigarette Smoking Act of 1969, which banned all electronic advertising of cigarettes as inherently misleading and harmful. The act took effect in 1971 and survived a court challenge that same year. The law remains in effect today. No federal laws or FCC rules ban alcohol advertising, however.

Unlike other areas of telecommunications law, Congress has allowed states to adopt their own regulations governing false and deceptive advertising. Many states have responded by adopting the Uniform Deceptive Trade Practices Act (UDTPA), which prohibits three specific types of representations: (1) false representations that goods or services have certain characteristics, ingredients, uses, benefits, or quantities; (2) false representations that goods or services are new or original; and (3) false representations that goods or services are of a particular grade, standard, or quality. Under UDTPA, liability may arise for advertisements that are only partially accurate, if the inaccuracies are likely to confuse prospective consumers. Ambiguous representations may require clarification to prevent the imposition of liability. For example, a business that accuses a competitor of being "untrustworthy" may be required to clarify that description with additional information if consumer confusion is likely to result.

## Children and Television

The 1990 Children's Television Act (CTA) was passed to increase the amount of educational and informational television programming for children. CTA requires broadcast stations to serve the educational and informational needs of children through its overall programming, including programming specifically designed to serve these needs ("core programming"). Core programming is programming specifically designed to serve the educational and informational needs of children ages 16 and under. CTA requires that broadcasters:

- Provide parents and consumers with advance information about core programs being aired.

- Define the type of programs that qualify as core programs.

- Air at least three hours per week of core educational programming.

- Limit the amount of time devoted to commercials during children's programs.

Fueled in part by growing public sentiment against the increasingly violent nature of television programming, NTIA and FCC officials recommended that federal law give parents greater control over the programming viewed by their children. The Telecommunications Act of 1996 introduced a ratings system that requires television shows to be rated for violence and sexual content. The act also created the so-called V-chip, a receptor inside television sets that gives parents the ability to block programs they find unsuitable for their children. Under the act, authority to establish TV ratings is given to a committee comprised of parents, television broadcasters, television producers, cable operators, **public interest** groups, and other interested individuals from the private sector.

In 2004, the FCC imposed children's educational and informational programming obligations on digital multicast broadcasters. Effective January 1, 2006, at least three hours per week of core programming must be provided on the main programming stream, for digital broadcasters. The minimum amount of core programming increases for digital broadcasters that multicast; it increases in proportion to the amount of free video programming offered by the broadcaster on multicast channels. The FCC also limited the amount of commercial matter on all digital video programming, whether free or pay, that is aimed at an audience 12 years old and under.

Beginning January 1, 2006, the FCC also imposed rules governing and limiting the display of Internet web site addresses during programs directed at children 12 and under. The requirements apply to both analog and digital programming. Moreover, FCC rules prohibit "host-selling". According to the FCC, host-selling is any character endorsement that may confuse a child viewers from distinguishing between program and non-program material.

## Additional Resources

*American Jurisprudence* West Group, 1998.

*http://caselaw.lp.findlaw.com/data/constitution/ amendment01* U..S. Constitution: First Amendment.

*West's Encyclopedia of American Law* West Group, 1998.

## Organizations

### *Federal Communications Commission*
445 12th Street S.W.
Washington, DC 20554 USA
Phone: (888) 225-5322
Fax: (202) 835-5322
URL: http://www.fcc.gov
Primary Contact: Kevin J. Martin, Chairman

### *National Telecommunications and Information Administration*
1401 Constitution Ave. N.W
Washington, DC 20230 USA
Phone: (202) 482-7002
Fax: (202) 482-1840
URL: http://www.ntia.doc.gov
Primary Contact: Michael D. Gallagher, Administrator

# TORT AND PERSONAL INJURY ACTIONS

## ASSAULT

*Sections within this essay:*

## Background

Assault is an intentional attempt or threat to inflict injury upon a person, coupled with an apparent, present ability to cause the harm, which creates a reasonable apprehension of bodily harm or offensive contact in another. Assault does not require actual touching or bodily harm to the victim. Assault and battery are sometimes used interchangeably, but battery is an unjustified harmful or offensive touching of another. Battery also differs from assault in that it does not require the victim to be in apprehension of harm.

Assault developed in **common law**, meaning it developed through usage, custom, and judicial decisions rather than from legislative enactment. Modern-day assault statutes closely reflect the ancient common-law definition. An assault is both a crime and a **tort**. Therefore, an assailant may face both criminal and civil liability. A criminal assault conviction may result in a fine, imprisonment, or both. In a civil assault case, the victim may be entitled to monetary damages from the assailant.

## Elements

Assault requires:

- An act intended to cause an apprehension of harmful or offensive contact.

- An at that casues apprehension in the victim that harmful or offensive contact is imminent.

Words, without an act, cannot constitute an assault. For example, no assault has occurred where a person waves his arms at another and shouts, "I'm going to shoot you!" where no gun is visible or apparent. However, if the threatening words are accompanied by some action that indicates the perpetrator has the ability to carry out a threat, an assault has occurred. It is an assault where a person threatens to shoot another while pointing a gun, even where the victim later learns that the gun was not loaded. Moreover, pointing a gun without an accompanying verbal threat is still an assault, assuming the victim saw the gun.

Assault requires **intent**, meaning that there has been a deliberate, unjustified interference with the personal right or liberty of another in a way that causes harm. In the tort of assault, intent is established if a reasonable person is substantially certain that certain consequences will result; intent is established whether or not he or she actually intends those consequences to result. Pointing a gun at someone's head is substantially certain to result in apprehension for the victim. In criminal law, intent means acting with a criminal or wrongful purpose. Criminal assault statutes often speak of acting "purposely," "knowingly," "recklessly," or "negligently." Acting negligently means to grossly deviate from the standards of normal conduct. Some criminal assault statutes recognize only "purposely," "knowingly," and "recklessly" as the level of intent required to establish that an offense occurred.

The victim must have a reasonable apprehension of imminent injury or offensive contact. This element is established if the act would produce apprehension in the mind of a reasonable person. Apprehension is not the same as fear. Apprehension means awareness that an injury or offensive contact is imminent. Whether an act would create apprehension in the mind of a reasonable person varies depending upon the circumstances. For example, it may take less to create apprehension in the mind of a child than an adult. Moreover, if a victim is unaware of the threat of harm, no assault has occurred. An assailant who points a gun at a sleeping person has not committed an assault. Finally, the threat must be imminent, meaning impending or about to occur. Threatening to kill someone at a later date would not constitute an assault.

## Criminal Assault

All states and the federal government have statutes making assault a crime. A criminal assault may be either a **felony** or a **misdemeanor**, depending upon the seriousness of the offense. Aggravated assault is a felony in all jurisdictions. It is an assault that goes beyond merely an intention to frighten the victim; it is committed with intent to commit some additional crime or is particularly egregious in some way. Examples of aggravated assault are assaults committed with the intent to kill, rape, or rob. Assault with a dangerous or deadly weapon is an aggravated assault where the assailant points a loaded gun at the victim. An assailant who points an unloaded gun at a victim has committed an assault, but not an aggravated assault.

## Civil Assault

Separate from any criminal prosecution for assault, a victim may pursue civil **damages** for injuries caused by it. After a determination by a judge or jury that an assault was committed, the next step is to determine what compensation is appropriate. Three types of damages may be awarded. **Compensatory** damages, such as medical expenses, are meant to compensate for the injury sustained. **Nominal** damages are a small sum. Nominal damages act as an acknowledgment that a person has suffered a technical invasion of rights. They are awarded in cases where no actual injury has resulted, or where an injury occurred, but the amount has not been established. Finally, **punitive** damages may sometimes be awarded. Punitive damages may be awarded in particularly egregious circumstances, as a way to further punish the wrongdoer. Punitive damages go above and beyond compensatory damages.

## Additional Resources

*Criminal Law: Model Penal Code.* Dubber, Markus, Foundation Press, 2002.

# TORT AND PERSONAL INJURY ACTIONS

## BATTERY

*Sections within this essay:*

- Background
    - Criminal Battery
    - Civil Battery (Tort)

- Elements of a Battery
    - Intent
    - Contact
    - Harm
    - Damages

- Special Applications
    - Medical Battery
    - Toxic Battery
    - Sports
    - Domestic Violence

- Defenses

- Additional Resources

## Background

In both criminal and civil law, a battery is the intentional touching of, or application of force to, the body of another person, in a harmful or offensive manner, and without consent. A battery is often confused with an assault, which is merely the act of *threatening a battery, or of placing another in fear or apprehension of an impending and immediate battery.* A battery is almost always preceded by an assault, which is why the terms are often used transitionally or combined, as in "assault and battery."

The Restatement (Second) of Torts, Sections 13 and 18, states that an actor commits a battery if he acts intentionally *either* to cause a harmful or offensive contact *or* to cause imminent apprehension of such a contact *and* a harmful or offensive contact actually occurs.

### Criminal Battery

The difference between battery as a crime and battery as a civil tort is merely in the type of intent required. A criminal battery requires the presence of **mens rea,** or a criminal intent to do wrong, i.e., to cause a harmful or offensive contact. Accordingly, a defendant found guilty of the crime of battery is often sued by the defendant in a civil action for the same offense/incident.

Simple criminal battery is most often prosecuted as a misdemeanor. Repeat offenses or the specific nature of the offense may warrant more severe treatment. For example, in some states, a second or third offense against the same individual is a felony. In cases of domestic violence, many states do not permit battery charges to be dropped against the defendant, even at the request of the victim, because of the potential for repeat or escalated harm.

Most sexual crimes include elements of battery (since they are basically non-consensual contacts), and some states actually have penal codes listing the specific crime of "sexual battery."

Aggravated battery is a simple battery with an additional **element** of an aggravating factor. This is most often the addition of a weapon (whether use was real or merely threatened), and is almost always a felony offense. Other aggravated batteries include those committed against protected persons (children, the elderly or disabled, or governmental agents); those in which the victim suffers serious injury; or those occurring in a public transit vehicle or station, or school zone, or other protected place. These are all aggravating factors that will enhance simple misdemeanor batteries to the level of felonies.

### Civil Battery (Tort)

A battery is an intentional tort. The elements to establish the tort of battery are the same as for criminal battery, excepting that **criminal intent** need not be present. For a tortious battery to occur, the requisite intent is merely to touch or make contact without consent. It need not be an intention to do wrong, and the wrongdoer need not intend to cause the particular harm that occurs.

## Elements of a Battery

### Intent

Battery is a **general intent** offense. This means that the actor need not intend the specific harm that will result from the unwanted contact, but only to commit an act of unwanted contact. This also means that **gross negligence** or even **recklessness** may provide the required intent or (in criminal matters) **mens rea** to find a battery.

The doctrine of **transferred intent** is also applicable. If one person intends to strike another, but the person moves out of the way to avoid being struck, causing the blow to hit a third person, both an assault (against the second person) and a battery (against the third person) have occurred, in both criminal and civil law.

This is important in the distinction between a battery and an assault. A battery involves actual contact. An assault is, in actuality, an incomplete battery; a person commits an assault if he or she intentionally places a person in apprehension of an impending battery. Conversely, if a persons intended only an assault (to cause apprehension of an imminent battery), and harmful or offensive contact actually occurs, the person has committed a battery as well as an assault.

This is also important in distinguishing accidental conduct. If a person violently slams into a fellow passenger on a moving public bus, there is no liability. But if, on the same public bus, there is only the slightest *intentional* touching of another, which is harmful or offensive and also non-consensual (such as reaching out and touching a woman's thigh), a battery has occurred.

Conversely, if there was only an intended *assault,* as in a person gesturing toward another in a menacing manner, and the person trips and actually crashes into the other person, both an assault and battery have occurred.

### Contact

Non-consensual contact may be made with either a person *or* that person's extended personality. This means that if one person leans forward and yanks the jewelry necklace off another, a battery has occurred, even though the first person never actually touched the neck of the second person. If this act was preceded with an intent to cause the other to apprehend an impending violent yank of the necklace, both an assault and a battery have occurred. If the wrongdoer only intended an assault (causing the other to apprehend an impending violent yank of the necklace) but did not intend to actually complete the violent yank, and yet his hand made contact with, and actually yanked off the necklace, both an assault and a battery have occurred. In other words, if in the process of physically gesturing to violently yank the necklace off, contact is actually made and the necklace is pulled from the other's neck, a battery has occurred.

The tort rule of "extended personality" applies to both civil and criminal battery. For example, if a person threatens to spit into another's cup of coffee (clearly offensive and possibly harmful), and then proceeds to do so, both a criminal and civil battery have occurred. In another case involving the issue of extended contact, a Texas hotel manager was found guilty of a battery when he snatched away a patron's dinner plate in a "loud and offensive manner," even though the contact did not result in any physical harm to the diner.

### Harm

A plaintiff or complainant in a case for battery does not have to prove an actual physical injury. Rather, the plaintiff must prove an unlawful and unpermitted contact with his or her person or property in a harmful or offensive manner. This, in and of itself, is deemed injurious. As in the case of the Texas hotel manager above, the harm may be offensive rather than physical, but equally worthy of compensation under the law.

### Damages

Once there is palpable harm (be it physical, emotional, or monetary) all elements of a battery are present, and an aggrieved person may file charges. Of course, in criminal law, the state will file charges for battery, and the victim becomes a witness for the prosecution. In criminal court, the focus is on the guilt or innocence of the defendant and generally, no damages are available to the victim. However, harm may be so severe that he or she may qualify for assistance through a **"victims' compensation fund."**

Conversely, the victim of a battery may file a civil lawsuit stemming from the same incident, in which the defendant is charged with the tort of battery. In such a case, damages are typically compensatory (a monetary award), along with special relief such as injunctive or punitive. Substantial harm is not required, but nonetheless, there must be palpable harm. Compensatory damages may be for either/both economic and non-economic (emotional) harm. In the case of the necklace (above), the plaintiff may ask for monetary damages to cover property (the broken necklace); physical harm to her neck (economic damages for medical bills, if any, and non-economic damages for pain and suffering, if any); and emotional harm caused from the incident (the apprehension of a battery; the embarrassment when it actually occurred, etc.). In the case of transferred intent involving an assault and battery, there will likely be two plaintiffs: the person who was the intended victim of the battery (who sues for assault) and the person who was actually physically harmed (who sues for battery).

In medical malpractice cases involving unauthorized treatments or lack of informed consent (see below), the patient may sue for all costs and treatments/procedures associated with the treatment received. This is true, in many cases, even where the patient ultimately benefited from the unauthorized treatment (although this may be argued as a **mitigating factor** by defense).

## Special Applications

### Medical Battery

Virtually all states have recognized, either by express **statute** or **common law**, the right to receive information about one's medical condition, the treatment choices, risks associated with the treatments, and prognosis. The information must be in plain language terms that can readily be understood and in sufficient amounts such that a patient is able to make an "informed" decision about his or her health care. If the patient has received this information, any consent to treatment that is given will be presumed to be an "informed consent." A doctor who fails to obtain **informed consent** for non-emergency treat-

ment may be charged with a civil and/or criminal offense, including a battery, for the unauthorized touching of the plaintiff's person.

### Toxic Battery

Toxic torts (toxic exposure cases) typically involve claims of negligence or strict liability. However, in recent years, cognizable claims for toxic battery have succeeded in many courts. Again, the intent necessary to constitute a tortious battery need not be an intent to cause harm, but rather, the intent to do the act which ultimately causes the harm. Companies that manufacture chemicals that are known to be volatile or known to ultimately result in human contact are vulnerable to such claims. They may be sued for illegal disposal of toxic/hazardous materials as well as toxic battery if persons are harmed by leached chemicals or fumes in the air, ground, or water. The intent was not to harm others, but to dump the material in an illegal manner or location. This is a good example of gross negligence or recklessness so egregious as to constitute the requisite intent to commit battery under law.

Cases of toxic batteries began appearing in the late 1900s. In the early case of **_Gulden v. Crown Zellerbach Corp._** (9th Circuit, 1989), the court held that exposing workers to PCBs (known carcinogens and harmful agents) at 500 times the maximum exposure allowed under EPA standards could constitute a battery. Toxic battery also became an element in many of the tobacco and breast implant cases. Obviously, such cases often involve multiple plaintiffs and multiple defendants, and may become class action suits in the case of widespread exposure to harm.

### Sports

Most sports injuries, which are common in competitive, contact sports, are accidental. However, viable causes of action have been found in cases where sports players used excessive force in their tactics, to the detriment or harm of other players. Of course, the infamous fights among hockey players have resulted in numerous multi-party claims for battery.

### Domestic Violence

Of all torts and crimes involving domestic relations, the most recurring ones involve charges of battery. This is true not only in spousal relations, but also in child abuse cases. Sexual offenses against other persons (including children) are both specific crimes as well as batteries. Unfortunately, spousal batteries often escalate into situations involving serious physical harm and property damage. Some courts permit batteries to the "extended personality," committed in the presence of the victim, because intentional destruction of items personal to a spouse are not uncommon in situations involving highly emotionally-charged marital discord. Moreover, in criminal battery, authorities recognize that victims may not want to press charges for fear of future harm or retaliation, especially in spousal battery. For this reason, prosecution may proceed even where the spousal victim is compelled to testify, or becomes an **adverse witness** for the state.

## Defenses

Viable defenses to both tortious and criminal battery are similar. A defendant may raise lack of intent, especially in criminal battery, and in those circumstances tending to show accidental behavior. Another commonly-invoked defense, especially where a battery results in physical injury, is self-defense or the defense of others or property. These are the only true defenses, and other issues raised (lack of harm or injury, provocation, etc.) are merely mitigating factors. A defense of **contributory negligence** cannot be raised in a claim for intentional tort.

## Additional Resources

Diamond, John L., et al. *Understanding Torts.* 2000.

Prosser. W. *Prosser and Keeton on Torts.* 5th ed., 1984. Sections 13-18.

Weaver, Russell L., John H. Bauman, et al. *Torts: Cases, Problems, and Exercises.* 2003.

## Organizations

### National Coalition Against Domestic Violence
P.O. Box 18749
Denver, CO 80218
Phone: (303) 839-1852
Fax: (303) 831-9251
URL: www.ncadv.org

# TORT AND PERSONAL INJURY

## LIBEL AND SLANDER

*Sections within this essay:*

## Background

The law of defamation protects a person's reputation and good name against communications that are false and derogatory. Defamation consists of two torts: libel and slander. Libel consists of any defamation that can be seen, most typically in writing. Slander consists of an oral defamatory communications. The elements of libel and slander are nearly identical to one another.

Historically, the law governing slander focused on oral statements that were demeaning to others. By the 1500s, English courts treated slander actions as those for damages. Libel developed differently, however. English printers were required to be licensed by and give a bond to the government because the printed word was believed to be a threat to political stability. Libel included any criticism of the English government, and a person who committed libel committed a crime. This history carried over in part to the United States, where Congress under the presidency of John Adams passed the Sedition Act, which made it a crime to criticize the government. Congress and the courts eventually abandoned this approach to libel, and the law of libel is now focuses on recovery of damages in civil cases.

Beginning with the landmark decision in *New York Times v. Sullivan* (1964), the U.S. Supreme Court has recognized that the law of defamation has a constitutional dimension. Under this case and subsequent cases, the Court has balanced individual interests in reputation with the interests of free speech among society. This approach has altered the rules governing libel and slander, especially where a communication is about a public official or figure, or where the communication is about a matter of public concern.

## Elements of Libel and Slander

Specific requirements that a plaintiff must prove in order to recover in a defamation action differ from jurisdiction to jurisdiction. Under the Restatement (Second) of Torts, which is drafted by the American Law Institute and has been influential among state courts, a **plaintiff** must prove four elements. First, the plaintiff must prove that the defendant made a false and defamatory statement concerning the plaintiff. Second, the plaintiff must prove that the defendant made an unprivileged publication to a third party. Third, the plaintiff must prove that the publisher acted at least negligently in publishing the communication. Fourth, in some cases, the plaintiff must prove special damages.

## Defamatory Statements

One essential element in any defamation action is that the defendant published something defamatory about the plaintiff. The Restatement defines a communication as defamatory "if it tends so to harm the reputation of another as to lower him in the estimation of the community or to deter third persons from associating with him." Examples of defamatory statements are virtually limitless and may include any of the following:

- The communication that imputes a serious crime involving moral turpitude or a felony

- A communication that exposes a plaintiff to hatred

- A communication that reflects negatively on the plaintiff's character, morality, or integrity

- A communication that impairs the plaintiff's financial well-being

- A communication that suggests that the plaintiff suffers from a physical or mental defect that would cause others to refrain from associating with the plaintiff

One question with which courts have struggled is how to determine which standard should govern whether a statement is defamatory. Many statements may be viewed as defamatory by some individuals, but the same statement may not be viewed as defamatory by others. Generally, courts require a plaintiff to prove that he or she has been defamed in the eyes of the community or within a defined group within the community. Juries usually decide this question.

Courts have struggled to some degree with the treatment of statements of opinions. At **common law**, statements of opinion could form the basis of a defamation action similar to a statement of pure fact. Generally, if a statement implies defamatory facts as the basis of the opinion, then the statement may be actionable.

## Publication Requirement

Another requirement in libel and slander cases is that the defendant must have published defamatory information about the plaintiff. Publication certainly includes traditional forms, such as communications included in books, newspapers, and magazines, but it also includes oral remarks. So long as the person to whom a statement has been communicated can understand the meaning of the statement, courts will generally find that the statement has been published.

## Meaning of a Communication

In some instances, the context of a statement may determine whether the statement is defamatory. The Restatement provides as follows: "The meaning of a communication is that which the recipient correctly, or mistakenly but reasonably, understands that it was intended to express." Courts generally will take into account extrinsic facts and circumstances in determining the meaning of the statement. Thus, even where two statements are identical in their words, one may be defamatory while the other is not, depending on the context of the statements.

## Reference to the Plaintiff

In a defamation action, the recipient of a communication must understand that the defendant intended to refer to the plaintiff in the communication. Even where the recipient mistakenly believes that a communication refers to the plaintiff, this belief, so long as it is reasonable, is sufficient. It is not necessary that the communication refer to the plaintiff by name. A defendant may publish defamatory material in the form of a story or novel that apparently refers only to fictitious characters, where a reasonable person would understand that a particular character actually refers to the plaintiff. This is true even if the author states that he or she intends for the work to be fictional.

In some circumstances, an author who publishes defamatory matter about a group or class of persons may be liable to an individual member of the group or class. This may occur when: (1) the communication refers to a group or class so small that a reader or listener can reasonably understand that the matter refers to the plaintiff; and (2) the reader or listener can reasonably conclude that the communication refers to the individual based on the circumstances of the publication.

# Fault

One of the more difficult issues in a defamation case focuses on whether the defendant is at fault for publishing defamatory comments. Common law rules created strict liability on the part of the defendant, meaning that a defendant could be liable for defamation merely for publishing a false statement, even if the defendant was not aware that the statement was false. Cases involving an interpretation of the First Amendment later modified the common law rules, especially in cases involving public officials, public figures, or matters of public concern.

## *Common Law Rules*

At common law, once a plaintiff proved that a statement was defamatory, the court presumed that the statement was false. The rules did not require that the defendant know that the statement was false or defamatory in nature. The only requirement was that the defendant must have intentionally or negligently published the information.

## *Public Officials and Public Figures*

In *New York Times v. Sullivan,* the Supreme Court recognized that the strict liability rules in defamation cases would lead to undesirable results when members of the press report on the activities of public officials. Under the strict liability rules of common law, a public official would not have to prove that a reporter was aware that a particular statement about the official was false in order to recover from the reporter. This could have the effect of deterring members of the press from commenting on the activities of a public official.

Under the rules set forth in *Sullivan*, a public official cannot recover from a person who publishes a communication about a public official's conduct or fitness unless the defendant knew that the statement was false or acted in reckless disregard of the statements truth or falsity. This standard is referred to as "actual malice," although malice in this sense does not mean ill-will. Instead, the actual malice standard refers to the defendant's knowledge of the truth or falsity of the statement. Public officials generally include employees of the government who have responsibility over affairs of the government. In order for the First Amendment rule to apply to the public official, the communication must concern a matter related directly to the office.

Later cases expanded the rule to apply to public figures. A public figure is someone who has gained a significant degree of fame or notoriety in general

or in the context of a particular issue or controversy. Even though these figures have no official role in government affairs, they often hold considerable influence over decisions made by the government or by the public. Examples of public figures are numerous and could include, for instance, celebrities, prominent athletes, or advocates who involve themselves in a public debate.

## *Private Persons*

Where speech is directed at a person who is neither a public official nor a public figure, the case of *Gertz v. Robert Welsh, Inc.* (1974) and subsequent decisions have set forth different standards. The Court in *Gertz* determined that the actual malice standard established in New York Times v. Sullivan should not apply where speech concerns a private person. However, the Court also determined that the common law strict liability rules impermissibly burden publishers and broadcasters.

Under the Restatement (Second) of Torts, a defendant who publishes a false and defamatory communication about a private individual is liable to the individual only if the defendant acts with actual malice (applying the standard under New York Times v. Sullivan) or acts negligently in failing to ascertain whether a statement was false or defamatory.

# Defenses

A defendant in a defamation case may raise a variety of defenses. These are summarized as follows:

## *Truth*

The common law traditionally presumed that a statement was false once a plaintiff proved that the statement was defamatory. Under modern law, a plaintiff who is a public official or public figure must prove falsity as a prerequisite for recovery. Some states have likewise now provided that falsity is an element of defamation that any plaintiff must prove in order to recover. Where this is not a requirement, truth serves as an affirmative defense to an action for libel or slander.

A statement does not need to be literally true in order for this defense to be effective. Courts require that the statement is substantially true in order for the defense to apply. This means that even if the defendant states some facts that are false, if the "gist" or "sting" of the communication is substantially true, then the defendant can rely on the defense.

### Consent

Where a plaintiff consents to the publication of defamatory matter about him or her, then this consent is a complete defense to a defamation action.

### Absolute Privileges

Some defendants are protected from liability in a defamation action based on the defendant's position or status. These privileges are referred to as absolute privileges and may also be considered immunities. In other words, the defense is not conditioned on the nature of the statement or upon the intent of the actor in making a false statement. In recognizing these privileges, the law recognizes that certain officials should be shielded from liability in some instances.

Absolute privileges apply to the following proceedings and circumstances: (1) judicial proceedings; (2) legislative proceedings; (3) some executive statements and publications; (4) publications between spouses; and (5) publications required by law.

### Conditional Privileges

Other privileges do not arise as a result of the person making the communication, but rather arise from the particular occasion during which the statement was made. These privileges are known as conditional, or qualified, privileges. A defendant is not entitled to a conditional privilege without proving that the defendant meets the conditions established for the privilege. Generally, in order for a privilege to apply, the defendant must believe that a statement is true and, depending on the jurisdiction, either have reasonable grounds for believing that the statement was true or not have acted recklessly in ascertaining the truth or falsity of the statement.

Conditional privileges apply to the following types of communications:

- A statement that is made for the protection of the publisher's interest

- A statement that is made for the protection of the interests of a third person

- A statement that is made for the protection of common interest

- A statement that is made to ensure the well-being of a family member

- A statement that is made where the person making the communication believes that the public interest requires communication of the statement to a public officer or other official

- A statement that is made by an inferior state officer who is not entitled to an absolute privilege

## State Statutes of Limitations in Defamation Actions

ALABAMA: A two-year statute of limitation applies to defamation actions.

ALASKA: A two-year statute of limitation applies to defamation actions.

ARIZONA: A one-year statute of limitation applies to defamation actions.

ARKANSAS: A one-year statute of limitation applies to slanders actions, while a three-year statute of limitation applies to libel actions.

CALIFORNIA: A one-year statute of limitation applies to defamation actions.

COLORADO: A one-year statute of limitation applies to defamation actions.

CONNECTICUT: A two-year statute of limitation applies to defamation actions.

DELAWARE: A two-year statute of limitation applies to defamation actions.

DISTRICT OF COLUMBIA: A one-year statute of limitation applies to defamation actions.

FLORIDA: A two-year statute of limitation applies to defamation actions.

GEORGIA: A one-year statute of limitation applies to defamation actions.

HAWAII: A two-year statute of limitation applies to defamation actions.

IDAHO: A two-year statute of limitation applies to defamation actions.

ILLINOIS: A one-year statute of limitation applies to defamation actions.

INDIANA: A two-year statute of limitation applies to defamation actions.

IOWA: A two-year statute of limitation applies to defamation actions.

KANSAS: A one-year statute of limitation applies to defamation actions.

KENTUCKY: A one-year statute of limitation applies to defamation actions.

LOUISIANA: A one-year statute of limitation applies to defamation actions.

MAINE: A two-year statute of limitation applies to defamation actions.

MARYLAND: A one-year statute of limitation applies to defamation actions.

MASSACHUSETTS: A three-year statute of limitation applies to defamation actions.

MICHIGAN: A one-year statute of limitation applies to defamation actions.

MINNESOTA: A two-year statute of limitation applies to defamation actions.

MISSISSIPPI: A one-year statute of limitation applies to defamation actions.

MISSOURI: A two-year statute of limitation applies to defamation actions.

MONTANA: A two-year statute of limitation applies to defamation actions.

NEBRASKA: A one-year statute of limitation applies to defamation actions.

NEVADA: A two-year statute of limitation applies to defamation actions.

NEW HAMPSHIRE: A three-year statute of limitation applies to defamation actions.

NEW JERSEY: A one-year statute of limitation applies to defamation actions.

NEW MEXICO: A three-year statute of limitation applies to defamation actions.

NEW YORK: A one-year statute of limitation applies to defamation actions.

NORTH CAROLINA: A one-year statute of limitation applies to defamation actions.

NORTH DAKOTA: A two-year statute of limitation applies to defamation actions.

OHIO: A one-year statute of limitation applies to defamation actions.

OKLAHOMA: A one-year statute of limitation applies to defamation actions.

OREGON: A one-year statute of limitation applies to defamation actions.

PENNSYLVANIA: A one-year statute of limitation applies to defamation actions.

RHODE ISLAND: A one-year statute of limitation applies to slander actions. A three-year statute of limitation applies to libel actions.

SOUTH CAROLINA: A two-year statute of limitation applies to defamation actions.

SOUTH DAKOTA: A two-year statute of limitation applies to defamation actions.

TENNESSEE: A six-month statute of limitation applies to slander actions. A one-year statute of limitation applies to libel actions.

TEXAS: A one-year statute of limitation applies to defamation actions.

UTAH: A one-year statute of limitation applies to defamation actions.

VERMONT: A three-year statute of limitation applies to defamation actions.

VIRGINIA: A one-year statute of limitation applies to defamation actions.

WASHINGTON: A two-year statute of limitation applies to defamation actions.

WEST VIRGINIA: A one-year statute of limitation applies to defamation actions.

WISCONSIN: A two-year statute of limitation applies to defamation actions.

WYOMING: A one-year statute of limitation applies to defamation actions.

## Additional Resources

*Law of Defamation, Second Edition.* Smolla, Rodney A., Thomson/West, 1997.

*The Law of Torts.* Dobbs, Dan B., Thomson/West, 2000.

*Sack on Defamation: Libel, Slander, and Related Problems, Third Edition.* Sack, Robert D., Practising Law Institute, 2005.

*Torts in a Nutshell.* Kionka, Edward J., Thomson/West, 2005.

*West's Encyclopedia of American Law, 2nd Edition,* Thomson/Gale, 2004.

## Organization

### *Media Law Resource Center, Inc.*

80 Eighth Avenue, Suite 200
New York, NY 10011 USA

Phone: (212) 337-0200
URL: http://www.medialaw.org

## Organization

### *Reporters' Committee for Freedom of the Press*

1101 Wilson Blvd., Suite 1100
Arlington, VA 22209 USA
Phone: (800) 336-4243
URL: http://www.rcfp.org

# TORT AND PERSONAL INJURY ACTIONS

## NEGLIGENCE

*Sections within this essay:*

## Background

The law of negligence requires that persons conduct themselves in a manner that conforms with cer-

tain standards of conduct. Where a person's actions violate those standards, the law requires the person to compensate someone who is injured as a result of this act. In some instances, the law of negligence also covers a person's omission to act.

In **tort law**, negligence is a distinct cause of action. The Restatement (Second) of Torts defines negligence as "conduct that falls below the standard established by law for the protection of others against unreasonable risk of harm." Negligence generally consists of five elements, including the following: (1) a duty of care owed by the **defendant** to the **plaintiff**; (2) a breach of that duty; (3) an actual causal connection between the defendant's conduct and the resulting harm; (4) proximate cause, which relates to whether the harm was foreseeable; and (5) damages resulting from the defendant's conduct.

In some instances, a statute or other law may define specific duties, such as the duty of a person to rescue another. Professionals, such as doctors and lawyers, are also required to uphold a standard of care expected in their profession. When a professional fails to uphold such a standard of care, the professional may be liable for **malpractice**, which is based on the law of negligence.

## Standards of Care

The standard of care required in negligence law typically relates to a person's conduct, rather than a person's state of mind. In most instances, a defendant is required to exercise the same "ordinary care" or "due care" that a reasonable person would exercise in the same or similar circumstances. Negligence cases often focus on the reasonableness requirement.

### Reasonable Person

The so-called reasonable person in the law of negligence is a creation of legal fiction. Such a "person" is really an ideal, focusing on how a typical person, with ordinary prudence, would act in certain circumstances. The test as to whether a person has acted as a reasonable person is an objective one, and so it does not take into account the specific abilities of a defendant. Thus, even a person who has low intelligence or is chronically careless is held to the same standard as a more careful person or a person of higher intelligence.

A jury generally decides whether a defendant has acted as a reasonable person would have acted. In making this decision, the jury generally considers the defendant's conduct in light of what the defendant actually knows, has experienced, or has perceived. For example, one may consider a defendant working on a loading dock and tossing large bags of grain onto a truck. In the process of doing this, the defendant notices two children playing near the truck. The defendant throws a bag towards the truck and unintentionally strikes one of the children. In this instance, a jury would take into account the defendant's actual knowledge that children were playing in the area when the jury determines whether the defendant acted reasonably under the circumstances. One must note, however, that the defendant would be liable for negligence only if the defendant owed a duty to the child.

In addition to the defendant's actual knowledge, a jury also considers knowledge that should be common to everyone in a particular community. Accordingly, the defendant in the example above would be charged with knowing that a bag of grain could injure a child, as well as with knowing the natural propensities of children.

### Standards of Care for Children

A child generally is not expected to act as a reasonable adult would act. Instead, courts hold children to a modified standard. Under this standard, a child's actions are compared with the conduct of other children of the same age, experience, and intelligence. Courts in some **jurisdictions**, however, apply the adult standard of care to children who engage in certain adult activities, such as snowmobiling.

## Elements of a Negligence Case

### Duty

The outcomes of some negligence cases depend on whether the defendant owed a duty to the plaintiff. Such a duty arises when the law recognizes a relationship between the defendant and the plaintiff, and due to this relationship, the defendant is obligated to act in a certain manner toward the plaintiff. A judge, rather than a jury, ordinarily determines whether a defendant owed a duty of care to a plaintiff. Where a reasonable person would find that a duty exists under a particular set of circumstances, the court will generally find that such a duty exists.

In the example above involving the defendant loading bags of grain onto a truck, the first question that must be resolved is whether the defendant owed a duty to the child. In other words, a court would need to decide whether the defendant and the child had a relationship such that the defendant was required to exercise reasonable care in handling the bags of grain near the child. If the loading dock were near a public place, such a public sidewalk, and the child was merely passing by, then the court may be more likely to find that the defendant owed a duty to the child. On the other hand, if the child were trespassing on private property and the defendant did not know that the child was present at the time of the accident, then the court would be less likely to find that the defendant owed a duty.

### Breach of Duty

A defendant is liable for negligence when the defendant breaches the duty that the defendant owes to the plaintiff. A defendant breaches such a duty by failing to exercise reasonable care in fulfilling the duty. Unlike the question of whether a duty exists, the issue of whether a defendant breached a duty of care is decided by a jury as a question of fact. Thus, in the example above, a jury would decide whether the defendant exercised reasonable care in handling the bags of grain near the child.

### Cause in Fact

Under the traditional rules in negligence cases, a plaintiff must prove that the defendant's actions actually caused the plaintiff's injury. This is often referred to as "but-for" causation. In other words, but for the defendant's actions, the plaintiff's injury would not have occurred. The child injured by the defendant who tossed a bag of grain onto a truck could prove this element by showing that but for the defendant's negligent act of tossing the grain, the child would not have suffered harm.

### Proximate Cause

Proximate cause relates to the scope of a defendant's responsibility in a negligence case. A defendant in a negligence case is only responsible for those harms that the defendant could have foreseen through his or her actions. If a defendant has caused damages that are outside of the scope of the risks that the defendant could have foreseen, then the plaintiff cannot prove that the defendant's actions were the proximate cause of the plaintiff's damages.

In the example described above, the child injured by the bag of grain would prove proximate cause by showing that the defendant could have foreseen the harm that would have resulted from the bag striking the child. Conversely, if the harm is something more remote to the defendant's act, then the plaintiff will be less likely to prove this element. Assume that when the child is struck with the bag of grain, the child's bicycle on which he was riding is damaged. Three days later, the child and his father drive to a shop to have the bicycle fixed. On their way to the shop, the father and son are struck by another car. Although the harm to the child and the damage to the bicycle may be within the scope of the harm that the defendant risked by his actions, the defendant probably could not have foreseen that the father and son would be injured three days later on their way to having the bicycle repaired. Hence, the father and son could not prove proximate causation.

### Damages

A plaintiff in a negligence case must prove a legally recognized harm, usually in the form of physical injury to a person or to property. It is not enough that the defendant failed to exercise reasonable care. The failure to exercise reasonable care must result in actual damages to a person to whom the defendant owed a duty of care.

## Proof in a Negligence Case

A negligence case is usually proven through one of two types of evidence: direct and circumstantial. Evidence derived from the personal knowledge of a witness or from images in a photograph or video constitutes direct evidence. Circumstantial evidence, by comparison, requires a fact-finder to draw an inference based on the evidence that has been produced.

Courts have formulated special rules that govern proof in specific instances. In a slip-and-fall case, where a plaintiff's injury occurs when the plaintiff slips and falls due to a condition on the defendant's property, courts require the plaintiff to prove that the condition existed for such a length of time that the defendant should have discovered and remedied

the condition. Thus, a plaintiff who sues a supermarket when she slips on spilled liquid laundry soap could not recover from the supermarket without showing that the liquid had been on the floor long enough for the supermarket to have discovered it. Evidence that the soap was smeared across the floor due to the number of customers walking on the liquid may be sufficient proof in this type of case.

A plaintiff in some instances may rely on the doctrine of *res ipsa loquitur*, which is Latin for "the thing speaks for itself." This doctrine allows a jury to infer that a defendant acted negligently, even without other proof of misconduct. In order for this doctrine to apply, the plaintiff must prove that the event that occurred usually does not happen in the absence of negligence and that the defendant had exclusive control of the instrument that caused injury. For example, the child who was injured by the bag of grain on a public sidewalk may not have any direct or circumstantial proof that the defendant was negligent in handling the bag. However, a bag of grain typically does not fly onto a public sidewalk in the absence of negligence, and the defendant had exclusive control over the bag at the time of the accident. In this instance, the jury may infer negligence on the part of the defendant by employing *res ipsa loquitur*.

## Negligence Per Se

In some instances, a plaintiff in a negligence action may rely on a statute to prescribe a certain standard of care. Under the doctrine of negligence per se, a standard of conduct required under a statute is adopted by a court as defining the conduct of a reasonable person. In other words, rather than asking a jury what a reasonable person would have done under certain circumstances, the statute establishes what a reasonable person would have done under those circumstances. A statutory violation under this rule is conclusive on the issue of whether the defendant violated a standard of care.

## Specific Duties

Courts have developed special rules regarding the duty that a defendant may have in a specific case. Where a duty does exist, it is based on specific circumstances or the nature of the relationship between the parties.

### Duty to Rescue

The general rule is that a person has no duty to rescue another person who is in peril. Even in an extreme situation, such as where an adult sees a child trapped on top of railroad tracks, courts generally hold that a person is under no duty to come to the aid of another. Courts, however, recognize several exceptions. These include the following:

- The Defendant Created the Peril: Where the defendant's negligence created the need for the plaintiff to be rescued, the defendant is generally under a duty to rescue the plaintiff.

- Undertaking to Act: If a defendant begins to rescue a person but then stops, in some instances the defendant may be under a duty to continue the rescue. Most courts require that the defendant act reasonably once the rescue has begun. If a reasonable person would have continued to rescue the victim, then the defendant may have been under a duty to continue the rescue.

- Special Relationship: A defendant may have the duty to rescue a person where the defendant has a special relationship with the victim, such as in an employer-employee or a school-student relationship.

### Duty to Control

A person generally has no duty to control the actions of another person. However, in some relationships, this duty may arise. The most common example involves a parent and child. If a parent is aware of a child's dangerous propensities, then the parent is generally under a duty to exercise reasonable care in controlling the child.

### Duty to Protect

A defendant may have a duty to protect a plaintiff based on the defendant's relationship with the plaintiff. This most clearly applies in cases involving jailors and prisoners or innkeepers and guests. Some courts have imposed a duty to protect based on other relationships, including landlord-tenant and business-patron relationships, but the law is less clear about duties in these instances.

## Professional Malpractice

Members of certain professions, such as doctors, lawyers, and accountants, may be liable for professional negligence, also known as malpractice. Professional negligence occurs when a professional fails to exercise a degree of care that is exercised by well-qualified professionals in the same field. This standard is based on how well-qualified professionals or-dinarily and customarily perform, rather than on how reasonable professionals should have performed.

## Premises Liability

One of the more complex areas of law related to negligence focuses on the standard of care that a land possessor owes to a person injured on the land. In some jurisdictions, the law requires the possessor of the land to act reasonably in the maintenance of his or her land. In other jurisdictions, whether the person who is injured may recover from the land possessor depends on the person's status when he or she was on the property.

If a person is invited onto a property, the land possessor is generally obligated to exercise some care with respect to the person's safety. At the least, the land possessor must warn the person about dangers that are present on the property. A possessor of land does not, however, owe a duty to a person who enters the land without the occupier's permission. Possible exceptions to the rule regarding trespassers apply when the trespasser frequently enters the land or when the trespasser is a child.

## Products Liability

Another distinct area of law related to negligence is products liability. A person may bring a products liability action when the person suffers physical harm as a result of an unsafe product. In this type of suit, the injured person attempts to prove that the manufacturer of the product is at fault for the unsafe condition of the product. One basis for proving that the manufacturer is at fault is by proving that the manufacturer was negligent in the production or distribution of the product. Where a products liability suit is based on allegations of negligence, the plaintiff must prove that the manufacturer failed to exercise reasonable care in the design or manufacturing of a product or failed to provide adequate warnings regarding potential dangers associated with the product.

## Defenses in Negligence Actions

A defendant in a negligence suit typically tries to negate one of the elements of the plaintiff's cause of action. In other words, the defendant introduces evidence, for example, that he or she did not owe a duty to the plaintiff, exercised reasonable care, did not cause the plaintiff's damages, and so forth. In addition to negating one or more of these elements, a defendant may rely on one of a few doctrines that may eliminate or limit liability based on alleged negligence. Two of the more common doctrines are comparative fault and assumption of the risk.

### Comparative Fault

Under traditional tort law, a defendant could avoid liability by proving contributory negligence on the part of the plaintiff. Contributory negligence occurs when a plaintiff's conduct falls below a certain standard necessary for the plaintiff's protection, and this conduct cooperates with the defendant's negligence in causing harm to the plaintiff. Where the plaintiff's negligence for his or her own protection is the cause-in-fact and proximate cause of the plaintiff's damages, then the doctrine of contributory negligence would bar recovery.

Contributory negligence has led to harsh results in some cases, and the vast majority of states have replaced the doctrine with an alternative called comparative negligence. The doctrine of comparative negligence reduces a plaintiff's recovery by the percentage in which the plaintiff is at fault for his or her damages. A majority of states have modified this rule, barring a plaintiff from recovering if the plaintiff is as much at fault (in some states) or more at fault (in other states) than the defendant.

### Assumption of the Risk

Another defense that traditionally has barred recovery for a plaintiff applies when a plaintiff has assumed the risk involved in an obviously dangerous activity but proceeded to engage in the activity anyway. In order for this doctrine to apply, the plaintiff must have actual, subjective knowledge of the risk involved in the activity. The plaintiff must also voluntarily accept the risk involved in the activity. An ex-

ample might involve an amusement park ride that flips passengers completely upside-down. A passenger who saw the ride and knew what would happen on the ride assumed the risks associated with the ride. On the other hand, a plaintiff does not assume the risk of something unexpected related to the ride, such as where a loose bolt causes the ride to throw the plaintiff in a violent manner.

## Additional Resources

*The Law of Torts.* Dobbs, Dan B., West Group, 2000.

*Principles of Tort Law.* Shapo, Marshall S., Thomson/West, 2003.

*Torts in a Nutshell.* Kionka, Edward J., Thomson/West, 2005.

*Understanding Torts.* 2d Edition. Diamond, John L., Lawrence C. Levine, and M. Stuart Madden, Lexis Publishing, 2000.

## Organizations

### Association of Trial Lawyers of America
1050 31st Street, NW
Washington, DC 20007 USA
Phone: (800) 424-2725
URL: http://www.atla.org/

### National Association of Personal Injury Lawyers
23945 Calabasas Rd. Suite 106
Calabasas, CA 91302 USA
URL: http://www.napil.com/

### American Bar Association
321 North Clark Street
Chicago, IL 60610 USA
Phone: (312) 988-5000
URL: http://www.abanet.org

# TORT AND PERSONAL INJURY ACTIONS

## PRODUCT LIABILITY

*Sections within this essay:*

- Background
- Basis for Liability
    - Negligence
    - Tortious Misrepresentation
    - Warranty
    - Strict Liability
- Defects in Products
    - Defects in Manufacturing
    - Defects in Design
    - Defects in Warnings
- Liability for Used Products
- Defenses
- Statutes of Limitations in Products Liability Cases
- Additional Resources

## Background

A **plaintiff** in a products liability case asserts that the manufacturer of a product should be liable for personal injury or property damage that results from a defect in a product or from false representations made by the manufacturer of the product. A **defendant** often tries to disprove the plaintiff's case by showing that the product was not defective or that the plaintiff's misuse of the product was what caused harm to the plaintiff.

Products liability law consists of a mixture of **tort law** and contract law. Aspects of this area of law relat-

ed to tort include strict liability, **negligence**, and deceit. Aspects that relate to contract law relate mostly to the laws governing warranties. Because this area of law is really hybrid in nature, a plaintiff may assert a number of possible claims, such as negligence, breach of implied **warranty** of fitness, breach of express warranty, or **fraud**.

The basis for products liability law developed over several centuries. English courts developed the doctrine of *caveat emptor*, meaning "let the buyer beware." Under this doctrine, a buyer was expected to protect himself against both obvious and hidden defects in a product and could not recover from the manufacturer for damages caused by these defects. Over time, however, English courts began to recognize a rule that a seller implied warrants that a product does not contain a hidden defect. On the other hand, American courts continued to employ the caveat emptor rule for most of the nineteenth century.

When courts in the United States began to impose implied warranties of merchantability in the late 1800s, the rule required that the plaintiff have privity of contract with the defendant. This meant that the buyer must have purchased a product directly from the manufacturer in order to recover from the manufacturer. During that time, manufacturers had begun to rely more heavily on retailers to sell products. Since many buyers did not actually purchase the products directly from the manufacturers, though, those buyers could not recover for breach of implied warranty from the manufacturers due to a lack of privity of contract.

Courts opened the doors to modern products liability cases in the 1950s and 1960s by allowing remote plaintiffs to recover against the manufacturers of defective products. The American Law Institute (ALI) included rules pertaining to products liability in the Restatement (Second) of Torts, which was official promulgated in 1965. Since the 1960s, the law of products liability has continued to expand and develop. The ALI recognized this development by approving the Restatement (Third) of Torts: Products Liability, in 1998.

## Basis for Liability

A plaintiff may rely on one or more of several theories upon which to base his or her argument for recovery in a products liability case. The primary theories for recovery include the following: negligence, tortious misrepresentation, breach of warranty, and strict liability in tort.

### Negligence

The tort of negligence remains a central part of the law of products liability. In order to recover under a theory of negligence, a plaintiff must prove five basic elements, including the following: (1) the manufacturer owed a duty to the plaintiff; (2) the manufacturer breached a duty to the plaintiff; (3) the breach of duty was the actual cause of the plaintiff's injury; (4) the breach of duty was also the proximate cause of the injury; and (5) the plaintiff suffered actual damages as a result of the negligent act.

In a products liability case, the law requires that a manufacturer exercise a standard of care that is reasonable for those who are experts in manufacturing similar products. However, even if a plaintiff can prove that a manufacturer has failed to exercise the proper standard of care, the plaintiff cannot recover without proving two aspects of causation. The plaintiff must first show that but for the manufacturer's negligence, the plaintiff's would not have been injured. The plaintiff must also show that the defendant could have foreseen the risks and uses of the product at the time of manufacturing.

### Tortious Misrepresentation

A claim in a products liability suit may be based on false or misleading information that is conveyed by the manufacturer of a product. A person who relies on the information conveyed by the seller and who is harmed by such reliance may recover for the misrepresentation. This basis for recovery does not depend on a defect in the product, but rather depends on the false communication.

Tortious misrepresentation may appear in one of three basic forms. First, a person may commit fraud-ulent misrepresentation, or deceit, in which the person knows that a statement is false and intends to mislead the plaintiff by making the statement. Second, a person may commit negligent misrepresentation, where the person was negligent in ascertaining whether a statement was true. Third, some jurisdictions allow for strict liability in instances where a manufacturer makes a public statement about the safety of a product.

### Warranty

A warranty is a type of guarantee that a seller gives regarding the quality of a product. A warranty may be express, meaning that the seller makes certain representations regarding the quality of a product. If the product's quality is less than the representation, the seller could be liable for breach of express warranty. Some warranties may also be implied due to the nature of the sale.

The **Uniform Commercial Code** (U.C.C.), which has been adopted in part by every state, provides the basis for warranties in the United States. The U.C.C. recognizes express warranties and two types of implied warranties: the implied warranty of merchantability and the implied warranty of fitness for a particular purpose. An implied warranty of merchantability is a promise that a product sold is in good working order and will do what it is supposed to do. An implied warranty of fitness for a particular purpose is a promise that a seller's advice on how to use a product will be correct.

### Strict Liability

Section 402A of the Restatement (Second) of Torts included a provision that created strict liability on the part of a manufacturer. Under this section, a manufacturer is liable for product defects that occur during the manufacturing process, notwithstanding the level of care employed by the manufacturer. Courts later extended the strict liability principles to include cases that did not involve errors in manufacturing, such as cases involving a failure of a manufacturer to provide ample warnings.

The Restatement (Third) of Torts: Products Liability applies strict liability rules to cases involving errors in manufacturing, but applies negligence rules to other types of products liability cases. Nevertheless, many states continue to apply the strict liability rules that were developed in older cases.

# Defects in Products

In order to recover for harm caused by a product, a plaintiff in a products liability suit must prove that a product possessed some sort of defect or hazard. This is true irrespective of the theory or theories of recovery that the plaintiff attempts to prove. The vast majority of states recognize three types of defects that may give rise to a products liability suit. These include defects in manufacturing, design, and warnings.

### Defects in Manufacturing

A defect in manufacturing is one that the manufacturer did not intend. A manufacturing defect is the clearest instance in which strict liability applies. Under the Restatement (Third) of Torts: Products Liability, a product "contains a manufacturing defect when the product departs from its intended design even though all possible care was exercised in the preparation and marketing of the product."

An example of a manufacturing defect would be a car's braking system that does not work properly and causes a plaintiff to have an accident. Even though the manufacturer of the car did not intend for the brakes to malfunction, and even though the manufacturer was not negligent in the design of the brakes, the strict liability doctrine in products liability law could render the manufacturer liable.

A plaintiff may have difficulty proving that a product caused the plaintiff's injuries. For example, even if a car had some defect in the braking system, the driver's poor reaction to driving conditions may have been the actual cause of an accident. Additionally, in some circumstances, it may be difficult for a plaintiff to prove that a defect caused an accident due to the damage to the product. A car may be so heavily damaged in an accident, for instance, that it is impossible to prove what caused the accident to occur.

In some instances, a plaintiff can rely on the "malfunction doctrine" to prove causation. Under this doctrine, if the circumstances of an accident indicate that a defect caused the accident, and the plaintiff can produce evidence that removes other possible causes, then the plaintiff can prove causation even if the product is damaged or destroyed. This doctrine is similar in application to *res ipsa loquitur* in the law of negligence.

### Defects in Design

A defect in a products liability suit may be based on the product's design. The Restatement (Third) provides that a design defect occurs "when the foreseeable risks of harm posed by the product could have been reduced or avoided by the adoption of a reasonable alternative design by the seller or other distributor, or a predecessor in the commercial chain of distribution, and the omission of the alternative design renders the product not reasonably safe."

Cases involving design defects generally focus on the manufacturer's decisions in making a product, especially with respect to decisions regarding a product's safety. Unlike manufacturing defect cases, which focus on errors that a manufacturer made while actually making the product, design defect cases focus on the manufacturer's plans in producing the product.

Modern courts employ a cost-benefit analysis in resolving design defect cases, as captured in the Restatement (Third). A plaintiff must identify an alternative design that could have made a product safer in order to prove a case based on a design defect. If a plaintiff can demonstrate that a practicable alternative to the design employed by the manufacturer could have prevented the plaintiff's harm, then the court will determine whether the alternative was cost-efficient.

For example, assume that a metal fan was covered by a guard, but the openings in the guard were three-quarters of an inch wide. In using the fan, the plaintiff's hand slips between the gaps in the guard, and the plaintiff is injured by the blades of the fan. The plaintiff may base a product liability suit on the design of the fan, arguing that if the guard's openings were a half-inch or less, the plaintiff's hand would not have been injured.

### Defects in Warnings

The last type of defect focuses on the warnings that a manufacturer fails to give regarding the dangerousness of a product. Under the Restatement (Third), a product may be defective "because of inadequate instructions or warnings when the foreseeable risks of harm posed by the product could have been reduced or avoided by the provision of reasonable instructions or warnings by the seller or other distributor,... and the omission of the instructions or warnings renders the product not reasonably safe."

A manufacturer is under two related duties. First, the manufacturer is required to warn users of hidden dangers that may be present in a product. Second, the manufacturer must instruct users how to use a product so that the users can avoid any dangers and use the product safely. An example could involve a fan that is prone to overheating if operated for more than three hours continuously. After three hours, the fan could present a fire risk. If the manufacturer fails to provide a warning about the potential danger of the product, then a plaintiff who is injured in a fire started by the product could recover not only for a defect in the design of the fan, but also for the inadequate warnings regarding the danger posed by the fan.

A warning generally must be clear and specific. It should also be conspicuous and placed in a location that the user can easily find. Many manufacturers now provide warnings in foreign languages and by using symbols so that children and non-English speaking users are aware of dangers associated with a product.

## Liability for Used Products

Different rules have developed in products liability law for those who sell or repair used products. In most instances, a person who repairs, rebuilds, or reconditions a product is liable if the person is negligent in treating the product, but the person is not subject to strict liability for defects. In some instances, however, a person who remanufactures a product may be subject to the same products liability rules as the original manufacturer.

States are split regarding the bases of liability of sellers of used products. Some states expressly exclude sales of used products from products liability rules. In other states, the general products liability rules apply.

## Defenses

A defendant in a products liability suit may employ one of several defenses to liability. One of the more common defenses is that the plaintiff misused the product in a manner that was not reasonably foreseeable to the manufacturer. For instance, assume that a plaintiff wanted to sweep a number of rocks in his driveway back into a bed of rocks. The plaintiff decides to use his lawnmower to shoot the rocks back into the rock bed. One of the rocks strikes and injures the plaintiff. The defendant could argue that using the lawnmower to move the rocks off of the driveway was not a reasonably foreseeable use of the product.

Other defenses may be based on the plaintiff's own negligence in using a product or on the plain-

tiff's assumption of the risk associated with the product. Similar defenses apply in breach of warranty claims. In a tortious misrepresentation claim, the primary defense centers on whether a plaintiff's reliance on a seller's statement is justifiable. If a plaintiff's reliance is not justified, then the lack of reliance defeats an essential element of the plaintiff's claim.

## Statutes of Limitations in Products Liability Cases

A plaintiff in each state must bring an action within a certain period of time prescribed in the state's statute of limitations. In most states, the time period begins when the plaintiff discovered or should have discovered his or her injury, under what is known as the discovery rule. A few states begin this time period when the injury actually occurred. Some states have also enacted statutes of repose, which bar actions that are not brought within a specified period of time after some event has occurred, such as the initial sale of a product.

ALABAMA: An action must be brought within one year from the time when the injury is or should have been discovered.

ALASKA: An action must be brought within two years from the time when the injury is or should have been discovered.

ARIZONA: An action must be brought within two years from the time when the injury is or should have been discovered. The state has enacted a 12-year statute of repose that begins to run once the product is first sold. The statute of repose does not apply to actions based on negligence or breach of warranty.

ARKANSAS: An action must be brought within three years from the time when the injury is or should have been discovered.

CALIFORNIA: An action must be brought within two years from the time when the injury is or should have been discovered.

COLORADO: An action must be brought within two years from the time when the injury is or should have been discovered.

CONNECTICUT: An action must be brought within two years from the time when the injury is or should have been discovered. The state has enacted a 10-year statute of repose that begins to run once the manufacturer or seller has last parted with the product.

DELAWARE: An action must be brought within two years from the time when the injury is or should have been discovered.

DISTRICT OF COLUMBIA: An action must be brought within three years from the time when the injury is or should have been discovered.

FLORIDA: An action must be brought within two years from the time when the injury is or should have been discovered. The state has enacted a 12-year statute of repose, subject to various exceptions.

GEORGIA: An action must be brought within two years from the time when the injury is or should have been discovered or one year from the date in which death has occurred. The state has enacted a 10-year statute of repose, subject to various exceptions.

HAWAII: An action must be brought within two years from the time when the injury is or should have been discovered.

IDAHO: An action must be brought within two years from the date in which the occurrence of the injury took place. The state has enacted a 10-year statute of repose, subject to various exceptions.

ILLINOIS: An action must be brought within two years from the date in which the occurrence of the injury took place. The state has enacted a 12-year statute of repose that begins to run once the product is sold and a 10-year statute of repose that begins to run once the product is delivered to the first owner.

INDIANA: An action must be brought within two years from the date in which the occurrence of the injury took place. The state has enacted a 10-year statute of repose.

IOWA: An action must be brought within two years from the date in which the occurrence of the injury took place.

KANSAS: An action must be brought within two years from the date in which the occurrence of the injury took place.

KENTUCKY: An action must be brought within one year from the date in which the occurrence of the injury took place. If injury, death, or property damage does not occur within eight years of the product's use, then this creates a rebuttable presumption that the product does not contain a defect.

LOUISIANA: An action must be brought within one year from the date in which the occurrence of the injury took place. This statute does not apply to minors.

MAINE: An action must be brought within six years from the date in which the occurrence of the injury took place.

MARYLAND: An action must be brought within three years from the date in which the occurrence of the injury took place.

MASSACHUSETTS: An action must be brought within three years from the date in which the occurrence of the injury took place.

MICHIGAN: An action must be brought within two years from the date in which the occurrence of the injury took place. If a product is in use for more than 10 years, then liability cannot be based on strict liability.

MINNESOTA: An action must be brought within four years from the date in which the occurrence of the injury took place.

MISSISSIPPI: An action must be brought within two years from the date in which the occurrence of the injury took place.

MISSOURI: An action must be brought within five years from the date in which the occurrence of the injury took place.

MONTANA: An action must be brought within three years from the date in which the occurrence of the injury took place.

NEBRASKA: An action must be brought within four years from the date in which the occurrence of the injury took place. The state has enacted a 10-year statute of repose, which begins to run from the date in which a product is first sold.

NEVADA: An action must be brought within four years from the date in which the occurrence of the injury took place.

NEW HAMPSHIRE: An action must be brought within three years from the date in which the occurrence of the injury took place, except where a legal duty has been imposed by the government, in which case the action must be brought within six years. The state has enacted a 12-year statute of repose, which begins to run once the product is manufactured and sold.

NEW JERSEY: An action must be brought within two years from the date in which the occurrence of the injury took place.

NEW MEXICO: An action must be brought within three years from the date in which the occurrence of the injury took place.

NEW YORK: An action must be brought within three years from the date in which the occurrence of the injury took place.

NORTH CAROLINA: An action must be brought within six years from the date of the initial purchase.

NORTH DAKOTA: An action must be brought within 10 years from the date of the initial purchase or within 11 years of the date of manufacture.

OHIO: An action must be brought within two years from the date in which the occurrence of the injury took place.

OKLAHOMA: An action must be brought within two years from the date in which the occurrence of the injury took place.

OREGON: An action must be brought within two years from the date in which the occurrence of the injury took place. The state has enacted an eight-year statute of repose.

PENNSYLVANIA: An action must be brought within two years from the date in which the occurrence of the injury took place.

RHODE ISLAND: An action must be brought within three years from the date in which the occurrence of the injury took place.

SOUTH CAROLINA: An action must be brought within three years from the date in which the occurrence of the injury took place.

SOUTH DAKOTA: An action must be brought within three years from the date in which the occurrence of the injury took place. The state has enacted a six-year statute of repose, which begins to run after purchase.

TENNESSEE: An action must be brought within four years from the date in which the occurrence of the injury took place. The state has enacted a statute of repose that runs six years after an injury and 10 years after the initial purchase of a product.

TEXAS: An action must be brought within two years from the date in which the occurrence of the injury took place.

UTAH: An action must be brought within two years from the date in which the occurrence of the injury took place.

VERMONT: An action must be brought within three years from the date in which the occurrence of the injury took place.

VIRGINIA: An action must be brought within two years from the date in which the occurrence of the injury took place.

WASHINGTON: An action must be brought within two years from the date in which the occurrence of the injury took place. The state has enacted a 12-year statute of repose.

WEST VIRGINIA: An action must be brought within two years from the date in which the occurrence of the injury took place.

WISCONSIN: An action must be brought within three years from the date in which the occurrence of the injury took place.

WYOMING: An action must be brought within four years from the date in which the occurrence of the injury took place.

## Additional Resources

*Personal Injury Statutes of Limitations: A Legal Guide.* Parker & Waichman, LLP. Available at http://www.statutes-of-limitations.com.

*Products Liability in a Nutshell..* 7th Edition. Owen, David G. and Jerry J. Phillips, Thomson/West, 2005.

*Products Liability Law.* Owen, David G., Thomson/West, 2005.

*Restatement of the Law Third: Torts: Products Liability.* American Law Institute, 1998.

## Organizations

### Association of Trial Lawyers of America
1050 31st Street, NW
Washington, DC 20007 USA
Phone: (800) 424-2725
URL: http://www.atla.org/

### National Association of Personal Injury Lawyers
23945 Calabasas Rd. Suite 106
Calabasas, CA 91302 USA
URL: http://www.napil.com/

### American Bar Association
321 North Clark Street
Chicago, IL 60610 USA
Phone: (312) 988-5000
URL: http://www.abanet.org

# TRAVEL

## CHILDREN TRAVELING ALONE

*Sections within this essay:*

- Background

- Why Children Travel Alone

- Train and Bus Travel

- Air Travel
    - Airline Regulations
    - Other Air Travel Issues
    - International Flights

- Common Sense

- Additional Resources

## Background

The number of children between the ages of 5 and 12 traveling alone, particularly by air, has risen steadily over the years. Estimates for how many children travel alone by plane in the United States per year run as high as 7 million. Children traveling alone, known in the travel industry as "unaccompanied minors," raise a number of issues, the most important being liability and safety. In most cases, solo child travelers neither create nor encounter difficulties. Even the best-planned trip, however, can go wrong, and when unaccompanied children are involved the issues can be particularly problematic.

Many air travelers, for example, have had the frustrating experience of finding out that their luggage was accidentally placed on the wrong plane, and they may have to spend hours or even days tracking it down. But in August 2001, two girls ages 11 and 8 wound up in Toronto instead of San Diego because

airline personnel placed them on the wrong connecting flight in Phoenix. While many airlines have strict rules about allowing unaccompanied children to transfer to connecting flights, others do not. (The airline that placed the two girls on the wrong plane quickly revised its policy.)

There are no official guidelines regarding the transport of unaccompanied children. Train and bus regulations are more strict than air regulations, but in all cases it is the transportation providers' obligation to set the requirements. Neither the Air Transport Association nor the International Air Transport Association provides detailed guidelines or even statistics on the number of children traveling alone. The American Society of Travel Agents (ASTA) does note in its "Traveler's Bill of Rights" that unaccompanied children have a right to "timely and courteous assistance" and that they should "never be abandoned or put in fear of being abandoned."

These omissions do not mean that the government is unconcerned about unaccompanied children. The self-imposed industry requirements that must be met are considered stringent enough. With the rise in concern for travel safety in general since the fall of 2001, the government has taken a more active role. Still, airlines, trains, and bus lines are all still allowed to set their own rules for children traveling alone.

The necessary precaution for sending children on trips unaccompanied is that those making the travel arrangements should get as much information before the trip as possible about travel policies and procedures for children. Because rules are subject to change and in order to avoid potential difficulties, it is important to check each time a child travels.

## Why Children Travel Alone

The most common reason children travel alone is to visit relatives. As families spread out it is more likely that grandparents, aunts, uncles, and cousins may live across the country or overseas. Children whose parents are divorced also travel alone. In years past, divorced couples with children would tend to stay in the same geographic location to be able to spend time with those children. Today, job opportunities or remarriage may mean that a child's mother and father may live on opposite coasts.

Clearly, some children are more comfortable traveling than others. A child who flies several times a year will likely be more comfortable on a plane than one who has never flown alone. That is not a given, however. Just as some frequent passengers never get over their fear of flying, neither do some children. A 6-year-old who has never flown before may find the experience one big enjoyable adventure. An 11-year-old who dislikes plane travel, on the other hand, might actually be a difficult and demanding passenger.

Since the attacks in New York and Washington, D.C., on September 11, 2001, airline, train, and bus security have all increased. While this may not affect children as directly as it affects adults, the travel process is longer and involves a considerable amount more time standing in line and waiting. Not only that, children who are old enough to understand what happened in the plane attacks may be frightened of flying even if they were never afraid in the past.

Relatively few unaccompanied children travel by train or bus, in part, because train and bus trips may be too long for children. Also, railroad and bus companies have stricter regulations about who is old enough to travel solo.

## Train and Bus Travel

Amtrak estimates that no more than 5,100 children per year travel unaccompanied on its trains. Greyhound estimates far fewer unaccompanied children on its bus routes. In part this low number reflects the fact that most long-distance travel is done by plane, but it also has to do with strict train and bus regulations.

Amtrak will not allow children under the age of 8 to travel unaccompanied, subject to the following restrictions:

- All trips must be scheduled for daylight hours

- Unaccompanied children cannot transfer to another train or to a bus

- Children must depart from and arrive at fully staffed stations; an Amtrak stop with only a ticketing machine is off limits

- Whoever takes the child to the train must fill out a form authorizing Amtrak to let the child travel alone

- The Amtrak agent who makes the arrangements must ask the child who is meeting him or her

- Children traveling unaccompanied pay the full adult fare

Greyhound's requirements are similar, with the following additional restrictions:

- The child's trip cannot be for more than 250 miles

- The child must sit in the first two rows of the bus and must get the driver's permission to get off the bus at rest stops

## Air Travel

Travel by air presents a number of challenges where unaccompanied children are concerned. One reason is that so many more children travel solo by plane than by any other means. Another is that, while there are age guidelines and restrictions, maturity levels can differ dramatically among children. It is not just whether a child likes to fly. Some children are fearful of not being with their parents. Others may not want to travel to the place where they happen to be going. The Independent Traveler, Inc., an organization that provides travel advice, reported on its website the case of an 11-year-old boy whose father saw him board the plane that was to take him to his grandparents' home. After the father left, the boy got off the plane, left the airport, and walked 30 miles back to his house. Clearly he did not want to take this trip. Yet his behavior is surprising in view of his age.

### Airline Regulations

No airline will allow a child under the age of 5 to travel alone, although some will allow a child under 5 to travel with a companion as young as 12. Most airlines will not allow a child under the age of 8 to take a flight that requires changing planes to make a connection. Any child under 12 who has to make a connecting flight will be escorted by an employee of the airline. Southwest Airlines does not allow any child under the age of 12 to take connecting flights. Although children between the ages of 12 and 15 are not automatically escorted, the parent or **guardian** making the travel arrangements can ask the airline to assist the child.

Accompanied minors usually pay half or reduced fare when flying. Unaccompanied minors are required to pay full fare, as well as an additional service fee of between $30 and $75 each way (the price is higher when the child has to make a connection). On most airlines, that fee will cover more than one minor traveling within the same party.

Airlines usually require that a parent or guardian fill out a form with all relevant information about the child. While the airline does not generally take actual guardianship of the child during the flight, one of the personnel is generally assigned to look after the child. Solo child travelers usually have to wear a button or badge to make them easy to identify by airline staffers.

Some children are required to take medication. Airline personnel will not dispense medication to the child, but if the child is able to administer his or her own medication, the airline will allow the child to carry that medicine. The form that parents and guardians fill out asks for a list of medications or other medical issues that may be important for staffers to know.

Most airlines will not allow minors to take the last flight of the day. The reason is that, air travel being subject to such unforeseen circumstances as weather, there is always a chance of delay. If a late evening flight is delayed, it means passengers will probably have to wait until the next morning to catch another flight. A stranded child clearly presents more difficulties to the airline than a stranded adult.

### Other Air Travel Issues

In the event that a child is stranded at the airport overnight despite everyone's best efforts, different airlines have different procedures, all of which are subject to the approval of the parent or guardian. Usually, the airline will put the child up in a hotel room. An airline staffer may stay in the room with the child or in an adjoining room. Some airlines will post a guard outside the room. In most cases the airline assigns a staffer of the same sex as the child to serve as an escort. Some airlines may turn a stranded child over to a local child welfare agency for the night.

One of the biggest challenges for those in charge of watching children is keeping those children amused. Doing so is particularly difficult in the case of long flights. Many of the larger airlines have established facilities designed for children at major airports, where children can wait for their connecting flights. These rooms have games and other activities for children. They also will have other children, so that young travelers will feel less lonely.

Under no circumstances will airline personnel turn a child over to a waiting adult without seeing definitive identification and matching that carefully to the information filled out on the pre-departure form.

### International Flights

Children traveling alone on international flights face even closer scrutiny, in part because of the fear of child abductions. In fact, children traveling with only one parent are subject to strict regulations to ensure that a parent is not **kidnapping** the child from a custodial parent. Any child under the age of 18 who is traveling with one parent to Mexico must show notarized consent from the other parent or a sole **custody decree** from the accompanying parent. If the other parent is dead, the airline requires the travelers to show a death certificate.

Children need the same documentation, whether passports, visas, or other official paperwork, as adults. It is a good idea to contact the consulate of the country being visited to determine whether there are any special requirements for children traveling alone.

## Common Sense

The most important rule for both parents and children to remember is to plan ahead. Parents should explain to children exactly what will be expected of them as solo travelers. They should also let children know that inappropriate behavior by adult passengers (such as unwanted physical contact) should be reported to airline personnel. If the child has traveled alone before on a different airline, it is not a good idea to assume that the current airline has the same policies. Most airlines list their policies clearly and comprehensively on their websites.

Increased concern for flight security has made the travel process slower and more cumbersome. These new procedures should be explained to the child. It should also be made clear that no matter how accommodating airline personnel may be, they have no obligation to children traveling alone before or after a flight.

Checking out the airlines' websites is a good way to become familiar with each carrier's policies on solo child travelers. Groups such as ASTA (http://www.asta.org) and the U. S. Department of Transportation (http://www.usdot.gov) can provide additional information. The Department of Transportation offers a free publication, *Kids and Teens Traveling Alone*, which can be obtained by writing to 400 Seventh Street SW, Washington, D. C., 20590.

## Additional Resources

*Fun on the Run: Travel Games and Songs.* Cole, Joanna, and Stephanie Calmerson, Morrow Junior Books, 1999.

*Trouble-Free Travel with Children: Helpful Hints for Parents on the Go.* Lansky, Vicki, Book Peddlers, 1996.

## Organizations

### Air Transportation Association of America, Inc. (ATA)
1301 Pennsylvania Avenue, Suite 1100
Washington, DC 20004 USA
Phone: (202) 626-4000
URL: http://www.airline.org
Primary Contact: Carol Hallett, President and CEO

### American Society of Travel Agents (ASTA)
1101 King Street, Suite 200
Alexandria, VA 22314 USA

Phone: (703) 739-2782
Fax: (703) 684-8319
URL: http://w ww.asta.org
Primary Contact: Richard M. Copland, President and CEO

### International Air Transport Association (IATA) (Regional Office, United States)
1776 K Street NW
Washington, DC 20006 USA
Phone: (202) 293-9292
Fax: (202) 293-8448
URL: http://w ww.iata.org
Primary Contact: Pierre Jeanniot, Director General and CEO

### National Center for Missing and Exploited Children
699 Prince Street
Alexandria, VA 22314 USA
Phone: (703) 274-3900
Fax: (703) 274-2200
URL: http://w ww.missingkids.com
Primary Contact: Ernie Allen, President and CEO

### U. S. Department of Transportation, Office of Aviation and International Affairs
400 Seventh Street SW
Washington, DC 20590 USA
Phone: (202) 366-4000 (General Information)
Phone: (202) 366-2220 (Aviation Consumer Protection Division)
URL: http://ostpxweb.dot.gov/aviation
Primary Contact: Read van de Water, Assistant Secretary for Aviation and International Affairs

# TRAVEL

## HOTEL LIABILITY

*Sections within this essay:*

- Background
- Key Points to Remember
- Authority
- Duty to Receive Guests
- Guest Reservations
- Right to Evict Persons Admitted as Guests
- Duty to Persons Who Are Not Guests
- Duty to Provide Safe Premises
  - Harm or Damage Caused by Other Guests
  - Harm or Damage Caused by Third Persons
  - National Disasters, Acts of God, Public Enemies, Catastrophic Exposures
  - Responsibility for Personal Property
  - Statutory of Contractual Limitations on Liability
- Innkeepers' Liens
- Good Samaritan Acts
- Unusual Cases
- State Innkeeper Laws
- Additional Resources

## Background

Hotel guests should be aware of certain laws and regulations or policies that could impact their visits.

Special concerns affect the "hospitality industry" because its establishments hold their property open to the public at large. For hotels (collectively referred to as "innkeepers" under many state laws), duties owed to the public at large are based on the historic consideration that when weary travelers reached wayside inns as night approached, they were not to be arbitrarily turned away into the dark (the roads were filled with robbers) or otherwise subjected to the arbitrary mercy of the innkeeper with regard to prices or adequacy of quarters. Modern innkeepers' laws are mostly based on old English **common law**.

## Key Points to Remember

- Hotels are not liable for every accident or loss that occurs on the premises, nor do they insure the absolute safety of every guest.

- Hotels have a general duty to exercise "reasonable care" for the safety and security of their guests.

- Hotels have a general duty to reasonably protect guests from harm caused by other guests or non-guests.

- Hotels have an affirmative duty to make the premises reasonably safe for their guests. This obligation includes a two-fold duty either to correct a hazard or warn of its existence. The hotel must not only address visible hazards but must make apparent hidden dangers or hazards.

- Hotels are not liable for harm to person or property unless "fault" can be established against the hotel.

- Hotels may be "vicariously liable" for the **negligence** of their employees.

- Hotels are generally liable for damages if they cannot honor a confirmed reservation because of "overbooking."

- Hotels may generally sue for damages or retain deposits if confirmed reservations are not honored by prospective guests.

- Hotels may generally evict registered guests for a variety of well-established reasons.

- Hotels may retain personal possessions of evicted guests as security for room charges.

- Hotels are generally not required to have lifeguards on duty at hotel swimming pools, except by state **statute**. However, conspicuous "No Lifeguard" warning signs are minimally required.

- Hotels are generally not liable for valuables that are not secured in the hotel safe, if conspicuous notice is posted.

- Hotels are generally not liable for harm to guests caused by criminal acts of others, unless hotel fault is established.

- Hotels may generally limit their liability for losses if conspicuous notice is given to hotel guests.

## Authority

The federal government has limited involvement in the private relationships between hotels and guests.

- Title 42 of the U. S. Code, Chapter 21, Subchapter II (Public Accommodations) makes prohibited **discrimination** under the **Civil Rights** Act of 1964 applicable to "any inn, hotel, motel, or other establishment which provides lodging to transient guests."

- Under a phase-in provision, hotels must meet the requirements of the Americans With Disabilities Act (ADA); any new or renovated hotel facility must comply with the Act's mandates for public access and/or removal of physical barriers.

- The Hotel and Motel Fire Safety Act of 1990 (as amended in 1996) imposes additional safety requirements upon hotel facilities above and beyond those found in local building codes.

Generally, most day-to-day liability issues affecting hotels are based on early English common law theories of contract and tort (negligence). States are free to enact their own statutes regarding innkeepers' rights and duties, so long as they do not abridge federal rights and most states have done so. Waivers or limitations to liability are also generally permitted, where not deemed "unconscionable" in law or fact.

## Duty to Receive Guests

The very first and most important "public duty" of the hotel is the duty to receive guests. But the duty is not absolute and is subject to lawful excuses. Hotels may generally deny accommodations to a prospective guest for the following reasons:

- if the person is unwilling or unable to pay for a room or other establishment privileges

- if the person is visibly under the influence of alcohol or other drugs or creating a public nuisance

- if the person's use of a room or accommodation would violate the facility's maximum capacity

- if the innkeeper reasonably believes the person will use the room or facility for an unlawful purpose

- if the innkeeper reasonably believes the person will bring in something that would create an unreasonable danger or risk to others

Generally speaking, to avoid liability for refusal to receive a prospective guest, hotels must reasonably believe a person is unable or unwilling to pay, plans to use the room or premises for an unlawful purpose; or plans to bring a potentially dangerous object onto the premises.

### Guest Reservations

Most hotels have well-established policies for making, confirming, and holding reservations placed by prospective guests. A confirmed reservation generally constitutes a binding agreement (in essence, a "reservation contract") between the hotel and prospective guest. If the guest fails to use the reservation, the hotel is generally entitled to damages. On the other hand, if the hotel breaches a reservation contract, the guest can sue the hotel for damages. If the hotel actually has accommodations available but fails to supply them as agreed, it may be liable for breach of its duties as an innkeeper.

Hotel overbooking often presents problems, and many hotels have adopted a pledge that requires their assistance in securing comparable accommodations, if, for any reason, a room should not be available for a patron who holds a valid confirmed reservation. A few states have enacted legislation that addresses hotel overbooking. Florida's law, for example, makes the hotel responsible for "every effort" to find alternate accommodations and up to a $500 fine for each guest turned away because of the overbooking.

## Right to Evict Persons Admitted as Guests

Hotels may generally evict a guest and keep the room rental payment, despite the **eviction**, for the following reasons:

- disorderly conduct

- nonpayment

- using the premises for an unlawful purpose or act

- bringing property onto the premises that may be dangerous to others

- failing to register as a guest

- using **false pretenses** to obtain accommodations

- being a minor unaccompanied by an adult registered guest

- violating federal, state, or local hotel laws or regulations

- violating a conspicuously posted hotel or motel rule

- failing to vacate a room at the agreed checkout time

Generally speaking, to avoid liability for evicting a guest, the guest must have refused to pay; or the innkeeper must reasonably have believed that the person used the room or premises for an unlawful purpose or brought a potentially dangerous object onto the premises.

## Duty to Persons Who Are Not Guests

A person who is not a guest (or intending immediately to become a guest) generally has no right to enter or remain on the premises over the objection of the hotel. Nor can a non-guest resort to public areas of the premises, such as lobbies or hallways, without the consent of the hotel. Despite the fact that the hotel has held itself out to the public with an invitation to enter and seek out accommodations, any person who enters without the intention of accepting an invitation for accommodations remains on the premises only by the consent of the hotel.

A widely-acknowledged exception to this general rule is that a non-guest or stranger coming to the hotel at the request or invitation of an existing guest has a right to enter the premises for that purpose; otherwise, the guest would unfairly be deprived of a privilege necessary for his or her comfort while at the hotel. However, the hotel may revoke such permission if the non-guest engages in conduct which would justify his or her eviction.

There is no duty to permit non-guests into the hotel public areas for the purpose of soliciting business from hotel guests. To the contrary, there is a duty to protect guests from bothersome or troublesome non-guests. Accordingly, most hotels have posted notices that prohibit **solicitation** of any kind on the premises.

## Duty to Provide Safe Premises

The duty of an hotel to provide safe premises is based on the common law duty owed to business and social invitees of an establishment. Under common law, hotels must exercise reasonable care for the safety of their guests. Hotels may be found negligent if they knew or should have known, upon reasonable inspection, of the existence of a danger or hazard and failed to take action to correct it and/or warn guests about it. Accordingly, hotels have an affirmative duty to inspect and seek out hazards that may not be readily apparent, seen or appreciated by patrons and guests. In addition, they may have an affirmative duty to warn guests of dangers or hazards. If the risk of harm or damage was foreseeable, and the hotel failed to exercise reasonable care to either eliminate the risk or warn guests of its existence, the hotel may be liable for any resulting harm or damage caused by its negligence ("proximate cause").

However, the law does not protect hotel guests from their own negligence. An "open and obvious" hazard, such as a bathroom tile floor that becomes slippery when wet after reasonable use, is not a basis for liability. On the other hand, if a poorly maintained bathroom fixture results in standing water on the tile floor, and an unsuspecting guest enters the bathroom and slips on the tile, the hotel would most likely be liable for damages. Likewise, standing water on any floor in the hotel, if left standing beyond a reasonable time for management to have detected and eliminated it, may result in liability for the hotel.

Hotel swimming pools are a major topic for **litigation** battles. After a rash of lawsuits in the 1970s, diving boards have disappeared from almost all hotel pools. But that has not stopped diving accidents from occurring as a result of swimmers leaping from the edges of pools, piers, and docks. It is important that "NO DIVING" signs are posted in highly visible areas. There is no minimum requirement regarding the number or nature of posted warnings, but a hotel's diving-accident history is key in establishing what would be considered "adequate," "sufficient," or "satisfactory" posted warnings in any legal matter. Statutes in most states do not require the presence of lifeguards at hotel pools. However, "NO LIFE-GUARD" warnings should be posted and visible from all angles of the pool. All water recreational facilities must have emergency telephone service.

### Harm or Damage Caused by Other Guests

Hotels have an affirmative duty to exercise reasonable care for the safety and security of their patrons. This obligation may include the duty to evict or otherwise restrain drunken or disorderly guests or patrons who may possibly cause harm to other guests or their property. However, the hotel also has a duty not to cause foreseeable injury or harm to the drunken or disorderly guest as a result of the eviction. Under those circumstances, hotels must seek more reasonable alternatives, such as contacting police and arranging safe transport of the drunken or disorderly guest or escorting the person back to his/her room (if this can be done safely without the risk of recurring problems).

A major area of liability exposure is in the serving of alcohol to guests and non-guests. If the hotel actually creates the risk of harm by serving alcohol to an already-intoxicated person, other laws come into play, most notably, state "dram-shop" acts. These laws generally provide that persons injured by intoxicated persons may sue the seller/provider of the alcohol (in this case, the hotel). Hotels can also lose their liquor licenses for serving minors, and, in many states, can be sued for a subsequent drunken driving accident caused by the minor.

Hotels also may be liable for the **personal injury** of guests caused by the criminal act of another patron or guest, if it can be established that the hotel was negligent or at fault. Criminal acts of other patrons do not always fall into the category of foreseeable risks that hotels can protect against. Nonetheless, in assessing potential fault of the hotel, several factors will be considered. Was the injury or harm reasonably preventable? Who was in charge of security? Were security personnel properly trained? Is there a past history of crime at the hotel? Were assessments of security risks ever established for the hotel? Were security personnel uniformed? Were there an adequate number of security persons on hand to handle routine matters as well as potential emergencies or crises?

### Harm or Damage Caused by Third Persons

Hotels have an affirmative duty to exercise reasonable care for the safety and security of their patrons. Therefore, they must protect their guests and employees from foreseeable criminal acts of third parties. In most states, a greater burden of protection is placed upon hotels than upon landlords and other business owners. However, the law in this area varies greatly from state to state. Most states hold that hotels are not liable for third-party crimes unless at fault (negligent) in reasonably protecting guests from foreseeable harm.

For example, numerous court decisions nationwide have found hotels liable for failing to provide adequate locks on doors and windows. While the lodging industry does not recognize an official "standard of security," there are several minimum safety and security measures that indicate compliance with "standard practices," and have in fact been used to establish legal precedent. These would include deadbolt locks, viewing devices (peepholes) on room doors, chain locks, communication devices (telephones to enable emergency calls for assistance), and track bars for sliding glass doors. Closed circuit television has been found to be fundamental to reasonable security in facilities with several entrances, high-risk parking lots, or remote locations.

It is fair to say that the ultimate test in establishing hotel liability is to ask whether the hotel had taken reasonable steps to prevent certain crimes, in light of the relevant facts and circumstances surrounding the particular incident. Often, the hotel is simply the location of a random crime. Other times, it is the preferred location for a particular type of crime, thereby enhancing the probability of its recurrence, and raising questions of potential liability.

Generally, the same or similar **assessment** of hotel security will be appropriate for crimes committed by third parties as for those committed by other guests or patrons. Ultimately, there must be fault on the part of the hotel in failing to prevent harm caused by foreseeable risks. The probability of occurrence of a particular crime or type of crime, as well as the level of care required from the hotel, are questions of fact which may vary from case to case.

### Natural Disasters, Acts of God, Public Enemies, Catastrophic Exposures

Common law and most state statutes excuse hotels from liability if guests are injured or harmed as the result of an act of God or natural disaster. Hotels are likewise not liable for terrorist acts or harm caused by public enemies. Most hotel insurance policies exclude coverage for catastrophic or widespread disasters which affect a great number of insureds or an unmanageable number of claimants. Acts of war, damages arising from nuclear energy, and certain exposures to pollutants are routinely eliminated from coverage. Notwithstanding, hotels are keenly sensitive to enabling guests to vacate the premises, in an orderly and speedy fashion, in the event of a catastrophe.

## Responsibility for Personal Property

To avoid liability, most hotels exempt themselves or substantially limit their liability for loss or damage to valuables kept in hotels rooms. Most will post conspicuous notices declaring that valuables worth more than a certain amount of money (e.g., $250) must be stored in the hotel safe in order to be covered for loss. When a hotel requests that a guest state a "declared value" for valuables, the hotel generally has the right, on behalf of its insurer, to inspect the valuables for stated value. Room safes are generally recommended only if they contain digital keypads, and the guest assumes all responsibility for getting into the safe and keeping the combination confidential.

A hotel is generally not liable for loss of luggage or other personal items belonging to guests of the hotel and lost in areas other than the guest's private room, unless the hotel or its employees are at fault.

## Statutory or Contractual Limitations on Liability

Hotels may waive, exclude, or limit liability coverage for certain losses or harms, including dollar amount limitations on loss of valuables, and may exclude from coverage any assaults or crimes committed by third parties. It is imperative that guests check their hotel's policies prior to checking in, to review its liability limitations.

All states have enacted legislation that permits hotels to limit their liability for damage to guests or their **personal property**. This action even may include limits placed on damages resulting from the hotel's own negligence ("exculpatory clauses"), unless found to be "unconscionable" in certain jurisdictions.

Whenever hotels intend to limit their liability, it is almost always required that they notify guests in a conspicuous manner. Failure to post adequate notices in conspicuous locations may result in a court finding that the limits are not in effect and that the hotel must cover the entire loss, if applicable.

## Innkeepers' Liens

Many states have retained the common law right of an "innkeeper's lien." If a hotel has properly evicted a guest, or if a guest refuses to leave or pay, the hotel may take into its possession the personal property of the guest and hold it as security for hotel charges. Innkeepers' liens differ from others in that the hotel need not take physical possession of the guest's personal property, but may simply prevent its removal from the hotel until the debt is satisfied. Hotels cannot sell the goods or personal property until there has been a final judgment in an action to recover charges.

## Good Samaritan Acts

Laws regarding Good Samaritan acts generally apply to hotel personnel in emergencies. Most states have Good Samaritan Acts that generally shield persons from liability if they try to save a life but fail. Florida was one of the first states to enact new legislation allowing hotel desk clerks, among others, to revive heart attack victims using automated defibrillators, without the fear of exposure to unreasonable lawsuits.

## Unusual Cases

In the 1996 case of Woods-Leber v. Hyatt Hotels of Puerto Rico, Inc., a federal district court found that the posh oceanfront Cerromar Beach Hotel in Dorado, Puerto Rico was not liable for damages caused by a rabid mongoose that entered upon the hotel grounds and bit a guest. The hotel had no control over adjacent bordering swamplands, and no history of recurrent visits from mongooses.

Nor was there liability in two bizarre swimming pool cases: one involved the death of a 12-year-old girl whose hair was caught in a whirlpool's suction; the other involved a Scottish Inn guest's **entrapment** when his genitals became stuck in the pool's suction hole. There is no duty to warn of unique hazards.

In 1999, several pre-lawsuit notices were filed against California hoteliers for alleged violations of California's controversial "Proposal 65 of 1986." The statute was intended to provide warnings about hazardous waste sites and contaminated water. However, lawyer Morse Mehrban, on behalf of the California Consumer Advocacy Group, sued Hilton Hotels, Fairfield Inns, and Residence Inns by Marriot for alleged violations of "Prop 65" involving guest exposure to chemicals in alcoholic beverages, chemicals in second-hand tobacco and cigar smoke, and noxious fumes in enclosed parking structures. Under the law, violations must be corrected within 60 days of notice. Prop 65 places primary burden on the manufacturer or packager of alcoholic and tobacco products, but responsibility shifts to hotels when products are separated from their original packaging, such as when hotels serve "house wine" or "house cigars" from hotel humidors. In such cases, liability can be avoided if hotels post required warning signs or correct the defect within the notice period.

## Selected State Innkeepers Laws

ALABAMA: See Title 34 of the Alabama Code of 1975, ACA 34-15. Hotel owners may eject guests for **intoxication**, **profanity**; lewdness, brawling, or otherwise disturbing the peace and comfort of others. Hotels must give oral notice to leave the premises and return the unused portion of any advance payment. Refusal to leave upon request is a **misdemeanor**.

ALASKA: See Title 8 of the Alaska Statute, Chapter 56, "Hotels and Boardinghouses." which discusses such issues as registration, refusal to register, liability for valuables, and baggage liability.

ARIZONA: See Title 44 of the Arizona Revised Statutes, Chapter 15. Arizona has special provisions for the posting of minimum and maximum rates, and a **statutory** requirement to have advertised accommodations available.

CALIFORNIA: See California Civil Code, Sections 1861-1865. Hotels may evict guests who refuse to depart at checkout, with proper notice of check-out time and a need to accommodate another arriving guest. Moreover, if a guest refuses to leave, the hotel owner may enter the room and take possession of the guest's personal property, re-key the door, and make the room available to new guests. The personal possessions may be sold to enforce an innkeeper's **lien**.

COLORADO: See Title 12 of the Colorado Revised Statutes Annotated, 12-44-302 codifies common law with respect to refusing accommodations to certain persons.

FLORIDA: See Florida Statutes Annotated, FSA 509.141. In addition to the usual reasons for evicting guests, Florida hotels may evict a person for injuring the facility's reputation, dignity, or standing.

GEORGIA: See Chapter 43 of the Georgia Code, 43-21-2, et seq; 48-13-50, et seq. Georgia has a very comprehensive statute that expressly outlines the rights and duties of hotels; much of it is carried over from common law.

IDAHO: See Titles 39 of the Idaho Code, Sections 39-1805 and 1809. The statute follows the common law general reasons for denying accommodations to or evicting guests. The statute expressly permits hotel owners to enter the rooms of guests who fail to pay and leave and remove personal property to be held by lien.

IOWA: See Iowa Code Annotated 137C.25C and 137C.25. Iowa follows the general rules for denying accommodations and for evictions.

KANSAS: See Kansas Statutes Annotated, 36-604 and 602. Kansas adds a few more categories to the general rights to evict guests: failing to register as a guest, using false pretenses to obtain accommodations, exceeding the guest room **occupancy** limits, or being a minor unaccompanied by a parent or **guardian**.

LOUISIANA: See Louisiana Statutes Annotated 21:75 and 76. Louisiana expressly requires that a hotel owner notify a guest at least one hour before the time to leave, before he may legally evict the guest. After this, the hotel may have law enforcement personnel remove the guest and personal belongings.

MINNESOTA: See Minnesota Statutes Annotated 327.73. Minnesota follows the general rules for denying accommodations and for evictions.

MISSOURI: See Missouri Revised Statutes, 315.075 and 315.067. Missouri follows the general rules for denying accommodations and for evictions.

MONTANA: See Montana Code Annotated 70-6-511 and 70-6-512. Montana follows the general rules for denying accommodations and for evictions and expressly adds the right to evict guests for refusing to abide by reasonable hotel standards or policies.

NORTH CAROLINA: See Chapters 72 of the North Carolina General Statutes, Article 1. North Carolina has express provisions that address liability for lost baggage, losses by fire, safeguarding of valuables, and hotel rights for negligence of the guest. North Carolina also has an express provision for the admittance of pets to hotel rooms.

OKLAHOMA: See Title 15 of the Oklahoma Statutes Annotated, OSA 15-5-8 and 506. Oklahoma follows the general rules for denying accommodations and for evictions.

OREGON: See Chapters 699 of the Oregon Revised Statutes, "Innkeepers and Hotelkeepers." Oregon's thorough statutory provisions cover liability for valuables, baggage, and other property. Special provisions address personal property left in a hotel for more than 60 days. Guests who refuse to leave or pay are deemed "trespassers" under Oregon law and may be removed by force without the hotel incurring liability.

PENNSYLVANIA: See Pennsylvania Statutes Annotated, PSA 37-106 and 103. Pennsylvania follows the general rules for denying accommodations and for evictions.

RHODE ISLAND: See RIGL 5-14-4 and 5-14-5. Rhode Island follows the general rules for denying accommodations and for evictions.

SOUTH CAROLINA: See South Carolina Statutes Annotated, SCSA 45-2-60 and 45-2-30. South Carolina follows the general rules for denying accommodations and for evictions.

TENNESSEE: See Tennessee Code Annotated 68-14-605 and 68-14-602. Tennessee follows the general rules for denying accommodations and for evictions.

UTAH: See the Utah Code Annotated, UCA 29-2-103. Utah follows the general rules for denying accommodations and for evictions.

## Additional Resources

"ADA Compliance Needs Practical Approach." Dawson, Adam, and Charles Sink. *Hotel & Motel Management,* 15 September 1997.

"California Hoteliers Fend Off Lawsuits Alleging Harmful Chemical Exposure." Carolyn Woodruff. *Hotel & Motel Management,* 19 July 1999.

*Hotel and Motel Fire Safety Act of 1990,* P.L. 101-391; 104 Stat. 747, as amended, P.L. 104-316, 1996.

"Innkeepers' Rights Regarding Guests." Sandra Norman-Eady. Available at http://www.law.cornell.edu/topics/civil_procedure.html

*The Laws of Innkeepers* Sherry, Jophn H. Cornell University Press, 1972.

"Protect Guests Against Third-party Crimes." James R. Butler, Jr. *Hotel & Motel Management,* 3 June 1996.

"Security Standards for the Lodging and Residential Industries." Published by the Foreseeable Risk Analysis Center. Available at http://www.frac.com/lodging.htm

*The Court TV Cradle-to-Grave Legal Survival Guide.* Little, Brown and Company. 1995.

*The Laws of Innkeepers.* John H. Sherry. Cornell University Press: 1972.

*U. S. Code, Title 42: Public Health and Welfare, Chapter 21: Civil Rights, Subchapter II: Public Accommodations.* U. S. House of Representatives, 1964. Available at http://uscode.house.gov/title_42.htm

"Your Uniform, Nametag and Defibrillator." *Lodging Hospitality,* 15 July 2001.

## Organizations

### The American Hotel & Motel Association (AH & MA)
1201 New York Avenue. NW, #600
Washington, DC 20005-3931 USA
Phone: (202) 289-3100
Fax: ()
URL: http://www.ahma.com

### The Educational Institute of American Hotel & Lodging Association
800 North Magnolia Avenue, #1800
Orlando, FL, FL 32803 USA
Phone: (800) 752-4567

# TRAVEL

## INTERNATIONAL TRAVEL

*Sections in This Essay:*

## The U. S. Government's Representatives Abroad

Embassies are the official diplomatic representation of one sovereign government to another. The principal person in charge of an embassy is usually an ambassador. An ambassador is the official representative from the head of state of one country to the host country. Embassies are primarily responsible for maintaining government-to-government communications and business. Embassies generally do not perform functions directly for nationals from their home country who may be travelling or residing in their host country.

Supervision of U. S. embassies is the job of the U. S. Department of State (DOS), under the administration of the U. S. Secretary of State. The DOS is the large governmental department that manages relations with foreign governments and helps to interpret and implement U. S. policies around the world. It also assists U. S. citizens abroad. The DOS divides its embassies, consulates, and other diplomatic posts into six geographical regions. These are:

- Africa

- East Asia and the Pacific

- Europe

- Near East

- South Asia

- The Western Hemisphere

There is an embassy in almost every country with which the United States maintains diplomatic relations; the embassy is usually located in the capital. Each embassy contains a consular section. Consular officers in consular sections of embassies perform two primary functions:

- they issue visas to foreigners wishing to travel to the United States, and

- they help U. S. citizens abroad.

In some countries, the United States may have a consulate general or a consulate to assist the embassy in handling its business. These are different from the consular section within embassies. Consulates General or consulates are regional offices of embassies. When U. S. citizens travel abroad, they may want to register at the U. S. embassies or consulates at the countries they visit. When they register at an U. S. embassy or consulate, it makes their presence and whereabouts are known, in case it is necessary for a consular officer to contact them. It is a good idea for them to register at the Consular Section of the nearest U. S. embassy or consulate, especially if their stay in a country will be longer than one month. They should also consider registering at the nearest U. S. embassy or consular office if they are traveling in a country or area that is experiencing civil unrest, is politically unstable, or has experienced a recent natural disaster.

American consular officers can help evacuate U. S. citizens from a country were that to become necessary, but they cannot help them if they do not know where the travelers are. Registration also makes it easier for travelers to apply for a replacement **passport**, if theirs becomes lost or stolen. Sometimes, registration will be done for them if they are traveling with an organized tour to areas experiencing unrest or political upheaval.

## Consulates

U. S. consulates are a special division or office located at U. S. embassies and sometimes in other important cities or regions in foreign countries. The officials who work at consulates are known as consular officers. They can give advice and assistance if travelers are in serious trouble. Their services are loosely grouped into none-emergency services and emergency services. Non-emergency services include providing information about Selective Service registration, travel safety, **absentee voting**, and how to acquire or lose U. S. citizenship. Also, they can arrange for the transfer of Social Security and other Federal benefits to beneficiaries residing abroad, provide U. S. tax forms, and notarize documents.

Emergency services are often the most crucial functions of the consulate. Travelers may need the emergency services of a consulate in the following situations:

- If travelers need emergency funds, consulates can help them get in touch with their families, friends, bank, or employer and tell them how to arrange for money to be sent.

- If travelers become ill or injured, the nearest U. S. embassy or consulate can provide them with a list of local doctors, dentists, medical specialists, clinics and hospitals. If the illness or injury is serious, they can help travelers find medical assistance and can inform their family or friends of their condition. Because travelers must pay their own hospital and other expenses, they may want to consider purchasing additional or supplemental medial insurance before they travel abroad.

- If travelers get married abroad, their marriage must be performed according to local law. There will be documentary requirements to marry in a foreign country, and in some countries, they may be asked to complete a lengthy residence requirement before their marriage may take place. Before traveling, U. S. citizens need to ask the embassy or consulate of the country in which they plan to marry about the marriage regulations and how best to prepare to marry abroad. Once abroad, the Consular Section of the nearest U. S. embassy or consulate may be able to answer some of their questions, but it is the travelers' responsibility to comply with local laws and to interact with local civil authorities.

- If a U. S. citizens child is born abroad, their children generally acquires U. S. citizenship at birth. As soon as possible after the birth, they should contact the nearest U. S. embassy or consulate to obtain a Report of Birth Abroad of a Citizen of the United States of America. This document will serve as proof of U. S. citizenship, and is acceptable **evidence** for obtaining a U. S. passport for a child. It is also acceptable for most other purposes where parents must show a birth certificate or proof of citizenship for their child.

- If U. S. citizens plan to adopt a child overseas, they should know that the U. S. government looks on foreign adoptions as private, legal matters subject to the sovereign **jurisdiction** of the nation in which the child is residing. U. S. embassy or consular officers may not intervene on prospective parents' behalf in the courts of the country where the **adoption** takes place. Even so, there are a ways in which U. S. embassies and consulates can assist them in an overseas adoption.

These officials can provide them with information on the adoption process in that particular country, inquire about the status of their case in the foreign court, help to explain the requirements for documents, try to ensure that they will not be discriminated against by foreign courts, and provide them with information about the **visa** application process for their adopted child.

- If the death of a U. S. citizen occurs abroad, the consular officer reports the death to the **next of kin** or **legal representative**. The consular officer will prepare a Report of the Death of An American Citizen. This document will provide the facts concerning the death and the **custody** of the personal effects of the deceased. The consular officer also arranges to obtain from them kin the necessary private funds for local burial or return of the body to the United States because the U. S. Government will not pay for local burial or shipment of human remains to the United States. However, travelers may purchase private insurance to cover these expenses. As a first step toward simplifying the process for their loved ones in the event of a death while traveling abroad, travelers should complete the address page in the front of their passports, and do provide the name, address and telephone number of someone to be contacted in an emergency.

## Other Travel Information

### Health and Immunizations

Depending on their destination abroad, travelers may need to show proof that they were immunized against certain diseases. It is a good idea to check with representatives of the countries they intend to visit to make sure they comply with any immunization requirements they may have. The requirements vary based on specific diseases. Travelers may find that countries with more tropical climates may require international certificates of vaccination against yellow fever and cholera. Generally, typhoid vaccinations are not required for international travel, but may be recommended for countries where there is a risk of exposure. Smallpox vaccinations are not required anywhere. And it is a good idea for travelers to check their health care records to make sure that their measles, mumps, rubella, polio, diphtheria, tetanus, and pertussis immunizations are current. Pre-

ventative measures are advisable for certain areas, such as quinine in areas prone to outbreaks of malaria. Regardless of where U. S. citizens travel, the United States currently requires no immunizations for citizens returning from travel abroad.

If travelers must receive vaccinations, they should keep a record of them on approved forms. An increasing number of countries require that people entering their countries be tested for Human Immune deficiency Virus (HIV) prior to entry. The HIV test is usually included in a medical exam for long term visitors (i.e., students and workers). Before people travel abroad, check with the embassy or consulate of the country that they intend to visit to learn about the health or immunization requirements for visiting their countries, and whether they require an AIDS/HIV test as a condition to enter their countries.

### Foreign Laws

When U. S. citizens are in a foreign country, they are subject to its laws. It helps to learn about local laws and regulations and to obey them. Travelers should learn the local laws and customs before they consider selling their personal effects like clothing, cameras, or jewelry. The penalties for disobeying local laws can be quite severe, regardless of how such an act would be viewed or treated in the United States. Some governments are especially sensitive about tourists taking photographs. Basically, it is a good idea to avoid photographing police, and anything to do with the military and industrial facilities, including harbors, railroads, and airports. Taking pictures of these subjects may result in travelers' being detained, their cameras and film being confiscated, and their being fined. People need to check with the country's embassy or consulate for information on restrictions on photography.

### Drug Arrests

About 1,000 Americans are arrested abroad on drug charges each year. Many countries strictly enforce their drug laws and impose very severe penalties for drug violations. When people travel abroad, they are subject to the laws of the countries in which they travel, not to U. S. laws. **Criminal procedure** in other countries can be very different from U. S. criminal procedure, especially in cases of drug-related offenses. If travelers are arrested, they will find the following is the case:

- Jury trials are often not allowed.

- Trials can be very long, with many delays and unaccountable postponements.

- Most countries do not have a system for accepting bail.

- Pre-trial detention, which is often carried out in solitary confinement, may last for many months.

If U. S. citizens are convicted on a drug charge, they face the possibility of the following:

- 2 - 10 years in jail,

- In some countries, there is a minimum of 6 years hard labor and a steep fine, and, in a number of countries,

- Tthe death penalty (e.g. Malaysia, Pakistan, Turkey, Thailand, and Saudi Arabia).

### Getting Legal Assistance

If U. S. citizens become involved in legal difficulties abroad, there is little that the U. S. embassy or a consular officer can do for them. American officials are limited by foreign as well as U. S. laws. In short, a consular officer cannot get them out of a foreign jail, nor can they serve as their attorney or give them legal advice. They can, however, provide them with a list of local attorneys. These lists of attorneys are compiled from local **bar association** lists and responses to United States Department of State questionnaires, although the embassy or consular staff cannot vouch for the competence of any particular local attorney.

If U. S. citizens are arrested, they should ask the local authorities to inform a consular officer at the nearest U. S. embassy or consulate. International agreements and diplomatic practice give them the right to talk to the U. S. consul. If the local authorities refuse to inform the nearest U. S. embassy or consular office, try to have someone else get in touch with the U. S. consular officer for. Once they know that U. S. citizens has been arrested, U. S. officials will visit them, advise them of their rights under the local laws, and contact their family and friends, if they wish. Additionally, U. S. consuls can arrange to send money, food, and clothing to the appropriate authorities from their family or friends. If they are being held in unhealthy or inhumane conditions, they will work to get relief for them.

## Passports

A passport is "a document issued by competent authority (which is a state or the United Nations Organization), evidencing the right, arising from law, of the person named and described in the document to travel abroad, and, in relation to a state, authenticating his right to diplomatic protection and consular services" (Stephen Krueger, Krueger on United States Passport Law [Hong Kong: Crossbow Corporation, 2001], 6). "State" in this sense means a nation state or country, not one of the fifty states in the United States.

### Who Needs a Passport

U. S. citizens need passports to depart or enter the United States and to enter and depart most foreign countries. There are a few exceptions for short-term travel between the United States and Mexico, Canada, and some countries in the Caribbean, where a U. S. birth certificate or other proof of U. S. citizenship may be accepted. But even if people need not have a passport to visit a foreign country, the United States requires one to prove U. S. citizenship and identity to reenter the United States. Hence, travelers need to provide documentation when they pass through United States **Immigration** upon their return. U. S. passports are the best proof of U. S. citizenship. Travelers may also use one of the following:

- an expired U. S. passport

- a **certified copy** of a U. S. birth certificate

- a Certificate of Naturalization

- a Certificate of Citizenship

- a Report of Birth Abroad of a Citizen of the United States

All U. S. citizens must have their own passport. Family members may not be included on any passport. This applies to everyone, even newborn babies. To obtain their first passport, citizens must appear in person at one of the 13 U. S. passport agencies, along with a completed Form DS-11, Passport Application. They may also apply for a passport at one of many federal and state courts, **probate** courts, county/municipal offices, or at U. S. post offices authorized to accept passport applications.

If applying for the first time, applicants who are 16 and older must appear in person when applying for a passport. Minors aged 13, 14, and 15 must also appear in person, and must be accompanied by a parent or legal **guardian**. Applicants ages 16 and 17 may apply on their own as long as they have acceptable identification. The passport agency may contact their parent or legal guardian to confirm that the parent or legal guardian gives permission to issue the passport. If a passport applicant is a minor and has no identification, then the parent or legal guardian must accompany the applicant. For children under age 13, a parent or legal guardian may appear and apply for a passport on their behalf. If individuals previously had a U. S. passport and wish to obtain a new one, they may be able to apply by mail.

It may take many weeks to process the application for a passport. If possible, individuals should apply for their passport several months before they plan to depart on their trip abroad. If they also need to apply for visas, they need to allow approximately two weeks per visa. Finally, if their U. S. passport becomes altered or mutilated, it may be invalid. If they alter or mutilate it themselves, they may be prosecuted (Section 1543, Title 22 of the **U.S. Code**).

### Keep a Passports Safe

Carelessness is the principal reason travelers lose their passports. People may need to carry their passport with them because they must show it to cash traveler's checks or the country that they are visiting requires them to carry it as an identity document. When they must carry their passport, they must conceal it securely on their person. It should not be put it in a purse, handbag, or in an outer pocket. When possible, it should be deposited passport in the hotel's safe. It should not be left Do not leave it in the hotel room or m, and do not try to conceal it in pieces of luggage. One member of a group should not carry all the passports for the entire group.

Criminals sometimes use stolen U. S. passports to enter the United States illegally or to help them establish false identities. This can cause distress and embarrassment to innocent U. S. citizens whose names become associated with illegal activity. Travelers should be aware that consular officers overseas may take certain precautions to process lost passport cases. Should they lose their passport while traveling abroad, these precautions may in turn cause them some delay before their new passport is issued.

If their passports is are lost or stolen abroad, travelers should report the loss immediately to the local police and to the nearest U. S. embassy or consulate. It will help speed the replacement process if travelers can provide the consular officer with the information contained in their passport. Their passport is the most important document that they will carry abroad. It is proof of their U. S. citizenship. It should never be used it as **collateral** for a loan, nor should someone lend it to anyone. It is the best form of identification. Travelers may need it when they pick

up mail or check into hotels, or when they register at embassies or consulates.

When entering some countries or registering at hotels, travelers may be asked to fill out a police card listing their names, passport numbers, destinations, local addresses, and reasons for travel. They may be required to leave their passport at the hotel reception desk overnight so that the local police may check it. These are normal procedures required by local laws. However, if the passport is not returned the following morning, immediately report the seizure to the local authorities and to the nearest U. S. embassy or consulate.

### Passport Records

Passport Services maintains records of passport information on individuals for the period from 1925 to the present. These records contain applications for U. S. passports and supporting evidence of U. S. citizenship. The records' contents are protected by the Privacy Act. The Privacy Act permits individuals to obtain copies of passport records in their own name. The National Archives and Records Administration maintains records for passports issued prior to 1925.

## Visas

A visa is an endorsement by a foreign country that permits individuals to visit that country for a defined purpose and for a specific duration. It usually comes in the form of a stamp placed in their passport. Their visa to visit a foreign country will indicate the length of time of their visit, as well as the scope of activities they may perform while in that country. Probably the most common visas are travel visas that identify people as a tourists visiting the country for leisure purposes. But, there are also visas that permit them to work and earn income in a country or visas that allow them to attend a college or university in that country, or possibly a visa that indicates they are a members of the U. S. diplomatic corps on official business. It is best to apply for visas before individuals leave the United States. They may not be able to obtain visas for some countries after they have left the United States.

U. S. citizens should apply for a visa directly to the embassy or nearest consulate of each country they plan to visit. Visas are stamped directly onto a blank page in their passport, so they will need to give their passport to an official of each foreign embassy or consulate along with their application for a visa.

When applying for a visa, individuals will usually be asked to fill out a form and submit one or more photographs with the form. They should also be aware that many countries require a fee to accompany visa applications. The application process may take several weeks, depending on the country where they apply for a visa.

## Customs

U. S. customs laws help regulate the conduct of business, protect U. S. citizens from harmful diseases, and protect U. S. crops and livestock from damaging foreign diseases, infections, and other pests. The customs laws also reflect U. S. policy on environmental issues. The United States Customs Service is the agency with primary responsibility for protecting the nation's borders. It has an extensive air, land, and marine interdiction force and with an investigative branch supported by its own intelligence resources. Among its areas of responsibility, the U. S. Customs Service is charged with overseeing the importation of goods into the country.

### Before Departing the United States

Before individuals travel abroad, it is helpful to learn about U. S. Customs regulations. The regulations apply to things they take from the United States as well as items they bring into the United States from abroad. Foreign-made items taken abroad (e.g. a Swiss watch or Japanese camera) are subject to U. S. Customs duty and tax upon return, unless they have proof they possessed them before they left the United States. A receipt, **bill of sale**, insurance policy, or a jeweler's **appraisal** usually is sufficient proof of prior ownership. In some cases, it may be necessary to register their foreign-made goods that they intend to take on their trip abroad. If they do not have sufficient proof of prior ownership, but their property includes foreign-made items that can be identified by serial number or some other permanent marking, travelers can take them to a Customs office or to the port of departure for registration. There they can obtain a certificate of registration, which can expedite free entry of these items when they return to the United States.

### Bringing Foreign Products into the United States

The United States prohibits travelers from bringing many fruits, vegetables, meats, plants, soil, and other products from abroad into the United States. These products may carry harmful insects or diseases that could damage U. S. crops, forests, gardens, and

livestock. In general, travelers may not bring the products in person, nor can they import them through the mail. In addition to these items, it is a crime to bring many wildlife souvenirs into the United States. These crimes are specified in U. S. laws and in international treaties. The list of prohibited items is long, and includes those made from sea turtle shell, reptile skins or leathers, ivory, furs from endangered species, as well as items manufactured from coral reefs. Consequently, travelers should not purchase wildlife souvenirs, especially if they are unsure about being able to bring them legally into the United States. The penalties for violating these laws are severe; at the very least, the purchases could be confiscated.

When returning to the United States from a trip abroad, if travelers needed their passport for their trip, they will need it when they go through U. S. Immigration and Customs. If they took other documents with them such as an International Certificate of Vaccination, international driver's license, medical documents, a customs certificate of registration for foreign-made personal articles, they will need them upon their re-entry to the United States.

### Tax Considerations

When individuals buy goods abroad and bring them back to the United States, they are subject to **taxation** on the value of those goods. Currently, travelers may bring back $400 worth of foreign-acquired goods without having to pay a duty on those goods, known as "duty free" merchandise. There are some important limitations to the duty free exemption:

- travelers must have been outside the United States for at least 48 hours,

- they may not have imported duty free goods within 30 days, and

- they must be able to present the purchases for inspection upon their arrival at the port of entry.

After travelers have used their exemption on their first $400 worth of duty free goods, the next $1,000 worth of items they bring back for personal use or gifts are subject to duty, taxed at 10%. For some products, there are additional limits on the quantity they may bring into the United States duty free:. For example,

- 100 cigars,

- 200 cigarettes, and

- one liter of wine, beer, or liquor.

Depending on where travelers purchased some items, their duty free exemption may be higher. The exemption is $600 for goods purchased in any of 24 specific countries in the Caribbean and Central America. For a group of U. S. possessions (the U.S. Virgin Islands, American Samoa, and Guam), the exemption is $1,200.

## Additional Resources

*http://travel.state.gov/americansabroad.html.* "Americans Abroad." U. S. Department of State, 2002.

*http://travel.state.gov/asafetripabroad.html.* "A Safe Trip Abroad." U. S. Department of State, 2002.

*http://travel.state.gov/foreignentryreqs.html.* "Foreign Entry Requirements." U. S. Department of State, 2002.

*Krueger on United States Passport Law.* Hong Kong: Crossbow Corporation, 2001.

*http://travel.state.gov/passport_services.html.* "Passport Services." U. S. Department of State, 2002.

*http://www.embassyworld.com/.* "Directory & Search Engine of the World's Embassies & Consulates." EmbassyWorld.com, 2002.

*http://travel.state.gov/americansabroad.html.* "Americans Abroad." U.S. Department of State, 2002.

*http://travel.state.gov/asafetripabroad.html.* "A Safe Trip Abroad." U.S. Department of State, 2002.

*http://travel.state.gov/foreignentryreqs.html.* "Foreign Entry Requirements." U.S. Department of State, 2002.

*http://www.customs.ustreas.gov/index.htm.* "U. S. Customs Service." U. S. Customs Service, 2002.

*http://www.customs.ustreas.gov/travel/travel.htm.* "Traveler Information." U. S. Customs Service, 2002.

*Krueger on United States Passport Law* Crossbow Corporation, 2001.

*http://www.customs.ustreas.gov/travel/travel.htm.* "Traveler Information." U.S. Customs Service, 2002.

## Organizations

### United States Department of State
2201 C Street NW
Washington, DC, DC 20520 USA
Phone: (202) 647-4000
URL: http://www.state.gov

### U.nited States. Department of State
Public Inquiries, Visa Services
Washington, DC, DC 20522-0106 USA
Phone: (202) 663-1225

### United. States Customs Service
1300 Pennsylvania Ave., N.W.
Washington, D.C., DC 20229 USA
Phone: (202) 927-1000
URL: http://www.customs.ustreas.gov/index.htm

# TRAVEL

## PASSPORTS AND VISAS

*Sections within this essay:*

- Background

- Obtaining a Passport
    - Applying in Person
    - Proof of Citizenship
    - No-Fee Passports
    - Photographs
    - Children Under 14

- National Passport Information Centers (NPIC)

- Visas
    - From the United States
    - To the United States

- Additional Resources

## Background

The U. S. Department of State issues nearly seven million passports to U. S. citizens every year. For most people, obtaining a **passport** is a fairly routine experience. In fact, a passport is more than just a personal identification document. A passport is actually a guarantee to the bearer that he or she can travel freely and securely through other countries.

Not all countries are willing or able to grant unimpeded travel and protection to others. Countries that are at war with each other or whose diplomatic ties are strained or broken will likely not permit their citizens to travel to territory designated as dangerous or unfriendly. Visas, or endorsements, indicate that a government has examined the traveler's passport

and that the traveler can continue on. Some countries do not require a formal **visa** process; others insist that visitors obtain visas, sometimes well in advance of their trips.

Because a passport is an important identification document, applicants must prove that they are who they are, and they also must prove citizenship. Proof can be established through birth or baptismal certificates or other documents; sometimes **affidavit** from people who know the applicant are necessary. Passports are the property of the governments that issue them and must be returned on demand.

## Obtaining a Passport

Anyone who wishes to travel abroad needs a passport, as does anyone whose work requires overseas travel. Some countries, such as Canada and Mexico, do not require U. S. citizens to show passports upon crossing the border; other forms of identification such as a driver's license will suffice. Still, it is a good idea to have a passport because it is a much more reliable means of establishing identity and nationality.

The fee for a first-time passport is $60, which includes a $45 passport fee and a $15 **execution** fee. Applicants under 16 pay $40 (the passport fee is $25). Renewing a passport costs $40.

The average wait for a passport is six weeks. For those who need a passport sooner, expedited service is available (the waiting period is only two weeks) for an additional $35. Passport officials recommend that to further expedite a passport, the application should be sent via overnight delivery and the applicant should include a pre-paid overnight delivery envelope in which the passport can be sent. This cost must be paid by the applicant in addition to the expedited service fee.

### Applying in Person

Individuals can apply for their passports by mail unless they are applying for the first time. If a previous passport was issued more than 15 years ago or when a person was under the age of 16, the individual will also need to apply in person; likewise if the person's name has changed or if the old passport was lost, stolen, or damaged. Minors under the age of 14 do not need to appear as a matter of course, but passport officials have the right to ask the child to appear.

There are 13 Regional Passport Agency offices across the country; they are located in Boston, Chicago, Honolulu, Houston, Los Angeles, Miami, New Orleans, New York, Norwalk (Connecticut), Philadelphia, San Francisco, Seattle, and Washington, DC. These offices are open to the public by appointment only, and appointments are usually only granted to people who need urgent action on a passport application (for example, if they need a passport in less than two weeks). For routine passport applications, there are 4,500 designated passport application acceptance facilities across the United States.

### Proof of Citizenship

To obtain a U.S. passport, individuals must prove that they are U. S. citizens. A previous U. S. passport will suffice, but if they do not have one they will need to supply either a certified birth certificate, a naturalization certificate, or a consular report of birth abroad. A birth certificate must have been issued within one year of their births to be acceptable. A later, or delayed certificate may be valid if it comes with affidavits from an attending physician or midwife or the parents.

If individuals do not have certified birth certificates, they will need a "letter of no record" issued by the state and listing their name and date of birth while also noting that there is no birth record. In addition they will need as many other documents as they can provide, including baptismal certificates, school or family Bible records, or physician's records. A parent or other older relative can submit an "Affidavit of Birth" claiming personal knowledge of when the individual was born. In addition, individuals can ask a friend to vouch for them. This friend must be a U. S. citizen and a permanent resident, have a valid identification, and have known them for

at least two years. He or she must fill out a special form in the presence of the passport agent.

### No-Fee Passports

Certain travelers may be able to receive a passport free of charge, known as a "no- fee" passport. Those eligible for no-fee passports include members of the armed services and their dependents, diplomats or other government officials, family members of a deceased member of the U. S. Armed Forces, and Peace Corps volunteers. (Anyone who applies for a no-fee passport in person may have to pay the $15 execution fee, but that fee can be waived.) Essentially these passports are sponsored by the agency or group that the applicant represents.

The no-fee passport is valid only for specific travel. Peace Corps volunteers can use no-fee passports to go to and from the countries in which they are working. Members of a deceased soldier's family must be traveling to visit that soldier's grave. Diplomats and other government officials must be traveling on government business. For personal travel, a regular passport is required. It is acceptable to hold both a regular and a no-fee passport. No-fee passports are not sent directly to the applicant; they are mailed to the sponsoring organization and applicants must pick them up.

### Photographs

Two copies of a current (no older than six months) photograph are required as part of the passport application. It should be full face, front view, and be 2x2 inches in size. (There should be between 1 inch and 1 3/8 inches from the bottom of the chin to the top of the head.) Passport photos should be taken in normal street attire, and officials remind applicants that photos showing the applicant smiling or looking relaxed are welcome. Hats are not acceptable, nor are non-prescription glasses that are dark or tinted. Uniforms are not allowed although members of the clergy can wear religious attire if it is worn daily. Photos can be either color or black-and-white.

Photos from vending machines are usually not acceptable for passport photos. It is usually quite easy to find a photo service near a passport acceptance center, where photos are taken for a nominal fee. Regarding application for a passport for a baby or youngster, be aware that some photographers will not take pictures of infants or toddlers because it can be difficult to get them to cooperate.

### Children Under 14

Children are required to submit the same forms for passport application as adults, but their parents or guardians must submit identification to ensure that they are in fact the child's parents or guardians. Each parent must submit identification forms; if only one parent is submitting forms he or she must have **evidence** that the other parent has consented or a court order showing sole **custody** of the child or a valid death certificate if the other parent is deceased.

For adoptive parents whose children were born overseas and who do not acquire U. S. citizenship at birth, the Child Citizenship Act confers citizenship automatically as soon as the **adoption decree** is final. A **certified copy** of this decree needs to be presented to obtain a U. S. passport for the child. Because this law has only been effect since February 2001, there is still some lack of familiarity, and occasionally there might be confusion as far as which documents to submit and in what form. It is probably best to err on the side of caution; for example, adoptive parents should not send originals of any adoption document when mailing material to a passport agency office. It is probably a good idea to speak to the adoption agency and someone knowledgeable in **immigration** law, as well as passport officials, when applying for a passport for an adopted child.

## National Passport Information Centers (NPIC)

In the 20 years between 1975 and 1995 the number of passports issued by the U. S. Department of State more than doubled, from just over 2.3 million to nearly 5.3 million. The workload increased more that 70 percent, but the number of employees handling the work remained unchanged. In 1996 the State Department opened the National Passport Information Center (NPIC) to answer the public's questions about passports. NPIC is a fee-based service; callers either dial a 900 number for up to $1.05 per minute or an 888 number for a flat rate of $4.95 per call. The money collected goes toward running NPIC; the State Department receives no income from the center, nor does the government provide it with tax dollars. The reason the State Department decided to create NPIC was service. With more passport-related calls coming in but no additional staff to handle the volume, callers often had to wait on hold, sometimes for lengthy periods. While there was no charge for the service, many callers were frustrated at what they saw as a waste of their time. Thanks to NPIC, waits are shorter and callers are greeted by people who are not nearly so overextended. Today, people calling for anything other than the most basic

information about passports will need to call NPIC. The phone numbers are 1-900-225-5674 or 1-888-362-8668. (For the hearing impaired, the TDD numbers are 1-900-225-7778 and 1-888- 498-3648.)

## Visas

### From the United States

Each country has different passport and visa requirements for U. S. citizens. The most commonly visited countries, such as those in Western Europe, generally do not require visas; other countries do require visas, sometimes with specific stipulations. Still other countries require some sort of additional or substitute documentation, usually to ensure that the traveler is merely visiting as a tourist.

Countries with which the United States has troubled relations may require more documentation, from both that country and from the United States. The United States will not allow its citizens to travel to certain countries except for clearly defined business purposes. Because governmental changes in some countries can happen with remarkable speed, it is advisable for travelers to know whether their visit will put them at risk. The Bureau of Consular Affairs at the U. S. State Department keeps an updated list of visa requirements for traveling to every country at its web site http://travel.state.gov/foreignentryreqs.html. Travelers should also contact the foreign embassy or consulate of the country they wish to visit; most often these offices are in Washington, D. C., or New York. Although some countries, such as Canada, Mexico, and certain Caribbean nations, do not require a U. S. passport, it is still a good idea to carry one because of its value as an identification document.

### To the United States

Overseas visitors who wish to visit the United States usually require a visa. Most people come to the United States for business or tourism; others, taking advantage of highly skilled American medical facilities, may come to the United States for medical treatment. In general, a visa application asks the individual to state the purpose and length of the visit. It also asks for proof that the applicant has a domicile outside the United States, along with binding ties such as family members; this is to ensure that he or she plans to return home after the visit.

To obtain a visa, a foreign visitor must submit an application form with a nonrefundable $45; a valid passport, and two photographs 1.5 inches square.

Some 29 countries around the world participate in the Visa **Waiver** Program, which allows visitors to travel without applying for a visa. These countries include most of Western Europe, as well as such countries as Australia, New Zealand, Singapore, Argentina, and Iceland. Travelers visiting under the Visa Waiver Program may only stay for 90 days and must submit proof of financial **solvency**. Overseas travelers can get information from the nearest U. S. Embassy office, or they can visit http://travel.state.gov/visa;visitors.html.

Travel agents are often able to provide many of the forms and applications necessary, in addition to updated travel guidelines and advisories.

## Additional Resources

*The United States Passport: Past, Present, Future.* U. S. Department of State, 1976.

## Organizations

### American Society of Travel Agents (ASTA)
1101 King Street, Suite 200
Alexandria, VA 22314 USA
Phone: (703) 739-2782
Fax: (703) 684-8319
URL: http://www.ast a.org
Primary Contact: Richard M. Copland, President and CEO

### United States Customs Service
1300 Pennsylvania Avenue, NW
Washingtona, DC 20229 USA
Phone: (202) 927-1000
URL: http://customs.ustreas.gov
Primary Contact: Robert C. Bonner, Commissioner of Customs

### U. S. Department of State, Bureau of Consular Affairs
2201 C Street NW
Washington, DC 20520 USA
Phone: (202) 647-4000
Fax: (202) 647-5225 (Overseas Citizens Services)
URL: http://travel.state.gov/passport_services.html
Primary Contact: Georgia Rogers, Deputy Assistant Secretary for Passport Services

# TRAVEL

## SAFETY

*Sections within this essay:*

- Background

- Federal and Global Protections

- The Travel Industry
    - Liability of Travel Agencies
    - Airline Travel
    - Cruise Line Travel
    - Bus and Rail Tours and Packaged Tours

- Special Considerations for International Travel

- Select State Provisions for the Licensing and Regulation of Travel Agents or Sellers

- Additional Resources

## Background

Both domestic and international travelers are often exposed to unique risks and dangers not common to other activities or industries. In the course of travel, direct control over the safety and welfare of travelers is effectively transferred to others (often unknown third parties). In some instances, the law imposes "strict liability" upon these third parties, whereas in other circumstances, there must be fault on the part of the third party before a traveler may recover damages for injury or harm.

However, the issue of travel safety invokes more consideration than merely the identification of potentially liable parties. Of particular concern is the myriad of complex bodies of law that affect different

aspects of travel safety, e.g., maritime law, aviation law, hotel law, consumer law, etc. This is further complicated in instances of international travel, which may invoke questions of **jurisdiction** and choice of law rules.

## Federal and Global Protections

At the global level, one must consider the many provisions contained in international treaties and federal statutes which address issues of travel safety. Among them are the following:

- The Warsaw Convention (Convention for the Unification of Certain Rules Relating to International Carriage by Air Signed at Warsaw on 12 October 1929): Among other things, this body of law governs the legal rights of international travelers to sue airlines for physical injuries or death suffered on an airliner. The amended Warsaw Convention provides that airlines have strict liability (providing an automatic entitlement without proof of fault) up to $100,000 SDRs ("Special Drawing Rights," equivalent to approximately $135,000 U.S. dollars).

- The Athens Convention and The Hague Convention.

- The Death on the High Seas Act (DOHSA), 49 **USC** 40120, governs crashes occurring more than one marine league (approximately three miles) from land. The DOHSA limits recovery to pecuniary damages only.

- The Ford Federal Aviation Reauthorization Act of 2000, PL 106-181, which, among other things, amends provisions of the above DOHSA to clarify that crashes within 12 nautical miles ("territorial waters") from U.S. shores will be adjudicated by domestic state and federal laws and not DOHSA.

- The Foreign Sovereign Immunities Act, 28 USC 1330, governs the **waiver** of **sovereign immunity** for foreign governments whose airlines cause injuries in the United States.

Domestically, major issues of travel safety fall under the Department of Transportation (DOT) and the DOT's Federal Aviation Administration (FAA), and to a lesser degree, the National Transportation Safety Board (which is not affiliated with the DOT but is responsible for investigating air accidents), the Department of State, U.S. Customs, and the Department of Health's Center for Disease Control (CDC).

As part of the Aviation and Transportation Security Act of 2001, P.L. 107-71, the Bush Administration created the Transportation Security Administration (TSA), an arm of the Department of Homeland Security. These entities are concerned with traveler safety from a security perspective. They include initiatives such as airport passenger screening and color-coded homeland security alerts for travelers.

## The Travel Industry

Congress has used the Commerce Clause as authority to enact other laws affecting travel safety. One such law is the Air Carrier Access Act of 1986 (49 CFR 382), which prohibits **discrimination** and requires physical accommodation of passengers with disabilities. Airlines may not require advance notice that a person with a **disability** is traveling (with certain exceptions involving special equipment or hook-ups), and airlines are prohibited from restricting the number of **disabled persons** on a flight.

As a general rule, "common carriers," such as airlines, cruise line, bus and rail operators, are held to a higher standard of care owed to passengers and travelers. Common carriers cannot require or request patrons to sign contracts that purport to disclaim liability caused by the **gross negligence** or intentional misconduct of the common carrier or its agents/employees. Nor may common carriers attempt to enforce such a disclaimer even if it appears on a passenger ticket.

### Liability of Travel Agencies

Several state courts have ruled that travel agents are agents of the consumer and not the travel service providers. According to these states (including Arizona, California, Illinois, Louisiana, New Jersey, New York, Ohio, Oklahoma, Pennsylvania, and the District of Columbia), travel agents are fiduciaries owing a high standard of care. This makes their obligations and duties to the consumer independent from their relationship with airlines, cruise lines, hotels or tour operators. In addition, it exposes them to potential liability for harm or injury to their customers caused by travel arrangements made by them.

Some of the legal theories under which travel agents or agencies have been sued (in addition to the travel supplier or tour operator actually providing the service or accommodation) include:

- Failure to Disclose Identity of Supplier: A travel agent must disclose the identity of a supplier or tour operator ultimately responsible for delivering the travel services. If the agent fails to make such a disclosure, the agent may be jointly liable for any harm or injury caused to the traveler by the supplier or tour operator.

- Vouching for the Reliability of Suppliers or Tour Operators: By doing so, the travel agent may be jointly responsible for harm or injury to the traveler under a variety of legal theories, including breach of **warranty** and negligent or **fraudulent** misrepresentation.

- Failure to Disclose Health and Safety Hazard Information: While the travel agent generally has no duty to investigate ultimate service providers for compliance with safety and health laws, the agent may be jointly liable in circumstances where the agent knew or should have reasonably known of specific risks and did not communicate them to the traveler. Some jurisdictions have found travel agents liable for failure to investigate crime levels in destination areas or advise of epidemics or needed shots/vaccines, or advise of need for travel insurance.

### Airline Travel

Although air disasters are quite rare, they are of such magnitude and consequence that applicable laws and regulations should be addressed.

Under its International Aviation Safety **Assessment** Program (IASA), the FAA, as part of its responsibility to inform the public about safety issues, assesses the civil aviation authority of each country with service to the United States. The assessments are to determine whether or not the civil aviation authority (CAA) overseeing airline operations to and from the United States meets the safety standards set by the United Nations body known as the International Civil Aviation Organization (ICAO). The FAA has established two ratings for the status of these civil aviation authorities at the time of the assessment: compliance with ICAO standards, noncompliance with ICAO standards. CAAs are the FAA's foreign counterparts. The IASCA assessment program began in 1992.

The FAA also conducts domestic Flight Operational Quality Assurance Programs (FOQA) through the use of in-flight recorders. The data logged by the recorders is used to evaluate in-flight operations, including standard operating procedures (SOPs), flight training, and cockpit workload. In the event of an accident, the FOQA program assists in interpreting the events leading up to the accident in order to determine causation.

In the unfortunate event of a domestic air accident, the NTSB is called in to investigate. Based upon its findings, injured persons or victims' survivors may have causes of action based on several legal theories including products liability against the aircraft manufacturers; negligent maintenance and repair; **negligence** of pilot and crew; negligence of ground support/air traffic control departments; negligent maintenance of airport runways or facilities, etc.

The Warsaw Convention applies to airlines passengers ticketed on an international itinerary, whether or not the accident occurs on the domestic part of a continuous international trip. In *El AL Israel Airlines, Ltd. v. Tsui Yuan Tseng*, 97-475 (1999), the U.S. Supreme Court confirmed the Warsaw Convention's "exclusive" control over a passenger's right of recovery in U.S. courts for "physical injuries" sustained on international flights.

This created an inequity among passengers on the same flight, as those who were ticketed for a shorter (domestic) leg of the international trip (i.e., traveling between two U.S. cities on an international itinerary that continued beyond the second city) did not fall under the purvey of the Warsaw Convention. Until 1997, the maximum allowable recovery for damages against the airlines subject to the 70-year-old Warsaw Convention provisions was $75,000 (excepting actions grounded in "willful misconduct"). Families of domestic passengers on the same flight, conversely, could recover millions of dollars.

In 1997, the International Air Transport Association (IATA) joined with the U.S. DOT to sponsor an international agreement which removes the $75,000 limit of liability and permits passengers to recover full **compensatory damages** according to the laws of their place of permanent residence (domicile). More than 120 airlines have signed the agreement.

### Cruise Line Travel

An area of more limited and restrictive legal rights is that of cruise line travel. In addition to accidents or injuries occurring on the vessels themselves, passengers may also be injured while being transported from ship to shore (embarking or disembarking), shopping in a port of call, on local excursion trips, or at a hotel owned by the cruise line. (The U.S. Supreme Court held, in *Kenward v. The Admiral Peoples,* 295 U.S. 649, (1935) that admiralty jurisdiction applied to an injury sustained on a gangplank leading to a ship.)

Title III of the Americans with Disabilities Act of 1990 (ADA), 42 U.S.C. 12181 et seq., which prohibits discrimination based on disability in places of "public accommodation," and in "specific public transportation services," is applicable to foreign-flag ships temporarily in U.S. waters, i.e., departing from, and returning to, U.S. ports. *Spector v. Norwegian Cruise Line Ltd.,* No. 03-1388, (2005). This requires such entities to make reasonable modifications and accommodations for disabled persons, as well as to remove architectural barriers and communication barriers that are structural in nature.

Admiralty (maritime) law (46 USC 183b) permits very short statutes of limitations for filing claims or lawsuits. For injuries occurring while on board cruise vessels that touch U.S. shores, passengers are generally required to file claims within six months and commence a lawsuit within one year, but **case law** suggests that the limitations must be "reasonably communicated" to passengers.

The passenger ticket is a very important document in the event of injury. It must disclose any limitations periods for filing suits or claims. Again, maritime law governs the rights and remedies of cruise passengers and preempts any state laws requiring "fine print" on consumer contracts to be printed in a certain print type or size.

The passenger ticket may also contain a "forum selection" clause. Such clauses generally provide that any disputes, claims, or lawsuits must be brought in the local court ("forum") in the country of the ship's registry or where the cruise line is head-quartered. Again, these clauses are generally enforceable if notice to passengers is deemed adequate and fair. Forum selection clauses may be subject to **judicial review** for fundamental fairness or reasonableness.

Passenger tickets may also contain "choice of law" clauses, which are extremely important to a passenger's right to recover damages for injury or death. In such clauses, a statement of notice is made to the passenger that all disputes or claims will be resolved according to the laws of a certain country, state, or principality, etc. Choice of law clauses are generally enforceable but can be subjected to judicial review for **patent** unreasonableness or unjustness (such as fraudulent misrepresentation or overreaching). The application of foreign law may greatly impact the monetary damages or types of actions available to an injured traveler.

Waivers or limitations on liability may be contained in passenger tickets. Under maritime law (46 USC 183c), cruise vessels touching U.S. shores may not disclaim liability for physical injury or loss caused or contributed to by the vessel's negligence. However, in 1996, Congress enacted a provision (46 USC 183(b)(1)) permitting limitations on liability for infliction of emotional distress, mental suffering, or psychological injury.

Finally, if passengers are injured or need medical treatment while on board, cruise lines are generally not liable for **medical malpractice** of a ship's doctors or medical staff. Some courts have found liability when medical staff are touted or advertised by the cruise lines as an added benefit or advantage during the cruise.

### Bus and Rail Tours and Packaged Tours

Generally speaking, the same rights and protections afforded passengers of other common carriers are extended to bus and rail travelers, as bus and rail systems are also considered "common carriers." Often, bus and rail tours are integral parts of total "package tours" arranged by a single tour operator or sponsor. U.S. based tour operators may not disclaim liability for injuries caused by their own negligence or the negligence of their agents or employees, but they may disclaim liability for injuries caused by a foreign supplier. Such disclaimers may be overcome by the application of certain theories of liability such as the following:

- Breach of warranty of safety: This may occur if the bus or rail tour operator promises that

a particular travel service will be rendered in a safe manner, such as statements that recreational areas are "perfectly safe," or that buildings are "suitable for disabled persons."

- Negligent supervision: this theory applies for escorted tours handled by "qualified" or "trained" (etc.) tour directors or guides. When injuries occur as the result of the negligence of the guide, bus and rail tour companies may be held liable for negligent supervision, negligent hiring or selection, etc.

- Assumed ownership or control: this theory may apply in a minority of jurisdictions that hold tour operators liable for negligent travel services if they incorporate possessive language such as "our" or "we" when describing the availability or quality of travel services.

- Negligent or unreasonable exposure to risk: a minority of jurisdictions permit causes of action premised on a tour operator's failure to design or prepare an itinerary with safety risks considered, such as disease epidemics, political unrest, or inclement weather (for which the tour should be canceled or delayed).

- Motor vehicle accidents involving fault of a bus tour driver almost always results in liability on the part of the tour operators or providers.

### Special Considerations for International Travel

- The FAA has limited air travelers to one carry-on bag and one personal item. All other luggage must be checked in. New Transportation Security Administration (TSA, an arm of the Department of Homeland Security) airport security procedures require all passengers (domestic and international) to remove outer coats and jackets for X-ray before proceeding through the metal detectors. Included are suit and sport coats, athletic warm-up jackets and blazers.

- A government-issued photo identification (federal, state, or local) is generally required for passenger check-ins (domestic and international). The regulation under which the

Transportation Safety Administration (TSA) instructs the airlines to collect such identification is classified as "Sensitive Security Information.".

• Travelers should check their passenger tickets for such items as waivers of liability, time limits for filing claims, choice of law clauses, jurisdiction limits, etc., prior to implicitly accepting the terms by boarding the airplane, cruise ship, bus, or train.

• The State Department's Consular Information Sheets are available for every country in the world. They include information regarding unusual entry or currency regulations, drug penalties, unusual health conditions or high crime areas, political disturbances and areas of instability, etc. They are available at the 13 regional **passport** agencies, all U.S. embassies, and consulates abroad, and by electronic or first class mail (see below).

• Travelers are subject to the laws and customs of the countries they are in. Some of the offenses that U.S. travelers have been arrested abroad for include: drug violations; possession of firearms; photography of certain buildings, locations, or operations; and purchasing relics or antiques that were considered national treasures by host countries.

• Registration with the Consular Section of the nearest U.S. embassy or consulate makes things easier in the event of a natural disaster, civil unrest, or terrorist attack. At a minimum, travelers should locate and be aware of the location of these entities wherever they travel.

## Select State Provisions for the Licensing and Regulation of Travel Agents or Sellers

Under the laws of those states with express laws, travel sellers generally include tour operators and consolidators, travel agents, pseudo travel agents, time share salespersons, telemarketing representatives, Internet web sites, and travel discount clubs.

CALIFORNIA: See California Business and Professional Code Section 17554.

FLORIDA: See Florida Statutes Annotated, Sections 559.927(10) and (11).

HAWAII: See Hawaii Revised Laws, Section 486L.

ILLINOIS: See Illinois Annotated Statutes, Chapter 121 1/2, Section 1857.

IOWA: See Iowa **Statute** 120.4.

MASSACHUSETTS: See Massachusetts General Laws, Chapter 93A.

NEW YORK CITY: See General Business Law Sections 157 and 158.

OHIO: See Ohio Revised Code Annotated, Section 1333.99.

OREGON: See Oregon Revised Statute Section 642.218.

RHODE ISLAND: See Rhode Island Revised Laws Annotated, Section 5-52-12.

VIRGINIA: See Virginia Statutes, Section 59.1-448 et seq.

WASHINGTON: See Washington Revised Code Sections 19.138 et seq.

## Additional Resources

*"Death on the High Seas Act"* Available at http://www.condonlaw.com/march2000.htm.

*Guide to Consumer Law* American Bar Association. Random House:1997.

*Law for Dummies.* Ventura, John. IDG Books Worldwide, Inc. 1996.

*"Recent Developments in Airline Disaster Law"* Available at http://www.avweb.com/articles/disaslaw/.

*"The Cruise Passenger's Rights & Remedies"* Dickerson, Thomas A., 2000. Available at http://courts.state.ny.us/tandv/cruiserights.html.

*"The Legal Status of Travel Agents"* Dickerson, Thomas A., 2000. Available at http://courts.state.ny.us/tandv/travelagent.html.

*"The Licensing and Regulation of Travel Sellers in the United States"* Dickerson, Thomas A., 2000. Available at http://courts.state.ny.us/tandv/Aqtaed1.htm.

*"Tips for Travelers in a Time of War."* Jackson, Kristin, The Seattle Times, October 22, 2001.

## Organizations

### Better Business Bureau
4200 Wilson Blvd., Suite 800
Arlington, VA 22203-1838 USA
Phone: (703) 276-0100

Fax: (703) 525-8277
E-Mail: feedback@cbbb.bbb.org
URL: http://www.bbb.org

**Transportation Security Administration (TSA)**
URL: http://www.tsa.gov

# STATE AND FEDERAL AGENCY CONTACTS

*The following is a list of state and federal contacts—websites only. Due to the constantly shifting landscape of the Internet, websites acknowledged by authors in this section may no longer operate, or may operate at a different URL. The editors are not responsible for obsolete or changed URLs.*

## Official State Websites

Every state can be accessed by going to www.state.[2 digit postal code].us

For Example—Alabama: www.state.al.us

## Federal Websites

FedStats—A comprehensive site providing links to statistical databases of many federal agencies
http://www.fedstats.gov/

Fed Forms—Links to official forms of many federal agencies
http://www.fedforms.gov/

Thomas—A Legislative database from the Library of Congress, which includes links to full text of recent Congressional Record, Bills, Reports and Hearings
http://thomas.loc.gov

## Legislative Branch

United States Code
http://uscode.house.gov/
http://www4.law.cornell.edu/uscode/

U.S. Senate
http://www.senate.gov/

U.S. House of Representatives
http://www.house.gov/

Might also include "Federal Judicial Branch" links:

U.S. Courts Homepage
http://www.uscourts.gov/

Official Supreme Court Web Site
http://www.supremecourtus.gov/

## Federal Courts Decisions

U.S. Supreme Court Decisions from Cornell Legal Information InstituteU.S.
http://supct.law.cornell.edu:8080/supct/

Supreme Court Decisions from FindLaw
http://www.findlaw.com/casecode/supreme.html

U.S. Supreme Court Briefs from Findlaw (1999–present)
http://supreme.lp.findlaw.com/supreme_court/briefs/index.html

U.S. Court of Appeals (1st Circuit)
http://www.law.emory.edu/1circuit/

U.S. Court of Appeals (2d Circuit)
http://csmail.law.pace.edu/lawlib/legal/us legal/judiciary/second circuit.html

U.S. Court of Appeals (3d Circuit)
http://vls.law.vill.edu/Locator/3/index.htm

U.S. Court of Appeals (4th Circuit)
http://www.law.emory.edu/4circuit/index.html

U.S. Court of Appeals (5th Circuit)
http://www.ca5.uscourts.gov/

U.S. Court of Appeals (6th Circuit)
http://www.law.emory.edu/6circuit/index.html

U.S. Court of Appeals (7th Circuit)
http://www.kentlaw.edu/7circuit/

U.S. Court of Appeals (8th Circuit)
http://www.ca8.uscourts.gov/opinions/
opinions.html

U.S. Court of Appeals (9th Circuit)
http://www.ce9.uscourts.gov/

U.S. Court of Appeals (10th Circuit)
http://www.law.emory.edu/10circuit/index.html

U.S. Court of Appeals (11th Circuit)
http://www.law.emory.edu/11circuit/index.html

U.S. Court of Appeals (D.C. Circuit)
http://www.ll.georgetown.edu:80/Fed Ct/cadc.html

U.S. Court of Appeals (Federal Circuit)
http://www.ll.georgetown.edu/Fed Ct/cafed.html

A map of the states covered by each circuit with links.
http://www.ll.georgetown.edu:80/Fed Ct/

## Executive Branch and Agency Links

The White House
http://www.whitehouse.gov/

Code of Federal Regulations
http://www.access.gpo.gov/nara/cfr/

Office of Homeland Security
http://www.whitehouse.gov/homeland/

## Cabinet Department Websites

Department of Agriculture
http://www.usda.gov/

Department of Commerce
http://home.doc.gov/

Department of Defense
http://www.defenselink.mil/

Department of Education
http://www.ed.gov/

Department of Energy
http://www.energy.gov/

Department of Health and Human Services
http://www.dhhs.gov/

Department of Housing and Urban Development
http://www.hud.gov/

Department of the Interior
http://www.doi.gov/

Department of Justice
http://www.usdoj.gov/

Department of Labor
http://www.dol.gov/

Department of State
http://www.state.gov/

Department of Transportation
http://www.dot.gov/

Department of the Treasury
http://www.dot.gov/

Department of Veterans Affairs
http://www.va.gov/

## Sub Cabinet Agencies

Bureau of Alcohol, Tobacco, Firearms
http://www.atf.treas.gov/

Bureau of Economic Analysis
http://www.bea.doc.gov/

Bureau of Indian Affairs
http://www.doi.gov/bureau indian affairs.html

Bureau of Justice Statistics
http://www.ojp.usdoj.gov/

Bureau of Land Management
http://www.blm.gov/

Census Bureau
http://www.census.gov/

Centers for Disease Control
http://www.cdc.gov/

Coast Guard (Transportation Dept.)
http://www.uscg.mil/

Customs Service
http://www.customs.treas.gov/

Federal Aviation Administration
http://www.faa.gov/

Federal Bureau of Investigation (FBI) (Justice Dept.)
http://www.fbi.gov

Federal Bureau of Investigation (TRAC FBI Web)
(Transactional Records Access)
http://trac.syr.edu/tracfbi

Federal Energy Regulatory Commission
(FERC)(Energy Dept.)
http://www.ferc.fed.us

Fish and Wildlife Service (FWS)(Interior Dept.)
http://www.fws.gov

Food & Drug Administration
http://www.fda.gov/

Health Care Financing Administration (HCFA) (HHS
Dept.)
http://www.hcfa.gov

Immigration & Naturalization Service
http://www.ins.usdoj.gov/

Internal Revenue Service (IRS) (Treasury Dept.)
http://www.irs.ustreas.gov

Mine Safety and Health Administration (MSHA) (Labor Dept.)
http://www.msha.gov/

National Highway Traffic Safety Administration (NHTSA) (Transportation Dept.)
http://www.nhtsa.dot.gov/

National Institutes of Health (NIH) (HHS Dept.)
http://www.nih.gov/

National Park Service (Interior Dept.)
http://www.nps.gov/

National Technical Information Service (NTIS) (Commerce Dept.)
http://www.ntis.gov/

National Telecommunications Information Administration(NTIA) (Commerce Dept.)
http://www.ntia.doc.gov

Occupational Safety and Health Administration (OSHA) (Labor Dept.)
http://www.osha.gov

Public Health Service
http://www.hhs.gov/phs/

## Independent and Quasi Federal Agencies

Agency for International Development (USAID)
http://www.info.usaid.gov

Arms Control and Disarmament Agency (ACDA)
http://www.acda.gov/

Central Intelligence Agency
http://www.cia.gov

Commodity Futures Trading Commission (CFTC)
http://www.cftc.gov/

Consumer Information Center
http://www.pueblo.gsa.gov

Consumer Product Safety Commission (CPSC)
http://www.cpsc.gov/

EDGAR (SEC electronic filings)
http://www.sec.gov/edgarhp.htm

Environmental Protection Agency (EPA)
http://www.epa.gov

Equal Employment Opportunity Commission (EEOC)
http://www.eeoc.gov

Export Import Bank of the U. S. (Ex Im Bank)
http://www.exim.gov/

Federal Communications Commission (FCC)
http://www.fcc.gov

Federal Deposit Insurance Corporation (FDIC)
http://www.fdic.gov/

Federal Election Commission (FEC)
http://www.fec.gov

Federal Emergency Management Agency (FEMA)
http://www.fema.gov

Federal Labor Relations Authority (FLRA)
http://fedbbs.access.gpo.gov/flra01.htm

Federal Maritime Commission
http://www.fmc.gov:80/

Federal Mediation and Conciliation Service
http://www.fmcs.gov

Federal Reserve System Board of Governors
http://www.federalreserve.gov

Federal Trade Commission
http://www.ftc.gov

General Accounting Office (GAO)
http://www.gao.gov

General Services Administration (GSA)
http://www.gsa.gov

Legal Services Corp.
http://www.lsc.gov/index2.htm

Merit Systems Protection Board (MSBP)
http://www.mspb.gov/

National Archives and Records Administration (NARA)
http://www.nara.gov/

National Capital Planning Commission (NCPC)
http://www.ncpc.gov/

National Credit Union Administration (NCUA)
http://www.ncua.gov/

National Labor Relations Board
http://www.nlrb.gov/

National Performance Review (NPR)
http://www.npr.gov

National Railroad Passenger Corporation (AMTRAK)
http://www.amtrak.com/

National Science Foundation (NSF)
http://www.nsf.gov/

National Security Agency (NSA)
http://www.nsa.gov

National Security Council (NSC)
http://www.whitehouse.gov/WH/EOP/NSC/html/
nschome.html

National Transportation Safety Board (NTSB)
http://www.ntsb.gov/

Nuclear Regulatory Commission
http://www.nrc.gov/

Office of Government Ethics (OGE)
http://www.usoge.gov

Office of Management and Budget (OMB)
http://www.whitehouse.gov/omb/

Office of Personnel Management (OPM)
http://www.opm.gov/

Office of Special Counsel (OSC)
http://www.osc.gov/

Peace Corps
http://www.peacecorps.gov/

Pension Benefit Guaranty Corporation (PBGC)
http://www.pbgc.gov/

Postal Rates Commission
http://www.prc.gov/

Securities and Exchange Commission (SEC)
http://www.sec.gov

Selective Service System
http://www.sss.gov/

Small Business Administration (SBA)
http://www.sba.gov/

Tennessee Valley Authority (TVA)
http://www.tva.gov/

U.S. Commission on Civil Rights
http://www.usccr.gov/

U.S. Information Agency (USIA)
http://www.usia.gov

U.S. Trade Representative (USTR)
http://www.ustr.gov

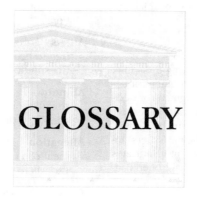

# GLOSSARY

## A

**Abandonment** The surrender, relinquishment, disclaimer, or cession of property or of rights. Voluntary relinquishment of all right, title, claim, and possession, with the intent of not reclaiming it. The giving up of a thing absolutely, without reference to any particular person or purpose, as vacating property with the intention of not returning, so that it may be appropriated by the next comer or finder. The voluntary relinquishment of possession of thing by owner with intention of terminating ownership, but without vesting it in any other person. The relinquishing of all title, possession, or claim, or a virtual, intentional throwing away of property. Term includes both the intention to abandon and the external act by which the intention is carried into effect. In determining whether one has abandoned property or rights, the intention is the first and paramount object of inquiry, for there can be no abandonment without the intention to abandon. *Abandonment* differs from surrender in that surrender requires an agreement, and also from forfeiture, in that forfeiture may be against the intention of the party alleged to have forfeited.

**Abatement** A reduction, a decrease, or a diminution. The suspension or cessation, in whole or in part, of a continuing charge, such as rent.

**Abolition** The destruction, annihilation, abrogation, or extinguishment of anything, but especially things of a permanent nature—such as institutions, usages, or customs, as in the abolition of slavery.

**Abortion** The spontaneous or artificially induced expulsion of an embryo or fetus. As used in legal context, usually refers to induced abortion.

**Absentee voting** Participation in an election by qualified voters who are permitted to mail in their ballots.

**Accessory** Aiding or contributing in a secondary way or assisting in or contributing to as a subordinate. In criminal law, contributing to or aiding in the commission of a crime. One who, without being present at the commission of an offense, becomes guilty of such offense, not as a chief actor, but as a participant, as by command, advice, instigation, or concealment; either before or after the fact or commission. One who aids, abets, commands, or counsels another in the commission of a crime.

**Accusation** A formal criminal charge against a person alleged to have committed an offense punishable by law, which is presented before a court or a magistrate having jurisdiction to inquire into the alleged crime.

**Accused** The generic name for the defendant in a criminal case. A person becomes accused within the meaning of a guarantee of speedy trial only at the point at which either formal indictment or information has been returned against him or her, or when he or she becomes subject to actual restraints on liberty imposed by arrest, whichever occurs first.

**Acquiescence** Conduct recognizing the existence of a transaction and intended to permit the transaction to be carried into effect; a tacit agreement; consent inferred from silence.

**Acquit** To set free, release or discharge as from an obligation, burden or accusation. To absolve one from an obligation or a liability; or to legally certify the innocence of one charged with a crime.

**Acquittal** The legal and formal certification of the innocence of a person who has been charged with a crime.

**Actual cash value** The fair or reasonable cash price for which a property could be sold in the market in the ordinary course of business, and not at forced sale. The price it will bring in a fair market after reasonable efforts to find a purchaser who will give the highest price. What property is worth in money, allowing for depreciation. Ordinarily, *actual cash value, fair market value,* and *market value* are synonymous terms.

**Ad hoc** [*Latin, For this; for this special purpose.*] An attorney ad hoc, or a guardian or curator ad hoc, is one appointed for a special purpose, generally to represent the client or infant in the particular action in which the appointment is made.

**Ad valorem** According to value.

**Adjudication** The legal process of resolving a dispute. The formal giving or pronouncing of a judgment or decree in a court proceeding; also the judgment or decision given. The entry of a decree by a court in respect to the parties in a case. It implies a hearing by a court, after notice, of legal evidence on the factual issue(s) involved. The equivalent of a determination. It indicates that the claims of all the parties thereto have been considered and set at rest.

**Adjusted gross income** The term used for income tax purposes to describe gross income less certain allowable deductions such as trade and business deductions, moving expenses, alimony paid, and penalties for premature withdrawals from term savings accounts, in order to determine a person's taxable income.

**Adjuster** A person appointed or employed to settle or arrange matters that are in dispute; one who determines the amount to be paid on a claim.

**Admissible** A term used to describe information that is relevant to a determination of issues in any judicial proceeding so that such information can be properly considered by a judge or jury in making a decision.

**Adoption** A two-step judicial process in conformance to state statutory provisions in which the legal obligations and rights of a child toward the biological parents are terminated and new rights and obligations are created in the acquired parents.

**Adultery** Voluntary sexual relations between an individual who is married and someone who is not the individual's spouse.

**Affidavit** A written statement of facts voluntarily made by an affiant under an oath or affirmation administered by a person authorized to do so by law.

**Affirmative action** Employment programs required by federal statutes and regulations designed to remedy discriminatory practices in hiring minority group members; i.e., positive steps designed to eliminate existing and continuing discrimination, to remedy lingering effects of past discrimination, and to create systems and procedures to prevent future discrimination; commonly based on population percentages of minority groups in a particular area. Factors considered are race, color, sex, creed, and age.

**Age of consent** The age at which a person may marry without parental approval. The age at which a female is legally capable of agreeing to sexual intercourse, so that a male who engages in sex with her cannot be prosecuted for statutory rape.

**Age of majority** The age at which a person, formerly a minor or an infant, is recognized by law to be an adult, capable of managing his or her own affairs and responsible for any legal obligations created by his or her actions.

**Aliens** Foreign-born persons who have not been naturalized to become U.S. citizens under federal law and the Constitution.

**Alimony** Payment that a family court may order one person in a couple to make to the other person when that couple separates or divorces.

**Allegation** The assertion, claim, declaration, or statement of a party to an action, setting out what he or she expects to prove.

**Allege** To state, recite, assert, or charge the existence of particular facts in a pleading or an indictment; to make an allegation.

**Amendment** The modification of materials by the addition of supplemental information; the deletion of unnecessary, undesirable, or outdated information; or the correction of errors existing in the text.

**Ancillary** Subordinate; aiding. A legal proceeding that is not the primary dispute but which aids the judgment rendered in or the outcome of the main action. A descriptive term that denotes a legal claim, the existence of which is dependent upon or reasonably linked to a main claim.

**Annual percentage rate** The actual cost of borrowing money, expressed in the form of a yearly measure to allow consumers to compare the cost of borrowing money among several lenders.

**Annuity** A right to receive periodic payments, usually fixed in size, for life or a term of years that is created by a contract or other legal document.

**Annulment** A judgment by a court that retroactively invalidates a marriage to the date of its formation.

**Antitrust law** Legislation enacted by the federal and various state governments to regulate trade and commerce by preventing unlawful restraints, price-fixing, and monopolies, to promote competition, and to encourage the production of quality goods and services at the lowest prices, with the primary goal of safeguarding public welfare by ensuring that consumer demands will be met by the manufacture and sale of goods at reasonable prices.

**Appellant** A person who dissatisfied with the judgment rendered in a lawsuit decided in a lower court or the findings from a proceeding before an administrative agency, asks a superior court to review the decision.

**Appellate** Relating to appeals; reviews by superior courts of decisions of inferior courts or administrative agencies and other proceedings.

**Appellate court** A court having jurisdiction to review decisions of a trial-level or other lower court.

**Apportionment** The process by which legislative seats are distributed among units entitled to representation. Determination of the number of representatives that a state, county, or other subdivision may send to a legislative body. The U.S. Constitution provides for a census every ten years, on the basis of which Congress apportions representatives according to population; but each state must have at least one representative. *Districting* is the establishment of the precise geographical boundaries of each such unit or constituency. Apportionment by state statute that denies the rule of one-person, one-vote is violative of equal protection of laws. Also, the allocation of a charge or cost such as real estate taxes between two parties, often in the same ratio as the respective times that the parties are in possession or ownership of property during the fiscal period for which the charge is made or assessed.

**Appraisal** A valuation or an approximation of value by impartial, properly qualified person; the process of determining the value of an asset or liability, which entails expert opinion rather than express commercial transactions.

**Appraiser** A person selected or appointed by a competent authority or an interested party to evaluate the financial worth of property.

**Appreciation** The fair and reasonable estimation of the value of an item. The increase in the financial worth of an asset as compared to its value at a particular earlier date as a result of inflation or greater market demand.

**Appropriation** The designation by the government or an individual of the use to which a fund of money is to be applied. The selection and setting apart of privately owned land by the government for public use, such as a military reservation or public building. The diversion of water flowing on public domain from its natural course by means of a canal or ditch for a private beneficial use of the appropriator.

**Arbiter** [*Latin, One who attends something to view it as a spectator or witness.*] Any person who is given an absolute power to judge and rule on a matter in dispute.

**Arbitration** The submission of a dispute to an unbiased third person designated by the parties to the controversy, who agree in advance to comply with the award—a decision to be issued after a hearing at which both parties have an opportunity to be heard.

**Arrears** A sum of money that has not been paid or has only been paid in part at the time it is due.

**Arrest warrant** A written order issued by authority of the state and commanding the seizure of the person named.

**Arson** At common law, the malicious burning or exploding of the dwelling house of another, or the burning of a building within the curtilage, the immediate surrounding space, of the dwelling of another.

**Articles of Confederation** The document that set forth the terms under which the original thirteen states agreed to participate in a centralized form of government, in addition to their self-rule, and that was in effect from March 1, 1781, to March 4, 1789, prior to the adoption of the Constitution.

**Articles of incorporation** The document that must be filed with an appropriate government agency, commonly the office of the secretary of state, if the owners of a business want it to be given legal recognition as a corporation.

**Artificial insemination** The process by which a woman is medically impregnated using semen from her husband or from a third-party donor.

**As is** A term used to describe a sales transaction in which the seller offers goods in their present, existing condition to prospective buyers.

**Assault** At common law, an intentional act by one person that creates an apprehension in another of an imminent harmful or offensive contact.

**Assault and battery** Two separate offenses against the person that when used in one expression may be defined as any unlawful and unpermitted touching of another. *Assault* is an act that creates an apprehension in another of an imminent, harmful, or offensive contact. The act consists of a threat of harm accompanied by an apparent, present ability to carry out the threat. *Battery* is a harmful or offensive touching of another.

**Assent** An intentional approval of known facts that are offered by another for acceptance, agreement.

**Assessment** The process by which the financial worth of property is determined. The amount at which an item is valued. A demand by the board of directors of a corporation for the payment of any money that is still owed on the purchase of capital stock. The determination of the amount of damages to be awarded to a plaintiff who has been successful in a lawsuit. The ascertainment of the pro rata share of taxes to be paid by members of a group of taxpayers who have directly benefited from a particular common goal or project according to the benefit conferred upon the individual or his or her property. This is known as a special assessment. The listing and valuation of property for purposes of fixing a tax upon it for which its owner will be liable. The procedure by which the Internal Revenue Service, or other government department of taxation, declares that a taxpayer owes additional tax because, for example, the individual has understated personal gross income or has taken deductions to which he or she is not entitled. This process is also known as a deficiency assessment.

**Attorney-client privilege** In law of evidence, client's privilege to refuse to disclose and to prevent any other person from disclosing confidential communications between the client and his or her attorney. Such privilege protects communications between attorney and client made for the purpose of furnishing or obtaining professional legal advice or assistance. That privilege that permits an attorney to refuse to testify as to communications from the client though it belongs to the client, not the attorney, and hence the client may waive it. In federal courts, state law is applied with respect to such privilege.

**Audit** A systematic examination of financial or accounting records by a specialized inspector, called an auditor, to verify their accuracy and truthfulness. A hearing during which financial data are investigated for purposes of authentication.

**Authentication** The confirmation rendered by an officer of a court that a certified copy of a judgment is what it purports to be, an accurate duplicate of the original judgment. In the law of evidence, the act of establishing a statute, record, or other document, or a certified copy of such an instrument as genuine and official so that it can be used in a lawsuit to prove an issue in dispute.

# B

**Bad faith** The fraudulent deception of another person; the intentional or malicious refusal to perform some duty or contractual obligation.

**Bail** The system that governs the status of individuals charged with committing crimes, from the time of their arrest to the time of their trail, and pending appeal, with the major purpose of ensuring their presence at trial.

**Bailiff** An individual who is entrusted with some authority, care, guardianship, or jurisdiction over designated persons or property. One who acts in a managerial or ministerial capacity or takes care of land, goods, and chattels of another in order to make the best profit for the owner. A minor officer of a court serving primarily as a messenger or usher. A low-level court official or sheriff's deputy whose duty is to preserve and protect orderly conduct in court proceedings.

**Bankruptcy** A federally authorized procedure by which a debtor—an individual, corporation, or municipality—is relieved of total liability for its debts by making court-approved arrangements for their partial repayment.

**Bar association** An organization of lawyers established to promote professional competence, enforce standards of ethical conduct, and encourage a spirit of public service among members of the legal profession.

**Beneficiary** An organization or a person for whom a trust is created and who thereby receives the benefits of the trust. One who inherits under a will. A person entitled to a beneficial interest or a right to profits, benefit, or advantage from a contract.

**Bequest** A gift of personal property, such as money, stock, bonds, or jewelry, owned by a decedent at the time of death which is directed by the provisions of the decedent's will; a legacy.

**Beyond a reasonable doubt** The standard that must be met by the prosecution's evidence in a criminal prosecution: that no other logical explanation can be derived from the facts except that the defendant committed the crime, thereby over-coming the presumption that a person is innocent until proven guilty.

**Bias** A predisposition or a preconceived opinion that prevents a person from impartially evaluating facts that have been presented for determination; a prejudice.

**Bigamy** The offense of willfully and knowingly entering into a second marriage while validly married to another individual.

**Bilateral contract** An agreement formed by an exchange of promises in which the promise of one party is consideration supporting the promise of the other party.

**Bill of rights** The first ten amendments to the U.S. Constitution, ratified in 1791, which set forth and guarantee certain fundamental rights and privileges of individuals, including freedom of religion, speech, press, and assembly; guarantee of a speedy jury trial in criminal cases; and protection against excessive bail and cruel and unusual punishment. A list of fundamental rights included in each state constitution. A declaration of individual rights and freedoms, usually issued by a national government.

**Bill of sale** In the law of contracts, a written agreement, previously required to be under seal, by which one person transfers to another a right to, or interest in, personal property and goods, a legal instrument that conveys title in property from seller to purchaser.

**Birth control** A measure or measures undertaken to prevent conception.

**Blackmail** The crime involving a threat for purposes of compelling a person to do an act against his or her will, or for purposes of taking the person's money or property.

**Bonds** Written documents by which a government, corporation, or individual—the obligor—promises to perform a certain act, usually the payment of a definite sum of money, to another—the obligee—on a certain date.

**Boundaries** Natural or artificial separations or divisions between adjoining properties to show their limits.

**Boycott** A lawful concerted attempt by a group of people to express displeasure with, or obtain concessions from, a particular person or company by refusing to do business with them. An unlawful attempt that is prohibited by the Sherman Anti-Trust Act (15 U.S.C.A. § 1 et seq.), to adversely affect a company through threat, coercion, or intimidation of its employees, or to prevent others from doing business with said company. A practice utilized in labor disputes whereby an organized group of employees bands together and refrains from dealing with an employer, the legality of which is determined by applicable provisions of statutes governing labor-management relations.

**Bribery**   The offering, giving, receiving, or soliciting of something of value for the purpose of influencing the action of an official in the discharge of his or her public or legal duties.

**Burglary**   The criminal offense of breaking and entering a building illegally for the purpose of committing a crime therein.

**Bylaws**   The rules and regulations enacted by an association or a corporation to provide a framework for its operation and management.

# C

**Canon law**   Any church's or religion's laws, rules, and regulations; more commonly, the written policies that guide the administration and religious ceremonies of the Roman Catholic Church.

**Capital asset**   Property held by a taxpayer, such as houses, cars, stocks, bonds, and jewelry, or a building owned by a corporation to furnish facilities for its employees.

**Capital punishment**   The lawful infliction of death as a punishment; the death penalty.

**Case law**   Legal principles enunciated and embodied in judicial decisions that are derived from the application of particular areas of law to the facts of individual cases.

**Casualty**   A serious or fatal accident. A person or thing injured, lost, or destroyed. A disastrous occurrence due to sudden, unexpected, or unusual cause. Accident; misfortune or mishap; that which comes by chance or without design. A loss from such an event or cause, as by fire, shipwreck, lightning, etc.

**Caveat**   [*Latin, Let him beware.*] A warning; admonition. A formal notice or warning given by an interested party to a court, judge, or ministerial officer in opposition to certain acts within his or her power and jurisdiction.

**Cease and desist order**   An order issued by an administrative agency or a court proscribing a person or a business entity from continuing a particular course of conduct.

**Censorship**   The suppression or proscription of speech or writing that is deemed obscene, indecent, or unduly controversial.

**Census**   An official count of the population of a particular area, such as a district, state, or nation.

**Certified check**   A written order made by a depositor to a bank to pay a certain sum to the person designated—the payee—which is marked by the bank as "accepted" or "certified," thereby unconditionally promising that the bank will pay the order upon its presentation by the payee.

**Certified copy**   A photocopy of a document, judgment, or record that is signed and attested to as an accurate

and a complete reproduction of the original document by a public official in whose custody the original has been placed for safekeeping.

**Certiorari**   [*Latin, To be informed of.*] At common law, an original writ or order issued by the Chancery of King's Bench, commanding officers of inferior courts to submit the record of a cause pending before them to give the party more certain and speedy justice. A writ that a superior appellate court issues on its discretion to an inferior court, ordering it to produce a certified record of a particular case it has tried, in order to determine whether any irregularities or errors occurred that justify review of the case. A device by which the Supreme Court of the United States exercises its discretion in selecting the cases it will review.

**Chief justice**   The presiding, most senior, or principal judge of a court.

**Child abuse**   Physical, sexual, or emotional mistreatment or neglect of a child.

**Child care**   The supervision and nurturing of a child, including casual and informal services provided by a parent as well as more formal services provided by an organized child care center.

**Child custody**   The care, control, and maintenance of a child, which a court may award to one of the parents following a divorce or separation proceeding.

**Child labor laws**   Federal and state legislation that protects children by restricting the type and hours of work they perform.

**Child support**   A payment that a noncustodial parent makes as a contribution to the costs of raising her or his child.

**Children's rights**   The opportunity for children to participate in political and legal decisions that affect them; in a broad sense, the rights of children to live free from hunger, abuse, neglect, and other inhumane conditions.

**Circumstantial evidence**   Information and testimony presented by a party in a civil or criminal action that permit conclusions that indirectly establish the existence of nonexistence of a fact or event that the party seeks to prove.

**Citation**   A paper commonly used in various courts—such as a probate, matrimonial, or traffic court—that is served upon an individual to notify him or her that he or she is required to appear at a specific time and place. Reference to a legal authority—such as a case, constitution, or treatise—where particular information may be found.

**Civil action**   A lawsuit brought to enforce, redress, or protect rights of private litigants (the plaintiffs and the defendants); not a criminal proceeding.

**Civil procedure**   The methods, procedures, and practices used in civil cases.

**Civil rights**  Personal liberties that belong to an individual owing to his or her status as a citizen or resident of a particular country or community.

**Civil rights cases**  A landmark decision, which was a consolidation of several cases brought before the Supreme Court of the United States in 1883 that declared the Civil Rights Act of 1875 (18 Stat. 336) unconstitutional and ultimately led to the enactment of state laws, such as Jim Crow Laws, which codified what had previously been individual adherence to the practice of racial segregation. The cases were *United States v. Stanley, United States v. Ryan, United States v. Nichols,* and *United States v. Singleton,* 109 U.S. 3, 3 S. Ct. 18, 27 L. Ed. 835.

**Class action**  A lawsuit that allows a large number of people with a common interest in a matter to sue or be sued as a group.

**Clayton Act**  A federal law enacted in 1914 as an amendment to the Sherman Anti-Trust Act (15 U.S.C.A. § 1 et seq. [1890]), prohibiting undue restriction of trade and commerce by designated methods.

**Clemency**  Leniency or mercy. A power given to a public official, such as a governor or the president, to in some way lower or moderate the harshness of punishment imposed upon a prisoner.

**Code of Federal Regulations**  A set of books published by the federal government and containing the regulations of federal agencies currently in effect.

**Codicil**  A document that is executed by a person who had previously made his or her will, to modify, delete, qualify, or revoke provisions contained in it.

**Coercion**  The intimidation of a victim to compel the individual to do some act against his or her will by the use of psychological pressure, physical force, or threats. The crime on intentionally and unlawfully restraining another's freedom by threatening to commit a crime, accusing the victim of a crime, disclosing any secret that would seriously impair the victim's reputation in the community, or by performing or refusing to perform an official action lawfully requested by the victim, or by causing an official to do so. A defense asserted in a criminal prosecution that a person who committed a crime did not do so of his or her own free will, but only because the individual was compelled by another through the use of physical force or threat of immediate serious bodily injury or death.

**Cohabitation**  A living arrangement in which an unmarried couple live together in a long-term relationship that resembles a marriage.

**Collateral**  Related; indirect; not bearing immediately upon an issue. The property pledged or given as a security interest, or a guarantee for payment of a debt, that will be taken or kept by the creditor in case of a default on the original debt.

**Collective bargaining**  The process through which a labor union and an employer negotiate the scope of the employment relationship.

**Collective bargaining agreement**  The contractual agreement between an employer and a labor union that governs wages, hours, and working conditions for employees and which can be enforced against both the employer and the union for failure to comply with its terms.

**Commerce**  The exchange of goods, products, or any type of personal property. Trade and traffic carried on between different peoples or states and its inhabitants, including not only the purchase, sale, and exchange of commodities but also the instrumentalities, agencies, and means by which business is accomplished. The transportation of persons and goods, by air, land, and sea. The exchange of merchandise on a large scale between different places or communities.

**Commercial Code**  A colloquial designation for the body of law known as the Uniform Commercial Code (UCC), which governs the various business transactions that are integral parts of the U.S. system of commerce.

**Commercial paper**  A written instrument or document such as a check, draft, promissory note, or a certificate of deposit, that manifests the pledge or duty of one individual to pay money to another.

**Common law**  The ancient law of England based upon societal customs and recognized and enforced by the judgments and decrees of the courts. The general body of statutes and case law that governed England and the American colonies prior to the American Revolution. The principles and rules of action, embodied in case law rather than legislative enactments, applicable to the government and protection of persons and property that derive their authority from the community customs and traditions that evolved over the centuries as interpreted by judicial tribunals. A designation used to denote the opposite of statutory, equitable, or civil; for example, a common-law action.

**Common stock**  Evidence of participation in the ownership of a corporation that takes the form of printed certificates.

**Community property**  The holdings and resources owned in common by a husband and wife.

**Compensatory damages**  A sum of money awarded in a civil action by a court to indemnify a person for the particular loss, detriment, or injury suffered as a result of the unlawful conduct of another.

**Compound interest**  Interest generated by the sum of the principal and any accrued interest.

**Comptroller**  An officer who conducts the fiscal affairs of a state or municipal corporation.

**Computer crime**  The use of a computer to take or alter data, or to gain unlawful use of computers or services.

**Conciliation** The process of adjusting or settling disputes in a friendly manner through extrajudicial means. Conciliation means bringing two opposing sides together to reach a compromise in an attempt to avoid taking a case to trial. Arbitration, in contrast, is a contractual remedy used to settle disputes out of court. In arbitration the two parties in controversy agree in advance to abide by the decision made by a third party called in as a mediator, whereas conciliation is less structured.

**Condominiums and cooperatives** Two common forms of multiple-unit dwellings, with independent owners or lessees of the individual units comprising the multiple-unit dwelling who share various costs and responsibilities of areas they use in common.

**Confession** A statement made by an individual that acknowledges his or her guilt in the commission of a crime.

**Conflict of interest** A term used to describe the situation in which a public official or fiduciary who, contrary to the obligation and absolute duty to act for the benefit of the public or a designated individual, exploits the relationship for personal benefit, typically pecuniary.

**Conjugal** Pertaining or relating to marriage; suitable or applicable to married people.

**Conspiracy** An agreement between two or more persons to engage jointly in an unlawful or criminal act, or an act that is innocent in itself but becomes unlawful when done by the combination of actors.

**Constitutional amendment** The means by which an alteration to the U.S. Constitution, whether a modification, deletion, or addition, is accomplished.

**Consumer Credit Protection Act** A federal statute designed to protect borrowers of money by mandating complete disclosure of the terms and conditions of finance charges in transaction by limiting the garnishment of wages and by regulating the use of charge accounts.

**Consumer Price Index** A computation made and issued monthly by the Bureau of Labor Statistics of the federal Labor Department that attempts to track the price level of designated gods and services purchased by the average comsumer.

**Consumer protection** Consumer protection laws are federal and state statutes governing sales and credit practices involving consumer goods. Such statues prohibit and regulate deceptive or unconscionable advertising and sales practices, product quality, credit financing and reporting, debt collection, leases and other aspects of consumer transactions.

**Consummate** To carry into completion; to fulfill; to accomplish.

**Contempt** An act of deliberate disobedience or disregard for the laws, regulations, or decorum of a public authority, such as a court or legislative body.

**Continuance** The adjournment or postponement of an action pending in a court to a later date of the same or another session of the court, granted by a court in response to a motion made by a party to a lawsuit. The entry into the trial record of the adjournment of a case for the purpose of formally evidencing it.

**Contraband** Any property that it is illegal to produce or possess. Smuggled goods that are imported into or exported from a country in violation of its laws.

**Contract** Agreements between two or more persons that create an obligation to do, or refrain from doing, a particular thing.

**Conviction** The outcome of a criminal prosecution which concludes in a judgment that the defendant is guilty of the crime charged. The juncture of a criminal proceeding during which the question of guilt is ascertained. In a case where the perpetrator has been adjudged guilty and sentenced, a record of the summary proceedings brought pursuant to any penal statute before one or more justices of the peace or other properly authorized persons.

**Cooling-off period** An interval of time during which no action of a specific type can be taken by either side in a dispute. An automatic delay in certain jurisdictions, apart from ordinary court delays, between the time when divorce papers are filed and the divorce hearing takes place. An amount of time within which a buyer is permitted to cancel a contract for the purchase of consumer goods—designed to effect consumer protection. A number of states require that a three-day cancellation period must be allowed purchasers following door-to-door sales.

**Copyright** An intangible right granted by statute to the author or originator of certain literary or artistic productions, whereby, for a limited period, the exclusive privilege is given to the person to make copies of the same for publication and sale.

**Corporate** Pertaining to or possessing the qualities of a corporation, a legal entity created—pursuant to state law—to serve the purposes set out in its certificate of incorporation.

**Corporations** Artificial entities that are created by state statute, and that are treated much like individuals under the law, having legally enforceable rights, the ability to acquire debt and pay out profits, the ability to hold and transfer property, the ability to enter into contracts, the requirement to pay taxes, and the ability to sue and be sued.

**Counsel** An attorney or lawyer. The rendition of advice and guidance concerning a legal matter, contemplated form of argument, claim, or action.

**Counterclaim** A claim by a defendant opposing the claim of the plaintiff and seeking some relief from the plaintiff for the defendant.

**Counterfeit** To falsify, deceive, or defraud. A copy or imitation of something that is intended to be taken as authentic and genuine in order to deceive another.

**Counterfeiting** The process of fraudulently manufacturing, altering, or distributing a product that is of lesser value than the genuine product.

**Counteroffer** In contract law, a proposal made in response to an original offer modifying its terms, but which has the legal effect of rejecting it.

**Court of appeal** An intermediate federal judicial tribunal of review that is found in thirteen judicial districts, called circuits, in the United States. A state judicial tribunal that reviews a decision rendered by an inferior tribunal to determine whether it made errors that warrant the reversal of its judgment.

**Court of claims** A state judicial tribunal established as the forum in which to bring certain types of lawsuits against the state or its political subdivisions, such as a county. The former designation given to a federal tribunal created in 1855 by Congress with original jurisdiction—initial authority—to decide an action brought against the United States that is based upon the Constitution, federal law, any regulation of the executive department, or any express or implied contracts with the federal government.

**CPA** An abbreviation for certified public accountant. A CPA is a trained accountant who has been examined and licensed by the state. He or she is permitted to perform all the tasks of an ordinary accountant in addition to examining the books and records of various business organizations, such as corporations.

**Credibility** Believability. The major legal application of the term *credibility* relates to the testimony of a witness or party during a trial. Testimony must be both competent and credible if it is to be accepted by the trier of fact as proof of an issue being litigated.

**Credit union** A corporation formed under special statutory provisions to further thrift among its members while providing credit for them at more favorable rates of interest than those offered by other lending institutions. A credit union is a cooperative association that utilizes funds deposited by a small group of people who are its sole borrowers and beneficiaries. It is ordinarily subject to regulation by state banking boards or commissions. When formed pursuant to the Federal Credit Union Act (12 U.S.C.A.§ 1751 et seq. [1934]), credit unions are chartered and regulated by the National Credit Union Administration.

**Creditor** An individual to whom an obligation is owed because he or she has given something of value in exchange. One who may legally demand and receive money, either through the fulfillment of a contract or due to injury sustained as a result of another's negligence or intentionally wrongful act. The term *creditor* is also used to describe an individual who is engaged in the business of lending money or selling items for which immediate payment is not demanded but an obligation of repayment exists as of a future date.

**Criminal procedure** The framework of laws and rules that govern the administration of justice in cases involving an individual who has been accused of a crime, beginning with the initial investigation of the crime and concluding either with the unconditional release of the accused by virtue of acquittal (a judgment of not guilty) or by the imposition of a term of punishment pursuant to a conviction for the crime.

**Cross-examination** The questioning of a witness or party during a trial hearing, or deposition by the party opposing the one who asked the person to testify in order to evaluate the truth of that person's testimony, to develop the testimony further, or to accomplish any other objective. The interrogation of a witness or party by the party opposed to the one who called the witness or party, upon a subject raised during direct examination—the initial questioning of a witness or party—on the merits of that testimony.

**Cruel and unusual punishment** Such punishment as would amount to torture or barbarity, and cruel and degrading punishment not known to the common law, or any fine, penalty, confinement, or treatment so disproportionate to the offense as to shock the moral sense of the community.

**Custody** The care, possession, and control of a thing or person. The retention, inspection, guarding, maintenance, or security of a thing within the immediate care and control of the person to whom it is committed. The detention of a person by lawful authority or process.

# D

**Debit** A sum charged as due or owing. An entry made on the asset side of a ledger or account. The term is used in bookkeeping to denote the left side of the ledger, or the charging of a person or an account with all that is supplied to or paid out for that person or for the subject of the account. Also, the balance of an account where it is shown that something remains due to the party keeping the account. As a noun, an entry on the left-hand side of an account. As a verb, to make an entry on the left-hand side of an account. A term used in accounting or bookkeeping that results in an increase to an asset and an expense account and a decrease to a liability, revenue, or owner's equity account.

**Debtor** One who owes a debt or the performance of an obligation to another, who is called the creditor; one who may be compelled to pay a claim or demand; anyone liable on a claim, whether due or to become due. In bankruptcy law, a person who files a voluntary petition or person against whom an involuntary petition is filed. A person or municipality concerning which a bankruptcy case has been commenced.

**Declaration of trust** An assertion by a property owner that he or she holds the property or estate for the benefit of another person, or for particular designated objectives.

**Decree**  A judgment of a court that announces the legal consequences of the facts found in a case and orders that the court's decision be carried out. A decree in equity is a sentence or order of the court, pronounced on hearing and understanding all the points in issue, and determining the rights of all the parties to the suit, according to equity and good conscience. It is a declaration of the court announcing the legal consequences of the facts found. With the procedural merger of law and equity in the federal and most state courts under the Rules of Civil Procedure, the term *judgment* has generally replaced *decree*.

**Deductible**  That which may be taken away or subtracted. In taxation, an item that may be subtracted from gross income or adjusted gross income in determining taxable income (e.g., interest expenses, charitable contributions, certain taxes).  The portion of an insured loss to be borne by the insured before he or she is entitled to recovery from the insurer.

**Deduction**  That which is deducted; the part taken away; abatement; as in deductions from gross income in arriving at net income for tax purposes.  In civil law, a portion or thing that an heir has a right to take from the mass of the succession before any partition takes place.

**Deed**  A written instrument, which has been signed and delivered, by which one individual, the grantor, conveys title to real property to another individual, the grantee; a conveyance of land, tenements, or hereditaments, from one individual to another.

**Deed of trust**  A document that embodies the agreement between a lender and a borrower to transfer an interest in the borrower's land to a neutral third party, a trustee, to secure the payment of a debt by the borrower.

**Defamation**  Any intentional false communication, either written or spoken, that harms a person's reputation; decreases the respect, regard, or confidence in which a person is held; or induces disparaging, hostile, or disagreeable opinions or feelings against a person.

**Default**  An omission; a failure to do that which is anticipated, expected, or required in a given situation.

**Default judgment**  Judgment entered against a party who has failed to defend against a claim that has been brought by another party. Under rules of civil procedure, when a party against whom a judgment for affirmative relief is sought has failed to plead (i.e., answer) or otherwise defend, the party is in default and a judgment by default may be entered either by the clerk or the court.

**Defendant**  The person defending or denying; the party against whom relief or recovery is sought in an action or suit, or the accused in a criminal case.

**Defraud**  To make a misrepresentation of an existing material fact, knowing it to be false or making it recklessly without regard to whether it is true or false, intending for someone to rely on the misrepresentation and under circumstances in which such person does rely on it to his or her damage. To practice fraud; to cheat or trick. To deprive a person of property or any interest, estate, or right by fraud, deceit, or artifice.

**Deportation**  Banishment to a foreign country, attended with confiscation of property and deprivation of civil rights.  The transfer of an alien, by exclusion or expulsion, from the United States to a foreign country. The removal or sending back of an alien to the country from which he or she came because his or her presence is deemed inconsistent with the public welfare, and without any punishment being imposed or contemplated. The grounds for deportation are set forth at 8 U.S.C.A. § 1251 and the procedures are provided for in §§ 1252-1254.

**Deposition**  The testimony of a party or witness in a civil or criminal proceeding taken before trial, usually in an attorney's office.

**Depository**  The place where a deposit is placed and kept, e.g., a bank savings and loan institution, credit union, or trust company. A place where something is deposited or stored as for safekeeping or convenience, e.g., a safety deposit box.

**Depreciation**  The gradual decline in the financial value of property used to produce income due to its increasing age and eventual obsolescence, which is measured by a formula that takes into account these factors in addition to the cost of the property and its estimated useful life.

**Detainer**  The act (or the juridical fact) of withholding from a lawfully entitled person the possession of land or goods, or the restraint of a person's personal liberty against his or her will; detention. The wrongful keeping of a person's goods is called an unlawful detainer although the original taking may have been lawful.  A request filed by a criminal justice agency with the institution in which a prisoner is incarcerated asking the institution either to hold the prisoner for the agency or to notify the agency when release of the prisoner is imminent.

**Direct examination**  The primary questioning of a witness during a trial that is conducted by the side for which that person is acting as a witness.

**Directed verdict**  A procedural device whereby the decision in a case is taken out of the hands of the jury by the judge.

**Disability**  The lack of competent physical and mental faculties; the absence of legal capability to perform an act.  The term *disability* usually signifies an incapacity to exercise all the legal rights ordinarily possessed by an average person. Convicts, minors, and incompetents are regarded to be under a disability. The term is also used in a more restricted sense when it indicates a hindrance to marriage or a deficiency in legal qualifications to hold office. The impairment of earning capacity; the loss of physical function resulting in diminished efficiency; the inability to work.

**Disabled persons** Persons who have a physical or mental impairment that substantially limits one or more major life activities. Some laws also include in their definition of disabled persons those people who have a record of or are regarded as having such an impairment.

**Discovery** A category of procedural devices employed by a party to a civil or criminal action, prior to trial, to require the adverse party to disclose information that is essential for the preparation of the requesting party's case and that the other party alone knows or possesses.

**Discrimination** In constitutional law, the grant by statute of particular privileges to a class arbitrarily designated from a sizable number of persons, where no reasonable distinction exists between the favored and disfavored classes. Federal laws, supplemented by court decisions, prohibit discrimination in such areas as employment, housing, voting rights, education, and access to public facilities. They also proscribe discrimination on the basis of race, age, sex, nationality, disability, or religion. In addition, state and local laws can prohibit discrimination in these areas and in others not covered by federal laws.

**Dismissal** A discharge of an individual or corporation from employment. The disposition of a civil or criminal proceeding or a claim or charge made therein by a court order without a trial or prior to its completion which, in effect, is a denial of the relief sought by the commencement of the action.

**Disposition** Act of disposing; transferring to the care or possession of another. The parting with, alienation of, or giving up of property. The final settlement of a matter and, with reference to decisions announced by a court, a judge's ruling is commonly referred to as disposition, regardless of level of resolution. In criminal procedure, the sentencing or other final settlement of a criminal case. With respect to a mental state, denotes an attitude, prevailing tendency, or inclination.

**Dissolution** Act or process of dissolving; termination; winding up. In this sense it is frequently used in the phrase dissolution of a partnership.

**Dissolve** To terminate; abrogate; cancel; annul; disintegrate. To release or unloose the binding force of anything.

**Dividend** The distribution of current or accumulated earnings to the shareholders of a corporation pro rata based on the number of shares owned. Dividends are usually issued in cash. However, they may be issued in the form of stock or property. The dividend on preferred shares is generally a fixed amount; however, on

common shares the dividend varies depending on such things as the earnings and available cash of the corporation as well as future plans for the acquisition of property and equipment by the corporation.

**Divorce** A court decree that terminates a marriage; also known as marital dissolution.

**Docket** A written list of judicial proceedings set down for trial in a court. To enter the dates of judicial proceedings scheduled for trial in a book kept by a court.

**Documentary evidence** A type of written proof that is offered at a trial to establish to existence or nonexistence of a fact that is in dispute.

**Domestic violence** Any abusive, violent, coercive, forceful, or threatening act or word inflicted by one member of a family or household on another can constitute domestic violence.

**Donor** The party conferring a power. One who makes a gift. One who creates a trust.

**Double jeopardy** A second prosecution for the same offense after acquittal or conviction or multiple punishments for same offense. The evil sought to be avoided by prohibiting double jeopardy is double trial and double conviction, not necessarily double punishment.

**Down payment** A percentage of the total purchase price of an item that is proffered when the item is bought on credit.

**Drunkenness** The state of an individual whose mind is affected by the consumption of alcohol.

**Dual nationality** An equal claim, simultaneously possessed by two nations, to the allegiance of an individual.

**Due process of law** A fundamental, constitutional guarantee that all legal proceedings will be fair and that one will be given notice of the proceedings and an opportunity to be heard before the government acts to take away one's life, liberty, or property. Also, a constitutional guarantee that a law shall not be unreasonable, arbitrary, or capricious.

**Duress** Unlawful pressure exerted upon a person to coerce that person to perform an act that he or she ordinarily would not perform.

**Durham rule** A principle of criminal law used to determine the validity of the insanity defense asserted by an accused, that he or she was insane at the time of committing a crime and therefore should not be held legally responsible for the action.

**DWI** An abbreviation for *driving while intoxicated,* which is an offense committed by an individual who operates a motor vehicle while under the influence of alcohol or drugs and narcotics. An abbreviation for *died without issue,* which commonly appears in genealogical tables.

# E

**Earned income**  Sources of money derived from the labor, professional service, or entrepreneurship of an individual taxpayer as opposed to funds generated by investments, dividends, and interest.

**Easement**  A right of use over the property of another. Traditionally the permitted kinds of uses were limited, the most important being rights of way and rights concerning flowing waters. The easement was normally for the benefit of adjoining lands, no matter who the owner was (an easement appurtenant), rather than for the benefit of a specific individual (easement in gross).

**EEOC**  An abbreviation for Equal Employment Opportunity Commission.

**Emancipation**  The act or process by which a person is liberated from the authority and control of another person.

**Employee Retirement Income Security Act**  The name of federal legislation, popularly abbreviated as ERISA (29 U.S.C.A. § 1001 et seq. [1974]), which regulates the financing, vesting, and administration of pension plans for workers in private business and industry.

**Encroachment**  An illegal intrusion in a highway or navigable river, with or without obstruction. An encroachment upon a street or highway is a fixture, such as a wall or fence, which illegally intrudes into or invades the highway or encloses a portion of it, diminishing its width or area, but without closing it to public travel.

**Entrapment**  The act of government agents or officials that induces a person to commit a crime he or she is not previously disposed to commit.

**Equal protection**  The constitutional guarantee that no person or class of persons shall be denied the same protection of the laws that is enjoyed by other persons or other classes in like circumstances in their lives, liberty, property, and pursuit of happiness.

**Equal Rights Amendment**  A proposed addition to the U.S. Constitution that read, "Equality of rights under the law shall not be denied or abridged by the United States or by any State on account of sex," and that failed to receive ratification by the required number of states.

**Equity of redemption**  The right of a mortgagor, that is, a borrower who obtains a loan secured by a pledge of his or her real property, to prevent foreclosure proceedings by paying the amount due on the loan, a mortgage, plus interest and other expenses after having failed to pay within the time and according to the terms specified therein.

**ERISA**  The name of federal legislation, popularly abbreviated as ERISA (29 U.S.C.A. § 1001 et seq. [1974]), which regulates the financing, vesting, and administration of pension plans for workers in private business and industry.

**Escrow**  Something of value, such as a deed, stock, money, or written instrument, that is put into the custody of a third person by its owner, a grantor, an obligor, or a promisor, to be retained until the occurrence of a contingency or performance of a condition.

**Espionage**  The act of securing information of a military or political nature that a competing nation holds secret. It can involve the analysis of diplomatic reports, publications, statistics, and broadcasts, as well as spying, a clandestine activity carried out by an individual or individuals working under a secret identity for the benefit of a nation's information gathering techniques. In the United States, the organization that heads most activities dedicated to espionage is the Central Intelligence Agency.

**Estimated tax**  Federal and state tax laws require a quarterly payment of estimated taxes due from corporations, trusts, estates, non-wage employees, and wage employees with income not subject to withholding. Individuals must remit at least 100 percent of their prior year tax liability or 90 percent of their current year tax liability in order to avoid an underpayment penalty. Corporations must pay at least 90 percent of their current year tax liability in order to avoid an underpayment penalty. Additional taxes due, if any, are paid on taxpayer's annual tax return.

**Estoppel**  A legal principle that precludes a party from denying or alleging a certain fact owing to that party's previous conduct, allegation, or denial.

**Eviction**  The removal of a tenant from possession of premises in which he or she resides or has a property interest, done by a landlord either by reentry upon the premises or through a court action.

**Evidence**  Any matter of fact that a party to a lawsuit offers to prove or disprove an issue in the case. A system of rules and standards used to determine which facts may be admitted, and to what extent a judge or jury may consider those facts, as proof of a particular issue in a lawsuit.

**Examination**  A search, inspection, or interrogation. In criminal procedure, the preliminary hearing held to decide whether a suspect arrested for a crime should be brought to trial.   In trial practice, the interrogation of a witness to elicit his or her testimony in a civil or criminal action, so that the facts he or she possesses are presented before the trial of fact for consideration.   In the law governing real property transactions, an investigation made into the history of the ownership of and conditions that exist upon land so that a purchaser can determine whether a seller is entitled to sell the land free and clear of any claims made by third persons.   In patent law, an inquiry made at the Patent and Trademark Office to determine the novelty and utility of an invention for which a patent application has been filed and whether the invention interferes with any other invention.

**Examiner** An official or other person empowered by another—whether an individual, business, or government agency—to investigate and review specified documents for accuracy and truthfulness. A court-appointed officer, such as a master or referee, who inspects evidence presented to resolve controverted matters and records statements made by witnesses in the particular proceeding pending before that court. A government employee in the Patent and Trademark Office whose duty it is to scrutinize the application made for a patent by an inventor to determine whether the invention meets the statutory requirements of patentability. A federal employee of the Internal Revenue Service who reviews income tax returns for accuracy and truthfulness.

**Excise** A tax imposed on the performance of an act, the engaging in an occupation, or the enjoyment of a privilege. A tax on the manufacture, sale, or use of goods or on the carrying on of an occupation or activity, or a tax on the transfer of property. In current usage the term has been extended to include various license fees and practically every internal revenue tax except the income tax (e.g., federal alcohol and tobacco excise taxes).

**Exclusionary rule** The principle based on federal constitutional law that evidence illegally seized by law enforcement officers in violation of a suspect's right to be free from unreasonable searches and seizures cannot be used against the suspect in a criminal prosecution.

**Exculpatory** Clearing, or tending to clear, from guilt.

**Execution** The carrying out of some act or course of conduct to its completion. In criminal law, the carrying out of a death sentence (see also capital punishment). The process whereby an official, usually a sheriff, is directed by an appropriate judicial writ to seize and sell as much of a debtor's nonexempt property as is necessary to satisfy a court's monetary judgment. With respect to contracts, the performance of all acts necessary to render a contract complete as an instrument, which conveys the concept that nothing remains to be done to make a complete and effective contract.

**Executive branch** The branch of the U.S. government that is composed of the president and all the individuals, agencies, and departments that report to the president, and that is responsible for administering and enforcing the laws that Congress passes.

**Executive orders** Presidential policy directives that implement or interpret a federal statute, a constitutional provision, or a treaty.

**Extortion** The obtaining of property from another induced by wrongful use of actual or threatened force, violence, or fear, or under color of official right.

**Extradition** The transfer of an accused from one state or country to another state or country that seeks to place the accused on trial.

# F

**Fair Credit Reporting Act** Legislation embodied in title VI of the Consumer Credit Protection Act (15 U.S.C.A. § 1681 et seq. [1968]), which was enacted by Congress in 1970 to ensure that reporting activities relating to various consumer transactions are conducted in a manner that is fair to the affected individual, and to protect the consumer's right to privacy against the informational demands of a credit reporting company.

**Fair hearing** A judicial proceeding that is conducted in such a manner as to conform to fundamental concepts of justice and equality.

**Fair Labor Standards Act** Federal legislation enacted in 1938 by Congress, pursuant to its power under the Commerce Clause, that mandated a minimum wage and forty-hour work week for employees of those businesses engaged in interstate commerce.

**Fair market value** The amount for which real property or personal property would be sold in a voluntary transaction between a buyer and seller, neither of whom is under any obligation to buy or sell.

**Fairness doctrine** The doctrine that imposes affirmative responsibilities on a broadcaster to provide coverage of issues of public importance that is adequate and fairly reflects differing viewpoints. In fulfilling its fairness doctrine obligations, a broadcaster must provide free time for the presentation of opposing views if a paid sponsor is unavailable and must initiate programming on public issues if no one else seeks to do so.

**Fair Use** Legal doctrine by which a non-copyright holder can make use of copyrighted material without owner's consent.

**False advertising** "Any advertising or promotion that misrepresents the nature, characteristics, qualities or geographic origin of goods, services or commercial activities" (Lanham Act, 15 U.S.C.A. § 1125(a)).

**False arrest** A tort (a civil wrong) that consists of an unlawful restraint of an individual's personal liberty or freedom of movement by another purporting to act according to the law.

**False pretenses** False representations of past or present material facts, known by the wrongdoer to be false, made with the intent to defraud a victim into passing title in property to the wrongdoer.

**Family law** Statutes, court decisions, and provisions of the federal and state constitutions that relate to family relationships, rights, duties, and finances.

**Fatal** Deadly or mortal; destructive; devastating.

**Felon** An individual who commits a crime of a serious nature, such as burglary or murder. A person who commits a felony.

**Felony** A serious crime, characterized under federal law and many state statutes as any offense punishable by death or imprisonment in excess of one year.

**Fiduciary** An individual in whom another has placed the utmost trust and confidence to manage and protect property or money. The relationship wherein one person has an obligation to act for another's benefit.

**Finance charge** The amount owed to a lender by a purchaser-debtor to be allowed to pay for goods purchased over a series of installments, as opposed to one lump sum at the time of the sale or billing.

**Financial statement** Any report summarizing the financial condition or financial results of a person or an organization on any date or for any period. Financial statements include the balance sheet and the income statement and sometimes the statement of changes in financial position.

**Fingerprints** Impressions or reproductions of the distinctive pattern of lines and grooves on the skin of human fingertips.

**Fiscal** Relating to finance or financial matters, such as money, taxes, or public or private revenues.

**Foreclosure** A procedure by which the holder of a mortgage—an interest in land providing security for the performance of a duty or the payment of a debt—sells the property upon the failure of the debtor to pay the mortgage debt and, thereby, terminates his or her rights in the property.

**Forfeit** To lose to another person or to the state some privilege, right, or property due to the commission of an error, an offense, or a crime, a breach of contract, or a neglect of duty; to subject property to confiscation; or to become liable for the payment of a penalty, as the result of a particular act. To lose a franchise, estate, or other property, as provided by the applicable law, due to negligence, misfeasance, or omission.

**Forfeiture** The involuntary relinquishment of money or property without compensation as a consequence of a breach or nonperformance of some legal obligation or the commission of a crime. The loss of a corporate charter or franchise as a result of illegality, malfeasance, or nonfeasance. The surrender by an owner of her or his entire interest in real property mandated by law as a punishment for illegal conduct or negligence. In old English law, the release of land by a tenant to the tenant's lord due to some breach of conduct, or the loss of goods or chattels (articles of personal property) assessed as a penalty against the perpetrator of some crime or offense and as a recompense to the injured party.

**Forgery** The creation of a false written document or alteration of a genuine one, with the intent to defraud.

**Fraud** A false representation of a matter of fact—whether by words or by conduct, by false or misleading allegations, or by concealment of what should have been disclosed—that deceives and is intended to deceive another so that the individual will act upon it to her or his legal injury.

**Fraudulent** The description of a willful act commenced with the specific intent to deceive or cheat, in order to cause some financial detriment to another and to engender personal financial gain.

**Freedom of Information Act** A federal law (5 U.S.C.A. § 552 et seq.) providing for the disclosure of information held by administrative agencies to the public, unless the documents requested fall into one of the specific exemptions set forth in the statute.

**Freedom of speech** The right, guaranteed by the First Amendment to the U.S. Constitution, to express beliefs and ideas without unwarranted government restriction.

**Freedom of the press** The right, guaranteed by the First Amendment to the U.S. Constitution, to gather, publish, and distribute information and ideas without government restriction; this right encompasses freedom from prior restraints on publication and freedom from censorship.

**Friend of the court** A person who has a strong interest in a matter that is the subject of a lawsuit in which he or she is not a party.

**Frisk** A term used in criminal law to refer to the superficial running of the hands over the body of an individual by a law enforcement agent or official in order to determine whether such individual is holding an illegal object, such as a weapon or narcotics.

# G

**Gerrymander** The process of dividing a particular state or territory into election districts in such a manner as to accomplish an unlawful purpose, such as to give one party a greater advantage.

**GI Bill** Federal legislation that created a comprehensive package of benefits, including financial assistance for higher education, for veterans of U.S. military service.

**Glass-Steagall Act** Legislation passed by Congress in 1933 that prohibits commercial banks from engaging in the investment business.

**Good faith** Honesty; a sincere intention to deal fairly with others.

**Grace period** In insurance law, a period beyond the due date of a premium (usually thirty or thirty-one days) during which the insurance is continued in force and during which the payment may be made to keep the policy in good standing. The grace period for payment of the premium does not provide free insurance or operate to continue the policy in force after it expires by agreement of the parties. *Grace period* may also refer to a period of time provided for in a loan agreement during which default will not occur even though a payment is overdue.

**Grand jury** A panel of citizens that is convened by a court to decide whether it is appropriate for the government to indict (proceed with a prosecution against) someone suspected of a crime.

**Grandfather clause** A portion of a statute that provides that the law is not applicable in certain circumstances due to preexisting facts.

**Green card** The popular name for the Alien Registration Receipt Card issued to all immigrants entering the United States on a non-temporary visa who have registered with and been fingerprinted by the Immigration and Naturalization Service. The name *green card* comes from the distinctive coloration of the card.

**Gross income** The financial gains received by an individual or a business during a fiscal year.

**Gross negligence** An indifference to, and a blatant violation of, a legal duty with respect to the rights of others.

**Guaranty** As a verb, to agree to be responsible for the payment of another's debt or the performance of another's duty, liability, or obligation if that person does not perform as he or she is legally obligated to do; to assume the responsibility of a guarantor; to warrant. As a noun, an undertaking or promise that is collateral to the primary or principal obligation and that binds the guarantor to performance in the event of nonperformance by the principal obligor.

**Guardian** A person lawfully invested with the power, and charged with the obligation, of taking care of and managing the property and rights of a person who, because of age, understanding, or self-control, is considered incapable of administering his or her own affairs.

**Guardian ad litem** A guardian appointed by the court to represent the interests of infants, the unborn, or incompetent persons in legal actions.

**Gun control** Government regulation of the manufacture, sale, and possession of firearms.

# H

**Habeas corpus** [*Latin, You have the body.*] A writ (court order) that commands an individual or a government official who has restrained another to produce the prisoner at a designated time and place so that the court can determine the legality of custody and decide whether to order the prisoner's release.

**Habitability** Fitness for occupancy. The requirement that rented premises, such as a house or apartment, be reasonably fit to occupy.

**Habitual** Regular or customary; usual.

**Head of household** An individual in one family setting who provides actual support and maintenance to one or more individuals who are related to him or her through adoption, blood, or marriage.

**Hearing** A legal proceeding where an issue of law or fact is tried and evidence is presented to help determine the issue.

**Hearsay** A statement made out of court that is offered in court as evidence to prove the truth of the matter asserted.

**Heir** An individual who receives an interest in, or ownership of, land, tenements, or hereditaments from an ancestor who has died intestate, through the laws of descent and distribution. At common law, an heir was the individual appointed by law to succeed to the estate of an ancestor who died without a will. It is commonly used today in reference to any individual who succeeds to property, either by will or law.

**Holding company** A corporation that limits its business to the ownership of stock in and the supervision of management of other corporations.

**Homestead** The dwelling house and its adjoining land where a family resides. Technically, and pursuant to the modern homestead exemption laws, an artificial estate in land, created to protect the possession and enjoyment of the owner against the claims of creditors by preventing the sale of the property for payment of the owner's debts so long as the land is occupied as a home.

**Homicide** The killing of one human being by another human being.

**Human rights** Personal liberties that protect individuals and groups against individual or state conduct prohibited by international law or custom.

**Hung jury** A trial jury duly selected to make a decision in a criminal case regarding a defendant's guilt or innocence, but who are unable to reach a verdict due to a complete division in opinion.

# I

**Immigration** The entrance into a country of foreigners for purposes of permanent residence. The correlative term *emigration* denotes the act of such persons in leaving their former country.

**Immunity** Exemption from performing duties that the law generally requires other citizens to perform, or from a penalty or burden that the law generally places on other citizens.

**Impartial** Favoring neither; disinterested; treating all alike;; unbiased; equitable, fair, and just.

**Impeach** To accuse; to charge a liability upon; to sue. To dispute, disparage, deny, or contradict; as in to impeach a judgment or decree, or impeach a witness; or as used in the rule that a jury cannot *impeach its verdict*. To proceed against a public officer for crime or misfeasance, before a proper court, by the presentation of a written accusation called articles of impeachment.

**Impeachment** A process used to charge, try, and remove public officials for misconduct while in office.

**Implied consent** Consent that is inferred from signs, actions, or facts, or by inaction or silence.

**Implied warranty**   A promise, arising by operation of law, that something that is sold will be merchantable and fit for the purpose for which it is sold.

**Imprisonment**   Incarceration; the act of restraining the personal liberty of an individual; confinement in a prison.

**In re**   [*Latin, In the matter of.*] Concerning or regarding. The usual style for the name of a judicial proceeding having some item of property at the center of the dispute rather than adverse parties.

**Inadmissible**   That which, according to established legal principles, cannot be received into evidence at a trial for consideration by the jury or judge in reaching a determination of the action.

**Incarceration**   Confinement in a jail or prison; imprisonment.

**Incest**   The crime of sexual relations or marriage taking place between a male and female who are so closely linked by blood or affinity that such activity is prohibited by law.

**Income tax**   A charge imposed by government on the annual gains of a person, corporation, or other taxable unit derived through work, business pursuits, investments, property dealings, and other sources determined in accordance with the Internal Revenue Code or state law.

**Incompetency**   The lack of ability, knowledge, legal qualification, or fitness to discharge a required duty or professional obligation.

**Incriminate**   To charge with a crime; to expose to an accusation or a charge of crime; to involve oneself or another in a criminal prosecution or the danger thereof; as in the rule that a witness is not bound to give testimony that would tend to incriminate him or her.

**Independent contractor**   A person who contracts to do a piece of work according to her or his own methods and is subject to another's control only as to the end product or the final result of the work.

**Indictment**   A written accusation charging that an individual named therein has committed an act or omitted to do something that is punishable by law.

**Individual Retirement Account**   A means by which an individual can receive certain federal tax advantages while investing for retirement.

**Informed consent**   Assent to permit an occurrence, such as surgery, that is based on a complete disclosure of facts needed to make the decision intelligently, such as knowledge of the risks entailed or alternatives.   The name for a fundamental principle of law that a physician has a duty to reveal what a reasonably prudent physician in the medical community employing reasonable care would reveal to a patient as to whatever reasonably foreseeable risks of harm might result from a proposed course of treatment. This disclosure must be afforded so that a patient—exercising ordinary care for his or her own welfare and confronted with a choice of undergoing the proposed treatment, alternative treatment, or none at all—can intelligently exercise judgment by reasonably balancing the probable risks against the probable benefits.

**Infraction**   Violation or infringement; breach of a statute, contract, or obligation.

**Infringement**   The encroachment, breach, or violation of a right, law, regulation, or contract.

**Inherit**   To receive property according to the state laws of intestate succession from a decedent who has failed to execute a valid will, or, where the term is applied in a more general sense, to receive the property of a decedent by will.

**Inheritance**   Property received from a decedent, either by will or through state laws of intestate succession, where the decedent has failed to execute a valid will.

**Insanity defense**   A defense asserted by an accused in a criminal prosecution to avoid liability for the commission of a crime because, at the time of the crime, the person did not appreciate the nature or quality or wrongfulness of the acts.

**Insolvency**   An incapacity to pay debts upon the date when they become due in the ordinary course of business; the condition of an individual whose property and assets are inadequate to discharge the person's debts.

**Installment**   Regular, partial portion of the same debt, paid at successive periods as agreed by a debtor and creditor.

**Intellectual property**   Intangible rights protecting the products of human intelligence and creation, such as copyrightable works, patented inventions, trademarks, trade secrets, and rights against unfair competition. Although largely governed by federal law, state law also governs some aspects of intellectual property.

**Internal audit**   An inspection and verification of the financial records of a company or firm by a member of its own staff to determine the accuracy and acceptability of its accounting practices.

**Interrogatories**   Written questions submitted to a party from his or her adversary to ascertain answers that are prepared in writing and signed under oath and that have relevance to the issues in a lawsuit.

**Intestacy**   The state or condition of dying without having made a valid will or without having disposed by will of a segment of the property of the decedent.

**Intestate**   The description of a person who dies without making a valid will or the reference made to this condition.

**Intestate succession**   The inheritance of an ancestor's property according to the laws of descent and distribution that are applied when the deceased has not executed a valid will.

**Intoxication**   A state in which a person's normal capacity to act or reason is inhabited by alcohol or drugs.

**Involuntary manslaughter**   The act of unlawfully killing another human being unintentionally.

**Irreconcilable differences**   The existence of significant differences between a married couple that are so great and beyond resolution as to make the marriage unworkable, and for which the law permits a divorce.

**IRS**   An abbreviation for the Internal Revenue Service.

**Itemize**   To individually state each item or article.

# J

**Jeopardy**   Danger; hazard; peril. In a criminal action, the danger of conviction and punishment confronting the defendant.

**Joint venture**   An association of two or more individuals or companies engaged in a solitary business enterprise for profit without actual partnership or incorporation; also called a joint adventure.

**Judicial review**   A court's authority to examine an executive or legislative act and to invalidate that act if it is contrary to constitutional principles.

**Jurisdiction**   The geographic area over which authority extends; legal authority; the authority to hear and determine causes of action.

**Jurisprudence**   From the Latin term *juris prudentia,* which means "the study, knowledge, or science of law"; in the United States, more broadly associated with the philosophy of law.

**Just cause**   A reasonable and lawful ground for action.

**Justice Department**   The Department of Justice (DOJ) is the executive-branch department responsible for handling the legal work of the federal government.

**Justice of the peace**   A judicial officer with limited power whose duties may include hearing cases that involve civil controversies, conserving the peace, performing judicial acts, hearing minor criminal complaints, and committing offenders.

# K

**Kidnapping**   The crime of unlawfully seizing and carrying away a person by force or fraud, or seizing and detaining a person against his or her will with an intent to carry that person away at a later time.

# L

**Labor law**   An area of the law that deals with the rights of employers, employees, and labor organizations.

**Labor union**   An association, combination, or organization of employees who band together to secure favorable wages, improved working conditions, and better work hours, and to resolve grievances against employers.

**Landlord**   A lessor of real property; the owner or possessor of an estate in land or a rental property, who, in an exchange for rent, leases it to another individual known as the tenant.

**Landlord and tenant**   An association between two individuals arising from an agreement by which one individual occupies the other's real property with permission, subject to a rental fee.

**Lanham Act**   A federal statute enacted in 1946 and subsequently amended to revise trademark law.

**Larceny**   The unauthorized taking and removal of the personal property of another by a person who intends to permanently deprive the owner of it; a crime against the right of possession.

**Leading question**   A query that suggests to the witness how it is to be answered or puts words into the mouth of the witness to be merely repeated in his or her response.

**Lease**   A contractual agreement by which one party conveys an estate in property to another party, for a limited period, subject to various conditions, in exchange for something of value, but still retains ownership.

**Legal age**   The time of life at which a person acquires full capacity to make his or her own contracts and deeds and to transact business or to enter into some particular contract or relation, such as marriage.

**Legal proceedings**   All actions that are authorized or sanctioned by law and instituted in a court or a tribunal for the acquisition of rights or the enforcement of remedies.

**Legal representative**   In its broadest sense, one who stands in place of, and represents the interests of, another. A person who oversees the legal affairs of another. Examples include the executor or administrator of an estate and a court appointed guardian of a minor or incompetent person.   This term is almost always held to be synonymous with the term *personal representative.* In accident cases, the member of the family entitled to benefits under a wrongful death statute.

**Legal residence**   The place of domicile—the permanent dwelling—to which a person intends to return despite temporary abodes elsewhere or momentary absences.

**Legal right**   An interest that the law protects; an enforceable claim; a privilege that is created or recognized by law, such as the constitutional right to freedom of speech.

**Lemon laws**   Laws governing the rights of purchasers of new and used motor vehicles that do not function properly and which have to be returned repeatedly to the dealer for repairs.

**Lessee**   One who rents real property or personal property from another.

**Lessor**   One who rents real property or personal property to another.

**Libel and slander**   Two torts that involve the communication of false information about a person, a group, or an entity such as a corporation. Libel is any defamation that can be seen, such as a writing, printing, effigy, movie, or statue. Slander is any defamation that is spoken and heard.

**Libelous**   In the nature of a written defamation, a communication that tends to injure reputation.

**Lien**   A right given to another by the owner of property to secure a debt, or one created by law in favor of certain creditors.

**Life or limb**   The phrase within the Fifth Amendment to the U.S. Constitution, commonly known as the Double Jeopardy Clause, that provides, "nor shall any person be subject for the same offence to be twice put in jeopardy of life or limb," pursuant to which there can be no second prosecution after a first trial for the same offense.

**Limited liability company**   A noncorporate business whose owners actively participate in the organization's management and are protected against personal liability for the organization's debts and obligations.

**Limited liability partnership**   A form of general partnership that provides an individual partner protection against personal liability for certain partnership obligations.

**Line of credit**   The maximum borrowing power granted to a person from a financial institution.

**Lineup**   A criminal investigation technique in which the police arrange a number of individuals in a row before a witness to a crime and ask the witness to identify which, if any, of the individuals committed the crime.

**Liquidate**   To pay and settle the amount of a debt; to convert assets to cash; to aggregate the assets of an insolvent enterprise and calculate its liabilities in order to settle with the debtors and the creditors and apportion the remaining assets, if any, among the stockholders or owners of the corporation.

**Liquidation**   The collection of assets belonging to a debtor to be applied to the discharge of his or her outstanding debts.   A type of proceeding pursuant to federal bankruptcy law by which certain property of a debtor is taken into custody by a trustee to be sold, the proceeds to be distributed to the debtor's creditors in satisfaction of their claims.   The settlement of the financial affairs of a business or individual through the sale of all assets and the distribution of the proceeds to creditors, heirs, or other parties with a legal claim.

**Litigation**   An action brought in court to enforce a particular right. The act or process of bringing a lawsuit in and of itself; a judicial contest; any dispute.

**Living trust**   A property right, held by one party for the benefit of another, that becomes effective during the lifetime of the creator and is, therefore, in existence upon his or her death.

**Living will**   A written document that allows a patient to give explicit instructions about medical treatment to be administered when the patient is terminally ill or permanently unconscious; also called an advance directive.

**Lobbying**   The process of influencing public and government policy at all levels: federal, state, and local.

**Loco parentis**   [*Latin, The place of a parent.*] A description of the relationship that an adult or an institution assumes toward an infant or minor of whom the adult is not a parent but to whom the adult or institution owes the obligation of care and supervision.

# M

**M'Naghten Rule**   A test applied to determine whether a person accused of a crime was sane at the time of its commission and, therefore, criminally responsible for the wrongdoing.

**Magistrate**   Any individual who has the power of a public civil officer or inferior judicial officer, such as a justice of the peace.

**Magnuson-Moss Warranty Act**   The first federal statute to address the law of warranty. The act (15 U.S.C.A. § 2301 et seq.) mandates that a written warranty on any consumer product that costs more than $5 must completely and conspicuously disclose, in easily understood words, the terms and conditions of the warranty. A warranty may guarantee several things, such as that the item will perform in a certain way or that the manufacturer will repair or replace the item if it is defective.

**Mail fraud**   A crime in which the perpetrator develops a scheme using the mails to defraud another of money or property. This crime specifically requires the intent to defraud, and is a federal offense governed by section 1341 of title 18 of the U.S. Code. The mail fraud statute was first enacted in 1872 to prohibit illicit mailings with the Postal Service (formerly the Post Office) for the purpose of executing a fraudulent scheme.

**Malice**   The intentional commission of a wrongful act, absent justification, with the intent to cause harm to others; conscious violation of the law that injures another individual; a mental state indicating a disposition in disregard of social duty and a tendency toward malfeasance.

**Malpractice**   The breach by a member of a profession of either a standard of care or a standard of conduct.

**Managed care**   A general term that refers to health plans that attempt to control the cost and quality of care by coordinating medical and other health-related services.

**Manslaughter**   The unjustifiable, inexcusable, and intentional killing of a human being without deliberation, premeditation, and malice. The unlawful killing of a human being without any deliberation, which may be involuntary, in the commission of a lawful act without due caution and circumspection.

**Market value** The highest price a willing buyer would pay and a willing seller would accept, both being fully informed, and the property being exposed for sale for a reasonable period of time. The market value may be different from the price a property can actually be sold for at a given time (market price). The market value of an article or piece of property is the price that it might be expected to bring if offered for sale in a fair market; not the price that might be obtained on a sale at public auction or a sale forced by the necessities of the owner, but such a price as would be fixed by negotiation and mutual agreement, after ample time to find a purchaser, as between a vendor who is willing (but not compelled) to sell and a purchaser who desires to buy but is not compelled to take the particular article or piece of property.

**Mediation** A settlement of a dispute or controversy by setting up an independent person between two contending parties in order to aid them in the settlement of their disagreement.

**Medicaid** A joint federal-state program that provides health care insurance to low-income persons.

**Medical malpractice** Improper, unskilled, or negligent treatment of a patient by a physician, dentist, nurse, pharmacist, or other health care professional.

**Medicare** A federally funded system of health and hospital insurance for persons age sixty-five and older and for disabled persons.

**Mental anguish** When connected with a physical injury, includes both the resultant mental sensation of pain and also the accompanying feelings of distress, fright, and anxiety. As an element of damages implies a relatively high degree of mental pain and distress; it is more than mere disappointment, anger, worry, resentment, or embarrassment, although it may include all of these, and it includes mental sensation of pain resulting from such painful emotions as grief, severe disappointment, indignation, wounded pride, shame, despair, and/or public humiliation. In other connections, and as a ground for divorce or for compensable damages or an element of damages, it includes the mental suffering resulting from the excitation of the more poignant and painful emotions, such as grief, severe disappointment, indignation, wounded pride, shame, public humiliation, despair, etc.

**Militia** A group of private citizens who train for military duty to be ready to defend their state or country in times of emergency. A militia is distinct from regular military forces, which are units of professional soldiers maintained both in war and peace by the federal government.

**Minimum wage** The minimum hourly rate of compensation for labor, as established by federal statute and required of employers engaged in businesses that affect interstate commerce. Most states also have similar statutes governing minimum wages.

**Misdemeanor** Offenses lower than felonies and generally those punishable by fine, penalty, forfeiture, or imprisonment other than in a penitentiary. Under federal law, and most state laws, any offense other than a felony is classified as a misdemeanor. Certain states also have various classes of misdemeanors (e.g., Class A, B, etc.).

**Mistrial** A courtroom trial that has been terminated prior to its normal conclusion. A mistrial has no legal effect and is considered an invalid or nugatory trial. It differs from a "new trial," which recognizes that a trial was completed but was set aside so that the issues could be tried again.

**Mitigating circumstances** Circumstances that may be considered by a court in determining culpability of a defendant or the extent of damages to be awarded to a plaintiff. Mitigating circumstances do not justify or excuse an offense but may reduce the severity of a charge. Similarly, a recognition of mitigating circumstances to reduce a damage award does not imply that the damages were not suffered but that they have been partially ameliorated.

**Money laundering** The process of taking the proceeds of criminal activity and making them appear legal.

**Monopoly** An economic advantage held by one or more persons or companies deriving from the exclusive power to carry on a particular business or trade or to manufacture and sell a particular item, thereby suppressing competition and allowing such persons or companies to raise the price of a product or service substantially above the price that would be established by a free market.

**Mortgage** A legal document by which the owner (buyer) transfers to the lender an interest in real estate to secure the repayment of a debt, evidenced by a mortgage note. When the debt is repaid, the mortgage is discharged, and a satisfaction of mortgage is recorded with the register or recorder of deeds in the county where the mortgage was recorded. Because most people cannot afford to buy real estate with cash, nearly every real estate transaction involves a mortgage.

**Mutual fund** A fund, in the form of an investment company, in which shareholders combine their money to invest in a variety of stocks, bonds, and money-market investments such as U.S. Treasury bills and bank certificates of deposit.

# N

**Negligence** Conduct that falls below the standards of behavior established by law for the protection of others against unreasonable risk of harm. A person has acted negligently if he or she has departed from the conduct expected of a reasonably prudent person acting under similar circumstance. Negligence is also the name of a cause of action in the law of torts. To establish negligence, a plaintiff must prove that the defendant had a duty to the plaintiff, the defendant breached that duty by failing to conform to the required standard of conduct, the defendant's negligent conduct was the cause of the harm to the plaintiff, and the plaintiff was, in fact, harmed or damaged.

**Net** The sum that remains following all permissible deductions, including charges, expenses, discounts, commissions, or taxes.

**Next of kin** The blood relatives entitled by law to inherit the property of a person who dies without leaving a valid will, although the term is sometimes interpreted to include a relationship existing by reason of marriage. See also descent and distribution.

**No fault** A kind of automobile insurance that provides that each driver must collect the allowable amount of money from his or her own insurance carrier subsequent to an accident regardless of who was at fault.

**Notary public** A public official whose main powers include administering oaths and attesting to signatures, both important and effective ways to minimize fraud in legal documents.

# O

**Obscenity** The character or quality of being obscene; an act, utterance, or item tending to corrupt the public morals by its indecency or lewdness.

**Occupancy** Gaining or having physical possession of real property subject to, or in the absence of, legal right or title.

**Open court** Common law requires a trial in open court; "open court" means a court to which the public has a right to be admitted. This term may mean either a court that has been formally convened and declared open for the transaction of its proper judicial business or a court that is freely open to spectators.

**Ordinance** A law, statute, or regulation enacted by a municipal corporation.

**Out-of-court settlement** An agreement reached between the parties in a pending lawsuit that resolves the dispute to their mutual satisfaction and occurs without judicial intervention, supervision, or approval.

# P

**Pardon** The action of an executive official of the government that mitigates or sets aside the punishment for a crime.

**Parole** The conditional release of a person convicted of a crime prior to the expiration of that person's term of imprisonment, subject to both the supervision of the correctional authorities during the remainder of the term and a resumption of the imprisonment upon violation of the conditions imposed.

**Passport** A document that indicates permission granted by a sovereign to its citizen to travel to foreign countries and return and requests foreign governments to allow that citizen to pass freely and safely. With respect to international law, a passport is a license of safe conduct, issued during a war, that authorizes an individual to leave a warring nation or to remove his or her effects from that nation to another country; it also authorizes a person to travel from country to country without being subject to arrest or detention because of the war. In maritime law, a passport is a document issued to a neutral vessel by its own government during a war that is carried on the voyage as evidence of the nationality of the vessel and as protection against the vessels of the warring nations. This paper is also labeled a *pass, sea-pass, sea-letter, or sea-brief.* It usually contains the captain's or master's name and residence; the name, property, description, tonnage, and destination of the ship; the nature and quantity of the cargo; and the government under which it sails.

**Patent** Open; manifest; evident.

**Patents** Rights, granted to inventors by the federal government, pursuant to its power under Article I, Section 8, Clause 8, of the U.S. Constitution, that permit them to exclude others from making, using, or selling an invention for a definite, or restricted, period of time.

**Paternity** The state or condition of a father; the relationship of a father.

**Patients' rights** The legal interests of persons who submit to medical treatment.

**Penalty** A punitive measure that the law imposes for the performance of an act that is proscribed, or for the failure to perform a required act.

**Pension** A benefit, usually money, paid regularly to retired employees or their survivors by private business and federal, state, and local governments. Employers are not required to establish pension benefits but do so to attract qualified employees.

**Per capita** [*Latin, By the heads or polls.*] A term used in the descent and distribution of the estate of one who dies without a will. It means to share and share alike according to the number of individuals.

**Per se** [*Latin, In itself.*] Simply as such; in its own nature without reference to its relation.

**Peremptory challenge** The right to challenge a juror without assigning, or being required to assign, a reason for the challenge.

**Perjury** A crime that occurs when an individual willfully makes a false statement during a judicial proceeding, after he or she has taken an oath to speak the truth.

**Perpetrator** A term commonly used by law enforcement officers to designate a person who actually commits a crime.

**Personal injury** Any violation of an individual's right, other than his or her rights in property.

**Personal property** Everything that is the subject of ownership that does not come under the denomination of real property; any right or interest that an individual has in movable things.

**Piracy** The act of violence or depredation on the high seas; also, the theft of intellectual property, especially in electronic media.

**Plaintiff** The party who sues in a civil action; a complainant; the prosecution—that is, a state or the United States representing the people—in a criminal case.

**Plea** A formal response by the defendant to the affirmative assertions of the plaintiff in a civil case or to the charges of the prosecutor in a criminal case.

**Plea bargaining** The process whereby a criminal defendant and prosecutor reach a mutually satisfactory disposition of a criminal case, subject to court approval.

**Plurality** The opinion of an appellate court in which more justices join than in any concurring opinion. The excess of votes cast for one candidate over those votes cast for any other candidate.

**Polygamy** The offense of having more than one wife or husband at the same time.

**Polygraph** An instrument used to measure physiological responses in humans when they are questioned in order to determine if their answers are truthful.

**Pornography** The representation in books, magazines, photographs, films, and other media of scenes of sexual behavior that are erotic or lewd and are designed to arouse sexual interest.

**Power of attorney** A written document in which one person (the principal) appoints another person to act as an agent on his or her behalf, thus conferring authority on the agent to perform certain acts or functions on behalf of the principal.

**Preferred stock** Stock shares that have preferential rights to dividends or to amounts distributable on liquidation, or to both, ahead of common shareholders.

**Preliminary injunction** A temporary order made by a court at the request of one party that prevents the other party from pursuing a particular course of conduct until the conclusion of a trial on the merits.

**Premarital agreement** A contract made in anticipation of marriage that specifies the rights and obligations of the parties. Such an agreement typically includes terms for property distribution in the event the marriage terminates.

**Pretrial conference** A meeting of the parties to an action and their attorneys held before the court prior to the commencement of actual courtroom proceedings.

**Price-fixing** The organized setting of what the public will be charged for certain products or services agreed to by competitors in the marketplace in violation of the Sherman Anti-Trust Act (15 U.S.C.A. § 1 et seq.).

**Privilege against self-incrimination** The right, under the Fifth Amendment to the U.S. Constitution, not to be a witness against oneself in a criminal proceeding.

**Pro bono** Short for *pro bono publico* [*Latin, For the public good*]. The designation given to the free legal work done by an attorney for indigent clients and religious, charitable, and other nonprofit entities.

**Pro se** For one's own behalf; in person. Apearing for oneself, as in the case of one who does not retain a lawyer and appears for himself or herself in court.

**Probable cause** Apparent facts discovered through logical inquiry that would lead a reasonably intelligent and prudent person to believe that an accused person has committed a crime, thereby warranting his or her prosecution, or that a cause of action has accrued, justifying a civil lawsuit.

**Probate** The court process by which a will is proved valid or invalid. The legal process wherein the estate of a decedent is administered.

**Probation** A sentence whereby a convict is released from confinement but is still under court supervision; a testing or a trial period. It can be given in lieu of a prison term or can suspend a prison sentence if the convict has consistently demonstrated good behavior. The status of a convicted person who is given some freedom on the condition that for a specified period he or she act in a manner approved by a special officer to whom he or she must report. An initial period of employment during which a new, transferred, or promoted employee must show the ability to perform the required duties.

**Probationer** A convict who is released from prison provided he or she maintains good behavior. One who is on probation whereby he or she is given some freedom to reenter society subject to the condition that for a specified period the individual conduct him or herself in a manner approved by a special officer to whom the probationer must report.

**Procedural law** The body of law that prescribes formal steps to be taken in enforcing legal rights.

**Product liability** The responsibility of a manufacturer or vendor of goods to compensate for injury caused by a defective good that it has provided for sale.

**Profanity** Irreverence towards sacred things; particularly, irreverent or blasphemous use of the name of God. Vulgar, irreverent, or course language.

**Progressive tax** A type of graduated tax that applies higher tax rates as the income of the taxpayer increases.

**Property settlement** An agreement entered into by a husband and wife in connection with a divorce that provides for the division of their assets between them.

**Proprietary** As a noun, a proprietor or owner; one who has the exclusive title to a thing; one who possesses or holds the title to a thing in his or her own right; one who possesses the dominion or ownership of a thing in his or her own right. As an adjective, belonging to ownership; owned by a particular person; belonging or pertaining to a proprietor; relating to a certain owner or proprietor.

**Prosecute** To follow through; to commence and continue an action or judicial proceeding to its ultimate conclusion. To proceed against a defendant by charging that person with a crime and bringing him or her to trial.

**Prosecutor** One who prosecutes another for a crime in the name of the government.

**Protective order** A court order, direction, decree, or command to protect a person from further harassment, service of process, or discovery.

**Provisional** Temporary; not permanent. Tentative, contingent, preliminary.

**Public defender** An attorney appointed by a court or employed by the government to represent indigent defendants in criminal actions.

**Public domain** Land that is owned by the United States. In copyright law, literary or creative works over which the creator no longer has an exclusive right to restrict, or receive a royalty for, their reproduction or use but which can be freely copied by the public.

**Public figure** A description applied in libel and slander actions, as well as in those alleging invasion of privacy, to anyone who has gained prominence in the community as a result of his or her name or exploits, whether willingly or unwillingly.

**Public interest** Anything affecting the rights, health, or finances of the public at large.

**Public lands** Land that is owned by the United States government.

**Public law** A general classification of law concerned with the political and sovereign capacity of a state.

**Public policy** A principle that no person or government official can legally perform an act that tends to injure the public.

**Public utilities** Businesses that provide the public with necessities, such as water, electricity, natural gas, and telephone and telegraph communication.

**Punitive damages** Monetary compensation awarded to an injured party that goes beyond that which is necessary to compensate the individual for losses and that is intended to punish the wrongdoer.

# Q

**Quid pro quo** [*Latin, What for what or Something for something.*] The mutual consideration that passes between two parties to a contractual agreement, thereby rendering the agreement valid and binding.

# R

**Ratification** The confirmation or adoption of an act that has already been performed.

**Real evidence** Probative matter furnished by items that are actually on view, as opposed to a verbal description of them by a witness.

**Reasonable doubt** A standard of proof that must be surpassed to convict an accused in a criminal proceeding.

**Redress** Compensation for injuries sustained; recovery or restitution for harm or injury; damages or equitable relief. Access to the courts to gain reparation for a wrong.

**Relevancy** The tendency of a fact offered as evidence in a lawsuit to prove or disprove the truth of a point in issue.

**Repeal** The annulment or abrogation of a previously existing statute by the enactment of a later law that revokes the former law.

**Res** [*Latin, A thing.*] An object, a subject matter, or a status against which legal proceedings have been instituted.

**Rescind** To declare a contract void—of no legal force or binding effect—from its inception and thereby restore the parties to the positions they would have occupied had no contract ever been made.

**Restitution** In the context of criminal law, state programs under which an offender is required, as a condition of his or her sentence, to repay money or donate services to the victim or society; with respect to maritime law, the restoration of articles lost by jettison, done when the remainder of the cargo has been saved, at the general charge of the owners of the cargo; in the law of torts, or civil wrongs, a measure of damages; in regard to contract law, the restoration of a party injured by a breach of contract to the position that party occupied before she or he entered the contract.

**Restraining order** A command of the court issued upon the filing of an application for an injunction, prohibiting the defendant from performing a threatened act until a hearing on the application can be held.

**Retainer** A contract between attorney and client specifying the nature of the services to be rendered and the cost of the services.

**Roe** A fictitious surname used for an unknown or anonymous person or for a hypothetical person in an illustration.

GLOSSARY

# S

**S corporation** A type of corporation that is taxed under subchapter S of the Internal Revenue Code (26 U.S.C.A. § 1 et seq.).

**Sales tax** A state or local-level tax on the retail sale of specified property or services. It is a percentage of the cost of such. Generally, the purchaser pays the tax but the seller collects it as an agent for the government. Various taxing jurisdictions allow exemptions for purchases of specified items, including certain foods, services, and manufacturing equipment. If the purchaser and seller are in different states, a use tax usually applies.

**Sanction** To assent, concur, confirm, approve, or ratify. The part of a law that is designed to secure enforcement by imposing a penalty for violation of the law or offering a reward for its observance. A punitive act taken by one nation against another nation that has violated a treaty or international law.

**Savings and loan association** A financial institution owned by and operated for the benefit of those using its services. The savings and loan association's primary purpose is making loans to its members, usually for the purchase of real estate or homes.

**School desegregation** The attempt to end the practice of separating children of different races into distinct public schools.

**Search and seizure** In international law, the right of ships of war, as regulated by treaties, to examine a merchant vessel during war in order to determine whether the ship or its cargo is liable to seizure. A hunt by law enforcement officials for property or communications believed to be evidence of crime, and the act of taking possession of this property.

**Search warrant** A court order authorizing the examination of a place for the purpose of discovering contraband, stolen property, or evidence of guilt to be used in the prosecution of a criminal action.

**SEC** An abbreviation for the Securities and Exchange Commission.

**Securities** Evidence of a corporation's debts or property.

**Segregation** The act or process of separating a race, class, or ethnic group from a society's general population.

**Self-defense** The protection of one's person or property against some injury attempted by another.

**Self-incrimination** Giving testimony in a trial or other legal proceeding that could subject one to criminal prosecution.

**Separate but equal** The doctrine first enunciated by the U.S. Supreme Court in *Plessy v. Ferguson,* 163 U.S. 537, 16 S. Ct. 1138, 41 L. Ed. 256 (1896), to the effect that establishing different facilities for blacks and whites was valid under the Equal Protection Clause of the Fourteenth Amendment as long as they were equal.

**Settlement** The act of adjusting or determining the dealings or disputes between persons without pursuing the matter through a trial.

**Sex discrimination** Discrimination on the basis of gender.

**Sex offenses** A class of sexual conduct prohibited by the law.

**Sexual abuse** Illegal sex acts performed against a minor by a parent, guardian, relative, or acquaintence.

**Sexual harassment** Unwelcome sexual advances, requests for sexual favors, and other verbal or physical conduct of a sexual nature that tends to create a hostile or offensive work environment.

**Social Security Act of 1935** Legislation (42 U.S.C.A. § 301 et seq.) designed to assist in the maintenance of the financial well-being of eligible persons, enacted in 1935 as part of President Franklin D. Roosevelt's New Deal.

**Sodomy** Anal or oral intercourse between human beings, or any sexual relations between a human being and an animal, the act of which may be punishable as a criminal offense.

**Sole proprietorship** A form of business in which one person owns all the assets of the business, in contrast to a partnership or a corporation.

**Solicitation** Urgent request, plea, or entreaty; enticing, asking. The criminal offense of urging someone to commit an unlawful act.

**Solicitor general** An officer of the U.S. Department of Justice who represents the U.S. government in cases before the U.S. Supreme Court.

**Solvency** The ability of an individual to pay his or her debts as they mature in the normal and ordinary course of business, or the financial condition of owning property of sufficient value to discharge all of one's debts.

**Sovereign immunity** The legal protection that prevents a sovereign state or person from being sued without consent.

**Stalking** Criminal activity consisting of the repeated following and harassing of another person.

**Status offense** A type of crime that is not based upon prohibited action or inaction but rests on the fact that the offender has a certain personal condition or is of a specified character.

**Statute** An act of a legislature that declares, proscribes, or commands something; a specific law, expressed in writing.

**Statute of limitations** A type of federal or state law that restricts the time within which legal proceedings may be brought.

**Statutory** Created, defined, or relating to a statute; required by statute; conforming to a statute.

**Stop payment order** Revocation of a check; a notice made by a depositor to his or her bank directing the bank to refuse payment of a specific check drawn by the depositor.

**Subcontractor** One who takes a portion of a contract from the principal contractor or from another subcontractor.

**Subletting** The leasing of part or all of the property held by a tenant, as opposed to a landlord, during a portion of his or her unexpired balance of the term of occupancy.

**Subpoena** [*Latin, Under penalty.*] A formal document that orders a named individual to appear before a duly authorized body at a fixed time to give testimony.

**Substantiate** To establish the existence or truth of a particular fact through the use of competent evidence; to verify.

**Succession** The transfer of title to property under the law of descent and distribution. The transfer of legal or official powers from an individual who formerly held them to another who undertakes current responsibilities to execute those powers.

**Summary judgment** A procedural device used during civil litigation to promptly and expeditiously dispose of a case without a trial. It is used when there is no dispute as to the material facts of the case and a party is entitled to judgment as a matter of law.

**Summons** The paper that tells a defendant that he or she is being sued and asserts the power of the court to hear and determine the case. A form of legal process that commands the defendant to appear before the court on a specific day and to answer the complaint made by the plaintiff.

**Surrogate motherhood** A relationship in which one woman bears and gives birth to a child for a person or a couple who then adopts or takes legal custody of the child; also called mothering by proxy.

**Surtax** An additional charge on an item that is already taxed.

**Suspended sentence** A sentence given after the formal conviction of a crime that the convicted person is not required to serve.

# T

**Taft-Hartley Act** The amendments to the National Labor Relations Act, also known as the Wagner Act of 1935 (29 U.S.C.A. § 151 et seq.), which were enacted to counteract the advantage labor unions had gained under the original legislation by imposing corresponding duties on unions.

**Tangible** Possessing a physical form that can be touched or felt.

**Tax evasion** The process whereby a person, through commission of fraud, unlawfully pays less tax than the law mandates.

**Tax return** The form that the government requires a taxpayer to file with the appropriate official by a designated date to disclose and detail income subject to taxation and eligibility for deductions and exemptions, along with a remittance of the tax due or a claim for a refund of taxes that were overpaid.

**Taxable income** Under the federal tax law, gross income reduced by adjustments and allowable deductions. It is the income against which tax rates are applied to compute an individual or entity's tax liability. The essence of taxable income is the accrual of some gain, profit, or benefit to a taxpayer.

**Taxation** The process whereby charges are imposed on individuals or property by the legislative branch of the federal government and by many state governments to raise funds for public purposes.

**Tenancy** A situation that arises when one individual conveys real property to another individual by way of a lease. The relation of an individual to the land he or she holds that designates the extent of that person's estate in real property.

**Terrorism** The unlawful use of force or violence against persons or property in order to coerce or intimate a government or the civilian population in furtherance of political or social objectives.

**Testament** Another name for a will.

**Testate** One who dies leaving a valid will, or the description of this status.

**Testator** One who makes or has made a will; one who dies leaving a will.

**Testify** To provide evidence as a witness, subject to an oath or affirmation, in order to establish a particular fact or set of facts.

**Testimony** Oral evidence offered by a competent witness under oath, which is used to establish some fact or set of facts.

**Timeshare** A form of shared property ownership, commonly in vacation or recreation condominium property, in which rights vest in several owners to use property for a specified period each year.

**Title insurance** A contractual arrangement entered into to indemnify loss or damage resulting from defects or problems relating to the ownership of real property, or from the enforcement of liens that exist against it.

**Title search** The process of examining official county records to determine whether an owner's rights in real property are good.

**Tort law** A body of rights, obligations, and remedies that is applied by courts in civil proceedings to provide relief for persons who have suffered harm from the wrongful acts of others. The person who sustains injury or suffers pecuniary damage as the result of tortious conduct is known as the plaintiff, and the person who is responsible for inflicting the injury and incurs liability for the damage is known as the defendant or tortfeasor.

**Tortfeasor** A wrongdoer; an individual who commits a wrongful act that injures another and for which the law provides a legal right to seek relief; a defendant in a civil tort action.

**Trade dress** A product's physical appearance, including its size, shape, color, design, and texture.

**Trade name** Names or designations used by companies to identify themselves and distinguish their businesses from others in the same field.

**Trademarks** Distinctive symbols of authenticity through which the products of particular manufacturers or the salable commodities of particular merchants can be distinguished from those of others.

**Transfer of assets** The conveyance of something of value from one person, place, or situation to another.

**Transfer tax** The charge levied by the government on the sale of shares of stock. A charge imposed by the federal and state governments upon the passing of title to real property or a valuable interest in such property, or on the transfer of a decedent's estate by inheritance, devise, or bequest.

**Treason** The betrayal of one's own country by waging war against it or by consciously or purposely acting to aid its enemies.

**Trespass** An unlawful intrusion that interferes with one's person or property.

**Tribunal** A general term for a court, or the seat of a judge.

**Trust company** A corporation formed for the purpose of managing property set aside to be used for the benefit of individuals or organizations.

**Trustee** An individual or corporation named by an individual, who sets aside property to be used for the benefit of another person, to manage the property as provided by the terms of the document that created the arrangement.

# U

**U.S. Code** A multivolume publication of the text of statutes enacted by Congress.

**Unemployment compensation** Insurance benefits paid by the state or federal government to individuals who are involuntarily out of work in order to provide them with necessities, such as food, clothing, and shelter.

**Unfair competition** Any fraudulent, deceptive, or dishonest trade practice that is prohibited by statute, regulation, or the common law.

**Unfair labor practice** Conduct prohibited by federal law regulating relations between employers, employees, and labor organizations.

**Uniform acts** Laws that are designed to be adopted generally by all the states so that the law in one jurisdiction is the same as in another jurisdiction.

**Uniform commercial code** A general and inclusive group of laws adopted, at least partially, by all the states to further uniformity and fair dealing in business and commercial transactions.

**Unilateral contract** A contract in which only one party makes an express promise, or undertakes a performance without first securing a reciprocal agreement from the other party.

**Unlawful detainer** The act of retaining possession of property without legal right.

**USC** An abbreviation for U.S. Code.

**Use tax** A charge imposed on the use or possession of personal property.

**Usury** The crime of charging higher interest on a loan than the law permits.

# V

**Vagrancy** The condition of an individual who is idle, has no visible means of support, and travels from place to place without working.

**Vandalism** The intentional and malicious destruction of or damage to the property of another.

**Visa** An official endorsement on a passport or other document required to secure an alien's admission to a country.

**Voir dire** [*Old French, To speak the truth.*] The preliminary examination of prospective jurors to determine their qualifications and suitability to serve on a jury, in order to ensure the selection of fair and impartial jury.

**Voting Rights Act of 1965** An enactment by Congress in 1965 (42 U.S.C.A. § 1973 et seq.) that prohibits the states and their political subdivisions from imposing voting qualifications or prerequisites to voting, or standards, practices, or procedures that deny or curtail the right of a U.S. citizen to vote because of race, color, or membership in a language minority group.

**Voucher** A receipt or release which provides evidence of payment or other discharge of a debt, often for purposes of reimbursement, or attests to the accuracy of the accounts.

# W

**Wage assignment**   The voluntary transfer in advance of a debtor's pay, generally in connection with a particular debt or judgment.

**Waiver**   The voluntary surrender of a known right; conduct supporting an inference that a particular right has been relinquished.

**Warrant**   A written order issued by a judicial officer or other authorized person commanding a law enforcement officer to perform some act incident to the administration of justice.

**Warranty**   An assurance, promise, or guaranty by one party that a particular statement of fact is true and may be relied upon by the other party.

**Warranty deed**   An instrument that transfers real property from one person to another and in which the grantor promises that title is good and clear of any claims.

**Weight of evidence**   Measure of credible proof on one side of a dispute as compared with the credible proof on the other, particularly the probative evidence considered by a judge or jury during a trial.

**Whistleblowing**   The disclosure by a person, usually an employee, in a government agency or private enterprise; to the public or to those in authority, of mismanagement, corruption, illegality, or some other wrongdoing.

**Wiretapping**   A form of electronic eavesdropping accomplished by seizing or overhearing communications by means of a concealed recording or listening device connected to the transmission line.

**Workers' compensation**   A system whereby an employer must pay, or provide insurance to pay, the lost wages and medical expenses of an employee who is injured on the job.

**Writ**   An order issued by a court requiring that something be done or giving authority to do a specified act.

**Wrongful death**   The taking of the life of an individual resulting from the willful or negligent act of another person or persons.

**Wrongful discharge**   An at-will employe's cause of action against his former employer, alleging that his dischargee was in violation of state or federal antidiscrimination statutes, public policy, an implied contract or an implied covenant of good faith and fair dealing.

# Z

**Zoning**   The separation or division of a municipality into districts, the regulation of buildings and structures in such districts in accordance with their construction and the nature and extent of their use, and the dedication of such districts to particular uses designed to serve the general welfare.

# INDEX

# B

# G

## H

# I

INDEX

INDEX

# L

# M

# N

# O

INDEX

# S

INDEX

INDEX

INDEX

INDEX

INDEX